C000276651

## 🕮 Let's Go writers travel on your budget.

"Guides that penetrate the veneer of the holiday brochures and mine the grit of real life."

—*The Economist*

"The writers seem to have experienced every rooster-packed bus and lunar-surfaced mattress about which they write."

—*The New York Times*

"All the dirt, dirt cheap."

—*People*

## 🕮 Great for independent travelers.

"The guides are aimed not only at young budget travelers but at the independent traveler; a sort of streetwise cookbook for traveling alone."

—*The New York Times*

"Flush with candor and irreverence, chock full of budget travel advice."

—*The Des Moines Register*

"An indispensible resource, *Let's Go*'s practical information can be used by every traveler."

—*The Chattanooga Free Press*

## 🕮 Let's Go is completely revised each year.

"Only *Let's Go* has the zeal to annually update every title on its list."

—*The Boston Globe*

"Unbeatable: good sightseeing advice; up-to-date info on restaurants, hotels, and inns; a commitment to money-saving travel; and a wry style that brightens nearly every page."

—*The Washington Post*

## 🕮 All the important information you need.

"*Let's Go* authors provide a comedic element while still providing concise information and thorough coverage of the country. Anything you need to know about budget traveling is detailed in this book."

—*The Chicago Sun-Times*

"Value-packed, unbeatable, accurate, and comprehensive."

—*Los Angeles Times*

# Let's Go Publications

Let's Go: Alaska & the Pacific Northwest 2001
Let's Go: Australia 2001
Let's Go: Austria & Switzerland 2001
Let's Go: Boston 2001 **New Title!**
Let's Go: Britain & Ireland 2001
Let's Go: California 2001
Let's Go: Central America 2001
Let's Go: China 2001
Let's Go: Eastern Europe 2001
Let's Go: Europe 2001
Let's Go: France 2001
Let's Go: Germany 2001
Let's Go: Greece 2001
Let's Go: India & Nepal 2001
Let's Go: Ireland 2001
Let's Go: Israel 2001
Let's Go: Italy 2001
Let's Go: London 2001
Let's Go: Mexico 2001
Let's Go: Middle East 2001
Let's Go: New York City 2001
Let's Go: New Zealand 2001
Let's Go: Paris 2001
Let's Go: Peru, Bolivia & Ecuador 2001 **New Title!**
Let's Go: Rome 2001
Let's Go: San Francisco 2001 **New Title!**
Let's Go: South Africa 2001
Let's Go: Southeast Asia 2001
Let's Go: Spain & Portugal 2001
Let's Go: Turkey 2001
Let's Go: USA 2001
Let's Go: Washington, D.C. 2001
Let's Go: Western Europe 2001 **New Title!**

## Let's Go *Map Guides*

Amsterdam
Berlin
Boston
Chicago
Florence
Hong Kong
London
Los Angeles
Madrid

New Orleans
New York City
Paris
Prague
Rome
San Francisco
Seattle
Sydney
Washington, D.C.

**Coming Soon:** Dublin and Venice

# Let's Go

# AUSTRALIA

# 2001

**Thomas P. Windom** editor
**Megan V. Strackbein** associate editor
**Brian R. Walsh** associate editor

researcher-writers

Amanda Beck   Jonathan L. Lee
Noah Bloom   Abigail Mnookin
Niki Christoff   Jen Mrowka
T.J. Kelleher   David Sivak
Eliot Wadsworth

**Anna Malsberger** map editor

**Macmillan**

**HELPING LET'S GO** If you want to share your discoveries, suggestions, or corrections, please drop us a line. We read every piece of correspondence, whether a postcard, a 10-page email, or a coconut. Please note that mail received after May 2001 may be too late for the 2002 book, but will be kept for future editions. **Address mail to:**

Let's Go: Australia
67 Mount Auburn Street
Cambridge, MA 02138
USA

Visit Let's Go at **http://www.letsgo.com,** or send email to:

feedback@letsgo.com
Subject: "Let's Go: Australia"

In addition to the invaluable travel advice our readers share with us, many are kind enough to offer their services as researchers or editors. Unfortunately, our charter enables us to employ only currently enrolled Harvard students.

❧

Published in Great Britain 2001 by Macmillan, an imprint of Macmillan Publishers Ltd, 25 Eccleston Place, London, SW1W 9NF, Basingstoke and Oxford.
Associated companies throughout the world
www.macmillan.com

Maps by David Lindroth copyright © 2001, 2000, 1999, 1998, 1997, 1996, 1995, 1994, 1993, 1992, 1991, 1990, 1989, 1988 by St. Martin's Press.

Published in the United States of America by St. Martin's Press.

**Let's Go: Australia.** Copyright © 2001 by Let's Go, Inc. All rights reserved. Printed in the United States of America. No part of this book may be used or reproduced in any manner whatsoever without written permission except in the case of brief quotations embodied in critical articles or reviews. For information, address St. Martin's Press, 175 Fifth Avenue, New York, NY 10010, USA.

ISBN: 0-333-90116-9
First edition
10 9 8 7 6 5 4 3 2 1

**Let's Go: Australia** is written by Let's Go Publications, 67 Mount Auburn Street, Cambridge, MA 02138, USA.

**Let's Go®** and the thumb logo are trademarks of Let's Go, Inc.
Printed in the USA on recycled paper with biodegradable soy ink.

**ADVERTISING DISCLAIMER** All advertisements appearing in Let's Go publications are sold by an independent agency not affiliated with the editorial production of the guides. Advertisers are never given preferential treatment, and the guides are researched, written, and published independent of advertising. Advertisements do not imply endorsement of products or services by Let's Go, and Let's Go does not vouch for the accuracy of information provided in advertisements.
  If you are interested in purchasing advertising space in a Let's Go publication, contact: Let's Go Advertising Sales, 67 Mount Auburn St., Cambridge, MA 02138, USA.

# ACKNOWLEDGMENTS

**TEAM OZ 2001 THANKS:** To the most energetic, most perplexing, and most endearing RWs in the history of Let's Go; to Walter, Erica, Jordana, Jack, LB3, Alicia, Jeremy, Milo, Toby, Franklin, VB, Carolyn Tobgui, Neecia, Sharon, Joe, Maggie, Molly, the kangaroo from Aldinga, SA, Christie in Perth, Mark in Albany, Barry in Karratha, Andrea; to Brady, Andrea, and Sunny for proof of commitment; to Eli Ceryak and Erica Levy for long-distance RWing; to Anne Chisholm for making the world go 'round; to our friends and family; and to all the people who gave us cups of coffee and good cheer along the way.

**TPW:** Booyah! Thanks to a stellar bookteam; Megs for cranking and staying with me; Bri for dealing (and very well) with getting split; mappa Malsy for not hitting (hating?) my overbearing self; Nick for keeping us cool and pushing our 8 to a perfect 10; Dawid for sarcasm; 60 Banks for giving weekends meaning; Reuland for good cheer; Cordell for a constant laugh (at not with); Dilley for midnight snacks; the wolves for keeping me on my toes; Ma Go for shelter from the wolves; and ASR for guiding me to this great job and 4 years of friendship. To my fam for everything; JP for getting me in shape; the Cabal for things to come; TW for the initials; WGC for mid-week meaning; and finally to BFRW for dealing with my spring and living the best years of my life with me.

**MVS:** To Thomas for picking my name out of a stack and making that a good thing, Brian, for comedic stylings, Nick, for elegant editing, Ann, for spicing things up, Dawid, for winning the title of pod curmudgeon. Aly, Beth, Dani, Delayne, and Kristin, for being the best roommates ever. Tova, for keeping me sane. Richie, Jason, Ollie, Matt, Laura, Kat, Beth S., Sara, Kate, and Shannon, for always being just a phone call away. Russ, for being the best bro a girl could ask for. Mom and Dad, for your love and suppport.

**BRW:** First to TW, for encouraging my vices but making me start at a reasonable hour; Megan, my comrade in arms; Ann, for the ficus and half-sneezes; Dawid, for the sarcasm; Bede for money and a day off; Kaya for a generous spirit; Maya, we'll get Dan someday; Arock, Jdwill for being there; RL for 6 yrs of English; Brady and Hely-my two favorite Steves. Mum and Dad, for an open ear and mind; Tom Tim Mat and Meg for laughs, and God for seeing me through to the end.

**Editor**
Thomas P. Windom
**Associate Editors**
Megan V. Strackbein, Brian R. Walsh
**Managing Editor**
Nicholas Grossman
**Map Editor**
Anna L. Malsberger

**Publishing Director**
Kaya Stone
**Editor-in-Chief**
Kate McCarthy
**Production Manager**
Melissa Rudolph
**Cartography Manager**
John Fiore
**Editorial Managers**
Alice Farmer, Ankur Ghosh, Aarup Kubal, Anup Kubal
**Financial Manager**
Bede Sheppard
**Low-Season Manager**
Melissa Gibson
**Marketing & Publicity Managers**
Olivia L. Cowley, Esti Iturralde
**New Media Manager**
Daryush Jonathan Dawid
**Personnel Manager**
Nicholas Grossman
**Photo Editor**
Dara Cho
**Production Associates**
Sanjay Mavinkurve, Nicholas Murphy, Rosalinda Rosalez, Matthew Daniels, Rachel Mason, Daniel Visel
**Some Design**
Matthew Daniels
**Office Coordinators**
Sarah Jacoby, Chris Russell

**Director of Advertising Sales**
Cindy Rodriguez
**Senior Advertising Associates**
Adam Grant, Rebecca Rendell
**Advertising Artwork Editor**
Palmer Truelson

**President**
Andrew M. Murphy
**General Manager**
Robert B. Rombauer
**Assistant General Manager**
Anne E. Chisholm

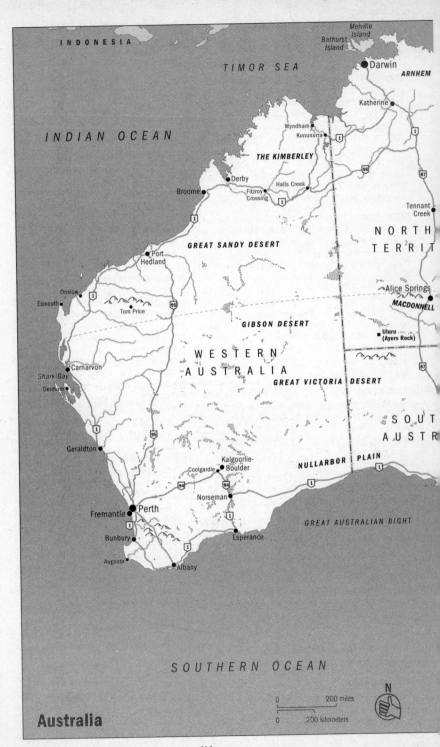

**Australia**

# HOW TO USE THIS BOOK

A good travel guide, like the Wizard of Oz, has a little something for everyone. Although we can't provide a heart or a brain, we strive to provide useful and candid guidance in whatever it is that you may be seeking in Australia—hiking, diving, clubbing, sightseeing, adventure, you name it. As much as we'd like to, however, we can't take your vacation for you. Much of the adventure of traveling is having the courage the Lion lacked to strike out on your own, and part of our job is to provide the basic information you need to be ready to do that. So take our suggestions as starting points, not as the Munchkins orders, and don't be afraid to stray a bit from the Yellow Brick Road.

The first chapter of this book, **Discover Australia**, presents an overview of the country, including **Suggested Itineraries** that give you an idea of what you shouldn't miss. The **History and Culture** chapter is a general introduction to—you guessed it— the history and culture of Australia. If you find yourself remarking, "I don't think we're in _____ (your home region here) anymore" as you think about your upcoming trip, this chapter is a fantastic way to start learning about the people, music, sports, beer, food, and wildlife of Oz. Next, the **Essentials** section is everything Auntie Em always wanted to be and more; it provides heaps of traveling information, from entrance requirements to safety tips. Reading it will ensure that you tip your waiter the proper amount (nothing) and drive on the right side of the road (er, the left).

The heart of the book is the eight chapters arranged alphabetically by **state** or **territory**, with the **capital city** always first. The black tabs in the margins will help you search between chapters easily. Our nine researchers hauled themselves all over the continent, dodging flying monkeys, in search of the year's best **accommodations, food, sights, activities, entertainment,** and **nightlife.** Each of the listings in these sections is arranged in order of preference, though sometimes we broke things up by region to help you navigate more easily. A perky little thumb is thrust to the left of our 🖐**favorite listings.** To help you move along, every chapter and capital city contains a **Highlights** box filled with great finds and must-dos. The absolute best of the best can be found in the **Let's Go Picks** (see p. 5).

Unfortunately, someone in research confused the Scarecrow's need for a brain with a need for an **appendix**—but the appendix at the back of our book (see p. 673) is still incredibly useful, filled with **beer terminology**, a phrasebook of 'strine (so you're not bewildered the next time an Aussie at a barbie shouts you a XXXX from the esky), useful **conversions**, and a **distance chart** to help you find the end of the Yellow Brick Road. So that's it—good luck and say hey to the Wizard for us!

## A FEW NOTES ABOUT LET'S GO FORMAT

A few terms may appear throughout the book that may seem unclear; many are just Australian lingo. **Return**, as in "4km return," means round-trip. All listed prices are in **Australian dollars**, unless otherwise noted. In hostel listings, you'll often see something at the end like **YHA, VIP,** or **NOMADS.** These hostels give discounts (usually $1 per night) to people carrying that type of card (see p. 48). **BYO** means you are allowed to "**B**ring **Y**our **O**wn" alcohol into a restaurant; sometimes these places charge **corkage** fees. **Licensed** means a restaurant sells alcohol. If you're not sure where or what something is check out the **Index** or the **Glossary.**

---

**A NOTE TO OUR READERS** The information for this book was gathered by Let's Go researchers from February through August of 2000. Each listing is based on one researcher's opinion, formed during his or her visit at a particular time. Those traveling at other times may have different experiences since prices, dates, hours, and conditions are always subject to change. You are urged to check the facts beforehand to avoid inconvenience and surprises.

---

# CONTENTS

**DISCOVER AUSTRALIA 1**
When to Go
Things to Do 2
Suggested Itineraries 6

**HISTORY AND CULTURE 9**
History 9
The People 15
Culture 18
Environment 26

**ESSENTIALS 31**
Facts for the Traveler 31

**AUSTRALIAN CAPITAL TERRITORY 76**
CANBERRA 76

**NEW SOUTH WALES 88**
SYDNEY 89
BLUE MOUNTAINS 138
Glenbrook to Katoomba 139
Katoomba 141
NEW ENGLAND 150
Hunter Valley 150
Tamworth 153
WATERFALL WAY 157
NORTH COAST 159
Newcastle 160
Port Stephens Bay Area 165
Port Macquarie 172
Nambucca Heads 177
Coffs Harbour 181
Lismore 188
Nimbin 191
Byron Bay 192
SOUTH COAST 200
Wollongong 201
SOUTH FROM BATEMANS BAY 208
SNOWY MOUNTAINS 212
Kosciuszko National Park 215
HUME CORRIDOR 218
Albury 220
RIVERINA 223
CENTRAL WEST 226
Dubbo 231
NORTHWEST: BACK O' BOURKE 232
Broken Hill 237

**NORTHERN TERRITORY 242**
DARWIN 244
THE TOP END 256
Kakadu National Park 257
Arnhem Land 266
DOWN THE TRACK 268
Litchfield National Park 268
Katherine 270
Nitmiluk National Park 272

Tennant Creek 275
THE RED CENTRE 277
Alice Springs 277
The MacDonnell Ranges 284
Yulara (Ayers Rock Resort) 289
Uluru-Kata Tjuta National Park 290

**QUEENSLAND 294**
BRISBANE 298
MORETON BAY AND ISLANDS 313
North Stradbroke Island 313
GOLD COAST 317
Coolangatta and Tweed Heads 317
Surfers Paradise 319
Gold Coast Hinterland 326
SOUTHERN & DARLING DOWNS 328
Stanthorpe 329
SUNSHINE & FRASER COASTS 332
Maroochy 332
Noosa 334
Near Noosa 339
Hervey Bay 341
Fraser Island 343
Bundaberg 347
CAPRICORN AND WHITSUNDAY
COASTS 349
Rockhampton 349
Great Keppel Island 353
Mackay 355
Near Mackay 358
Airlie Beach 360
Whitsunday Islands 364
NORTH COAST OF QUEENSLAND 368
Townsville 368
Magnetic Island 373
Mission Beach 378
FAR NORTH QUEENSLAND 381
Cairns 381
Atherton Tablelands 392
Port Douglas 395
Cooktown 401
Cape York 403
CENTRAL & WESTERN QUEENSLAND 405
The Warrego Highway 405
Capricorn and Landsborough Hwys 406
The Flinders Highway 408
Mount Isa 410
The Gulf Savannah 412

**SOUTH AUSTRALIA 413**
ADELAIDE 415
NEAR ADELAIDE 428
Adelaide Hills 428
FLEURIEU PENINSULA 429
KANGAROO ISLAND 433
CENTRAL WINE REGIONS 440
Barossa Valley 440
SOUTHEAST OF THE MURRAY RIVER 446
YORKE PENINSULA 449

FLINDERS RANGES 451
Southern Flinders 453
Central Flinders 453
Northern Flinders 456
OUTBACK SOUTH AUSTRALIA 457
Coober Pedy 458
EYRE PENINSULA 460

**TASMANIA 466**
HOBART 468
THE SOUTH 477
D'ENTRECASTEAUX CHANNEL 480
DERWENT VALLEY
AND THE SOUTHWEST 482
THE WESTERN WILDERNESS 484
THE NORTHWEST 490
Devonport 490
THE NORTHEAST 495
Launceston 495
THE SUNCOAST 501
CENTRAL EAST 505

**VICTORIA 507**
MELBOURNE 508
PORT PHILLIP AND WESTERNPORT
BAYS 545
Phillip Island 545
GREAT OCEAN ROAD 550
Warrnambool 556
Portland 559
Near Portland 560
THE GRAMPIANS
AND OUTBACK VICTORIA 561
Grampians (Gariwerd) National Park 562
Little Desert National Park 567
GOLDFIELDS 568
Ballarat 569

Bendigo 576
**MURRAY RIVER 580**
Echuca 580
Swan Hill 583
Mildura 585
**HUME CORRIDOR 587**
Mount Buller 589
**HIGH COUNTRY 592**
GIPPSLAND 598
Wilsons Promontory National Park 598
Lakes Entrance 606
Snowy River National Park 608
Croajingolong National Park 611

**WESTERN AUSTRALIA 615**
PERTH 616
Near Perth 628
SOUTHWEST 630
Margaret River 632
GREAT SOUTHERN 636
GOLDFIELDS 643
Kalgoorlie-Boulder 645
BATAVIA COAST & MIDLANDS 648
OUTBACK COAST & GASCOYNE 651
Shark Bay 651
THE PILBARA 656
THE KIMBERLEY 660
Broome 661
Great Northern Highway 666
Gibb River Road 669
Kununurra 670

**APPENDIX 673**

**INDEX 677**

**MAP INDEX 689**

# MAPS

Australia vi-vii
**Australian Capital Territory**
Canberra 77

**New South Wales**
New South Wales 90-91
Sydney 94-95
Greater Sydney 97
Kings Cross 105
Glebe 107
Manly 110
Homebush Bay Olympic Site 121
Katoomba and Leura 142
Newcastle 161
Port Stephens 167
Port Macquarie 173
Coffs Harbour 181
Byron Bay 193
Wollongong 201

Albury 221
Broken Hill 239

**Northern Territory**
Northern Territory 243
The Top End 245
Central Darwin 247
Kakadu National Park 259
Alice Springs 279
The MacDonell Ranges 284-285
Yulara 289
Uluru-Kata Tjuta NP 290
Kata Tjuta (The Olgas) 292
Uluru (Ayers Rock) 292

**Queensland**
Queensland 296-297
Greater Brisbane 301
Brisbane 302-303
Sunshine Coast and Gold Coast 317
Surfer's Paradise 321
Noosa 335
Rockhampton 351

Mackay 356
Airlie Beach 360
Townsville 371
Magnetic Island 374
Cairns 384
Port Douglas 397

**South Australia**
South Australia 413
Adelaide 417
Kangaroo Island 435
Barossa Valley 441

**Tasmania**
Tasmania 467
Hobart 469
The Tasman Peninsula 479
Launceston 495

**Victoria**
Victoria 509
Greater Melbourne 511
Central Melbourne 514-5
St. Kilda 517
Phillip Island 547

Great Ocean Road 551
Grampians NP 563
Ballarat 571
Bendigo 577
Wilsons Promontory NP 599

**Western Australia**
Western Australia 614
Perth and Vicinity 617
Central Perth 621
Fremantle 625

Far Southwest 630
Kalgoorlie 647
The Kimberley 661
Broome 663

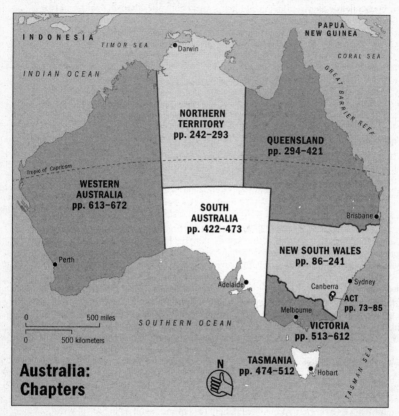

Australia: Chapters

NORTHERN TERRITORY pp. 242–293

QUEENSLAND pp. 294–421

WESTERN AUSTRALIA pp. 613–672

SOUTH AUSTRALIA pp. 422–473

NEW SOUTH WALES pp. 86–241

ACT pp. 73–85

VICTORIA pp. 513–612

TASMANIA pp. 474–512

| | | | | | |
|---|---|---|---|---|---|
| ✛ Hospital | ✈ Airport | 🏛 Museum | | Pedestrian Zone | |
| ✪ Police | 🚌 Bus Station | ♦ Hotel/Hostel | | Park | |
| ✉ Post Office | 🚂 Train Station | ▲ Camping | | | |
| ⓘ Tourist Office | ✝ Church | Food & Drink | | Beach | |
| 💲 Bank | ✡ Synagogue | Shopping | | | |
| Embassy/Consulate | ⚓ Ferry Landing | ♪ Nightlife & Clubs | | Water | |
| ▪ Site or Point of Interest | Theater | Bars | | | |
| ☎ Telephone Office | ▲ Mountain | 🖥 Internet Access | | The Let's Go thumb always points NORTH. | |

100 meters (m) = 328 feet (ft.)     500m = 1640 ft. = 0.31 miles (mi.)
1 kilometer (km) = 0.625 mi.     50km = 31.25 mi.     1 hectare (ha) = 2.47 acres

# RESEARCHER-WRITERS

**Amanda Beck** *Northern Queensland*

Not even death-defying flips could keep Amanda from venturing to the outback and conquering the coast. A true diving diva, she did for the Great Barrier Reef what Fitzgerald did for the great American novel. With Calliope as her guide, Amanda bypassed bones for sunken treasure and cities for hills and islands.

**Noah Bloom** *Southern Queensland*

As if questing for the Holy Grail, Noah relentlessly pursued the mythic ideal of perfectly thorough research. From diving with sharks to sailing the islands, he did it all at the lowest possible price. Noah sorted the seedy from the magic and offered up only pearls. We raise to him a Kangaroo Kicker and down it in one.

**Niki Christoff** *Sydney and Northern New South Wales*

After sweet-talking her way through Sydney, our latté-loving Biscuit sank her teeth into country life. From modeling shoots to livestock auctions, this Cold Warrior became a local celeb while sending back kickass prose. Equal parts swank and cowgirl, hipster Nikster never minced words and never failed to impress.

**T.J. Kelleher** *South Australia and Great Ocean Road, Victoria*

T.J., editor of *Let's Go: USA 2000*, decided to forgo his patriotism to explore the Australian outback. Written with a pen as sharp as lemon cordial, even the wittiest prose appeared effortless. Religiously avoiding the beaten path, TJ brilliantly conveyed a newfound passion for rural towns where local flavor presides.

**Jonathan L. Lee** *Melbourne, Victoria, and Far West New South Wales*

Redefining our Abercrombie stereotypes, Jonathan successfully ate up big city culture and the rugged Victoria outback. Neither clutch nor rain could stop the L, and when he polished off the land he took to the air. When he finally conquered the heart of Melbourne, we discovered that the city had won his heart instead.

**Abigail Mnookin** *Tasmania and Gippsland, Victoria*

A zealous writer, Abbie could have filled an entire *Let's Go: Tasmania* with her fine prose. Though occasionally stepping to the touristy coast, our hiker always kept to the trail in pulling back the veil on enviro-debates. Never straying from supporting local shops, Abbie set Tassie in order and faxed us beautiful work.

**Jen Mrowka** *ACT, Southern and Coastal NSW, and Victoria Skifields*

Jen handled mountains as if they were molehills, and we're not just telling a furphy. Our snow queen only once overdosed on adventure. Her thirst for action (don't worry, she passed the breathalizer with flying colors) was matched only by her hunger to have a good time. Jen, third time's the charm—want a cookie?

**David Sivak** *Northern Territory and The Kimberley, WA*

Never hesitating to bare the naked truth, David redefined our take on P.C. Even when sneaking around at dawn, Crazy Dave still found time to give tips to the fledgling NT tourist industry. Above all, our pickup artist followed a spiritual calling to tell the story of the true outback spirit. David, thanks for stopping the tape.

**Eliot Wadsworth** *Western Australia*

Eliot took his travels through Australia's back door to discover good, friendly folks. Journeying from hardened mining towns to welcoming vineyards, he researched with cool confidence and formed concise, carefully-crafted prose with debonair ease as he discovered his rightful home in the no worries west.

# DISCOVER AUSTRALIA

The experience of the Land Down Under is part physical and part psychological. The British convicts who settled this land were sent against their will into presumed desolation, a vast emptiness on the other side of the world. But the Aboriginals who had occupied Australia for tens of thousand of years recognized the full beauty that the rest of the world is only now discovering. For the indigenous people, the stark terrain which had scared so many others was actually a vibrant landscape carved and populated by sacred spirits: the deserts, canyons, rainforests, and valleys were embodied by these Dreaming creatures. The Australia of myth is big, hot, and empty, but the reality, like the Dream, presents endless possibility. The outback—the *never never*—is only a little distant from the populated coasts, allowing travelers to zig zag between the underwater majesty of the Great Barrier Reef and the eerily calm beauty of the Red Centre, or seek a middle ground in the 37,000 kilometers of pristine beach. Unlike in other places, in Australia the ends of exploration are left to the limits of the individual. You can splice the mystery of the outback into a coastal journey or completely live it with a rugged bushwalk through Tasmanian wilderness or a solitary drive on the world's longest straightaway. This problem-free paradise promises that you will be left alone—or bothered—as much as you want; the people aren't pushy, and the great cities are welcoming oases of civilization in which you will never feel left out. In the end, Australia is not for someone else, it is for you—to lose and find yourself, to make it up as you go along, to travel in a pure sense that more trafficked travel destinations can no longer offer. Visitors come for a full view of it all—the outback, the coast, the Aboriginal lore, the modern culture—and leave with at least a glimpse of themselves. Australia used to be on the other side of what early explorers deemed a flat world; fear prevented them from heading over the oceans. But today we know the world is round. *Never never?* Now.

## FACTS AND FIGURES

| | |
|---|---|
| **CAPITAL:** Canberra | **KINDS OF KANGAROOS:** 60 |
| **HUMAN POPULATION:** 18.6 million | **AMOUNT OF FOLIAGE KOALAS MUST EAT EACH DAY TO SURVIVE:** 9 kg (about 20lb) |
| **SHEEP POPULATION:** 37 million | |
| **NUMBER OF BEACHES:** about 7000 | |
| **WEST-TO-EAST DISTANCE:** 4000km | **AMOUNT OF DAMAGE TO CROPS CAUSED BY RABBITS EACH YEAR:** over AUS $1 billion |
| **PERCENT LARGER THAN BRITAIN, ITS FORMER COLONIALIST RULER:** 3152% | **AMOUNT THE MOVIE "CROCODILE DUNDEE" GROSSED IN 1986:** about AUS $200 million |
| **PERCENT OF THE WORLD'S OPALS:** 90% | **NUMBER OF ABBREVIATIONS ENDING IN THE SOUND "EE":** Infinite—midgie, bluey, barbie, esky, dummy, mozzie... |
| **BEER PER AUSTRALIAN:** 96L beer/yr. | |

# WHEN TO GO

Australia is big. Really big. When to travel depends on where you want to go and what you want to do. Most of the country is in a temperate climate zone, with the **seasons** reversed from those in the Northern Hemisphere. Summer lasts from December to February, autumn from March to May, winter from June to August, and spring from September to November. In general, Australian winters are mild, comparable to the southern U.S. or southern Europe; snow is infrequent except in the mountains, though in winter it's far too cold to have much fun at the beach. The north is an entirely different story—many people forget that over one-third of Australia is in the tropics, where it's always hot. Seasons are defined not by the almost-constant temperature but by the wildly varying precipitation. **"The Wet"** lasts from November to April, and **"the Dry"** is from May to October (see p. 257). Traveling in the Wet is not recommended for the faint of heart; the heavy rains tend to wash out unsealed roads, making driving a huge challenge in non-urban areas.

Crowds and prices of everything from flights to hostel bunks tend to be directly proportional to the quality of the weather. If you plan on traveling in the high season, start planning your trip and booking accommodations months ahead of time if possible. As a general rule, tourism peaks when school is out of session. Summer holidays for primary and secondary schools generally include December and January; for universities, they're from the end of November to the middle of February. Winter break runs from the end of June through early July. From Christmas to New Year's is ultra-peak season.

Diving on the Great Barrier Reef is seasonal as well; January and February are rainy months, and the water is clearest between April and October. The toxic box jellyfish is most common near the east coast between October and April. Ski season in New South Wales and Victoria runs from late June to September, and the famous wildflowers of Western Australia bloom from September to December. For help planning when and where to go, read below, and see the list of major holidays and festivals and the chart of temperature and rainfall data on p. 31.

# THINGS TO DO

Australia's abundant wilderness and unique geography could keep almost any traveler busy for years. Every topography and natural wonder can be explored in Oz, from rainforests abuzz with the chatter of wildlife to eerily quiet red deserts, from jagged mountains to tamed beaches. This chapter offers a brief glimpse at some of Australia's most popular attractions. For more specific regional attractions, see the **Highlights of the Region** section at the beginning of each chapter.

## SAND AND SURF

Great beaches are everywhere—Australia is an island continent, after all. Beachlife can mean lounging in the sun with cool drinks and swarms of happy sunbathers or quiet solitude among expansive dunes and gently lapping waves. **Bondi** and **Coogee** beaches in **Sydney** (p. 89) are crowded and glamorous. The ocean off Queensland's **Fraser Island** (p. 343) lets you look at pristine beauty but not touch. **Whitehaven Beach** in the **Whitsunday Islands** (p. 364) paints perfect white sand against azure waters. The green hills at Broome's **Cable Beach** (p. 661) tumble softly into the Indian Ocean.

Surf's up in the land down under, and the east coast takes center stage. The waves at **Surfers Paradise** (p. 319) are perfect for beginners, and a little farther south, **Coolangatta** (p. 317) is the place for pros—**Duranbah** for fast waves, **Kirra** and **Snapper Rocks** for some of the best surfing in the world. In New South Wales, **Byron Bay** (p. 192) and Newcastle's **Nobby's Beach** (p. 160) are among the country's most popular spots, whereas **Lennox Head** (p. 198) is home to one of the longest right-hand breaks in the world. On the southern coast, Victoria's **Bell's Beach** in **Torquay** (p. 552) hosts the annual Rip Curl Classic. Though not as popular as the east coast's veritable surfing carnivals, the crowds love **Yallingup** (p. 632) in Western Australia and Bruny Island's **Cloudy Bay** (p. 480) in Tasmania. For even more options, see **surfing** in the index.

# SCUBA DIVING

Whether you're a seasoned scuba diver or a determined beginner, you've probably got "see the Great Barrier Reef" scrawled on your list of things to do in your lifetime. And for good reason—off the coast of Queensland, the 2000km reef system encompasses hundreds of islands and cays and thousands of smaller coral reefs, rendering the marine wonderland available to anyone. Most choose to venture out from **Cairns** (p. 381), unmistakably the main gateway to the reef. Further south, on the doorstep of the reef, the sunken **S.S. Yongala** near **Townsville** (p. 368) is one of the best wreck dives in the world. **Airlie Beach** (p. 360) draws backpackers ready to leave the bars for the real thrill of the water. Though the Great Barrier Reef is quintessential, most coasts have good diving spots. In New South Wales, the diving in **Batemans Bay** (p. 208) is second only to the Reef. In South Australia, **Innes National Park** (p. 451) yields access to the Southern Ocean's depths. In Western Australia, giant whale sharks patrol **Ningaloo Reef** in **Exmouth** (p. 654), making for an exhilarating dive. For those looking to learn how to dive, the cheapest certification courses can be found in Queensland at **Hervey Bay** (p. 341), **Bundaberg** (p. 347), and **Magnetic Island** (p. 373). For additional diving and more information, see **diving** in the Index and **The Great Barrier Reef** (p. 295).

# THE OUTBACK

The draw of the outback is mythical, yet magnetic. Geographically confined by the continent's more developed coasts, Australia's outback seems like the most never-ending place on earth. Every year, both travelers and Aussies take on the *never never*, hoping to find a little piece of adventure and a lot of peace of mind. In the west, the red dust and bushland of the **Pilbara** (p. 656) extend limitlessly on every horizon. During the Dry season, the **Kimberley** (p. 660) opens to the insanely courageous who rumble along the **Gibb River Road** (p. 669), the roughest but most stunning drive in the world. In the Northern Territory, **Kakadu National Park** (p. 257) is a gateway to another world of thundering waterfalls, snapping crocs, and mystical beauty. The Aboriginal homeland **Arnhem Land** (p. 266) is the essence of the outback, yet virtually inaccessible. In Australia's Red Centre, imposing **Uluru (Ayers Rock)** (p. 291) keeps a dignified 360° watch over the rest of the outback. Its cousin **Kata Tjuta** (p. 293) revels in solitude, yielding its more poignant beauty only to those who haven't gone Rock-crazy. Down into South Australia, **Coober Pedy** (p. 458) playfully affirms the Down Under mentality—scorching temperatures force residents to carve their homes underground. The **Nullarbor** (p. 463 and p. 644) is a desolate blight, perfect for true solitude. For travelers who won't make it out of the east, Queensland's outback **mining towns** (p. 408) and New South Wales's **Broken Hill** (p. 237) are on the fringe but offer a taste of what lies within.

# NATIONAL PARKS AND UNTAMED WILD

Australia literally has a national park around every corner. The parks preserve all types of terrain—from rainforest to desert, from mountain to coast. Hands-down, the Northern Territory has the best national parks in Australia. The itinerary-topping **Uluru (Ayers Rock)** (p. 291) and timeless **Kakadu** (p. 257) ensure the other, some say better, Territory parks stay more pristine and untrammeled. The **Macdonnell Ranges** (p. 284) have some of the continent's best hiking, and just next door is the spectacular **Kings Canyon** (p. 288). Up the track, the write-home-to-Ma lookouts of **Nitmiluk (Katherine Gorge)** (p. 272) are equalled by the surprising waterfalls of **Litchfield** (p. 268). In Queensland, lush rainforest complements the nearby reef from the tip of **Cape York** (p. 403) all the way down to **Eungella** (p. 359). In New South Wales, the **Blue Mountains** (p. 138) attracts avid abseilers and in winter **Kosciuszko** (p. 215) becomes a warren of ski bunnies and bums. **Wilsons Promontory** (p. 598) in Victoria is the most beautiful part of the southern coast. Tasmania is Australia's hiking mecca; the **Overland Track** (p. 489) is one of the best bushwalks in the world. South Australia's **Flinders Ranges** (p. 451) cater to the truly hardcore. Struggling not to be denied, Western Australia showcases marine life instead of mountains—whales and dolphins defend the hype behind **Bunbury** (p. 630) and **Monkey Mia** (p. 652). For more hiking adventures, look under **national parks** in the Index.

# ABORIGINAL CULTURE

Aboriginals traditionally see a strong connection between the earth and its inhabitants. During the "Dreaming," they believe, spirits carved the canyons and gorges and came to life as animals and trees. The spirituality of the Aboriginals will never be fully incorporated in modern Australian culture, but the significance of their people and beliefs is everywhere. In New South Wales, **Mungo National Park** (p. 241) records the earliest Aboriginal presence. Sacred regions and timeless rock art sites penetrate from **Tasmania** (p. 466) in the far south to **Kakadu National Park** (p. 257) in the Northern Territory's Top End. Though lore has become popular among tourists, increasing the chances of glitz overwhelming tradition, **Tjapukai** (p. 391) near Cairns, **Brambuk Living Cultural Centre** (p. 562) in Grampians National Park, and **Warradjan Cultural Centre** in Kakadu National Park all present intelligent and fair histories of "Dreaming" stories and European interaction. Modern Aboriginal art can be found in small galleries in larger cities, but the **National Gallery** in Canberra (p. 83) has the continent's best collection.

# CITY SIGHTS

Australia's mythical outback spirit and dominant rugged beauty might have made it easy for travelers to bypass city life altogether. But instead, Australia's cosmopolitan meccas shine from under the veneer of obscurity. **Sydney** (p. 89) thrives under several influences—the city center demonstrates European roots; Haymarket is the city's fast-growing Chinatown; bohemian Glebe speaks up for university life; and the sands of Bondi play home to the beach crowd. Melding international culture with a typical Aussie laid-back attitude, **Melbourne** (p. 508) offers more style than Sydney with less hype. With incredible nightlife, a chill daytime café society, and a bustling budget food scene, all as backdrop to the mad and venerable Melbourne Cricket Ground, Melbourne is truly the continent's best city. **Canberra** (p. 76), the orderly capital, gives travelers a sense of Aussie business and government. Like the smooth jazz notes of its clubs, **Brisbane** (p. 298) eases coastal backpackers into urban culture. **Hobart** (p. 468) is a civilized bastion in the Tasmanian wild. The antithesis of a tourist trap, the country town of **Adelaide** (p. 415) lives at a slower pace. Farther from the east, **Perth** (p. 616) and **Darwin** (p. 244) grant relaxing coastal stretches and hopping nightlife on the other edge of the never never.

# WINE

Though not known for its cuisine, Australia has recently acquired an international reputation for the quality of its victual spirits. All throughout Australia, scores of tiny boutique vineyards dot random small towns and river banks. Just follow your nose and keep your wallet in your pocket—most wine tastings are absolutely free. The premier, and most touristed, wine region is New South Wales's **Hunter Valley** (p. 150). West across the Victoria border, **Rutherglen** (p. 591) is smaller but it's proximity to the **Milawa Cheese Region** will whet your nouveau-ritzy palette. Just south, the **Yarra Valley** (p. 543) is Victoria's best donation to the wine scene. At the end of the wine trail, SA's **Barossa** (p. 440) and **Clare Valleys** (p. 444) rival the quality of the Hunter without the hype.

## ▚ LET'S GO PICKS

**BEST BACKPACKERS:**
So many! Buchan Lodge, Buchan, VIC (p. 607). Dreamtime, Cairns, QLD (p. 385). Ozzie Pozzie Backpackers, Port Macquarie, NSW (p. 173).

**BEST FARMSTAY:** Riverslea Backpackers Farmstay, near Cowra, NSW (p. 228).

**BEST PLACE TO ACQUIRE OBSCURE OUTBACK SKILLS:** Leconfield Jackaroo and Jillaroo School, near Tamworth, NSW (p. 154).

**BEST FISH-AND-CHIPS:** Port Albert Fish-and-Chips, Port Albert, VIC (p. 602).

**BEST MEAT PIE:** The Pinnacle Hotel, Pinnacle, QLD (p. 358).

**BEST MILKSHAKE:** The Mars Bar Milkshake at the Hideout Café, Melbourne, VIC (p. 527).

**BEST CUPPA:** Caffe 567, Lakes Entrance, VIC (p. 606).

**CHEESIEST PLACE:** Milawa Cheese Company, near Wangaratta, VIC (p. 591).

**BEST PORTRAYAL OF ABORIGINAL CULTURE:** Warradjan Cultural Centre, Kakadu National Park, NT (p. 265).

**BEST VIEW AT THE END OF THE YELLOW BRICK ROAD:** The Barrk Marlam walk overlooking Jim Jim Falls, Kakadu National Park, NT (p. 265).

**BEST REASON TO GET STUCK UP A CREEK WITHOUT A PADDLE:** Sunset at the top of Surprise Creek Falls, Litchfield National Park, NT (p. 269).

**BEST OFTEN-BYPASSED SIGHT:** Kings Canyon, Watarrka National Park, NT (p. 288).

**BEST END-OF-THE-EARTH SPOT:** Cape Leeuwin, Augusta, WA (p. 635).

**BEST SWANK IN THE OUTBACK:** Tie. Charlie's Mine, Coen, QLD (p. 404). Chateau Hornsby, the NT's only vineyard, outside Alice Springs (p. 282).

**BEST SIGHT WITH NO REDEEMING TOWN:** Taggerty Bush Settlement, VIC (p. 587).

**HIGHEST POINT ON THE CONTINENT:** Nimbin, NSW (p. 191).

**BEST WAY TO GET HYPOTHERMIA:** Swimming past Handrail pool into the gorge and to the top of the 30m waterfall, Karijini National Park, WA (p. 659).

**BEST DRIVE (PAVED):** The Great Ocean Road, VIC (p. 550).

**BEST DRIVE (NOWHERE NEAR PAVED):** Gibb River Road, The Kimberley, WA (p. 669).

**BEST SCUBA DIVING:** The *S.S. Yongala* wreck, off Townsville, QLD (p. 371).

**BEST ADRENALINE RUSH:** The 60m abseil from The Ledge, Grampians National Park, VIC (p. 566).

**BEST CELEBRATION OF THE MIDDLE OF NOWHERE:** Big Galah, Kimba, SA (p. 465).

**BEST SNUB TO THOMAS EDISON:** The Electric Light Parade, Hervey Bay, QLD (p. 343).

**BEST SIMULTANEOUS EXAMPLE OF LOVE OF SPORT AND UTTERLY INEXPLICABLE INSANITY:** Footy at the Melbourne Cricket Ground (p. 531).

**SAFEST PLACE TO VIEW A TASMANIAN DEVIL:** As roadkill on the side of the road.

**BEST EXCUSE TO DRINK:** Australia Day Cockroach Races, Story Bridge Hotel, Brisbane, QLD (p. 312).

**BEST BAR:** Prairie Hotel, Parachilna, SA (p. 455).

**BEST SCOPE-AND-SCAM SCENE:** Metro nightclub, Melbourne, VIC (p. 542).

**MOST ROMANTIC SPOT:** The mudflats at sunset, Derby, WA (p. 666).

**MOST UNFORGETTABLE CHARACTER:** The Lego Man, Angaston, SA (p. 444).

**MOST UNFORGETTABLE MEMORY:** A sincere "G'day mate," everywhere in Oz.

**DISCOVER**

# SUGGESTED ITINERARIES

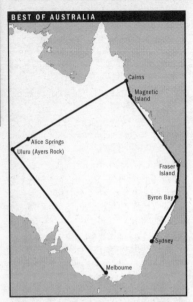

**BEST OF AUSTRALIA**

crash course that will serve you well up the coast. **Brisbane's** (p. 298) smoky jazz clubs are a debonair break from backpacker culture. For a return to natural beauty, travel off the coast to the gorgeous beaches of **Fraser** (p. 343) and **Great Keppel Islands** (p. 353). After recuperating from a big night in **Airlie Beach** (p. 360), go scuba diving or sailing to the **Whitsunday Islands** (p. 364). The next necessary stops, **Townsville** (p. 368) and **Magnetic Island** (p. 373) promise not only a vacation where the sun is always shining, but also some of the cheapest and best diving on the Great Barrier Reef. **Mission Beach** (p. 378) maintains a long sliver of sparkling white silica and popular diving charters. Tropical **Cairns** (p. 381) sums the whole coastal route with unlimited diving, adventure activities, and hearty backpacker nightlife. If you've got another day, investigate the rainforests and less crowded reef just north in **Port Douglas** (p. 395).

## BEST OF AUSTRALIA (3 WEEKS).
Cosmopolitan **Sydney** (p. 89) begins this tour of the continent's highlights. Heading north up the coast, get a taste of the surf before having your aura read in **Byron Bay** (p. 192). Hop into Queensland and across to the constantly-changing sand dunes of **Fraser Island** (p. 343). Check out what you came to Oz for, the Great Barrier reef, on a dive from **Magnetic Island** (p. 373) before heading farther north to **Cairns** (p. 381). Perhaps snorkel a day or two or check out the World Heritage rainforest before catching a flight to the Northern Territory's **Alice Springs** (p. 277). From this most famous of Outback towns, it's just a short trip to the most famous of Australian icons: **Uluru (Ayers Rock)** (p. 290). Catch a flight back in Alice to **Melbourne** (p. 508), the cultural heart of the continent. To make a loop, bus directly back to Sydney or reverse the All Points South itinerary.

## SUN, SURF, AND SHOUTS (3-4 WEEKS).
The beaches and nightlife of **Sydney** (p. 89) set a high standard from the start, and the vineyards of the **Hunter Valley** (p. 150) bring an air of sophistication to the effort of getting housed. People like to tie one on in **Coffs Harbour** (p. 181), while chill **Byron Bay** (p. 192) brings surfing and relaxation. For those who want to learn how to party, **Surfers Paradise** (p. 319) offers a

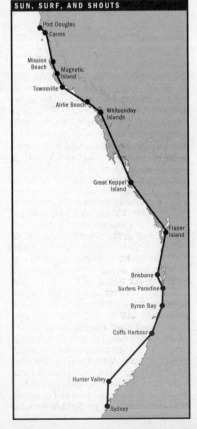

**SUN, SURF, AND SHOUTS**

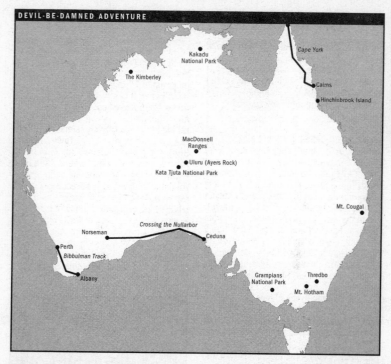

**DEVIL-BE-DAMNED ADVENTURE (UP TO A LIFETIME).** Think you're hardcore? Think again. Start just outside of **Perth, WA** (p. 616) to hike the 964km **Bibbulman Track** (p. 630) to **Albany, WA** (p. 639). Now prepare for the grueling desert haul crossing the **Nullarbor Plain** from **Norseman, WA** (p. 644) to **Ceduna, SA** (p. 463). Stretch your legs and attack the hikes of **Grampians National Park, VIC** (p. 562). Tired of climbing? Going down can be even more challenging on the ski mountains of **Mt. Hotham, VIC** (p. 597) and **Thredbo, NSW** (p. 215). Headed north, the most daring can stop at **Mt. Cougal National Park, QLD** (p. 327) to try the natural waterslide. Go where few have gone before, but be sure to book way ahead, to mountaineer on **Hinchinbrook Island, QLD** (p. 377). Continue up the coast—ALL THE WAY up the coast—to conquer the tip of the continent at **Cape York, QLD** (p. 403). Now travel west to the **MacDonnell Ranges, NT** (p. 284) to tackle more hikes. The next stop is pretty much on the beaten track, but if you think a sunset at **Uluru (Ayers Rock)** (p. 290) isn't worth a detour, then you've clearly never been there. Return to the wilderness at Australia's largest national park and every outdoor enthusiast's dream: **Kakadu National Park** (p. 257). Finally, round out your trip on the severe turn-offs and ruts of the **Gibb River Road** (p. 669) in **The Kimberley, WA** (p. 660). We hope you survived. Only now does *Let's Go* recognize you as hardcore!

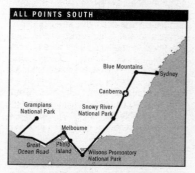

**ALL POINTS SOUTH (2 WEEKS).** After exploring **Sydney** (p. 89), head out for some abseiling and sightseeing in the **Blue Mountains** (p. 138). The nation's capital, **Canberra** (p. 76), offers insights into the higher cultural, and lower political, aspects of the country. Stop to do some hiking in the rugged **Snowy River National Park** (p. 608) on your way to the coastal wonders of

**Wilsons Promontory National Park** (p. 598). Stop at **Philip Island** (p. 545) to watch the adorable penguins at dusk before sliding west into **Melbourne** (p. 508) for an injection of funk, nightlife, and café culture. Further west, fall in love with the **Great Ocean Road** (p. 550) before taking a break for another natural high, the jagged peaks of **Grampians National Park** (p. 562).

---

**WILD WILD WEST (2-3 WEEKS).** This itinerary is particularly ideal between August and November when Western Australia is carpeted in wildflowers. Base yourself in **Perth** (p. 616) while you get lost in history in **Fremantle** (p. 626), bike around beautiful **Rottnest Island** (p. 628), and daytrip out to the eerie limestone pillars rising from the dunes at the **Pinnacles** (p. 649). Heading north, learn to windsurf in **Geraldton** (p. 649), before frolicking with the dolphins of **Monkey Mia** in Western Australia's only World Heritage Area, **Shark Bay** (p. 651). Dive into the ocean off of **Exmouth** (p. 654), then swim in the plunge pools within the red gorges of **Karijini National Park** (p. 659). The wayward tourist destination of **Broome** (p. 661) entices backpackers with pristine beaches and serves as a gateway to the indescribable wilderness adventure that is **The Kimberley** (p. 660).

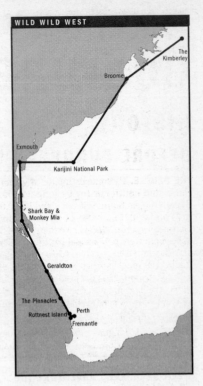

WILD WILD WEST

The Kimberley

Broome

Exmouth

Karijini National Park

Shark Bay & Monkey Mia

Geraldton

The Pinnacles

Rottnest Island

Perth

Fremantle

# HISTORY AND CULTURE

## HISTORY

### BEFORE EUROPEAN SETTLEMENT

**THE PEOPLE.** By some estimates, the **Aboriginal** people of Australia have inhabited the island continent for as long as 100,000 years. The Aboriginals probably migrated from Southeast Asia, and by 30,000 years ago had settled across most of the continent. Estimates of the Aboriginal population of Australia just prior to European colonization vary widely, from 300,000 to over one million. The Aboriginal people were **hunters and gatherers,** migrating seasonally in search of food. Men usually hunted large game, while women gathered vegetables. The large prey were divided among band members, while smaller food was kept for the family. Although Aboriginals did not farm, they did increase the land's productivity by setting controlled fires (see **Burn, Baby, Burn,** p. 263) which replaced nutrients in the soil and allowed seeds that opened only under intense heat to germinate.

**TRIBAL LIFE.** The Aboriginal people formed tribes, largely based on territorial claims. While language did not determine the boundaries of these tribes, it has been estimated that there were more than 200 languages, with up to 600 dialect groups. Most Aboriginals could speak at least two different languages. Within their tribes, Aboriginals divided into smaller groups, called bands, which were made up of two or three different families. Aboriginals were generally accepting of polygamy, and families used inter-band marriages to solidify communities.

**COMMUNITY AND SOCIAL STRUCTURE.** Aboriginals, because of the nomadic nature of their lives, did not develop a system of private land ownership. Instead, a sort of unwritten charter existed, tying together a particular tribe and the territory they covered in their travels, known as a "range." The relationship between these caretakers and their area was considered one of reciprocal responsibility. In addition to strong ties to the land, there was also a strong cultural emphasis on expansion through personal relationships such as kinship, marriage, and ceremony.

**THE DREAMING.** Aboriginals believe the world was created during the Dreaming, or Creation Time, a mythological period of time with no beginning or end, when the acts and deeds of powerful ancestral beings shaped the land and populated it with humans, animals, and plants. There are three categories of land in Aboriginal culture: ceremonial sites, *djang* (Dreaming), and *djang andjamun* (Sacred Dreaming). Ceremonial sites are now used for burials, rites of passage, and other events. At *djang* sites, a creator passed through, took shape, or entered or exited the Earth, leaving the site safe to visit. *Djang andjamun* sites, however, where the ancestor still lingers, are considered spiritual hazard zones. Laws prohibit entry to the latter group of sites. Because features of the land are linked to the ancestors, the land is not an inherited possession, but a sacred site.

The Dreamtime stories defined the Aboriginals' interactions with each other and the environment. The relationships of social units and their geographic home were determined by interactions of Traveling Dreaming Beings and localized Dreaming Beings. In ceremonies, Aboriginals celebrated, integrated, and regenerated the travels of the Dreamings, bringing together social groups, the land, resources, and languages, and uniting the timeless Dreaming and the present. For more information on the Dreaming, flip through **Kakadu National Park,** p. 257.

# EUROPEAN SETTLEMENT

## COLONIZATION

**TAKE A LOOK.** Although Australia is often inextricably linked with Britain, the British were not the first outsiders to stumble upon the continent. **Chinese** explorers were almost certainly among the first non-Aboriginals to arrive; both Chinese and Arabic documents from the early 1400s speak of an island south of Asia. **Portuguese** sailors in the 15th century were also aware of the existence of a *terra australis incognita* ("unknown southern land"). The Spanish, too, visited Australia in the early 1600s. Dutch explorers included a misshapen Australia on 16th century maps, and left a memorial at Shark Bay (see p. 651) in 1616 proving their discovery. It was not until 1642 that **Abel Tasman,** a Dutch explorer under the commission of Governor **Anthony van Diemen** of the Dutch Indies, sailed south to spot the rest of Australia—a "new" southern island. Although he modestly dubbed it Van Diemen's Land, it nonetheless came to be known as Tasmania. Tasman explored Australia's coastline but never established a settlement.

**TAKE A CLOSER LOOK.** As early as 1573 occasional English documents suggested exploring the southern hemisphere. The move to colonize did not come until **William Dampier,** an English pirate who explored the Australian coast in 1688, published his records, *Voyages* and persuaded the English Admiralty to let him return. In 1699-1700, he explored the coastline extensively, but his evaluation was so harsh that little interest was generated for settlement. In 1770, while observing the transit of Venus across the sun, the English captain **James Cook** in his ship *Endeavour*, explored the eastern coast of what would become Australia. The other sides of the island continent had all been explored and mapped, but the Great Barrier Reef had previously deterred explorers from the east. Cook and his crew of astronomers and scientists discovered and named **Botany Bay** (see p. 132), and returned to England with stories of strange animals and plants.

**SETTLE DOWN.** The motives for the British colonization of Australia have been a matter of debate. The traditional explanation is that Britain needed to solve the problem of overcrowding in its prisons. Another explanation suggests that the English hoped to establish a base for a global navy with plentiful natural resources, particularly timber, and an available work force, particularly prisoners. In any case, the prisons in London were full, and Australia, by all accounts, was empty. Preparations for convict settlement began in 1786. On May 13, 1787, the 11-ship **First Fleet** left from England with its unwilling cargo. **Lord Sydney,** the British home secretary, appointed **Arthur Phillip** to command the fleet. About 730 convicts were on board, with more than 250 others who were mostly wardens and their families. The fleet arrived at Botany Bay on January 20, 1788 after a grueling eight-month voyage. When the local resources were deemed insufficient for a colony, Commander Phillip headed north to Port Jackson. The English flag was raised on January 26, on the spot where Sydney stands today.

## CONVICT(ION)S AND PERSISTENCE

**LET'S GO AGAINST OUR WILL.** Upon arrival in Australia, the convicts and their guards faced a foreign, unyielding land. And, to put it lightly, the first years of the colony went poorly: half the workforce was occupied guarding the other half; livestock escaped into the bush; relations with Aboriginals deteriorated; most subsequent supply ships wrecked; and the land seemed impossibly inhospitable. The convicts were mostly undesirables from the slums of London deported to Australia for small crimes (see **Budget Travel in the Old Days,** below), and had no agricultural experience. Moreover, the seeds and cuttings that the fleet had so carefully carried across the sea did not thrive in the strange climate. Captain Phillip's grandiose plans for 200-foot-wide streets had to be scrapped; the colony had only manpower to rely on. No mill or team of cattle would be available for over eight years.

**BUDGET TRAVEL IN THE OLD DAYS** In the late 18th and early 19th centuries, it didn't take much to win a free trip to Australia, as long as you didn't mind traveling aboard a convict ship. Most of the convicts were guilty of petty thievery—and of being poor, ill-connected, and often Irish. Many had originally been sentenced to death, with those sentences commuted to "transportation beyond the seas" and seven years' service upon arrival. Records show that the disappearance of one coffee pot, one guinea, 28 lb. of hair powder, six live turkeys, five woolen blankets, one piece of yellow canvas, three petticoats, 11 yards of printed cotton, 8 lb. of cheese, or one sheep was enough to send a convict to Australia. One man was convicted of destroying 12 cucumber plants, while another "unlawfully cut down one maiden ash timber tree." One woman was convicted of "spoiling, burning, and defacing the garment of a female." Another woman received a sentence of death, commuted to Australian transportation, for stealing two linen aprons. A boy, age 11, was shipped out for stealing one pair of silk stockings. A stiff price to pay for that smooth, silky feel...

**EARLY ABORIGINAL INTERACTION.** Australia's history of white settlement is, as often is the case, partly a history of genocide. When the British landed in Australia and claimed the land for the Crown, they did so under a doctrine of **terra nullius,** (empty land), which meant either that there were no people on the continent, or that inhabitants were mere occupants, and did not actually own the land. This doctrine gave the British free reign (or so they rationalized) to take what land they wished, without the hassle of treaties or agreements. Most Aboriginals were displaced, if not eradicated; European settlement disrupted hunting territories, destroyed watering holes, and brought influenza, measles, smallpox, tuberculosis, and venereal diseases. Many Aboriginal children were kidnapped and forced into assimilation programs, a practice not officially ended until the twentieth century (see **Stolen Children,** p. 17). Some Europeans even took to deliberately and savagely killing the Aboriginals. The history of Aboriginal and white interaction in Tasmania, where the Aboriginals had remained isolated for over thousands of years, is particularly horrid; systematic genocide of the Aboriginal population caused their near-complete disappearance within 70 years of contact.

**POWER POLITICS.** Arthur Phillip became the first governor of New South Wales and saw the colonists through the worst times before returning to England in 1792. After some time, a growing number of convicts were finishing their sentences and looking for their piece of the power pie. The **New South Wales Corps,** a group of officers that assigned jobs to the convicts and maintained order, soon became engaged in a power struggle with Australia's governors to curb the growing influence of former convicts. The tension came to a climax in 1808 when **John Macarthur,** a former officer of the Corps, forced **William Bligh** from the governorship. In 1809, the imperial government appointed **Colonel Lachlan Macquarie** to the position of the new governor. Macquarie again fought with officers and English citizens who had come to Australia due to the promise of large land grants (and influence). Eventually, Macquarie extended full citizenship to convicts who served their seven years and remained in Australia.

# EXPANSION

**THE NEVERENDING STORY.** The costs for maintaining convict colonies became an increasingly onerous economic burden for England, since most were not self-supporting (and were located halfway around the world). After 1815, as more convicts continued arriving, the government began hiring convicts to private employers to lighten the load. Abolitionist crusades in the 1830s convinced some that the practice smelled suspiciously of **slavery.** In 1840, the practice was abolished, and almost no more convicts were sent to eastern Australia. However, a steady stream continued to pour into Tasmania and, in 1850, convicts began to arrive in Western

Australia. Finally, in January 1868, the last convict ship arrived in Australia. In all, approximately 160,500 convicts had been sent to Australia.

**WORTH A SHOT.** In addition to sending convicts, England encouraged settler migration with **land grants** until 1831, and offered cheap passage to women to equalize the gender imbalance. **Wool** was Australia's major export, and by 1845, **sheep farming** was the most profitable business in the country. Despite land grants and economic improvements, the population remained stagnant. The discovery of **gold** in 1851 accomplished what the promise of land could not. By the end of 1851, the non-Aboriginal population numbered around 450,000, eight times that of a quarter-century earlier. Ten years later, the number was 1,150,000. The fierce competition for gold inevitably led to conflict, Australia's closest brush with civil war. During the 1854 **Eureka Stockade Rebellion,** miners in **Ballarat,** Victoria (see **Our Proudest Defeat,** p. 572), formed a collective and built a stockade to protest miner licensing fees. Government forces crushed the uprising in a violent fifteen-minute melee that cost two dozen miners their lives.

**HOW WIDE IS IT?** Four of the six states (the Northern Territory is not a state) were formed between 1829 and 1859. The English parliament first ratified New South Wales' and Victoria's constitutions in 1855, bringing **self-government** to Australia for the first time, and creating a more cohesive feel to the country. Previous to the formation of a central government, each individual colony had little to do with other colonies and instead communicated directly with London. Australia's rail system is a classic case of colonial confusion: in the 19th century, when the country's original six colonies started building railroad tracks, each colony conferred with London instead of its neighbors. By 1901, the year of Australian federation, the six areas of the country had tracks of six different widths.

# TWENTIETH CENTURY

## UNIFICATION AND SEGREGATION

**FEDERATION.** The Commonwealth of Australia was founded on January 1, 1901. Federation had been a difficult process for Australia; the new constitution was only ratified after a decade of debate among the six different colonies over issues such as representation and tax collection. The six states of Australia were (and are) New South Wales, Victoria, Queensland, South Australia, Western Australia, and Tasmania. The Northern Territory and the Australian Capital Territory are two self-governing territories within Australia that still do not have state status.

**SUFFRAGE.** The year after federation, Australia became only the second country in the world, after New Zealand, to grant federal **suffrage to women.** In 1921, **Edith Dircksey Cowan** of Western Australia became the first female in a state parliament in Australia. Her only predecessor in the British Empire was Lady Astor who served in the House of Commons in 1919. The new national government gradually consolidated its power over the states. As a compromise between the urban centers of Sydney and Melbourne, the capital was located in a brand-new city between the two. **Canberra** formally became the nation's capital in 1927. For more on the federation today, see **Government,** p. 16.

**RACE.** Despite the progressive moves forward in gender relations, Australia still had a ways to go. When convicts stopped arriving, Europeans began encouraging the immigration of Chinese laborers. Race-based immigration restrictions were soon adopted, especially when **Chinese immigrants** started working the goldfields. In 1879, an Intercolonial Trade Union Congress, one of the first national meetings with representatives from all of the states, published a warning that Chinese immigration "supplanted white labor, and would leave no work or hope for the rising generation, who would fill the jails in consequence." By 1888, the "Chinese question" had emerged onto the political front stage, and a Queensland journal first

**THE FIGHT OVER THE FLAG** On September 3, 1901, the first **Australian flag** flew over the Exhibition Building in Melbourne, the winner of a design contest that had attracted 32,823 entries from all over the world. The blue flag has the Union Jack in the upper left corner, with the star of Australia underneath, today with seven points, one for each state or territory in the federation. The Southern Cross star formation is to the right. Since then, much debate has ensued over whether the flag is an appropriate national symbol for Australia. Criticism of the current flag include its similarity to other flags (especially New Zealand's) and the Union Jack's implication of subordination or loyalty to Britain. The main argument for the current flag is that thousands of men and women fought and died under it, giving it historical value. Many others simply find nothing wrong with the flag. However, recent polls show that support for a new flag is increasing. Throughout the past 15 years, over 50,000 new designs have been submitted to Ausflag, the lead organization fighting the current flag.

coined the rallying cry **"White Australia."** In 1896, immigration restrictions were extended to include all non-whites. With Federation came the **Immigration Restriction Act of 1901,** which required immigrants to pass a 50-word dictation test in any European language chosen at the discretion of the immigration officers.

## WORLD WAR

**WWI.** At the outset of **World War I,** Australia's Prime Minister declared support for the mother country, saying: "Our duty is quite clear—to gird up our loins and remember that we are Britons." About 330,000 Australians girded up their loins and 60,000 lost their lives. About 165,000 more soldiers were wounded. While these figures pale in comparison to casualties from other countries, they were a shocking percentage of the country's relatively small population. The single worst day of battle was April 25, 1915, when 2000 members of the **Australian and New Zealand Army Corps** (ANZAC) were killed at **Gallipoli,** Turkey, initiating a campaign that eventually took 8500 Australian lives and forced evacuation of the troops. Australia celebrates **Anzac Day** (April 25) each year to remember the heroism of these troops. Economically, though, the war helped industries by opening Western markets to Australian exports.

**WWII.** A generation later, **World War II** allowed Australia to reiterate its commitment to Great Britain and its allies. The Royal Australian Air Force defended Great Britain, while other troops won victories at Tobruk and El-Alamein in North Africa. After the Japanese attack on the United States' Pearl Harbor (Dec. 7, 1941) and the fall of British-protected Singapore (Feb. 15, 1942), Australian citizens became increasingly concerned about safety on their own shores. On February 19, 1942, **Darwin,** the capital of the Northern Territory, suffered the first of many destructive bombings by the Japanese. The US, with its commitment to the Pacific theater, became a closer ally to Australia than the more distant Britain. Over the course of the war, about 30,000 Australian soldiers died fighting.

## AFTERMATH AND ALLIANCE

**HELL NO.** After 1945, the country enjoyed a time of relative peace and prosperity marked by rapid immigration; in the thirty years following the end of the war, the population nearly doubled from 7 million to 13.5 million. In the meantime, Australia and American formalized relations in 1951 with the signing of the **Australia-New Zealand-United States (ANZUS)** pact. But when the United States became embroiled in the **Vietnam** conflict, Australians were conscripted to serve, touching off a slow-gathering storm of anti-war protest. Violent protests broke out among university students in Sydney and Melbourne in 1968, just as anti-war protests were heating up in the US as well. Dissent culminated in 1969, when Australian students stormed the US consulate in Melbourne.

**MONEY MATTERS.** In 1967, Australia broke its currency link with Britain in deciding not to devalue the pound sterling. Within the same year, **Japan** replaced the United Kingdom as the primary recipient of Australian exports, and eventually passed the United States to become Australia's largest supplier of imports by 1984. Australia today is a member of the **Asia Pacific Economic Cooperation (APEC)** forum.

**GIVE A HOOT.** The 1970s also saw the beginnings of **environmental activism** in Australia, echoing movements the world over. The first case to create a nationwide impact was a disagreement over **Lake Pedder** in Tasmania. Despite environmentalists' protests, a hydroelectric dam was erected in 1973. The loss galvanized environmentalists to organize and protest, and eventually to put the Green political party in power in Tasmania in 1989.

# CURRENT EVENTS

## DAMN REPUBLICANS

**WHAT HAPPENED.** The most ground-breaking political news of the 90s was when Queen Elizabeth won her first election. On November 6, 1999, in response to a **national referendum vote,** 55% of Australians voted to officially keep ties with the British Crown and not become a republic. Under the reforms proposed, the duties of monarch would have been performed by a non-political President appointed by a two-thirds vote of the parliament. Despite a strong Republican sentiment in the country, the Australian people voted to continue as a constitutional monarchy rather than have a parliament-appointed president. Some believe that the vote was evidence of a break between a forward-looking urban middle class who supported the republic and rural voters and workers who were hostile to any change. Others instead point to Australians' preference for a democratically elected president and a general distrust of politicians. But almost all agree that the referendum did not resolve the debate once and for all.

**...AND WHY.** In November 11, 1975, the Governor General, acting in response to a deadlock over government finances, exercised his right to dissolve parliament in times of crisis. The deadlock occurred after two states replaced outgoing Labor members of parliament with Liberals, swaying the balance in their favor. The Governor General responded by dismissing the Labor Prime Minister, **Edward Gough Whitham,** and appointing **Malcolm Fraser,** a Liberal, to lead. This act shocked the Australian people and raised popular support for **republicanism,** a movement geared toward gaining full independence from the British Crown. In the election a year after the dissolution, the Liberals under Fraser were voted into power anyway, and remained there for eight years.

**AH, POLITICS!** In 1983, the Labor Party once again took control of parliament under Prime Minister **Bob Hawke,** who retained power through four terms. He was succeeded by **Paul Keating,** also a member of the Labor Party, who tried to use the Labor dominance to improve economic relations with Asia and transform Australia into a republic. In 1996, after 13 years of uninterrupted Labor rule, the Liberals finally regained control of parliament under **John Howard,** a social conservative and constitutional monarchist. His platform included industrial relations reform and, of course, the reversal of some of the more liberal policies of the Labor administration. On February 13, 1998, a constitutional convention voted overwhelmingly in favor of severing Australia's 210-year-old links to the British monarchy and making the country a republic. Many republicans who had favored election of a president by popular ballot compromised, and accepted a proposal by the Australian Republican Movement to have the president elected by parliament. And so, the national referendum was born.

# NEWS BRIEFS

**GUN CONTROL AND FIRE SAFETY.** No traveler should venture into Australia without brushing up on certain news stories that shook the nation. On April 28, 1996, at **Port Arthur,** Tasmania (see **Recent News,** p. 478), deranged citizen Martin Bryant shot and killed 35 strangers. The event fueled Australia's gun-control movement, and led to a much-touted plan to ban rapid-fire weapons. The issue is still a sensitive one, so be wary of any politically-charged remarks you make, especially in the Port Arthur area. In June 2000, a hostel in **Childers,** Queensland (see **Hostel Fire,** p. 348) burned down, resulting in the death of 15 backpackers. Though investigators have suspected arson was the cause of the fire at the old wooden pub, the tragedy has nevertheless drawn attention to the need for official guidelines—especially for strict fire regulations—over the hostel industry.

**ENVIRONMENT.** For the most part, Australia has shown an intense commitment to the preservation of its natural beauty, and the environment in general. In 1995, French President Jacques Chirac decided to sponsor **nuclear weapons testing** in the South Pacific. Protesters fire-bombed the French consulate in Perth, and demonstrations were held all over the country. In May 1997, the Australian government funded a $1.3 billion project to clean up the Murray and Darling Rivers, by selling **Telstra,** the previously state-owned telecommunications company. Recent protests about a **uranium mining** project on Aboriginal lands in Kakadu National Park, reveal two of the most important issues in contemporary Australian politics: race and the environment. The controversy has unsatisfied the question of native land rights and government intervention (see **Land Rights,** p. 17).

**ECONOMY.** Despite struggling with addressing the problem of racism, Australia for the most part has increasingly emphasized its role as a member of the Pacific economic and security community. International trade is vital to Australia's economy, particularly within the region; hence, the financial **Asian currency crisis** that began in the summer of 1997 has had damaging spillover effects. While Australia's economy has not collapsed, its dollar's value has spiraled downward and exports to Asia have declined.

**POLITICS. Pauline Hanson,** a former Queensland member of the federal parliament, has received a great deal of negative press for her inflammatory political platform as a reactionary conservative and the leader of the **One Nation Party.** The party supports isolationist policies, charges that Asian interests have corrupted Australian business, calls for strict limits on immigration, and challenges social programs for Aboriginals arguing that they represent unfair preferences. Hanson did not regain her seat in parliament in the general election at the end of 1998, and the One Nation Party has little power in the national legislature today. But some political analysts have predicted a resurgence in the party's political standing within the next few years, and nationwide polls still show a substantial population of supporters.

# THE PEOPLE

**POPULATION COMPOSITION.** The Commonwealth of Australia is home to 19.2 million people. Immigration has defined the narrative of the Australian population and 23% of the current population was born overseas. The **White Australia Policy** (see p. 5) created a fairly homogenous population. In the 1996 census, whites made up 95.2% of the population, Aboriginals less than 1%, and Asians, 4.3%. In recent years, Asian immigration has increased faster. **English** (better known as **'Strine;** see p. 673) is Australia's only national language and is spoken in 84% of Australian homes. Virtually 100% of the population is **literate.**

**RELIGION.** The religious composition of the population generally reflects the immigrant's backgrounds. Just over 70% of Australians declared themselves **Christians** in the 1996 census. Roman Catholics make up about 27% of the population, Anglicans account for 22%, and other Christian denominations make up 22%. **Non-Christian** religions comprise 3.5%, with Buddhism, Muslim, and Judaism leading the list. Roughly a quarter of Australians reject organized religion.

**DEMOGRAPHICS.** Australia's population density is 2.4 people per square kilometer. In comparison, the United States squeezes 28.1 people in an average square kilometer, and, for a particularly tight fit, the United Kingdom has 241.4 people per square kilometer. Eighty-five percent of Australians live in urban areas, and the suburbs are still growing. The vast majority live on or relatively near the coasts, particularly the east coast—some radical theories point to the vast, inhospitable desert in the center of the country.

# GOVERNMENT

**REPRESENTATION.** Since federation in 1901, Australia's government has been a constitutional monarchy in which federal and state governments share power. The British monarch is Australia's official head of state, and appoints a primarily ceremonial **Governor General Sir** (the current Governor General is **William Deane**) to exercise authority. The **Federal Parliament** is a bicameral legislature comprised of the **House of Representatives,** which is populated by a certain number of delegates from each state and territory based upon population, and the **Senate,** which is made up of 12 delegates from each state and two from each territory. Voter participation is nearly 90%, partly due to a system of compulsory voting, under which eligible voters who abstain can be fined. Voting is **preferential,** meaning that a voter must rank all the candidates in order of preference.

**LEGISLATION.** The Governor General appoints the leader of the majority party in the House of Representatives to the position of **Prime Minister.** The Prime Minister then acts as the head of the legislative body. Supreme judicial power rests in the **High Court,** which consists of seven judges. This body may declare legislative and executive actions unconstitutional. Most appointments and decisions under the jurisdiction of the Governor General, including **cabinet** members and high court judges are made with the advice of the Prime Minister. State governments are particularly strong and active, and are organized like the central government. Each state has its own Governor General, who is advised by a Premier and cabinet, and a legislative body to make laws. The federal government defers many duties to the state governments, and thus laws and policies can vary greatly from state to state.

**LABOR AND LIBERAL.** The two main parties in the federal parliament are the **Labor Party** and the **Liberal Party.** The Labor Party advocates the recognition of Aboriginal lands, socialist economic policies, and severing ties with the English monarchy in order to form an Australian republic. The party's former leader, **Paul Keating,** a staunch advocate for Australia's becoming a republic, was Australia's Prime Minister until 1996. That year's election brought a new Liberal majority, and **Kim Beazley** took over the reigns. The Liberal Party currently holds the most power in parliament, led by Prime Minister **John Howard.** Its platforms advocate free enterprise, conservative financial policies, and a strong relationship with the British Commonwealth. These two parties were most responsible for the debate over turning Australia into a republic (see p. 14).

**OTHER POLITICAL PARTIES.** Several smaller parties hold some weight in parliament, including the **National Party,** which often forms a coalition with the Liberals. The **Green Party** is very active in the **Tasmanian** state government and fights for liberal platforms and environmental concerns. The **Australian Democrats,** holding a moderate socialist agenda, have maintained a small faction in the Senate. The **One Nation Party** also had a controversial stint in Parliament (see **Current Events,** p. 14).

# ABORIGINAL RIGHTS

## GRIEVANCES

**STOLEN CHILDREN.** In the early 1800s, some missionaries began to try to make Aboriginals "employable" by converting them to Christianity and teaching them European skills and customs. Some of the program leaders decided that this was impossible if Aboriginal children were raised by Aboriginal parents, and the children were moved out of their homes to live with European families. This removal became state policy in New South Wales in 1883 and, astonishingly, was not officially discontinued until 1969. Aboriginals refer to these children as "taken" or "stolen," and it is estimated that there may be 100,000 people of Aboriginal descent today who do not know their families or the communities of their birth. Many are still seeking restitution or merely an overdue government apology.

**GROWING DISSENT.** The land rights issue has become a hot topic in Australia during the last few decades, as Aboriginal peoples demand land rights and compensation for the loss of land and the abuse they have endured. In 1933, the Aboriginal population of Australia hit a low of 73,828. By 1981 this had risen to just over 171,000, and the most recent census (1996) counted 353,000 Aboriginals, making up two percent of the total population. Finally, Aboriginals have gathered enough clout to band together and organize politically to fight for their rights. Some Australians of European descent—particularly those with mining and other industry interests—vehemently defend their control of the land. The courts and the government have taken up the issue, and legal developments and legislation continue to fuel the controversy.

## LAND RIGHTS

**NATIVE TITLE.** In 1966, the **Gurindji** Aboriginal people from the Northern Territory formed the first Aboriginal-owned and -operated cattle station, **Daguragu.** Although it took a long and difficult 20 years, the Gurindji were officially given permanent title to the land in a 1986 court decision. This Aboriginal legal success paved the way for the controversial **Mabo** decision in 1992. The Mabo case originated with a claim by Koiki (Eddie) Mabo, a Torres Straits Islander who successfully argued for the return of Murray Island to the Mer people (its original inhabitants) through the legal system. The High Court struck down the legal fiction of *terra nullius*, recognizing that the principle of native title—defined as the traditional Aboriginal right of access, use, or occupation of the land—had existed before the arrival of the British. The Mabo decision, however, left ambiguities as to where and to whom native title was applicable, and as to what exactly it meant. The **Native Title Act** of 1993 sought to clarify the decision by establishing guidelines to reassure farmers, miners, and conservatives that the Aboriginals could not claim Native Title to the whole continent. It also set out a means of compensating Aboriginals, placed limitations on future acts affecting Native Title land and waters, and created a Land Fund to help Aboriginal and Torres Strait Islanders acquire and manage land.

**ONGOING DISPUTES.** The effectiveness of the Act is still in doubt. Many believe that it was a token gesture, granting few substantial new rights to Aboriginals and leaving many of the ambiguities in place. Several amendments have been proposed, partly in response to the issues emerging from the 1996 **Wik** case. In December of 1996, the Wik and Thayorre peoples of western Cape York obtained a ruling that a **pastoral lease** (where the Crown rents land to a farmer for a long, long time) does not necessarily require Aboriginals to leave who are living on that land. In fact, both farmer and Aboriginals can claim rights to the same land under Australian law. A pastoral lease can co-exist with Native Title. In the case of conflict, however, the former takes precedence, thus limiting the practical implementation of Native Title throughout the 42% of Australia that is under pastoral lease.

**FURTHER SETBACKS.** Following the Court's decision, the government developed a **10-point plan on Native Title** that eliminated Native Title in certain circumstances. The **Native Title Amendment Bill of 1997** incorporates this plan and has been resoundingly condemned by Aboriginal leaders and their supporters. Other bills related to Aboriginal land rights are currently under consideration, and new cases continue to come before the High Court. Each bill attempts to clarify the one before, but it is clear that the Aboriginals' struggle for land rights is far from over. Some Aboriginal leaders used the Sydney Olympics to attract international attention to their grievances. For updated information on Aboriginal political events and Native Title claims, check out the web site of the Aboriginal and Torres Strait Islander Commission at www.atsic.gov.au, and that of the Australian Institute for Australian and Torres Strait Islander Studies at www.aiatsis.gov.au.

**RECONCILIATION.** Indigenous people continue to experience poorer health, limited employment opportunities, and educational disadvantages. Aboriginals too often face prejudice when trying to rent a home, find a job, thumb a cab, and other everyday activities which many citizens take for granted. Official efforts have been made to eliminate the prejudice including the **Racial Discrimination Act of 1975,** and there has been progress towards recognizing the culture, history, and rights of the Aboriginals. In 1991 the Council for Aboriginal Reconciliation was established to help foster a national dialogue on reconciliation. At a recent council event, Corroboree 2000, former Prime Minister Keating claimed: "Much more needs to be done for, with and by Aboriginal and Torres Strait Islander Australians to repair the damages of the past and to set a better course for the future. But saying sorry is the gesture of integrity; the fundamental and necessary first step." But as of August 2000, the current Prime Minister has yet to make an official apology.

# CULTURE

## ARTS

Australia is a young nation and its artistic identity is still growing. Historically, European arts exerted a strong influence on non-Aboriginal Australian artists and writers, and the artists responded by defining an Australian identity and experience. Many Australian artists focus particularly on their relationship with their unique—some might say solitary—landscape and climate. Though modern artists are branching out to explore new themes, the most popular national arts are still those that depict traditional themes, sustain an Australian mythology, or explore some facet of the nation's cultural and natural heritage.

## THE ORAL TRADITION

**THE FIRST FORMS.** Even before Europeans settled in Australia, the **Aboriginal** people developed a rich **oral tradition** that was the precursor to written literature. By mixing song, dance, and the spoken word, the Aboriginals could pass on traditional stories and religious expressions through generations. Although modern writers like **Sally Morgan** in her book *My Place* and **Paddy Roe** in *Gularabulu* have tried to capture some of this oral tradition on paper, the artistry of the original storytellers may never be fully recreated.

**HISTORICAL AND EARLY WORKS.** During the early nineteenth century, the Australian literary world began to expand through the creative efforts of newly settled Europeans. Most of the works were in the form of short written histories and accounts of pioneer life. A few writers wove themes of convict exile and settler life into their poetry. **Barron Field,** an author with a more fertile mind than his arid name suggests, wrote the first volume of original Australian poetry entitled *First Fruits of Australian Poetry.* **Adam Lindsay Gordon** was a popular poet during the

1870s and the author of *Bush Ballads and Galloping Rhymes*. His works evoked Australian camaraderie and stoicism.

Australian literature found a wider audience with the **The Bulletin,** a literary journal founded in Sydney in 1880. Thought to be the most famous and significant of its kind, it started a tradition of publishing new and original works, encouraging local artists and writers with a regular outlet for their work to promote **nationalism.** *The Bulletin's* contributions to literature continued through the 20th century, but as its politics became increasingly conservative and anachronistic, sales fell. The journal became *The Bulletin with Newsweek* under new ownership, but its significance has faded in the past three decades. Aussie pride lives on, and numerous other literary magazines have emerged, catering to a wider variety of genres.

**BUSH BALLADS, POETRY, AND SHORT WORKS.** Possibly the first uniquely Australian literature was the **bush ballad,** a form of poetry frequently published in *The Bulletin* that celebrated the working man and the superiority of life in the bush to urban life. The most famous of these ballads is **Banjo Paterson's** *Waltzing Matilda*, a song often considered even more representative of the independent Australian pride than the national anthem (see p. 228). Despite the popularity of the ballad, a strong division existed between popular and intellectual poetry; intellectual poets were often seen as too pseudo-European. At the end of the nineteenth century, some poets began to shift their focus from the landscape of bush ballads to more urban concepts. Early in the twentieth century, **C.J. Dennis** began to explore the Australian city lifestyle. More recently, **Judith Wright** has led a movement towards a re-examination of colonial literature, establishing a continuity of identity with the poets of the past. In this vein, **A.D. Hope's** *Australia* condemns the country's insularity but still expresses hope for the future.

The **short story** was popularized with stories of life in the bush as well. **Henry Lawson** and **Barbara Baynton** are two writers who captured the essence of this experience. Many short story writers still strive to define the relationship between person and landscape, and their work represents a search for cultural identity and historical continuity. In recent years the prose style has diversified with increased overseas influences, and short stories today explore social issues and express the realities of urban life.

# MODERN LITERATURE

**THE AUSTRALIAN NOVEL.** Modern written literature has a complicated history, in part because many of the early novelists spent most of their adult lives outside Australia looking in. **Henry Savory** wrote the first Australian novel, *Quintus Servinton*, in 1831. Like other early novelists, he struggled with the mindset of most Australians accustomed to a life shadowed by the British penal system. The convict experience had a profound presence in Australian literature. Perhaps the first real classic, **Marcus Clarke's** *His Natural Life* (1869), was centered around this theme. The fictional Australian character was respected for his independent ruggedness and simultaneously misunderstood and condemned for his rough manners. The most famous work of Australian literature is *Voss* (1957), by Nobel Prize-winning author **Patrick White.** A love story about the idiosyncrasies of Australia—the vacancy at the center, life on the perimeter, urban residents' (particularly male) obsession with the bush—*Voss* was the basis for a play and an opera of the same name. In fact, it is hard to believe that *Voss* focuses on Australia 150 years ago since the same concepts still fascinate authors and readers today.

**GENDER AND ETHNICITY.** The tradition and misogyny in early bush ballads and short stories provoked a conflict between male and female writers in the twentieth century. Among the better-known female writers is **Miles Franklin,** author of *My Brilliant Career* (1901), a book influenced by her rejection of traditional female roles as wife and mother to work as a journalist and feminist in Sydney. Today's names in literature still introspectively examine the meaning of being Australian, but the meat of their work is increasingly varied. **Peter Carey** is best known as the author of *Bliss* (1981), a humorous exploration of the Australian national character. **Tim Winton**, a Western Australian short-story writer and novelist, writes about the everyday lives of the Westralians. Both Carey and Winton write with concern for the effects of colonialism on the Australian environment and people. The attention given to "ethnic" writing, Aboriginal literature, and song-cycles has also been growing in the twentieth century. A growing number of **Aboriginal writers** are beginning to gain national recognition. For samplings of contemporary Aboriginal literature, check out the anthology *Paperbark*.

## POPULAR MUSIC

Australia's early colonial period relied heavily on British folk music, with lively fiddle and drum bushdances held in cleared-out sheep-shearing sheds. Popular music of the last few decades was greatly influenced first by British rock and later by American New Wave and Alternative music. More recently, some Aboriginal sounds have come in vogue. You can now find virtually any music from around the world in Sydney or Melbourne. Australia's youth radio, **JJJ (Triple J),** plays a lot of contemporary local music, and is always promoting new acts.

**ORIGINS.** US soldiers brought big band jazz to Australia during WWI, and the American music has found increasingly firm footing. Don Burrows and Graeme Bell were inspired leaders of big and small groups in the 60s, establishing an **Australian jazz** scene that gained mainstream attention with the likes of too-hip singer Vince Jones, instrumental wizard James Morrison, and genius pianist Paul Gabowsky in the 80s. Each capital city has a flourishing live scene, nourished by intensively creative jazz programs in the conservatories of Perth and Sydney and the Victorian College of the Arts in Melbourne, all excellent places to look for music and musicians.

**ROCK AND ROLL.** The Australian pop of the late 50s was epitomized by rocker **Johnny O'Keefe** whose sound, inspired by the musical blend emerging from the American south, took the country by storm. Television hit Australia at the same time as rock and roll, creating a booming youth culture based around shows like **Australian Bandstand.** A lively folk music scene, heavily influenced by groups like Peter, Paul, and Mary, thrived in the 50s and 60s, but few names gained international recognition.

**HARD ROCK AND NEW WAVE.** In the late 70s, **AC/DC** hit the charts with blues-influenced heavy metal grown out of pub culture. But after making it big, the group moved its headquarters to Europe. They are no longer considered truly Australian (especially since they were originally Scottish immigrants). Refusing to emulate American and English sounds, **Cold Chisel, Goanna,** and **Australian Crawl** gained local fame with Aussie-themed hits that still get radio airtime.

The 80s saw the advent of bands like **Midnight Oil,** a group born out of hard rock pub culture and known for its support of social causes. While many popular Australian bands never managed to sell their sound outside of Australia, there are a few notable exceptions. **Men At Work** came from the land down under with a Vegemite sandwich to break into the American music scene for a short while. Following in their quickly disappearing footsteps, **Crowded House** briefly became a well-known international band at the height of New Wave. **INXS** became one of the most successful Australian bands, but a recent planned comeback tour was cut short by the suicide of lead singer Michael Hutchence.

Today's Australian music is very diverse, influenced by grunge and world music. Recently, **Savage Garden** flew to the moon and back, leaping onto the international pop scene, while **Nick Cave and the Bad Seeds** carry a fair-sized European following. Both **Kylie Minogue** and **Natalie Imbruglia** graduated from the Australian TV show *"Neighbours"* to take a shot at pop music.

**BUSH ROCK AND COUNTRY.** Aboriginal groups have just recently entered the mainstream music culture. **Yothu Yindi,** a band out of Arnhem Land in the Northern Territory, has combined traditional Aboriginal musical styles with dance music and rock, and respects Midnight Oil's tradition of using the spotlight to further political causes. Other similarly politicized Aboriginal "bush rock" groups are the **Coloured Stones,** the **Warumpi Band,** and **Archie Roach,** whose country-influenced tunes reflect on his background as a "stolen child" and the problems of Aboriginals in urban Australia.

Country music is big in Australia, and is celebrated at an annual **Country Music Festival** in Tamworth, the "country capital" of Australia (see p. 153). The music takes its cues from its American counterpart, but is strongly influenced by the peculiarities of Australian rural life. **Slim Dusty** is the style's founding father, having sold over three million albums since he began songwriting at age 12.

# VISUAL ARTS

**ABORIGINAL PAINTING.** The nation's original visual art, although its intent was not exclusively artistic, was educational, spiritual, and functional. Before the 1970s, public perception of Aboriginal art was restricted to "bark paintings"— paintings on strips of eucalyptus that were traditionally ceremonial and generally destroyed during or after the ceremony. After becoming collector's items in the 1940s, bark paintings have since been widely reproduced. During the 1970s, other forms of Aboriginal art, such as mural art, body painting, and rock painting, were rediscovered and became popular, partly because of government support. Among Aboriginal artists today, there exists a division between **contemporary traditional art,** which focuses primarily on Aboriginal culture and customs, and **urban Aboriginal art,** which focuses on themes connected to general life experience, using western art techniques and avoiding images that have ritual significance. In the 80s and 90s, contemporary traditional art has achieved more international popularity, probably because it appears more "authentic" to the rest of the world.

**ART IN MODERN TIMES.** Visual arts of the modern era began, much like other arts, with a search for Australian identity. Especially in the work of early Australian impressionists such as **Tom Roberts** (1856-1931), whose *Break Away* depicts the red, dry, dusty land of the cattle station, and **Frederick McCubbin** (1850-1917), whose *Lost Child* portrays the thin forests of smoky green gum trees. Later landscape paintings by artists like **Hans Heysen, Robert Juniper,** and **Russell Drysdale** focused on similar natural features, with a greater variety of style, color, and mood. **Sidney Nolan's** series on Ned Kelly illustrates the folk hero's exploits, final capture, and execution. Completed between 1945 and 1954, these pieces are on display in Australia's National Galleries (see **Canberra,** p. 87 and **Glenrowan,** p. 590). Nolan has also done emotional and provocative series on the Eureka Stockade, Gallipoli and drought.

**OTHER CONTEMPORARY ARTISTS.** Other prominent contemporary artists include **John Perceval,** expressionist **Albert Tucjer,** abstract artist **John Colburn,** and **Arthur Boyd,** who depicts popular figures of Australian legend. Younger Australian painters such as **Mandy Martin, Susan Norrie,** and **Neil Taylor** are flooding the scene with eclectic collections and explorations of post-industrial Australia.

# FILM

**"EARLY" WORKS.** Although responsible for producing the world's first feature length film—*The Story of the Kelly Gang* in 1906—the Australian cinema industry was fairly inactive until the 1970s when the federal government created the **Australian Film Development Corporation** (later called the **Australian Film Commission**) to fund original Australian films. In the last few decades, the rest of the world has begun giving greater respect to Australian talent in the film industry. The **Australian Film School** opened in 1973 and began training the likes of **Gillian Armstrong, Paul Cox,** and **Bruce Beresford.** In 1976, **Peter Weir's** acclaimed *Picnic at Hanging Rock* hit the international scene, followed by *Gallipoli* in 1980 (which starred Australian-born and bred superstar **Mel Gibson**). Other popularly recognized and appreciated Australian films of this time period include **Phillip Noyce's** *Newsfront* and **Gillian Armstrong's** *My Brilliant Career.* The 80s brought the *Mad Max* trilogy as well as the *The Year of Living Dangerously.* Australia has sent a spate of hits in the past ten years that include *Strictly Ballroom, Death in Brunswick, Muriel's Wedding, The Adventures of Priscilla, Queen of the Desert* and *Shine.* The same Australian creative team that produced *Strictly Ballroom* also produced the well-received modern interpretation of *Romeo and Juliet.*

**RECENT HITS.** Several Australian movie directors and actors have found international success recently. **Geoffrey Rush,** after being nominated for a best actor Oscar for Australian-made *Shine,* endeared himself to audiences in *Shakespeare in Love.* Aussie-lass **Cate Blanchett** recently starred in *Elizabeth,* and **Peter Weir** directed *The Truman Show.* Sydney was the prominent backdrop for last summer's blockbuster *Mission: Impossible 2* starring Tom Cruise who, of course, is married to everybody's favorite glossy Aussie **Nicole Kidman. George Lucas,** the producer of *Star Wars* has chosen Australia as the film set for parts two and three of the new prequel trilogy. In the Australian spirit of the independent macho man, **Russell Crowe** played a tough cop in *L.A. Confidential,* a courageous witness in the critically acclaimed *The Insider,* and the head-hewing title character in *Gladiator.* The only Aussie who can beat that is *Braveheart* himself.

# FOOD AND DRINK

## THE BASICS

**WHAT ARE YOU EATING?** Australians eat four meals a day: breakfast, lunch, dinner and beer. Aussies hardly ever eat their **"brekkie"** out, and most restaurants don't open until noon except in the larger cities. The evening meal is sometimes called **"tea,"** but shouldn't be confused with the diminutive British version; it's the largest meal of the day. Beware of ordering only an **"entree,"** an appetizer in Australia. A **"cuppa"**—tea or coffee—should tide you over between meals. The pub is the place to go to relax and grab a quickie after work. And whatever the country may lack in gourmet cuisine it makes up for in delectable beer (see p.24). **Vegetarians** shouldn't go hungry despite Australia's meat-hungry reputation. Trendy urban eateries frequently cater to special diets, but traditional establishments rarely will. **Tipping** in Australian restaurants and pubs is rare and never expected.

**WHERE AND HOW TO EAT.** As is to be expected from the island-continent, **seafood** is a highlight. From the British come cholesterol-heavy **pub meals,** such as steak and eggs, and the Aussie institution of **fish-and-chips.** A popular meal for families on Friday nights, the fish is fried, battered, rolled in newspaper, and served with British-style chips (thick french fries). **Chook** (chicken) is often substituted for fish to create much-needed variety. **"Chippers"** are the quintessential Aussie eating establishments, and most specialize in **takeaway** (take-out).

---

**KEEP YOUR KIWIS OFF!** Sweet and white, creamy and light, **pavlova** is, was, and forever shall be *the* Australian dessert. Some consider the ability to make this chewy meringue covered in whipped cream and fresh fruit a prerequisite for marriage—if one's spouse can't make a decent pav, he or she just isn't fit to bring little Aussies into the world. The term "pavlova" is of debatable origin. Rather, its origin has been debated. Let's set the record straight. The delectable dessert came into existence in 1935 when the chef of Perth's Esplanade Hotel, Bert Sachse, decided to create a new dish in honor of their famous Russian guest: the ballerina Anna Pavlova. Nevertheless, some poor misguided souls on neighboring New Zealand seem to believe that *they* invented the dessert. Utter hogwash. (For the deluded Kiwi myth of pavlova's origins, see *Let's Go: New Zealand 2001*).

# AUSTRALIAN "CUISINE"

**WATCH WHAT YOU EAT.** Australia's origin as a convict colony didn't endow the country with a subtle palate. **Meat pies** are the ultimate Australian fare. Inexplicably popular, these doughy shells contain meat of dubious origin and often a mushy vegetable filling. Most consumers douse them in **tomato sauce** (a sweet ketchup-like concoction) to disguise the taste. Let us say that again, tomato sauce is not ketchup. Use Australian condiments sparingly until you are familiar with them. Aussie mustard delivers a horseradishy kick, and the infamous **Vegemite**, a yeasty by-product of the beer-brewing process, should be scraped thinly rather than spread liberally. Or is it the other way around? You'll just have to try both.

**SPICE UP YOUR DIET.** Australia may suffer from a reputation of having a notoriously dull national cuisine, but it has been remarkably successful at adding layers of flavor with each wave of immigration. Recent European and Middle Eastern arrivals have spiced up Australian menus with Greek souvlaki, Italian pasta, and Lebanese tabbouleh. The cheapest way to sample these flavors is at any of numerous takeaway joints. Influxes of immigrants from Asian and Pacific countries have added further variety. Chinese dishes first arrived with Chinese gold prospectors in the 1850s and have so infiltrated the menu that even their names have taken a uniquely Australian twist: **"dim sims"** are Australian *dim sum*. Japanese, Thai, Malay, and Vietnamese restaurants also are abundant, particularly in Darwin and cosmopolitan centers in the southeast.

**NOT UNTIL YOU FINISH DINNER.** Australia has plentiful pickings when it comes to fruit for desserts; its tropical north supports fruit industries that other western countries can only fantasize about. Travelers from fruit-deprived countries will encounter exotic offerings such as custard apples, lychees, passionfruit, star fruit, coconuts, mangoes, and pineapples. Queensland is the main fruit-producing region. Of the typical prepared desserts, there's the ubiquitous **lamington**—a coconut-covered chunk of pound cake dipped in chocolate, and the festive **pavlova** meringue (see **Keep Your Kiwis Off!**, opposite).

# BUSH TUCKER

**THE REAL THING.** Coastal Aboriginals have eaten crayfish, **yabbies** (freshwater shrimp), and fish for centuries, and the first English settlers rapidly followed suit. But in the harsh environments of the bush, Aboriginal foragers exploited food resources that early colonists found a little too unorthodox to stomach. **Witchetty grubs** are the most well-known of the bush foods that make first-timers recoil in horror. If you want to sample **goanna** or **ants,** however, you might have to catch dinner yourself or join one of the Red Centre tours that feature real bush tucker.

**FOR THE TOURISTS.** These days the appeal of bush tucker has grown and is no longer limited to the adventurous and brave of heart (read: tourist). Australia has recently discovered a taste for is own "exotic" indigenous food. And "bush tucker" is the new urban catch phrase. Each year, more restaurants spring up offering hip urban menus that incorporate aboriginal wild foods like bunya nuts, Kakadu plums, and wild rosella flowers with specialty meats such as kangaroo filet, crocodile meat, Northern Territory buffalo, and wild magpie geese.

**TASTES LIKE CHICKEN** Kangaroo has a tangy slam to it, not unlike grilled liver. The meat is tough and demands a thick peanut sauce. Crocodile is indifferent: bleached and as tasteless as virgin sand, it must be regarded from a respectful distance. Buffalo, with its wandering edges of gristle and chewy texture, is sanguine and can only be penetrated under the spell of soy sauce. Emu has a curious flavor that becomes clear to the tongue when presented with pineapple, or a more vigorous fruit like mango. Otherwise it is tasteless and gray.

AUSTRALIA

## MORE THAN JUST DRINKIN'

**COFFEE.** In Australia, ordering drinks is an art that takes time to perfect. Nothing better illustrates this than ordering a simple cup of coffee. In fact, ordering "just coffee" is nearly impossible. Though they are a long way from Italy, Australia's major cities harbor a cappucino culture that can deliver caffeine into your bloodstream in more ways than there are letters in cappucino. If you need some help getting what you want, see the guide to **Coffee Confusion** on p. 114. And whatever you do, don't let any Aussie know that you needed to ask for directions.

**BEER.** Let's move on to the more important skill of choosing a beer. For many, a close association (if not love) exists between Australia and **beer,** and with good reason. Australia produces some of the world's best brews, and Australians over the legal drinking age of 18 consume it readily (we can't speak for those under the legal age). Some Australians despise **Fosters,** which owes its international name-recognition to saturation advertising. Instead, loyalty goes to the state brew. Queensland makes **XXXX** ("four-ex"), but **Victoria Bitter,** known as "VB," is much better. **Cooper's Ale,** from South Australia, is a terrific drop-brewed beer in the bottle (roll the bottle back and forth for 30 seconds to mix the sediment left in every bottle) and promises a different taste with each sip. While many beers have a relatively high alcoholic content (around 5%), there has been a recent trend toward "light" beers, which have less alcohol (not fewer calories). **Strongbow,** Australia's favorite cider, is quietly gaining popularity in pubs as a potent and tasty alternative, but many Aussie blokes wouldn't be seen dead holding a stubbie of it (the favorite excuse is "I was holding it for my girlfriend"). Beer unequivocally prevails. The best place to share a coldie with your mates is the omnipresent Aussie **pub.** Traditional payment etiquette is the **shout,** in which drinking mates alternate rounds. If the beach is more your style, throw a **slab** (24 containers of beer) in the **Esky** (ice chest). For more beer terminology, consult the **glossary,** p. 673.

**WINE.** Simply put, Australian **wines** rival those the world over. Overseas export started soon after the first vineyards began to produce wine in the early 1800s, and the industry has gained renown after a post-WWII influx of European talent. The **Hunter Valley** (see p. 150), the **Barossa** and **Clare Valleys** (see p. 440), the **Swan** and **Margaret Rivers** (see p. 632), and the **Derwent** and **Tamar Valleys** (see p. 482), possess some of the best Aussie vineyards. Many cafés and low-end restaurants advertise that they are **BYO,** or "bring your own." Though typically not licensed to serve alcohol, these establishments permit patrons to furnish their own bottle of wine with the meal and charge only a small **corkage fee,** if anything.

# SPORT

**WHERE TO FIND IT.** Australians take sport very seriously. Seriously. The 1956 Melbourne Olympics inaugurated national television broadcasting in Australia, and televisions in public places have been tuned to sporting events ever since. While the big event on everyone's calendar in late 2000 was the Sydney Olympics, the national team-sports melodrama extends year-round. You can't walk into a bar without a sports event from somewhere in Oz on TV. Unfortunately, much of it revolves around gambling (see **Pokies vs. The People,** p. 125). In winter, Western Australia, South Australia, and Victoria catch **footy fever** for **Australian Rules Football,** while New South Wales and Queensland traditionally follow **rugby.** In summer, **cricket** is the spectator sport of choice across the nation. Throughout the year, star Aussie Rules football players and top cricketers enjoy hero status similar to that accorded baseball players in the US or soccer players in Europe. For good insight into Australian sport culture, tune in to H. G. Nelson and Roy Slaven's Sunday afternoon Triple-J radio show *This Sporting Life*.

**WHAT IS IT?** Even if you missed the Olympics, cricket seems eternally confusing, or Aussie Rules football is still incomprehensible, just join in the crowds, cheer for the home team, and remember the old adage that many an Australian sports fan takes to heart: **It's all fun and games until somebody loses an eye—then it's sport.**

# CRICKET

**INTERNATIONAL MATCHES.** The uninitiated may have trouble making sense of a sport where people can "bowl a maiden over of five flippers and a googly," but visitors won't be able to avoid the enthusiasm. Two teams of 11 players face off in a contest that can last anywhere from an afternoon to five days. Each summer, international cricket overshadows the national competition. A "test match" is not just a scrimmage; it is the most lengthy and serious form of international cricket. In 1877, Australia's cricket team headed to England for its first international test against the mother country, and, surprisingly, the colonials won. The Australians, as a shocked English reporter wrote, had "taken off with the ashes" of English cricket. Ever since then, the England and Australian Test teams have been in noble competition for **"the Ashes"** (the trophy is actually a small, symbolic urn).

**NATIONAL MATCHES.** In December and January, different international teams arrive for a **full tour,** consisting of five test matches, one each in Melbourne, Sydney, Perth, Adelaide, and Brisbane. The five-day tests are accompanied by smaller, titillating one-day matches, and are over by February, in time for the country to turn its attention to national cricket and the Sheffield Shield finals in March.

# AUSTRALIAN RULES FOOTBALL

**HOW TO PLAY.** Good question. In Victoria, South Australia, and Western Australia, the **Australian Football League (AFL)** teams fill the winter void that the end of the cricket season might otherwise leave. Played on cricket ovals, the game was originally designed (if there is any actual design involved) to keep cricket players in shape in the off-season. Teams attempt to get the red leather ball from one end of the field to the other and kick it through the opposing team's posts to score. Each team of 18 players defends three sets of posts for four 20-minute quarters: six points are earned for scoring in the middle goal, and one point for reaching either side goal. Confused yet? Just wait until you actually see a match.

**HOW TO WIN.** The basic move in AFL is the **punt,** used for both passing and scoring; good players can punt the ball over 70m. The best move to make, though, is the **mark.** If a player can catch the ball on the kick before it bounces, he is entitled to unobstructed possession of that ball. Consequently, just after a kick, the players all pack together and run, jump, and soar (though not gracefully) under and over each other, in an effort to snatch the ball from the sky. The AFL grand final, in early September, is a marvelous spectacle at the home of Australian sport, the **MCG (Melbourne Cricket Ground,** see p. 537).

# RUGBY

**RUGBY UNION.** According to legend, **rugby** was born one glorious day in 1823 when one inspired (or perhaps frustrated) student in Rugby, England, picked up a soccer ball and ran it into the goal. Since then, rugby has evolved (or devolved) into an intricately punishing game, with two variants: **rugby union** involving 15-man teams, and **rugby league** with 13-man teams. Despite the international reputation of the national union team, the **Wallabies,** rugby union sometimes carries a muted following. Since they defeated France to win the World Cup in 1999, though, rugby union has grown in popularity. Larger matches such as the **Super 12** tournament and **Tri-nation** series (Australia, South Africa, and New Zealand) often pack stadiums and pubs alike. Part of the Tri-nation series, the **Bledisloe Cup** perpetuates a healthy animosity with Australia's down-under cousin, New Zealand.

**RUGBY LEAGUE.** Rugby league attracts a much larger following, especially in New South Wales and Queensland. The national league competition culminates in the **National Rugby League (NRL) final** in September. The only match that comes close to the intensity or popularity of the NRL final is the **State of Origin** series in June, when Queensland takes on New South Wales. Both games promise a mix of blood, mud, and plenty of drinking. For all the rugby action you can handle (if you're tough enough), check out www.rugbyworld.com.

## OTHER SPORT

Australia sport is not cricket shots or footy marks. Melbourne hosts one of tennis' Grand Slam events, the **Australian Open,** each January. Grassy tennis courts, bowling greens, and golf courses pepper the cities coast-to-coast. Most towns also have a horse racing track, and on the first Tuesday in November, the entire country stops to watch jockeys jockey for the prestigious **Melbourne Cup.** On Boxing Day, even as the Melbourne cricket Test gets underway, half of Australia's amateur sailing community fills Sydney Harbour with billowing white sails to begin the **Sydney-to-Hobart yacht race,** the highlight in a full calendar of water sports. Australia is, of course, famous for its **surfing,** which for some is a competitive sport in addition to a great way to spend a summer morning. People attempt to surf virtually everywhere, but especially up and down the East Coast.

# ENVIRONMENT

Simply put, Australia has benefited from millions of years of isolation on a very large island. The sheltered existence has helped breed some of the world's most peculiar plants and animals. When plants and animals landed on a continent nearly devoid of competition, they grew fast from a limited number of ancestral groups. However, Australia's inevitable contact with the outside has presented an enormous challenge to its unique biology. The introduction of animals and colonization by Europeans upset Australia's delicate ecology. It is estimated that 13 species of mammals and one species of bird have already become extinct since European settlement. In recent years, environmental policy has begun to recognize the importance of protecting Australia's precious biodiversity.

## PLANTS

**STRANGE GROWTHS IN SECRET PLACES.** There is one plant you are guaranteed to find in Australia. Dominating forests from coast to coast, the **eucalypts,** also known as **gum trees,** amaze biologists with their successful adaptation to diverse environments, taking on many different shapes and sizes across the continent. The majestic **karri** soars to over 50m in ancient stands along well-watered valleys, while the **mallee** gum tends to grow in stunted copses across scrubland, like that of western Victoria. The characteristically bulging trunk and splayed branches of the **boab** mark the horizon, particularly in the arid Kimberley in Western Australia. In the drier areas of the southeast, a common species of the **acacia** tree (which has over 600 species), known as the **golden wattle,** is distinguished by its fragrant flowers. Perhaps the most unusual—and most rare—tree is the **Wollemi pine.** The pine was discovered by scientists a few years ago, who had previously thought that the species was extinct (see **Wollemi National Park,** p. 148).

**BRING ME A SHRUBBERY.** Gums aren't the only plant dominating the landscape. Other regulars in the bush and coastal thickets include **banksias, tea trees,** and **grevillias.** Feathery and almost pine-like in appearance, **casuarinas** also exist in multiple habitats. In temperate, rain-fed stretches of Victoria and Tasmania, valleys of tall, dinosaur-era **tree ferns** are dwarfed by towering **mountain ash,** the tallest flowering plant in all of nature. A remarkable feature found along parts of Australia's tropical coasts, the **mangrove** has adapted readily to its unfavorable environment, and stilt-like trunks cling tenaciously to the briny mud of alluvial swamps. Meanwhile, Australia has wide swaths of land that grow nary a tree. The arid outback is dominated by dense tufts of **spinifex** grasses. Another common plant is the **saltbush,** a hearty shrub that grows in soil too salty for other plants and that has been pivotal in converting harsh habitats to livestock pastures.

**FLOWER POWER.** Although Australia has a tough plant life, wildflowers are abundant in more fertile areas. Western Australia is home to **swamp bottlebrush, kangaroo paw,** and **Ashby's banksia,** along with nearly 10,000 other species. Yellow and pink **everlastings** cover fields across the country, to the delight of casual wild-flower viewers, but rare **spider orchids** hidden in the forests reveal themselves only to the most dogged of investigators. The **Sturt pea** adds a distinctive splash of red and black to the inland deserts of South Australia and Western Australia. Elsewhere, **orchids** and **begonias** provide extra visual garnish.

# ANIMALS

When most people think of Australia, they picture kangaroos and cuddly koalas. But the country has much more to offer than those tourist symbols. Between 200,000 and 300,000 species of animals call Australia home. While most of these are insects, larger and more exotic creatures make the island continent their breeding ground. Marsupials, of course, are the stars of the Australian menagerie. Marsupials had few mammalian competitors on the continent and inhabited many different ecosystems. Thus, early naturalists named marsupials by the habitat in which other mammals would be found; the koala is not a bear; the marsupial "rat" is not a rat; and the marsupial "cat" and "mole" are more closely related to each other than their given names would suggest.

**KANGAROOS.** Bounding about everywhere, kangaroos are synonymous with Australia and, like most indigenous Australian mammals, they are marsupials. At any time after the age of two, a female kangaroo is likely to have one offspring in the womb, one living in the pouch, and one making occasional visits to the pouch. This style of reproduction, combined with the kangaroo's ability to suspend gestation for up to two years, ensures survival in harsh desert environments, but also results in a markedly lower life span for females. Kangaroos have thrived on the fringes of human communities since colonization, leading the Australian government to conduct an annual program of kangaroo culling.

Kangaroos travel in groups known as mobs, which can have over 20 members. The many species are in two basic groups: grey kangaroos and the larger and more aggressive red kangaroos. Male red 'roos can grow to be 3m long, nose to tail, and are capable of propelling themselves nearly 9m at a single bound. Contrary to popular myth, kangaroos do not feed marmalade sandwiches to small bears or send their young out to play with tree-dwelling pigs and tail-bouncing tigers. The kangaroo's look-alike cousin, the wallaby, is another common outback critter. Other native marsupials include wombats, possums, bandicoots, and quolls.

**KOALAS.** Australia's other most-loved marsupials live on and among the leaves of certain eucalypt trees. Sleeping an average 18 out of every 24 hours and existing on a diet made up exclusively of the intoxicating and semi-toxic eucalyptus leaves (with the nutrition equivalent of cardboard), the koala lives every college student's dream. It has little energy for hunting, gathering, or even moving. Seeing a koala is often just a matter of being patient enough to scan the treetops for a familiar fur-ball, or impatient enough to find the nearest zoo or nature preserve.

**REPTILES.** The most fearsome reptiles, saltwater crocodiles **("salties")** actually live in both brine and freshwater and grow to lengths of 7m. For a primer on discriminating between the salty and its less threatening freshwater relative—and avoiding becoming croc fodder—take a look at **Freshies and Salties,** p. 255. In addi-

---

**I'M-A GOANNA GET YA!** Goannas are large lizards, growing in length up to 3 or 4 meters. Should you encounter one, the old maxim applies: it's more afraid of you than the other way 'round. Be aware, however, that goannas protect themselves from danger by scurrying up trees, and if a scared goanna comes running toward you (away from whatever scared it), there's the off-chance that it will try to seek refuge on you! Crouch down or lie flat to avoid being climbed. Once your pursuer realizes you're not a tree and offer no protection, it should leave you alone.

tion to its crocodiles, Australia's reptiles include aggressive **goannas** (see **I'm-A Goanna Get Ya!,** below), and a wide array of **poisonous snakes,** including the **taipan, smooth snake, tiger snake, brown snake,** and the **death adder** (for advice on what to do in the case of an adverse meeting with one of these **nasties,** see p. 54).

**BIRDS.** Outshining Australia's mammals in vividness of color is the continent's tremendous diversity of **birds.** The **emu** is related to other flightless birds such as the African ostrich and the extinct moa of New Zealand. Flightless hordes of **little** (or **fairy**) **penguins** can be spotted at sites on the south coast, where they wade ashore each night. Australia's flight-endowed birds include noisy flocks of **galahs,** colorful **rainbow lorikeets,** and large **cassowaries.** Songs and poems have immortalized the unmistakable laugh of the **kookaburra.** Both **crimson rosellas** and **cockatoos** are common in the southeast.

**MONOTREMES.** Australia's list of peculiar mammals does not end with marsupials. Two families of **monotremes,** or egg-laying mammals, call Australia home. **Echidnas** are small ant-eaters that resemble porcupines with protruding snouts. When threatened, the echidna buries itself in the ground, leaving only long spines exposed. Strangest of all, the **platypus** sports a melange of zoological features: the bill of a duck, the fur of an otter, the tail of a beaver, and webbed claws. So outrageous did this anatomy seem to colonists that early naturalists refused to consider stuffed specimens real (see **Magnificent Mammalian Monotreme,** p. 28).

**MEGAFAUNA.** Giant marsupials once roamed the landscape of prehistoric Australia. Now extinct, these megafauna included towering relatives of kangaroos called diprotodons (not Optimus Prime's nemesis). The megafauna died off soon after the arrival of humans, due to hunting or climatic changes (see **Cenozoic Megafauna,** p. 241). The **thylacine,** or **Tasmanian tiger,** is a more recent loss. Resembling a large wolf with stripes, the predator was driven to the edge of extinction by competition with dingoes, then hunted by white settlers who feared for livestock. One infamous marsupial carnivore has survived, however. Fierce in temperament, **Tasmanian devils** are nocturnal scavengers. They also hunt small prey and have been known to kill livestock with their powerful jaws (see **Marsupials from Hell,** p. 486).

**PESTS.** Humans have been responsible for the introduction of animals to Australia since prehistoric times, and many are now considered pests. The **dingo,** a lithe, wild canine with a vicious bite but no bark, crossed the Timor Sea with ancestors of Aboriginal populations several thousand years ago. The creatures mainly hunt small, wild prey, but may also menace livestock. Although dingoes pose no threat to adults, ranchers detest them and kill those they encounter near their flocks. The massive overpopulation of **rabbits,** purportedly introduced to Australia to provide practice targets for marksmen (see **Believe It Or Not,** p. 550), has become one of Australia's gravest wildlife problems. (But at least the rich Brits didn't play the Most Dangerous Game...) Accidental introductions such as European **rats** and **Cane toads** present serious threats to native fauna as well.

---

# MAGNIFICENT MAMMALIAN MONOTREME

Oh yes, we're talking about that milk-bearing, web-footed wonder, the platypus. The result of an evolutionary mix-and-match game, these furry water dwellers have been swimming around for at least 190 million years. In addition to anatomical non-sequiters such as a duck's bill and a beaver's tail, the male platypus also has a venomous spur under its ankle. Both genders have an all-purpose cloaca, an organ usually found in birds and reptiles. Solid waste, urine, sperm and eggs are all released from this one hole (hence "monotreme"). The platypus swims with its eyes, ears and nostrils shut, but uses special sensors on its bill to detect the electrical signals of other, potentially tasty animals. These timid creatures inhabit eastern waters from Tasmania up to Cooktown and are quite common in the bends of creeks within the Atherton Tablelands.

**LIVESTOCK.** More recent (and intentional) arrivals accompanied European colonists to help settle the land. Domesticated **cattle** and **sheep** have always been of tremendous economic importance in Australia, with ranches across the continent. These species have had a dramatic impact on the landscape and ecological balance of the nation; vast tracts have been converted to pasture to support the meat industry. In recent years, the farming of non-native **honeybees** has also become a growing part of the economy.

# MARINE LIFE

**THE GREAT BARRIER REEF.** Fur seals, elephant seals, and sea lions populate Australia's southern shores during summer breeding seasons, but it's the Great Barrier Reef that makes Australia's sea life unique. It's also one of Australia's biggest tourist draws and a diving wonderland. A comprehensive overview on **diving and snorkeling** the reef is in the introduction to the Queensland chapter (see **The Great Barrier Reef,** p. 295). The longest coral formation in the world, it is actually a series of many reefs that stretches more than 2000km along the eastern coast of Queensland from the Tropic of Capricorn to Papua New Guinea. Although adult **coral polyps** are sedentary, corals actually belong to the animal kingdom. Thus, the Great Barrier Reef is the only community of animals visible to the eye from space.

Corals rely on sunlight filtering down from the ocean surface and cannot grow at depths greater than 50m. Reef accumulates whenever a coral polyp dies and leaves behind its skeletal legacy of calcium carbonate. As layers of limestone build, the reef rises toward the surface. Once the coral reaches the top of the waves, the surf pounds it into sand-size bits. Add some more years and the bits form a little mound, called a **cay,** that sticks out of the water. Birds come along, land on the cay, and ingloriously deposit seeds from the mainland, and vegetation turns the cay into an island. Sea turtles and birds come to nest, and soon a whole ecosystem has literally risen from the water.

Colonies of coral grow by asexual reproduction, but new colonies propagate by **sexual reproduction**—quite a feat for creatures fixed to one spot. Using the moon for synchronization, all of the corals along the whole reef release their gametes at once so as to maximize the chance of fertilization. On a single night each October, the water fills with an dense fog of reproductive cells.

**CORAL.** Coral reefs take a number of different forms. Closest to the shore are **patch reefs,** comprised of patches of **hard** and **soft coral.** The former is often dried, bleached and sold to tourists in shops (beware of national marine park rules against removing living creatures from the sea). Soft corals, however, lose their shape and turn to sludge when taken out of water. Long, slender **sea whips** and delicate, intricate **fan corals** are some of the most plentiful and beautiful soft corals. Hard corals come in hues ranging from purple to emerald to red, and are mostly categorized as either branched, boulder, or plate coral. The fast-growing **branched coral** is named for its appearance; its most common varieties are the thin, brittle **needle coral,** the antler-like **stag coral,** and **finger coral,** also appropriately named. **Boulder coral** is sturdier and slower-growing, including the **honey-comb, golfball** and **brain boulders;** in areas where cyclones are frequent, these are the species that tend to survive. **Plate corals,** such as **sheet** and **table corals,** also look like they sound.

Further out than the patch reefs are **fringe reefs,** which contain the same types of coral. Their arrangement in circular patterns deeply entrenched in the sea floor means that they frequently fill with silt, meaning bad visibility for divers. The far outer reef is made up of 710km of **ribbon reef;** this includes some of Australia's best diving, but is accessible only to boats that venture out for four days or longer.

**FISH.** The reef also houses a spectacular variety of colorful, sometimes otherworldly fish, from the enormous **potato cod** to the **fusaleres,** a family of fish that change color at night. The **parrotfish** eats bits of coral by cracking it in its beak-like mouth, and at night envelops itself in a protective mucus sac, a phenomenon that might be a highlight of a night dive. If you're diving, taking a **briefing course** on marine life is an excellent way to familiarize yourself with what you'll see. While it's impossible to memorize every species, many shops sell **fish identification cards** that you can take down with you. A few terms to know: the **wrasse** is a long, slender, cigar-like fish; **angel** and **surgeon fish** have similar oblong shapes, but the surgeon has a razor-sharp barb close to its tail; the **butterfly** and **bat fish** are round, but the latter is a larger and has a black stripe across the eye. Despite Australia's reputation for **sharks,** only grey **reef sharks** (and the very occasional **tiger shark**) are seen around the Reef and are typically harmless when unprovoked. Besides fish, the reef houses **turtles, porpoises, dolphins,** and **whales,** as well as **echinoderms:** sea cucumbers, sea stars, feather stars, and brittle stars.

**POISONOUS SEA CREATURES.** If an Aussie is somewhat scared of something, that means you should probably be terrified. If you're told that the unidentified creature you're holding is a **nasty**—drop it. Better yet, **don't touch unfamiliar objects.** Many benign-looking creatures are poisonous, some even deadly. The most infamous nasty is the **box jellyfish,** a near-transparent creature which tends to live near the coast, particularly near river mouths or estuaries. Its up-to-3m tentacles contain a toxin that can kill you within three minutes; carrying a vinegar-based antivenom is wise. The best option is to avoid coastal diving (and swimming) altogether during box jellyfish season (Oct.-Apr.) and to obey all posted warnings. The **cone shell** has brightly patterned shells that look as though they would make excellent souvenirs, but the stingers inside are packed with enough venom to kill an adult human. The **stone fish** lies motionless and camouflaged against the coral, waiting for prey. If you're unlucky enough to step on its poison-filled spines, seek medical attention pronto. It takes a lot of weight to step on one of these and get hurt, so it is danger only in shallow water. **Sting rays, lion fish,** and **sea snakes** are all poisonous as well, but aren't likely to attack except in retaliation. Some nasties are irritating but not deadly. If you pick up the inert **sea urchin,** you may get small pieces of its spines embedded in your skin, causing swelling and pain. A prick from the **crown of thorns,** a type of sea star, will send a low-grade poison into your bloodstream. However, its effects on the reef itself are far worse, as it feeds on coral. A recent population explosion has led to the legalization of removal of sea stars by dive boats.

# ESSENTIALS

## FACTS FOR THE TRAVELER

### HOLIDAYS AND FESTIVALS

| PUBLIC HOLIDAYS AND FESTIVALS IN 2001 | |
|---|---|
| January 1 | New Year's Day |
| January 26 | Australia Day |
| January 19-29 | Tamworth Country Music Festival, NSW (see p. 153) |
| January | Sydney Festival, NSW (see p. 126) |
| March 2-18 | WOMADELAIDE (World Music Art Dance) Adelaide, SA (see p. 426) |
| March 3 | Sydney Gay and Lesbian Mardi Gras, NSW (see p. 126) |
| April 21-24 | Good Friday through Easter Monday |
| April 25 | Anzac Day |
| June 8-11 | Queen's Birthday weekend |
| July 7 | Camel Cup Carnival, Alice Springs, NT (see p. 283) |
| July 18-August 5 | Melbourne International Film Festival, VIC (see p. 538) |
| December 25 | Christmas Day |
| December 26 | Boxing Day |

For Australia's most important other holidays—when *everything* shuts down—see **Sport,** p. 24.

Each state capital also includes a list of major local festivals. Banks, museums, and other public buildings are often closed or operate with reduced hours during these times. During **school holidays,** accommodations fill up and prices rise. Public transportation may run on weekend schedules during school holidays. Vacations differ between schools and regions, but school holidays are typically from Christmas to the end of January, Easter Week, and in early July and early October.

### TEMPERATURE CHARTS

To convert from °C to °F, multiply by 1.8 and add 32. For a rough approximation, double the Celsius and add 26. To convert from °F to °C, subtract 32 and multiply by 0.55. For a rough approximation, subtract 26 and cut it in half.

| °CELSIUS | -5 | 0 | 5 | 10 | 15 | 20 | 25 | 30 | 35 | 40 |
|---|---|---|---|---|---|---|---|---|---|---|
| °FAHRENHEIT | 23 | 32 | 41 | 50 | 59 | 68 | 77 | 86 | 95 | 104 |

| Av. Temp. lo/hi Precipitation | January | | | April | | | July | | | October | | |
|---|---|---|---|---|---|---|---|---|---|---|---|---|
| | °C | °F | mm | °C | °F | mm | °C | °F | mm | °C | °F | mm |
| **Adelaide** | 16/28 | 61/82 | 19 | 12/22 | 54/72 | 43 | 7/15 | 45/59 | 65 | 10/21 | 50/70 | 43 |
| **Alice Springs** | 21/36 | 70/97 | 40 | 13/28 | 55/82 | 17 | 4/19 | 39/66 | 12 | 15/31 | 59/88 | 20 |
| **Brisbane** | 21/29 | 70/84 | 161 | 17/26 | 63/79 | 89 | 10/20 | 50/68 | 57 | 16/26 | 61/79 | 77 |
| **Cairns** | 24/31 | 75/88 | 407 | 22/29 | 72/84 | 200 | 17/26 | 63/79 | 27 | 20/29 | 68/84 | 38 |
| **Canberra** | 13/28 | 55/82 | 58 | 7/20 | 45/68 | 53 | 0/11 | 32/52 | 40 | 6/19 | 43/66 | 67 |
| **Darwin** | 25/32 | 77/90 | 393 | 24/33 | 75/91 | 103 | 20/31 | 68/88 | 1 | 25/34 | 77/93 | 52 |
| **Hobart** | 12/22 | 54/72 | 48 | 9/17 | 48/63 | 52 | 4/12 | 39/54 | 54 | 8/17 | 46/63 | 64 |
| **Melbourne** | 14/26 | 57/79 | 48 | 11/20 | 52/68 | 58 | 6/13 | 43/55 | 49 | 9/20 | 48/68 | 68 |
| **Perth** | 18/30 | 64/86 | 9 | 14/25 | 57/77 | 46 | 9/18 | 48/64 | 173 | 12/22 | 54/72 | 55 |
| **Sydney** | 18/26 | 64/79 | 98 | 14/23 | 59/72 | 129 | 8/16 | 46/61 | 100 | 13/22 | 55/72 | 79 |

## TIME ZONES

The following table should help you convert time between different Australian states, New York City, London, and Greenwich Mean Time. Daylight savings time makes everything complicated, especially since some states use it and some don't. To use the following table, imagine it is noon, Greenwich Mean Time (GMT), and then look at what time it would be in the two cities you are comparing, take the difference between them, and then apply it to whatever the real time is. (GMT is an international standard time; it is not affected by daylight savings.) Remember that the **date** is affected too—Australia is ahead of the Western Hemisphere, so Monday evening in New York is Tuesday morning in Sydney.

| AT NOON GMT | OCT. 29-MAR. 25 | MAR. 26-SEPT. 31 | OCT. 1-OCT. 28 |
| --- | --- | --- | --- |
| ACT | 11pm | 10pm | 10pm |
| New South Wales | 11pm | 10pm | 10pm |
| Northern Territory | 9:30pm | 9:30pm | 9:30pm |
| Queensland | 10pm | 10pm | 10pm |
| South Australia | 10:30pm | 9:30pm | 9:30pm |
| Tasmania | 11pm | 10pm | 11pm |
| Victoria | 11pm | 10pm | 10pm |
| Western Australia | 8pm | 8pm | 8pm |
| New York City | 7am | 8am | 8am |
| London | noon | 1pm | 1pm |
| Greenwich Mean Time | noon | noon | noon |

# DOCUMENTS AND FORMALITIES

**ENTRANCE REQUIREMENTS** Unlike during the convict era, a criminal record is no longer required for entry into Australia.

**Passports** (p. 33). Required for all visitors.

**Visas** (p. 34). Required of all citizens except holders of Australian and New Zealand passports.

**Working Visa** (p. 35). Required for all foreigners planning to work in Australia.

**Inoculations** (p. 43). Only necessary for those who come from or have just visited yellow fever-infected areas (parts of South America and Central Africa).

**Driving Permit** (p. 68). Recommended; required for many car rental agencies.

# AUSTRALIAN CONSULAR SERVICES ABROAD

**Canada:** All visa applications should go to: High Commission, 50 O'Connor St #710, **Ottawa**, ON K1P 6L2 (visas ☎(613) 783-7665; general ☎236-0841; fax 236-4376; www.ahc-ottawa.org). Consulate, 888 Dunsmuir St #1225, **Vancouver**, BC V6C 3K4 (☎(604) 684-1177; fax 684-1856). Consulate, 175 Bloor St E #314, **Toronto**, ON M4W 3R8 (☎(416) 323-1155; fax 323-3910).

**Ireland:** Fitzwilton House, 2nd fl., Wilton Tce, **Dublin** 2 (☎(01) 676 1517; fax 678 5185; www.australianembassy.ie).

**New Zealand:** Visa requests should be sent to Auckland. 72-78 Hobson St, Thorndon, **Wellington** (☎(04) 473 6411; fax 498 7135). Union House, 132-138 Quay St, Private Bag 92023, **Auckland** 1 (☎(09) 303 2429; fax 377 0798).

**South Africa:** High Commission, 292 Orient St, Arcadia, **Pretoria** 0083 (☎(012) 342 3781; fax 342 8442).

**United Kingdom:** High Commission, The Strand, **London** WC2B 4LA (☎(171) 379 4334; fax 240 5333; www.australia.org.uk). Consulate, Chatsworth House, Lever St, **Manchester** MI 2QL (☎(161) 228 1344; fax 236 4074).

**United States:** Visa requests should go to Washington, DC or Los Angeles. Embassy, 1601 Massachusetts Ave NW, **Washington, D.C.** 20036 (☎(202) 797-3000; fax 797-3168; www.austemb.org). Consulate, 150 E. 42nd St, 34th fl., **New York,** NY 10017 (☎(212) 351-6500; fax 351-6501). Consulate, 2049 Century Park E #1900, 19th fl., **Los Angeles,** CA 90067 (visas ☎(310) 229-4840; fax 277-5620; general ☎229-4800; fax 277-2258).

# EMBASSIES AND CONSULATES IN AUSTRALIA

**Canada:** High Commission (☎(02) 6270 4000; fax 6273 3285), Commonwealth Ave, **Canberra** ACT 2600. Consulate, Level 5, Quay West Building, 111 Harrington St, **Sydney** NSW 2000 (☎(02) 9364 3000; fax 9364 3098). Consulate, 267 St. George's Tce, 3rd fl., **Perth** WA 6000 (☎(08) 9322 7930; fax 9261 7706).

**Ireland:** Embassy, 20 Arkana St, Yarralumla, **Canberra** ACT 2600 (☎(02) 6273 3022; fax 6273 3741). Consulate, P.O. Box 250, Floreat Forum, Floreat **(Perth)** WA 6014 (☎/fax (08) 9385 8247).

**New Zealand:** High Commission, Commonwealth Ave, **Canberra** ACT 2600 (☎(02) 6270 4211; fax 6273 3194). Consulate, GPO Box 365 (Level 10, 55 Hunter St), **Sydney** NSW 1041 (All passport queries: ☎(02) 9247 7500; fax 9223 0223; visa queries: ☎9247 1511; fax 9223 0166).

**South Africa:** High Commission, State Circle, Yarralumla, **Canberra** ACT 2600 (☎(02) 6273 2424; fax 6273 4994).

**United Kingdom:** High Commission, Commonwealth Ave, Yarralumla, **Canberra** ACT 2600 (☎(02) 6257 5857; fax 6273 3236). Consul-General, 17th fl., 90 Collins St, **Melbourne** VIC 3000 (☎(03) 9650 4155; fax 9650 2990). Consul-General, Level 26, Allendale Square, 77 St. Georges Tce, **Perth** WA 6000 (☎(08) 9221 5400; fax 9221 2344). Consul-General, Level 16, The Gateway, 1 Macquarie Pl, **Sydney Cove** NSW 2000 (☎(02) 9247 7521; fax 9251 6201).

**United States:** Embassy, Moonah Pl, Yarralumla, **Canberra** ACT 2600 (☎(02) 6214 5900; fax 6214 5970). Consulate, Level 59, MLC Centre, 19-29 Martin Pl, **Sydney** NSW 2000 (☎(02) 9373 9200; fax 9373 9125). Consulate, 553 St Kilda Rd, P.O. Box 6722, **Melbourne** VIC 3004 (☎(03) 9526 5900; fax 9510 4646). Consulate, 13th fl., 16 St. Georges Tce, **Perth** WA 6000 (☎(08) 9231 9400; fax 9231 9444).

# PASSPORTS

## REQUIREMENTS

All visitors need valid passports to enter Australia and return home. Australia prohibits entrance if the holder's passport expires in under six months; returning home with an expired passport is illegal and may result in a fine.

## PHOTOCOPIES

Be sure to photocopy the page of your passport with your photo, passport number, and other identifying information, as well as any visas, travel insurance policies, plane tickets, or traveler's check serial numbers. Carry one set of copies in a safe place, apart from the originals, and leave another set at home. Consulates also recommend that you carry an expired passport or an official copy of your birth certificate in a part of your baggage separate from other documents.

## LOST PASSPORTS

Your passport is a public document belonging to your nation's government. You may have to surrender it to a foreign government official, but if you don't get it back in a reasonable amount of time, inform the nearest mission of your home country. If you lose your passport, immediately notify the local police and the nearest embassy or consulate of your home government. To expedite its replacement, you will need to know all information previously recorded and show ID and proof of citizenship. In some cases, a replacement may take weeks to process, and it may be valid only for a limited time. Any visas stamped in your old passport will be irretrievably lost. In an emergency, ask for immediate temporary traveling papers that will permit you to re-enter your home country.

## NEW PASSPORTS

File any new passport or renewal applications well in advance of your departure date. Most passport offices offer rush services for a steep fee. Citizens living abroad who need a passport or renewal should contact the nearest consular service of their home country.

**Canada:** Canadian Passport Office, Department of Foreign Affairs and International Trade, Ottawa, ON K1A 0G3 (☎(613) 994-3500 or ☎(800) 567-6868; www.dfait-maeci.gc.ca/passport). Applications available at passport offices, Canadian missions, and post offices. Passports CDN$60; valid for 5 years (non-renewable).

**Ireland:** Pick up an application at a *Garda* station or post office, or request one from a passport office. Then apply by mail to the Department of Foreign Affairs, Passport Office, Molesworth St, Dublin 2 (☎(01) 671 1633; fax 671 1092; www.irlgov.ie/iveagh), or the Passport Office, Irish Life Building, 1A South Mall, Cork (☎(021) 27 25 25). Passports IR£45; valid for 10 years. Under 18 or over 65 IR£10; valid for 3 years.

**New Zealand:** Send applications to the Passport Office, Department of Internal Affairs, P.O. Box 10526, Wellington, New Zealand (☎(0800) 22 50 50 or ☎(4) 474 8100; fax 474 8010; passports@dia.govt.nz; www.passports.govt.nz). Standard processing time is 10 working days. Passports NZ$80; valid for 10 years. Children NZ$40; valid for 5 years. 3 day "urgent service" NZ$160; children NZ $120.

**South Africa:** Passports are issued only in Pretoria, but all applications must still be submitted or forwarded to the nearest South African consulate. Processing time is 3 months or more. Passports around SAR80; valid for 10 years. Under 16 around SAR60; valid for 5 years. For more information, check out http://usaembassy.southafrica.net/VisaForms/Passport/Passport2000.html.

**United Kingdom:** Info ☎(0870) 521 0410; www.open.gov.uk/ukpass/ukpass.htm. Get an application from a passport office, main post office, travel agent, or online (for UK residents only) at www.ukpa.gov.uk/forms/f_app_pack.htm. Then apply by mail or in person at a passport office. Passports UK£28; valid for 10 years. Under 15 UK£14.80; valid for 5 years. The process takes about 4 weeks; faster service (by personal visit to the offices listed above) costs an additional £12.

**United States:** Info ☎(202) 647-0518; www.travel.state.gov/passport_services.html. Apply at any federal or state courthouse, authorized post office, or US Passport Agency (in most major cities); see the "US Government, State Department" section of the telephone book or a post office for addresses. Processing takes 3-4 weeks. New passports US$60; valid for 10 years. Under 16 US$40; valid for 5 years. Passports may be renewed by mail or in person for US$40. Add US$35 for 3-day expedited service.

# VISAS, ETA, AND WORK PERMITS

## VISAS

Australia **requires all visitors** except Australian citizens and New Zealand passport holders to have a visa. A visa system called the **Electronic Travel Authority (ETA),** is used by about 80% of Australia's visitors. Quick, simple, and free, the fully-electronic ETA replaces a standard visa, and is available from most travel agencies and airports. The ETA allows three months on each visit within a one-year period. It is free for those staying less than three months. To extend a visit over three months, contact the nearest office of the Department of Immigration and Multicultural Affairs in Australia before the end of your 3 month stay period. There is no provision for obtaining a further ETA when you are in Australia. For more info, go to www.immi.gov.au/wwi/aust-off.htm. Standard **visas** (US$40) may be obtained from the nearest Australian high commission, embassy, or consulate. If you register in person, it will take two days to process; allow 21 working days by mail.

US citizens can take advantage of the **Center for International Business and Travel** (**CIBT; ☎** (800) 925-2428), which secures visas for travel to almost all countries for a variable service charge.

Be sure to double-check on entrance requirements at the nearest embassy or consulate of Australia for up-to-date info before departure. US citizens can also consult www.pueblo.gsa.gov/cic_text/travel/foreign/foreignentryreqs.html.

## WORK PERMITS

Those ages 18 to 25 from Canada, Ireland, Japan, Korea, Malta, the Netherlands, the UK, and Germany are eligible for a **working holiday visa,** which may be granted only under certain conditions for a fee of AUS$150. Any work done in Australia must be solely to support your vacation. You must have a good chance of finding work, you may not enroll in formal studies, and you must show either a return ticket or sufficient funds to leave the country. To obtain a **student visa,** you must complete an application form, pay the application charge, have a confirmation of enrollment issued by a registered provider, and meet health and character requirements. Working and studying visas vary according to your plans; contact the Australian embassy or consulate in your home country with questions. For more information, see **Work,** p. 74. Rates on **extending** your ETA or visa depend on length of desired stay and type of visa; an application to extend a standard visa is AUS$150. Contact the **Department of Immigration and Multicultural Affairs** at their toll-free inquiries line (**☎** 13 18 81) before your stay period expires. Otherwise, contact an Australian consulate or embassy.

# IDENTIFICATION

When you travel, always carry two or more forms of identification on your person, including at least one photo ID; a passport combined with a driver's license or birth certificate is usually adequate. Many establishments, especially banks, require several IDs to cash traveler's checks. Never carry all your forms of ID together; split them up in case of theft or loss. It is useful to bring extra passport-size photos to affix to the various IDs or passes you may acquire along the way.

## STUDENT AND TEACHER IDENTIFICATION

The **International Student Identity Card (ISIC),** the most widely accepted form of student ID, provides discounts on sights, accommodations, food, and transport. Present the card wherever you go, and ask about discounts even when none are advertised. The ISIC is preferable to an institution-specific card (such as a university ID) because it is more likely to be recognized (and honored) abroad. All cardholders have access to a 24-hour emergency helpline for medical, legal, and financial emergencies (in North America call **☎** (877) 370-ISIC, elsewhere call US collect **☎** +1 (715) 345-0505). US cardholders are also eligible for insurance benefits (see **Insurance,** p. 47). Many student travel agencies issue ISICs, including STA Travel in Australia and New Zealand; Travel CUTS in Canada; USIT in the Republic of Ireland and Northern Ireland; SASTS in South Africa; Campus Travel and STA Travel in the UK; and Council Travel (www.counciltravel.com/idcards/default.asp) and STA Travel in the US (see p. 61). The card is valid from September of one year to December of the following year and costs AUS$15, CDN$15, or US$22. Applicants must be degree-seeking students of a secondary or post-secondary school and must be at least 12 years of age. Because of the proliferation of fake ISICs, some services (particularly airlines) require additional proof of student identity, such as a school ID or a letter attesting to student status, signed by your registrar and stamped with your school seal. The **International Teacher Identity Card (ITIC)** offers the same insurance coverage as well as similar but limited discounts. The fee is AUS$13, UK£5, or US$22. For more info, contact the **International Student Travel Confederation (ISTC),** Herengracht 479, 1017 BS Amsterdam, Netherlands (**☎** +31 (20) 421 28 00; fax 421 28 10; email istcinfo@istc.org; www.istc.org).

**ESSENTIALS**

## YOUTH IDENTIFICATION

The International Student Travel Confederation issues a discount card to travelers 25 years or under but who are not students. This one-year **International Youth Travel Card** (**IYTC**; formerly the **GO 25** Card) offers many of the same benefits as the ISIC. Most places that sell ISIC also sell the IYTC (US$22).

## DISCOUNTS

"Concessions" is the Australian catch-all phrase for discounts always given to specific groups, most often students and senior citizens. However, it may be limited to holders of specific Australian concession cards. "Pensioners" are Australian senior citizens, and discounts for pensioners may or may not apply to non-Australians who otherwise fit the bill. Student discounts often require that you show an ID, and may only apply to Australian University students, or even to university students within the particular state. Discounts on accommodations are regularly given to VIP, YHA, ISIC, or NOMADS card holders. Play it safe and carry a couple forms of ID with you at all times.

# CUSTOMS

Because of the isolation afforded by being an island nation, Australia has been able to avoid some of the pests and diseases that plague other countries. But with increased tourism, there is an increased risk of contamination from imported goods. Customs is therefore taken extremely seriously. Australia expressly forbids the entry of drugs, steroids, and weapons. Articles subject to quarantine may include live animals, food, animal products, plants, plant products, and protected wildlife. These articles are not automatically forbidden, but they will undergo a **quarantine inspection.** Camping equipment is also subject to a quarantine inspection, so be prepared to declare these items as well. Don't risk large fines or hassles when entering Australia—throw out questionable items in the big customs bins as you leave the plane, and declare anything about which you have the slightest suspicion. The beagles in orange smocks know their stuff, and they WILL find you out. If you are planning to stay a while and must bring your **pets** with you, contact the **Australian Quarantine and Inspections Service,** GPO Box 858, Canberra, ACT 2601 (☎(02) 6272 3933; fax 6272 3399) to obtain a permit. Pick up **Customs Information for Travellers** at an Australian consulate or any travel agency for more information.

Visitors over 18 may bring into Australia up to 1125ml alcohol, 250 cigarettes, and 250g tobacco **duty-free.** For other goods intended as gifts, the allowance is AUS$400 (over 18) or AUS$200 (under 18).

Upon returning home, you must declare articles acquired abroad and pay a **duty** on the value of articles that exceeds the allowance established by your country's customs service. Goods bought at **duty-free** shops abroad are not exempt from duty tax at your return; you must declare these items as well. "Duty-free" merely means that you need not pay a tax in the country of purchase. Australia recently implemented a **Tourist Refund Scheme** (TRS) that refunds the **Goods and Services Tax** (GST) on items bought in Australia (see **Taxes and Tipping,** p. 41). For more information on customs requirements, contact the following information centers:

**Australia:** Australian Customs National Information Line (in Australia call ☎(01) 30 03 63, from elsewhere call ☎+61 (2) 6275 6666; www.customs.gov.au).

**Canada:** Canadian Customs, 2265 St. Laurent Blvd, Ottawa, ON K1G 4K3 (☎(800) 461-9999 (24hr.) or ☎(613) 993-0534; www.revcan.ca).

**Ireland:** Customs Information Office, Irish Life Centre, Lower Abbey St, Dublin 1 (☎(01) 878 8811; fax 878 0836; taxes@revenue.iol.ie; www.revenue.ie/customs.htm).

**New Zealand:** New Zealand Customhouse, 17-21 Whitmore St, Box 2218, Wellington (☎(04) 473 6099; fax 473 7370; www.customs.govt.nz).

**South Africa:** Commissioner for Customs and Excise, Private Bag X47, Pretoria 0001 (☎(012) 314 9911; fax 328 6478; www.gov.za).

ESSENTIALS

**United Kingdom:** Her Majesty's Customs and Excise, Passenger Enquiry Team, Wayfarer House, Great South West Road, Feltham, Middlesex TW14 8NP (☎(020) 8910 3744; fax 8910 3933; www.hmce.gov.uk).

**United States:** US Customs Service, 1330 Pennsylvania Ave NW, Washington, D.C. 20229 (☎(202) 354-1000; fax 354-1010; www.customs.gov).

## TOURIST BOARDS

The government-sponsored **Australian Tourist Commission** promotes tourism internationally (but not within Australia), distributing literature and sponsoring helplines. The ATC carries books, magazines, and fact sheets for backpackers, younger people, disabled travelers, and others with special concerns. Check out their fairly comprehensive web page at www.australia.com. Requests for information should be directed to the addresses and phone numbers below.

**Australia (Head Office):** Level 4, 80 William St, Wolloomooloo, NSW 2011, GPO Box 2721, Sydney 1006 (☎(02) 9360 1111; fax 9331 6469).

**Ireland:** Helpline (☎(01) 402 9896); send faxes to London office, below.

**New Zealand:** Level 13, 44-8 Emily Place, Auckland 1 (helpline (☎(0800) 65 03 03 or ☎(09) 379 9594; fax 307 3117).

**United Kingdom:** Gemini House, 10-18 Putney Hill, London SW156AA (☎(181) 780 2229; fax (181) 780 1496).

**U.S./Canada:** 2049 Century Park E, Suite 1920, CA 90067 (helpline ☎(310) 229-4870; fax 552-1215; general information ☎(800) 333-4305).

# MONEY

No matter how low your budget, you should keep handy a larger amount of cash than usual. Carrying it around is risky but necessary; personal checks are seldom accepted and even traveler's checks may not be accepted in some locations.

 **LET'S GO: AUSTRALIA LISTS ALL PRICES IN AUSTRALIAN DOLLARS UNLESS OTHERWISE STATED.**

## CURRENCY AND EXCHANGE

The Australian currency is in dollars and cents. Notes come in $5, $10, $20, $50, and $100 denominations, and coins are 5¢, 10¢, 20¢, 50¢, $1, and $2. The currency chart below is based on August 2000 exchange rates between local currency and US dollars (US$), Canadian dollars (CDN$), British pounds (UK£), Irish pounds (IR£), Australian dollars (AUS$), New Zealand dollars (NZ$), South African Rand (SAR), and European Union euros (EUR€). Check a large newspaper or the web (e.g. finance.yahoo.com or www.bloomberg.com) for the latest exchange rates.

| CURRENCY | | |
| --- | --- |
| US$1 = AUS$1.75 | AUS$1= US$0.57 |
| CDN$1 = AUS$1.18 | AUS$1= CDN$0.85 |
| UK£1 = AUS$2.59 | AUS$1= UK£0.39 |
| IR£1 = AUS$1.99 | AUS$1= IR£0.50 |
| NZ$1 = AUS$0.75 | AUS$1= NZ$1.33 |
| SAR1= AUS$0.25 | AUS$1= SAR3.99 |
| EUR€ = AUS$1.57 | AUS$1= EUR€0.64 |

As a general rule, it's cheaper to convert money in Australia. It's good to bring enough foreign currency to last for the first 24 to 72 hours of a trip to avoid being penniless after banking hours or on a holiday. In the U.S., **International Currency Express** (☎(888) 278-6628; www.foreignmoney.com) will deliver foreign currency for over 120 countries or traveler's checks overnight to your home (US$15) or second-day (US$12) at competitive exchange rates.

Watch out for commission rates, and check newspapers for the standard rate of exchange. When changing money abroad, try to go only to banks or bureaus of change that have at most a 5% margin between their buy and sell prices. The largest and most widespread banks in Australia are ANZ, Commonwealth, National, and Westpac. Since you lose money with every transaction, **convert large sums** (unless the currency is depreciating rapidly), **but no more than you'll need.** Using an ATM card or a credit card (see p. 39) often gets you the best possible rates as well.

If you use traveler's checks or bills, carry some in small denominations (the equivalent of US$50 or less) for times when you are forced to exchange money at disadvantageous rates, but bring a range of denominations since charges may be levied per check cashed. Store your money in a variety of forms; ideally, you will at any given time be carrying some cash, some traveler's checks, and an ATM (see p. 39) and/or credit card (p. 39).

> **BUT I WANNA PAY MORE!**
> On July 1, 2000, Australia implemented a new 10% goods and services tax (GST). Parts of *Let's Go: Australia 2001* were researched before the GST was implemented, so some prices in this book (particularly in South Australia and Tasmania) could differ from the actual current price by up to 10%. Our savvy researchers usually got the post-GST price even before the GST was implemented, but at the time many retailers had not yet decided exactly how much their prices would rise, if at all. For more info, see **Tipping and Taxes,** p. 41.

# TRAVELER'S CHECKS

Traveler's checks (**American Express** and **Visa** are the most recognized) are one of the safest and least troublesome means of carrying funds, since they can be refunded if stolen. Several agencies and banks sell them, usually for face value plus a small commission. Members of the American Automobile Association, and some banks and credit unions, can get American Express checks commission-free (see **Driving Permits and Insurance,** p. 68). Each agency provides refunds if checks are lost or stolen, and many provide additional services, like toll-free refund hotlines, emergency message services, and stolen credit card assistance.

While traveling, keep check receipts and a record of which checks you've cashed separate from the checks themselves. Also leave a list of check numbers with someone at home. Never countersign checks until you're ready to cash them, and always bring your passport with you to cash them. If your checks are lost or stolen, immediately contact a refund center (of the company that issued your checks) to be reimbursed; they may require a police report verifying the loss or theft. Less-touristed, rural areas may not have refund centers at all, so you might have to wait to be reimbursed. Ask about toll-free refund hotlines and the location of refund centers when purchasing checks, and always carry emergency cash.

**American Express:** Call ☎(1800) 25 19 02 in Australia; in New Zealand ☎(0800) 44 10 68; in the UK ☎(0800) 52 13 13; in the US and Canada ☎(800) 221-7282. Elsewhere call US collect ☎+1 (801) 964-6665; www.aexp.com. Traveler's cheques are available in Australia at 1-4% commission at AmEx offices and banks, commission-free at AAA offices (see p. 67). *Cheques for Two* can be signed by either of 2 people together.

**Citicorp:** In the US and Canada call ☎(800) 645-6556; in Europe, the Middle East, or Africa call the UK ☎+44 (020) 7508 7007; elsewhere call US collect ☎+1 (813) 623-1709. Traveler's checks available in 7 currencies at 1-2% commission. Call 24hr.

**Thomas Cook MasterCard:** In the US and Canada call ☎(800) 223-7373; in the UK call ☎(0800) 62 21 01; elsewhere call UK collect ☎+44 (1733) 31 89 50. Checks available in 13 currencies at 2% commission. Thomas Cook offices cash checks commission-free.

**Visa:** In the US call ☎(800) 227-6811; in the UK call ☎(0800) 89 50 78; elsewhere call UK collect ☎+44 (1733) 31 89 49. Call for the location of their nearest office.

# CREDIT CARDS

Credit cards are generally accepted in all but the smallest businesses in Australia. Credit cards often offer superior exchange rates—up to 5% better than the retail rate used by banks and other currency exchanges. Credit cards may also offer services such as insurance or emergency help and are sometimes required to reserve hotel rooms or rental cars. **MasterCard** and **Visa** are the most welcomed; **American Express** cards work at some ATMs and at AmEx offices and major airports.

Credit cards are also useful for **cash advances,** which allow you to withdraw cash from associated banks and ATMs throughout Australia instantly. However, transaction fees for all credit card advances (up to US$10 per advance, plus sometimes a 2-3% extra on foreign transactions after conversion) tend to make credit cards a more costly way of withdrawing cash than ATMs or traveler's checks. In an emergency, however, the transaction fee may prove worth the cost. To be eligible for an advance, you'll need to get a **Personal Identification Number (PIN)** from your credit card company (see **Cash (ATM) Cards,** below).

## CREDIT CARD COMPANIES

**Visa** (US ☎ (800) 336-8472) and **MasterCard** (US ☎ (800) 307-7309) are issued in cooperation with banks and other organizations. **American Express** (US ☎ (800) 843-2273) has an annual fee of up to US$55. AmEx cardholders may cash personal checks at AmEx offices abroad, access an emergency medical and legal assistance hotline (24hr.; in North America call ☎ (800) 554-2639, elsewhere call US collect ☎ +1 (202) 554-2639), and enjoy American Express Travel Service benefits (including plane, hotel, and car rental reservation changes; baggage loss and flight insurance; mailgram and international cable services; and held mail). The **Discover Card** (in US call ☎ (800) 347-2683, elsewhere call US ☎ +1 (801) 902-3100) offers small cashback bonuses on most purchases, but it may not be readily accepted in Australia.

# CASH (ATM) CARDS

Cash cards—popularly called ATM cards—are widespread in Australia. Depending on the system that your home bank uses, you can most likely access your personal bank account from abroad. ATMs get the same wholesale exchange rate as credit cards, but there is often a limit on the amount of money you can withdraw per day (around US$500), and computer networks sometimes fail. There is typically also a surcharge of US$1-5 per withdrawal. Be sure to memorize your PIN code in numeric form since machines often don't have letters on their keys. Also, if your PIN is longer than four digits, ask your bank whether you need a new number.

## ELECTRONIC BANKING

The two major international money networks are **Cirrus** (US ☎ (800) 424-7787) and **PLUS** (US ☎ (800) 843-7587). To locate ATMs around the world, call the above numbers, or consult www.visa.com/pd/atm or www.mastercard.com/atm. **Cirrus** is the most widespread ATM network in Australia; **Plus** is almost as good, and **Visa** is probably third best. **Mastercard** and **American Express** are found less often but are possibilities. **NYCE** is not found in Australia. Though ATMs are increasingly prevalent in smaller towns and rural areas, they are scarce in northern Western Australia and more remote interior areas.

**Visa TravelMoney** (for customer assistance in Australia, call ☎ (0800) 12 51 61) is a system allowing you to access money from any Visa ATM, common throughout Australia. You deposit an amount before you travel (plus a small administration fee), and you can withdraw up to that sum. The cards, which give you the same favorable exchange rate for withdrawals as a regular Visa, are especially useful if you plan to travel through many countries. Check with your local bank to see if it issues TravelMoney cards. **Road Cash** (US ☎ (877) 762-3227; www.roadcash.com) issues cards in the US with a minimum US$300 deposit.

## EFTPOS

Electronic Funds Transfer at Point Of Sale (EFTPOS) is an extremely common way for Australians to pay for goods. ATM cards (from Australian banks only) swiped at the register work as debit cards, withdrawing money directly from your bank account. This means that travelers can carry less cash, without worrying about credit card bills. If you'll be in Australia for a while, the convenience of this service, among other reasons, may justify opening an Australian bank account. The most widespread banks in Australia are ANZ, Commonwealth, National, and Westpac, and most offer online banking as well. A permanent Australian address and two or three forms of identification are required to open an account; your home driver's license and your passport are the most sure-fire bets. Banks accept cash or traveler's checks to open an account. You can expect the bank to perform a routine check on your credit history. Bringing along home bank statements from the last three months can expedite the process enormously; accounts can be ready in as little as an hour.

# GETTING MONEY FROM HOME

## AMERICAN EXPRESS

Cardholders can withdraw cash from their checking accounts at any of AmEx's major offices and many representative offices (up to US$1000 every 21 days; no service charge, no interest). AmEx "Express Cash" withdrawals from any AmEx ATM in Australia are automatically debited from the cardholder's checking account or line of credit. AmEx Green card holders may withdraw up to US$1000 in any seven-day period (2% transaction fee; minimum US$2.50, maximum US$20). To enroll in Express Cash, cardmembers may call ☎ (800) 227-4669 in the US; elsewhere call the US collect ☎ +1 (336) 668-5041. The AmEx national number in Australia is ☎ (0800) 23 01 00.

## WESTERN UNION

Travelers from the US, Canada, and the UK can wire money abroad through Western Union's international money transfer services. In the US, call ☎ (800) 325-6000; in Canada, ☎ (800) 235-0000; in the UK, ☎ (0800) 83 38 33; in Australia, ☎ (0800) 64 95 65. The rates for sending cash are generally US$10-11 cheaper than with a credit card, and the money is usually available at the place you're sending to within an hour. To locate the nearest Western Union, see www.westernunion.com.

## FEDERAL EXPRESS

Some people choose to send money abroad in cash via FedEx to avoid transmission fees and taxes. In the US and Canada, call ☎ (800) 463-3339; in the UK, ☎ (0800) 12 38 00; in Ireland, ☎ (0800) 53 58 00; in Australia, ☎ 13 26 10; in New Zealand, ☎ (0800) 73 33 39; and in South Africa, ☎ (021) 551-7610. While FedEx is fairly reliable, note that this method is illegal and somewhat risky.

## US STATE DEPARTMENT (US CITIZENS ONLY)

In dire emergencies only, the US State Department will forward money within hours to the nearest consular office, which will then disburse it according to instructions for a US$15 fee. Contact the Overseas Citizens Service, American Citizens Services, Consular Affairs, Room 4811, US Department of State, Washington, D.C. 20520 (☎ (202) 647-5225; nights, Sundays, and holidays 647-4000; http://travel.state.gov).

# COSTS AND TIPS FOR STAYING ON BUDGET

The cost of your trip will vary considerably, depending on where you go, how you travel, and where you stay. The single biggest cost of your trip will probably be your round-trip (return) **airfare** to Australia (see p. 58). A **railpass** (or **bus pass**) would be another major pre-departure expense as well as **domestic airfare** for travel within Australia (see p. 62). Before you go, spend some time calculating a reasonable per-day **bud-**

**get** that will meet your specific needs. To give you a general idea, a bare-bones day in Australia (sleeping in hostels, buying food at supermarkets) would cost about US$20-30; a slightly more comfortable day (sleeping in hostels and the occasional budget hotel, eating one meal a day at a restaurant, going out at night) would run around US$40-50; and for a luxurious day, the sky's the limit. Don't forget to factor in emergency reserve funds (at least US$200) when planning how much money you'll need.

Considering that saving just a few dollars a day over the course of your trip might pay for days or weeks of additional travel, the art of penny-pinching is well worth learning. Learn to take advantage of freebies: for example, **museums** will typically be free once a week or once a month, and cities often host free open-air **concerts** and/or **cultural events** (especially in the summer). Bring a **sleepsack** (see p. 48) to save on sheet charges in hostels, and do your **laundry** in the sink (unless you're explicitly prohibited from doing so). You can split **accommodations** costs (in hotels and some hostels) with trustworthy fellow travelers; multi-bed rooms almost always work out cheaper per person than singles. The same principle will also work for cutting down on the cost of **restaurant** meals. You can also buy food in **supermarkets** instead of eating out; you'd be surprised how tasty (and cheap) simple bread can be with cheese or spread.

With that said, don't go overboard with your budget obsession. Staying within your budget is important, but don't do so at the expense of your sanity or health.

## TIPPING AND TAXES

In Australia, tipping is not required at restaurants or bars, in taxis, or hotels—service workers are fully salaried and do not rely on tips for income. Tips are occasionally left at more expensive restaurants, if you think the service was exceptionally good. In this case, 10% is more than sufficient. Taxes are already included in the bill, so only pay the advertised price.

On July 1, 2000, Australia implemented a **10% Goods and Services Tax (GST).** Some retail goods such as basic foods and medicines are not subject to the new tax. To offset some of the GST price increases, the country's wholesale sales tax was reduced. As part of The New Tax System, the Government also introduced a **Tourist Refund Scheme (TRS)**. Under the TRS, tourists and Australian overseas travelers may be entitled to a refund of the goods and services tax (GST) and of the **Wine Equalisation Tax (WET)** on purchases of goods bought from Australian retailers. The refund is only good for GST and/or WET paid on purchases of AUS$300 or more. The GST refund is calculated by dividing the total amount (after tax) of the purchase by 11. The WET refund is 14.5% of the price paid for wine. Travelers can claim the refund from customs officers when departing Australia by presenting tax receipts from retailers along with a valid passport and proof of travel at TRS booths in international airports or cruise terminals. For more information on the TRS, see the Australia Customs service web page (www.customs.gov.au).

## SAFETY AND SECURITY

| **EMERGENCY PHONE NUMBER** Anywhere in Australia, dial ☎**000.** |

Although Australia is a relatively safe country, it is always important to keep personal safety in mind. Tourists are particularly vulnerable to crime because they often carry large amounts of cash and are not as street savvy as locals. To avoid unwanted attention, try to blend in as much as possible. The gawking camera-toter is a more obvious target than the low-profile traveler. Familiarize yourself with your surroundings before setting out; if you must check a map on the street, duck into a café or shop. If you are traveling alone, be sure that someone at home knows your itinerary and **never admit that you're traveling alone.** The **Australian Department of Foreign Affairs and Trade** (☎(02) 6261 1111) offers travel information and advisories at their website (www.dfat.gov.au).

# GENERAL PRECAUTIONS

## EXPLORING

Extra vigilance is always wise, but there is no need for panic when exploring a new city or region. Find out about unsafe areas from tourist offices, from the manager of your hotel or hostel, or from a local whom you trust. You may want to carry a **whistle** to scare off attackers or attract attention; memorize the emergency number of the city or area. Anywhere in Australia, **dial ☎ 000 for emergency medical help, police, or fire.** Whenever possible, *Let's Go: Australia* warns of unsafe neighborhoods and areas.

## SELF DEFENSE

There is no sure-fire set of precautions that will protect you from all of the situations you might encounter when you travel. A good self-defense course will give you more concrete ways to react to different types of aggression. **Prepare & IMPACT Personal Safety** (www.prepareinc.com) can refer you to local self-defense courses in the United States (☎ (800) 345-5425) and Canada (☎ (604) 878-3838). Workshops (2-3hr.) start at US$50 and full courses run US$350-500. Both women and men are welcome. Their Australian affiliate can be reached at Worth Defending, c/o Sharon Crossno, PO Box 734, Mudgeerab QLD 4213.

**FURTHER INFORMATION.** The following government offices provide travel information and advisories by telephone or on their websites:

**Australian Department of Foreign Affairs and Trade.** ☎ (02) 6261 1111. www.dfat.gov.au.

**Canadian Department of Foreign Affairs and International Trade (DFAIT).** ☎ (800) 267-8376 or ☎ (613) 944-4000 from Ottawa. www.dfait-maeci.gc.ca. Call for their free booklet, *Bon Voyage...But.*

**United Kingdom Foreign and Commonwealth Office.** ☎ (020) 7238 4503. www.fco.gov.uk.

**United States Department of State.** ☎ (202) 647-5225. http://travel.state.gov. For their publication *A Safe Trip Abroad,* call ☎ (202) 512-1800.

## PROTECTING YOUR VALUABLES

To prevent easy theft, don't keep all your valuables (money, important documents) in one place. **Photocopies** of important documents allow you to recover them in case they are lost or filched. Carry one copy separate from the documents and leave another copy at home. Label every piece of luggage both inside and out. **Don't put a wallet with money in your back pocket.** Never count your money in public and carry as little as possible. If you carry a purse, buy a sturdy one with a secure clasp, and carry it crosswise on the side, away from the street with the clasp against you. Secure packs with small combination padlocks which slip through the two zippers. A **money belt** is the best way to carry cash; you can buy one at most camping supply stores. A nylon, zippered pouch with a belt that sits inside the waist of your pants or skirt combines convenience and security. A **neck pouch** is equally safe, although far less accessible. Refrain from pulling out your neck pouch in public; if you must, be very discreet. Avoid keeping anything precious in a fanny-pack (even if it's worn on your stomach): your valuables will be highly visible and easy to steal. Keep some money separate from the rest to use in an emergency or in case of theft.

# BOWLS, BOOZE, AND BUTTS

Australia has fairly strict drug laws, and **illegal drugs** are best avoided altogether. There is a debate currently ensuing over whether or not to legalize marijuana. At this point, the law remains unchanged. Australia does not differentiate between "hard" drugs and more mainstream ones such as marijuana; all are illegal to possess in any quantity. If you carry **prescription drugs** while you travel, take a copy of the prescription with you to show at customs.

Very strict **drunk-driving** (or "drink-driving" as they say in Australia) laws apply, and most states operate frequent random breath-testing. The maximum legal blood-alcohol limit for drivers is .05%. For learner drivers, P-plate holders, and drivers under 25 who have had their licence for less than three years, the maximum blood-alcohol limit is .02%. You must be 18 years old to purchase alcohol or consume it in public.

**Smoking** is prohibited in government buildings and on most public transportation in Australia, including domestic flights. Some international airlines even prohibit smoking while flying in Australian airspace.

# HEALTH

In the event of a serious illness or emergency, call ☎**000 from any phone**—this is a free call—to connect to police, an ambulance, or the fire department.

Common sense is the simplest prescription for good health on the road. Travelers complain most often about their feet and their gut, so take precautionary measures: drink lots of fluids to prevent dehydration and constipation, wear sturdy, broken-in shoes and clean socks, and use talcum powder to keep your feet dry.

## BEFORE YOU GO

Preparation can help minimize the likelihood of contracting a disease and maximize the chances of receiving effective health care in the event of an emergency.

For minor health problems, bring a compact **first-aid kit,** including bandages, aspirin or other pain killer, antibiotic cream, a thermometer, a Swiss army knife with tweezers, moleskin, decongestant for colds, motion sickness remedy, medicine for diarrhea or stomach problems (Pepto Bismol tablets or liquid and Immodium), sunscreen, insect repellent, burn ointment, and a syringe for emergency medical purposes (get a letter of explanation from your doctor). **Contact lens** wearers should bring an extra pair, extra solutions, a copy of the prescription, eye-drops, and a pair of glasses. Those who use heat disinfection might consider switching to chemical cleansers for the duration of the trip.

In your **passport,** write the names of any people you wish to be contacted in case of a medical emergency, and also list any **allergies** or medical conditions you would want doctors to be aware of. Allergy sufferers might want to obtain a full supply of any necessary medication before the trip. Matching a prescription to a foreign equivalent is not always easy, safe, or possible. Carry up-to-date, legible prescriptions or a statement from your doctor stating the medication's trade name, manufacturer, chemical name, and dosage. While traveling, be sure to keep all medication with you in your carry-on luggage. Australian pharmacies, called chemists, can fill most prescriptions written by an Australian doctor.

### IMMUNIZATIONS

Take a look at your immunization records before you go. Travelers over two years old should be sure that the following vaccines are up to date: MMR (for measles, mumps, and rubella); DTaP or Td (for diptheria, tetanus, and pertussis); OPV (for polio); HbCV (for haemophilus influenza B); and HBV (for hepatitus B). Check with a doctor for guidance through this maze of injections.

 **INOCULATION REQUIREMENTS.** Vaccinations are not required unless you have visited a yellow fever infected country or zone within six days prior to arrival. You do not need any other health certificate to enter Australia.

### USEFUL ORGANIZATIONS

The US **Centers for Disease Control and Prevention** (**CDC;** ☎(877) FYI-TRIP; www.cdc.gov/travel), is an excellent source of information for travelers, and maintains an international fax information service. The CDC's comprehensive booklet *Health Information for International Travelers*, an annual rundown of disease, immunization, and general health advice, is free on the website or US$22 via the Government Printing Office (☎ (202) 512-1800). The **US State Department** (http:// travel.state.gov) compiles Consular Information Sheets on health, entry requirements, and other issues for various countries. For quick information on health and other travel warnings, call the **Overseas Citizens' Services** (☎ (202) 647-5225; after-hours ☎ 647-4000). The **British Foreign and Commonwealth Office** also gives health warnings for individual countries (www.fco.gov.uk).

## MEDICAL ASSISTANCE ON THE ROAD

Australia offers a high quality of medical care in both public and private facilities. If you are concerned about being able to access medical support while traveling, there are special support services you may employ. The *MedPass* from **Global Emergency Medical Services (GEMS)**, 2001 Westside Dr., #120, Alpharetta, GA 30004, USA (☎ (800) 860-1111; fax (770) 475-0058; www.globalems.com), provides 24-hour international medical assistance, support, and medical evacuation resources. The **International Association for Medical Assistance to Travelers** (IAMAT; US ☎ (716) 754-4883, Canada ☎ (416) 652-0137, New Zealand ☎ (03) 352 2053; www.sentex.net/ ~iamat) has free membership, lists English-speaking doctors worldwide, and offers detailed info on immunization requirements and sanitation.

Medical assistance is often costly, however, and it may be worthwhile to research various insurance opportunities. With the exception of Medicare, most American health insurance plans cover members' medical emergencies for trips abroad; check your insurance carrier to be sure. If your regular **insurance** policy does not cover travel abroad, you may want to purchase additional coverage. For more information, see **Insurance,** p. 47.

## MEDICAL CONDITIONS

Those with medical conditions (e.g. diabetes, allergies to antibiotics, epilepsy, heart conditions) may want to obtain a stainless steel **Medic Alert** identification tag (US$35 the first year, and $15 annually thereafter), which identifies the condition and gives a 24-hour information number. Contact the Medic Alert Foundation, 2323 Colorado Ave, Turlock, CA 95382 (☎ (800) 432-5378; www.medicalert.org). Throughout Australia, the Medic Alert number is ☎ (0800) 88 22 22 (www.medica-lert.com.au). Diabetics can contact the **American Diabetes Association,** 1071 N. Beauregard St, Alexandria, VA 22311 (☎ (800) 342-2383; www.diabetes.org), to get a copy of "Travel and Diabetes" and a diabetic ID card, which has messages in 18 languages explaining the carrier's diabetic status.

If you are **HIV** positive, contact the Bureau of Consular Affairs, #4811, Department of State, Washington, D.C. 20520 (☎ (202) 647-1488; auto-fax 647-3000; http:// travel.state.gov). Travelers applying for a permanent visa must first be tested for HIV and AIDS; tests taken in the US are acceptable.

## JET LAG

Many Travelers to Australia will arrive after a flight of over 12 hours. In such cases, jet lag can be rather severe and take a few days to overcome. To minimize the effects of jet lag, "reset" your body's clock by adopting the time of your destination as soon as you board the plane. While it may be tempting to sleep, some say it is best to force yourself to make it at least through the early evening. If you will be arriving in the morning, one strategy is to stay up all night before your departure and sleep on the plane. On long flights, search for and claim an open row for a better sleep. Some travelers also take herbal supplements such as melatonin (or a few glasses of free in-flight wine) to help reset their body clocks.

# ENVIRONMENTAL HAZARDS

## HEAT EXHAUSTION AND DEHYDRATION

Heat exhaustion, characterized by dehydration and salt deficiency, can lead to fatigue, headaches, and wooziness. Avoid heat exhaustion by drinking plenty of clear fluids and eating salty foods, like crackers. Always drink enough liquids to keep your urine clear. Alcoholic beverages are dehydrating, as are coffee, strong tea, and caffeinated sodas. Wear a hat, sunglasses, and a lightweight longsleeve shirt in hot sun, and take time to acclimate to a hot destination before seriously exerting yourself. Continuous heat stress can eventually lead to **heatstroke,** characterized by rising body temperature, severe headache, and cessation of sweating. Heatstroke is rare but serious, and victims must be cooled off with wet towels and taken to a doctor as soon as possible.

## SUNBURN

Since there is so much outdoor fun in Australia, apply sunscreen liberally and often to avoid burns and lower the risk of skin cancer, a disease which is no stranger to Australia. Queensland has the highest rate of skin cancer cases in the world. If you are planning on spending time near water, in the desert, or in the snow, you are at risk of getting burned, even when it is cloudy. If you get sunburned, drink more fluids than usual and apply Calamine or an aloe-based lotion.

## HYPOTHERMIA AND FROSTBITE

A rapid drop in body temperature is the clearest warning sign of overexposure to cold. Victims may also shiver, feel exhausted, have poor coordination or slurred speech, hallucinate, or suffer amnesia. Seek medical help, and *do not let hypothermia victims fall asleep*—their body temperature will continue to drop and they may die. To avoid hypothermia, keep dry, wear layers, and stay out of the wind. In wet weather, wool and synthetics such as pile retain heat. Most other fabric, especially cotton, will make you colder. The Australian climate is fairly temperate for most of the year, but during the winter months, especially in areas like the Snowy Mountains, it can get cold. When the temperature is below freezing, watch for **frostbite.** If a region of skin turns white, waxy, and cold, do not rub the area. Drink warm beverages, get dry, and slowly warm the area with dry fabric or steady body contact until a doctor can be found.

# PREVENTING DISEASE

## INSECT, ANIMAL AND FOOD-BORNE DISEASES

Many diseases are transmitted by insects—mainly mosquitoes, fleas, ticks, and lice. Be aware of insects in wet or forested areas (such as northern Queensland and Kakadu, NT), while hiking, and especially while camping. **Mosquitoes** are most active from dusk to dawn. Use insect repellents, such as DEET. Wear long pants and long sleeves (fabric need not be thick or warm; tropic-weight cottons can keep you comfortable in the heat) and buy a mosquito net. Wear shoes and socks, and tuck long pants into socks. Soak or spray your gear with permethrin, licensed in the U.S. for use on clothing. Natural repellents can be useful supplements: taking vitamin B-12 pills regularly can make you smelly to insects, as can garlic pills. Calamine lotion or topical cortisones (like Cortaid) may stop insect bites from itching, as can a bath with a half-cup of baking soda or oatmeal. **Ticks**—responsible for Lyme and other diseases—can be particularly dangerous in rural and forested regions. While walking, pause periodically to brush off ticks from exposed parts of your body using a fine-toothed comb. Do not try to remove ticks by burning them.

Prevention is the best cure for food- and water-borne diseases: be sure that everything you eat is cooked properly and that the water you drink is clean. To purify your own water, bring it to a rolling boil or treat it with **iodine tablets,** available at any camping goods store. Other culprits are raw shellfish, unpasteurized milk, and sauces containing raw eggs. Always wash your hands before eating, or bring a quick-drying purifying liquid hand cleaner like Purrell.

> **Encephalitis** is a rarely occurring disease transmitted in regions of Western Australia by mosquitoes. Carriers breed annually north of Port Hedland between February and April. Symptoms include headaches, neck stiffness, and nausea. Wearing long-sleeved clothing and using topical DEET to fend off bites is recommended.

ESSENTIALS

**Ross River and Barmah Forest Virus (epidemic polyarthritis)** is a disease transmitted by mosquitoes in regions of Victoria. Symptoms include fever, aching joints and sometimes small purple blotches that look like bruises. Symptoms will disappear after a few weeks, although they may return even after the virus is gone. Full recovery can take up to several months to complete.

**Dengue Fever** is an "urban viral infection" transmitted by *Aedes* mosquitoes, which bite during the day rather than at night. Dengue has flu-like symptoms and is often indicated by a rash 3-4 days after the onset of fever. Symptoms for the first 2-4 days include chills, high fever, headaches, swollen lymph nodes, muscle aches, and in some instances, a pink rash on the face. If you experience these symptoms, see a doctor, drink plenty of liquids, and take fever-reducing medication such as acetaminophen (Tylenol). *Never take aspirin to treat dengue fever.*

**Parasites** such as microbes and tapeworms hide in unsafe water and food. **Giardia,** for example, is acquired by drinking untreated water from streams or lakes all over the world, including Australia. Symptoms of parasitic infections in general include swollen glands or lymph nodes, fever, rashes or itchiness, digestive problems, eye problems, and anemia. Boil your water, wear shoes, avoid bugs, and eat only cooked food.

**Rabies** is transmitted through the saliva of infected animals. It is fatal if untreated. Australia is officially rabies free, but there have been reports of rabies-like diseases among the country's indigenous bats. If you are bitten, clean your wound thoroughly and seek medical help to determine whether you need to be treated.

## AIDS, HIV, STDS

**Acquired Immune Deficiency Syndrome (AIDS)** is a growing problem around the world. The World Health Organization estimates that there are around 30 million people infected with the HIV virus, and women now represent 40% of all new HIV infections. In Australia, 11,000 adults are currently diagnosed with HIV—0.14% of the population. Since the start of the AIDS epidemic, 8300 cases of AIDS have been recorded. Visitors or students applying for a permanent or long-term visa will be tested for AIDS. Contact the Australian consulate for details about the AIDS and HIV policies regarding permanent and temporary entrance to the country.

**Sexually transmitted diseases** (STDs) such as gonorrhea, chlamydia, genital warts, syphilis, and herpes are easier to catch than HIV, and some can be just as deadly. **Hepatitis B** and **C** are also serious sexually transmitted diseases. Warning signs for STDs include: swelling, sores, bumps, or blisters on sex organs, rectum, or mouth; burning and pain during urination and bowel movements; itching around sex organs; swelling or redness in the throat; or flu-like symptoms with fever, chills, and aches. If these symptoms develop, see a doctor immediately. When having sex, condoms may protect you from certain STDs, but oral or even tactile contact can lead to transmission.

## WOMEN'S HEALTH

Women travelers may be vulnerable to **urinary tract** and **bladder infections,** common and very uncomfortable bacterial diseases that cause a burning sensation and painful and frequent urination. To minimize risk, drink plenty of vitamin-C-rich juice and clean water and urinate frequently, especially right after intercourse. Untreated, these infections can lead to kidney infections, sterility, and even death. If symptoms persist, see a doctor.

**Tampons** and **pads** are sometimes hard to find when traveling, especially in Australia's less populated areas like parts of the Northern Territory, so it may be advisable to take supplies along. **Reliable contraceptive devices** may also be difficult to find. Women on the pill should bring enough to allow for possible loss or extended stays. Bring a prescription, since forms of the pill vary a good deal.

# INSURANCE

Travel insurance generally covers four basic areas: medical/health problems, property loss, trip cancellation/interruption, and emergency evacuation. Although your regular insurance policies may well extend to travel-related accidents, you may consider purchasing travel insurance if the cost of potential trip cancellation/ interruption is greater than you can absorb.

Be aware that many **medical insurance** policies (especially university policies) often cover costs incurred abroad; check with your provider. **US Medicare does not cover foreign travel.** Australia's national health insurance scheme, Medicare, is available for travelers from New Zealand, the United Kingdom, Ireland, Malta, Sweden, Italy, Finland, and the Netherlands. Visitors from these places can enroll at any Medicare office in Australia. Canadians are protected by their home province's health insurance plan for up to 90 days after leaving the country; check with the provincial Ministry of Health or Health Plan Headquarters for details.

**ISIC** and **ITIC** provide basic insurance benefits, including US$100 per day of in-hospital sickness for a maximum of 60 days, US$3000 of accident-related medical reimbursement, and US$25,000 for emergency medical transport (see **Identification,** p. 35). Cardholders have access to a toll-free 24-hour helpline whose multilingual staff can provide assistance in medical, legal, and financial emergencies overseas. (US and Canada ☎ (877) 370-4742, elsewhere call US collect +1 (713) 342-4104). **American Express** (☎ (800) 528-4800) grants most cardholders automatic car rental insurance (collision and theft, but not liability). AmEx also includes accidental death and dismemberment coverage of US$100,000 when you purchase the flight, train, boat, or bus ticket with the card.

Prices for travel insurance purchased separately generally run about US$50 per week for full coverage, while trip cancellation/interruption may be purchased separately at a rate of about US$5.50 per US$100 of coverage. **Homeowners' insurance** (or your family's coverage) often covers theft during travel and loss of travel documents (passport, plane ticket, railpass, etc.) up to US$500.

**INSURANCE PROVIDERS. Council** and **STA** (see p. 59 for complete listings) offer a range of plans that can supplement your basic coverage. Other private insurance providers in the **US** and **Canada** include: **Access America** (☎ (800) 284-8300); **Berkely Group/Carefree Travel Insurance** (☎ (800) 323-3149; www.berkely.com); **Globalcare Travel Insurance** (☎ (800) 821-2488; www.globalcare-cocco.com); and **Travel Assistance International** (☎ (800) 821-2828; www.worldwide-assistance.com). Providers in the **UK** include **Campus Travel** (☎ (01865) 258 000) and **Columbus Travel Insurance** (☎ (020) 7375 0011). Additionally, for Australia specific information, contact **Travel Insurance on the Net** (☎ (02) 6293 3764; www.travelinsurance.com.au), which offers Smart Cover, Worldcare Assist, Australia Visitors Travel Insurance, and Travel Insurance, the complete insurance cover.

# PACKING

Pack light: lay out only what you absolutely need, then take half the clothes and twice the money. The less you have, the less you have to lose (or store, or carry on your back). Save any extra space left for souvenirs or items you pick up along the way. If you plan to do a lot of hiking, see **Camping And The Outdoors,** p. 52.

**LUGGAGE.** Toting a suitcase or trunk is fine if you plan to stay in one or two cities and explore from there, but a very, very bad idea if you're going to be trekking through the Kimberly or hiking through the rainforest. In addition to your main vessel, a small backpack, rucksack, or courier bag may be useful as a daypack for sight-seeing expeditions; it doubles as an airplane carry-on. An empty, lightweight duffel bag packed inside your luggage may also be useful. Once abroad you can fill your luggage with purchases and keep your dirty clothes in the duffel. For advice on choosing a backpack, see p. 52.

**CLOTHING.** No matter if it's the Wet or the Dry, it's always a good idea to bring a **warm jacket** or wool sweater, a **rain jacket** (Gore-Tex® is both waterproof and breathable), sturdy shoes or **hiking boots,** and **thick socks. Flip-flops** or waterproof sandals are crucial for grubby hostel showers. You may also want to add one outfit beyond the jeans and t-shirt uniform, and maybe a nicer pair of shoes if you plan to do any clubbing in the bigger cities.

**SLEEPSACKS.** Many hostels require that you either provide your own linen or rent sheets from them. Save cash by making your own sleepsack: fold a full-size sheet in half the long way, then sew it closed along the long side and one of the short sides. Also, keep in mind that some hostels in larger cities prohibit sleeping bags.

**WASHING CLOTHES.** *Let's Go* attempts to provide info on laundromats in the Practical Information and hostel listings. Most cities have laundromats, but sometimes it may be cheaper and easier to use a sink. Bring a small bar or tube of detergent soap, a small rubber ball to stop up the sink, and a travel clothes line.

**ELECTRIC CURRENT.** In Australia, electricity is 220/240 volts, and AC is 50Hz, enough to fry 110V North American appliances. 220V electrical appliances don't like 110V current, either. Hardware stores sell adapters (to change the shape of the plug) and converters (to change the voltage). Don't make the mistake of using only an adapter (unless appliance instructions explicitly state otherwise).

**CONTACT LENSES.** Machines which heat-disinfect contact lenses will require a small converter (about US$20) to 220 volts AC. Consider switching temporarily to a chemical disinfection system, but check with your lens dispenser to see if it's safe to switch; some lenses may be damaged by a chemical system. Contact lens supplies may be expensive and difficult to find in less populated areas; bring enough saline and cleaner for your entire vacation.

### OTHER USEFUL ITEMS

No matter how you're traveling, it's always a good idea to carry a first-aid kit including sunscreen, insect repellent, and vitamins. Other useful items include: an umbrella; sealable plastic bags (for damp clothes, soap, food, shampoo, and other spillables); alarm clock; waterproof matches; sun hat; moleskin (for blisters); sunglasses; pocketknife; plastic water bottle; compass; towel; padlock; whistle; flashlight; earplugs; electrical tape (for patching tears); tweezers; garbage bags; a small calculator for currency conversion; a pair of flip-flops for the shower; a money-belt for carrying valuables; deodorant; razors; tampons; and condoms. Never forget condoms.

# ACCOMMODATIONS

## HOTELS

While **hotels** in large cities are similar to those in the rest of the world, "hotels" in rural Australia, particularly in Victoria and New South Wales, are simple furnished rooms above local pubs. Some smack of fancy Victorian-era lodging with grand back staircases, high tin ceilings, and wrap-around verandas. Others have been converted to long-term worker housing, and are thus less conducive to brief overnight stays. Singles in these hotels usually cost AUS$15-30. This generally includes a towel, a shared bathroom, and a private bedroom (no bunks, usually). A simple breakfast may be included, and there's occasionally a common kitchen. The pubs are fully functional downstairs, so it's a good idea to choose a quieter one if you're fond of tucking in early. **Motels** in Australia are accommodations with parking.

## HOSTELS

Get ready for more Down Under lingo. In Australia, a "youth hostel" is more commonly known as a "backpackers." Hostels are generally dorm-style accommodations, often in single-sex large rooms with bunk beds, although most hostels do offer private rooms or doubles for families and couples. They sometimes have kitchens and utensils for your use, bike rentals, storage areas, and laundry facilities. Remember that crime occurs in even the most demure-looking hostel; bring your own **padlock** for your storage locker. Many hostels allow guests to leave valuables in a safe at the front desk. Some hostel owners provide transportation to and from bus stations and airports. In Australia, a bed in a hostel will average around AUS\$15-20. A **VIP** discount card offered by Backpackers Resorts International gets AUS\$1 off per night at many hostels. Let's Go designates these hostels with a VIP at the end of the listing. A list of many hostels, regardless of affiliation, can be found at www.hostels.com.

**A HOSTELER'S BILL OF RIGHTS.** There are certain standard features that we do not include in our hostel listings. Unless we state otherwise, you can expect that every hostel has: no lockout, no curfew, free hot showers, secure storage, and no key deposit.

## HOSTELLING INTERNATIONAL

Joining the youth hostel association in your own country (listed below) automatically grants you membership privileges in **Hostelling International (HI),** a federation of national hosteling associations. Australia's over 140 **YHAs** are members of HI, and some in larger cities accept reservations via the **International Booking Network** (Australia ☎(02) 9261 1111; Canada ☎(800) 663-5777; England and Wales ☎(1629) 58 14 18; Northern Ireland ☎(1232) 32 47 33; Republic of Ireland ☎(01) 830 1766; New Zealand ☎(09) 379 4224; Scotland ☎(541) 55 32 55; US ☎(800) 909-4776). HI's umbrella organization's web page (www.iyhf.org), which lists the web addresses and phone numbers of all national associations, is a great place to begin researching hostelling in a specific region. Most student travel agencies (see p. 59) sell HI cards, as do all of the national hosteling organizations listed below. All prices listed are valid for **one-year memberships** unless otherwise noted.

**Australian Youth Hostels Association (AYHA),** 422 Kent St, Sydney NSW 2000 (☎(02) 9261 1111; fax 9261 1969; www.yha.org.au). AUS\$49, under 18 AUS\$14.50.

**Hostelling International-Canada (HI-C),** 400-205 Catherine St, Ottawa, ON K2P 1C3 (☎(1800) 663-5777 or ☎(1613) 237-7884; fax 237-7868; email info@hostelling-intl.ca; www.hostellingintl.ca). CDN\$25, under 18 CDN\$12.

**An Óige (Irish Youth Hostel Association),** 61 Mountjoy St, Dublin 7 (☎(1) 830 4555; fax 830 5808; email anoige@iol.ie; www.irelandyha.org). IR£10, under 18 IR£4.

**Youth Hostels Association of New Zealand (YHANZ),** P.O. Box 436, 173 Cashel St., Christchurch 1 (☎(03) 379 9970; fax 365 4476; email info@yha.org.nz; www.yha.org.nz). NZ\$40, ages 15-17 NZ\$12, under 15 free.

**Hostels Association of South Africa,** 3rd fl. 73 St. George's St Mall, P.O. Box 4402, Cape Town 8000 (☎(021) 424 2511; fax 424 4119; email info@hisa.org.za; www.hisa.org.za). SAR50, under 18 SAR25, lifetime SAR250.

**Scottish Youth Hostels Association (SYHA),** 7 Glebe Crescent, Stirling FK8 2JA (☎(01786) 89 14 00; fax 89 13 33; www.syha.org.uk). UK£6, under 18 UK£2.50.

**Youth Hostels Association (England and Wales) Ltd.,** Trevelyan House, 8 St. Stephen's Hill, St. Albans, Hertfordshire AL1 2DY, UK (☎(01727) 85 52 15; fax 84 41 26; www.yha.org.uk). UK£12, under 18 UK£6, families UK£24.

**Hostelling International Northern Ireland (HINI),** 22-32 Donegall Rd, Belfast BT12 5JN, Northern Ireland (☎(01232) 32 47 33; fax 43 96 99; email info@hini.org.uk; www.hini.org.uk). UK£7, under 18 UK£3.

**Hostelling International-American Youth Hostels (HI-AYH),** 733 15th St NW, #840, Washington, D.C. 20005 (☎(1202) 783-6161 ext. 136; fax 783-6171; email hiayhserv@hiayh.org; www.hiayh.org). US\$25, under 18 free.

ESSENTIALS

ESSENTIALS

# Your gateway to Australia!

## We invented backpacking...

**YHA is the world's leading budget accommodation network. We offer you 150 of the best places to stay in Oz – from the beach to the bush to the cities.**

### Great hostels!

- Affordable, secure and friendly
- 24 hour access
- Informed staff for travel tips
- Free hostel-to-hostel reservation
- Open to all ages

## Get a bed on-line!

Want to have a place to stay confirmed before you leave home?

Go to **www.yha.com**

**1** > Pick your hostel
**2** > Fill in the form
**3** > Hit the SEND button
Done! It's that easy!

HOSTELLING INTERNATIONAL

**For HI membership in the US call (202) 783 6161**

**Great value Accommodation/Coach Passes available online**
# www.yha.com

## NOMADS

Another large hosteling chain in Australia is NOMADS Backpackers. Though it has only about one third as many locations as YHA, the services and amenities are similar. You don't have to be a member to stay at a NOMADS hostel. Their website (www.nomadsworld.com) not only lists all hostels, but also gives advice on finding work. Bookings can be made through the respective hostel or by calling. The NOMADS Adventure Card (AUS$25) offers discount international calling, cheaper rates at many Internet cafés, and either $1 off per night or 7th night free at NOMADS. For reservations, call ☎ (1800) 73 73 78 (from overseas, ☎ +61 8 8224 0919; fax 8224 0972), or email bookings@nomads-backpackers.com.

## BED AND BREAKFASTS

For a cozy alternative to impersonal hotel rooms, B&Bs (private homes with rooms available to travelers) range from the acceptable to the sublime. Hosts will sometimes go out of their way to be accommodating by giving personalized tours or offering home-cooked meals. On the other hand, many B&Bs do not provide phones, TVs, or private bathrooms. Rooms in B&Bs generally cost AUS$40-80 for a single and AUS$60-100 for a double, but are more expensive in touristed areas.

Several travel guides and reservation services specialize in B&Bs. **Travel-Link International** has a website at www.travel-link.org/bbpages/bbau/bbau00masterset.html with over 1500 B&B listings in Australia. Run in partnership with HomeLink International, Travel-Link uses its extensive network to help travelers plan their itineraries. **Bed and Breakfast Australia,** PO Box 448 Homebush St, Sydney NSW, 2140 (☎ (02) 9763 5833; fax (02) 9763 1677; email bnb@bedandbreakfast.com.au) can plan itineraries and make advance bookings.

## DORMS

Many **colleges and universities** open their residence halls to travelers when school is not in session—some do so even during term-time. These dorms are often close to student areas—good sources for information on things to do—and are usually very clean. Getting a room may take a couple of phone calls and require advanced planning, but rates tend to be low. *Let's Go* lists colleges which rent dorm rooms among the accommodation listings for appropriate cities.

Typical university holidays include most of September and the summer break from December to mid- February. Easter break lasts for two weeks, while winter break encompasses the first two weeks of July. The Universities of Canberra, Sydney, and Queensland, as well as Flinders University of South Australia, Melbourne University, and Monash and LaTrobe Universities in Melbourne are among those occasionally offering accommodation. No one policy covers all institutions. Contact the universities directly; the Australian Tourist Commission has contact info on their website www.australia.com, under "Traveller's Resources," then "Special Interest Fact Sheets," then "Student Travel." Demand is high, so book ahead.

## HOME EXCHANGE AND RENTALS

Home exchanges offer the opportunity to live like a native and to cut down dramatically on accommodation fees—usually only an administration fee is paid to the matching service. Once you join or contact one of the exchange services listed below, it is then up to you to decide with whom you would like to exchange homes. Most companies have pictures of member's homes and information about the owners. A great site with many exchange companies is www.aitec.edu.au/~bwechner/Documents/Travel/Lists/HomeExchangeClubs.html. Home rentals are much more expensive than exchanges, but can be cheaper than comparably-serviced hotels. Both home exchanges and rentals are ideal for families with children or travelers with special dietary needs; you often get your own kitchen, maid service, TV, and telephones.

**HomeLink International,** P.O. Box 1388, Byron Bay, NSW 2481 (☎ (02) 6680 8071; fax 6680 8073; email homelink@nor.com.au; www.homelink.org). 25 offices worldwide;

ESSENTIALS

contact the one in your home country to facilitate home exchange. Listing of 11,000 homes worldwide, and 400 homes throughout Australia. Paid subscribers have access to a comprehensive web page; on-line registration available.

**Latitudes Home Exchange,** P.O. Box 436, South Perth WA 6951 (☎(08) 9367 9412; fax 9367 9576; www.home-swap.com). Offers temporary home exchange for 1-24 months. Computerized matching service (USD$50 lifetime membership; USD$250 fee when the member approves a match) or directory listings (USD$50 per year).

**Intervac International Home Exchange,** has home exchanges in 34 countries. Check out www.intervac.com to find your home country listing.

# CAMPING AND THE OUTDOORS

If your travels take you to Australia when the weather is agreeable, camping is by far the cheapest way to go. The ubiquitous caravan parks offer sites without power for tent campers, and some hostels have camping facilities or at least allow guests to pitch tents in the yard. Unpowered campsites can vary in price from free to AUS$20 for a prime spot during Christmas holidays, but are generally at the lower end of the scale. The flexibility of camping allows you to access the more remote corners of the country's numerous wilderness areas, including most of the 13 World Heritage Sites in Australia.

World Heritage Sites have been determined to have significant ecological or cultural value for the world. Some of the World Heritage Sites in other countries are the Acropolis, Stonehenge, the Serengeti, and Yellowstone. Australia's include **The Great Barrier Reef, Fraser Island** in Queensland; **Kakadu National Park** and **Uluru** (Ayers Rock in Kata Tjuta National Park) in Northern Territory; **Lord Howe Island Group** and **Willandra Lakes Region** in New South Wales; **Shark Bay** in Western Australia; as well as Tasmanian wilderness, Heard and McDonald Islands, Macquarie Island, fossil sites in Queensland and South Australia, and the wet tropics of Queensland. For more information on World Heritage Sites, check out www.unesco.org/whc/nwhc/pages/sites/main.htm.

## USEFUL PUBLICATIONS AND WEB RESOURCES

Other publications about camping and hiking are available from the **NSW National Parks and Wildlife Service Head Office,** Level 1, 43 Bridge St, Hurstville NSW 2220 (☎(02) 9585 6333; fax 9585 6527; email feedback@npws.nsw.gov.au; www.npws.nsw.gov.au; open M-F 9am-5pm). **Australia Outdoor Connection** (http://flinders.com.au/home.htm) is sponsored by Flinders Camping in Adelaide which provides camping and environmental information and links. For **topographical maps of Australia,** contact the Australian Surveying & Land Information Group (☎(02) 6201 4201, in Australia ☎(0800) 80 01 73; fax 6201 4366; www.aus-lig.gov.au), or write to P.O. Box 2, Belconnen, ACT 2616. AUSLIG publishes over 500 maps (most run $7.50; plus shipping).

## CAMPING AND HIKING EQUIPMENT

### WHAT TO BUY...

Good camping equipment is both sturdy and light. Camping equipment is generally more expensive in Australia than in North America, so if you have your own, you might want to bring it with you. However, customs officials will inspect used camping equipment to be sure that it is clean and free of any dirt or foreign soil.

**Sleeping Bag:** Most good sleeping bags are rated by "season," or the lowest outdoor temperature at which they will keep you warm ("summer" means 30-40°F at night and "four-season" or "winter" often means below 0°F). Sleeping bags are made either of down (warmer and lighter, but more expensive, and miserable when wet) or of synthetic material (heavier, more durable, and warmer when wet). Prices vary, but might range from US$80-150 for a summer synthetic to US$150-250 for a good down winter bag. **Sleeping bag pads,** including foam pads (US$10-20) and air mattresses (US$15-50) cushion your back and neck and insulate you from the ground. **Therm-A-Rest** brand self-inflating sleeping pads are part foam and part air-mattress and partially inflate when you unroll them, but are costly at US$45-80. Bring a **"stuff sack"** (US$5-15) or plastic bag to store your sleeping bag and keep it dry.

**Tent:** The best tents are free-standing, with their own frames and suspension systems; they set up quickly and only require staking in high winds. Low-profile dome tents are the best all-around. When pitched their internal space is almost entirely usable, which means little unnecessary bulk. If you're traveling by car, go for the bigger tent, but if you're hiking, stick with a smaller tent that weighs no more than 5-6 lbs (2-3kg). Good 2-person tents start at US$90, 4-person tents at US$300. Seal the seams of your tent with waterproofer, and make sure it has a rain fly.

**Backpack:** If you intend to do a lot of hiking, you should have a frame backpack. **Internal-frame packs** mold better to your back, keep a lower center of gravity, and can flex adequately to allow you to hike difficult trails that require a lot of bending and maneuvering. **External-frame packs** are more comfortable for long hikes over even terrain since they keep the weight higher and distribute it more evenly. Whichever you choose, make sure your pack has a strong, padded hip belt, which transfers the weight from the shoulders to the legs. Any serious backpacking requires a pack of at least 4000 cubic inches (16,000cc). Allow an additional 500 cubic inches for your sleeping bag in internal-frame packs. Sturdy backpacks cost anywhere from US$150-450. This is one area where it doesn't pay to economize—cheaper packs may be less comfortable, and the straps are more likely to fray or rip. Before you buy any pack, try it on and imagine carrying it, full, a few miles up a rocky incline. Better yet, insist on filling it with something heavy and walking around the store to get a sense of how it distributes weight before committing to buy it. A **waterproof backpack cover** will prove invaluable. Otherwise, plan to store all of your belongings in plastic bags inside your backpack.

**Boots:** Get hiking boots with good **ankle support** which are appropriate for the terrain you plan to hike. Your boots should fit snugly and comfortably over one or two wool socks and a thin liner sock. Break in boots properly by wearing them for several weeks to spare yourself painful and debilitating blisters.

**Other Necessities: Raingear** either in two pieces, a top and pants, or a poncho is absolutely essential, even when a destination is reputed to be sunny. **Synthetics,** like polypropylene tops, socks, and long underwear, along with a pile jacket, will keep you warm even when wet. Plastic water bottles keep water cooler than metal ones do, and are virtually shatter- and leak-proof. Large, collapsible **water sacks** will significantly improve your lot in primitive campgrounds and weigh practically nothing when empty, though they are bulky and heavy when full. Bring **water-purification tablets** (US$5 for 50 tablets) for when you can't boil water. Though most campgrounds provide campfire sites, you may want to bring a small **metal grate** or **grill** of your own. For those places that forbid fires or the gathering of firewood, you'll need a **camp stove.** The classic Coleman stove starts at about US$40. You will need to purchase a **fuel bottle** and fill it with propane to operate it. A **first aid kit, pocket knife, insect repellent, calamine lotion,** and **waterproof matches** or a **lighter** are other essential camping items.

## ...AND WHERE TO BUY IT

The mail-order/online companies listed below offer lower prices than many retail stores, but a visit to a local camping or outdoors store will give you a good sense of the look and weight of certain items.

**Campmor,** Upper Saddle River, NJ USA (US ☎(1888) 226-7667; from abroad call US ☎+1 (201) 825-8300; www.campmor.com).

**Discount Camping,** 880 Main North Rd, Pooraka, South Australia 5095, Australia (☎(08) 8262 3399; fax (08) 8260 6240; www.discountcamping.com.au).

**Eastern Mountain Sports (EMS),** 327 Jaffrey Rd, Peterborough, NH 03458, USA (☎(1888) 463-6367 or ☎(1603) 924-7231; www.shopems.com).

**L.L. Bean,** Freeport, ME USA (US and Canada ☎(1800) 441-5713; UK ☎(0800) 96 29 54; elsewhere, call US ☎+1 (207) 552-6878; www.llbean.com).

**Mountain Designs,** P.O. Box 1472, Fortitude Valley, Brisbane, Queensland 4006, Australia (☎(07) 3252 8894; www.mountaindesign.com.au).

**Recreational Equipment, Inc. (REI),** Sumner, WA USA (☎(1800) 426-4840 or ☎(1253) 891-2500; www.rei.com).

**YHA Adventure Shop,** 14 Southampton St, London, WC2E 7HA, UK (☎(020) 7836 8541). The main branch of one of Britain's largest outdoor equipment suppliers.

# WILDERNESS SAFETY

**Stay warm, stay dry, and stay hydrated.** The vast majority of life-threatening wilderness situations result from a breach of this simple dictum. On any hike, however brief, you should pack enough equipment to keep you alive should disaster befall. This includes **raingear, hat, mittens,** a **first-aid kit,** a **reflector,** a **whistle, high energy food,** and extra **water.** Dress in warm layers of **synthetic materials** designed for the outdoors, or **wool.** Pile fleece jackets and Gore-Tex® raingear are excellent choices. Never rely on **cotton** for warmth. This "death cloth" will be absolutely useless should it get wet. Make sure to check all equipment for any defects before setting out, and see **Camping and Hiking Equipment,** p. 52, for more information.

Check **weather forecasts** and pay attention to the skies when hiking. Weather patterns can change suddenly. Whenever possible, let someone know when and where you are going hiking—either a friend, your hostel, a park ranger, or a local hiking organization. Do not attempt a hike beyond your ability—you may be endangering your life.

See **Health,** p. 43, for info on outdoor ailments such as heatstroke, hypothermia, giardia, rabies, and insects, as well as basic medical concerns and first-aid.

For **further reading,** consult *How to Stay Alive in the Woods* by Bradford Angier (Macmillan, US$8).

# DANGEROUS WILDLIFE

When Gondwanaland split up into continents ages ago, Australia got more than its fair share of extremely dangerous animal life. With a few precautions, travelers should be able to avoid the nastiest creatures, but hospitals do stock anti-venoms. If you get bitten or stung, it is best to take the offending creature to the hospital with you (if you are not in danger of being bitten or stung again) so that doctors can administer the correct anti-venom.

**Sea life** can be deadly during certain times of year, and warnings to stay out of the water should be strictly observed. The most notorious of these beasts is the **box jellyfish,** which inhabits the waters of northern Australia from November to April. Swimming on beaches north of Rockhampton QLD during these months is forbidden (see p. 388). The sting is potentially lethal to adults, and almost certainly lethal to children. Box jellyfish that have washed up on shore are still dangerous, so walking barefoot at the water's edge is discouraged. The **stonefish** and **blue-ringed octopus** also present danger at the beach. **Sharks** are common to some Australian shores, but lifeguards at heavily visited beaches keep a good look out—don't swim outside the red and yellow flagged areas.

Freshwater and saltwater **crocodiles** present another water and water's-edge hazard in north and northwest Australia. "Salties" are the more dangerous of the two. They can be found in fresh and salt water, are hard to see, and attack without provocation. Heed local warning signs; don't swim or paddle in streams, lakes, the ocean, or other natural waterways, and keep kids away from the water's edge. "Freshies" are found in freshwater and will not attack unless provoked, but they are also hard to see, and you may provoke one without knowing it's there.

**Snakes** are perhaps the most feared Australian animals, and while most hikers will never run across these venomous slitherers, there are certain precautions and safety information that travelers should know. Several species of poisonous snakes live in Australia; most are scared enough of humans that they will slide away at the sound of tramping feet. If cornered, though, a few might attack in self-defense. To prevent a bite, wear boots and long pants when walking through the wilderness, and never approach, attempt to step over, or try to kill a snake. Instead, walk around it at a safe distance. If bitten, tightly wrap the wounded area and work the bandage down to the tip of the limb and back up to the next joint to help slow the spread of venom. If possible, keep the infected area immobile, and seek medical attention immediately. Do not try to suck out the venom or clean the bite. Don't panic—most snake bites can be treated effectively.

The two most dangerous **spiders** in Australia are the funnel-web (found in eastern Australia including Tasmania) and the redback (common throughout Australia, particularly in urban areas). Stinging **insects** abound in Australia, including the bull-ant, wasp, bee, and bush-tick, and although these may hurt a lot, they are not life-threatening. If you know that you are allergic to bee stings or other insect bites, carry your own epinephrine kit. After a period of time in the bush, check for lumps on your skin to find and remove bush-ticks.

## CARAVANS AND CAMPERVANS

Caravanning is popular in Australia where most campgrounds double as caravan parks, consisting of both tent sites and powered sites for caravans. On-site caravans (also called on-site vans) are a frequent feature at caravan parks, and are anchored permanently to the site and rented out. "Cabins" at caravan parks are often analogous to an on-site van, with a toilet inside.

There is a distinction between **caravans** and **campervans (RVs).** The former is pulled as a trailer, while the latter has its own cab. Renting a caravan is more expensive than tenting or hosteling, but cheaper than renting a car and staying in hotels. The convenience of bringing along your own bedroom, bathroom, and kitchen makes it an attractive option, especially for older travelers and families.

It's not difficult to arrange a campervan rental, although you should start gathering information several months before departure. Rates vary widely by region, season (Dec.-Feb. are the most expensive months), and type of van. It always pays to contact several different companies to compare vehicles and prices. **Hertz** (☎(1800) 654-3001) is a US firm which arranges caravan rentals in Australia. **Maui Rentals** (☎(03) 9415 1069; fax 9415 1208; www.maui-rentals.com) and Britz Campervan Rentals and Tours (☎(03) 9417 1888; www.brits.com.au) rent RVs as well.

# KEEPING IN TOUCH

## MAIL

### SENDING MAIL TO AUSTRALIA

Mark envelopes "air mail" or "par avion" to avoid having letters sent by sea.

**Canada:** Allow 4-10 days for regular **airmail** to Australia. Postcards and letters up to 20g cost CDN75¢; packages up to 0.5kg CDN$8.50, up to 2kg CDN$28.30. www.canadapost.ca/CPC2/common/rates/ratesgen.html#international.

**Ireland:** Allow 5-7 days for regular **airmail** to Australia. Postcards and letters up to 25g cost IR£0.45. Add IR£2.30 for Swiftpost International (one day faster). www.anpost.ie.

**New Zealand:** Allow approximately 7 days for regular **airmail** to Australia. Postcards NZ$1. Letters up to 20g cost NZ$1.20-1.80; small parcels up to 0.5kg NZ$5.85-24, up to 2kg NZ$15.09-39. www.nzpost.co.nz/nzpost/inrates.

**UK:** Allow 4-8 days for airmail to Australia. Letters up to 20g cost UK£0.65; packages up to 0.5kg UK£4.95, up to 2kg UK£19.20. UK Swiftair delivers letters a day faster for an extra UK£2.85. www.royalmail.co.uk/calculator.

**US:** Allow 7-10 days for regular **airmail** to Australia. Postcards/aerogrammes cost US55¢/60¢; letters under 1 oz. US$1; packages under 1 lb. cost US$15.11. **US Global Priority Mail** delivers small/large flat-rate envelopes to Australia in 4 business days for US$5/9. http://ircalc.usps.gov.

Additionally, **Federal Express** (Australia ☎ 13 26 10; US and Canada ☎ (1800) 463-3339; New Zealand ☎ (0800) 73 33 39; UK ☎ (0800) 12 38 00) handles express mail services from most of the above countries to Australia; they can get a letter from New York to Sydney in three business days for US$30.68. Rates among non-US locations are prohibitively expensive (for example, London to Sydney costs £30).

## RECEIVING MAIL IN AUSTRALIA

There are several ways to arrange pickup of letters sent to you by friends and relatives while you are abroad.

**General Delivery:** Mail can be sent via **Poste Restante** (General Delivery) to almost any city or town in Australia with a post office. Address *Poste Restante* letters as in the following example: William GRAYSWOOD, Poste Restante, London SW1, United Kingdom. The mail will go to a special desk in the central post office unless you specify a post office by street address or postal code. It's best to use the largest post office, since mail may be sent there regardless. Poste Restante mail is held for usually only 30 days; bring your passport or other photo ID for pick up. If the clerks insist that there is nothing for you, have them check under your first name as well. *Let's Go* lists post offices in the **Practical Information** section for each city and most towns.

**American Express:** AmEx travel offices around the world offer a free **Client Letter Service** (mail held up to 30 days and forwarded upon request) for cardholders who contact them in advance. Address letters in the same way shown above. Some offices will offer service to non-cardholders (especially AmEx Traveler's Cheque holders), but call ahead to make sure. *Let's Go* lists AmEx office locations for most large cities in **Practical Information** sections. A complete list is available from AmEx (in the US ☎ (1800) 528-4800, in Australia ☎ (1800) 23 01 00, or visit www.americanexpress.com).

## SENDING MAIL HOME FROM AUSTRALIA

General post offices (GPO) are usually open Monday through Friday from 9am to 5pm. Larger branches sometimes have extended hours and are also open on Saturday mornings. Domestic letters require AUS45¢ and take up to two business days. **Airmail** letters (up to 50g) from major cities in Australia to North America averages 7-10 days (AUS$1.50); to New Zealand, 3-5 days (AUS$1); to the UK or Ireland, 4-5 days (AUS$1.50); to South Africa, 5-6 days (AUS$1.50). **Postcards** to any destination cost AUS$1. **Aerogrammes,** printed sheets that fold into envelopes and travel via airmail, are available at post offices (AUS78¢). Most post offices will charge exorbitant fees or simply refuse to send aerogrammes with enclosures. **Surface mail** is by far the cheapest and slowest way to send mail. It takes two to four months to cross the Pacific and one to three months to cross the Atlantic—appropriate for sending large quantities of items you won't need to see for a while.

# TELEPHONES

## CALLING HOME FROM AUSTRALIA

Increasing competition is beating out the calling card as the best way to call home. Cheap international calling stores such as Global Gossip appear in the major cities. Prepaid phone cards can be bought and used throughout Australia, usually at cheaper rates than the regular international carriers, though sometimes these cards have restrictions on what times you can place calls. A newer and possibly better option is to purchase your own mobile phone in Australia ($80-160). Once you own the phone, international calls can be expensive and usually require prepaid phone cards; however, incoming calls are usually free (check before purchasing the phone), so people at home can call you and you don't have to pay the bill. Shop around while you're down there, as prices drop and incredible deals appear unexpectedly. Throughout Australia, though, a **calling card** might be your most convenient option. **To obtain a calling card** from your national telecommunications service before leaving home, contact:

### CALLING AUSTRALIA FROM HOME

If you need to find an Australian number from abroad, call international directory assistance in your home country or check out Telstra's online directory at www.whitepages.com.au. To call Australia direct from home, dial:

1. The **international access code in your home country**. (**Canada** or the **US,** 011; the **Republic of Ireland, New Zealand,** or the **UK,** 00; **South Africa,** 09)
2. 61 (Australia's **country code**)
3. The **area code.** *Let's Go* lists the phone codes at the end the **Practical Information** section for most cities and towns in Australia alongside the following icon: ☎. Although area codes are listed with a zero in front, when dialing from outside Australia drop the first zero after dialing Australia's country code. Australia has 4 area codes: 02 in the Central East (including ACT, most of NSW, and some VIC and QLD border towns), 03 in the South East (including TAS, VIC, and some NSW border towns), 07 in the North East (QLD and some NSW border towns), and 08 in the Central and West regions (NT, SA, WA, and some NSW border towns).
4. The **local number.**

**Australia:** Telstra **Australia Direct** (☎ 13 22 00).

**Canada:** Bell Canada **Canada Direct** (☎ (800) 565-4708).

**Ireland:** Telecom Éireann **Ireland Direct** (☎ (0800) 25 02 50).

**New Zealand: Telecom New Zealand** (☎ (0800) 00 00 00).

**South Africa: Telkom South Africa** (☎ 09 03).

**UK:** British Telecom **BT Direct** (☎ (0800) 34 51 44).

**US: AT&T** (☎ (1888) 288-4685), **Sprint** (☎ (1800) 877-4646), or **MCI** (☎ (1800) 444-4141).

**To call home with a calling card,** contact the operator of your service provider in Australia by dialing:

**AT&T:** ☎ (1800) 88 10 11.

**Sprint (Global One):** ☎ (1800) 55 11 10 or ☎ (1800) 88 18 77.

**MCI WorldPhone Direct:** Using OPTUS, ☎ (1800) 55 11 11; using TELSTRA ☎ (1800) 88 11 00.

**Canada Direct:** ☎ (1800) 55 11 77 or ☎ (1800) 88 11 50.

**BT Direct:** Using OPTUS, ☎ (0800) 89 06 11; using TELSTRA, ☎ (0800) 89 00 61.

**Ireland Direct:** ☎ (800) 88 19 71.

**Telecom New Zealand Direct:** Using OPTUS ☎ (1800) 55 11 64; using TELSTRA, ☎ (1800) 88 16 40.

**Telkom South Africa Direct:** Using OPTUS, ☎ (1800) 55 11 48; using TELSTRA ☎ (1800) 88 12 70.

You can usually make **direct international calls** from pay phones, but if you aren't using a calling card you may need to drop your coins as quickly as your words. Prepaid phone cards and occasionally major credit cards can be used for direct international calls, but they are less cost-efficient. Although incredibly convenient, in-room hotel calls invariably include an arbitrary and sky-high surcharge.

The expensive alternative to dialing direct or using a calling card is using an international operator to place a **collect call;** sometimes in an emergency, though, this is the only way to reach home. An operator from your home nation can be reached by dialing the appropriate service provider listed above, and they will typically place a collect call even if you don't possess one of their phone cards.

## CALLING WITHIN AUSTRALIA

**Public phones** are easy to find nearly everywhere you go in Australia. Some phone booths in Australia are coin-operated, some are phone-card operated, and some accept either coins or phone cards. Local calls from phone booths cost AUS40¢. In addition to phone booths, public phones (often small blue or orange boxes) can sometimes be found in bars and hotels, and local calls on these often cost AUS50¢.

Australia has two main telecommunications companies: Optus and Telstra. Telstra rules every local market and much long-distance, while Optus concentrates on mobile phone service and long-distance. **Pre-paid phonecards** are available in $5, $10, $20, and $50 denominations from many newsagents and pharmacies. Most must be inserted into the phone, whereas others have a toll-free access telephone number and a personal identification number (PIN). As phone cards have grown in popularity, so have the number of booths accepting cards only. A very few public phones (at airports, city center locations, and major hotels) even take **credit cards.**

For **directory assistance,** you can call ☎013 from any public phone at no charge. Six-digit phone numbers beginning with **13** are information numbers that can be dialed from anywhere in Australia for the price of a local call. Numbers beginning with **(1300)** operate similarly. Numbers beginning **(1800) or (0800)** are **toll-free.**

**Mobile phones** are everywhere in urban Australia; people walk down the street talking on the phone, just like anywhere else. Mobile phone numbers are either nine or 10 digits; the nine-digit phone numbers begin 01* and ten-digit numbers begin 04**. Usually the caller picks up the charges when calling a mobile phone, and charges run about AUS80¢ per minute. Some hotel owners ask guests to register their mobile phones when they check in.

**Long-distance calls** within Australia use STD (Subscriber Trunk Dialing) services. You have to dial an **area code** (listed above) before the eight-digit number.

## EMAIL AND INTERNET

Finding Internet access in Australia is simple. Most big cities in Australia have **Internet Shops** that also offer discounted international calling. These coffee-less counterparts to **cybercafés** offer access from as low as **free** to as high as $8 per hour. Coin-operated Internet kiosks are an expensive (usually $2 per 10min.), yet common, option in cities and in many hostels. In addition, virtually all public libraries now offer free access to the web, though sometimes you are restricted from checking email or must have a prior reservation. *Let's Go* lists Internet access option in the Practical Information section of towns and cities. Lists of cybercafés and Internet access in Australia can also be found at www.netcafeguide.com and www.cyberiacafe.net/cyberia/guide/ccafe.htm.

Free, web-based email providers include Hotmail (www.hotmail.com) and Yahoo! Mail (www.yahoo.com). Most Internet search engines have affiliated free email service. If you have a Telnet account, you can forward that email to the web-based account. Travelers who have the luxury of a laptop with them can use a **modem** to call an Internet service provider. Some Internet providers also have access phone numbers in other countries so you only need pay for a local call; contact your own provider for more information. Otherwise, long-distance phone cards specifically intended for such calls can defray normally high phone charges. Check with your long-distance phone provider to see if they offer this option.

## GETTING THERE

### BY PLANE

When it comes to airfare, a little effort can save you a bundle. The key is to hunt around, be flexible, and persistently ask about discounts. Students, seniors, and those under 26 should never pay full price for a ticket.

#### DETAILS AND TIPS

**Timing:** Airfares to Australia peak between Dec. and Feb., and holidays are also expensive periods in which to travel. Midweek (M-Th morning) flights run cheaper than weekend flights. Return-date flexibility is usually not an option for the budget traveler;

traveling with an "open return" ticket can be pricier than fixing a return date when buying the ticket and paying later to change it.

**Route:** Round-trip flights are by far the cheapest; "open-jaw" (arriving in and departing from different cities) and round-the-world, or RTW, flights are pricier but reasonable alternatives. Patching one-way flights together is the least economical way to travel. Flights between capital cities or regional hubs will offer the most competitive fares.

**Round-the-World (RTW):** If Australia is only 1 stop on a more extensive globe-hop, consider a RTW ticket. Tickets usually include at least 5 stops and are valid for about a year; prices range US$1200-5000. Try **Northwest Airlines/KLM** (US ☎(800) 447-4747; www.nwa.com) or **Star Alliance**, a consortium of 13 airlines including United Airlines (US ☎(800) 241-6522; www.star-alliance.com).

**Boarding:** Whenever flying internationally, pick up tickets for international flights well in advance of the departure date, and confirm by phone within 72hr. of departure. Most airlines require that passengers arrive at the airport at least 2hr. before departure. One carry-on item and 2 pieces of checked baggage is the norm.

**Fares:** The privilege of spending 24 hours or more on an airplane doesn't come cheap. Full-price round-trip fares to Australia from the United States or Canada can run between US$900 and $2000, depending upon which coast of each continent you are heading to and from; special deals can knock that price down. Flights from the United Kingdom are usually even pricier; London to Sydney return usually runs £500-1100.

# BUDGET AND STUDENT TRAVEL AGENCIES

A knowledgeable **travel agent,** or an agent specializing in flights to Australia or the Asia-Pacific region can make your life easy and help you save, too, but agents may not spend the time to find the lowest possible fare—they get paid on commission. Students and those under 26 holding either **ISIC** or **IYTC cards** (see **Identification,** p. 35), qualify for big discounts from student travel agencies. Most flights from budget agencies are on major airlines, but in peak season some may sell seats on less reliable chartered aircraft.

**Campus/Usit Youth and Student Travel,** 52 Grosvenor Gardens, London SW1W 0AG (in the U.K. call ☎(0870) 240 10 10, worldwide call ☎+44 (020) 7730 8111; www.usit-campus.co.uk). Other offices include: 19-21 Aston Quay, O'Connell Bridge, **Dublin** 2 (☎(01) 602 1600; www.usitnow.ie) and **Belfast** (☎(02890) 327 111).

**Council Travel** (www.counciltravel.com). US offices include: Emory Village, 1561 N. Decatur Rd, **Atlanta**, GA 30307 (☎(1404) 377-9997); 273 Newbury St, **Boston,** MA 02116 (☎(1617) 266-1926); 1160 N. State St, **Chicago,** IL 60610 (☎(1312) 951-0585); 931 Westwood Blvd, Westwood, **Los Angeles,** CA 90024 (☎(1310) 208-3551); 254 Greene St, **New York,** NY 10017 (☎(1212) 822-2700); 530 Bush St, **San Francisco,** CA 94108 (☎(1415) 566-6222); 3301 M St NW, **Washington, D.C.** 20007 (☎(1202) 337-6464). **For US cities not listed,** call ☎(1800) 2-COUNCIL (226-8624). Also 28A Poland St (Oxford Circus), **London,** W1V 3DB (☎(020) 7437 7767). Australian offices include: 39 Lake St, **Cairns** (☎(07) 4041 4500); 315 Wellington St, **Perth** (☎(08) 9321 8330); Level 8, 92 Pitt St, **Sydney** (☎(02) 9232 8444).

**CTS Travel,** 44 Goodge St, **London** W1 (☎(020) 7636 0031; fax 7637 53 28; email ctsinfo@ctstravel.com.uk).

**STA Travel,** 6560 Scottsdale Rd #F100, Scottsdale, AZ 85253 (☎(800) 777-0112; fax (602) 922-0793; www.sta-travel.com). A student and youth travel organization with over 150 offices worldwide. Ticket booking, travel insurance, railpasses, and more. US offices include: 297 Newbury St, **Boston,** MA 02115 (☎(617) 266-6014); 429 S. Dearborn St, **Chicago,** IL 60605 (☎(312) 786-9050); 7202 Melrose Ave, **Los Angeles,** CA 90046 (☎(323) 934-8722); 10 Downing St, **New York,** NY 10014 (☎(212) 627-3111); 4341 University Way NE, **Seattle,** WA 98105 (☎(206) 633-5000); 2401 Pennsylvania Ave, Ste. G, **Washington, D.C.** 20037 (☎(202) 887-0912); 51 Grant Ave, **San Francisco,** CA 94108 (☎(415) 391-8407). In Australia: 224 Faraday St, **Melbourne** VIC 3053 (☎(03) 9347 6911).

ESSENTIALS

ESSENTIALS

Spend less,
EXPLORE MORE!

LOW STUDENT AIRFARES
EURAIL PASSES
BUS PASSES
STUDY ABROAD

800.272.9676

www.studentuniverse.com

**Why wait in line when you can go online?**
Low student airfares the easy way.
Go ahead... put your feet up and
plan your trip.

student universe.com
IT'S YOUR WORLD. EXPLORE IT

**Travel CUTS** (Canadian Universities Travel Services Limited), 187 College St, **Toronto,** ON M5T 1P7 (☎(416) 979-2406; fax 979-8167; www.travelcuts.com). 40 offices across Canada. Also in the UK, 295-A Regent St, **London** W1R 7YA (☎(020) 7255 1944).

# COMMERCIAL AIRLINES

The commercial airlines' lowest regular offer is the **APEX** (Advance Purchase Excursion) fare, which provides confirmed reservations and allows "open-jaw" tickets. Generally, reservations must be made seven to 21 days ahead of departure, with seven- to 14-day minimum-stay and up to 90-day maximum-stay restrictions. These fares carry hefty cancellation and change penalties (fees rise in summer). Book peak-season APEX fares early. Use **Microsoft Expedia** (expedia.msn.com) or **Travelocity** (www.travelocity.com) to get an idea of the lowest published fares, then use the resources outlined here to try and beat those fares. Popular carriers to Australia include:

**Air New Zealand** (www.airnz.com) offers flights to Australia, including the option of stopovers in New Zealand or the Pacific Islands. In **Australia** (☎ 13 24 76) offices are: **Sydney** (☎(02) 9223 4666); and **Melbourne** (☎(03) 9602 5900). In **New Zealand** (☎(0800) 73 77 67): **Auckland** (☎(09) 336 2488) and **Wellington** (☎(04) 382 2000). In the **UK** ☎(020) 8741 2299; in the **US** ☎(1800) 262-1234; in **Canada** ☎(80) 663-5494.

**British Airways** (www.british-airways.com) flies from Europe. In **Australia** offices include: **Brisbane** (☎(07) 3223 3133); **Sydney** (☎(02) 8904 8800); and **Melbourne** (☎(03) 9603 1199). In **Ireland** ☎(1800) 62 67 47. In the **UK** (☎(084) 5773 3377).

**Cathay Pacific** (www.cathaypacific.com) connects major Australian cities with Asia, Europe, and North America. In **Australia** ☎ 13 17 47; in **Canada** ☎(800) 268-6868; in the **UK** ☎(0345) 58 15 81; and in the **US** ☎(1800) 233-2742.

**Qantas** (www.qantas.com.au) is Australia's main airline, and has the most international connections. Nationwide in **Australia** ☎ 13 13 13. *Let's Go* also lists local Qantas offices in the Practical Information section of cities. In **Canada** and the **US** ☎(1800) 227-4500. In **New Zealand** ☎(0800) 80 87 67, or in **Auckland** (☎(09) 357 8900). In **South Africa:** (☎(011) 441 8550). In the **UK** contact: (☎(0845) 74 77 67).

**South African Airlines** (www.saa.co.za) flies from points in southern Africa to Perth and Sydney. In **Australia:** in **Sydney** (☎(02) 9223 4402); or in **Perth** (☎(08) 9322 7388). In **South Africa:** (☎(011) 978 1000).

**United** (www.ual.com) flies from North America to Sydney and Melbourne, often codesharing with Air New Zealand, with some routes via Auckland, New Zealand. In **Australia** ☎ 13 17 77, and offices include: in **Sydney** (☎(02) 9292 4111); in **Melbourne** (☎(03) 9654 4488). In **New Zealand: Auckland** (☎(09) 379 3800). In the **UK** ☎(0845) 844 4777. In **Canada** and the **US** ☎(1800) 241-6522.

# OTHER CHEAP ALTERNATIVES

## AIR COURIER FLIGHTS

Couriers help transport cargo on international flights by guaranteeing delivery of the baggage claim slips from the company to a representative overseas. Generally, couriers must travel light (carry-ons only) and deal with complex restrictions on their flight. Most flights are round-trip with short fixed-length stays and a limit of a single ticket per issue. Most of these flights also operate only out of the biggest cities, like New York. Generally, you must be over 21 (in some cases 18), have a valid passport, and procure your own visa. Groups such as the **Air Courier Association** (☎(800) 282-1202; www.aircourier.org) and the **International Association of Air Travel Couriers,** P.O. Box 1349, Lake Worth, FL 33460 (☎ (561) 582-8320; www.courier.org) provide their members with lists of opportunities and courier brokers worldwide for an annual fee. For travel to Australia, however, courier options are limited.

**FLIGHT PLANNING ON THE INTERNET**

The Web is a great place to look for travel bargains—it's fast, convenient, and you can spend as long as you like exploring options without driving your travel agent insane. Just one last note—to protect yourself, make sure that the site uses a secure server before handing over credit card details. Happy hunting!

**STA** (www.sta-travel.com) and **Council** (www.counciltravel.com) provide quotes on student tickets, while **Expedia** (msn.expedia.com) and **Travelocity** (www.travelocity.com) offer full travel services.

Many airline sites offer special last-minute deals on the Web. Other sites do the legwork and compile the deals for you—try www.bestfares.com, www.one-travel.com, www.lowestfare.com, and www.travelzoo.com.

**Priceline** (www.priceline.com) allows you to specify a price, and obligates you to buy any ticket that meets or beats it; be prepared for red-eye flights and multiple layovers. **Skyauction** (www.skyauction.com) allows you to bid on both last-minute and advance-purchase tickets.

## TICKET CONSOLIDATORS

Ticket consolidators, or **"bucket shops,"** buy unsold tickets in bulk from commercial airlines and sell them at discounted rates. The best place to look is in the Sunday travel section of any major newspaper, where many bucket shops place tiny ads. Call quickly, as availability is typically extremely limited. Not all bucket shops are reliable establishments, so insist on a receipt that gives full details of restrictions, refunds, and tickets, and pay by credit card (in spite of the 2-5% fee) so you can stop payment if you never receive your tickets. For **more information,** check the website **Consolidators FAQ** (www.travel-library.com/air-travel/consolidators.html) or the book *Consolidators: Air Travel's Bargain Basement*, by Kelly Monaghan (Intrepid Traveler, US$8).

## FURTHER READING AND WEBSITES

*The Worldwide Guide to Cheap Airfare*, by Michael McColl (Insider Publications, US$15).

*Discount Airfares: The Insider's Guide*, by George Hobart (Priceless Publications, US$18).

**Travelocity** (www.travelocity.com) and Expedia (www.expedia.com) are searchable online databases of published airfares with online reservations.

**TravelHUB** (www.travelhub.com) is a directory of travel agents that includes a searchable database of fares. Also available on the web is the **Air Traveler's Handbook** (www.cs.cmu.edu/afs/cs.cmu.edu/user/mkant/Public/Travel/airfare.html).

# GETTING AROUND

## BY PLANE

Because Australia is so large, many travelers, even many budget travelers, take a domestic flight at some point while touring the country. Qantas and Ansett Australia (recently acquired by Air New Zealand) are the two major domestic carriers. Oz Experience (p. 65) and Qantas offer an Air-Bus Pass with which travelers can fly one-way, and bus back (or vice versa) around Australia. Passes are valid for six months with unlimited stops; all dates are can be changed.

**Qantas:** Reservations ☎ 13 13 13 in Australia, ☎(800) 227 4500 in the U.S. and Canada, ☎0845 7 747 767 in the U.K.; www.qantas.com.au. Qantas boomerang passes allow travelers to change flight dates free of charge on domestic flights; cities can be changed for $50. For international travelers (with the exception of New Zealanders and Fijians, who are not eligible), a boomerang pass may be the best domestic flight option (min. 2, max. 10). One-way passes within zones are US$155, between zones US$195. Zones are roughly broken down into east (including Sydney, Melbourne, Brisbane, Cairns, and Adelaide), middle (including Ayers Rock, Alice Springs, and Darwin) and west (including Perth). The $195 travel passes can also be used for travel to New Zealand and Fiji. The first two segments must be purchased before arriving in Australia.

**Ansett Airlines:** Reservations ☎ 13 13 00 in Australia, ☎ (888) 426-7388 in the U.S., (0181) 741 2299 in the UK; www.ansett.com.au. With a wink at monopolistic price collusion, Ansett offers a domestic flight option similar to the boomerang pass called the G'day airpass (with only an east and west zone, $155 within zones, $195 between). Has the most extensive domestic routes in Australia and New Zealand, although it flies internationally to Japan, Hong Kong, Fiji, and Bali, Indonesia.

# BY TRAIN

Each state runs its own rail service, and transfers between services may require a bus trip to the next station. The main rail companies are **Countrylink** (☎ 13 22 32; bookings@countrylink.nsw.gov.au; www.countrylink.nsw.gov.au), based in New South Wales, **V/Line** (☎ 13 61 96; www.vline.vic.gov.au) in Victoria, **Queensland Rail** (☎ 13 22 32; res.traveltrain@qr.com.au; www.qr.com.au) in Queensland, **Westrail** (☎ 13 10 53; timetables@westrail.wa.gov.au; www.westrail.wa.gov.au) in Western Australia, and **Great Southern Railways** (☎ 13 21 47; salesagent@gsr.com.au; www.gsr.com.au) in South Australia and the Northern Territory. For reservations and ticketing from the US, call ☎ (1800) 423-2880. Wheelchair access on interstate trains can be poor, as the corridors are often too narrow for wheelchairs. Some larger stations provide collapsible wheelchairs, but not all do. Also, some stations have platforms which make it difficult to disembark.

The **Austrail Pass** allows unlimited travel over consecutive days within a given period (14 days US$436, 21 days US$568, 30 days US$683). The **Austrail Flexipass** allows you to purchase eight (US$363), 15 (US$521), 22 (US$733), or 29 (US$950) traveling days to be used over a six-month period. Both passes are only available to non-Australians and must be bought overseas. Rail Australia has agents in the US (☎ (1800) 423-2880), Canada (☎ (416) 322-1034), New Zealand (☎ (09) 639 0515), South Africa (☎ (021) 419 9382), and in the UK (☎ (87075) 002 22). The **East Coast Discovery Pass** allows unlimited stops in one direction on the Eastern Seaboard within six months (Sydney-Cairns AUS$162, Melbourne-Cairns AUS$215). For information on more passes, go to www.railpage.org.au/pass.html.

# BY BUS

Buses cover more of the desolate intermediate landscape of Australia than do trains. Buses run regularly to major cities, but journeys off the beaten track may require a wait of a few days. It may be more cost efficient to buy a kilometer or multi-day pass if you are planning on doing a large amount of travel by bus

**GREYHOUND PIONEER.** Greyhound (☎ 13 20 30; outside Australia, ☎ +61 7 3258 1800) covers the whole country, with dozens of travelpass options. Seven- to 21-day passes allow you to travel on any Greyhound route within 30 to 60 days, depending on the length of your pass; days of travel do not have to be consecutive. These passes cost between AUS$565 and AUS$1113. The **Aussie Explorer Pass** allows you to predetermine a route and take up to 12 months to get there, while an **Aussie Kilometer Pass** lets you choose a number of kilometers to be used on any Greyhound route (minimum 2000km, AUS$233). Most of these passes can be used to take **Greyhound Pioneer Tours,** which offer combinations of tours for National Parks and scenic spots in Central Australia, Western Australia, and the Top End. A VIP, Euro26, ISIC, and NOMADS card holders; maybe more if purchased overseas.

**MCCAFFERTY'S COACHLINES.** McCafferty's (☎ 13 14 99; email infomcc@mccaffertys.com.au; www.mccaffertys.com.au/home1.html) runs through most of the country, with the exception of Western Australia. **Travel Australia** passes are valid for six to 12 months (up to AUS$915), and let travelers ride with unlimited stops one way along any of seven predetermined routes. Passes can be purchased from a local travel agent or at any McCafferty's terminal. A 10% discount is available for international students, pensioners, and backpacker card holders; the discount is 15% if the purchase is made outside of Australia. McCafferty's also offers an **Australian Roamer** pass, which allows long-distance travelers to pay by the kilometer

ESSENTIALS

(2000km AUS$192, 10,000km AUS$743); the Roamer pass is available only to back-packer card and ISIC card holders. Non-Australians are also to get the **Discover Australia Day Pass,** but it must be purchased before arrival in Australia. Allowing for unlimited travel on the McCafferty's network for a set number of days within the life of the pass, you can choose among many options between seven (US$314) and 30 (US$753) days worth of travel within a range of 30 to 60 days.

**OZ EXPERIENCE.** This popular bus company offers backpacker packages with a lot of flexibility, and charismatic drivers who double as tour guides. The packages must be purchased for predetermined routes (cheaper if bought outside of Australia), and travelers can usually take up to six months to finish with unlimited stop-overs. Be prepared for a younger, more party-heavy crowd. 5% YHA discount. (Shop 401, Kingsgate Shopping Centre, Darlinghurst Rd, Kings Cross, Sydney NSW 2011. ☎(02) 9368 1766, or nationwide ☎(1300) 30 00 28; www.ozexperience.com.)

# BY CAR

Some regions of Australia are virtually inaccessible without a car, and in many sparsely populated areas public transportation options are simply inadequate. One of the major dilemmas of traveling in Australia, at least beyond the main coastal cities, is that the road system is in many areas basic and often poorly maintained. To travel on most outback roads and in many national parks, you will often need a **four-wheel-drive (4WD),** which unfortunately can double the cost of renting or buying. Shopping around well ahead of time is advisable.

## RENTING

Although the cost of renting a car can be prohibitive for an individual traveler, rentals can become cost-efficient when traveling with a group.

**RENTAL AGENCIES.** There are three basic categories: multinational companies with hundreds of branches, national companies with tens of branches, and local agencies which serve only one city or region. Budget, Hertz, Avis, National and Thrifty are Australia's largest multinational companies. You can generally make reservations before you leave by calling their offices in your home country. However, occasionally the price and availability information they give doesn't jive with what the local offices in Australia will tell you. Try checking with both numbers to make sure you get the best price and accurate information. Local desk numbers are included in town listings; for home-country numbers, call your toll-free directory or check the web. The larger national companies are Delta and Britz. These complement dozens of smaller local agencies, which usually have lower prices. Australia numbers and web addresses are listed below:

**Avis** (☎(02) 9353 9000, nationwide ☎(1800) 22 55 33; www.avis.com). YHA member discounts available; quote code P081600 when making reservations.

**Budget** (☎(03) 9206 3333, nationwide ☎(1300) 36 28 48; www.budget.com.au). YHA discounts available; quote code E013609.

**Hertz** (☎(03) 9698 2555, nationwide ☎13 30 39; www.hertz.com). YHA discounts available; quote CDP code 317961.

**Thrifty** (☎(1300) 36 72 27; www.thrifty.com.au).

To rent a car from most establishments in Australia, you need to be at least 21 years old. Some agencies require renters to be 25, and most charge those aged 21-24 an additional insurance fee (around AUS$10-18 per day). Policies and prices vary from agency to agency. Small local operations occasionally rent to people under 21, but be sure to ask about the insurance coverage and deductible, and always check the fine print.

**COSTS AND INSURANCE.** Rental car prices start at around AUS$45 a day from national companies, AUS$30 from local agencies. Expect to pay more for larger cars and for 4WD. Cars with **automatic transmission** can cost up to AUS$15 a day more than standard manuals (stick shift), and in Western Australia, Northern Territory, and more remote areas of the eastern states, automatic transmission is hard to find in the first place. It is virtually impossible, no matter where you are, to find an automatic 4WD.

Many rental packages offer unlimited kilometers, while others offer 100-200km per day with a surcharge of approximately AUS25¢ per kilometer after that. Return the car with a full tank of petrol to avoid high fuel charges at the end. Be sure to ask whether the price includes **insurance** against theft and collision. Remember that if you are driving a conventional vehicle on an **unsealed road** (Australian for unpaved) in a rental car, you are almost never covered by insurance; ask about this before leaving the rental agency. Beware that cars rented on an **American Express** or **Visa/Mastercard Gold or Platinum** credit cards in Australia might *not* carry the automatic insurance that they would in some other countries; check with your credit card company. Insurance plans almost always come with an **excess** (or deductible) of around AUS$1000 for conventional vehicles; excess ranges up to around AUS$2500 for younger drivers and for 4WD. This means you pay for all damages up to that sum, unless they are the fault of another vehicle. The excess you will be quoted applies to collisions with other vehicles; collisions with non-vehicles, such as trees or kangaroos, ("single-vehicle collisions") will cost you even more. The excess can often be reduced or waived entirely if you pay an additional charge, between AUS$5-20 per day.

National chains often allow one-way rentals, picking up in one city and dropping off in another. There is usually a minimum hire period and sometimes an extra drop-off charge of several hundred dollars.

## ON THE ROAD

Australians drive on the **left side** of the road. In unmarked intersections, a driver must yield to vehicles entering the intersection from the right. In some big cities, right turns often must take place from the farthest left lane, after the light has already turned red—keep your eyes peeled for signs to that effect. By law, **seat belts** must be worn. Children under 40lbs. should ride only in a special kind of carseat, available for a small fee at most car rental agencies. The speed limit in most cities is 60kph (35mph) and on highways 100 or 110kph (62 or 68mph). Radar guns are often used to patrol well-traveled roads; sly speed cameras nab offenders on less populated paths. **Petrol (gasoline)** prices vary by state, but average about AUS78¢-88¢ per liter in cities and from AUS90¢-$1.10 per liter in outlying areas.

**PRECAUTIONS.** When traveling in the summer or in the outback, bring substantial amounts of water (a suggested 5 liters of **water** per person per day) for drinking and for the radiator. For long outback drives, travelers should register with police before beginning the trek, and again upon arrival at the destination. Check with the local automobile club for details. In the north, **four-wheel-drive (4WD)** is essential for seeing the parks, particularly in the Wet, when dirt roads turn to mud. When traveling in the outback or for long distances, make sure tires are in good repair and have enough air, and get good maps. A **compass** and a **car manual** can also be very useful. You should always carry a **spare tire** and **jack, jumper cables, extra oil, flares, a torch (flashlight),** and **heavy blankets** (in case your car breaks down at night or in the winter). If you don't know how to **change a tire,** learn before heading into the outback. Blowouts on dirt roads are exceedingly common. If you do have a breakdown, **stay with your car;** if you wander off, there's less likelihood trackers will find you.

**DANGERS.** Australia's highway system can be tough, and road conditions are not consistent. Find out ahead of time whether roads are sealed, especially if you're driving a conventional vehicle. Unsealed roads dominate rural Australia, ranging from smooth, hard-packed sand to an eroded mixture of mud, sand, and stones. Locals are a good source of information on the road conditions in the immediate vicinity. When driving on unsealed roads, call regional tourist boards ahead of time for road conditions, especially in the North, as the wet season sometimes makes roads impassible for months after the rains stop. Furthermore, you should allow at least twice as much time as you would for travel on paved roads. One can skid on gravel almost as badly as on ice.

**Kangaroos are a serious danger** to drivers; they may be cute, but they are large and will jump in front of or into the side of cars. Dusk and dawn are particularly dangerous times when 'roos are usually hopping about.

**CAR ASSISTANCE.** The **Australian Automobile Association (AAA)** is the national umbrella organization for all of the local automobile organizations. You won't often see it called the AAA, though; in most states, the local organization is called the **Royal Automobile Club (RAC)**. In New South Wales and the ACT, it's the **National Royal Motorist Association (NRMA)**. In the Northern Territory, it's the **Automobile Association of the Northern Territory (AANT)**. Services—from breakdown assistance to map provision—are similar to those offered by automobile associations in other countries. Most overseas organizations have reciprocal membership with AAA (including AAA in the US; AA and RAC in the UK; NZAA in New Zealand; and AASA in South Africa). Bring proof of your membership to Australia, and you'll be able to use AAA facilities free of charge. To join in the US, dial ☎ (1800) 222-4357. **AAA roadside assistance** can be reached at ☎ 13 11 11, except in the Northern Territory, where it's ☎ (08) 8941 0611. It's possible to join AAA through any state's organization. *Let's Go* lists the location of the state automobile organization in each state introduction.

## BUYING AND SELLING USED CARS

Buying used cars and then reselling them is popular among long-term travelers or those too young to rent. Automotive independence costs around AUS$1600-5000. Buying from a dealer is often more expensive than from a private owner or fellow traveler. In many cities, hundreds of private sellers rent space at used car lots, as buyers stroll around and haggle. Hostel or university bulletin boards are another good bet. In Sydney, check the *Weekly Trading Post* on Thursdays for used car advertisements, and the *Daily Telegraph Mirror* and *Sydney Morning Herald* on Saturdays. When selling a car back, consider the high tourist season for the region you're in. Vehicles are also easier to sell if they are registered in the state where they are being sold—new owners need to register the car, and some states don't allow registration transfer by mail. If you buy a car privately, check the registration papers against the license of the person who is selling the car.

**WHAT TO LOOK FOR.** The **Ford Falcon, Holden Kingswood,** and **Holden Commodore** are among the most popular large cars, while the **Toyota Corolla** and **Mazda 626** have cornered much of the small-car market. Those who buy campervans report having the most luck with **Toyota.** Buying popular automobiles can pay off if you end up needing parts in the middle of nowhere. Holden, Ford, Nissan, Toyota, Mazda, and Mitsubishi are all fairly safe bets. Keep in mind the low resale value of used cars—you probably won't turn a profit or finance your ticket home at the end of your trip. Another option is to purchase a car from a dealer who guarantees to buy the car back at the end of your trip, but be wary of small print when contemplating **buy-back deals.**

Before buying a used car, check in with the local branch of the AAA, as states have varying requirements for a transfer of ownership, and local organizations can advise you on how to get your money's worth. For example, the NRMA in New South Wales publishes brochures entitled *International Tourists Car Buying Advice* and *Worry-free Guide to Buying a Car.* In Victoria, all cars are required to carry a Road Worthiness Certificate, and it's probably unwise to purchase a car without one. Local auto clubs also do mechanical inspections (NRMA vehicle inspections ☎ 13 21 32).

**BEFORE YOU BUY.** When considering buying a car, call the **Register of Encumbered Vehicles** to confirm that a vehicle is unencumbered—that it has not been reported as stolen and has no outstanding financial obligations nor traffic warrants. For cars registered in NSW, VIC, ACT, QLD, or NT, dial ☎ (02) 9600 0022 or ☎ (1800) 42 49 88. For cars registered in TAS, dial ☎ (03) 6233 5201. For cars registered in SA, dial ☎ 13 10 84. For cars registered in WA, dial ☎ (1300) 30 40 24. You'll need to provide the registration-, engine-, and VIN/chassis-numbers of the vehicle. In New South Wales, a car must have a pink inspection certificate to guarantee that it is roadworthy. It is valid for 20 days, and is available at most service stations.

**INSURANCE AND REGISTRATION. Third-party personal injury insurance,** sometimes called a green slip, is automatically included with every registered vehicle. In the event of an accident, this covers any person who may be injured except the driver

ESSENTIALS

at fault, but does not cover damage or repairs to any cars or property. Even travelers trying to save money should consider purchasing additional insurance. **Third-party property damage insurance** covers the cost of repair to other people's cars or property if you're responsible for an accident. **Full comprehensive insurance,** which covers damage to all vehicles, including your own, is more expensive, but provides more peace of mind. Within two weeks after purchase, you'll need to **register** the car in your name at the Motor Vehicle Registry. Although requirements vary between states, re-registration costs about AUS$15, and must be completed within about two weeks. The local automobile organization can always help.

American Express and the Gold/Platinum Visa and Mastercard cover standard insurance; most other credit cards do not. If you rent, lease, or borrow a car, you will need a **green card,** or **International Insurance Certificate,** to prove that you have liability insurance. Obtain it through the car rental agency; most include coverage in their prices. If you lease a car, you can obtain a green card from the dealer. Some travel agents offer the card; it may also be available at border crossings. Verify whether your auto insurance applies abroad; even if it does, you will still need a green card to certify this to foreign officials. If you have a collision abroad, the accident will show up on your domestic records if you report it to your insurance company. Rental agencies may require you to purchase theft insurance in countries that they consider to have a high risk of auto theft. Ask your rental agency about Australia.

## INTERNATIONAL DRIVING PERMITS

If you plan to drive a car while in Australia, your home country's driver's license will suffice. After driving in the same state for three months, you must have an International Driving Permit (IDP). If your home country's driver's license is not printed in English, you must have an English translation with you. Your IDP, valid for one year, must be issued in your own country before you depart; AAA affiliates cannot issue IDPs valid in their own country. You must be 18 years or older to receive the IDP. A valid driver's license from your home country must always accompany the IDP. An application for an IDP usually needs to include one or two photos, a current local license, an additional form of identification, and a fee.

**Canada:** Contact any Canadian Automobile Association (CAA) branch office or write to CAA, 1145 Hunt Club Rd, #200, K1V 0Y3. (☎(1613) 247-0117; www.caa.ca/CAAInternet/travelservices/internationaldocumentation/idptravel.htm). Permits CDN$10.

**Ireland:** Contact the nearest Automobile Association (AA) office or write to the UK address below. Permits IR£4. The Irish Automobile Association, 23 Suffolk St, Rockhill, Blackrock, Co. Dublin (☎(01) 677 9481), honors most foreign automobile memberships (24hr. breakdown and road service ☎(800) 66 77 88; toll-free in Ireland).

**New Zealand:** Contact your local Automobile Association (AA) or their main office at Auckland Central, 99 Albert St (☎(9) 377 4660; www.nzaa.co.nz). Permits NZ$8.

**South Africa:** Contact the Travel Services Department of the Automobile Association of South Africa at P.O. Box 596, 2000 Johannesburg (☎(11) 799 1400; fax 799 1410; http://aasa.co.za). Permits SAR28.50.

**UK:** To visit your local AA Shop, contact the **AA Headquarters** (☎(0990) 44 88 66), or write to: The Automobile Association, International Documents, Fanum House, Erskine, Renfrewshire PA8 6BW. To find the location nearest you that issues the IDP, call ☎(0990) 50 06 00 or ☎(0990) 44 88 66. For more info, see www.theaa.co.uk/motoringandtravel/idp/index.asp. Permits UK£4.

**US:** Visit any American Automobile Association (AAA) office or write to AAA Florida, Travel Related Services, 1000 AAA Drive (mail stop 100), Heathrow, FL 32746 (☎(1407) 444-7000; fax 444-7380). You don't have to be a member to buy an IDP. Permits US$10. AAA Travel Related Services (☎(1800) 222-4357) provides road maps, travel guides, emergency road services, travel services, and auto insurance.

# BY BICYCLE

Australia has many **bike tracks** to attract cyclers. Much of the country is flat, and road bikers can travel long distances without needing to huff and puff excessively. In theory, bicycles can go on **buses and trains,** but most major bus companies require you to disassemble your bike and pay a flat AUS$15 fee. You may not be allowed to bring your bike into train compartments.

The **Bicycle Federation of Australia (BFA)**, GPO Box 3222, Canberra, ACT 2601 (☎(02) 6355 1570; email secretary@bfa.asn.au; www.bfa.asn.au), a nonprofit bicycle advocacy group, publishes *Australian Cyclist* magazine and has a list of regional bicycling organizations on its web page. Member groups include the **Pedal Power ACT** (☎(02) 6248 79950, **Bicycle Institute of South Australia** (☎(08) 8411 0233), **Bicycle Transportation Alliance** (Western Australia, ☎(08) 9420 7210), **Bicycle New South Wales** (☎(02) 9283 5200), **Bicycle Tasmania** (☎(03) 6233 6619), **Victoria Bicycle Association** (email jch@sci.vu.edu.au),and the **Bicycle Institute of Queensland** (☎(07) 3844 1144) among others. Some cyclists say that some of these organizations focus more on resources for daytrips and short excursions than on long-distance riding, but they are definitely the place to begin.

Safe and secure cycling requires a quality helmet and lock. A good **helmet** costs about AUS$40—much cheaper than critical head surgery. Helmets are required by law in Australia. Travel with good **maps** from the state Automobile Associations.

## BY THUMB

 **LET'S GO DOES NOT RECOMMEND HITCHHIKING.** *Let's Go* strongly urges you to seriously consider the risks before you choose to hitch. We do not recommend hitching as a safe means of transportation and none of the information printed here is intended to do so.

Given the infrequency of public transport to several popular destinations, travelers often need to find other ways to get where they're going. Hostels frequently have message boards where those seeking rides and those seeking to share the cost of gas can meet up. If you are looking to travel with a stranger, car-less travelers report having a good deal of luck meeting willing drivers in roadhouses. This arrangement gives them an opportunity to size up potential lifts before accepting a ride. On the east coast, backpacker traffic moves from Sydney to Brisbane (and possibly as far north as Cairns), and those who go with the flow are sure to make friends who have wheels.

Standing on the side of the highway with your thumb out is much more dangerous than making a new friend at your hostel. Safety issues are always imperative, even when you're traveling with another person. Hitching means risking assault, sexual harassment, and unsafe driving, all while entrusting your life to a random person who happens to stop beside you on the road. If you're a woman traveling alone, don't hitch. It's just too dangerous. A man and a woman are a safer combination; two men will have a harder time finding a ride, as drivers also must keep watch for their safety. Avoid getting in the back of a two-door car (as there is little chance of escape if in trouble), and never let go of your backpack. Hitchhiking at night can be particularly dangerous. Don't accept a ride that you are not entirely comfortable with. If you ever feel threatened, insist on being let off, but keep in mind that the vast distances between towns on some stretches of highway increase your chance of being left literally in the middle of nowhere.

If you decide to hitch, choose a spot on the side of the road with ample space for a car to pull over, where traffic is not moving too fast. The edges of town are ideal as people have not yet accelerated to highway speed. Dress nicely and keep your backpack in full view, as it tells people you're a backpacker and justifies your reason for hitching. A sign with your destination marked in large letters can also help.

## SPECIFIC CONCERNS

## WOMEN TRAVELERS

Women exploring on their own inevitably face some additional safety concerns, but it's easy to be adventurous without taking undue risks, and these warnings and suggestions should not discourage women from traveling alone. If you are concerned, you might consider staying in hostels which offer single rooms or in accommodations that offer rooms for women only. Stick to centrally located accommodations and avoid solitary late-night treks.

Conditions for women in Australia have improved greatly in recent years, but vestiges of a male-dominated culture remain. Outback pubs, especially, can be chauvinistic and uncomfortable places to some. In general, though, it is safe for women to travel alone in Australia.

When traveling, always carry extra money for a phone call, bus, or taxi. **Hitching** is never safe for lone women, or even for two women traveling together. Generally, the less you look like a tourist, the better off you'll be. Dress conservatively, especially in rural areas. Look as if you know where you're going (even when you don't) and consider approaching older women or couples for directions if you're lost or feel uncomfortable.

Your best answer to verbal harassment is no answer at all; feigned deafness, sitting motionless and staring straight ahead at nothing in particular will do a world of good that reactions usually don't achieve. Don't hesitate to seek out a police officer or a passerby if you are being harassed. Carry a **whistle** or an airhorn on your keychain, and don't hesitate to use it in an emergency. *Let's Go* lists emergency numbers (including rape crisis lines) in the Practical Information listings of most cities. Memorize the emergency numbers in the places you visit. A **Prepare & IMPACT** model mugging self-defense course will both prepare you for a potential attack and raise your levels of confidence (see **Self Defense,** p. 42). Women also face some specific health concerns when traveling (see **Women's Health,** p. 46).

### FURTHER READING

*A Journey of One's Own: Uncommon Advice for the Independent Woman Traveler,* by Thalia Zepatos (Eighth Mountain Press, US$17).

*Adventures in Good Company: The Complete Guide to Women's Tours and Outdoor Trips,* also by Thalia Zepatos (Eighth Mountain Press, US$17).

*Active Women Vacation Guide,* by Evelyn Kaye (Blue Panda Publications, US$18).

*Gutsy Women: Travek Tips and Wisdom for the Road,* by Marybeth Bond (Traveler's Tales, US$8).

*A Foxy Old Woman's Guide to Traveling Alone,* by Jay Ben-Lesser (Crossing Press, US$13).

## TRAVELING ALONE

There are many benefits to traveling alone, among them greater independence and challenge. As a lone traveler, you have greater opportunity to interact with the residents of the region you're visiting. Without distraction, you can write a great travel log in the grand tradition of Mark Twain, John Steinbeck, and Jack Kerouac. On the other hand, any solo traveler is a more vulnerable target of harassment and street theft. Lone travelers need to be well-organized and look confident at all times. Try not to stand out as a tourist, and be especially careful in deserted or very crowded areas. If questioned, never admit that you are traveling alone. Maintain regular contact with someone at home who knows your itinerary. For **further reading,** consult *Traveling Solo,* by Eleanor Berman (Globe Pequot, US$17).

A number of organizations supply information for solo travelers, and others find travel companions for those who don't want to go alone. A few are listed here.

**Connecting: Solo Traveler Network,** P.O. Box 29088, Delamont RPO, Vancouver, BC V6J 5C2, Canada (☎(604) 737-7791; email info@cstn.org; www.cstn.org). Bi-monthly newsletter features going solo tips, single-friendly tips, and travel companion ads. Annual directory lists holiday suppliers that avoid single supplement charges. Advice and lodging exchanges facilitated between members. Membership US$28-46.

**Travel Companion Exchange,** P.O. Box 833, Amityville, NY 11701 (☎(631) 454-0880 or ☎(800) 392-1256; www.whytravelalone.com). Publishes the pamphlet *Foiling Pickpockets & Bag Snatchers* (US$4.70) and *Travel Companions,* a bi-monthly newsletter for single travelers seeking a travel partner (subscription US$48).

# OLDER TRAVELERS

Senior citizens are eligible for a wide range of discounts on transportation, museums, theaters, restaurants, and accommodations. If you don't see a senior citizen (or "pensioner") price listed, ask, and you may be surprised. Agencies for senior group travel are growing in enrollment and popularity. These are only a few:

**Elderhostel,** 75 Federal St, Boston, MA 02110-1941 (☎(617) 426-7788 or ☎(877) 426-8056; email registration@elderhostel.org; www.elderhostel.org). Programs in Australia on subjects like National Parks, trains, wildlife, and wine, lasting 1-4 weeks. Must be 55 or over (spouse can be of any age).

**The Mature Traveler,** P.O. Box 50400, Reno, NV 89513 (☎(775) 786-7419 or ☎(800) 460-6676). Adventure tours for seniors. Subscription $30.

## FURTHER READING

*No Problem! Worldwise Tips for Mature Adventurers,* Janice Kenyon (Orca Book Publishers, US$16).

*A Senior's Guide to Healthy Travel,* Donald L. Sullivan (Career Press, US$15).

*Unbelievably Good Deals and Great Adventures That You Absolutely Can't Get Unless You're Over 50,* by Joan Rattner Heilman (NTC Publishing Group, US$13).

# BISEXUAL, GAY, AND LESBIAN TRAVELERS

The profile of bisexual, gay, and lesbian community in Australia has risen in recent years, most notably in the popularity of the **gay and lesbian Mardi Gras** in Sydney each year, which is now the largest gay and lesbian gathering in the world (see p. 126). Though pockets of discrimination exist everywhere, the east coast is especially gay-friendly—Sydney ranks in the top most gay-friendly cities on earth. The farther into the country you get, the more homophobia you may encounter. Homosexual acts are now legal in every state except Tasmania.

**Gay and Lesbian Tourism Australia (GALTA)** is a nonprofit nationwide network of tourism industry professionals who are dedicated to the welfare and satisfaction of gay and lesbian travelers to, from, and within Australia. They can be reached at ☎(08) 8379 7498 or on the web at www.galta.com.au. Listed below are relevant contact organizations, mail-order bookstores, and publishers:

**Gay/Lesbian Visitor Information Sydney,** P.O. Box 7, Darlinghurst NSW 2010 (☎(02) 9331 1333; fax 9331 1199; email pride@rainbow.net.au).

**Silke's Travel.** (☎(02) 9361 6244; www.silkes.com.au). Travel agency that specializes in planning gay and lesbian holidays.

**Friend's of Dorothy Travel,** 2nd Floor, 77 Oxford St, Darlinghurst NSW (☎(02) 9360 3616; fax (02) 9332 3326; www.fod.com.au/travel). Gay and lesbian owned travel agency, recently took over Break Out Travel and Tours.

**International Gay and Lesbian Travel Association,** 4331 N. Federal Hwy. #304, Fort Lauderdale, FL 33308 (☎(954) 776-2626; fax 776-3303; email IGLTA@iglta.org; www.iglta.com). A travel trade association that serves gay and lesbian travelers worldwide. Call for lists of travel agents, accommodations, and events

## FURTHER READING

*G'Day Guide/G'day Accommodation Guide,* a guide for gay travelers to Australia (published May and December; contact 4 Baker St, St. Kilda, VIC 3182).

*Spartacus International Gay Guide* by Bruno Gmunder Verlag (US$33).

# TRAVELERS WITH DISABILITIES

Travelers with disabilities should inform airlines and hotels of their disabilities when making arrangements for travel; some time may be needed to prepare special accommodations. Call ahead to restaurants, hotels, parks, and other facilities to find out about the existence of ramps, the widths of doors, the dimensions of elevators, etc. With the arrival of the 2000 Sydney Olympics and Paralympics, many locations in Australia (particularly the east) became wheelchair accessible, and budget options for the disabled are increasingly available. The following organizations provide information or publications that might be of assistance:

## USEFUL ORGANIZATIONS

**National Information Communication Network (NICAN),** P.O. Box 407, Curtin ACT 2605 Australia (☎(02) 6258 3713; fax (02) 6258 3714; www.nican.com.au). National database of accommodations, recreation, tourism, sport and arts for the disabled.

**Australian Quadriplegic Association,** P.O. Box 397, Mantraville NSW 2036 Australia (☎(02) 9661 8855; fax (02) 9661 9598; www.aqa.com.au). Network of community services for individuals with spinal cord injuries.

**IDEAS,** P.O. Box 786, Tamut NSW 2720 Australia (☎(02) 9647 3377; fax (02) 6947 3723; www.ideas.org.au). Organization which provides information about the needs and rights of all people with disabilities.

**Travelers Aid Disability Access (TADAS),** Level 2, 169 Swanston St, Melbourne VIC 3000 Australia (☎(03) 9654 7690; fax (03) 9654 1926; home.vicnet.net.au/~tadas). Support and information for people visiting Melbourne.

**Accessibility.com.au, The Access Information Supermarket,** provides information about accessible opportunities in Sydney.

**Wheelabout Van Rental,** P.O. Box 3180, Erina NSW 2250 Australia (☎(02) 4367 0900; fax 4365 5840; www.wheelabout.com) Wheelchair accessible van rentals and sales.

## FURTHER READING AND WEBSITES

*Easy Access Australia* by Bruce Cameron (order at www.vicnet.net.au/~bruceeaa).

*The Wheelie's Handbook of Australia,* by Colin and Diane James (order at home.vicnet.net.au/~wheelies/?S=A).

# MINORITY TRAVELERS

Australia is a generally tolerant and diverse country, but fear of losing jobs to **Asian** immigrants has inflamed racism in some areas. This may well extend to Asian travelers. White Australians are often described as racist in their attitudes toward the **Aboriginals,** and this assessment is not unfounded. Blacks of African descent are likely to get a few stares in smaller towns, and may encounter some hostility in outback areas, but will probably not be discriminated against in cities. As always, cities tend to be more tolerant than small towns, but don't let this dissuade you from venturing off the beaten track. *Let's Go* asks that its researchers exclude from the guides establishments that discriminate. Please let us know by mailing us a letter if you encounter discrimination in any establishment we list.

# TRAVELERS WITH CHILDREN

Family vacations often require that you slow your pace, and always require that you plan ahead. When deciding where to stay, remember the special needs of young children; if you pick hostels or motels, call ahead and make sure it's child-friendly. If you rent a car, ask that the rental company provides a car seat for younger children. Consider using a papoose-style device to carry a baby on walking trips. Be sure that your child carries some sort of ID in case of an emergency or he or she gets lost, and arrange a reunion spot in case of separation when sightseeing. Virtually all museums and tourist attractions in Australia have a children's rate. Children under two generally fly for 10% of the adult airfare on international flights (this does not necessarily include a seat). International fares are usually discounted 25% for children from two to 11. Finding a private place for **breast feeding** is often a problem while traveling, so pack accordingly.

## FURTHER READING.

*Backpacking with Babies and Children,* by Goldie Silverman (Wilderness Press, US$10).

*How to take Great Trips with Your Kids,* by Sanford and Jane Portnoy (Harvard Common Press, US$10).

*Have Kid, Will Travel: 101 Survival Strategies for Vacationing With Babies and Young Children,* by Claire and Lucille Tristram (Andrews and McMeel, US$9).

*Trouble Free Travel with Children,* by Vicki Lansky (Book Peddlers, US$9).

## DIETARY CONCERNS

Despite the prevalence of meat pies, **vegetarians** should have little problem finding suitable cuisine in Australia. Most restaurants have vegetarian selections on their menus, and some cater specifically to vegetarians. *Let's Go* often notes restaurants with good vegetarian selections in city listings. Small towns may present more of a problem. Travelers who keep **kosher** should contact synagogues in larger cities for information on kosher restaurants; your own synagogue may have access to lists of Jewish institutions in Australia. If your observance is strict, you may have to prepare your own food on the road. For more information, contact:

**Australian Vegetarian Society,** (www.moreinfo.com/au/avs). Vegetarian shopping guide and listings of vegetarian restaurants.

**The Kosher Grocer,** (☎(02) 9388 8970; www.koshergrocer.com.au). Provides a source of Kosher food and catering information for both Aussies and travelers.

**Koshernow.com,** (☎(02) 9371 3837; www.koshernow.com.au). Australia's self-proclaimed largest on-line kosher grocery store.

# ALTERNATIVES TO TOURISM

## STUDY

Foreign study programs vary in expense, academic quality, living conditions, degree of contact with local students, and exposure to local culture. High school students can usually find exchange programs. For university students, most American undergraduates enroll in programs sponsored by U.S. universities. However, some local universities can be much cheaper than an American university program, though it can be hard to receive academic credit (and sometimes housing). Schools that offer study abroad programs to foreigners are listed below. For a more complete list, check out www.studyabroadlinks.com/search/Australia.

**University of New South Wales,** aside from semester offerings, hosts 6-week study programs during Northern Hemisphere summer for undergraduates, graduate students, and adults. To find out more about courses in Australian history, Outback art, biogeography, and screen acting (among others), contact Russ Alexander, Project Manager, University of New South Wales, Study Abroad, Sydney NSW 2052, Australia (☎(02) 9385 3727; fax 9385 1265; email r.alexander@unsw.edu.au; www.unsw.edu.au/studyabroad).

**University of Melbourne,** International Center, Parkville, VIC 3010, Australia; ☎(03) 8344 6890; fax 8344 4424. Semester abroad offerings in ten academic disciplines, including campus housing ten minutes from the city center.

**American Institute for Foreign Study,** College Division, River Plaza, 9 West Broad St, Stamford, CT 06902, USA (☎(800) 727-2437, ext. 5163; www.aifsabroad.com). Organizes programs for high school and college study in universities in Australia.

**Association of Commonwealth Universities (ACU),** John Foster House, 36 Gordon Sq., London WC1H OPF (☎(020) 7387 8572; www.acu.ac.uk). Publishes information about Commonwealth universities including 39 Australian universities.

**Beaver College Center for Education Abroad,** 450 S. Easton Rd, Glenside, PA 19038, USA (☎(888) 232-8379; www.beaver.edu/cea). Operates programs with many Australian universities.

**School for International Training, College Semester Abroad,** Admissions, Kipling Rd, P.O. Box 676, Brattleboro, VT 05302, USA (☎(800) 336-1616 or ☎(802) 258-3267; www.sit.edu). Semester- and year-long programs in Australia run US$12,300-12,900. Also runs the **Experiment in International Living** (☎(800) 345-2929; fax (802) 258-3428; email eil@worldlearning.org), a 5-week summer program that offers high-school students cross-cultural homestays, community service, ecological adventure, and language training in Australia that costs US$5000.

**Council on International Educational Exchange (CIEE),** 205 East 42nd St, New York, NY 10017 (☎(888) 268-6245 or ☎(800) 407-8839; www.ciee.org/study) sponsors work, volunteer, academic, and internship programs in Australia.

## FURTHER READING

www.studyabroad.com.

*Academic Year Abroad 2000/2001 (*Institute of International Education Books, US$45).

*Vacation Study Abroad 2000/2001 (*Institute of International Education Books, US$43).

*Peterson's Study Abroad 2001 (*Peterson's, US$30).

*Peterson's Summer Study Abroad 2001 (*Peterson's, US$30).

# WORK

There's no better way to immerse yourself in a foreign land than to become part of its economy. Call the Consulate or Embassy of Australia to get more information about work permits. Working holiday visas can be issued to British, Irish, Canadian, and Dutch citizens, though people of many nationalities have been known to acquire them. The visas are intended to allow visitors to supplement their vacation funds for up to a year, and do not allow full time work for more than three months. While working in Australia technically requires a permit, travelers can generally find jobs in cities and towns if they are willing to try their hands at menial clerical work, or seasonal jobs like fruit picking, collecting for charity, or working on a sheep station. For **work** options around the country, consult the Index.

If you are a **U.S. citizen** and a full-time student at a U.S. university, the simplest way to get a job abroad is through work permit programs run by **Council on International Educational Exchange (Council)** and its member organizations. For a US$400 application fee, Council can procure three- to six-month work permits for Australia and a handbook to help you find work and housing (plus US$106 visa application fee; ☎ (888) 268-6245).

The **Commonwealth Employment Service's** offices provide information, and backpacker magazines or hostels usually have info on seasonal work. If you are planning to work for an extended period of time or want to open a bank account in Australia, you should apply for a Tax File Number. These are not required, but without one, tax will be withheld at the highest rate. Contact a local branch of the Australian Taxation Office.

## TEACHING

**International Schools Services,** Educational Staffing Program, P.O. Box 5910, Princeton, NJ 08543 USA (☎ (609) 452-0990; www.iss.edu). Recruits teachers and administrators for a few schools in Australia. Applicants must have a bachelor's degree and 2 years of relevant experience (nonrefundable $150 application fee; applications available online). Publishes *The Directory of Overseas Schools* (US$35).

**Office of Overseas Schools,** US Department of State, Room H328, SA-1, Washington, D.C. 20522 USA (☎ (202) 261-8200; fax 261-8224; www.state.gov/www/about_state/schools). Keeps a comprehensive list of schools abroad and agencies that arrange placement for Americans to teach abroad.

## AGRICULTURE

**Willing Workers on Organic Farms (WWOOF),** Mt. Murrindal Co-op, Buchan, VIC 3885 (☎/fax 5155 0218; email wwoof@ozemail.com.au). WWOOF grants a cheap opportunity to live and learn on organic farms. Membership ($35) in WWOOF allows you to receive a handbook of WWOOF partners throughout Australia. There can be stipulations on minimum stays and work expected from a WWOOFer, but each site has its own expectations. Bed and board are provided in exchange. Memberships can be purchased from Melbourne Student Uni Travel, 440 Elizabeth St (☎ 9662 4666) or many other places throughout Australia (for a complete list, see www.wwoof.com.au/agents.html.)

# VOLUNTEER

Throughout Australia, small organic farms agree to sponsor volunteers in exchange for a few hours of work each day. See **WWOOF,** above. Volunteer jobs are readily available almost everywhere. You may receive room and board in exchange for your labor. You can sometimes avoid the high application fees charged by the organizations that arrange placement by contacting the individual workcamps directly; check with the organizations.

**Australian Trust for Conservation Volunteers,** Box 423, Ballarat VIC 3353 (☎(03) 5333 1483 or nationwide ☎(1800) 03 25 01; email info@atcv.com.au; www.atcv.com.au), offers travel volunteer packages (6 weeks, AUS$840) that include service opportunity as well as accommodations, food, and project-related transport.

**Involvement Volunteers,** P.O. Box 218, Port Melbourne VIC 3207 (☎(03) 9646 5504; email ivworldwide@volunteering.org.au; www.volunteering.org,au) offers volunteering options in Australia as well as New Zealand, Fiji, Malaysia, Japan, and several other areas that might be accessible on your way into or out of the country.

**Volunteers for Peace,** 1034 Tiffany Rd, Belmont, VT 05730 USA (☎(802) 259-2759; fax 259-2922; email vfp@vfp.org; www.vfp.org). A nonprofit organization that arranges speedy placement in 2-3 week workcamps in Australia comprising 10-15 people. Complete, up-to-date listings provided in the annual *International Workcamp Directory* (US$20). US$200 registration fee per workcamp includes meals and accommodations.

## FURTHER READING.

*International Jobs: Where they Are, How to Get Them,* by Eric Koocher (Perseus Books, US$17).

*Work Abroad: The Complete Guide to Finding a Job Overseas,* by Clayton Hubbs (Transitions Abroad, US$16).

*International Directory of Voluntary Work,* by Louise Whetter (Vacation Work, US$16).

*Teaching English Abroad,* by Susan Griffin (Vacation Work, US$17).

*Overseas Summer Jobs 2001, Work Your Way Around the World,* and *The Directory of Jobs and Careers Abroad* (Peterson's, US$17-18 each).

*The Alternative Travel Directory,* by Clayton Hubbs (Transitions Abroad, US$20).

# THE WORLD WIDE WEB

Almost every aspect of budget travel (with the most notable exception, of course, being experience) is accessible via the web. Even if you don't have Internet access at home, seeking it out at a public library or at work would be well worth it; within 15min. at the keyboard, you can make a reservation at a hostel in Australia, get advice from other travelers who have just returned from Perth, or find out exactly how much a train from Melbourne to Cairns costs.

The following is a short list of useful sites about travel and the Land Down Under. Region-specific pages appear throughout the guide. Because website turnover is high, use search engines (like www.excite.com.au) to explore on your own. But keep in mind that most travel web sites simply exist to get your money.

## OUR PERSONAL FAVORITE...

**www.letsgo.com** Our recently revamped website features photos and streaming video, info about our books, a travel forum buzzing with stories and tips, and links that will help you find everything you could ever want to know about Australia.

## LEARNING THE ART OF BUDGET TRAVEL

**www.artoftravel.com** A compendium of great travel tips, from cheap flights to self defense to interacting with local culture.

**www.travel-library.com** Fantastic set of links for information and personal travelogues.

**www.stratpub.com** An e-zine focusing on budget travel.

## INFORMATION ON AUSTRALIA

**www.australia.com** The tourist commission website has information about Australia and travel including climate, economy, health, and safety concerns.

**www.ausemb.org** The website of the Australian Embassy has facts about Australia and travel information related to Australian law and politics.

**www.atn.com.au** The Australian Tourism Net, has tons of service listings and Oz facts.

**www.odci.gov/cia/publications/factbook/index.html** CIA World Factbook. Tons of vital statistics on Australia's geography, government, economy, and people.

**www.whitepages.com.au** If you ever need a phone number or address, this is the place.

# AUSTRALIAN CAPITAL TERRITORY

The Australian Capital Territory (ACT) contains a metropolitan population living in the heart of bushland. Carved out of New South Wales in 1908, the ACT was a geographic and political compromise between Sydney and Melbourne in the competition to host the capital of the newly-federated Australia. Designed and constructed at the very beginning of the 20th century, the ACT is not even a fully-qualified state, yet its center—Canberra—is the political heart of the country. Neatly-designed satellite towns, home to commuters and shopping areas, creep outward from Canberra into the bush. The ACT's combination of a cosmopolitan center and outlying natural refuges promises visitors a capital look at high culture and government at an easygoing pace.

## CANBERRA

For a city that is home to 313,000 people and the government of an entire continent, Canberra's streets are, for the most part, amazingly quiet. Wide avenues, huge tracts of green spaces, and modern architecture offer a utopian vision of metropolis; yet it feels empty, as if someone expected a lot more people to show up. The city houses a myriad of tourist attractions from space centers to dinosaur museums, but it's unfortunate that there is a shortage of tourists to visit them because Canberra is a beautifully planned city. The unique city design can be attributed to Walter Burley Griffin, the American architect whose design proposal was selected from a pool of competitors before construction began in 1913. The first Canberra Parliament convened in 1927, and since then, life has picked up pace a bit, but even today Canberra keeps a low profile and a refined lifestyle to match. Regardless of its dull reputation, Canberra is both a national exhibition and the international face of the Australian political body, while its blend of culture and class may qualify it as one of Australia's most underrated destinations.

### CANBERRA HIGHLIGHTS

**EXPANSE.** The city view from Mt. Ainslie (p. 83).

**POLITICAL ANTICS.** Question Time—a spectacle of wit and persuasion (p. 83).

**BICYCLING.** The paths around Parliamentary Triangle (p. 83).

**INTERACTIVE LEARNING.** The National Science and Technology Centre (p. 84).

**REMEMBRANCE.** The elegant Australian War Memorial (p. 84).

**STARGAZING.** The Mt. Stromlo Observatory (p. 86).

## GETTING THERE

### BY PLANE

Located in Pialligo, 7km east of the city center, the **Canberra International Airport** is an easy ride by car. From Commonwealth Ave, take Parkes Way east past the roundabout at Kings Ave. The name of the road changes first to Morshead Dr, then to Pialligo Ave, en route to the airport. For weekend transit, a **taxi** ($13-15 from the city center) is your best bet. The misnamed airport still only handles domestic flights to four cities; international transport requires a stop in nearby Sydney. **Impulse Airlines** (☎ 13 13 81 or ☎ 9317 5400) is the new kid on the block, and their

TO ⬆️ 🏢 AND
AUSTRALIA INSTITUTE
OF SPORTS

TURNER

Masson St

Haig Park

TO 🏢 🏢 🏢
AND VISITOR
INFORMATION
CENTRE

BRADDON

Girrahween St

N

Australian
National
Botanic
Gardens

Barry Dr

University Ave

Barry Dr

Cooyong St

Northbourne Ave

Mort St

Rugby
Park

Donaldson St

Currong St

## Canberra

**ACCOMMODATIONS**
Blue and White Lodge, 4
Canberra Carotel, 6
Canberra Central Apartments, 7
Canberra City Backpackers, 15
Canberra Motor Village, 1
Canberra YHA, 2
City Walk Hotel, 10
Fenner Hall, 3
Kingston Hotel, 22
Macquarie Hotel, 18
Northbourne Lodge, 5
Victor Lodge B&B, 21

Entrance to
Gardens

ACTON

Australian
National
University

ScreenSound
Australia

Rudd St

Alinga St

Childers St

Marcus Clarke St

London

Circuit

Petrie Pl Petrie St
Ainslie Ave
Petrie Pl
CITY
WALK
Akuna St

CIVIC

VERNON
CIRCLE

Glebe
Park

Cooranderrk St

Ballumbir St

Boolindoonda St

REID

Elimatta St

Currong St

Cure St

Reid

**Australian
War Memorial**

Park

Fairbairn Ave

ACT

TO BLACK MT. &
TELSTRA TOWER

Carruthers Rd

McCoy Ct

Gordon St

Edinburgh

Footbridge

Bamain Cres

Liversidge St

London

Circuit

Allan St

Amaroo St

Constitution Ave

St. John
the Baptist

Anzac Park West

Anzac Park

Parkes Way

Lennox

**Archbishop's
Residence**

Regatta
Point

Parkes

Way

**Commonwealth
Park**

**Captain Cook
Memorial Water Jet**

**Blundells' Cottage**

Wentworth Dr

Russell Dr

RUSSELL

TO AUSTRALIAN
AMERICAN
MEMORIAL (5m)

*Lake
Burley Griffin*

**National Museum
of Australia**

**National
Library**

Commonwealth Ave

Langton Cres

King Edward Tce

**National Science
and Technology Centre**

**High
Court**

Parkes

Parkes Pl

**National
Carillon**

**National Gallery
of Australia**

Kings
Park

TO ✈️
Morshead Dr

*Lake
Burley Griffin*

STIRLING PARK

Coronation Dr

Pimm Dr

**National
Rose Garden**

Parkes Place

King George Tce

**United
Kingdom**

**Canada**

Forster Cr

**Portrait
Gallery**

Queen Victoria Tce

**Old Parliament
House**

Kings Ave

Blackall St

Bowen Dr

BARTON

Brisbane Ave

Hunter St

Perth Ave

**South
Africa**

State Circle

Capital Circle

Arkana St

**Ireland**

**United
States**

Turrana St

Schlich St

YARRALUMLA

CAPITAL
HILL

**Parliament
House**

Federation Mall

Blackall St

Sydney Ave

Telopea Park

Mugga Way

Wentworth Ave

Adelaide Ave

**Prime
Minister's
Lodge**

Grey St

Hotham St

DEAKIN

Melbourne Ave

Hobart Ave

State Circle

National Circuit

Canberra Ave

Kennedy St

Giles St

Leichhardt St

Eyre St

KINGSTON

FORREST

Dominion Circuit

Empire Circuit

**FOOD**
La Capanna, 19
Fisho Café, 20
Little Saigon, 9
Mama's Trattoria, 14
The Pancake Parlour, 12
Supabarn
  Supermarket, 16
**NIGHTLIFE**
Casino Canberra, 17
Gypsy Bar, 11
Mooseheads, 13
Meridian Club, 8

*Collins
Park*

Tasmania Circle

MANUKA

*Manuka
Park*

Manuka Circle

Oxley Dr

Eyre St

Cunningham St

Arthur Circle

Torres St

Mildura St

Captain Cook Cres

La Perouse St

Monaro Cr

Canberra Ave

GRIFFITH

HUME
PLACE

0 _____ 300 yards
0 _____ 300 meters

super low prices (Sydney $131; Brisbane $218) are blowing their competition away. Both Qantas (☎13 13 13 or ☎6250 8211) and Ansett (☎13 13 00 or ☎6249 7641) connect Canberra to: **Adelaide** (1½hr., 8-10 per day, $375); **Brisbane** (2hr., 6-8 per day, $379); **Melbourne** (1hr., 12-20 per day, $258); and **Sydney** (50min., 20-30 per day, $182); they offer **discounts for students, seniors, and advance reservations.**

## BY TRAIN

The **Canberra Railway Station,** on Wentworth Ave in Kingston, 6km from the city center, is on ACTION bus route #39 (bus to Civic 25min., at least 1 per hr.). Alternatively, a taxi ride to the city will cost $12-14. The station houses little more than a Countrylink office. (☎13 22 32 or ☎6239 7039. Open M-Sa 6:20am-5:30pm, Su 10:30am-5:30pm.) **Trains** leave for: **Brisbane** (23hr., 1 per day, $110) via **Sydney** (4hr., 3 per day, $45). **Train/coach** service extends to: **Melbourne** (8½hr., 1 per day, $90); **Bega** (3½hr., 1 per day, $33); **Cooma** (1¼hr., 1-2 per day, $16); **Goulburn** (1¼hr., 3 per day, $13); and **Wollongong** via **Moss Vale** (4hr., 1 per day, $38). Fourteen-day advance purchase can yield up to a 40% discount.

## BY BUS

Intercity **buses** are based at **Jolimont Tourist Centre,** 65-67 Northbourne Ave, just north of Alinga St in Civic. (Open daily 6am-10:30pm; winter 5am-10:30pm. Lockers $4 per day; overnight storage available at Jolimont Bistro.) Several bus companies, both major domestic airlines, and Countrylink have desks in the building.

Greyhound Pioneer (☎13 20 30) provides frequent service to: **Adelaide** (17hr., 1 per day, $109); **Melbourne** (8-10hr., 2 per day, $52-62); **Sydney** (4-5hr., 4-6 per day, $32); **Albury** (5-6hr., 2-5 per day, $34-39); **Goulburn** (1hr., 2 per day, $20); **Griffith** (6hr., 1 per day, $40); **Gundagai** (1¾hr., 2 per day, $23); **Parramatta** (3½hr., 4-6 per day, $32); **Wagga Wagga** (3hr., 1 per day, $29); and June to October to the snowfields at **Thredbo** (3½hr., $48) via **Jindabyne** ($45), **Perisher** ($59), and **Cooma** ($30). **McCafferty's** (☎13 14 99) covers an almost identical route at comparable prices. McCafferty's and Murray's offer great deals on a **ski packages** which include return transport, lift tickets, ski hire, and park entrance for $100. **Murray's** (☎13 22 51) also runs to: **Sydney** (4hr., 3-4 per day, $35); **Bateman's Bay** (2½hr., 1 per day, $24); **Goulburn** (1¼hr., 1 per day, $15.50); **Narooma** (4¼hr., 1 per day, $36); and **Wollongong** (3½hr., 1 per day, $31); as well as ski-season service to **Cooma** (1¼hr., 1-2 per day, $26), **Jindabyne** (3¼hr., 1-2 per day, $26), **Perisher** (3hr., 1-2 per day, $26), and **Thredbo** (3hr., 1-2 per day, $32). **Rendell's** (☎(1800) 02 33 28) trundles out to **Dubbo** (6 hr.; M, F 3pm; $50), and **Transborder Express** (☎6241 0033) runs to **Yass** (1hr., 1-4 per day, $12). Always ask about **student and senior discounts.**

## BY CAR

The **NRMA automobile club,** 92 Northbourne Ave, is the place to turn for road service or car problems. (☎13 21 32. Open M-F 9am-5pm.) For 24-hour **emergency road service,** call ☎13 11 11. **Budget** (☎13 27 27; open M-F 7am-10pm, Sa 8am-noon), on the corner of Mort St and Girrahween St; **Avis,** 17 Lawnsdale St (☎6249 6088; open M-F 8am-6pm, Sa 8am-2pm, Su 9am-noon); **Hertz,** 32 Mort St (☎6257 4877; open M-F 8am-6pm, Sa 8am-noon); and **Thrifty,** 29 Lawnsdale St (☎6247 7422; open M-F 8am-5:30pm, Sa-Su 8am-5pm), all have offices in Braddon and at the airport. Local outfit **Value Rent-a-Car,** in the Rydge's Capital Hill Hotel on Canberra Ave and National Circuit, charges about $35 per day; weekly $195. (☎6295 6155. Open daily 8am-6pm.) **Noss Car and Van Rentals,** 41 Whyalla St in Fyshwick, rents used cars from $175 per week. (☎6280 0320. Open M-F 8:30am-5pm, Sa 9am-noon.)

# ✦ ORIENTATION

**Lake Burley Griffin,** formed by the damming of the Molonglo River, splits Canberra in two; on each side is a central hill with concentric roads leading outwards. **Commonwealth Ave** is the major thoroughfare spanning the lake to connect these points. To the north is **Vernon Circle,** the center of Canberra City and the southern edge of the area known as **Civic.** This area hosts the city's social center and bus interchange. The street called **City Walk** (the eastern part of Alinga St) is the middle of a pedestrian mall where restaurants, shops, and nightclubs form the heart of Canberra. North of Civic, **Northbourne Ave** continues in the line of Commonwealth Ave. To the south of the lake is the "official" part of the capital. **Capital Hill's** huge four-pronged flagpole reaches up from the new Parliament House. One corner of the area known as **Parliamentary Triangle** encloses most of the city's museums and government-related attractions. Commonwealth Ave and Kings Ave are the roads that make up the two arms of the triangle as it stretches across the lake to Parkes Way.

The key to understanding the city plan is the system of roundabouts surrounded by concentric streets ("circuits") and the wheel-spoke offshoots. If you drive, a good map is invaluable. Roundabouts are well marked, but signs often refer to districts rather than to streets. The railway station and budget lodging are in **Kingston,** southeast of Capital Hill. The embassies populate **Yarralumla,** west of Capital Hill. **Dickson,** northeast of Civic via Northbourne Ave and Antill St, and **Manuka** ("MA-nik-uh"), southeast of Capital Hill, have clusters of reasonably priced restaurants.

# ▐ GETTING AROUND

Canberra's public transit system, **ACTION** (☎ 13 17 10), centers on the city bus interchange on East Row at Alinga St, one block south of the Jolimont Tourist Centre. Purchase tickets on the bus or at the sales desk in the interchange. The invaluable *Bus Pack* ($2) has full maps and timetables for all routes and is available at the bus interchange, the Canberra Visitors Centre, and newsagents. Route maps are posted at the city bus interchange. ACTION bus fares are based on a zone system, but the airport and the majority of the city's attractions and budget accommodations fall within the central zone, so you'll probably only need the **one-zone fare** ($2.30; concessions $1.20). These are valid for a single trip; if you ask for a **transfer ticket** from the bus driver, the single ticket is good for 1hr. **Fare-saver tickets** ($17, $8.50) are available for 10 one-zone rides. Buses run M-Sa 6am-12:30am, Su 7am-8:15pm; some routes have limited hours.

City Sightseeing's **Canberra Tour** makes 12 stops covering all major tourist attractions. The ticket is valid for 24 hours and unlimited stops. Tickets can be bought on the bus, in most hotels, or at the visitors center. (☎ (0500) 50 50 12, $25 per person.) **Canberra Cabs** (☎ 6285 9222) covers the city and suburbs at all hours.

Thanks to a superb system of **bicycle paths,** the capital can also be covered easily on a bike. A ride along the shores of Lake Burley Griffin is an excellent way to take in Parliamentary Triangle without having to find parking. For **bike rental,** the best deal is **Capital Bike Hire** run through the YHA in O'Connor. (☎ 6248 9155. Open daily 7am-10pm. Full-day $25; YHA guests $16; cheaper in winter.) Closer to the city center is **Mr. Spokes Bike Hire and Café** on Barrine Dr in Acton Park, near the Ferry Terminal. (☎ 6257 1188. Open W-Su 9:30am-6pm, in winter W-Su 9am-5pm. 1hr. $9.)

# ▐ PRACTICAL INFORMATION

## TOURIST AND FINANCIAL SERVICES

**Tourist Offices: Canberra Visitors Centre,** 330 Northbourne Ave (☎ 6205 0044, freecall ☎ (1800) 02 61 66; fax 6205 0776; www.canberratourism.com.au). About 3km north of Vernon Circle. Take bus #30, 31, 32, 39, 50, 80. Maps and the ever-useful *Bus Pack* for sale ($2 each). Accommodations booking (☎ (1800) 10 06 60). Open M-F 9am-5:30pm, Sa-Su 9am-4pm. Wheelchair accessible. Smaller volunteer-staffed **Canberra Tourism Booth,** inside Jolimont Tourist Centre, is 2 blocks from the city bus interchange. Open M-F 9am-5pm, Sa-Su 11am-3pm. Another volunteer booth is at the **airport.**

**Budget Travel Office: STA Travel,** 13 Garema Place (☎ 6247 8633), on the corner of City Walk. Open M-Th 9am-5pm, F 9am-7pm, Sa 10am-2pm.

**Embassies and High Commissions:** Unless specified, all locations are in Yarralumla. **Canada** (☎ 6270 4000; fax 6273 3285), on Commonwealth Ave south of the lake. Open for consular services M-F 8:30am-12:30pm and 1-4:30pm. **Ireland,** 20 Arkana St (☎ 6273 3022; fax 6273 3741). Open M-F 9:30am-12:45pm and 2-5pm. **New Zealand** (☎ 6270 4211; fax 6273 3194), on Commonwealth Ave, south of the lake. For consular services, contact the consulate in Sydney. **South Africa** (☎ 6273 2424; fax 6273 4994), on the corner of State Circle and Rhodes Pl. Open M-F 8:30am-5pm. **United Kingdom** (☎ 6270 6666, emergency ☎ 6285 6171; fax 6257 5857), on Commonwealth Ave. Consular services downtown, SAP building, Level 10, corner of Bunda and Akuna St. Open M-F 9am-3pm. **USA,** Moonah Pl (☎ 6214 5600, emergency ☎ 6214 5900). Contact the consulate in Sydney for routine consular services.

**Currency Exchange: American Express:** Shop 1, Centrepoint, 185 City Walk (☎ 6247 2333). Cardholders and travelers cheque users can have mail held for 3 weeks at no charge. Send mail (Name), Attn: Client Mail, P.O. Box 153, Civic Square ACT 2608. No fee for AMEX traveler's cheque transactions. Currency exchange incurs a 1% fee. Open M-F 9am-5pm, Sa 9am-noon. **Thomas Cook** (☎ 6247 9984), Canberra Centre shopping mall, Bunda St, corner of Petrie Plaza. No fee for cashing Thomas Cook checks, flat fee $7 on other checks and currency exchange. Open M-F 9am-5pm, Sa 9:30am-12:30pm.

## LOCAL SERVICES

**Bookstore: Travelers Maps and Guides** (☎ 6249 6006), inside the Jolimont Tourist Centre. Open M-Th 8am-6pm, F 8am-7pm, Sa 9am-5pm, Su 10am-5pm.

**Library: ACT Library Service** (☎ 6207 5155), inside the Civic shopfront, on East Row between Alinga St and London Circuit. Open M-Th 10am-5pm, F 10am-7pm, Sa 9:30am-5pm. See also **National Library of Australia,** p. 84.

**Ticket Agencies: Ticketek** (☎ 6219 6666; www.ticketek.com.au), GIO building, Akuna St, Civic. Tickets to sport and music events and **Royal Theater.** Open M-F 9am-5pm, Sa 9am-noon. **Canberra Ticketing** (☎ 6257 1077, freecall ☎ (1800) 80 20 25), on London Circuit, covers the **Canberra Theatre** and **Playhouse.** Open M-Sa 9am-5:30pm.

**Public Markets: Gorman House Markets** (☎ 6249 7377), on Ainslie Ave between Currong and Doonkuma St, swims in crafts, clothing, and miscellany. Open Sa 10am-4pm. The **Old Bus Depot Markets,** 49 Wentworth Ave (☎ 6292 8391), features many food and arts-and-crafts stalls. Open Su 10am-4pm.

---

**MEDIA AND PUBLICATIONS**

**Newspapers:** The main newspaper is the *Canberra Times* ($1.10). They also put out a local newspaper, *The Chronicle.*

**Entertainment:** *Good Times,* released on Thursdays in the Canberra Times, has a list of entertainment options.

**Radio:** Lite Rock, 106.3FM; Mix, 104.7FM; Rock, Triple J 101.5FM; News, 1440AM; Tourist Info, 88FM.

---

## EMERGENCY AND COMMUNICATIONS

**Emergency:** ☎ 000.

**Police:** on London Circuit opposite University Ave (☎ 6213 1777).

**Crisis Lines: Drug and Alcohol Crisis Line** (24hr. ☎ 6205 4545). **Poison Information Centre** (24hr. ☎ 13 11 26). **Gay/Lesbian Line** (☎ 6247 2726), M-F 6-10pm, after-hours recording. **Women's Info and Referral Service** (☎ 6205 1075), M-F 9am-5pm.

**Late-Night Pharmacy: Day and Night Chemist,** 9 Sargood St (☎ 6248 7050), in the O'Connor Shopping Centre. Open daily 9am-11pm. **Urgent Prescription Service** (☎ 6249 1919) operates after 11pm for emergencies.

**Hospital/Medical Services: Canberra Hospital** (☎ 6244 2222, 24hr. emergency ☎ 6244 2324), on Yamba Dr, Garren. Follow signs to Woden southwest from Capital Hill.

**Internet Access:** For a big city, cheap access is not common. The **ACT Library Service** (see **Local Services,** above) and the **National Library** (see **National Library of Australia,** p.

84) offer free 1hr. and 30min. sessions, but **book ahead. Café Cactus** (☎6248 0449) on Bunda St offers internet access $10 per hr., or 20¢ per min. Open M-F 8am-8:30pm or later, Sa-Su 9:30am-late. YHA 20% discount. The kiosk at the **Jolimont Tourist Centre, Canberra YHA and Australia Post** costs $2 per 10min.

**Post Office: General Post Office (GPO),** 53-73 Alinga St (☎6209 1680). Open M-F 8:30am-5:30pm. **Australia Post** at Civic Square, outside Canberra Centre mall, has stamps and counter service. Open M-F 8:45am-5:15pm. **Postal Code:** 2601 (City).

**Phone Code:** 02.

# ▛ ACCOMMODATIONS

Book ahead during public holidays. Check-out is generally at 10am.

## HOSTELS AND DORMS

▓ **Canberra YHA Hostel,** 191 Dryandra St, O'Connor (☎6248 9155; fax 6249 1731). Five kilometers northwest of the city center. Bus #35 (20min., at least 1 per hr.) from the city interchange, stops out front. By car, follow Northbourne Ave north from city center. Go left on Macarthur, go 2km, and right on Dryandra. The pleasant family-friendly hostel is impeccably clean with a wonderfully helpful staff. Great place for meeting other travelers. Multiple kitchens, 3 daily shuttles to the city, TV/pool room, great movie selection, bike rental (full-day $16), small store. Laundry. Internet (10min. $2). Key deposit $10. Reception daily 7am-10pm. Dorms $19.50, under 18 $13; twins $46-50.

**City Walk Hotel,** 2 Mort St (☎6257 0124; fax 6257 0116). Across from the bus interchange. Privacy is scarce in the men's dorms. Still, it is within walking distance of the interchange and nightlife. Kitchen, TV, laundry. Key deposit $10. Reception M-Sa 7:30am-10pm, Su 7:30am-8pm. Dorms $21-23; singles $46, with bath $66; doubles $60, en suite $71; 7th night free. Wheelchair accessible.

**Victor Lodge Bed and Breakfast,** 29 Dawes St, Kingston (☎/fax 6295 7777). Six kilometers south of the city center. Free pickup in Civic by arrangement at Jolimont Tourist Centre. Bus #38 or 39 from the city bus interchange stops 2 blocks away on Eyre St (15min.). Kitchen, TV, laundry. In biking distance of Parliamentary Triangle. Bike hire $12. All-you-can-eat breakfast included. Key deposit $10. Reception daily 7:30am-9:30pm. Dorms $23; singles $44, weekly $230; doubles $56. VIP.

**Canberra City Backpackers,** 2 Akuna St (☎6230 1177). This centrally-located four-star hostel opens in 2001. Gym, heated pool and rooftop garden. Reception 24hr. at the Waldorf. Bunks $24-25; twins $60; doubles $70.

**Australian National University** (☎6249 3454). Accommodation available in several residence halls. The clean and recently refurbished **Fenner Hall,** 210 Northbourne Ave (☎6279 9000, afterhours ☎6279 9017; fax 6257 4926), generally has more rooms during university holidays, though it's worth calling during term-time as well. Unlimited Internet access in lab. Reception M, W, F 8:30am-12:30pm and 1:30-5pm; Tu, Th 8:30am-12:30pm and 2-7:30pm. Singles $30, students $25.

**Kingston Hotel,** 73 Canberra Ave, Kingston (☎6295 0123; fax 6295 7871). On the corner of Giles St, about 7km from Civic. Take bus #38 or 39. Canberra's least expensive pub stay, the "Kingo" provides basic, clean dorms. The mattresses and shared bathrooms could use an upgrade, but for the price, no one's complaining. Linen $5. Key deposit $10. Dorms $15.

## MOTELS AND GUESTHOUSES

**Macquarie Hotel,** 18 National Circuit, Barton (☎6273 2325; fax 6273 4241). On the corner of Sydney Ave, a stone's throw from the Parliament building and on the #35 bus line. The huge complex is full of reasonable rooms with shared facilities. This is the best option for tourists. Reception daily 6am-10:30pm. Basic singles with sink $44; spiffier refurbished singles $55 with TV and fridge; twins and doubles $77 with TV and fridge; includes full breakfast. Book ahead, especially in January.

**Canberra Central Apartments,** 79-81 Northbourne Ave (☎6230 4781, freecall ☎(1800) 62 97 00), 1km from Civic. Breakfast included. Key deposit $20. Reception Su-Th 7am-9:30pm, F-Sa 7am-midnight. Singles $65; twins and doubles $73.

**Northbourne Lodge,** 522 Northbourne Ave (☎/fax 6257 2599). Next door to the Blue and White. Slightly more upscale; all rooms are ensuite. English breakfast. Reception daily 7:30am-midnight. Singles $85; doubles $99; without breakfast $10 less.

**Blue and White Lodge,** 524 Northbourne Ave, and affiliated **Canberran Lodge,** 528 Northbourne Ave, Downer (both ☎6248 0498; fax 6248 8277). Four km north of the city center. Bus #50 stops in front. It's hard to differentiate between the string of B&Bs, but each guesthouse offers TV, fridge, and kettle in a large, clean room. Full breakfast included. Reception daily 7am-8:30pm. Singles $60, ensuite $83; doubles $94-99.

## CAMPING

**Canberra Motor Village,** Kunzea St, O'Connor (☎6247 5466, freecall ☎(1800) 02 61 99; fax 6249 6138). 4km northwest of the City Center. Take Bus #34 or 35 to Miller and Macarthur Ave. By car, follow Northbourne Ave north from Civic, turn left on Macarthur, then right on Dryandra, and take an immediate left on Kunzea. Toilets, showers, laundry, BBQ, pool, store, restaurant, playground. Key deposit $10. Reception 24hr. Sites $10, for 2 $12; family of 4 $17; with power and water $14, $18, $22.

**Canberra Carotel,** Federal Hwy, Watson (☎6241 1377; fax 6241 6674). 7km north of the City Center, on the #36 bus line. By car, follow Northbourne Ave until it becomes Federal Hwy. Swimming pool, store, playground, BBQ, toilets, showers, and laundry. Reception M-F 7am-9pm, Sa-Su 7am-8pm. Sites for 2 $13.20, powered $16.50; extra person $2.20. On-site caravans for 1 $39; extra person $3.30. Cabins for 2 $50, with cooking facilities for up to 5 $77. Prices rise during public holidays.

## 🖸 FOOD

In a city populated by government officials, cheap food is never easy to find. Cafés in the city center and the food court at Canberra Centre provide welcome exceptions. In Dickson, Woolley St off Northbourne Ave has excellent mid-range cuisine, much of it Asian. On Bunda St, Canberra Centre holds a vast Supabarn **supermarket.** (☎6257 4055. Open M-Th 8am-9pm, F 8am-10pm, Sa-Su 8am-8pm.) Across from Canberra Centre, the **City Market** complex packs in fruit stands, butcher shops, and prepared food stalls.

▧ **Dickson Asian Noodle House,** 29 Woolley St, Dickson (☎6247 6380). Take bus #38 or 35 Sa-Su. Natives recommend the succulent stir-fry noodles and the spicy Thai dishes ($9-12). Dine in or takeaway. Vegetable mains $8. Open daily 11:30am-10pm. BYO.

**La Capanna,** 32 Giles St, Kingston (☎6239 6712). Low prices for big portions (most mains under $12) blow away competitors but cause long lines. Foccaccia ($7.50) is a good value. Open daily noon-2:30pm and 6-10:30pm. BYO. Corkage $1.50 per person.

**The Pancake Parlour,** downstairs at 121 Alinga St, Civic (☎6247 2982). Wednesday night 5-course, all-you-can-eat pancake and crepe feast ($14). Mains from $11-16, from steak to fish on pancakes. Open Su-Th 7am-10:30pm, F-Sa 24hr.

**Little Saigon Restaurant and Café** (☎6230 5003). At the corner of Alinga and Northbourne. This Vietnamese restaurant has tempting food at tantalizing prices. Vegetarian mains from $8, a few dollars more for carnivores. Open daily for lunch and dinner.

**Mama's Trattoria,** 7 Garema Pl, Civic (☎6248 0936). Satisfying cuisine, a bubbly atmosphere, and outdoor dining are the perfect ingredients for a bella noche. Pastas from $10.50 and meat dishes from $14. Open daily 10am-late.

**Fisho Café,** 54 Giles St (☎6295 3153). Across from Tench St. Take bus #38 or 39. Amid the bustle of the Kingston Shops, the café quietly earns rave reviews for fresh fish and elegant preparation. Risottos $14-15; pastas $13-15. Open Su-F 10am-2pm and 5-10pm, Sa 5-10pm. Licensed and BYO. Corkage $4.50.

# ☎ SIGHTS

## LOOKOUTS

A stop at one of the city's lookouts can give you a general idea of what's in store on a sightseeing tour. On a hill in Commonwealth Park at Regatta Point on the north shore of Lake Burley Griffin, the **National Capital Exhibition** provides a panorama of Canberra and exhibits on the planning and growth of the city. (☎ 6257 1068. Open daily 9am-5pm. Free. Wheelchair accessible.) Farther back from the city's center, **Mt. Ainslie** and **Black Mountain** offer broader views of the city and are—for the energetic—within walking distance. North of Lake Burley Griffin and east of the city center, Mt. Ainslie rises 845m over the lake, the Parliamentary Triangle, and the Australian War Memorial, providing the classic postcard view down Anzac Pde. To reach the summit by car, turn right onto Fairbairn Ave from the Memorial end of Anzac Pde, to Mt. Ainslie Dr. Trails lead to the top from behind the War Memorial. Two lookout points above the city on Black Mountain are a vigorous walk away. The first, on Black Mountain Dr, accessible by taking Barry Dr to Clunies Ross St and heading left, faces southeast and takes in the Parliamentary Triangle and Lake Burley Griffin. The second viewpoint faces north toward the surrounding countryside and the **Australian Institute of Sport.** From the peak of Black Mountain, **Telstra Tower** climbs a 195m to ensure viewers an unobstructed gaze in every direction. Exhibits in the tower catalogue the history of Australian telecommunications. (☎ (1800) 80 67 18. Open daily 9am-10pm. Admission $3.)

## PARLIAMENTARY TRIANGLE

A showpiece of grand architecture and cultural attractions, Canberra's Parliamentary Triangle is the center of the capital. The triangle is bordered by Commonwealth Ave, Kings Ave, and across the lake, Parkes Way.

**PARLIAMENT HOUSE.** The focal point of the triangle, Parliament House takes the ideal of unifying architecture and landscape to a new level. The building is actually built *into* Capital Hill so that two sides jut out of the earth, leaving the grassy hilltop on its roof undisturbed and open to the public 24 hours. The tour stresses the symbolic nature of the walkway, which places the people above Parliament. Perched on this landmark is a four-pronged stainless steel flagpole visible from nearly every part of Canberra. Inside, free guided tours conducted every 30min. give an overview of the unique features of the building and the workings of the government housed inside. Visitors can even observe both houses of Parliament in action from galleries. The House of Representatives, which meets more often than the Senate, allows advance booking. The televised **Question Time** provides some viewer-friendly acrimony. Every day that both the House and the Senate are sitting (M-Th in approximately 2-week blocks, except during recess in Jan. and July), the floor is opened up at 2pm for on-the-spot questioning of the Prime Minister and other ministers, thus keeping government responsible. (☎ 6277 5399; to reserve tickets for viewing gallery, call ☎ 6277 4889. Open daily 9am-5pm. Free. Wheelchair accessible.)

**OLD PARLIAMENT HOUSE AND THE NATIONAL PORTRAIT GALLERY.** This building, aligned with the front of Parliament House, served as Australia's seat of government from 1927-88, until the current Parliament House was completed. It is now a political history museum and home to the **National Portrait Gallery.** (☎ 6270 8222. Gallery ☎ 6270 8236. Daily tours every 45min. 9:30am-3:15pm. Open daily 9am-5pm. $2, concessions $1, families $5. Wheelchair accessible.)

**NATIONAL GALLERY OF AUSTRALIA.** The third side of the Parliamentary Triangle is comprised of the four large modern buildings on Parkes Place, just off King Edward Tce. On the southeastern end, nearest Kings Ave, the National Gallery displays an extensive Australian art collection, including paintings by famed postmodernist Arthur Boyd, Aboriginal works, and a good contemporary collection. Keep your eyes out for a few big-name French impressionists, too. The surround-

ACT

ing sculpture garden is free and open 24hr. (☎6240 6502, *recorded message* ☎6240 6501. *Open daily 10am-5pm. Free 1hr. guided tours daily 11am and 2pm. Aboriginal art tour Th and Su 11am. Free; separate fees for special exhibits $8-15. Wheelchair accessible.*)

**HIGH COURT OF AUSTRALIA.** Australia's highest court is encased in a seven-story wall of seemingly impregnable glass and steel. You almost expect the justices to yell, "Help, let us out!" When court is in session, visitors may watch proceedings from public galleries in the courtrooms. (*Next door to the National Gallery.* ☎6270 6811. *Open M-F 9:45am-4:30pm. Free. Wheelchair accessible.*)

**NATIONAL SCIENCE AND TECHNOLOGY CENTRE (QUESTACON).** Entertaining, interactive devices mete out science lessons to people of all ages. Free displays at the entrance let you sample before you pay. (*On the northwest side of the High Court.* ☎6270 2800. *Open daily 9am-5pm. $10, concessions $6.50, ages 4-16 $5.*)

**NATIONAL LIBRARY OF AUSTRALIA.** The nation's largest library (6 million volumes) is the final stop on Parkes Place. Open for research and visitation, it houses copies of Australian publications and exhibits on Australian topics, but why go except for the **free Internet access.** (☎6262 1111. *Exhibition program* ☎6262 1156. *Tours Tu 12:30pm. Open M-Th 9am-9pm, F-Sa 9am-5pm, Su 1:30-5pm. Wheelchair accessible.*)

**LAKE BURLEY GRIFFIN.** The last two attractions in the Parliamentary Triangle are actually located in the *middle* of Lake Burley Griffin. The **Captain Cook Memorial Jet** blows a six-ton column of water to heights of up to 147m to commemorate Captain James Cook's arrival at the east coast of Australia. Might as well celebrate in style, right? The bell tower of the **National Carillon** is located on Aspen Island at the other end of the lake's central basin. A gift from Britain on Canberra's 50th birthday in 1963, the Carillon is rung several times per week for 45min. bell concerts. (*Summer concerts M-F 12:45pm, Sa-Su 2:45pm. Winter W 12:45pm, Sa-Su 2:45pm.*)

# NORTHEAST

Anzac Pde extends northeast from Parkes Way, continuing the line formed by the old and new Parliament Houses across the lake.

**AUSTRALIAN WAR MEMORIAL.** The popular crucifix-shaped memorial, with its artifacts, photos, and depictions by major Australian artists of wartime life, make a moving tribute. Exhibits are organized according to military campaign. The Hall of Memory holds the tomb of an unknown Australian soldier underneath a beautiful handmade mosaic dome. (*Anzac Pde, on bus route #33 from Civic.* ☎6243 4211. *Open daily 10am-5pm. Free. 1½ tours daily 10, 10:30, 11am, 1, 1:30, 2pm. Wheelchair accessible.*)

**ST. JOHN THE BAPTIST CHURCH.** This church has given services since 1845, long before the current city rose up around it. Its former schoolhouse is now a museum of pioneer life in Canberra. (*On the corner of Anzac Pde and Constitution Ave.* ☎6248 8399. *Open daily 9am-5pm. Museum open W, Sa-Su 2-4pm. $2.*)

**BLUNDELLS' COTTAGE.** An 1860 house built by the people who once farmed the land where Lake Burley Griffin is today. Blundells' has a "please touch" philosophy regarding its relics. Don't apply the same philosophy to fellow visitors, or you may find yourself in serious trouble. (*On Wendouree Dr off Constitution Ave.* ☎6273 2667. *Open Tu-Su 10am-4pm, last entry 3:30pm. $2, families $5.*)

# NORTHWEST

**SCREENSOUND AUSTRALIA.** Formerly the **National Film and Sound Archive,** Screensound is one of Canberra's least-known but most enjoyable attractions. The bonanza of sight-and-sound relics of Australian radio, film, and television ranges from the 1800s to today. (*On McCoy Circuit in Acton; catch bus #34 to Liversidge St.* ☎6248 2000. *Open daily 9am-5pm. $2, concessions $1. Wheelchair accessible.*)

**AUSTRALIAN INSTITUTE OF SPORT (AIS).** After Australia left the 1976 Olympics empty-handed, the disgruntled nation took action and established the AIS as a training facility for the nation's top athletes in 1981. Tours led by resident athletes take regular humans through the world of the aerobically superhuman, with a stop at the hands-on Sportex exhibit where you can try rowing, wheelchair basketball, or golf. If you're ashamed of your performance, get to work. A pool and several tennis courts are open for your muscle-toning pleasure. *(On Leverrier St just northwest of O'Connor. ☎6252 1444. Reservations ☎6252 1281. Take bus #80 from Civic. Pool $3.50. Outdoor Tennis Courts 1hr. $8. Open M-F 8:30am-5pm, Sa-Su 10am-4pm. Tours M-F 10:20, 11:30am, 2:30pm; Sa-Su 10am, 11:30, 1, 2:30. $11.)*

**AUSTRALIAN NATIONAL BOTANIC GARDENS.** Running along the northwestern border of the campus on Clunies Ross St at the foot of Black Mountain, the Botanic Gardens' flora includes 30% of all Australian species and a rainforest. You know, it's just your basic urban rainforest. *(Bus #34 stops nearby on Daley Rd, leaving a 15min. walk toward the lake along Clunies Ross Rd. ☎6250 9540. Concerts Sa evenings in the summer months. Free guided walks daily 11am and 2pm. Open daily 9am-5pm. Visitors center open 9:30am-5:30pm. Free. Two electric walkabout chairs available.)*

**NATIONAL AQUARIUM AND AUSTRALIAN WILDLIFE SANCTUARY.** The mediocre aquarium-sanctuary combo probably won't justify the trip from the city center unless you are a kid (or have one). The nearly seven-hectare sanctuary for native Australian fauna does have some redeeming features, but it boils down to your average animal park. From Parkes Way, heading out of the city to the west, Lady Denman Dr branches south toward the aquarium at Scrivener Dam. *(☎6287 1211. Open daily 9am-5pm. $10, concessions $8, families $32.)*

## SOUTHWEST

West of Capital Hill on the south side of the lake, **Yarralumla** is peppered with **embassies** of over 70 nations, displaying a multicultural melange of architecture. **The Lodge,** home to the Australian Prime Minister, is on Adelaide Ave, but heckler's be warned—it's closed to the public. Farther down Adelaide, at the **Royal Australian Mint,** on Denison St in Deakin, you can watch coins being minted. Push a button to "press your own" dollar coin...for $2. *(☎6202 6999. Open M-F 9am-4pm, Sa-Su 10am-4pm; coin production M-F 9am-noon and 12:40-4pm. Free. Wheelchair accessible.)*

# 🎵 ENTERTAINMENT

**Casino Canberra,** 21 Binara St, can help you strike it rich or, more likely, lose it all. The upstairs nightclub, **Déjà Vu,** allows people to lounge around or get down on weekends. *(☎6257 7074. Cover F $4, Sa $5. Open F-Sa 9pm-late. Casino open daily noon-6am.)* In addition to the usual first-run cinemas, Canberra has some funky art-house alternatives, including **Electric Shadows,** on Akuna St near City Walk. *(☎6247 5060. Tickets $13.50, students $8.50.)* The **National Gallery** *(☎6240 6502)* shows free videos, films, and talks on art and artists (F 12:45pm).

Housing several venues in varying shapes and sizes, and dedicated more to pure theater and dance shows, the **Canberra Theatre** on London Circuit is the best place to start looking for live entertainment. Register for the free Under 27 Club and take advantage of great savings on tickets. *(☎(1800) 80 20 25. Ages 18-27 tickets $22.)*

Canberra's calendar is packed with minor **festivals,** but there are two annual events that temporarily transform the city. For 16 days in March (March 4-20, 2001), **Canberra Festival** brings the capital to life with musical productions, a hot-air balloon show, and street parties. The last day of the festival is a public holiday, Canberra Day. Mid-September (Sept. 15-Oct. 14, 2001) ushers in **The Floriade** *(☎(1800) 02 01 41)*, which paints the shores of Lake Burley Griffin with thousands of springtime blooms and relieves the city of all accommodation (book ahead).

# ◪ NIGHTLIFE

Canberra's after-hours scene is surprisingly vibrant. The student population supports a solid range of bars and clubs, while relaxed licensing allows boozing to continue until 4am. Most places claim to close "late," meaning midnight on slow nights and until whenever people stop partying on busier nights. Canberra has fewer pub-style watering holes than most Australian cities, but more dance clubs and sleeker bars; on weekend nights just wander from Civic, following the pounding music and scurrying clubgoers. The clientele at hot spots can usually be characterized as one of three different crowds: raging uni students, posh government officials, or unwinding defense school students. The Thursday *Good Times* supplement in the *Canberra Times* ($1.10) has a full roster of entertainment options.

**Gypsy Bar,** 131 City Walk (☎6247 7300). A Canberra institution with live music Tu-Sa, from acoustic to heavy, from local acts to big Australian artists. The atmosphere is always jovial. Cover $5-20. Open Tu-F 5:30pm-late, Sa 7pm-late, Su 3pm-midnight.

**Mooseheads,** 105 London Circuit (☎6257 6496). A rare Canadian bar, but without maple-leaf flags over your head it can be difficult to tell. Lively scene of uni and defense school students lasts through the week in the downstairs bar. The upstairs nightclub **The Moose Upstairs** gyrates with retro dance (70s-early 90s) and Top-40 until 5am Th-Sa (cover Sa $5). Bottle of the bar's Canadian namesake $4.50. Open M-Sa 11am-late.

**Heaven Nite Club** (☎6257 6180). On Bunda St in the center of Canberra's eating district. The funkiest place around, with a mixed crowd. House and trance beats are so persistent they sometimes outlast the dark hours. Open Tu-F 9pm-late, Sa 10pm-morning, Su 8pm-late.

**The Meridian Club,** 34 Mort St, Braddon (☎6248 9966). A short walk from the center of activity. Canberra's only exclusively gay/lesbian club, with a large bar, pool table, and raised dance floor. Not too packed or loud to be unpleasant; hopping on F-Sa nights. Cover F-Sa $5, students $3. Open M-Th 6pm-late, F 5pm-late, Sa 8pm-late.

**The Wig and Pen** (☎6248 0171). On Alinga St, 2 blocks west of the bus interchange. A laid-back pub named for its location in the solicitors district. The club is a good rendezvous point to start the night with good homebrews (schooners $4) and pub food. Live bands W-Sa nights. Open M-F noon-late, Sa 2:30pm-late.

**ANU Student Uni Bar** (☎6249 0786). On the corner of North Rd and University Ave in the student union building. The big student hangout, cheapest pub in Canberra, and host to some of the biggest names in music. Open M-Sa noon-late, except during uni holidays.

**Tilley's Devine Café** (☎6247 7753). On the corner of Briglow St and Wattle. Take #33 or #35 bus to Lyncham. The plush red-velvet interior and sidewalk café are magnets for the mellow clientele. Live shows weekly. Open daily 8am-10pm, later on show nights.

**P.J. O'Reilly's** (☎6230 4752). On the corner of West Row and Alinga St, in the Melbourne Building. The local Irish Pub. Enter a non-smoking pub area and into the dark bar thronging with people dancing to live music Th-Su. Open daily 11am-late.

# ◪ DAYTRIPS FROM CANBERRA

## SOUTH OF CANBERRA

Bushland pushes on Canberra's borders with the promise of an easy retreat from urban refinement. The Tourist Drive 5 loop hits the major southern attractions on a full day of sightseeing. Traveling along the tourist drive loop in a counter-clockwise direction, the first two stops will transport you to worlds beyond.

**MT. STROMLO EXPLORATORY.** The Exploratory serves as the visitors center for **Mt. Stromlo Observatory** and has hands-on exhibits that give a look at the work of astronomers. On occasional Wednesday nights, visitors can stargaze through the powerful telescopes. *(Off Cotter Rd, 15min. west of Canberra. ☎6249 0232. Open daily 9:30am-4:30pm. $6, concessions $5. Telescope $16, children $11.)*

**CANBERRA DEEP SPACE COMMUNICATIONS COMPLEX.** One of the most powerful antenna centers in the world, Canberra Deep Space Communications Complex will awe novices and serious space cadets alike. The 70m radio dish tracks signals from orbiting spacecraft. The visitors center, the **Canberra Space Centre,** has displays on the history of space exploration. An old Telstra phone booth now serves as the NASA hotline, a visitors' link to the latest space mission information. *(Off Paddy's River Rd. ☎ 6201 7800. Open daily 9am-8pm, in winter 9am-5pm. Free.)*

**TIDBINBILLA NATURE RESERVE.** Dedicated to preserving the natural gum-forest habitat of the kangaroos, wallabies, koalas, emus, and other animals that roam the area, the reserve loosely monitors its residents to better your chances of encountering them. Bushwalks in the park range from 30min. strolls to full-day outings. The walk to **Gibraltar rock** (3hr.) rewards not-so-easy rock climbing with stupendous views. The **Birrigai Time Trail** (3km) is an easy trail that allows bush walkers to see a 21,000-year-old rock shelter. The **Tidbinbilla Visitor Centre,** off Paddy's River Rd, a 40min. drive southwest of Civic, has info on bushwalks and ranger-led activities throughout the 5500-hectare park. *(☎ 6205 1233. Park open daily 9am-6pm. $8.50 per car, full-year pass $11. Centre Open M-F 9am-4:30pm, Sa-Su 9am-5:30pm. Tours Sa-Su: Koala Walk 1pm; Bushbird and Wetland tour 2:30pm; Red 'Roos and Wallaroos walk 3:30pm.)*

**NAMADGI NATIONAL PARK.** The expansive Namadgi National Park is the western border of Tidbinbilla Nature Reserve and fills almost all of the southern arm of the ACT with preserved alpine wilderness traversed by only one major road, Naas/Bobayan Rd. Though the park has tracks for all experience levels, it is most famous for its untrammeled recesses accessible only to serious hikers. **Campsites** at Orroral River, Mt. Clear, and Honeysuckle Creek, each with parking nearby, have firewood, untreated water, and toilets. The **Namadgi Visitor Centre,** on the Naas/Bobayan Rd 3km south of **Tharwa,** sells maps and has info about Aboriginal rock painting and camping options. *(☎ 6207 2900. Park open daily 9am-6pm. Centre open daily 9am-4pm. Camping $3.30 per person; register at the Visitor Centre.)*

**LANYON HOMESTEAD.** Built in the 1800s, the buildings at Lanyon Homestead survey Canberra's European architectural history from the days of convict labor through the colonial era. An Aboriginal canoe tree gives evidence of earlier habitation at the same site. Lanyon's greatest draw may be the **Nolan Gallery,** which has many of Sidney Nolan's paintings of bushranger Ned Kelly (see **Glenrowan,** p. 590). *(Tharwa Dr., 30km south of Canberra. Homestead ☎ 6237 5136. Gallery ☎ 6237 5192. Open Tu-Su 10am-4pm. Homestead $6.50; Gallery $3.50; both $7.50. Wheelchair accessible.)*

# NORTH OF CANBERRA

**NATIONAL DINOSAUR MUSEUM.** The privately run National Dinosaur Museum includes 10 full-sized dinosaur skeletons and three reconstructions, complete with skin and teeth. *(Barton Hwy at the corner of Gold Creek Rd. Follow Northbourne until the turn-off to Barton Hwy. ☎ 6230 2655. Open daily 10am-5pm. $8.50, families $24.)*

**COCKINGTON GREEN.** Set among winding garden paths, miniature reproductions of buildings from Britain and elsewhere transport visitors to a Kingdom far, far away. *(☎ (1800) 62 72 73. Open daily 9:30am-4:30pm. $11.50, families $32.50.)*

**GINNINDERRA FALLS.** Just over the New South Wales border on the Murrumbidgee River, a privately-owned park holds the Ginninderra Falls, which spill 200m down into the Ginninderra Ravine. The park is also known for its **rock-climbing** faces. *(☎ 6278 4222. Open daily 10am-5pm. $4.40.)*

ACT

# NEW SOUTH WALES

From a historical perspective, there's no disputing that New South Wales is Australia's premier state. It was here that British convicts lived through the first bitter years of colonization, dreaming of what might lie beyond the impassable Blue Mountains, and here that explorers first broke through the Great Dividing Range, opening the interior of the country for settlement and ensuring the stability of the colony. In the central plains and on the rich land of the Riverina, Merino wool and agricultural success provided the state with its first glimpses of prosperity. Then, in 1851, prospectors struck gold just west of the mountains, and Australia's history changed forever. No longer the desolate prison of exiled convicts, New South Wales became a place that promised a new life and a chance to strike it rich. Although the gold rush days are long gone, New South Wales has continued to grow. Today, it's the most populous state and—thanks largely to Sydney—the well-touristed, diverse, and sophisticated center of modern Australia.

## NEW SOUTH WALES HIGHLIGHTS

**BUMPIN' AND GRINDIN'.** Sydney's King Cross and Oxford St (p. 127).

**ESCAPE.** The great outdoors of the Blue Mountains (p. 138).

**GLITZ.** Free fine wines in the Hunter Valley (p. 150).

**INDULGENCE.** The coastal pleasures of Port Macquarie (p. 172).

**UNWIND.** Peaceful Nambucca Heads (p. 177).

**COUNTERCULTURE.** The wily ways of Nimbin (p. 191).

**INDIVIDUALITY.** The unexamined life in Byron Bay (p. 192).

**EXPLORATION.** The underwater world of Jervis Bay (p. 206).

**CHEAT DEATH.** The ski slopes at Thredbo (p. 215).

**STUPOR.** Ancient archaeology in Mungo National Park (p. 241).

The country's biggest and flashiest city, Sydney sits midway along the coast, brimming with new-found Olympic popularity. North and south of Sydney, sandy surfing and swimming beaches string together in an almost unbroken chain. The trip up the coast is the be-all-and-end-all of backpacker party routes, with the large coastal towns of Port Macquarie and Coffs Harbour whetting appetites for the full-on delights awaiting in the legendary counter-culture of Byron Bay. The south coast is colder but refreshingly far less crowded and every bit as beautiful. Directly west of Sydney's suburban reaches, the Blue Mountains encompass some of the state's favorite getaways and separate the coastal strip from the expansive Central West and outback regions. The New England Plateau, along the Great Dividing Range north of the wineries of the Hunter Valley, achieves an unusually lush and high-altitude setting for a cozy collection of small Australian towns and stunning national parks. Just below the carved-out enclave of the Australian Capital Territory, the Snowy Mountains offer winter skiing and superb summer hiking.

The attractions of New South Wales are as varied as the terrain. Whether it's the cosmopolitan fun of Sydney, the challenging bushwalks of the Blue Mountains, the laid-back surf culture, or the post-apocalyptic simplicity of the outback, most visitors find plenty to write home about.

# ▐ GETTING AROUND

New South Wales has an excellent **public transportation** system, especially in the eastern part of the state. For timetables or route info regarding bus, rail, or ferries in Sydney and throughout the state, call **CityRail** (☎ 13 15 00) or **Countrylink** (☎ 13 22 32; www.countrylink.nsw.gov.au). Countrylink, New South Wales' sole rail transport, gives a 40% discount for Australian students and ISIC-holders. The three major bus companies are **McCafferty's** (☎ 13 14 99; www.mccaffertys.com.au), **Greyhound Pioneer** (☎ 13 20 30; www.greyhound.com.au), and **Premier** (☎ 13 34 10). Greyhound and McCafferty's have a 10% discount for YHA members and a 20% discount for students and ISIC-holders; Premier has a 20% discount for ISIC and YHA.

The **National Roads and Motorists Association (NRMA)** headquarters at 74-76 King St, Sydney, is a comprehensive driver's resource. Anyone doing extensive driving in Australia should consider joining; benefits include roadside and accident assistance. (☎ (1300) 13 11 22 or ☎ 9292 9267. Open M-F 8:30am-5pm. First-time annual membership $98, renewal or if a member of an international partner agency $50.) For more information, see **On The Road,** p. 66.

# SYDNEY

Sometimes elegant, sometimes bizarre, and always amazing, Sydney pulses with energy and swaggers with the self-assurance that stems from being one of the world's great cities. Nearly 4 million Sydney-siders (about 20% of the total national population) make this Australia's unofficial capital. Sydney is where it all goes down, where most international visitors first touch Australian soil and find themselves in a cosmopolitan whirlwind of fashion, finance, and culture. But it isn't quite as overwhelmingly fast-paced as some cities of equal size; this is Australia, after all, famous for its "no worries" attitude.

Fresh from its Olympic showcasing, Sydney is an optimistic, cutting-edge, internationally influential hotbed of activity. But beneath all its shiny newness, Sydney contains as old a history as any city in Australia. In 1788, its stupendous natural harbor, then called Port Jackson, drew the First Fleet of colonists and convicts north of their intended settlement at Botany Bay. Today, the iconic Harbour Bridge and Sydney Opera House occupy the foreshores of Sydney Cove and draw every visitor to the water's edge for a few photo-framing moments. On sunny days, when sailboats skim across the water and the sidewalk cafés buzz with chatter, those few moments easily become hours.

Though geographically bounded by water and mountains, Sydney cannot be culturally contained—its international presence is both Western and Eastern. The city is home to a massive Asian population that flavors a culture whose food, language, and especially attitude are so clearly of European heritage. The economic diversity of the city is somewhat less inspirational: certainly a social chasm exists between the wealthy, wisteria-lined avenues of the North Shore, the bland neighborhoods of the Western suburbs, and the poverty-stricken areas that are home to Aboriginals.

Nonetheless, after the construction, beautification, and general economic boom brought by last summer's Olympic games, spirits are high. Australians are notorious for their obsession with sports, and the world's greatest celebration couldn't have found a more appropriate home than the multi-ethnic, athlete-worshipping, environmentally conscious Sydney. Eager to serve as a springboard to the continent, the locals are glad you came; after raging at the clubs, relaxing by the water, and marveling at the taste of Down Under history and culture, you will be too.

# ▩ GETTING THERE

## BY PLANE

Sydney's **Kingsford-Smith Airport** (☎ 9667 6056), 10km southwest of the Central Business District, serves most major international carriers. **Qantas** (☎ 13 13 13) and **Ansett** (☎ 13 13 00) cover most domestic destinations. **Luggage storage** is available

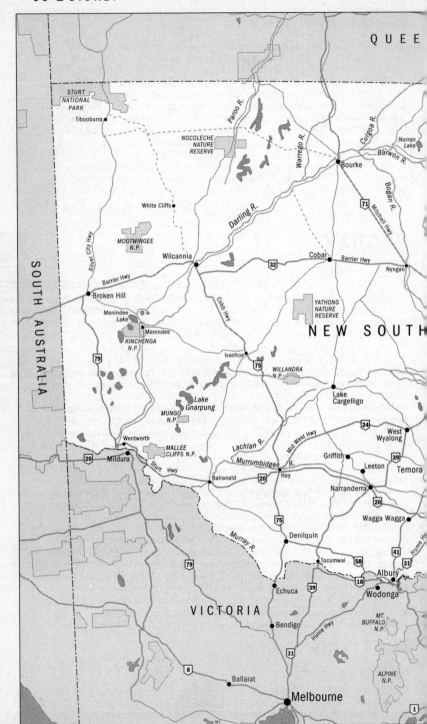

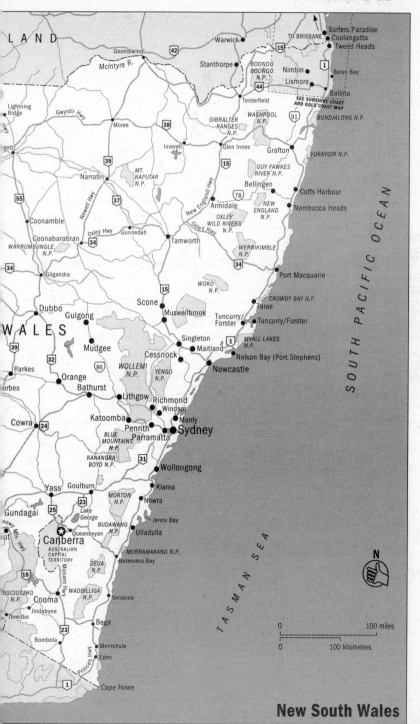

**New South Wales**

### SYDNEY HIGHLIGHTS

**UNBEATABLE VIEWS.** The Harbour from Mrs. Macquaries Point (p. 96).

**SEEING AND BEING SEEN.** The it-crowd cafés of Glebe and Newtown (p. 113).

**UP-AND-COMING ENERGY.** Fresh Darling Harbour (p. 119).

**CHEEKY BEACHLIFE.** The world-renowned Bondi Beach (p. 122).

**COASTAL WALKS.** Spotlighting Harbour life and the endless ocean (p. 123).

**ACOUSTIC CULTIVATION.** Inside the Opera House (p. 124).

**FLAMBOYANCE.** The gay and lesbian Mardi Gras Festival (p. 126).

**CROWDS, MUSIC, AND WARES.** The lively Rocks weekend market (p. 126).

**CHIC BOUTIQUES.** Tailored life for the fashion-forward in Paddington (p. 126).

**NONSTOP PARTYING.** Kings Cross—'nuff said. (p. 128).

($4-6 per day). The **New South Wales Tourism Centre,** in the international terminal, offers a booking service and free calls to all area youth hostels. (☎9667 6050; fax 9667 6059. Open daily from 5:30am until after the last flight lands.)

Transportation into the city is readily available directly outside the terminal. **Local bus #100** goes to the city center, but can be cramped for travelers with luggage (every 20min. M-F 6:30am-6:30pm; $2.50, students $1.25). **Airport Express** runs to the city center (#300), Kings Cross (#350), and the northern and eastern beaches. (☎13 15 00. Runs daily 5:30am-11pm. $6.50). **Kingsford-Smith Transport** runs to accommodations in the city or the inner suburbs. (☎9667 3221. Runs every 20min. daily 5am-10pm; $6.) A variety of independent shuttles run to the city for around $6. A **CityRail** link (☎13 15 00) at the airport runs to the city center and the outer suburbs. Many hostels offer free pickup with a one- or two-night booking. A **taxi** to the city center costs about $20 from the domestic terminal, $25 from the international area; the drive takes 20-45min., depending on traffic.

## BY TRAIN

Countrylink (☎13 22 32) **trains** depart from the **Central Railway Station** on Eddy Ave. Branch offices at **Town Hall Station, Bondi Junction Station,** in the **Countrylink New South Wales Travel Centre** next door to Wynyard Station, and on Alfred St at Circular Quay also sell tickets. Fares include all meals. To Perth, Adelaide, or Alice springs, holiday class is about twice as expensive as coach and includes a sleeping berth, while a luxurious first-class trip (sleeping berth, private bathroom, and steward service) is about three times as much as coach. Return fares are generally double the price of one-way. Countrylink gives 40% ISIC discounts; all other services generally give 20% ISIC discounts. Seniors and children aged 4-16 pay half price; children under 4 ride free.

### FROM SYDNEY TO:

| DESTINATION | COMPANY | DURATION | TIMES | PRICE |
|---|---|---|---|---|
| Adelaide | Great Southern | 26hr. | Su, M, Th | $168 |
| Alice Springs | Great Southern | 45hr. | Su | $372 |
| Brisbane | Countrylink | 13½-15hr. | 2 per day | $110 |
| Byron Bay | Countrylink | 12½hr. | 2 per day | $98 |
| Cairns | Countrylink | 50hr. | 2 per day | $265 |
| Canberra | Countrylink | 4hr. | 3 per day | $47 |
| Coffs Harbour | Countrylink | 8hr. | 3 per day | $78 |
| Melbourne | Countrylink | 10½hr. | 2 per day | $110 |
| Surfers Paradise | Countrylink | 13hr. | 2 per day | $105 |
| Perth | Great Southern | 4 days | M, Th | $439 |

# BY BUS

Fifteen bus companies operate from the **Sydney Coach Terminal,** Central Station, on the corner of Eddy Ave at Pitt St. (☎9281 9366. Open daily 6am-10:30pm.) **Luggage storage** is available ($4-8 per day). Because special rates and concessions vary, consult a travel agent for the lowest rate on any given itinerary—the folks at the Central Station coach terminal are well-informed. The two major national companies, McCafferty's (☎13 14 99; www.mccaffertys.com.au), and Greyhound Pioneer (☎13 20 30; www.greyhound.com.au), generally offer more frequent trips to major destinations than the smaller regional carriers, but their rates are not always the best. Be sure to shop around. Both McCafferty's and Greyhound have a number of two- to 12-month pass options that can be cheaper for the more nomadic traveler, and Greyhound has an Aussie Kilometer Pass that allows more flexible travel paid for by the kilometer. Both companies offer discounts to students, seniors, and children, and also give 10% YHA discounts and 20% ISIC discounts. For more info, see **Essentials,** p. 63. For a more guided tour, **Oz Experience,** Shop 401, Kingsgate Shopping Ctr, Kings Cross (☎9368 1766; www.ozexperience.com) is popular with backpackers for its stop-and-go service, well-planned itineraries, and youthful partyers; rates vary by trip.

## FROM SYDNEY TO:

| DESTINATION | COMPANY | DURATION | TIMES | PRICE |
|---|---|---|---|---|
| Adelaide | McCafferty's/ Greyhound | 21hr. | 3 per day | $104 |
| Alice Springs (via Adelaide) | McCafferty's/ Greyhound | 41-48hr. | 3 per day | $231-284 |
| Brisbane | McCafferty's/ Greyhound | 15-16hr. | 12 per day | $75 |
| Byron Bay | McCafferty's/ Greyhound | 12-13½hr. | 7 per day | $75 |
| Cairns | McCafferty's/ Greyhound | 46hr. | 10 per day | $200-221 |
| Canberra | McCafferty's/ Greyhound | 4-4½hr. | 8 per day | $29-35 |
| Coffs Harbour | McCafferty's/ Greyhound | 10hr. | 9 per day | $57 |
| Darwin (via Adekaide) | Greyhound | 64hr. | daily 5:45pm | $408 |
| Darwin (via Adelaide) | McCafferty's | 74hr. | Su, Tu, W, F 2:45pm | $409 |
| Darwin (via Brisbane) | McCafferty's | 68hr. | daily 9:15pm | $372 |
| Melbourne | McCafferty's/ Greyhound | 12-14½hr. | 7 per day | $55-60 |
| Mt. Isa (via Brisbane) | McCafferty's/ Greyhound | 38hr. | 1 per day | $176 |
| Perth | McCafferty's/ Greyhound | 54hr. | 1 per day | $295 |
| Surfers Paradise | McCafferty's/ Greyhound | 15-15½hr. | 8 per day | $75 |

# ✹ ORIENTATION

The Sydney metropolitan area is immense—Aussies all want their own car and plot of land. The city seems to be contained only by the forces of nature, with **Ku-Ring-Gai Chase National Park** to the north, the **Blue Mountains** to the west, **Royal National Park** to the south, and the **Pacific Ocean** and **Sydney Harbour** to the east. Much of this area, however, is made up of largely quiet, residential outer suburbs.

The standard city map creates the impression that Sydney's center is far larger than it actually is. In truth, the walk from Central Station to Circular Quay along Pitt St takes only 30min., and from Kings Cross only 15min. Inside the city itself

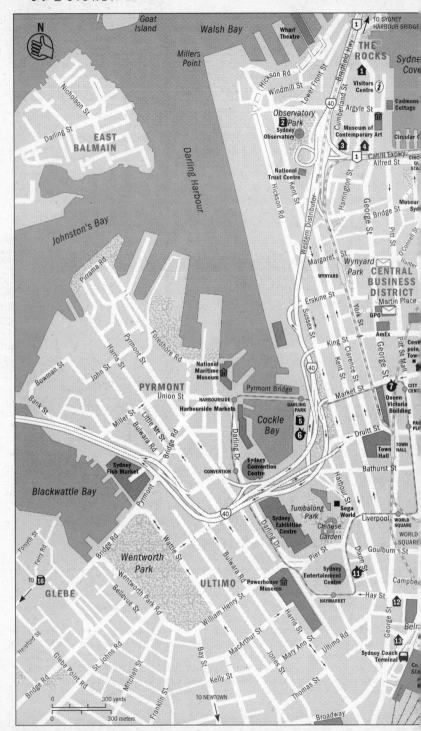

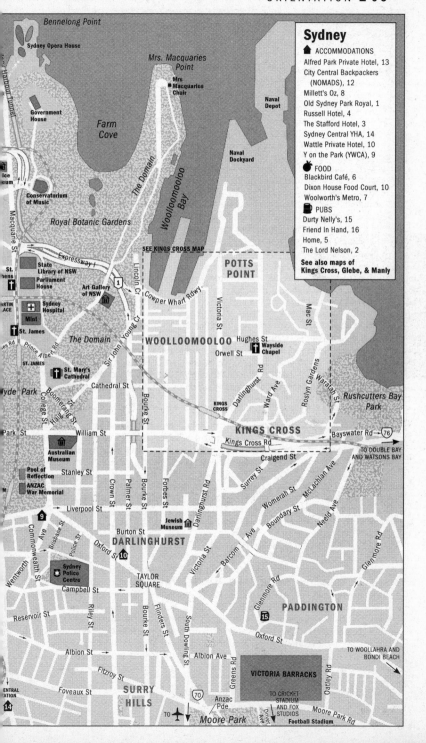

# Sydney

## 🏠 ACCOMMODATIONS
Alfred Park Private Hotel, 13
City Central Backpackers
  (NOMADS), 12
Millett's Oz, 8
Old Sydney Park Royal, 1
Russell Hotel, 4
The Stafford Hotel, 3
Sydney Central YHA, 14
Wattle Private Hotel, 10
Y on the Park (YWCA), 9

## 🍴 FOOD
Blackbird Café, 6
Dixon House Food Court, 10
Woolworth's Metro, 7

## 🍺 PUBS
Durty Nelly's, 15
Friend In Hand, 16
Home, 5
The Lord Nelson, 2

**See also maps of
Kings Cross, Glebe, & Manly**

are areas that Sydney-siders call "suburbs"; don't worry, you haven't wandered out of Sydney—these are sections of town that others might call large neighborhoods or precincts. For a bird's eye view of it all, ascend **Centrepoint Tower** (see p. 117).

## SYDNEY COVE AND THE CITY CENTER

Sydney's most famous sights lie on the Harbour at **Sydney Cove,** directly north of the city center. The southern end of the **Sydney Harbour Bridge** is anchored in **The Rocks,** a somewhat theme-park feeling restored historic neighborhood surrounded by upscale boutiques. Drivers entering downtown Sydney from the north have two options—the **Harbour Bridge** and the **Harbour Tunnel** (southbound toll for either $2). Though less scenic, the tunnel is a more convenient route for anyone heading into the eastern suburbs. Opposite the bridge and on the other side of the cove, the **Sydney Opera House** perches prominently on Bennelong Point. The sprawling **Royal Botanic Gardens** and an emerald gem of a park called the **Domain** are at its back. For the best views of the Harbour Bridge and Opera House, take a stroll down to **Mrs. Macquaries Point,** the tip of the peninsula that forms the northeast corner of the Botanic Gardens; or take a ferry ride from the wharves at **Circular Quay.**

Sydney proper, or the **city center,** is bounded by Circular Quay to the north, **Central Station** to the south, **Darling Harbour** to the west, and the **Royal Botanic Gardens** and **Hyde Park** to the east. **George St** and **Pitt St** are major avenues that run parallel from Circular Quay straight through the heart of the city to Central Station in the south. Street numbers begin at the water and increase proceeding from The Rocks to Central Station, near the 800s. Martin Place, a pedestrian mall spanning the five blocks between George and Macquarie St, is the heart of the **Central Business District (CBD).** Moving south, the next major center of activity is **Town Hall,** located on Druitt St between George and Kent St. The area around **Central Station** supports several backpacker accommodations and a number of cheap restaurants. Sydney's rapidly growing **Chinatown** can be found immediately northwest of the station, radiating from the intersection of Hay, Sussex, and George St; this area, home to the famous weekend-discount **Paddy's Market,** is also known locally as **Haymarket. Redfern,** the area directly south of Central Station, may be unsafe at night.

## INNER SUBURBS

Many tiny municipalities (or "neighborhoods") known as the **inner suburbs** populate the rest of Sydney's central urban area. Despite their proximity to one another, the suburbs do maintain distinct characters and special attractions. Just to make it more confusing, many areas overlap, and some are known by more than one name. West of the city center, **Pyrmont** covers the point of land between Darling Harbour and Blackwattle Bay. The waterside here is also called **Darling Harbour** and is serviced by the Sydney Monorail. South of Pyrmont, **Ultimo** approaches the west side of Central Station and ultimately reaches the Chinatown area. **Glebe,** southwest of Ultimo and just north of the **University of Sydney,** benefits from the presence of students in all the usual ways: casual cafés, cheap food, crowded pubs, and well-supplied bookstores. Glebe Point Rd is the center of activity in this district and home to a number of hostels. **Newtown,** just south of the university, is a bohemian neighborhood centered around King St whose mix of rambunctious students and eclectic gay and lesbian shop owners create the atmosphere.

The infamous inner suburb of **Kings Cross,** east of the city center at the far end of William St, reigns as the center of Sydney backpacker culture. Lively and crowded hostels and cafés line Victoria St north of William St, while busy nightclubs and pubs are packed in along Bayswater Rd. The bawdy strip shows and solicitors on Darlinghurst Rd explain the neighborhood's seedy reputation. Travelers should watch all belongings while in the Cross and avoid walking alone at night. Female backpackers on their own should probably steer clear of the entire area from dusk until dawn (not because you're not a badass, just because there is a relatively high concentration of sickies there). Just be careful.

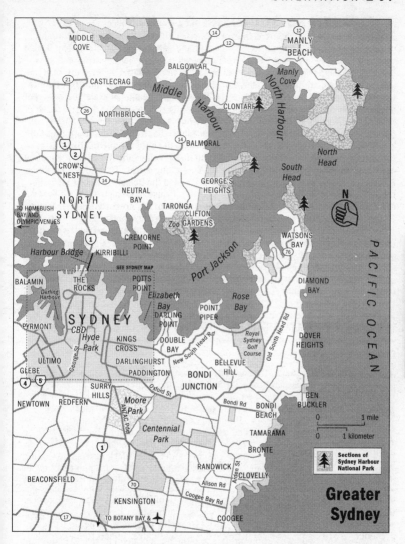

**Greater Sydney**

Near Kings Cross, **Woolloomooloo** gets down to the business of shipping while **Potts Point** and **Elizabeth Bay** nourish Sydney's wealthier denizens. Here again, suburban borders get fuzzy; a posh Potts Point address may be across the street from your Kings Cross hostel. To the south of Kings Cross, **Victoria St** goes chic with some of the city's coolest cafés lining the way to **Darlinghurst.** Along with **Surry Hills** to the south and **Paddington** to the east, Darlinghurst provides fashionable housing for young, creative types. Much of Sydney's nightlife revolves around the outrageous clubs along **Oxford St,** the main road through Darlinghurst, Paddington, and Woollahra to the east. Just south of the army's stately Victoria Barracks, **Moore Park** and **Centennial Park** to its east form the city's largest swath of greenery and house Sydney's major athletic facilities, including the **Sydney Football Stadium** and **Cricket Ground.**

## FAR EAST AND SOUTHERN BEACHES

Outside of these central areas, surroundings get less urban. East of Paddington, **Woollahra's** terrace houses provide a nice change of scenery. To the north, **Double Bay** and **Rose Bay** are among Sydney's most exclusive residential areas and are the location of Sydney's elegant, resort shopping areas. **Bondi Junction,** south of Wool-lahra, is the last train stop on the eastern end of the subway system. Ten minutes east by bus or subway is the famous if smallish **Bondi Beach** (BOND-eye), model of many a surf movie and home to the majority of Sydney's celebrity types. Farther south, the beaches of **Tamarama, Clovelly,** and **Bronte** offer low-key alternatives for families and quieter sunbathers. **Coogee Beach** lies farthest south and rivals Bondi with its popular beachlife and young residents. Decide for yourself by taking the hour-long walk along the coastline between Bondi and Coogee Beaches, sampling all the beaches in between.

## NORTH SHORE

The second half of Sydney's professional district fronts the **north shore** of Sydney Harbour, at the other end of Harbour Bridge. **North Sydney** was originally settled by wealthy merchants and its upper-class heritage gleams through today. It's the play-ground of wealthy urbanites and posh business people. While tourist attractions on the north shore are essentially limited to **Taronga Park Zoo** in Mosman and the beach community of **Manly** (both accessible by ferry), the beautiful, more secluded north shore beaches are worthy escapes from the city proper. The meandering ferry rides to Manly and Taronga are interesting enough in themselves to justify the trip on a pleasant day.

# ▐▀ GETTING AROUND

## OVERVIEW

Sydney's well-oiled public transportation machine makes for simple traveling in town. Comprised of **Sydney Buses, CityRail Trains,** and **Sydney Ferries,** the **Sydney Transit Authority (STA)** network stops just about anywhere. For information or route advice on any part of the STA system, call ☎ 13 15 00. A **bus information kiosk** is at Circular Quay, on the corner of Alfred and Loftus St (open M-F 6:30am-7:45pm, Sa-Su 6:30am-6pm), as well as outside the Queen Victoria Building on York St (open M-F 8am-6pm, Sa 9am-5pm). There's a **ferry kiosk** near Wharf 4, Circular Quay (open M-F 7am-5:45pm, Sa-Su 8am-5:45pm), and a **train kiosk** at Central Station (open daily 6am-10pm). Check out various available passes, frequently cheaper than paying individual fares. For $12, the **DayPass** grants unlimited use of Sydney Ferries and local buses for one day. The **TravelPass** for the four centermost zones includes unlimited seven-day access to buses, trains, and ferries for just $26.

The **Sydney Pass** includes unlimited bus, train, and ferry use within the basic TravelPass zone, return Airport Express service, access to both Explorer Buses, and passage on Sydney Harbour cruises and the higher-speed ferries to Manly and Parramatta. The Sydney Pass can be purchased for use on three, five, or seven days within any seven-day period (3-day pass $85, ages 4-16 $45, families $215; 5-day pass $115, $60, $290; 7-day pass $135, $70, $340).

The free brochure *Sydney: The Official Book of Maps*, available from all Countrylink offices and most tourist info outlets, contains detailed route maps. Similar information is available in the seasonal *Sydney Visitors Guide* and the *Sydney Map Guide: CITY HOST*. For a full-colored map of the city, beaches, and surrounding areas, as well as transportation routes, *Let's Go* also produces a handy pocket-sized **Sydney Map Guide.**

## BY BUS

Drivers don't automatically stop at bus stops; hail them as you would a taxi. Fares range between $1.20 and $4.60 depending on distance (children half-price, seniors

$1-3, ask for student concessions). Pay when boarding. Color-coded **TravelTen** passes cover 10 trips at a significant discount and can be purchased from most news agencies ($9.50 for a Blue TravelTen allows for 10 trips within the city and inner suburbs). The **Bus Tripper** ($8.30) covers one day of unlimited bus travel. Most buses run between 5am and 11:30pm, but there is 24hr. service between the city center, Kings Cross, and other central locales. The STA info line (☎ 13 15 00) has schedule details.

In addition to local commuter bus service, the STA operates two sightseeing buses, the **Sydney Explorer** and the **Bondi & Bay Explorer,** that allow passengers to get on and off at major attractions along designated routes. The Explorer services are expensive, but can be an excellent way to do concentrated touring ($30 for a 1-day pass for either route, ages 4-16 $15, families $75; tickets combining both routes over 2 non-consecutive days are $55, children $30, families $140; purchase tickets on a bus at any stop along the route). The Sydney Explorer covers sights between the Harbour and Central Station, moving as far east as Woolloomooloo Bay and as far west as Darling Harbour, originating in Circular Quay every 15min. between 8:40am and 5:25pm. The Bondi & Bay Explorer service visits the eastern bays and southern beaches down to Coogee, departing from Circular Quay every 30min. between 9:15am and 4:20pm. Start early to get the most bang for your buck.

# BY SUBWAY AND TRAIN

Sydney's **CityRail** subway system rumbles down under from Bondi Junction in the east to the most distant corners of the suburban sprawl in the north, west, and south. Service is fast, frequent, easy to navigate, and safe. CityRail's lowest one-way fare is $1, but most trips cost a little bit more. Weekdays before 9am, return fares are double the one-way price. At all other times, the purchase of a round-trip "off-peak return" ticket gets you a sizeable discount. The combined service **Travel-Pass** detailed above is generally a bargain for regular subway users. CityRail trains run 24hr., although service is infrequent during the wee morning hours.

Both the **Monorail** and **Light Rail** (☎ 9552 2288) provide futuristic if impractical methods of transportation (although one has less calories). Riding above the city bustle is a nice change if you are going from one point directly to another and don't mind the slightly heftier fee to ride above the city bustle. The Monorail linking the City Centre with Darling Harbour and Chinatown. (Runs every 3-5min. M-F 7am-10pm, Sa-Su 7am-midnight. $3, seniors $1.80, under 6 free; day pass $6, families $19.) The Light Rail connects Chinatown, Darling Harbour, Star City, and Ultimo. (Runs every 8-15min. 24hr. $2-3 depending on distance traveled, ages 4-15 $1-2; adult unlimited day pass $6, concessions $4, families $18; signal the driver from designated stopping areas.)

# BY FERRY

The good ol' STA green 'n' gold ferries provide passengers with a magnificent view of the Harbour; aimless cruising is highly recommended. Ferries embark from the **Circular Quay** wharves between the Opera House and the Harbour Bridge daily 5am-midnight. The **information office** (☎ 9207 3170) is opposite Wharf 4. Short one-way trips in the harbor cost $3.20; a **FerryTen** pass for the same area costs $19 and works much like the TravelTen bus pass described above. The fare for the high-speed JetCat to Manly is $5.20 (FerryTen pass $48). The STA's fastest and longest commuter ferry service is the RiverCat to Parramatta ($5, FerryTen $35). Children ages 4-16 ride all these ferries for half-price.

STA administers several **Sydney Ferries Harbour Cruises:** the Morning Cruise (1hr.; departs daily 10am and 11:15am; $14, ages 4-16 $9.50, families $37.50); the Afternoon Cruise (2½hr.; departs M-F 1pm, Sa-Su 1:30pm; $21, $12.50, $54.50); and the after-dark Evening Harbour Cruise (1½hr.; departs M-Sa 8pm; $18.00, $11.50, $47.50). The Sydney Ferries **information** line has details. (☎ 9207 3170. Operates M-Sa 7am-5:45pm, Su 8am-5:45pm.)

# BY CAR

The **National Royal Motorist Association (NRMA),** 74-76 King St, is a comprehensive driver's resource (see **Essentials,** p. 66). Anyone doing extensive driving in Australia should consider joining—benefits include roadside and accident assistance, knowledgeable staff, accurate maps, and passenger transport and accommodation in emergencies. (☎13 21 32. Open M-F 8:30am-5pm. $86 first-time annual membership, $46 renewal or if a member of an international partner agency.)

All major **car rental** companies have desks in Kingsford-Smith Airport, and most appear again on William St near Kings Cross. The big names include: **Avis,** 214 William St (☎9357 2000); **Budget,** 76 Anzac Pde (☎13 27 27 or ☎9217 0222); **Hertz,** corner of William and Riley St (☎13 30 39 or ☎9360 6621); **Thrifty,** 78 William St (☎9331 1385); and **Dollar,** on Sir John Young Crescent (☎9223 1444). All rent cars starting from $55 per day. Dollar cuts a little lower than the others with small, manual transmission cars starting at $40 per day ($28 per day with longer rentals) with unlimited kilometers, and automatic transmission cars for $45 per day, with no surcharge for 21-25 year olds. However, it is a smaller chain, which can make interstate travel and drop off more difficult.

In general, local and regional outfits offer much better monetary deals than the big companies, but consider the possible downsides: fewer locations translates to more difficult interstate travel and drop off. **Delta Car Rentals,** 77 William St, has small, manual cars from $35 per day and automatics from $48. (☎9380 6288, freecall ☎(1800) 63 13 90; www.deltacarrentals.com.au. Open M-F 8am-6pm, Sa 8am-5pm, Su 9am-5pm. Ages 21-24 $12 surcharge.) **Bayswater Car Rental,** 120 Darlinghurst Rd, Kings Cross (☎9360 3622), is cheap and has the lowest age limit, 20. All companies offer reduced long-term rental rates, and most offer free pickup from the airport or Central Station.

Hostel notice boards overflow with fliers for privately-owned cars, campers, and motorcycles **selling** for as little as several hundred dollars. When purchasing a car this way, it's a good idea to make sure it's registered to the seller so the registration can be transferred. For more information on car sales, see **Essentials,** p. 67. **Kings Cross Backpackers Car Market,** Level 2, Kings Cross Car Park, on the corner of Ward Ave and Elizabeth Bay Rd, brings buyers and sellers together. They offer third party insurance for travelers—meaning that in the case of an accident that is your fault, they will pay for the other person's damages, a feature difficult to get elsewhere—and their knowledgeable staff has invaluable information on registration and other matters for car-buyers. (☎9358 5000, freecall ☎(1800) 80 81 88; www.carmarket.com.au. Open daily 9am-5pm. Weekly charge from $35. Required vehicle inspection $23.) **Travellers Auto Barn,** 177 William St, offers guaranteed buyback agreements on cars over $3000. Minimum buy-back rates are 40-50% of purchase price, depending on the length of time you take the car. Cheaper cars are also available, but do not come with warranties and buy-back guarantees, whereas purchases over $3000 include 5000km engine warranties and free NRMA Service membership. (☎9360 1500. Open M-Sa 9am-6pm, Su 10:30am-4pm.)

# BY BICYCLE

For taking in lots of scenery at a manageable pace, cycling is hard to beat; by complementing cycling with ferries and trains, in a single day it's possible to tour the Harbour and northern and eastern beaches, or venture out to Royal or Ku-Ring-Gai Chase National Park. **Bicycles in the City,** 722 George St (☎9252 2229), near Chinatown, hires bikes from $25 per day and provides cycling maps and comprehensive information for day and longer adventure tours. **Inner City Cycles,** 151 Glebe Point Rd, rents bikes starting at $30 per day. (☎9660 6605. Open daily 9am-5pm, later Th.) For a coastal ride, visit **Manly Cycle Centre,** 36 Pittwater Rd, at Denison St in Manly. (☎9977 1189. Open M-F 9am-6pm, Sa 9am-4:30pm, Su 11am-3pm. First 2hr. $10; each additional hour $5; full-day $25.) **Bicycle NSW,** Level 2, 209 Castlereagh St, has 10,000 members and organizes weekly rides. (☎9283 5200. Annual dues $38.)

## BY TAXI

Like in every big city, taxis can be hailed from virtually any street. Initial fare is $2.20 ($4 with call-in request), plus $1.07 per km. Tipping is not expected, though rounding up the fare is appreciated. Some companies are: **Legion Cabs** (☎13 14 51 or ☎9211 2300); **RSL Cabs** (☎13 22 11 or ☎9698 3511); **Taxis Combined** (☎9332 8888); **St. George Cabs** (☎13 21 66); and **Premiere Taxi** (☎13 10 17).

# 🛈 PRACTICAL INFORMATION

## TOURIST AND TRAVEL INFORMATION

**Tourist Office:** The **Sydney Visitors Centre,** 106 George St (☎9255 1788, freecall ☎(1800) 06 76 76; fax 9241 5010), located in the white, historic sailors' building in the Rocks. The 17min. presentation on the Rocks area is an entertaining introduction to the city's history. Open daily 9am-6pm.

**Travel Offices: Travellers Contact Point,** Level 7, 428 George St (☎9221 8744; fax 9221 3746; email sydney@travellers.com.au), between King and Market St. Internet access and word-processing 1hr. $4. Mail forwarding and holding in Australia, including your own email address, $40 per year. Employment board with recruiting officers for travelers with work visas. Open M-F 9am-6pm, Sa 10am-4pm. **Student Uni Travel,** Level 8, 92 Pitt St (☎9232 8444; fax 9231 1254; email sydney@backpackers.net), near Martin Pl. Free email and Internet access. Mail forwarding. Luggage storage $1 per day. Job agency and visa assistance. Open M-F 8:30am-6pm, Sa 10am-2pm. Student discounts, YHA, VIP. **Australian Travel Specialists,** Jetty 2 and Jetty 6, Circular Quay (24hr. ☎9555 2700; fax 9555 2701; email quayside@ozemail.com.au), on the waterfront. Comprehensive information on trips around Sydney and beyond. Open daily 8am-6:30pm. Locations also at Manly Ferry Wharf, Harbourside Shopping Centre (Darling Harbour), Centrepoint Shopping Centre, and Koala Oxford Hotel in Paddington. **YHA Membership and Travel Center,** 422 Kent St (☎9261 1111; fax 9261 1969; www.yha.org.au), behind Town Hall, between Market and Druitt St. Open M-W, F 9am-5pm, Th 9am-6pm, Sa 10am-2pm.

**Consulates: Canada,** Level 5, 111 Harrington St (☎9364 3000). Open M-F 8:30am-4:30pm. **New Zealand,** Level 14, 1 Alfred St, Goldfields Building, Circular Quay (☎9247 1344). Passport office open M-F 9am-4pm (☎9247 7500). Visa office open M-F 10am-4pm (☎9247 1511); phones answered M-F 10am-1pm. **U.K.,** Level 16, 1 Macquarie Pl (☎9247 7521; fax 9233 1826). Open M-F 10am-12:30pm and 1:20-4:30pm; phones answered 9am-5pm. **U.S.,** 59th floor, 19-29 Martin Pl, MLC Centre (☎9373 9200). Open M-F 8am-12:30pm; phones answered 8am-4:30pm.

## FINANCIAL SERVICES

Banks and exchange offices are crammed on the streets of Sydney, particularly in the Central Business District (**CBD**). They are generally open M-F 9am-5pm. **ATMs** are equally ubiquitous and usually accept Plus, MasterCard, Visa, and Cirrus. Be sure that you know both the number and corresponding letters of your password—some machines only have one or the other on the keypad.

**Singapore Money Exchange:** 67A Darlinghurst Rd, Kings Cross (☎9368 0972). 5% commission on traveler's checks in Australian dollars. Other offices at 304-308 George St (☎9223 6361), opposite Wynyard Station; 401 Sussex St, Chinatown (☎9281 0663); on Eddy Ave near Central Station, Shop #10 by the Greyhound office (☎9281 4118); in Darling Harbour's Harbourside Mall (☎9212 7124); and Centrepoint Tower's Castlereagh St level (☎9223 9222). All offices open M-Sa 9am-6pm, Su 9am-5pm.

**Thomas Cook:** (☎(1300) 72 87 47). Several locations in the international terminal of the airport. $7 charge on traveler's checks and currency exchanges; $10 for Australian traveler's checks. Open daily 5:30am-10:30pm. There are dozens of offices throughout the city, including 175 Pitt St (☎9231 2877). Open M-F 9am-5pm, Sa 10am-2pm.

**NEW SOUTH WALES**

**Money Change:** On the mall at Darlinghurst Rd and Springfield Ave, Kings Cross. 5% commission on traveler's checks and currency. Open Su-F 8am-11:30pm, Sa 8am-1am.

**American Express Office:** Dozens of locations around the city, including 92 Pitt St (☎9239 9226), around the corner from Martin Pl. Traveler's cheques cashed and currency changed with no commission; 1% commission to buy cheques. Mail held for card and traveler's cheque holders up to a month. Open M-F 8:30am-5:30pm, Sa 9am-noon.

## LOCAL SERVICES

**Bookstores: Dymocks Booksellers,** 424-430 George St (☎(1800) 68 83 19; www.dymocks.com.au). Open M-W 9am-6pm, Th 9am-9pm, F 9am-6pm, Sa-Su 9am-5pm. Australia's largest bookstore has franchise locations all over Sydney City.

**Library: Sydney City Library,** Town Hall House, 456 Kent St (☎9265 9470), at the corner of Kent and Druitt St. From Town Hall Station, walk through the arcade and enter off Sydney Sq. Open M-F 8am-7pm, Sa 9am-noon. The **State Library of New South Wales** (☎9273 1414), part of the former hospital complex on Macquarie St, houses galleries and research facilities. Open M-F 9am-9pm, Sa-Su 11am-5pm.

**Gyms: City Gym,** 107 Crown St, East Sydney (☎9360 6247), is central and open 24hr. M-Sa until 10pm, Su 8am-10pm. $10 per visit, $12 between 4-8pm, $110 per month.

**Ticket Agencies: Ticketek** (☎9266 4800; www.ticketek.com.au), has offices in retail stores and an information kiosk between Castlereagh and Elizabeth St, or you can buy on-line. Full-price advance booking for music, theater, sports, and selected museums. Phone lines are open for credit card purchases M-Sa 7:30am-10pm, Su 8am-8pm. **Ticketmaster** (☎13 61 00 or ☎9320 9000), covers many concert and theatrical venues. Phones answered M-Sa 9am-9pm, Su 10am-5pm.

**Weather:** For conditions 24hr., dial ☎11 96.

> **MEDIA AND PUBLICATIONS.**
> **Newspapers:** The main newspapers are the (more white-collar) *Sydney Morning Herald* (85¢) and (more blue-collar) *Daily Telegraph* (88¢).
> **Nightlife:** *Streetpress, The Revolver,* or *3-D World* (all free). For gay nightlife, check out *Capital Q Weekly* (free). See **Nightlife,** p. 127.
> **Entertainment:** The *Metro* section of Friday's *Sydney Morning Herald*, as well as free weeklies *Beat* and *Sydney City Hub*. See **Entertainment,** p. 124.
> **Radio:** Rock, Triple J 105.7FM and Triple M 104.9FM; News, ABC 630AM; Tourist Info, 88FM.

## EMERGENCY SERVICES

**Emergency:** Dial ☎000 anywhere in Australia for police, ambulance, or fire assistance.

**Police:** Kings Cross police station (☎9265 6233), on Fitzroy Gardens.

**Crisis Lines: Alcohol and Drug Information Service:** 24hr. ☎9361 2111. **Rape Crisis Centre:** 24hr. ☎9819 6565, outside Sydney ☎(1800) 42 40 17. **HIV/AIDS Information Line:** ☎9332 4000 or ☎9332 1090, phones answered M-F 8am-7pm, Sa 10am-6pm. **Suicide prevention:** ☎9331 2000.

**Late-Night Pharmacy (Chemist): 24hr. Prescription and Delivery Service:** ☎9235 0333. **Crest Hotel Pharmacy,** 60A Darlinghurst Rd, Kings Cross (☎9358 1822), opposite the rail station. Open Su-M 8am-midnight, Tu-Sa 8am-2am. **Wu's Pharmacy,** 629 George St, Chinatown (☎9211 1805). Open M-Sa 9am-9pm, Su 9am-7pm.

**Medical Services: Sydney Hospital** (☎9382 7111, emergency ☎9382 7009), on Macquarie St opposite the Martin Pl station. **Traveller's Medical and Vaccination Centre,** Level 7, 428 George St (☎9221 7133). Consultation fee $38. Open M-W, F 9am-6pm, Th 8:30am-8pm, Sa 9am-1pm. **Kings Cross Travellers' Clinic,** 13 Springfield Ave (☎9358 3066). Provides travel medical services and vaccinations. Consultation fee $35. Open M-F 9am-1pm and 2-6pm, Sa 9am-noon. **Contraceptive Services,** Level 3, 195 Macquarie St (☎9221 1933). Open M-F 8:30am-4:30pm, Sa 8am-1pm.

## POST AND COMMUNICATIONS

**Internet Access:** Internet cafés are as copious as pubs and McDonald's. Cheap rates abound, especially near Chinatown and Kings Cross; common charges in the city center are $3 per hr. and $4 for unlimited use, but rates fluctuate. **Global Gossip** shops are franchised across the city and offer 2min. free access. Locations include: 770 George St (☎9212 1466), near Sydney Central YHA; 111 Darlinghurst Rd, Kings Cross (☎9326 9777); 108 Oxford St, Darlinghurst (☎9380 4588); 14 Wentworth, Sydney City (☎9263 0400); 37 Hall Street, Bondi Beach (☎9365 4811); and 317 Glebe Point Rd (☎9552 6966). They also offer postboxes and mail-forwarding ($5 per month) and super-cheap **international call rates** in their on-site phone booths. Open daily 8am-1am (except the Oxford St location, which opens at 10am). There are also about half a dozen competitively priced places on George St near Chinatown and the Sydney YHA. **Student Uni Travel** offers free access but few terminals (see **Travel Offices,** p. 101).

**Post Office:** Sydney General Post Office **(GPO),** 159-171 Pitt St (☎ 13 13 17), on Martin Pl. Open M-F 8:15am-5:30pm, Sa 9am-1pm. *Poste Restante* awaits at 310 George St, inside Hunter Connection across from Wynyard Station. They will hold mail for up to a month. Enter under the "Through to Pitt St" sign on the east side of the street. Computers allow you to check whether you've got mail. No, this isn't a bad Tom Hanks movie. Open M-F 8:15am-5:30pm. Many hostels will also hold mail for up to a month. **Postal Codes:** 2000 for city center, 2001 for *Poste Restante.* Suburbs have their own post offices and postal codes.

**Directory Assistance:** ☎013.

**Phone Code:** 02.

---

### CYBER-SYDNEY ;-)

The following web sites have great information on what's hot in Sydney.

**www.cityofsydney.nsw.gov.au** The homepage of the city of Sydney. Visitor guide and information on services provided by the local government.

**http://sydney.citysearch.com.au** A business directory, entertainment listings, and latest attractions.

**http://sydney.sidewalk.com.au** Entertainment options, restaurant listings, shopping guides, and gay and lesbian information.

**www.sydney.com.au** Info on Sydney's sights, accommodations, and transportation system.

**http://australiavideo.com/sydney/index.htm** Pictures and videos.

**http://australia.craigslist.org/syd** This newcomer is a community notice board, with work, housing, and events listings.

---

# WORKING IN SYDNEY

Sydney is infested with backpackers seeking jobs, especially young Brits taking advantage of working-holiday visa agreements (for info on **work visas,** see p. 34). Fortunately, in economically optimistic Sydney, there is generally plenty of work available for the persistent. Those who arrive without prior arrangements report a 10-20 day or shorter lag before finding semi-permanent employment. Virtually all Sydney hostels have services to help guests find work (Sydney Central YHA distributes lists of employment agencies at their employment desk), and travel magazines like *TNT* and *OVG* contain work advice and listings of work agencies.

It pays to start preparing before leaving home. Have a resumé typed and saved on a PC floppy; you can print it at most Internet shops. Don't get stuck shelling out a lot to prepare a shabby document in a public facility. The best way to prepare for job hunting in Sydney is to do research and establish contacts before arriving. Spend time searching the web. Qualified applicants in computer fields enjoy the most success in landing high-quality positions. If you don't have the opportunity to set up house before commencing your search, it is advisable *not* to list hostel numbers as contact information, or you'll look transient. Instead, use a friend, get a cellular phone, or set up a mailbox at **Global Gossip** (see **Internet Access**, p. 103) or **Travellers Contact Point** (see **Travel Offices**, p. 101); both are good sources of job search ideas and allow you to receive incoming faxes. **Student Uni Travel** is another useful job agency (see **Travel Offices,** p. 101).

On the web, **Cowley's Job Centre** (www.cowleys.com.au) allows you to advertise yourself, and provides access to employment news groups and links to other employment-related packages. Also try the **Monster Board** (www.monster board.com.au), where you can post your resumé and search a list of employers. Newspapers are always an essential resource. The *Sydney Morning Herald* is stuffed with job classifieds on Wednesday and Saturday. *The Australian* is especially strong for computer opportunities in its Tuesday listings.

For tax info, visit the **Australian Taxation Office,** 100 Market St, GPO Box 9990, at the Centrepoint shopping plaza in the Central Business District. There you can grab the annual *TaxPack.* The helpful officers at this office report that the biggest misunderstanding for foreigners is that they believe they will be charged the 50% income tax while their tax number is being processed by immigration. In fact, travelers are given a 28-day grace period and are taxed at the 29% non-resident rate. However, it is essential to apply for a tax file number to get the lower rate and many employers will not even consider your application until you've filed the paperwork. (☎ 13 28 61; www.ato.gov.au. Open M-F 8:30am-4:45pm.)

# ▛ ACCOMMODATIONS

As most travelers' gateway to Australia, Sydney supports a thriving budget accommodation market. The first question most travelers must answer when looking for a bed in Sydney is whether or not to stay in Kings Cross. Well-located, traveler-friendly, and party-ready, Kings Cross has become an established backpacker mecca, and the high concentration of steadily improving hostels ensures that beds are almost always available. However, the omnipresence of prostitutes and go-go bars make many travelers uncomfortable. In addition, tales of theft are rampant. If you do opt to stay in the Cross, be sure you feel comfortable with your hostel's security measures before letting your valuables out of your sight.

While staying in the city center brings the benefit of convenient transportation, many travelers sing the praises of more remote suburbs, as the nightlife and good-value restaurant options around the CBD are quite limited. Glebe offers the second-highest concentration of backpackers (after the Cross), but with a safer feel. While Bondi is Sydney's high-profile beach, the accommodations at Coogee Beach are generally nicer. The accommodations listings are generally divided by neighborhood, though there is a special section entitled **Upscale Bargains** (p. 111) for those willing to pay a little more to really live it up.

Unless stated otherwise, hostels accept major credit cards, have 24hr. access, no linen fee, and a 10am check-out. Laundry, when available, is generally $2.50 per load. Prices listed are **winter rates** and most dorm beds increase in price by a few dollars ($2-5) during peak season (Nov.-Feb.). The most expensive time to travel, by far, is during Christmas and Easter vacations.

## KINGS CROSS AND AROUND

Some accommodations in the Cross can be seedy and run-down, but plenty of clean, well-maintained rooms exist. The shabbier places have been left out of our listings. The Victoria St locations are rather stately, as hostels go. **CityRail** runs from Martin Pl in the city to Kings Cross Station. **Bus** #311 runs from Circular Quay through Central Station to Kings Cross and on to Elizabeth Bay; buses #324 and 325 run from Circular Quay to Watson's Bay via Kings Cross; bus #327 runs from Circular Quay to Darling Point and Bondi Junction via Kings Cross; and bus #200 runs from Chatswood on the North Shore to Bondi Junction via Kings Cross. It's a 10min. walk from the east side of Hyde Park down William St to Darlington St—you've arrived when you reach the world's largest Coca-Cola sign.

NEW SOUTH WALES

## Kings Cross

🏠 ACCOMMODATIONS
Cross Court, 8
Eva's Backpackers, 1
Funk House Backpackers, 10
Jolly Swagman, 2
Highfield Private Hotel, 5
Original Backpackers, 4
Pink House, 11
Virgin Backpackers, 3
🍎 FOOD
Govinda's, 7
Shakespeare's, 6
🍺 PUBS
O'Malley's Hotel, 9

🗾 **Eva's Backpackers,** 6-8 Orwell St (☎9358 2185; fax 9358 3259; www.evasbackpack ers.com.au). Cozy, homey feel, with tidy rooms and family management. Picnic tables in kitchen and rooftop garden provide great meeting places—the rooftop view is mesmerizing. Hourly security patrols. Free luggage storage. Laundry $3. Internet (16min. $2). Key deposit $10. Reception daily 7am-1pm and 5:30-7pm. Bunks in 4- to 10-bed dorms $20; twins and doubles $50. 7th night free during winter. Book ahead.

🗾 **Funk House Backpackers,** 23 Darlinghurst Rd (☎9358 6455; fax 9358 3506; www.funkhouse.com.au). Above Hungry Jack's; enter via Llankelly Pl, an alley off the main drag. A very young, badass backpacker feel. In the middle of all the action, with an interior as bizarre as its surroundings. Murals of Jimi Hendrix, Jim Morrison, and Ray Charles done in a sort of narcotic spray paint job cover the doors and much of the walls. Doubles and twins have TV and fridge; all rooms have fans. Laundry. Reception daily 7am-10pm. 3- to 4-bed dorms $22, weekly $126; twins $56, $336. VIP.

**The Pink House,** 6-8 Barncleuth Sq (☎9358 1689, freecall ☎(1800) 80 63 84; email thepinkh@qd.com.au). Off Ward Ave. Unlike most other Kings Cross hostels, the Pink House feels like a house—a big, fun, light pink house. Copious group activities (daytrips, pub outings, skydiving, inter-hostel soccer) promote a family atmosphere. Brick kitchen opens onto garden terrace. Luggage storage $5 per week, $15 per month. Laundry. Reception daily 8:30am-12:30pm and 4-9pm. Dorms $17-22, weekly $99-132; twins and doubles $51, $306. YHA, VIP. Book ahead. Discounts for long-term stays.

**Jolly Swagman Backpackers,** 27 Orwell St (☎9358 6400, freecall ☎(1800) 80 58 70). Dorms get messy, but ample lounges and kitchens make up for it. All the primary colors lend a bit of a circus feel. Jolly offers everything: travel agency, bus trips to nearby beaches, videos, pub crawls, café (meals from $5), and Internet (1hr. $4). Free 24hr. pickup. Free luggage storage. Jolly 24hr. reception. Check-out 9am. Dorms $21, weekly $120; doubles $52, $300. Jolly good.

**The Virgin Backpackers,** 144 Victoria St (☎9357 4733; fax 9357 4434). Don't fret—this is not the latest Dirk Diggler cinema venture, but rather a swanky, tightly-knit hostel offering a painless first-time experience. The top floor has an action-packed common room with jukebox, pool table, and free weekly beer and BBQ. Internet café and travel desk downstairs. Free airport or city pickup. Luggage storage $2. Reception daily 8am-8pm. Dorms $20, weekly $119; twins $23, $139; doubles $49, $297. VIP.

**Cross Court,** 201-203 Brougham St (☎9368 1822; fax 9358 2595; email sales@cross court.hotel.com). Off William St. A quiet place without much common space. Shared bathrooms are clean and private. Microwave, no kitchen. Immaculate rooms, all with TV and fridge. Ideal for couples. Reception daily 8am-7pm. Dorms $18; singles $50, weekly $315; doubles $60, $385; triples $90.

**Original Backpackers,** 160-162 Victoria St (☎9356 3232; fax 9368 1435; www.origi nalbackpackers.com.au). Wrap-around front porch, kitchen, and dining area make for the most spacious hostel common area in the Cross. Cable TV, Internet (15min. $2), safe for valuables, security patrols, and laundry. Luggage storage $1 per day. Reception 24hr. Dorms $20, weekly $120; singles $35, $210; twins and doubles $55, $330. Discounts for long-term stays.

**Highfield Private Hotel,** 166 Victoria St (☎9326 9539; fax 9358 1552; www.highfield hotel.com). A backpacker might not appreciate the long hallways and lack of common space, but it's ideal for less hectic, comfortable long-term stays. Pristine bathrooms, small kitchen and TV room, security-coded lock, and a safe for valuables. Scandinavian-owned. Linen $3. No laundry. Reception M-F 7:30am-7pm, Sa-Su 8am-noon and 5-7pm. 3-bed dorms $20, weekly $120; singles $44, $265; doubles $55, $330.

**Travellers Rest,** 156 Victoria St (☎9358 4606). This job-oriented hostel provides contacts and lists of potential employers—and not much else. Reception daily 8am-noon and 4:30-6pm. Dorms $18, weekly $118. No advance bookings.

# CITY CENTER AND NEAR CENTRAL STATION

These accommodations are conveniently located near the city center and main lines of transportation. Excluding the first two listings, nicer accommodation can generally be found in Kings Cross or Glebe.

▨ **Sydney Central YHA,** corner of Pitt St and Rawson Pl (☎9281 9111; fax 9281 9199; email sydneycentral@yhansw.org.au). Visible from Central Station's Pitt St exit. The mothership has landed. The world's busiest hostel is the ideal spot for getting your bearings in Sydney. 532 beds and every possible service: pool, sauna, game room, employment and travel desks, TV rooms, Internet (30min. $2), parking ($9 per night, by advance arrangement), multiple kitchens, arranged activities, attached bar and café, and on and on. Its size is both amazing and a little alienating, more like a hotel than a cozy hostel. No sleeping bags allowed. Lockers $3, linen $2, towels $1. 14-day max. stay. Reception 24hr. Check-in from noon. Dorms $20-25; twins $60, ensuite $70. Under 18 half-price. Non-YHA add $3. Wheelchair accessible.

**Y on the Park (YWCA),** 5-11 Wentworth Ave (☎9264 2451, freecall ☎(1800) 99 49 94; fax 9285 6288; www.ywca-sydney.com.au). On the southeastern corner of Hyde Park; Wentworth Ave is at the junction of Liverpool and Oxford St. Dorms are more like barracks à la Martha Stewart—loads of carpeting, closet space, and pastels. Everything's sparkling and spacious. Women-only floor. A/C, heat, TVs, kitchen. Free short-term luggage storage. Laundry. Cheap Internet café (open daily 7am-8:30pm). Reception 24hr. Check-in from 1pm. 4-bed dorms $29; singles $68, ensuite $108; twins $93, $132; triples $105, $142. 10% YWCA discount. Wheelchair accessible.

**Alfred Park Private Hotel,** 207 Cleveland St (☎9319 4031; fax 9318 1306; www.oze mail.com.au/~hotels). A 10min. walk south on Chalmers St from Central Station, off Prince Alfred Park. Not in the best area of town. Former home of a sea captain with 14

**NEW SOUTH WALES**

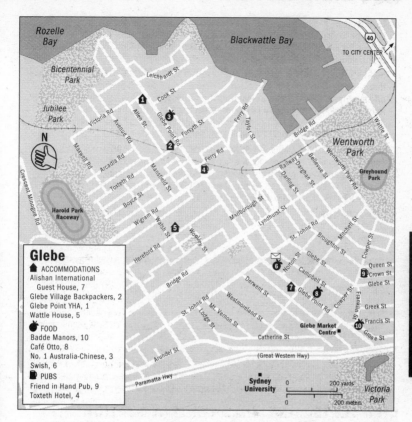

**Glebe**

🏠 ACCOMMODATIONS
Alishan International
  Guest House, 7
Glebe Village Backpackers, 2
Glebe Point YHA, 1
Wattle House, 5

🍎 FOOD
Badde Manors, 10
Café Otto, 8
No. 1 Australia-Chinese, 3
Swish, 6

🍺 PUBS
Friend in Hand Pub, 9
Toxteth Hotel, 4

children. The best rooms available in the budget range feature TVs, fridges, fans, and armoires. Kitchen. Free pickup. Airport shuttle $5. Laundry. Reception daily 7:30am-11pm. Check-out 9am. Dorms $19-22, ensuite with TV and fridge $27.50; singles $66, ensuite $77; twins and doubles $88, $99. Limited wheelchair access.

**City Central Backpackers (NOMADS),** 752 George St (☎9212 4833, freecall ☎(1800) 24 99 10; fax 9212 5753). Exit Central Station on Pitt St and take Rawson Pl from the north corner of the station to George St. The hostel's entrance has security bars on the door, and traffic can be noisy. Freshly painted, TV lounge, clean kitchen, reasonably clean bathrooms. Dorm rooms are large and carpeted, with fans and lockers. Free luggage storage. Reception daily 7am-10pm. Dorms $19.50. Wheelchair accessible.

**Millett's Oz,** Level 1, 161 Castlereagh St (☎9283 6599; fax 9283 8655; www.millettsoz.com.au). Near Centrepoint Tower, Millett's is one of the city's most centrally-located hostels—but certainly not its best. Reception M-F 8am-11pm, Sa 8am-10pm, Su 8am-8pm. Check-out 9:30am. Dorms $22, weekly $132; singles $41, $264; twins and doubles $60, $363. Wheelchair accessible.

# GLEBE

To get to Glebe Point Rd, take bus #431, 432, 433, or 434 from the eastern side of George St. By car, follow George St south towards Central Station until it feeds into Broadway, then turn right onto Glebe Pt Rd opposite Victoria Park.

🏠 **Wattle House,** 44 Hereford St (☎9552 4997; fax 9660 2528; www.wattle house.com.au). A 5min. walk from Glebe Point Rd. A hostel with a B&B feel, this is Sydney's smallest—and one of its nicest—backpackers. Restored Victorian decor includes lace curtains, brick kitchen, and manicured garden. Plush bean bags fill the small TV room, where guests get acquainted over complimentary hot chocolate. Laundry. Deposit $20. 4-week max. stay. Reception M-F 9am-noon, Sa-Su 10am-noon. 3- to 4-bed dorms from $25; doubles $50-60. Weekly rates available. Book way ahead.

**Alishan International Guest House,** 100 Glebe Point Rd (☎9566 4048; fax 9525 4686; www.alishan.com.au). Neat Victorian house features new rooms with TVs and fridges. The dorms are a bit less sparkling than the sparkling private rooms, but both are great values. Parking. Reception daily 8am-10:30pm. Dorms $27-37; ensuite singles $94; ensuite twins and doubles $104; ensuite family room for 4 $154, each extra person $16. Wheelchair accessible room available.

**Glebe Point YHA,** 262-264 Glebe Point Rd (☎9692 8418; fax 9660 0431; email glebe@yhansw.org.au). With long narrow halls and box-like rooms, the hostel feels like a university dorm but with cleaner bathrooms. Guests hang out on the roof for BBQs and in the subterranean lounge to play pool. Spacious kitchen and dining area. Sinks in rooms. Regular free bus service to the airport and city center. No sleeping bags allowed. Linen $2. Laundry. Internet (12min. $2). Reception daily 7am-10:45pm. Dorms $22-25, weekly $155; twins and doubles $50. Non-YHA add $3.

**Glebe Village Backpackers,** 256 Glebe Point Rd (☎9660 8133, freecall (1800) 80 19 83; fax 9552 3707; email glebevillage@bakpak.com). Come to hang hardcore or don't come at all. For the purist backpacker, it has decent-sized rooms in Glebe center and an unbeatable scene for meeting other dred-locked folks with fruit-picking jobs. For compulsively clean types, this is probably not the best choice. Laundry. Internet (15min. $2). Reception M-Sa 7:30am-9pm, Su 7:30am-1pm and 5-9pm. Check-out 9:30am. Dorms $23-24, weekly $143-148. VIP.

# NEWTOWN

Buses #422, 423, 426, and 428 run through Central Railway Sq via Castlereagh St to Newtown's central artery, King St. Buses running from Newtown to the city go to Circular Quay via George St.

**Billabong Gardens,** 5-11 Egan St (☎9550 3236; fax 9550 4352; www.billabonggardens.com.au). Off King St 2 blocks past Missenden Rd, coming from the city. Medium-sized, quietly bustling hostel with tiny dorms and comfortable motel-style rooms. Swimming pool-billabong, BBQ, kitchen, Internet, and free airport pickup. Reception daily 8:30am-noon and 6-10pm. Dorms $18-19, weekly $125; doubles from $66, ensuite $88, weekly $390; triples from $75, weekly $520. VIP. Wheelchair accessible.

# BONDI BEACH

Take bus #380, 382, or L82, which run from Circular Quay via Oxford St; or drive east along Oxford St. CityRail trains run to Bondi Junction, where a bus can be caught to the waterfront. Accommodations in Bondi are generally better than those in the CBD or the Cross.

**Indy's Bondi Beach Backpackers,** 35A Hall St (☎9365 4900; fax 9365 4994). 1½ blocks inland from Campbell Pde, set back from the street beyond the Commonwealth Bank. Large screen TV and video library. Free use of bikes and boards. Dorm partitions available for improvised privacy. Breakfast included. Laundry. Internet (12min. $2). Key deposit $20. Reception M-Sa 7:30-11am and 4-8pm, Su 8-11am. Check-out 10:30am. A more family- and couples-oriented location is at 252 Campbell Pde on the north end of the beach. Book through main office. Large dorms $20-22, weekly $120; doubles at 252 Campbell Pde $45 ($40 per night for 4-6 day stay), weekly $235. YHA, VIP.

**The Biltmore Private Hotel,** 110 Campbell Pde (☎9130 4660; fax 9365 0195; email biltmore@magna.com.au). As close as you can get to Bondi's waves without sleep-surfing. Kitchen and an in-house chef (M-F $5 dinners). Comfy common room with big TV. Free boogie board use. Luggage storage. Laundry $2.50. Internet (12min. $2). Reception daily 7:30am-10pm. Dorms $18-21, weekly $115-135; singles $35, $210; doubles $49, $295; beachfront doubles $55, $300; triples $65, $360.

**Noah's Bondi Beach,** 2 Campbell Pde (☎9365 7100, reservations freecall ☎(1800) 22 66 62; fax 9365 7644). Up the hill on the beach's south end. According to reception, it can get a bit rowdy. Rooftop balcony with BBQ and a view of the whole beach. Free surf and boogie board use. Pool table, TV, $2-10 dinners in adjacent restaurant. Ensuite female-only dorm available (rare in beach hostels). Key deposit $20. Dorms $21-24, weekly $126-144; twins and doubles $55, $330; beachside double $65, $390.

**Bondi Beachside Inn,** 152 Campbell Pde (☎9130 5311; fax 9365 2646; www.bondi inn.com.au). Seven stories of well-kept rooms overlooking the beach; ideal for families or couples. Rooms have kitchenette, TV, balcony, and phone. No laundry. Reception 24hr. Oceanview singles and doubles $110, land-side $100. Wheelchair accessible.

## COOGEE BEACH

Take bus #373 or 374 from Circular Quay, #372 from Central Station, or #314 from Bondi Junction.

▓ **Surfside Backpackers,** 186 Arden St (☎9315 7888, fax 9315 7892; www.surfside backpackers.com.au). Entrance off street behind McDonald's; buzz to be let in. You couldn't ask for a better location, with the shops of Coogee Bay Rd to one side, professional athletic fields to the other, and the beach right out in front. Balconies connecting the sunny rooms encourage socializing. The bigger dorms, especially the 16-bed dinosaur, are somewhat cramped, but that's par for the course at the beachside hostels. Female-only dorm available. Laundry. Internet (15min. $2). Deposit $20. Reception M-F 8am-12:30pm and 5-8pm, Sa-Su 8:30-12:30pm and 5-8pm. Check-out 9:30am. Dorms $20-22, weekly $104-112; doubles $48, $275. No doubles in summer. VIP.

**Original Coogee Beach Backpackers,** 94 Beach St (☎9315 8000 or ☎9665 7735; fax 9664 1258; www.millettsoz.com.au). Atop the steep hill at the north end of the beach. Surfside cottage with a view worth the hike. Spacious bedrooms. Two common rooms with TVs, 3 kitchens, big windows, and good vibes. Free airport and city pickup. Laundry. Key deposit $20. Reception 8am-1pm and 5-8pm; check-in 24hr. Check-out 9:30am. Dorms $20-22, weekly $110; twins and doubles $50. VIP. No credit cards.

**Coogee Beach Wizard of Oz,** 172 Coogee Bay Rd (☎9315 7876, freecall ☎(1800) 01 34 60; fax 9315 8974; www.sydneybeachside.com.au). 1½ blocks from the center of the beach. Hardwood floors, fresh paint, and lots of open common space allow for relaxation and socializing with the Munchkins. Free Th BBQs in summer. Free pickup. No smoking. Laundry. Key deposit $20. Reception daily 8am-noon and 6-8pm. Check-out 9:30am. Dorms $20, weekly $120; doubles $55, $300. VIP.

**Aegean Coogee Bay Road Backpackers,** 40 Coogee Bay Rd (☎9314 5324; www.pip.com.au/aegean). A 10min. walk inland. A bit crowded, but with a relaxed communal feel. Brims with amenities: 6 full kitchens, heated outdoor pool, sauna, rooftop balcony and BBQ. Free airport pickup with 2-night stay. No smoking or alcohol. Luggage storage $3. Linen $2 in summer. Laundry. Internet (10min. $12). Key deposit $20. Reception daily 8am-10pm, in winter 8am-noon and 5-10pm. Check-in 24hr. Dorms $20-25, weekly $90-120; doubles $25-35. Wheelchair accessible.

## MANLY

To get to Manly from Circular Quay, take either the **ferry** (25min.; M-F 6am-7pm, Sa-Su 8am-7pm; $10 return) or **Jetcat** (15min; M-Sa 6am-midnight, Su 7:15am-11pm; $12 return, $10 when ferry is not operating). See **Getting Around,** p. 99.

**Manly Beach Resort,** 6 Carlton St (☎9977 4188, freecall ☎(1800) 25 23 43; fax 9977 0524; www.manlyview.com.au). From the ferry, walk 10min. down Belgrave St, which becomes Pittwater St, and turn right onto Carlton St. A nicer-than-budget accommodation that also has backpackers dorms. Apartments available. Free pickup from the wharf 9am-noon. Heated pool, TV room, laundry. Key deposit $20. Reception 24hr. Dorms $22, weekly $143; doubles $42, $283. VIP. Motel rooms: singles $115; twins $140; 10% off weekly stays. Advance motel room bookings require $100 deposit.

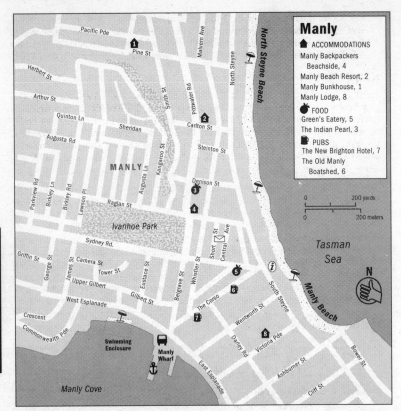

**Manly Backpackers Beachside,** 28 Raglan St (☎9977 3411; fax 9977 4379; email manlybackpack@bigpond.com.au). From the ferry, cross the Esplanade to Belgrave St, which becomes Pittwater St, and turn right onto Raglan St. Despite the blank, narrow hallways, the hostel manages to have an open, friendly atmosphere and clean, cozy dorms. Small TV room. Free use of body boards. Safe at reception; small lockers, but not in rooms. Linen $2, free for multi-night stays. Laundry. Reception M-F 9am-1pm and 4-8pm, Sa-Su 9am-1pm and 4-7pm; holidays 9am-noon only. Check-out 9:30am. Dorms $23-24, weekly $136-147; twins and doubles $55, ensuite $60.

**Manly Bunkhouse,** 35 Pine St and 46 Malvern Ave (☎9976 0472, freecall ☎(1800) 65 71 22; fax 9977 0692). Check-in for both locations at 35 Pine St. From the ferry, cross the Esplanade to Belgrave St, which becomes Pittwater St, then turn left onto Pine St (10min.). This small and quiet hostel is one of the best-kept in Manly. No common room, but each 4-bed dorm has its own kitchenette, bathroom, TV, heater, lockers, and closet space. At 46 Malvern Ave, there's an outdoor courtyard and eating area, plus a rooftop perfect for contemplative nights. Free wharf pickup. One-time $2 linen fee. Check-out 9:30am. Dorms $22, weekly $143; twins $55. VIP. Wheelchair accessible.

# COLLAROY

To get to Collaroy, take bus #183, 187, 188, 189, 190, 151, or any of the Northern Beach expresses which originate at Wynyard Station (Carrington St side), or take the ferry to Manly and catch buses #151, 155, or 157.

☒ **Sydney Beachouse/Collaroy Beach YHA,** 4 Collaroy St, Collaroy (☎9981 1177; fax 9981 1114; www.sydneybeachouse.com.au). This is precisely why you came to Sydney. A chic contemporary house 100m from the water, with tons of activities and free surf boards, snorkeling gear, and bikes. Buses to bush walks, national parks, and to Palm Beach, where the Aussie soap opera "Home and Away" is filmed. Luggage storage $4. Reception daily 8am-9pm. Dorms $24-25, weekly $154; family rooms for 5 $104.

# KIRRIBILLI

Kirribilli is a slightly upscale, quiet, residential neighborhood. Most travelers who stay here are older and many are on working holidays. Kirribilli offers a welcome haven from the constant din of the city. In North Sydney, Kirribilli is most easily accessed by taking the Neutral Bay ferry from Wharf 4, Circular Quay. Alternately, the train stops at nearby Milson's Point. From Milson's Point, walk down Ennis Rd towards the harbor, turn left onto Kirribilli St, and then left onto Carabella St.

**Tremayne Private Hotel,** 89 Carabella St (☎9955 4155; fax 9922 5228). From the Neutral Bay ferry, walk up Holbrook St, turn right and take a 5min. walk up Carabella St. Balconies have an unobstructed view of Careening Cove and Neutral Bay. Rooms have fridges, some with TV. Kitchen. Laundry. Dorms $18; singles $160, ensuite $215; twins and doubles $260; includes daily breakfast and M-F dinner. No credit cards.

**Glenferrie Lodge,** 12A Carabella St (☎9955 1685; fax 9929 9439; www.sydney-accom-group.com). From the ferry, walk up Holbrook St, and take a left onto Carabella St. More expensive than its budget neighbors, although it's money well-spent. A stately house with ample balcony space and a courtyard. Breakfast and country-style dinner included. TV hire $5.50, weekly $16.50. Reception daily 7am-10pm. Dorms $38, weekly $180; singles $75, $350; doubles $55, $120.

# UPSCALE BARGAINS

**⊠ Russell Hotel,** 143A George St, The Rocks (☎9241 3543; fax 9252 1652; www.therus sell.com.au). A small, inviting hotel with exquisitely-furnished, brightly painted rooms and a rooftop garden overlooking The Rocks. Relaxing downstairs sitting room with bar is well-suited for reading, socializing, or gloating to less fortunate comrades via post-card. Continental breakfast included. Reception daily 6am-10pm. Check-in from 1pm. Check-out 11am. Singles $115-165, ensuite $200-245; doubles $130-180, $215-260; suite or studio $285. Not wheelchair accessible.

**Wattle Private Hotel,** 108 Oxford St, Darlinghurst (☎9332 4118; fax 9331 2074; email mikeyu@riv ernet.com.au). On the corner of Palmer St. Cozy and elegant rooms with TV and fridge. Reception daily 7am-9pm. Singles $88; twins $110; doubles $99.

**Hotel 59,** 59 Bayswater Rd, Kings Cross (☎9360 5900; fax 9360 1828; www.inter space.net.au/inns/hotel59.html). A brothel less than a decade ago, Hotel 59 is still a fantastic deal for your dollar; it now offers 8 thoughtfully-arranged ensuite family rooms with TV. Full breakfast included. Reception daily 7:30am-7:30pm. Check-out 11am. Rooms $100-135.

**De Vere Hotel,** 46 Macleay St, Kings Cross (☎9358 1211, freecall ☎(1800) 81 87 90; fax 9358 4685; www.devere.com.au). On the corner of Crick St. Elegant rooms have TV, fridge, A/C, and phone. Laundry. Internet (10min. $2.50). Reception 24hr. Check-in from 1pm. Check-out 10:30am. Standards run $99-149, extra person $30.

**Manly Lodge,** 22 Victoria Pde, Manly (☎9977 8655; fax 9976 2090). Luxurious ensuite rooms are a steal for families or couples. A/C, TV, VCR, and fridge; some have hot tubs. Communal sauna, spa, gym, laundry. Twins from $120-159; doubles $110-144; deluxe $130-168. Extra person $35, children under 10 $20. For Sa only bookings, rates increase $30. Cheaper weekly rates in winter.

**Landmark Parkroyal,** 81 Macleay St, Kings Cross (☎9368 3000, freecall ☎(1800) 02 36 65; fax 9357 7600; www.parkroyal.com.au). Contemporary hotel with great views of Rushcutters Bay, the Pacific, or the Harbour Bridge. TV, fridge, and mini-bar. Continental breakfast, parking, city shuttles, sauna, and gym use all included. Reception 24hr. Check-in from 2pm. Check-out 11am. Rooms start at $174.

# ☐ FOOD

Sydney's streets overflow with eateries of every flavor for any budget. Asian options, most notably Thai and Chinese cuisine, rank highly among the international selections. The Central Business District, the northern half of Sydney proper, is rife with quick lunch stops for the professional masses still dreaming of three-martini lunch status. Sandwiches, meat pies, and focaccias run $2.50-6 at sandwich counters throughout these blocks. Slightly south, the feeding frenzy of **Chinatown** lurks west of Central Station, around Hay St, Little Hay St, and the Dixon St Plaza. Just east of the center, the Oxford St social artery runs between Surry Hills in the south (where many of the city's best **Thai** kitchens line up on Crown St), and the (very) **Little Italy** on Stanley St, between Crown and Riley St, in Darlinghurst. Cafés in Little Italy serve excellent **coffee** and hearty hot sandwiches. Continuing east through Darlinghurst, the strip of restaurants on Oxford St near St. Vincent's Hospital (at Victoria St) is known for a quality variety of **Asian** and **European flavors.** Victoria St runs north from Oxford at the hospital into **the land of high cappuccino chic** before depositing the last of its café class amidst the hostels of Kings Cross. In the Cross, Darlinghurst Rd and Bayswater Rd offer fare abiding by the local atmosphere: **late-night cheap bites,** fast-food chains, and little else.

As usual, a large student population means good, **cheap cafés** and restaurants on both Glebe Point Rd in Glebe and Kings St in Newtown. Blues Point Rd on McMahons Point and Fitzroy St in Kirribilli lead the North Shore's attempts at affordability with style, featuring several cafés well-loved by the locals. **Breakfast** is big on the beachfront drives of Manly, Bondi, and Coogee. At most coastal cafés, $6-7 buys a large cooked breakfast and an excuse to appreciate the view over the morning paper. Manly offers even less expensive carnival-style food counters along the Corso. Though the neighborhoods vary in their offerings, none disappoint.

## KINGS CROSS

☑ **Govinda's,** 112 Darlinghurst Rd (☎9380 5155, showtimes ☎9360 7853). A unique, can't-miss restaurant and cinema. $15 covers a mostly Indian, wholly vegetarian, all-you-can-eat buffet, and a current movie in the upstairs theater, which features cushy, reclining sofas for total viewing bliss or dark room flirtation. Open daily from 6pm.

☑ **Shakespeare's Sydney Pie Co.,** 87 Darlinghurst Rd (☎8354 0995). This city-wide sweets chain is the missing link of fast-food cuisine—where else can you get an entire pie and a jug of coffee at 3am after you've been out boozing all night? Open Su-W 9am-10:30pm; open Th-Sa 24hr. (except closed 4:30-5am).

**@Potts Point,** corner of Challis and Macleay St, Potts Point (☎9356 2223). A happening place. Burgers, fish, lamb, or veal scallopini (all from $11). Open daily 7am-11pm.

**Harry's Café de Wheels,** Cowper Wharf Roadway, Woolloomooloo (☎9357 3074). Northeast of the Cross in a stand near the Navy shipyard. Easy late-night stagger on Brougham St for a post-party pastie. The house special, meat pie and peas (from $4), reflects Harry's 50 years of pie-making expertise. Open Su-Th 7am-2am, F-Sa 7am-4am.

## CITY CENTER

☑ **Dixon House Food Court,** 80 Dixon St, Chinatown. Downstairs, on the corner of Little Hay St. Cheap-feed East Asian meals that taste much better than the convenience store frozen eggrolls you'd get for the same price. Meals $5-10. Open daily 10:30am-8:30pm.

☑ **Blackbird Café,** Balcony Level, Cockle Bay Wharf (☎9283 7385). Very trendy eatery with a great view of Darling Harbour. The prices are average for coffee, cakes, and a wide variety of alcohol, but the ambiance is posh enough to justify full-price. Board games, comfy leather couches, outside heaters, and books make for an unbeatable lounging atmosphere. Open daily 8am-1am.

**Soup Plus,** 383 George St, CBD (☎9299 7728). With a $25 cover, this smoky jazz bar is an expensive dinner option, but the value-per-dollar is unbeatable. The price covers entertainment and a 2-course dinner: an entree (from *mousaka* to lasagna to stuffed pumpkin), and an appetizer or dessert. Open daily noon-midnight (cover from 8pm).

**Baker's Oven Coffee Lounge,** 121 George St., The Rocks (☎9247 9978). Healthy gourmet sandwiches (from $4), salads, and fruit. The Turkish vegetable-and-cheese foccaccia is a scrumptious way to funnel nutrients into a vending-machine sustained backpacker bod. Open daily 6am-8:30pm.

**Mamma Mia's Italian Restaurant,** 580 George St, CBD (☎9261 4622). Above Pavillion Hotel. This is one of the truly inexpensive places downtown to get a filling pasta dish. Meals from $6. Open M-Th noon-2:30pm and 5-9pm, F noon-2:30pm.

**Chinta Ria—Temple of Love,** Roof Terrace, Cockle Bay Wharf (☎9264 3211). A fantastic spot for soaking in the trendy wharf neighborhood. Yummy, if pricey, Malaysian fare from $13. Tu: jazz outside. Open daily noon-2:30pm and 6-11pm (10:30pm on Su).

**Harbour Plaza Food Court,** corner of Dixon and Goulburn St. Several restaurants offer hearty $5 meals; Chinese eateries are especially prevalent. Open daily 10am-10pm.

## GLEBE

Glebe could be called Sydney's restaurant district. It is home to a variety of bohemian cafés, exotic eateries, and great pub meals.

**Swish,** 131-145 Glebe Point Rd (☎9552 6800). The elegant outdoor patio and vibrantly decorated interior provide the setting, while the kitchen crew provide the most thoughtfully prepared and finely presented $6-8 breakfast and lunch specials around. Both eggs Benedict and tortellini are sure to please. Open W-M 8am-11pm.

**Café Otto,** 79 Glebe Point Rd (☎9552 1519). High-ceilinged diner with an insulated outdoor courtyard, serving everything from popular pastas ($10-14) and pizza ($8-10) to pricier meat dishes. Separate kids menu. For dessert, try the local fave: sticky date pudding ($8). Open Su-Th 9am-11pm, F-Sa 9am-midnight. BYO.

**Badde Manors,** 37 Glebe Point Rd (☎9660 3797). World music plays in the background as the scent of freshly ground coffee permeates the air in this all vegetarian café. Gourmet coffee, fresh sorbet, and smoothies. Lentil burger $7.50. Open M-Th 8am-midnight, F 8am-1am, Sa 9am-11pm, Su 9am-10pm.

**No. 1 Australia-Chinese Take-Away,** 245 Glebe Point Rd (☎9571 9588). Hey, it's number one! Well sort of. A surprisingly unassuming place given the audacious name, but with substantial meals for around $6. Open daily 8am-9pm.

## NEWTOWN

King St bisects Newtown and provides backpacker style cheap eats, from Indian takeaways and Thai restaurants to filling brekkie deals. Newtown is a very young and bohemian place—cheap and tasty options are endless. It's the new hot place for uni-backpackers.

**Simply Thai,** 186 King St (☎9565 5111). A merely typical King St ethnic option as far as atmosphere is concerned—but the food is very cheap and very fresh. $6 lunch special. Open M 4-10pm, Tu-Th noon-3pm and 4-10pm, F-Su noon-3pm.

**Kilimanjaro African Eatery,** 280 King St (☎9557 4565). Re-creates the flavors of several African nations with meals cooked in glazed clay pots and served in a simple dark-wood setting. Lots of couscous dishes. Filling mains from $9. Appetizers and sides $6. Open daily noon-3pm, and Su-Th 6-10pm, F-Sa 6-11pm. BYO.

**Happy Chef,** 264 King St (☎9550 3423). One of King St's best Chinese take-aways. Piled-high plates from $6. Open M-Th 11am-10pm, F-Sa 11am-11pm.

**Stingy Lil's,** 549 King St (☎9565 2526). Huge, cheap, filling brekkie for a growling tummy $5-10. Open for gorging daily 8:30am-5pm.

**Tamana's North Indian Diner,** 196 King St (☎9519 2035). Also a smaller location at 236 King St. It's rare to find a fast-food joint with such a faithful following. Tamana's keeps local favor with its generous curry portions for under $7. Open daily 11:30am-10:30pm.

**COFFEE CONFUSION** Just after arriving in Australia, sleepy-eyed and weary from your travels, you stumble into a coffee lounge in great need of a nice, big cup of coffee. Only trouble is, upon ordering, you're asked what kind. "Flat white?" the barista queries, and you stare back, blankly, quite confused and a bit anxious for that dose of caffeine. Don't panic—there are a few things you should know. Perhaps most importantly, coffee drinks are all made with espresso, as opposed to the automatic-drip style brewing machines. This means that if you drink it black, it tastes quite a bit stronger. The most common drinks are: **short black** (about 60ml of espresso); **long black** (120-200ml espresso); and **flat white** (espresso with cold milk). Then there are the fancier, but more commonly known, espresso drinks: café latte (espresso, hot milk, and froth); cappuccino (espresso, hot milk, and heaps of froth); macchiato (espresso with a bit of froth); and vienna coffee (espresso, whipped cream, and powdered chocolate). Any of these drinks can be made weak, medium, or strong. And you'll get whole milk unless you ask for something different, like cream or lowfat milk (referred to as "skinny," "rev," or "physical." Though coffee may not be Australia's specialty (to put it mildly), there are some delicious caffeinated drinks. So go out there, hold your head high, and order yourself a flat white that's strong and physical.

## DARLINGHURST AND PADDINGTON

Oxford St addresses start at the street's origin on Hyde Park, but confusingly begin again once the street runs southeast from Darlinghurst into Paddington at the intersection with Victoria and Dowling St. Noting whether an address is in Darlinghurst or Paddington is the easiest way to locate an Oxford St property.

**Micky's Café,** 268 Oxford St, Darlinghurst (☎9361 5124). Every combination under the sun: noodles, stirfry, burgers, burritos, cheesecakes, pasta, risotto, chicken satay, and the best Caesar salad in Sydney. Meals from $10. Open 9am-midnight (1am F-Sa).

**Arthur's Pizza,** 139 Oxford St, Paddington (☎9389 4432). In a city with surprisingly few good pizza options, Arthur's hits the spot. Pizzas from $5-15. Open daily 8am-10pm.

**Burgerman,** 116 Surrey St, Paddington (☎9361 0268). Off Victoria St, near Willam St. Also at 249 Bondi Rd (☎9130 4888). A 70s-style American burger joint with a metallic-techno-hip identity crisis. The clashing decor goes as well with the soundtrack as the french fries ($3-5) go with the tomato-shaped ketchup bottles. For a truly Aussie treat, get a burger with beetroot. Open daily noon-10pm. Licensed and BYO (corkage $4).

**Green Chillies,** 113-115 Oxford St, Darlinghurst (☎9361 3717). Despite the address, the entrance is around the corner on Crown St. Traditional Thai dishes with far more style than you pay for. Dishes are flavored liberally with chili, lime, mint, and coriander. Mains $9-10. $6 takeaway lunch specials Tu-F. Open Tu-F 11:30am-3:30pm and daily 6-10:30pm. BYO wine only (corkage $2 per person).

## SURRY HILLS

**Uchi Lounge,** 15 Brisbane St (☎9261 3524). A reasonably-priced place for a night of self-indulgence. Japanese menu with speciality items like chrysanthemum sushi and grilled eggplant parmesan. Entrees $10-18. Open M-Sa 6-10:30pm.

**Prasits Northside Thai Take Away,** 395 Crown St (☎9332 1792). Several blocks south of Oxford St, near Fitzroy St. Hot, fresh, hot, creative, hot dishes. The green peppercorn stir-fry might be used to melt iron if it weren't so yummy ($11.50). Tasty spring rolls ($2). Limited seating. Open Tu-Su noon-3pm and 5:30-10pm. BYO (corkage $1).

**Mehrey Da Dhaba Indian Street Restaurant,** 466 Cleveland St (☎9319 6260). Named for the roadside food stalls of north India, the Dhaba brings a tradition of hearty, inexpensive, and filling food across the ocean without losing any of the flavor. Whole tandoori chicken $9. Vegetarian meals from $8; meat dishes $7-12. *Naan* or *roti* 90¢. Open W-Su noon-3pm and daily from 5:30pm. BYO.

# BONDI BEACH

Outdoor eateries line Campbell Pde, allowing the savvy traveler to choose from an array of cheap culinary delights.

**Bondi Tratt,** 34b Campbell Pde (☎9365 4303). Mod-Oz cuisine with some Italian influence. Try some kangaroo, if you dare. Hey, it's supposed to be low-fat, if chewy. Entrees from $13. Open daily 7am-11pm.

**Gabby's Café,** 94 Campbell Pde (☎9130 3788). Gabby's has satisfied customers with its filling breakfasts ($7) for more than 20 years. Molly Ringwald take heed: it's sometimes referred to as the "Breakfast Club." Open daily 7am-5pm.

**Flavour of North India,** 138 Campbell Pde (☎9365 6239). Warm and ready curries $6-8. Fresh *naan* ($1.50-2) tempers the spicier options. Open daily noon-10:30pm.

# COOGEE BEACH

**Coogee Bay Hotel** (☎9665 0000). Corner of Coogee Bay Rd and Arden St. An entertainment complex with a nightclub, full-size concert hall, 3 bars, and a restaurant. Cook your own juicy T-bone or chicken breast for $10-12, including salad and a roll. $6 kids meals of chicken nuggets or fish-and-chips. Open daily noon-3pm and 6-9:30pm.

**Barzura,** at the end of Carr St (☎9665 5546). At the south end of the beach, a 2min. walk from Coogee central. Outdoor seating. Breakfast until 1pm $8, mains $11-17. Open daily 7am-11pm. Licensed and BYO wine only (corkage $2 per person).

# MANLY

Cheap cafés, takeaways, and American imperialist fast-food chains colorfully line the Corso, which connects the harbor to the Pacific, while more expensive, image-conscious cafés can be found on Steyne St running parallel to the ocean.

**Green's Eatery,** 1-3 Sydney Rd (☎9977 1904). On the pedestrian stretch of Sydney Rd near the ocean side of the Corso. Sunny, vegetarian café serves amazingly hearty meals, with rice and interesting vegetable combos for $4-6. Try the chick pea casserole or the sauteed vegetables with tofu. Open daily 8am-6:30pm. BYO.

**The Indian Pearl,** 26-28 Pittwater Rd (☎9977 2890). North of the town center. Savory curry and tandoori dishes include chicken, lamb, and beef dishes from $10. Tandoori chicken entree for just $7.50. Open daily 5:30-11pm. BYO wine only. Free delivery.

# 🔘 SIGHTS

Sydney's sights range from architectural landmarks to beaches, from museum tours to neighborhood strolls. Because of the city center's manageable size, most cultural attractions could be seen in less than a week of serious sightseeing. However, while many of Sydney's neighborhoods do not have specific "sights" per se, their attraction lies in their tasty cafés, off-beat stores, and local nooks and crannies. There's architecture to appreciate in Paddington, markets to rummage through in Glebe and Newtown, and tanned and toned beach action on Bondi and Coogee. Find adrenaline-fixes and pulse-quickeners in **Activities** (p. 122) and the best spots for retail-therapy in **Shopping and Markets** (p. 126).

## THE ROCKS AND CIRCULAR QUAY

▨**SYDNEY OPERA HOUSE.** Standing like a fleet of sailboats beating into the wind, the Sydney Opera House is the city skyline's defining aspect. Designed by Danish architect Jørn Utzon, Sydney's pride and joy took 14 years to construct. A saga of bureaucracy and broken budgets (planned at $7 million, the building cost $102 million by the time it was finished) surrounded the construction and eventually led the architect to divorce himself from the project prior to its completion. In 1973, Queen Elizabeth opened the building, despite strong winds, a false fire alarm, and 1400 spectator seats initially set up facing the wrong way. By starring in thousands of tourist photographs every day and hosting operas, ballets, classical concerts, plays, and films, the Opera House has come to symbolize Sydney itself. (On Bennelong Point, opposite the base of the Harbour Bridge. ☎9250 7250; www.soh.nsw.gov.au. For box office info, see **Entertainme**nt, p. 124. 1hr. tours every 30min. daily 9am-4pm. $13, concessions $9; 200 steps on the tour.)

■**SYDNEY HARBOUR BRIDGE.** Spanning the harbor, the arching steel lattice-work of the massive Harbour Bridge has been a visual symbol of the city since its opening in 1932. It is the best place to get a look at the Harbour and the cityscape. Pedestrians can enter the bridge walkway from a set of stairs on Cumberland St just south of Argyle St in The Rocks. At the bridge's southern pylon, there is an entry on the walkway which leads up to solid photo-ops. **The Harbour Bridge Museum** inside the pylon tells the baffling story of the bridge's construction. (☎9240 1100 for more info. Open daily 10am-5pm. Admission to lookout and museum $2.) For high adventure, **Bridgeclimb** will take you up to the apex for a gut-wrenching view of the city and Harbour. Only mildly strenuous and hyper-safe, this is maximum bragging potential with minimum stress—though it will noticeably lighten your wallet. (☎8274 7777. Open daily 7am-7pm. M-F $117, age 12-16 $96; Sa-Su $142, $118.)

**THE ROCKS.** At the base of the bridge, The Rocks is the site of the original Sydney Town settlement. Built during the lean years of the colony's founding, the area remained quite rough-and-tumble well into this century. In the 1970s, when plans to raze the slums were revealed, a movement to preserve the historic area began. Today, The Rocks bustles with tourists wandering from charming cafés to historic storefronts. Street performers and live bands liven-up the The Rocks Market, held every Saturday and Sunday (see **Shopping,** p. 126). **Sydney Visitors Centre** and the **Rocks Walking Co.** share the white, three-story Sailors' Home at 106 George St. The former has info on local attractions and displays on the history of the Rocks, and the latter conducts informative walking tours of The Rocks. (Visitors Centre: ☎9255 1788, freecall ☎(1800) 06 76 76. Open daily 9am-6pm. Walking Co.: ☎9247 6678. 80min. tours depart M-F 10:30am, 12:30, and 2:30pm; Sa-Su 11:30am and 2pm. $12, ages 10-16 $8.50, under 10 free.)

**CIRCULAR QUAY.** Of course it's pronounced "key." How else would you say it? Between Dawes Point and Bennelong Point is the departure point for both the city ferry system and numerous private cruise companies. The Quay becomes a lively hub of tourist activity on weekends, with street performers, souvenir shops, and easy access to many major sights. It's also a prime place for those sun-worshippers who find the concrete jungle of the CBD blocks their rays.

**SYDNEY OBSERVATORY.** This huge sandstone building atop Observatory Hill caters to the starry-eyed (there's no Beatrice here). Guided tours of the heavens (through the telescopes, that is) take place nightly 8:15pm, with a 6:15pm session during the winter season of early sunsets. In the daytime, the observatory functions as a museum of astronomy with displays, films, talks, and simulated skyscapes. (On Miller's Point, a quick walk west of George St via Argyle St. ☎9217 0485. Open daily 10am-5pm. Museum free. Tours $10, concessions $5, families $25; book ahead. Wheelchair access via Cumberland St.)

**MUSEUM OF CONTEMPORARY ART.** Injecting a little modernity into an area largely absorbed with its past, the smallish museum is a playground for an uber-hip artsy crowd. The extensive collection of Aboriginal work is worthwhile. (140 George St. ☎9252 5876; recorded info 9241 5865; www.mca.com.au. Free guided tours 11am and 2pm. Open daily 10am-6pm. $12, concessions $7, families $24.)

**MUSEUM OF SYDNEY.** Unable to escape, even history has succumbed to the technology age. Located in the site of the first Government house, this new and stylish museum celebrates the city's past through films and high-tech exhibits. (37 Phillip St. ☎9251 5988. Open daily 9:30am-5pm. $6, concessions $3, families $15.)

NEW SOUTH WALES

## PACIFIC RIM          PACIFIC HEIGHTS

AT&T Direct Service access numbers are the easy way to call home from anywhere.

Global connection with the AT&T Network | **AT&T** direct service

**www.att.com/traveler**

---

# AT&T Direct®Service

The easy way to call
home from anywhere.

### AT&T Access Numbers

| | |
|---|---|
| Amer. Samoa .....633-2-872 | Greece ● .......00-800-1311 |
| Argentina ...0800-555-4288 | Guam .......1-800-2255-288 |
| Australia.....1-800-881-011 | Hong Kong .....800-96-1111 |
| Bangladesh ▲ ........157-001 | India ▲ ...............000-117 |
| Brazil ..............000-8010 | Indonesia ▲ .....001-801-10 |
| Cambodia ✚...1800-881-001 | Ireland✓ ....1-800-550-000 |
| China, PRC ▲ ..........10811 | Israel ......1-800-94-94-949 |
| Fiji.............004-890-1001 | Italy ● ...............172-1011 |
| France .......0800-99-00-11 | Japan ▲ ● .......005-39-111 |
| Germany ....0800-2255-288 | Korea, Republic ● 0072-911 |

# AT&T Direct®Service

The easy way to call
home from anywhere.

### AT&T Access Numbers

| | |
|---|---|
| Amer. Samoa .....633-2-872 | Greece ● .......00-800-1311 |
| Argentina ...0800-555-4288 | Guam .......1-800-2255-288 |
| Australia.....1-800-881-011 | Hong Kong .....800-96-1111 |
| Bangladesh ▲ ........157-001 | India ▲ ...............000-117 |
| Brazil ..............000-8010 | Indonesia ▲ .....001-801-10 |
| Cambodia ✚...1800-881-001 | Ireland✓ ....1-800-550-000 |
| China, PRC ▲ ..........10811 | Israel ......1-800-94-94-949 |
| Fiji.............004-890-1001 | Italy ● ...............172-1011 |
| France .......0800-99-00-11 | Japan ▲ ● .......005-39-111 |
| Germany ....0800-2255-288 | Korea, Republic ● 0072-911 |

The best way to keep in touch when you're traveling overseas is with **AT&T Direct**® Service. It's the easy way to call your loved ones back home from just about anywhere in the world. Just cut out the wallet guide below and use it wherever your travels take you.

For a list of AT&T Access Numbers, tear out the attached wallet guide.

**AT&T**

---

| | |
|---|---|
| Macao ...............0800-111 | Reunion Isl.....0800-99-0011 |
| **Malaysia●▲...1-800-80-0011** | **Saipan●** .....**1-800-2255-288** |
| Marshall Isl....1800-225-5288 | Singapore ......800-0111-111 |
| Micronesia ..................288 | Solomon Islands ..........0811 |
| Nepal●▲ ........0800-77-001 | **Spain** .............**900-99-00-11** |
| **Netherlands ●...0800-022-9111** | Sri Lanka ...............430-430 |
| **New Zealand ●** .......**000-911** | **Switzerland ●**..**0800-89-0011** |
| Pakistan▲ ......00-800-01001 | **Taiwan**..........**0080-10288-0** |
| Palau .....................02288 | Thailand **‹** ....001-999-111-11 |
| Papua New Guinea...0507-12880 | **U.K.** .............**0800-89-0011** |
| **Philippines ●** ..........**105-11** | Vietnam ● .........1-201-0288 |

**FOR EASY CALLING WORLDWIDE**
*1.* Just dial the AT&T Access Number for the country you are calling from.
*2.* Dial the phone number you're calling.   *3.* Dial your card number.

For access numbers not listed ask any operator for **AT&T Direct**® Service.

In the U.S. call 1-800-331-1140 for a wallet guide listing all worldwide AT&T Access Numbers.

Visit our Web site at: **www.att.com/traveler**

Bold-faced countries permit country-to-country calling outside the U.S.

● Public phones require coin or card deposit to place call.

▲ May not be available from every phone/payphone.

✔ Use U.K. access number in N. Ireland.

✦ Available from payphones in Phnom Penh and Siem Riep only.

● Available in select hotels in Ho Chi Minh City, calling centers in Hanoi, post offices in Da Nang, Ho Chi Minh City and Quang Ninh.

‹ When calling from public phones, use phones marked "Lenso."

When placing an international call *from* the U.S., dial 1 800 CALL ATT.

AP                                         © 8/00 AT&T

---

| | |
|---|---|
| Macao ...............0800-111 | Reunion Isl.....0800-99-0011 |
| **Malaysia●▲...1-800-80-0011** | **Saipan●** .....**1-800-2255-288** |
| Marshall Isl....1800-225-5288 | Singapore ......800-0111-111 |
| Micronesia ..................288 | Solomon Islands ..........0811 |
| Nepal●▲ ........0800-77-001 | **Spain** .............**900-99-00-11** |
| **Netherlands ●...0800-022-9111** | Sri Lanka ...............430-430 |
| **New Zealand ●** .......**000-911** | **Switzerland ●**..**0800-89-0011** |
| Pakistan▲ ......00-800-01001 | **Taiwan**..........**0080-10288-0** |
| Palau .....................02288 | Thailand **‹** ....001-999-111-11 |
| Papua New Guinea...0507-12880 | **U.K.** .............**0800-89-0011** |
| **Philippines ●** ..........**105-11** | Vietnam ● .........1-201-0288 |

**FOR EASY CALLING WORLDWIDE**
*1.* Just dial the AT&T Access Number for the country you are calling from.
*2.* Dial the phone number you're calling.   *3.* Dial your card number.

For access numbers not listed ask any operator for **AT&T Direct**® Service.

In the U.S. call 1-800-331-1140 for a wallet guide listing all worldwide AT&T Access Numbers.

Visit our Web site at: **www.att.com/traveler**

Bold-faced countries permit country-to-country calling outside the U.S.

● Public phones require coin or card deposit to place call.

▲ May not be available from every phone/payphone.

✔ Use U.K. access number in N. Ireland.

✦ Available from payphones in Phnom Penh and Siem Riep only.

● Available in select hotels in Ho Chi Minh City, calling centers in Hanoi, post offices in Da Nang, Ho Chi Minh City and Quang Ninh.

‹ When calling from public phones, use phones marked "Lenso."

When placing an international call *from* the U.S., dial 1 800 CALL ATT.

AP                                         © 8/00 AT&T

**JUSTICE AND POLICE MUSEUM.** Directly inland from the southeastern corner of Circular Quay, the museum indulges Sydney's outlaw past with exhibits on convict life and punishment. *(Corner of Albert and Phillip St. ☎9252 1144. Open Jan. Su-Th 10am-5pm; Feb.-Dec. Sa-Su 10am-5pm. $6.50, concessions $3.30, families $16.40.)*

**ROYAL BOTANIC GARDENS.** All of the city center's greenery is concentrated in charmingly landscaped plants, flowers, and trees filling 30 hectares around Farm Cove. Not for the heartsick—couples shamelessly lounge everywhere. Within the gardens, attractions such as the Aboriginal plant trail and the formal rose garden are free, but the **Tropical House** greenhouses charge admission. **Government House,** in the northeast corner of the Gardens, served as the home of the governor of New South Wales as recently as 1996. On the eastern headland of Farm Cove, the Botanic Gardens end at **Mrs. Macquarie's chair.** The chair, carved from the stone at the point, was fashioned for the wife of Governor Lachlan Macquarie and is now a classic Sydney photo-op. Daily guided walks begin at a visitors center, located in the southeast corner of the park near Art Gallery Rd. *(Gardens open sunrise to sunset. Free. Visitors Centre: ☎9231 8125. Open daily 9:30am-4:30pm. 2hr. guided walks daily 10:30am. Tropical House: Open daily 10am-4pm. $5, concessions $2.20. Government House: ☎9931 5222. Grounds open daily 10am-4pm; house open F-Su 10am-3pm. Free.)*

# THE HARBOUR

The **Sydney Harbour National Park** preserves four harbor islands, several south shore beaches, a few green patches on the northern headlands, and North and South Head. Meander around the waterways on **Captain Cook Cruises.** (☎9206 1111. More than 20 departures per day from 9:30am. Departs from Circular Quay.) Guided visits to the Harbour islands themselves must be booked ahead through the **National Park Information Centre,** 110 George St, The Rocks, in **Cadman's Cottage.** (☎9247 5033. Open daily 9am-5pm. Tours depart from the Cottage.) The Heritage Tour focuses on history (M, F-Su 12:30pm; $20, concessions $15.40). The Water Rats tour visits the sets of this popular TV show (M, F-Su 11:45am; $20, concessions $15.40). The Gruesome Tales tour focuses on the grisly aspects of convict history (Sa 5:45pm, daylight savings 6:45pm; $24; unsuitable for children).

**▓ FORT DENISON.** The early colony's most troublesome convicts were once isolated on Pinchgut Island, off Mrs. Macquarie's Point. The name came from the habit of punishing unruly convicts by isolating them on the exposed rock with a diet consisting of only bread and water. The island was later renamed to Fort Denison for the fort that was built to protect the city from a feared Russian invasion. Ah, the paranoia of the Cold War...

**▓ GOAT ISLAND.** West of the city center, near the shore at Balmain, the sandstone gunpowder station and barracks of Goat Island were the site of cruel punishments for the convicts who built them.

**▓ BEACHES.** The park's south shore beaches—**Nielson Park, Camp Cove,** and the nude beach **Lady Jane**–are situated on Vaucluse Bay, accessible by bus #325, which runs to Watsons Bay. Popular North Shore Harbour beaches include **Balmoral Beach,** on the north side of Middle Head, a 15min. walk from Military Rd; **China-man's Beach,** north of Balmoral, a 7min. walk from Spit Rd; and **Manly Cove,** at the Manly Wharf ferry port. To get to Balmoral Beach, take bus #178, 180, or 182 to Spit Junction, then take #257 or 229 to Balmoral. To get to Manly, take a ferry or Jetcat; or bus #143 or 144 from Spit Junction. Up the coast from Manly are **Freshwater, Coogee,** and **Narrabeen**—all of which are less commercial and less crowded.

# CITY CENTER AND THE DOMAIN

**▨ SYDNEY CENTREPOINT TOWER.** Rising 325m above sea level (and four floors of shopping mall), the tower affords a stunning panoramic view of the city and surrounds. The 40sec. ride to the top of Australia's highest building is steep in grade and price, so don't waste a trip on a cloudy day. When the sky is clear, views extend as far as the Blue Mountains to the west, the New South Wales central coast to the north, and Wollongong to the south. Sydney's only revolving restaurant spins on the second-highest floor. *Let's Go* does not recommend looking down from the top after eating—it could get messy. *(100 Market St. ☎9229 7444. Open Su-F 9am-10:30pm, Sa 9am-11:30pm. $20, concessions $16, families $55.)*

**TOWN HALL.** Sydney's age insures that architecture in the center is far from uniformly modern. The French Renaissance-style Town Hall was built in the prosperity of the late 1800s; the building's ostentation merits at least a passing look. The wood-lined concert hall fields an 8000-pipe organ; free midday concerts are held regularly. *(483 George St. ☎9265 9007. Open daily 9am-5pm. Tours ☎8223 3815.)*

**QUEEN VICTORIA BUILDING.** The imposing statue of Queen Victoria, visible from the north corner of Town Hall, guards the entrance to its namesake's lavish building. The Byzantine edifice was constructed in 1898 as a home for the plebeian city markets, but recent renovations have brought in ritzier shopping venues. Still, a stroll in the fantastic wood and brass interior doesn't cost a cent. *(455 George St.)*

**SYDNEY HOSPITAL AND NEW SOUTH WALES PARLIAMENT HOUSE.** The 1814 hospital building is a landmark of colonial architecture. In 1854, with new wealth coming in from the recent gold rush, Sydney Hospital's south wing became a branch of the Royal Mint. The central section of the building is still Sydney's main medical facility, while the **NSW Parliament House** occupies the north wing. Visitors are welcome in the building, with access to public viewing galleries during parliamentary sessions and free tours. *(Parliament: Faces Macquarie St at the end of Martin Pl. ☎9230 2637. Open M-F 10am-4pm. Tours M-F 10, 11am, and 2pm when Parliament is not in session; book ahead for Parliamentary session viewing.)*

**AUSTRALIAN MUSEUM.** The, um, creatively titled museum succeeds with its unique mix of natural and cultural history. Stuffed re-creations of prehistoric Australian megafauna cast shadows over popular Aussie animals such as the koala and kangaroo. Though the science exhibits are fun for kids only, the museum's treatment of the cultures of indigenous Australian peoples, both historically and as part of Australian society today, is superb for all ages. *(6 College St. On the east side of Hyde Park. ☎9320 6000. Open daily 9:30am-5pm. $8, students $4, ages 5-12 $3, Aussie seniors and under 5 free, families of 4 $19. Special and temporary exhibits cost extra.)*

**HYDE PARK.** Between Elizabeth and College St at the eastern edge of the city center, Hyde Park was set aside in 1810 by Governor Lachlan Macquarie, and is still Sydney's most structured public green space, complete with fountains and stately trees. A buzzing urban oasis during the day, the park warrants some caution for those strolling at night. In the southern half, below Park St, the Art Deco-style **ANZAC Memorial** commemorates the service of the Australian and New Zealand Army Corps in WWI, as well as that of the Australians who have fought in the nation's eight other overseas conflicts. *(☎9267 7668. Open daily 9am-4:30pm.)* On the park's east sits **St. Mary's Cathedral,** a Neo-Gothic structure undergoing renovations to better integrate into its urban setting. The original structure was erected in 1833, burned to the ground in 1865, and completed again in 1928. To heighten its symbolism, the cathedral is currently constructing the originally-planned two Gothic towers on the southern end. An exhibit placed not so aptly in the crypt gives an informative and thoughtful account of the cathedral's place in a modern city. *(☎9220 0400. Crypt open daily 10am-4pm. Tours Su noon after mass, or by arrangement.)*

**HYDE PARK BARRACKS.** The 1819 barracks house a museum devoted to the daily lives of former convict inhabitants. If you're a masochist, overnight hammock accommodations are available. *(Queen Sq. ☎9223 8922. Open daily 9:30am-5pm. $6.50, concessions $3.50, families $16.40.)*

**THE DOMAIN.** Behind the buildings on Macquarie St, the unmanicured, grassy expanse of the Domain stretches east along the south edge of the Royal Botanic

Gardens. Concerts fill the area during January's **Sydney Festival** (see p. 126). During the rest of the year, the park is most popular for corporate weekday lunch breaks and Sunday-morning rabble-rousing at **Speakers' Corner,** modeled after London's traditional weekly public speaking in the park.

**ART GALLERY OF NEW SOUTH WALES.** Sydney's major art museum's strength lies in its contemporary Australian works and its extensive Aboriginal and Torres Straight Islander gallery. (*Northeast corner of the Domain, on Art Gallery Rd.* ☎ 9225 1744; *www.artgallery.nsw.gov.au. Open daily 10am-5pm. Free.)*

# DARLING HARBOUR

The site of several events of the XXVII Olympiad, Darling Harbour, on the west side of the city center, is a popular tourist stop reminiscent of Disneyland with its immaculate brick walkways, trams, squealing children, and opportunities to spend money. The concentration of tourist attractions in this small area makes it a perfect outing for afternoon sightseeing and a popular spot for families. On foot, Darling Harbour is only 10min. from Town Hall Station. Follow George St north, then turn left on Market St to Pyrmont Bridge. Bus #456 approaches Darling Harbour from Circular Quay by way of Town Hall, and ferries run from Circular Quay to the Aquarium steps. For transport as tourist-oriented as the destination, hop on the **monorail** from Pitt St, at Park or Market St in the CBD (runs M-F 7am-10pm, Sa-Su 7am-midnight; $3, seniors $1.80, under 6 free; day pass $6, family day pass $19). For more info on 2000 Olympic sites, see p. 121.

**POWERHOUSE MUSEUM.** The largest museum in the southern hemisphere explores the breadth of human ingenuity through exhibits, interactive displays, and demos with a focus on technology and applied art and science. From decorative arts to space exploration, from communication to transportation advances, the museum's astounding variety makes it popular with visitors of all ages. (*500 Harris St. Just south of Darling Harbour, between Ultimo and Haymarket.* ☎ 9217 0444. *Open daily 10am-5pm. $9, students $3, ages 5-15 $2, families $20, Aussie seniors and under 5 free.)*

**SYDNEY AQUARIUM.** Over 11,000 marine animals from Australia's many aquatic regions inhabit the tanks on the pier at Darling Harbour's eastern shore. If you need more evidence that Australia has the weirdest fauna on earth, stop at the mudskipper containment where these freaks of the fish world display their ability to live out of water by absorbing moisture from the air. More conventional attractions include the recently-opened Great Barrier Reef exhibit, a seal pool, and a small touching pool. The underwater Oceanarium, a plexiglass walking tunnel through a huge fish enclosure, makes the pricey admission less bothersome. (*Aquarium Pier.* ☎ 9262 2300; *www.sydneyaquarium.com.au. Open daily 9am-10pm, last entry 9pm. $20, students $13, ages 3-15 $8.50, under 3 free, families of 5 $40. Wheelchair accessible. Seal sanctuary closes at sunset.)*

**CHINESE GARDEN.** This serene garden was a bicentennial gift to New South Wales from her sister province in China, Guangdong. The delicately manicured plot in traditional southern Chinese style provides a break from the hubbub of the city. (*On the corner of Harbour and Pier St.* ☎ 9281 6863. *Open daily 9:30am-sunset. $4.50, concessions $2, families $10, wheelchair-bound persons free.)*

**SEGA WORLD.** The yin to the yang of the next-door Chinese Garden (see above), Sega World jumps with over 100 arcade games and nine rides. (*1-25 Harbour St.* ☎ 9273 9273. *Open M-F 11am-10pm, Sa-Su 10am-10pm. $28, concessions $22.)*

**NATIONAL MARITIME MUSEUM.** Docked opposite the aquarium are the massive destroyer *HMAS Vampire* and submarine *HMAS Onslow.* Both were in active service during the Cold War years, and are now part of the Maritime Museum. On land, the museum provides a fascinating survey of Australia's maritime history from the times of early Aboriginal trading to the present. More importantly, you can climb all over submarines and battle ships. (*2 Murray St.* ☎ 9298 3777;

**NEW SOUTH WALES**

*www.anmm.gov.au. Open daily 9:30am-5pm. Admission to submarine or destroyer with audio tour $9, concessions $5, families $22.50; to both vessels and the museum $15, concessions $8, children $5, families $34. The museum is wheelchair-accessible but the ships are not.)*

# INNER EAST

The suburbs just east of the city center are some of Sydney's most vibrant areas for shopping, eating, and meandering. Although Kings Cross tends to be a bit seedy, the neighborhood is not without a certain vibrance and charm. Oxford St slides through Surry Hills, Darlinghurst, and Paddington in an endless string of cafés, boutiques, and hip homeware outlets. Sydney's large, outgoing gay community calls much of this strip home. Buses #378, 380, and 382 run the length of Oxford St, connecting the city center to the inner eastern suburbs.

**FOX STUDIOS AUSTRALIA.** This state-of-the-art theme park and studio only opened in Moore Park in late 1999. *The Matrix* and *Mission Impossible: II* were filmed on location here, as will the next two editions of *Star Wars*. The park features 16 movie screens, pubs, and restaurants, not to mention a **backlot tour** with interactive exhibits on the film and TV industry and a special effects re-enactment of (yuck) *Titanic* scenes with visitors participating as extras. (☎ *9383 4000; www.foxstudios.com.au. Backlot tours $40, ages 6-15 $25.)*

**MOORE PARK.** South of Paddington and east of Surry Hills, Moore Park contains the **Sydney Football Stadium** and the city's major **cricket oval.** For a tour of the Stadium and a small museum of Aussie sports history, call **Sportspace**. (☎ *9380 0383. Tours M-Sa 10am, 1, and 3pm during non-game days. $19.50, concessions $13, family $52.)*

**CENTENNIAL PARK.** The city's largest park abuts Moore Park's east side and stretches north to meet Oxford St between Paddington and Woollahra. The park includes eight small lakes, a bird sanctuary, athletic fields, and cycling tracks.

**SYDNEY JEWISH MUSEUM.** This moving and informative museum is a remarkable exhibition of Australia's Jewish heritage and the horrors of the Holocaust. *(148 Darlinghurst Rd. Across William St from Kings Cross. ☎ 9360 7999. Open Su 11am-5pm, M-Th 10am-4pm, F 10am-2pm. $6, concessions $4, children $3, families of 4 $15.)*

**ELIZABETH BAY HOUSE.** Near the Cross, this colonial mansion provides a window into upper-class life in the 19th century. If you're into that sort of thing... *(7 Onslow St. ☎ 9356 3022. Open Tu-Su 10am-4:30pm. $6.50, concessions $3.30.)*

# NORTH SHORE

Coastal amusements at the northern beach resort of **Manly** have a tacky boardwalk feel unusual for an Australian beach. For less contrived pleasure, the **Manly to Spit Bridge** walk (9.5km; 3hr.) offers uncluttered harbor coastline, sandy beaches, national park, and bayside homes. The walk originates at the Manly Visitors Centre, where maps are available. (☎ *9977 1088. Open daily 10am-4pm.)* From the Spit Bridge, bus #132 returns to Manly and #144 runs to Sydney.

**TARONGA PARK ZOO.** The koalas, kangaroos, and tigers at Taronga Zoo enjoy million-dollar harbor views. The impressive collection includes animals from all over Australia and the world. To reach the zoo, take a 12min. ferry ride from Circular Quay, then a short jaunt on a bus. Admission includes an enclosed chair-lift safari ride, widely considered the best part of a visit. *(At the end of Bradley's Head Rd in Mosman. ☎ 9969 2777; www.zoo.nsw.gov.au. Open daily 9am-5pm. $21, students $15, ages 4-15 $11.50, families $55. A Zoopass, purchased at Circular Quay, covers admission and ferry and bus transport. $25, concessions $12.50, ages 4-15 $10.50.)*

**OCEAN WORLD.** This aquatic playground earns rave reviews for its strange and rare specimens of tropical fish. There is a snake show daily, and weekends bring an extensive array of tours and presentations geared especially toward children. *(On the West Esplanade at Manly Cove. ☎ 9949 2644. Open daily 10am-5:30pm. $16, concessions $11, families of 4 $25. Shark feeding: M, W, F 11:15am.)*

# HOMEBUSH BAY OLYMPIC SITE

Built to host the greatest athletes in the world and remaining as a tribute, the impressively huge Homebush Bay Olympic Site is where most events took place, 14km west of the city center along the Parramatta River. To get to Homebush Bay, take a CityRail train to the Olympic Park Station; do not take the train to "Homebush." Bicycles can also enter the area from near the Concord West train station and enjoy a scenic pathway that carves through the surrounding wetlands of Bicentennial Park and into the heart of Homebush Bay. Call the Olympic Coordination Authority's Information Centre (☎9735 4800) for information on tours.

**HISTORY AND TRADITION.** Australia and Greece are the only two countries that have participated in every Summer Olympics since the beginning of the modern games in 1896, and the September 2000 Games marked the second time Australia hosted the event (the first was in Melbourne, in 1956). The Paralympic Games followed in the month of October ("para" is for parallel, not paraplegic) with athletes

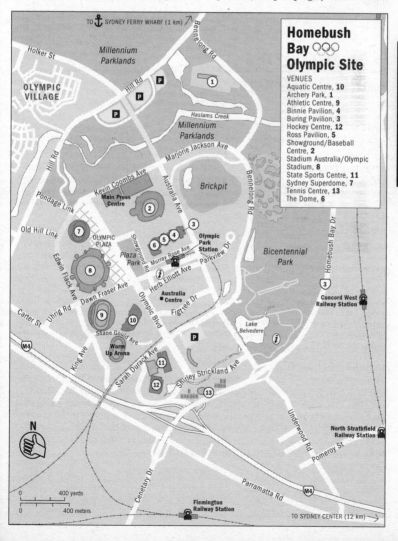

NEW SOUTH WALES

**Homebush Bay ◯◯◯ Olympic Site**

VENUES
Aquatic Centre, **10**
Archery Park, **1**
Athletic Centre, **9**
Binnie Pavilion, **4**
Buring Pavilion, **3**
Hockey Centre, **12**
Ross Pavilion, **5**
Showground/Baseball Centre, **2**
Stadium Australia/Olympic Stadium, **8**
State Sports Centre, **11**
Sydney Superdome, **7**
Tennis Centre, **13**
The Dome, **6**

**PLAYING WITH FIRE** As with all modern Olympic Games, the Sydney 2000 games were preceded by the relay of the Olympic torch around the country. With over 10,000 torchbearers and a route in excess of 27000km, the 2000 Torch Relay was the longest in history. The lighted torch arrived in Yulara, NT, and zig-zagged across the continent for 100 days before reaching the opening ceremonies in Sydney. The route was thoughtfully designed to run within an hour's drive from the homes of 85% of the Australian population.

competing in archery, track-and-field, basketball, boccia, fencing, football (soccer), goalball, judo, powerlifting, rugby, swimming, table tennis, tennis, volleyball, cycling, equestrian, sailing, and shooting events.

**OLYMPIC VILLAGE.** At the Homebush Site, you can visit the largest **Olympic Stadium** to date (110,000 seats), **Stadium Australia,** as well as the other venues that hosted basketball, gymnastics, tennis, tae kwon do, volleyball, judo, hockey, wrestling, weightlifting, boxing, field hockey, and archery contests. (☎9373 0870.) The **Sydney International Aquatic Centre** is open to the public for both swimming and diving. *(1 Herb Elliot Ave. ☎9714 7888. Open M-F 8am-5:30pm.)*

## 🏄 ACTIVITIES

## NAUTICAL DIVERSIONS

Sydney's most popular pastimes are inspired by the Harbour and the coastline's natural playgrounds.

**SAILING.** On any sunny day, white sails can be seen clipping across the waters. **East Sail Sailing School** caters to all experience levels and offers intimate courses and trips. *(At D'Albora Marina on Rushcutters Bay. Follow William St until it merges with Bayswater Rd, then turn left on Beach Rd. ☎9327 1166. Open daily 8am-6pm. 2½hr. sailing trips depart daily at 10am; up to 12 passengers but usually less, $66.)* **Sydney by Sail** runs introductory sailing lessons from the National Maritime Museum. *(☎9280 1110, mobile ☎(0419) 36 71 80. Trips daily depending on weather and demand; 25-person max. 1½hr. lesson at 11am $54; 3hr. lesson at 1pm $98; book ahead.)*

**DIVING.** Sydney's rocky shores include several worthwhile spots for both shore and boat diving. With over 20 different dive sites, it's possible to dip in all along the coast. **ProDive** has excellent advice on local diving spots and all the gear you'll ever need. They also offer certification courses. *(City center: Level 7, 428 George St. ☎9232 5788, freecall ☎(1800) 82 08 20. Coogee: 27 Alfreda St. ☎9665 6333. Both open M-F 9am-5:30pm, Sa-Su 8:30am-5pm. 4-day courses from $295; trips and courses for other Australian locations can be arranged from George St. Boats and gear for a full-day $120; gear alone $75.)*

**SURFING.** Surfing at **Bondi Beach** makes all the postcards, but Sydney has other beaches with equally appealing waves and smaller crowds. **Coogee** can be just as crowded as Bondi, and **Tamarama** is smaller but with trickier rips. The locals are protective of **Maroubra**, south of Coogee, and to an extent the beaches north of the Harbour. Up north, **Manly** ranks with Bondi and Coogee as a popular city beach. Farther up the coast, **Curl Curl, Dee Why, North Narrabeen, Newport Reef,** and **Palm Beach** are well worth the relative seclusion they offer. To get to the northern beaches, take bus #183, 187, 188, 189, 190, 151, or any of the northern beach expresses that originate at Wynyard Station (Carrington St side); or take the ferry to Manly and catch bus #151, 155, or 157. The **Manly Surf School** gives surf lessons to everyone from beginners to more experienced surfers. *(At North Steyne Surf Club. ☎9970 6300. Open daily dawn-dusk. 2hr. $45, twice $70, thrice $95, four times $115; prices include wetsuit and board. Bookings essential.)* In Manly, **Aloha Surf** rents boards and wetsuits. *(44 Pittwater Rd. ☎9977 3777. Open F-W 9am-7pm, Th 9am-9pm. Short and long boards half-day $25, full-day $35; bodyboards $20.)* **Bondi Surf Co.** rents surfboards and bodyboards with wetsuits. *(72 Campbell Pde. ☎9365 0870. Open daily 9am-6pm, longer summer hours. 3hr. $20-30; credit card or passport required.)*

NEW SOUTH WALES

**FISH AND WHALES.** A number of charter boats run guided deep-sea **fishing** trips; groups get cheaper rates. **Whale watching season** is from June-July and Sept.-Oct. **Halicat** has both fishing and whale watching tours for up to 23 people running from Rose Bay and Cremorne. *(410 Elizabeth St, Surry Hills. ☎9212 5911, freecall ☎(1800) 67 96 29. Reef fishing $75. Sport fishing $160, trips go farther out and find bigger fish. Trips depart 6:30am and return mid-afternoon. Whale watching 4hr. weekend trips $42, children $25.)* **Zane Grey** offers similar rates. *(☎9565 4949. Reef fishing $100; sport fishing $160. Trips depart 7am and return mid-afternoon.)* Award-winning **Broadbill** runs a smaller operation (their boat holds 6) at competitive prices from Sans Souci Wharf. *(☎9534 2378. Sport fishing $150-180. Trips depart 7am and return 5-6pm.)* Departing from The Rocks, **Aqua Queen** offers only whale watching. *(☎9955 4911. 4hr. trips $45, concessions $25.)*

**CRUISES. Ferry cruises** are a great way to take in the harbor. In addition to those offered by Sydney Ferries (see p. 99), **Australian Travel Specialists** book a number of 1-3hr. Harbour cruises that run out of Circular Quay and Darling Harbour between 9:30am and 8pm and cost from $13-116. *(☎9555 2700; for more info see p. 101.)* **Matilda Cruises** has lots of options: ferries between Darling Harbour and Circular Quay; the **Rocket Harbour Express** between Sydney Aquarium, Circular Quay, the Opera House, Taronga Zoo, and back to Darling Harbour; and sailing tours. *(Pier 26 near the Aquarium. ☎9264 7377. Harbour to Quay: $3.25, concessions $1.60. Express: $18, concessions $9, families $44. Sail: from $24, concessions $12.)* **Captain Cook Cruises** also runs a number of sightseeing and meal cruises. *(Jetty 6, Circular Quay. ☎9251 1281.)*

**CANOES.** To explore the area's inland waterways or to get a more in-depth look at the harbor coast from the seat of a canoe, call **Balmoral Marine.** *(On Awaba St at Balmoral Beach. Take bus #244 or 247 toward Mosman from Wynyard Station. ☎9969 6006. Open daily 8:30am-5pm. 1hr. $10, full-day $50; deposit $10.)*

## AERIAL EXPLOITS

**SKYDIVING.** Skydiving in Australia is relatively cheaper than at home, if you come from Britain or the U.S. Thank you, oh God of the Exchange Rate. Take advantage. **Simply Skydive Australia** throws people out of planes from 4300 feet—with an instructor and parachute attached, of course. *(Goulburn Airport. ☎9970 5037. With Sydney pickup $295, from Wollongong or Hunter Valley $265.)* **Skydive Tandem** does the same from Bankstown Airport. *(☎9791 9056. $295, backpackers $250.)*

**SCENIC FLIGHTS.** For views of Sydney without having to plummet towards it, a couple places offer scenic flights around Sydney and environs—but it'll hurt your wallet. **Sydney Air Scenic Flights** runs from the Bankstown Airport. *(☎9790 0628. Blue Mountains 1hr. $175; Sydney Harbour 1hr. $175; coastal tour 1¼hr. $340; day tours also available to Hunter Valley, Snowy Mountains, and Coffs Harbour. Backpacker discounts available.)* **Dakota National Air** also operates out of the Bankstown airport. *(☎9791 9900, freecall ☎(1800) 24 67 47. F night Sydney Harbour 1hr. $135, with champagne; Su morning Harbour 1hr. $65-95; other tours available.)* **Heli-Aust** tools you around by 'copter. *(Bankstown Airport. ☎9317 3402. Harbour $105, children $92; Twilight Harbour $150, children $105; Blue Mountains $325, $249.)* **Blue Sky** also runs many 30- to 60-minute helicopter tours. *(Sydney Airport. ☎9700 7888. $130-380.)*

## EXTRA TERRESTRIAL ADVENTURES

**WALKING TOURS.** Walking tours of The Rocks depart from the Visitors Centre. *(106 George St. ☎9247 6678. See p. 116.)* Additionally, Unseen Sydney conducts 1½hr. walking tours entitled *History, Convicts, and Murder most Foul* that include a complimentary drink from the historic Hero of Waterloo's cellar. *(☎9907 8057. Tu, Th-Sa 6:30pm; $19, students $15.)* The Original Sydney Walking Tours runs five different tours delving into the sensational past of The Rocks and Kings Cross. *(☎9380 2059, mobile (0413) 13 91 62. $14, concessions $10.)*

**SELF-GUIDED WALKS.** They don't cost a cent and are a better way for the purist to enjoy Sydney's beautiful landscape. The walk from the Opera House to Mrs. Macquarie's Chair through the Royal Botanic Gardens is deservedly popular, while the walk from Watson's Bay to the Gap provides equally beautiful serenity with even more isolation from the urban center. The walk from Manly to Spit Bridge is a bit rigorous and provides views and lush flora from the other side of the Harbour, while the walk from Bondi to Coogee Beach has a city beach at every valley and a breathtaking Pacific view at every peak. Which sounds more appealing?

**RAW POWER. Australian Travel Specialists** book a number of chauffeured Harley-Davidson motorcycle tours, ranging from a 1hr. $80 Harbour tour to a mammoth 8hr. $395 tour of the Hunter Valley and Blue Mountains. (☎9555 2700. See p. 101.)

**OTHER RENTALS.** Several places rent **in-line skates** or **skateboards.** In Bondi, visit **Bondi Boards and Blades.** (148 Curlewis St. ☎9365 6555. Open daily 10am-6pm. 1hr. $11, $5.50 per hr. afterwards.) In Manly, try **Manly Blades.** (49 North Steyne St. ☎9976 3833. Open M-W 9am-7pm, Th 9am-9pm, F-Sa 9am-7pm, Su 9am-6pm. 1hr. $12, full-day $25, 24hr. $30.) In Paddington, try **Total Skate.** (36 Oxford St, Woollahra, close to Centennial Park. ☎9380 6356.)

# 🎭 ENTERTAINMENT

## PERFORMING ARTS

The iconic **Sydney Opera House** is the linchpin of Sydney's creative culture, operating as its primary venue. With five stages (described below), the Opera House nimbly hosts a variety of the city's artistic endeavors. (Box office for all venues ☎9250 7777; www.soh.nsw.gov.au. Open M-Sa 9am-8:30pm and only for ticket pick-up Su 2hr. prior to show.)

**Opera Theatre** (☎9319 1088). The excellent **Sydney Opera Company** performs here. Reserved seats range $82-165 and sell out fast, even though there are 1547 of them. Partial-view seats (blocking more than ¼ of the stage) are from $48. Standing room and listening-only (totally obstructed stage "view") are $28 and available over-the-counter only at 9am the morning of the performance and are limited to 2 per person. Leftover tickets are sometimes sold after 7pm on performance night during student rush for $33 (ISIC required). **Australian Ballet Company** (☎(1300) 36 97 41) shares the same theater space; ballet season alternates with opera season. Call for ticket prices and info.

**Concert Hall** (24hr. ☎9334 4600). The 2678-seat Concert Hall is the one-stop shop for symphony, chamber, and orchestral music performances. **Sydney Symphony Orchestra** performs here Feb.-Dec. Call for ticket info.

**Drama Theatre.** Home to many shows and play companies throughout the year, the Drama Theatre most frequently stars the **Sydney Theatre Company** (☎9250 1777). The Theatre seats 544. Advance seating from $50, student rush tickets from $17 available 30min. prior to show. Also hosts the **Sydney Dance Company** (☎9221 4811).

**Playhouse Theatre.** A traditional round-stage forum with 398 seats, the Playhouse is the place to come for plays in Sydney. Call the **Bell Shakespeare Company** (☎9241 2722) for information on which of Will's classics they might be presenting.

**Studio Stage.** This catch-all, transformable stage seats 364 and exhibits less traditional Opera House offerings, including cabaret shows and contemporary performances.

## SPECTATOR SPORTS

Australia is a land of beer-guzzling, meatpie-gorging, obscenity-hurling mega-fans (see **Sport,** p. 24). Check out a sports match for an unforgettable lesson in social psychology, mob action, and VB-induced testosterone rituals. All events below sell tickets through Ticketek (☎9266 4800; www.ticketek.com.au), and are played in stadiums in Moore Park, accessible by bus #349, 373, 393, and 395.

**Rugby League.** The **Sydney Football Stadium** (☎9360 6601), home to the **South Sydney** and **Sydney City Side** teams, draws rowdy, fiercely-loyal urbanite fans throughout the winter season and in Sept. for the Wynfield Cup. Tickets $15-30, children $5-25.

**Australian Rules Football.** This head-crushing, uniquely Aussie game is held at the Sydney Football Stadium. Root, root, root for the home team: 1995 Grand Final participants, the **Sydney Swans.** Tickets cost more and are harder to get than rugby tickets ($10-60).

**Cricket.** The games feel perpetual, the rules are maddeningly complicated, and the "athletes" are men wearing white straw hats and sweater vests. Head to the **Sydney Cricket Ground** (☎9369 6601). Tickets $10-40, depending upon the game.

# CINEMAS

Sydney doesn't have a great film scene. It's American. It's Hollywood. Ticket prices are obscene. It's the same as everywhere else on this green Earth. But here, Tuesdays are **bargain day,** often half price. Go then. Prices during the rest of the week hover around $13-14, children $10-11. Call **Movieline** (☎13 27 00) for show times at all theaters. For info on the **Sydney Film Festival,** see p. 126.

**Hoyts Centre,** 505 George St (☎13 27 00). The largest mainstream theater, located midway between Chinatown and the CBD.

**Greater Union Cinemas,** 525 George Street (☎9267 8666). Mostly blockbusters, but the occasional foreign or art film.

**Reading Cinemas,** Market City Mall, Chinatown (☎9280 1202). Undercuts other theaters by a buck or two and has Sunday double-features.

**Govinda's,** 112 Darlinghurst Rd, Darlinghurst (☎9360 7853). Reaps cult, classic, and contemporary films, and throws in an all-you-can eat buffet (see **Food,** p. 112).

**Chauvel Cinema,** Paddington Town Hall, Paddington (☎9361 5398). At Oxford and Oatley St. Specializes in indie, arthouse, and un-dubbed foreign films.

**Panasonic IMAX Cinema,** Southern Promenade, Darling Harbour (☎9281 3300). The eight-story high movie screen is the largest in the world. A different film is shown every hour. Open daily 10am-10pm.

**Fox Studios Australia,** Moore Park (☎9383 4000). A monolithic movie complex with 12 theaters and stadium seating. There's also a four-screen arthouse.

# POKIES VS. THE PEOPLE

Australians are fond of saying how obsessed they are with fads. For instance, in Melbourne cellular phones are so prevalent that all types of stores from booksellers to barbershops carry them. But sooner or later, fads end up going the way of the hula hoop—pleasantly embarrassing nostalgia. A few years ago, the Victorian government deregulated gambling, basically allowing video poker (called "pokies") free reign and increasing the prevalence of tabaret simulcast racing halls. Many bars and most R.S.L.s (Aussie war veteran clubs) depend on them. And Victoria wasn't the only state to legalize gambling; the whole country followed suit. A July 1999 draft report by the Australian Productivity Commission is quite damning. According to the report, 330,000 adults (2.3% of the population) are problem gamblers, losing an astounding average of $12,000 each per year. They're not alone: with 82% of Australians having gambled in the last year and 40% playing the odds weekly, the total losses amount to $11 billion per year, a vast sum for a population of barely 18 million. Forgetting the social and economic costs, the report's conclusion that Oz has the world's highest rate of gambling addiction is not shocking once you walk down Main St in Smalltown, Anywhere, Australia, where every third store is a gaming stop. Now, many people are praying the gambling craze is just another fad that will soon disappear.

# GAMBLING

Okay, so gambling destroys marriages, depletes hard-saved nest eggs, and is a tax on people who are bad at math. But games of chance can't be all bad: public lottery revenues financed the Sydney Opera House after all. Australia, with just 1% of the world's population, fields 20% of its gaming machines (known locally as "pokies"). These video poker machines allow you to compete against a computer very effectively programmed to kick your ass. New South Wales lays claim to more than half of the continent's collection; pokies fill pub rooms across the state and the city (see **Pokies vs. The People,** above). But it might be the state governments that are the real gambling addicts. The New South Wales treasury takes a healthy cut from Sydney's $1.2 billion **Star City Casino,** 80 Pyrmont St, Pyrmont (☎9777

9000), in West Darling Harbour. The twinkling complex entices the punters 24hr. with an unlucky 13 restaurants, 12 bars, a nightclub, PVC trees, and an endless (okay, a mere 145,000 square meters) gaming room with 1500 poker machines and 160 gaming tables. The casino can be accessed by light rail or shuttle bus to the casino, or monorail to Harbourside.

## ❄ FESTIVALS

Sydney-siders aren't as gung-ho as Melburnians when it comes to flaunting random festivals, but they sure know how to party anyway.

**Sydney Festival,** all throughout Jan. Features arts and entertainment events. Check the *Daily Telegraph* for details on free concerts in The Domain, street theater in The Rocks, and fireworks in Darling Harbour.

**Gay and Lesbian Mardi Gras,** Mar. 3, 2001 (☎9557 4332; www.mardigras.com.au). Late-Feb. through early-Mar. brings the rip-roaring, no-holds-barred festivities of this huge international event. The festival climaxes on its final day with a parade attended annually by over 500,000 people and a gala party at the RAS Show Ground in Moore Park. Though the party is restricted and the guest list fills up way, way ahead of time, travelers can get on the list by becoming "International Members of Mardi Gras" well in advance. Membership $40, tickets around $95.

**Royal Agricultural Society's Easter Show,** the two weeks surrounding Easter, 2001 (☎9704 1111; www.eastershow.com.au). Held at the Homebush Olympic Site. The carnival atmosphere makes it fun even for those with no interest in farming.

**Sydney Film Festival,** mid-June 2001 (☎9660 3844; www.sydfilm-fest.com.au). The ornate State Theatre, 49 Market St, between George and Pitt St, showcases documentaries, retrospectives, and art films from around the world.

**City to Surf Run,** Aug. 12, 2001 (☎9282 3606). Draws 50,000 contestants for a semiserious 14km trot from Park St to Bondi Beach. Some are world-class runners; others treat the race as a lengthy pub crawl. Entries ($20) are accepted up to race day.

**Manly Jazz Festival,** Oct. 5-8, 2001 (☎9977 1088; www.pcn.com.au/manlyjazz). Oz's biggest jazz festival, featuring national and international artists and all types of jazz.

**Kings Cross Carnival,** late-Oct., 2001 (www.kingscross.nsw.gov.au). Fairly self-explanatory, don't you think?

**Bondi Beach Party,** Dec. 25 each year. Bondi sets the pace for debauchery all along the coast as people from around the world gather for a foot-stomping Christmas party.

**Sydney-to-Hobart Yacht Race,** Dec. 26 each year. Brings the city's hungover attention (see above) back to civilized entertainment.

## 🛍 SHOPPING AND MARKETS

While conspicuously lacking a large number of world-worshipped chains (the Gap, for example), there is still some serious shopping to be done in Sydney. Crammed with consumers, the **Queen Victoria Building** and **Centrepoint Shopping Centre** are in the city center, **Harbourside** on Darling Harbour is a yuppie magnet, and **Market City** in the heart of Haymarket is a bargain shopper's haven. **Oxford St** has some funky finds; **Glebe Point Rd** offers more alternative commodities as well as U.K. and U.S. brandnames. Newtown's **King St** is the place to go for vintage bins and colorful boutiques. Those who can afford it should venture to **Double Bay** or **Castlereagh St**, where designer fashion houses, jewelers, and other indulgences await. To get to Double Bay, take a ferry or buses #323, 324, or 325 from Circular Quay.

Sydney has numerous year-round weekend markets, all of which tend to specialize in arts, crafts, and souvenirs. Haggling is fun, the food is reasonably priced, and there's generally at least one cart selling fresh fruit. **Paddington Bazaar,** 395 Oxford St, is Sydney's best known and most lively market, featuring entertainment, food, and a variety of crafts. (☎9331 2923. Open W-F 10am-4pm.)

NEW SOUTH WALES

**THE 30¢ CONE** A good deal is hard to pass up, even when it's being offered by an organization gradually achieving world domination through global capitalism. And McDonald's—the American behemoth rumored to have more restaurants per capita in Australia than anywhere else in the world—offers one of the best in its 30¢ soft-serve ice cream cone. A sizeable mound of luscious vanilla ice cream can be had for a couple of those silver coins jangling in your pocket. Just 150 cones (much like 42 pints of Guinness) are said to be enough to sustain a healthy human life for a single day, and a savvy traveler can survive on considerably less.

**Paddy's Markets,** on Ultimo Rd at Hay St, is legendary and as old as the city itself. Be sure to head up to the second level; it's not just a food court, but also home to a handful of brand name factory outlets. (☎(1300) 36 15 89. Open Th-Su 9am-4:30pm, rain or shine.) **Paddy's Flemington,** run by Paddy's Markets, is off Parramatta Rd in the Sydney Markets across from the Homebush Bay Olympic Site (open F 10am-4:30pm, Su 9am-4:30pm; see p. 121). **The Rocks Market,** at the north end of George St under the bridge, is more upmarket with antiques, jewelry, and collectibles designed by local artists, as well as street performers and live musicians (open Sa-Su 9am-5pm, rain or shine). **Glebe Markets,** at Glebe Public School, on the corner of Glebe Point Rd and Derby Pl, sells new and secondhand crafts (Sa 10am-4pm, weather permitting). The hip **Bondi Beach Market,** at Bondi Beach Public School on Campbell Pde, features locally made arts and crafts. (☎9315 8988. Open Su 9am-4pm.)

# ⊠ NIGHTLIFE

Whether they're out on the town for drinks and dancing or huddling around a TV for the latest crucial sports telecast, many Sydney-siders hit the pub and club scene four or five times per week. Different neighborhoods have distinctly different scenes, and the scenes vary from night to night. Bars in **Kings Cross** attract a large, straight male crowd, which quickly spills over from the strip joints into the pubs and dance clubs. Backpackers round out the mix in this neighborhood, giving several spots an international feel. Outside Kings Cross, travelers generally congregate in pubs to avoid the high cover charges and inflated drink prices of Sydney's high-profile dance venues. **Gay Sydney** struts its stuff on Oxford St in Darlinghurst and Paddington, where some establishments are specifically gay or lesbian and many others are mixed. Because the gay clubs provide much of the city's best dance music, flocks of young, beautiful club scenesters of all persuasions fill any extra space on their vibrant, vampy dance floors. **Taylor Square,** at the intersection of Oxford, Flinders, and Bourke St, is the heart of this district. Suits clog the bars in the **Central Business District,** and night spots in **The Rocks** tend toward the expensive. For more casual pub crawling, wander on Bourke and Flinders St in **Surry Hills.** Large student populations in **Glebe** and **Newtown** make for a younger crowd and cheaper drinks on special nights at pubs in these areas.

Major concerts are held in the **Sydney Entertainment Centre,** Harbour St, Haymarket (☎9320 4200; www.sydentcent.com.au; box office open M-F 9am-5pm, Sa 10am-1pm); the **Hordern Pavilion,** in Moore Park; and the **Enmore Theatre,** 130 Enmore Rd, Newtown (☎9550 3666). Sydney's daily **live music** scene consists largely of local bands casting their pearls before pub crowds. The *Metro* section of the Friday *Sydney Morning Herald* and free weeklies such as *Beat* and *Sydney City Hub* contain listings for upcoming shows, along with info on art showings, movies, theater, and DJ appearances city-wide. The bible of the Sydney clubber is *3-D World* (www.threedworld.com.au), a free Tuesday publication that can be found in hostels, music stores, and trendy clothing stores. It gives the lowdown on special events for each night of the week. Look for the free *Streetpress* or *The Revolver*, which highlight the weekly hotspots for shaking your groove thang; *Drum Media* covers music. *Capital Q Weekly* focuses on the gay community.

# BARS AND PUBS

## KINGS CROSS

**Fitzroy Hotel,** 129 Dowling St (☎9356 3848). On the corner of Cathedral St, 3 blocks west of Victoria St. A neighborhood pub comfortably sequestered from the more hectic Cross. Upstairs is popular with backpackers for its casual atmosphere and pool tables. Frequent discounts through local hostels. Schooners $3. M: $2 Happy Hour. Tu: Free pool. Open M-Sa 10:30am-midnight, Su 3-10pm.

**O'Malley's Hotel,** 228 William St (☎9357 2211). On the corner of Brougham St. Upscale style in a casual pub atmosphere. The row of TVs makes O'Malley's into something of an Irish sports bar, but its nightly live music is the best in the Cross. Eclectic crowd proves that backpackers, business-types, and locals can indeed mix. Schooners of Toohey's $3. Open M-Th 11am-2am, F-Sa 11am-2:30am, Su noon-midnight.

**Barons,** 5 Roslyn St (☎9358 6131). Smoky and open 24hr.—it doesn't even really get hopping until 2 or 3am (just about the time those multiple lounges come in handy...)

**Darlo Bar,** 306 Liverpool St (☎9331 3672). On the corner of Darlinghurst Rd. A crowd of starving actors, students, and the tragically hip come to drink lots of beer. All ages and income brackets represented. Open M-Sa 10am-midnight, Su noon-10pm.

**Bourbon and Beefsteak,** 24 Darlinghurst Rd (☎9358 1144). It's 7am, there is nowhere that you *haven't* had a drink, but you can still stomach the neon and excessive Australian flag regalia. A bit of a bottom-feed, but somehow everybody ends up here at one time or another while carousing in the Cross. Open 24hr. Breakfast from 6am.

## PADDINGTON AND SURRY HILLS

▨ **Durty Nelly's,** 9-11 Glenmore Rd, Paddington (☎9360 4467). Off Oxford St at Gipps St. Sydney's best traditional Irish pub takes its Guinness very seriously; those in the know claim it's hands-down the best around (schooner $3.50). Even on weekends when it's packed, the dark wood decor and the jovial staff create a relaxing refuge from the nearby Oxford St melee. Su nights feature a musical contest with traditional Irish sing-alongs. Open M-Sa 11am-midnight, Su noon-10pm.

**Grand Pacific Blue Room,** corner of Oxford and S. Dowling St, Paddington (☎9331 7108). A very cool lounge bar with live acoustic performances. Shed the backpack for a night to join a young and sophisticated crowd wearing tank tops and shiny pants, and drinking Cosmopolitans. Open Tu-Su 6-11:30pm.

**Woolloomooloo Bay Hotel,** 2 Bourke St, Surry Hills (☎9357 1177). Bring your mates for pool and some very tasty (possible indeed) pub food. Karaoke nights, good DJs, and live retro bands draw crowds F-Sa. Open Th-F 8pm-2am, Sa 2pm-2am, Su 6pm-2am.

**The Fringe Bar,** 106 Oxford St, Paddington (☎9360 3554). Upscale bar housing a cohesive hybrid of young execs, sports fans, and locals. Schooners daytime $3.20, night $3.70. Su: pool competition; M: comedy night; F-Sa: hip-hop DJs. Open M-W 11am-1am, Th 11am-2am, F-Sa 11am-3am, Su noon-midnight or later.

**Albury Hotel,** 6 Oxford St, Paddington (☎9361 6555). A classic drag venue: a bit touristy, but when you go to Rome, you see the Vatican, right? Two large rooms provide separation between the 10:30pm drag show entertainment and dancing, and the less-energized bar scene. Together, these halves comprise a fully functioning meat market—surely you will leave with a story to tell your friends. A mixed gay-and-straight crowd revel in the debauchery. Happy Hour daily 2-8pm. Open 11am-4am, though hours vary.

## THE ROCKS

▨ **The Lord Nelson,** 19 Kent St (☎9251 4044). On the corner of Argyle St west of The Rocks center. Nautical flags drape from sturdy wooden beams in this colonial building. Sydney's oldest hotel and pub, first licensed in 1841 to a former convict landlord, shelters a young crowd. A very chill place for an after-work pint from one of Sydney's only microbreweries. Try the award-winning Old Admiral (pint $6). Open daily 11am-11pm.

**The Hero of Waterloo,** 81 Lower Fort St (☎9252 4553). One block off Argyle St west of The Rocks center. Since 1843, this pub has been an Australian favorite; its underground tunnels were once used for rum smuggling. The older group of regulars has been drinking here since before you were born (so they must be very drunk by now). Live entertainment F-Su. Open M-Sa 10am-11pm, Su 10am-9:45pm.

## CITY CENTER

The CBD is mainly a professional crowd, but backpacker options can be found.

**Scruffy Murphy's,** 43-44 Goulburn St (☎9211 2002). On the corner of George St. It may not be the most authentic Irish pub, but it's the best live music venue in the city center. And it's always chockers. This bar's popularity prompted management to recently open another full floor. Pub, disco dance, and terrace. Schooners $3. M: Backpacker night, $6 jugs. No cover. Open 24hr.

**Scubar,** 4 Rawson Pl (☎9212 4244; www.scubar.com.au). In the YHA basement; 1min. west of Central Station. Pool competitions, big screen cable TVs, and periodic jug-and-pizza dinner deals bring backpackers over from next door in droves. Not really a place to meet Sydney-siders, but a mecca for international travelers. Open daily noon-late.

**Forbes Hotel,** 30 York St (☎9299 3703). A multi-level afterwork pub and restaurant teeming with young worker-bees. DJ downstairs on weekends; cheap pasta on the top floor for carbo-loading between grinds on the dance floor. Open M-Th 10am-midnight, F-Sa 10am-late.

**Jackson's on George,** 176 George St (☎9247 2727). Near Circular Quay. Grown-up nightclub has 4 swanky levels—danceclub, pool bar, games, and restaurant. Open 24hr.

## GLEBE

▧**Friend In Hand Pub,** 58 Cowper St (☎9660 2326). Off Glebe Point Rd. The name is ripe for jokes, so we'll just skip to the skinny. Tu: poetry competition; W: legendary crab races and eating contests prove that it's possible to earnestly bet on pretty much anything; Th: trivia night, promising "absolutely pathetic prizes." Somewhat tamer on weekends. Open M-Sa 10am-midnight, Su noon-10pm.

▧**Toxteth Hotel,** 345 Glebe Point Rd (☎9660 2370). On the corner of Ferry Rd. Lively atmosphere, right near most of Glebe's hostels, and always packed. Schooners of VB $3.50. M: $2.50 schooner of the beer-of-the-month; Tu, Th: pool competitions; W: free movies in the courtyard. Open M-Sa 11am-midnight, Su 11am-11:45pm.

## NEWTOWN

▧**Kuletos Cocktail Bar,** 157 King St (☎9519 6369). Deliciously fruity liqueurs go down smooth during Kuletos' daily 6-7:30pm Happy Hour, with 2-for-1 drinks. Mixed drinks are normally pricey (from $10), but the immense range provides mouth-watering flavors. The Toblerone, Red Corvette, and Peach Passion are the house favorites. Open M-W 4pm-midnight or 1:30am, Th-Sa 4pm-3am; extra Happy Hour Th 9:30-10:30pm.

**Marlborough Hotel,** 145 King St (☎9519 1222). When Happy Hour is over next door at Kuletos, the Marley is the place to be. Tu: lounge night; F: DJ; Sa-Su: jazz and blues bands. No sandals. Open M-Sa 10am-1 or 3am, Su noon-midnight.

## NORTH SHORE

Sydney-siders call going to the North Shore "OTB"—"over the bridge."

**The Old Manly Boatshed,** 40 The Corso, Manly (☎9977 4443). A nice alternative to DJs and clubbin'. Cityslickers deem it a must-stop during a night out OTB. Live music most weeknights. M: comedy. Open daily 6pm-3am.

**Coogee Bay Hotel,** corner of Coogee Bay Road and Arden St, Coogee Beach (☎9665 0000). Large and swanky, supplying the juice for the Coogee scene. Backpackers and UNSW students swarm to the cheap drinks like frenzied, happy bees. Multiple bars, beer garden, and a nightclub with no cover. Selina's Entertainment Center, in the hotel, is one of Sydney's more popular concert venues and sometimes gets international acts. Schooners $3. Open Su-W 9am-midnight, Th-Sa 9am-3am or later.

**The New Brighton Hotel,** 71-73 The Corso, Manly (☎9977 3722). In the center of Manly. The downstairs of this lively 2-part bar is primarily for workers; the upstairs is youth-oriented. Free pool upstairs M after 8pm and Su from noon-4pm. DJ upstairs Wednesday. Schooner of VB $2.90. Open M-Sa until 3am, Su until 11:30pm.

**Newport Arms Hotel,** Kalinya St, Newport (☎9997 4900). A mostly family-oriented hotel with large gardens. A nice traditional-feeling pub—definitely not a raging scene. Restaurant and bar open from 10am-late.

# NIGHTCLUBS

▨ **Home,** 101 Cockle Bay Wharf (☎9266 0600). Looks like the ruby slippers finally worked. The cover charge is highway robbery, but hey, supply-and-demand, baby. The scene is ultra-trendy and very happening. Th: one level is open for funk/house dancing from 10pm (cover $8, students $6); F-Sa: four dance floors and 15 DJs have the place grinding with everything from disco to break-beat from 11pm (F $20, Sa $25). Discounts for members. Absolutely 18+; photo I.D. required.

▨ **Imperial Hotel,** 35 Erskineville Rd, Erskineville (☎9519 9899). Take a train to Erskineville, take a taxi, make the hike. The costumes at the outrageous weekend drag shows make it well worth it. The "Priscilla Queen of the Imperial" show adds one more layer to the parody and homage surrounding Swedish super-group ABBA; scenes from *Priscilla* were filmed here. The crowd is straight, gay, lesbian, and huge by showtime. Schooners of VB $3.30. Open M-Tu 4pm-2am, W 2pm-3am, Th 4pm-6am or later, F-Sa 1pm-8am, Su 4pm-midnight. Shows F-Sa 10:30pm, 11:30pm, 1:15am, and 2:15am. No cover.

**Q-Bar,** Level 2, 44 Oxford St, Darlinghurst (☎9360 1375). Entering Q-Bar is a bit like navigating into the Bat Cave—before you can find the club, you'll need to locate the "Synergy Hair" sign, go underneath it through an unmarked corridor, and hop onto an old elevator to the party upstairs. The stealthy entrance gives way to a head-spinning, body-thumping dance floor where the tightly clad bounce to techno beats. Th "Prom Nights" are the exception—rock sing-alongs own the night. Open daily 4pm-4am or later, but the dance floor action rarely heats up until midnight.

**Midnight Shift,** 85 Oxford St, Darlinghurst (☎9360 4463). The boy-toy pictures downstairs come to life on the video screens up above, where VJs spin hot dance tunes for an almost exclusively gay male audience. While the door policy is not strictly male-only, the "no open shoes under any circumstances" mantra manages to sift out most curious women. The showy, sexual atmosphere, enhanced by a catwalk and dancing stands, gets deeper and dirtier as the night progresses, attracting a very mixed mob—testimony to the club's 20+ years of popularity. Draft beers $3-3.80. Sa cover $15. Open M-Th noon-6am or later, F-Su 24hr.

**Taxi Club,** 40 Flinders St, Darlinghurst (☎9331 4256). Waves of intrigue emanate from one of Sydney's most notorious alternative bars. Locals fill the bar early to play the pokies. Evenings are dominated by a largely gay crowd, from transvestites and transsexuals to muscle-bound bouncers, but the club maintains a straight-friendly ambiance and a mixed crowd. Open 24hr. Dance club open F-Sa midnight-7am; cover $5, beers $2.50.

**Arq,** Taylor Sq, Darlinghurst (☎9380 8700). Ultra-trendy dance club with a mixed gay and straight crowd. Upstairs, bump to techno with buff and beautiful boys on podiums. Downstairs, an alternative crowd jams to soul and funk in the bar. Cover $15, Sa $17. Open W 5-10pm, Th 5pm-6am, F 5pm-9am, Sa 5pm-noon, Su 5pm-9am ($5).

**Rhino Bar,** 24 Bayswater Rd, Kings Cross (☎9357 7700). The subdued African safari lodge theme makes weekend dance parties a little incongruous, but that's the last thing on anyone's mind. Cream-color and wrought-iron gates outside smack of colonialism, but colored capitalist lights flash throughout the small, smoky dance area as DJs spin house and progressive music Th-Sa. Jugs $8 (usually $6 on Th). Beers $2 F all night, Sa until midnight. Cover Th-Sa $5. Open M-Th 3pm-late, F-Sa 3pm-4am or later.

**Gas,** 477 Pitt St, Haymarket (☎9211 3088). The place to break it down in the CBD. With hip-hop, heavy house, and a bit of disco spinning, the place is far from delphic. Open Th 10pm-4am, cover $10; F 10pm-5am, $20; Sa 10pm-6am, $25.

**The Burdekin Hotel,** 2 Oxford St, Darlinghurst (☎9331 3066). On the Hyde Park end of Oxford St. Part bar and part upscale nightclub, the Burdekin's 5 levels each have a slightly different feel, from the chill-out level with the original Space Invaders to the dance-crazy main level. Schooners of VB $4; cocktails are popular with those who can afford $10-12 per drink. Open M-Th 11am-midnight, F-Sa 11am-4am. No cover.

# ⚡ DAYTRIPS FROM SYDNEY

Sydney's attractions are not just limited to the city proper. The surrounding hills and valleys contain a sampling of the greater natural beauty for which the continent is known. As well, the small towns outside Sydney give a feel for, well, small town life that the lights of the big city often drown. If your stay in Oz is confined to Sydney, each of these daytrips at least give a flavor of the rest of the continent.

## ROYAL NATIONAL PARK

Just 30km south of Sydney's city center, Royal National Park is an easy and glorious escape from city life. The park, Australia's oldest and the world's second-oldest (after the United States's Yellowstone), consists of over 16,000 hectares of beach, heath, rainforest, swamp, and woodland. The range of activities available in the park is as diverse as the habitat—bushwalkers, birdwatchers, swimmers, and surfers all find favorite getaways in different corners of the park. Across the Princes Hwy on the west side of the park, the smaller, often-forgotten **Heathcote National Park** contributes another 2000 hectares of heathland to the cause of travelers trying to lose themselves in green.

▐ **TRANSPORT.** CityRail **trains** from **Sydney** connect to: **Loftus** in the northwest (35min., 4 per day M-F, $4); **Waterfall** in the west (40min., 12-17 per day, $5); **Otford** (45min, 12-17 per day, $6) and **Heathcote** at the park's southern point (1hr., 12-17 per day, $4). From Waterfall or Otford, walk east to enter the park. For the northeast corner, take CityRail to **Cronulla** (50min., approx. every 30min., $4) then catch a Cronulla National Park **ferry** (☎9523 2990) to **Bundeena** (13 per day, $3). **By car,** follow the Princes Hwy.

▐ **PRACTICAL INFORMATION. The Audley Visitor Centre,** 2km from the park's entrance and 4km south of Loftus, distributes information on trails, ranger-led activities, and camping in the park. The indispensable maps cost only $1. (☎9542 0648. Open daily 8:30am-4:30pm.) The main park road runs from the northwest entrance to Otford and stays open 24 hours, but turn-offs have locked gates from 8pm to 7am. Entrance to the park costs $10 per car (pedestrians and cyclists free).

▐ **ACCOMMODATIONS AND CAMPING. The National Parks and Wildlife Service (NPWS)** administers one car-accessible serviced camping area in Royal National Park, **Bonnie Vale,** just inside the park at Bundeena. From Audley, take the main park road to Bundeena Rd and follow the signs to Bonnie Vale. The spot has parking, toilets, showers, water, and phones. (Sites for 2 $11; no powered sights or individual water supplies. Gates open 6am-9:30pm.) The NPWS also oversees **free campsites** in five locations throughout Royal National Park and in nearby Heathcote National Park (including the popular Kingfisher Pool camping area). No open fires are permitted in the park. Permits for any of these areas must be obtained at the Audley Visitors Centre or by mail. For bushcamping permits or to put in an application during the Bonnie Vale **lottery period** (during school holidays), write to NPWS, P.O. Box 44, Sutherland NSW 1499.

Royal National Park's only public accommodation with a roof is in the **Garie Beach YHA Hostel,** a three-room house overlooking Garie Beach. It's idyllic, but rugged—bring your own toilet paper and flashlights (12 beds; $8, under 18 $4; YHA membership required). Reservations and key pickup must be arranged in advance through the YHA Travel and Membership Centre, 422 Kent St, Sydney (☎9261 1111), or at any of the Sydney YHA hostels.

▲ **ACTIVITIES.** The breathtaking **Coastal Track** (26km; 10hr.) tops Royal National Park's list of bushwalking trails. Running along the sandstone cliff line between Bundeena and Otford, the trail is generally approached as a two-day affair, allowing time to enjoy the wildflowers of the heath, the depths of the coastal caves, and the expanse of the ocean views. Particularly in June, Humpback and Right whales swim off the shore during their migration (Providential Head is a great vantage point). Overnighters usually bushcamp at North Era or stop at the YHA hostel. Hikers with less time often tackle a piece of the trail from one of the park roads and then return to their starting point. The park's only **wheelchair accessible trail** (1km) runs up to Bungoona Lookout from the Audley Visitors Centre. The **Uloola Track** (11km) from Waterfall station to Audley in the north traverses ecosystems from rainforest and woodlands to heathlands. The walk rewards hikers with wildflower strewn paths, the inviting Blue Pools, and the cascading Uloola Falls. The short **Aboriginal rock engravings** walk begins at Jibbon Beach, on Port Hacking, east of Bundeena. The engravings, believed to be between 200 and 5000 years old, depict animals important to the local tribe's diet. Although Aboriginal carvings appear on rocks throughout the park, officials only direct tourists to the Jibbon site. Defacement at the site makes their reasoning obvious. Inquire at the Visitors Centre about ranger-guided walks ($7-14) to the park's Aboriginal sites.

From **Otford Lookout,** at the park's southern tip, **Werrong (Hellhole) Track** (1km; 5min.; steep return) leads to the only **nude swimming beach** in Royal National Park. When the wind is right, Werrong is also an excellent **body boarding** spot. The Visitors Centre has maps and directions to other walking trails, many of which lead to swimming holes, waterfalls, or secluded beaches. The water off of Bonnie Vale, Jibbon Beach, Wattamolla, and Little Marley is suitable for swimming. Marley Beach, just north of Little Marley, is considered unsafe. Inland, freshwater swimming holes, such as Deer Pool, near Marley Beach, and the Karloo Pool in Heathcote, offer more placid and secluded settings for a dip. Most **surfers** favor the beaches at Garie, North and South Era, or the secluded Burning Palms area. Surf Life Saving Clubs overlook the beaches at both Garie and Burning Palms during most holidays and weekends. Wattamolla is a fun area 30min. into the park and just off the main artery, with a lagoon and cove beach. Jibbon Point, Wattamolla, Garie, and Burning Palms are all popular spots for fishing.

The **Audley Boatshed** off Farnell Ave about 2km beyond the Audley Visitors Centre rents rowboats, canoes, kayaks (2hr. $20, half-day $20, full-day $26.50), **mountain bikes** (1hr. $11, full-day $26.50), and **aqua bikes** (30min. $11). All rentals require a $10 deposit. (☎9545 4967. Open daily Aug.-Apr. 9am-6pm; May-July 9am-5pm.) Bikes are only permitted on management tracks. The 10km **Lady Carrington Drive** is an excellent mountain biking day trip. From Waterfall station, a 5km ride along McKell Ave places bikers at the trailhead. Access is relatively easy for bikers with the route ending in Audley 5km away from Lotus along the busy Princes Highway.

# BOTANY BAY NATIONAL PARK

Botany Bay takes its name, strangely enough, from the wide spectrum of plant life that European explorers originally found on its shores. The national park that now occupies the northern and southern headlands of the bay was created not only to preserve species of flora now endangered by urban expansion, but also to memorialize the voyages of Captain James Cook and French explorer Count de Laperouse. Cook's landing at Kurnell on the southern headland of the bay was the origin of British colonization. The park itself is relatively small in contrast to Royal National Park but the shorter trails are more accessible and manage to pack a ton of nature into each kilometer. The Laperouse expedition, to which the northern half of the park is dedicated, ended less successfully with the mysterious disap-

**"L'AUSTRALIE"** On January 26, 1788, members of the British First Fleet were surprised to see two ships approach the shore at Botany Bay. The French Laperouse expedition arrived just six days after the British brought the first convicts to the planned penal colony. Three years into an around-the-world exploratory mission, the French crew needed time to rest and repair their vessels. The British Captain Phillip moved north to Port Jackson, later renamed Sydney, while Laperouse stayed at Botany Bay for six weeks. On March 10, Laperouse and his party set sail and cruised into the South Pacific, never to be seen again. The French government sent out a search party in 1791, and Louis XVI's last request before his death in 1793 was "any news of Monsieur de Laperouse?" Forty years passed before any trace of his wreck was found.

pearance of two ships and scores of men. Despite popular impressions of Botany Bay as either sleepy and suburban or ugly and industrial, visitors often remember the ocean views and beaches best.

**SOUTHERN SECTION.** The **Discovery Centre,** 450m beyond the toll gate inside the park's southern section, has an exhibit on the eight-day landing of Cook's ship, the *Endeavour.* There are also exhibits on the history of Aboriginal life in the area. (☎9668 9111. Open M-F, hours vary. $2.20.) Nearby, **Monument track** (1km; 20min.) passes several historical markers related to Cook's landing. **Cape Bailey Coast Walk** takes those up for a moderately difficult trek from the end of Solander Drive past sand dunes, along the cliffs up to Cape Bailey lighthouse. Most of the ocean shoreline is dangerous for water activities, but fishing and diving are possible on the bayside shore near the Discovery Centre. Natural rock pools in Cronulla have excellent swimming, but **surfers** should move down the beach to **Cronulla.**

To get to the park's southern section from Sydney, take the **train** (Illawarra line) from Town Hall or Central Station to Cronulla (45min., approx. every 30min., $4). **Kurnell Bus Service** (☎9523 4047) runs from Cronulla Railway Station to the park on Rte 987 (20min.; 8-11 per day M-Sa, 3 per day Su; $3.30). By **car,** follow the Princes Hwy south and branch left at Rocky Point Rd. Cross the Captain Cook Bridge, where it becomes Taren Point Rd, then turn left on Captain Cook Dr to Kurnell and the park. (Gates open daily 7am-7:30pm. $5.50 per car, pedestrians free.)

**NORTHERN SECTION.** In the northern half of Botany Bay National Park, the **Laperouse Museum,** on Anzac Pde, recounts the tale of Laperouse and his mysterious last voyage (see **"L'Australie,"** above). The mystery is not huge—the poor guy sank (and his boat did too)—but the museum does an excellent job of building suspense. (☎9311 2765. Open W-Su 10am-4pm. $5.50, concessions $3.30.) Part of the museum contains a timeline exhibit of local Aboriginal history, evidence of the park's increasing emphasis on indigenous culture. Local Aboriginals come on Sundays to display and sell crafts. Another popular attraction is the "Snake Man of Laperouse," who visits the park Sundays around 1:30pm to show off his prowess with an assortment of reptiles. Across a footbridge from the main visitors area, **Bare Island Fort**—featured in the film *Mission: Impossible II*—once guarded Sydney's southern approach from the none-too-likely threat of attack. In fact, it was later revealed that soldiers would have been safer outside than inside the poorly crafted fort. The fort is accessible via guided tours run through Cadman's Cottage. (☎9247 5033. Tours 40min.; 4 per day Sa-Su; $7.70, concessions $5.50.)

The **Henry Head Trail** (3.5 km; 1hr.) leads from Anzac Pde past beautiful views of the city, bay, and south coast, all the way to the fortifications at Henry Head. Those seeking the "botany" part of Botany Bay will find the rare Eastern Suburbs Banksia Scrub in Jennifer St Park. A 350m boardwalk leads visitors to the endangered plant with only 1% of its original cover left. If you have tired of land, rent a boat from **First Fleet Marine,** inside the Boatshed Café Building, on the water in front of the museum. Fisherfolk will find bait for sale, but there is no equipment to rent. (☎9661 9522. Motorboats 2hr. $50; kayaks 1hr. $10.) The beach below the café is clean, sandy, and suitable for swimming.

NEW SOUTH WALES

Sydney **buses** #393 from Railway Square and #394 from Circular Quay make the trip to this end of Botany Bay (the Laperouse stop) about every 25min. (50min., $2.80 each way). **Drivers** need only take Anzac Pde until it ends at the Laperouse Museum. There are a couple of virtually indistinguishable seafood cafés near the museum, as well as a few other eateries. The **Boatshed Café** is a convenient spot to grab lunch and watch the windsurfers on Botany Bay. (☎9661 9315. Open Tu-Su 9am-5pm, in winter closes at 5pm. Fish-and-chips $5.50.)

## PARRAMATTA

In April 1788, Governor Phillip led an expedition to discover what lay upriver from the new settlement of Sydney, and Australia's second town was established as a result. Parramatta is now a suburban extension of the city, complete with a nearby theme park for daytripping Sydney-siders. The five-floor Westfield mall is said to be the largest in the Southern Hemisphere. Parramatta also maintains several buildings from the early days of colonization. Most notable is the **Old Government House** in Parramatta Park at the west end of town. Originally a plaster cottage built by Governor Phillip in 1790, the house grew into Georgian grandeur through renovations made by Governor Macquarie between 1812 and 1818. The oldest public building in Australia contains the country's largest collection of pre-1855 colonial furniture. (☎9635 8149. Open M-F 10am-4pm, Sa-Su 11am-4pm. $6, concessions $4.) **Elizabeth Farm,** 70 Alice St, in Rosehill, east of the town center, was the home of John and Elizabeth Macarthur, founders of the Australian Merino wool industry. (☎9635 9488. Open daily 10am-5pm. $6.50, concessions $3.30.) In 1789, the colonial government made its first land grant in the colony to convict James Ruse at the site of **Experiment Farm Cottage,** 9 Ruse St. (☎9635 5655. Open Tu-Th 10am-4pm, Su 11am-4pm. $5.) West of Parramatta, in Doonside, **Featherdale Wildlife Park,** 217 Kildare Rd, provides wonderful interactive animal fun, allowing visitors to cuddle koalas, feed kangaroos, and see close-up the country's largest collection of native Australian animals. (☎9622 1644. Open daily 9am-5pm. $14, students $11, families $36.) The park is 40min. from Sydney by car (Reservoir Rd exit from M4) and also accessible by bus #725 from the Blacktown train station ($5 return from Central Station). Attractions at **Wonderland Sydney** range from wombats to waterslides to rollercoasters galore. (☎9830 9100. Open daily 10am-5pm. $42.90.) Take the Wallgrove Rd exit from the M4 or catch Busways bus #738 (return $6) from the Rooty Hill train station (from Central Station off-peak return $6).

Parramatta is 20min. from Sydney along Parramatta Rd. Before reaching Parramatta, the road becomes the M4 Tollway at Strathfield, the most direct route to the Blue Mountains. Both **trains** and **ferries** make the trip to **Sydney.** The 1hr. cruise on the sleek RiverCat pontoon (every hr. from wharf 2, $5.50), is preferable to the 30min. train ride ($3.40). CityRail also runs to: **Blackheath** ($9.80); **Katoomba** ($9.40); **Lithgow** ($12.60); and **Penrith** ($4). The **Parramatta Visitors Centre,** 346 Church St, is within the Parramatta Heritage Center. (☎9630 3703; fax 9630 3243. Open M-F 10am-5pm, Sa-Su 10am-4pm.) Parramatta's accommodation scene does not cater to budget travelers, but Sydney is close enough to make commuting worthwhile. **The Sushi Train,** 188 Church St, whirls plates of sushi around on a conveyer belt tempting customers to sample the color coded samples. (☎9891 1399. Open M-Sa 11:30am-9pm, Su 11:30am-8pm.)

## PENRITH

The town of Penrith, 35km west of Parramatta along the Great Western Hwy, hovers at the edge of Sydney's sphere of suburban influence at the base of the Blue Mountains. Running through the west half of town, the **Nepean River,** a wide, placid corridor, is one of Penrith's best features. The **Nepean Belle** paddlewheel riverboat makes leisurely trips through the Nepean Gorge in **Blue Mountains National Park.** (☎4733 1274. Departs **Tench Reserve Park,** off Tench Ave, on an irregular schedule. Shortest cruise 90min., $18.) **Penrith Regional Gallery and the Lewers Bequest,** 86 River Rd in Emu Plains, is devoted to the promotion of Australian modernist art. (☎4735 1100. Open Tu-Su 11am-5pm. $2.) Just 5km north of town along Castlereagh Rd, the **Sydney International Regatta Centre** and **Penrith Whitewater Stadium** served as the **Olympic** venues for all rowing and canoeing events. The landscaped grounds (open daily 9am-5pm) around the Regatta Centre's water course are good for picnicking or just frolicking in the grass (see **contraceptive devices,** p. 46).

CityRail **trains** come in from: **Sydney** (1hr., 23-33 per day, $6.40); **Blackheath** (1½hr., 15-21 per day, $7.60); **Katoomba** (1hr., 15-21 per day, $5.60); **Lithgow** (2hr., 12-14 per day, $9.80); and **Parramatta** (30min., 23-34 per day, $4). The **Penrith Valley Visitors Centre,** on Mulgoa Rd, in the carpark of the Panther's World Entertainment Complex, provides info on Penrith and the Blue Mountains. (☎4732 7671; fax 4732 7690; www.penrithvalley.com.au. Open daily 9am-4:30pm.) **Nepean River Caravan Park,** on MacKellar St in Emu Plains, provides inexpensive sleeping arrangements. Creature comforts include kitchen, swimming pool, games room, and TV lounge. (☎4735 4425. Reception M-F 8am-7pm, Sa-Su 8am-6pm. Key deposit $20. Dorms $16.50; sites for 2 $16, powered $19.50; cabins for 2 $45.) **Explorer's Lodge,** 111 Station St, targets the herds of athletes frequenting the area and accordingly provides extra long beds, a rock climbing machine, a small gym, and laundry facilities to wash all those sweaty workout clothes. (☎4731 3616. Reception daily 9am-9pm. Dorms $25.) The **Oz Family Restaurant,** at the corner of Mulgoa and Blaikie Rd, spreads a hearty all-you-can-eat smorgasbord for $12-$16. (☎4733 3833. Open W-Su lunch 11:30-3pm, Tu-Su dinner 5pm-10pm.)

## THE UPPER HAWKESBURY

The fertile farmland of the Upper Hawkesbury has been cultivated from the first Australian colonization, but it was not until 1810 that towns were first established in the area. Governor Lachlan Macquarie selected sites for five towns: **Windsor, Richmond, Wilberforce, Castlereagh,** and **Pitt Town.** Today, these towns, collectively known as the **Macquarie Towns,** lie at the east end of Bells Line of Road (see p. 147), a scenic alternative to the freeway between the outskirts of Sydney and the Blue Mountains. **Hawkesbury Heritage Farm** on Rose St in Wilberforce, 6km northeast of Windsor off Putty Rd, recreates colonial life with historical buildings and antiques. (☎4575 1457. Open Th-Su 10am-5pm. $11, concessions $7.) **Richmond,** 10km northwest of Windsor via Richmond Rd, has a nice collection of 1800s buildings. A **National Parks and Wildlife Service** office covering the Blue Mountains is also in Richmond. (☎4588 5247; fax 4588 335. Open M-F 9:30am-12:30pm and 1:30-5pm.)

CityRail **trains** from Sydney's Central Station reach both Windsor ($6, off-peak return $7) and Richmond ($6.40, $7.40). **Tourism Hawkesbury,** on Windsor St between Windsor and Richmond, has information on the entire area. (☎4588 5895; fax 4588 5896. Open M-F 9am-5pm, Sa 10am-3pm, Su 9am-1pm.)

Cheap places to stay are rare in this resort area. One of the more interesting is the **Alpaca Bed & Breakfast** outside Pitt Town, a farmstay with spacious self-contained rustic cabins among curious alpacas (llively llama-llike animals). Follow the signs to Pitt Town and then to the B&B. (☎4573 6643. Double-bed cabins from $70; 2-bedroom cabins from $90. Book ahead.)

## WINDSOR

The town of **Windsor** is well-preserved. The refurbished center at Thompson Square holds several historical buildings. On the square, the Daniel O'Connell Inn houses the **Hawkesbury Museum of Local History** and a small **tourist information office.** (☎4577 2310. Both open daily 10am-4pm; museum admission $2.50.) The 1815 **Macquarie Arms Hotel** (☎4577 2206) claims to be "the oldest pub in Australia," and the owner is fond of leading ghost tours into the cellar, where smuggling once took place. **St. Matthew's Anglican Church,** on Moses St at the corner of Greenway Crescent, built between 1817 and 1822, is considered one of the greatest achievements of ex-convict architect Francis Greenway. (☎4577 3193. Open daily dawn-dusk.) The 1809 **Ebenezer Church,** outside town on Coromandel Rd, is Australia's oldest church still used for public worship. (☎4579 9350. Open daily 10am-3:30pm.)

NEW SOUTH WALES

## KU-RING-GAI CHASE NATIONAL PARK

The country's second-oldest national park, Ku-Ring-Gai Chase (named after a local Aboriginal group) was seven years old when the Australian colonies federated in 1901. The Park came close to serving a far more central role in the new nation's development as the site of the capital city. However, the proposal to build the city on the park land in medieval English style—as a moated fortress capital to be called **Pacivica**—was eventually passed over in favor of the plan that led to the creation of Canberra. The park, 24km north of Sydney, includes over 15,000 hectares covering most of the southern headlands of Broken Bay. Waterways leading out to the ocean carve their way through the park's sandstone rock landscape giving the park a rugged beauty. Many Sydney-siders come for the numerous Aboriginal rock engravings and the exotic wildflowers that bloom early in winter.

**TRANSPORT.** Ku-Ring-Gai Chase is effectively sectioned in two by access roads. Ku-Ring-Gai Chase Rd from the Pacific Hwy and Bobbin Head Rd from Turramurra provide access to this area of the park (entry $9.90 per car). By public transport from Sydney, you can reach the Bobbin Head Rd entrance by first taking the **train** to Turramurra (35min., $3.40) and then catching bus #577 of **Shorelink Bus Company** (☎ 9457 8888; 15min.; M-Sa every hr., Su limited service; $3.40) to just outside the park gates. Palm Beach **Ferry** Service (☎ 9918 2747) stops at the **Basin** (8 per day, $8 return). Palm Cruises (☎ 9997 4815) runs to **Bobbin Head** (scenic cruise at 11am, $30) and **Patonga** (at least 1 per day, $13). Sydney Bus #L90 goes from Central Station to Palm Beach near the ferry wharf (1½hr., approx. every 30min.). The Bobbin Head section of the park has access roads with no gates, but the park is closed from sunset to sunrise.

**PRACTICAL INFORMATION.** The Bobbin Head area in the southwest is home to the **main visitors center,** a picnic area, and lush views of the valley and peaceful headwaters of Cowan Creek. The volunteer-run **Kalkari Visitors Centre,** on Ku-Ring-Gai Chase Rd, 4km inside the park gates, distributes free hiking maps, and offers educational information on the park's wildlife. (☎ 9457 9853. Open daily 9am-5pm.) Volunteers from the center run an irregular program of **guided walks** highlighting Aboriginal engraving sites and the park's scenic gems. **Bobbin Head Information Centre,** inside the Wildlife Shop, at the bottom of the hill at Bobbin Head, is the official information outlet for the park. (☎ 9472 8949. Open daily 10am-4pm.)

**ACCOMMODATIONS.** Possibly the most refreshing and remote hostel in the greater Sydney area, the **Pittwater YHA Hostel,** enjoys lush green scenery from its lofty, terraced perch over Pittwater. Take bus #156 from Manly (1hr.), bus #E86 from Wynyard (1¼hr.), or follow Pittwater Rd to the ferry at Church Point wharf ($6.50 return). The open, outdoorsy hostel provides a retreat without the distraction of TV or radio. Hosts encourage guests to get out and use any of the 16 walking trails which start in the immediate area, or to swim in the nearby bay. Canoe hire is $8 for length of stay, and bikes are $15 per day. (☎ 9999 2196; fax 9997 4296. Linen $2. Reception daily 8-11am and 5-8pm. Dorms $19; twins $48. Sa only $25, $58. Non-YHA add $3. Bookings required.) The **campground** at the Basin is accessible by ferry from Palm Beach or by a 3km hike on the Basin track from West Head Rd. The site has cold showers, toilets, gas BBQs, and a public phone, but all supplies, except bait and drinks, must be carried in. Bookings must be arranged through the NPWS automated reservation service. (☎ 9974 1011. Open 24hr. Sites for 2 $11, each additional person $2.20; holidays $15.50, $3.30.) Both the park's **hostel** and **camping area** can be approached by car from the east side of the park, but each requires that you leave the car behind somewhere along West Head Rd.

**HIKING.** Ku-Ring-Gai Chase has **bushwalks** for any level of expertise. The discovery walk (20min.; wheelchair accessible) just outside the Kalkari Visitors

Centre is a quick, easy way to spot a few kangaroos and emus as well as some native plant life. An easily accessible bush walk (10km) begins at the Bobbin Head Rd entrance to the park and follows the **Sphinx-Warrimoo Track** for 6.5km to Bobbin Head. The hike can be made into a circuit by taking the Bobbin Head Track (3.5km) back to the park entrance. The bushwalk passes through mangroves, along a creek, and near an Aboriginal engraving site. The **Aboriginal Heritage Walk** (3.5km) at West Head is a moderately difficult hike which incorporates the Red Hands Cave, a Shelter Site, and an engraving site (access through West Head Road). Rock engravings in the park include mythical beings and whales reaching 8km long. For the best views of the Hawkesbury River as it feeds out into **Broken Bay,** proceed north along West Head Rd until you reach a picnic lookout area.

◖ **BEACHES.** There are no patrolled swimming **beaches** in the park, but the protected coves of Pittwater along **West Head,** in particular at the **Basin,** are less turbulent than the open waters of Broken Bay. **Halvorsen Boats,** at Bobbin Head near the Wildlife Shop, rents motorboats (1hr. $48, each additional hr. $8; deposit $30) and rowboats ($13, $4.50, $10). On Sundays call ahead to check availability, and get there early. (☎9457 9011. Open daily 8am-4pm.)

## GOSFORD

Gosford lies 65km north of Sydney, along the Pacific Hwy. Its proximity and transit-hub status are its main appeal. For those who actually come for the sights, Gosford is best attacked by car, though some can technically be reached by public transport. The two best attractions sit next to each other 13km west of town on the Pacific Hwy. **Old Sydney Town** time warps to the era between 1788-1810. The park's 150 hectares include many olde-tyme shoppes, a windmill, and the modern day Macquarie, Hunter, York, and Argyle St. The actors put on street theater and presentations, including bullock yoking and horse shoeing. Swarms of school groups mob the site, but luckily, you can often find the little dearies in the stockade. (☎4340 1104. Open W-Su 10am-4pm. $21, ages 5-16 $12, families $57.) Next door, the **Australian Reptile Park** is home to multiple Burmese pythons and Eric the 4.8m saltwater crocodile. The park also has its share of 'roos, wombats, and fowl. Don't miss the daily 1pm koala feedings, when the bleary-eyed little cuddlies are at their playful best. (☎4340 1146. Open daily 9am-5pm. $14, concessions $7, families $36.) Both parks are wheelchair accessible. From the train station, take bus #38 (call **Busways,** ☎4362 1030, for schedules).

The Gosford area has many nature reserves—Kincumba Mountain, Katandra, and Rumbalara. Call the **National Park and Wildlife Service** (☎4324 4911) for specifics. The mostly-sandstone **Brisbane Water National Park,** home to many marsupials and platypuses, is the most popular park in the area. The most interesting feature is the **Bulgandry Aboriginal Site,** containing 10 rock engravings from about 200 years ago. From Gosford, head 4km west on Pacific Hwy and turn onto Woy Woy Rd. The turn-off for the carpark is poorly marked about 2.5km down on the right.

East of Gosford along the Pacific shore are some bodacious **surf beaches,** most notably **Avoca, Terrigal,** and **Wamberal.** (If you want to learn to hang ten, the tourist office supplies brochures on surf schools.) The best launching point is the town of **Terrigal,** 15km east of Gosford, accessible by bus #80, 81, and 82. **Avoca Beach** can be reached directly by bus #75 or 79.

To get to Gosford's main thoroughfare, **Mann St,** follow the signs to the city center. Here sits the **train station** (☎13 15 00). CityRail trains run 24hr. more than twice per hour to **Sydney** (1½hr.; $7) and **Newcastle** (1½hr.; $9). **Bus** service runs from in front of the train station. **Taxis** (☎4323 6444) are always on-call. The **Tourist Information Centre,** 200 Mann St, is directly in front of the train station. (☎4385 4074; http://cctourism.com.au. Open M-Sa 9am-4:30pm, Su 9:30am-2:30pm.)

# BLUE MOUNTAINS

The motto of the Blue Mountains region, "come up for air," bespeaks the get-away-from-it-all attitude of this tourist wonderland. Although a variety of adventure activities such as abseiling (rappelling) and canyon rafting have become popular in recent years, the major attractions of the Blue Mountains remain their excellent hiking trails and lookouts. Sunlight filtering through eucalyptus oil suspended in the air gives the forest its tint. From the lookout points, the earth falls away into endless blue foliage speckled with white bark and bordered by distant sandstone cliffs. Whether you have a hankering for drenching waterfalls, serene rainforest, or jaw-dropping panoramic views, you'll find it here.

Because the so-called mountains are actually a series of canyons separated by several high plateaus, colonialist explorers found impassable cliffs at the edges of the valleys instead of hills. A successful route was not found until 1813, when the bitter white guys finally cried "uncle" and asked the Aboriginal community, which had lithely crossed the mountains for centuries, how to get across—walk along the ridges. Today, the mountains are the first stop on most backpacker trips west from Sydney and an easy getaway for Sydney-siders. The short trip inland, a 1½hr. drive or a 2hr. train ride, grants summertime visitors a reprieve from the oppressive heat that hangs over the coast. In winter, crisp sunny days, occasional snowfalls, and Yulefest (Christmas in July) festivities draw travelers.

## ✳ ORIENTATION

Three national parks divide the wild stretches of the region. **Blue Mountains National Park,** the largest and most accessible of the three, spans most of the Jamison Valley (south of the Great Western Hwy between Glenbrook and Katoomba), as well as the Megalong Valley (south of the Great Western Hwy west of Katoomba) and the Grose Valley (north of the Great Western Hwy and east of Blackheath). The Grose and Jamison Valleys appeal primarily to hikers, while horseback riders tend to favor the Megalong Valley (for more information on horse-riding, see **Blackheath,** p. 145). **Kanangra-Boyd National Park** (see p. 147), tucked between two sections of Blue Mountains National Park in the southwest reaches of the mountains, is reserved for skilled bushwalkers. The park, accessible by partially paved roads from Oberon and from Jenolan Caves, has only one 2WD road. **Wollemi National Park** (see p. 148) contains the state's largest preserved wilderness area. It's a place so unspoiled and untrafficked that a species of pine tree thought to be long extinct was found here, alive and well, in 1994. Access to the park, the southern edge of which abuts the north side of **Bells Line of Road,** is possible at Bilpin and at several points north of the central Blue Mountains.

The national parks of the Blue Mountains are divided into regions and administered by different branches of the **National Parks and Wildlife Services (NPWS).** If you are planning to bushcamp or even to drive into these parks, contact the appropriate NPWS office (see specific park listings) a few days in advance to ensure that roads are drivable and that no bushfire bans are in place. Additionally, it is recommended that you leave a bushwalk plan filed with the appropriate NPWS office before you go.

## ▣ TRANSPORT

The Blue Mountains are an easy 1½hr. drive west of Sydney. Take George St until it becomes Parramatta Rd, then head west to the Western Motor Tollway. The tollway goes to Penrith, becoming the **Great Western Hwy,** the main route through the mountains. All service centers and attractions lie on or near this road. Alternatively, the northern route, **Bells Line of Road** (see p. 147), roams west from Windsor, northeast of Parramatta, providing a more beautiful and less developed passage.

CityRail **trains** stop throughout the Blue Mountains at most of the towns along the Great Western Hwy, offering the least expensive option for travelers who are willing to walk sizable distances from rail stations and bus stops to trailheads. Within the towns, most distances are walkable, and local bus companies cover those that aren't (for bus info, see **Katoomba**, p. 141). There is **no public transportation** to Kanangra-Boyd National Park or Wollemi National Park.

There are two above-par smaller bus **tour** companies. **Wonderbus** offers a basic tour including stops at Euroka Clearing Campground, Wentworth Falls, Katoomba's Echo Point, and Blackheath's Govett's Leap. The aim is to allow time for wilderness bushwalks with the experienced advice of the driver-guide; if you want to stay the night, you can call to get a ride home on a later bus. (☎9555 9800. Daily pickup from city hostels 7:30-8:30am, return approximately 7pm. $61.) **Wildframe Ecotours** provides an exclusive trip into the challenging **Grand Canyon,** a rainforest walk in Blackheath. (☎9314 0658 or ☎(0500) 50 50 56. $71.50, concessions $60.) Wildframe has a partnership with the local YHA, so it runs overnight trips that include YHA accommodation (canyon and overnight $104). Both companies offer other trips as well, including **spelunking** and **abseiling.**

Several companies run bus **tours** to the mountains from Sydney. A common one-day package includes stops at Katoomba's Echo Point, the Scenic Railway and Skyway, and Blackheath's Govett's Leap; some throw in visits to the Edge Maxvision Cinema in Katoomba and the Australian Wildlife Park at Wonderland Sydney. Trips focusing on bushwalking stop at Echo Point, the Wentworth Falls Conservation Hut, and Govett's Leap. **AAT Kings,** Jetty 6, Circular Quay, has a basic Blue Mountains tour along the Great Western Hwy. (☎9518 6095. Departs 9am, returns 5:45pm. Basic tour $85, concessions $82; bushwalking package with cattleman's lunch and horseriding or 4WD $113, $104; Jenolan caves package with 6:45pm return $104, $95; 10% YHA discount.) **Great Sights,** on Circular Quay, offers a more scenic trip down Bells Line of Road with a visit to the Australian Wildlife Park. (☎9241 2294. Basic $94; Jenolan caves $105; more advanced spelunking $120.)

# GLENBROOK TO KATOOMBA

CityRail **trains** from **Sydney** (20-30 per day) run parallel to the Great Western Hwy through the Blue Mountains to **Glenbrook** (1¼hr.), **Leura** (2hr.), and points further west, including **Blaxland, Springwood, Faulconbridge, Woodford,** and **Wentworth Falls.** Trips from Sydney to this part of the mountains will cost $8-10. Tickets between these towns range $3-5 and last no more than 1hr.

## NEAR GLENBROOK

On the Great Western Hwy (going west) outside the easternmost section of Blue Mountains National Park, **Blue Mountains Tourism's** Glenbrook office, serves as the gateway to the Blue Mountains from Sydney. (☎(1300) 65 34 08; fax 4780 5729. Open M-F 9am-5pm, Sa-Su 8:30am-4:30pm.) The **NPWS Glenbrook** gate, south of Glenbrook on Bruce Rd, is the nearest entrance to the park (car entrance fee $6, cyclists and pedestrians free). From the highway, take Ross St until it dead-ends, then turn left on Burfitt Pde, which becomes Bruce Rd and leads to the park.

Inside the park, 4km over mostly paved roads beyond the Bruce Rd entrance, is the **Euroka Clearing Campground.** The site has pit toilets, BBQ plates, and pumped creek water. Kangaroos congregate close by at dawn and dusk. The entrance is locked 6pm-8:30am, and campers are advised to bring ample firewood, food, and water. Call the NPWS in Richmond to arrange permits in advance. (☎4588 5247. Open 9am-12:30pm and 1:30-5pm. Sites for 2 $12.50 first night, subsequent nights much cheaper; includes park entrance fee.) Bushcamping is free.

The **Red Hands Cave trail** (8km) from the Glenbrook Visitors Centre runs an easy circuit through patches of rainforest to an Aboriginal **hand-stencil** site and the **Jellybean Pool** (named for its shape, not its contents), a popular swimming hole near the park's entrance. At **Blaxland,** less than 1km west of Glenbrook, Layton Ave turns off on a pleasant 2km detour toward **Lennox Bridge,** constructed between

1832-1833, the **oldest bridge** on the Australian mainland. As you approach the bridge, take note of the **Glenbrook Lagoon,** which marks the spot where the team of Blaxland, Lawson, and Wentworth set up their first camp before tackling the peaks. The National Trust-owned **Norman Lindsay Gallery,** 14 Norman Lindsay Crescent, **Faulconbridge,** houses a large collection of work by the controversial and multitalented artist who once inhabited the house. By using female nudes as his primary subjects, Lindsay drew intense criticism in the first half of the century, though his popular children's book *The Magic Pudding* (not featuring nudes) has been in continuous publication since 1918. The turn-off for the gallery, onto Grose Rd, is just east of Faulconbridge in Springwood. (☎4751 1067. Open daily 10am-4pm. $8, concessions $5.50.)

## NEAR WOODFORD

**Wentworth Falls,** renowned for its picturesque waterfall walks and record foliage diversity (more varieties of plants exist in the Blue Mountains than in all of Europe), hugs the highway 4km beyond Woodford. To find the starting points of the walks, turn off the highway at Falls Rd, and proceed south through the town's center. For the most direct access to the falls, continue along Falls Rd to a trailhead area offering short paths (under 1hr.) to the smaller upper falls, more challenging trails to the base of the falls, and a short walk (1km; 30min.) to **Princes Rock Lookout,** which provides an excellent vantage point for appreciating the full scale of the drop. If you're willing to devote half a day to a walk in this area, turn right off Falls Rd, following signs to the **National Park Conservation Hut** at the end of Fletcher St. Perched on the rim of the Jamison Valley, the hut is primarily a tea house with a killer view, but it also sells pamphlets on tourist facilities and walking tracks in the Blue Mountains. (☎4757 3827. Open daily 9am-5pm.) From the hut, try the **Valley of the Waters walk** (4km; 3hr.), which has stunning views of several nearby waterfalls and connects to the longer, more difficult **National Pass circuit** (6km; 3½hr.), a gorgeous walk hewn into the side of the cliff line. The return trail offers the best views of Wentworth Falls, though it involves a steep ascent.

An **NPWS campsite** can be found at **Murphy's Glen,** 10km south of the Great Western Hwy outside of Woodford. Take Park Rd from the highway to Railway Pde, turn left and proceed less than 1km, then turn right onto Bedford Rd. The road is unpaved for most of the way, and the campground, located in a thick eucalypt forest, has only pit toilets (free camping; no permits required). For camping in Wentworth Falls, the **Ingar Campground** is 13km farther southeast along Tableland Rd and the unsealed Queen Elizabeth Dr. The campground has bush toilets, no water, and no cooking facilities (free; no permits required). Nearby, a small pond makes the spot popular for picnics and camping.

## NEAR LEURA

The likeable and affluent town of Leura (pop. 8500), 3km west of Wentworth Falls and adjacent to Katoomba, offers shops, cafés, and galleries along its central street, Leura Mall. As one tour guide put it, "Leura is a latte and an afternoon at antique stores, and Blackheath is a flat white and a stop-off at second hand shops." (For translation help, see **Coffee Confusion,** p. 114.) **Everglades Gardens,** 37 Everglades Ave, is a lush example of the floral cultivation for which the town is known. (☎4787 1938. Open daily Sept.-Feb. 10am-5pm, Mar.-Aug. 10am-4pm. $6, concessions $4.) Nearby, Fitzroy St leads east to Watkins Rd, which soon turns into Sublime Point Rd and ends at the breathtaking overlook at **Sublime Point.** Coming south down Leura Mall from the highway, turn left on Craigend St, right onto Everglades Ave, then left onto Fitzroy St, proceeding from there as explained above. For travelers continuing west, the 8km **Cliff Drive** begins at Gordon Rd near the south end of Leura Mall and provides a scenic escape from the highway. The loop skirts the south edge of Katoomba, passing many lookouts and a handful of trailheads. If you're up quite early in the morning, turn south off of the Great Western Highway down **Mt. Hay** road and travel 12km to a brilliantly majestic sunrise over the cliffs (the last 2km are unsealed.)

# KATOOMBA

The image most widely associated with the Blue Mountains is that of the Three Sisters, a trio of towering stone blocks crumbling from the cliffs down into the dark blue-green velvet of the silent valley below. A first-hand view of the spectacular rock formation brings tourists from parts distant to the linchpin of the Blue Mountains, the mountain town of Katoomba (pop 30,000). In addition to its natural grandeur, Katoomba offers excellent hiking, climbing, and biking opportunities and a very convenient rail-accessible location; the result is a backpacker's and lay-mountaineer's dream. Though it's touristy, the town retains a distinctively liberal flavor, replete with VW vans, vegetarian eateries, and dredlocked 'dos.

## ⌷ TRANSPORT

**Trains: Katoomba Railway Station** (☎ 4751 5444) is on Main St, at the north end of Katoomba St. CityRail **trains** and Countrylink (☎ 13 22 32) trains and **buses** run to: **Sydney** (2hr., 20-29 per day, $11); **Bathurst** (2hr., 1 per day, $19); **Blackheath** (13min., 17-23 per day, $3); **Dubbo** (5hr., 1 per day, $52); **Glenbrook** (50min., 18-28 per day, $5); **Lithgow** (45min., 12-15 per day, $5.60); **Mt. Victoria** (20min., 12-15 per day, $3); **Orange** (3hr., 1 per day, $29); **Parramatta** (1½hr., 20-29 per day, $9); **Penrith** (1hr., 19-26 per day, $6); and the **Zig Zag railway** on demand (45min., $5).

**Buses:** Greyhound Pioneer (☎ 13 20 30) runs from opposite the Gearin Hotel to: **Sydney** (2½hr., 2 per day, $28.60); **Adelaide** (21hr., 1 per day, $108.90); **Bathurst** (2hr., 2 per day, $28.60); **Broken Hill** (14hr., $108.90); **Dubbo** (4¾hr., 1 per day, $48.40); **Lithgow** (40min., 1 per day, $15.40); **Orange** (3hr., 1 per day, $30.80); **Parramatta** (1½hr., 2 per day, $28.60); and **Penrith** (40min., 2 per day, $15.40). 10% YHA, VIP, ISIC discount. For day-touring at your own pace, the **Blue Mountains Explorer Bus** runs an 18-stop circuit allowing passengers to get on and off as often as they choose. Stops include Echo Point, the Scenic Railway and Scenic Skyway, Leura Cascades, Gordon Falls, Everglades Gardens, and the Edge Maxvision Cinema. Buses run every hr., daily 9:30am-4:30pm. (24hr. ☎ 4782 1866. $22, ages 5-15 $11.)

**Local Transportation: Blue Mountains Bus Company** (☎ 4782 4213) runs between Katoomba and **Woodford** with stops at Katoomba Station, near Echo Point, the Edge Cinema, Leura Mall, the Valley of the Waters trailhead, the Scenic Skyway, and Wentworth Falls. Fares $1.80-3. Regular service daily approximately 7:30am-6pm. Buses pickup outside Carrington Hotel on Main St, Katoomba. **Mountainlink** (☎ 4782 3333) runs to Leura, Blackheath, and Mt. Victoria. Fares from $1.20. Timetables for both services are available at the Blue Mountains Tourism Authority center on Echo Point.

**Taxis: Katoomba Leura Radio Cars** (☎ 4782 1311) picks up 24hr. anywhere between Wentworth Falls and Mt. Victoria. Initial fare $4, plus $1.07 per km.

**Automobile Clubs: NRMA** (road service ☎ 13 11 11).

**Bike Rental: Cycletech,** 182 Katoomba St (☎ 4782 2800), rents excellent mountain bikes. Half-day $27.50, full-day $49.50. Non-front suspension bikes half-day $19, full-day $27.50. Helmets, locks, and repair kits included. YHA and backpackers 10% discount. Open M-F 8:30am-5:30pm, Sa 8:30am-5pm, Su 9am-4pm.

## ◼◪ ORIENTATION AND PRACTICAL INFORMATION

Katoomba sits just south of the Great Western Hwy, 2km west of Leura and 109km from Sydney. The town's main drag, **Katoomba St,** runs south from the **Katoomba Railway Station** through town toward **Echo Point.** Echo Point Rd brings visitors to the Blue Mountains' most famous view, the **Three Sisters.**

**Tourist Office: Blue Mountains Tourism** (☎ (1300) 65 34 08; fax 4739 6787; www.bluemountainstourism.org.au), at the end of Echo Point Rd, on Echo Point. Take Lurline St south and veer left onto Echo Rd when Lurline St ends. The center has an

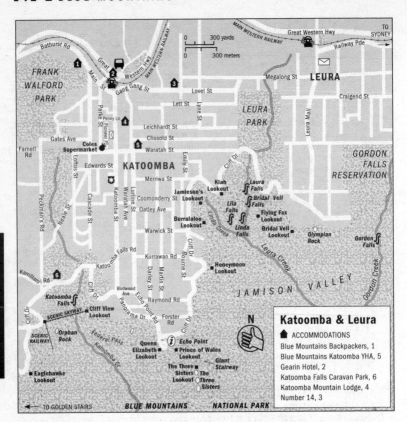

Katoomba & Leura

♠ ACCOMMODATIONS
Blue Mountains Backpackers, 1
Blue Mountains Katoomba YHA, 5
Gearin Hotel, 2
Katoomba Falls Caravan Park, 6
Katoomba Mountain Lodge, 4
Number 14, 3

amazing clifftop view and tons of info on the Blue Mountains area. Open daily 9am-5pm. For hiking advice from park rangers, try NPWS in Blackheath (see p. 145).

**Hospital: Blue Mountains District Anzac Memorial Hospital** (☎4780 6000), on the Great Western Hwy, 1km east of the railway station.

**Internet Access: Barcode 6ix Internet Caffé,** 6 Katoomba St (☎4782 6896), brews coffee ($2.20) and provides info, discounts, phone cards, storage, and Internet (30min. $5, 1hr $6.50). Open daily 9am-8pm.

**Post Office:** Shop 3, Pioneer Pl (☎4782 1005). Open M-F 9am-5pm. **Postal Code:** 2780.

**Phone Code:** 02.

# ▗ ACCOMMODATIONS

Katoomba increasingly hosts larger numbers of budget travelers than anywhere else in the Blue Mountains, and this trend is coupled with diminishing options outside the town line. Although beds here are plentiful, so are the vacationers that swamp the town Nov.-Apr. and on winter weekends. Advance bookings are highly recommended, especially on school holidays and long weekends.

▨ **Blue Mountains Katoomba YHA** (☎4782 1416; fax 4782 6203; email bluemoun tains@yhansw.org.au). On the corner of Lurline and Waratah St. From the train station, go down Katoomba St, turn left on Waratah St, and look for the YHA sign. Convenient location down the street from both Echo Point and downtown. Tons of common space, clean facilities, ample dorms, kitchen, gameroom, lockers ($1), Internet, and great security. Bike hire $24 per day. Key deposit $10. Reception daily 7am-10pm. Dorms $16-20; ensuite twins and doubles $60. Non-YHA $3 extra. **NOTE:** In March 2001, the YHA will be moving to Homesdale, 207 Katoomba St, an art-deco house with 200 beds.

**Number 14,** 14 Lovel St (☎4782 7104; www.bluemts.com.au/no14). A 5min. walk east of the train station via Gang Gang St. Luxurious, quiet homestay pad. Outstanding kitchen, modern decor, hardwood floors, sunny veranda, central heating. Reception daily 8-10am and 5-9pm. Unisex dorms $18; twins and doubles $48.

**Katoomba Mountain Lodge,** 31 Lurline St (☎/fax 4782 3933l; email kmt lodge@pnc.com.au). From the train station, walk down Katoomba St and go left down the alley marked "Hostel" just before the Uniting Church. This convenient budget guest-house has the cheapest rates in town, though dorms may feel crowded. Kitchen and social TV lounges (smoking and non-). Fireplace, electric blankets, and heat for cold winter nights. Free pickup from train station. Luggage storage $1. Reception daily 7:30am-10pm. Dorms $11-15; doubles from $42. YHA, VIP, ISIC.

**Blue Mountains Backpackers,** 190 Bathurst Rd (☎4782 4226; fax 4782 4236; email bluemountains@hotmail.com). A 5min. walk west of the train station. It's a fun, friendly, mellow accommodation aimed at a young crew. Small kitchen, dining area, common room with VCR, and a travel desk. Less than stellar bathrooms and a bit disorienting decor (tropical fish duvets and olive green shag carpet). Abseiling and canyon rafting from $45. Rides to trailheads $2. Free luggage storage. Bike hire $25 per day. Linen $1. Key deposit $10. Reception daily 9am-noon and 5-9pm (winter 5-8pm). Tentsites $10, weekly $63; dorms $15-17, $90; twins and doubles $50, $300. YHA, VIP.

**Gearin Hotel,** 273 Great Western Hwy (☎4782 4395). Behind the train station. Raucous pub and gaming lounge downstairs make it rather noisy (live entertainment W, F-Sa). Free lockers and comforters. Dorms $16.50; singles $27.50; doubles $55.

**Katoomba Falls Caravan Park,** on Katoomba Falls Rd (☎4782 1835). South of town via Katoomba St. Well-positioned for several bushwalks and the Scenic Skyway and Scenic Railway. Toilets, hot showers, indoor BBQ area. No linen. Key deposit $20. Reception daily 8am-6pm. Sites $12 per person, families $26; powered for 2 $26.40, family $30; ensuite cabins for 2 $81, each extra person $10.

## 🛒 🎵 FOOD AND ENTERTAINMENT

Katoomba St is littered with cafés, takeaways, and nicer restaurants serving a variety of cuisines at all price levels. The **Blues Café,** 55-57 Katoomba St, serves high-class veggie cuisine. (☎4782 2347. Open daily 9am-5:30pm. Meals $7-11.) **Tom's Eats,** 200 Katoomba St, is the best food-for-dollar value in town, serving specialty milkshakes, pizza, burgers, spicy chicken dishes, and pastas. (☎4782 3182. Open Su, Tu-Th 11am-9pm, F-Sa 11am-10pm. Meals $5-8. Delivery W-Su.) **Siam Cuisine,** 172 Katoomba St, has spicy, delicious Thai food and $6 lunch specials. (☎4782 5671. Open Tu-Su 11:30am-2:30pm and 5:30-10pm. BYO.) Coles **supermarket** is next to K-Mart on Parke St (open daily 6am-midnight).

Katoomba's nightlife revolves around two main downtown pubs. The **Gearin Hotel,** 273 Great Western Hwy (☎4782 6028), can get rowdy. The crowd varies in age but tends to be more alternative than other nightspots in town. On Wednesdays, the Gearin hosts a very popular local band Jam Night. The tamer, more yuppie option, is the **Carrington Hotel,** 15-47 Katoomba St, where the crowds sway to Top-40 and dance hits. If you lack rhythm, try the billiards and two separate bars. (☎4782 1111. DJs F-Sa. Nightclub upstairs open F-Sa until 4 am. Cover $5.)

The **Edge Maxvision Cinema,** 225 Great Western Hwy, projects *The Edge,* a 38min. film on the Blue Mountains, onto a six-story screen. The movie takes viewers to several places in the mountains that cannot be accessed by visitors, including the secret grove where the recently-discovered Wollemi pine species grows. The cinema also shows other giant-format films and screens recent feature films every evening. (☎4782 8900. *Edge:* Six shows daily 10am-5:45pm. $13.50, concessions $11.50. Other films: $12.50, Tu $7.)

**NEW SOUTH WALES**

**FUN WITH TRIPLETS** According to Aboriginal legend, Katoomba's Three Sisters are more than just pretty rocks; they are beautiful maidens trapped since the Dreamtime (the Aboriginal time of creation) in stone pillars. Once upon a time, three exquisite sisters lived at home with their father, the Witchdoctor of their Katoomba tribe. Word of their beauty spread far and wide, reaching three brothers of the Nepean tribe, who were so enamored that they simply had to marry the mistresses. Ancestral law prohibited the women from marrying outside their tribe. Undaunted by this obstacle, the brothers attempted to capture their objects of affection by force and waged war on the Katoomba tribe. The Katoombans were no match for the mighty Nepeans; when the Witchdoctor realized this, he magically transformed his daughters to stone for protection. The sisters awaited the end of the war and their father's return. But the Witchdoctor of Katoomba fell in battle, and his daughters are still waiting at Echo Point for someone to release them from their imprisonment...

## ◣ LOOKOUTS, WALKS, AND ACTIVITIES

**ECHO POINT.** Nearly everyone ventures out to Echo Point on the southernmost tip of town to take in the tectonic majesty of the **Three Sisters** cliff line. From dusk until 10:30pm, strategically placed floodlights lend new brilliance to these three golden sisters. From Echo Point, the steep and taxing 860-step **Giant Stairway Walk** makes a dramatic descent to the floor of the Jamison Valley down the back of the Three Sisters to meet the **Federal Pass trail.** The Federal Pass snakes its way through the trees in the valley, passing Cook's Crossing picnic area at the base of **Katoomba Falls** and continuing on past **Orphan Rock,** a beautiful free-standing pillar that erosion has separated from the nearby cliff. Just beyond Orphan Rock are two ways to get back to civilization: the **Furber Steps** (30min.; moderate, 1040 steps), and the **Scenic Railway** (5km; 2½hr; moderate). The passage to the Steps winds through overhanging sandstone and clay rock formations, past the spray of waterfalls, and through rainforest foliage.

**SCENIC RAILWAY.** The Scenic Railway is a tourist attraction in its own right since it is the **world's most steeply inclined railway**—hold on tight; there are no seatbelts. Originally for hauling coal, it's now a short rollercoaster through Jamison Valley's rainforest scenery. Many bus tours and individual travelers approach the railway from Katoomba Falls Rd and take the short trip. For hikers coming from either the Federal Pass or the Ruined Castle Track (see below), the ride is a restful way to cover the last 250 vertical meters after a long day-hike. (☎4782 2699. Open daily 9am-5pm; last ride 4:50pm. Return 7min.; one-way $3, return $8.) The **Scenic Skyway** is a cable gondola that departs from the Scenic Railway station for a quick trip over Katoomba Falls Gorge. Go in the morning or afternoon to avoid crowds. (☎4782 2699. Open daily 9am-5pm; last ride 4:50pm. Return 7min., $5.)

**NARROW NECK PLATEAU.** On the west side of town, the easy walk along Narrow Neck Plateau beyond the gate on Glenraphael Dr leads to fabulous views of the Megalong and Jamison Valleys on either side of the clifftop trail. Before the gate, about 1km out onto the plateau from Cliff Dr, the **Golden Stairs** run down the cliff face to the Ruined Castle Track. The walk to **Ruined Castle** (8km; 5hr. return including the Stairs), a distinctive rock formation reminiscent of crumbling turrets, is difficult. At the Ruined Castle, a short climb to the top yields views straight across the valley to distant parts of the Blue Mountains and Kanangra-Boyd National Parks. Because of the stairs' taxing grade, many walkers tack on an extra 1hr. and walk east to the Furber Steps or the Scenic Railway on the return trip.

**TOURS.** Several companies in Katoomba organize adventure activity trips throughout the Blue Mountains, from guided bushwalking to **abseiling** (rappelling) and **canyoning** (abseiling and swimming in the area's unique sandstone caves). The

**Australian School of Mountaineering,** 166B Katoomba St, inside the Paddy Pallin outdoor shop, offers the best resources and introductory courses. Book ahead. (☎4782 2014; www.ausmtn.com.au. Open daily 8:15am-5:30pm. Abseiling $99, concessions $89; canyoning Oct.-Apr. only, from $100 per day.) **High 'n' Wild Mountain Adventures,** 3/5 Katoomba St, across from the train station, also offers many packages. (☎4782 6224; www.high-n-wild.com.au. Open daily 8am-5:30pm. Mountain bike tours: half-day from $65, full-day $115; abseiling $55, $99; year-round canyoning courses from $99.) For an unbeatable guided **ecotour,** try **Tread Lightly** (☎4788 1229; www.treadlightly.com.au. Bushwalk, midnight hike, or 4WD.)

The **Blue Mountains Highlights Tour** covers the area's star attractions. (24hr. ☎4782 1866. 3hr.; 3 per day; $36, concessions $28, families $80.) The same guide runs tours to **Jenolan Caves** (see p. 146), including views of Echo Point and Govett's Leap (3hr.; $60, $52, $160). Overnight trips to the caves, not including accommodation or cave tours, cost $40 each way (families $105). Serious hikers might want to combine a one-way ticket with 2-3 days of walking and camping on the poorly-named **Six Foot Track,** actually a 42km trail from Jenolan Caves to Nellies Glen Rd off the Great Western Hwy at the west end of Katoomba.

# BLACKHEATH

Behind the facade of restaurants, pubs, and upscale shops lining the highway, Blackheath is a small, friendly, and residential town in a great location. To the northeast of this plateau-top town lies the beautiful Grose Valley, which offers many of the area's best lookouts and most challenging walks. The Megalong Valley to the south of the town is popular for horseback riding. Given its prime position between these two areas and its easy accessibility, Blackheath is a natural choice as a Blue Mountains base, though its services are more limited than Katoomba's.

**⊟ TRANSPORT.** The Great Western Hwy snakes 11km west and north from Katoomba to the town of Blackheath on the way to Mt. Victoria and Lithgow. Mountainlink runs **buses** from **Katoomba** to **Mt. Victoria** by way of Blackheath, coming as close as possible to the town's major trailheads. (☎4782 3333. Service M-F 7:30am-6pm, Sa 6:30am-4:30pm; from $4.) Blackheath is on the convenient **CityRail** runs to: **Sydney** (2½hr., 15-20 per day, $12); **Glenbrook** (1hr., 15-22 per day, $70); **Katoomba** (11min., 15-23 per day, $4); **Lithgow** (30min., 12 per day, $5); **Parramatta** (2hr., 15-20 per day, $10); and **Penrith** (1¼hr., 15-20 per day, $8).

**⚑ PRACTICAL INFORMATION.** Pure tourist information falls under the auspices of **Blue Mountains Tourism,** at Echo Point, Katoomba (☎(1300) 65 34 08). The **Blue Mountains Heritage Centre,** at the end of Govett's Leap Rd just inside the national park, is the main NPWS visitors center for the Blue Mountains. Staffed by park officials who know their stuff, it also carries detailed trail guidebooks ($2-4). (☎4787 8877. Open daily 9am-4:30pm.)

**⌂⌂ ACCOMMODATIONS AND FOOD.** The **New Ivanhoe Hotel,** at the corner of the Great Western Hwy and Govett's Leap Rd, has clean, tasteful, and not-at-all-pub-like rooms. (☎4787 8158. Reception at bar 6am-midnight, later F-Sa. Twins and doubles $66, ensuite $88; light breakfast included.) The tent camping area at **Blackheath Caravan Park,** on Prince Edward St off Govett's Leap Rd, lies in a tree-covered grove secluded from the rest of the park and down a steep hill. (☎4787 8101. Reception daily 8am-7pm. Toilets, showers, BBQ. Key deposit $10. Sites $8.80 per person, powered $12.10; trailers for 2 $42, each extra person $5.) The nearest **free national park camping areas** are at **Perry's Lookdown,** at the end of the partially paved Hat Hill Rd, 8km from the Great Western Hwy; and at **Acacia Flat,** on the floor of the Grose Valley, a hefty 4hr. hike from Govett's Leap (shorter from Perry's Lookdown). Both sites have pit toilets and no other facilities. Water from Govett's Creek is available at Acacia Flat, but it must be treated before use.

If small Blackeath is too big for you, head 7km west on the Great Western Hwy to **Mt. Victoria,** a quiet village that serves as an alternate Blue Mountains base. It has several historical buildings, including **Manor House,** on Montgomery St, the former summer home of John Fairfax, built in 1876. **Victoria and Albert Guesthouse,** 19 Station St, has a pool, spa, and sauna. (☎4787 1241. B&B with shared bath Su-Th $50, F-Sa $66.)

Blackheath's limited food options line the Great Western Hwy. Among the small eateries, the **Wattle Café,** 240 Great Western Hwy, serves breakfast all day. (☎4787 8153. Open daily 7:30am-7pm. Burgers from $4.)

▨ **HIKES AND LOOKOUTS.** Walks in the Blackheath area vary widely in length and level of difficulty. The **Fairfax Heritage Walk** (2km; 1hr.) is a wheelchair-accessible alternative to the 350m drive between the Blue Mountains Heritage Centre and **Govett's Leap,** one of the most magnificent lookouts in the national park. From Govett's Leap, the moderate walk to the lookout at **Pulpit Rock** (3hr.; 5km) follows the cliff line north for an almost non-stop display of breathtaking views of the grand canyon of the Grose Valley. Following the moderate cliffs in the other direction to **Evans Lookout** (2hr.; 3km) leads past the majestic **Bridal Veil Falls,** a thin and wispy stream that takes nearly 10 seconds to tumble to the valley below. Since most of Blackheath's walks start at Govett's Leap or Evans Lookout, this walk allows you to connect to others, thereby sampling Blackheath's best in but a day.

One of two possible trailheads for the popular **Grand Canyon** hike, Evans Lookout gives way to a manageable descent to the canyon floor. The trail then runs along Greaves Creek through the wet, forested, narrow canyon and up to **Neates Glen,** the other possible entry point. A short walk on the unpaved portion of Evans Lookout Rd completes the moderate circuit back to Evans Lookout (4hr.; 5km).

From the Great Western Hwy, Hat Hill Rd runs parallel to Govett's Leap Rd, which leads north of town to **Perry's Lookdown,** then branches off to the superb lookout at **Anvil Rock.** Perry's Lookdown provides the steepest descent into the valley 600m below; a difficult trail from the valley leads to the beautiful **Blue Gum Forest** (2½hr.; 2.5km). Once at the forest, another option is to turn toward Govett's Leap and make a full day of walking through the forest along Govett's Creek; this strenuous walk is more appropriate in summer when the days are longer (10hr. using cliff-top track and Hat Hill Rd circuit).

The **scenic drive** (there's no public transport) into the **Megalong Valley** begins on Shipley Rd, across the Great Western Hwy from Govett's Leap Rd. Cross the railroad tracks from the highway and take an immediate left onto Station St, following it until it turns right to become Shipley Rd. Megalong Rd is a left turn from Shipley Rd, leading down to a picturesque farmland area that contrasts nicely with the surrounding wilderness. In the valley, outfitters conduct guided **trail rides** or supply horses. **Werriberri Trail Rides** is on Megalong Rd near Werriberri Lodge. (☎4787 9171. Open daily 9am-3:30pm; reservations 7:30am-8:30pm. 30min. $19, 3hr. $57.) The **Megalong Australian Heritage Centre,** a bit farther south on Megalong Rd, has longer guided rides, unguided outings, livestock lassoing shows, and 4WD forays into the bush. (☎4787 8188. Open daily 8:30am-6pm. Horse rides daily 10am-4pm. 3hr. ride with lunch $82, full-day $95. Unguided: $25 for first hr., each additional hr. $22. 4WD $25 per hr.)

# JENOLAN CAVES

The amazing limestone and crystal formations of Jenolan ("Je-NO-lan") Caves, on Jenolan Caves Rd, 45km south of the Great Western Hwy from Hartley, have beguiled visitors since first introduced to the general public in 1838. The caves can be reached by bus from Katoomba (see p. 141). The cave system, overseen by the **Jenolan Caves Reserve Trust,** contains nine open caves, accessible through the trust's extensive program of **guided tours,** and many more unexplored recesses. (☎6359 3311; www.jenolancaves.org.au. Ticket office open daily 9am-5pm, winter 9am-4:30pm. M-F 14 tours per day, Sa-Su 25; $13-22.) Because it displays a broad range of features seen throughout the caves, **Lucas Cave** is generally presented as the place to start but is rather touristy, and the large crowds detract somewhat from the experience (1½hr. tour, $13). **Orient Cave** and **Imperial Cave** both have a more tolerable flow of visitors as well as several eye-catching rock formations (Orient: 1½hr., $17; Imperial: 1hr., $13). The **Temple of Baal** is under-visited in spite of its delightful jagged patterns. Three **arches** are open for unguided viewing as well; ask for a map of the area from the tour ticket office. Orient Cave and **Chifley Cave** are partially wheelchair accessible. **Adventure tours** run by the Trust take small groups (limited to 8-12 people) through some of the cave system's less accessible areas—the hard way. These tours involve moderate to strenuous climbing, some crawling, and a healthy dose of darkness. The minimum age for adventure tours is generally 16, although ages 10+ can head into **Elder Cave.** The Trust also offers theme tours through areas that other tours don't cover, such as ghost tours and off-track adventures with miner's lights and overalls (2-8hr., from $50).

## KANANGRA-BOYD NATIONAL PARK

The 68,000 hectares that comprise Kanangra-Boyd National Park awe with stark wilderness punctuated by rivers and creeks, still-developing caves, and the dramatic sandstone cliffs that mark the edges of the Boyd Plateau. The park's remote location and rugged terrain attract serious bushwalkers looking for long-term solitude. The park is nonetheless worthwhile for the casual visitors who follow its only 2WD road across the **Boyd Plateau** to the famous lookouts at **Kanangra Walls.**

Sandwiched between sections of Blue Mountains National Park to the east and south, Kanangra-Boyd National Park extends one small arm north to nearly surround Jenolan Caves. A dirt road continues from the end of Jenolan Caves Rd, entering Kanangra-Boyd only 5km past the caves. This path, through Jenolan Caves from the Great Western Hwy, is the only car-accessible eastern approach to the park. From the west, another road also called Jenolan Caves Rd and paved for only half its length, comes in from the town of **Oberon.** These roads meet at the edge of the park to become Kanangra Walls Rd, the direct 26km route to the cliff-top lookout of the same name. The **National Parks and Wildlife Service** office, 38 Ross St, Oberon, has details on the park's longer tracks; be sure to call before visiting or you may find the branch unattended. Cave exploration permits must be obtained at least four weeks in advance. (☎ 6336 1972. Open M-F 9am-4:30pm.)

The **Boyd River Campground,** on Kanangra Walls Rd 5km before Kanangra Walls, has the park's only car-accessible camping. There are pit toilets, potable water from the Boyd River (boil before drinking), and fireplaces (bring wood and fuel). There is no fee for camping throughout the park, but bushcampers must follow two rules: stay 500m from any major path and always minimize your impact.

Three **scenic walks** begin at the Kanangra Walls carpark. **Lookout Walk** (20min. return) is a wheelchair-accessible path leading first to the lookout over the Kanangra Creek gorge and then to the view over the eight-tiered 400m **Kanangra Falls.** The **Waterfall Walk** (20min. one-way with steep return) leads from the second lookout to the deep pool at the bottom of **Kalang Falls.** The moderate **Plateau Walk** (2hr.) branches from the Lookout Walk between the parking lot and the first lookout, descending briefly from the plateau before ascending to Kanangra Tops for views of Kanangra Walls. Along the way, **Dance Floor Cave** contains indented floors and other signs of old-time recreation in the park. A water container placed in the cave in 1940 catches pure, drinkable water dripping from the cave ceiling. Longer walks, like the overnight trip to **Batsch Camp** (pit toilets, no water), on the park's southern border, should be planned in advance with help from the Oberon NPWS.

## BELLS LINE OF ROAD

The difference between taking the Great Western Hwy and taking Bells Line of Road through the Blue Mountains is similar to the difference between setting out to get drunk with a tumbler of cheap gin and doing so with a bottle of fine wine. You wind up in the same place, but one route allows you to savor the experience a bit more along the way. This 87km drive between Windsor and Lithgow provides rambling, scenic passage through the mountains, perfect if you have a little time.

**KURRAJONG HEIGHTS.** At the top of the Heights, 16km west of Richmond, the **Kurrajong Heights Grass Ski Park** rents specially designed "grass karts" (made of little more than a board, four rubber wheels, and a hand brake) and grass skis, both of which allow you to careen down a mountainside regardless of the weather or season. An uphill lift ensures that visitors get the most out of their time. (☎4567 7184. Open Sa-Su and public holidays 9am-5pm. 1hr. $11, each extra hour $6.)

**BILPIN.** The town of Bilpin, 5km west of Kurrajong Heights, has several active orchards and roadside fruit stands that sell fresh-picked produce most of the year. The **Pines Orchard** allows travelers to pick their own fruit—peaches, plums, nectarines, and apples as in season. (☎4567 1195. Open daily 8am-5pm.)

**MT. TOMAH BOTANIC GARDEN.** A couple kilometers west of Berambing, Mt. Tomah Botanic Garden is the cool-climate and high-altitude plant collection of Sydney's Royal Botanic Garden. The plants thrive on the rich volcanic soil and grow in naturalistic arrangements, with the exception of the herbs and roses in the formal terrace garden. The garden's best moments are in spring (Sept.-Nov.), when the large collection of rhododendrons and other flowers bloom, and in autumn (Mar.-May) when the deciduous forest areas change their colors. Free tours depart the visitors center during the week. (☎4567 2154. Open daily Mar.-Sept. 10am-4pm, Oct.-Feb. 10am-5pm. Entrance fee $6 per car, $3 per pedestrian or cyclist.)

**MT. WILSON.** People come from far and wide to see the formal, European-style gardens and unspoiled rainforest of the small town of Mt. Wilson, 8km north of Bells Line of Road, between Mt. Tomah and Bell. For a sample of the fern-laden rainforest, turn right onto Queens Ave off the main road through town and proceed about 500m until you reach a park area on the left. From there, follow signs to a moderate 45min. circular walk (steep steps) that leads to the base of two small waterfalls. Three gardens stay open throughout the year: **Sefton Cottage,** on Church Ln (☎4756 2034; open daily 10am-6pm; $3); **Merry Garth,** on Davies Ln, 500m from Mt. Irvine Rd (☎4756 2121; open daily Sept.-Nov. and Apr.-May 9am-6pm, call for times during other months; $3); and **Lindfield Park,** on Mt. Irvine Rd, 6km northeast of Mt. Wilson (☎4756 2148; open daily 10am-6pm; $3).

**ZIG ZAG RAILWAY.** The Zig Zag Railway, 10km east of Lithgow at Clarence, is a functional train operating on a piece of the 1869 track that first made regular travel possible across the Blue Mountains and down into the Lithgow Valley. (☎6351 4826. 1½hr.; 3-4 per day; $14 return, concessions $11, ages 5-18 $7.) By request, CityRail **trains** from Sydney's Central Station stop near the bottom of the track ($13).

# WOLLEMI NATIONAL PARK

New South Wales's largest remaining wilderness area, Wollemi ("WO-lem-eye") National Park, sprawls from the Blue Mountains in the south to the Hunter and Goulburn River valleys in the north. There are relatively few access points to the park, and 4WD is recommended as the unsealed roads leading to the trail are narrow and long. With limited vehicle access and a largely undeveloped interior, the park still has many pockets of undiscovered land. One such area yielded an amazing find in 1994, when scientists found a species of pine tree that was a close relative to pines previously seen only in fossil form. Although the location of the **Wollemi Pine** grove is a closely-guarded secret, most visitors find the park's deep forests, sandstone gorges, and rainforests sufficiently unique and awe-inspiring. Entrance and campgrounds are free. Those who wish to camp outside of designated sites should be aware that **quicksand** and fickle weather accompany any trip into the depths of the Wollemi. Attempts to cross the park on extended week-long trips should only be made in a latitudinal direction. North-south passes are available to those equipped to handle many rock climbs and abseils.

The southernmost entrance point is at Bilpin on Bells Line of Road. In this corner of the park, also accessible from Putty Rd north of Windsor, the **Colo River** slices the landscape along the 30km Colo Gorge. The car-accessible **camping area** at **Wheeny Creek** lies near good walking tracks and swimming holes. The nearest **National Parks and Wildlife Service** information office, 370 Windsor Rd, is in Richmond. (☎4588 5247. Open M-F 9:30am-12:30pm and 1:30-5pm.)

Farther west, roads from Lithgow and Wallerawang enter the park at **Newnes.** The moderately difficult **Newnes Historic Ruins Track** (5km; 3hr.) tours the remains of the oil shale mining village along the banks of the Wolgan River. The large, unserviced camping area and the rocky faces which surround the Wolgan Valley make Newnes one of Wollemi's more popular stops. A 37km unsealed road from Lithgow takes starry-eyed observers within 1.5km of **Glow Worm Tunnel**, an abandoned railway tunnel housing hundreds of tiny bioluminescent worms. Be sure to bring a flashlight; keep in mind that what you're looking at is not a beautiful constellation but a wall plastered with shining excrement. The Tunnel can also be reached by a walking track from Newnes (22km return). **Capertee Valley** is the second largest enclosed valley in the world, after the USA's Grand Canyon. The area is home to more birds per square kilometer than anywhere in the Southern Hemisphere. **Lithgow Visitors Centre,** 1 Cooerwull Rd, off the Great Western Hwy in Lithgow, has maps and info. (☎6353 1859; fax 6353 1851. Open daily 9am-5pm.)

The **Mudgee NPWS office,** 160 Church St, administers the northwest section of the park, including the **campground** at **Dunn's Swamp,** 1½hr. from Mudgee by way of Rylstone. (☎6372 7199; fax 6372 7850. Open M-F 8:30am-4:30pm.) From Mudgee, roads (some paved) arc along the park's north edge to Bulga in the northeast. Along the way, they dip into the park, providing access to breathtaking views of the **Widden Valley** and the creeks which lace the region. These routes often pass through private property, however. Inquire at the **Bulga NPWS office** on Putty Rd before venturing into this part of the park. (☎6574 5275; fax 6574 5274. Open Tu-Th 8:30am-4pm.) There are no marked trails in the northern section of Wollemi National Park; bushwalkers should carry a compass and a topographic map available at the Bulga NPWS office. South of Bulga, Putty Rd traces the east edge of the park with several 4WD access points along the way.

# LITHGOW

The Great Western Hwy and Bells Line of Road meet on the west side of the Blue Mountains at Lithgow, a medium-sized, vaguely industrial town, at the end of the Sydney's CityRail train line. Once a center for steel production, the town has little charm beyond its utility for exploring nearby wilderness areas such as Wollemi National Park to the north and the Jenolan Caves and Kanangra-Boyd National Park to the south.

**⌨☎ TRANSPORT AND PRACTICAL INFORMATION.** Lithgow is 40km west of Katoomba and 61km east of Bathurst on the Great Western Hwy. **Trains** stop at the Main St station. CityRail and Countrylink (☎13 20 32) **train** and **bus** services head to: **Sydney** (2½hr., 12-14 per day, $25.30); **Bathurst** (1¼hr., 1-5 per day, $11); **Blackheath** (30min., 11-15 per day, $4.40); **Dubbo** (3½hr., 4 per week, $42); **Forbes** and **Parkes** (4hr., 6 per week, $40); **Katoomba** (45min., 11-14 per day, $5.50); **Mudgee** (2½hr., 1-2 per day, $22, reservations required); **Orange** (2½hr., 1-5 per day, $22); and **Parramatta** and **Penrith** (2¼hr., 12-15 per day, $15.40-22). The **Lithgow Visitor Information Centre,** 1 Cooerwull Rd, occupies the old Bowenfels Railway Station, off the Great Western Hwy at the Bathurst end of town. (☎6353 1859; fax 6353 1851. Open daily 9am-5pm.) **Post office:** on Main St across from the train station (☎6351 3562. Open M-F 9am-5pm.) **Postal code:** 2790.

**⌨☎ ACCOMMODATIONS AND FOOD. Grand Central Hotel,** 69 Main St, is the pick of the litter with its spacious singles and TV lounge. Take a left out of the train station and walk two blocks. (☎6351 3050. Singles $23.) The **pub** and adjacent **bistro** are pleasant. (Open daily noon-2pm and 6-9pm.) **Turon Gates** has affordable lodging, and with horse riding, canoeing, swimming, and biking, it is almost impossible to run out of things to do. From Lithgow, follow signs to Mudgee until you hit Capertee and the turn-off for Turon. (☎6359 0142. Camping $15 per car. Cabins $26

NEW SOUTH WALES

per person, minimum 3 people.) For camping, try **Lithgow Caravan Park,** 58 Cooerwull Rd, with clean showers and laundry. (☎6351 4350. Reception daily 8am-7pm. Sites $12, powered $16. On-site caravans for 2 $39.)

At **Sand-Witches at the Plaza,** 117 Main St, your mouth will water over the sandwich combos from $3.50-$7.50. (☎6353 1066. Open M-F 7:30am-5pm, Sa 8:30am-2pm.) The **Blue Bird Café,** 118 Main St, prepares huge omelets and great milkshakes. (☎6352 4211. Open daily 6:30am-7:30pm.) The Food For Less **grocery store** is on Railway Pde. (☎6352 2011. Open M-Sa 7am-10pm, Su 7am-6pm.)

◪ **SIGHTS. Blackfellows Hands Reserve,** 24km north of Lithgow, off Wolgen Road to Newnes, was a meeting place for Aboriginal tribes, and paintings adorn the walls of the cave. **Gardens of Stone National Park,** 30km north of Lithgow, features pagoda-like formations from millions of years of erosion. The highest lookout in the Blue Mountains (1130m) is indisputably worth the 5min. detour along the **Hassans Walls Link** drive. The spectacular granite formations of **Evans Crown Nature Reserve** (☎6354 8155), 32km west of Lithgow, is a climbers' playground.

# NEW ENGLAND

A lovely, scenic alternative to the coast, with simple beauty and a cooler year-round climate, the New England Hwy branches west from the Pacific Hwy in Newcastle and continues along Hwy 15 to Brisbane. Most of this 566km stretch of road is dotted with inviting country towns serviced by many of the area's major bus lines. The highway traverses the Hunter Valley, along west of Maitland (tantalizingly close to the vineyards), past Singleton's army base and mines, and through Muswellbrook's coal mines and Scone's horse stud farms, lapsing into Tenterfield's nature reserves. It then begins the dramatic climb up the Dividing Range from Tamworth to Armidale, in New England proper. The national parks in New England (clustered in southern Queensland and northern New South Wales) are worth re-routing an itinerary. Unfortunately, most are only accessible by vehicle (some only by 4WD), although there are companies attempting to start cheap shuttle service; call the Armidale Visitors Centre (☎6772 4655) for an update.

## HUNTER VALLEY

Although the notion of budget travel seems like it should simply not apply to the Hunter Valley, one of the world's premiere wine regions, it is easily possible. The Hunter is home to over 80 wineries, packed together like sardines—but with a much finer aroma and taste. The region specializes in the almost uniquely Australian Shiraz, a spicy, peppery number (known sometimes as Syrah outside Australia). The area's international reputation comes from its vast options—the dry Semillion, the varietal Chardonnays, through more standard Merlots, Cabernet Sauvignons, and on and on. Most of the wineries are in the lower Hunter, clustered northwest of Cessnock; nine are in the upper Hunter, centered in Denman, 1hr. northwest. Paying tribute to the Hunter Valley's heavenly nectars is a mandatory part of any coastal itinerary. For other Aussie wine regions, see Barossa Valley SA, p. 440; Rutherglen VIC, p. 591; and Yarra Valley VIC, p. 543.

Some traveling tips: don't be tempted to buy a wine because it's won an award. The efficient tourism industry has created enough competitions that virtually every winery has been recognized for some "outstanding" achievement. Find your own taste. Many a so-called expert's sobriquet is mere snobbery. Let your own palette be your guide and don't shy away from individuality. Finally, the narrow roads, high-speed traffic, and random police search points and breathalyzers don't mix well with wine. Be smart: choose a designated driver, or hop on one of the inexpensive, informative day tours.

# ▐ TRANSPORT AND TOURS

The best time to visit wine country is mid-week, when both population and prices are lower than on the weekends. By car, Cessnock is 30km west of the Sydney-Newcastle Fwy along Aberdare Rd. Countrylink (☎ 13 22 32) choo-choos daily from **Sydney** to **Scone** (4½hr., $45) via **Muswellbrook** (3½hr., $39). Return to Sydney daily at 1:18pm (arriving at 5pm). Keans Travel Express (☎ (1800) 04 33 39) departs from Bay 14 in Sydney Central Station's coach terminal (M-Sa 3pm, F also 6pm, Su 6:40pm) en route to: **Cessnock** (2¼hr., $24); **Singleton** (2¾hr., $28); **Muswellbrook** (3½hr., $31); and **Scone** (3¾hr., $37). Rover Motors, 231 Vincent St (☎ 4990 1699), in **Cessnock**, shuttles to **Newcastle** throughout the day (1¼hr.; M-Sa only; $9).

Unless you have a car, you'll need to book a tour to see the wineries. Each of the various companies picks up and drops off at all area accommodations. The usually 10- to 20-person tours generally last from 10am to 5pm and visit around five wineries. The **Vineyard Shuttle Service** is cheapest, and is run by an entertaining and informative tee-totaler who lets his passengers suggest wineries rather than following a strict itinerary. (☎ 4991 3655. $20, with evening restaurant transfer $28). **Shadows** tours a variety of both boutique and large, commercial wineries, and offers door-to-door bus service for Newcastle and surrounding addresses. (☎ 4990 7002. $30, with lunch $48.) **Hunter Vineyard Tours** (☎ 4991 1659) picks up from Cessnock ($34, with lunch $50) and Newcastle and Maitland ($39, $55). **Trekabout** creates a more intimate setting with tours limited to six people. (☎ 4990 8277. Half-day $25, full-day $40). **Bicycle rental** is available from the **Hermitage Lodge** in Pokolbin. (☎ 4998 7639. Half-day $15, full-day $25). **Horse-drawn carriage tours** are available through **Paxton Brown** (☎ 4998 7362) and **Brokenback Trail Tour** (☎ 4998 7305) and begin at $48. Alternatively, **Hertz**, 1A Aberdare Rd (☎ 4991 2500), is the only car rental company in Cessnock. For safety's sake, remember **taxis** (☎ 4991 1659).

Several companies offer daytrips from Sydney. **Wonderbus** runs straight to the Hunter. (☎ 9555 9800. $100, with lunch $120.) **Oz Trails** throws in Lake Macquarie and the Hawkesbury River. (☎ 9387 8390. $99.) **Hunter Valley Day Tours** (☎ 4938 5031) does Sydney group pickup by arrangement.

## WINERIES

Most wineries are open for free tastings and occasional tours daily 10am-5pm (some 9:30am-4:30pm), although some of the smaller ones are only open on weekends. Of the 80-plus wineries, the largest are **McGuigan's, Lindemans, Tyrrell's, Drayton's, Rothbury Estate, Wyndham Estate,** and **McWilliams-Mount Pleasant Estate.** The smaller ones, called "boutiques," only sell the wines they produce on their private premises. They are not as glitzy but are generally more relaxed. Check with the Cessnock visitors center (see **Cessnock,** below) about free tours of individual wineries. Wine prices start around $10-12 and move up with age and flavor.

## CESSNOCK AND THE LOWER HUNTER VALLEY

Most visitors to the Hunter only stay in the lower valley, the closest and most-accessible part of the valley to Sydney and Newcastle.

▐▌ **ORIENTATION AND PRACTICAL INFORMATION.** The best and most popular launching point to see the vineyards is the centrally-located town of **Cessnock.** The well-marked **Cessnock Visitors Centre,** 1.2km off Vincent St on Aberdare Rd in Turner Park, has oodles of info on the wineries and weekly specials on accommodations and meals. It also books most tours and lodging. (☎ 4990 4477; fax 4991 4518; email info@www.winecountry.com.au. Open M-F 9am-5pm, Sa 9:30am-5pm, Su 9:30am-3:30pm.) Don't leave without the indispensable (and free) *Hunter Valley Wine Country* booklet, covering every wine-affiliated option and containing all-important guide maps. The visitors center also has a wheelchair mobility map covering the entire Cessnock area and wineries.

## MATH SURE IS HARD WITH A HANGOVER

One ton of grapes—once squished, crunched, and processed—yields roughly 1000 bottles of wine. The typical acre in the Hunter Valley yields 3.5 tons in a good year. Thus, even the smaller wineries of thirty acres can produce upwards of 70,000 bottles per vintage. The cooler climes of more southerly regions, like the Barossa Valley SA (p. 440) and the Yarra Valley VIC (p. 543), produce 5-6 tons per acre. Ever at its immodest best, the Hunter Valley is quick to claim quality over quantity. The real success of the region is probably more its proximity to Sydney—but the wines are still damn good.

**Maitland** is 30min. east of Cessnock along the Hunter River. An historic city, it once rivaled Sydney as a potential state capital. The **Visitor's Information Centre** is in Ministers Park, near the junction of High St and the New England Hwy. (☎4933 2611; email maitland.tourism@maitland.nsw.gov.au. Open daily 9am-5pm.)

**⌐⌐ ACCOMMODATIONS AND FOOD.** The **Chardonnay Sky Motel,** 210 Allandale Rd, about a 10min. drive north of town, has the best atmosphere of the accommodations options. Motel rooms are $20 cheaper if you tandem sky dive next door. People are always dropping in here. (☎4991 4812; fax 4991 2259. Backpacker heated bunks $20; spacious ensuite motel doubles with TV $59, weekends $95; continental breakfast included. Wheelchair accessible.) **Cessnock Caravan Park,** on O'Connors Rd near the intersection of Allandale Rd and about five minutes north of town, has a pool, BBQ, and a wheelchair accessible cabin. (☎4990 5819; fax 4991 2944. Tent sites $7; on-site caravans $35; cabins $55, weekends $65-70.) If these are booked, the pubstays in Cessnock charge about $20 for singles.

At the **Tallawanta Hotel and Motel,** on Broke Rd, you can cook your own meat for $10-16 including an unlimited salad and pasta bar. (☎4998 7819. Open daily 11:30am-3pm and 6-9pm. $8.50 for salad and pasta bar only.) **Amico's,** 138 Wollombi Rd, specializes in Italian, Mediterranean, and Mexican food; its huge servings of pasta on Monday are the best deal in town. (☎4911 1995. Open daily from 6pm, also F 11:30am-2:30pm. Delivery. BYO.) **Hunter Gourmet Pizza,** 146 Vincent St, is open later and delivers. (☎4990 8883. Pizzas $7-13.) Coles **supermarket** is at the intersection of Wollombi and Allandale Rd.

**WINERIES OF THE LOWER HUNTER VALLEY.** The vineyards of the lower Hunter are spread on close-knit tangled roads, so the free map from the Cessnock visitors center is the best way to navigate. Even so, the entire area is well-signposted, and large billboard maps are located at the major intersections. You couldn't ask for a better starting point than **Tyrrell's** (☎4993 7000). The enigmatic, self-deprecating guides give 1hr. free tours daily at 1:30pm revealing the entire wine-making process of the 141-year-old family business. They don't skimp on filling your glass at the free tastings, so make sure you keep in mind the other stops. **McGuigan's** (☎4998 7402) is an all-purpose stop. Alongside the great vines, they also have a cheese shop with free tastings; a souvenir shop with wine accessories at tourist-inflated prices; and a cheap bakery with fudge, pies, and pasties to keep you going. **Wyndham Estate** (☎4938 3444) has by far the nicest tasting room: a huge space with wine casks for tables. **Petersons Champagne House** (☎4998 7881) is the only place in New South Wales strictly devoted to the bubbly, including an interesting selection of sparkling red wines. The 1998 sparkling Merlot has a good smoky aftertaste, with only a light lilt of bubbly in the body. Who would have thought the **Golden Grape Estate** has sprawling grounds for a stroll between swigs? It also hosts a German-inspired Octoberfest in the fall. **Pepper Tree Winery** (☎4998 7539; www.peppertreewines.com.au) is another great choice. If you'd like a running start on wine tasting, take a lesson at **Hunter Cellars School of Wine.** (☎4998 7466. Th-Su 10am-12:30pm. $20.)

**ACTIVITIES.** The expansive views and adrenaline rush are well worth the cost at **NSW Skydiving Centre** (☎4990 1000) at the Chardonnay Sky Motel, 210 Allendale Rd ($265; with 2 nights of backpacker bunks and Sydney pickup, $295). **Balloon Aloft**

(☎ (1800) 028 568), **Cloud Nine** (☎ 9686 7777), and **Hunter Valley Ballooning** (☎ (1800) 81 81 91) all have dawn hot air balloon flights that last roughly 1hr. ($185-225; usually includes champagne breakfast).

## THE UPPER HUNTER VALLEY

A few towns well northwest of Cessnock are great bases from which to explore the Upper Hunter Valley vineyards. **Singleton** (pop. 18,000), on the New England Hwy, doesn't have much to offer, but it is the home of the **world's largest sundial**.

**MUSSWELLBROOK.** On the New England Hwy, Muswellbrook is closest to the action. The tiny town is most proud of its abundance of historical buildings, many of them visible on the 4.5km Muswellbrook Heritage walk which begins at the Old Tea House on Bridge St (New England Hwy). The highway is also the site of a living Vietnam Memorial, a grove of 519 trees that represent each of the Australian casualties of that conflict. The tourist office, 87 Hill St, just off Bridge St, shares a building with the Upper Hunter Wine Centre. (☎ 6541 4050. Open daily 9:30am-5pm.) Accommodation in Muswellbrook is neither luxurious nor plentiful. **Eatons Hotel,** on Bridge St, has basic singles, twins, and doubles. (☎ 6543 2403. $15 per person.) **Pinaroo Caravan Park** is 3km south on the New England Hwy. (☎ 6543 3905. Tent sites for 2 $10, powered $15; caravan sites $35.)

**SCONE.** A better choice for accommodation is in Scone, 26km north on the New England Hwy, a small but pretty town which prides itself on being the horse capital of Australia. The distinction is owed to the annual week-long Scone Horse Festival in mid-May, which includes an air show featuring WWII fighter jets. The week culminates in three days of thoroughbred racing for the Scone Cup. The race course is 5min. from the town center. Large thoroughbred stud farms sprawl alongside the New England Hwy near the town; some are open for tours. The tourist information center is at the corner of Kelly (New England Hwy) and Susan St, in front of the train station. (☎ 6545 1526; email sconesc@brooknet.com.au. Open daily 9am-5pm.) The **Scone YHA**, 1151 Segenhoe Rd, 8km off the highway in a converted country schoolhouse surrounded by horse stud farms, has a kitchen, BBQ, warm fireplace and friendly hosts. (☎/fax 6545 2072. Dorms $14; twins and doubles $30; family rooms $42). The **Highway Caravan Park,** 248 New England Hwy, is a place to pitch a tent and that's about it. (☎/fax 6545 1078. Sites for 2 $10, powered $12; caravan sites $20.) The **Station Café,** in the railroad station, makes a delectable tomato soup. (☎ 6545 2144. Open M-F 11am-6pm, Sa-Su 10am-6pm.)

**WINERIES OF THE UPPER HUNTER VALLEY.** The Upper Hunter Valley has fewer wineries, is more spread out, and has less tourists, though it has many great wines. Pick up the humorously titled *Vineyards of the Upper Hunter Valley* brochure from any area tourist centers. It includes listings and a small map. All the wineries can easily be visited in one day; the well-marked trail starts off the New England Hwy a few kilometers north of Muswellbrook. Unfortunately, no tour groups operate here, so you need your own car. **Rosemount** (☎ 6547 2310) is the largest vineyard and has extraordinary varieties from a light Sauvignon Blanc to a mild Shiraz to a more peppery Cabernet Sauvignon. Since it exports 70% of its 2.5 million cases, you're likely to see some at home too. **Arrowfield** (☎ 6576 4041) is also big. **Cruikshank's** (☎ 6547 8149) specializes in Cabernet Sauvignon, while **Reynolds Yarraman** (☎ 6547 8127) has an excellent 1998 Semillon.

# TAMWORTH

Yee-haw! Welcome to country, folks. Tamworth (pop. 35,000) annually hosts a **Country Music Festival,** which brings famous crooners and hordes of people to town (January 19-29 in 2001). The rest of the year, weekends see local country bands playing the pubs, but no more so than rock or dance. The country spirit is otherwise maintained by gallon-hatted city slickers and cheesy tourist attractions such as a giant golden guitar and a concrete slab with handprints of country artists.

NEW SOUTH WALES

**TRANSPORT.** The **train station,** corner of Brisbane and Marius St, has a travel center that sells all bus and train tickets. (☎6766 2357, afterhours ☎13 22 32. Open M-F 8:30am-5:30pm, Sa 9:30am-5pm.) Countrylink (☎13 22 32) runs express trains to **Sydney** (6hr.; 1 per day; $71.50, ISIC $43). All buses run from the **coach terminal** adjoining the tourist information center. Greyhound Pioneer (☎13 20 30) and McCafferty's (☎13 14 99) travel to: **Sydney** (6-8hr., 2 per day, $53); **Brisbane** (9-10hr., 3 per day, $55); **Melbourne** (18hr., 1 per day, $134) via **Dubbo** (4¾hr., $65); and **Scone** (1½hr., 1 per day, $29); 20% ISIC discount. Kean's Travel Express (☎6543 1322) meanders to **Port Macquarie** (8¼hr.; M, W, F 1 per day; $64.50).

**■? ORIENTATION AND PRACTICAL INFORMATION.** Tamworth is 412km north of Sydney on the New England Hwy (which enters the town from the east and departs south) and is a convenient rest stop on a journey to Brisbane (578km north). The town center lies along **Brisbane St,** which crosses the Peel River, becoming **Bridge St** in West Tamworth. The **information center** is at the corner of Peel and Murray St. (☎6755 4300; www.tamworth.nsw.gov.au. Open M-F 8:45am-4:35pm, Sa-Su 9am-5pm.) Several **banks** and **ATMs** are in the center of Peel St. The **library,** 203 Marius St, has **Internet access.** (☎6755 4457. Open M-Th 10am-8pm, F 10am-6pm, Sa 9am-noon. 30min. $2.50.) The **post office,** in the center of town at Peel and Fitzroy St, has a giant clock (open M-F 8:30am-5pm). **Postal code:** 2340.

**▐▐ ACCOMMODATIONS AND FOOD.** Most rooms for January's Country Music Festival are gone by the previous March, but throughout the rest of the year, beds are plentiful. The **YHA Country Backpackers,** 169 Marius St, opposite the train station, is the only hostel in town and perhaps the cleanest one in New South Wales (think: obsessive compulsive disorder). (☎6761 2600; fax 6761 2002. No heat. Linen, towels, and breakfast included. Dorms $15-18; doubles $35; family rooms available.) **Tamworth Hotel,** 147 Marius St, also opposite the train station, is the most upscale pubstay. (☎6766 2923. Singles $28; doubles $40.) **Paradise Caravan Park,** next to the info center along the creek, has laundry, BBQ, and a playground. (☎/fax 6766 3120. Sites for 2 $13, powered $19; on-site vans $34; cabins for 2 $55.)

The **Coffee Bean,** Shop 18, Tamworth Arcade, takes coffee-brewing seriously; they also have a more whimsical line of pastries and cakes, as well as **Internet access.** (☎6766 3422. Open M-W, F 8am-5pm; Th 8am-7pm; Sa 8:am-3pm. Internet 1hr. $6.70.) The **Inland Café,** 407 Peel St, is a local fave, with tasty sandwiches and meaty or veggie mains (open M-W 7am-6pm, Th-Sa 7am-11pm, Su 9am-5pm; meals $5-15). There are a number of Thai and Chinese eateries on the main drag (a bit baffling in a country-western town). Coles **supermarket** is at 436 Peel St (open 24hr. except closed Sa noon-M 6am).

**☐ SIGHTS AND ACTIVITIES.** You don't have to be a country music fan to enjoy Tamworth—you just need a high tolerance for kitsch. The turn-off for **The Golden Guitar Complex,** south of town on the New England Hwy, is marked by, predictably enough, a gaudy 12m golden guitar. Inside, a realistic "Gallery of Stars" **wax museum** dresses 21 replicas in the donated clothes of the crooning stars themselves, including Slim Dusty. In an odd juxtaposition, a large gem and mineral display shares the complex. (☎6765 2688. Open daily 9am-5pm.) The popular **Hands of Fame Cornerstone** is on the corner of the New England Hwy and Kable Ave; make sure to also check out **Joe Macguires' Noses of Fame,** 148 Peel St (☎6766 2114), a 15min. walk west of town. For real devotees, the **Australian Country Music Foundation,** 93 Brisbane St (☎6766 1577), is an archive with a small museum display.

A town with a legendary preoccupation with country and western ballads would be remiss without providing **line dancing** lessons for visitors. **Maverick Line Dancers,** Tamworth RSL Club (☎6766 4661) offers free lessons Sunday at 5:30pm.

Bring out the inner cowboy or cowgirl at one of the **"Jackaroo and Jillaroo schools"** in the Tamworth area, with crash courses on how to ride horses, train dogs, milk cows, lasso, operate farm equipment, and muster cattle from the saddle. Certificates and, often, help finding **jobs** are given upon completion. **Leconfield** runs a highly recommended school of this type. If you're lucky, they'll even let you castrate a baby lamb the old fashioned way—with your teeth. (☎6769 4328. 5-day course from $341 begins M. Free Tamworth pickup.)

The **Oxley Scenic Lookout** at the top of White St gives a bird's-eye view of the bustling city. It also marks the start of the **Kamilaroi Walking Track** (6.2km), a scenic tour that passes by the **Endeavour Drive Marsupial Park,** past the top end of Brisbane St, with its free roaming 'roos, echidnas, and red-necked wallabies (open daily 8am-5pm). A lighter **Heritage Walk** (4.7km) loops through town, starting at the corner of Kable and Brisbane St. Parallel to Peel St, one block south along the river, is **Bicentennial Park,** a reclusive stretch of greenery, ponds, and picnic tables with a delightful bit of masonry on its rocks. More than a dozen well-hidden reliefs of animals jutting off the stones near the water fountain (open daily 8am-4:45pm).

**🎵🎭 ENTERTAINMENT AND NIGHTLIFE.** Nightlife in Tamworth is amusing. Teenagers too young to drink cruise Peel St in their parents cars and climb about on public landmarks making eyes at each other. Meanwhile, their older siblings fill their bellies with enough liquid courage to make them feel tough even though they wear cowboy hats and have adopted lingo exported from Texas. Never mind that most are city folk. The **RSL Club,** behind Peel St on Kable Ave, is really the only constantly country live venue. (☎6766 4661. Th-Sa 7:30pm, Su 2:30pm. No cover.) The **Imperial Pub,** on the corner of Marius and Brisbane St, draws a mix of ages. (☎6766 2613. Live mainly rock music Th-Su.) Most pubs close around midnight, but the **Tudor,** 327 Peel St (☎6766 2930), doesn't even get rolling until 10pm and then parties until 3am. Downstairs an older crowd chats while the younger set gets sloshed at the disco upstairs, dancing to heavy bass rhythms.

# ARMIDALE

The town of Armidale (pop. 25,000) has two claims to fame: it has four distinct seasons, and it has a number of self-guided historical walks. If you are on a crusade to see leaves fall or if you are a fan of power-walks, Armidale is the comfortable but common place for you. The University of New England's campus, 5km from Armidale's center, brings energy and business to a healthy number of pubs. Conveniently positioned at the beginning of "Waterfall Way" (see p. 157), the city is also a base for many surrounding national parks.

**🚌 TRANSPORT.** The **bus terminal,** 82 Marsh St, behind Pizza Hut, holds McCafferty's (☎13 14 99) and Greyhound (☎13 20 30). To: **Sydney** (8hr., 2 per day, $60.50); **Brisbane** (7½hr., 3 per day, $55); **Glen Innes** (1hr., 3 per day, $30); and **Tenterfield** (2hr., 3 per day, $35). Keans (☎(1800) 04 33 39) runs three times per week to: **Coffs Harbour** (3½hr., $26.50); **Nambucca Heads** (4hr., $29.50); **Port Macquarie** (6hr., $45.50); and **Tamworth** (3hr., $22). **Harvey World Travel,** corner of Beardy and Dangar St, books tickets. (☎6772 1177. Open M-F 9am-5:30pm, Sa 9:30am-12:30pm.)

**🛈 ORIENTATION AND PRACTICAL INFORMATION.** Armidale's main drag is **Marsh St.** The **Visitors Centre,** 82 Marsh St, is by the bus terminal. (☎6772 4655, freecall (1800) 62 77 36; www.new-england.org/armidale. Open M-F 9am-5pm, Sa 9am-4pm, Su 10am-4pm.) One block up Marsh St is the start of the **Beardy St Mall,** Armidale's cluster of upscale shops and cafés, which holds a **supermarket, banks, ATMs,** and the **post office** (158 Beardy St). **UNE Students Association,** 173A Beardy St, has **Internet access.** (☎6771 2180. Open M-F 9am-5pm. 1hr. $7, students half-price.)

**🏠🍴🎭 ACCOMMODATIONS, FOOD, AND ENTERTAINMENT.** The **Pembroke Caravan Park,** 2km east of town on Grafton Rd, past the racecourse, has an adjoining **YHA hostel.** The grounds have a swimming pool, tennis courts, and a gorgeous hilly backdrop. (☎6772 6470, freecall ☎(1800) 35 55 78; pembroke@mail.north net.com.au. Sites $14; dorms $15, non-YHA $18.) **Country Comfort,** 86 Barney St near Faulkner St, has pleasant motel rooms. (☎6772 8511. From $81.) **Tattersall's Hotel,** 174 Beardy St, is a town center pubstay. (☎6772 2247. Singles $25.)

Many of the pubs have bistros with cheap or all-you-can-eat meals. The Wicklow Hotel, nicknamed, and better known as **The Pink Pub** for its salmon-pink facade, is opposite the tourist office on the corner of Marsh and Dumarsq St. (☎ 6772 2421. Open daily 10:30am-2am. Country style dinners $12-15.) The historic **New England Hotel,** corner of Faulkner and Beardy St, has great steak dinners and has been serving beer since it opened in 1857. **Rumours** is the Mall's most popular café, if curiously bourgeois for a small town. The café window displays fliers for concerts, raves, and temporary employment. (☎ 6772 3084. Open for all 3 meals M-Sa.)

**🎦 📷 SIGHTS AND ACTIVITIES.** The visitors center has free 2hr. electric **trolley tours** of Armidale that are rich in local history and stop at the New England Regional Art Museum, the Railway Museum, and the Booloominbah mansion on the UNE campus. (Book ahead at ☎ (1800) 62 77 36. Departs M-F 10am, Sa-Su 10:30am from the visitors center. Donation requested.) The center also has guides for the 3km or 6.2km **Heritage Walking Tours,** covering 35 National Trust buildings; the 2hr. **Heritage Drive** is a self-guided 25km tour of many of the same buildings and more. Following Marsh St south, up the hill to the corner of Kentucky St, leads to the much-praised **New England Regional Art Museum** (☎ 6772 5255; open daily 10:30am-5pm; free). As you exit the art museum, on your right is the **Aboriginal Cultural Centre and Keeping Place** (☎ 6771 1249; open M-F 9am-5pm, Sa-Su 2-5pm; $3).

A 5.7km scenic cycleway runs along Dumaresq Creek to the **University of New England. Armidale Bicycle Center,** 244 Beardy St, rents bikes. (☎ 6772 3718. 1hr $5.; helmet and locks included.) By car, follow signs from Marsh St for 5min. to Madgwick Dr and Trevenna Rd. To reach the **Sports Union,** follow signs left off Trevenna Rd before reaching the academic campus. For a small fee, visitors can play squash, tennis, swim indoors, use the gym, play basketball, and rent mountain bikes. (☎ 6773 2316. Open M-F 7am-10pm, Sa-Su 8am-7pm.)

**Waterfall Way Tours,** 5 Canambe St, travels by 4WD to up to six national parks along the Waterfall Way, focusing on natural history, with some Aboriginal and European background as well. (☎ 6772 2018. Half-day $40; full-day with lunch $65; overnight tours available.) Horseback riding and fishing are also popular area activities; the visitors center has details.

## NEAR ARMIDALE: OXLEY HIGHWAY

The New England Hwy (15) reaches a juncture at Bendemeer, 41km north of Tamworth. Here, you can head coastward along the Oxley Hwy (follow signs to Walcha), a stretch of raw and remote national parks that are nothing short of spectacular. From Armidale, follow the New England Hwy south for 22km to Uralla where a tourist route takes a shortcut directly to Walcha along the Oxley Hwy. The Oxley meets Port Macquarie at the coast, 178km east from Walcha.

**APSLEY AND TIA GORGES.** The highlights of the eastern end of **Oxley Wild Rivers National Park** (see p. 157) are the must-see waterfalls of the Apsley and Tia Gorges, which are most easily accessed from the Oxley Hwy. The larger part of the park is usually accessed from Waterfall Way, closer to Armidale (see p. 157). About 20km east of Walcha and 83km from Armidale is the turn-off for the **Apsley Gorge,** 1km off the highway. This mighty gorge will take your breath away. At the far carpark is a stairway leading part of the way into the gorge with a good view of the falls. Swimming in the pool is permitted at your own risk. Beware of sometimes-submerged boulders just in front of the falls. The 2km **Oxley Walk** (45min.) takes you around the rim of the gorge and across a bridge over the Oxley River. Camping and fresh water are available. Nineteen kilometers south of the Apsley Falls entrance is the small picnic and camping area of **Tia Falls.** A nearby walk shows off the **Tia Gorge.**

Small and unexciting, Walcha is still a useful jumping-off point for Apsley and Tia Gorges and the rest of Oxley Wild Rivers National Park. You'll find the **tourist information center** in the Old School Art Gallery on the Oxley Hwy. (6777 2713.

Open daily 8am-5pm.) For basic pub stay and food, try the **Commercial Hotel**, on Churchill Ln also off the highway. (☎6777 2551. Singles $27.50.)

**WERRIKIMBE NATIONAL PARK.** Remoteness and poor access roads have preserved the rugged wilderness of Werrikimbe National Park. This is a camper's paradise, and many choose to stay for days and weeks, gleefully veering from the paths into the depths of temperate and subtropical rainforest, eucalypt forest, and snow gum woodlands. District Managers in Armidale (☎6776 4260; email armidale@npws.gov.au) or Port Macquarie (☎6583 5518) have info on expeditions beyond the western section of the park. Look closely for the sign for Werrikimbe National Park and Moorback Rd, which appears 40km south of Walcha. The first 15km of this track isn't bad, but the twisting, climbing, and loose gravel may wear on conventional vehicles. Inside the park, the tracks crumble but remain flat and direct. You can either go left a few kilometers to Moorback Rest Area or right to Cobcroft's Rest Area. **Moorback** is set amid snow gum woodlands and by the Moorback Creek. Walks meander along the creek and deeper into the forest. Campsites at **Cobcroft** are set in open eucalypt forest with a few tree ferns for seasoning. The **Carrabeen Walk** (1hr.) passes through an adjacent warm temperate rainforest. The vivid passage crosses through gullies of Antarctic Beeches with gnarled, web-like bases that on take astounding shapes. The campsites have pit toilets and firewood.

# WATERFALL WAY

Waterfall Way (Rte 78) runs east-west between Armidale and the north coast of New South Wales. Along the way, the aptly-named tourist route passes four excellent national parks with accessible campgrounds, several tiny hamlets, and the charming town of Bellingen (see p. 179). The 169km route is worth the trip, but be cautious on the sometimes steep highway. In addition to the parks below, the Ebor Falls, approximately 42km west of Dorrigo and 600m off the highway, are a killer photo-op. A 600m walk from the carpark leads to a scintillating lookout. Waterfall Way Tours (☎6772 2018) runs to the national parks (see Armidale, p. 155).

## OXLEY WILD RIVERS NATIONAL PARK

Oxley is an extensive park of rough, rocky terrain with a network of gorges, campsites, bushwalks, and appropriately wild rivers. Useful pamphlets with photos and maps can help you choose a site to camp or picnic; contact the Armidale **NPWS** (☎6773 7211; fax 6771 1894; email armidale@npws.nsw.gov) or **Armidale Visitors Centre** (☎(1800) 62 77 36; email visit@northnet.com.au). For information on **Apsley and Tia Gorges** at the more remote eastern end of the park, see p. 156.

**Dangars Gorge** is an easy 22km trip from Armidale, with the 120m Dangars Falls as the centerpiece. Take Gangarsleigh Rd (Kennedy St) from Armidale for about 11km, then go left at the Perrott's War Memorial; 10km of gravel lead to the gorge. The rest area there is equipped with BBQ, firewood, and pit toilets, and is the trailhead for a series of walks ranging from the Gorge Lookout path (100m) to 10-14km half-day treks. An eroding, unofficial path from the rest area leads down to the Gorge riverbed and a deep pool, zig-zagging along a steep gradient (2hr.).

**Long Point** is a secluded wilderness area in an open eucalypt forest adjacent to a rare dry rainforest, a fact that has earned it World Heritage status. Dry rainforest sounds oxymoronic, but the main criterion for rainforest classification is a closed canopy forest ceiling. The turn-off for Long Point appears 40km east of Armidale along Waterfall Way. A 7km stretch of sealed track passes through the two-horse town of Hillgrove where a left turn skips onto an adequate dirt track that reaches the park 20km down. The attached campsite has pit toilets, picnic tables, and fresh water, and is the trailhead for the excellent **Chandler Walk** (5km; 2-2½hr.), leading through a grove of mosses, vines, and yellow-spotted Hillgrove Gums, which are found only in this area. A tremendous lookout along the walk surveys the valley and Chandler River.

The **Wollombi Falls** gorge is severe and the surrounding forest rugged and dry. Turn-off 40km east of Armidale onto a 2km bitumen road leading to the Falls. The strenuous **Chandler River Track** (5.6km; 4hr.) starts here. Alternately, a moderately strenuous 1.2km walk leads to the river, or a 700m path heads to a gorge lookout. There is a bush camping site near the entrance to the gorge area.

## NEW ENGLAND NATIONAL PARK

New England National Park offers some fabulous bushwalking trails. Its densely-vegetated basalt cliffs formed from several lava flows from the Ebor volcano over 18 million years ago. The park gets chilly in summer and down-right cold in winter. Near the park entrance, 85km from Armidale and 75km from Dorrigo, is the **Thungutti Campground.** Nearby begin the Wright's Lookout Walk (2½hr.) and Cascades Walk (3½hr.). Most people skip these outskirts to head for the **Point Lookout Picnic Area,** the park's hub, with toilets, fire pits, and ample parking. Point Lookout Rd heads up to the area; about 11km is gravel, 2.5km sealed. Point Lookout marks the start of nine walks ranging from 5min. to 3½hr., all of which can be linked for nearly a full day of walking. The Point Lookout, a vertical escarpment rising 1564m from sea level, surveys dense forest often shrouded in mist. **Eagles Nest Track** (2hr.) passes straight down and along the steep cliffside. It takes some ingenuity to negotiate the rocky areas through moss-covered beeches, snow gum woodland, and water sprays that turn to icicles in winter. The difficult **Lyrebird Walk** links with the Eagles Nest Track and can be made a 2km (1hr.) route or a 7km (3½hr.) circuit.

## GLEN INNES

Glen Innes (pop. 9000), 1hr. from both Armidale and Tenterfield on the New England Hwy, has a Celtic heritage and constantly finds cause to celebrate its rural nature. A full slate of annual festivals complement the changing seasons as markers of the passage of time. Glen Innes's most striking monument is a collection of vertical megalithic **Standing Stones** overlooking the town and valley, an homage to an ancient Celtic form of timekeeping. Resting solemnly on **Martins Lookout,** 1km east of the visitors center on Meade St (Gwydir Hwy), the Stones bear an uncanny resemblance to Stonehenge.

The main commercial street in town is **Grey St,** parallel to and one block west of the **New England Hwy** (called Church St as it runs through town). The **Gwydir Hwy,** known in town as **Meade St** and **Ferguson St,** runs west 65km to Inverell and east 160km to Grafton and the Pacific Hwy. Greyhound (☎ 13 20 30) and McCafferty's (☎ 13 14 99) send **buses** to: **Sydney** (9hr., 2 per day, $60.50); **Brisbane** (5hr., 3 per day, $55); **Armidale** (1hr., 3 per day, $30); and **Tenterfield** (1hr., 3 per day, $23). All buses stop at the **Visitors Centre,** 152 Church St, near the intersection of the New England and Gwydir Hwy. (☎6732 2397; email gitourne@northnet.com.au. Open M-F 9am-5pm, Sa-Su 9am-3pm.) Grey St is home to several banks with **ATMs, supermarkets,** pubstays, greasy eateries, and the library with **free Internet access** (open M-F 9:30am-5:30pm, Sa 9am-noon). **Post office:** 321 Grey St, on the corner of Meade St. **Postal code:** 2370.

Cheap rooms are available at the pubs on Grey St (singles $20; twins and doubles $35). **New England Motor Lodge,** on the northern end of Church St, has much nicer rooms and a swimming pool for a bit more coin. (☎6732 2922. Singles $75-85; doubles $80-90; family rooms $125.)

## TENTERFIELD AND NEARBY PARKS

It was in Tenterfield in 1889 that Sir Henry Parkes made his "one nation" speech that foresaw Australian federation. Although it clings to its history with some preserved buildings, travelers today know Tenterfield as a base for exploring nearby parks and a stop on the way into Queensland's Darling Downs region.

**▇▌ TRANSPORT AND PRACTICAL INFORMATION.** The New England Hwy becomes **Rouse St** in town. Greyhound and McCafferty's **do not stop** at the town's bus station, but south of town near the BP and Ampol petrol stations. Several of the buses barrel in late at night or early in the morning. Greyhound (☎ 13 20 30) and McCafferty's (☎ 13 14 99) **buses** run to: **Sydney** (10-11½hr., 2 per day, $60.50); **Brisbane** (4½-5hr., 3 per day, $45); **Armidale** (2hr., 3 per day, $35); and **Glen Innes** (1hr., 3 per day, $23). Crisp's undercuts the big companies with its daily **Brisbane** service. (☎ 6736 1074. 4½hr., $38.) Kirkland's (☎ (1800) 15 04 67) services **Lismore** (4hr., $24), where a connection can be made to **Byron Bay** (1hr., $12). Countrylink (☎ 13 22 32), operating locally as Edward's Coaches with a **train** transfer in **Armidale,** travels to **Sydney** (11hr., daily 6:10am, $87) via **Glen Innes** (1hr., $13) and **Armidale** (2hr., $32). **T&T Travel,** 228 Rouse St, books all coaches. (☎ 6736 1074. Open M-F 10am-5pm.) The **tourist office,** 157 Rouse St, keeps park info. (☎ 6736 1082. Open M-F 9am-5pm, Sa 9am-4pm, Su 9am-3:30pm.) **Commonwealth Bank,** on Rouse St, has an **ATM. Post office:** 225 Rouse St (open M-F 9am-5pm). **Postal code:** 2372.

**▛▟ ACCOMMODATIONS AND FOOD.** The YHA-affiliated **Tenterfield Lodge** is essentially a caravan park with dorms. From the tourist office turn left off Rouse on Manners St and walk 1km to the end of the road. (☎ 6736 1477. Dorms $18; doubles $40; tent sites $12, powered $15; on-site vans $30-40; ensuite cabins $45.) The **Famous Pie Shop** on Rouse St has reasonably priced tasty hot pies, thick milkshakes, and fresh bread. (☎ 6736 3556. Open M-F 7:30am-5:30pm, Sa 7:30am-2pm.) There's a **supermarket** on Rouse St.

**▟ PARKS.** Tenterfield lies near three national parks; a great map ($8) is available at the visitors center or the NPWS, 68 Church St, Glen Innes (☎ 6732 5133). **Boonoo Boonoo National Park** (pronounced, inexplicably, "Bunner Bernoo") is 27km away; take Rouse St south, turn right on Nas St, then quickly bear left on Mt. Lindesay Rd. The next 27km to the park entrance is mostly unsealed. From the entrance, 14km of gravel leads to **Boonoo Boonoo Falls,** the park hub and overnight camping area (no water; $5). The park is dominated by eucalypts and has a few rock pools. There's a swimming hole 5km back from the falls toward the park entrance. If you can't reach Uluru (Ayers Rock), you'll have to make do with **Bald Rock National Park,** featuring the largest exposed granite rock in Australia. To reach it, head down Mt. Lindesay Rd for 29km to a gravel road that runs 5km to the park's camping area. The **Burgoona Walk** (5km) takes you to the 1277m summit, with a view of the McPherson Ranges and the Clarence River. **Girraween National Park** (see p. 328) is Queensland's extension of Bald Rock National Park, and is 9km down a paved road 11km north of Wallangara on the New England Hwy. **Woollol Woollol Aboriginal Culture Tours** runs an Aboriginal-guided trip to both Boonoo Boonoo and Bald Rock National Parks ($55, for 2 $105; book at visitors center).

# NORTH COAST

Called the Holiday Coast by Sydney-siders, the sandy fantasyland of the northern New South Wales coast caters to meandering backpackers, die-hard surfers, and swarms of families. Existing somewhere between the rat-race of the big city and the permanent-vacation attitude of points north, this area offers locals easy access to both bright lights and holiday hot-spots, with a slightly slower pace of life. Newcastle and Port Macquarie draw travelers itching to sunbathe, water-ski, or hang-ten. At the other end of the spectrum, inland eco-activist centers Lismore and Bellingen thrive on highly productive agricultural land punctuated by scenic national parks and fast-flowing rivers. With virtual cult status, Byron Bay synthesizes these two distinct flavors, magnetically pulling sunburned, party-ready mobs and detaining them for a spell (or a bender) before they head for the Queensland beaches. For coverage of Tweed Heads, see **Tweed Heads and Coolangatta,** p. 317.

# NEWCASTLE

Newcastle (pop. 265,000) is a city with a complex. As the world's largest coal exporter, Newcastle exports over one million tons each week and if you stand in the center of town long enough, you will probably get graffitied. But as the second-largest city in New South Wales, Newcastle stubbornly insists that it is not just a smokestack-ridden industrial metropolis (which it is). In all fairness, Newcastle does offers high-adrenaline surfing, a spectacular view of the Pacific, and easy access to the nearby Hunter Valley wineries and wetland reserves.

## ■ ORIENTATION

**Hunter St,** at the heart of the city, is Newcastle's commercial district and is (as one hostel owner put it) "not very inspirational." The mostly-pedestrian street, south of the harbor and parallel to the wharf, is overrun with chintzy stores and gangs of boys on skateboards. Unless you want to mail a letter, get cash, visit the tourist office, or bet on horses, stay away from Hunter St and stick to the outer edges of town. On the eastern end of the main drag, atop a peninsular hill, lies **Fort Scratchley,** a number of hostels and seaside bars, the crashing waves, and the emerald-green **Harbour Foreshore Park. Queen's Wharf** runs the distance of the city, starting with the Convict Lumberyard on east Scott St, next to the train station and near the shore. Climb the **Queen's Wharf Tower** to get a 360° view of the city to the south and the harbor to the north. Follow it to the western end of town, near Hamilton, and look for the perpendicular (north/south) **Darby St** and **Beaumont St** to find Newcastle's hip happenings. Westward on Hunter St is also where the highway splits; the New England Hwy heads west toward the **Hunter Valley wineries** (see p. 150) and the Pacific Hwy climbs north up the coast. Take a ferry from Newcastle's town center to cross the river to the residential area of **Stockton.**

## ▐ TRANSPORT

**Trains: Newcastle Railway Station,** Wharf Road, Queen's Wharf (☎ 13 15 00). Trains chug to **Sydney** (3hr., at least 1 per hr. 2:15am-11:15pm, $15) via **Maitland** (40min., $4). Other destinations on the CityRail network usually route back through Sydney. The main transfer station for access to the northern coast is **Broadmeadow,** a 5min. train ride on CityRail. From Broadmeadow: **Brisbane** (14hr., 2 per day, $85); **Coffs Harbour** (6-8hr., 3 per day, $57); and **Surfers Paradise** (12hr., 2 per day, $85). Luggage storage ($1.50; open daily 8am-5pm). Station open daily 6am-7:15pm; after-hours ticket machines outside. Ask for student discounts.

**Buses:** The bus depot butts up against the wharf side of the railway station. Several bus lines including Greyhound and McCafferty's zip to: **Sydney** (3hr., at least 6 per day, $22); **Brisbane** (14hr., 6 per day, $60); **Byron Bay** (10hr., 4 per day, $59); **Cairns** (45hr., 1 per day, $204); **Coffs Harbour** (6hr., 6 per day, $42); **Port Macquarie** (4hr., 3 per day, $31); **Surfers Paradise** (13hr., 6 per day, $60); and **Taree** (3hr., 5 per day, $30). Rover Motors (☎ 4990 1699) goes to **Cessnock** (1¼hr., M-Sa 4-6 per day, $9).

**Local transportation:** City buses (☎ 4961 8933) run along Hunter St every 15min. during the day, less frequently at night; some run as late as 4am. Hail buses like you would a taxi. Tickets allow unlimited travel for a specified length of time (1hr., $2).

**Ferries:** Passenger ferries (☎ 4929 2106) depart from the tip of the wharf, just west of the train station, and cross the river north to **Stockton** (15min.). The ferry leaves at least once every 30min. (M-Sa 5:15am-10:45pm, Su and holidays 8:30am-10:05pm.) Tickets ($1.40, children 70¢) can be bought from a machine on the dock or onboard.

**Taxis: Newcastle Taxi Services** (☎ 4961 5555).

**Car and Motorcycle Rental: ARA,** 86 Lawson St, Hamilton (☎ 4962 2488), rents 2-door hatches from $44. **Thrifty Car Rental,** 113 Parry St (☎ 4942 2266), is only a little bit pricier ($8 surcharge for drivers under 25).

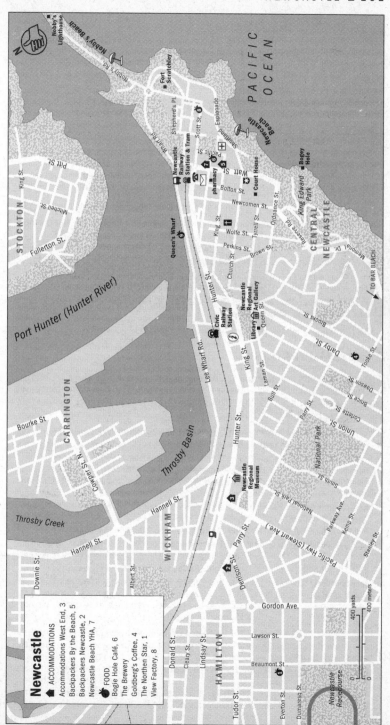

NEW SOUTH WALES

**Newcastle**

⏏ ACCOMMODATIONS
Accommodations West End, 3
Backpackers By the Beach, 5
Backpackers Newcastle, 2
Newcastle Beach YHA, 7

🍴 FOOD
Bogie Hole Café, 6
The Brewery
Goldberg's Coffee, 4
The Northen Star, 1
View Factory, 8

NEW SOUTH WALES

## ▼ PRACTICAL INFORMATION

**Tourist Office:** 363 Hunter St, (☎4974 2999; fax 4929 6732). As you stand in front of the Civic rail station (the next one west of the Newcastle terminal), with the wharf at your back, the tourist office is across the street. Free maps of Newcastle and the MacQuarie area. Open M-F 9am-5pm, Sa-Su 10am-2pm.

**Currency Exchange:** In the city center on Hunter St between Newcomen and Perkins St, are a number of banks and 24hr. ATMs.

**Library:** (☎4921 3000), on Laman St behind Civic Park, just off Darby, in the Newcastle Memorial Cultural Centre. **Internet access** free for non-email sites, email $2.50 per 30min. Book ahead at ☎4974 5344. Open M-F 9:30am-8pm, Sa 9:30am-2pm.

**Surfing: Pacific Dreams,** 7 Darby St (☎4926 3355), rents boards (from $20 per day and $100 per week, plus a refundable deposit) and wetsuits. Open M-F 9am-5:30pm, Sa 9am-5pm, Su 10am-3pm. Credit card and driver's license required.

**Police:** (☎4929 0999). A gray concrete monstrosity on the corner of Church and Watt St.

**Hospital: Shortland Esplanade,** by the shore. Or larger and full-serviced **John Hunter Hospital** (☎4921 3000), New Lambton, accessible by bus #363, 232, or 332.

**Pharmacy: City Pharmacy,** 53 Hunter St (☎4929 2866). Also sells prepaid phone cards and is, um, conveniently located next to a liquor store. Open daily 8:30am-5:30pm.

**Internet Access: The Store,** 854 Hunter St (☎4961 0310), has access at $5 per 10min.; ask about their 2-for-1 backpacker special. Open M-W, F-Sa 9am-5pm, Th 9am-7:30pm, Su 9am-4pm. **Newcastle Regional Museum,** 787 Hunter St, has a few free terminals. Also see public **library,** above.

**Post Office:** 96 Hunter St. Open M-F 7:30am-5pm. **Postal Code:** 2300.

## ▐ ACCOMMODATIONS

With tourism (and a hankering for backpackers' business) on the rise, budget accommodation has flourished in Newcastle. Inquire about negotiable long-term rates, especially in winter. Other than the listings below, pub rooms abound too. Remember to book ahead in summer, on weekends, and around national holidays.

■ **Newcastle Beach YHA,** 30 Pacific St (☎4925 3544; fax 4925 3944). Just around the corner from the breaking surf and local train station lies this crown jewel of hostels in a breezy, bricked, and retro-feeling remodeled heritage building. This hostel offers cavernous accommodations, compulsively cleaned facilities, steaming hot showers, and a countryclub-worthy common area with a TV, pool table, and fireplaces for chilly winter months. Co-ed facilities throughout, except a unisex large dorm. Cheapish winery tour for $30 and occasional BBQ. Kitchen. Linen $1. Laundry $2. Internet access $2 per 15min. Key deposit $10. Reception 7am-10:30pm. Dorms $17-$18; twins and doubles $44; non-YHA members $3 extra. Reservations recommended in summer.

**Backpackers Newcastle,** 42-44 Denison St, Hamilton (☎4969 3436; fax 4968 4095). A 30min. walk west of the city center and within drunken hollering distance of happening Beaumont St. The rooms are not great, but the laid back, familial, surfer-funky atmosphere in the common areas more than makes up for it. Books winery tours and occasional outings. Two kitchens, TV area, reading room, laundry, and co-ed bathrooms. Free pickup and drop off in town. Free surf lessons. Free linen. Unrestricted parking. Reception 8am-8pm. Dorms $18; doubles $38-42. YHA, VIP.

**Backpackers by the Beach (NOMADS),** 34-36 Hunter St (☎4926 3472; fax 4926 5210; email backbeach@hunterlink.net.au). Less than a 5min. walk north of the train station, this hostel occupies its own yellow corner of Hunter and Pacific St. Modern but small dorms, heaps of bright light, high ceilings, and an echoing steel stairwell create the ambiance of a converted warehouse. The larger rooms have a bathroom attached, otherwise shared facilities. All-female/male dorm rooms have single-sex bathrooms. Unbeatable access to beaches, transportation, and the wharf. Free surfboard loans.

**ESCAPE RUN AGROUND** Newcastle was originally a colony to which the most troublesome convicts were sent—this is where the baddest of the bad ended up. In November 1800, a band of 15 men determined to escape seized a supply ship, the *Norfolk*, pirate-style. However, the clever convicts were not able to navigate through a gale and wrecked their getaway ship on the shore of what is now Stockton. Six decided they'd learned their lesson and stayed put, but nine were only frustrated by the failure and snatched another, smaller ship from shore. Proudly sailing past Nobby's Point to freedom, they were later captured by a naval boat. Two men were hanged and the other seven were sent elsewhere for further punishment. Ironically, two of the less adventurous pirates who remained on shore after the shipwreck successfully made it to Sydney by other means.

Kitchen. TV room. Weekly BBQ. Key deposit $10. Reception 7am-11pm. Dorms $15; doubles $40; non-YHA/VIP/NOMADS members $2-3 extra. With a membership card, a week in a dorm room is $14 per day if paid in advance. No credit cards.

**Accommodation West End,** 775 Hunter St (☎4961 4446; fax 4961 0766). At the corner of the Pacific Hwy. A 20min. walk from the city center and another 10min. from any serious nightlife. Sunshine yellow and thistle purple painted rooms feel like a children's story come to life. Kitchen. Private sinks in most rooms. Two-ply toilet paper feels like heaven. Free daytime pickup from Newcastle Station. Laundry $4. Free linen. Reception 24hr. Dorms $25 first two nights, $20 after; singles $40; doubles $50; twins $60.

## 🍴 FOOD

**Darby St** is popular for its bakeries, takeaways, coffeehouses, and trendy ethnic restaurants. If, all in the name of a buck, you can sacrifice atmosphere and don't mind breathing bus fumes while eating, **Hunter St** has $5-6 lunch specials. If you're trying to sneak a cheap dinner, go early, as many places close at 6pm. Over 80 restaurants line Hamilton's **Beaumont St,** a popular hang-out for students, and home to tasty, cheap, and bustling restaurants just a 1min. walk southwest of the city center. The **Oasis,** on the corner of Beaumont and Cleary St, is a small food court with an outdoor patio. The huge **Bi-Lo supermarket** (☎4926 4494) in the Marketown shopping center at the corner of National Park and King St is open 24hr.

☒ **Bogie Hole Café,** corner of Hunter St and Pacific Hwy (☎4929 1790). Just a short jaunt directly north of the train station, this sidewalk café and restaurant offers healthy, monstrous meals in a trendy atmosphere just minutes from the water's edge. Ample seating allows for guiltless loitering. Ask for a voucher and take advantage of the special "Backpackers Breakfast": bacon, eggs, toast, and tea for $5. Open daily 7am-late.

**The Brewery Restaurant,** 150 Wharf Rd (☎4929 6333). On the water, this is the designated neighborhood drink spot. A gourmet menu has a wild range of prices. Entrees $6-20. Management hosts free BBQ, beer, and trivia contests for hostelers on advertised nights. Dress "smart.' Open Su-Tu and Th 11am-midnight, W and F-Sa until 3am.

**Goldberg's Coffee House,** 137 Darby St (☎4929 3122). This place has the feel of an old English pub where everybody knows each other and meets up before heading out for a night of carousing. While you're cruising down Darby St, swing in for a cup of coffee ($3-5) or a glass of wine, to scope and be seen. Open 7am-midnight or later.

**The View Factory,** corner of Telford and Scott St (☎4929 4580). Meters from the water's edge on the eastern part of town, this place has an artsy feel with its brick, stone, and colored glass decor. Specialty salads, pastas, and lighter lunch options, including vegetarian. Entrees $6-18. Buy one, get one free Monday/Tuesday dinner deal. YHA discounts. Opens daily 11am-9pm.

**The Northern Star,** corner of Beaumont and James St (☎4961 5963). Really good, cheap food. The right part of town if you want to go out for drinks after dinner. Heaping $9-10 pasta entrees will keep you full for at least two meals. Frequent jazz and funk bands. Open M-Th 9:30am-9pm, F-Sa 8am-9pm.

**The Tongue and Groove,** 196 Union St, The Junction (☎4940 8133). With inside and outside seating and cozy floor cushions, this is a very cool place to hang out and nosh. Sit under the sparkling Christmas tree lights, and enjoy a warm Aussie evening with the local "it" crowd. BYO. Open Su-M 8am-6pm, Tu-Sa 8am-8pm.

## ▣ ⌒ SIGHTS AND ACTIVITIES

Newcastle's public image problems are nothing new: the city was established in 1804 as a settlement for the most egregious of convicts and was dubbed "Sydney's Siberia." However, looking closely, one finds that this hard-luck town has a number of compelling redemptions. Its ornate **heritage buildings,** built by convicts, are the architectural highlights of the town, along with the **Cathedral** in the city center. **Newcastle's Famous Tram** offers a delightful, informative city overview and tells of the devastation from a freak earthquake in 1989. The weekday tours focus on architecture, while the weekend tours specialize in history. (☎4963 7954. 45min.; departs from Newcastle Railway Station every hour 10am-3pm. $8.50, children $5.50, family $22.) But people don't come to Newcastle for the architecture—they come for the seaside parks, the gut-wrenching crash of the sea against the rocky shore, and the hardcore surf where a world champ once cut his teeth.

**FORT SCRATCHLEY.** Climb the hill for the best view in the city. Play around on the cannons, pretend to shoot your friends (er, WWII Japanese assailants), and take a tour of the underground tunnel system for $1.50. The fort has been an inactive military site since the 1970s and now houses the Military Museum and, next door, the Maritime Museum. *(Military Museum: open Sa-Su noon-4pm. Free. Maritime Museum: ☎4929 2588. Open Tu-F 10am-4pm, Sa-Su noon-4pm.)*

**BEACHES.** Newcastle's shore is lined with white sand beaches, tidal pools, and landscaped parks. At the tip of Nobby's Head peninsula is Nobby's Lighthouse, surrounded by (you guessed it) **Nobby's Beach,** a terrific surfing spot. Walking clockwise around the peninsula from Nobby's leads to a surf pavilion and public beaches, then to **Bogey Hole,** a convict-built ocean bath at the edge of the manicured **King Edward Park.** Farther along, you'll see a cliff walk leading to the **Susan Gilmore nude beach;** farther still is the large **Bar Beach,** popular with surfers.

**BLACKBUTT RESERVE.** A 200-acre tree sanctuary with walking trails, small caves, and many animals. There's a koala enclosure and kangaroo and emu reserves. If you're lucky, you can pat a koala Sa-Su 11:30am and 2:30pm. Bring your own picnic food; no food is available. *(Catch bus #232 or 363 in the city center for 35min. to Lookout Rd Cardiff Heights and follow signs down the hill. ☎4952 1449. Open daily 9am-5pm. Free.)*

**WETLANDS CENTRE.** As well as offering sanctuary to birds and reptiles, the center offers respite to humans with walking and cycling paths and a creek and swamp for canoeing. Guided walks are conducted at twilight on Sundays. *(Take the CityTrain to Sandgate, in the suburb of Shortland, and then walk 10min. ☎4951 6466. Canoe rental $15 per 2hr. Bikes $6 per hr. Open daily 9am-5pm. $5.)*

**NEWCASTLE REGIONAL MUSEUM.** A collection of hands-on science exhibits and heritage displays that fills three floors. You just might catch a glimpse of it as you head up to the top level for **free Internet access.** *(787 Hunter St. ☎4974 1400; www.amol.org.au/newcastle. Open Tu-Su 10am-5pm. Free.)*

**NEWCASTLE REGION ART GALLERY.** The gallery displays Australian and international art and ceramics and hosts traveling exhibitions. However, the surrounding leafy, cloistered neighborhood may be the highlight. *(☎4974 5100. Laman St, off Darby St, behind Civic Park. Open Tu-Su 10am-5pm. Free.)*

**FESTIVALS. Surfest** rides into town in late February for a two-week international surfing spectacular, drawing crowds from all of Oz. The **Newcastle Jazz Festival** plays out in late August. The **King St Fair** is a city-wide carnival in December. **Newcastle Maritime Festival's** boat races and watersports are the last week of January.

## ♪🎤 ENTERTAINMENT AND NIGHTLIFE

The *Newcastle Herald* (80¢) publishes an entertainment guide with Thursday's paper. For info on clubs and pubs, peruse the free local guide *TE (That's Entertainment)* at the tourist office. **SJ's,** 8 Beaumont St (☎4961 2537), is a gaming room and pub that gets swamped on weekend nights and specializes in rock bands W-Su. The **Northern Star Hotel,** 112 Beaumont (☎4961 1087), is a popular jazz spot, while the **Kent Hotel,** 59-61 Beaumont (☎4961 3303), fronts more mainstream bands. The **Newcastle Workers Club,** at the corner of King and Union St, sizzles Saturday until 3am with the "World's Biggest Disco." (☎4926 2700. $2 cover.). Go to **Mercury** for dancing ($6 cover). Attracting a backpacker crowd, the classy **Brewery,** (see **Food,** above) brews its own (they're trying to take their Ginger Beer national). If it's raining, catch a movie at the **Kensington Cinema,** 299 Hunter St (☎4929 3893).

## 🏞 DAYTRIPS FROM NEWCASTLE

Fifteen minutes south of Newcastle is **Lake Macquarie,** Australia's largest coastal saltwater lake (four times the size of Sydney Harbour) and a weekend-vacation hot spot. The shore is popular with surfers, backpackers, and families on holiday, with hefty waves, deep caverns at **Caves Beach,** and an old mining village at **Catherine Hill Bay.** Spelunkers must go at **low tide** so as not to get trapped in the caves. Find tide tables at the **Lake Macquarie information center,** 72 Pacific Hwy, in the Blacksmiths. (☎4972 1172. Open M-F 9am-5pm, Sa-Su 9am-4pm.)

The mountainous **Watagans National Park** separates Lake Macquarie from the Hunter River. An hour from Newcastle and the Hunter Valley, it's ideal for hikes, picnics, or camping. There are six campsites, most with firewood, BBQs, toilets, and water. Call the **NPWS Hunter** office (☎4987 3108) for more info.

Many visitors use Newcastle as a "gateway to the Hunter," or as springboard to tipsiness via wine sampling at the many nearby vineyards (see p. 215).

# PORT STEPHENS BAY AREA

North of Newcastle, Port Stephens is a placid, secluded bay and a collection of rural townships defined by blue-green water and the **Tomaree National Park.** During the summer, surfing beaches and luxury resorts draw backpackers and families alike, clogging central shopping areas with traffic. The ocean beyond the surf also attracts visitors of the aquatic kind: bottlenose dolphins are visible twelve months of the year in the harbor and, quite cheeky—they'll come right up to your legs. The whale watching season runs from June to October as the giants head north to warmer waters for breeding. On the coastal edge of the national park, abandoned Australian-American forts are left over from WWII training camps.

## ⬅ TRANSPORT

**Port Stephens Buses** (☎4982 2940) run from **Sydney** (3½hr., 1 per day, $25) and **Newcastle** (1½hr.; 11 per day M-F, 3 per day Sa-Su; $8.50, $7.55 roundtrip for students) to four of the townships. The main stop in Nelson Bay is at the **Bi-Lo** on Stockton St. **Local buses** run hourly (around $2; 1 day unlimited travel $10). The Port Stephens **Ferry** Service (☎4981 3798) makes three trips daily to **Tea Garden,** across the water from Nelson Bay (8:30am, noon, 3:30pm; $17). For a **taxi,** call ☎13 10 08.

## 🎆🏨 ORIENTATION AND PRACTICAL INFORMATION

**Nelson Bay Rd** leads from Newcastle to four local residential townships of the Port Stephens area. The road forks onto **Gan Gan Rd,** which leads to the seaside township of **Anna Bay,** home to **Stockton Bight,** the largest sand dune area in the southern hemisphere, and close to the popular surfing destination of **One Mile Beach,** known simply as "The Big Beach" to locals. Gan Gan and Nelson Bay Rd rejoin en route to three other townships: **Nelson Bay** (the largest), **Shoal Bay,** and finally the quite

---

**YANKS IN OZ** Although Port Stephens' harbor is nearly 2½ times the size of the Sydney Harbour, it has historically enjoyed a clandestine existence. During WWII, American General Douglas MacArthur took advantage of this hidden, and very deep, body of water to train his fleets. Through the entire Pacific phase of the war, the area remained successfully out of sight of the Japanese. The American soldiers, in exchange for covert amphibious training grounds, helped the local townships build infrastructure and roads that still exist today.

---

rural and out of the way **Fingal Bay.** The marina, shopping complex, and cafés are located on **Victoria Parade** and **Stockton St** in Nelson Bay. The **Salamander Shopping Centre,** a 5min. bus ride west, is home to the Tomaree public **library** (☎ 4982 0670. **Internet access** free, email $2.50 per 30min. Book ahead. Open M, W, F 10am-6pm; Tu, Th 10am-8pm; Sa 9:30am-2pm.)

The **tourist office,** on Victoria Pde, by the wharf in Nelson Bay, arranges bookings for local attractions. (☎ 4981 1579; www.portstephens.org.au. Open M-F 9am-5pm, Sa-Su 9am-4pm.) Other services include: **banks** with **ATMs,** near the tourist office on Stockton and Magnus St; the **police** (☎ 4981 1244), on Government Rd, Nelson Bay; and the **post office** (☎ 4981 1240), corner of Stockton and Magnus St, or in the Salamander Shopping Center. **Postal Code:** in Nelson Bay, 2315.

# ACCOMMODATIONS

Winter often brings great deals, but available beds drop and prices rise in the summer. Book 4-6 weeks ahead on weekends, in summer, in January, and around holidays. Beware of significant price spikes on weekends in the hotel/motel market. All of the following are on the Port Stephens local bus route.

**Samurai Beach Bungalows Backpackers** (☎/fax 4982 1921, freecall (1800) 04 59 49). On Robert Connell Circle, reached by Frost Rd, off of Nelson Bay Rd just outside Anna Bay. Solidly in the bush, this is a city-weary traveler's dream; don't let the strapping pet rottweiler scare you—he's friendly. There's a volleyball court, a campfire where guests share stories and roast marshmallows among the koalas, an outdoor kitchen, TV, pool table, free surfboards, and boogie boards. Ask the owner about "sandboarding" the local dunes. Beaches nearby. Bike rentals $10 per day, free use for those staying 3 or more days. Linen included. Sparse 5-bunk dorms with shared bath $16; doubles with TV, bath, coffee maker and mini-kitchen from $40; family room $60. VIP.

**Sandy Point Motor Lodge,** 19-21 Sandy Point Rd, Corlette (☎/fax 4981 1744; email sandypointmotel@bigpond.com.au). A stop on the route of the daily Sydney Coach. Family-owned and operated with possibly the cleanest rooms in New South Wales. Ensuite, TV, BBQ, toaster, and fridge. Continental breakfast included. Reception 8am-7pm. Singles $50, more during peak-season; doubles $45, $60; family rooms with full kitchen $70, $100.

**Shoal Bay Holiday Park** (☎ 4981 1427 or (1800) 60 02 00; email shoal@portst ephens.nsw.gov.au). On Shoal Bay Rd on the way to Fingal Bay, within hearing distance of the ocean. Laundry $2. New kitchen. Common television, tennis courts, trivia contests, and movie nights. Reception 8am-6pm. Powered tent and caravan sites for 2 adults $16-19, additional adult $12; 7th night free. Bright family cabins for 5 with bathroom $44-104. Ask about backpacker discount.

**Shoal Bay YHA,** 59-61 Shoal Bay Beachfront Rd (☎ 4981 0982). In the Shoal Bay Motel, across from the beach and a 15min. walk west of the Tomaree trails. Rooms have TV, fridge, heat and A/C. The 6-bed women's dorm has an attached bathroom, as does the 6-bed men's dorm which is separated from the common room by partitions and a curtain. Kitchen, TV lounge, sauna, BBQ. $10 key deposit includes linen rental. Reception 7:30am-10pm. Dorms $17, non-YHA members $20; ensuite family rooms $42.

NEW SOUTH WALES

## Port Stephens

▲ ACCOMMODATIONS
Samurai Beach Bungalows, 6
Sandy Point Motor Lodge, 1
Shoal Bay YHA, 5
Shoal Bay Holiday Park, 4
● FOOD
Chez Jules, 3
Bi-Lo, 2

Port Stephens

Tasman Sea

South Head

Tomaree National Park

Tomaree Head

Zenith Beach

Stephens Peak

Wreck Beach

Box Beach

Fly Roads

The Spit

Fingal Bay

TO POINT STEPHENS

FINGAL BAY

Shoal Bay

Messines St.

Tomaree Rd.

Rigney St.

Horace St.

Government Rd.

Tomaree Rd.

Marine Dr.

SHOAL BAY

Govern Hill

Nelson Head Lighthouse

Nelson Head

Gowrie Ave.

Shoal Bay Rd.

Harris St.

Dixon Dr.

Little Nelson Bay

Austral St.

Parkes St.

NELSON BAY

600 yards

600 meters

Fly Point

Victoria Pde.

Magnus St.

Donald St.

Church St.

Dowling St.

i

Nelson Bay

West Point

Tallean Rd.

Stockton St.

TO ANNA BAY & 6

Dutchmans Bay

Wahgunyah Rd.

Galoola Dr.

Gan Gan Lookout

Nelson Bay Rd.

Red Patch

Government Rd.

Sandy Point Rd.

Sandy Point

CORLETTE

N

## ✔ FOOD

Nelson Bay—the Port Stephens hub—is the best place to find cheap food. On Stockton St in the **Twin Cinema Mall** (opposite the Bi-Lo), **Chez Jules,** an award-winning local hole-in-the-wall, has a few modestly-priced choices, such as $5 gourmet sandwiches and $5 Devonshire tea service. (☎4981 4500. Open M 10am-4pm, Tu-Sa 10am-10pm.) Try breakfast near the water at the **Great Escape Café,** 19 Stockton St, Nelson Bay (☎4984 3322), next to the harbor. Trusty supermarket **Bi-Lo** has locations on the corner of Stockton and Donald St (☎4981 1666) and in the Salamander Shopping Center. There's also a **Woolworth's** in Salamander. As in many Australian towns, locals recommend registered clubs with bistros as good inexpensive eating options.

## ▨◖ SIGHTS AND ACTIVITIES

You've probably seen sport-utility-vehicle ads on TV and wondered if anyone really drives off-road like that. Now's your chance to use a 4WD like God intended. The fun-loving folks at Port Stephens Council (☎4980 0255) will let you buy a day pass for $5 so you and your 4WD can go play on **Stockton Bight,** the biggest sand dune in the Southern Hemisphere; passes available at the Mobil station in Anna Bay. Follow signs to Anna Bay from Nelson Bay Rd; the Mobil is past the beach access sign. For renting or participating in more organized group-duning, try the **Bushmobile Dune Adventure** and conquer the deserts for just $25 per person (☎(0500) 55 00 66). **Surfing**, **camel rides**, and **nude bathing** are also available on the Anna Bay shore (just don't try all three at once); inquire at the Nelson Bay tourist office for information.

**Dolphin** and **whale watching cruises** depart twice per day in the summer and once in the winter. The cheapest of the lot is the large *Tamboi Queen*, which cruises the harbor for sightings of the over 150 dolphins that live there year-round. (☎4981 1959. 1½hr. dolphin cruise $9.) On the ocean side, try Moonshadow cruises, which has a whale-sighting guarantee (☎4984 9388). Book a **high speed jet boat ride** at the tourist office or call ☎4984 9811.

For second-to-none views of the bay's rippling blue-green waters and stark headlands, and the expanse of the South Pacific horizon, it's worth making the 30min. walk to the summit of **Tomaree Head** at the end of Shoal Bay. Follow Shoal Bay Rd until it ends at the Tomaree National Park; signs direct you to the tracks.

**Nelson Bay Sports,** 77 Victoria Pde, opposite the tourist office, rents equipment for outdoor activities (☎/fax 4981 2333; open daily 8:30am-5pm): Cycles (2hr. $15, day $25), snorkeling gear (4hr. $10, day $15), body boards (4hr. $10, day $20), in-line skates (2hr. $12, day $25), and fishing gear (day $6). **Shoal Bay Bike Hire,** 63 Shoal Bay Rd, near the YHA, is a somewhat cheaper bike option. (☎4981 4121. 2hr. $10; day $20. Open W-M 9am-5pm. Hours vary in winter.)

**Sahara Trails** offers spectacular 2hr. dune and beach **horse rides** and 1hr. beginners bush rides starting at $15. (☎4981 9077. Open daily, but bookings required.) **Toboggan Hill Park,** in Nelson Bay, off Salamander Way behind the Aquatic Center, is a small theme park with a 700m downhill toboggan run, a 19-hole mini golf course, indoor rock climbing, and many other diversions. (☎4984 1022. Open daily 9am-6pm, off-season 10am-4:30pm. All activities $3-5.)

## MYALL LAKES NATIONAL PARK

If you consider yourself an ecotourist, you may well find paradise in the Myall Lakes National Park among over 10,000 hectares of lakes, 40km of beaches, and walking tracks traversing coastal rainforest, heath, and paperbark swamp. With only two major vehicular access points, the lake area enshrouds a large number of restive outdoor spots if you're willing to look for them. To find seclusion, pick up the park notes at the visitor center, and explore the various ways to access the park from The Lakes Way. Most people enter via **Bulahdelah,** 83km north of Newcastle and 70km south of Taree along the Pacific Hwy, and 60km southwest of Forster by The Lakes Way. **Bulahdelah Visitor Centre** (☎4997 4981) at the corner of Pacific Hwy and Crawford St, is the park's only "interpretive center," with comprehensive maps and information. From Bulahdelah, take the Myall Way (Lakes Rd), a one-lane sometimes-paved road with an absurd 100kph speed limit. Beware of cars, caravans, and boat tugs barreling along.

The road finishes at **Bombah Point,** a center of activity for both the Myall Lake and Bombah Broadwater. Here, the office and kiosk of **Myall Shores Ecotourism Resort** (☎4997 4495) distribute maps and some supplies. They also sell gasoline and rent canoes ($10 per hr.) and outboards (2hr. $30). The facilities within this **campground** include BBQs, laundry, a store, and a restaurant. (Campsites $16.50-23, powered $20-26, varying with the season.) A **toll ferry** carries vehicles over to the Mungo Brush area of the park. (5 min. one-way, every 30min., $3.) The almost-all-paved **Mungo Brush Rd** extends 25km along the coast to the park's southern edge. The lake side of the road has various entrances to the usually-crowded Mungo Brush **campgrounds** that have water, toilets, BBQs, and access to the shallow lake. (NPWS office ☎4987 3108. Sites for two $12.50. First-come first-served. Pay a ranger if one comes by, or use the honesty box.) On the other side of the park, accessible via Seal Rocks Rd (turnoff after Bungwahl on The Lakes Way) is the secluded **Yagon** park campsite where you can camp out on the ocean headland.

Access points all along the road lead to the **beach.** At the northern end of Mungo Brush begins the poorly signposted **Mungo Brush Rainforest Walking Track,** a 1.5km loop through a rainforest that is unusually fertile for this stretch of coast. This track has its share of interestingly large and intimidating vegetation, and koalas snooze in the trees year round. Other tracks on this side of the ferry can be walked consecutively to make up the hardy **Mungo Track,** which will take the day if you're moving along reasonably quickly; pick up the trail map before setting out.

# FORSTER AND TUNCURRY

Small they may be, but Forster and its lesser twin town Tuncurry, situated on twin isthmuses, are the height of civilization in the popular Great Lakes region—Aussie holiday spots frequently passed over by international travelers. Blessed with a temperate climate and endless stretches of empty beaches nearby, the Forster area is a nice break from the party scenes of Sydney or Byron Bay.

**🖃📶 TRANSPORT AND PRACTICAL INFORMATION.** From the south via the Pacific Hwy, **The Lakes Way** turn-off heads east right after Buladelah, and Forster is an hour down the road. From the north, The Lakes Way turn-off is east at Rainbow Flat, and Forster is a 15min. drive. Great Lakes Coaches (☎4983 1560) connects to **Sydney** (5½hr., 2-4 per day, $43) via **Newcastle** (3hr., 2-3 per day, $27); and **Bluey's Beach** (3-4 per day, 2 per day Sa-Su; $9). Eggins Comfort Coaches (☎6552 2700) goes to **Taree** (1hr., 2-4 per day M-Sa; $10, 50% student and YHA discounts). The **Great Lakes Visitors Centre,** on Little St by the wharf, is the **coach terminal** and a booking agency. (☎6554 8799. Open daily 9am-5pm.) **Post office:** on Wallace St at the end of Wharf St. (☎6554 6144. Open M-F 9am-5pm.) **Postal code:** 2428.

**📠📋 ACCOMMODATIONS AND FOOD.** Do you like nice people? If not, you will after meeting the owners of the █**Dolphin Lodge (YHA),** 43 Head St, who treat you to surf and boogie boards, a kitchen, and a TV lounge, all just a stone's throw from the beach and town. They make pre-arranged pickup at the bus stops in Nabiac on the Pacific Hwy, rent bikes, and have Internet access. (☎/fax 6555 8155. Dorms $18; singles $28; ensuite doubles $42.) **Smugglers Cove Holiday Village,** 45 The Lakes Way, has top notch facilities—a pool, a kitchen, and canoe hire. (☎6554 6666. Sites $27, powered $34; winter $13, $19.50; cabins $81-146, $43-$86.) The **Great Lakes Motor Inn,** 24 Head St, has budget accommodation with a pool and TVs. (☎6554 5555. Twins $44; doubles $52.) For food, try the small **market** on Wharf St. On Beach St at the end of Wharf St, **Beach Street Seafood** (☎6557 5300) serves a substantial $6 fish-and-chips meal, with a two-for-one special on Tuesday. When work gets out on Friday, **Lakes and Ocean Hotel** gets its taps running full volume. In this pub on the corner of Little and Lake St, Shannon Lee wrote her locally famous novel *The Dog House*. Live bands play on weekends. **Fat Ant Café,** 32 Wharf Street (☎6555 3444), transforms into a groovy nightclub on Friday nights (from 10pm).

**SIGHTS AND ACTIVITIES. Tobwabba,** 10 Breckenridge St, means "place of clay" to the Worimi Aboriginals who welcome visitors to this studio and art gallery. For those seeking souvenirs that are a little more original than the ubiquitous stuffed kangaroos and koalas, the beautiful prints and canvasses are an interesting alternative. (☎6554 5755. Open daily 10am-4:30pm. Another location is on Beach St at the end of Wharf St.) At the north end of **Forster Beach,** at the end of West St off Head St, there's a gas BBQ, a saltwater swimming pool, and the beach. For stunt skiing, seaplane flights, fishing cruises, or diving, consult the Visitors Centre. **Biking** to the beaches of Booti Booti National park is the best way to go. Beach after beach provide ample rest stops, and the treasured **Green Cathedral** is an easy turn-off from the road. Bike hire is available from the Dolphin Lodge YHA (see above; 4hr. $10, full-day $16; guests $8, $12). Boat and tackle rental sheds line the lake shore. A **swim with dolphins** cruise lowers passengers near the mammals on a boom net. (☎6554 6321. 2hr $33.) Near Forster, **Eureka Trails** offers **horseriding.** (☎6554 1281. 1hr. $20, 2hr. $35.) **Forster's Dive School,** at Fisherman's Wharf opposite the post office, runs a variety of trips, including trips to the shipwreck *S.S. Satara*. (☎6554 7478. Rates vary; 2 dives with equipment $127; advanced divers only for shipwreck.) **Action Divers,** 1-5 Manning Street offer slightly cheaper rates. (☎6555 4053. 2 dives with equipment $115.) The **Edith Breaker** and **Big Seal Rock** dives take thrill-seekers right into shark hangouts.

# NEAR FORSTER: GREAT LAKES REGION

**BOOTI BOOTI NATIONAL PARK.** For a piece of Booti Booti, follow The Lakes Way south of Forster along the coastline of Elizabeth Bay. Wallis Lake, the forest between the road and beach, and the hinterland on the road's other side comprise **Booti Booti National Park.** Aww, yeah! **Tiona Park,** 10min. south of Forster, rents sites on both the lake and beach sides of the road. (☎6554 0291. Sites $18; cabins $38-67.) Tiona Park is also home to the popular **Green Cathedral** set along the lake's edge. The sheltered waters of Lake Wallis can be affordably enjoyed with **Lakeside Family Boat Hire,** off Lakes Way. (☎6554 0309. Sea buggies 1hr. $5, paddle boats 30min. $5, double canoes 1hr. $10, motor boats 1hr. $25.) A walk (1hr.) around the lake through cabbage tree palms and eucalypts will lead you to the ocean and **Elizabeth Beach.** You can camp with less clutter at **The Ruins Camping Area,** known as the "Bull Ring" to locals, by the soft white sand of **Seven-Mile Beach** next to a mangrove forest (BBQ, toilets, and showers; pay camping fees in slots at the entrance to the Bull Ring; $17.50). Good **surfers** should travel 1km north to Janice's Corner.

**BLUEY'S BEACH AND PACIFIC PALMS.** Approximately 20min. along The Lakes Way south of Forster, a sign appears for Bluey's Beach. The road, Boomerang Dr, passes several beaches and continues through the small town of Pacific Palms before rejoining The Lakes Way a few kilometers south. **Elizabeth's Beach** is the first turn-off on the left. Patrolled by pelicans and lifeguards, the waves usually die down in summer, making the surf ideal for swimmers. Farther along Boomerang Dr is **Shelly's Beach,** a calm secluded stretch with clothing-optional bathing permitted. **Boomerang Beach,** home of myriad **surfer** dudes, is just a couple minutes farther. You can crash at **Moby Dick,** a plain caravan park with a kiosk and hot junk food. (☎6554 0292. Sites $17-25, powered $20-30; cabins $45-125.) From here, Boomerang Dr loops through **Pacific Palms,** which has a small strip of shops selling junk food, sundries, and magazines. At its end is the **Info Center.** (☎6554 0123, freecall ☎(1800) 99 69 94. Open daily 9am-4pm.) A bit farther on, you can camp in style at the **Oasis Caravan Park.** There's petrol, a market, and a small pool on the premises. (☎6554 0488; fax 6554 0268. Reception daily 8am-8pm, later in summer. Sites $14-18; cabins $73-125.) **Great Lakes Sea Planes** (☎6555 8771) offers scenic flights departing from Forster Marina and Pacific Palms for as low as $40 per per-

NEW SOUTH WALES

son. Pacific Palms is also home to the 6,500 hectare **Wallingat State Forest** which adjoins the Wallis Lake system. **Whoota Whoota lookout** is spectacular with panoramic views of the endless coastline.

**SANDBAR.** A kilometer south of the southern end of Boomerang Dr along The Lakes Way is the turn-off for a dirt road that takes you 2km to **Celito Beach.** The 300m boardwalk leads through dry littoral forest to a beach to drool over, whether you're a surfer or a sunbather. Take a left off on the main dirt road to the **Sandbar Caravan Park,** to reach a wilderness site on **Smith's Lake.** (☎6554 4095. Sites $16-22; cabins $38-76; prices vary with season.)

**SEAL ROCKS.** South of Pacific Palms and Bluey's Beach, The Lakes Way turns westward to skirt **Myall Lakes National Park** on its way to rejoining the Pacific Hwy at Buladelah. Between Smith's Lake and Myall Lake, there is an easterly turn-off from The Lakes Way onto **Seal Rocks Rd.** The community of Seal Rocks has insisted that most of the road (15km) remain unpaved to protect its seclusion from tourism. Beyond this road, a narrow dirt track leads to **Boat Beach.** Swimmers, windsurfers, and fishermen share this spot. The **Seal Rocks Camping Reserve** is near Number One Beach. (☎4997 6164. Tent sites $11.55; vans $35-44; cabins $46-54.)

# TAREE

Taree, on the Manning River and Pacific Hwy, is a small run-of-the-mill base for nearby beaches, state parks, and forests. The many budget hotels, motels, and caravan parks lining the Pacific Hwy in Taree and surrounding areas make it a convenient stop on long road trips, although northbound travelers should consider pushing on a little farther to the welcoming arms of Port Macquarie.

Taree is 200km south of Coffs Harbour, 83km south of Port Macquarie, and 310km north of Sydney. The **beaches** near Taree are gorgeous and inviting, but have unexpected currents: swim only where patrolled. The closest is **Old Bar Beach** in the little village of Old Bar, a 15min. drive from the town center on Old Bar Rd. **Wallabi Point,** to the south, has a swimming lagoon. **Diamond Beach** and **Hallidays Point,** two well-known beaches farther south, both offer **camping.** To the north is Crowdy Head, site of a lighthouse lookout.

Taree's main street, **Victoria St,** overlaps the Pacific Hwy, but you must take a turn-off; going straight leads off the Pacific Hwy to nearby **Wingham.** Most shops are on Victoria St or the streets between Pulteney and Macquarie St. Countrylink (☎13 22 32), Greyhound Pioneer (☎13 20 30), Premier (☎13 34 10), Eggins Comfort Coaches (☎6552 2700), Great Lakes Coaches (☎(1800) 04 32 63), and McCafferty's (☎13 14 99) run **buses** to: **Sydney** (5-6hr., 5 per day, $55-57); **Brisbane** (10-11hr., 5 per day, $62-74); **Byron Bay** (7hr., 2 per day, $60.50); **Coffs Harbour** (3-3½hr., 5 per day, $33-36); **Forster** (1hr.; 2-6 per day; $10, $5 YHA); and **Port Macquarie** (1-1½hr., 5 per day, $30-32). The **bus station** is on Victoria St and Pacific Hwy in front of the Crazy Prices store. Other services include: a **tourist office** on the Pacific Hwy, 4km north of town, just past the Big Oyster (☎(1800) 80 15 22; open daily 9am-5pm); and a **post office** on Albert St (☎6552 1099; open M-F 8:30am-5pm). **Postal code:** 2430.

Accommodations are cheap and plentiful. **The Exchange Hotel,** on the corner of Victoria and Manning Street offers basic but clean rooms. (☎6552 1160. Reception at bar 10am-late. Singles $18; doubles $30.) Motel after indistinguishable motel line the Old Pacific Highway offering doubles starting at $34. On Pacific Hwy, **Taree Caravan Park,** near the tourist office and across from the Arlite Motor Inn, has a pool, laundry, TV, and wheelchair access. (☎6552 1751. Sites for 2 $10, powered $15.40; cabins for 2 $30-35, ensuite $37-44.)

# FROM TAREE TO PORT MACQUARIE

**CROWDY BAY NATIONAL PARK.** Home to some of the area's most popular beaches, bushwalks, picnic areas, and a healthy supply of kangaroos, Crowdy Bay has something for every visitor. The park supposedly derives its name from Captain Cook's passing observation that the headland was crowded with Aboriginals. The southern entrance is at Moorland on the Pacific Hwy. Coralville Rd leads into the park. Wild eastern grey kangaroos live at all three of the **camping sites: Diamond Head, Indian Head,** and **Kylie's Rest Area** (named for Australian author Kylie Tennant). There are septic toilets and cold showers at Diamond Head; all other sites have pit toilets. Whereas groups of kangaroos hop within feet of astounded visitors, and **whales** can be spotted off the headlands, it often takes an expert to spot more elusive **koalas** at **Indian Head** and **Kylie's Hut.** There are three reasonably tame **bushwalks** in the park which pass through delicate habitats stunted from exposure to wind and subject to harsh salt sprays. The shortest walk is along the base of the cliff of the headland, accessible from Diamond Head at low tide. The **Cliff Base Walk** passes rock pools abounding with marine life. A longer walk links Diamond Head and Indian Head, while a third goes from Kylie's Hut to the beach at Crowdy Bay. Visitors must bring their own fresh water into the park. The roads are 2WD-accessible dirt tracks. (One-time camping charge for 2 $13.)

**BULGA STATE FOREST.** The site of a 99km tourist drive, and a 190km, full-day trip from Taree, The Bulga Forests are actually four separate forests: the Bulga, Doyles River, Dingo, and Knorrit. The Bulga is home to the **Tirrill Creek Flor Reserve,** with walking trails, picnic areas, and the **Blue Knob Lookout,** from which even Taree is sometimes visible. **Maxwells Flat,** with toilet and BBQ facilities, has **camping.**

   The most spectacular sight of the Bulga drive is **Ellenborough Falls.** Created by a fault line 30 million years ago, it's the largest drop in the southern hemisphere (160m). There are multiple **walking** tracks, the most difficult of which leads to the bottom of the gorge. At the top of the Falls, there are picnic tables, restrooms, and a **refreshment kiosk** (open Sa-Su 10am-4pm). The falls can be reached without the Bulga drive, by an east-west trip through **Comboyne.** This route also gives access to the **Boorganna Nature Reserve.** Both this and the Bulga drive are along rough, unsealed roads. For more info, call the **State Forests Office** in Taree (☎ 6551 0249).

**ALTERNATE ROUTES.** A different coastal drive runs through **Crowdy Bay National Park** and **Laurieton,** rather than taking the Pacific Hwy; the change adds negligible time. A quick drive through **Dooragan National Park** leads to the amazing lookout at **North Brother** mountain, with a panorama of the surrounding valley and bodies of water. There are also walking trails in Dooragan.

   East of the Pacific Hwy en route from Taree to Port Macquarie, there's another series of drives and parks. The **Middle Brother State Forest** and **Coopernook Forest** are accessible from Moorland. Middle Brother, near **Kendall,** contains many trails, lookouts, the two largest blackbutt trees in the state, and the equally huge **Big Fella Gum Tree.** The Coopernook drive, 25km northeast of Taree, goes through the **Coorabakh National Park,** and **Landsdowne** and **Comboyne State Forests.** Along with walks and lookouts, there is the **Big Nellie** volcanic plug, a 20min. climb to the top, and the swimming spot of **Waitui Falls.** Forestry offices in Taree (☎ 6551 0249), Kendall (☎ 6559 4108), and Port Macquarie (☎ 6583 7100) have info.

# PORT MACQUARIE

Travelers with their blinders on en route to Sydney and Byron Bay make the sad mistake of bypassing Port Macquarie (pop. 34,000), once a lock-up for Sydney's worst offenders. Today, it is one of the best places to exercise your freedom (and exercise in general); the coastal town is growing into a veritable action-sport capital. Though hard-core partiers don't dominate the town, worn-out backpackers still go strong in the cafés and bars on Clarence St well into the evening, to recover for another day of fun in the sun. In the summer, as crowds swarm to the surrounding beaches and nature reserves, Port Macquarie's population triples in size.

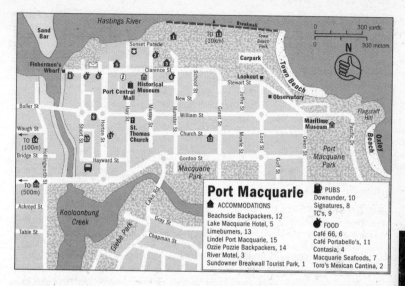

**Port Macquarie**

⌂ ACCOMMODATIONS
Beachside Backpackers, 12
Lake Macquarie Hotel, 5
Limeburners, 13
Lindel Port Macquarie, 15
Ozzie Pozzie Backpackers, 14
River Motel, 3
Sundowner Breakwall Tourist Park, 1

▯ PUBS
Downunder, 10
Signatures, 8
TC's, 9

🍴 FOOD
Café 66, 6
Café Portabello's, 11
Contasia, 4
Macquarie Seafoods, 7
Toro's Mexican Cantina, 2

# 🖥 TRANSPORT

McCafferty's (☎ 13 14 99), Premier (☎ 13 34 10), and Greyhound (☎ 13 20 30) **buses** each pass through once per day. **Cars** are available through **Budget** (☎ 13 27 27), at the corner of Gordon and Hollingsworth St; **Hertz,** 102 Gordon St (☎ 6583 6599); or **Thrifty** (☎ 6584 2122), at the corner of Horton and Hayward St.

# 🔆🛈 ORIENTATION AND PRACTICAL INFORMATION

Port Macquarie's town center is bordered on the north by the Hastings River and on the west by a small bridged creek. **Horton St,** parallel to **Hay St,** is the main commercial drag, and the area in the surrounding one- to two-block radius comprises the central business district. Perpendicular to Hay, running along the water to the Marina, is **Clarence St,** which houses the tourist office and many restaurants to the west, and accommodations to the east. To the northwest, across the bridge, is **Settlement City,** an upmarket residential district with its own shopping center. The well-organized **Visitor Information Centre** is at the corner of Clarence and Hay St. (☎ 6581 8000, freecall ☎ (1800) 02 59 35. Open M-F 8:30am-5pm, Sa-Su 9am-4pm.) Other services include: **police,** on Hay St by the water; cheap **Internet access** at the **library,** on the corner of Grant and Gordon St (☎ 6581 8755; 1hr. $5.40; open M-F 9:30am-6pm, Sa 9am-noon); and the **post office** at the corner of Horton and Clarence St (☎ 6583 2300; open M-F 9am-5pm). **Postal code:** 2444.

# 🏠 ACCOMMODATIONS

Port Macquarie has a range of good budget options; most offer the seventh night free. Peak season is during summer holidays and Easter, when motels and caravan parks can double their prices; booking ahead becomes essential.

▨ **Ozzie Pozzie Backpackers (NOMADS),** 36 Waugh St (☎ 6583 8133, freecall ☎ (1800) 62 00 20; ozziepozzie@bigpond.com). Off Gore St between Buller and Bridge St. The newest hostel in town, and closest to downtown. Friendly owners go way beyond the call of duty. Clean bedrooms with lockers are decorated with prints from the owners' European adventures. The common room has a VCR (movies free). Free use of boogie boards, bikes, and fishing gear. Laundry, Internet. Free pickup from bus stop. Dorms from $18; twins and doubles from $44. YHA, VIP, NOMADS, ISIC.

**Lindel Port Macquarie,** 2 Hastings River Dr (☎/fax 6583 1791, freecall ☎(1800) 68 88 82; email lindel@midcoast.com.au). On the corner of Hastings River Dr and Gordon St, 10min. from the town center. This relaxed, social Heritage house has modern facilities. Pool, BBQ, TV room, billiards, Internet, kitchen and pickup. Owners organize not-to-be-missed 10km morning beach walks. Free use of bikes, boogie boards, and fishing gear. Quiet time at 11pm, but kitchen and common room remain open 24hr. Key deposit $10. Dorms $20; twins and doubles $44. VIP.

**Beachside Backpackers (YHA),** 40 Church St (☎/fax 6583 5512; portmacqyha@hot mail.com). The closest hostel to the beaches and a 5min. walk from the town center. Clean and friendly, with a large kitchen, Internet, and cable TV lounge. Most bathrooms are in a separate building behind the hostel. You're welcome to join the owner on his daily swimming/surfing trips at 7:30am. Free use of bikes, boogie boards, and fishing rods. Exercise bike and stairmaster keeps health nuts from causing a ruckus. Lockers available. Common area has lights-out at 11pm. Free pickup from bus stop. Reception daily 8am-10pm. Dorms $18; twins $40.

**Limeburners** (☎6583 3381; www.limeburnerslodge.com.au). On Shoreline Dr, 10km from town, in a house on a lagoon, accessible from the Settlement Point Ferry. Comfy TV lounge and kitchen. A BBQ, stone pool, and 35 acres of land and wandering peacocks, await outside. Free pickup and drop off from Port Macquarie center by arrangement. Laundry. Caters to groups and families more than backpackers. Dorms $19.

**Sundowner Breakwall Tourist Park,** 1 Munster St (☎6583 2755; email sund owner@midcoast.com.au). A huge waterfront park near Town Beach. Pool, BBQ, convenience store, tackle shop, and food stand. No linen. Tent sites $26, winter $17; powered $32, $19. Caravans $124, $45; cabins $90-140, $50-68; deluxe 2-bedroom cottages $215, $104. Each additional person $30, $8. Book far in advance in summer.

**Lake Macquarie Hotel** (☎6583 1011). At the corner of Horton and Clarence St. The cheapest and most centrally located pub hotel. Basic singles $28, ensuite $33; doubles $44, $49; includes breakfast.

**River Motel,** 5-9 Clarence St (☎6583 3744). Conveniently in the heart of town, River is an alternative to hostels with access to beaches and waterways. Pool, BBQ, TV, tea and coffee, and toasters. Doubles with water view $66. Reception daily 7am-9:30pm.

## ▒ FOOD

Clarence St has many restaurants with specials or daily low prices. The best bet for fresh healthy seafood takeaway is **Macquarie Seafoods,** at the corner of Clarence and Short St. (☎6583 8476. Open daily 11am-9pm. Fish-and-chips $5.30) If you plan to cook, visit the **Fish Market,** (☎6583 8348), at the marina on the bottom of Clarence St, where the catch comes straight off the boat. Mouth-watering sandwiches await at **Café Portabello's,** in Shop 6-124 on Horton St. (☎6584 1171. Open Tu-Sa 10am-10pm. Lunch $4.50-5.50.) The otherwise elegant **Café 66** (☎6583 2484) becomes budget-accessible with two-for-one pasta dinners on Tuesdays. **Contasia,** 14 Clarence St (☎6584 9638), on the corner of Munster St, serves a huge $7 all-you-can-eat lunch buffet with continental and Asian foods. The **Port Central Mall** to the left of the tourist office has a cheap, typical food court. Get into a festive mood with colorful **Toro's Mexican Cantina** in Shop 2 on Murray St. (☎6583 4340. Open 5pm-late. Mains $12-14; YHA discount.)

There are some other spots popular among locals that are not in the city center. **Flynn's Beach Pasta Place,** 53 Pacific Dr, across from Flynn's Beach, features homemade pastas ($8-10) that are often big enough for two. (☎6584 0720. Open Su-Th 5-8:30pm, F-Sa 5-9pm; closed Su in winter; BYO.) **Lotus at Lighthouse,** 42 Watonga St, off of Riverside Dr near Lighthouse Beach, serves Chinese and Malaysian food. Mains begin at $10, but the huge, delicious *laksas* (from $16) are worth a splurge. (☎6582 3233. Open Tu-Su noon-2pm, and from 5pm.)

## ◉ ⚫ SIGHTS AND ACTIVITIES

### AROUND TOWN

**HISTORY.** The beautiful **St. Thomas Church** was built by convicts between 1824 and 1828. The jail's former superintendent is buried under one of the pews, because he feared that, if he was buried in the cemetery, his body would be exhumed by vengeful convicts. *(On the corner of Hay and William St. ☎ 6584 1033. Open M-F 9:30am-noon and 2-4pm.)* The history of a thousand shipwrecks along the coast is kept alive in the **Port Macquarie Maritime Museum.** *(6 William Street. Open M-Sa 11am-3pm. $2.)* Take a trip back in time with the characters in **Timbertown,** a turn-of-the-century Australian country town. *(☎ 6585 2322. Open 9:30am-3:30pm. Free; steam train ride $5.)*

**KOALAS.** You're in luck if you like **koalas**—the Port Macquarie area has the biggest urban population in the country. The secret to spotting them in the wild is to look through the trees and not at individual forks in the trees. At one of Australia's few **Koala Hospitals,** there are usually four or more injured or sick koalas on site. *(On Lord St, 20min. from the town center on Lord St. ☎ 6584 1522. Open daily 9am-4:30pm; feedings at 8am and 3pm. Gold coin donation requested.)* You can pet not just koalas, but also wallabies and kangaroos at the **Billabong Koala Breeding Centre.** *(61 Billabong Dr, on the way to Kempsey. ☎ 6585 1060. $8.50, $7 backpackers, children $5. Feedings 10:30am, 1:30pm, 3:30pm.)* Additional cuddly koalas await at **Kingfisher Park,** outside town on the Oxley Hwy. *(On Kingfisher Rd past the race course. ☎ 6581 0783. $9, children $6.)*

### PLACES TO GO

**BEACHES.** An 8km walk includes all nine area beaches and begins at the **Lighthouse Beach** lookout (hostels usually drop you here). Go down Lighthouse Beach Rd (5-10min.) to the sign for **Miner's Beach** (a nude beach) on the right; an entrance by a forest path leads to the beach and up hidden cliff paths. **Shelly's Beach,** 3km down and home to huge **goannas,** is Port Macquarie's best. **Nobby's Beach** is to the north by Nobby's Headland. The obelisk here stands in memory of those who died swimming in the dangerous blowhole—don't even think about it. Continuing north, **Flynn's Beach** is popular with surfers. The south end of **Town Beach** is good for swimming, sunbathing, and fishing.

**PARKS.** Over 70 hectares of the last subtropical rainforest on the coast is preserved at **Sea Acres Rainforest Center,** a few minutes out of town at Miner's Beach. A 1.3km boardwalk circles through the forest. The last guided walk leaves at 3pm. *(☎ 6582 3355. Open daily 9am-4:30pm. Admission $10.)* At the end of Horton St is the entrance to the peaceful bushland of **Kooloonbung Creek Nature Park,** where several kilometers of footpaths wind through mangroves and rainforest. A short trip across the bay leads to **Point Plomer and Limeburner Creek Nature Reserve,** the site of Aboriginal artifacts and the Big Hill walking track. From Settlement Point, a vehicle ferry runs across the river. The 16km coastal road to Point Plomer is unsealed and rough, but bikeable. There are **campsites** at Barries Bay and Point Plomer. *(☎ 6583 8805. Book ahead in summer.)* The tourist office has a list of nearby national parks and nature reserves.

### SIGHTS TO SEE

**BY WATER. Port Macquarie Kayak Adventures** leads tours past submerged Mangrove forests and the wildlife of the Hastings River. *(☎ 6583 9388. Daily at 9am and 2pm, $35.)* **Port Macquarie Canoe Safaris** also runs tours of the Hastings River. *(☎ 6585 6231. Full day $85.)* **M.V. Port Venture** has the largest boat, and runs Devonshire tea and dolphin-spotting cruises. *(3/74 Clarence St. ☎ 6583 3058. 2hr. dolphin cruise Th-Tu. $20, backpackers $13.50.)* **Waterbus Everglade Tours** also offers similar cruises. *(☎ 6582 5009. Dolphin watching $20. Oyster World Party Day $29, includes lunch and wine.)*

**THONG TH-THONG THONG THONG** Although goannas roam the sand and fruit bats flutter around at night, Shelly's Beach used to have a more famous resident wandering about. The beach was once home to Harry, the Port's legendary citizen-squatter who had camped in a small caravan on the beach since 1960. The somewhat eccentric Harry kept an autograph and souvenir book and was a delight to chat with. Sadly, Harry passed away three weeks after being recognized as the honorary mayor of his hometown. Though his footsteps may no longer cross the sand, the amiable beach bum will always be remembered. True, the remains of his famous "thong tree" still exist. But Harry has left an even greater legacy (if that's possible): the railed footpath up to Harry's Lookout. The view from the lookout is so gorgeous that it's been the site of more than 100 weddings; many locals have the pictures to prove it. Next time you wander down Shelly's Beach or up to the lookout, think of the pleasant man who once called this place home.

**BY LAND.** Aussie extrordinaire Greg leads **Port Macquarie Camel Safaris,** with jaunts to Lighthouse Beach and wild koala sightings. Pickup in the camel car can be arranged. (☎6583 7650. 20min. $13, children $9; 1hr. $25, $15; 1hr. tours must be booked in advance.) **Bicycles** can be rented from **Graham Seers Cyclery.** (In the marina. ☎6583 2333. 1 hr. $6.50, $22 per day, $55 per week.) **Macquarie Mountain Tours** visits the three nearby **vineyards,** all of which offer free tastings. (☎6585 9242. $24.)

**BY SKY. Port Aero Transport & Training** allows passengers to fly under supervision as part of their scenic flights over the Hastings. (☎6583 4198. $50.) **Johnston Aviation Services** runs daily aerial beach patrols and scenic flights. (☎6584 0484. From $55.)

## THINGS TO DO

**ON THE DEEP BLUE. Sea Quest Fishing Charters** runs reef fishing. (On the wharf. ☎6583 3463. 6½hr., $95.) **Gypsy Boat Hire** can provide many water vehicles for your recreation pleasure. (52 Settlement Point Rd. ☎6583 2353. Fishing boats 2hr., $20; cabin cruisers 2hr., $30; BBQ boats 2hr., $45.) **Settlement Point Boatshed** has similar deals for similar prices. (Next to Settlement Point Ferry. ☎6583 6300.) **Port Macquarie Dive Centre** can help you create personalized adventure weekends. (In Port Marina. ☎6583 8483.)

**FROM THE BEACH.** For beach adventures, **Dawn Light Surf School,** rents wetsuits and surfboards. Group surf lessons are a steal at $20 or 3 for $50. They usually have a blue trailer set up at Town Beach. (53 Pacific Dr, Opposite Flynn's Beach. ☎6584 1477. 4hr. $16.50, 24hr. $27.50.) **Surfing Australia** does surfing lessons too. (☎(04) 1747 9972. 1½hr. $30; with free pickup.) **C-Spray Jet Ski Hire** is the place for jet skiing. (On the Town Wharf. ☎(018) 65 69 33. Double seaters 30min. $50.) Many companies offer cruises up the Hastings River and to the Everglades.

**IN THE SKY. Skydive Port Macquarie** has the cheapest backpacker prices for tandem skydiving in NSW. (☎6584 3655. $290, backpackers $225.) **High Adventure Air Park** offers everything from live-in courses to tandem flights. (☎6556 5265. On-site accommodation $15; tandem para-gliding $130; hang gliding $160, motorized $88.)

## ◪ NIGHTLIFE

The local watering hole is **Hotel Macquarie** (☎6583 1011), on the corner of Clarence and Horton St. Three nightclubs cater to the younger crowd. Party-goers in their Saturdays-best flock to the **Beach House,** on the town green. (☎6584 5692. Open until 3am. $5 cover after 10pm.) Look for the recently renovated **TC's,** on William St upstairs in the Galleria Building. (☎6583 5466. Cover after 11pm F-Sa.) **Downunder** (☎6583 4018), on Short St next to Coles Supermarket, has karaoke on Wednesday and rocks on weekends. **Signatures,** 2-72 Clarence St (☎6584 6144), has 2-for-1 drink vouchers which make a good start to the night. **Finnian's Irish Tavern,** 97 Gordan St (☎6583 4646), and the weekend bands attract a slightly older crowd. A free entertainment guide, *Hastings Happenings*, is published on Wednesdays.

## NEAR PORT MACQUARIE: SOUTH WEST ROCKS

South West Rocks is *way* off the backpacker trail. Although the lack of accommodations and transport can make an uncomfortable overnight stay for the impatient backpacker, it is a wonderful daytrip. Until the 1970s, the region's virtues—the best year-round climate, beachside scenery, and beaches on the north coast of NSW—were known only to locals.

**◢ PRACTICAL INFORMATION.** Coming from the south, the turn-off for South West Rocks and **Hat Head National Park** is about 10km after Kempsey. You approach town by way of **Gregory St.** At its end, go left to find the **tourist information center**, on Ocean St in old Boatman's Cottage. The volunteers know the area's trails, beaches, and history inside and out. (☎6566 7099. Open daily 10am-4pm.) Cavanagh's Coaches (☎6562 7800) has **buses** departing from Kempsey (3 per day M-F, $7). In this part of town you'll find food shops, an **ATM,** and the **post office** (**postal code:** 2431).

**◤ ACCOMMODATIONS.** Below the tourist office, **Horseshoe Bay Beach Park** is just paces from a surf and swim beach. (☎6566 6370. Powered sites $28, winter $18; vans $61, $34; cabins $77, $53.) **Bay Motel** on the corner of Livingston and Prince of Whales St, provides basic pub accommodation with private bathrooms. (☎6566 6999. Reception at bar. Singles $50; doubles $61.)

**◉ SIGHTS.** In 1887, the New South Wales government sent convicts to South West Rocks to build a prison (for themselves) and a break wall so ships could moor in Trial Bay without wrecking. In a classic example of British colonial governance, planners ordered that the break wall be built at a 90° angle to the northwest swell. When the wall was half-built, it was destroyed by the first swell that hit it. The **Trial Bay Gaol** is now one of the best convict historical sites in the country. The government last used the granite building to hold potential dissidents—German immigrants and a few Buddhist monks—during WWI. (☎6566 6168. Open daily 10am-4pm. $4.40.) **Front Beach** curves around Trial Bay to create a warm-water swimming hole (campsites $11). **Wilay Bijarr Aboriginal Tours** (☎6562 5959) offers activities including cleansing smoke ceremonies, campfire dreaming stories, and ecotours. **Brandybrook Lavender Farm** is an aromatic rest stop along the Pacific Highway between Kempsey and Macksville. (☎6565 0000. Open M-F 10am-4pm.)

**◣ ACTIVITIES.** The best **surfing** waves break beyond the tourist office at **Back Beach. South West Rocks Dive Centre,** (☎6566 6474) 5/98 Gregory St, takes divers out to **Fish Rock Cave,** one of Australia's top cave dives. The eastern cape of South West Rocks is just as beautiful, if not more so. Take Philip Dr 5km until it turns into Wilson St after the Lagoon View Caravan Park. Turn left at the juncture of Wilson and Caldwell St toward the Trial Bay Gaol (see below), or follow signs to **Little Bay.** A narrow opening guarded by two cliffs on either side opens to rushing waves and deep water. BBQs are by the carpark. A short hike up the headland leads to spectacular views of the cliffs. From here, you can enter **Hat Head National Park** via **Gap Beach Track** (1km to Gap Beach; 5km to **Smoky Beach**). Also, beyond the BBQs, a stairway leads to walking tracks toward the jail (40min.). The promontory at **Smoky Cape Lighthouse** is a great vantage point for spotting humpback whales. Smoky Cape was supposedly named by Captain Cook as he sailed past and observed bush fires.

# NAMBUCCA HEADS

For the traveler in need of a break from relentless tourist attractions and constant activities, peaceful Nambucca Heads ("nam-BUH-kuh"; pop. 6500) provides a welcome break. Nambucca's allure is its natural attributes, especially the Nambucca River winding through lush hills into the Pacific, and its dazzling beaches. Residents, who may very well be the friendliest folks on the East Coast, often refer to it as "our paradise," and, with more days of sunshine per year than any other town in New South Wales, you can understand why. Surfing, fishing, and strolling along strips of isolated beach are all favorite pastimes in the summer, when parents bring their families back to this vacation spot that they had enjoyed as children.

## ▣ TRANSPORT

The **railway station** is a few kilometers out of town; from Mann St, bear right at the roundabout to Railway Rd. Countrylink (☎13 22 32) **trains** go to **Coffs Harbour** a few times per day ($5.50). Newman's Coaches (☎6568 1296) **buses** to **Coffs Harbour** (4 per day M-F, $5), and Joyce's (☎6655 6330) serves **Bellingen** (3 per day M-F, $5.10). Greyhound (☎13 20 30), McCafferty's (☎13 14 99), and Premier (☎13 34 10) stop daily on their **Sydney-Brisbane** route. **Radio Cabs** (☎6568 6855) run 24hr.

## ✳🛈 ORIENTATION AND PRACTICAL INFORMATION

The Pacific Hwy splits off to the right to **Riverside Dr,** the main road. Riverside has more names than the artist formerly known as Prince: when it inclines steeply at the RSL club it becomes **Fraser St,** at the town center it becomes **Bowra St,** and on the way back out to the Pacific Hwy, it's **Mann St. Shelly Beach** and **Beilby's Beach** are to the east of town. **Ridge St** forks as it leaves town. **Liston St,** to the left, leads to the **Headland** and **Main Beach. Parkes St,** to the right, leads to **Shelly Beach.** The tiny **Nambucca Valley Visitor Information Centre** (☎6568 6954; open daily 9am-5pm) and nearby **long-distance bus terminal** are on the Pacific Hwy, just south of the turn-off into the town. Behind the terminal is a shopping center with a **supermarket** and a movie theater. For an email fix, go to **Café Internet,** 1/40 Bowra St (☎6568 9030. 1hr. $7.50.) The **police station, bank,** and **post office** (**postal code:** 2448) are in the town center on Bowra St.

## ▮ ACCOMMODATIONS

Nambucca and the surrounding townships of Bowraville, Scotts Head, and Valla Beach are chock-full of places to sleep. To be safe, there are few lodgings in the town center, but most mass around the beaches or along the Pacific Hwy near the tourist office. Book ahead for summer holidays, when prices rise.

▨ **Beilby's Beach House,** 1 Ocean St (☎/fax 6568 6466; email beilbys@mid coast.com.au). Near Beilby's Beach. From downtown, take Ridge St toward the beaches, turn left on Liston St and follow the signs. This romantic guesthouse with a pool and garden is ideal for families and couples, but backpackers should check out the $52 triple. Kitchen and free pickup. Bikes and boogie boards available. Twins and doubles $42; ensuite queen $65; ensuite family room $70; includes large breakfast.

**Nambucca Heads Backpackers,** 3 Newman St (☎6568 6360; www.midcoast.com.au/ ~jpilgrim). After the second speed bump on Bowra St, turn right onto Rosedale St, continue 2 long blocks to Newman St, and turn right; the hostel is on the left. A small hostel with a mountain lodge atmosphere. The hostel's painting supplies are a definite bonus if the V-wall inspires you to leave your mark. Two kitchen areas and common rooms with TV. Owners offer advice on bushwalks. Courtesy pickup. Reception daily 7am-11pm. Dorms from $18, off-peak 3-night special $45; twins and doubles $40. VIP.

**White Albatross Holiday Resort** (☎6568 6468; fax 6568 7067). At the ocean end of Wellington Dr, next to the popular V-Wall Tavern. A sprawling caravan park with a gorgeous setting near a swimming lagoon and the Nambucca River. Picnic and BBQ areas, small game room, convenience store, takeaway café. Linen $5.50. All prices for 2 people: sites $19; on-site vans $27.50; flats and mobile homes $46; service units $77.

## ◖🎵 FOOD AND ENTERTAINMENT

Bowra St has an assortment of quick, cheap food possibilities. Nambucca Plaza, across from the bus stop and south of the tourist office on the Pacific Hwy, also has some good options. **The Bookshop and Internet Café,** on the corner of Bowra and Ridge St, is the perfect place to trade in your old books and have a delicious lunch. The café serves sandwiches and unusual juices including spinach and watermelon. (☎ 6568 5855. Open daily 9am-5pm. Internet 1hr. $9.) The **RSL Club,** at the bottom of Back St, has a gorgeous view of the river. (☎ 6568 6288. Meals $3-11.) **V-Wall Tavern,** at the mouth of the Nambucca River on Wellington Dr, also has unbeatable views and a monopoly on the night scene, with discos on Fridays and Saturdays. (☎ 6568 6344. Open daily 10am-midnight. Meals $3-9.) The **Bluewater Brasserie** (☎ 6568 6344), the tavern's restaurant, is pricier ($7-18), but worth it, while the **White Albatross Kiosk,** the holiday park's takeaway in the same building, is the cheapest of the three. **Golden Sands Tavern,** 31 Bowra Street, doubles as a cheap bistro eatery and a popular pub. (☎ 6568 6000. Lunch $5.50. Pints $4. W pool competition; F disco.)

## 👁 SIGHTS AND ACTIVITIES

Nambucca is full of delightful and spontaneous artwork. Don't miss the **mosaic wall** in front of the police station on Bowra St, a glittering, 3-D, 60m-long sea serpent scene made completely of broken crockery, including a toilet. Many of the town's lampposts are painted with colorful underwater scenes. Hundreds of rocks along the breakwater wall, called the **V-Wall** because of its shape, are painted and inscribed with dates and rhyming ditties from years of tourists, honeymooners, and families. It's one of the few places in the world where graffiti artists are welcomed and even provided with an outdoor gallery; travelers are encouraged to contribute to this creative legacy.

The **Nambucca Boatshed Boathire,** 1 Wellington Dr (☎ 6568 5550), and **Beachcomber Marine** (☎ 6568 6432), on Riverside Dr, both have a good selection of fishing gear and boats. **East Coast Adventures,** 5 Mann St, has on-site **scuba** certification courses with accommodation and runs trips to the Solitary Islands and Fishrock Cave. (☎ 6569 4422. Double dives with equipment from $90, intro dives $90.)

There are **walks** of varying difficulty throughout the beach and bush, many of which begin at the backpackers on Newman St. Park at the end of Wellington Dr. There are three gorgeous lookouts along the way: **Rotary, Captain Cook,** and **Lions.** The Foreshores Boardwalk starts at the RSL carpark down to the V-Wall. Kyeewa Bushwalkers conducts walks on Wednesdays and Saturdays (☎ 6569 5627).

**Main Beach** and **Grassy Head** attract malibu men, whereas Bellwood park with its still-water is a popular swimming spot. To get the inside edge, the **Loggerheads Malibu Board Riding Club** (☎ 6568 7314). A 16km beach separates Nambucca Heads and **Scotts Head,** an excellent surfing beach and small residential town to the south. **Bowraville,** 25min. west, and Macksville, 20min. southwest along the Pacific Hwy, are both small residential towns. **Taylors Arm,** home of the deceptive **Pub With No Beer** (☎ 6564 2101), is a 40min. drive from Nambucca Heads, and west of Macksville. The tavern is featured in the hit country song by Slim Dusty.

## BELLINGEN

Bellingen (pop. 2350) is a calm, scenic town between Coffs Harbour and Nambucca Heads, 30min. from **Dorrigo National Park** (see p. 180). Although its heyday was 50 years ago, when it was the financial and commercial center for the Coffs Harbour region, Bellingen has recently earned a reputation as an artsy community where craft shops and organic cafés thrive.

**█ TRANSPORT. Hyde St** forms the city center and leads in one direction to Urunga (20min. away), Coffs Harbour, and the ocean. Dorrigo and Armidale are close by in the other direction. **Buses** stop at Hyde and Church St. Jessups (☎ 6653 4552) services **Coffs Harbour** (1hr., 3 per day M-F, $5.20), while Joyce's (☎ 6655 6330) runs to **Nambucca Heads** (3 per day M-F, $5.10). Keans (☎ (1800) 04 33 39) travels to: **Tamworth** (5hr.; Tu, Th, Su; $49) via **Armidale** (3hr., $26); and **Port Macquarie** (3hr.; M, W, F; $28) via **Nambucca Heads** (1hr., $21) and **Coffs Harbour** (30min., $11.50). Hail a cab from **Bellingen Taxi** (☎ (018) 65 35 35). **Tourist information** is avail-

NEW SOUTH WALES

able at **Traveland**, 42 Hyde St (☎6655 2055). They book seats on various bus services. The **library** (☎6655 1744), in the park across from the post office, has **Internet access**. The **post office**, 41 Hyde St (☎6655 1020), is across the street from the tourist office (open M-F 9am-5pm). **Postal code:** 2454.

■■□ **ACCOMMODATIONS AND FOOD.** ▨**Bellingen Backpackers (YHA),** 2 Short St, is in a gorgeous house 1½ blocks off Hyde St. If you ever meet anyone critical of hostels, just send them a photo of the huge verandas, earthy tones, and incredible decorations. The floors are polished wood, and the downstairs lounge/kitchen has oversized floor pillows, a pool table, and a TV. Gregarious owners pick up guests from the Urunga train or bus stations, arrange group trips to Dorrigo National Park ($17) and treat guests with seasonal fresh veggies. They also rent bikes ($5) and canoes ($15). Work is sometimes available in surrounding farmlands. (☎6655 1116; email belloyha@midcoast.com.au. Dorms $18; twins and doubles $42; tent sites for 2 $14.) **Church St** has a row of cafés and eateries. **Cool Creek Café,** 5 Church St, seats you under the soft glow of orange snapdragon walls and old photos. (☎6655 1886. Sea perch and salad $10. Open M and Th 4:30-10pm, F-Su 11am-10pm.) On the top end of town, the **Lodge 241 Gallery Café,** 117-121 Hyde St, combines panoramic views, art displays, and generous portions of local cuisine. (☎6655 2470. Open daily 8am-5pm, later F-Sa. Famous ricotta hotcakes $8.50.) **Old Butter Factory Café** (☎6655 9599), opposite the playing fields on Hyde St, has outdoor seating and tasty meals; try the scones with jam and cream.

■□▨ **SIGHTS AND ACTIVITIES.** Behind the Bellingen Caravan Park, across the river, is the entrance to **Bellingen Island,** summer home to an active colony of "flying foxes," or **fruit bats.** A walking trail loops through the subtropical rainforest around the peninsular "island." The **Promised Land** and the **Never Never River,** lovely spots with BBQs and excellent **swimming holes,** are easier to reach than their names imply. Both are an easy 10-15km bike ride from town. Cross the Bellingen Bridge and take a left at the first rotary. Continue straight until you see a sign for Glennifer; bear right at this sign and continue for 6km. The route passes the humble abode of David Helfgott, the inspiration for the movie *Shine,* and the house of the young actor who will star in *Crocodile Dundee 3.* The river is behind the church. Cross the bridge and take the first right to the Promised Land. Platypuses live in the river; it's possible to see them in the early morning or late afternoon.

**Bellingen Canoe Adventures** has rentals and tours. (☎6655 9955. $11 per hr.; half-day tour $44.) **On the Wallaby** provides 4WD tours through the valley and Dorrigo Plateau. (☎6655 2171. Half-day $30.) **Gambaarri Tours** offers half-day local tours with an Aboriginal guide and an introduction to traditional dance and spear throwing. (☎6655 4195. $50, children $25.) The **Bellingen YHA** has equipment hire and canoe outings. The **Jazz Festival** (☎6655 9345), with ticketed performances and street performers, will be held August 18-20 in 2001. Every third Saturday, Bellingen is host to the **markets.**

# NEAR BELLINGEN: DORRIGO NATIONAL PARK

Dorrigo National Park is close enough to a prosperous town (Bellingen) to set up and support a **Rainforest Centre,** complete with educational displays, audio visuals, and a café. (☎6657 2309. Open daily 9am-5pm.) Allow 40 minutes to drive from Bellingen, 42km east, or one hour from Coffs Harbour. Dorrigo is lush rainforest, with sections of multi-layered canopy and wet eucalypt forest. When the rain makes things sloppy, the **leeches** have a field day. Pick them off, or buy a cream stick from the Centre that repels them. Do not rub them with salt, as this has a negative effect on the health of the rainforest. Adjacent to the Centre, the well-known 100m **Skywalk** boardwalk allows an aerial *birds-eye* view of the forest canopy. The **Walk with the Birds** stroll (2.5km) gives the opposite perspective of the rainforest from below the magnificent canopy. Just behind the Centre, pademelons, miniature wallabies, can be found hopping through the picnic area. You're likely to soak your shoes on the **Wonga Walk** (5.8km), a satisfying rainforest journey past waterfalls. To get deeper into the park, take the well-maintained gravel **Dome Rd** (10km) to **Never Never Picnic Area,** the origin of a network of tracks that wind among loping vines and yellow clay soils. From the town of Dorrigo, follow Megan Rd to **Dangar Falls,** which offers breathtaking views. A sealed walking track takes visitors down to the base of the falls for even more picture-perfect scenery.

# COFFS HARBOUR

Situated along a gorgeous coastline backed by hills covered in lush banana plantations, Coffs Harbour (pop. 66,000) is a popular resort for partiers, located a boat ride away from the stunning Solitary Islands National Marine Park. Coffs' rapid expansion in the past decade has come at the expense of its coastal charm, but four social and tight-knit hostels make it a worthwhile backpacker stop. Much of the town's tourism industry aims to please adrenaline-seekers with cash to spare—although it does have the cheapest scuba certification courses on the east coast. The entire city seems to subscribe to a play hard, party hard philosophy and even the most sedentary find themselves unable to resist. Just watch out for the potential activities overdose while in this action capital.

## ⌐ TRANSPORT

**Trains:** The **railway station** is at the end of Angus McLeod St by the jetty. From High St, turn right on Camperdown St and take your first left. Countrylink (☎ 13 22 32) passes through Coffs several times per day en route to: **Sydney** (8½hr., 4 per day, $79); **Bris-**

NEW SOUTH WALES

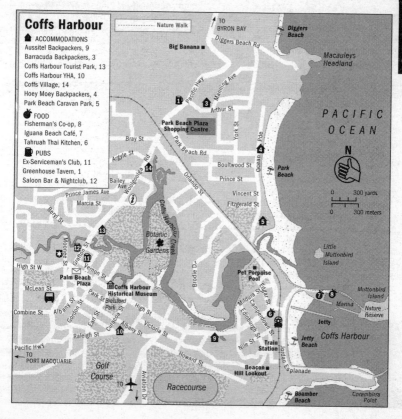

### Coffs Harbour

🏠 **ACCOMMODATIONS**
Aussitel Backpackers, 9
Barracuda Backpackers, 3
Coffs Harbour Tourist Park, 13
Coffs Harbour YHA, 10
Coffs Village, 14
Hoey Moey Backpackers, 4
Park Beach Caravan Park, 5

🍴 **FOOD**
Fisherman's Co-op, 8
Iguana Beach Café, 7
Tahruah Thai Kitchen, 6

🍺 **PUBS**
Ex-Serviceman's Club, 11
Greenhouse Tavern, 1
Saloon Bar & Nightclub, 12

**bane** (6-7hr., 2 per day, $71.50); **Byron Bay** (4hr., 3 per day, $42); and **Nambucca Heads** (40min., 4 per day, $5.50).

**Buses:** The long-distance bus stop is at Elizabeth St, near the corner of High and Grafton St; hostel owners meet nearly all arrivals. McCafferty's (☎13 14 99), Greyhound (☎13 20 30), Jessup's (☎6653 4552), Newman's (☎6568 1296), and Premier (☎(1300) 36 81 00) go to: **Byron Bay** (4hr., 9 per day, $26-43); **Brisbane** (7hr., 9 per day, $45); **Port Macquarie** (2½hr., 9 per day, $29-34); **Newcastle** (6½hr., 3 per day, $45); **Sydney** (9-10½hr., 9 per day, $62); **Bellingen** (3 per day M-F, $5.20); **Nambucca Heads** (4 per day M-F, $5). Running a few times weekly, Keans (☎(1800) 04 33 39) also visits: **Armidale** (3½hr., $26.50); **Dorrigo** (1hr., $15); and **Tamworth** (5½hr., $51).

**Car Rental: Coffs Harbour Rent-A-Car** (☎6652 5022), at the Shell Roadhouse, on the corner of Pacific Hwy and Marcia St, rents from $44. **A Little Car and Truck Hire,** 32 Alison St (☎6651 3004), rents cars from $22; 4WD from $80.

## ◾🛈 ORIENTATION AND PRACTICAL INFORMATION

Three large shopping centers divide the focus of the town: the **Palm Centre Mall** on Grafton St in the center of town; the **Jetty Village Shopping Centre** by the water; and the **Park Beach Plaza** on the Pacific Hwy in the northern part of town. **Muttonbird Island Nature Reserve** is accessible by walking down the marina boardwalk.

**Tourist Office: Visitor Information Centre** (☎6652 1522, freecall ☎(1300) 36 90 70; email tourism@coffscoast.com.au). As you head north through town, it's to the right just off Woolgoolga Rd, at the corner of Rose Ave and Marcia St. Open daily 9am-5pm.

**Currency Exchange: ANZ bank,** corner of Moonee and High St. Other banks with 24hr. international **ATMs** are in the Palm Centre Mall and the Park Beach Plaza.

**Police:** 16 Moonee St (☎6652 0299). **Water Police** (☎6652 0257), on the wharf.

**Hospital:** (☎6659 1599).

**Post Office:** (☎6652 2022), in the Palm Centre. Open M-F 8:30am-5pm, Sa 8:30am-noon. **Postal Code:** 2450.

**Internet: Coffs Harbour City Library** (☎6648 4905) has free access but must be booked at least a day in advance. **Computer Discounts,** 27 Orlando St (☎6650 0773), near the Jetty. 1hr. $4.50. Open M-F 9am-5pm.

**Phone Code:** 02.

## ▌ ACCOMMODATIONS

All four hostels in Coffs Harbour are good quality and most offer 24hr. courtesy pickup, winter discounts, and good laundry and kitchen facilities. Coffs has three central caravan parks; one near the beach and two near the town center. **Park Beach Caravan Park,** near the Surf Club on Ocean Pde, is near the beach. (☎6648 4888. Tent sites $15, powered $18; on-site vans $32.50; cabins $41-63. 7th night free.) **Coffs Harbour Tourist Park,** 123 Pacific Hwy, is just south of the visitors center (☎6652 1694. Sites $13, powered $15; on-site caravans $29; cabins $42; 7th night free.) **Coffs Village,** 215 Pacific Hwy, is just north of the visitors center in the Clog Barn complex. (☎6652 4633; fax 6651 5009. Sites $13, powered $16.50; cabins $44; 7th night free.) Dozens of motels are clustered along the highway just outside of town, along Grafton St and Woolgoolga Rd, and along Park Beach Rd.

🏅**Aussitel Backpackers,** 312 High St (☎6651 1871, freecall ☎(1800) 33 03 35; fax 6651 5335; email chb@tpgi.com.au), 20min. walk down High St from the town center. Social, clean, and wholesome, Aussitel is proof that the family which eats, drinks and makes merry together, stays together. A word of caution: many find themselves staying for weeks on end. People constantly mill about the kitchen/common area, complete with Internet, ping-pong, pool table, darts, and video games. Amenities include an outdoor heated pool, luggage storage, surfboards, boogie boards, wetsuits, bikes, and canoes. Discounts on activities like diving, surfing, and whitewater rafting. Quiet time after 11pm. Free pickup and drop off. Dorms $18; twins and doubles $42. 7th night free. YHA, VIP, NOMADS.

**Coffs Harbour YHA,** 110 Albany St (☎/fax 6652 6462; email coffsyha@keynet.com.au). 5min. walk from the town center down High St, right onto Curacoa St and left on Albany. Closest hostel to town and main bars. Everything's clean and everyone's active—both the crew and guests of the lively hostel will make you feel right at home. It's even easier to settle into the play hard, party hard atmosphere with chalkboards and murals of local activities. Outdoor pool, billiards, ping-pong, and satellite TV. Tons of equipment is available for use for $5 maintenance fee and $15 deposit. Bus runs to the beaches and on request to local attractions. Kitchen. Breakfast $3-6. Dorms $18; twins and doubles from $40; family rooms for 4-6 from $60.

**Barracuda Backpackers,** 19 Arthur St (☎6651 3514, freecall ☎(1800) 11 15 14; fax 6651 4575; email bbarracud@key.net.au). Near the corner of Arthur St and the Pacific Hwy; the first street past Park Beach Plaza. This small hostel, just a 5min. walk from the beach, is immaculate and amazingly welcoming. Each 4-bunk dorm has linen, lockers, and a fridge. Free use of BBQ, pool, spa, didgeridoos, fishing gear, boogie boards, and surfboards. Frequent activities and rides to local sights. Internet access. Dorms $18; twins $40; doubles $44, ensuite $46. 7th night free. YHA, VIP, ISIC, NOMADS.

**Hoey Moey Backpackers,** Ocean Pde (☎6651 7966; fax 6651 4434; email hoeymoey@midcoast.com.au). 3km from the center, at the end of Park Beach Rd, 50m from the beach. A backpackers, motel, and pub all rolled into one. Lively pub has weekly bands, a beer garden, and meals starting at $4.50. Four-bed ensuite rooms are functional, but the motel arrangement minimizes socializing. Free bikes, surfboards, boogie boards. Internet. Courtesy shuttle to town. Reception 6am-8pm, earlier in winter. Key deposit $10. Dorms $16.50; doubles $35.50. In the motel: singles $36.50; doubles $41.50; each extra person $5.50. 7th night free. YHA, VIP.

## ▮ FOOD

Dining options are wholly unspectacular, save the **Fisherman's Co-op**, at the end of the jetty, which serves delicious seafood straight off the boat. (☎6625 2811. Fish counter open daily 8:30am-5pm; cooked counter open daily 10am-6pm.) For another jetty seafood option, try the **Iguana Beach Café** (☎6652 5725), at the Yacht Club on Marina Dr. The outdoor deck has a somewhat obscured view of the bay. Lunch specials (noon-3pm) are $6.50; dinners from 7pm start at $10.50.

Near Coffs Promenade along High St is a series of inexpensive restaurants. A local favorite is **Tahruah Thai Kitchen**, 366 High St (☎6651 5992), where filling mains run $7-16. Grab a quick lunch at **Beach Hut Café** on Ocean Parade across the street from the beach. Hotcakes $3.50, steak sandwich with chips $6.50. (☎6651 2773. Open daily 7:30am-3pm, dinner Sept.-Mar.) The **City Centre Mall** and **Palm Beach Plaza** each offer **supermarkets,** cheap takeaways, and sit-down cafés. The Hoey Moey Hotel, Pier Hotel, Plantation Hotel, and Greenhouse Tavern (see **Nightlife,** below) all have cheap pub meals.

## ◢ DIVING IN THE SOLITARY ISLANDS

Coffs Harbour's **Solitary Islands** were recently declared a national marine park, and have since been respected as a top diving spot. The less crowded Islands may even be more enjoyable than the Great Barrier Reef. The Islands are composed of at least 19 protected beaches, headlands, creeks, and rocks. For more info contact the **Marine Parks Office** (☎6652 3977) on the jetty. Visibility is often better during the winter, but the water is chilly. You can swim with harmless gray nurse sharks year-round; they breed from June to September. Coffs has three dive shops, all of which rent equipment and conduct lessons and trips to the Solitary Islands. A PADI course or open-water course is a requirement for independent diving. A "resort" or introductory dive is done one-on-one with an instructor and does not result in any certification. For an overview on diving, see p. 295.

**Divers Depot** (☎6652 2033). On the jetty. An unbeatable deal on PADI certification, the 4-day course, including off-shore dives, costs $165 for backpackers staying at any Coffs Hostel. Manuals are not included, minimum class size is 4, and the company is known to give extra practice dives until it deems beginners ready. Divers Depot has collaborated with the hostels to offers a 5-day $219 PADI course including 4 nights accommodation. Two dives with gear supplied $95, intro dives $120.

**The Jetty Dive Centre,** 398 High St (☎6651 1611). Weekend dive packages with 4 dives and 2 nights accommodation from $274. PADI course $299. Two dives with gear from $107; intro dive $109, for 2 $137. Snorkeling charters $65.

**Pacific Blue Dive Center,** 321 High St (☎6652 2759). In the Coffs Promenade. They offer pickup. Two dives with gear $105; intro dive $135. 4-day PADI course $286.

##  SIGHTS

The Coffs Harbour **jetty,** built in 1890, was the center of a busy marine industry at the start of the century. At the end of the jetty is **Muttonbird Island,** a high-elevation nature reserve and a terrific lookout for spotting **whales.** The island was sacred to the region's Aboriginals, whose adolescent males would swim out to the island for several weeks of initiation into manhood. The jetty foreshore has BBQ facilities and is an easy walk from **Jetty Beach,** popular with families. **Park Beach** and the beach on the other side of the marina are also popular, but have dangerous currents. The best **surfing** is at **Diggers Beach,** north of Macauleys Headland and accessible off the Pacific Hwy by Diggers Beach Rd, opposite the Big Banana.

The **Botanic Gardens** is 1km east down High St from the City Centre Mall; park at the end of Hardacre St. Take yourself on a self-guided walk through mangroves and rainforests of the lovely 20-hectare gardens. The gardens can also be visited via a detour off the **Coffs Creek Walk** (5.4km; 2hr.), which leads from Rotary Park at Coff St in the city center to Muttonbird Island. (☎6648 4188. Gardens open daily 9am-5pm. Orchid house open W, F, Su 10am-2pm. Admission by donation.)

At the **Pet Porpoise Pool** (also known as the **Oceanarium**), on Orlando St by Coffs Creek, dolphins and seals perform tricks daily in the Sea Circus (10:30am-noon and 2:15-4pm), and you can talk to cockatoos, watch kangaroos, and see peacocks strut their stuff. (☎6652 2164. Open daily 9am-5pm. $15.50, concessions $11, backpackers $13, children $7, families $47.) See 80 species of mammals at the **Coffs Zoo,** 12km north of Coffs past Moonee Beach. (☎6656 1330. Open daily 8:30am-5pm; winter 8:30am-4pm. $14.50, concessions $10.50, families $36.)

The **Coffs Harbour Historical Museum,** 191 High St, documents the history of the area with a model banana plantation, the optic from South Solitary Island Lighthouse, and other displays. (☎6652 5794. Open Tu-Th and Su 1:30-4pm. $2.) The **Bunker Cartoon Gallery,** at the corner of Hogbin Dr and Albany St near the airport, is Australia's first and only collection of contemporary and classic original cartoons. (☎6651 7343. Open daily 10am-4pm. $2.) Meanwhile, the **Big Banana,** on the Pacific Hwy north of town, is quintessential kitsch. Zoom around the plantation on a monorail, learn more than you need to know about banana cultivation methods, and try your luck at ice-skating or tobogganing. Or just gawk at the giant banana in front. (☎6652 4355. Open daily 9am-4pm. Monorail tour $11. Ice skating $11. Tobogganing $4 per ride. Admission and feelings of inadequacy free.)

## ▲ ACTIVITIES

There's no shortage of activities and the field is ever-increasing. Hostels can offer good rates, but don't hesitate to call companies and ask about commission-free fun. Some companies may offer cheaper rates during the winter months.

### WATER SPORTS

**WHITEWATER RAFTING.** The **Nymboida River,** 2hr. west of Coffs, is the most popular place to raft; the rapids are mostly grade 3 to 4, with some grade 5 sections, and pass through dense rainforest. The **Gwydir River,** only flowing Nov.-Feb., is a constant grade 4. The **Goolang River,** a man-made kayaking course, is a steady grade 3. A few companies offer shuttles from Coffs and include lunch; most pick up from Coffs and Byron, but the drive from Byron can be three times as long. Always ask for backpacker discounts. ■ **Liquid Assets Adventure Tours,** the pioneers of sea rafting, runs unbeatable whitewater rafting on the Goolang. (☎6658 0850. Half-day, $77. Sea kayaking 3hr., $35. Surf-rafting 3hr., $35.) **WOW Rafting Professionals** does a trip with BBQ dinner and amusing commentary. (☎6654 4066, freecall ☎(1800) 64 03 30. 10hr. $153, two-day $325.) Award-winning **Wildwater Adventures,** 754 Pacific Hwy, 5km south of Coffs, also conducts rafting journeys. (☎6653 3500. Nymboida full-day $148; two-day $312, including camping. Gwydir two-day $335, including camping.) **Rapid Rafting** also leads trips on the Nymboida or Goolang River. (☎6652 1741, freecall ☎(1800) 62 97 97. Full-day $121, half-day $77, and one-hour $44. Backpacker discounts.)

**ADVENTURE PACKAGES. Liquid Assets** (see above) runs the **Big Day Out** which lets thrill-seekers sea kayak, surf raft, and whitewater raft all in one day. (☎6658 0850. $125.) **Rope Pack and Paddle** can customize your ultimate adventure weekend. Free pickup. (☎6654 5454. Full-day abseiling $110, biking/abseiling combo $125. Canyoning full-day $130. Kayaking full day $130.) **Coffs Water Sports** offers both jet skiing and parasailing separately and in combination. (☎(04) 1866 5656. Jet ski 30min. $82. Parasailing $62. Combo parasailing and jet skiing packages $99. Book in advance.)

**SURFING. Coopers Surf Centres** rents surfboards at the Coffs Harbour jetty by the day. (380 High St. ☎6652 1782. Surfboards $22-30, bodyboards $12. Open M-W, F 9am-5:30pm, Th 9am-8pm, Sa 9am-4pm, Su 10am-2pm.) With the sand as its chalk board, **East Coast Surf School** has a remarkable success rate with novices. Classes for advanced surfers are also available. Call to arrange pickup from hostels. (☎6651 5515. 2hr. lesson and private 1hr. lesson $34 each.)

**FISHING AND WHALE WATCHING. Adriatic III** is your best bet for fishing in Coffs Harbour. (On the jetty at the Marina Booking Centre. ☎6651 1277. Reef fishing $66. Whale watching $35.) **Whales** swim by Coffs from June to July and again (in the other direction) from September to November. Many chartered boats convert to whale watching cruisers during these times. **Pacific Explorer** can be booked at the Marina Booking Centre. (On the jetty. ☎6651 4612. From $44, children $33.)

## OTHER ACTIVITIES

**IN THE SKY. Coffs City Skydivers** offers tandem skydiving from 3000m. (☎6651 1167. Backpacker special rate $231; shorter dives $205. Free pickup.) **Skylink** does scenic helicopter flights. (At the airport. ☎6658 0899. From $58.)

**ON HORSE. Wyndyarra Estate** does 2hr. horseback rides which include swimming with the horses. (418 Loop Island Rd, in Upper Orara. ☎6653 8488; mobile ☎(015) 65 72 68. $35, with pick-up in Coffs Harbour $40.) **Valery Trails,** in Valery, offers 2hr. horseback rides with tea, but no transport. (☎6653 4301. Sa-Th 10am and 2pm. $30.)

**ON WHEELS. Coffs Harbour Mountain Trails 4WD Tours** tours through rainforests and past waterfalls. (☎6658 3333. Full-day $84.) **Bob Wallis Bicycle Centre,** at the corner of Collingwood and Orlando St, rents mountain bikes. (At Coffs Harbour jetty. ☎6652 5102. $15 per day, $50 deposit. Open Jan.-Sept. M-F 8:30am-5pm, Sa 8:30am-1pm; Oct.-Dec. also Su 9am-1pm.) Personalized mini-bus tours aimed at backpackers are offered by **Blue Tongue Tours,** with trips to Dorrigo, Bellingen, wineries, rainforests, and national parks. (☎6651 8566, freecall ☎(1800) 25 83 86. $49.50, BBQ lunch included.)

**ON ROCKS.** If adventure activities have done a job on your body, try taking a more relaxed (and slower) look around you. Try **Coffs Rock,** for active—but not entirely draining—indoor rock climbing. (13 GDT Seccombe Close. ☎6651 6688. Open W-Th 1-8pm, F 1-5pm, Sa-Su noon-5pm. $13 per visit.)

## ♫ ▣ ENTERTAINMENT AND NIGHTLIFE

Coffs nightlife, centered around Grafton St (be sure to say hello to Monica), has not quite been able to keep up with the rest of the town, but finding the party crowd isn't too difficult; people often meet while rafting, and hostels sometimes organize nights out for their guests. Most pubs have cover bands on weekends.

The popular **Saloon Bar & Nightclub,** 76 Grafton St (☎6658 0877), has no cover before 11pm. It's a pick-up scene lacking subtlety, but does have frequent drink specials and money-saving 4-drinks-for-$10 backpacker/student cards available at the coat check. **Hoey Moey Backpackers pub** (☎6652 3833), on Ocean Pde, has live entertainment a few nights a week, usually hard rock. It's also got a beer garden, pool table, and gaming room. **Coffs Harbour Hotel,** across from the City Centre Mall on Grafton St, pours the best drink in town—$4.50 pints of Guinness. (☎6652 3817. Live bands W-Su.) Some of the cheapest drinks in town are at the **Ex-Serviceman's Club** (☎6652 3888), on the corner of Grafton and Vernon St, although you'll need a passport to get in. On Friday nights, the club comes alive as non-members rush to get in by 10:30pm. Other nights, many people start their evenings here before moving on to more lively pastures. **Fitzroy Hotel** (☎6652 3007), a block south of the Coffs Hotel on Grafton St, has a 24hr. license, and often does not close until the last person leaves. **Plantation Hotel** (☎6652 3855), on Grafton St, has a relaxed sports bar and live music on weekends with an occasional cover. The **Greenhouse Tavern** (☎6651 5488), on the Pacific Hwy across from the Park Beach Plaza, is a great developing place. It has two well-decorated bars, live music weekly, and pool tables; Barracuda Backpackers offers free drink vouchers.

## WOOLGOOLA

Don't be deterred by the two large, tacky, artificial elephants at the north entrance to town—Woolgoola has a gorgeous coastline and weather that allows you to enjoy it all year. After your senses have been tricked by the tusked monuments (advertising the Indian restaurant), trick them again by heading straight to the **Woolgoola Headland.** This spot has a bird's eye view of the **Solitary Islands Marine Reserve,** small islands with marine biodiversity approaching that of the Great Barrier Reef. Dolphin and whale sightings are common from May to October. Two beaches flank the headland. The surfing- and fishing-friendly **Back Beach** stretches right when facing the ocean; the patrolled **Front Beach** is off to the left. If you have a hankering to stroll in the rainforest, leave town past the elephants and cross the highway onto Woolgoola Creek Rd; a picnic area 3km down marks the beginning of a short walk toward a waterfall. **Island Snorkel & Dive** (☎6654 2860) does affordable diving ($44) and snorkeling ($16.50) trips to the Solitary Islands.

Ryan's buses (☎6652 3201) run to **Coffs Harbour** (40min., 5 per day M-F, $7.40) and **Grafton** (1½hr., 3 per day M-F, $11.30). The **Tourist Information Centre,** in the Neighborhood Centre at the corner of Boundary Rd and Beach St, the main drag, hand out fun, detailed, artist-designed maps. (☎6654 0800. Open daily 10am-3pm.) The **post office** is at Woolgoola Plaza on Beach St, as is an **ATM.**

To sleep in the bush—or near it, anyway—veer left when entering town; at the end of the road you'll arrive at the **Lakeside Holiday Park,** with direct access to the beach and a lake. (☎6654 1210. Sites $11-15.50, powered $15.40-22; on-site vans $24.20-44; cabins $40-66.) The ornate **Raj Mahal,** behind the elephants, serves vindaloo for $14.50. (☎6654 1149. Open M from 6pm, Tu-Su noon-3pm and from 6pm.)

## MINNIE WATER AND YURAGYIR NATIONAL PARK

The **Wooli Rd** branches off the Pacific Hwy and passes through the raw **Glenngie State Forest.** A fork in the road gives the option of heading for Wooli or Minnie Water, both set in central **Yuragyir National Park.** The area is uncommercialized with an expansive bush coastal area. In the village of Minnie Water, there's a beach, a general store, and a few houses. The **BP General Store** (☎6649 7586) sells petrol and groceries. You can walk along the beach to the **Minnie Water Lagoon** or take the

Hyawath Rd (just outside of town) and second left to the parking area. The **Headlands Walking Track** sprouts from here.

To enter Yuragyir National Park, continue past the BP store and climb onto the dirt track. Less than a kilometer into the park is the **Ilaroo Camping Area,** on the beach. There's fresh water at the entrance and it accesses the **Angaphora Grove** trail. From here you can walk to the secluded **Rocky Point Camp.** Continuing into the park will lead to **Wilson's Headland,** a 500m walk across dunes to the beach, and, 2km farther along, to the **Boorkroom Rest Area.** Wilson's Headland Walking Track (2km one-way) takes in ocean blue, intertidal rock platforms, and coastal banks. Robins and eagles are plentiful, but beware of large spiders that prey on small birds. We're serious—these guys are nasty. **Diggers Camp Village** is at the end of the park road ($5; firewood, no water).

## YAMBA AND NORTHERN YURAGYIR

The raw earth and sea of this 43km stretch of the Princes Hwy are simply fascinating. The Iluka Rd leads 3km east off the Pacific Hwy and through a spooky forest. Two roads diverge in this wood, and the one most traveled heads southeast to **Yamba** (7km), a hick-meets-surfer town, with the feel of a village that wants to be big business. A road running south along the coast brings you to a three-way dead end into the bush: **Angourie.** Only **hard-core surfers** venture into this desolate terrain. In Angourie's front yard are two **natural pools** and a surf beach. The Green Pool and the Blue Pool (more popular for no real reason) are side by side. A merciless shore of rocks leads to **Spooky Beach.** Nearly next door in northern **Yuragyir National Park** are swimming beaches. There is no camping allowed in this area. You must hike 3km on the **Angourie Walk** to **Shelley Head** to camp. Beware of predatory fauna—the spiders, birds, and reptiles abound. Perhaps the most alluring activity in Yamba is simply a short drive or long walk beginning at the **Pacific Parade.**

**The Pacific Hotel** sits atop the cliff overlooking the ocean. (☎6646 2466. Singles $22; ensuite doubles $44.) The other road at the aforementioned Iluka Rd fork heads toward **Iluka;** the main reason to turn here is the **Woody Head Camping Area** in **Bundjalong National Park.** Approximately 3km from Iluka, it fills quickly in summer and Easter. **Campervans** are allowed, and there are hot showers, BBQs, and a kiosk. Visitors take advantage of surf and swim beaches, as well as swamp forest and littoral rainforest for bushwalking. (☎6646 6134. Reception daily 8:30am-4pm. Sites $14, winter $11; cabins for 2-8 $8.50-12 per person.) There's a **post office** on Yamba St (☎6646 2402), and the BP station rents outboards (5hr. $30; $20 deposit).

## BROADWATER AND EVANS HEAD

The best time to visit **Broadwater National Park** is springtime (Sept.-Dec.), when wildflowers burst into bloom in pinks, blues, whites, yellows, and reds. The park is interesting year-round, however, due to the thick vegetation that has survived the harsh conditions and poor soils of the coastline. Most of the park is beach and heath growing atop windswept dunes, speckled with the distinctive red and orange flowers of the wedding bush banksia. The **beach** can be accessed at several points along the Broadwater-Evans Head Rd, which runs the 8km length of the park. A couple of kilometers into the park from the north end is the **Broadwater Lookout,** the best place for surveying the park. Drive 4km south to the start of the **Salty Lagoon Track** (3km), a flat path that ends at a lagoon and is colorful in spring.

To reach the park from the north, take Broadwater-Evans Head Rd from the Princes Hwy in Broadwater, 20km south of Ballina. From the south, take Woodburn-Evans Head Rd 11km east to **Evans Head,** between Broadwater and Bundjalong National Parks. There is camping at the beachside **Koinina recreation park,** on Terrace St at the north end of Evans Head. (☎6682 4329. Sites $10, powered $12.)

At Evans Head is a little-known entrance to **Bundjalong National Park;** cross the Evans River Bridge and turn right. The road narrows into dirt track, and several turn-offs lead to rest stops and boat launches on the estuary. Continue 2km to the road's end at the **Gamma Garra Picnic Area.** Three walks begin across the footbridge next to the park and finish at an Aboriginal midden. The **Dirrawong Track** hugs the river and passes through swamp and dry littoral forest. The **Jenna Jenna Track** crosses an Aboriginal campsite, and the **Guweean** leads through a dry forest. Camping is forbidden in these sections of the park. Two kilometers south of the river is **Chinamans Beach,** a favorite among serious surfers.

## BALLINA

Technically an island, Ballina is a peaceful port and beach town 30 minutes south of Byron Bay with popular cycling paths and great vantage points for whale watching. Angels Beach in East Ballina packs dolphins, intertidal zones and dune ecology into 68 hectares. Flat Rock has incredible marine life diversity with three distinct areas changing with the tidal flows. Sea anemones, sea stars, octopus, and neptune's necklace are just some examples of the thriving underwater world.

**TRANSPORT AND PRACTICAL INFORMATION.** McCafferty's (☎13 14 99), Greyhound (☎13 20 30), and Premier (☎13 34 10) stop in Ballina on their Sydney-Brisbane runs. The long-distance **bus stop** at the **Transit Centre** is a good 4km from town center, in a large building complex known affectionately as **The Big Prawn** for the enormous pink shrimp nailed to the roof. **Ballina Taxi Service** (☎6686 9999) will take you into town for about $11. Regional companies stop in town at the Tamar St bus zone. Blanch's Coaches (☎6686 2144) travel daily to **Lennox Head** ($4.40) and **Byron Bay** ($7).

In the town center, the **Information Centre,** on the corner of Las Balsa Plaza and **River St,** can provide more details on fishing trips and river cruises. (☎6686 3484; fax 6686 0136; email balinfo@balshire.org.au. Open M-F 9am-5pm, Sa-Sun 9am-4pm.) Cyber-licious **Internet access** is at the **Ballina Ice Creamery Internet Café,** 178 River St. (☎6686 5783. 1hr. $6.)

**ACCOMMODATIONS AND FOOD. Ballina Travelers Lodge (YHA),** 36-38 Tamar St, is a motel and hostel. Go one block up Norton St from the tourist office, then turn left. The friendly Kiwi owners keep the lodge quiet and meticulously clean. The YHA half has a large communal kitchen, BBQ area, and laundry. Larger motel rooms have TVs and lots of amenities. There's a small pool, free bikes, surfboards, and fishing gear, and courtesy pick up from the Transit Centre. (☎6686 6737. Dorms $18; twins and doubles $40; non-YHA add $2. Motel rooms $58-95.) **Ballina Central Caravan Park,** 1 River St, is just north of the information center. (☎6686 2220. Tent sites $14-16.50, powered $16-20; cabins $33-72). River St is home to a few watering holes. **Paddy McGinty's,** 56 River St (☎6681 4638), is the local Irish pub and serves lunch and dinner. On the corner of River and Cherry St, the **Australian Hotel** has a variety of entertainment options with jam sessions on Wednesdays, Karaoke on Thursdays and bands on Fridays. (☎6686 2015. Schooners $3.30. Open until 1am.) Fine foods await at **Sasha's** in the Wigmore Arcade off River St. (☎6681 1118. Open M-F 8:30am-5pm, Sa 8:30am-12:30pm. Pastas $4-6.)

**ACTIVITIES. Ballina Ocean Speed Parasail** (☎6686 3999) offers beach fun, including parasailing ($66). Learn to surf or just perfect your technique with **Ballina & Evans Head Surf School** (☎6682 4393; $20). **Forgotten Country** offers tours to nearby rainforests, waterfalls, and an ancient volcano shield. (☎6687 7845. $55-330, 10% student discount.) **MV Richmond Princess** does mid-week cruises of the Richmond River (☎6687 5688. 2hr. $11.) For self-guided exploring, **Jack Ransom Cycles,** 16 Cherry St, just off River St, rents bikes. (☎6686 3485. Full-day $16.50.)

## LISMORE

Lismore (pop. 45,500) is a large country town with a significant Aboriginal presence. Wide, tree-bordered boulevards, brick sidewalks, and well-preserved buildings give the town the charm of a slower era, while students at nearby Southern Cross University help to sustain Lismore's cultural venues. An emphasis on environmental protection follows naturally from its surroundings: three world heritage rainforests, volcanic remains, and a disproportionately high number of rainbows (due to the position of valleys), earn it the nickname "Rainbow Region." Lismore is refreshingly suburban, one of the few places where you can walk through the business district without feeling like a tourist target.

# TRANSPORT

The **railway station** is on Union St, across the river. Countrylink (☎13 22 32) hugs the rails to **Sydney** (12hr., 2 per day, $85) and **Brisbane** (4hr., 2 per day, $29). The new **Transit Centre** is on the corner of Molesworth and Magellan St. It's the stop for **buses** run by Kirkland's (☎6622 1499) and Marsh's (☎6689 1220) to: **Brisbane** (4½hr., 2-4 per day, $31.50) via **Byron Bay** (1hr., $12) and **Surfers Paradise** (3hr., $29.40); **Nimbin** (3 per day M-F, $9.40) via **Murwillumbah** ($16.20); and **Tenterfield** (4hr., 1 per day, $23). Greyhound Pioneer buses stop at the **Ampol Roadhouse**, 136 Woodlark St, and run once a day to **Sydney** (11½hr., $78) and **Brisbane** (5½hr., $33). **Nimbin Shuttle Bus** (☎6687 2007) has free pickup and is $22 return. The best way to get around might be to rent a car. Options include **Hertz**, 49 Dawson St (☎6621 8855), and **Thrifty**, 147 Woodlark St (☎6622 2337). For a **taxi**, call ☎13 10 08.

# ORIENTATION AND PRACTICAL INFORMATION

In the hinterlands west of Ballina, Lismore lies off the Bruxner Hwy (called **Ballina St** in town) just east of the **Wilson** (or **Richmond**) **River**. Approaching the river from the east, Ballina St crosses **Dawson, Keen,** and **Molesworth St,** the busiest part of town. Perpendicular to these streets in the town center are small **Conway** and **Magellan St** and the main thoroughfare **Woodlark St,** accessible from the Dawson St roundabout and leading across the river to **Bridge St** and **Nimbin.**

At the corner of Molesworth and Ballina St, the **tourist office** has a small indoor tropical rainforest (admission $1) and a handy topographical map of the national parks. (☎6622 0122 or ☎(1300) 36 97 95; fax 6622 0193; email tourism@liscity.nsw.gov.au. Open M-F 9:30am-4pm, Sa-Su 10am-3pm.) Other services include: **ATMs** everywhere; **police** on Molesworth St (☎6623 1599); **Internet access** at Myra **Computer Services** on the corner of Ballina and Dawson St. (☎6621 2875; open M-F 8:30am-5pm; 1hr. $5); and **post office** on Conway St between Molesworth and Keen St (☎6622 1855; open M-F 8:30am-5pm).

# ACCOMMODATIONS

**Currendina Lodge/Lismore Backpackers,** 4 Ewing St (☎6621 6118; email currendi@nor.com.au). From the tourist office, go left on Ballina, cross Molesworth and Keen St, and turn left on Dawson St. Ewing is halfway down Dawson. The Lodge has neat rooms with all the amenities that make you feel welcome. The kitchen opens to a sunny eating area. Reception daily 8am-10pm. Dorms $17, weekly $100; singles $22-28, $116-135; twins and doubles $35, $155.

**Lismore City Motor Inn,** 129 Magellan St (☎6621 4455). On the corner of Dawson St. Comfortable rooms, swimming pool and $5.50 all-you-can-eat breakfast. Reception daily 7:30am-9pm. Singles $55; twins and doubles $60; family rooms $72.

**Lismore Palms Caravan Park,** 42-58 Brunswick St (☎6621 7067). Follow Dawson north and make a right onto Brunswick. Basic and cheap. Tent sites $12, powered $15.

# FOOD

Lismore's students' demand for vegetarian cheap eats has turned out some terrifically funky cafés. The cheapest **grocery store** in town is Woolworth's on Keen St (back entrance on Carrington St; open M-Sa 7am-10pm, Su 9am-6pm). Many pubs offer cheap lunch and dinner meals.

**Dr. Juice Bar** (☎6622 4440). On Keen St. An all-vegetarian student haunt. The Doctor prescribes marvelous smoothies, veggie burgers, and wildly popular apricot tofu cheesecake, all for less than $5. Open M-F 9am-6pm, Sa 9am-1pm.

NEW SOUTH WALES

**Northern Rivers Hotel** (☎6621 5797). At the corner of Bridges and Terania St. Follow Woodlark St to the bridge, cross it, and veer right at the Winsome Hotel. The best deal in town. A choice of about 10 dishes, including lasagna, steak, and roast chicken with vegetables or salad for lunch ($2.20) or dinner ($3.30). You can also cook your own T-bone for $7.70, and there's a leafy courtyard and a quieter backroom.

**20,000 Cows,** 58 Bridge St (☎6622 2517). No cows are served at this vegetarian restaurant, with wildly patterned tablecloths pinned down with tall candlesticks. Fresh pasta, Indian, and Middle Eastern food (most mains $6-10). Open W-Su from 6pm.

**Caddies Coffee,** 20 Carrington St (☎6621 7709). The indoor deck, outdoor patio, and beautiful stained glass make this a sure shot, with sandwiches, pasta, focaccia. And how can you hit a hole in one without bagels? Open M-F 8am-6pm, Sa 8am-1:30pm.

## ■ SIGHTS

Two blocks up Molesworth St from Ballina St is the **Lismore Regional Art Museum** (the white building), 131 Molesworth St. (☎6622 2209. Open Tu-Sa 10am-4pm, Su 11am-3pm; donation requested). Farther along the street is the fabulous **Richmond River Historical Society,** 165 Molesworth St, in the Municipal Building. There's a natural history room with preserved baby crocs and mummified tropical birds, and a hallway with Aboriginal boomerangs. (6621 9993. Open M-F 10am-4pm. $2.)

For a breath of fresh air, there are many parks nearby. **Rotary Park,** is a hoop pine and giant fig rainforest equipped with an easy boardwalk. The **Boatharbour Nature Reserve,** 6km northeast of Lismore on Bangalow Rd, sports 17 hectares of rainforest trees, the remnants of the "Big Scrub Forest." The original 75,000 hectares of lowland forest throughout northern New South Wales has been almost completely deforested. **Tucki Tucki Nature Reserve,** which doubles as a koala sanctuary, is 15 minutes from Lismore on Wyrallah Rd. Lismore's water supply comes from the **Rocky Creek Dam,** home to a waterfront boardwalk and a platypus lagoon.

## ■♫ NIGHTLIFE AND ENTERTAINMENT

Like any hard-working town, Lismore knows how to kick back and have a few. The town's nightlife centers around the hotel pubs in the town center. With **Powerhouse** nightclub and **Main St Bar** under the same roof, the **Canberra Hotel,** 77 Molesworth St, is the main nightspot in town. The bar has live music gigs Thursday through Saturday and plenty of pool tables. (☎6622 4736. Open Th-F until 3am, Sa 3:30am.) **Mary Gilhooleys Irish Bar,** on the corner of Woodlark and Keen St at the roundabout, has live music Th-Sa, but pricey pints of Guinness at $6.30. (☎6622 2924. Open until 1am.) On Keen St, the **Lismore Workers Club** (open F and Sa till midnight) offers cheap drinks as does the **Lismore RSL,** 1 Market St.

## NEAR LISMORE: THE VILLAGES

Though the roads to the 10 small villages within the Lismore region are indirect and confusing, each hamlet yields some unique feature to draw visitors, if only for an afternoon. **Bexhill's** main attraction is an open-air cathedral and periodic organ recitals. **Dunoon,** near the Whian Whian State Forest, has rows of macadamia nut factories, some with free samples. Scenic **Rosebank** is particularly beautiful in late October when the jacarandas are in bloom.

**The Channon,** 20 minutes from Lismore, is home every second Sunday to the **Channon Markets,** the largest in the region, with spectacular displays of music and homemade food. It's also the closest village to the lovely **Protestor's Falls,** named for a group of activists who, in 1979, were determined to prevent logging of the Terania Creek Forests. They arrived for a one-day demonstration and stayed for six weeks. Their efforts paid off: the tall, elegant stands of intertwined limbs were declared a national park, and the falls still empty into a shaded swimming hole.

# NIMBIN

A popular day trip from Byron, Nimbin is an experience you won't forget. Numerous galleries and psychedelic streetscape facades attest that the area's artistic talents are as rich as the surrounding soil. Since thousands of university students descended on Nimbin (pop. 700) for the 1973 Aquarius festival—Australia's answer to Woodstock—the community has retained an image as Australia's hippie and drug capital. Cookie? Cookie? While the presence of mumbling, shifty-eyed drug dealers downtown can be an immediate turn-off, the area's natural beauty and pure living hold a degree of promise. More than 350 communes, some open to the public, are sheltered by the volcanic valley around the town, and residents' lives are closely intertwined with the land and its fruits, most of which are legal.

**TRANSPORT.** The Nimbin Shuttle Bus (☎6680 9189) departs daily to Nimbin from **Byron Bay** at 10am, returning at 2:30pm ($22). For visitors who just want a glimpse of the spectacle, Byron-based tours to nearby national parks often stop in town for an hour or two. **Jim's Alternative Tours** (☎6685 7720) is the most engaging, and costs $25. **Mick's Bay to Bush** (☎6685 6889) has $20 tours, and **Peterpan** (☎(1800) 25 24 59) starts around $12. **Nimbin Explorer Eco-Tours** (☎6689 1557) runs 2hr. tours of the sacred rocks, Permaculture Education Center, Rainbow Power Company, and rainforest (2-3hr., $17).

**PRACTICAL INFORMATION.** Nimbin's commercial district and center is on **Cullen St** between the police station and the corner hotel. You'll know you're there by the vivid murals, wild storefront displays, and thin wisps of smoke. Cookie? **The Nimbin Tourist Connexion,** at the end of Cullen St, has info on national parks and Nimbin's "straight" side, and is also a booking agency. (☎6689 1764. Open M-F noon-5pm, Sa-Su noon-2pm.) **Perception Books,** 47 Cullen St, has a terminal for **Internet access** (☎6689 1766. Open M-F 10am-5pm, Sa 10:30am-4:30pm. 1hr. $7.50.)

**ACCOMMODATIONS AND FOOD. Granny's Farm** is a 10min. walk from the town center north on Cullen St. Turn left just before the bridge. The creekside lodge has two pools, showers, a kitchen, frequent BBQs, loose horses, and laundry facilities; platypuses frolic in the creek. Nightly outdoor fires are great icebreakers. (☎6689 1333. Dorms $17; doubles $38; tent sites $8 per person.) For pure living, the **Rainbow Retreat,** 75 Thorburn St, lies 10 minutes from the town center and miles from anywhere else. Take a left onto Thorburn from Cullen St just across a green stream; the hostel is up a rocky driveway through a horse pasture. (☎6689 1262. Dorms $13; brightly colored VW $28; wagon double $33; tentsites $9.) **Nimbin Tourist Caravan Park,** 29 Sibley St, has basic facilities. (☎6689 1402. Reception 7am-9:30pm. Sites $16, powered $18; caravan $39.) Many of the area communes are part of **WWOOF** (☎(03) 5155 0218), in which **W**illing **W**orkers exchange their labor for homestays **O**n **O**rganic **F**arms (for more info, see p. 74).

Nimbin has a few good eateries, all on Cullen St. **Rick's Café,** 60 Cullen St (☎6689 1296), makes veggie burgers and lasagna ($4.40). The **Rainbow Café,** 64A Cullen St, was the first alternative café in Nimbin. (☎6689 1997. Focaccia sandwiches $7. Open daily 8am-5pm.) Cookie? Nearby, **Nimbin Emporium** sells health and bulk foods. (☎6689 1205. Open M-F 8:30am-6:15pm, Sa-Su 9am-6pm.) **Bush Theatre/Picture Factory** has put together a movie/meal deal including wine (F-Su, special backpackers nights Tu-W through Granny's Farm; $13). The **Cave,** 81 Cullen St, doubles as a vegetarian café and groovy nightclub. (☎6689 0007. Open daily 8am-late.)

**SIGHTS AND FESTIVALS.** The mural-covered **Nimbin Museum,** on Cullen St, redefines creativity and historical interpretation. It's complete drug-induced strangeness, but at the same time ingenious (or is that redundant?). Party vans burst through the front facade, and the 3D tangle of cobwebs, clocks, psychedelic fans, and tree branches lend credence to Einstein's quotation, found in the second room: "Imagination is more important than knowledge." The rooms relate the founders' version of regional history, with proportionate coverage of all three major historical periods: the first room is about Aboriginals, the second about European settlers, and the next five about the hippies. This last group is illustrated by dollhouses, fluorescent-lit cave rooms, melted skeletons (presumably illustrating nuclear meltdown), and marijuana legalization propaganda. (☎6689 1123. $2 donation requested.) The Hemp Party (which must be one raging party) has its base at the **Hemp Embassy,** 51 Cullen St. (☎6689 1842. Open daily 9am-5pm.) Cookie? Cookie? On the first weekend of every May, crowds flock to the tiny town for the annual **Mardi Grass,** the brainchild of the Hemp Embassy. Events include the Hemp Olympics where contestants battle it out in everything from a bong-throwing competition to a joint-rolling contest.

In 1973, the Australian Union of Students created the **Aquarius Festival** as a forum for a new future. The most direct outcome of the festival, and a major employer in Nimbin, is the **Rainbow Power Company,** a 10min. walk from the city center down Cullen St to Alternative Way, on the right. The building, made of mud bricks, is a remarkable achievement in energy production; they even sell their excess generated power to the electricity grid for general consumption. One-hour factory tours are available with advance booking. (☎6689 1430. Open M-F 9am-5pm, Sa 9am-noon. Tours by arrangement; 1hr. $2.) Oh come on, have a cookie!

## NEAR NIMBIN: NIGHTCAP NATIONAL PARK

An 8000-hectare park with the highest rainfall in the state and containing the southern rim of the 20-million-year-old **Mt. Warning** volcano crater, Nightcap has two main areas: **Mt. Nardi,** 12km out of Nimbin, and the **Terania Creek/Protestors Falls** area, 15km out of **The Channon** (20km from Nimbin). Mt. Nardi, one of the highest peaks, is accessible on sealed roads and has BBQ and picnic facilities. The viewing platform has info on the walk to nearby **Mt. Matheson** (1.5km) and the **Pholi's Walk** (2km), with a lookout to the **Tweed Valley.**

Gravel Terania Creek Rd leads to Protestor's Falls in the Terania Creek basin and to a picnic area with BBQ, toilets, wood, and shelter. **Camping** is limited to one night. The track to Protestor's Falls (1.4km return) passes **Waterfall Creek** on the way (see **The Villages,** p. 190). **Tuntable Falls** in the Tuntable Falls commune is a 120m waterfall (from the parking lot, 3-4hr. return). From Nimbin, the turn-off is 6km down Sibley St; then go another 6km. The **Nimbin Rocks,** and Aboriginal sacred site, are the other way out of town, toward Lismore. **Hanging Rock Falls** is just 25min. from Nimbin near Wadeville. The natural swimming hole is perfect for picnics and bordered by basalt columns.

# BYRON BAY

The "come for a day, stay for a week" coastal malaise that infects many a wandering traveler on the Holiday Coast of Australia hits its peak in Byron Bay, one of the most popular stops on the Sydney-to-Cairns route. Here, everyone stays longer than they had planned. With Byron's excellent family and surfing beaches and refreshing lack of high rises and mass consumerism, it's not hard to see why. While Byron feeds its indignant-granola masses with palm reading, massage classes, and bead shops, it's more than just commercialized karma. The relaxed, rejuvenating coastal town with a famously "alternative" attitude is nirvana for its diverse devotees: aged hippies, dredlocked backpackers, bleached surfers, ravers, young families, sharp businessmen, and yoga gurus. Although many are high, few are "tuned out;" a passion for environmentalism, liberalism, vegetarianism, and sunshine is manifest, and each finds a home on this beautiful section of beach.

## ▗ TRANSPORT

**Trains:** Countrylink (☎13 22 32) runs 2 per day to: **Sydney** (10½hr., $98); **Brisbane** (5hr., $26); **Coffs Harbour** (4hr., $42); and **Surfers Paradise** (4½hr., $15). 50% discount with 15-day advance purchase.

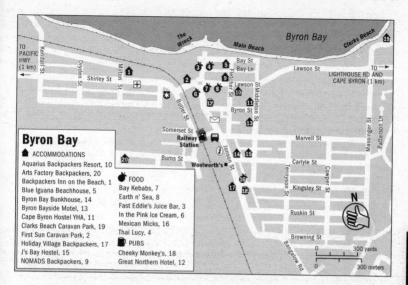

**Byron Bay**

⌂ ACCOMMODATIONS
Aquarius Backpackers Resort, 10
Arts Factory Backpackers, 20
Backpackers Inn on the Beach, 1
Blue Iguana Beachhouse, 5
Byron Bay Bunkhouse, 14
Byron Bayside Motel, 13
Cape Byron Hostel YHA, 11
Clarks Beach Caravan Park, 19
First Sun Caravan Park, 2
Holiday Village Backpackers, 17
J's Bay Hostel, 15
NOMADS Backpackers, 9

🍎 FOOD
Bay Kebabs, 7
Earth n' Sea, 8
Fast Eddie's Juice Bar, 3
In the Pink Ice Cream, 6
Mexican Micks, 16
Thai Lucy, 4

🍺 PUBS
Cheeky Monkey's, 18
Great Northern Hotel, 12

**Buses:** Between Greyhound (☎ 13 20 30), McCafferty's (☎ 13 14 99), Kirkland's (☎ (1300) 36 70 77), Blanch's Coaches (☎ 6686 2144), and Premier (☎ 13 34 10), buses run to: **Sydney** (13hr., 9 per day, $79); **Brisbane** (3-3½hr., 10 per day, $29); **Ballina** (3-7 per day, $18); **Coffs Harbour** (4-5hr., 9 per day, $45); **Lennox Head** (3-7 per day, $5); **Lismore** (1hr., 2-4 per day, $18); **Murwillumbah** (1hr., 2-4 per day, $18); **Port Macquarie** (6-7½hr., 9 per day, $57); and **Surfers Paradise** (2hr., 2-4 per day, $21).

**Car Rental: Earth Car Rentals,** Shop 6, 1 Carlyle St (☎ 6685 7472), rents from $33 per day. **JetSet Travel,** on Marvell St (☎ 6685 6554), starts at $38.50 per day.

## ✳🛈 ORIENTATION AND PRACTICAL INFORMATION

Byron is not on the Pacific Hwy, but is accessible from it through nearby Bangalow. From the latter, **Bangalow Rd** enters Byron Bay from the south. Turn off a roundabout onto Browning St, which leads to **Jonson St,** the southern boundary of the city center. **Lawson St** is to the north of town, running at times along **Main Beach.** To the east, Lawson St becomes **Lighthouse Rd,** running past **Clarks Beach, The Pass** surfing spot, **Wategos Beach,** the **lighthouse,** and the Cape Byron lookout. To the west, Lawson becomes **Shirley St** and curves off to **Belongil Beach.** Farther west it becomes **Ewingsdale Rd** and passes the **Arts and Industrial Estate** before reaching the Pacific Hwy.

**Tourist Office: Tourist Information Centre,** on Jonson St (☎ 6685 8050), by the railway station. Luggage storage $3 per day. Open daily 9am-4:30pm.

**Budget Travel:** Most hostels book activities, and there are a few travel agencies in town. **Byron Bus and Backpacker Centre** (☎ 6685 5517), behind the long-distance bus stop, is a booking agency. Service fee $3. Backpack storage $3 per day. Open daily 7am-7pm.

**Currency Exchange: ANZ,** 57 Jonson St (☎ 6685 6502); **National,** 33 Jonson St (☎ 6613 2265); **Westpac,** 73 Jonson St (☎ 6685 7407). All open M-Th 9:30am-4pm, F 9:30am-5pm. Other **ATMs** are across the street from the tourist office.

**Taxis:** Byron Bay Taxis (☎ 6685 5008). 24hr.

**Police:** on the corner of Butler and Shirley St (☎ 6685 9499).

**Hospital: Byron District Hospital,** on Wordsworth St (24hr. ☎ 6685 6200).

**Internet Access: Global Gossip,** 84 Jonson St (☎ 6680 9140), at the bus stop. 1hr. $5.50. Open daily 8am-midnight. **Peterpan Tours,** 107 Jonson St. 1hr. $3. Internet cafés literally line the streets of backpacker-ready Byron Bay.

NEW SOUTH WALES

**Post Office:** 61 Jonson St. Open M-F 9am-5pm. **Postal Code:** 2481.
**Phone Code:** 02.

# ✦ ACCOMMODATIONS

In summer, especially around Christmas, Byron floods with thousands of tourists; everything gets packed, and some accommodation prices go up 150-200%. The best advice is to book early, but demand is so high that many hostels do not take reservations in summer. Many unlucky would-be Byron dwellers make do with Ballina (see p. 188) or Lennox Head (see p. 198).

## HOSTELS

Byron has numerous hostels, and the standard of quality is amazingly high. Most of the hostels have strict 11pm lights-out in the common room and 10am check-out. In peak season, rates can increase by as much as 200%.

🏅 **Arts Factory Backpackers Lodge,** on Skinners Shoot Rd (☎6685 7709; fax 6685 8534; www.omcs.com.au/artsfactory). Cross the railroad tracks behind the bus stop and take a right on Burns St to Skinners Shoot Rd. Welcome to Wonderland, Alice. Sprawling grounds with weirdly wonderful sleeping options from teepees to island bungalows in a lake. Daily activities include didgeridoo-making, yoga, fire-twirling, and drum workshops ($8-15). Weekly talent shows and BBQ. Free use of volleyball courts, pool, and sauna. Internet 30min. $5. Surfboard and bodyboard hire. Reception daily 7am-9pm. Dorms $16-21; weirdly wonderful options $18-22; twins and doubles $44-58; tent sites $8. Off-season, multi-night, and student discounts. YHA, VIP.

🏅 **The Blue Iguana Beachouse,** 14 Bay St (☎6685 5298; fax 6680 9150). Opposite the Surf Club, on the corner of Bay and Fletcher St. True relaxation in an intimate beachhouse near the town center. Sundeck and screened front porch with couches and TV; porch and kitchen open 24hr. Free surfboards and bodyboards. Off-street parking. Reception daily 9am-noon and 4-9pm. Dorms $20; doubles $40. 7th night free.

🏅 **Aquarius Backpackers Resort,** 16 Lawson St (☎6685 7663, freecall ☎(1800) 02 89 09; fax 6685 7439; www.qai.com.au/backpackers/nsw.html). At the corner of Middleton St, 2 blocks off Jonson St. Many of the spacious rooms have 2 levels, porches, sinks, and fridges; all have beautiful rosewood beds. Pool, kitchen, café (dirt-cheap meals; pancakes $3), bar, parking, and Internet. Each night, guests get a complimentary $5 voucher for use at the on-site bar or café. Free boogie boards, bikes, and shuttle bus. Reception daily 7am-9pm. Ensuite dorms $22; doubles $50. YHA, VIP.

**Byron Bay Bunkhouse,** 1 Carlyle St (☎6685 8311; fax 6685 8258). Opposite the Jonson St Woolworth's. Crowded and loud, but it's the cheapest hostel in town. $3 dinners (tacos, pasta, etc.) every night that can be eaten on the beautiful, candle-lit terrace. Free pancake breakfast, bikes, and boogie boards. Live entertainment W. Reception daily 7:30am-2:30pm and 4:30-10pm. Dorms $15-22. Wheelchair accessible.

**NOMADS Main Beach Backpackers,** corner of Lawson and Fletcher St (☎6685 8695; fax 6685 8609). Take a right on Lawson from the beach end of Jonson St. It's a beaut, with high ceilings, wood paneling, fireplace, and rooftop deck. Friendly, but surfer-centric and usually quiet. Patio, saltwater pool, secured parking, BBQ, comfortable common room with TV and pool table. Clean bedrooms have individual lockers. Internet 12min. $2. Reception daily 8am-9:30pm. Dorms from $14, weekly $98; twins and doubles $40-45. YHA, VIP, NOMADS. Wheelchair accessible.

**Backpackers Inn on the Beach,** 29 Shirley St (☎6685 8231; fax 6685 5708). Follow Jonson St, veer left onto Lawson St, cross the railroad tracks, and continue on Shirley St to the corner of Milton St. The only hostel in Byron with direct beach access. Large, functional, and social. Loft kitchen, volleyball, heated pool, BBQ, pool table, and Internet. Free bikes and boogie boards. Small café sells food for under $6. Reception daily 8am-8pm. Dorms $19-21; doubles from $54. Rates drop $1 nightly after 3 days, and another $1 after a week. YHA, VIP, NOMADS, ISIC. Wheelchair accessible.

**J's Bay Hostel (YHA),** 7 Carlyle St (☎6685 8853; email jbay@nor.com.au). Clean, colorful, and cozy, J's has one of the best all-you-can-eat-and-drink BBQ deals, with live music and lots of wine (Tu, F $6). Billiards and picnic tables in an upstairs covered pavilion, very large kitchen, heated pool. Family-friendly. Free use of bikes and boogie boards. Internet (10min. $2). Reception daily 8am-9pm. Dorms $16-20; twins and doubles $45, ensuite $50; separate family building $60. Wheelchair accessible.

**Cape Byron Hostel (YHA),** corner of Middleton and Byron St (☎6685 8788; fax 6685 8814; email byronyha@nrg.com.au). From the bus stop, go 2 blocks down Byron St and take a left on Middleton. Great owners lend a homey atmosphere, except at home there aren't pinball machines, a pool table, and video games in the living room. Unless you're obscenely rich, in which case you'd just buy your own house in Byron (see **Bloody Hell,** p. 197). Upstairs deck and eating area overlooks a pool bordered by palm trees. $9 all-you-can-down BBQ and wine twice per week. Family-friendly. Secured parking. Internet 10min. $2. Reception daily 6:45am-10pm. Dorms $18-22; twins and doubles $50-55, ensuite $65. Wheelchair accessible.

**Holiday Village Backpackers,** 116 Jonson St (☎6685 8888, freecall ☎(1800) 35 03 88; fax 6685 8777). 2 blocks from the tourist center. Rooms are a bit musty. Large courtyard, picnic tables, heated pool, spa, TV and video room. Internet 1hr. $4. Free use of bikes, surfboards, and boogie boards. All-you-can-eat BBQ M, F $10. Reception daily 7am-9:30pm. Dorms $21; doubles $55; apartments $24 per person. YHA, VIP.

## MOTELS AND CAMPING

**Byron Bayside Motel,** 14 Middleton St (☎6685 6004; fax 6685 8552). Take Byron St from Jonson St. Great location near the town center and beaches. Large, clean rooms with new furniture, full kitchen, TV, laundry, and sparkling private bathroom. Off-season singles $66; twins and doubles $70, each extra person $15. Prices increase $5 for weekends, $20 for holidays, $60 Christmas and Easter. Wheelchair accessible.

**First Sun Caravan Park** (☎6685 6544). On Lawson St, between Jonson and Butler St. On the main beach, and thus popular with backpackers. Kitchen, BBQ, laundry. Public pool next door. Sites $17, peak $17-30; cabins $57, $105. Wheelchair accessible.

**Clarks Beach Caravan Park** (☎6685 6496). On Clarks Beach, off Massinger St. Well-kept sites. Lights out 9:30pm. Sites for 2 $17, school holidays $19; weekly $102, $165. Ensuite cabins $69, $75; weekly $410, $525.

## ◖ FOOD

▨ **Thai Lucy** (☎6680 8083). On Bay Lane. In the alley opposite Hog's Breath Café on Jonson St. You'll have to wait to get in, but the food is fantastic. Indoor and outdoor seating. Prices are medium range (main dishes $8-14) but worth it for every savory bite. Takeaway available. Open Tu-Su noon-3pm and 5:30-10pm. BYO.

▨ **Mexican Micks,** 109 Jonson St (☎6680 9050). One of the few non-seedy, really quality Mexican places in the area that is also a good value. A heaping plate of beans, rice, and two enchiladas will only set you back $9. Open daily for dinner from 6-9pm.

**Earth n' Sea,** 11 Lawson St (☎6685 6029). Cheesy, doughy, comfort food. It caters to "pastaholics," hitting a nerve with anyone who wants to stuff their face with carbo-goodness. Pastas from $8, pizza pies from $12. Delivery available. Open daily 5:30-9pm.

**Fast Eddie's Juice Bar,** 11 Jonson St (☎6685 8805). The name is a bit misleading, as Fast Eddie's serves up stylish and healthy full meals just as frequently as they concoct iced juicy nectars. The soy-dominated menu has a wide range of veggie options, including vegetarian pizzas (from $9) and tofu burgers. Open daily 8:30am-9pm.

**Supernatural Foods,** at the Arts Factory (☎6685 5833). Hare Krishna staff prepares delicious, fabulously popular "karma free" vegetarian dinners ($5-12.50). Candles and lights are suspended by ropes from the lofty ceiling; long wooden tables are surrounded by stone statues, sculptures, and a splashing waterfall. Open for dinner from 6pm.

**In the Pink Homemade Ice Cream,** on Jonson St near the Lawson St roundabout. It just wouldn't be the beach without ice cream, now would it?

**Bay Kebabs,** corner of Jonson and Lawson St (☎6685 5596). The marinated chicken kebab is addictive ($4.90). Open daily 10am-late.

## ◉ SIGHTS

Built in 1901, the **Byron Bay Lighthouse,** at the end of Lighthouse Rd, is Cape Byron's crowning glory. A steadily rotating beam pierces through 40km of darkness every night. The interior is red cedar, the outside concrete. The last lighthouse keeper left in 1988, long after the lighthouse became fully automated. The keepers' cottages are still standing, however; one is a small museum and the other is available for private holiday rental. (Grounds open daily year-round 8am-5:30pm. Tours during school holidays.) A boardwalk leads to the lighthouse, passing along Main Beach to Clarks Beach and the **Captain Cook Lookout.** From here, a walking circuit follows the beach to **The Pass,** and winds up a steep gradient past Wategos Beach to the **Headland Lookout,** the easternmost point in Australia and an excellent place for spotting dolphins and whales. The lighthouse is just a short distance farther; the track then heads through forest back to Captain Cook Lookout.

Byron's artistic community is flourishing and growing; the best example is the **Michael Commerford Gallery,** in the Byron Arcade at 4/13 Lawson St (☎6680 8433; open daily 11am-6pm). **Gondwana Gifts,** 7-9 Byron St (☎6685 8866), has Aboriginal art and free weekly didgeridoo lessons. West of town, the **Arts and Industrial Estate,** off Ewingsdale Rd (called Shirley Rd in town), houses paintings, sculptures, and crafts, and sells shoes cheap. Colin Heaney **blows glass** at 6 Acacia St (☎6685 7044; open M-F 9am-5pm, Sa-Su 10am-4pm).

## ◗ ACTIVITIES

**SURFING.** Boards slung over their shoulders, herds of bleach-blond surfers trudge dutifully to Byron's beaches every morning at sunrise. Surf schools entice novices by providing all equipment and soliciting through hostels. **Black Dog Surfing** has a stand-up guarantee. (☎6685 5352, afterhours ☎6680 9828. 2hr. lesson $25; half-day with lunch $30, full-day with lunch $50.) The **East Coast Surf School** has group lessons. (☎6685 5989. 2½hr. $20.) Its agent, **Bay Action,** 14 Jonson St, rents equipment. (☎6685 7819. Surfboards full-day $22, weekly $66; wetsuits $10, $40; boogie boards $15, $45.) **Style Surfing** offers an all-inclusive beginner package with free pickup; the accompanying photographer captures the real you instead of the vision of grace and loveliness you think you are. (☎6685 5634. 4hr. $33.)

Byron has excellent surfing spots all around the bay, so no matter the wind conditions there are always good waves somewhere. A crowded spot off Main Beach, **The Wreck** is known for fast waves that break close to the beach. Working down the beach toward the lighthouse, **The Pass** promises long, challenging rides, but can be dangerous because of overcrowding, sharp rocks, and boats. The water off **Wategos Beach,** close to The Pass, is best for longer surfboards, since the waves are slow and rolling. Again, the rocks can be dangerous. **Cosy Corner,** on the other side of the headland from Wategos, has great northern-wind surfing. On the other side of Main Beach, southern winds bring **Broken Head** and **Belongil Beach** alive.

**KAYAKING AND RAFTING.** Ocean kayaking is a great way to exercise (who wants to do that?) and *also* see the dolphins. **Ocean Kayaking Byron Bay** runs half-day trips past the area's wrecks and reefs to a snorkeling site. (☎6685 7651. $30.) **Dolphin Kayaking** provides a guided tour of Byron's marine life, taking guests right up to a school of local dolphins or whales in season. (☎6685 8044. Half-day $30.) For those who prefer to kayak at their own pace, **Coastal Fishing Tackle,** at Byron and Middleton St, hires vessels. (☎6685 5344. Single half-day $33, full-day $55; double $45, $65.) **Wildwater Rafting** does trips on the nearby Goolang, Nymboida, and Gwydir rivers, with pickup in Byron Bay and Coffs Harbour. (☎6653 4469.)

NEW SOUTH WALES

**BLOODY HELL!** Certain beachfront properties in Byron Bay that are currently worth millions couldn't even be given away less than 20 years ago. An acre near Clarks Beach in 1970 only cost $100, and is now worth a thousand times that. Why? Well, Byron used to be the home of a whaling station that dumped truckloads of whale blood and parts into the water, transforming the bay into a shark extravaganza during the 1960s. Since no tourists came to stick their toes in the water, the town itself subsisted on the rather unpleasant business of pig slaughtering. All in all, Byron was a rather rough and unpleasant place. Then whaling became illegal, the piggery closed, and mellow drug trafficking became the profession of choice. Now, too cool for its own good, baby Byron is an exploding tourist destination—trying to balance its granola goodness with the bucks and backpackers that are scrambling up the coast from Sydney in droves. The lesson? Always buy cheap property on the water. Always.

**DIVING.** Most diving is done at **Julian Rocks Marine Park,** 2.5km off Main Beach, widely considered one of the 10 best dive sites in Australia. Julian Rocks has both warm and cold currents and is home to 500 species of fish, including the occasional grey nurse shark. Required medical clearances are $35-50. Dive certification courses can go up by $70-100 or more during the summer. **Sundive,** on Middleton St, next to the YHA, has an on-site pool and offers many types of dives. Courses usually start on Mondays, but weekend certification courses are sometimes offered. (☎6685 7755. *5-day PADI certification $470, winter $275; intro dives $110; day dives $75, additional trips $35; snorkeling trips $44.*) **Bayside Scuba** is at the corner of Lawson and Fletcher St. (☎6685 8333. *4-day SSI certification $325; intro dives $120; day dives $66, additional trips $38; snorkeling trips $44.*)

**INDOORS.** The small but wildly colored **Wave Rock,** 1/91 Centennial Circuit at the Arts and Industrial Estate, is a well-plotted indoor rock climbing room with over 50 different climbs. (☎6680 8777. *Open daily 10am-10pm, but call if you plan to go after 8:30pm. 2hr. $10. Boot rental $5. Chalk bag $1.*) After all that work, **Samadhi Flotation Centre,** opposite Woolworth's on Jonson St, has massages and cheap, great-value massage classes. (☎6685 6905. *Open daily 9am-6pm. Intro massage classes $30; 1hr. massage $60, backpackers $45. Book ahead; cash only; BYO towel.*) The other major massage center, **Relax Haven,** at the rear of Belongil Beachhouse, 2km from town, is much smaller. (☎6685 8304. *1hr. float and 1hr. massage $40).*

**OUTDOORS.** **Rockhoppers** runs mountain bike tours through the nearby rainforest. (☎6685 7142. *$45, includes lunch and pickup.*) **Byron Bay Bicycles,** 93 Jonson St, hires bikes. (☎6685 6067. *Half-day $12, full-day $26, weekly $85.*) For horseback riding or canoe tours, **Pegasus Park Equestrian Centre,** 15min. west of Byron, leads rides and rows along Byron Creek. (☎6687 1446. *$33-38; 3hr. sunset rides $45.*)

**OUT OF THE SKY. Skylimit** offers hang gliding and motorized ultralight tours from $55. (☎6684 3711.) For tandem skydiving, **Skydive** costs $250-340 depending on height; it's cheaper if paid in cash and booked directly. (☎6684 1323.) Closer to the ground, but more unusual, the **Byron Bay Beach Club Flying Trapeze and Circus School,** on Bayshore Dr, has trapeze classes and also squeezes in some tumbling, juggling, and trampoline jumping. (☎6685 8000. *$25, with pickup.*)

**TOURS. Peterpan** offers tours to nearby **Nimbin** that also run past Minyon Falls. (☎(1800) 25 24 59. *$22-25.*) Those interested in a bit more local color should try **Jim's Alternative Tours,** a great trip through Minyon Falls, Nimbin, Protestor's Falls, and the half-crazy but entirely delightful **Fruit Spirit Botanical Gardens.** The gardens are cultivated by Dr. Paul Recher, a New York City "environmental refugee" and a first-class character. He walks visitors through his estate and slices open some of his hundreds of fruit species for sampling, all the while explaining the importance of energy conservation. (☎6685 7720. *9hr., $20.*) **Mick's Bay to Bush Tours** has similar day tours through Nimbin, Minyon Falls, and the rainforest, including a stop at a swimming hole. (☎6685 6889. *$17.*) Jim's and Mick's tours both provide shuttle ser-

NEW SOUTH WALES

**WHAT'S IN A NAME?** The North Coast Steam Navigation Company's 2240-ton vessel *T.S.S. Wollongbar* was once the fastest ship on the east coast of Australia. It ran bi-weekly to Sydney and could hold up to 300 passengers. On May 14th, 1921, however, it became a permanent part of Byron Bay, and is now known simply as **The Wreck**. On that fateful day, the ship's captain decided to lift anchor and go to sea. Bad timing—a gale sprang up, and six waves in rapid succession knocked the ship sideways onto the shore and split its back while it was grounded. Hoping to recover some of their losses, the owners sold off whatever they could; some of the ship's furniture is on display around town. The unmoved ship has itself become a Byron landmark, with the stern still visible at low tide. Perhaps it's just an unlucky name: the next *Wollongbar* was torpedoed by a Japanese submarine during World War II.

vice to the **Channon** and **Bangalow** markets. The **Nimbin Shuttle Bus** departs Byron Bay at 10am and returns from Nimbin at 2:30pm. (☎ 6680 9189. $18.) **The Pioneering Spirit** offers a full-day guided climb of Mt. Warning. (☎ 6685 7721. $20, with pickup.)

## 🎭🎵 NIGHTLIFE AND ENTERTAINMENT

Byron Bay's three pubs have an atmosphere that is both mellow and lively; Jimmy Buffet would be at home here. The newest addition to Byron nightlife is also one of the most hopping these days. **Cheeky Monkey's,** on the corner of Jonson and Kingsley St, is brand-new and packed with backpackers and locals, dancing on the tables, and generally being cheesy and rowdy. (☎ 6685 5886. Open daily 7pm-3am.) The **Great Northern Hotel,** on the corner of Jonson and Byron St, draws a laid-back crowd and is a good place to grab a VB early in the evening. (☎ 6685 6454. Open daily until 1:15am. Live music M-Sa; W-Sa cover varies depending on the band.) The **Beach Hotel,** on Jonson St overlooking the beach, is a favorite of slightly older drinkers, with a garden bar and huge patio. (☎ 6685 6402. Live music W-Su; usually no cover.)

There are two nightclubs that advertise specials heavily through hostels. Cover charges are $3-5 and both are open until 3am. The **Carpark Nightclub,** on Jonson St, in the Woolworth's parking lot, is hot, sweaty, loud, and techno-heavy. Expect a haze of smoke (both manufactured and second-hand), bright lights, and a raver atmosphere. **Cocomangas,** 32 Jonson St, has a slightly calmer and smaller dance floor, and, despite tons of drink specials, is invariably more expensive than local pubs. (☎ 6685 8493. M 70s night; Tu industrial and techno; W one free drink for the first 75 women; Th three DJs. No cover before midnight.)

Out of the town center on the way to the Arts and Industrial Estate is the enormous **Epicentre** studio complex, home once or twice a month to wild **all-night no-alcohol raves** (what about illicit substances?) that attract 1500 or more partyers. (☎ 6685 6979. $15-20. Concerts $15-50.) **Pighouse Flicks,** at the Piggery on Skinners Shoot Rd next to the Arts Factory, shows art and foreign (read: American) films three times nightly. (☎ 6685 5828, after 4:30pm. 4 shows Sa. $9.50; movie-and-dinner deal with nearby vegetarian restaurant $14.)

### NEAR BYRON BAY: LENNOX HEAD

Lennox Head (pop. 2300) lies between Ballina and Byron Bay. It's renowned for its excellent **surf**—it has one of the longest right-hand surf breaks in the world, and from Jun.-Aug., it's rated one of the top 10 areas in the world. Lennox is a great spill-over location if Byron gets too crowded. The highway enters the town on Tourist Rd. The town center is accessible by taking the roundabout to coastal Ballina St, which becomes Pacific Pde and runs along **Seven Mile Beach,** prime dolphin-spotting territory. **Lake Ainsworth** is at the north end of Pacific Pde. **Lennox Point,** 2km south, is an excellent but crowded surf area. Blanch's Coaches run through Lennox Head a few times daily to **Byron Bay** and **Ballina;** the bus stop is on Ballina St near the town center, or flag them down along Pacific Pde. (☎ 6686 2144. $5.)

**ATMs,** food stores, eateries, and the local pub are clustered within one minute's walk of each other at the southern end of Ballina St. **All Above Board,** 68 Ballina St (☎6887 7522), rents surfboards ($16.50), Malibus ($22), and body boards ($9).

The **Lennox Head Beach House,** 3 Ross St, is north of the town center, just off Pacific Pde and a short walk from Lake Ainsworth. The intimate beachouse has surfboards, boogie-boards, bicycles, and fishing rods; unlimited use of windsurfers and catamarans is just $5, and lessons are free. Aspiring gourmets can help themselves to the herb garden and dine in the open courtyard. Once a week, enjoy a massage from their "natural healing center." Bedrooms are small but tidy. (☎6687 7636. Dorms $21; doubles $42-44. Non-YHA add $2. Ask about weekly rates.) **Lake Ainsworth Caravan Park** is across Ross St next to the lake. (☎6687 7249. Sites $14, powered $16.50; cabins $33-50; peak season add $5-10.)

# MURWILLUMBAH

Located in a mountain valley, Murwillumbah ("more-WOOL-um-bah") is a small country town dissected by the mud-colored Tweed River. The town's name has several suggested meanings, including "place of high mountain which catches sun" and "place of many possums and people." The residents have seized on the second definition and have begun to paint possum murals on their Art Deco public buildings. There are four national parks near Murwillumbah: **Nightcap** (30km southwest), **Border Ranges, Lamington,** and **Mt. Cougal.** It's also a popular base for exploring the enormous, spectacular volcanic rim of **Mt. Warning,** the first place on the continent to greet the dawn. The area's main attraction is the splendid **Mt. Warning.** In town, the small but worthwhile **Art Gallery** down Tumbulgum Rd, awards the world's biggest portraiture prize, a whopping $100,000 prize. (☎6672 0409. Open W-Su 10am-5pm.)

Murwillumbah is halfway between Byron Bay and Tweed Heads. The **Tweed River** runs through the east side of town, and the Pacific Hwy and the **railway station** are on the east bank. The Pioneer and Kirkland's **bus depot** is on Murwillumbah St, next to Tweed Valley Travel. Kirkland's (☎(1300) 36 70 77) runs to **Brisbane** (2hr., $20.70); **Byron Bay** (1hr., $12.40); and **Surfers Paradise** (1hr., $14.90). Northbound Greyhound and McCafferty's buses stop at the Stafford St BP station; southbound buses stop outside the info center. In **Budd Park,** at the corner of the highway and Alma St, is the **Tourist Information Centre,** in the **World Heritage Rainforest Centre** (☎6672 1340; fax 6672 5948. Open M-Sa 9am-4:30pm, Su 9:30am-4pm.) The town centers on the west bank of the Tweed River, which is crossed by the **Alma St bridge** behind Tweed Tavern. Alma St crosses Commercial St and becomes **Wollumbin St** which has eateries and a shopping center with a 24hr. Coles **supermarket** at the end of the block. The **post office** is at the corner of Brisbane and Murwillumbah St. **Postal code:** 2484.

The **Mt. Warning/Murwillumbah YHA,** 1 Tumbulgum Rd, is the second oldest YHA in NSW, and is a well-kept, family-oriented lodge. From the info center, cross the Alma St bridge, turn right on Commercial St, and follow the river. The lodge rests on the riverbank, with a deck facing Mt. Warning. The YHA offers free use of rowboats, canoes, fishing gear, and inner tubes for lazing in the river. Ask the owner about the plentiful biking routes ranging from 16-70km. (☎6672 3763. Occasional drop off at Mt. Warning. Ice cream in the evening. Bike rental available. Dorms $18; twins and doubles $34.)

# WHIAN WHIAN AND MULLUMBIMBY

Adjoined to Nightcap National Park to the east, **Whian Whian State Forest** is another rainforest and waterfall showcase, accessible through Dunoon, Mullumbimby, or some of the villages around Lismore. The best way to see the park is the **Forest Drive** (30km; 2hr.) begins at **Minyon Falls** or Gibbergunyah Range Rd. **Minyon Grass** is a picnic area with many walking trails and toilets, 2km before Minyon Falls. The **Minyon Loop** (4km) begins at the Minyon Grass and brings hikers to the base of the waterfall. **Rummery Park** is a popular camping spot, with access to the 16km Nightcap track which ends at **Mt. Nardi.** The next stop along that trail, **Peates Mountain**

**Lookout,** is a 10min. walk. Along with blackbutt and flooded gum plantations, the drive passes through **Gibbergunyah** and **Big Scrub Flora Reserves** before reaching **Rocky Creek Dam,** a favorite family picnic stop.

The town of **Mullumbimby** (pop. 2700) is so small and tranquil it doesn't even have a tourist office. Dalley St is the main thoroughfare and Burringbar St has most of the shops. Brunswick Valley Coaches (☎6685 1385) runs to **Brunswick Heads** daily ($5), where riders can transfer via Kirklands (☎(1300) 36 70 77) to **Byron Bay** ($7). A convenient stopping place for trips to Whian Whian as well as the **Border Ranges National Park,** Mullumbimby has a string of motels on Dalley St. **Mullumbimby Motel,** 121 Dalley St, is a bit less expensive than the average. (☎6684 2387. Singles $48; twins and doubles $58.) The cheapest option is **Maca's Camping Ground.** From Dalley St head to the Pacific Hwy and turn left onto Main Arm Rd. Follow it 12km out and Maca's will be on your right. (☎6684 5211. Kitchen laundry, showers, and general store. Sites $6.) Tucked in the hills around Mullumbimby is the **Crystal Castle,** on Monet Dr. If you ever wonder what kind of aura you are radiating (and who doesn't on a daily basis?), here's your chance. A photograph and interpretation of your aura costs $25. (☎6684 3111. Open daily 10am-4:30pm.)

## MT. WARNING AND BORDER RANGES

The spire that caps **Mt. Warning,** which catches the sun's rays before any other spot on the coast, is the centerpiece of a bowl-shaped landform born of an eroded, extinct volcano that once stood twice its current height. The climb to the peak offers a fantastic 360° view of the coast and surrounding forest. The **Summit Track** (8.8km return; 4-5hr.) is moderately strenuous. The last segment of the trail is a vertical rock scramble with a necessary chain handrail. Watching the sunrise is spectacular although you'll need a flashlight for the climb. Bring your own water; there are toilets at the **Breakfast Creek** picnic area at the start of the walk. To reach the Summit Track from Murwillumbah, take Kyogle Rd 12km west, turn on Mt. Warning Rd, and go about 6km to Breakfast Creek. *Let's Go* doesn't recommend **hitchhiking,** but it is a popular way to get from town to the mountain. **Mount Warning Caravan Park** makes a great base for exploring the mountain. (☎6679 5120. Kitchen, TV room, pool, BBQ, and friendly wallabies. Sites $13, powered $16.50; vans $33.)

If you find Mt. Warning too touristed, the gorgeous **Border Ranges National Park** is an ideal getaway. It takes some work to get there, but its seclusion rewards you with the shade of a lush canopy and a great vantage point for viewing the volcano region. Take the Kyogle Rd west from Murwillumbah for 44km; the Barker Vale turn-off leads 15km along gravel road to the park entrance. Inside the park, the road becomes the **Tweed Range Scenic Drive** (60km; 4-5hr.). The drive exits the park at **Wiangaree,** 13km from Kyogle and 66km from Murwillumbah.

The first picnic area in the park is **Bar Mountain,** with a lovely beech glade. Less than 1km farther is the more remarkable **Blackbutts** picnic area, with striking views of Mt. Warning and the basin. If heights don't scare you, try the **Pinnacle Lookout,** another 8km north. For the **Forest Tops** camping area, go another 4km and turn left, then go 4km and turn left again. Here, a right turn leads to the **Brindle Creek** picnic area, the departure point for a walk (3hr.) among rainforests and waterfalls that ends at the **Antarctic Beech** picnic area, home to 2000-year-old trees.

# SOUTH COAST

The Princes Hwy south of Sydney is the string that binds the pearls of the southern coastal towns. While industry dominates larger towns such as Wollongong and Bega, the smaller coastal towns in between are some of New South Wales' undiscovered treasures. With a succession of beautiful beaches on one side and bordered by mountain ranges on the other, the South Coast is a refreshing escape from the city and other tourist-mobbed places.

# WOLLONGONG

Directly down the coastline about 80km from Sydney, Wollongong ("WOOLEN-gong"; pop. 200,000) suffers from the city-versus-town identity crisis that plagues many of Australia's mid-sized cities. New South Wales's third-largest metropolitan area, Wollongong has a city center small enough to be walkable yet urban enough to be unattractive. The easy view of Port Kembla's steel, coal, and grain plants compounds Wollongong's image problems. Still, because of Wollongong's niche between the peaks of the Illawarra Escarpment and the blue ocean, plenty of diversions allow outdoor entertainment. Adrenaline-pumping activities, decent nightlife, and some of the best surfing around are within easy reach of the city.

## ⌐ TRANSPORT

CityRail **trains** (☎ 13 15 00) stop at Wollongong City Station on Station St, and continue on to: **Sydney** (1½hr., 12-28 per day, $9); **Bomaderry,** the closest stop to **Nowra** (1½hr., 4-10 per day, $7); and **Kiama** (45min., 11-16 per day, $4.50). **Buses** arrive at the City Coach Terminus (☎4226 1022), on the corner of Keira and Campbell St. Between Premier (☎13 34 10), Greyhound (☎13 20 30), and Murray's (☎13 22 51) buses service: **Sydney** (1½-2hr., 4-5 per day, $11-19); **Canberra** (3½hr., 1 per day, $28); **Melbourne** (15hr., 1 per day, $60); **Batemans Bay** (3-3¾hr., 3-4 per day, $28-31); **Bega** (5½-6hr., 2-3 per day, $42-45); **Bermagui** (4¾hr., 1-2 per day, $39); **Kiama** (20-35min., 3-4 per day, $11-19); **Narooma** (4¾hr., 3-4 per day, $38-40); **Nowra** (1¼hr., 3-4 per day, $11-19); and **Ulladulla** (2¼hr., 3-4 per day, $22-23).

NEW SOUTH WALES

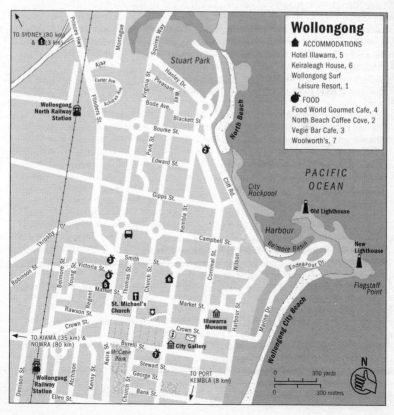

**Wollongong**

🛏 ACCOMMODATIONS
Hotel Illawarra, 5
Keiraleagh House, 6
Wollongong Surf
  Leisure Resort, 1

🍎 FOOD
Food World Gourmet Cafe, 4
North Beach Coffee Cove, 2
Vegie Bar Cafe, 3
Woolworth's, 7

## ✦ ❷ ORIENTATION AND PRACTICAL INFORMATION

The Princes Hwy leads directly into Wollongong, becoming **Flinders St** just north of the city center and merging into **Keira St** downtown. The **pedestrian shopping mall** on Crown St, between Keira and Kembla St, is the city's commercial heart. **Tourism Wollongong,** 93 Crown St, is on the corner of Kembla St (☎ 4227 5545, freecall ☎ (1800) 24 07 37; fax 4228 0344; open M-F 9am-5pm, Sa 9am-4pm, Su 10am-4pm). **Post office:** in the Gateway Shopping Centre, on Keira St between Crown and Burelli St (☎ 4228 9322; open M-F 9am-5pm). **Postal code:** 2500. **Internet access: Boomerang Software Exchange,** Shop 3, 176-192 Keira St (☎ 4228 8686; 1hr. $6; open M 10am-5:30pm, Tu-Sa 9:30am-5:30pm, Su 10am-4pm).

## ▛ ACCOMMODATIONS

**Keiraleagh House,** 60 Kembla St, between Market and Smith St, is Wollongong's cheapest, friendliest option, though the greenhouse and backyard show their age, and facilities are less than immaculate. TV lounge, kitchen, laundry. (☎ 4228 6765; fax 4228 6216; email backpack@cyberelectric.net.org.au. Key deposit $10. Bunk rooms $15; singles $25; doubles $35-46; light breakfast included.) Rooms in the **Hotel Illawarra,** on the corner of Market and Keira St, are not as swanky as the nightclub downstairs, but they're tidy. Rooms get noisy on weekend evenings due to the bar below. (☎ 4229 5411; fax 4229 5140. Laundry $2. Key deposit $20. Bunks $30; singles $35; doubles $65.) **Wollongong Surf Leisure Resort,** Pioneer Rd in Fairy Meadow, 4.5km north of downtown, is the nearest campground, a 13min. walk from the Fairy Meadow CityRail. Inquire at Tourism Wollongong for directions. Pool, spa, and indoor tennis courts. (☎ 4283 6999; fax 4285 1620. Bicycle hire 1hr. $4. Laundry $2. Key deposit $10. Hot water 5min. 10¢. Open M-Sa 8am-9pm, Su 8am-6pm. Tent sites for 2 $15-30, powered $18-35; varies according to season.)

## ◓▤ FOOD AND NIGHTLIFE

Downtown Wollongong has a handful of cheap eateries. **Woolworth's,** on the corner of Kembla and Burelli St, sells **groceries.** (☎ 4228 8066. Open M-Sa 7:30am-midnight, Su 8am-8pm.) The restaurants lining Keira St north of Market St cover an astonishing variety of Asian cuisines with main dishes around $9-12. The most affordable and always packed **Food World Gourmet Café,** 148 Keira St, serves healthy and tasty Chinese dishes. (☎ 4225 9655. Open Su-W 11am-8pm, Th-Sa 11:30am-9pm. Mains $6-9.) For a picnic lunch at North Beach, stop in at **North Beach Coffee Cove,** on Bourke St half a block from the beach, and pick up sandwiches ($3-5) or energize for $2.50 with a fresh fruit salad. (☎ 4229 7876. Open daily 7am-4pm.) The menu at the **Vegie Bar Café,** 130 Kiera St, features a delicious range of vegetarian dishes. (☎ 4227 1033. Mains $8-11.)

The **Hotel Illawara** (see **Accommodations** above) draws a twenty-something crowd in the early evening for cocktails and conversation, but loud music interrupts the crowd with some happening dance on weekends. (☎ 4229 5411. F-Sa cover $5, back room after 1am $10. Open M-W 10am-1am, Th 10am-3am, F-Sa noon-5am, Su noon-late.) The hottest spot around for younger crowds, **Bourbon Street Night Club,** 150 Kiera St, has hundreds of party-goers lined up as early as 8pm, doing anything to join the in-crowd. (Open W-Sa 8pm-3am.) **Cooney's Tavern** (☎ 4229 1911), on the corner of Keira and Burelli St, rocks Thursday and Friday nights with bands that usually draw a good crowd. The **Glasshouse Tavern** on the corner of Crown and Kembla St, is more of a dancing nightclub than a tavern. Its adjoining late-night café is a nice break from the loud music. (Cover $5 F-Sa til 2am.) Up-and-coming rock bands play from 9pm at the student-dominated **Oxford Tavern,** at 47 Crown St. (☎ 4228 3892. Bands W, F, Sa. Open M-Sa 10am-3am, Su 10am-10pm.)

NEW SOUTH WALES

# SIGHTS AND ACTIVITIES

Wollongong's **harbour** is by far its best feature. The small, sandy cove shelters both sailboats and the fishing fleet that docks in Belmore Basin. The old lighthouse, visible from the beach, adds an air of old-time charm absent from the rest of the city. A beautiful jogging and cycling path forces fitness freaks to keep running kilometers along the coast. Just north, **surfers** wait for waves at **North Beach.** If you want to break into the surfing scene or just refine your technique, **Pines Surfriders School** can help. (☎4274 0400. $30; students $25; $15 group booking, 3-person minimum.)

The **Wollongong City Gallery,** on the corner of Kembla and Burelli St, displays regional, Aboriginal, and contemporary art. (☎4228 7500. Open Tu-F 10am-5pm, Sa-Su noon-4pm. Free.) **Hangdog Climbing Gym,** 130 Auburn St, offers outdoor rock-climbing courses and 100 different climbs on 40 ropes. (☎4225 8369. Open M-F 10am-9pm, Sa-Su 9am-6pm. Entry $10; gear hire $8; outdoor climbing course with gear hire $75.) For those attractions just beyond walking distance, bikes can be rented from **Spearman Cycles,** 302 Crown St (☎4229 2317). The lazy or lame can go to **Leisure Coast Scootcar Hire** if they are prepared to pay the price for their sloth. (☎(0419) 29 43 09. Open daily. Two-seater 3hr. $80, full-day $135.) For those especially susceptible to the drag of gravity, **Sydney Microlight Centre** at Illawarra Regional Airport gives you the chance to fly an open-cockpit two-seater microlight aircraft. (☎4294 1031. Open daily. Intro flight $100.)

South of Port Kembla, **Lake Illawarra** draws crowds from Wollongong when the weather is good. Motorboats (4hr. $40) and rowboats (4hr. $25) are available from **Windang Boat Shed,** 1 Judbooley Pde, on the lake in Windang. (☎4296 2015. Open daily 9am-5pm. **Trains** ($2) run to Port Kembla station, a short walk to the lake. Otherwise, John J. Hill **buses** #50 and 51 run from the Wollongong City Station or the Gateway Shopping Center to Windang Bridge, also a short walk to the lake. From Port Kembla Station, **Port Beach** and **MM Beach** are nearby.

# DAYTRIPS FROM WOLLONGONG

The **Bulli Pass** goes inland to the Southern Fwy, 12km north of Wollongong, and uncovers a magnificent panoramic view of the area from its crest. Down at sea level, Wollongong's biggest attractions await at **Bulli Point** (also know as Sandion Point), **Headland,** and farther north, **Austinmer Beach.** Beach bums flock to Bulli or **Thirroul** for some of the area's best **surfing.** (CityRail from Wollongong $2.) English writer **D.H. Lawrence** resided in Thirroul, between Bulli and Austinmer, for several months in 1922, and described the area in his novel *Kangaroo.* The home is privately owned and inaccessible to the public, but the beach is open for strolling and literary speculation. Lawrence Hargrave Dr winds along the coast north of Bulli Pass, providing tantalizing glimpses of the shore below, before reaching the lookout at **Bald Hill** north of Stanwell Park, perhaps the best of all the views on this stretch of coast. It was here that **Lawrence Hargrave** contributed to the development of aviation by experimenting with box kites. Today, the hill continues its service as an aeronautical jumping-off point in the employment of skilled hang gliders.

The **Illawarra Escarpment** defines Wollongong's inland border. The nearest peak, **Mt. Keira,** is a short drive from town on Mt. Keira Rd. Take #39 bus to get within 8km of Mt. Keira's peak. At the top, await bushwalking trails and a fantastic view. In the southern suburb of **Berkeley** on the north shore of Lake Illawarra, the **largest Buddhist Temple** in the Southern Hemisphere, Nan Tien Temple, towers above the horizon and welcomes visitors. (☎4272 0600. Open Tu-Su 9am-5pm. Museum $1, with tour $2. Wheelchair accessible.) Rutty's bus #34 goes right to the temple from the Gateway Shopping Centre ($2.40). The **Cockatoo Run,** a scenic mountain railway, offers day-long excursions which climb over the escarpment, into the highlands and back. (☎(1300) 65 38 01. Operates Mar.-Nov. Tu, Th, Sa and Su. $30; children $20; family $80.)

# KIAMA AND AROUND

Under the right conditions, when the wind is high and the seas surge from the southeast, water washing into a rock cave in Kiama ("KAI-amma") is forced upward through a hole in the rocks to heights of 20-35m. Visitors arrive from miles around to shower—metaphorically, at least—in the awesome spray of **Kiama's Blowhole.** But even if the wind doesn't comply, Kiama and the surrounding area make for a pretty coastal stop. Accordingly the word *Kiama* means "sound of the sea." But be careful of the lulling crash and sharp rocks. Dangers abound around the precipice. Forty kilometers south of Wollongong via the Princes Hwy or F6 Fwy, Kiama and the nearby beaches at Gerringong and Gerroa lie within daytrip range of Sydney.

█ **TRANSPORT.** From the CityRail station, on Bong Bong St just west of Blowhole Point, **trains** run to: **Sydney** (2hr., 11-14 per day, $12); **Bomaderry/Nowra** (30min., 10-15 per day, $4); and **Wollongong** (45min., 14-21 per day, $5). Premier Motor Service (☎ (1300) 36 81 00), and the generally more expensive and slower Greyhound Pioneer (☎ 13 20 30) **buses** depart from the Kiama Leagues Club, on the corner of Terralong and Collins St, to: **Sydney** (2½hr., 3-4 per day, $16-19); **Melbourne** (15hr., 2 per day, $60); **Batemans Bay** (2½-3¼hr., 3-4 per day, $31); **Bega** (5-5½hr., 3-4 per day, $42-45); **Bermagui** (4¼hr., 1 per day, $39); **Narooma** (3½-4¼hr., 3-4 per day, $38-40); **Nowra** (40min., 3-4 per day, $11-19); **Ulladulla** (1¾-2½hr., 3-4 per day, $12-23); and **Wollongong** (35min., 3-4 per day, $11-19).

█ **PRACTICAL INFORMATION.** Dotted with pines, palms, heritage buildings, and takeaways, Manning St is the main street in town. The center of tourist life is **Blowhole Point,** down Terralong St from Princes Hwy toward the coast. On Blowhole Point lies the **Visitors Centre** (☎ 4232 3322, freecall ☎ (1300) 65 42 62; fax 4226 3260; open daily 9am-5pm). **Internet Access:** Kiama Library, 1hr. $2. (☎ (1800) 80 38 97. Open M-Sa.) **Post office:** on the corner of Terralong and Manning St (☎ 4232 1389). **Postal code:** 2533.

█ **ACCOMMODATIONS AND FOOD.** The **Kiama Backpackers Hostel,** 31 Bong Bong St, a few steps downhill from the CityRail Station, has an uninspiring feel of a university dormitory but manages to preserve the hostel spirit. Free use of bikes, fishing reels, and surfboards. TV, kitchen. Internet access 1hr. $5. (☎/fax 4233 1881. Key deposit $10. Dorms $15; singles $20, F-Sa $22; twins and doubles $35, $40.) Twelve kilometers south, a walk from Werri Beach in Gerringong, the **Nestor House YHA,** 28 Fern St, 1.5km from the bus and train, occupies a building on the grounds of Uniting Church. The rooms are clean and comfortable but sparse. (☎/fax 4234 1249. Open 5-8pm. Dorms $19.) Behind the visitors center, the **Blowhole Point Caravan Park** leans over the quiet ocean. (☎ 4232 2707; fax 4232 4290. Sites for 2 $19, peak season $22; simple cabins $66-99.)

For a tasty coastal treat, locals recommend the fish and chips ($6) at the **Kiama Harbour Takeaway,** at the front of the beige building nearest the mainland as you head onto Blowhole Point. (☎ 4232 2911. Open daily 10:30am-6:30pm, later during summer.) **Coffee Table Bookshop,** 2/3 Railway Parade, has a small but interesting selection of gourmet sandwiches. (☎ 4233 1060. Open daily 9am-4:30pm.)

█ **SIGHTS AND ACTIVITIES.** Every visitor to Kiama should give the **Blowhole** a chance to do its trick. The **natural rock pool** on the northern face of Blowhole Point is a good swimming spot. A second, deeper rock pool, across Kiama Harbour from Blowhole Point covers the rocks of Pheasant Point. On the other side of Pheasant Point, experienced **surfers** brave the riptides at **Bombo Beach.** The protected area inside the next headland to the north goes by two names. Sightseers interested in the striking rock formations which mark the spot call it **Cathedral Rock.** Surfers know it as the **Boneyard,** and, despite the menacing nickname, it's a popular spot for catching waves, but still no place for neophytes. To the south, surfers and swimmers frequent the patrolled **Surf Beach** at Kendalls Point. **Little Blowhole** may be a good insult to level at your enemies, but it is also redemption for disappointed Blowhole-watchers. It works on the opposite swell, on Marsden Head at the end of Tingira Ctr, and erupts more regularly than its neighbor. The next stop on a surfer's tour of the Kiama area lies 5km south at **Werri Beach** in Gerringong. If you get tired of just blandly watching water (who would?), **Kiama Charter Service** can send you out on the deep sea for some sport fishing. (☎4237 8496. 7hr. $50-60.) **Signa Charter** (☎4233 1020) offers smaller 6-hour trips for 1-2 people, complete with a local guide for $60.

Climb the **Saddleback Mountain Lookout** for a vista that can extend from Wollongong to Jervis Bay on clear days. Follow Manning St south until it bends inland, then proceed straight onto Saddleback Mountain Rd at the edge of town. The steep path up the mountain is signposted from Saddleback Mountain Rd.

Farther west, the **Barren Grounds Nature Reserve** is accessible by Jamberoo Mountain Rd by way of Tourist Dr 9 through Jamberoo and contains several moderate **hiking trails** from 2km to 19km. The area is known as the home to over 160 species of birds. Turning off Jamberoo Mountain Rd leads you to **Minnamurra Rainforest** (☎4236 0469) in **Budderoo National Park,** a rare tract of subtropical rainforest with two delightful bushwalks originating from the Visitors Centre. (Open daily 9am-5pm; rainforest access until 4pm. $9 per car, or $4 per person.) The 1.6km (45min.) **Rainforest Walk,** a looping, boardwalked track, tours the unusual plant life in the park. The longer, steeper 2.6km **Minnamurra Falls Walk** (2hr.) branches off from the Rainforest Walk and rewards hikers with, strangely enough, waterfalls.

# NOWRA AND BOMADERRY

Every sign in the Shoalhaven directs you to Nowra. Smaller sibling Bomaderry lies immediately north, across the Shoalhaven River. Together, they are the population centers of the Shoalhaven. Rockies come from all over for what many claim to be the best sport climbing in Australia.

**TRANSPORT AND PRACTICAL INFORMATION.** CityRail's last stop is in Bomaderry on Railway St. **Trains** run to: **Sydney** (2¾hr., 11 per day, $13); **Kiama** (30min., 10-15 per day, $4); and **Wollongong** (1½hr., 4-10 per day, $7). There are plenty of **bus** options among Greyhound Pioneer (☎13 20 30), Premier Motor Services (☎13 34 10), and Kennedy's Coaches (☎4421 7596). Services to: **Sydney** (3-3¼hr., 3-4 per day, $16-19); **Melbourne** (14hr., 1-2 per day, $57-60); **Batemans Bay** (1¾-2hr., 3-4 per day, $18-24); **Bega** (4¼hr., 3-4 per day, $28-32); **Bermagui** (3½hr., 1 per day, $29); **Fitzroy Falls** (1hr., 1 per day, $10); **Kangaroo Valley** (35min., 1 per day, $7); **Kiama** (40min., 3-4 per day, $11-19); **Narooma** (2¾-3hr., 3-4 per day, $27-34); **Ulladulla** (1-1¾hr., 3-4 per day, $12-17); and **Wollongong** (1½hr., 3-4 per day, $11-19). The new **Shoalhaven Visitors Centre,** lies on the corner of Princes Hwy and Pleasant Way, south of the bridge to Nowra on the left (☎4421 0778, freecall ☎(1800) 02 42 61; fax 4423 2950; www.shoalhaven.nsw.gov.au; open daily 9am-4:30pm). The **National Parks and Wildlife Service,** 55 Graham St in Nowra, has info on the parks (☎4423 2170; fax 4423 3122; open M-F 8:30am-5pm). **Internet access:** Flatearth Internet café, Level 1, Nowra Mall. (☎4423 7771; 1hr. $6.)

**ACCOMMODATIONS.** Due to its proximity to Berry, Kangaroo Valley, and Jervis Bay, many choose to stay in Nowra when exploring the area. **M&M's Guesthouse,** 1A Scenic Dr, on the grounds of the Riverhaven Motel on the right across the bridge from Bomaderry, is run by a friendly couple with a passion for motorcycles. (☎4422 8006; fax 4422 8007. TV, pool table, laundry. No kitchen. Dorms or private rooms with hall bathrooms $20, including light brekkie.) Take a right on Illaroo Rd just before the grey metal bridge to Nowra, follow McMahon's Rd left from the roundabout, and take a left on Rockhill Rd for cheap and scenic camping sites at the **Nowra Animal Park.** The owner can also direct travelers to local rock climbing sites. (☎/fax 4421 3949. Open daily 8am-5pm. Toilets. Hot showers. Sites for 2 $16, powered $18.)

**⚠ ROCK CLIMBING AND OTHER ACTIVITIES.** Although the liability-shy tourist office refrains from directing travelers to the best local rock-climbing areas, most area climbers recommend **Thompson's Point,** on the southern shore of the river. Many also find PC, Grotto, and South Central to be challenging. Entrepreneurs take note—climbers must bring their own gear because no one has had the business sense to open a mountaineering-equipment store. **The Gym** (☎4421 3708), at the corner of McMahons and Illaroo Rd, offers indoor rock climbing. On weekends, the more adventurous should try **RAN Gliding** at the Naval Air Station (☎4423 3744). For beginners, the best choices are the trial instructional flight ($55) or a full-day course that includes three flights and basic weather and aerodynamics instruction ($99). **Skydive Nowra** (☎(0500) 88 55 56) and **Southern Cross Skydivers** (☎4423 3121) have tandem skydives and freefall courses.

## KANGAROO VALLEY

The fading Caltex petrol station in the middle of Kangaroo Valley's main thoroughfare is probably the last vestige of the original one-marsupial town. Subsequently, Kangaroo Valley (pop. 280) has gone decidedly arts-and-crafts touristy, but the area is still remote, pleasant, and rightfully popular for B&B and camping retreats.

At the northwest end of town, the sandstone **Hampden Bridge** spans the Kangaroo River. Built in 1898, it's Australia's oldest suspension bridge. Located on the north side of the bridge, **Kangaroo Valley Safaris,** 2210 Moss Vale Rd, organizes canoe camping trips and rents **canoes** ($35 per day), **kayaks** ($25-45 per day), and **camping gear.** (☎4465 1502. Open daily dawn to dusk. Tents $18 per day.)

Twenty kilometers beyond Kangaroo Valley on Moss Vale Rd, **Fitzroy Falls** greets visitors at one of the few places where they can enter **Morton National Park** on its eastern side. The NPWS-run **Fitzroy Falls Visitor Centre** has maps for bushwalking trails. (☎4887 7270; open daily 8:30am-5pm.) **Kennedy's Coaches** takes you there from the Kangaroo Valley post office on the way to Moss Vale, but the next bus back leaves the following morning (☎4421 7596; 25min., 1 per day, $4).

By car, avoid the steep, winding Kangaroo Valley Rd leading west from Berry and opt for the Moss Vale Rd which leads northwest from Bomaderry, off the Princes Hwy. Check road conditions ahead of time for both routes before deciding. Prior's (☎(1800) 81 62 34) runs **buses** to **Sydney** (3½hr.; M, Tu, Th, Sa; $17); **Batemans Bay** (2¼hr.; M, W-F, Su; $16); **Narooma** (4hr.; M, W-F, Su; $22); **Parramatta** (3hr.; M-Tu, Th-Sa; $17); and **Ulladulla** (1½hr., $12).

The **Bendeela Picnic Area,** 7km outside town provides plenty of **free** camping, toilets, BBQ, and water. Reach it by driving north out of town and turning left on Bendeela Rd, following signs to the entrance. For campers looking for showers or a roof, there is **Glenmack Caravan Park** on the main road just east of town. (☎4465 1372. Open 8am-6pm. Tent sites $7 per person; cabins for 2 $45-70.)

## JERVIS BAY

Almost entirely enclosed by its northern headland, the Beecroft Peninsula, Jervis Bay is a serene body of water surrounded by strikingly white beaches. It teems with marine life and rock formations that make for arguably the **best diving** in Australia outside of the Great Barrier Reef. To take in the Bay, stop at any of the towns along the shore and wander down the beach until the scenery suits your taste.

**HUSKISSON.** Twenty-four kilometers southeast of Nowra lies Huskisson. **Nowra Coaches** (☎4423 5244) goes out to Huskisson a few times a day. Buses run to Booderee at least once a day Tu and F. For tourist info, visit the **Huskisson Trading Post** on the corner of Tomerong and Dent St. (☎4441 5241; fax 4441 5198. Open daily 9am-5:30pm.) **Leisure Haven Caravan Park,** 1km outside of town along Currambene Creek on Woollamia Rd, provides tent sites in the woods. (☎4441 5046. Laundry facilities. Key deposit $20. Open daily 8am-evening. Sites for 2 $14, powered $16.) **The Husky Pub,** on Owen St overlooking the Bay, is the town's pubstay. (☎4441 5001; fax 4441 6754. Open M-F noon-2pm, Sa-Su noon-2:30pm; bar open daily 11am-late. Singles $35; doubles $55)

**THE BAY.** Underwater, Jervis Bay is exquisite. The bay is a natural meeting place for tropical marine life coming down from the north as well as a variety of southern species not found at the Great Barrier Reef. Divers rave about the massive archways and rock shelves which characterize the aquatic scenery. The only things cooler than the diving itself are the names of the many diving haunts. Cathedral Cave and Smuggler's Cave are perfect for **cave diving.** The Arch, Stoney Creek Reef, and the Ten Fathom Dropoff make good places for **deep diving.** Steamers Beach Seal Colony is recommended for **open-water dives** and even **snorkeling.** Despite chillier waters, visibility is best from April to the beginning of August. **Jervis Bay Sea Sports** (☎4441 5012) takes certified divers out for a day including two dives ($55, with equipment $105), or for $380 they'll certify you in four days. **Pro-Dive** (☎4441 5255) also located on Owen Street in Huskisson offers similar services.

For those content to enjoy marine life from a drier vantage point, **Baywatch Cruises,** 62 Owen St (☎4441 5455, freecall ☎(1800) 44 43 30), separates the explorations into a 2½hr. dolphin cruise ($25) and a 3hr. whale watch ($40) during peak whale migrations (June-Nov.). (David Hasselhoff not included.)

**Fishermen** work for their dinner at nearby Curramberry Creek, and **Husky Hire-a-Boat** will rent out and deliver an aluminum boat. (☎4441 6200. 2hr. $30. Open dawn-5pm.) If you just want to wander around, **Jervis Bay Kayak Company** stretches your arms in sleek style. (☎4443 3858. Half day $72, includes transport, snack, tuition, park user fees.) **Jet Ski and Canoe Hire** can also get you nowhere fast. (☎(018) 67 17 30. Weekends and holidays only; jets ski 30min. $55; canoe 1hr. $15.)

**BOODEREE NATIONAL PARK.** On the southern end of the bay, **Booderee National Park,** formerly Jervis Bay National Park, which is under joint management with the Aboriginal people, has **camping** areas: **Greenpatch** on Jervis Bay (toilets, water, hot showers; tent sites $14-16.25), and **Cave Beach** near Wreck Bay to the south (cold showers, no electricity; sites $9-10). The **Visitors Centre,** just beyond the park entry gates, accepts campsite bookings. (☎4443 0977. Open daily 9am-4pm. Park entrance $5 per car per week.) The Visitors Centre can provide you with a guide to the various walking trails. The **Botanic Gardens** are inside the park as well. (☎4442 1122. Open M-F 8am-4pm, Sa-Su 10am-5pm. Free.) A variety of walks from 1-3km pass through the different ecosystems. **Greenpatch beach** offers kangaroos and **snorkeling**—but not together. **Chinaman's beach** is also a popular **swimming** spot.

## ULLADULLA

Moving south through the Shoalhaven, the next major service center is Ulladulla. The 1870 wreck of the Walter Hood can be found off Ulladulla's coast along with a fair number of other decent dives.

**⊏⃠ TRANSPORT AND PRACTICAL INFORMATION.** Premier Motor Service (☎(1300) 36 81 00), Murray's (☎13 22 51), and the more expensive Greyhound Pioneer (☎13 20 30) **buses** stop at the Marlin Hotel (southbound) and the Traveland Travel Agency (northbound) on the way to: **Sydney** (4½hr., 1-2 per day, $24); **Canberra** (3¾hr., 1 per day, $30); **Batemans Bay** (45min., 3-4 per day, $9); **Bega** (3¼hr., 3-4 per day, $25); **Bermagui** (2hr., 1-2 per day, $22); **Kiama** (2hr., 3-4 per day, $22); **Narooma** (1¾hr., 3-4 per day, $17); **Nowra** (1hr., 3-4 per day, $12); and **Wollongong** (2½hr., 3-4 per day, $22). The **Visitors Centre** is on the Princes Hwy in the Civic Centre complex (☎4455 1269; fax 4454 0889; open M-F 10am-5pm, Sa-Su 9am-5pm). **Internet access** is available at the Visitors Centre and the adjacent **library** (30min. $1; open M-F 10am-7pm, Sa 9am-noon).

**⌐ ACCOMMODATIONS.** The local hostel, **South Coast Backpackers,** 63 Princes Hwy between Nurrawallee and North St, is a small operation with an unexciting roadside location but a nice sundeck and kitchen area and clean facilities. TV, laundry, off-street parking. (☎4454 0500. Key deposit $5. Dorms $20; twins and doubles $40. VIP.) At the end of South St, centrally located **Ulladulla Tourist Park**

has ample oceanfront camping space. Hot showers, toilets, gas BBQs, laundry, pool, and access to a secluded nearby beach. (☎/fax 4455 2457. Open 8am-9pm. Sites $8 per person, powered $14; cabins $44-89; peak season $14, $16; $100-165.)

■ SIGHTS AND ACTIVITIES. The people at the **Ulladulla Dive Shop,** 10 Wason St, can give seasoned advice on **diving** in the area or take you out themselves. (☎4455 5303. Open Nov.-Apr. daily 7am-7pm; May-Oct. M-F 9am-5pm, Sa-Su 8am-5pm. Equipment $55 per day; intro dives $85; for qualified divers 1 dive $80, 2 dives $115.) Bushwalkers generally stop in Ulladulla on the way out to the **Pigeon House Walk.** Turn off the Princes Hwy onto Wheelbarrow Rd 3km south of Burrill Lake. The trailhead is located 27km farther at a picnic area. The walk, which involves some ladder climbing, is a strenuous 5km affair (about 3hr.), but the view at the top is a knock-out. The **Coomee Nulunga Cultural Trail** (access to park is on Deering St across from the Lighthouse Oval car park) combines natural beauty and Aboriginal history. The beautiful 30-45min. walk is dotted with hand-painted dream posts and garawanga daran that depict local plant and wildlife. Take the guided walk arranged by the local Land Council to get the most out of your visit. (☎4455 5883. $5.) **Lakes Burrill** and **Conjola** nearby have nice **swimming** beaches, and **Mollymook Beach,** just north of town, is good for **surfing.**

## MURRAMARANG NATIONAL PARK

With expansive views of the Pacific and tame kangaroos all over, the coastline in the Murramarang National Park makes a great detour from the highway or a good place to stay and enjoy the beaches. The shore itself is at the far end of a 15min. drive over mostly unpaved roads. **Pebbly Beach** is a superb spot where many 'roos lazily congregate. A number of worthy campgrounds and caravan parks are speckled throughout the park, but tent **camping** sites are cheapest at the Pebbly Beach camping area. (☎4478 6006. Sites for 2 $10, plus a one-time park fee $7.50; book ahead over Christmas holidays.) At the southernmost point in the Shoalhaven half of Murramarang Park, **Durras North** looks onto Durras Lake and a beautiful windswept ocean beach. **Durras Lake North Caravan Park,** the first of several caravan parks at the end of Durras Rd, is clean and quite a kangaroo gathering place in its own right. (☎/fax 4478 6072. Store and reception 8:30am-9:30pm. Powered tent sites $6; caravan for 1 $35, each extra adult $5.)

# SOUTH FROM BATEMANS BAY

Batemans Bay, 10km south of Durras Lake on the Princes Hwy and just inland from Murramarang National Park, has some of the best places to dive in Australia. On the way out of Shoalhaven and into the Eurobodalla shire, the larger towns center around industries like fishing and dairy farming and are less touristed. Smaller, quieter villages hidden in the countryside, such as Mogo and Central Tilba, are the most compelling reasons to follow the Princes Hwy along the coast.

## BATEMANS BAY

The town begins where the Kings Hwy from Canberra (152km inland) meets the Princes Hwy at the coast. Situated south of the junction at the mouth of the Clyde River, upmarket tourists visit Batemans Bay on holiday from the capital. Nevertheless, the town is suitable for budget travelers too. The azure waters of Batemans and Malua Bay are so beautiful, just reading about them makes you wish you were certified to dive. In fact, between Jervis Bay and the Batemans Bay area, the diving is second only to the Great Barrier Reef.

■ TRANSPORT AND PRACTICAL INFORMATION. **Buses** leave from Batemans Bay outside the Promenade Plaza on Orient St. Premier Motor Service (☎(1300) 36 81 00) goes to: **Sydney** (5½hr., 2-3 per day, $30); **Bega** (2½hr., 2-3 per day, $19); **Bermagui** (1¾hr., 1 per day, $15); **Kiama** (2¾hr., 2-3 per day, $28);

NEW SOUTH WALES

**TELLING A FURPHY** In Australia, the expression "telling a Furphy" describes a story that has been exaggerated as it passes by word of mouth to become a tall tale. It is much like the children's game "Telephone" where the message at the end is usually very different from the original. The term dates back to the 1850s gold rush during which Furphy's Farm Water Cart was used to deliver water to farmers and miners. The carts usually brought the news along with their water delivery. By the end of the day the news was usually sensational. The story of Doc Ladmore's record find—an eight-pound hunk of the purest gold around—is the perfect example of a Furphy. While the measurement may have been true, the story alleges that he stumbled upon the nugget in his front yard. If you ask one of the locals in Mogo to direct you to the famous patch of grass, you'll be sent to a massive mine in the ground. At least Doc Ladmore never had to worry about mowing his "lawn."

Narooma (1hr., 2-3 per day, $12); **Nowra** (2hr., 2-3 per day, $18); **Ulladulla** (45min., 2-3 per day, $9); and **Wollongong** (3½hr., 2-3 per day, $28). Greyhound Pioneer (☎ 13 20 30) makes most of the same stops Su-F for a bit more money. **Canberra** (2½hr., 1-2 per day, $22) is **Murray's** territory (☎ 13 22 57). The staff at **Batemans Bay Tourist Information Centre,** on Princes Hwy at Beach Rd, give good advice on the local beaches (☎4472 6900; fax 4472 8822; open daily 9am-5pm).

**⌐ ACCOMMODATIONS.** For award-winning hostel accommodation, stay with the friendly crew at the YHA-affiliated **Batemans Bay Backpackers** inside a caravan park on the corner of Old Princes Hwy and South St, off the new Princes Hwy. The hostel runs daily trips to Pebbly Beach ($10) and Mogo ($3), rents bikes ($10 per day), and lends boogie boards. TV, kitchen, laundry. Pickup from the Greyhound stop. (☎4472 4972; fax 4472 4045. Dorms $16; twins and doubles $36.) Small and friendly, **Beach Road Backpackers** is within easy walking distance of town. Bike hire ($7.50 per day), and trips to Pebbly beach ($10). TV, kitchen. Free pickup and drop off at bus stop. (☎4472 3644. Dorms $19. VIP.)

**◨◪ SIGHTS AND ACTIVITIES.** The 1880 wreck of the Lady Darling is considered the **best wreck dive** around. Other dives include the Burrawarra Wall, the Maze, and Montague Island perfect for all levels, and for snorkeling too. The **Dive Shop,** 33 Orient St, can be your link to the water world. (☎4472 9930. Single boat dive $35; double $60. Equipment hire $30.) The **Opal and Shell Museum,** 142 Beach Rd, hosts an extensive display of shells from Australia and around the world. (☎4472 7248. Open daily 10am-6pm. $1.50, family $3.) To buy or rent a surfboard try **Kaffir Surfboards.** (☎4472 3933. Single fin $25, thrusters $35.)

To indulge in a spot of bushwalking, join the locals from **Batemans Bay Bushwalkers** on an outing ($2). Contact Bruce Cox (☎4471 1434) or ask the tourist office for a schedule. Traveling south on the coastal road, there's good **surf** at Malua Bay and Broulee (naturally, Surf Beach is no good for surfing). **U-Canoe** has canoe and kayak hire. (☎4474 3348. 1-man $25; 2-man $35; includes pickup or delivery.)

Further inland lies **Mogo,** 10km south of Batemans Bay, an 1850s gold rush town currently riding the craft craze. Take the tour at ◪**Old Mogo Town,** James St off Princes Highway, a reconstructed 19th-century mining town, and experience the gold rush yourself. Where else can you go panning for gold, see Tasmanian death masks, and even get hitched? (☎4474 2123. Open daily 10am-5pm. $12, includes tea and biscuit, gold panning, and tour; 10% off with Let's Go guide.) **Mogo Zoo,** 222 Tomakin Rd, off Princes Hwy in Mogo, houses endangered and exotic animals like snow leopards, red pandas, and pythons. (☎4474 4930. Open daily 9am-5pm. $11.)

# NAROOMA

With several free parks within an hour's drive, the town of Narooma is a place for outdoor exploration. One popular 2WD-accessible park is **Eurobodalla National Park,** which conserves coastline along a 30km stretch from Moruya Head in the north to Tilba Tilba Lake in the south with one campground at Congo, near the town of **Moruya** (sites for 2 $6). Just 7km offshore, fur seals, crested terns, and some 10,000 pairs of fairy penguins inhabit the **Montague Island Nature Reserve.** Since only 70 people are allowed to visit each day, the reserve is only accessible through official NPWS-sanctioned tours; most say the thrill outweighs the cost. (3½hr.; 1-2 per day; $66, families $198. Book through NPWS or the Visitors Centre.)

On Wagonga Head off of Bar Rock Rd, ocean waves and coastal winds have left one rock, known as **Australia Rock,** with a hole in the shape of Australia. Whether or not you see the "hole continent," the area is pretty. **Glasshouse Rocks,** another locally famous rock formation, lies at the south end of Narooma Beach. Depending on the winds, **surfers** will head out to Hankerchief, Bar, Carter's or Josh's Beaches.

**Pioneer Motor Service** (☎(1300) 36 81 00) stops in Narooma, outside the St. George Bank (northbound) and the Westpac Bank (southbound), and runs to: **Sydney** (6½-7½hr., 2-3 per day, $40); **Batemans Bay** (1hr., 2-3 per day, $12); **Bega** (1½hr., 2-3 per day, $13); **Bermagui** (40min., 1 per day, $7); **Kiama** (3¾hr., 2-3 per day, $38); **Nowra** (3hr., 2-3 per day, $27); **Ulladulla** (1¾hr., 2-3 per day, $17); and **Wollongong** (4¼hr., 2-3 per day, $38). **Greyhound Pioneer** (☎13 20 30) also does the coastal run once per day, but is more pricey. **Murray's** (☎13 22 51) travels from Narooma Plaza to **Canberra** (4½hr., 1-2 per day, $33). The **Narooma Visitors Centre,** on Princes Hwy, handles advance bookings for some campgrounds and tours (☎4476 2881; fax 4476 1690; open daily 9am-5pm). The free **Narooma Lighthouse Museum,** attached to the Visitors Centre, houses the original light mechanism from the Montague Island Lighthouse. The **National Parks and Wildlife Service** office is a block away on the corner of Princes Hwy and Field St. (☎4476 2888; fax 4476 2757; open M-F 9am-5pm.)

The new **Bluewater Lodge (YHA),** 8 Princes Hwy, is surrounded by water, and still under renovation. (☎4476 4440; fax 4476 5444; naroomayha@narooma.com. Bikes and canoes $5 per day. Internet. Open 8am-noon and 3-10pm; dorms $18; non-YHA add $3.) **Narooma Leisure Resort Caravan Park,** on Ballingala St, has great ocean views and beach access. (☎4476 2275; fax 4476 2336. Open 9am-5pm, later in summer. Sites for 2 $16-21, powered $18-25.)

## CENTRAL TILBA AND TILBA TILBA

You know you're in a small town when you ask about the population, and in response a local begins counting as people pass. **Central Tilba** (pop. 70) was 80 years old and fading into the hillsides in 1974 when the National Trust took the whole village under its wing and began a process of partial restoration. Central Tilba sits 15km south of Narooma off Princes Hwy. Blink and you'll miss **Tilba Tilba** (pop. 30), literally consisting of a bend in the road, a few kilometers away. **Pam's Village Store,** (☎4473 7311; open M-F 7am-7pm, Sa 7am-6pm, Su 8am-6pm), marks the center of local life and the start of a moderate 11km (4hr.) walking track up **Gulaga (Mt. Dromedary)** (4hr.; moderate) through forest in the company of lyrebirds. A guided tour from the **Umbarra Aboriginal Cultural Centre** presents more secluded areas and includes explanations of local Koori culture along the way. (☎4473 7232. 4-5hr., departs 9:30am, call ahead. $50.) The Cultural Centre, a few kilometers down the road to Bermagui from the Princes Hwy, features educational activities like spear throwing and Dreaming stories. (Centre open M-F 9am-5pm, Sa-Su 9am-4pm. Activities $7 each, conducted Sept.-June daily 9:30am-3pm. June-Aug. M-F 9:30am-3pm.) At the lower end of Tilba Tilba, flora bloom year round at the peaceful **Foxglove Spire Gardens.** (☎4473 7375. Open daily 9am-5pm. $5.)

**Premier Motor Services** offers limited bus service to Tilba (☎13 34 10; call for timetable and fares). The **Bates General Store** just off the highway on Bates St, is the source of good tourist info (☎/fax 4473 7290; open M-Sa 8am-5pm, Su 8:30am-5pm). They'll help you find accommodation and point you down the road to free tastings at the award-winning **ABC Cheese Company.** (☎4473 7387. Open daily 9am-5pm.) Visit **Tilba Valley Winery,** 5km North of Tilba off Princes Highway, and stop for a ploughman's lunch or a wine tasting. (☎4473 7308. Open M-Sa 10am-5pm, Su 11am-5pm. Picnic and BBQ facilities). The only pub in Central Tilba, **The Dromedary**

**Hotel,** on Bates St, has reasonably priced rooms with a TV lounge and laundry. Space is often limited so call ahead. (☎4473 7223; fax 4473 7238. Singles $30; doubles $60.) **Farmstays** and **B&Bs** make up the rest of accommodations in the area.

## BERMAGUI

Southeast of Tilba Tilba, 30min. from the Princes Hwy, **Bermagui** is a great place to fish and unwind in a seaside town. The catch is best Nov.-May, with game fish around Jan.-June. Those who prefer **swimming** cluster at Horseshoe Bay between Bermagui Point and Shelly Beach or at **Blue Pool,** the rock pool on Scenic Dr. The **surf** is good at Camel Rock and Cuttagee.

Premier Motor Services (☎13 34 10) is the only **bus** to come directly to town, offering one bus a day from the Village Store to: **Sydney** (6¾hr., $42); **Batemans Bay** (1¾hr., $15); **Bega** (1hr., $12); **Kiama** (4¼hr., $39); **Narooma** (40min., $7); **Nowra** (3½hr., $29); **Ulladulla** (2½hr., $22); and **Wollongong** (4¾hr., $39). Greyhound Pioneer (☎13 20 30) stops at **Cobargo** back out on the Princes Hwy, but it would be one heck of a walk. The volunteer-run **Tourist Information Centre** faces the park toward the end of Lamont St (☎6493 3054; open M-F 10am-4pm, Sa-Sun 10am-1pm). The BP **gas station,** 8 Wallaga Road, also serves as an information center and may be the better choice. (☎(1800) 64 58 08. Open daily 7am-7pm.)

The kind owner at **Blue Pacific Flats,** 73 Murrah St, gives great deals. (☎6493 4921. Pickup from bus stops outside Narooma $5. Kitchen. Laundry. $18-$20 per person, includes bikes and fishing gear.) Taste the catch of the day at the **Bermagui Fishermans Co-Op** on the waterfront on Cutajo St. (☎6493 4239. Fish and chips $5; dozen oysters $8. Open Su-Th 9am-6pm, F-Sa 9am-7pm.)

## BEGA

If you've been to the dairy section of an Australian grocery store, you've heard of Bega ("BEE-ga"). In the heart of dairy country, about 50km south of Cobargo where the road from Bermagui rejoins the Princes Hwy, Bega is the town that produces Bega cheese. While little goes on in the town itself, from Bega it is just a quick jaunt to the coast and the bushwalking, abseiling, and skiing of the Snowies.

**⬛🔁 TRANSPORT AND PRACTICAL INFORMATION.** Several bus companies pass through Bega, making stops opposite the tourist office. Premier Motor Service (☎13 34 10) heads to: **Sydney** (7¾hr., 2-3 per day, $44); **Batemans Bay** (2½hr., 2-3 per day, $19); **Bermagui** (2¼hr., 1 per day, $12); **Kiama** (5¼hr., 2-3 per day, $42); **Narooma** (1½hr., 2-3 per day, $13); **Nowra** (4½hr., 2-3 per day, $32); **Ulladulla** (3¼hr., 2-3 per day, $25); and **Wollongong** (5¾hr., 2-3 per day, $42). Greyhound Pioneer (☎13 20 30) does about the same Su-F for higher prices, but will stop at the door of the Bega YHA. The volunteer **Information Centre,** 91 Gipps St, also books bus tick-

---

# THE AUSTRALIAN HOTEL
White Australia came into being very fast. The explosion of explorers and settlers (and convicts) moving to the continent occurred in bursts: a gold rush here, a railway installation there. Thousands found themselves in makeshift tent cities. The first semi-permanent structures to arise quickly needed to put a roof over the heads of these original budget travelers, serving as meeting places and providing recreation when the work had been done. Thus, the Great Australian Pub (or Hotel) was born. Unique to the then-upstart country, this necessary combination drinking-establishment and overnight-stay ran against the long standing British trend of separate inns and taverns. Today, many of the 'hotels' built in the 19th and early 20th centuries have shed their upstairs beds, conceding victory to the blossoming motel industry. But some pubs, particularly in smaller towns with fewer alternatives, still rent their basic rooms to weary travelers. Pubstays, as the current revival trend calls them, are almost always less expensive than motels or guest houses, but then, they were certainly never meant for luxury.

ets. From the north, follow the highway into town and turn right onto Gipps St; the office will be on the right with the small clocktower island on the left (☎/fax 6492 2045; open M-F 9am-5pm, Sa-Su 9am-noon).

**▟ ACCOMMODATIONS.** Coming in north of town on the Princes Hwy, it's hard to miss the rooftop with the huge lettering that crowns the **Bega YHA Hostel,** on Kirkland Crescent off Kirkland St. The comfortable mud-brick building keeps clean dorms. TV, pool table, kitchen, laundry. (☎6492 3103; fax 6492 2335. Free pickup from bus. Open daily 8am-10pm. Dorms $13, under 18 $10; one double $34.) Uninspired but inexpensive accommodation can be found at the **Bega Caravan Park,** 256 Princes Hwy south of town. (☎/fax 6492 2303. Tent sites for 2 $16, powered $19; caravans $30; cabins $35; ensuite $44, extra person $8. Prices higher in peak season.)

**▣▟ SIGHTS AND ACTIVITIES.** The Bega Co-Operative Creamery Company has been making cheese here since 1899, and the **Bega Cheese Factory and Heritage Centre,** off the Princes Hwy northwest of town, offers visitors a behind-glass view of the cheese-making process. Don't miss the slightly disturbing **auto-milker** display. Cheese tastings and free entry make it palatable even for non-dairy enthusiasts. (Open daily 9am-5pm.) At **Grenvillea Estate Winery,** on Buckajo Rd just off Princes Highway, you can sample wines from the vineyard or watch cows being milked at 3pm daily at this family estate. (☎6492 3006. Open daily 9am-5pm. Free.)

Twenty-two gravel kilometers northeast of Bega, **Mimosa Rocks National Park** contains over 5000 hectares of coastal land and lagoon. In addition to several short walking tracks and picnic areas, the park has **camping.** The camping areas at Aragunnu and Picnic Point, north of Wapengo Lake at Middle Beach (trail access only) and Gillards Beach, have no facilities or drinking water, but you can always have a mimosa on the rocks. Just don't get too drunk and fall off. (Narooma NPWS ☎4476 2888. Sites for 2 $6; collector at site.)

# SNOWY MOUNTAINS

The Snowies, Australia's highest mountains, are a winter wonderland for skiers and snowboarders, while the warmer months bring swarms of hikers. Kosciuszko National Park, home of Mt. Kosciuszko (2228m), Australia's highest peak, covers most of the area. The Snowy Mountains Hwy and the Alpine Way ramble past the boulder-strewn countryside where the skiing industry is king. Compared to other mountain ranges around the world, the runs are shorter and less challenging.

Conditions on each mountain can vary wildly: Thredbo is a black diamond paradise. Perisher's name is a little deceiving; those content to wander aimlessly over the Australian slopes will love this ominous-sounding mountain. Snowbunnies will find unbeatable deals and easier slopes at Selwyn. Wherever you go, be careful of "death cookies." They're worse than the burnt treats you used to try to bake; these icy chunks of snow will burn your thighs to crisps as you ride over them.

## COOMA

Often considered the capital of the Snowies, Cooma links together Canberra, other coastal towns and skiing country. The town barely hangs on the eastern edge of the Snowy Mountains region, but it keeps a safe enough distance from the snowfields for bargain accommodations and reasonable rental rates in the ski season—for those willing to commute.

**▛▟ TRANSPORT AND PRACTICAL INFORMATION. Sharp St** forms the downtown area of Cooma with its two flanking routes, Massie St and Commissioner St. **Buses** come through three times per day during ski season, but service is severely curtailed the rest of the year. Countrylink (☎13 22 32) and Greyhound Pioneer

(☎13 20 30) cover: **Sydney** (9hr., $52); **Canberra** (2hr., $28.60); **Jindabyne** (1hr., $41); and **Thredbo** (1¾hr., $41). See the staff at **Harvey World Travel,** 114 Sharp St, opposite the visitors center, for reservations and info. (☎6452 4677. Open M-F 9am-5pm, Sa 9am-noon). The **Cooma Visitors Centre,** 119 Sharp St, is in the center of town. (☎6450 1742; fax 6450 1798; email cvc@snowy.net.au. Open daily mid-Oct. to May 9am-5pm; June to mid-Oct. 8am-5:30pm.) Several **ATMs** are downtown on Sharp St. **Internet access** can be found at the **Monaro Regional Library,** on the corner of Vale and Commissioner St. (☎6450 1730. Open M-F 9:30am-5:30pm, Sa 9am-12:30pm. 1hr. $5.) **Family Motel** (see below) has the same prices but better hours. The **post office** is on Massie at Vale St (open M-F 9am-5pm). **Postal code:** 2630.

**▓▓ ACCOMMODATIONS AND FOOD. Cooma Bunkhouse Backpackers,** 28-30 Soho St, on the corner of Commissioner St, has great year-round hostel accommodation with bathrooms, kitchens, and TVs. (☎/fax 6452 2983. Reception 7am-10pm. Dorms $20; singles in adjacent motel $30; doubles $50; triples $75. VIP.) **Family Motel,** 32 Massie St, offers friendly service and ski season steals. (☎6452 1414; fax 64542 5536; email family@snowy.net.au. Reception 8am-10pm. Internet 1hr. $5 Ensuite rooms $19 per person.) On Sharp St, **Snowtels Caravan Park,** provides a kitchen and on-site caravans and cabins. (☎6452 1828. Tent sites $15, powered $20; sites for 4 $33, ski season $44).

**Hideaway Café,** in the Woolworth's carpark, was around long before the supermarket popped up to obscure it. The cottage offers cheap eats from gourmet sandwiches and foccacias to smoothies and burgers. (☎6452 1509. Open daily 8am-5pm. Meals $3-5.) Another one of Cooma's better-kept secrets is **Rose's Restaurant,** serving Lebanese takeaway in Nassar's Four Mile Roadhouse, 6km west of Cooma across the Snowy Mountain Hwy from the Mountain View Caravan Park. Delicious *shish tawook* (chicken kebab) goes for $5.50. (☎6452 4512. Open until 9pm most days.) Stock up on relatively cheap food at Woolworth's **supermarket** (☎6452 3638), the corner of Vale and Massie St, as well as 228 Sharp St. (☎6452 3806. Both open daily 7am-10pm.)

**▓▓ SIGHTS AND SKIING.** The ski resorts of Thredbo, Perisher, and Selwyn radiate 100km from Cooma. **Rental shops** clutter the streets. Flashing signs advertising 'round-the-clock rentals may remind you of a casino town that depends on gambling for its livelihood. Rates are comparable to those closer to the mountains. For skis, poles, and boots, expect to pay about $30 the first day and $10-15 per day thereafter, or about $40 for the first day of a snowboard-and-boots rental. Look for brochures in the visitors center with 10%-15% discount coupons.

The **Snowy Mountains Hydro-Electric Scheme,** one of the world's greatest engineering feats of its kind, has its administrative center in Cooma. The Scheme diverts snowmelt waters from the east of the Dividing Range to the west, where it irrigates the fertile but dry plains. Simultaneously, huge quantities of hydro-electric power can be generated at peak times if necessary. Carried out between 1949 and 1974, the Scheme included the construction of 16 large dams and is responsible for nearly every body of standing water in the Snowy Mountains. The **Snowy Mountains Hydro-Electric Authority Visitors Centre,** on the Monaro Hwy just north of town, has models, brochures, and a 15-minute film explaining the grand plan. (☎6453 2004. Open M-F 8am-5pm, Sa-Su 8am-1pm. Free.)

As with most man-made achievements, advances come at a cost. The system has put Australia's legendary **Snowy River** in serious jeopardy. With only 1% of its original volume, the mighty river has been reduced to a trickle. There are huge campaigns currently lobbying the government to restore the parched waterway to at least 30% of its original flow to keep it from running dry.

# JINDABYNE

On the scenic shores of man-made **Lake Jindabyne,** the town of Jindabyne is a logical stopping point for those who can't afford to sleep in chalets at the foot of the

Thredbo chairlifts. During ski season the town plays its part as a satellite ski town, with the corresponding services and high seasonal prices. After the ski season, bushwalkers and backpackers stop through for park exploration. The original town was flooded as part of the hydro-electric scheme, and people can swim up the steps of the old church when the water level is low. Jindabyne is a goldmine for job-seekers arriving early in the season, providing decent wages (from $13) and a fun-loving **working community.** For job inquiries, check the employment bulletin at the IGA supermarket. Encounters with true ski bums who alternate seasons between the northern and southern hemispheres are not infrequent; many have been living for years in a perpetual state of winter.

**TRANSPORT AND PRACTICAL INFORMATION.** Jindabyne Coaches (☎6457 2117) runs **shuttles** to the Skitube train station for **Perisher Blue** ($13 return) throughout the ski season. Transport into Jindabyne from the northeast passes through **Cooma** (see p. 212) and operates only during the ski season. The **Snowy Region Visitors Centre** (☎6450 5600; fax 6456 1249), on the Alpine Way at the east end of town, combines a NPWS office and a multi-million-dollar tourist center. For road conditions dial ☎6450 5551; for snow reports dial ☎6450 5553. **Internet Access: Snowy Mountain Backpackers** (see below) plugs people into the web (1 hr. $10). The **Jindabyne NETcafé,** hidden in the left end of the Town Centre plaza, offers Internet access. (☎6457 1722. Open June-Oct. daily 10am-9pm; Nov.-May M-F 10am-5pm. 1hr. $12.) **Post office:** at the corner of Snowy River Rd and Gippsland St. (☎6456 2394. Open M-F 9am-5pm.) **Postal code:** 2627.

**ACCOMMODATIONS.** Even in the height of ski madness, affordable accommodation in Jindabyne does exist, but availability may be a problem; book well in advance. ◾**Snowy Mountain Backpackers,** 7 Gippsland St, behind the visitors center, combines an unbeatable location with brand-new facilities, laundry, Internet, and kitchen. (☎6456 1500. Reception daily 7:30am-10pm. Key deposit $5. Bunks $18, winter $30; doubles $70; Wheelchair accessible. VIP.) The **Station Resort** (see **Perisher Blue,** p. 216) offers package deals with lodging as low as $15 night. **The Jindy Inn,** 18 Clyde St, has private rooms with bathrooms, TVs, and fridges. There's a well-equipped kitchen downstairs and a nice adjoining restaurant. (☎6456 1957; fax 6456 2057. 24hr. reception. Bunks from $17 per person; singles $22, June-Oct. $25-80.) **Jindabyne Holiday Park** is in the center of town on a choice stretch of Lake Jindabyne shoreline. (☎6456 2249; fax 6456 2302. Key deposit $20. Ski-and-boot rental $30; snowboard-and-boot $40. Tent sites $10, powered $14. Extra person $5. On-site caravans Oct.-June from $30, July-Aug. from $65.)

**FOOD.** Cheap food is hard to come by in this alpine town that seems compelled to match the sky-high resort prices. **Wrap A Go-Go,** 2 Snowy River Ave, warms up visitors with spicy Mexican dishes and tasty wraps. (☎6457 1887. Open daily noon-9pm; summer closed M. Mains $8-13.) For those unwilling to venture into the cold, **Dial A Bits & Pizza** (☎6456 2439) will deliver any one of their 17 pizzas (large pies $15-$18) as far as Jindabyne Town Center. IGA **supermarkets** can be found in the Nuggets shopping center as well as the Town Centre. In the evenings, people relax at the **Lake Jindabyne Hotel,** on Kosciuszko Rd in the center of town, where entertainment ranges from old-fashioned drinking to concerts by top-notch rock bands. It's not surprising that Friday and Saturday nights are big. But Wednesday night is payday and LJH is the first stop for many employees. (☎6456 2203. Open M-Sa 10am-late, Su 10am-10pm. Schooners of VB $3.50.)

**ACTIVITIES.** To get to the slopes from Jindabyne, take the **Alpine Way,** which leads to the Skitube station (23km) that services Perisher Blue resorts, then continues on to Thredbo (30km). From there it extends its curvaceous and sometimes treacherous path through the mountains to **Khancoban,** a full-service town on the western edge of **Kosciuszko National Park.** Cars traveling to Khancoban are required to carry **snow chains.** The Shell station rents snow chains for $20, and has a drop-off program with the Shell station in Khancoban. The experts at **Wilderness Sports** (☎6456 2966), Nuggets Crossing, handle **cross-country skiing** adventures in the Thredbo area. Their **Backcountry Centre** is at the top of the Crackenback chair at Thredbo. (☎6457 6955. Open daily 8am-8pm; summer daily 9am-6pm. Snowshoe hire $30 per day; half-day telemarking lesson and tour $79, includes all equipment; half-day abseiling $69; full-day Mt. Kosciuszko tour $110, with lunch.)

Adventure activities in the area make the town a fun place in the summer. **Paddy Pallin** at the Thredbo turn-off next to the Shell station organizes **abseiling,** and rents **mountain bikes** and **kayaks.** It's the place for all your outdoor needs from hired clothing to equipment and activities. (☎6456 2922. Abseiling half-day $66, full-day $121. Mountain bike rental 1hr. $11, full-day $38. Kayak rental half-day $33, full-day $48.) For an organized thrill ride rafting down the Murray River, contact **Upper Murray White Water Rafting.** (☎6457 2002. Sept.-Apr. full-day $130.)

# KOSCIUSZKO NATIONAL PARK

Named after the heroic Polish nationalist but horribly mispronounced, Kosciuszko ("Kaw-zee-AW-sko") National Park marches along the New South Wales and Victoria border. Within the park, Australia's highest peaks loom over some of the country's largest power and irrigation projects. Skiers and hikers traipse about the mountaintops, oblivious to hydro-electric activity under their feet. While Kosciuszko National Park may forever be associated with ski resorts, tourists have begun to appreciate the year-round beauty of attractions such as Yarrongobilly Caves and the wildflower-strewn hikes leading to the rooftop of Australia. There's an entry fee for the park ($15 per car per day). Cars just passing through are exempt from the hefty entrance fee, although snow chains are required. The Shell station allows drop off of chains at either end ($20). Pick up park stickers at the Snowy Mountain Visitors Centre in Jindabyne (see p. 213) or the NPWS office on Scott St in Khancoban. (☎6076 9373. Open daily 8:30am-noon and 1-4pm.)

## THREDBO

Home of the country's longest ski runs, Thredbo is still considered by many to be *the* place to go for Australian snow. With a busy schedule of outdoor events and activities, the upscale resort village has established itself as a year-round entertainment venue rather than just a set of slopes. Its efforts haven't gone unnoticed; it was recently awarded the NSW Tourist Destination of the Decade.

**TRANSPORT AND PRACTICAL INFORMATION.** Thredbo-bound hitchhikers can often be found standing at the roundabout just outside town. From June to early October, Deanes Coaches runs **shuttles** between Thredbo and **Jindabyne** (☎9319 4666 or ☎(1300) 85 03 80. $24 return.) Greyhound Pioneer (☎13 20 30) also runs June-Oct. from **Cooma** (1hr., 2 per day, $41). During the summer, Mushwandry Bus Services (☎6452 3802, freecall ☎(1800) 63 65 25) runs from Cooma thru Jindabyne to Thredbo. Book ahead. **Thredbo Information Centre** is at 6 Friday Dr. (☎6459 4198; www.thredbo.com.au. Open ski season daily 8am-6pm; summer 9am-4pm.) **SKE Café,** in Kellar Plaza, connects skiers to the Internet. (☎6457 7333. 1hr. $10.)

**ACCOMMODATIONS.** With its nearest competitors charging hundreds of dollars more per night, the **Thredbo YHA Lodge,** 8 Jack Adams Path, is the best deal in town. Though less luxurious than its neighbors, the lodge has a comfortable chalet feel with ample common space, a big kitchen, and an Internet kiosk. TV-less rooms foster a social atmosphere. Five minutes of morning chores are expected of guests to keep costs down. **Reservations** for the ski season are made by ballot the first week in May. Applications must be submitted through the YHA Travel Centre, 422 Kent St, Sydney (☎9261 1111). For a more impromptu visit, contact the man-

NEW SOUTH WALES

ager at the lodge, Kerry Muller, about single night openings from cancellations. (☎6457 6376; fax 6457 6043; email thredbo@yhansw.com.au. Reception 7-10am and 4:30-9pm. June dorms $20; July-Oct. $44; Oct.-May $18. Seven-night package $326; F-Sa weekend package $107.) Other lodges can be booked through **Thredbo Resort Centre.** (☎6459 4294. Open daily Mar.-Aug. 9am-6pm; Sept.-Feb. 9am-5pm.)

🍴 **FOOD.** Eating on the mountain can burn a hole through your pocket. *Let's Go* does not recommend burning holes in one's pockets. Across the bridge, cafés and pizza parlors are slightly cheaper, less scarring alternatives. **Alfresco Pizzeria,** just below the Thredbo Alpine Hotel, serves pastas and pizza that will satisfy the biggest appetite. **Altitude 1380,** on Mowamba Pl., has lunches ranging from $7-10. Their coffee is famous and the Tom Yum chicken baguette ($7.50) is popular among locals. (☎6457 6190. Open 8-9:30pm daily.) After a tiring day on the slopes, hit the **Schuss Ski Club** in Palmers Lodge (☎6457 6297), for an afternoon of live entertainment. Later in the evening, the Schuss bar is so much fun that many skiers don't end up making it to the slopes the next day.

⛷ **SKIING.** Thredbo has 12 lifts and a healthy number of challenging blue and black runs to complement the easier slopes. All levels of skiers can handle the variety of bowls above treeline and trails lined with snowcovered gums. Experienced skiers brave Michael's Mistake—a mix of moguls, obstacles, and steep inclines. **Lift tickets** will set you back $73 per day (under 15 $40), and group ski lessons go for $39. Night skiing on Tuesday and Saturday nights is free with a valid lift pass. Charges for ski and snowboard rentals at **Thredbo Sports,** at the base of the Crackenback Chairlift and at the east end of the village near the Friday Flat lift, are higher than in Jindabyne or Cooma. (☎6459 4100. Skis, stocks, and boots $49.)

For the use of hikers and ganderers, the **Crackenback Chairlift** runs year-round. (All-day summer pass $18. Operates daily 8:30am-4:30pm.) Several excellent walks depart from the top of the mountain for sweeping views of Kosciuszko National Park. From the top of the chairlift, the **Mt. Kosciuszko Walk** is a 12km return to the summit of Australia's tallest mountain, but only a 4km return to reach another lookout point. At the village level, spring opens the way for mountain biking. The **Dead Horse Gap Walk** and **Wildflower Walk** are among the most beautiful walks around Thredbo. Free maps of all trails are available throughout the village. **Snowy Mountains Climbing School** (☎6076 9101) offers relatively cheap thrills (four abseils for $44). For more info, inquiries at **Thredbo Sports** (see above).

## PERISHER BLUE

New South Wales' other premier ski resort, Perisher Blue (☎(1300) 65 58 22; www.perisherblue.com.au), is actually four resorts in one. One lift ticket buys entry to the interconnected slopes leading down to the **Perisher Valley, Blue Cow, Smiggins,** and **Guthega** alpine villages. With 51 lifts and over 95 trails, Perisher is Australia's largest ski resort. Surprisingly, access between the seven peaks is relatively easy. While the runs aren't quite as long as those at Thredbo, they're more plentiful, and the total skiing area is much larger. Situated above the natural snow line, with a slightly higher elevation than its competitors, Perisher offers some of the best snow around. Snow comes right down to the parking lot, making daytrips less of a hassle with park-and-ski convenience. **Zali's Run,** named after the Australian World Cup skier, is a popular intermediate slope. **Kamikaze** and **Double Trouble** will really put skiers and boarders to the test.

**Lift tickets** cost $73 per day (under 17 $40), plus a same-day return ticket ($86, $48) to the Skitube. Perisher Blue also has **night skiing.** (Available Tu and Sa 6:30-10pm. $21, children $14. 2hr. group lesson $35.) All lift tickets include unlimited use of the Perisher-Blue Cow segment of the Skitube. Purchase tickets at Bullocks Flat or at the **Perisher Blue Jindabyne Ticket Office** in the **Snowy Mountains Plaza** shopping center. (☎6456 1659. Open daily 7am-7pm.) **Murray's** (☎13 22 51) and **Lever Coachlines** (☎6262 3266) offer a daytrip skiing package from Canberra. ($99; under 13 $80. Includes return bus, park entry, lift ticket, and ski hire.)

Unlike Thredbo, Perisher is not a full-service village, and has no budget accommodation or overnight parking. On busy days, the Perisher Valley day lot fills up quickly (and is often entirely inaccessible due to road conditions), but the **Skitube** (☎6456 2010) is an all-weather train that makes the 8km journey from **Bullocks Flat,** located on the Alpine Way, into the Perisher Valley Alpine Village. You can either start your adventures here, or keep riding the skitube halfway up the mountain to the Blue Cow terminal. There, lifts take more advanced skiers and 'boarders to the blue and black runs atop **Guthega Peak** and **Mt. Blue Cow.** At the Perisher Station, follow your nose to **Lil' Orbits Donuts** where you can grab 12 mini-donuts for $3. To get to the Skitube station at Bullocks Flat, take Jindabyne Coaches (☎6457 2117), which runs shuttles from **Jindabyne** (4 per day, $13 return). By **car,** drive along the Alpine Way from Jindabyne until you reach the station; there's plenty of parking.

For Perisher-bound skiers, **The Station Resort** is a popular destination for the cheapest lodging and the least hassle. The self-contained village is located 6km outside of town, but there is little reason to leave; bars, restaurants, and bus services are all on the premises. With cars lined up along the streets, the place looks like a house party. Packages vary from basic accommodation and lifts (5 days $479) to all inclusive deals (5 days $719, includes lifts, accommodation, ski tube, ski hire and 8 meals). Package deals range from 2-5 days and become increasingly cheaper with more people sharing the room.

## YARRANGOBILLY CAVES

Hidden near a valley floor in the beautiful northern scrub wilderness of the Kosciuszko National Park, the Yarrangobilly Caves attract curious visitors and hardcore spelunkers alike. The **Yarrangobilly River,** located off the Snowy Mountains Hwy 77km south of Tumut and 109km northwest of Cooma, runs through a 12km-long stretch of limestone, riddled with formation-filled caves. The caves are a well-signposted 6.5km from the highway, downhill on a windy unsealed road. **Jillabenan** is the shortest (3km; 1hr.) and only wheelchair-accessible cave. Its array of stalactite and stalagmite formations amid crystal-lined nooks is spectacular. The slightly longer 1½hr. **Jersey Caves** tour passes equally stellar sights. After wandering around the caves, take a load off in the 27°C **thermal pools** near the river, a 700m steep downhill walk from the carpark (free). All of the caves are open daily from 9am to 5pm. Marked walking trails help tourists better understand the beauty of the caves and the surrounding canopies. The NPWS **Visitor Centre** (☎6454 9597) at the site is an essential first stop. Only one cave (South Glory) is open for a **self-guided tour,** but even then you'll need a token from the visitor center to explore beyond the unusual and pretty "glory arch" entrance. (About 45min. $8.80, children $5.50.) The remaining caves are open to **guided tours.** (Daily at 11am, 1, and 3pm; other times with advance scheduling. $11, children $8.)

## MOUNT SELWYN

Along the Snowy Mountains Hwy, halfway between Cooma and Tumut, the **Selwyn Snowfields** offer beginner budget skiing steals. (☎6454 9488; fax 6454 9482; http://selwynsnow.com.au). Primarily a family resort, Selwyn has a small number of trails, minimal amenities, and only a couple advanced runs. Elevation at the base is 1492m; the summit is 122m higher (this means extensive snowmaking when necessary to offset lack of the real stuff). **Lift tickets** are inexpensive. (Full-day $44, under 15 $22. Half-day $33, $19; valid 8:30am-12:45pm or 12:45-4:30pm. Over 65 and under 6 free.) Forty-five kilometers of marked trails and no lift fee make **cross-country skiing** another attractive option.

**Ski hire** for alpine or cross-country skis and snowboards is pretty reasonable on the mountain. (Half-day $20, full-day $28; snowboards $33, $44.) **Toboggans** are also available. ($8 per day; toboggan lift ticket $5 per 10 rides.) Or try out a **lift and lesson** package. (1½hr. lesson $66, under 15 $44. Includes full-day lift ticket.) There is no accommodation at Mt. Selwyn, but Cooma (see p. 212) is an hour's commute.

# HUME CORRIDOR

As the major route between Australia's two largest cities, the Hume Hwy provides fast travel without too much in the way of scenery. In fact, to get to Sydney or Melbourne is really the only reason to travel the Hume or to stop in any of the towns along the way. It takes 9-10hr. to cover the 872km between Sydney and Melbourne, but scenic detours along stretches of the Old Hume Hwy where it parts from the new to some historic villages tucked away in the countryside can periodically spruce up the monotony. For towns in the Hume Corridor in Victoria, see p. 587.

## SYDNEY TO GOULBURN

As the state capital recedes in the rearview mirror, the Hume Hwy leads into an area known as the "Cow-pastures," a name given for its use as grazing land for the young colony of Sydney. Now divided into the towns of **Liverpool, Campbelltown, Camden,** and **Narellan,** this area was the site of some of Australia's first colonial land grants, including the 1805 grant to John Macarthur, whose wildly successful investment in wool and wine is popularly considered the starting point of the nation's wealth. Housed at **Mt. Annan Botanic Garden,** off the F5 freeway between Camden and Campbelltown along Tourist Dr 18, the native-plant collection of Sydney's **Royal Botanic Garden** includes flora from throughout Australia on 410 hectares. Outside the visitors center you can look at a young specimen of the recently-discovered rare **Wollemi pine.** (☎ 4648 2477. Open daily Apr.-Sept. 10am-4pm; Oct.-Mar. 10am-6pm. Admission $4.40.) For a day of Australiana, **Gledswood,** on Camden Valley Way closer to Camden, entertains visitors with farm activities including sheep-shearing and boomerang-throwing. (☎ 9606 5111. Tour 11am; shearing show noon. Open daily 10am-4pm. $14.)

Two budget accommodations are available in the town of **Mittagong,** 40min. south of Campbelltown. There's a **caravan park,** with basic facilities. (☎ 4871 1574. Sites for 2 $14, powered $17.) The **Lion Rampant Hotel,** is a clean and comfy pub stay. (☎ 4871 1090. Singles $27; doubles $38.) **Bowral,** 3km farther south, was the childhood home of legendary cricketer **Sir Donald Bradman.** The **Bradman Museum,** on Saint Jude St, documents the history of Australian cricket. (☎ 4862 1247. Open daily 10am-5pm. $8.) Between the two towns, a long detour (2hr. one-way) from the Hume Hwy leads to the deep and beautiful **Wombeyan Caves.** (☎ 4843 5976. Open daily 8:30am-5pm. Admission $11, guided tour $13.)

Thirty kilometers south of Mittagong lies the turn-off for **Morton National Park,** off the Hume Hwy by way of the Bundanoon/Exeter exit. Thick forests stretch toward the sandstone cliffs at the park's interior, carved by scenic walking tracks. At the park's edge, the town of **Bundanoon** has one lovely accommodation: the **Bundanoon YHA Hostel,** a spacious old guesthouse on Railway Ave on the north end of town. The hostel has warm management, a full kitchen, and a game room. (☎ 4883 6010; fax 4883 7470. Reception 8-10am and 5-8:30pm. Dorms $17; twins and doubles $42; family rooms $50. Non-YHA members $3 more.) From the hostel, a short trail (1hr.) leads to the bioluminescent bliss of the **Glow Worm Glen,** best seen at night. Trails from the glen cross into the National Park. Hiking maps available at the hostel cover the entire area. CityRail **trains** from Sydney's Central Station stop at Bundanoon's railway station daily (return $16, off-peak $17).

## GOULBURN

Settled in the early 1830s, Goulburn (pop. 22,000) has long been a regional center, once of agriculture and the judicial system, now of enterprises like the Merino wool industry. The city still has buildings that date from the 1800s. This connection with history, and easy access to parks and adventure activities, gives Goulburn a feeling of continuity unusual among the towns of New South Wales.

■■🛈 **ORIENTATION AND PRACTICAL INFORMATION.** Goulburn is on the Hume Hwy between Yass (87km) and Sydney (195km) and 10km east of the junction with the Federal Hwy. Countrylink (☎ 4827 1485), Fearnes Coaches (☎ (1800)

02 99 18), Greyhound Pioneer (☎13 20 30), and McCafferty's (☎13 14 99) run service to area towns and major destinations such as Sydney and Canberra. **Trains** and **buses** stop at the **Goulburn Railway Station** on Sloane St, or the **Big Merino** (see above). Across from Belmore Park, the **Goulburn Visitor Information Centre,** 201 Sloane St, distributes the *Self-Guided Heritage Walking Tours* guide to the city's historic buildings. (☎4823 4492; email visitor@goulburn.nsw.gov.au. Open daily 9am-5pm.) **Auburn St** is the major street in town on which lies the **post office,** 165 Auburn St (☎4821 1422; open M-F 8:30am-5pm). **Postal code:** 2580. **Internet access** is available at the **Southern Tablelands Regional Library** in the Civic Centre on Bourke St. (☎4823 4435. Open M, W, F 10am-6pm, Tu, Th 10am-7pm, Sa 10am-5pm, Su 2-5pm. Free access for 20min.)

**▐▜▐▘ ACCOMMODATIONS AND FOOD.** The **Goulburn Gateway Service Station** (☎4821 9811), on the corner of Common St and the Hume Hwy, has cheap accommodations. The owners converted the defunct bus depot behind their petrol station complex into a small **dormitory.** The location is disconcerting, but the bedroom is clean and livable. (Reception 24hr. Beds $14.50.) Across Sloane St from the railway station, the aging but tidy **Coolavin Hotel,** 188 Sloane St, rents basic rooms with electric blankets and TVs. (☎4821 2498. Singles $22; twins $33.) The smattering of eateries includes **Antiques & Eats,** 193 Auburn St, which combines, as the name suggests, an antique shop and a café. (☎4821 1511. Open W-Su 9:30am-5pm. Sandwiches from $7.) The **Goulburn Deli,** 140 Auburn St, offers fast, tasty sandwiches from $4-5 and melts from $6. (☎4821 8818. Open M-F 8am-5pm, Sa 8am-2pm.)

**◙ SIGHTS.** An enduring, if tacky, monument to the city's livelihood, the 97-ton **Big Merino,** a three-story Merino Ram, stands next to the Hume Hwy at the southwest end of town. Climb up into his head and look out over Goulburn through the eyes of the Big Merino; perhaps enlightenment will come, or maybe just an intense desire to eat grass. (☎4821 8800. Open daily 8am-8pm. Enlightenment free, but intermittent.) The high points of the historic walking tour lie on Montague St in the center of town. On one end, the dome of the **1887 Court House** towers over stately grounds. Two blocks up the street is **St. Saviour's Cathedral,** built between 1874 and 1884. (☎4821 2206. Open M-Sa 10am-4pm. Small donation requested with tour.) The **Goulburn Brewery** on Bungonia Rd, southeast of the city center, is open daily for visitation, but tours and tastings happen only on Sundays. The restaurant and bar serve lunch, dinner, and, of course, beer. (☎4821 6071. Open M-Th 11am-7pm, F-Sa 11am-7pm or later, Su 11am-5pm. 45min. tours Su 11am and 3pm, $5.50. Tastings $1. Free.) **Bungonia State Park,** 35km East of Goulburn, has plenty of natural wonders. Experienced cavers can put their skills to the test while **adventure caving** in some of the deepest caves in Australia. (☎4844 4277. Car entry fee $5.50.)

# GUNDAGAI

Sure, Gundagai ("GUN-dah-GUY") *could* brag about its historic buildings, or perhaps its notoriety as the site of Australia's most devastating flood (1852, death toll 83), but this little town off the Hume Hwy instead draws visitors with some of the more bizarre attractions in the state.

Entering town from the east, it's hard to miss the **Dog On The Tuckerbox** monument just next to the highway, honoring loyal pioneer dogs. The tourist center also houses a stunning tribute to craftwork and neurosis: **Frank Rusconi's Masterpiece in Marble,** a fantastical model building composed of 20,948 pieces of handcrafted marble constructed between 1910 and 1938. (Open M-F 8am-5pm, Sa-Su 9am-noon and 1-5pm. Admission $2.) Also of interest are the **Historic Bridges,** just off of the eastern end of Sheridan St, with numerous striking vistas. South of Sheridan, the **Gundagai Historical Museum,** on Homer St, houses a hodgepodge of old machinery, farm equipment, and even a Model T. (☎6944 1995. Open daily 9-5pm. $3.)

Gundagai is a node in several transport networks. V/Line (☎13 61 96), McCafferty's (☎13 14 99), Greyhound Pioneer (☎13 24 14), Firefly Express (☎(1800) 63 11 64), and Fearnes (☎(1800) 02 99 18) can take you to: **Sydney** (5-6¾hr., 7 per day,

$32-40); **Canberra** (2hr., 3 per day, $20-25); **Melbourne** (6-6½hr., 7 per day, $45-49); **Albury/Wodonga** (2-2½hr., 7 per day, $20-27); **Goulburn** (2-3¾hr., 6 per day, $30-34); **Narrandera** (2¼hr., 2 per day, $32); **Wagga Wagga** (1¼hr., 3 per day, $23). The **Tourist and Travel Centre,** on Sheridan St east of the Hume Hwy, serves as the bus depot. (☎ 6944 0250; fax 6944 1409. Open M-F 8am-5pm, Sa-Su 9am-noon and 1-5pm.)

The **Criterion Hotel,** 172 Sheridan St, at the corner of Byron St, has comfortable lodging. The pub has some funky nude paintings, but the rooms stick to practical amenities. (☎ 6944 1048. Reception at bar 10am-10pm. Singles $20.) **Gundagai Caravan Village,** close to town on Junee Rd, has sites with private bathrooms. (☎ 6944 1057. Sites for 2 $14, powered $19; on-site vans $33.) The local food is just pub grub with some takeaways, though the **Niagra Café,** 142 Sheridan St, boasts of having served the Prime Minister in 1942. How many restaurants today can (or want to) say that? (☎ 6944 1109. Open daily 9am-9:30pm.) **IGA supermarket** is at 152 Sheridan S. (☎ 6944 1499. Open M-F 8am-6pm, Sa 8am-12:30pm, Sun 9am- noon.)

# ALBURY

Spanning the Murray River, which marks the border between New South Wales and Victoria, the Albury-Wodonga metropolitan area (pop. 90,000) belongs to both states. Right on the Hume Hwy, it breaks the transit between Sydney and Melbourne and provides an excellent base for daytrips to nearby wineries, alpine retreats, and the neighboring Riverina. The preponderance of quality budget accommodations and cheap eats makes Albury the most backpacker-friendly pit-stop along the Hume. Many linger a while, especially during the summer months when the river is high and ripe for outdoor excursions.

## ▌▛ TRANSPORT

**Trains and Buses:** The impressive **Albury railway station** is at the eastern end of Dean St. Inside, the **Countrylink Travel Centre** can book all rail and most bus transport. (☎ 6041 9555. Open M-F 9am-5pm, Sa 9:30am-4:30pm.) Countrylink (☎ 13 22 32) **trains** run to: **Sydney** (6¾hr., 2 per day, $86); **Melbourne** (3hr., 2 per day, $56); **Goulburn** (5hr., 2 per day, $66); **Wagga Wagga** (1hr., 2 per day, $22); **Wangaratta** (45min., 2 per day, $13); and **Yass** (3¾hr., 2 per day, $47). V/Line (☎ 13 61 96) services destinations in Victoria far more frequently and cheaper. To: **Melbourne** (3-3½hr., 4-6 per day, $40); **Wangaratta** (50min., 4-6 per day, $10); **Echuca** (3-4hr., 1-2 per day, $21-34); **Swan Hill** (5½-7hr., 1-2 per day, $35-42); **Mildura** (10hr.; M, W, Th, Sa mornings; $56); and **Rutherglen** (40min; M, W, Th, Sa mornings; $6). McCafferty's (☎ 13 14 99) **buses** service: **Sydney** (9hr., 3 per day, $38); **Brisbane** (23hr., 3 per day, $115); **Canberra** (4¼hr., 4 per day, $27); **Melbourne** (4hr., 3 per day, $32); **Gundagai** (2hr., 2 per day, $21); **Wagga Wagga** (8hr., 1 per day, $54); and **Wangaratta** (1hr., 2 per day, $18). Greyhound (☎ 13 20 30) offers direct service to **Coonabarabran** (10hr., 2 per day, $104); **Cowra** (5hr., 1 per day, $71.50); **Dubbo** (3½hr., 2 per day, $86); and **Forbes** (5¾hr., 2 per day, $79).

## ▚▐ ORIENTATION AND PRACTICAL INFORMATION

The **Hume Hwy** (Hwy 31) from Sydney enters Albury from the northeast, runs through town, and then turns sharply west to bypass Wodonga. The **Murray Valley Hwy** (Hwy 16) runs along the Victorian side and enters Wodonga from the southeast, running through town before uniting with the Hume Hwy. Along the river on the New South Wales side, the **Riverina Hwy** (Hwy 58) runs from Corowa toward Khancoban. Albury's main street, **Dean St,** runs east-west from the railroad tracks and is crossed by (the easternmost) **Young St** (Hume Hwy), Macauley, David, Olive, Kiewa, and Townsend St. **Smollett St** runs parallel to Dean St one block south.

**Tourist Office: Gateway Visitors Information Centre** (☎ 6041 3875, freecall (1800) 80 07 43; fax 6021 0322; email info@cow.mav.asn.au). In the Gateway Village no-man's land between Albury and Wodonga on the east (Melbourne-bound) side of the Hume Hwy. Open daily 9am-5pm. 24hr. computer information station outside.

**Currency Exchange: Westpac Bank,** 613 Dean St (☎6041 1111). Open M-Th 9:30am-4pm, F 9:30am-5pm. **ATMs** line Dean St.

**Police:** 539-543 Olive St (☎6023 9299), near Swift St.

**Post Office:** (☎6021 1755), at the corner of Dean and Kiewa St. Open M-F 9am-5pm. **Poste Restante** services available. **Postal Code:** 2640.

**Internet Access: Albury City Library** (☎6041 6633), in the city block behind the Regional Art Centre, has 2 terminals. Free for research, but email costs $2.75 per 30min. Book ahead. Open M-F 9am-7pm, Sa 9am-2pm.

**Laundry:** 461 Smollett St. Wash $3, dry $1 for 10min. Open daily 5am-10:30pm.

**Phone Code:** 02.

## ACCOMMODATIONS

▨ **Albury Backpackers,** 452 David St (☎6041 1822; fax 6031 6335; www.alburyback packers.com.au). At the corner of Smollett St. The backpacker spirit lives on at this comfy hostel near the train station. Travelers bond through karaoke nights, pub crawls, and the popular overnight canoe trips run by the affable owner (1-day Murray trip $26, 2-day $59). Kitchen. Internet (1hr. $5). Bike hire ($6 per day). Check-out noon. Dorms $16; twins and doubles $34. Seasonal weekly rates. VIP.

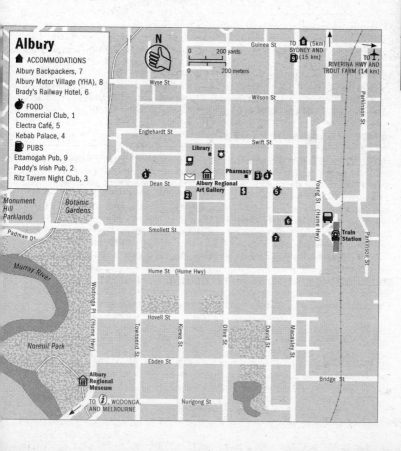

**Albury**

🏠 ACCOMMODATIONS
Albury Backpackers, 7
Albury Motor Village (YHA), 8
Brady's Railway Hotel, 6

🍴 FOOD
Commercial Club, 1
Electra Café, 5
Kebab Palace, 4

🍺 PUBS
Ettamogah Pub, 9
Paddy's Irish Pub, 2
Ritz Tavern Night Club, 3

**Albury Motor Village (YHA),** 372 Wagga Rd, Hume Hwy (☎ 6040 2999; fax 6040 3160; albury@motorvillage.com.au). 5km north of the city in Lavington across from the KFC and Cal-Tex. Greyhound and McCafferty's will drop off here; $10 cab ride from train station. Quiet, clean, family-friendly, but with little character. Pool, kitchenette, TV lounge, parking, laundry. Reception 7:30am-10:30pm. Dorms $16; powered sites for 2 $18; cabins for 2 $51-100 (all but deluxe cabins are BYO linens). Book ahead in summer.

**Brady's Railway Hotel,** 450 Smollett St (☎ 6021 4700). 2 blocks from the railway station. Reception at bar M-Th 7am-midnight, F-Sa 10am-midnight, Su 7am-9pm. Singles $20.

## FOOD AND NIGHTLIFE

Dean St proffers a fine collection of international cuisines at good prices. The **Commercial Club,** 618 Dean St, serves a $10 all-you-can-eat lunch and dinner with a rich variety of vegetables, meat dishes, and surprisingly gourmet desserts. Provided you don't get lured into the casino next door, it's the best deal in town. (☎ 6021 1133. Open daily for lunch noon-2pm, dinner 6-9pm. Neat dress.) **Electra Café,** 441 Dean St, has a selection of large open foccacias ($8) for lunch and an ephemeral "pasta of the moment" dinner ($14). Live music Tu nights, brekkie on weekends. (☎ 6021 7200. Open M-F 10am-11pm, Sa 9am-11pm, Su 9am-3pm.) Kebabs, souvlakis, and falafels come in all sizes ($4-7) at the **Kebab Palace,** 462 Dean St. (☎ 6041 6220. Open Su-Th 11am-10pm, F-Sa 11am-11pm.) Coles **supermarket** is on the corner of Kiewa and Smollett St (open daily 7am-midnight).

Albury's one and only nightclub, **The Ritz Tavern Nightclub,** 480 Dean St, is a high-budget, high-class dance venue fit for a big city. It's always a mad party on Wednesday Uni Nights, when $2 spirits and beers suck the local students in like a black hole. Thursdays are notoriously silent, but Friday and Saturday nights kick off around midnight to the latest dance music. (☎ 6041 4484. Open W-Th 4pm-4am, F-Sa 4pm-5am. Strict neat casual dress code. No cover downstairs with live band every night. Cover upstairs W $5, Th-F $8, Sa $10; $2 discount with student ID.) **Paddy's Irish Bar,** 491 Kiewa St, in the New Albury Hotel, is the local upscale jig joint with a 30-something clientele and Guinness on tap (pints $6.20). Irish bands play fortnightly. (☎ 6021 3599. Open M-Sa 8:30am-late, Su 10am-late.)

## SIGHTS AND ACTIVITIES

On Wodonga Pl between Smollett and Dean St, the **Albury Botanic Gardens** (☎ 6023 8241) have diverse arboreal displays and plenty of grassy picnic space. To take in a sweeping view of the region, climb to the top of the **Monument Hill Bushlands** and gaze out on Albury-Wodonga from the base of the Deco obelisk Albury War Memorial. Walk uphill from Dean St, or follow the street up and around the back of the hill. The **Albury Regional Art Gallery,** 546 Dean St, presents a changing array of contemporary art exhibitions, including a collection of works by Australian artist Russell Drysdale. (☎ 6023 8187. Open M-F 10:30am-5pm, Sa-Su 10:30am-4pm. Free.)

On the Riverina Hwy 14km east of Albury, the **Hume Weir Trout Farm** raises Rainbow Trout for commercial and recreational purposes. You can pet baby trout (if you really, really miss your puppy), catch trout (rod and bait free, fish caught cost $8-9 per kg, cleaning 20¢ per fish, BBQ $1) and sample smoked trout. (☎ 6026 4334. Open daily 9am-5pm. Admission $5.50, students $4.50, children $3.)

**FOLLOW THAT MOTH** Occurring on November 24 in 2001, the annual **Ngan Girra festival** is a cultural celebration held in Mungabareena Reserve near Albury. The festival celebrates the traditional confluence of several local Aboriginal groups, who gathered to follow the springtime Bogong moth migration. The moths, after being smoked out and cooked, were a high-nutrient feast. The indigenous term for this particular "meeting place" is *ngan girra*, or *kamberra*, which was only altered slightly when it was used to create the name of the Australian capital city, Canberra.

**NEW SOUTH WALES**

## 🏛 DAYTRIP FROM ALBURY: ETTAMOGAH PUB

Just 15km north of Albury along the Hume Hwy, the **Ettamogah Pub** explodes in goofy fun as it caters to gawking tourists and satirizes and stereotypes all things Aussie. Cartoonist Ken Maynard had been drawing the place for years before someone decided to actually construct it. The amusement-park-style village is composed of eye-popping, off-kilter buildings decorated with a running stream of witticisms. The centerpiece is the hilariously constructed and fully-operational Ettamogah Pub itself, capped with a vintage Fosters beer truck on the roof, a crashed airplane next door, and filled with business-card-slathered walls (pub open Su-Th 10am-9pm, F-Sa 10am-10pm). Other sights include a hollowed-out tree sealed with jail bars and dubbed Lock Up, a police "office" covered in corny cop punnery, a real pottery studio, a picnic area, and bumper cars ($2 per ride). The Ettamogah Winery predates the pub but is now part of the complex, and it has free tastings and wine sales. Next door is a restaurant and souvenir shop (open daily 8:30am-5pm). There's no admission to tour the site, and signs will clearly direct you from the highway.

# RIVERINA

Dry, brown, and flat, much of the Riverina's terrain doesn't look like a land suited for farming. Heavy irrigation has turned the soil into fertile plains. Although not a prime sightseeing destination, the Riverina attracts budget travelers seeking seasonal farm or fruit-picking work in order to save up for more exciting destinations. Two rivers fertilize the system: the Murrumbidgee starts as a trickle in the Snowy Mountains and then widens into a major waterway that joins the Murray.

**PICKING WORK.** Seasonal picking jobs abound in the Riverina year-round, although December to April is the easiest time to find work. Conditions can be tough—even the basics such as water and toilets are unusual, and pay is typically based on how much you pick, not how long you work. To find out more about seasonal work, contact **Employment National** (☎ 13 34 44) or check out the "Seasonal Work" section of the **Australian Jobsearch** web site (http://jobsearch.deetya.gov.au). **Pickers Plus,** 20 Olympic St (☎ 6964 0080; email miacha@webfront.net.au), in Griffith, links growers with laborers free of charge. Riverina tourist offices keep copies of the useful booklet Working Holidays in the Riverina, also available online at www.riverinatourism.com.au.

## WAGGA WAGGA

New South Wales' largest inland city (pop. 58,000), sprawling Wagga Wagga (mercifully abbreviated and pronounced "WAU-guh") is more of a commercial and residential center than a tourist destination. With Walla Walla, Gumly Gumly, Book Book and Grong Grong as neighboring towns, you wonder whether the cartographer covering this region suffered from a serious stuttering problem (or maybe he was extremely drunk). Located along the Murrumbidgee River, Wagga Wagga is home to Charles Sturt University, and consequently thousands of uni students.

On the Baylis side of the river lies the new **Civic Centre,** which houses the **Wagga Wagga Regional Art Gallery** (featuring local and touring exhibitions), the **National Art Glass Collection,** and the **Carnegie Print Collection.** (☎ 6926 9660. Gallery open M-Sa 10am-5pm, Su noon-4pm. Glass collection open W-Su 10am-5pm.) **Taste of the Riverina,** the premier food event during the long weekend in June, alternates each year between Wagga Wagga and Griffith. With the Chef's Challenge, food courts, and the "Golden Plate" awards, the 2001 Wagga Wagga festival will not disappoint. Next door, the attractive **Botanic Gardens** are arranged across nine hectares. An **aviary** envelops visitors in native birdlife, and pathways wind pleasantly among the brooks and trees. (☎6925 4065. Open daily 7:30am-dusk. Free.) The **Wiradjuri Walking Track** meanders for 30km, covering many of the city's natural highlights. The trail runs through the Botanic Gardens, along the Murrumidgee River past Lake Albert to many panoramic views of the region.

**Baylis St** is the town's main strip, and it goes over a bridge to become **Fitzmaurice St.** Countrylink (☎13 22 32) and Fearnes Coaches (☎(1800) 02 99 18) operate **bus** and **train** service from the railway station on the south end of Baylis St to: **Sydney** (6½-7¼hr., 3 per day, $75); **Albury** (1½hr., 2 per day, $22); **Gundagai** (1hr., 1 per day, $22); and **Wangaratta** (2hr., 1 per day, $37.40). Greyhound Pioneer (☎13 20 30) departs from the terminal on the corner of Gurwood and Trail St for: **Sydney** (8¼hr., 2 per day, $40); **Canberra** (3hr., 2 per day, $29.70); **Albury** (2hr., 2 per day, $31); **Cowra** (2¾hr., 1 per day, $60.50); **Dubbo** (5hr., 2 per day, $82.50); **Forbes** (3hr., 2 per day, $67); **Griffith** (2hr., 2 per day, $30); **Gundagai** (1hr., 2 per day, $23); and **Wangaratta** (2¾hr., 2 per day, $32). The **Visitor Information Centre** is on Tarcutta St. (☎6926 9621; www.wagga.nsw.gov.au. Open daily 9am-5pm.) **Post office:** on Baylis St, in the **Wagga Wagga Marketplace** mall between Forsyth and Morgan St (open M-F 8:30am-5pm, Sa 9am-noon.) **Postal code:** 2650. Basic **pubstays** (singles $22) line Baylis St, as do restaurants. There's a Coles **supermarket** (☎6921 5377) on the corner of Baylis and Forsyth St.

## NARRANDERA

Downtown Narrandera ("na-RAN-dra") feels refreshingly like an intimate Anytown, Australia. This low-key transportation hub (pop. 5000) doesn't try to trip over itself to nab tourists. About halfway between Adelaide and Sydney off the Sturt Hwy, and a day's drive from Melbourne en route to Brisbane along the Newell Hwy, Narrandera provides excellent budget beds for commuters.

No visit to the town would be complete without seeing the **world's second largest playable guitar**—Bristol, England recently reclaimed the title with one slightly larger—in the Tourist Centre. The adjacent **Tiger Moth Memorial** houses a WWII plane, a reminder of Narrandera's use as a training site for the Royal Australian Air Force. (Open daily 9am-5pm. Free.)

Two blocks east of East St, Countrylink (☎13 22 32) **buses** run from the **railway station** to **Griffith** (1¼hr., 1 per day, $12) and **Wagga Wagga** (1½hr., 1-2 per day, $8). McCafferty's (☎13 14 99) runs daily from the Mobil Roadhouse on the highway to: **Sydney** (9¼hr., $44); **Canberra** (4¾hr., $32); **Melbourne** (5hr., $65); **Dubbo** (4½hr., $55); **Griffith** (1¼hr., $16); **Gundagai** (2¼hr., $27); and **Wagga Wagga** (1hr., $16). From the Shell Auto Port, Greyhound (☎13 20 30) goes to the same places.

The main street, **East St,** runs north-south one block east of Cadell St. The **Tourist Information Centre** is on Cadell St in the park. (☎6959 1766. Open daily 9am-5pm.) **Internet access:** at the **library,** 39-51 East St. (☎6959 2129. Open M-Tu and Th-F 10am-5:30pm, W 1-5:30pm, Sa 9:30am-noon. 1hr. $3.30.) **Post office:** on the corner of Twynam and East St. (Open M-Th 9am-4:45pm, F 9am-5pm.) **Postal code:** 2700.

For a decent bed, the **Royal Mail Hotel** is a pubstay that's a fair deal. (☎6959 2007. Singles $15; doubles $30.) Above the popular pub, the **Charles Sturt Hotel,** on the corner of East and Douglas St, offers nicely furnished rooms. (☎6959 2042. TV lounge, BBQ. Reception at bar 10am-late. Singles $20; doubles $25.)

**Venice Pizza & Pasta** serves super-tasting—you guessed it—pastas and pizzas from $7. (☎6959 3066. Open M-W 6-9pm, Th-Su 6pm-late. BYO.) **Hing Wah,** 94-96 East St, has an endless Chinese menu. (☎6959 2059. Open daily 5-9pm, also Tu-F noon-2pm. Mains $10-18.) Foodworks **supermarket** is at the corner of East and Bolton St. (☎6959 2388. Open M-F 8am-6:30pm, Sa 8am-2pm, Su 9am-1pm.)

## GRIFFITH

Griffith (pop. 22,800) is an anomaly in rural Australia. Bustling as a residential and commercial center out in the heartlands, Griffith has none of the small-town charm that pervades many villages in the region—it can feel downright urban. The layout of the town is strikingly similar to that of Canberra; both were designed by Walter Burley Griffin. Development of the irrigation scheme in the early part of the century attracted Italian miners from Broken Hill, whose farming efforts helped transform the once-barren Griffith into the agricultural center it is today. It is the undoubtable hub of the food and wine country. With such plentiful fruit trees, the area experiences a constant demand for work. Its 60% Italian population ensures a cosmopolitan edge. The community's influence on the town's food scene means that dining cheaply doesn't just mean choosing between fish-and-chips shops.

**TRANSPORT.** McCafferty's (☎ 13 14 99), Greyhound (☎ 13 20 30), V/Line (☎ 13 61 96), and Countrylink (☎ 13 22 32) **buses** stop, often late at night, at the Mobil station, 121 Banna Ave, enroute to: **Sydney** (11-11½hr., 3 per day, $54); **Canberra** (6-7hr., 3 per day, $37); **Melbourne** (18hr., 1 per day, $50.50); **Dubbo** (7hr., 1 per day, $70.40); **Gundagai** (4¼hr., 3 per day, $32); and **Narrandera** (1¼hr., 1 per day, $15).

**ORIENTATION AND PRACTICAL INFORMATION.** The main axis through Griffith is Banna Ave, which runs east-west and is lined with shops and restaurants. With the Firefly Fighter Bomber **WWII airplane** hovering above, the **Visitors Information Centre,** located on the corner of Jondaryan and Banna Ave, is hard to miss. (☎ 6962 4145, freecall ☎ (1800) 68 11 41; fax 6962 7319. Open M-F 9am-5pm, Sa-Su 9am-3pm.) **Internet access: Western Riviera Public Library,** 233-7 Banna Ave. (☎ 6962 2515. Open M-F 9am-5:30pm, Sa 9am-12:30pm. Free.) **Post office:** 245-263 Banna Ave. (☎ 6962 1599. Open M-F 9am-5pm, Sa 9am-noon.) **Postal code:** 2680.

Fruitpicking and seasonal work can be had in Griffith and nearby Leeton (see **Picking Work,** p. 223). To find work, ask the hostel manager, or call **Pickers Plus,** 20 Olympic St (☎ 6964 0080; email miacha@webfront.net.au), which links growers with laborers. **Out Source Personnel,** 170 Yambil St, matches job-seekers with temporary, seasonal, or long-term work and can provide transportation. (☎ 6962 9888 or (1300) 65 52 92. Open daily 8am-5pm.)

**ACCOMMODATIONS AND FOOD.** Intended to accommodate fruit pickers, Griffith has basic, dirt-cheap lodging. The **Griffith International Hostel,** 112 Binya St, is the place to be if seeking harvesting work. The unheated rooms are cramped, and the place is in a general state of disrepair, but it is livable and the price unbeatable for those trying to put away some cash. The catch is that you must be 18-25 years old and have an overseas passport and **work visa,** as their goal is to attract foreign labor to the area. Call ahead and the manager will arrange work in advance and even drop you off at work in the mornings. (☎ 6964 4236; fax 6964 4236. Reception daily 7-11am and 4-6pm. Key deposit $5. Dorms $17.50, weekly $107.50. YHA, VIP $15, $92.) Downtown, the **Area Hotel,** 208 Banna Ave, offers pub lodging in a modern facility. (☎ 6962 1322. Singles $35; twins $50. Breakfast included.) The **Griffith Tourist Caravan Park,** four blocks south of the info center on the corner of Jondaryan St and Willandra Ave, offers camp sites and motel-style units. (☎ 6964 2144; fax 6964 1126. Reception daily 7am-10pm. Linen $5. Tent site for 2 $16.50, powered $17.60; ensuite cabins $55.)

For flavorful cuisine, try any of the Italian restaurants or cafés along Banna Ave. Among the best is **Il Corso Café & Pizza Restaurant,** 232 Banna Ave, with a huge range of saucy pastas for $9 and lunch focaccias for $4.50. (☎ 6964 4500. Open M-Sa 8am-10pm, Su 5-10pm.) **Bertoldo's Bakery,** 324 and 150 Banna St, lures customers with whiffs of scrumptious cakes, fresh sandwiches, and refreshing Italian-style Gelati. (☎ 6962 3275. Open M-F 8am-6pm, Sa 8am-3pm, Su 8am-2pm.)

**SIGHTS AND ACTIVITIES.** Griffith's attractions cluster around the **bush reserve** on the town's northern bluffs. The aptly named **Scenic Dr** heading east offers two lookouts of the surroundings before passing the **Griffith Pioneer Park Museum,** at the corner of Scenic and Remembrance Dr. The largest museum west of the Blue Mountains contains a village of over 40 historical structures from the Griffith region. (☎ 6962 4196. Open daily 9am-5pm. $7.) Disgusted with humanity, Valerio Recitti, Griffith's legendary Italian immigrant-turned-hermit, spent years of his life in the **hermit cave** below the Sir Dudley Chair lookout in the Park.

NEW SOUTH WALES

Although some of the town's **wineries** produce a higher volume of wine than the entire Hunter Valley region, they are slightly less geared to tourists than wineries in other areas. **DeBortoli Winery,** off Yenda Rd northeast of the town center, has several generations of tradition—and more importantly—free tastings. (☎6964 9444. Open M-Sa 9am-5pm, Su 9am-4pm.) **McWilliams Winery,** on Jack McWilliams Rd off Kidman Way, attracts visitors to its enormous barrel-shaped cellar door and offers a guided tour through the modern grape-crushing facilities. (☎6963 0001. Open M-Sa 9am-5pm. Tours M-F 10am.)

# CENTRAL WEST

The cities and towns of the Central West lie between the rugged plateaus of the Blue Mountains and the stark dryness of outback New South Wales. The major route into the region from the east is the Great Western Hwy, which crosses through the Blue Mountains to Bathurst. From Bathurst, the Mitchell Hwy heads northwest to Dubbo, Bourke, and beyond, and the Mid Western Hwy runs southwest to Cowra and eventually Hay. Both of these roads intersect the Newell Hwy, the major route between Melbourne and Brisbane, which cuts a long path across the Central West. Most towns of the Central West, surrounded by miles of rolling agriculture, are regarded as waystations between grander destinations. Even with a short stay in this region, you'll notice an extraordinary degree of hospitality in locals who have chosen to live the less hectic life.

## BATHURST

The first inland settlement, Bathurst features wide avenues and large, ornate lamp-posts, which suggest that it was once slated for greatness. It is an unadorned route, though, on the southwest corner of town that has brought the city notoriety. Originally built as a scenic drive in 1938, the 6km circular road up Mt. Panorama and back down does double duty as a public road and the track for the annual touring car races **AMP Bathurst 1000** (for V-8 engines) and **Australian 1000 Classic** (2-litre class). In mid-November and early October, respectively, these events draw crowds of over 40,000 to this otherwise low-profile town. Largely thanks to the races and the large population of students at Charles Sturt University, Bathurst has a certain vibrance that the industrial towns of the region lack.

■🖪 **TRANSPORT AND PRACTICAL INFORMATION.** Bathurst is 101km west of Katoomba on the Great Western Hwy. **Trains** and **buses** leave the **Railway Station** at the corner of Keppel and Havannah St. Countrylink (☎13 22 32) and Greyhound (☎13 20 30) go to: **Sydney** (3½-4½hr., 2 per day, $37.40); **Cowra** (1½hr., 2-6 per day, $16.50); **Dubbo** (2½-3½hr., 3 per day, $33); **Forbes** and **Parkes** (3½hr., 6 per week, $29); **Katoomba** (2hr., 2 per day, $29); **Lithgow** (1-1¼hr., 3-7 per day, $19); **Orange** (1hr., 1-2 per day, $10-28); and **Parramatta** and **Penrith** (2½-3½hr., 2 per day, $31).

The **Bathurst Visitors Centre,** 28 William St, has brochures and free maps. (☎6332 1444, freecall ☎(1800) 68 10 00; fax 6332 2333. Open daily 9am-5pm.) **Post office:** 230 Howick St (☎6331 3133; open M-F 9am-5pm). **Postal code:** 2795.

🖪🖪 **ACCOMMODATIONS AND FOOD.** Bathurst has a few pubstays downtown. **Bathurst Explorer's Hotel,** 357 Stewart St, recently embraced the backpacker market, offering luxurious rooms with TV, fridge, heat, A/C, and a $10 dinner coupon for area restaurants. (☎6331 2966; freecall ☎(1800) 04 79 07. Reception 24hr. Key deposit $10. Singles $30; twins and doubles $50.) Bathurst's year-round camping area, **East's Bathurst Holiday Park,** is on Sydney Rd (the Great Western Hwy), 4km east of town. (☎6331 8286; fax 6332 6439. Reception daily 8am-8pm. BBQ, showers, laundry, TV room. Tent sites for 2 $15; powered $17.50; cabins $48.)

**Ziegler's Café,** 52 Keppel St, has a range of salads, grilled veggie dishes, and burgers. (☎6332 1565. Open M-Sa 9am-9pm, Su 10am-3pm. Dinners from $9.50. BYO.)

On the upstairs veranda at **Bernard's Bakery,** 81 George St, indulge in delicious pastries or gourmet sandwiches for $4.50-6. (☎ 6331 2042. Open daily 6am-7pm.) Coles **grocery store,** 47 William St, has a deli with sandwiches and pizza. (☎ 6332 9566. Deli open daily 8am-3:30pm; store open M-F 24hr., Sa 7am-10pm, Su 8am-8pm.)

⬛ **SIGHTS.** A trip to Bathurst would be incomplete without a spin round the **Mt. Panorama circuit,** southwest on William St until it becomes Panorama Ave. As you twist your way up and down the steep hill, you'll gain an appreciation for the pros who do it in excess of 200kph. Don't let the banner ads and tire piles seduce you; local police patrol the area frequently, looking for tourists who edge above the 60kph speed limit. The recently expanded **National Motor Racing Museum,** near the starting line, keeps the thrill of the race alive year-round. (☎ 6332 1872. Open daily 9am-4:30pm; $6.60.) At the top, the signs to "Nature Park" lead to the **Sir Joseph Banks Nature Park,** a 52-hectare animal enclosure criss-crossed by walking tracks. (☎ 6333 6285. Open daily 9am-4pm; $3, concessions $2, families $8.) The **courthouse** on Russell St was considered so grand when it was built in 1880 that residents of the town thought there must have been a mistake putting it in Bathurst. Rumors circulated that the building had been meant for a more prominent colony in India or Africa; the massive railings encircling the building could easily have kept elephants out. (Open M-F 9am-5pm, but hours vary when in use.) The east wing houses a **museum** with Bathurst artifacts ranging from Aboriginal weapons to penny-farthing bicycles. (Open Tu-W, Su 10am-4pm, Sa 9:30am-4:30pm; $2.) Don't miss the **Abercrombie Caves,** 70km south of Bathurst via Trunkey Creek. The majestic Grand Arch is the largest limestone archway in the Southern Hemisphere. (☎ 6368 8603. Open daily 9am-4pm. $11; guided tour 2pm $13.20.)

# ORANGE

Ironically famous for its apples, Orange (pop. 36,000) is a pleasant town in the shadow of nearby Mt. Canobolas (an extinct volcano). Dubbed "Australia's Colour City," it sits at the heart of an agricultural district that produces grain, livestock, and fruit (but no oranges) on the volcanic soil. Orange is most famous for Andrew Barton "Banjo" Paterson, the man who penned the lyrics to *Waltzing Matilda*.

⬛⬛ **TRANSPORT AND PRACTICAL INFORMATION.** From the east, Orange is 55km beyond Bathurst on the Mitchell Hwy, and Dubbo lies 150km further down the road. Smaller roads lead directly to the smaller regional hubs of Cowra, Forbes, and Parkes. From Orange, **buses** run from the railway station on Peisley St to: **Sydney** (5hr., 2-5 per day, $45); **Melbourne** (9hr., 1 per day, $90); **Broken Hill** (11hr., 1 per day, $98); **Dubbo** (2hr., 1-2 per day, $22); and **Lithgow** (2½hr., 2-5 per day, $22). **Orange Visitor Centre,** on Byng St, has a lot of good information. (☎ 6361 5226; fax 6361 5200. Open daily 9am-5pm.) **Post Office:** 222 Summer St (☎ 6362 3088; open M-F 9am-5pm). **Postal code:** 2800.

⬛⬛ **ACCOMMODATIONS AND FOOD. Marshall's Carrington Club Hotel,** on the corner of Lord's Pl and Byng St, has simple but tidy rooms; don't be put off by the appearance of the pub floor downstairs. (☎ 6362 2919. Singles $30; twins and doubles $50.) The **Colour City Showground Caravan Park,** on Margaret St at the end of McLachlan St, about 2km from the town center, is functional. (☎ 6362 7254. Tent sites for 2 $7.50, powered $11; simple cabins $33, ensuite $40.)

There's a Woolworth's **supermarket** at 197 Anson St (☎ 6362 4655; open M-Sa 7am-10pm, Su 8am-8pm), and a number of pleasant cafés on Summer St. **Café 48,** 48 Sale St, has chic international cuisine with a leafy outdoor dining area. (☎ 6361 7748. Open M 10:30am-4pm, W-F 10:30am-late, Sa-Su 7am-late. Lunch $6.50-14. BYO.) For a chance to sample the local produce in a fancier setting, locals dine at the award-winning **Selkirks Restaurant,** 179 Anson St, one block past Woolworth's, heading out away from town. (☎ 6361 1179. Open for dinner Tu-Su.)

NEW SOUTH WALES

**⏺ SIGHTS.** In the summer (Nov.-Feb.), backpackers have luck finding fruit-picking jobs (the tourist office keeps a list). In the annual April **F.O.O.D. festival,** you can crush your own grapes for practice. **Borenore Caves Reserve,** located 17km west of Orange on the Orange-Forbes Road, offers caving for experienced novice adventurers. The Arch Cave is suitable for beginners, but unfortunately vandalism over the years has taken its toll on the beauty. **Ophir Gold Fields,** 30km from Orange, was the site of Australia's first gold rush in 1851 (the region was also the exclusive gold supplier for **Sydney's Olympic medals**). For a country retreat, join the Wythes family at the **Uralba Homestead,** 40km southwest of Orange. Guests are welcome to give the day-to-day farm activities a whirl or use the homestead to explore local attractions. (☎ 6364 3124. $25 per adult per night. BYO food, linen and sleeping bag.)

## COWRA

On August 5, 1944, over 1000 Japanese soldiers staged an escape at the **Prisoner of War camp** in Cowra; in the failed attempt, 231 perished. Cowra has since formed strong ties, including a regular exchange of gifts and visits, with a Japan grateful for Cowra's help in caring for the graves of Japanese servicemen.

**⏺⏺ TRANSPORT AND PRACTICAL INFORMATION.** Cowra sits on the banks of the Lachlan River in the Lachlan Valley, 109km southwest of Bathurst. The Mid Western Hwy cuts through town west toward Grenfell, while Rte 81 heads north to the Mitchell Hwy. Countrylink (☎ 13 22 32), Greyhound Pioneer (☎ 13 20 30), McCafferty's (☎ 13 14 99), and Rendell's (☎ (1800) 02 33 28) **buses** zip to: **Sydney** (6 hr., 1 per day M-F, $52); **Canberra** (3hr., 2 per week, $31); **Melbourne** (9hr., 1 per day, $80); **Albury-Wodonga** (5hr., 1 per day, $72); **Bathurst** (2½hr., 0-3 per day, $16.50); **Coonabarabran** (6hr., 1 per day, $75); **Dubbo** (3hr., 1 per day, $51); **Forbes** (1½hr., 1 per day, $41); **Lithgow** (3hr., 1 per day M-F, $65); **Orange** (1½hr., 5 per week, $15.40); **Parkes** (2½ hr., 1 per day, $47); and **Wagga Wagga** (2½hr., 1 per day, $60.50). **Cowra Tourism** is on the corner of Boorowa Rd and the Mid Western Hwy. They have a tacky, yet bizarrely compelling, free nine-minute hologram presentation about the breakout. (☎ 6342 4333. Open daily 9am-5pm.)

**⏺⏺ ACCOMMODATIONS AND FOOD.** Perhaps the best reason to come here is the ⏺**Riverslea Backpackers Farmstay,** south of Cowra toward Darby's Falls, in an area not unlike the Elysian Fields. Sheep and horses graze on meadows spotted with eucalyptus trees and blue-green boulders. Come here for jillaroo and jackaroo courses, horseriding, bushwalking, and a taste of farm life. Country living is peppered with tech savvy (rooms are wired for Internet) and New Age spiritualism. Wonderbus (www.wonderbus.com) can pick you up from Sydney hostels and bring you on the 4hr. trip. (☎ 6345 1835; www.backpackers-farmstay.com.au. B&B

---

**WALTZING MATILDA** No song—not even Australia's official national anthem—is as deeply ingrained in the hearts of Aussies as *Waltzing Matilda*. The folk ballad originated in the social upheaval of the shearing disputes between unionist woolworkers and wealthy landowners during the late 19th century. Conflict erupted in September 1894 at Dagworth Station, when laborers and police fired at each other, and a shed containing 100 "jumbucks" (colloquial for sheep, derived from an Aboriginal term) with hundreds of bales of wool was burned to the ground. Banjo Paterson, a wealthy man who sided with the workers, adapted an old Scottish folk song to commemorate the event. Completed in 1895, the song still strikes a chord in the Australian psyche, recalling the tough frontier spirit of the bushmen and shearers (who were overcome by the police). Its sentiments are best expressed in the final stanza, where the swagman (the song's hero), cornered and facing certain capture at the hands of the squatter (rich landowner), chooses death rather than surrender: "But the swagman, he up and he jumped into the waterhole/Drowning himself by the Coolabah tree/And his ghost may be heard as it sings in the Billabong/'Who'll come a-waltzing Matilda with me?'"

cottage (up to 6) from $75; homestead rooms from $90; camping $35. Meals included.) If you have to stay in town, the **Imperial Hotel**, 16-18 Kendal St, has refurbished rooms above a popular wood-paneled pub. (☎6341 2588; fax 6341 3970. Reception at the bar 10am-midnight. Singles $27.50; doubles $44; family rooms $60.50. Breakfast included. Reservations recommended.) Just under the Kendal St bridge, **Cowra Van Park** on Lachlan St, provides riverside camping. (☎6340 2110. Reception daily 8am-10pm. Sites for 2 $13, powered $18.) A **supermarket** is on Macquarie at Kendal St. (☎6342 3283. Open M-F 7am-9pm, Sa 7am-7pm, Su 8am-5pm.)

🄜 **SIGHTS.** Three monuments commemorate the **Cowra Breakout.** The first memorial is a **monument** at the site of the breakout, on Sakura Ave at the corner of Farm St. The foundations of the camp's buildings still divide the field, and a photograph shows the camp in 1944. Two kilometers north of the actual memorial on Doncaster Dr, the adjoining **Japanese and Australian War Cemeteries** make a powerful sign of mourning. The **Japanese Gardens and Cultural Centre,** on Scenic Dr north of downtown, was opened in 1979 as a statement of friendship between Australia and Japan. The gardens are punctuated by ponds, rock gardens, and benches for contemplation. (☎6341 2233. Open daily 8:30am-5pm. $8, concessions $5.50.)

# FORBES

An overall feeling of timelessness and the nearby Parkes Radio Telescope compensate somewhat for a lack of compelling sights. Once the stomping grounds of famed bushranger **Ben Hall,** Forbes shows little evidence of its checkered past.

🄵🄷 **TRANSPORT AND PRACTICAL INFORMATION.** The **Newell Hwy** runs through Forbes, with Dubbo 153km to the northeast. There are also fairly direct routes east to Orange (93km) and southeast to Cowra (90km). The downtown, anchored by Lachlan St, is surrounded by the flood-prone **Lake Forbes,** which looks suspiciously like a river to the untrained eye. From the old **railway station** on Union St, Countrylink (☎13 22 32) runs **buses** to: **Sydney** (7hr., 1 per day M-Sa, $63); **Dubbo** (2hr., 3-4 per week, $19); **Orange** (2hr., 13 per week, $16.50); and **Parkes** (30min., 1-3 per day, $5.50). From the Cal-Tex 24 Roadhouse, 1km north of town on the Newell Hwy, Greyhound Pioneer (☎13 20 30) handles services to: **Albury-Wodonga** (5hr., 2 per day, $79); **Coonabarabran** (4hr., 2-3 per day, $56); **Cowra** (1hr., 1 per day, $47); **Parkes** (30min., 2-3 per day, $37.50); and **Wagga Wagga** (3hr., 2 per day, $67). **Harvey World Travel**, 6 Templar St, sells all bus tickets. (☎6852 2344. Open M-F 9am-5pm, Sa 9am-noon.) The old railway station on Union St has been converted into the **Forbes Railway Arts and Tourist Centre** now that passenger trains no longer service the town. (☎6852 4155; fax 6852 4433. Open daily 9am-5pm.) **Complete Insite Solutions,** on the corner of Rankin and Templar St, has **Internet access.** (☎(1300) 30 30 74. Open M-F 9am-5:30pm, Sa 9am-12:30pm. 1hr. $4.) **Post office:** 118 Lachlan St (☎6852 2315). **Postal code:** 2871.

🄰🄵 **ACCOMMODATIONS AND FOOD.** Pubstays in Forbes are some of the best and cheapest in the area. Everything's huge at the **Albion Hotel,** 135 Lachlan St, from the clean rooms to the men's showers that could house a town meeting. (☎6851 1881. Singles $16.50.) **Apex Caravan Park,** 86 Reymond St, 2km south of the town center via Bridge St and Flint St, is along the river. (☎6851 1929. Showers, laundry, BBQ. Sites for 2 $13.20, powered $16.50; cabins from $33.) Buy **groceries** at Woolworth's, at the corner of Rankin and Grenfell St. (☎6852 2421. Open M-Sa 7am-9pm, Su 9am-6pm.)

🄜 **SIGHTS.** Back in the gold rush days when Forbes had 80,000 prospector residents, Ben Hall was reputedly head of an outlaw gang known for robbery, whippings, arson, kidnapping, and murder. Among the locals, the debate continues over whether Hall was forced into crime by injustice or whether he was a dirty-dealing bushranger at heart from the beginning. The **Albion Hotel** (see above), formerly the Cobb & Co. Stage Coach stop, recently opened its doors as the **Bushrang-**

ers **Hall of Fame and Underground Tour.** Guided tours go through the honeycomb of tunnels where gold and money were transported between banks in an attempt to dodge robberies. (Open daily 10am-6pm. $5.) **Lachlan Vintage Village,** off Newell Hwy, recreates the 1860's gold rush with exhibits including a replica of Ben Hall's home. (☎6852 2655. Open daily 8am-5pm. $8.) The **Forbes Museum,** on Cross St, has a small collection of local artifacts and displays on Ben Hall. (Open daily Oct.-May 3-5pm; June-Sept. 2-4pm. $2.)

## NEAR FORBES: PARKES RADIO TELESCOPE

The **64m dish,** visible from the Newell Hwy, 55km northeast of Forbes (20km north of Parkes) on the road to Dubbo, belongs to the **Parkes Radio Telescope.** The combination of low radio interference, proximity to Sydney, and a cream-of-the-crop staff puts Parkes at the forefront of research. A major contributor to astronomy since its opening in 1961, the Parkes Telescope has participated in high-profile projects including the televising of the first moon walk and the rescue of NASA's Apollo 13. Recently, the telescope has been used to seek out **hidden galaxies** in the southern skies and to understand mysterious cosmic **dark matter.** The **Visitors Discovery Centre** is a surprisingly low-tech facility with displays on the telescope. The knowledgeable staff and a 20min. film make it interesting even for non-scientists. (☎6861 1777. Open daily 8:30am-4:15pm. Free. Film $3.)

## MUDGEE

A land of wine and honey cradled in the foothills of the Great Dividing Range, Mudgee (from the Aboriginal "nest in the hills") has over 20 vineyards—and not much else to offer the tourist, though locals proudly proclaim that Mudgee is "tasting better each year."

**■⚫ TRANSPORT AND PRACTICAL INFORMATION.** Mudgee is a 3½hr. drive from Sydney on Hwy 86, between Lithgow (159km) and Dubbo (109km). Countrylink **buses** (☎13 22 32) run 1-2 times per day to: **Sydney** (5hr., $45); **Coonabarabran** (3hr., $30); and **Lithgow** (2½hr., $18). Book at Harvey World Travel, Shop 28-29, Town Centre, Church St. (☎6372 6077. Open M-F 8:30am-5:30pm, Sa 9am-noon.)

The **Mudgee Visitors Centre,** 84 Market St, is armed with maps and advice. (☎6372 5875; fax 6372 2853. Open M-F 9am-5pm, Sa 9am-3:30pm, Su 9:30am-2pm.) The **NPWS office,** 160 Church St, administers the northwest section of Wollemi National Park (☎6372 7199. Open M-F 9am-5pm. See p. 148.) **Post office:** 80 Market St (open M-F 9am-5pm). **Postal code:** 2850.

**▌⚫ ACCOMMODATIONS AND FOOD.** Pubstay accommodation is the cheapest and most readily available in town. **The Woolpack Hotel,** 67 Market St, is near the visitors center; turn left and go one block down Market St. (☎6372 1908. Reception 7am-3pm. Singles $20; doubles $35.) The slightly dreary **Mudgee Riverside Caravan and Tourist Park,** 22 Short St, behind the visitors center, has showers and laundry. (☎6372 2531. Reception daily 8am-8pm. Sites for 2 $13, powered $17.)

**Red Heifer Grill and Carvery,** 1 Church St, inside the Lawson Park Hotel, is a great spot for good grub—steak dinner $11, bottle of local wine from $10. (☎6372 2183. Open daily noon-2:30pm and 6-9pm.) Through an archway behind the bustle of Market St, the cute **Tramp Café,** 61 Market St, offers slightly pricey but decent melted sandwiches and quiches. (☎6372 6665. Open M-Sa 7:30am-6pm, Su 7:30am-3pm.) A Bi-Lo **supermarket** is on Church St (open M-Sa 7am-10pm, Su 9am-6pm).

**WINERIES.** Mudgee's calling cards are its victual offerings, ranging from small vineyards that share their wine-making facilities to large, self-sufficient wineries. There are many vineyards in the area; consult the tourist office for extensive information. Travelers passing through in September will find the streets hopping with the Mudgee Wine Festival. If you want to do the wine-tasting circuit but also wish to avoid running afoul of stringent drink-driving laws, a number of companies offer tours. Try **Mudgee Transit Corporation** (☎6372 0091; half-day $38, full-day $60), or **Mudgee Valley Tours** (☎6372 6766; Su-F 4hr. tour $45, full-day including lunch $50). **Poet's Corner Wine Cellar,** which is a conglomeration of Craigmoor, Montrose, and Poet's Corner labels, has been making tawny Rummy Port for 70 years. To reach the winery, bike or drive 7km northwest of Mudgee on Henry Lawson Dr, then turn onto Craigmoor Rd. (☎6372 2208. Open M-Sa 10am-4:30pm, Su 10am-4pm.) **Huntington Estate Wines,** past the airport on Cassilis Rd, has a savory array of reds and a self-guided tour. (☎6373 3825. Open M-F 9am-5pm, Sa 10am-5pm, Su 10am-3pm.) **Botobolar,** 89 Botobolar Rd, 16km northeast of town, is an organic winery. Guests are not allowed to wander through the vineyards for fear they might spread disease to the fragile vines, but tastings are scheduled each day. (☎6373 3840. Open M-Sa 10am-5pm, Su 10am-3pm.)

Local honey is another elixir of the area. You can sample some at **Mudgee Honey Haven,** on the corner of Gulgong and Hargraves Rd, if you still want to after you find out how honeybees swallow and then regurgitate the concentrated nectar that you know and love. Yum. (☎6372 4478. Open daily 9am-5pm.)

# DUBBO

The hub of the Central West, Dubbo is a busy, workmanlike service town filled with down-to-earth Australians. It's easy to forget that just on the far side of that last roundabout is nothing but empty agricultural lands for a very, very long way. It's not quite the outback, but venture past the city limits by night, with only the stars lighting the desolate road, and you might feel like it is. Headlined by the awesome Western Plains Zoo, Dubbo's recent interest in luring tourists beyond the zoo has resulted in an impressive roster of attractions.

**E TRANSPORT.** Countrylink **trains** and **buses** (☎13 22 32) depart from the **railway station** on Talbragar St to: **Sydney** (11hr., 2 per day, $94); **Melbourne** (10½hr., 1 per day, $94); **Albury** (7hr., 1 per day, $68); **Broken Hill** (8½hr., 1 per day, $83); **Forbes** (2hr., 2-3 per day, $23); **Orange** (2hr., 1-2 per day, $21); and **Wagga Wagga** (5hr., 1 per day, $50). The **Shell Station,** at the intersection of Newell and Mitchell Hwy, is the drop off point for Greyhound Pioneer (☎13 20 30), Rendell Coaches (☎6884 2411), and McCafferty's (☎13 14 99). They service: **Adelaide** (15½-18hr., 2 per day, $90-150); **Brisbane** (11½hr., 2 per day, $88); **Melbourne** (11½hr., 3 per day, $92); **Broken Hill** (8hr., 1 per day, $95); **Coonabarabran** (2hr., departs 7:55am, $36); and **Cowra** (3hr., 2:20am, $62). Drop off in Dubbo frequently occurs in the wee hours of the morning as coaches ramble on to further destinations. To reach accommodations, rely on 24hr. **taxis** (☎6882 1911). **Wheelers Cycles,** 193 Brisbane St (☎6882 9899), hires bikes for $17 per day. Bike trails criss-cross town and head out to the zoo.

**ORIENTATION AND PRACTICAL INFORMATION.** Dubbo sits at the intersection of the Newell Hwy (39) between Melbourne and Brisbane, and the Mitchell Hwy (32), leading from Sydney and Bathurst to points west. The town's sprawling layout could make life difficult for those without a car, but major sights are in two clusters, so plan accordingly. **Talbragar St** runs east-west, parallel to the two major highways that sandwich the town. The intersection of Talbragar and **Macquarie St** marks the town center, with most of the action running down Macquarie St.

For a map of the biking trails, river cruise bookings, and plenty of other good information, visit the **Dubbo Visitors Centre,** on the corner of Erskine and Brisbane St, in the northwest corner of the small downtown area. (☎6884 1422; email tour ism@dubbo.nsw.gov.au. Open daily 9am-5pm.) Find **Internet access** at Dubbo Regional **Library,** on the southwest corner of Macquarie and Talbragar St (1hr. $5.50; open M-F 10am-6pm), or the Grapevine Café (see below). The **Post office** is at 65-69 Talbragar St, near Brisbane St (open M-F 9am-5pm). **Postal code:** 2830.

**ACCOMMODATIONS AND FOOD.** Plenty of hotels cluster around Talbragar St in the city center with singles from $20. The cheapest beds are at the **Dubbo YHA Hostel,** 87 Brisbane St, close to the old inter-city bus station. Walk out onto Erskine St, turn right and walk a block, then turn right on Brisbane St. The talking pet cockatoo adds flavor to an otherwise unglamorous place. Bike rental $6 per day. (☎6882 0922. Bunks $16.50; twins and doubles $33.) The **Amaroo Hotel,** 83 Macquarie St, is in the center of town. (☎6882 3533. Singles $55; doubles $77; includes breakfast.) The excellent **Dubbo City Caravan Park,** on Whylandra St just before it becomes the Newell Hwy northwest of the city center, has shaded sites overlooking the Macquarie River. (☎6882 4820; email dccp@dubbo.nsw.gov.au. Reception daily 7:30am-7:30pm. Sites from $12, powered $17-27; cabins from $39.)

Sandwich shops and bakeries are plentiful in the city center, but there is no real "cheap eats" restaurant, per se. For the best coffee concoctions in town, seek out the **Grapevine Café,** 144 Brisbane St. (☎6884 7354. Lunch $5-10. Internet 30min. $2.50.) Coles **supermarket** is inside a plaza on Macquarie St (open M-Sa 6am-midnight), as is Woolworth's (open 6am-midnight). The **Dubbo Markets,** on the corner of Darling and Erskine St, are in a small, covered marketplace. (☎6882 6699. Open M-W 8:30am-6pm, Th 8:30am-8pm, F 8:30am-6:30pm, Sa-Su 8:30am-4pm.)

🖼 **SIGHTS.** Dubbo's premier tourist attraction is the **Western Plains Zoo,** on Obley Rd, south of the city center off the Newell Hwy. It's all the animals you ever really wanted to see, all in one place. In addition to Australian native species, the zoo houses Bengal tigers, black rhinoceri, and Australia's only **African elephants.** Many of the animals wander unrestrained through loose enclosures. Enter at your own risk. On weekends and select days during school holidays, early morning zoo walks are available at 6:45am for an additional $3. (☎6882 5888; www.zoo.nsw .gov.au. Open daily 9am-5pm, last entry 3:30pm. $18, students $13, ages 4-16 $9.50. Bike rental 4hr. $11, plus $10 deposit.) On Obley Rd 2km past the zoo, **Dundullimal Homestead** is a National Trust-registered slab house dating from the 1840s, with a saddlery workshop and petting zoo. (☎6884 9984. Open daily 9am-5pm. $6, under 16 $3. Animal shows Tu, Th-Su 3:30pm.) In conjunction with the Homestead, **Macquarie River Cruises** offers trips on one of the biggest river boats in outback New South Wales, stopping for tea at the Homestead before a hay ride and trip down the river (2hr. cruises from $16; book through the Visitors Centre). The dough-faced animatronic models of **Old Dubbo Gaol,** on Macquarie St between Commonwealth and State Banks, tell the bygone convicts' sad, macabre stories in a way that proves any subject (including the hanging of eight men) can be funny when you add enough goofy talking mannequins. (☎6882 8122. Open daily 9am-4:30pm. $7, students $5.50, ages 5-18 $3.50.) Down the street, the **Dubbo Museum and History Centre** presents local history with a straighter face. (☎6882 5359. Open daily 9am-4:30pm. $5.50, concessions $4, families $12.) At the **Dubbo Observatory,** on Camp Rd off Newell Hwy, you can see the three galaxies only visible in the Southern Hemisphere. (☎6885 3022. Open nightly. $13.50, families $38.50.)

If you want a taste (and smell) of the real Central West Australia, do not miss the huge **livestock markets** 4km north on the Newell Hwy towards Gilgandra; look for the sign. Entering, watching, and mingling with the *cockies* (farmers) is free of charge. (Auctions M, Th-F 8am-1:30pm.)

Learn about aerodynamics, Aboriginal history, woodcraft, and flying sticks (that only sometimes come back to you) at **Jedda Boomerangs,** on Minore Rd, White Pines. Head southwest toward the zoo and turn right onto Minore before you get there; it's 4km down Minore Rd. The excellent and informative hourly tour culminates in burning your own design on a boomerang (costs extra to take it home) and learning how to throw one so that it really comes back to you. (☎6882 3110. Open daily 10am-4pm. Free admission. Tour $5.50, children $3.)

# NORTHWEST: BACK O' BOURKE

The empty stretches of northwest New South Wales are sparsely populated, difficult to reach, and largely untouched by the typical traveler. What's that you say? You're not the typical traveler? You want to explore and embrace the arid western lands—the dusty brown hills, dusty brown roads, and dusty brown cows? Ah, yes.

What deep and mysterious knowledge you will have gleaned when you have stepped one toe past Bourke's city limits merely for the sake of being able to say to your typical-traveler friends Sydneyside, "Yes, I have been "Back o' Bourke." I have seen desolation not unlike a nuclear winter. I know what life looks like after the road ends." And the day when you decide to take that road less traveled by (the Mitchell Hwy), will make all the difference.

## COONABARABRAN

For folks living in a tiny town in the middle of nowhere, the lifestyle of Coonabarabran ("coon-a-BAR-a-bran"; Aboriginal for "an inquisitive person;" pop. 3500) is surprisingly sophisticated: discreet, tasteful, and courteous. It embodies all that is good about the laid-back and friendly country life. The town is the astronomy capital of Australia, thanks to low-levels of urban light pollution, a large number of clear night skies, and relative proximity to major urban areas (Sydney and Brisbane are only a day's drive). It's also a base for Warrumbungle National Park.

**⊏ TRANSPORT.** Coonabarabran lies 159km northeast of Dubbo on the Newell Hwy. It's accessible from the northeast through Gunnedah on the Oxley Hwy, which joins the Newell and enters from the north. Countrylink (☎ 13 22 32) runs from the visitors center to **Sydney** (8hr.; Su-F 1 per day; $75, ISIC $45). Greyhound Pioneer (☎ 13 20 30) also runs from the visitors center to: **Sydney** (10hr.; 1 per day; $91, ISIC $74), connecting in **Dubbo; Brisbane** (9hr.; 2 per day; $81, $66); and **Melbourne** (15½hr.; 2 per day; $97, $78). McCafferty's (☎ 13 14 99) leaves from the Caltex Service Station outside of town heading to: **Brisbane** (9½hr.; 2 per day; $77, ISIC $62); **Melbourne** (13-15hr.; 2 per day; $97, $78); **Bendigo** (12½hr.; 1 per day, $97, $78); **Dubbo** (2hr.; 2 per day; $35, $28); **Echuca** (11hr.; 1 per day; $97, $78); and **Narrabri** (1½hr., $40). Companies have advance discounts of 30-50% subject to availability. **Harvey World Travel,** 79 John St (☎ 6842 1566) makes transport bookings. There is no public transport to Warrumbungle National Park, 30km from town.

**⊿ PRACTICAL INFORMATION.** The main drag is **John St** (the Newell Hwy), home to several motels and crossed by **Dalgarno, Cassilis,** and **Edwards St.** Warrumbungle National Park and the observatories are both east of town. The **Coonabarabran Visitors Centre** is at the south end of town on John St. It has a display on **Australian megafauna,** including the skeleton of a 33,000-year-old giant Diprotodon, the largest marsupial ever to roam the earth. (☎ 6842 1441, freecall ☎ (1800) 24 28 81; www.lisp.coona barabran.com.au. Open daily 9am-5pm.) Other services include: **National Parks and Wildlife Service,** 56 Cassilis St (☎ 6842 1311), with info on Warrumbungle National Park; **24hr. ATMs;** the **post office,** 71 John St (open M-F 8:30am-4:30pm); and an **Internet café** (see below). **Postal code:** 2357.

**⊓⊡ ACCOMMODATIONS AND FOOD.** Book ahead for accommodations during school holidays. Coonabarabran's motels average $50-75 per double, and the budget accommodations are uninspiring. The **Imperial Hotel,** corner of John and Delgarno St, is a YHA hostel over a pub with thin walls and floors through which to hear the cries (and crying) of pokies players downstairs. (☎ 6842 1023. Singles $20-28; doubles $34-44.) If you stay Friday, the entire town will be staked in front of a bitter downstairs. The other two pubstays, also on John St, are smaller but similar. At the **John Oxley Caravan Park,** 1km north of town on the Oxley Hwy, the affable hosts tend a shop, playground, and gas BBQ. (☎ 6842 1635. Reception daily 8am-8pm. Linen $11. Sites for 2 $10, powered $12.50; on-site vans $22; cabins $39.) A number of **bed and breakfasts** are also available in Coonabarabran and within Warumbungle. Singles start at $35. Ask at the visitors center.

The **Golden Sea Dragon Restaurant,** next to the visitors center, mixes a golden Buddha with instrumental Bette Midler but serves fantastic Chinese fare. (☎ 6842 2388. Spicy Szechuan Chicken $9.50; 2-course traveler's special $12.) There are plenty of tidy lunch counters on John St. The **Jolly Cauli Coffee Shop,** 30 John St, is one of the more stylish choices in the area, with reasonable prices and **Internet**

NEW SOUTH WALES

**access.** (☎6842 2021. Open M-F 8am-5pm, Sa 9am-1pm. Devonshire tea and focaccia $5. Internet 1hr. $6.) The IGA **supermarket** is on Dalgarno St (open M-F 8:30am-6pm, Sa 8:30am-4pm, Su 9am-1pm).

🔘 **SIGHTS.** The highlight of Coonabarabran is the 🌙**Skywatch Night and Day Observatory**, 2km from town on the road to Warrumbungle National Park. The effusive staff guides night viewing sessions that clarify the jumbled stars (there's a planetarium for cloudy nights). The accompanying **astro mini-golf** is cheesy but fun. (☎6842 3303; www.lisp.com.au./~skywatch. Open daily 2-5pm; night session Nov.-Jan. daily 9, 10pm; Feb. 9pm; Mar. 8:30, 9:30pm; April-Sept. 7, 8pm; Oct. 7:30, 8:30pm. Exhibition or golf $7, ages 5-16 $4, families $19; exhibition and nightshow $11, $6.50, $30.) Australia's largest optical telescope resides at **Siding Spring Observatory**, 28km from Coonabarabran on the road to Warrumbungle National Park. The observatory's visitor center offers an interactive, multimedia window onto the work of the resident astronomers, though no public viewing of the night sky. You'll see groundbreaking research here but will probably have more fun at Skywatch. (☎6842 6211. Open daily 9:30am-4pm. $5, concessions $3.)

The **sandstone caves** within the **Pilliga Nature Reserve** were hollowed out by wind and water erosion and are tricky to locate, requiring a brief rock scramble at the end of an unmarked road 30km north on Newell Hwy. Luckily, the visitors center has explicit directions. **Warrumbungle Scenic Flights Coonabarabran** runs guided flights over the nearby national park. (☎6842 3560. 30min. $55-60.)

# WARRUMBUNGLE NATIONAL PARK

The jagged spires and rambling peaks of the Warrumbungle Mountains are the result of volcanic activity millions of years ago. As the softer sandstone has worn away under the hardened lava rock, unusual shapes have been left to slice into the sky above the forested hills. The mountains sit at the juncture of the lush east and the barren west. Kangaroos and wallabies have long called the area home, while hikers, rock-climbers, and campers have more recently discovered its splendor.

A 75km **scenic drive** branches off from the Newell Hwy 39km north of Gilgandra and runs through the park, circling back to the highway at Coonabarabran (approximately 12km unsealed). The park entry fee should be paid at the **Warrumbungle National Park Visitors Centre**, on the park road 33km west of Coonabarabran. A light-up map highlights the park's unusual rock formations. The center also provides detailed info on facilities and walking tracks in the park and distributes $2 bush-camping and free rock-climbing permits. (☎6825 4364. Open daily 9am-4pm; outside drop-box for afterhours permit payers. Entry $5 per car; pedestrians free.) The **NPWS** has a district office in Coonabarabran, 56 Cassilis St (☎6842 1311).

Of the park's serviced **camping** areas, only four are open to individual travelers (sites for 2 $10, extra person $2). **Camp Blackman** is car-accessible and has toilets, rainwater, showers, and a pay phone (powered $15, extra person $3). **Camp Pincham** lies a short walk from the nearest carpark, while **Burbie Camp** requires a 4km hike from the park road (both areas have toilets and showers). **Gunneemooroo** (Aboriginal for "place of snakes") is reached by a much longer hike from Burbie Camp or by car on the unsealed road from **Tooraweenah** (toilets, water). Firewood cannot be collected in the park, so bring a fuel stove. Pets are also not allowed.

The **Gurianawa Track** (15min.) runs in an easy circle around the visitors center, gives a quick introduction to the park environment, passes fields of kangaroos, and includes views of the Siding Spring Observatory and the area's extinct volcanoes. The short walk (1km return) to **Whitegum Lookout**, 27km from Coonabarabran at the east end of the park, provides striking views of the surrounding mountains. The most popular of the park's longer walks, the hike to **Grand High Tops** (12.5km; 5-6hr.), starts at a carpark, 1km south of the main park road and 500m west of the visitors center turn-off. The steep circuit through the southern half of the park passes stunning views of **Breadknife**, an imposing 90m stone tower, and turn-offs for most of the park's other major sights. The walk via West Spiney adds 2km and provides a chance to see the eagles that often fly around **Bluff Mountain**. (Add 2hr. and 2.4km if you climb Bluff Mountain.)

**BETTER THAN A LET'S GO MAP!** Things really are different Down Under. The night sky is an entirely different panorama from the world's flip-side, yielding hours of neck-crimping stargazing. The Milky Way is a clear beacon, cutting a fiery swath directly through the center of the sky, and three galaxies are visible only in the Southern Hemisphere. Whereas Polaris, the North Star, guided European explorers for centuries, lost travelers in Australia have a trickier task. First, find the Southern Cross, which really looks more like a kite, its four points vibrantly marked. Check out the pattern on the Australian flag to get an idea of what you're looking for. Two bright "pointer" stars guide the way from their left side, if you're having trouble. Now gauge the distance of the long axis of the cross and extend it down and to the left one, two, three times. Fix that point and drag your finger down to the skyline. That point is due south. Got it? Neither do we.

## NARRABRI

Equidistant from Sydney and Brisbane (560km), Narrabri ("NEHR-uh-BRYE"; meaning "forked waters;" pop. 7500) is a wheat and cotton-growing center that has two major attractions: the six-dish **Australia Telescope** complex and the beautifully rugged scenery of **Mount Kaputar National Park.**

▣▟ **TRANSPORT AND PRACTICAL INFORMATION.** Countrylink (☎13 22 32) **trains** run to **Sydney** (7½hr.; 1 per day; $79, ISIC $47) from the train station at the east end of Bowen St, four blocks from Maitland St. McCafferty's **buses** (☎13 14 99) depart from the corner of Bowen and Maitland St, two blocks south of the post office for: **Brisbane** (8hr.; 2 per day; $54, ISIC $43); **Melbourne** (14½-16hr.; 2 per day; $104, $83), via **Coonabarabran** (1¼hr.) and **Dubbo** (3hr.). Greyhound (☎13 20 30) runs to the same places from the Mobil Roadhouse, several kilometers southwest along the Newell Hwy. All tickets can be booked through **Harvey World Travel,** 60 Maitland St (☎6792 2555; open M-F 8am-5:30pm, Sa 8:30am-11:30am).

▟ **PRACTICAL INFORMATION.** The **Narrabri Visitors Centre** lies on the Newell Hwy (Tibbereena St), which veers north in town along Narrabri Creek. (☎6792 3583. Open M-F 9am-5pm, Sa-Su 9am-noon.) The main drag is **Maitland St,** which runs parallel to Tibbereena one street farther from the creek. The **library,** corner of Doyle and Barwan, has **Internet access.** (☎6792 3562. 1hr. $5.50.) Other services include: the **NPWS** office, Level 1, 100 Maitland St (☎6799 1740; open M-F 8:30am-4:30pm; enter around the corner on Dewhurst St); **banks** with **ATMs;** and the **post office,** on the corner of Doyle St (open M-F 9am-5pm).

▛▙ **ACCOMMODATIONS AND FOOD.** All seven pubs along the central three-block stretch of Maitland St offer inexpensive accommodation, and there are a number of motels on the highway. A few dollars more than some of its competitors, but in the best location, the **Tourist Hotel,** 142 Maitland St, has great beds in small tidy rooms, and shared bathrooms. (☎6792 2312. Singles $20; doubles $33, ensuite $35.) The cheapest motel and camping are both at the **Narrabri Motel and Caravan Park,** 92 Cooma Rd, on the Newell Hwy toward Coonabarabran. (☎6792 2593. Tent sites for 2 $11, powered $15; singles $42; doubles $49; ensuite cabins $42-49.) There are several lunch counters and bakeries on Maitland St. **Watson's Kitchen,** 151 Maitland St, is a local fave. (☎6792 1366. Open M-F 6am-6pm, Sa 6am-1pm, Su 6am-noon.) A Woolworth's **supermarket** is on Maitland St (open M-Sa 7am-10pm, Su 8am-8pm).

▣ **SIGHTS.** Signs on the Newell Hwy heading toward Coonabarabran lead to the **Australia Telescope,** 20km west of Narrabri, a set of six large radio dishes which comprise the largest, most powerful telescope array in the Southern Hemisphere. The Australia Telescope Visitors Centre has a helpful staff, and its videos and displays are fun and simplified to layman's terms. When the dishes aren't in use, the staff is happy to show you their innards. (☎6790 4070. Open daily 8am-4pm; staffed M-F. Free.)

NEW SOUTH WALES

East of Narrabri, the peaks of the **Nandewar Range** beckon travelers to leave the paved road behind (either by hiking or unsealed action) and scale the summit of **Mt. Kaputar,** whose views encompass one-tenth of New South Wales. The entrance to the central section of **Mount Kaputar National Park** lies 31km east of Narrabri heading south on Maitland St and Old Gunnedah Rd. **Bark Hut Camping Area** is 14km inside the park, and **Dawsons Spring Camping Area** is 21km inside near the Mt. Kaputar summit. Both have hot showers, toilets, electricity, and BBQs (sites for 2 $15). The park's most famous attraction is **Sawn Rocks,** an amazing basalt rock formation, in the northern section accessible from the Newell Hwy north of Narrabri. The eerie organ-pipe geometry is best seen from down in the creek bed. The excellent *Park Guide* pamphlet available from the NPWS office in Narrabri has more hiking info ($3). The roads to and within the park are mostly unsealed and unstable after rain; call the NPWS office for updates (☎6799 1740).

# BOURKE

On a blistering hot day, Bourke ("BURK") can be an eerie place. It is dead quiet. Haze covering the unusually wide, naked streets distorts distance. At one end of the main drag, Oxley St, white office workers stroll past the immaculately restored Federation-style Courthouse, post office, and banks. At the other end, Aboriginal kids in worn clothing loiter beside the pub, convenience store, and public housing office. Bourke is a study in racial division of the sort that is often hidden beneath the surface of Australian society. That shouldn't scare you away; visiting Bourke is an educational experience in this and many other ways. An important inland port town in the 19th century, Bourke is rich with history, and today it's both a symbolic (as per the idiom "back o' Bourke") and a very real gateway to the outback.

**■▐ TRANSPORT AND PRACTICAL INFORMATION.** Bourke lies on the Mitchell Hwy (Hwy 71), 367km northwest of Dubbo and 142km south of the Queensland-NSW border. The Mitchell Hwy becomes Anson St through town; Richard St branches off to the north and runs all the way to the Darling River. Oxley St runs off Richard St to the left, and should be avoided at night. Mitchell St crosses Richard St a half block from Oxley St. Buses head to **Dubbo** (4½hr.; M, W, F, Sa 9:15am; $53), connecting to **Sydney** ($92) and elsewhere. Buy tickets at **Bourke Courier Service,** 37 Oxley St (☎6872 2092). Buses depart from the **Tourist Information Centre,** on Anson St a block west of Richard St. The center houses a small museum legendizing Bourke's most industrious tough guys. It can also refer farms for **year-round work.** (☎6872 2280; email Tourinfo@lisp.com.au. Open Easter-Oct. daily 9am-5pm, Oct.-Easter M-Sa 9am-5pm. Historical and farm tours: in winter M, W, F $10.) The **library,** 29 Mitchell St, has **Internet access.** (☎6872 2751. Open M-Tu, Th-F 9am-5pm, W 9am-noon and 1-5pm, Sa 9:30am-12:30pm. 1hr. $5.) **Post office:** 47 Oxley St (open M-F 9am-5pm). **Postal code:** 2840.

**▐▐ ACCOMMODATION AND FOOD. Port of Bourke Hotel,** 32 Mitchell St, has large rooms with gorgeous hardwood floors, sparkling shared baths, A/C, and heaters; many open onto the screened balcony. (☎6872 2544; fax 6872 2687. Singles $34; twins $51; doubles $57; triples $62; ensuite $83.) The **Bourke Riverside Motel,** 3 Mitchell St, is set on two acres along the river. It rents comfortable rooms with heat, A/C, and TV, and has a swimming pool, award-winning gardens, and rough tennis courts. (☎6872 2539. Reception daily 6:30am-10pm. Singles $50; doubles $55; suites for 2 $82.50, each extra person $15. Breakfast $6-9.) For a "real outback" experience, contact **Comeroo Camel Station,** Comeroo, in the red desert, where you can bushcamp, take a camel safari, or stay in cottages. You need 4WD to reach the 100,000-acre family-run station. (☎/fax 6874 7735. Doubles from $45).

In the outback, "cuisine" means anything hot and on the table. For basic pub food, try the **Port of Bourke Hotel** (see above). **Morall's Cappuccino Bakery** has superb sandwiches. (☎6872 2086. Open M-F 7am-4:30pm, Sa 7am-2pm.) An IGA **supermarket** is on Warraweena St just north of Mitchell St (open 8am-7:30pm daily).

NEW SOUTH WALES

**⬛ SIGHTS.** Around town, a few historical buildings merit a peek. The **Court House,** at Oxley and Richard St, dates to 1900 and can be visited when not in session. Australia's most inland maritime court in its day, the airy chamber and Italian marble fireplace warrant at least a quick free peek (open M-F 9:30am-1pm, 2-4pm). The **Post Office** and **London Bank** on Oxley St were also built during Bourke's heyday. The **Back o' Bourke Exhibition Center,** located 1km north of town off the North Bourke Rd, provides information on the city's history as well as its modern-day farming, fruit growing, and recreation attractions. Paddle boats will eventually run down the river from the center, but are temporarily docked behind the caravan park. (☎ 6872 1321. Open M-F 9am-5pm. Office at 29 Oxley St.)

The all-purpose guide *Back o' Bourke Mud Map Tours,* free at the tourist office, details trips just beyond the town borders or several thousand kilometers into the outback. Trips include **Mt. Oxley** with its eagles; **Gundabooka National Park's** Aboriginal rock art (NPWS ☎ 6872 2744); and **Brewarrina's** Aboriginal cultural museum (☎ 6839 2868). The manly **Darling River Run,** billed as "the last of the Great 4WD Adventures," is a 439km route tracing the Darling up to its junction with the Murray at Wentworth. It passes famous bush pubs, camping spots, and fishing holes. For a free kit, call the tourist center (☎ (1800) 24 72 21).

# BROKEN HILL

Broken Hill sits at the extreme western end of New South Wales, right on the edge of nowhere. It would take either insanity or the prospect of untold riches to convince people to live way the hell out here, and a healthy dose of both gave rise to Broken Hill. In 1883, Charles Rasp, a German-born boundary rider, discovered that the misshapen hill known locally as the "hog's back" was in fact the biggest lode of silver-lead ore in the world. Rasp and his associates opened the soon fabulously wealthy Broken Hill Proprietary (BHP), which in turn attracted thousands of people, transforming worthless scrubland into a booming city almost overnight.

Broken Hill's mining continues to this day, on the same giant lode of silver, zinc, and lead discovered by Rasp. However, the last operational mine is expected to shut its shafts in 2006, and the town's future is at best uncertain, since there is little else to hold people to this harsh land. Following the example of Victoria's Goldfield boom towns, Broken Hill hopes to lure tourists with its rich history, while attracting research institutions with its unique and inexplicable geological significance. For the time being, though, the town is a classical outback outpost with a quirky mineral obsession and a typically Australian sense of gritty independence.

## ▣ TRANSPORT

**Trains:** The **train station** (☎ 8087 1400, afterhours ☎ 13 22 32), is on Crystal St near the intersection with Chloride St. Countrylink (☎ 12 22 32) runs the *Indian-Pacific* to **Sydney** (16½hr.; W, Su 4:30pm; $116, ISIC $70). Great Southern Railway (☎ 13 21 47) runs the *Indian-Pacific* to **Perth** (48hr.; Tu, F 10am; $342, ISIC $274) via **Adelaide** (7hr.; $59, ISIC $47). Countrylink trains go to **Sydney** (16hr.; daily 4am; $116, ISIC $70).

**Buses:** The **bus depot** (☎ 8087 2735) is in the same building as the visitors center, at the corner of Blende and Bromide St. A Greyhound bus (24hr. ☎ 13 20 30) goes to: **Adelaide** (7hr., daily 10:30am, $68); other destinations are accessible via **Dubbo** (8hr., daily 3:35pm, $98). To connect with V/Line to **Melbourne** take the Tom Evans coach (☎ (03) 5022 1415) to **Mildura** (3½hr.; M, W, F 3:45pm; $50).

**Taxi:** Yellow Radio Cabs (☎ 13 10 08).

**Car Rental:** Sundry around-town rentals can go as low as $58 per day. **Thrifty,** 190 Argent St (☎ 8088 1928); **Hertz** (☎ 8087 2719), at the visitors center.

**Bike Rental:** A good way to get around town. **Town 'n Country Cycles,** 195B Argent St, (☎ 8087 3707). 24hr. $11, with $50 deposit. Open M-F 9am-5pm.

## ✦ 🛈 ORIENTATION AND PRACTICAL INFORMATION

Rather than use the points of the compass, Broken Hill's streets are aligned with the line of lode that is the city's lifeblood. Most shops and services congregate in the pedestrian-manageable rectangle bounded by **Bromide** (W), **Mica** (N), **Iodide** (E), and **Crystal** (S) Streets. Cutting west-to-east, one block above Crystal St, Argent St is the main thoroughfare, with most of the food and lodging. Several outlying attractions require motorized transport (particularly **Silverton, Mutawintji National Park,** and the **Living Desert**), but rental cars are extremely expensive. Organized tours are a reasonable option for seeing the sights.

**Tourist Office: Broken Hill Visitor Information Centre,** corner of Blende and Bromide St (☎8087 6077; fax 8088 5209; www.murrayoutback.org.au). From the railway station, turn left onto Crystal and walk 2 blocks west, then turn right onto Bromide; the office is 2 blocks down on the left. Tune your radio to 88FM for a recorded replay of the town's history. Open daily 8:30am-5pm.

**National Parks Information: New South Wales National Parks and Wildlife Service (NPWS),** 183 Argent St (☎8088 5933; fax 8088 4448).

**Bank: ANZ,** 357 Argent St (☎13 13 14). Open M-Th 9:30am-4pm, F 9:30am-5pm. 24hr. **ATMs** line Argent St.

**Library: Broken Hill Library** (☎8088 3317), on Blende St. Free **Internet access.** Open M-W 10am-8pm, Th-F 10am-6pm, Sa 10am-1pm, Su 1-5pm.

**Police:** 252 Argent St (☎8087 0299).

**Internet Access:** Slow but free at the library (see above). A faster, cheap alternative is **PC Professional,** 387 Argent St (☎8087 8686). 30min. $2.75.

**Post Office:** 260 Argent St (☎8087 7071). Open M-F 9am-5pm. **Postal Code:** 2880. *Poste Restante* available; pickup at the window around side of building.

**Phone Code:** 08. Broken Hill has adopted the phone code of South Australia, as well as its **time zone,** Central Standard Time (CST), 30min. behind the rest of NSW.

## ▌ ACCOMMODATIONS

If the establishments below are full, try a cheap pubstay on Argent St.

**The Tourist Lodge (YHA),** 100 Argent St (☎8088 2086; fax 8087 9511). This sprawling hostel has a swimming pool to beat the desert heat. A/C and heat will cost you a little more. The tourist center and bus depot are at the back door. Kitchen. Dorms and twins $16, non-YHA $18; singles $20, $22; singles with heat and A/C $30; doubles $42.

**West Darling Hotel,** 400 Argent St (☎8087 2691; fax 8087 1963). The hotel of choice for ore magnates back in the day, now a quality budget pub accommodation. The West D provides plain, neat rooms overlooking the town center. Some rooms have fridge and veranda; all have A/C, heat, and washbasin. TV lounge, parking. and continental breakfast. Reception open when bar is: M-Tu 11am-11pm, W-F 11am-midnight, Sa-Su 11am-10pm. Singles $28; twins and doubles $53, ensuite $60.

**The Grand Guest House,** 313 Argent St (☎/fax 8087 5305). Broken Hill's first hotel; slightly more upmarket digs right in the center of town. Recently refurbished. Rooms are bigger and a touch cleaner than standard budget fare, and have well-kept shared baths. Cozy common room with a roaring fireplace for cold desert nights. A great place for families. Off-street parking, continental breakfast. Singles $50; doubles $60, ensuite $70.

## 🍽 FOOD

Grizzled miners aren't known for their delicate palates, so most of Broken Hill's restaurants serve up what the scruffy-bearded pick-wielders want: meat, with a side of meat and some meat juice to wash it all down. Want something else? Then you must be spoilin' for a tussle, stranger. There are numerous takeaway joints along Argent St. **Schinella's Food and Liquor,** on Argent St across from the YHA hostel, has a solid variety of **groceries** and hooch (open M-F 8:30am-6pm, Sa 9am-

NEW SOUTH WALES

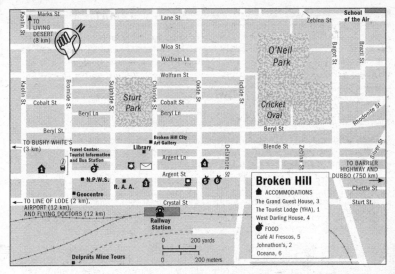

**Broken Hill**

**ACCOMMODATIONS**
The Grand Guest House, 3
The Tourist Lodge (YHA), 1
West Darling House, 4

**FOOD**
Café Al Frescos, 5
Johnathon's, 2
Oceana, 6

NEW SOUTH WALES

5:30pm, Su 9am-1pm). The pasta at **Café Al Fresco,** on the corner of Argent and Oxide St, is nothing special, but the $10 portions are huge. The funky pizzas are decent but depressingly small ($10-16). There's sidewalk dining for those who prefer their meals, well, al fresco. (☎8087 5599. Open 9am-9pm.) Non-vegiphobic fare can be had at the oddly-spelled **Johnathon's,** 198 Argent St. Brekkies go cheap, and the daily lunch board generally runs about $8. (☎8087 8344. Open M-W 7am-5pm, Th-Sa 7am-1pm.) Don't miss the $3.50 scrumptious fruit smoothies at **Ruby's Coffee Lounge,** 393 Argent St. (☎8087 1188. Open M-F 8am-5pm, Sa-Su 9:30am-5pm.) **Oceana,** 423 Argent St, has only one thing going for it: an $8 all-you-can-eat buffet. (☎8087 3695. Open Tu-F noon-2pm and 5-9:30pm, Sa-M 5-9:30pm.)

## SIGHTS

**DELPRAT'S MINE TOUR.** Mining is Broken Hill, and Broken Hill is mining. Gain insight into this intricate symbiosis with a tour of the original Broken Hill Proprietary mine. The fantastic 2hr. trip—all 130m underground—features equipment demonstrations and an insightful comparison of the mining labor system through time, with former miners-*cum*-annotative tour guides. Don your miner's hat and marvel at how they did it with only a candle 100 years ago. (*The BHP mine site is atop the Broken Hill. ☎8088 1604. Tours M-F 10:30am, Sa 2pm; during school holidays, also M-F 2pm and Sa-Su 10:30am. $26, concessions $22; book ahead during school holidays.*)

**LINE OF LODE BROKEN HILL.** As its ore reserves deplete, the city is turning to more historybased tourism. The Line of Lode Broken Hill is the driving body behind the revolution. Guided surface tours illuminate South Mine and the importance of miners to the city and Australia. Slated to open in 2001, the **Miner's Memorial Visitors Centre** lists the hundreds of individuals who have died mining the Lode, most in the days of 19th-century primitive techniques. (*The entire conglomerate is on Broken Hill's highest point, west on Crystal St toward the airport. ☎8088 6000; www.lineoflode brokenhill.com.au. 2hr. tours; 2 per day; $11, children $5.50, families $27.50.*)

**BUSHY WHITE'S MINING MUSEUM.** This former-miner's house has been turned into a unique museum with intricate dioramas of mining techniques through the ages. The museum's namesake goes out of his way to masterfully detail the course of mining over the past century. (*1 Allendale St. Off of Brookfield Ave, about 2km east of the city center. ☎8087 2878. Open daily 9am-5pm. $4, family $10.*)

**ALBERT KERSTEN GEOCENTRE.** Any questions you've ever had about geology, mettalurgy, and mining techniques will be answered in this sharp display of the science of the earth and its solids. Exactly. Regardless, the real highlight is an extensive display of just plain cool rocks. *(On the corner of Bromide and Crystal St.* ☎*8087 6538. Open M-F 10am-5pm, Sa-Su 1-5pm. $3, concessions $2.)*

**BROKEN HILL HERITAGE TRAIL.** This loop around much of the city center is marked with informational signs so you can do it yourself if you miss the guided tours. *(Depart from tourist center M, W, F 10am. Donation optional.)*

**ROYAL FLYING DOCTOR SERVICE.** The Flying Doctors provide health care to outback residents in over 80% of Australia; just a phone call will have them Victor-Sierra-Tango-ing your way. A museum and brief, exciting film detail the history and workings of this noble institution. *(At the Broken Hill Airport.* ☎*8080 1717. Open daily 9am-noon, also M-F 1-5pm. $3.30 admission supports the RFDS.)*

**SCHOOL OF THE AIR.** The School of the Air provides remote education for distant schoolchildren. Visitors can observe the proceedings on weekdays but must book at the tourist office the day before and be seated by 8:20am (demerits for tardiness). The worthwhile proceedings give a real feel for the quirks of life in the bush and outback. *(On Lane St, 2 blocks east of Iodide St. $3.30, children $2.20)*

**LIVING DESERT RESERVE.** Impressive eclectic art has been set up 5km north of town in the Living Desert Reserve. In 1993, the **Broken Hill Sculpture Symposium** commissioned a group of local and international sculptors to create stone works atop a hill. The masterful pieces blend Aboriginal with modern and international influence, creating an almost otherworldly nexus with the past. *(Head north 8km along Kaolin St. You can drive all the way by obtaining a gate key from the tourist office for $5.50 with a $10 deposit, but the 15min. hike from a nearby carpark is more fun and absolutely free.)*

**BROKEN HILL CITY ART GALLERY.** A variety of excellent local work and a strong collection of 20th-century Australian painting constitutes this small collection. *Silver Tree*, a delicately wrought arboreal centerpiece commissioned by Charles Rasp, is made of the first silver extracted from the Lode. *(Corner of Blende and Chloride St.* ☎*8088 5491. Open M-F 10am-5pm, Sa-Su 1-5pm. $3, concessions $2.)*

**TOURS OUT OF BROKEN HILL.** Many tour operators offer similarly priced day-trips to **Silverton** ($40-50), **Mutawintji National Park** (around $100), and multi-day outback safaris (many hundreds of dollars). Though pricey, the tours are the best option for lone risk-averse travelers and for those without their own vehicle; for groups, renting a car is more economical.

## ⁊ DAYTRIP FROM BROKEN HILL: SILVERTON

Diminutive Silverton makes Broken Hill, 25km to the south, look like a metropolis. The 1876 discovery of silver, zinc, and lead ore at Thackaringa brought Silverton into existence. Prospectors arrived in numbers, and the population peaked at around 3000 in 1885. Unfortunately for Silverton, most of the ore was gone by this point, just as Broken Hill's lode was revealing its precious potential. This combination of circumstances rendered Silverton a ghost town, home today to fewer than 60 hermits. Silverton revels in its emptiness and has been used in numerous bleak films, including the classic *Mad Max II*. But don't let concern over post-nuclear desert mutants keep you away from Silverton; it is an experience like no other.

Silverton's handful of buildings ranges from old brick ruins that have stood abandoned since the 1800s to some good art galleries specializing in outback naturalism. The **Silverton Gaol,** erected in 1889, was used infrequently after the evaporation of Silverton's population and was converted to a boys' reformatory in the 1930s. The buildings were closed in 1943 and then reopened as a museum in 1968. The former cells are packed with old-tyme geegaws, including a great array of daguerreotypes from the mining days and random assorted Australiana. (☎8088 5317. Open M-F 9:30am-4:30pm. $2.50.) The main social activity 'round these parts is getting sloshed, making the legendary **Silverton Hotel,** (☎8088 5313) the most important building in town. Filled to the rafters with a huge diversity of beer cans

**CENOZOIC MEGAFAUNA** Evidence collected throughout Australia strongly suggests that the early Aboriginals shared the continent with some fearsome beasts: giant mammals now termed megafauna. One of the more novel species, *Zygomaturus trilobus*, was sized like a buffalo, built much like a wombat, and possessed either a horn similar to a rhinoceros's or a short, flexible trunk. Strangest of all is *Procoptodon goliah*, a kangaroo twice as big as the largest red 'roos, which climbed trees and ate leaves. Its skull was flattened and its eyes were set forward in the head, giving it a snub-nosed, eerily humanoid visage. Unlike regular kangaroos, Goliah's arms and shoulders allowed it to manipulate objects and even reach overhead, much like the ancestors of human beings. If primates hadn't beaten out marsupials in the race toward human sentience, we might all be hopping today.

and signs with naughty sayings, the hotel serves simple food and drink until 8 or 9pm. Don't leave before taking "The Test," a super-secret outback initiation ritual.

The **Silverton Camel Farm,** on the road from Broken Hill, grants rides on the temperamental humped beasts. (☎8088 5316. 15min. $5; 2hr. sunset safari $40.) **Penrose Park,** just north of town, offers scandalously cheap accommodation: primitive campsites and unadorned, livable 6- to 8-person bunkhouses with kitchen, A/C, BBQ, and fridge. (☎8088 5316. Sites $3; $20 per bunkhouse; BYO linen.)

During the Ice Age, glaciers scraped the plains west of Silverton until they were as level as a freshly zambonied ice rink. If you still doubt that the world is round, drive 6km west to **Mundi Mundi Scenic Lookout.** The curvature of the planet is clearly visible. *Let's Go* does not recommend these plains to agoraphobes.

## MUNGO NATIONAL PARK

Ages ago, before the pyramids at Giza were even a sparkle in the eye of world history, hunter-gatherer communities flourished on the banks of Lake Mungo, in the extreme southwest corner of present-day New South Wales. Forty thousand years and 1600 Aboriginal generations later, life continues at **Mungo National Park,** one of the oldest continually inhabited sites in the world. Today the lake is dry (and has been for 15,000 years), and Mungo has undergone some spectacular weathering. Sand dunes on the edges of the lake bed have been sculpted into strange, otherworldly landforms by erosion, accelerated over the course of the past hundred years by settlers' unwitting introduction of harmful foreign species: grazing sheep and foraging rabbits. Known as the **Walls of China,** their erosion has revealed countless fossils and artifacts, including **Mungo Three,** a skeleton of a human male that is, at an estimated 40,000 years, the oldest remaining *Homo sapiens* relic in the world. (The skeleton was buried again in a secret location so that it wouldn't be plundered.) The colored layers of sand clearly demarcate periods of water change up to 120,000 years ago. The archaeological information uncovered here has earned the **Willandra Lakes** region status as a **World Heritage Site.** On a slightly less grandiose note, the shearing house, next to the **Visitors Centre,** dates to the mid-1800s but still contains some of the original sheep-shearing equipment.

Mungo is 110km northeast of Mildura, Victoria on the **Acumpo-Ivanhoe Rd.** Roads within and around the park are unsealed but accessible to 2WD vehicles in good weather. Road conditions can be checked with the NPWS (☎(03) 5023 1054). There is an excellent 60km driving tour that skirts the Walls of China and encompasses all of the park's best features. The **Visitors Centre** near the park entrance has maps and displays on megafauna and Aboriginal life in the area, as well as collects camping and lodging fees. A nature walk (1½hr.) through the Mallee scrub begins just outside the center. The shearer's quarters next to the Visitors Centre have been converted into bare-bones bunk rooms with surprisingly clean bathrooms with showers ($16.50). **Camping** is allowed near the Arump Rd entrance and at Belah Camp on the driving tour. Visitors must bring drinking water. Belah observes a strict total fire ban, excepting gas BBQs; firewood must be self-supplied at the Arump camp. (Campsites $5.50 per person for up to 2, $2.20 per additional person up to 6; honor system, but park rangers perform spot checks.)

# NORTHERN TERRITORY

A well-worn 4WD rumbles down an endless road toward a fiery sunset, bellowing pumpkin-colored dust behind its growling motor. The mud-caked license plate says "Northern Territory." Against the backdrop of a pastel sky, silver eucalyptus trees contort their limbs into ghost-like curves, and cockatoos squawk noisily from their branches. Sparse clumps of foliage and palm trees break the otherwise dry woodland. In the distance, the thick smoke of a bush fire bruises the horizon. If this is your image of the outback, and the outback is what you're after, you've come to the right place.

The Northern Territory stretches into the country's most extreme regions. In its 1.3 million square kilometer area, the 200,000 inhabitants could enjoy 6.5 square kilometers of land apiece. Instead, nearly 60% choose to settle in the population centers of Darwin in the tropical Top End or Alice Springs in the desert-like Red Centre. The rest scatter among three or four substantially-sized towns such as Katherine or Tennant Creek or upon the cattle stations, Aboriginal homelands, and national parks that give droplets of human life to the vast outback. Because towns and roadhouses can be up to a day's drive apart, residents proudly joke that "NT" stands not only for "Northern Territory" but also for "Not Today." Or Not Tomorrow, or Not in Three days.

With nearly 30% of the Territory's population indigenous, whites and Aboriginals live together in relatively mild, if indifferent, peace. However, separatism is rampant, and most businesses and services are predominantly run and staffed by whites. Though colonization began in the 17th century, the Territory's European population was slow to grow. Only telegraph and railway construction and the gold rushes brought an influx of hardy go-getters to this frontier land. Today, mining and cattle-breeding remain prominent sources of income, but are quickly being equalled or surpassed by tourism. With lush, tropical attractions like Kakadu and Litchfield National Parks in the Top End or Uluru and the MacDonnells in the barren Red Centre, the Northern Territory is a playground for adventurous travelers fed up with the overcrowded, overfed beach culture of the east coast.

In this land that necessitates and breeds independence, one might think that the push for statehood would be strong. But a Territory referendum for statehood in 1998 was voted down by a substantial margin. At least for now, the NT will continue to be financially run by Canberra. However, in spirit and in reality, southeast Australia is a long way away. The spectacular sunsets and overwhelming starscapes in the Northern Territory have a way of making governmental dictums and daily minutiae unimportant in the face of the realization that life goes on as it will.

## NORTHERN TERRITORY HIGHLIGHTS

**JUBILEE.** The multicultural Mindil Beach Sunset Market in Darwin (p. 253).

**THUNDERING.** The spectacular Jim Jim Falls in Kakadu National Park (p. 257).

**CONTEMPLATION.** Surprise Creek Falls in Litchfield National Park (p. 268).

**SILENCE.** Peace at Katherine River in Katherine Gorge National Park (p. 272).

**WIDE OPEN.** The awesome Ormiston Gorge in the Macdonnell Ranges (p. 284).

**ROCK SCRAMBLING.** The King's Canyon Walk in Watarrka National Park (p. 288).

**SHEER AWE.** Uluru—the rock will take your breath away (p. 291).

**FREE YOUR MIND.** Valley of the Winds at Kata Tjuta (p. 293).

# Northern Territory

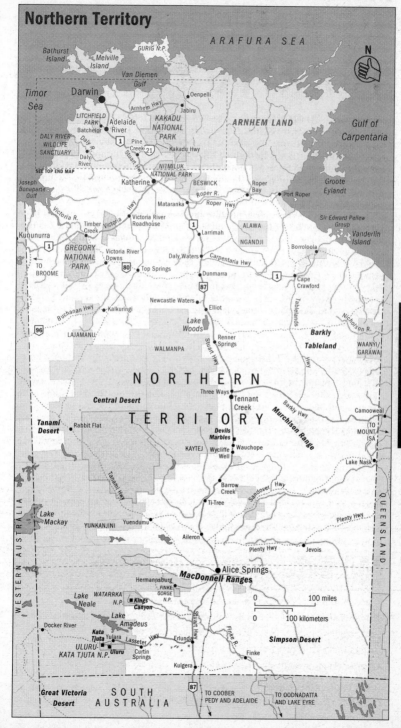

NORTHERN TERRITORY

# ⌐ GETTING AROUND

The NT's vast expanses make transportation a significant issue. Darwin, Alice Springs, and Yulara (Ayers Rock Resort) are most commonly reached by air. Smaller planes often fly to smaller destinations, but the price can be daunting. There is **no train** system traversing the Territory, except from Alice heading south to Adelaide. **Greyhound** (☎13 20 30) and **McCafferty's** (☎13 14 99) buses offer extensive service to most major tourist centers but not to the farther reaches of the national parks. **Renting a car** is the best way to retain freedom and flexibility, but it's also the most expensive, and you must be at least 21. There are many national chains which have offices all over the NT; **Territory-Thrifty Car Rental** (Darwin ☎8924 0000, Alice Springs ☎8952 9999) and **Budget** (☎13 27 27) are the cheapest, but limit kilometers (100km per day, each additional km $0.25), whereas **Britz** (☎(1800) 33 14 54) offers unlimited kilometers and rents 4WD to those under 25. Each company does one-way rentals, but there is a one-way fee, usually $300-400.

The major tourist centers in the area are accessible by sealed or gravel roads. You'll only need a 4WD to venture into the bush on dirt tracks; however, this is necessary to see many of the spectacular sights of Kakadu National Park and the MacDonnell Ranges. Furthermore, if you rent a conventional vehicle, it won't be insured on unsealed or gravel roads. If going to remote areas, ask for a high-clearance 4WD with two petrol tanks; trendier recreational vehicles often have 4WD but are too low to the ground to navigate many of the roads. Also, make sure the 4WD you rent is not so top-heavy that it could potentially flip over in rough terrain driving. There are many safari tours that operate in national parks and the bush for those who want the rugged experience without the hassle of renting. They usually run about $100 per day. **Wilderness 4WD Adventures** (☎(1800) 80 82 88) or **Gondwana** (☎(1800) 24 21 77) are good for Top End tours, and **Wayoutback Desert Safaris** (☎(1800) 22 43 24) for the Uluru area. These companies center around small groups and try to get off the beaten path. It's still best to do some research for a tour company that offers the price, length, and ruggedness that you're looking for.

If going beyond the highways, make sure to bring lots of extra water, food, emergency materials (tire, tools, rope, jack, etc.), and inform a friend, visitors center, or ranger station of your travel plans. Avoid driving at dusk and dawn, when kangaroos tend to loiter in the road. There are many sections of unfenced ranch land along the highways; beware of wandering cattle. Another risk is quite common: road trains (multi-part trucks) which carry supplies across the Territory. Slow down and give them plenty of room. When venturing onto unsealed roads, be sure to call ahead to find out **road conditions** (Territory-wide ☎(1800) 24 61 99); they vary tremendously, especially in the Top End during and soon after the Wet season (May-Oct.), when some tracks may be washed out entirely. For **weather reports** and forecasts, dial ☎8982 3826. The **Automobile Association of the Northern Territory (AANT)** (road service ☎8941 0611) can provide invaluable assistance, and is affiliated with national and international services (see **Essentials**, p. 66).

# DARWIN

Doused by rain half the year, flooded by visitors the rest, Darwin (pop. 90,000) is an energetically charged, nightlife-crazy, travelers' hub set in a tropical paradise. As the capital of the rugged Northern Territory and gateway to the cultures of Southeast Asia, Darwin blends raw outback grit with the eclectic flair of an international community. Serving both as a springboard to nearby overseas destinations, such as Bali, and as the front door to Australia, Darwin is home to numerous Asian immigrants and other international travelers who combine to produce one of Australia's newest, most diverse cities.

During the Dry, the incessant sunshine and azure beaches hypnotize mobs of midriff-baring backpackers to come to Darwin and play under the palm trees and stars, at the bars, with the didgeridoos, and with each other. However, Darwin's

NORTHERN TERRITORY

# The Top End

ARNHEM LAND

Cooper Cr.
E. Alligator R.
Oenpelli
Ubirr
Jabiru
Nourlangie Rock
Mt. Gilruth
Jim Jim Cr.
Jim Jim Falls
Twin Falls
Mt. Evelyn
S. Alligator R.
Coodinda
Aurora Kakadu Village
S. Alligator R.
KAKADU NATIONAL PARK
W. Alligator R.
Wildman
Gunlom Falls
Mary River Road House
Mt. Davis
Two Sisters (90km)
TO KATHERINE (90km)

21

36

Arnhem Hwy

MARY RIVER NAT'L PARK
Shady Camp
Bark Hut Inn
Mary R.
Mt. Douglas
Pine Creek
Umbrawarra Gorge
Kakadu Hwy

21

1

Van Diemen Gulf

SEE KAKADU NATIONAL PARK MAP

TO COBOURG PENINSULA

Annaburroo Billabong
Window on the Wetlands
Fogg Dam Conservation Reserve
Jumping Croc Cruises
Margaret R.
Butterfly Gorge
Hayes Creek
Douglas Hot Springs
Douglas R.

Howard Springs Nature Park
Humpty Doo
Berry Springs Nature Park
Lake Bennett Resort
Adelaide R.
Adelaide River
Stuart Hwy

1

23

Darwin
Palmerston
Territory Wildlife Park
Darwin River
Batchelor
LITCHFIELD NATIONAL PARK
Daly River
Daly R.
Fish R.

28

Beagle Gulf

Lee Point

TO THE TIWI ISLANDS

34

28

20 miles
20 kilometers

N

4WD track
Unsealed road (impassible in Wet season)

## Greater Darwin

Rocklands Dr
Lee Point Rd
Vanderlin Rd
McMillans Rd
Trower Rd
Marrara Swamp
CASUARINA
Charles Eaton Dr
Rapid Cr
DARWIN AIRPORT
Hospital
TO CROCODYLUS PARK (2km)
Tiger Brennan Dr
Frances Bay

Casuarina Beach

Beagle Gulf (Timor Sea)

Progress Dr
Bagot Rd
Dick Ward Dr
Stuart Hwy
Ross Smith

East Point Recreation Reserve

East Point Rd
Vestey's Beach
Fannie Bay
Mindil Beach
LARRAKEYAH
Botanic Gardens
McMinn St
Gilruth Ave
Mitchell St
SEE CENTRAL DARWIN MAP
Port Darwin

TIMOR SEA

character has not always been so footloose and fancy-free. In WWII, Darwin suffered nearly two years of intense Japanese bombing as Australia's hardest hit target. In 1974, Darwin sustained another bombardment—this time at the hands of Mother Nature. On Christmas Eve, Cyclone Tracy decimated the town. With true Territory grit, Darwin rebuilt, creating the convenient city center, manicured parks, and touristy outdoor mall that exist today.

The mining industry and tourism contribute to the city's current fortunes, with scores of new hostels luring backpackers. Still, visitors don't come to Darwin looking for refined, urban pleasures. They're on their way to explore the natural splendors of the Top End, including Kakadu and Litchfield National Parks, even if they may forget that for a few days while under Darwin's spell.

---

**DARWIN HIGHLIGHTS**

**CHAOS.** Arts, crafts, produce, and people at Mindil Beach Sunset Market (p. 252).

**SAY HEY TO YOUR SWEETHEART.** The croc at the Museum and Art Gallery of the Northern Territory (p. 252).

**JUST LOUNGIN'.** Deck Chair Cinema's avant-garde, avant-ceiling films (p. 253).

**TAKE ONE DOWN, PASS IT AROUND.** The great bar scene all over the city (p. 254).

---

# ✈ GETTING THERE

## BY PLANE

**Darwin International Airport** (☎8920 1850) is about 10km northeast of the city center on McMillans Rd. From Darwin city center, take a left on Bagot Rd off the Stuart Hwy. For arrivals, the easiest option is the **airport shuttle bus** that leaves from the terminal (☎(1800) 35 89 45). If notified in advance, many accommodations will pay or reimburse patrons for the $8 ride to the city center. **Taxis** (☎13 10 08) run to the airport for $13-15. **Qantas** and **Ansett** have domestic return services to: **Adelaide** ($683); **Alice Springs** ($397); **Ayers Rock** ($538); **Brisbane** ($708); **Broome** ($397); **Cairns** ($476); **Melbourne** ($719); **Perth** ($681); and **Sydney** ($719). Both offer 25% student discounts, and the cheapest tickets must be bought 21 days in advance. Numerous airlines offer international service to Southeast Asia, **Singapore** and **Bali.** Travel agencies can arrange the cheapest airline tickets. Airline offices include **Ansett Australia** in the Mall (☎13 13 00; www.ansett.com.au); **Qantas,** 16 Bennett St (☎13 13 13; www.qantas.com.au); **Singapore Airlines** in the Centrepoint arcade in the Mall (☎8941 1799); **Garuda Indonesia,** 9 Cavanagh St (☎(1300) 36 53 31); and the Territory-carrier **Airnorth,** at the airport (☎8945 2866).

## BY BUS

The **Transit Centre,** 69 Mitchell St, between Peel and Nuttall St, is the locus of intercity bus travel. **Greyhound Pioneer** (☎13 20 30; office open M-Sa 6am-6pm, Su 6am-2:30pm) runs to: **Adelaide** (39hr., 1 per day, $318); **Alice Springs** (20hr., 2 per day, $165) via **Katherine** (4hr., 2 per day, $44) and **Tennant Creek** (12hr., 2 per day, $115); **Broome** (12hr., 1 per day, $230); and **Cairns** (41hr., 1 per day, $329); **Melbourne** (51hr., 1 per day, $370); and **Sydney** (72hr., daily 8:45am, $408). **McCafferty's,** 71 Smith St (☎13 14 99), runs to **Adelaide** (46hr., 1 per day, $303); **Sydney** (68-74hr., 1-2 per day, $372-409); and **Alice Springs** (20hr., 1 per day, $162).

# ✦ ORIENTATION

Darwin is situated on a peninsula. Darwin Harbor runs north-south along the western edge of the peninsula. Parallel to the harbor, moving inland, are the **Esplanade, Mitchell St** (where most budget accommodations are), **Smith St,** and **Cavenagh St.** From the southern point of the peninsula moving northward, the major east-west streets are **Bennett St, Knuckey St, Peel St,** and **Daly St.** The **Mall** occupies the block

NORTHERN TERRITORY

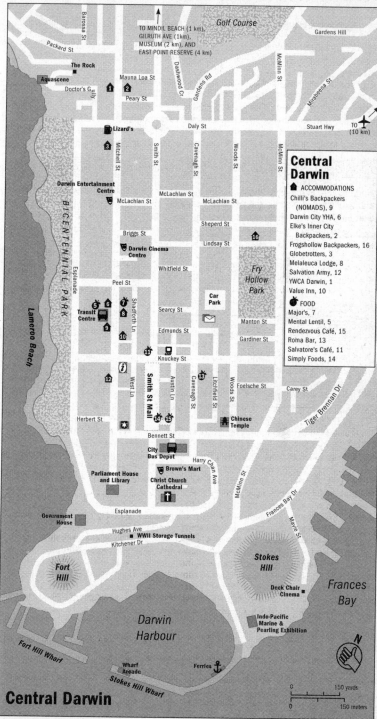

**Central Darwin**

TO MINDIL BEACH (1 km),
GILRUTH AVE (1km),
MUSEUM (2 km), AND
EAST POINT RESERVE (4 km)

Golf Course

Gardens Hill

Packard St

Barossa St

The Rock

Aquascene

Doctor's G____ully

Mauna Loa St

Peary St

Lizard's

Daly St

Stuart Hwy

TO ✈
(10 km)

Mitchell St

Smith St

Cavenagh St

Woods St

McMinn St

Mirambeena St

Gardens Rd

Dashwood Cr

McMinn St

Darwin Entertainment Centre

McLachlan St

McLachlan St

McLachlan St

Sheperd St

Lindsay St

BICENTENNIAL PARK

Briggs St

Darwin Cinema Centre

Whitfield St

Fry Hollow Park

Esplanade

Peel St

Lamaroo Beach

Transit Centre

Shadforth Ln

Searcy St

Car Park

Edmunds St

Manton St

Gardiner St

Knuckey St

West Ln

Smith St Mall

Austin Ln

Cavenagh St

Litchfield St

Woods St

Foelsche St

Carey St

Tiger Brennan Dr

Herbert St

Chinese Temple

Bennett St

City Bus Depot

Brown's Mart

Harry Chan Ave

Parliament House and Library

Christ Church Cathedral

Esplanade

McMinn St

Frances Bay Dr

Mavie St

Government House

Hughes Ave

WWII Storage Tunnels

Kitchener Dr

Fort Hill

Stokes Hill

Frances Bay

Deck Chair Cinema

Darwin Harbour

Darwin Harbour

Indo-Pacific Marine & Pearling Exhibition

Fort Hill Wharf

Wharf Arcade

Ferries ⚓

Stokes Hill Wharf

N

0        150 yards
0        150 meters

**Central Darwin**

**Central Darwin**

🏠 ACCOMMODATIONS

Chilli's Backpackers
  (NOMADS), 9
Darwin City YHA, 6
Elke's Inner City
  Backpackers, 2
Frogshollow Backpackers, 16
Globetrotters, 3
Melaleuca Lodge, 8
Salvation Army, 12
YWCA Darwin, 1
Value Inn, 10

🍴 FOOD

Major's, 7
Mental Lentil, 5
Rendezvous Café, 15
Roma Bar, 13
Salvatore's Café, 11
Simply Foods, 14

NORTHERN TERRITORY

**WHO'S FITTEST NOW?** Charles Darwin was not aboard the HMS Beagle in 1839 when it sailed into the harbor that his former shipmates named in his honor. He had been down under three years previously, but disembarked near modern-day Sydney. Darwin's tour of Australia included the Blue Mountains in New South Wales, which he described as having a "desolate and untidy appearance." He wrote of the continent, "Nothing but rather sharp necessity should compel me to emigrate."

of Smith St between Knuckey and Bennett St and is home to a multitude of shops and services. On the western side of the city center, The Esplanade is a pleasant, shady, tree-lined walk that provides access to the rocky Lameroo Beach.

Moving northeast out of downtown, Daly St eventually becomes the Stuart Hwy and heads out to the airport. Smith St continues north of the city center for a half-kilometer before converging with **Gilruth Ave**, which leads out to the **MGM Casino, Mindil Beach,** and **Vestey Beach.** At the **Museum and Art Gallery of the Northern Territory,** Gilruth Ave becomes **East Point Dr** which continues along the coast to **East Point Reserve**, where it ends 6km from the city center.

# ▐ GETTING AROUND

**Darwinbus** (☎8924 7666) is the public transportation that runs to outlying suburbs and beaches along the major thoroughfares. Fares are $1.40 ($1.80 for distant suburbs), and the bus terminal is between Bennett St and Harry Chan Ave, though there are stops along Mitchell and Cavenagh St. Tourcards allow unlimited travel for a day ($5) or a week ($25, concessions $12.50). There is a **city shuttle** (☎8985 3666 or ☎8982 1155) serving downtown ($2.50) and the suburbs ($5). For a **taxi,** dial ☎13 10 08 ($1.50 per km). **Bicycles** can be rented from most hostels (1hr. $3).

**Cars** are not a necessity to see the city, but many people rent cars to explore the rest of the Top End. **Territory Rent-a-Car,** 64 Stuart Hwy (☎8924 0000), has small sedans from $40 with 100km per day, and 4WDs from $80. **Nifty,** the "small car" specialist, 86 Mitchell St, is also a good budget choice. (☎8981 299. From $56, with 400km per day $86.) **Avis,** 145 Stuart Hwy (☎8981 9922), and **Hertz,** corner of Smith and Daly St (☎8941 0944) are larger operations, with sedans from $66, 4WD from $120. **Britz,** 44-66 Stuart Hwy, specializes in campervans and 4WDs. (☎(1800) 33 14 54. From $130 with unlimited km.) Most agencies require renters to be at least 21. Britz is the only company that rents 4WD to drivers under 25; for longer rentals, ask for the monthly lease plan. Most companies offer the first 100km per day free, with a 25¢ per km charge after that.

Travelers **purchasing a car** or selling one are in good company in Darwin. Check out the **Travelers Car Market,** at Peel and Mitchell St. Sellers pay $30 per week to cram into the lot, but buyers browse for free. Cars sell fastest May-Oct. (☎(0418) 60 08 30. Open daily 8am-4pm.) Also check out hostel bulletin boards. Newly purchased cars must be registered at the **Motor Vehicle Registry,** on Goyder Rd. (☎8999 3111. Open M-Th 8am-4pm, F 8am-5:30pm. Turn off the Stuart Hwy at Tom's Tyres.) Transferring registration costs 3% of the car cost, and must be done within 14 days of purchase. Stamp duty and registration fee may also apply. For more info, call **Auto Association of the Northern Territory (AANT),** 79-81 Smith St, Briggs (☎8981 3837; open M-F 8am-5pm) or dial ☎8941 0611. Also, see **Buying and Selling Used Cars,** p. 67.

# ▐ PRACTICAL INFORMATION

**Tourist Office: Darwin Region Tourism Association (DRTA)** (☎8981 4300; fax 8981 0653; email info@drta.com.au), in Beagle House Building at the corner of Mitchell and Knuckey St. From the Transit Centre, walk one block right on Mitchell. Open M-F 8:30am-5:45pm, Sa 9am-2:45pm, Su 10am-2:45pm. The airport also has a DRTA.

**Travel Office: STA,** Shop T-17 in Galleria, Smith St Mall (☎8941 2955). From the Transit Centre take Mitchell St to the right, turn left on Knuckey St, right into the Smith St Mall, then right at the second indoor court. Sells ISIC and VIP cards ($15). Open M-F 9am-5pm, Sa 9am-2pm. **Flight Centre,** 24 Cavanagh St (☎13 16 00), guarantees to beat any quoted current airfare price. Open M-F 9am-5pm, Sa 9am-1pm.

**Northern Territory Tourist Commission:** 43 Mitchell St (☎8999 3900; fax 8951 3888).

**Parks & Wildlife Commission of the Northern Territory:** (☎8999 5511; www.nt.gov.au/paw). Near Darwin, in Palmerston.

**Currency Exchange: Bank South Australia,** 13 Knuckey St (☎8981 1322). $5 or 1% charge to buy traveler's checks and foreign currency. Open M-Th 9:30am-4pm, F 9:30am-5pm. **ANZ Bank** (☎13 13 14), on Knuckey St by the Smith St Mall, processes bank cards and traveler's checks. Open M-Th 9:30am-4pm, F 9:30am-5pm.

**American Express: Travelers World,** 18 Knuckey St (☎8981 4699). Holds mail for 30 days (no packages) for card holders or traveler's check holders. Address mail "ATTN: Client Mail, GPO Box 3728, Darwin NT 0801." Open M-F 8:30am-5pm, Sa 9am-noon.

**Backpacking Supplies: NT General Store,** 42 Cavanagh St (☎8981 8242), at Edmunds St, has everything you need for the outdoors and sells Blundstones (from $60) and topo maps ($7.50). Open M-W 8:30am-5:30pm, Th-F 8:30am-6pm, Sa 8:30am-1pm.

**Bookstores: Read Back Book Exchange,** Darwin Plaza off Smith St Mall (☎8981 8885). Buys and sells used books. Open M-F 9am-5pm, Sa 8am-3pm. So does **Dusty Jackets,** Shop 3, 29 Cavanagh St (☎8981 6772). Open M-F 10:30am-5pm, Sa 9am-noon.

**Library: Northern Territory Library** (☎8999 7410), at the corner of Mitchell and Bennett St inside the Parliament building. Open M-F 10am-6pm, Sa-Su 1-5pm.

**Emergency:** Dial ☎000.

**Police:** 24 Mitchell St (24hr. ☎8922 3344), near Bennett St. Open M-F 8am-5pm, after-hours M-F 5-11pm, Sa-Su 8-11pm.

**Hotlines: Crisis Line** (☎(1800) 01 91 16). **Sexually Transmitted Diseases** (☎8922 8077). **NT Aids Council** (☎(1800) 88 08 99). **NT Police road report** (☎8922 3394).

**Pharmacy: Darwin Pharmacy,** Shop 46, Smith St Mall (☎8981 9202). Open M-Sa 8:30am-7pm, Su 9am-5pm.

**Hospital: Royal Darwin Hospital** (☎8922 8888), on Rocklands Dr in Tiwi, Casuarina 9km from the city center.

**Internet Access:** Everywhere. The cheapest option is **Didjworld Internet Shop,** 60 Smith St (☎8981 3510), in the Harry Chan Arcade. 1hr. $5. Open M-Sa 10am-10pm, Su 10am-8pm. **Global Gossip,** 44 Mitchell St (☎8942 3044), at Knuckey St, has daily 1hr. $5 "Happy Hour" from 8-11am and 11pm-midnight. Open daily 8am-midnight.

**Post Office: General Post Office Darwin,** 48 Cavenagh St (☎13 13 18), at Edmunds St. *Poste Restante* held 30 days. Open M-F 8:30am-5pm, Sa 9am-noon. **Postal Code:** 0800.

**Phone Code:** 08.

**MEDIA AND PUBLICATIONS.**
**Newspaper:** *NT News* (90¢).
**Entertainment:** The *NT News* publishes an Entertainment section in the Wednesday and Friday papers.
**Radio:** Rock, Triple J 103.3FM and HOT-100 101.1FM; News, ABC 105.7FM; Tourist info, 88FM.

# ▐ ACCOMMODATIONS

Darwin's budget accommodation scene centers around hostels. Most are clumped near the Transit Centre on Mitchell St. Beds fill up during the Dry, so call ahead. During the Wet, you'll be rewarded for your bravery with lower prices.

▨ **Darwin City YHA,** 69 Mitchell St (☎8981 3995; fax 8981 6674; email darwinyha@yhant.org.au). In the Transit Centre. La *crème de la crème* in a city drowning in hostels. Friendly, clean, and efficient, with a pool, TV room, kitchen, A/C, and luggage

NORTHERN TERRITORY

storage ($2 per day). Free airport shuttle. Linen $2. Laundry $2.20. Reception 24hr. Dorms $17; singles or doubles $39; ensuite doubles $50. Non-YHA $3-6 more.

**Melaleuca Lodge,** 50 Mitchell St (☎ 8941 3395, freecall ☎ (1800) 62 35 43; fax 8941 3368). Across from the Transit Centre. Really clean. Shady patio, pool, and garden create a relaxing environment despite the bustling location. A/C, lockers, 2 kitchens, TV rooms, laundry. Free airport pickup. Free pancake breakfast. Reception daily 5:30am-9pm. Dorms $20-22; twins $55; doubles $65. VIP. Wheelchair accessible.

**Chilli's Backpackers (NOMADS),** 69A Mitchell St (☎ 8941 9722, freecall ☎ (1800) 35 13 13; fax 8941 9835; www.nomads-backpackers.com). South of the Transit Centre. A good place to...chill, with spacious balconies to see and be seen by the Mitchell St throngs below. Their popularity has allowed the staff to exude an occasionally cold demeanor, but it's hard to argue with the location and facilities. Airport shuttle reimbursed. Key deposit $20. Reception daily 6am-9pm. Dorms $20; twins and doubles $51, ensuite $53. YHA, VIP, NOMADS.

**Salvation Army Red Shield Hostel,** 49 Mitchell St (☎8981 5994). South of Knuckey St. Great location, best prices in town, and all singles. But a much older crowd, no guests after 11pm, and absolutely no drugs or alcohol. Book way ahead. Laundry $1. Reception daily 8:30am-4:30pm. Singles: small $13, medium $14, large $16.

**YWCA Darwin "Banyan View Lodge,"** 119 Mitchell St (☎8981 8644; fax 8981 6104). 10min. from the Transit Centre, past Peary St. The spacious lodge offers clean, simple, if somewhat spartan, rooms. Large kitchen, spa, TV lounges, parking, laundry. Reception M-F 8am-6pm, Sa-Su 8am-4pm. Dorms $18; singles $38, with A/C $43; twins $48, $53; ensuite triple with A/C $61.

**Frogshollow Backpackers,** 27 Lindsay St (☎8941 2600, freecall ☎(1800) 06 86 86). 10min. from the Transit Centre, at Woods St. Better facilities than many Darwin hostels, and cool overhanging palm trees. Pool, laundry, spacious kitchen, Internet. Reception daily 6am-9pm. Dorms $20; doubles $48. YHA.

**Elke's Inner City Backpackers,** 112 Mitchell St (☎8981 8399; email elkes@dow nunder.net.au). 10min. from the Transit Centre, on the right past Peary St. Elke's offers a quieter, tropical environment. Patio, pool, spa, kitchens, TV room, laundry, Internet (1hr. $6). Reception daily 6am-9pm. Dorms $17; light brekkie included. YHA, VIP.

**Globetrotters,** 97 Mitchell St (☎8981 5385; fax 8981 9096). 5min. from the Transit Centre, before Daly St. Globetrotters lures innocent backpackers with nightly feasts, but its rooms are worn and more crowded than most hostels. Pool, kitchen, laundry, and in-house bar. Key deposit $20. Reception daily 6am-10:30pm. Bunks $20; twins and doubles $55. YHA, VIP.

**Value Inn,** 50 Mitchell St (☎8981 4733; fax 8981 4730). Near the Transit Centre. A quiet alternative. Reception daily 10am-9pm. Clean, cramped ensuite triples with TV, fridge, and A/C $74. Wheelchair accessible.

**Camping** options in town leave much to be desired. With harsh weather half the year and no campgrounds in central Darwin, die-hard campers should head out of town via the Stuart Hwy. **Lee Point Resort** is amazingly on Lee Point Rd. Take Bagot Rd to McMillans Rd. Lee Rd is at the second set of lights; turn left and take it to the end. (☎8945 0835. Sites $17, weekly $99; campervan sites $20, $105.) **Shady Glen** is off the Stuart Hwy at the intersection with Farrell Crescent, about 10km from central Darwin. (☎8984 3330. Sites $9 per person; campervan sites $21.50 per night.)

# ◖ FOOD

Darwin has a variety of options to feed the onslaught of budget travelers. The **Blue Heeler Bar,** on Mitchell St (☎8941 7945), just north of Herbert St, offers nightly free feedings with a drink purchase. The **Victoria Hotel,** 27 Smith St Mall (☎8981 4011), has all-you-can-eat greasy lunch for $8. For those who don't want to stand in line, or who are seeking more flavor, Darwin has heaps of international eateries including Asian, Italian, and Mexican. The food stalls inside the Transit Centre and in the

NORTHERN TERRITORY

side arcades off Smith St Mall offer hot, relatively cheap, mostly Asian cuisine. The markets at Mindil Beach (Th, Su night) and Parap (Sa morning) also offer cheap, delicious pan-Asian food in a great atmosphere ($6-8 for a full meal). The Parap market sells fresh fruit and veggies, too. The **Wharf Arcade,** at the end of Stokes Hill Wharf, is a popular sunset dining spot where slightly-better-than-average-take-away fetches high prices. Woolworth's **supermarket** is at the corner of Knuckey and Smith St (open M-Sa 6:30am-midnight, Su 8am-9pm).

▨ **The Mental Lentil,** in the Transit Centre (☎8981 1377). Vegetarians rejoice—you have reached the promised land. Scrumptious, creative cuisine and low, low prices. Try a soya smoothie ($3.50) or a three-inch-thick lentil burger ($5.50), but don't try any of that beef funny business here. We're onto you. Open M-Sa 11am-9pm, Su 5-9pm.

▨ **Simply Foods,** Star Village, Smith St Mall (☎8981 4765). Fresh, flavorful, and mostly organic vegetarian food for cheap. Creative sandwiches $4-5, falafel bursting with enticement $5, and the salads, oh the beautiful enormous salads (beautiful enormous salad $5). Open M-F 10:30am-2:30pm.

**Rendezvous Café,** Star Village, Smith St Mall (☎8981 9231). Better Malaysian and Thai cuisine than the Transit Centre food court and cheaper than the fancy Asian restaurants in town. Plan your own rendezvous with taste and value at this local fave. Delightful vegetable laksa $8. Open M-W 9am-2:30pm, Th-Sa 9am-2:30pm and 5:30-9pm.

**Roma Bar,** 30 Cavenagh St (☎8981 6729). A spot for locals who want good, reasonably priced lunches in a simple atmosphere. Sidewalk tables for sunny dining (except when it rains of course, smarty). Breakfast specials about $5, pick-your-ingredients sandwiches $3-5, lentil curry $6, pasta $8.50. Open M-F 7am-5pm, Sa-Su 8am-2pm.

**Salvatore's Café,** corner of Knuckey and Smith St (☎8941 9823). Popular for breakfast, but the real catch is the fresh pasta ($10). Open daily 7am-11pm.

**Pee Wee's at the Point,** at East Point Reserve (☎8981 6868). 4km from Darwin city. Spectacular ocean views and classy outdoor dining for a special evening. Mains $20; the "Better Than Sex White Chocolate Mudcake" is pretty damn close ($7.50). Open M-Tu 6pm-midnight, W-F 11am-2pm and 6pm-midnight, Sa 6pm-midnight, Su 11am-2pm.

**Major's,** on Mitchell St (☎8941 5741). Across from the Transit Centre. A popular place after a night of heavy boozing to sip $2.50 café lattes, chomp on overpriced breakfasts, and people-watch. Open 24hr.

# ◉ SIGHTS

Darwin's own attractions justify a diversion here even for travelers who are raring to hit Kakadu and Litchfield. Most sights are around Darwin's center, and even the more distant points are accessible by foot, bike, or a short public bus ride. The less industrious can take the **Tour Tub.** This trolley, popular with seniors, rounds up passengers at major accommodations or at the corner of Smith and Knuckey St and herds them to 10 popular sights from Stokes Hill Wharf to East Point Reserve. (☎8981 5233. Runs daily 9am-4pm. Full-day pass $22.)

# OCTOBER SHOWERS BRING...DEATH? Darwin's placid azure waters are a paradise for would-be swimmers...except that the world's most venomous animal inhabits these beaches from October to late spring. The box jellyfish, mistakenly called the Portuguese Man-O-War, is notable for its four sided box-like shape. From each corner dangles a group of tentacles which can reach 3-4m long. These terrifying weapons can kill victims within three minutes. If you feel tempted to swim in the wet season waters, treatment for a stung victim should involve 1) preventing drowning, 2) dousing the tentacles in vinegar (never alcohol!) to de-activate them, 3) removing the tentacles, 4) resuscitating the victim, and 5) calling a DOC-TOR!!! But, in the end, only abstinence is guaranteed to make the heart beat longer.

NORTHERN TERRITORY

# CENTRAL DARWIN

**AQUASCENE.** Lonely? Darwin's most unusual sight lets you snuggle up to a warm and friendly...fish. Each high tide, you can hand-feed bread to an enormous horde of surprisingly large fishies—watch those fingers—or take in the Scene from the concrete bleachers. Fishing punishable by $10,000 fine. *(28 Doctors Gully Rd. North off Daly St. ☎8981 7837. $5, under 15 $3.30. Call ahead for the feeding schedule or check the "Darwin and the Top End Today" guide.)*

**WWII OIL STORAGE TANKS.** These enormous underground tunnels, originally constructed to hold oil, now host ghostly-lit yet rather mundane WWII photos. ("Here's the 144th Australian Airborne taking a well-deserved break from drill. Here they are building a latrine.") Still, the spooky setting makes a visit worthwhile. *(Along Darwin Harbour, on Kitchener Dr. Open Apr.-Oct. daily 9am-5pm; Nov.-Mar. Tu-F 10am-2pm. $4, children $2.)*

**INDO PACIFIC MARINE.** A pool containing a fascinating ecosystem that is self-sustained (no feeding, no filters) is the main attraction here, but there are also many pretty fish and some (yawn) displays on plate tectonics. At the counter, ask in a hushed voice to see the movie "Sex on the Reef." *(On Stokes Hill Wharf. ☎8981 1294. Open in the Dry daily 9am-5pm; in the Wet M-Sa 9am-1pm, Su 10am-5pm. $14, concessions $12.60, under 14 $5, families $33. Free talks every 30min.)*

# EAST POINT ROAD AND BEYOND

■ **MINDIL BEACH SUNSET MARKET.** A jubilee of arts, crafts, and food, Mindil is the star of Darwin's market scene—heck, of Darwin, period. Outback goods, pottery, and clothes from Bali comprise many of the for-sale items. Make a dinner of samosa, laksa, and fruity ice cream for about $8, and watch the sunset with the rest of Darwin. *(Market active in the Dry Th 5-10pm, additionally June-Sept. Su 4-9pm.)*

■ **THE MUSEUM AND ART GALLERY OF THE NORTHERN TERRITORY.** If you only have time to visit one Darwin museum, this should be it. The seaside building contains comprehensive and intriguing exhibits of Aboriginal artwork and Territorial wildlife, including "Sweetheart," a gargantuan 5m croc famous for sinking fishing boats, though he never killed anyone. Another highlight is the Cyclone Tracy room, capturing the sounds and sights of the devastation. A maritime annex to the museum contains an awful lot of boats. Also part of the museum, the **Fannie Bay Gaol** served as Darwin's main jail from 1883-1979. The marked self-tour leads through eerie, empty rooms where prisoners once slept and where two were executed. *(Main museum is along the shore heading toward Vestey's Beach, away from Darwin; turn left on Conacher St off Gilruth Ave. Gaol is on the right farther up Gilruth, which becomes East Point Rd. ☎8999 8201. Open M-F 9am-5pm, Sa-Su 10am-5pm. Free. Wheelchair accessible.)*

**MINDIL BEACH AND VESTEY'S BEACH.** Prime locales for soaking up UV rays are just off Gilruth Ave. Heading away from downtown, take Smith St past Daly St and turn right on Gilruth Ave at the traffic circle. Mindil Beach is on the left behind the casino, and Vestey's Beach is a few hundred meters past it. The #4 or 6 public bus or city shuttles ($2.80 return) let beach-combers bypass a 30min. walk.

**PARAP MARKET.** Smaller and more mellow than its Mindil sister (and in a shopping mall parking lot), Parap caters to locals seeking fresh fruits and veggies. *(Catch bus #4 to Parap Shopping Plaza. Open Sa 8am-2pm.)*

**EAST POINT RESERVE.** Past the Gaol, away from downtown Darwin, East Point Rd enters the beautiful and tranquil peninsular park. The reserve itself draws city-loathers with an azure coastline, picnic areas, and predator-free swimming in Lake Alexander. You can often spot wallabies, especially in the evening. Admission is free, but there is no public bus into the reserve itself.

**EAST POINT MILITARY MUSEUM.** The huge 25cm-diameter guns at this site of a WWII anti-aircraft station attest to Darwin's efforts. Photos and a video reveal the

**NORTHERN TERRITORY**

decimation the Japanese ultimately wrought upon the city. *(At East Point Reserve, East Point Rd becomes Alec Fong Lim Dr, which leads to the museum. It's a 45min. bike ride from downtown. ☎8981 9702. Open daily 9:30am-5pm. $8, seniors $7, children $4, families $20.)*

**CROCODYLUS PARK.** Crocodylus theme park (which also holds lions, rheas, iguanas, and other assorted critters) doubles as an "educational adventure" and a research center. "Educational adventure" apparently means letting tourists hold baby crocs and look on as the adults (crocs, not tourists) devour hunks of meat. *(Take Local bus #5, then walk 10min. ☎8947 2510. Open daily 9am-5pm. Feedings and tours 10am, noon, 2pm. $19.50, concessions $16, ages 4-16 $10.)*

**DARWIN BOTANIC GARDENS.** Shaded paths wind through different sections of Australian ecosytems: rainforest, mangroves, and dunes. The gardens are old enough to have survived cyclones in 1897, 1937, and 1974. This peaceful, uncrowded park is an ideal picnic spot. *(Just past Mindil Beach, on the opposite side of Gilruth Ave; another entrance is on Geranium St off the Stuart Hwy. Free. Wheelchair accessible.)*

**CHARLES DARWIN NATIONAL PARK.** Soothing walking trails, picnic areas, and inspirational views of Darwin Harbour lie in wait at this underappreciated wetlands treasure. *(Bennett St eastbound becomes Tiger Brennan Dr. Follow this for 5km to the park entrance on the right. ☎8947 2305. Open 7am-7pm. Free.)*

**AUSTRALIAN AVIATION HERITAGE CENTRE.** This hangar's collection of old aircraft is crowned by an old American B-52 bomber. *(On the Stuart Hwy, in Winnellie.☎8947 2145. Open daily 9am-5pm. $11, children $6, concessions $9.50, families $28.)*

# 🟤 ACTIVITIES

Darwin, at least in the Dry, basks between sunny skies and blue waters. **Scuba diving** is popular; certified divers can rent equipment to explore sunken vessels in the harbor. While Darwin's waters teem with box jellyfish during the Wet, divers are usually safe farther from shore. To get out, try **Coral Divers** (☎8981 2686; charters $50; certification course $425) or **Cullen Bay Dive** (☎8981 3049). **Biking** is a convenient way to explore Darwin. A 45min. bike path extends from Darwin City all the way out to East Point Reserve. Take Mitchell St away from town; the bike path starts on the other side of the roundabout. Many hostels rent bikes ($15 per day).

For a vertical challenge, visit ▨**The Rock,** on Doctor's Gully Rd next to Aquascene. In the bowels of an old oil tanker, this climbing gym has an impressive variety of straight wall climbs, cracks, and overhangs for climbing connoiseurs. (☎8941 0747. Open daily 10am-8:30pm. Unlimited-length sessions $10; harness rental $3; shoe rental $4.) The truly wild at heart can go sky diving with **Pete's Parachuting** (☎(1800) 64 11 14; $289). **Parasailing** with **Odyssey Adventures** provides breathtaking aerial views for breathtaking prices. Sunset flights run Jun.-Sept.; book ahead. (☎(0418) 89 19 98. Single $65; tandem $60; about 10min. in the air.)

# 🎵🌺 ENTERTAINMENT AND FESTIVALS

You can blow your bus fare at the 24hr. **MGM Grand Casino** (☎(1800) 89 11 18). Feel slightly better about your value proposition at the **Darwin Cinema Centre,** 76 Mitchell St, which shows recent mainstream flicks. (☎8981 3111. $13, concessions $9.50.) If you're looking for something original, the infinitely more interesting ▨**Deckchair Cinema** shows offbeat, artsy films (many foreign) under the stars in a sunken amphitheater. Heading away from Darwin Harbor on Bennett St, turn right on McMinn and left on Frances Bay Dr. The cinema is 100m down on the right. Walking takes 20min., but go in groups or call the shuttle. (☎8981 0700. Dry season only. W-Su 7:30pm, additional shows F-Sa around 9:30pm. $11, concessions $9.)

Darwin has several venues for **theater.** The **Darwin Entertainment Centre,** 93 Mitchell St, between Peel and Daly St, with an imposing coral facade, hosts the noteworthy events. Call the box office for same-day 50% discounts and free shows. (☎8981 1222. Open M-F 10am-5:30pm.) The **Botanic Gardens Amphitheatre** has open-air theater in the midst of the lush gardens. **Brown's Mart,** 12 Smith St (☎8981 5222), near Bennett St, features local productions in one of Darwin's oldest buildings.

On the second and fourth Fridays of every month, the **Top End Folk Club** meets at 8pm at The Rock on Doctor's Gully Rd (see **Activities and Festivals,** above). For the buzz on all this biz, flip through the *NT News* or *Pulse*. Many bars also have live bands, especially on weekend nights.

Darwin celebrates the Dry season with a number of festivals. The **Darwin Beer Can Regatta,** held off Mindil Beach in early August, is decidedly not dry. Teams of devout beer-chuggers use their empties to construct vessels fit for America's Cup competition and race them across the harbor. In alternating Mays (the next being 2001), the **Arafura Sports Festival** brings athletes from all over the Pacific Rim to compete in 26 sports. On the second Sunday of June (June 10, 2001), the Greek population of Darwin stages the **Glenti Festival,** a musical and culinary event, on the Esplanade. Ask the tourist office for an **Aussie Rules Football** schedule; March holds several important competitions. Alas, when the Dry draws near its close in mid-August, Darwin goes for broke with the 17-day **Festival of Darwin.**

# ◪ NIGHTLIFE

Darwin has a *big* bar scene. People go out every night, and they go out late. The late-night booze scene caters primarily to backpackers and tourists, so a genuine flavor of "local Darwin" is difficult to locate. Many clubs offer specials to allure good-looking, scantily-clad backpackers; these places make themselves obvious with posters and brochures. Pubs and clubs with a little more character are farther out of the way.

Clubs are required by law to charge at least $5 cover after midnight F-Sa nights. Few exceed that or charge a cover on any other night. The distinction between pub and club blurs, as most pubs have a dance floor of varying crowdedness.

**◪ Lizards Outdoor Bar and Grill,** on Daly St (☎8981 6511). At the corner of Mitchell St. An outdoor bar at its very best, Lizards's patio is a haven of lush palm trees and good, live music (Th-Su). Half-pints $2.50. M: $6 jugs and free nibblies. F: great Latin band. Open M-Th 3pm-1am, F-Sa noon-2am, Su noon-midnight, with flexible closing hours.

**Nirvana,** on Smith St (☎8981 2025). Near Peary St. For only the price of a drink and some bar munchies, the upscale Southeast Asian restaurant Nirvana hosts a Tuesday jam session and Th-Sa jazz (for you to chill and think About a Girl). Music 9pm-1am)

**Discovery,** 89 Mitchell St (☎8942 3300). This new nightclub is popular with locals and backpackers. Theme nights range from retro to dance, and 80s tunes are always around. Cover every night $5-8; try to get a discount coupon at the door. Open W-Sa 8pm-4am. Next door, the **Lost Arc** is the place to drink, talk, and listen to live acoustic music. (Indiana Jones doesn't sing lead.) Open M-Th 10am-2am, F-Sa 10am-4am.

**Shenannigans Irish Pub,** 69 Mitchell St (☎8981 2100). A good, friendly, crowded place. Live music draws locals and backpackers to this hotspot packed with a boisterous, primarily male crowd. Irish music twice per week, rock music the other nights. Guinness or Kilkenny $5.70. Happy Hour F 4-6:30pm. Open M-Sa 10am-2am, Su noon-2am.

**Squires,** 3 Edmund St (☎8981 9761). Off Smith St behind Woolworth's. The place to go for a no-frills beer and a game of pool away from the backpacking hordes. W and F 5-7pm "Topless waitstaff"—leave the kids at home. Quarter pints $2.60, $1.60 during daily Happy Hour 12:30-1:30pm and 5-6pm. Open daily 11am-4am. Next door is **Time,** Darwin's original dance club, swinging with techno and 80s. Gay- and straight-friendly. Drafts and spirits around $5. Cover $5, occasionally $10. Open Th-Sa 10pm-4am.

**Rorke's Drift,** 46 Mitchell St (☎8941 7171). A mix of the backpackers scamming on the dance floor and placid middle-aged couples. The chintzy Wild West diorama doesn't really gel with the occasional male stripper. Open M-Sa 10am-2am, Su 11am-2am.

**The Victoria Hotel,** 27 Smith St Mall (☎8981 4011). But where's the hotel? Welcome to the sexually charged and raunchy outback-meets-blitzed-backpacker scene. At the Vic, skinny, sweaty travelers elbow their way into a dense crowd of Territorians. **Settlers** pub downstairs serves beer ($3.60, jugs $7.60) in a rough and rustic atmosphere. Live music every night. Open M-F 10am-4am, Sa 11am-4am, Su noon-4am. Upstairs **Banjo's** dancing and pool tables draw backpackers. Open M-F 11am-4am, Sa-Su 7pm-4am.

**Kitty O'Sheas,** on Herbert St (☎8941 7947). On the corner of Mitchell St. The Emerald Isle may be thousands of miles away, but the spirit of the Irish lives on in this relaxed, cavernous timber bar. Friendly staff serves a frigid Guiness ($5.40). Th-F: live Irish music; Sa: cover band. Cover $5 after midnight F-Sa. Open daily 11am-4am.

**Hippy Club,** on Mitchell St (☎8981 6511). South of Daly St. A relative newcomer, this club doesn't stick too strictly to its claimed allegiance, leavening the expected flower power with a healthy dose of 80s music. Far stricter dress code than Woodstock. Open Tu-Th 8pm-2am, F-Sa 8pm-4am.

**Blue Heeler Bar** (☎8941 7945). Near the corner of Mitchell and Herbert St. Farm tools, horse saddles, and tractor wheels create a strange mix with the bad, bad karaoke. Live music draws locals and backpackers Th-Su nights. $6 jugs and free dinners (with a drink purchase) keep 'em happy. Open daily 10am-2am.

# 🦅 OFF THE COAST: THE TIWI ISLANDS

In the Timor Sea, 80km north of Darwin, lie the Tiwi Islands, **Melville** and **Bathurst.** Melville is Australia's second biggest island, ranking behind only Tasmania. Together, the Tiwis represent 8000 square kilometers of Aboriginal-owned tropics. The main attractions are remoteness, contemporary Aboriginal communities, and relaxing beaches. **Tiwi Tours** (☎(1800) 18 36 30) and **Aussie Adventures** (☎(1800) 81 16 33) book pricey $300 tours, but they are the only way to see the islands.

## THE STUART HIGHWAY OUT OF DARWIN

The Stuart Hwy swings east and south out of Darwin through the town of **Palmerston,** which has been titled the "fastest-growing city in Australia." The highway connects Darwin to Adelaide and divides the continent in two. The first important junction is with the **Arnhem Hwy,** 33km south of Darwin. From here, the Arnhem Hwy heads east into some of the wildest wetlands in Australia (see **Kakadu,** p. 257). The Stuart Hwy continues south toward the towns of **Adelaide River** and **Katherine** (p. 270) and the Outback beyond.

About 25km south of Darwin off the Stuart Hwy is the turn-off for **Howard Springs Nature Park.** Once used as a WWII rest and recreation military camp but now popular among local civilians, the springs offer swimming (with barramundi) and a short 30min. nature hike. (☎8983 1001. Open daily 8am-8pm. Free.) About 10km farther south on the Stuart Hwy is the turn-off for **Cox Peninsula Rd,** which leads 11km west to **Territory Wildlife Park** and another 50km to **Litchfield National Park** (see p. 268). A cross between a large zoo and Jurassic Park, Territory Wildlife Park encompasses 400 hectares of various habitats and is a top-notch Top End experience. Visitors can enjoy direct contact with all sorts of marsupials, an enclosed tunnel aquarium, the Birds of Prey presentation, a reptile pavilion, and a house for nocturnal critters. Oh yes, emus too. (☎8988 7200. Open daily 8:30am-6pm, last admission at 4pm. $18, concessions $9, families $40.) **Darwin Day Tours** will take you

**FRESHIES AND SALTIES** The Top End has two different kinds of crocodiles: the freshwater crocodile, *Crocodylus johnstoni,* and the saltwater crocodile, *Crocodylus porosus,* which can live in fresh or salt water. It is easiest to learn the difference between "freshies" and "salties" through association. Salties are significantly larger than freshies and have rounded snouts, whereas freshies have narrow snouts. When you see a sign about freshies, it will probably refer to minimum risk and warn you merely to be cautious, since freshies nip only when provoked. When you see a sign about salties, it will most likely refer to death or danger and tell you to stay out—salties eat humans. Freshies have to mind the distinction, because salties eat freshies too. That's why many areas inhabited by salties don't have freshies. Or swimmers.

there as well. (☎8981 8696. Departs daily 7:30am. $46.) After animal gazing, relax the muscles 1km down the road at **Berry Springs Nature Park** with picnic spots and lukewarm soaking grounds. (Open daily 8am-6:30pm. Free.)

About 80km south of Darwin, 6km north of the turn-off for **Batchelor** (see p. 268) and 7km down an access road lies **Lake Bennett Resort,** which juxtaposes placid seclusion with the amenities of a suburban neighborhood. The recently refurbished resort provides immaculate facilities next to Lake Bennett. Swim, canoe, or fish in the water, and afterward have a game of golf before watching the sunset. Guest rooms include fridge, A/C, and TV, with shared bath and kitchen facilities. The affable staff will meet Greyhound bus travelers at the Stuart Hwy. (☎8976 0960. Tent sites $8 per person; twins and doubles $134; triples $158. Canoe hire 1hr. $15, $40 per day; BYO fishing and golf gear. All activities open to day visitors.)

# THE TOP END

A lush tropical crown atop a vast interior desert, the winterless Top End enjoys perpetually warm weather; like in other extreme northern parts of Australia, seasons here are divided only into the "Wet" monsoonal season and the semi-desertlike "Dry." Backpack-toting pilgrims descend on Darwin and use this oasis of civilization as a base from which to explore the region's prime natural wonders—Kakadu and Litchfield National Parks.

While very few do, brave souls who venture to the Top End during the November to May Wet may be rewarded with natural vibrance. Torrential rains drench the reddish dust and spark the growth of a velvet green blanket of vegetation, and mozzies (mosquitoes) become a bona fide weather pattern. Top Enders are openly willing to share their vast home for half the year, but they also seem to rejoice when their fierce outback spirit thrives in the face of nature's challenge as the rain drives out the trespassers.

## TOP END WETLANDS

Intersecting the Stuart Hwy 33km southeast of Darwin, the **Arnhem Hwy** glides for 120km through the **Adelaide** and **Mary River Wetlands** before hitting **Kakadu National Park.** During the Dry, these wetlands are a lush sanctuary for birds and crocs; during the Wet, much of the area floods into a virtual lake. The **Fogg Dam Conservation Reserve,** 25km east of the junction of the Stuart and Arnhem Hwy and 10km north on an access road, is a breathtaking yet peaceful spot to view the winged inhabitants of the area. No patience or binoculars is needed: flocks of cormorants, geese, herons, storks, egrets, and ibises fill the air with bird-song. The **Window on the Wetlands Visitor Centre** is another 4km east on the Arnhem Hwy. The out-of-place space-age design does little to disguise the fact that its mammoth windows provide stunning views of...a field. (☎8988 8188. Open daily 7:30am-7:30pm.)

Jumping crocodiles, Batman! Three kilometers farther east on the Arnhem Hwy is one of the Top End's overdone tourist experiences, the **Adelaide River Queen Jumping Crocodile Cruise.** Giving new meaning to takeaway cuisine, boat attendants dangle chunks of raw pork over the water and pester saltwater crocs until they give up and "jump" for the bait. The crocs' athleticism is impressive, but the whole spectacle is slick and off-putting. (☎8988 8144. 1½hr.; daily May-Aug. 9, 11am, 1, 3pm; Sept.-Apr. 9, 11am, 2:30pm. $31, children $18. Wheelchair accessible.) **AAT King's** (☎(1800) 07 71 86) and **Darwin Day Tours** (☎(1800) 81 16 33) run day tours from Darwin to the cruise site and other attractions (about $100, including cruise).

**Annaburroo Billabong,** 1km down an access road off the Arnhem Hwy, provides a genuine respite from modern civilization. More than 100 years ago, buffalo hunters established a homestead by this freshwater, "saltie free" oasis. The campground and rustic accommodations retain a timeless air. The billabong is home to five or six harmless "freshies" and offers swimming and canoeing. (☎8978 8971. Entrance fee $2; camping $7 per person; cabins for 2 $48, each extra person $10.) Across the highway, the touristy **Bark Hut Inn and Caravan Park** offers hot meals, baked good-

**IS IT WET HERE OR IS IT JUST ME?** Aboriginals, long acquainted with wildly diverse climatic patterns, break the year into six seasons. **Gunumeleng,** from mid-October to late-December, is the "whisper of the Wet," which comes in the form of drenching afternoon thundershowers punctuated by the greatest frequency of lightning strikes on the planet (an average of 10,000 per month Nov.-Jan.). Landscape browned by the Dry turns green again amid high temperatures and oppressive humidity. From January to March, the "real" Wet season—**Gudjewg**—brings monsoon rains with enormous amounts of water, peaked humidity, and green land with gushing waterfalls. While the ubiquitous spear grass shoots up 3m, the animals that live on the ground can get trapped in the swollen waterways. April comes, and with it **Banggerreng,** the "knock 'em down" storm season where the first glimpses of sunny skies peek through the clouds. The beginning of dry times is the cool **Yegge,** May to mid-June, when the wetlands begin to recede, leaving fields of water lilies in their wake. The coldest weather comes in **Wurrgeng,** from mid-June to mid-August. With no rains to replenish the floodplains, the land dries out and turns brown. This season slips into **Gurrung,** full of heat but little water, the end of which is signaled in October by the return of the thunderclouds of Gunumeleng.

ies, and simple accommodations with shared facilities. (☎8978 8988 or ☎8978 8932. Open daily 6am-9pm. Sites for 2 $13.50, powered $18; singles $33; doubles $50.) The **Shady Camp Billabong,** 19km farther east and 54km north on a mostly unsealed access road, is crawling with salties and mozzies (mosquitoes). It also has some of the best barramundi fishing in the Top End—the reason brave souls venture to camp there (no established accommodations available).

# KAKADU NATIONAL PARK

When the Aboriginal spirit Warramurrungundji set out on her daunting task to create much of Kakadu National Park, she had an immense vision. At 19,804 square kilometers, Australia's largest national park contains six distinct ecosystems, four river systems, abundant wildlife, and dozens of Aboriginal outstations and sacred sites where Aboriginal lifestyle and ceremony are still vibrantly practiced and protected. If you came to the Territory to get off the beaten track, to see a more primitive Australia, Kakadu is the place.

Kakadu's haunting landscape does at times appear deliberately created. With its burnt-cinnamon earth and blue-blanket sky (in the Dry, at least), Kakadu presents a surreal cross between the tropics and the desert. Quiet in the eastern stone escarpments and noisy with birds in the wetlands and low-lying woodlands, Kakadu's music is equally dichotomous. The grassy savanna woodlands filled with eucalyptus trees comprise 60% of the park and support the greatest variety of wildlife. Monsoon forests spot the park, and hills and ridges undulate throughout the southern region giving way to the rugged stone country that juts out of the park's eastern border. Floodplains and billabongs surround Kakadu's four major river systems and present a serene expanse of silver and green, while tidal flats and coast in the north offer some of the most diverse flora and fauna.

Intimately intertwined with this awe-inspiring landscape is the living legacy of the Aboriginal community that resides in Kakadu. Aboriginal people have inhabited this land for an estimated 50,000 years and have left the treasure of the world's largest, and possibly oldest, collection of rock art upon the stone escarpments. Aboriginal communities took shelter here during the wet seasons to escape the floods. Today's Aboriginal population in Kakadu has dwindled from its original 2000, recorded when Europeans first came to Australia, to 300. Those remaining live largely in the outlying bush, inaccessible to visitors, but some live in the relative civilization of Jabiru. The number of clans has likewise decreased from 20 to 12, and of the dozen languages once spoken here, only three remain active. "Gagudju," a language spoken here a century ago, lives on in the park's name.

Aboriginal people are active in the management and conservation of the park, and about 30% of the employees in Kakadu are of Aboriginal descent. Half of Kakadu is still owned by its traditional Aboriginal owners, who leased their land to the Australian National Parks and Wildlife Service in 1978. The other half is owned by the commonwealth and is under Aboriginal claim.

## THE SEASONS

Locals say they have a hard time describing Wet Kakadu to Dry season visitors, and vice versa. For most travelers, **the Dry**, from April to October, is the most convenient and comfortable season to visit. Dry highs average 30°C (86°F), lows 17°C (59°F), and the humidity is low. It can get cold at night; travelers should carry an extra layer and repellent to ward off commando mosquitoes. During the Dry, almost all roads are open except for a few unpaved ones early in the season. Check at the Bowali Visitor Centre for road openings (see **Practical Information,** p. 261). Most camping, accommodations, and attractions are also operating.

**The Wet** dramatically alters the landscape of Kakadu with its monsoon rains and floods. Locals insist that the Wet is the most beautiful time of the year, as the land teems with green foliage and flowers. Still, the oppressive humidity, heat—35°C (95°F) highs and 25°C (77°F) lows—and bugs make much of the park inaccessible. The famous falls, particularly Jim Jim and Twin, are at their most powerful but can only be seen from the air. One plus of the Wet—boat cruises are up and running, as the Ubirr drive becomes a river (see **East Alligator** sights, p. 263).

## ⌐ TRANSPORT

Armed with the *Kakadu National Park Visitor Guide and Map*, the most ideal way to do Kakadu is in your own 4WD. However, renting a 4WD can be even more costly than going on a tour. One economical way of getting to the park and its sites without a vehicle is a two-day tour from Darwin with **Greyhound Pioneer** or the **Blue Banana**, which can be expanded to three or more days. Greyhound Pioneer is a good deal for travelers with a Greyhound Kilometer Pass (see **Getting Around,** p. 63). The conductors double as knowledgeable, witty tour guides, and although the visit compresses the main sights without exploring the rugged, remote gems, it does give a memorable dose of Kakadu. The Blue Banana is also very flexible and highly recommended. For more information, see the **Transportation** listing, below.

If you're looking for a more rugged outback experience and have extra time and money, plenty of **tour companies** offer packages. Almost all 4WD operations work out of Darwin. Some rely on lodge accommodations, others camp under the stars, but all encourage more than two to three days to really see the park. **Wilderness 4WD Adventures** specializes in tours with biology-trained guides geared toward fit nature lovers. (☎(1800) 80 82 88. 3-5 days; $365-605.) **Kakadu Dreams** also offers 4WD "safaris." (☎(1800) 81 32 66. 2-5 days; $270-600; recommended age 16-35; max. 9 people.) **Gondwana Adventure Tours and Expeditions** gets kudos for super cheap prices. (☎(1800) 24 21 77. 3-day from $330.) All these tours involve a lot of hiking and hot sun. **AAT Kings** offers slightly less rugged tours of Kakadu in a coach. (☎8941 3844. 3-day; about $600, including indoor lodging.)

**Airport: The Jabiru Airport** (☎8979 2411), 6.5km east of Jabiru on the Arnhem Hwy, is the base for aerial tours of Kakadu. **Kakadu Air** offers bird's-eye **tours** of Kakadu (30min. flights $75, 1hr. $120). Flights during the Wet are popular since many roads close. Courtesy shuttles run between the airport and Jabiru.

**Car Rental: Territory Rent-a-Car** (☎(0418) 85 86 01), has a desk in the Gagudja Croc Hotel on Flinders St, Jabiru. Open M-F 7am-5pm, Sa-Su 7am-noon. Small sedans from $90 per day. **4WD unavailable.** Many people rent cars out of Darwin.

**Transportation: Greyhound Pioneer** (☎13 20 30) and the **Blue Banana** (☎8945 6800) run infrequently to the main sites in Kakadu. Return tickets from Darwin to Katherine via Kakadu

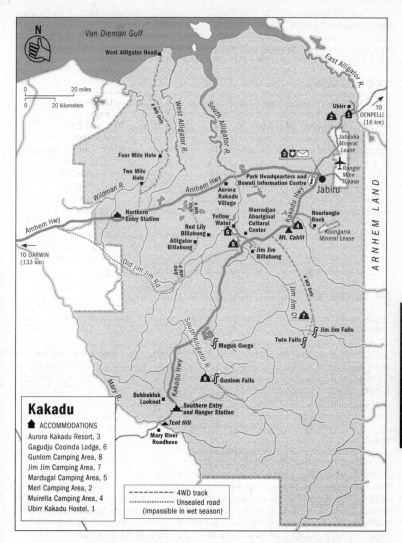

**Kakadu**

🏕 ACCOMMODATIONS
Aurora Kakadu Resort, 3
Gagudju Cooinda Lodge, 6
Gunlom Camping Area, 8
Jim Jim Camping Area, 7
Mardugal Camping Area, 5
Merl Camping Area, 2
Muirella Camping Area, 4
Ubirr Kakadu Hostel, 1

- - - - - 4WD track
·········· Unsealed road
(impassible in wet season)

are about $190. With the Blue Banana, travelers are free to take several weeks to complete the loop. No access to 4WD sites. **Kakadu Park Connection Cooinda** (☎(1800) 80 02 60) offers full-day trips to Jim Jim and Twin Falls ($105). Departs Cooinda at 7am, returns 5pm.

**Hitchhiking:** Kakadu has some extremely desolate roads, so hitching often becomes walking, and is strongly discouraged. However, people have been known to occasionally wait at the head of 4WD access roads to catch a ride to more remote sites. *Let's Go* does not recommend hitchhiking.

**Auto Services:** Diesel and unleaded **fuel stations** are at the Aurora Kakadu Village, Jabiru, Cooinda, the Border Store near Ubirr, and the Mary River Roadhouse at the south entrance. Jabiru's Mobil Station (☎8979 2001) has **auto repair.** Open daily 7am-8pm.

**Entrance Fee:** National Park admission is $16.25 per adult, under 16 free, and is good for 14 days. Pay at the Bowali Visitor Centre near Jabiru (see p. 261). Permit purchase includes the immensely informative *Kakadu National Park Visitor Guide and Map.*

## ⚡ ORIENTATION

**Kakadu National Park** is roughly rectangular. The two entries into the park are the **Arnhem Hwy** in the north, which runs east-west, and the **Kakadu Hwy** in the south, which runs northeast-southwest. These two fully paved roads converge in the park's northeastern interior near the township of **Jabiru** ("jabber-ROO"). They remain open year-round, except during the most severe floods in the Wet.

Kakadu is divided into seven regions. The **South Alligator Region** begins on the Arnhem Hwy eastbound at Kakadu's north gate, 120km east of the junction between the Arnhem and Stuart Hwy. It is marked by the flat woodlands and flood-plains that sprawl around the mighty South Alligator River, and includes the **Aurora Kakadu Village.** After another 81km, the Arnhem highway enters the **East Alligator Region,** and arrives at **Ubirr Rd,** the 39km turn-off to Ubirr Rock, a rock-art site and lookout. Ubirr Rd is the only paved road in the park that is routinely closed in the Wet, when it becomes a virtual river crossing. The junction of the Arnhem and Kakadu Hwy is about 1km past Ubirr Rd in the **Bowali Region.** Just 2km from the junction, tiny and tidy **Jabiru** (pop. 2000) is the primary town in Kakadu Park. It was built in 1982 for $100 million in order to accommodate the Ranger Mine workers and their families. The Arnhem Hwy ends 5km past Jabiru, and a secondary road goes 1km farther to the Jabiru Airport and the Ranger Uranium Mine.

Many of the park's tourist hot spots sit off the Kakadu Hwy. Starting from the junction with the Arnhem, the Kakadu Hwy heads southwest into the **Bowali Region** toward the **Bowali Visitor Centre,** just 2km down the Kakadu Hwy on the right. The turn-off for the **Nourlangie rock art site** and **Nourlangie Region** is 19km farther down the Kakadu, on the left. The paved Nourlangie Rd itself is 12km long and generally open in any season. The **Jim Jim/Twin Falls** turn-off is 20km farther. This 4WD-only road (impassable in the Wet) runs 60km to the Jim Jim Falls and camping area and 10km more to Twin Falls. Its opening day in the Dry season, eagerly awaited by tourists and tour guides alike, can be frustratingly uncertain. Nine kilometers past the Jim Jim/Twin Falls Road, the road to Gagudju Cooinda Lodge and the **Yellow Water Region** turns right off the Kakadu Hwy. This region is noted for the **Yellow Water Wetlands** (only accessible at erratic times during the Wet) and the **Warradjan Aboriginal Cultural Centre.** The south gate of Kakadu is 99km farther on the Kakadu Hwy through the **Mary River Region. Pine Creek** (p. 269) is an additional 59km on the Kakadu Hwy. *The Kakadu National Park Visitor Guide and Map* (available at the entry stations with an entry permit) also contains a reader-friendly map.

**KAKADU IN THE DREAMING** Aboriginals believe that Kakadu, like the rest of the world, was created during the Dreaming, or Creation Time, when the acts and deeds of powerful ancestral beings shaped the land. There are three categories of land in Aboriginal culture: ceremonial sites, *djang* (Dreaming), and *djang andjamun* (Sacred Dreaming). The ceremonial sites are now used for burials, rites of passage, and other events. At *djang* sites, a creator passed through, took shape, or entered or exited the Earth, leaving the site safe to visit. *Djang andjamun* sites, however, where the ancestor still lingers, are considered spiritual hazard zones, such as the 2000 square kilometer "Sickness Country" in the southern part of Kakadu. Laws prohibit entry to the latter group of sites. One of the primary Creation Ancestors in Kakadu is Warramurrungundji, or "Mother of the Earth." She traveled to Kakadu with her husband from the islands to the northeast. Upon arriving, she sent out her spirit children, teaching them various languages and how to hunt and gather, while she herself created river systems, billabongs, and wildlife. Her work completed, she sat down and became a rock. Similar stories involving the acts of ancestral spirits describe the creation of other features. A triangular rock at Nourlangie, for instance, is the stolen feather of a powerful spirit. Because the features of the land are linked to the ancestors, the land is not an inherited possession, but a sacred site.

## ⁊ PRACTICAL INFORMATION

**Tourist Information:** The **Bowali Visitor Centre** (☎ 8938 1120; fax 8938 1123), 2km west of Jabiru on the Kakadu Hwy, is an excellent source of information and a site unto itself. During the Dry, rangers give free daily talks and guided walks at different sites in the park. Open daily 8am-5pm. Wheelchair accessible. Reach the **Park Manager** at P.O. Box 71, Jabiru NT 0886. Outside the park, contact **Parks Australia North** (☎ 8946 4300; fax 8981 3497) at GPO Box 1260, Darwin NT 0801.

**Ranger Stations:** Ranger stations can relay information to the police and clinic from more remote areas, but are open to the public only sporadically (usually daily 8am-4pm, but often called away). **South Alligator Ranger Station** (☎ 8979 0194), 40km west of Bowali Centre near Aurora Kakadu Village; **East Alligator Ranger Station** (☎ 8979 2291), 40km north of Bowali Centre on the Ubirr Rd; **Jim Jim Ranger Station** (☎ 8979 2038), down a 2.5km road that turns off the Kakadu Hwy 45km south of Bowali; **Mary River Ranger Station** (☎ 8975 4578), 1km from the south entry station.

**Potable Water:** At Bowali, Jabiru, Cooinda, and Aurora Kakadu Village. Rangers recommend boiling water from any other source, including the campgrounds listed below.

**Travel Agency: Jabiru Tourist Centre,** Jabiru Plaza (☎ 8979 2548). Open M-F 9:30am-5:30pm, Sa-Su 9am-12:30pm and 3:30-5pm.

**Banks: Westpac Bank,** Jabiru Plaza (☎ 8979 2432), has currency exchange and a 24hr. **ATM.** Open M-Th 9:30am-4pm, F 9:30am-5pm. Cooinda Lodge has **eftpos** but no bank.

**Police: Jabiru Police,** 10 Tasman Crescent (**Emergency ☎ 000**, otherwise ☎ 8979 2122), across the street from **Jabiru Plaza** at the end of Flinders St.

**Health Clinic: Jabiru Community Health Clinic,** Jabiru Plaza (24hr. ☎ 8979 2018). Open M-Tu, Th-F 8am-noon and 1-4pm; W 9am-noon and 1-2:30pm.

**Swimming:** You'll need a cool dip here to soothe away the perma-dust and mozzie bites. The only 100% safe places to swim in Kakadu are the lodge pools and the mighty Olympic size **Jabiru Pool** (☎ 8979 2127; open daily 9am-7pm; $2). People have been known to **swim at their own risk** at Gubara, Jim Jim and Twin Falls, Maguk, Gunlom, Yurmikmik, Gimbat, and Jarrangbarnmi, although freshies do live in these places and salties occasionally enter the area. Check at Bowali for reports of saltie sightings.

**Internet Access: Library,** Jabiru Plaza (☎ 8979 2097). The server is slow. Open M-F 9am-5pm, Sa 9am-noon. 30min. $5.

**Post Office:** in Jabiru News Agency, Jabiru Plaza (☎ 8979 2727). Open Wet M-F 9am-5:30pm, Sa 9am-2pm, Su 9am-1pm, Dry 10am-2pm. **Postal code:** 0886.

**Phone Code:** 08.

## ┌ CAMPING

Camping is one of the best and cheapest ways to enjoy the outdoors in Kakadu. The park runs four large first-come, first-serve campgrounds with showers and toilets ($5.40 per person collected on site in the Dry, at Bowali in the Wet). **Merl Campground,** 4km from Ubirr, has spacious and shady lots made somewhat private by vegetation. In the Dry, ferocious swarms of mozzies make this campground inhospitable (some say uninhabitable). Check about Wet-season access—much of the road to Ubirr is closed in the Wet. The quiet **Muirella Park Campground** is located down a 6km gravel track from the Kakadu Hwy; the turn-off is 21.5km from the intersection with the Arnhem Hwy. Another 5km down a 4WD track is the Sandy Billabong. **Mardugal Campground,** 2km south of Cooinda turn-off on the Kakadu Hwy, is well placed near Yellow Water and the road to Jim Jim and Twin Falls. The relatively mozzie-free **Gunlom Campground** sits 11km from the southern entrance of the park, and 37km farther in on a gravel road. Close to the Gunlom Plunge Pool, it's a popular site. For private, more expensive full-facility campgrounds, try the **Aurora Kakadu Village** and the **Gagudju Lodge Cooinda.**

NORTHERN TERRITORY

The park also has free camping areas for those who want to rough it. These areas offer only the most basic facilities (outhouses) or none at all, but are generally uncrowded. Travelers should bring water. In the South Alligator area, **Two Mile Hole, Four Mile Hole,** and **West Alligator Head** are down an access road off the Arnhem Hwy about 1km east of the north entry station. (Four Mile Hole and West Alligator Head are accessible only by 4WD; this road is impassable in the Wet and early-Dry.) **Red Lily Billabong** and **Alligator Billabong** are also on a 4WD access road that turns off 4km west of the Aurora Kakadu Village. In the Bowali area, **Malabanjbandju** and **Burdulba** are near each other, but accessible only during the Dry via unsealed road. Their turn-offs are about 15km south of Jabiru on the Kakadu Hwy. **Sandy Billabong** in the Nourlangie area is 6km farther past Muirella campground on an unsealed road. **Jim Jim Falls** campsite draws crowds (4WD only). The Yellow Water area has **Black Jungle Spring,** 59km down the unsealed Old Jim Jim Rd (turn-off is 8.5km south of Yellow Water), and **Jim Jim Billabong,** on an unsealed road 3.5km past the Jim Jim Ranger Station (turn-off is 1km north of Yellow Water). In the Mary River area there is free camping at **Maguk,** on a 12km 4WD track 47km south of Yellow Water.

# ▌ ACCOMMODATIONS

Of course, there are more expensive options with four walls and real beds.

**Aurora Kakadu Resort and Caravan Park,** Jabiru (☎ 8979 2422; fax 8979 2254). The frontier never looked this resorty, mate. While lacking in personality, it has an abundance of comfort and cleanliness. A/C, linen and towels, swimming pool, laundry, bistro. There are several options: campsites with access to amenities $10 per person, powered for 2 $25; 4-bed concrete dorms with shared bath, kitchen, and BBQ $28; 5-person ensuite cabins with kitchen $175; lodge rooms $115. Wheelchair accessible. Book ahead.

**Gagudju Lodge Cooinda (YHA),** Cooinda (☎ 8979 0145; fax 8979 0148). Pricey motel rooms, crowded campgrounds, and budget rooms in a cul-de-sac of trailers. 2-bed budget rooms with A/C are compact but spotless. Shared bath, fridge, laundry, and coin-op BBQ. Reception daily 6am-10:30pm. Sites $9.50 per person, powered $12.50; budget rooms $25, non-YHA $30.50; motel rooms $ one arm + one leg. Book ahead in Dry.

**Kakadu Hostel** (☎ 8979 2232). 2km south of Ubirr. This hostel is more worn than just around the edges and has thin walls and no locks on the dorms. But it is laid-back, close to Ubirr, and cheap. Above-ground pool, laundry, kitchen. Dorms have A/C; twins and doubles have fans. All beds $18.

# ◖ FOOD

Kakadu is known for the game in the bush, not on the plate. Dining options, and groceries outside Jabiru, are sparse and expensive; bringing food is recommended. Prepared food in Kakadu is non-descript, meaty, or fried. The **Jabiru Café** in the shopping plaza has reasonably priced fare that provides a welcome respite from cereal and Vegemite sandwiches. (☎ 8979 2570. Open M-F 7:30am-4:30pm, Sa-Su 9am-2pm.) There are basic cafés and bistros at the Aurora Kakadu Resort, Aurora Kakadu Village, and Cooinda. The **supermarket** is in Jabiru plaza (☎ 8979 2077). Simple groceries can also be bought for big bucks at the **Border Store** in Ubirr (☎ 8979 2474; open daily 8:30am-5:30pm), or at the store in the **Gagudju Lodge Cooinda** (open daily in the Dry 6am-9pm, Wet 6am-7:30pm). The Border Store also has a BBQ that features barra, buffalo, or croc burgers (all around $7).

# ◉ ▲ SIGHTS AND HIKES

A natural and cultural wonderland, Kakadu offers a variety of well-established sights for nature lovers and history buffs. Several different short, marked, and relatively tame walking trails leave from the major sights; a few are wheelchair acces-

> # BURN, BABY, BURN! During the Dry, the horizon frequently billows with the purple-gray smoke of bush fires. Don't panic or call ☎ 000: Aboriginals have been using controlled bush burning for thousands of years for a variety of reasons such as hunting, communication, ceremony, and horticulture. Under the guidance of Aboriginal people, Kakadu National Park continues to widely and successfully use bush fires for, ironically, fire management. Burning is done in small patches during the Wet and early Dry season in order to prevent the build-up of thick undergrowth which could provide fuel for devastating late Dry season fires. Although Aboriginal people used to light bush fires by hand, this method has been replaced by high-tech satellite imagery and plane-dropped fire bombs. Seeing a bush fire up close is an eerie experience, especially at night. Bright orange tongues of flame devour the bases of trees and small plants, generating a thick, organic odor and a distinct crackling sound.

sible. A number of excellent, longer walks reward the fit and adventurous who choose to venture farther out into the bush.

All sights and walks are open during the Dry; many are subject to closure during the Wet, so check at the Bowali Visitor Centre for an update. The park brochure is a good supplement for descriptions and directions. Bring lots of water (at least 1L for every hour of walking), insect repellent, sunscreen, and sturdy shoes. Snakes and spiders live in these areas—long trousers and thick socks will help protect against bites. Salties are also common, so never swim or wade in water sources and stay away from the water's edge. For more detailed descriptions of these walks, check out *Kakadu By Foot* ($3) in the Bowali Visitor Centre.

For experienced hikers, unmarked and **overnight bushwalks** are the most genuine way to see Kakadu. These routes generally follow the creek lines and gorges along the escarpment. Routes and campsites on unmarked walks must be approved. For overnight camping permits and route plan approval, contact the Bowali Visitor Centre by phone, mail, or in person (see **Practical Information,** p. 261). Permits are free but require one week for processing. The Bowali Visitor Centre also sells topographic maps of Kakadu ($8).

**SOUTH ALLIGATOR REGION. Mamukala Wetlands** is a floodplain and bird-watching area off the Arnhem Hwy 8km east of the South Alligator River crossing and 1km down an access road. A 100m wheelchair-accessible path leads to a lookout where patient ornithologists can observe snowy egrets and Jabiru storks hunting for food. In late August and September, the plain comes to life as 25,000 *bamurru* (magpie geese) descend upon it. The birdhide and 3km circular trail are lackluster, though. The **Gungaree Walk** (3.6km; 2hr.) leaves from the Aurora Kakadu Village, extending through monsoon forests and skirting a billabong.

During the driest of the Dry, an 80km 4WD track 1km east of the northern entry station extends out to **Van Diemen's Gulf** (no swimming; the sea here is full of strange creatures). **West Alligator Campsite** is great for wildlife viewing at the coast. The 4WD, Dry-season-only road to **Red Lily and Alligator Billabong,** 4km west of the Aurora Kakadu Village, grants a glimpse of Kakadu at its most pristine. Check at the Bowali Visitor Centre for all road conditions.

**EAST ALLIGATOR REGION.** Because of the flooding of the Magela Creek, this area becomes restricted in the Wet. The gem of the East Alligator region is **Ubirr,** a collection of sandstone outliers on which Aboriginal ancestors created rock-art thousands of years ago. A wheelchair accessible circuit (1km; 1hr.) passes significant sights such as the **Namarrgarn Sisters,** which tells the story of the appearance of crocodiles, and the **Main Gallery,** which displays several different layers of rock art. A steep, rocky climb (250m; 30min.) leads to the top of Ubirr, with a spectacular view of the distant stone escarpment and the emerald floodplains. Sunsets on top of Ubirr are magical, but be prepared to share the experience with chattering tourists. Ubirr is open daily during the Dry 8:30am-sunset, conditionally during the Wet 2pm-sunset.

The **Bardedjilidji Sandstone Walk** (2.5km; 2hr.) through weathered sandstone pillars, arches, and caves is highly recommended; some of the sandstone cliffs are believed to have been formed over 1.5 billion years ago. From the base of the formations, tree roots extending 20m down the jagged cliffs to the ground are visible. The second half of the walk passes a small billabong and river. The trailhead is at the end of an access road a short distance from the campground turn-off. The **Rockholes** sandstone and riverside walk (6.5km), branching off Bardedjilidji, is moderately challenging and leads past floodplains and billabongs, arriving at the deep rocky pools of the sandstone outliers. The **Manngarre Monsoon Rainforest Walk** (1.6km; 1hr.) departs from the downstream boat ramp across from the Border Store for a primarily flat circular walk through monsoon rainforest. The trail comes close to the river banks here and there, and crocs can be spotted at low tide. The walk is only accessible in the Dry.

The **Cahills Crossing Picnic Area** features a wildlife viewing platform that is best used to watch (and laugh at) cars crossing the river when it is too deep to safely do so. The popular **Guyluyjambi Aboriginal Culture Cruise** journeys up the East Alligator River, providing insight into Aboriginal culture and tranquil views of the stony cliffs in the area. The tour runs from the upstream boat ramp near Ubirr. (☎8979 2411. 1¾hr.; May-Oct. daily 9, 11am, 1 and 3pm; $29.) A free shuttle connects to the Border Store and Merl Camping Area. Call for wet season tour times and bookings.

**BOWALI REGION.** The **Bowali Visitor Centre** is a good place to start a tour of the park, but most sights here are man-made. A captivating 8-screen slide-show displays the stunning visual beauty of the park; don't get caught up in the virtual because the real is right outside. The **Illigadjarr Walk** (3.8km; 2hr.), leaving from the Malabanjbanjdju or Burdulba camping areas, is Kakadu's unappreciated sunset spot. Wide-ranging grassy floodplains, flocks of snow-white egrets, the sky aflame, the Arnhemland Escarpment in the distance, and not another soul within sight: this is Kakadu. Far to the east, past the airport, the **Ranger Uranium Mine** is the most active such mine in Kakadu. (☎(1800) 08 91 13. Tours depart May-Oct. daily from the Jabiru Airport 10:30am, 1:30pm; $17; reservations essential.)

**NOURLANGIE REGION.** The principal pull of this part of the park is **Nourlangie** itself, a huge rock outlier used as a shelter and art studio by earlier Aboriginals. A wheelchair-accessible walking track (1.5km) passes the Main Gallery and ascends to a tame lookout. Many mystical images are painted on the walls of Nourlangie, including Nabulwinj-bulwinj, a dangerous spirit who eats females after striking them with a yam. **Anbangbang** rock shelter, formed by a gargantuan boulder leaning perilously over a narrow walkway, steals the show from the artwork. The farthest point on the loop is **Gunwarrdehwarrde Lookout,** a craggy climb with a view of the distant escarpment, where Aboriginals believe Lightning Man Namarrgon lives. The **Barrk Sandstone Bushwalk** (12km; 6-8hr.), one of the longest and most dramatic established walks in the park, branches off from the lookout walk and makes a loop past the sandstone cliffs of the Nourlangie region. Impressive views of surrounding lowlands, many ecosystems, rock art, and an untouristed, quiet atmosphere make it perfect for the curious and fit traveler. The lookout at **Nawurlandja** (600m; 40min.), a rock outlier next to Nourlangie, has the best views of the Nourlangie region. Take the second road to the left after leaving the Nourlangie parking lot. **Anbangbang Billabong** (2.5km; 1hr.), close to Nourlangie Rock, is an easy walk circling the water with delicate lilies and jagged cliffs—but be prepared to share your walk with every bus tourist. Only accessible in the Dry, take the first road to the left after leaving the Nourlangie parking lot. The **Mirrai Lookout** walk (1.8km; 1½hr.) is a short, steep hike leading to vast views of the stone escarpment, Nourlangie rock, and surrounding lowlands. The trail starts on the Kakadu Hwy 11km south of the Nourlangie turn-off. The **Gubara Pools Walk** (6km; 4hr.) passes dramatic rock outcroppings and peaceful forest pools. Leave the Nourlangie car park and take the first right 9km to the trailhead. The shorter **Nanguluwur walk** (2hr.) is 3.4km on the western side of Nourlangie rock. It passes several gal-

NORTHERN TERRITORY

leries of impressive ancient and modern rock art depicting non-Aboriginal settlers. Take the first right after Nourlangie car park.

**JIM JIM/TWIN FALLS REGION.** Perhaps the most beloved and most elusive sights in the park lie deep in this region. **Jim Jim Falls,** 59km up a tough road, cascade 150m down into a deep, clear green pool. Shy Jim Jim is not visible for much of the year—by late June its waters have decreased to a hesitant trickle; in the Wet, the falls rush with roaring intensity. However, the same rains that cause the awesome spectacle also prevent road access to it; the only way to see the falls during the Wet is by air. There is a lookout 20min. from the carpark. A boulder-ridden walk (1km) leads to the plunge pool, where a dip in the cool water will help ease the pain of the walk. Over the river (you must have a decent 4WD for this crossing) and 10km through the woods is **Twin Falls.** They are spectacular—two roaring cataracts down a steep cliff—but you'll have to earn the view; it is a 400m walk and a 500m swim or paddle (canoes reserved for tour groups; bring your inflatable flotation device if you don't want to get wet) up a narrow gorge to the plunge pool. Both Jim Jim and Twin are home to freshies, which tend not to bother people, although an occasional saltie makes its way into the pools. Swim at your own risk. The unheralded treasure of the region, though, is the stunning ■**Barrk Marlam walk** (3km; 4-6hr.), which branches off the path to Jim Jim Falls. It is a rugged one-way, straight up and across the escarpment, but the enjoyable exertion of the climb is dwarfed by the jaw-dropping, eye-bugging views of the gorge from the top.

**YELLOW WATER REGION.** Yellow Water, part of Jim Jim Creek, is the most popular billabong in Kakadu—not to swim in, but to cruise past meters-long crocodiles sunning themselves on the banks or floating ominously on the surface of the water. It is also famous for its less-threatening wildlife, visible on a circular walk (1.5km)—Jabiru storks, pied geese, and ducks pretend not to notice the clanking noise of the metal walkway. There's also a wheelchair-accessible platform to view the billabong. Still, the most popular way to do Yellow Water is on a **Yellow Water cruise,** where knowledgeable guides point out the variety of birds and the occasional croc. In the end, viewing Kakadu from a powerboat is a bit like watching a videotape of a sunset, so skip the hand-holding and get out on the trail! (☎8979 0111. In the Dry, 1½hr. and 2hr. tours each depart 3 per day; $29, $34. In the Wet, 1½hr. tours run every 2hr. 7am-5pm.)

Far more enlightening is the ■**Warradjan Aboriginal Cultural Centre,** 1km from the Cooinda Lodge, which shows visitors Kakadu's Aboriginal history. Built in the shape of a *warradjan* (turtle), the center contains fantastic displays of Aboriginal culture, ranging from tools and rock art to biographies of significant local figures. The exhibit is refreshing after being assaulted by repetitive, disconnected Aboriginal trivia on the trail. It concludes with moving statements by local Aboriginals on the future of their land and community. (☎8979 0051. Open daily 9am-5pm; free.)

**MARY RIVER REGION.** This is the land where the rivers begin. In the headwaters of the South Alligator River, a series of falls called **Gunlom** flow rapidly from December to May, but cease almost completely in the Dry. A wheelchair-accessible footbridge leads to the plunge pool, and a steep walk (1km; 1hr.) travels to the top of the falls and a series of enchanting smaller pools. Gunlom is the only escarpment cascade that conventional 2WD vehicles can reach in the dry season via the Gunlom Rd, a stone's throw from Kakadu's southern entry gate. **Maguk,** or **Barramundi Falls,** is a smaller cascade; the 4WD turn-off is located 32km north of the Gunlom turn-off on the Kakadu Hwy. It flows during both seasons and is reached via a 12km road and then a hike (2km; 1-2hr.) through monsoon forest. The **Yurmikmik Walking Tracks** pass Wet-season waterfalls. The trailhead is 21km down the Gunlom Rd off the Kakadu Hwy. There are three different circular day tracks (2km, 45min.; 5km, 2hr.; 7.5km, 4hr.) and two longer tracks which require overnight permits (see below). The 11km walk features a series of waterfalls and the 13.5km walk features plunge pools during the Wet. Both of these longer walks are

NORTHERN TERRITORY

**ANCIENT GRAFFITI** Over 5000 sites of Aboriginal rock art have been noted in Kakadu, most on the escarpment wall, and an estimated 10,000 sites remain undiscovered. The age of the art is difficult to determine, partly because pictures dating back thousands of years sit side-by-side with paintings done in the 1980s. Certain works have been "repainted" by descendants who are familiar enough with the old stories to "retell" them by the brush. Some recovered paintings date to 50,000 years ago, a few depicting extinct animals. Corresponding to the climatic changes that affected prehistoric Aboriginals, there are three general styles identified in the rock art. The pre-estuarine period (50,000-8000 BC) corresponds to a wooded Kakadu with an overall uniform style suggesting a small regional population. The estuarine period (8000-2000 BC), during the bountiful hunting era when the ocean was rising, shows previously unknown animals in an "X ray" art style, which depicts the insides as well as outlines of animals. Booming wildlife meant growing communities, reflected in a rise in artistic diversity. In the freshwater period (2000 BC-present), Aboriginals captured an even greater variety of species with more complex X ray images, eventually adding their own renditions of the first contact with the white colonists. Aboriginals now look to the rock art as a window into the past, and as a written history.

difficult, unmarked, and require good navigation and preparation. Near the Yurmikmik walks lies **Jarrangbarnmi,** one of the *djang andjamun* areas that bring catastrophic consequences if entered. This series of pools on **Koolpin Creek** is home to **Bula** and **Bolung,** two Creation Ancestors. Visitor numbers are restricted, and no one can enter the area without a permit and entry key. These can be organized by the southern entry station (☎8975 4859).

# ARNHEM LAND

Take the expansive wilderness, serenity, and the cultural spirit found in Kakadu, multiply it by ten, and you still won't be able to do justice to Arnhem Land's grandeur. Sprawling across the entire northeastern region of the Top End, and several times the size of Kakadu, this Aboriginal homeland was established in 1931. It remains largely uninhabited, save for four or five small settlements and about 100 Aboriginal outstations. The area's inland borders are cut square, but the endless coastline takes an untamed, jagged path from the Cobourg Peninsula in the west (location of Gurig National Park) to the Gove Peninsula in the east. Arnhem Land also includes the Groote and Elcho islands off-shore. The natural and cultural treasures here are incredible—but be aware that there are Aboriginals who welcome tourism and its revenues, and there are also those who would prefer to see their lands free of swarms of outsiders.

■ **PRACTICAL INFORMATION.** Venturing into Arnhem Land is a serious matter. There are very few roads (those that do exist are erratically navigable only in the Dry), and there are virtually no signs and services. Moreover, Arnhem Land is off-limits by law to non-Aboriginals, so a permit is required to enter. Permits can be applied for by contacting Darwin's **Northern Land Council** (☎8920 5100; fax 8945 2633; P.O. Box 42921, Casuarina NT 0811), or in Jabiru (☎(1800) 64 52 99; fax 8979 2650; P.O. Box 18, Jabiru NT 0886; open M-F 8am-4:30pm). Permits take 7-10 days to process and must be picked up in person at a Northern Land Council office. Even with a permit, travelers can only go to three places in Arnhem Land, and each destination must be paid for and marked accordingly on the permit.

The road into Arnhem Land from Ubirr crosses a tidal river **(Cahills Crossing).** It is very important to check with the Northern Land Council about tidal information before driving or you might find your car tipped over in the saltie-ridden East Alligator River. Driving into Arnhem Land, and especially beyond Injalak, should not

NORTHERN TERRITORY

be taken lightly. People occasionally have breakdowns or get mired in mud or sand, so it's wise to go with at least one other person. Bring a shovel, a kangaroo jack (higher than a normal jack), two spare tires, rope, and plenty of water. Telling the Oenpelli **police** (☎ 8979 0180) where you are going and when you plan to return is also a good precaution; people who live in Arnhem Land feel very responsible and concerned for those who travel in it. Road access into Arnhem Land is impossible during the Wet.

**◨ ⚠ SIGHTS AND ACTIVITIES.** The **Injalak** ("IN-yaluk") **Arts & Crafts Association** is located in Oenpelli (Gunbalanya), a short 16km dirt-road drive from Ubirr. The association has artists working on-site who create exquisite pieces such as pandanus baskets (from $15), limited edition bark and paper paintings (from $30), screen printed textiles, and didgeridoos (from $70). The works are distributed to art galleries around the world, but visitors can purchase pieces on-site. (☎ 8979 0190. Open year-round M-F 8am-noon and 1-5pm, also July-Sept. Sa 8am-noon. Call ahead for Sa.) Injalak also sponsors **Aboriginal-guided tours** through a local rock art gallery whose breadth, beauty, isolation, and rugged terrain put Ubirr and Nourlangie to shame—there are no crowds or roped-off galleries here. (2hr. tours $60; max. 6 people; book ahead.) The Injalak permit costs $12 per person.

Much more remote than Injalak are Sandy Creek and Wunyu Beach. **Sandy Creek,** on Arnhem's north shore, is popular for excellent barramundi, salmon, and tuna fishing. Ideally, anglers should have a boat, though people do fish from the shore. The drive to Sandy Creek (3hr.) is 4WD only. Also on the northern shore is **Wunyu Beach,** a long, virtually untouched, and often windy beach that is ideal for relaxing and strolling. Sunbathers and would-be swimmers beware—the water (and Sandy Creek as well) is teeming with **salties.** The drive to Wunyu takes at least 2½hr. on a 4WD road. Neither Sandy Creek nor Wunyu Beach have facilities, though people do camp at their own risk. Campers must bring their own water, food, and shelter. Stopping on the road to Injalak, Sandy Creek, and Wunyu is prohibited except in an emergency. To go to Sandy Creek or Wunyu with a permit costs $50 per vehicle, and Sandy Creek allows only seven vehicles to enter at a time.

Northern Arnhem Land is the site of **Gurig National Park,** the destination of many Arnhem Land visitors attracted by secluded beaches and wildlife. The park covers 2207 square kilometers of the Cobourg Peninsula and the adjacent islands. Travelers entering the park need a **permit** from the Parks and Wildlife Commission of the Northern Territory. (☎ 8979 0244; 1st floor, Gaymark Building, Palmerston NT 0831. Permits $211 per vehicle; 5 adults max.; includes 7 nights of full-facility camping with toilets and showers; 7-14 nights of camping $411. Number of vehicles allowed restricted.)

**TOURS.** For those seeking experienced guides and drivers, several companies run tours to Arnhem Land or Gurig National Park. Though pricey, multi-day tours can provide the most genuine Arnhem Land experience. **Venture North Australia** travels as far as Cobourg Peninsula on an Arnhem Land/Cobourg Peninsula Safari. The tour includes a stop at Injalak and boat exploration of Gurig National Park. (☎ 8927 5500. Departs from the Border Store in Ubirr. 3-day $530; includes meals and accommodation at Cobourg Beach Huts, permit fees, and fishing equipment.) **Wadda Safaris** four-day camping safari is highly recommended for its Aboriginal guides and remote sights. (☎ (0417) 81 56 82. Departs Tu and F from Katherine.)

One-day tours give a brief, less expensive taste of Arnhem Land, generally focusing on Injalak and the surrounding area. **Wilderness 4WD Adventures** cooperates with **Magela Tours.** (☎ 8941 2161. Departs Jabiru. $200.) **Lord of Kakadu Tours** (☎ 8979 2567; departs Jabiru, the Aurora Kakadu Village, and Cooinda; $165) and **Kakadu Parklink** also run one-day tours (☎ (1800) 08 91 13; departs Aurora Kakadu Resort and Gagudju Crocodile Hotel in Jabiru; $160).

# DOWN THE TRACK

Heading south down the Stuart Hwy from Darwin, the lush vegetation and cinnamon earth of the Top End give way to a deep, barren red that stretches for miles, broken only by occasional rock formations. The increasing desolation is reflected in mirages as well as the visages of stalwart residents who wouldn't trade their piece of "Never Never" for the world. On this stretch between Katherine and Tennant Creek, you'll never feel like you're close to anything. There isn't much to do besides gape at the expanse.

## LITCHFIELD NATIONAL PARK

Although shadowed in size and popularity by Kakadu, Litchfield National Park has natural wonders second to none. The park was established in 1986, and its 146,000 hectares encompass much of the Tabletop Range. Its spring-fed falls and close proximity to Darwin make it a popular daytrip, but its widespread paved access renders the sights more crowded and less wild than its big sibling. Litchfield is beautiful, but it's a more cultured, more catered beauty. Staying for more than the day allows you to explore the more isolated waterfalls, chiseled gorges, rock formations, and bush land plateaus that give Litchfield unique charm.

**GATEWAY TO LITCHFIELD: BATCHELOR.** Batchelor (pop. 350) is the entry point to Litchfield along the sealed Batchelor Rd, coming from the east. McCafferty's **buses** serve Batchelor twice daily from the Caravillage. The **Batchelor Store** supplies **food** and **petrol**. (☎8976 0045. Open M-F 7:30am-7pm, Sa-Su 8am-7pm.) The **post office** is next door. (☎8976 0020. Open daily 9am-7pm.)

Batchelor's sites are limited to a 6m replica of a 600-year-old **Bohemian castle** and a tropical **Butterfly Farm**. (☎8976 0199. Open M-F 9am-5:30pm, Sa 9am-noon. $5.50, children $2.50.) The **restaurant** at the Butterfly Farm has a shady porch (open daily 9am-4:30pm and 6-11pm). The **Batchelor Caravillage** has accommodations. (☎8976 0166. Sites $9, powered $23; cabins for 2 $84.) The **Jungle Drum Bungalows**, next door to the Butterfly Farm, has Balinese decor and a relaxing atmosphere. (☎8976 0555. Few dorms $15; doubles $65 and $85.) The **Banyan Tree Caravan Park**, 12km toward Litchfield, sells food and drinks. (☎8976 0330. Sites $6.)

**▐ TRANSPORT.** **Greyhound** arranges a daytrip three times per week from Darwin. (☎8981 8700. $99.) So does **Aussie Adventures**. (☎8981 1633. $104.) From Batchelor, try **Coo-ee Tours** (☎8981 6116; $105, includes a billabong cruise).

**▰▱ ORIENTATION AND PRACTICAL INFORMATION.** The park is located 100km southwest of Darwin. For paved access, go south on the **Stuart Hwy**, turn right on **Batchelor Rd** 90km out of Darwin, and head toward the park through the town of Batchelor. **Batchelor Rd** becomes the paved **Litchfield Park Rd** at the park boundary and runs to the southwest until it hits Greenant Creek, where it turns to the north, passing **Wangi Falls** and the most popular section of the park. The road becomes unsealed at the northern park boundary and leads 41km to the **Cox Peninsula Rd**, which heads east to Territory Wildlife Park and eventually the Stuart Hwy. A **4WD track** runs to the southern end of the park and the more secluded attractions; the turn-off is just west of Greenant Creek. Litchfield Park Rd is open most of the year to all vehicles; the 4WD tracks close in the Wet. Information is available through the **Parks and Wildlife Commission of the Northern Territory** in Darwin (☎8999 5511) or the ranger station in Batchelor (☎8976 0282). Entry is free, and detailed **maps** ($4.75) are available at the Batchelor Store. Call ☎8976 0282 for **road conditions**, especially during the Wet.

**▐ CAMPING.** Spending a night in Litchfield is highly recommended, if only for the superb stargazing. Camping costs $6.60 per person, payable in honor-boxes at campground entrances. Caravan camping is allowed only at Wangi Falls and generators are not permitted. Coming from Darwin on Batchelor Rd, **Buley Rockhole** is

NORTHERN TERRITORY

a quiet campground on a paved road 30km west of the park entrance. You can wade in small pools in the nearby creek. There are pit toilets, picnic tables, and a BBQ. Just north is **Florence Falls,** with spacious camp spots, flush toilets, showers, and access to the falls. **Tjaynera Falls** (Sandy Creek Falls) lies several kilometers south of the main road on the park's main 4WD track; look for the left turn after Tolmer Falls. Road conditions discourage many visitors, but the bold will be rewarded with pleasant bush camping (Emergency Call Device available). **Surprise Creek Falls** campsite is south on the 4WD track and also has tranquil bush camping and nearby swimming. This section of the park is for experienced 4WD drivers only. Back on Litchfield Park Rd heading north, **Wangi Falls** is more of a circus than a campground, and fills up early in the day. (Full facilities including food kiosk open daily 8am-5pm. Wheelchair accessible.) **Walker Creek**, 15km farther north, is a real gem, featuring private, beautiful riverside campsites strung out along 2km of the creek ($3.30 per person; open only in the Dry).

**⊙ ⚑ SIGHTS AND SHORT WALKS.** The spectacular falls at Litchfield are among the main attractions. At **Wangi** ("wong-GYE"), two dramatic falls plunge into a large, clear pool. Safe, croc-free swimming, a kiosk serving obligatory meat pies, and all of suburban Darwin dragging eskies behind them, combine to make Wangi more of a public beach than anything else. The walking trail (45min. return) to the top of the falls is nondescript; the spots with views are sacred, off-limits Aboriginal sites. The equally dramatic but more secluded **Florence Falls** is a pleasant trail (30min. return) through various habitats before coming to the plunge pool at the bottom of the falls, and culminates in a lookout over the impressive falls and surrounding terrain. A walk (3.2km) through lush monsoon forest connects Florence Falls with **Buley Rockhole,** featuring a number of soothing swimming spots. At **Tolmer Falls,** a short distance southwest from Florence Falls, there is another steep fall plunging from a sandstone gorge. Visitors are not allowed in the gorge due to the gentle ecosystem that is home to Ghost Bats. However, a commanding view awaits from the lookout deck. Next door is **Tjaetaba Falls,** accessible via a fairly steep but rewarding walking track through monsoon forests and eucalyptus woodlands. Tjaetaba is a sacred Aboriginal site; swimming is not permitted. Also worth seeing are the **magnetic termite mounds,** located about 20km down Litchfield Park Rd away from Batchelor. These mounds range in age from 50 to 100 years old, and are aligned so that their broad backs face east-to-west, in order to soak in the softer sunlight of the morning and evening.

For those with 4WD, **The Lost City** is a haunting arrangement of sandstone towers that turns everybody into amateur archaeologists. Early morning, with the structures shrouded in hazy mist and the place to yourself, is spellbinding. It is 10.5km down an access road 40km past the park entrance. The first 9km are fairly easy but are followed by a steep, rocky downhill to the city. Some visitors (wisely) choose to park and walk the last 1.5km. The track continuing on to **Blyth Homestead** is even worse. **Tjaynera Falls** (Sandy Creek Falls) lies about 7km off Litchfield Park Rd on a 4WD-track. A mild trail (1.7km) leads to the plunge pool, matching Wangi's beauty without the noisy crowds. For real seclusion, continue 20km farther on the track to ⧉**Surprise Creek Falls.** The 1hr. drive itself is a fascinating alternation of thick forest and grasslands dotted with ghostly cathedral termite mounds. The falls are typically deserted, and a scramble up the gently-sloping falls to a seat half-submerged in the creek above yields Litchfield's best (and least known) sunset spot.

# PINE CREEK

Bustling it's not, but Pine Creek (pop. 800) is more than a bump in the road. With cheap food and accommodations, Pine Creek is a popular base for nearby Kakadu. To get there, look for the turn on the Stuart Hwy at the junction of the Stuart and Kakadu Hwy. Near the center of town are the old **railway station** and **Miner's Park,** where mining machinery and memorabilia rust in peace. Gold-hungry visitors can go gold panning at **Gun Alley Gold Mining,** at the end of Moule St. (☎ 8976 1221. Open in the Dry daily 8:30am-3pm, in the Wet by appointment. $5.) **Copperfield Dam,** 6km southwest of town on a turn-off road on the Stuart Hwy, has swimming and picnic tables. **Umbrawarra Gorge,** 15km farther down the same turn-off road, is a favorite with locals and reputably better than its Katherine sister.

The **Diggers Rest Motel,** on Main Tce, near the intersection with Baxter Tce, serves as a **tourist center.** (☎8976 1442. Open 8am-8pm.) A few doors down is **Ah Toys,** which serves as the general store and **bus** depot. (☎8976 1202. Open M-F 9am-5:30pm, Sa 9am-12:30pm.) Greyhound and McCafferty's **buses** run to **Darwin** (3hr., 3 per day, $32), and **Alice Springs** (16-17hr., 1 per day) via **Katherine** (1hr.). There is **Internet access** in the library, on Railway Tce. (☎8976 1287. Open M-F 1-5pm. 30min. $2.50.) The **post office,** doubling as a **bank,** is on Moule St one block farther south. (☎8976 1220. Open M-F 9am-noon and 1-5pm.) **Postal code:** 0847.

**Kakadu Gateway Caravan Park,** at the end of Buchanan St off Millar Tce, has plain, clean rooms, A/C, showers, and free laundry. (☎8976 1166. Singles $30; doubles $55; rooms with no beds for up to 3 people $20, each extra person $5; powered caravan sites with bath $15, for 2 $25.) The **Diggers Rest Motel** offers cabins with kitchen, bath, TV, and A/C. (☎8976 1442. Reception daily 8am-8pm. $65, for 2 $75, for 3-5 $85.) The main restaurant is **Famished Café,** on Moule St. (☎8976 1241. Open M-F 7am-8pm, Sa-Su 8am-6pm.)

# KATHERINE

Between Darwin and Alice Springs, the Stuart Hwy covers 1500km with only one stoplight. That stoplight is in the pseudo-metropolis of Katherine (pop. 11,000). What was once a rough-and-tumble town has been refurbished and repainted since a 1998 flood sent 2m of water tearing down the main street, but downtown Katherine can still be rough around the edges, particularly once the sun goes down. Noisy conflict at night—often involving the Aboriginal community—is not unusual. Katherine is a refreshing blast of civilization after the wilderness of the Kimberley or the outback down south, but it is more of a stopover on the way to Alice Springs or Darwin, or a jumping-off point for nearby Nitmiluk National Park. In the end, it reminds one of the good and the bad that come with cities, and encourages one to "head bush" once again.

## ▐ TRANSPORT

The **Transit Centre** on Katherine Tce has Greyhound and McCafferty's **buses** (☎(1800) 08 91 03), and can also book accommodations and tours. Both companies run to: **Darwin** (4hr., 3 per day, $39); **Alice Springs** (15hr., 2 per day, $140); **Broome** (19hr., 1 per day, $189); and **Townsville** (eons, 1 per day, $227). Local car rental places are **Territory,** in the Transit Centre (☎8972 3183); **Hertz,** 392 Katherine Tce (☎8971 1111); and **Delta,** at Knotts Crossing Resort (☎(1800) 81 15 41). **Bike Shop,** on First St just west of Giles St, rents bikes for cheap. (☎8972 1213. Open M-F 9:30am-5:30pm, Sa 9am-1pm. 1hr. $3, half-day $10, full-day $15.)

## ✳ ▐ ORIENTATION AND PRACTICAL INFORMATION

The Stuart Hwy becomes **Katherine Tce** in town; most shops and services are here. The **Victoria Hwy** heading to the Kimberley leaves from the northern end of town, and the **Transit Centre** (for Greyhound and McCafferty's buses) is in the south, near **Lindsay St.** The Woolworth's shopping mall is on the southern end of Katherine Tce, diagonal from the Transit Centre. **Giles St** heads east from the middle of town, and goes out to **Nitmiluk National Park.** Parallel to Katherine Tce to the east, **First** through **Fourth Streets** support various tourist accommodations.

**Katherine Region Tourist Association,** on the corner of Lindsay St and Katherine Tce, across from the Transit Centre, is more impartial than the travel desk in the Transit Centre. (☎8972 2650; fax 8972 2969. Open in the Dry M-F 8:30am-6pm, Sa-Su 10am-3pm; in the Wet M-F 9am-5pm, Sa-Su 10am-3pm.) **Westpac, Commonwealth,** and **ANZ banks** and 24hr. **ATMs** are on Katherine Tce (all open M-Th 9:30am-4pm and

F 9:30am-5pm). The **police** (☎8972 0111) are 2.5km south of town on the Stuart Hwy, and the **hospital** (☎8973 9211) is on Giles St (Gorge Rd), 3km from Katherine Tce. Email from **Didj Shop Internet Café**, on Giles a block west of Katherine Tce. (☎8972 2485. Open daily in the Dry 10am-10pm, Wet 11am-7pm. 1hr. $7; 15min. free with coffee purchase.) The **post office** is on the corner of Katherine Tce and Giles St (open M-F 9am-5pm). **Postal code:** 0850.

# ACCOMMODATIONS

**Kookaburra Backpackers** (☎8971 0257, guestline ☎8971 1822). On the corner of Lindsay and 3rd St. Every group of 4 or 8 guests shares a clean bathroom, refrigerator, outdoor picnic table, and fully-stocked kitchenette in this extremely friendly (employees and guests) hostel. Free transport to and from Transit Centre (3 blocks). Laundry $3. Key deposit $10. Reception daily 7:30am-2pm and 4:30pm-7:30pm. Dorms $15; twins with TV and fridge $45; light brekkie included. Book ahead in the Dry. YHA, VIP.

**Victoria Lodge**, 21 Victoria Hwy (☎(1800) 80 88 75). A 10min. walk from Katherine Tce. The best deal in town, but more of a thirty-something crowd. Sparkling refurbished rooms with leather couches, microwave, bathroom, spacious kitchenette, and color TV. Free transport to Transit Centre. Dorms $13; singles $35; twins $40; doubles $50. YHA.

**Palm Court Backpackers** (☎(1800) 62 67 22). On the corner of 3rd and Giles St. Slightly dark but comfortable, clean, and mellow. Fridge and toilet in each room. Free transport to and from Transit Centre. Laundry $3. Key deposit $10. Reception daily 7am-8:30pm. Dorms $15; twins and doubles $42-45. YHA, VIP.

**Red Gum Caravan Park** (☎8972 2239). 1km down, right off the noisy Victoria Hwy. Laundry, pool, and BBQ. Sites for 2 $14; powered $18; each extra person $7. Self-contained cabins $50; each extra person $10.

**Frontier Katherine**, on Cyprus St (☎8972 1744). 3km south of town near the Stuart Hwy. Tennis, pool, laundry. Sites $7.50 per person, powered with bath $18.

# FOOD

A giant Woolworth's **supermarket** is across from the Transit Centre, on Katherine Tce. (☎8972 3055. Open daily 7am-10pm.)

**Café Enio's**, 385 Katherine Tce (☎8972 2255). Near the intersection with the Victoria Hwy. This upscale, health-conscious café and coffee bar provides a welcome respite from burgers and grease. Intriguing focaccia $8-10, Gleaming Gorge Salad with chicken and peanut sauce $6.50, fruit smoothies $4.50. Open M-F 9am-5:30pm, Sa 9am-1:30pm; will close if crowds are light.

**Popeye's Pizza**, 32 Katherine Tce (☎8972 3633). Just north of Giles St. The main event of this lively joint is the all-you-can-eat pizza buffet, including a smattering of vegetarian choices (Sa-Th 6-9pm; $7). 'Nuff said. Open M-Sa 9am-10pm, Su 11am-10pm.

**Tommo's Bakery**, 14 2nd St (☎8971 1155). On the corner of Giles St. This large, humble bakery sells sandwiches ($2-3) and makes a mean apricot pie ($1.80). Open M-F 5am-5pm, Sa 5am-1pm. Sandwiches and fish-and-chips available M-F 10am-9pm.

**Katherine Bakery**, on Katherine Tce (☎8971 2588). On the corner of Lindsay St. Open 24hr. for your pastry pleasure.

# SIGHTS AND ACTIVITIES

Two kilometers along the Victoria Hwy from the Stuart Hwy, **hot springs** bubble along the Katherine River—though "not hot, but warmer than I might expect" might be a better description. The springs have safe swimming, toilets, and wheelchair access along Croker St. Katherine's numerous art galleries display and sell regional Aboriginal work. **Coco's Place** (☎8971 2889), across from the cinema, has a large selection of locally made didgeridoos. An engaging conversationalist, Coco knows his stuff, but expect to pay more for his expertise. Make your own didgeridoo (and keep it) with **Whoop Whoop** overnight trips. (☎8972 2941. $220.) Or learn more about less "trendy" Aboriginal crafts at **Manyallaluk,** which provides in-depth and insightful **Aboriginal Cultural Tours.** (☎(1800) 64 47 27. Full-day $75, with transport $110; 2-day $250.) The visitors center publishes *Discovering Katherine: Arts & Culture* brochures for further exploration. The local extension of **School of the Air** is on Giles St about 2km from Katherine Tce, broadcasting lessons to rural schoolchildren. (☎8972 1833. Classes Apr.-Nov. M-F 9, 10, 11am, 1, 2pm. $5.) Evening **cruises** along the Katherine River provide wildlife spotting and lively dinner around a campfire. **Far Out Adventures** has BBQ-style meals with BYO. (☎8972 2552. $42, includes pickup.) **Travel North** runs a cruise that includes wine and stew. (☎(1800) 08 91 03. $39; $48, includes pickup.)

## ◪ NIGHTLIFE

**Kirby's Sports Bar,** on the corner of Katherine Tce and Giles St in the Katherine Hotel/Motel, is the center of local attention most nights, with a dance space out back (open Su-W 11:30am-11:30pm, Th 11:30am-12:30am, F-Sa 11:30am-1:30am). **Olympia,** 7 Victoria Hwy, one block west of Katherine Tce, lures backpackers with specials—check around hostels for cheap meal coupons—and a mellow atmosphere. (☎8971 0422. Open until "late.") **Rio** nightclub, on Katherine Tce just south of the Victoria Hwy, turns on in the wee hours (open F-Sa 10pm-4am).

# NITMILUK (KATHERINE GORGE) NATIONAL PARK

Nitmiluk (Katherine Gorge) National Park provides water and land activities in a setting as dramatic and striking as its bigger cousins, Kakadu and Litchfield National Parks. Composed of a sandstone plateau sliced by rivers and tributaries, its 292,008 hectares stretch over the region northeast of Katherine. Nitmiluk is actually a series of 13 gorges on the Katherine River. Plants grow thick, especially in the monsoon forest, and 168 species of birds decorate the skies. Rocky cliffs rise from the river, and visitors can hike through shady gorges or paddle a tranquil canoe. In the Wet, the individual cascades are subsumed by a single gushing current that largely restricts access to the gorge. Since 1989, the park has been owned by the local Jawoyn Aboriginals, who leased it for 99 years to the Northern Territory Government. Aboriginal livelihood remains a significant presence in the park, and the 450 recorded galleries of rock art dispersed throughout the region are physical reminders of the strong presence of the Jawoyn people.

## ◪◪ ORIENTATION AND PRACTICAL INFORMATION

**Travel North** runs buses from all accommodations in Katherine. (☎(1800) 08 91 03. 25min.; 4 per day; $16.50 return; book ahead.) There are two entrances into the park. To get to the northern entrance pointing to Edith Falls, turn off the Stuart Hwy 40km north of Katherine, and proceed 20km down an access road. From here, visitors can take two short day hikes. The park's southern entrance—where the longer treks begin—is 30km east of Katherine on Giles St, later called Gorge Rd. The **Nitmiluk Visitor Centre,** at the end of Gorge Rd, has a ranger desk that provides hiking info, camping permits, free slide shows, and campfire talks. A tourist desk in the gift shop gives out pamphlets, rents canoes, books helicopter tours and boat cruises, and serves as reception for the campground. There is an exhibit on the Jawoyn and natural history as well as a bistro that serves burgers for $6-7. (☎8972 3150. Ranger desk staffed daily 7am-7pm; store open daily 7am-7pm; bistro open 8am-4pm; restaurant in the Dry 6:30-8:30pm.) A winding concrete path connects the Centre with a carpark and the boathouse. Another path leads to the **campground,** with toilets, showers, laundry, and phones, which is also the trailhead for most of the park's walking tracks. (Sites $7 per person, powered $11.) Contact the **Parks and Wildlife Commission** in Katherine for more info on Katherine Gorge. (☎ 8972 1886; fax 8971 0702; PO Box 344, Katherine NT 0851.) Although some people drink water straight from the river, visitors are asked to bring water and to baste themselves in sunblock.

## 🌊 NITMILUK BY WATER

From May to September, quiet waters allow for canoeing, boating, and walking. **Nitmiluk Tours** (☎ 8972 1253) does all rentals for water activities, which can be booked at most accommodations in Katherine or at the Nitmiluk Visitor Centre. **Canoeing** is justifiably the most popular; it allows you to travel at your own pace and provides great views without racking up the expense of a boat cruise. Paddling on the cooler water is also more comfortable than hiking—temperatures here are sizzling year-round. No more than 75 canoes are permitted in the gorge at a time; book ahead. (Single canoes half-day $27, full-day $38; doubles $41, $56.) If traveling alone, it's a good idea to find a partner since paddling is only half the battle of the gorge tour—dragging the canoe across rocky portages is the other. Riverside campsites make longer trips possible (see **Overnight Camping and Extended Bushwalks,** below). Another popular aquatic activity is **swimming,** but keep in mind that you may be sharing the bath with freshwater crocs. Many people like to swim near the boathouse and at deep plunge pools at the end of some hikes. A **boat cruise** lets visitors zoom along the gorges in flat, shaded motor vessels; at the end of each gorge, passengers hike over to a new boat on the next gorge. The crowded arrangement makes it hard to enjoy the natural solitude of the area and destroys any chance of moving at one's own pace. (2hr.; departs from the boat jetty in the Dry 4 per day; $33, children $13.) Daily "adventure" and "safari" tours combine boating and hiking (departs 9am; 4hr. $47; 8hr. $82).

## 🪨 NITMILUK BY LAND

**Walking tracks** in the park fall in all difficulty levels and range from 2.5km to 66km. The abundant flora, fauna, and rocky outcroppings provide a different view from canoeing, but the sun can still be brutal. The main trail, starting from the Nitmiluk Visitor Centre, parallels the gorge at a 1.5km separation, with side trails branching off and heading directly for the gorge. Much of the main trail hiking is through unremarkable surroundings, but the scenery on the side trails more than makes up for it. The Southern Walks are usually open during the Wet; the Jatbula Trail is not.

### DAY WALKS
On the Southern Walks trail, the **Lookout Loop** (3.7km return; 2hr.; moderate) rewards with excellent views of the river and **17-Mile Valley.** The **Windolf** walk (8.4km; 3½hr.; moderate) has views of the lower gorge and occasional Aboriginal art, passes the panoramic **Pat's Lookout,** and ends at a gorgeous plunge pool. The **Butterfly Gorge** walk (12km; 4½hr.; difficult) provides a good overview of the region, with woodlands and rock formations giving way to a dense, tranquil monsoon forest in a side gorge that does, in fact, possess an unusually large population of butterflies. The walk ends at a deep swimming spot. **⚑Lily Ponds** trail (20km; 6½hr.; difficult) covers even longer distances and more treacherous terrain, but rewards with write-home-to-Ma vistas of the gorge and a fairy-tale plunge pool.

   On the Jatbula Trail, the **Northern Rockhole** walk (16km; 4hr.; moderate) winds through a valley, ending at a rock face and waterhole. The **Sweetwater Pool** walk (9km; 4hr.; moderate) leads to a waterhole and good camping. The **Leliyn Trail** (5.2km; 3hr.; easy) leads to the smaller but equally amazing upper pools.

### OVERNIGHT CAMPING AND EXTENDED BUSHWALKS
A permanent **campground** next to Edith Falls allows tents and reasonably-sized caravans, and has showers, BBQ, a food kiosk, and a picnic area, but no powered sites ($5 per person). Plenty of beautiful pools and waterfalls cool the grounds. The lower pool, a short walk from the carpark, is a huge, crystal-clear plunge pool with a waterfall.

**YUMMY?** Sausage Roll. Dim Sim. Chicko Roll. Wing Ding. Fisherman's Basket. Beef Pie. Kidney Pie. Chicken Pie. Beef and Mushroom Pie. Beef and Tomato Pie. The staples of a roadhouse hot-food counter. All of them either deep-fat-fried or else crammed full of mystery-meat goodness. The dazzling array of combinations of parts of a cow that one can find in a pie crust can boggle the mind, as can the fact that something as unassuming as a "tomato and onion pie" is in fact chock full of beef and gravy. Bon appetit.

The ranger desk at the Nitmiluk Center details all longer hikes, including the full-length hike of the popular **Jatbula Trail,** a 66km, 5-day, one-way-only sojourn between Nitmiluk Centre and Edith Falls. There are eight 1-4 day segments between the center and Edith Falls. The Southern Walks region has two overnight walks—**Eighth Gorge** and **Jawoyn Valley**—each a difficult 30-40km. Semi-detailed topographic maps are $7 at the desk. Register with the rangers before setting out.

Overnight camping in the depths of the park is permitted (register at the center; $3; $50 deposit, $20 if only going as far as Crystal Falls from Nitmiluk Centre). Areas, with toilets and (usually) a water source, are located along the Jatbula Trail and at the 4th, 5th, and 8th gorges in the Southern Walks area. Fires are permitted along the Jatbula, but not in the Southern Walks area.

## VICTORIA HIGHWAY: KATHERINE TO KUNUNURRA

From downtown Katherine, the "Vic" careens westward 512km to Kununurra WA (see p. 670). There isn't much in between, save two service areas and some stunning scenery. Two hundred kilometers west of Katherine, the **Victoria River Roadhouse** has petrol, a restaurant, and quiet campsites with breathtaking views of the nearby escarpment. (☎8975 0744. Sites for 2 $12, powered $18; budget rooms $35; motel rooms $70.) A Victoria River **cruise** also leaves from the Roadhouse (2½hr.; departs daily 9:30am, in peak season also 1 and 3pm; $35). The highway passes through **Gregory National Park** (☎8975 0888). The Territory's second-largest national park (after Kakadu) features 2WD-accessible bushwalks and lookouts over Victoria River Gorge, as well as rugged 4WD tracks through beautiful and isolated surroundings. **Timber Creek,** a rowdy roadside town, is 90km west of Victoria River. The **Wayside Inn** has a small restaurant and accommodations. (☎8975 0732. Sites for 2 $11, powered $17; budget rooms $39; motel rooms $91.) River cruises can be booked next door. (☎8975 0850. 4hr., $55.) **Big Horse Creek,** right on the Victoria River 10km west of town, is the better camping option, although there are no facilities besides an outhouse ($2.50 per person). About 480km west of Katherine is the border crossing into WA. There are strict quarantines against fruits, veggies, honey, and plant material. Western Australia clocks are 1½hr. behind the Territory's. Just before the border, **Keep River National Park** is home to Aboriginal rock art sites and a few bushwalks. Camping is permitted at two sites (15 and 28km down a gravel road); jokes about "keep"-ing the river clean are strictly forbidden throughout the park.

## STUART HIGHWAY: KATHERINE TO TENNANT CREEK

Twenty-seven kilometers south of Katherine is the 200km turn-off to an unsung gem, **Cutta Cutta Caves Nature Park** (☎8972 1940). Meaning "starry starry," the name refers to the delicate calcite crystals that grow within the dark, temperate passages. The cave extends 720m through an underground labyrinth of limestone columns and jagged ceilings, although visitors can only venture through the first 250m (the depths get too cold and reach 99% humidity). **Tours,** the only way to see the cave, are led by fun, knowledgeable guides, and proceed through five impressive chambers. (1hr. tours depart year-round, except during floods in the Wet. Daily 9, 10, 11am, 1, 2, and 3pm. $8.50, children $4.25.)

Another 79km south on the Stuart is the township of **Mataranka,** renowned for Elsey National Park and the thermal pool near Mataranka Homestead. "Only" 13,840 hectares, **Elsey National Park** features the emerald Roper River, perfect for canoeing, swimming, or fishing. To reach the park, continue 2km south past "downtown" Mataranka and take a left onto Homestead Rd. The turn-off for Elsey is 4km down this road. Another 11km farther on is picture-perfect **Jalmurark camp-ground,** where visitors can hike to the pristine pools at **Mataranka Falls** (4km) or rent a canoe and relax along the Roper River. (Canoe shop open daily in the Dry 8am-7pm. Single canoes 1hr. $5, $25 per day; doubles $7, $35.) The campground has private sites with showers and toilets ($6 per person).

Another 3km past the Elsey turn-off on Homestead Rd is **Mataranka Homestead** and its **thermal pool.** The homestead is a resort where travelers stay to dip in the crowded sapphire pool. Greyhound and McCafferty's **buses** between Katherine and Tennant Creek all stop at the Mataranka Homestead (northbound bus leaves daily, southbound twice daily; times vary). The Homestead holds a **general store,** takeaway eatery (open daily 7am-6pm), restaurant (open daily 6-8pm), and bar with live entertainment most nights (open daily 11am-11pm). You can also embark on a **free tour** of the historic homestead (departs daily in the Dry at 11am), or rent a canoe (1 hr. $9). **Camping** includes showers, laundry, and kitchen facilities at a budget lodge. (☎8975 4544. Sites $7.50 per person, powered $12; budget twins and triples $15, non-YHA $17; motel doubles $82; cabins for 2 $87.)

# TENNANT CREEK

The discovery of gold in the 1930s made Tennant Creek and the surrounding Barkly region the Northern Territory's mining prima donnas. Located 988km south of Darwin on the Stuart Hwy, the town is a rugged blip of urban development amid an expanse of bush and Aboriginal land. Through the years, mining continued to be the mainstay of Tennant Creek, though its last mine closed in 1999. Even with a prosperous $4 billion output of gold since the 1960s, Tennant Creek is very much a town that watches the road trains and travelers go by. No one seems to stay for long (except the locals), but Devil's Marbles, mining history, and the regional artistic flavor of the Warumungu Aboriginals all make the pause more engaging.

## ▐ TRANSPORT

**Buses:** The **transit centre** is on Paterson St, near the intersection with Stuart St, at the north end of town. Open 6am-3:30pm. Greyhound and McCafferty's **buses** run to: **Darwin** (13hr., $101); **Alice Springs** (5-6hr., $85); **Katherine** (8-9hr., $70); and **Mt. Isa** (7hr., $81). McCafferty's also runs to **Townsville** ($163). The travel agent in **Enterprise Electrics,** 62a Paterson St (☎8962 2211), books for both.

**Auto Club: AANT,** on Irvine St (☎8962 2468; afterhours ☎8962 3126), in Wyatt Motors.

**Bicycle Rental: Bridgestone Tyre,** 52b Paterson St (☎8962 2361), on the corner of Davidson St. Half-day $5, full-day $10. Open daily 8am-5pm.

## ✦▐ ORIENTATION AND PRACTICAL INFORMATION

The Stuart Hwy, called **Paterson St** in town, runs from north to south. Intersecting Paterson are, from the north, **Stuart St** (not to be confused with the Stuart Highway), **Davidson St,** then **Peko Rd** on the left side of Paterson, and **Windley St** on the right. Continuing south is **Memorial Dr** to the right.

**Tourist Office: Tennant Creek Battery Hill Information Centre** (☎8962 3388; fax 8962 2509), 1.5km up Peko Rd, provides info and tours. Open in the Wet daily 9am-5pm, Dry M-F 9am-5pm, Sa 9am-noon, and Su for tours.

**Currency Exchange: ANZ Bank** (☎13 13 14), on Paterson St. **Westpac Bank** (☎8962 2801), at the corner of Paterson St and Peko Rd. Both open M-Th 9:30am-4pm, F 9:30am-5pm, with 24hr. **ATMs.**

**Police:** on Paterson St (☎8962 4444), near Windley St.

**Hospital: Tennant Creek Hospital** (☎8962 4399, afterhours ☎8962 4232, ambulance ☎8962 1900), on Schmidt St. Take a left turn at the end of Memorial Dr.

**Internet Access:** at the **high school** (☎8962 2102). Take Peko Rd from town, then take a left before Outback Caravan Park. Open Feb.-Nov. M-F 3-6pm; Sa-Su 10am-6pm; Oct.-Jan. daily 9am-4:15pm. 1hr. $2. Also at the **public library,** on Peko Rd (☎8962 2256). 30min. $2.50. Open M-F 10am-1pm and 2-6pm, Sa 10am-noon.

**Post Office:** at the corner of Paterson St and Memorial Dr (☎8962 2196). Open M-F 9am-5pm. **Postal Code:** 0861.

**Phone Code:** 08.

## ACCOMMODATIONS AND FOOD

**Safari Backpackers YHA,** 12 Davidson St (☎8962 2207). West of Paterson St. Small, clean, and comfortable with a good location. Shared bath, kitchen, laundry, and lounge. Dorms $14; twins and doubles $36. Non-YHA add $2.

**Tourist's Rest Hostel** (☎8962 2719). On Leichardt St, walk south on Paterson and turn right on Windley St. Friendly and spacious, with an aviary and fun lawn decor. Kitchen, pool, TV. Free ride to transit center. Daytrips to Devil's Marbles $50, including one-night's stay $60. Dorms $17; twins $37; doubles $39. YHA, VIP, NOMADS.

**Outback Caravan Park** (☎8962 2459). On the left side of Peko Rd, 300m from Paterson St. Stellar swimming pool, small grocery, shared bath, kitchen, BBQ. Tent sites $8 per person; powered caravan sites for 2 $19; self-contained ensuite cabins $62.

Paterson St is lined with takeaway snack bars and restaurants. **Rocky's** provides tasty pizza in a no-frills setting. (☎8962 2049. Open M-Sa 11am-11pm, Su 5-11pm. Large pizzas $10-18.) **Bullwinkle's** does not exist. **Top of Town Café** has cheap veggie burgers and a sandwich bar. (☎8962 1311. Open M-W 8am-8pm, Th-Sa 8am-1:30am, Su 8am-2pm.) **Margo Miles Steakhouse,** across the street from the transit center, has more international fare and, of course, plenty of steak. (☎8962 1311. Open M-F noon-2pm and 6pm-late, Sa-Su 6pm-late. Mains around $15.) The **Tennant Food Barn,** on Paterson south of Memorial, offers the cheapest **groceries.** (☎8962 2296. Open M-Sa 8:30am-6pm, Su 9am-6pm.)

## SIGHTS AND ACTIVITIES

The **Dot Mine Tour** provides perspective on Tennant Creek mining and the men and women who struggled to make it work. A genuine prospector provides endless history around a nighttime fire before leading you through the mine that closed in 1942. (☎8962 2168. 2hr.; $20, children $10.) **Battery Hill** houses a working gold stamp battery (for crushing ore and extracting gold) and a gold mine replica. Each has history-heavy tours running twice daily. (☎8962 3388. Each $13, children $6.50.) History buffs can visit the **Tennant Creek Telegraph Station Historical Reserve,** 10km north of Tennant Creek, on the Stuart Hwy. Built in 1872, the station was integral in the overland telegraph project. There is a self-guided tour through the building. (Ranger-led talks May-Oct. F 9am-4pm.) The **Parks and Wildlife Commission** (☎8962 4599) manages the station as well as the nearby proposed **Davenport Range National Park** (4WD only). For a pleasant cycling trip, the **Ted Ryko Bike Trail** leaves from the north end of town and runs for 5km to the **Mary Ann Recreational Dam,** passing the **Honeymoon Ranges.** About 3km east of Paterson St on Peko Rd lies the **Bill Allen Lookout,** with impressive views of the entire Tennant Creek area. Manmade beauty is closer to town at the Aboriginal **Jurnkurakurr Mural,** on the corner of Paterson and Windley St.

## FROM TENNANT CREEK TO ALICE SPRINGS

As if dropped from the heavens onto the scrub-brushed desert, smooth 7m-thick boulders form idle piles atop the stretch of land 104km south of Tennant Creek on the Stuart Hwy. Wind-erosion is hardly a satisfying cause of the ethereal effect that the **Devil's Marbles** give to the barren landscape; the giant orange orbs are alien wonders against the blue sky. The local Aboriginals say they are eggs of the rainbow serpent. Camping at the Marbles is basic (pit toilets, BBQ, no water; $2.50 per

# Council *Travel*

America's Student Travel Leader for over 50 years

"Happiness is not a destination. It is a method of life"
-Burton Hills

Visit us at your nearest office or online @

# www.counciltravel.com

Or call: 1-800-2COUNCIL

**ISIC** *It's your world at a discount!*

*Accepted at over 17,000 locations worldwide.*
*Great benefits at home and abroad!*

# Call the USA

"feel free to call"

1 800
COLLECT

1-800-COLLECT

## When in Ireland
## Dial: 1-800-COLLECT (265 5328)

## When in N. Ireland, UK & Europe
## Dial: 00-800-COLLECT USA (265 5328 872)

*Member of*
**Dublin Tourism**

| Australia | 0011 | 800 265 5328 872 |
| Finland | 990 | 800 265 5328 872 |
| Hong Kong | 001 | 800 265 5328 872 |
| Israel | 014 | 800 265 5328 872 |
| Japan | 0061 | 800 265 5328 872 |
| New Zealand | 0011 | 800 265 5328 872 |

**DIDGERIDOO 101** So, you want to buy a "didge." The didgeridoo is the traditional musical instrument of the Yolngu Aboriginals of northern Australia, and has been used for thousands of years in *corroboree* dance ceremonies. Today the spirit of the didge reverberates as much as its bounding hum and has been combined with various percussion and electric instruments to create a tune for almost every preference. The didgeridoo itself is made from a eucalyptus tree naturally hollowed out by termites. Once cut, the bark is shaved from the outside and the mouthpiece is dipped in bee's wax. In the Aboriginal tradition, painted didges are only played in formal ceremonies honoring birth, marriage, or death, but their beauty and higher prices make them ubiquitous in tourist shops. Choosing a didge depends on what you want it for. If you're buying in hopes of one day mastering circular-breathing technique, droning your praises for minutes at a time, and imitating the cockatoo, there are some things to look for. Each didge has a unique sound, which depends on its length, diameter, bore-width, twists in the chamber, and the chamber wall texture created by the former termite inhabitants. Most stores allow wandering shoppers to have a go at their selection of didgeridoos, and many will package and send them home, where you can start your own didgeridoo band...if you can wait that long.

person paid at the entrance). **Garyo** (☎8962 2024) runs active, half-day tours that sacrifice quiet contemplation for numerous staged photo-ops; **Norm's Tours** (☎(0418) 89 17 11) are less let's-shimmy-up-this-rock, and place more emphasis on geologic info, attracting an older crowd. (Both $55 from Tennant Creek including evening BBQ back in town.) The closest town to Devil's Marbles is **Wauchope**, 9km south, which has petrol, food, and accommodations. (☎8964 1963. Motel singles $30; tentsites for 2 $10, powered $14.50.) Small towns farther along the highway have roadhouses that provide basic services including petrol, food, and accommodation: **Wycliffe Well** (☎8964 1966), rumored to receive frequent UFO visits; **Barrow Creek** (☎8956 9753); **Ti Tree** (☎8956 9741); and **Aileron** (☎8956 9703).

# THE RED CENTRE

The dry, desolate outback at the center of Australia takes its name from the color of the oxidized dust that stretches to the horizon. To many travelers, the Red Centre represents the essence of Australia. Flat lands perpetually bake under a scalding sun. The gnarled vegetation is weedy and sparse, and the wildlife is locked in a constant struggle for survival with the unforgiving climate and the unbearable bush flies. Out of this stark landscape, at the geographic center of the continent, rises Uluru (Ayers Rock), a celebrated symbol of the land down under.

Alice Springs is the outback's unofficial capital and the gateway to the desert beyond. The region's natural wonders include the MacDonnell Ranges, Watarrka (Kings Canyon), Uluru, and Kata Tjuta, all of which do their best to disrupt the red monotony of central Australia. These monuments have magnetic appeal, and tourists are attracted like little iron filings to the Red Centre, prepared to brave endless distances and remote disasters to experience the "real" outback.

## ALICE SPRINGS

The only city of any size for a long, long way in any direction, and inhabited by only 27,000 souls itself, Alice Springs is a desert outpost in the heart of the continent, connected to the world by endless, mirage-filled highways. In the midst of the MacDonnell Ranges where the usually waterless Todd River carves out a flat plain, sandstone hills and wallabies frame the city's humble skyline. Wilderness dominates here, and the town's lights can't hold a candle to the desert sky above.

Many travelers use Alice to explore the Red Centre, but the city works hard to be independently attractive. It's a relatively young town, only growing rapidly after 1929 when the Old Ghan Railway to Adelaide was completed. Today, tourism sur-

NORTHERN TERRITORY

passes the mining and cattle industries ("pastoralism"), and a plethora of attractions can easily fill up a three- or four-day visit. Downtown Alice is teeming with tourist shops that focus on Aboriginal art and opal jewelry, and cappuccino-selling cafés lure the outback traveler with a staid sense of cosmopolitan luxury.

## ▐▀ TRANSPORT

**Airplanes: Alice Springs Airport** (☎ 8951 1211), 20km south of the city on the Stuart Hwy, provides domestic service only, but has tourist information, currency exchange, and car rental agencies. Qantas (☎ 13 13 13) and Ansett (☎ 13 13 00) fly to: **Darwin** (2hr., 2 per day, $275); **Adelaide** (2hr., 1 per day, $290); **Brisbane** (4½hr., 2 per day, $440); **Melbourne** (4½hr., 2 per day, $403); **Perth** (3hr., 1 per day, $389); **Sydney** (3hr., 1 per day, $404); **Cairns** (3hr., 3 per day, $343); and **Yulara** (45min., 2 per day, $131). **Airnorth** (☎ (1800) 62 74 74) flies to NT destinations. **Airport shuttle bus** runs to accommodations. (☎ (1800) 62 11 88. $10, return $16.50; families $27.50, $44.)

**Trains: Alice Railway Station** is a 20min. walk from central Alice. Take Stott Tce across the Stuart Hwy, where it becomes Larapinta Dr. Take the first right onto George Tce; the station is at the end of the street. *The Ghan* runs to: **Adelaide** (Tu and F, $197); **Melbourne** (Tu, $271); and **Sydney** (F, $390). The tourist office and Traveland make reservations, or call ☎ 13 21 47.

**Buses:** Greyhound Pioneer (☎ 13 20 30) operates from the corner of Gregory and Railway Tce and runs **buses** to: **Darwin** (18-20hr., 1 per day, $158) via **Tennant Creek** (6hr., $85); **Adelaide** (19-20hr., 1 per day, $147) via **Yulara** (5hr., $65); **Sydney** ($251); and **Townsville** ($289) via **Cairns** ($248). A 3-day tour of **Uluru-Kata Tjuta** and **Watarrka** is $275. Open daily 4:45am-6:30pm. McCafferty's, on Gregory Tce (☎ 8952 3952), half a block toward the river from the Todd Mall, has similar destinations and prices. Both companies give a 10% discount with YHA, VIP, and ISIC.

**Public Transportation: ASBus** (☎ 8950 0500) is the infrequent public bus system, with routes to the outskirts of town. Runs M-F from about 8 or 9am to 6pm, on Sa only in the morning, and Su not at all. Fare $1.40 to most areas in the city.

**Taxis: Alice Springs Taxis** (☎ 8952 1877), queue on Gregory Tce just east of Todd Mall.

**Car Rental: Territory-Thrifty,** corner of Hartley St and Stott Tce (☎ 8952 9999), has cars from $80 per day, 4WD from $115. Open daily 8am-5:30pm. **Hertz,** 76 Hartley St (☎ 8952 2644), near Stott Tce, from $69. Both companies have airport locations open M-F 8am-5pm, Sa-Su 8am-1pm. **Britz,** corner of Stuart Hwy and Power St (☎ 8952 8814), rents 4WD with unlimited kilometers to those under 25, from $147. Open daily 8am-4:30pm.

**Roadside Assistance: AANT** (24hr. ☎ 8952 1087).

**Road Conditions:** (☎ (1800) 24 61 99).

**Bike Rental:** At most hostels. At **Pioneer YHA,** half-day $9.50, full-day $16.50.

## ✴ ORIENTATION

The Stuart Hwy runs through Alice on its way from Darwin (1486km) to Adelaide (1570km). Seen from the north, the **MacDonnell Ranges** form a backdrop to the town. A break in the ranges called **Heavitree Gap** permits both the highway and the **Todd River** to pass south. In the south, Todd St becomes **Gap Rd,** which eventually joins the Stuart Hwy at a traffic circle. Farther south, the southern outskirts of town lie beyond Heavitree Gap, as does the airport (20km south). The major routes to the city's outskirts are the Stuart Hwy (north and south) and **Larapinta Dr** (westward into the West MacDonnell Range). At the southern end of town, the Ross Hwy branches off the Stuart Hwy and leads to the East MacDonnells. Downtown, the major north-south streets are (from west to east) the Stuart Hwy, Railway Tce, Bath St, Hartley St, Todd St, and Leichhardt Tce; the major east-west streets are (from north to south) Wills Tce, Parsons St, Gregory Tce, Stott Tce, and Stuart Tce. Todd St becomes the pedestrian-only **Todd Mall** between Wills and Gregory Tce, while the two indoor malls are **Alice Plaza** (Todd Mall at Parsons St) and **Yeperenye Plaza** (Hartley St north of Gregory Tce).

NORTHERN TERRITORY

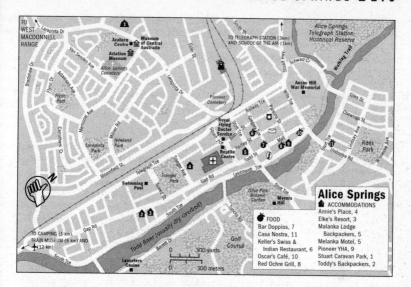

**Alice Springs**

🏠 ACCOMMODATIONS
Annie's Place, 4
Elke's Resort, 3
Malanka Lodge
   Backpackers, 5
Melanka Motel, 5
Pioneer YHA, 9
Stuart Caravan Park, 1
Toddy's Backpackers, 2

🍴 FOOD
Bar Doppios, 7
Casa Nostra, 11
Keller's Swiss &
   Indian Restaurant, 6
Oscar's Café, 10
Red Ochre Grill, 8

NORTHERN TERRITORY

## 🛈 PRACTICAL INFORMATION

**Tourist Office: Central Australian Tourism Industry Association** (☎ 8952 5800; fax 8953 0295), on Gregory Tce at the end of Todd Mall. Books transportation, tours, and accommodations, sells road and Larapinta Trail maps, and has National Park info. Grab their free excellent city map (yellow). Open M-F 8:30am-5:30pm, Sa-Su 9am-4pm.

**Budget Travel: Traveland** (☎ 8952 7186), on Gregory Tce at the end of Todd Mall. Open M-F 8:30am-5pm, Sa 9am-noon. **Flight Centre** (☎ 8953 4081), on Todd Mall near Parsons St, guarantees lowest airfares. Open M-F 9am-5pm, Sa 9:30am-12:30pm.

**Currency Exchange: National Australia** (☎ 8952 1611), and **ANZ** (☎ 8952 1144), are in Todd Mall, along with **ATMs.** Both open M-Th 9:30am-4pm, F 9:30am-5pm.

**Library:** next to the tourist office (☎ 8950 0555). Open M-Tu, Th 10am-6pm, W and F 10am-5pm, Sa 9am-1pm, Su 1-5pm.

**Police:** (☎ 8951 8888), on Parsons St, at the corner of Bath St.

**Pharmacy: Amcal Chemist** (☎ 8953 0089), in Alice Plaza on the Todd Mall at Parsons St. Open daily 8:30am-7:30pm.

**Hospital: Alice Springs Hospital** (☎ 8951 7777, emergency ☎ 8951 7529, ambulance ☎ 8952 2200), on Gap Rd south of Stuart Tce.

**Internet Access:** At the **library** (1hr. $6). Book ahead. Also at **Outback Travel,** on Gregory Tce west of Todd Mall (30min. $4). Open M-F 8am-8pm, Sa-Su 10am-6pm.

**Post Office: GPO,** on Hartley St south of Parsons St (☎ 8952 1020; fax 8953 4049). Open M-F 9am-5pm. **Postal Code:** 0870.

**Phone Code:** 08.

## 🛏 ACCOMMODATIONS AND CAMPING

The hostels of Alice are concentrated on or near Todd St and Gap Rd. All listings have air-conditioned rooms, a pool, $10 key deposit, and $2 laundry; all recommend booking in advance; most have bike rental from $12-15 per day; and *everybody* (hostelers, internet cafés owners, the little girl drinking from the water fountain) will be happy to book tours (and collect a handsome commission).

**🏠 Pioneer YHA** (☎ 8952 8855; fax 8952 4144). On the corner of Parsons and Leichardt St, one block off Todd Mall. Originally a deckchair cinema, guests now quietly relax around the pool and contemplate the large, blank screen. Coral-colored dorms, clean showers, large 24hr. kitchen, free safe and luggage storage. Linen $2. Reception daily 6:30am-9:30pm. 4- to 6-bed dorms $18, non-YHA add $3. Wheelchair accessible.

**Annie's Place** (☎ (1800) 35 90 89; fax 8952 8280), on Traegger Ave. Three long blocks south of Todd Mall and one block west of Todd St. Three daily courtesy shuttles to bus stations. This newcomer has a laid-back bohemian atmosphere. The kitchen has beautiful stone-work walls and there's an in-house café. Internet 1hr. $6. Reception daily 9am-noon and 4-8pm. 6-bed dorms $15; 4-bed dorms $16; doubles $45.

**Elke's Resort,** 39 Gap Rd (☎ (1800) 63 33 54; fax 8952 8143). At Baedem St, 1km south of Todd Mall. Elke's compensates for its hefty distance from town by providing 6 free shuttles daily. The efficient, professional folks here have converted a motel into a well-serviced and popular hostel. Each comfortable dorm room has its own bath, kitchenette, TV, and balcony. Reception daily 5am-8pm. 6- to 8-bed dorms $18; twins and doubles $50; motel doubles $83; light breakfast included. YHA, VIP.

**Melanka Lodge Backpackers,** 94 Todd St (☎ 8952 4744; fax 8952 4587). Reminiscent of a university dorm, complete with the party atmosphere and crowded unswept rooms, Melanka's lures tourists with a snack bar, sofa-strewn TV room, and their very own nightclub, the best nightspot in town. Just remember you came here to party. Free airport pickup; airport drop off $8. Reception daily 5am-8:15pm. 4- to 8-bed dorms $14; singles $38; twins and doubles $38. VIP.

**Toddy's Backpackers,** 41 Gap Rd (☎ 8952 1322; fax 8952 1767). At Hayes St, 1km south of Todd Mall, next to Elke's. The cheapest beds in town. Two buildings flank a pool, kitchen, and pool room. Courtesy bus meets most flights and buses. Reception daily 6am-8:30pm. Dorms $12-17; singles, doubles, and twins with sink and fridge $40; ensuite motel doubles with TV and fridge $57; light breakfast included. NOMADS.

**Melanka Motel,** 94 Todd St (☎ 8952 2233; fax 8952 2890). One block south of Todd Mall. The building's concrete hallways aren't too flattering, but rooms are clean and spacious, with large bathroom, fridge, and TV with free in-house movies. Laundry and nice pool. Reception daily 7:30am-9pm. Singles $83; doubles $88; family rooms $99.

**Stuart Caravan Park** (☎ 8952 2547). 2km west of town on Larapinta Dr across from the Araluen Centre. Reception daily 8am-8pm. Tent sites for 2 $16.50, powered $19.

**Heavitree Gap Outback Resort** (☎ 8950 4444). 3km south of central Alice; follow the Stuart Hwy south and take a left on Palm Circuit. A motel, bistro, and ranging wallabies. Reception daily 7am-8:30pm. Tent sites $8 per person, powered for 2 $18.

# 📷 FOOD

Alice has a heap of attractive, diverse restaurants that are a refreshing break from the roadhouse meat pies for 1000km in any direction. Unfortunately, they're not always budget—remember this is the most expensive town in the NT. A handful of overpriced outdoor cafés are at Todd Mall near Gregory Tce. **International Travellers Café,** in Annie's Place (see **Accommodations,** above), has excellent $5 dinners, including vegetarian stir-fry and lasagna, while **Toddy's** has all-you-can-gorge carnivorous mediocrity nightly 7-8pm for $7.50. **Coles supermarket** (open 24hr.) is on Bath St at Gregory Tce, and **Woolworth's** is in the Yeperenye Plaza (open M-Sa 7am-midnight, Su 7am-10pm).

**Bar Doppios,** Fan Arcade (☎ 8952 6525). At the Gregory Tce end of Todd Mall. Australian with a twist (salad and pies $10), Middle Eastern (falafel $9), and Southeast Asian (noodle soup $9), all for cheap make for one happy tummy. Vegetarian friendly. Open M-Th 7:30am-5pm, F 7:30am-9:30pm, Sa 7:30am-5pm, Su 10am-4pm. BYO.

**Red Ochre Grill,** Todd Mall (☎ 8952 9614). Near Parsons St. The scintillating outback cuisine delves deeply into regional ingredients. Aboriginal artwork and didgeridoo music round out the atmosphere for a memorable but pricey meal. But hey, this might be your only chance to eat "Wallaby Mignon" ($23). Smoked chicken with sun-dried tomatoes and native pasta ($16) is also delicious. Open daily 6:30am-9:30pm.

**SIGNS OF THE TIMES** You may notice that many restaurants throughout the Territory have signs outside demanding "No Thongs. No Singlets. Neat and Clean Dress," or something similar. In Alice Springs, the more subtle read simply "Dress Regulations Apply," but some signs go so far as urging those not following these strictures to "Bugger Off." Many see this as simply an attempt to take the edge off the Outback harshness, a variant on the American "No Shirt, No Shoes, No Service." But others see in it a thinly-veiled racism, an effort to keep Aboriginals, who are perceived as dressing much more shabbily, out of establishments. Shop owners will denigratingly point to a competitor who, with no dress regulations, "has *that* kind of crowd."

**La Casalinga,** 105 Gregory Tce (☎8952 4508). Near Todd Mall. Serves lots for little. Large specialty pizzas ($17), lasagna ($9.40), and diverse pasta selections (around $10) win over locals and Sicilians alike. Open daily 5pm-1am.

**Keller's Swiss and Indian Restaurant,** on Gregory Tce (☎8952 3188). East of Hartley St. Switzerland and India are exact opposites in geography, climate, political temperament, spelling, and cuisine, making for a titillating combination in one restaurant. *And* the food is really good. Spaetzle with mushroom-gruyere cream sauce or delicate vegetable curry, $13 takeaway. Open Sa-W 5:30pm-late, Th-F 11am-2pm and 5:30pm-late.

**Casa Nostra** (☎8952 6749). On Undoolya Rd at the corner of Sturt Tce, just across the river from downtown. Behind the closely-shuttered exterior lies a charming, cozy Italian restaurant with intriguing food at reasonable prices. Coming through the door here is like stepping out of a dark alley into a warm welcoming bar where everybody knows your name. Except you don't speak Italian, so you don't realize your appellation's familiarity to the crowd. Individual pizza and pastas $12-16. Open M-Sa 5pm-late.

**Oscar's Café,** Todd Mall (☎8953 0930). Swank, sophisticated, and proud of it, Oscar's spoils weary travelers with zesty Italian meals in a spacious, well-lit room with window walls. Mains $16-23. Open daily 9am-10pm.

## 👁 SIGHTS

Many sights are located near Todd Mall. Covering Alice's more distant sights is difficult without a vehicle. The **Alice Wanderer** shuttle service circles hourly past the major tourist sights in the Alice area. (☎8952 2211. Runs 9am-4pm, departing from the southern end of Todd Mall; no reservations required. All-day ticket $22.) The vigorous may prefer to hire a bike.

### CITY CENTER

**ANZAC HILL.** The best place to view a postcard sunset is atop Anzac Hill, which offers a panorama of the MacDonnell Ranges that should logically not be possible in a city. Walk to Wills Tce between Bath and Hartley St; a metal arch marks the start of the easy 10min. "Lions Walk" from the base to the obelisk at the top. Vehicle access is around the corner on the Stuart Hwy.

**REPTILE CENTRE.** Truly hands-on fun (leavened with a little fear) is yours at this recently-opened home to snakes, lizards (monitors and geckos and thorny devils, oh my), and coming soon...a saltie. Come let a python slither all over you. (*9 Stuart Tce. On the corner of Bath St. ☎8952 8900. Open daily 9am-5pm. $7, children $4.*)

**MUSEUM OF CENTRAL AUSTRALIA.** This new museum includes dinosaur casts, a display on meteorites, and an Aboriginal art gallery. (*2km west of town on Larapinta Dr. ☎8951 1121. $5.*) Next door, the **Araluen Centre** is a prime entertainment venue with two painting galleries, one of which features the work of the famous Aboriginal painter Albert Namatjira. (*☎8951 1120. Open daily 10am-5pm.*)

**ABORIGINAL ARTS AND CULTURE CENTRE.** Owned and operated by Arrernte, the Centre holds the "Didgeridoo University," where you can graduate with a 1hr.

degree in Didgeridoo Playing. Cap and gown extra. There's also a museum and tiny art gallery. *(86-88 Todd St. ☎ 8952 3408. Open M-F 9am-5pm, Sa-Su 8am-4pm. Degree $11.)*

**OLIVE PINK BOTANICAL GARDEN.** The desert scrub is hardly a "garden," but it's not a bad place for a picnic. Skip the walking trails and plant displays and head for the excellent lookout over the city. *(On the opposite bank of the Todd River, 2km from Todd Mall. This is Tuncks Rd; the Garden is ahead on the left. ☎ 8952 2154. Garden open daily 10am-6pm. Visitors center open daily 10am-4pm. Admission by donation.)*

**ROYAL FLYING DOCTOR SERVICE.** This 1939 building houses a gallery of medicine, transport, and communication. *(On a service lane to the right off Hartley St, just past Stuart Tce. ☎ 8952 1129. Open M-Sa 9am-4pm, Su 1-4pm. $5, children $2. Tours every 30min.)*

**NATIONAL PIONEER WOMEN'S HALL OF FAME.** In this frontier land of masculine bravado, this is a refreshing site that provides biographical sketches of over a hundred pioneer women. *(In the Old Courthouse on Parson St at the corner of Hartley St. ☎ 8952 9006. Open Mar.-Nov. daily 10am-2pm. $2.20.)*

## OUTSIDE THE CITY CENTER

**ALICE SPRINGS TELEGRAPH STATION HISTORICAL RESERVE.** Numerous walking paths with beautiful wildflowers meander along the riverside, through the surrounding desert hills where wallabies can be seen in the morning and late afternoon, and up to a superb lookout. The Reserve is the original location of Alice Springs, and an unremarkable handful of 19th-century buildings remain. *(4.5km north of town on the Stuart Hwy with a marked turn-off; or walk 4km (45min.) from downtown along the pleasant path that parallels the Todd River. ☎ 8952 3993. Park open daily 8am-9pm. Buildings open 8am-5pm. $6, concessions $4.50.)*

**DESERT PARK.** Fulfilling naive visitors' expectations by being neither a desert nor a park, this mini-zoo brings the self-guided explorer through three major Central Australian habitats, augmented by ranger presentations featuring a Birds of Prey show. Still, the show-stopper is the introductory film on the evolution of outback landscape. *(5km west of town off Larapinta Dr. For $5 shuttle from Alice, call ☎ 8952 4667. Park ☎ 8951 8788. Open daily 7:30am-6pm. $18, concessions $9.)*

**FRONTIER CAMEL FARM.** Alice Springs considers itself the camel capital of Australia, and the Camel Farm keeps the dream alive with camel rides. *(3km beyond where Palm Circuit crosses a traffic circle and emerges as the Ross Hwy. Open daily 9am-5pm. 1½hr. rides daily 10:30am-noon, Apr.-Oct. also 1-2:30pm. $10, children $5, families $25.)*

**TRAIN MUSEUM AND TRANSPORT HALL OF FAME.** The Old Ghan Train and Museum and the adjacent Road Transport Hall of Fame may be 10km from the city, but still two of Alice's definitive sights. The museum highlights the trials and tribulations of the enormous locomotive project, while the Hall of Fame is a spacious warehouse with a collection of vehicles from memory lane and many dashing pictures of handsome road trains to make your heart beat fast. Wait, that's just the gas fumes. *(Accessible by Norris Bell Ave off the Stuart Hwy. Train Museum: ☎ 8955 5047. $5.50, concessions $4.40. Hall of Fame: ☎ 8952 7161. $5, $3. Both open daily 9am-5pm.)*

**MECCA DATE GARDEN.** If you're expecting informative displays on the history of dates in Australia, you'll be disappointed; but, if you're expecting countless different date products for sale and a shady garden to eat them in, you demonstrate a cunning insight into the tourism industry. *(Left on Palm Circuit off the Stuart Hwy after Heavitree Gap; the garden is on the right. ☎ 8952 2111. Open M-F 9am-6pm, Sa 9am-1pm.)*

**CHATEAU HORNSBY.** It's a trek to get out here, but there's something to be said for sipping wine at the only vineyard in the Northern Territory. *(10km south of Alice on the Stuart Hwy, turn left on Colonel Rose Dr for 4km, then left on Petrick. ☎ 8955 5133. Open for tasting daily 10am-5pm. Free.)*

**SCHOOL OF THE AIR.** The school doubles as a visitors center where you can learn about the program and, during school hours, listen in on classes. *(Coming from Alice, before the turn-off to the Reserve, a sign on the Stuart Hwy points down Head St. ☎ 8951 6834. Open M-Sa 8:30am-4:30pm, Su 1:30-4:30pm. $3.50, concessions $2.50.)*

NORTHERN TERRITORY

**THE WORLD'S LARGEST CLASSROOM** It's Monday morning, and 140 children ages 4-13 are standing thousands of kilometers apart, yet singing their national anthem together. Forget virtual schools—the technology that carries these kids' lessons is nothing more complex than short-wave radios. The **School of the Air** is central Australia's educational answer to its vast geography and isolated families spread out on remote cattle stations, roadhouses, and Aboriginal lands. The program, stationed in Alice and a dozen other outback towns, brings children in contact with each other and their Alice-based teachers for three to four hours each week. Their makeshift classrooms are sheds, trailers, or rooms in homes. A parent or appointed instructor supplements their education with an additional five to six hours of weekly schooling. The closest student to Alice is 80km away; the farthest is 1000km. Founded in 1951, the Alice School is the oldest of its kind, though Australia now has 16. It covers 1.3 million sq km of land, and has been dubbed "the largest classroom in the world." And it turns cutting class from an artform into a walk in the park.

## 🎵🎭 ENTERTAINMENT AND NIGHTLIFE

The *Alice Spring News* (free at the library) has a "Dive Into Live" section listing upcoming events. The 500-seat **Araluen Centre,** on Larapinta Dr, presents artsy, independent flicks every Sunday, as well as live events. (☎8953 3111. Box office open daily 10am-5pm. $10, concessions $8.) The popular **Sounds of Starlight Theatre** is in the Todd St Mall a few doors down from Parsons St. This synth-laden, didgeridoo-led performance—part pulling at the heartstrings, part bringing back the worst of 80s music—is accompanied by striking slides of Red Centre landscape. (☎8952 0826. Open Apr.-Nov. Tu-Sa 7:30pm. $16.50, YHA $13, children $11.)

The setting of the climax of *Priscilla, Queen of the Desert,* **Lasseters Hotel Casino,** is across the Todd River on Barrett Dr, a $10 taxi ride from the city center. (☎(1800) 80 89 75. Open daily 10am until "very late.") The adjacent **Limerick Pub** is popular with young professionals. Don't walk; share a cab. (Open daily 4pm-3am.)

Afterhours Alice offers a small slew of lively pubs and clubs which don't charge a cover and are populated mainly by a middle-aged crowd. **Sean's Bar,** on Bath St just south of Gregory Tce, sets the standard with a relaxed setting, friendly clientele and weekend live music. (Open until "late." Guinness pints $6.60, mixed drinks $4.50.) **Desert Waterhole,** at the Melanka Lodge, draws backpackers with pool tables, a dance floor, and a DJ after 10pm. (☎8952 2233. Open nightly 6pm-4am. $6 jugs nightly until 10pm.) Cozy and smoky, **Scotty's Tavern,** on Todd Mall, draws a local crowd with nightly live music. (☎8952 7131. Open Su-Th 11am-midnight, F-Sa 11am-1am.) **Bojangles Saloon,** on Todd St south of Gregory Tce, is consistently jam-packed with hip travelers and outback cowboys, drawn by nightly live music and decor reminiscent of an Aussie cattle station. (☎8952 2873. Open daily 11:30am-late. Su: Blues Jam 1pm-late.)

## 🌺 FESTIVALS AND EVENTS

**Heritage Week** is a NT celebration held in late April featuring historical reenactments and displays. The horses head out of the gates at **Pioneer Race Park** on the Stuart Hwy on the first Monday in May for the lavish **Alice Springs Cup Carnival,** and on the same day the **Bangtail Muster** brings a parade and other entertainment to Alice's streets. Also in May, the 7.8km walking race **King of the Mountain** sends tourists and locals to the top of Mt. Gillen (off Larapinta, west of town). On the Queen's Birthday Weekend in early June, the plucky cars of the **Finke Desert Race** traverse 240km of roadless dusty desert from Alice to the town of Finke in the south. The not-so-traditional **Camel Cup Carnival** race is held the first Saturday in July, followed the next Saturday by the more traditional, agriculture-focused **Alice Springs Show.** The **Alice Springs Rodeo** and the **Alice Marathon** are both held in August. Early October brings the definitive Alice Springs festival, the **Henley-on-**

**Todd Regatta.** A good-natured mockery of the dry river, the race is in bottomless "boats" propelled Flintstones-style—by foot. The race is subject to cancellation: the river flowed in 1993. The **Honda Masters Games,** in September or October, is a friendly biennial (held next in 2002) 30-sport competition for elderly athletes. The **Corkwood Festival** in late November is a folk event featuring craft booths during the day and energetic bush dancing at night.

# THE MACDONNELL RANGES

To the north of the Uluru-Kata Tjuta and Watarrka area lie central Australia's mountains. The 460km-long MacDonnell Ranges roll west to east across the horizon. From a distance, the green shrub that covers its undulating ridges appears like a soft blanket of grass, but up close, Australia's rusty orange earth and rock, prickly ground-cover, and glowing white-ghost gums keep the range rugged. The MacDonnell's pastel colors have inspired painters and photographers, and numerous walking tracks cajole visitors to get out of the car and take a closer look. For hardy visitors bored with one-rock tourist acts, the MacDonnells are a must-see.

## WEST MACDONNELLS

More popular than their eastern counterparts, the sculpted gorges and waterholes of the West MacDonnells shelter vestiges of the bygone rainforest era and hardcore 4WD enthusiasts who know that this is where the good stuff is. **Larapinta Drive** heads out of Alice past the tame beginnings of the West MacDonnells, and **Namatjira Drive** veers off into deeper territory. A fulfilling loop can be made by continuing on Larapinta Drive, which passes by **Finke Gorge National Park** and connects with the western end of Namatjira Drive via **Tylers Pass.** If you're willing to brave rough, unsealed roads, hop on board.

### LARAPINTA DRIVE

The **John Flynn Memorial Grave** rests in peace 7km west of Alice on Larapinta Dr, celebrating the minister who brought the Royal Flying Doctor Service to the outback. The massive boulder atop the grave was taken from the Devil's Marbles formation near Tennant Creek. The Memorial is the starting point for a 17km bike path through the bush to **Simpson's Gap** (3-4hr. one-way). By road, Simpson's Gap is 9km beyond the grave on Larapinta Dr, and 8km up a paved access road. Ero-

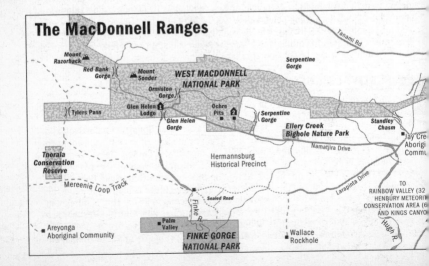

**The MacDonnell Ranges**

Tanami Rd

Mount Razorback

Red Bank Gorge

Mount Sonder

Serpentine Gorge

**WEST MACDONNELL NATIONAL PARK**

Ormiston Gorge

Glen Helen Lodge

Tylers Pass

Ochre Pits

Glen Helen Gorge

Serpentine Gorge

Ellery Creek Bighole Nature Park

Standley Chasm

Jay Cre Aborigi Commu

Tnorala Conservation Reserve

Namatjira Drive

Hermannsburg Historical Precinct

Mereenie Loop Track

Larapinta Drive

TO RAINBOW VALLEY (32 HENBURY METEORI CONSERVATION AREA (6 AND KINGS CANYO

Finke

Sealed Road

Areyonga Aboriginal Community

Palm Valley

**FINKE GORGE NATIONAL PARK**

Wallace Rockhole

Hugh R.

sion from millions of years of floods created this striking opening in the mountain ridges. Earlier on the access road, the **Cassia Hill Walk** (1.5km; 1hr.) culminates in expansive views of the range. (Gap open 5am-8pm; free entry.) **Standley Chasm**, 21km farther on Larapinta Dr, is an 80m-high fissure through the MacDonnells at the end of a 9km access road. When the sun shines directly into the crevasse at midday, the walls glow orange and the crowds gather to ogle. It took 100 million years to form, but a visit will only take 30min. That is, unless you are willing to wade a rockhole and scramble across rocky terrain, which brings you to a deserted and breathtaking second chasm with brilliant hues of red, brown, and gold gracing the walls. (☎8956 7440. Open 8am-6pm. Entry $5.)

Just 6km west of the Chasm, Larapinta Drive intersects **Namatjira Drive** which heads northwest to more isolated spots (see below). Another 46km west of the intersection is the turn-off to **Wallace Rockhole**, which is 18km down an access road, with **camping** and **rock art tours**. (☎8956 7993. Camping $8, children $4. Tours 1hr., 2 per day, $8.) Larapinta Dr continues in sealed sublimity only 34km more to ⊠**Finke Gorge National Park.** This 460 square kilometer park contains the Finke River, reputedly the oldest river on the planet; some stretches date back 350 million years. The park's main attraction is **Palm Valley**, whose palms, combined with the ancient river bed, create a timeless environment in which a dinosaur-spotting would hardly be a surprise. The 16km, 4WD-only access road arrives at a full-facility **campground** ($6.60 per person). Four more rough kilometers along the river bed lead into the valley proper, where the extremely rare Red Cabbage Palm makes its home; high-clearance 4WD is a must for this section. In the valley, the 6km **Mpulungkinya Walk** (6km; 2hr.) traipses among the palms the length of the valley, while the **Arankaia Walk** (2km; 1hr.) turns back halfway and returns by the valley rim. Back near the campgrounds the **Kalaranga Lookout Walk** quickly surmounts some steep crags to bring 360° vistas of the Park.

Just before the turn-off to Finke Gorge is the **Hermannsburg Historical Precinct,** which houses a collection of old broken-down houses from the early Lutheran mission. Hermannsburg is also the birthplace of the Aboriginal artist Albert Namatjira, and his legacy lives on at an art gallery next door. (☎8956 7402. Open daily Mar.-Nov. 9am-4pm, Dec.-Feb. 10am-4pm; precinct $4.50, gallery $3.50.) **Hermannsburg** itself is extremely littered and unappealing, and is restricted Aboriginal land to boot. **Petrol** and **groceries** are available at **Larapinta Service Station,** where you can also obtain the **Mereenie Tour Pass** for 4WD track to **Kings Canyon** (station open M-Sa 8:30am-5:30pm, Su 10am-5:30pm; cash only).

**NORTHERN TERRITORY**

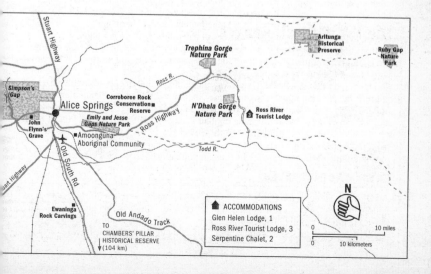

## NAMATJIRA DRIVE

Larapinta Dr forks 46km west of Alice Springs, and the right-hand path, Namatjira Dr, follows a northwesterly route into the heart of West MacDonnell National Park. **Ellery Creek Big Hole** is 42km down Namatjira Dr, and another 2km down an unpaved access road. The 18m-deep pool in a creek through a mountain gap makes for a very cold dip. The nearby **Dolemite Walk** traverses lush forest through spinifex while taking in striking vistas. Parking lot camping with basic facilities is available ($3.30 per person). The next stop is 11km later, at **Serpentine Gorge,** which slithers through the mountains. An easy walk (1hr.) leads to a slim and secretive gorge, while a shorter but steeper trail ascends to another amazing lookout. Six kilometers on, near the unremarkable ruins of the old **Serpentine Chalet,** there is free, isolated bush camping with no facilities, accessible on a rough 3km unsealed road. At the **Ochre Pits,** 6km after the Chalet, a 10min. stroll leads to swirly walls of ochre where Aboriginals still mine ceremonial paint supplies.

Another 17km on is **Ormiston Gorge.** With a permanent 14m-deep waterhole, popular basic camping facilities ($6.60 per person, families $15.40), and a small **ranger station** (☎ 8956 7799), Ormiston is a veritable MacDonnells happy meal—but the special toy is the gorge itself, with its spellbinding crags and colors. It was named by explorer Peter Warburton, who thought that the area looked a lot like his own Glen Ormiston back in Scotland. He's right, except for the gorge's dry vegetation, sand dunes, and steep orange cliffs. A 10min. walk leads from the parking lot into the gorge, but the real gems are the ▧**two longer hikes:** the circuitous **Pound Walk** (7km; 3hr.) meanders through constantly changing, constantly breathtaking wide-open expanses, hitting the MacDonnell's best lookout before returning through the gorge; the **Ghost Gum Walk** (1½hr.) works through the bottom of the gorge, then all of a sudden goes straight up the side, and then returns along the river bed. The Macs don't get any better than this.

Across the highway 4km farther on, the **Glen Helen Gorge** breaks grandly through the range as the **Finke River** winds south to disappear into the Simpson Desert. The gorge is a 10min. stroll from the **Glen Helen Lodge,** a restored homestead resort which provides petrol, phones, snacks, and accommodations. A $17.50 self-cook BBQ is the best dinner value. (☎ 8956 7489. Tent sites $9 per person, powered $11 per site; dorms $19.) At Glen Helen, the Namatjira Rd becomes a corrugated, unsealed track and continues 25km to **Redbank Gorge,** a narrow slit through mountains that shade a series of chilly pools. Two **campgrounds** are available along the bumpy 5km access road into the gorge. The first is free, with no facilities, and the second has a grand view into the valley ($3.30). **Gosse Bluff,** the site of an ancient comet crater, is 20km down Namatjira Dr. Staring at the enormous crater, one can only try to wrap one's mind around the sheer size of the comet. An 11km 4WD access track leads to the bluff. **West MacDonnell Lookout,** a turn-off near the north end of Tyler Pass, takes in the enormity of the crater from a distance.

Another way to see the West Macdonnells is to take the **Larapinta Trail,** an enormous, nearly-complete hiking trail that starts at the Telegraph Station in Alice and will extend 220km west to **Mt. Razorback.** The trail connects the main attractions and is usually hiked in two- to four-day pieces from one gorge to another. Before attempting the long hikes, seek info from the **Park and Wildlife Commission** in Alice (☎ 8951 8211; fax 8951 8258; P.O. Box 1046, Alice Springs NT 0871) and **register** at ☎ (1300) 65 07 30. A $50 refundable deposit is payable at the tourist center in Alice or at the Parks and Wildlife office on the Stuart Hwy. Pick up the flyer *Bushwalks* from the Tourist Office in Alice for a list of hikes—mostly on the Trail—organized by a small informal group (they only ask a contribution to vehicle costs).

## EAST MACDONNELLS

Just beyond Heavitree Gap south of Alice, **Palm Circuit** branches off the Stuart Hwy and heads east. After a few kilometers, it becomes the **Ross Hwy** and plunges into the East MacDonnells. The East Macs are less thrilling geologically than their western counterparts, but are also less crowded and see less tour buses. The **Emily**

**and Jessie Gaps,** 10km east of Alice on the Ross Hwy, are important sacred sites in the Aboriginal Dreaming. **Trephina Gorge Nature Park,** 59km east (plus 7km of access road), has two beautiful gorges. Trephina Gorge features the **Trephina Gorge Walk** (1hr.), an enjoyable trek along the gorge rim and riverbed; and the **Panorama Walk** (1hr.), an uneventful affair except for the incredible lookout. John Hayes Rockhole, 4km down a 4WD track, is home to the stunning **Chain of Ponds Walk** (1½hr.), a sojourn past a great lookout on the rim and through a picture-perfect series of ponds on the gorge floor. Camping with pit toilets and BBQs is available near both gorges (tent sites $3.30 per person; families $7.70).

The Ross Hwy continues another 29km east toward the **Ross River Homestead** (☎8956 9711), one of the most popular destinations in the East MacDonnells, offering hands-on outback activities such as camel-riding, bushwalking, and boomerang-throwing, and catering to an older crowd looking for a more sheltered "outback" experience. **N'Dhala Gorge,** the site of an estimated 6000 **Aboriginal carvings,** is 11km off the highway on a 4WD track. A walking track (1.5km; 1hr.) leads into the gorge and past a few carvings. Camping is available ($3.30; no water).

A left fork before the Homestead traverses 36km of unsealed road to the **Arltunga Historic Reserve,** the remains of central Australia's first official town. The usual assortment of decrepit stone chimneys and shacks is on display, and several short gold mines are open for your spelunking pleasure. Four-wheel-drive vehicles can push on 39km to the remote **Ruby Gap Nature Park,** with rugged scenery that includes a stunning gorge and excellent bush camping ($3.30; no water). The road is rough and registration with the ranger station at Arltunga is recommended. Ruby Gap was the site of the first mining rush in central Australia in 1886. What was believed to be precious ruby stones turned out to be relatively worthless garnets, bringing a swift and sudden death to the "ruby boom."

## THE SIMPSON DESERT

South of Alice, the Stuart Hwy passes Heavitree Gap and Palm Circuit. On the road to the airport, the unsealed and isolated **Old South Rd** veers right toward the **Simpson Desert.** Stock up on supplies before heading down it. Charles Stuart first explored this part of the Simpson in 1845, so bent on conquering the outback that he died trying. The first worthwhile spot is the **Ewaninga Rock Carvings,** 39km south of Alice. The weathered markings are a sacred site for modern Aboriginals, but a pleasant 30min. stroll allows respectful visitors to view the carvings.

The Aboriginal community of **Maryvale Station,** 62km more along the Old South Rd, marks the rough 4WD-only turn-off to **Chambers Pillar Historical Reserve** (4hr. one-way). This sandstone formation was a conspicuous landmark for early travelers and their carved initials (a practice now subject to high fines). The journey is more hard-core than stupendous, but sunsets at the rock are masterpieces of color. (Tent sites $3.30 per person. No water or facilities.)

**Rainbow Valley** is a jagged, U-shaped ridge standing in the desert like a Hollywood backdrop 22km east of the Stuart Hwy on a sandy unmarked 4WD track that begins 75km south of Alice. At sunset, the red, orange, yellow, and brilliant white of the rock formations, the green of the shrubbery, and the blues, indigoes, and violets of the sky illustrate the Valley's name. (Camping $3.30 per person. Toilets and BBQ, but no water.) Another 51km down the Stuart, the unsealed **Ernest Giles Rd** veers west toward Watarrka; 11km past the turn-off and 4km north on an access road lie the **Henbury Meteorite Craters.** This circular ridge of mountains is the remnant of a 4000-year-old meteorite impact site. Basic camping ($3.30) and a self-guided walk (20min.) are available. The Museum of Central Australia's meteorite exhibit, in Alice, makes this site much more meaningful (see p. 281). Back on the Ernest Giles Rd, the paved Luritja Rd, with eventual access to Watarrka, is 90km away, but the going is rough and time consuming. Heading farther south, all that lies along the Stuart Hwy until Coober Pedy SA are homogeneous and over-priced roadhouses, rising from endless miles of spiky spinifex shrub.

## WATARRKA (KINGS CANYON)

Watarrka National Park contains the wayward tourist mecca of Kings Canyon, cutting deep, sunburned grooves in a section of the George Gill Mountains. The canyon's knife-sliced, concave walls shelter waterholes that sustain tropical greenery. Erosion is visible across the canyon, especially in the eccentric domes atop both sides of the precipice. The weathered humps act as natural staircases to the fantastic views atop. Scattered on the flat canyon roof, the domes create an intimidating maze dubbed the Lost City.

**E TRANSPORT.** There are **three different ways** to get to Kings Canyon from Alice Springs. First, the fully-paved route runs 202km south to the roadhouse settlement of **Erldunda** on the Stuart Hwy at its junction with the Lasseter Hwy. Travelers changing buses here may end up spending the night. (☎8956 0984. Tent sites $8 per person; rooms for 2 $39.) From the junction, take the Lasseter Hwy west 110km and turn right on Luritja Rd, which goes north 163km to the Kings Canyon park entrance. Second, vehicles with 4WD can take a "shortcut" along Ernest Giles Rd, a 100km stretch of unpaved road that begins 132km south of Alice. The road is rough and can take 4hr., so highways may be the best bet. Ernest Giles meets Luritja Rd 100km south of the park entrance. Check local road conditions before attempting this road. Third, it's also possible to reach Kings Canyon from Alice Springs via Hermannsburg in the West MacDonnells. Take Larapinta Dr to the scenic but fiercely corrugated 4WD-only **Mereenie Loop Rd** (200km) which passes through Aboriginal land. There are no accommodations or camping allowed on the Mereenie, so plan to do the drive within one day. A $2 pass is required and can be obtained in Hermannsburg at Larapinta Service Station, at Glen Helen Lodge, or at Kings Canyon Resort.

**▛▜ ACCOMMODATIONS AND FOOD.** The **Kings Canyon Resort** (☎8956 7442; fax 8956 7410), 7km up the road from the canyon turn-off, is the beginning and the end of civilization in Watarrka. The resort has the **Desert Oaks Café** (open 5:30am-9pm), and a **grocery store** in the **fuel station** (open daily 7am-7pm). **Outback BBQ** (open daily 6-9pm) offers cook-your-own from $16, and **George Gill Bar** provides not-so-late-night entertainment (open daily noon-11pm). The **medical center** (☎8956 7807, afterhours ☎(0145) 11 51 98) can summon a Flying Doctor within 1hr. Rooms at the resort have A/C, heat, TV, fridge, and share a bath and kitchen. Comfortable, grassy **campsites** have flush toilets, showers, and a pool. The compact, tourist-bus-ridden resort's major drawback is the expense. (Tent sites for 2 $26, powered $29; dorms $40; quads $155. YHA. Beds are held for Greyhound passengers; otherwise book ahead.) Camping is also available at **King's Creek Station,** just outside the park's eastern entrance. (☎8956 7474. $10 per person, powered $12.) Otherwise, no camping is permitted.

**▟ HIKING.** The park has three well-marked paths. An easy walk (2.6km; 1hr.) follows **Kings Creek** along the bottom of the canyon. Cut loose with the challenging ▩**Kings Canyon Walk** (6km; 3hr.), scaling the rocky, steep slope around the top of the canyon, much of the Lost City, and the exhilarating rail-less edge. A side track (20min.) descends into the **Garden of Eden,** a waterhole shaded by palm trees and the narrow canyon walls. Water and tough hiking footwear are essential; there's an outhouse and an info display at the parking lot, but no other facilities at the trailhead. The long canyon walk has three emergency call boxes. The wheelchair-accessible **Kathleen Springs Walk** (2.6km; 1hr.) winds through sandstone valleys to a rockhole sacred to local Aboriginals. The access road is 20km south of the Canyon turnoff. The **Sunset Viewing** picnic area with water, toilets, and BBQ is 1km before the main parking lot, but is not as good as the resort's **Sunset Viewing Boardwalk,** with all-encompassing views of the George Gill Range.

# YULARA (AYERS ROCK RESORT)

Between the rock and a dry place stands the well-sculpted, immaculate community of Yulara. The municipal name shelters the employees of Ayers Rock Resort from the fact that they live on a tourist farm resembling a child's gameboard. The road that loops around Yulara curves in an effort to avoid looking pre-planned, and the town's facilities are carefully landscaped in an effort to blend into the outback. However, Yulara's monopoly on the tourist market is not as well disguised; be prepared for

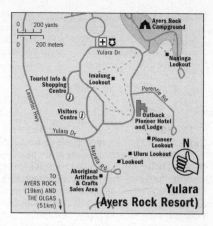

hefty mark-ups on food and more than a bit extra for prime real estate just 19km down the street from the world's largest monolith. If you want to forget that you're in the outback, this place is ideal. If not, keep glancing over at those distant rocks to remember where you are and why you came here.

◩ **TRANSPORT.** **Connellan Airport** lies 5km north of town. Airnorth, Qantas (☎ 13 13 13), and Ansett (☎ 13 13 00) fly to: **Darwin** ($372); **Adelaide** ($399); **Brisbane** ($432); **Melbourne** ($432); **Perth** ($371); **Sydney** ($391); **Alice Springs** ($131); and **Cairns** ($362). There are advance-purchase discounts and a 30% discount for international backpackers. A free **airport shuttle** run by AAT Kings meets all flights and picks up from all accommodations. Greyhound Pioneer and McCafferty's **buses** depart for **Alice Springs** twice daily from the Outback Pioneer Hotel (6hr., 9am and 12:30pm, $55-60). Ayers Rock Resort runs a free **village shuttle** around the resort loop (every 15min., daily 10:30am-6pm and 6:30pm-12:30am). **Territory Rent-a-Car** (☎ 8956 2030), **Hertz** (☎ 8956 2244), and **Avis** (☎ 8956 2266) have offices at the airport or at the **Tourist Information Centre** (☎ 8957 7324). The **Mobil** station on the resort loop rents **bicycles.** (☎ 8956 2229. Open daily 7am-9pm. $22 per day.)

A handful of walks around town lead to six different lookout points, all with impressive views of the usual suspects. To get to Uluru and Kata Tjuta from the resort, you'll need a vehicle. **Uluru Express** offers the most flexible transportation. (☎ 8956 2152. To Uluru $30, Kata Tjuta from $45.) **Anangu Tours** is owned by Aboriginals who can share some insider knowledge; book through the Cultural Centre. (☎ 8956 2123. 2hr. tours $47; children $24; families $142.) **Greyhound Pioneer** does a sunset run to Uluru from the resort (4hr., departs 3pm, $39) and also runs to Kata Tjuta (5½hr., departs 6am, $31). Book ahead.

◪ **PRACTICAL INFORMATION.** The **Tourist Information Centre,** in the main town square shopping center, has general info, a list of daily outdoors conditions, and several tour agencies. (☎ 8957 7324. Open daily 8:30am-8:30pm; service desks maintain shorter, variable hours.) The so-called **Visitors Centre,** with a grand set of stairs rising from the road near the entrance to the village, is actually little more than a gift shop and museum with a smattering of town info. (☎ 8957 7377. Open daily 8:30am-7:30pm.) Other services include: **police** (☎ 8956 2166); a 24-hour **medical center** (☎ 8956 2286; clinic open M-F 9am-5pm, Sa-Su 10-11am); an **ANZ bank** in the shopping center (open M-Th 9:30am-4pm, F 9:30am-5pm; 24hr. **ATM**); and the **post office** (☎ 8956 2288; open M-F 9am-6:30pm, Sa-Su 10am-2pm). The **library** has **Internet access** (☎ 8956 2531; open M-F 10:30am-5pm; 1hr. $10). **Postal code:** 0872.

NORTHERN TERRITORY

**ACCOMMODATIONS.** The resort offers little choice when it comes to accommodations within a given price range. For all lodge reservations call ☎ (1800) 08 96 22 or fax 8956 2260. The **Outback Pioneer Hotel** has a rather impersonal YHA hostel with barracks-type dorms. (Reception daily 4am-11pm. 20-bed dorms without door locks $30; 4-bed dorms $38. Reservations essential.) The uninspiring **Resort Campground** corners the market on camping, since it is not allowed elsewhere in the national park. Campers have access to a swimming pool, communal kitchen, laundry, hot showers, and free BBQ. (Tent sites $12 per person.) Free but less conveniently located camping is available 100km east of Yulara at **Curtin Springs,** or, unofficially, at the basic rest stops along the way—or in your car.

**FOOD AND ENTERTAINMENT.** The **Outback Pioneer Hotel** has a run-of-the-mill **snack bar** with $6 burgers (open daily 8am-9pm). Their nightly **BBQ** (open 7-9:30pm) ranges from beef or veggie burgers ($13) to emu sausages ($20). The restaurants listed on the back of the resort map have Uluru-sized prices, though the **Gecko Café** in the shopping center has creatively decorated wood-oven pizzas (that are still overpriced) at $17-21 (open daily 10am-10pm). The shopping center has a **Takeaway Food** counter (open 7am-8:30pm); an **ice creamery** (open daily 11am-7pm); and a pricey **supermarket** (open daily 8:30am-9pm). Entertainment within the resort is contrived and aimed at high-budget tourists. The auditorium behind the Visitors Centre shows second-run **films** (F-Su 8pm; $8). The main sights, of course, are the geologic ones.

# ULURU-KATA TJUTA NATIONAL PARK

Out of the flat, scrub-brush landscape of the Red Centre, where tumbleweed and dust funnels provide the only visible movement, Uluru (Ayers Rock) and Kata Tjuta (the Olgas) hulk like hibernating animals. These shockingly gigantic rock formations, with their smooth ridges and pocket-like caves, break not only the horizon but also the banks of many eager tourists who gather for their once-in-a-lifetime glimpse of "sunset at Uluru." As the largest single rock in the world, fiery-orange Uluru warrants the hype. Standing beside the monolith, it's impossible not to ogle at the towering walls while uttering "wow" through an open-mouthed gape. Nearby Kata Tjuta, a cluster of rounded hump-like mini-Ulurus, are less touristed

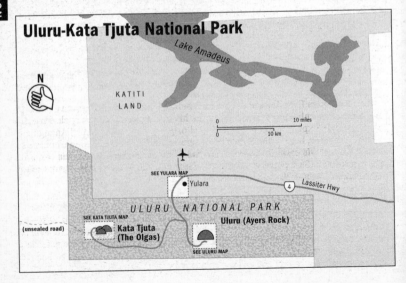

**Uluru-Kata Tjuta National Park**

but no less humbling. Together, Uluru, Kata Tjuta, and endless sand dunes and desert scrub comprise the 1325 square kilometer Uluru-Kata Tjuta National Park.

These natural wonders are a centerpiece for the local Anangu Aboriginals, who, for 22,000 years, have revered Uluru as a sacred site of the Dreaming. Since Uluru's European discovery in 1872 by Ernest Giles, the area has also become one of Australia's primary tourist meccas. A sense of indigenous loss off-set by industry gain is still present. Today, the park is managed jointly by the National Park Service and Anangu residents, and a strong effort is made to incorporate geologic and cultural information. Many think of Uluru-Kata Tjuta as the epitomizing symbol of the outback. With the natural splendor, cultural significance, and contemporary balancing-act between indigenous livelihood and visitor needs, it just might be. But the hard-earned solitude that lends the outback its true flavor is missing in this highly-marketed area. Still, Uluru and Kata Tjuta are so stunning that a visit is definitely worth it, even for travelers bent on keeping to the backroads.

# ⊏ TRANSPORT

To get to Uluru-Kata Tjuta by road, travel south on the Stuart Hwy 200km from Alice Springs, or north 483km from Coober Pedy to Erldunda, then 264km west on the **Lasseter Hwy.** Long before reaching Uluru, you'll see **Mt. Connor,** a big mesa in the distance. This tricky imitation, often mistaken for Ayers Rock, has its own viewing area right off the highway.

For those without a car, **Greyhound Pioneer** offers the cheapest three-day tour that includes Uluru, Kata Tjuta, and Kings Canyon. (☎ 13 20 30. Tours depart Alice Springs; $219; book ahead.) **Wayoutback** is a highly recommended company that offers off-the-beaten-path 4WD tours of the same area, with lots of walking and bush camping. (☎ 8952 4324. 3-day tours depart Alice Springs daily; $375.) **Northern Territory Adventure Tours** also offers popular 2- to 3-day tours. (☎ (1300) 65 46 04. Tours depart Alice Springs daily. 2-day $280; 3-day $375.)

# ⁊ PRACTICAL INFORMATION

The Uluru-Kata Tjuta National Park **entrance station** (☎ 8956 2252) lies 5km past the Yulara resort village, where all visitors must purchase a three-day pass ($16.25). Uluru is 14km ahead, and 4km farther is the turn-off to Kata Tjuta (42km). These roads are all paved. (Park open daily hour-before-sunrise to hour-after-sunset, i.e. Dec.-Feb. 5am-9pm; Mar. 5:30am-8:30pm; Apr. 6am-8pm; May 6am-7:30pm; June-July 6:30am-7:30pm; Aug. 6am-7:30pm; Sept. 5:30am-7:30pm; Oct. 5am-8pm; Nov. 5am-8:30pm.) **No camping** is permitted within the park. There are toilet facilities at the Cultural Centre, the main carpark at Uluru, and the sunset-viewing area at Kata Tjuta. Picnic facilities are at the Cultural Centre and the Kata Tjuta sunset-viewing area. As in the rest of the Red Centre, the **bush flies** can be unbearable in the late summer and fall. Bring mesh netting to cover your face.

The **Uluru-Kata Tjuta Cultural Centre,** 1km before Uluru, is an informative effort by the Anangu to enlighten tourists about the history surrounding the rock. Free displays include explanations of the mythical origins of the rock and of Anangu culture. The center, built with all-natural materials in the Aboriginal mode, contains a snack bar, an **info desk,** the **Maruku Arts and Crafts shop,** and the **Winkilun** ceramics shop. (☎ 8956 3138. Open daily Nov.-Mar. 7am-6pm; April-Oct. 7am-5:30pm. Gallery open daily 8:30am-5:30pm.)

# ULURU (AYERS ROCK)

The Uluru-hype is big, but Uluru is even bigger: 348m in height, 3.1km in length, 1.9km in width, and 9.4km around. The rock is actually only the summit of an enormous sandstone block that extends an estimated 3km beneath the surface. Eons of geological activity have tilted and eroded once-horizontal sedimentary layers into vertical grooves on the surface of the rock. Up close, the "grooves" become meters-long gorges, and the smooth rock walls reveal a rough, scaly exterior.

The strategically situated **sunset-viewing area,** 5km from the rock, is the place to hear the nightly oohs and aahs of awestruck travelers, punctuated by the clicking shutters and useless flashes of hundreds of cameras. The road continues on a **paved loop** around the rock. The **main carpark** and toilets are just to the left along the loop. A **sunrise-viewing area** lies on the opposite side of the rock.

The Anangu prefer people not climb because they feel responsible for those who are hurt, and because the spiritually significant

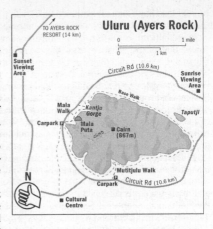

Mala Dreaming track follows the same ascent. It is a good idea to visit the Cultural Centre and understand Anangu motivations before deciding one way or the other. Still, they make it as safe as possible for those who choose to brave the ascent. A fixed chain helps with the brutal initial uphill, the steepest part of the track, but this climb is no easy jaunt; plaques memorialize people who have died (mostly of heart attacks). The climb (1.6km; 1¼hr.) requires rugged footwear and plenty of water: visitors should avoid climbing in the middle of the day or if they have medical conditions or loosely attached hairpieces. The summit affords a panorama of the Red Centre's expanse, broken by Kata Tjuta and Mt. Connor.

Several more humbling vantage-points allow visitors to enjoy the rock while obeying Anangu preferences. An ambitious **circuit walk** (9.4km; 4hr.) traces the base of the rock. The **Mala Walk** (1km; 1hr.) is a segment of this circuit which leads from the main parking lot past magnificent walls and a "stone wave" to **Kantju Gorge.** There is a free ranger-guided Mala Walk offering a look at Uluru from an Aboriginal perspective; meet the ranger at the **Mala Walk** sign at the base of Uluru, near the main parking lot (1½hr.; daily Oct.-Apr. 8am, May-Sept. 10am; free). A

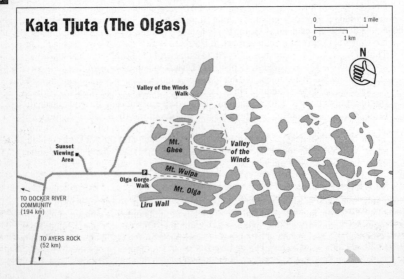

smaller parking lot to the right from the loop entrance serves the **Mutitjulu Walk** (1km), which leads to the waterhole home of the watersnake Wanampi. Both the Mala and Mutitjulu walks are wheelchair accessible. Grab *An Insight Into Uluru* ($1) at the Cultural Centre for an expanded self-guided tour of these two walks.

## KATA TJUTA (THE OLGAS)

Perhaps more beautiful than the Rock are the 36 undulating domes scattered over an area several times the size of Uluru. Kata Tjuta ("many heads") is the second conspicuous rock formation in the Red Centre, and it seems as though Uluru might just be a ploy to keep tourists away from this less-touted treasure that provides a fresh amazing perspective from each angle. The giant rocks sit like eggs on the horizon, and spaces between their steep walls allow entrance into their valleys. The 44km road to Kata Tjuta leaves the main road 4km after the park entrance station. The **Dune Viewing Area,** 25km down the road, is at the end of a wheelchair-accessible walk (300m) allowing relaxing and all-encompassing views of Kata Tjuta. This also is an underappreciated sunrise spot. The **sunset-viewing area** (toilets available) is just short of the starting points for the two walks. The **Olga Gorge walk** (2.6km; 1hr.) is an easy path between a pair of the most daunting domes. The dome on the right is **Mt. Olga** (546m), the highest peak in the range. With mind-blowing views around every corner, the winding ▨**Valley of the Winds walk** (7km; 3hr.) traces a majestic circuit through the outer wall of domes and into the inner sanctuary. Bring lots of water; there are plenty of shady spots and an emergency water source at the halfway point. The inner circuit of the walk closes at 11am on days hotter than 36°C, so morning jaunts are advised.

# QUEENSLAND

If the variety of the continent's natural attractions could be condensed into one state, the result would look something like Queensland, Australia's deliciously layered natural paradise. Queensland changes, east to west, from reef islands to sandy shores, from hinterland rainforest to the glowing red outback. At the base of this fantasyland sits the capital city of Brisbane, a diverse and manageable urban break from the surf and sun.

Queensland offers mega-tourist stops interspersed with country towns, subtle national parks, and isolated islands. Moving northward, Queensland's coastal side crawls with backpackers year-round—with the same faces popping up in every town, the journey often feels like a never-ending party. The downside for those on this heavily-touristed route is that real Aussies are hard to come by. Moving from one backpacker hot-spot to another can be mind-numbing as you wade through a never-ending swamp of brochures, billboards, and tourist packages.

The enjoyment of a Queensland visit will endlessly multiply the more you get off this beaten track. Those willing to temporarily trade sandals for hiking boots can explore the rainforest-drenched far north and the jewel-bedecked outback, where history, like tourism, proceeds at a koala's pace. Inland, you'll encounter charming country towns, pockets of thriving Aboriginal culture, and plenty of history—all without a hint of the rampant tourism of the coast. In Queensland, appreciating Oz at its extremes can be as simple as driving toward Cape Tribulation and watching the rainforest practically tumble into the pounding ocean.

## QUEENSLAND HIGHLIGHTS

**CAREFREE DRIFTING.** The vibrant Great Barrier Reef.

**TRUE INCENTIVES.** Race for rum in Moreton Bay (p. 316).

**CATCHING A BREAK.** The perfect wave of Coolangatta surf (p. 317).

**ROUGHING IT.** The sandy wonderland of Fraser Island (p. 343).

**SO THIS IS HEAVEN.** The white sand paradise of Great Keppel Island (p. 352).

**STARLIT SAILING.** The Whitsunday Islands (p. 364).

**DIVER'S DREAM.** The S. S. Yongala Wreck in Townsville (p. 371).

**PEEPING TOM.** Koalas in the lush forest of Magnetic Island (p. 373).

**WILDERNESS REDEFINED.** The rainforests of Hinchinbrook Island (p. 377).

**CULTURAL IMMERSION.** The Tjapukai Theatre, near Cairns (p. 391).

**SURVIVOR.** Wet Tropics Rainforest in Cape Tribulation (p. 399).

**THE THREE HOUR TOUR.** Unknown islands (p. ?).

## 🔳 GETTING AROUND

The Queensland coast as far north as Cairns, plus some locations farther north and in the interior, is comprehensively serviced by public transportation. Don't underestimate the distances involved; even within the state, many people choose to fly if they just want to get quickly from Brisbane to Cairns. If you've got the time for a leisurely trip, though, taking a bus up the coast allows you to stop at the innumerable great spots along the way. The major bus lines are **Greyhound** (☎ 13 20 30) and **McCafferty's** (☎ 13 14 99), and the train line is **Queensland Rail** (☎ 13 22 32). If you have a few friends to chip in for costs or if you're traveling with a family, **renting a car** provides the most convenience and freedom to wander off the beaten path. All the major car rental establishments are here, plus dozens of cheaper local ones listed throughout the chapter. To tackle the area from Cooktown north through Cape York as well as some of the desert roads, you'll need **4WD**. This is pricey; it's also tough to find an automatic transmission 4WD (try **Allcar Rentals** in Port Douglas, ☎4099 4123). Roads in the tropics are especially harrowing, and often impassible, during and immediately following the **Wet season** (Nov.-Apr.). It's best to call ahead for **road conditions** (☎3361 2406).

The central office of the **Royal Automobile Club of Queensland (RACQ)** is at 300 St. Paul's Tce, Fortitude Valley, Brisbane. Affiliated with clubs worldwide, RACQ provides excellent maps, car buying or selling info, and technical services. (☎3361 2444; statewide roadside service ☎13 11 11. Open M-F 8:30am-5:30pm. 1-year membership $67, overseas transfer free.) For more info, see **On the Road**, p. 66.

# 🔁 THE GREAT BARRIER REEF

The Great Barrier Reef, one of the world's greatest living wonders, stretches for 2300km from just offshore of Bundaberg to Papua New Guinea, encompassing hundreds of islands and cays and thousands of smaller coral reefs. This marine wonderland is easily accessible from the Queensland coast, but when, where, and how to explore it involve complicated and important decisions. Many people who don't plan sufficiently end up paying a lot for bad visibility or a mediocre dive site. It's important to first familiarize yourself with the types of reef and the life forms you'll see (for an overview see **Marine Life**, p. 29). *Let's Go* describes individual diving and snorkeling sites and operators throughout the book, but before making a choice, take some time to get a general sense of the options. With care and a touch of luck, your experience will be magical.

## WHEN, WHERE, AND HOW TO DIVE

The Great Barrier Reef is vast, and furthermore, many of Australia's very best dive sites aren't even on it—they're at more distant, smaller reefs in the **Coral Sea**. If you're a very serious diver with lots of time and money, you may want to invest in a trip for a week or two out to such sites as **Osprey, Flinders, Lihou**, or **Marion Reef**, superbly pristine spots with crystal-clear visibility. For most budget travelers, however, reaching these sites isn't an option, and it fortunately isn't necessary. There is excellent diving on the Great Barrier Reef if you plan it well.

**WHEN.** One crucial consideration: when comparing the quality of dive sites, it's not just about what's there—it's about how well you can see it, too. Bad weather or silt deposits can turn an underwater wonderland into a turbid, murky mess. For the best **visibility,** avoid diving for a day or two after a storm and a month after a cyclone if you're to the south of where it hit. Just north of a cyclone, on the other hand, the visibility is surprisingly excellent. Avoid the **wet season** altogether; the worst months are January through March, and the best are July through December. The very best time to dive is November, when the spawning reef is a shimmering spectacle. Throughout the year, weather is always unpredictable, but try not to go out if the windspeed is above 20 knots. Location-wise, visibility tends to increase with distance from shore. The reef recently suffered from coral bleaching near the shore, so the outer reef definitely provides better diving sites.

**WHERE. Cairns** (see p. 381), 27km from the reef, is the country's most popular diving destination because of its combination of superb weather, ample supply of dive-boats, urban amenities, and excellent sites close to shore. The best sites are the Norman Reef, Milin Reef, Saxon Reef, and Hastings Reef. Many popular tour operators go to the somewhat closer and less impressive sites of **Michaelmas Cay** and **Green Island**. Farther north, **Port Douglas** (see p. 395) and **Cape Tribulation** (see p. 399) offer similarly rich reefs, but with fewer tourists traversing the waters.

Below Cairns, the ecosystem slowly changes from tropical to subtropical around the southern end of the reef. **Beaver Cay** is **Mission Beach's** most popular site, home to numerous turtles and the occasional manta ray (see p. 378). Shore dives are cheap from **Magnetic Island** (see p. 373), but by far the best site in the

QUEENSLAND

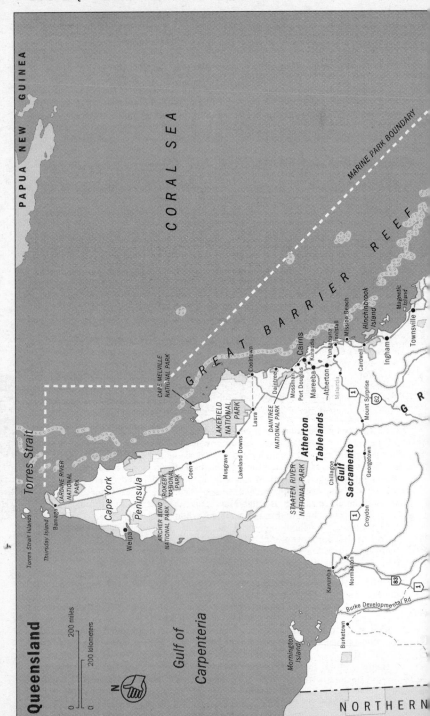

# Queensland

PAPUA NEW GUINEA

Torres Strait

CORAL SEA

MARINE PARK BOUNDARY

GREAT BARRIER REEF

Gulf of Carpenteria

Cape York Peninsula

JARDINE RIVER NATIONAL PARK

Torres Strait Islands

Thursday Island

Bamaga

Weipa

ARCHER BEND NATIONAL PARK

ROKEBY NATIONAL PARK

Coen

Musgrave

Lakeland Downs

Laura

LAKEFIELD NATIONAL PARK

CAPE MELVILLE NATIONAL PARK

DAINTREE NATIONAL PARK

STAATEN RIVER NATIONAL PARK

Cooktown

Mossman

Daintree

Port Douglas

Mareeba

Atherton

Cairns

Kuranda

Yungaburra

Ravenshoe

Innisfail

Mission Beach

Hinchinbrook Island

Cardwell

Ingham

Magnetic Island

Townsville

Atherton Tablelands

Mount Surprise

Chillagoe

Gulf Sacramento

Georgetown

Croydon

Karumba

Normanton

Mornington Island

Burketown

Burke Developmental Rd

62

1

83

1

G R

N

200 miles

200 kilometers

0

0

NORTHERN

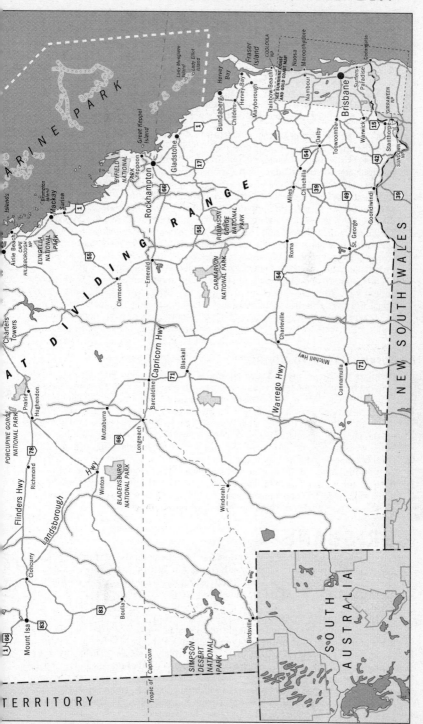

**Townsville** region is found on the wreck of the **S.S.Yongala** (see p. 371) which sank 33m one year before the *Titanic* disaster. Today, the ship is covered in coral polyps and other sealife and is the world's premier wreck site, but its challenging currents are suitable for experienced divers only. The **Whitsunday** area (see p. 364) has plenty of snorkeling and some island diving; most trips depart from **Airlie Beach** (see p. 360) or are linked to several-day sailing cruises. Other locations south of the reef offer far less to see, but can be great places to find **cheap certification courses; Hervey Bay** (see p. 341) and **Bundaberg** (see p. 347) have possibly the cheapest PADI courses in the state. **PADI** is the most recognized form of certification.

**HOW.** Australia is a great place to learn how to dive—it is cheap and safe. In Queensland, you need a **certification card** to go on all certified dives. Before you begin a certification course or set out for an extended trip, you might want to try an **introductory** or **"resort" dive,** with a trained guide. Resort dives may require time in the pool, and are always more expensive, but are an indispensable way to find out if you're willing to spend the big time and money required to pursue this sport.

If you decide to do a PADI open water course, try to get boat dives instead of shore dives. If you do an Advanced Open Water course, insist that the deep dive be to 30m and no shallower, and choose the electives you want—don't just take the ones offered. **Medical exams** are often demanded for certified dives, and are almost always necessary for certification courses. Such "dive medicals" cost about $50 and are generally cheapest in diving hotspots like Airlie Beach and Cairns.

Once you are choosing a dive operator, think about some questions: How long do you want to dive—a day-trip or a multi-day trip? How big of a boat do you want? For personal dive instruction and a group atmosphere, smaller boats may be the way to go. Finally, are you going with other divers or with friends who may prefer other water activities? If you are already certified, don't assume you're an expert—be honest with dive operators about your experience and ask questions.

### ALTERNATIVES TO DIVING

Diving is the ideal way to get an up-close view of the reef, but it's expensive, requires bulky, complicated equipment, and often requires time-consuming, costly training. By contrast, if you can swim, you can **snorkel.** Renting a mask and fins can be as cheap as $10 per day, and just a little more for a wetsuit. Gear is sometimes free with sailing trips or even hostel stays. Good snorkeling is often available just off the shore of islands or beaches; you can grab your gear and swim unguided. When wearing fins, be extremely aware of where you are flapping—if you hit the coral you may kill it, erasing hundreds of years of growth. Better yet, snorkel with your natural ten-toed flippers. **Reef walking** is an archaic and very destructive way to see coral; it can result in broken ankles, ruined coral, and dead creatures. If you don't want to get wet at all, an even tamer choice is to view the reef through one of the **glass-bottom boats** cruising from islands or beach towns.

# BRISBANE

Commonly unexplored (and unappreciated) by those on the northward pilgrimage, Brisbane (pop. 1,500,000) spreads around its central river with a wide spectrum of interests and attractions. Contrasting riverside to hillside, parkland to high-rise, alterna-chic to yuppie, and classy to seedy, Brisbane today is neither glamorous nor industrial—but practical, clean, and full of youthful energy.

The Brisbane River lends an easygoing grace to the city through which it weaves. River transportation is simple and pleasant—hulking ferries and slim kayaks glide between Chinatown and the South Bank Parklands, between investment banks in the Central Business District and the trendy West End. The sunny, warm climate has attracted artistic emigrés, eager to shed winter jumpers and rev up the city's cultural institutions. Always a good bet for temporary employment, Brisbane only recently earned a reputation as a tourist destination. Today, visitors to Brisbane enjoy not only the serene waterfront and peaceful parklands, but corner cafés, rocking nightclubs, and heaps of live local music.

**BRISBANE HIGHLIGHTS**

**STRESS, WHAT STRESS?** The tranquil South Bank Parklands (p. 309).

**FEAST LIKE TEN KINGS.** Garuva—an eating experience from a dream (p. 308).

**CULTURE BINGE.** Galleries aplenty at the Queensland Cultural Centre (p. 309).

**URBANE NATURE.** The gardens at Mt. Coot-tha Park (p. 310).

**GROOVE THANG.** Thumping techno with a funky crowd at the Beat (p. 312).

**WARM RAYS AND STINGRAYS.** First-rate diving and sunbathing on North Stradbroke Island (p. 313).

# ✈ GETTING THERE

## BY PLANE

**Brisbane International Airport,** 17km (25min.) northwest of the city center, has luggage storage (1 day $4-10). It's served by 23 airlines, including **Qantas,** 247 Adelaide St (☎ 13 13 13) and **Ansett** (☎ 13 13 00), on the corner of George and Queen St (both open M-F 8:30am-5pm).

The **Travellers Information Service** is located on level 2 of the international terminal, 3km from the domestic terminal aboard the $2.70 Coachtrans bus. (☎ 3406 3190. Open 5am until last flight of the night.) The **Roma Street Transit Centre** in town has info and books accommodations on level 3 (see below).

**SkyTrans** on level 3 of the Transit Centre, runs a daily **shuttle bus** between the airport and Transit Centre. (☎ 3236 1000. Every 30min. 5am-8:45pm, last bus to city 10:45pm. $9, return $15, same day return $12; children $5.) A trip to one of the major hotels costs $11. A **taxi** between the airport and downtown costs about $20.

## BY TRAIN

The **Roma Street Transit Centre,** 500m west of the city center, is Brisbane's main intercity bus and train terminal. (☎ 3236 2020. Open M-F 7am-6pm, Sa-Su 8am-5pm.) **Lockers** (24hr. $5) are on level 1 and 3, and showers are on level 2. **Queensland Rail** (☎ 3235 2222; bookings ☎ 13 22 32; reservations for packages including air and accommodations ☎ (1800) 62 76 55) has offices at Central Station on the corner of Ann and Edward St, diagonally opposite the Palace Backpacker, and on level 1 of the transit centre. Travel times can vary considerably depending on the train. The snazzy new Tilt Train is the fastest way to travel north along the coast from Brisbane as far as Rockhampton (book ahead). Trains run to: **Sydney** (14hr., 1 per day, $110); **Bundaberg** (4¼-6½hr., 2-3 per day, $49.50); **Cairns** (32hr., 4 per week, $193); **Gladstone** (5¾-9¼hr., 2-3 per day, $69); **Mackay** (17½hr., 4 per week, $158); **Maryborough West** (3½-4½hr., 2-3 per day, $43; connecting bus to **Hervey Bay**); **Prosperine** (19½hr., 4 per week, $158; connecting bus to **Airlie Beach**); **Rockhampton** (7-11hr., 2-3 per day, $77); and **Townsville** (24hr., 4 per week, $173).

For long travel itineraries, Queensland Rail's **Sunshine Rail Pass** is good for a given number of travel days within a six-month span on any Queensland service and unlimited travel on Citytrain, the intracity network. Passes available at the Queensland Rail booth at Roma Street Transit Centre or Central Station. (14-day $267, 21-day $309, 30-day $388; students and children half-price. Book ahead.)

## BY BUS

Greyhound Pioneer (☎ 13 20 30) and McCafferty's (☎ 13 14 99) cover destinations along the east coast. Both offer 10% concessions for YHA, VIP, and ISIC, and 20% for seniors and children. Adults receive 5% discount on return fares. Some routes are more frequently serviced Oct.-Mar. Kirkland's Coaches (☎ (1300) 36 70 77) offers 25% concessions for YHA and ISIC, and 50% for children. Coachtrans (☎ 13 12 30, ☎ 3236 1901) and Suncoast Pacific (☎ 3236 1901) also service the Queensland coast. To get to the Gold Coast for $1, hop on Conrad Jupiter's Shuttle, departing

Roma St at 9am, arriving at Jupiter Casino in **Broadbeach,** near **Surfers,** at 10:30am. Return for Brisbane departs the casino at 3pm. What's the catch? The ride costs $11, but when you arrive at Conrad's, you can join their Casino Rewards for free and receive $10 in gambling money (no luggage permitted; bookings essential)

# FROM BRISBANE TO:.

| DESTINATION | COMPANY | DURATION | TIMES | PRICE |
|---|---|---|---|---|
| Adelaide | McCafferty's | 30½hr. | 1 per day | $182 |
| Airlie Beach | McCafferty's | 18¼hr. | 5 per day | $122 |
| Bundaberg | McCafferty's | 6-7¾hr. | 7 per day | $49 |
| Byron Bay | Kirkland's | 3½hr. | 4 per day M-F, 2 per day Sa-Su | $28 |
| Byron Bay | McCafferty's | 3½hr. | 4-5 per day | $28 |
| Byron Bay non-express | Premier | 3½hr. | 3 per day | $25 |
| Cairns | McCafferty's | 25-30hr. | 9 per day | $163 |
| Coolangatta | CoachTrans | 2¼hr. | 12 per day | $16 |
| Hervey Bay | McCafferty's | 4½-6¼hr. | 10 per day | $36 |
| Hervey Bay | Suncoast Pacific | 5hr. | 8-10 per day | $33 |
| Lismore | Kirkland's | 4½hr. | 4 per day M-F, 2 per day Sa-Su | $31.50 |
| Mackay | McCafferty's | 15-16hr. | 9 per day | $106 |
| Maroochydore | McCafferty's | 1¾-2hr. | 6 per day | $17 |
| Maroochydore | Suncoast Pacific | 2hr. | 8-10 per day | $21 |
| Melbourne | McCafferty's | 24-28½hr. | 5 per day | $148 |
| Mission Beach | McCafferty's | 26hr. | 2 per day | $157 |
| Noosa | McCafferty's | 2¼-2¾hr. | 6 per day | $18 |
| Noosa | Suncoast Pacific | 3hr. | 8-10 per day | $24 |
| Rockhampton | McCafferty's | 10½-14¼hr. | 9 per day | $70 |
| Surfers Paradise | CoachTrans | 1¼-1½hr. | 12 per day | $14 |
| Surfers Paradise | Kirkland's | 1¼hr. | 4 per day M-F, 2 per day Sa-Su | $196 |
| Surfers Paradise | McCafferty's | 1½hr. | 6 per day | $15 |
| Surfers Paradise non-express | Premier | 1½hr. | 3 per day | $12 |
| Sydney | McCafferty's | 14-17½hr. | 12 per day | $81 |
| Sydney with one stop | Premier | 16-19hr. | 3 per day | $69 |
| Sydney with unlimited stops | Premier | 16-19hr. | 3 per day | $88 |
| Sydney with YHA, ISIC, VIP and one stop | Premier | 16-19hr. | 3 per day | $50 |
| Sydney with YHA, ISIC, VIP and unlimited stops | Premier | 16-19hr. | 3 per day | $79 |
| Toowoomba | McCafferty's | 2hr. | 15-17 per day | $19 |

# ✳ ORIENTATION

The Brisbane River meanders through the city, creating easily identifiable landmarks. The city's heart is cradled in the bottom of a sideways S-curve, connected to South Bank by the **Victoria Bridge.** The **Transit Centre** is on Roma St; a left turn out of the building and a 5min. walk down Roma St leads to the corner of Albert and Ann St and the grassy **King George Square** (a front lawn for the grand **City Hall**). Adelaide St runs along the opposite side of the square, and a block beyond is the **Queen St Mall,** a popular open-air pedestrian thoroughfare lined with shops and cafés, which was recently refurbished for $25 million. Underneath the mall and the adjoining **Myer Centre** shopping complex is the **Queen Street Bus Station.**

Brisbane's neighborhoods radiate out from the city center. A right turn out of the transit center leads to **Petrie Tce** and **Paddington,** both most easily reached by passing under the railway bridge and taking the first left up the hill. North of Boundary St is **Spring Hill,** bordered to the west by **Victoria Park** and 15min. from the Queen St Mall up steep Edward St. A 15min. walk down Ann St, the nightclub-heavy **Fortitude Valley** offers an alternative scene but contains some slightly seedy areas—use caution if walking alone at night. Fortitude Valley is also home to the small and authentic **Chinatown,** which has served as the film location for several Jackie Chan flicks. Down Brunswick St, at the intersection with Hardcourt St, officially begins **New Farm,** with its free art galleries and cafés.

South of the river, the Victoria Bridge footpath turns into Melbourne St and heads into **South Brisbane,** crossing Boundary St six blocks later into the heart of the **West End. South Bank** is to the east of the southern end of the bridge; further along the riverside, **Kangaroo Point** forms a peninsula into the River.

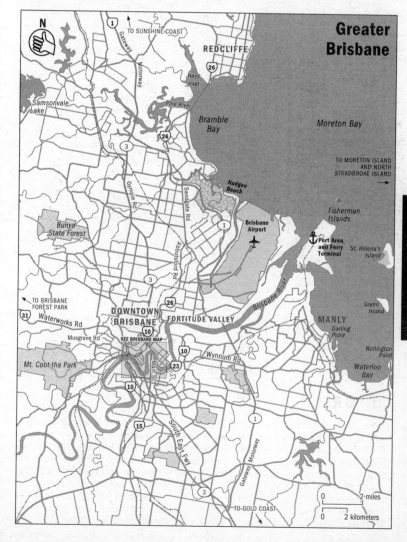

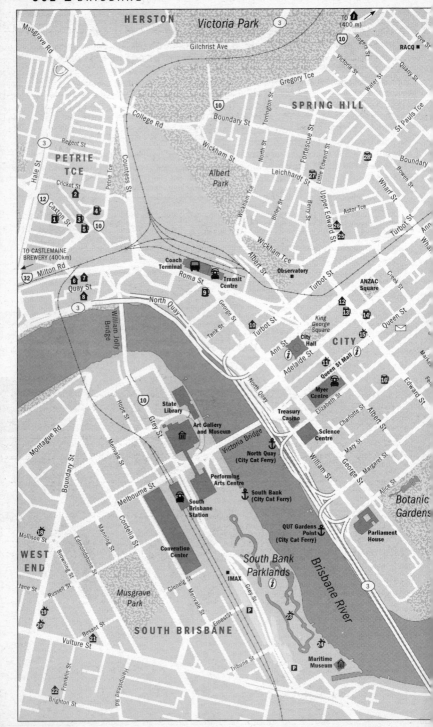

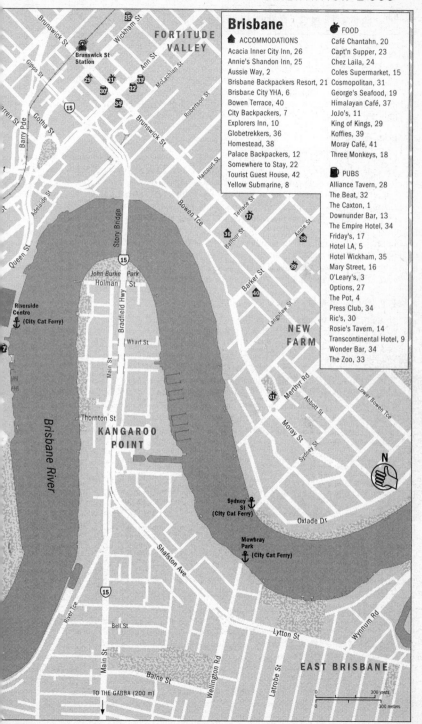

# Brisbane

## ACCOMMODATIONS
Acacia Inner City Inn, 26
Annie's Shandon Inn, 25
Aussie Way, 2
Brisbane Backpackers Resort, 21
Brisbane City YHA, 6
Bowen Terrace, 40
City Backpackers, 7
Explorers Inn, 10
Globetrekkers, 36
Homestead, 38
Palace Backpackers, 12
Somewhere to Stay, 22
Tourist Guest House, 42
Yellow Submarine, 8

## FOOD
Café Chantahn, 20
Capt'n Supper, 23
Chez Laila, 24
Coles Supermarket, 15
Cosmopolitan, 31
George's Seafood, 19
Himalayan Café, 37
JoJo's, 11
King of Kings, 29
Koffies, 39
Moray Café, 41
Three Monkeys, 18

## PUBS
Alliance Tavern, 28
The Beat, 32
The Caxton, 1
Downunder Bar, 13
The Empire Hotel, 34
Friday's, 17
Hotel LA, 5
Hotel Wickham, 35
Mary Street, 16
O'Leary's, 3
Options, 27
The Pot, 4
Press Club, 34
Ric's, 30
Rosie's Tavern, 14
Transcontinental Hotel, 9
Wonder Bar, 34
The Zoo, 33

FORTITUDE VALLEY

Brunswick St Station

Story Bridge

John Burke Park
Holman St

Riverside Centre
(City Cat Ferry)

Wharf St

NEW FARM

Brisbane River

Thornton St

KANGAROO POINT

Merthyr Rd
Abbott St
Lower Bowen Tce

Moray St
Sydney St

N

Sydney St
(City Cat Ferry)

Oxlade Dr

Mowbray Park
(City Cat Ferry)

Shafston Ave

River Tce

Main St

Bell St

Baine St

Wellington Rd

Lytton St

Latrobe St

Wynnum Rd

EAST BRISBANE

TO THE GABBA (200 m)

0        300 yards
0        300 meters

# ▣ GETTING AROUND

## BY TRAIN

**Citytrain,** Queensland Rail's intracity train network, has three major stations. The main transit center is at **Roma St; Central Station** is at Ann and Edward St; and the final station is at **Brunswick St.** One-zone journeys in the city area cost $1.65. One-day unlimited travel is $8.60. (Trains run M-Th 4:19am-12:09am, F 5am-2am, Sa 6am-1am, Su 6am-11pm. All return trips are free Sa-Su.)

## BY BUS

**Citybus** is the "all-stops" major service. Most buses depart from the **Queen St Bus Station,** a huge underground terminal beneath the Myer Center and the Queen St Mall. Platforms are named after Australian animals, while central city stops are sorted by color. Schedules organized by suburb and bus number are posted throughout the city, particularly frequently in the Queen St Mall. Suburban bus route schedules vary; call **TransInfo** (☎ 13 12 30) or stop by the Queen St Bus Station Info Centre on the ground floor of the Meyer Centre (open M-F 8:30am-5pm). Fares range from $1.60 to $3.60 (weekly $12-30; children half-price). The blue and white **City Circle bus** #333 runs a frequent city center circuit (70¢). The blue and yellow striped **Cityxpress** runs from the suburbs to the city every 30min. Buses #190 and #191 offer convenient routes from West End to New Farm.

## BY CAR AND TAXI

**ShoeString Car Rentals,** 360 Nudgee Rd, Hendra, near the airport, rents from $20 per day. (☎ 3268 3334. Open M-F 7:30am-6pm, Sa-Su 7:30am-4pm.) **Letz Rent-A-Car,** 925 Ann St, Fortitude Valley (☎ 3852 1188), rents from $35 per day and does 21-day minimum one-ways to Sydney and Cairns. **Budget,** 105 Mary St, isn't cheap, but they often have new cars. (☎ 3220 0699, airport ☎ 3860 4466. Open M-F 7:30am-6pm, Sa-Su 7:30am-noon. Airport booth open daily 5:30am-10pm.) The **RACQ** headquarters, 300 St. Paul's Tce, Fortitude Valley (☎ 3361 2444), provides 24hr. roadside assistance to members (overseas transfers free). See **Queensland Getting Around,** p. 294, for more information. For a **taxi,** try **Brisbane Cabs** (☎ 3360 0000), **Yellow Cab Company** (☎ 13 19 24), or **Black and White** (☎ 13 10 08), all of which operate 24hr.

## BY FERRY

Brisbane's excellent ferry system makes good use of the Brisbane River, providing practical transport and cheap sightseeing tours. The new, sleek **City Cat** ferry runs upstream to the University of Queensland and downstream to Bretts Wharf. North Quay near the Treasury Casino is the closest stop to the city center. The **City Ferry** operates around the city center and includes more stops than the City Cat (ferries run at least every 20-30min.). The **Crossriver** runs four routes connecting Brisbane's two banks, including downtown from the Holman St to the Edward St stops (every 15min. M-F 8:30am-11:45pm, Sa 5:30am-11:45pm, Su 8am-10:45pm). Schedules are posted at every dock and stop. Fares for all ferries are $1.60-3.60, depending on distance; Australian students get half-price concessions.

## BY BIKE OR IN-LINE SKATES

Bicycles are a great way to see Brisbane. Local public transportation carries them free of charge, and in Brisbane City alone there are 350km of cycling paths. You can also bike to sights like Mt. Coot-tha or Stradbroke Island. The Brisbane City Council publishes a pamphlet called *Brisbane Bicycle Maps.* **Brisbane Bicycle,** 87 Albert St, carries a range of bikes. (☎ 3229 2433. 1hr. $9, 24hr. $20. Open M-Sa 8:30am-5pm, Su 10am-5pm.) **Skatebiz,** 101 Albert St, rents in-line skates. (☎ 3220 0157. 2hr. $11, 24hr. $26. Open M-F 9am-5:30pm, Sa 9am-4pm, Su 10am-4pm.)

**QUEENSLAND**

# ⑦ PRACTICAL INFORMATION

**Tourist Office: Tourism Brisbane,** in City Hall (☎3221 8411, www.brisbanetour ism.com.au). Open M-F 9am-5pm. Another, more popular info booth (☎3229 5918) is in the middle of the Queen St Mall, but they can only provide info on companies that are part of their association. Open M-Th 9am-5pm, F 9am-8pm, Sa 9am-4pm, Su 10am-4pm. The *Brisbane Tourism* guide is available at most tourist booths.

**Budget Travel Offices: Flight Centre** (☎13 16 00) has 11 offices and a guarantee to beat any quoted current price. **STA Travel,** 111 Adelaide St (☎13 17 76 or ☎3221 3722; open M-F 9am-5:30pm, Sa 10am-4pm). **Backpackers Travel Centre,** 138 Albert St (☎3221 2225; open M-Th 9am-6pm, Sa 10am-4pm). **YHA Travel Centre,** 154 Roma St (☎3236 1680; open M-Tu, Th, F 8:30am-5pm, W 9am-5pm, Sa 9am-3pm).

**Banks:** Banks are clustered on Boundary St, in South Brisbane, and on Brunswick St in the Valley. Most are open M-Th 9:30am-4pm, F 9:30am-5pm. Typically no charge for cash exchange, $5 for traveler's checks. **ATMs** are ubiquitous. **American Express,** 131 Elizabeth St (☎3229 2729), is open M-F 9am-5:30pm, Sa 9am-noon.

**Employment:** Backpackers Employment Service (☎3236 4899; www.backpackersaus tralia.com.au), has a desk on level 3 of the Transit Centre.

**Backpacking and Camping Equipment: Globetrekker,** 142 Albert St (☎3221 4476), is open M-Th 9am-6pm, F 9am-9pm, Sa 9am-4:30pm, Su 10:30am-4:30pm. **Mountain Designs Australia,** 105 Albert St (☎3221 6756), offers YHA discounts. Open M-Th 9am-5:30pm, F 9am-9pm, Sa 9am-5pm, Su 10am-4pm.

**Bookstores:** The Queen St Mall area has many bookstores. **Pages Bookshop,** 217 Albert St (☎3221 4611), in the basement, has a wide selection at good prices.

**Library:** The **State Library** (☎3840 7666), in the Cultural Centre. Open M-Th 10am-8pm, F-Su 10am-5pm. Call ☎3840 7785 to book **free** 1hr. **Internet access.** The **John Oxley Library** (☎3840 7881) on level 4, is devoted to Queensland research and history, and holds historical exhibitions. Open Su-F 10am-5pm.

**Public Markets: South Bank Markets** (see **Sights,** p. 307). **Brunswick Markets,** Brunswick St, Fortitude Valley, is a hippie scene of second-hand items, clothes, and toys. Sa 9am-3pm. **Riverside Markets,** Eagle St (☎(0414) 88 80 41), Su 8am-4pm.

**Used Cars: Backpacker's Car Connection** (☎3392 0137)

**Emergency:** ☎000.

**Police:** ☎3364 6464.

**Hospital: Travellers Medical Service,** level 1, 245 Albert St (☎3211 3611; open 24hr.). **Brisbane Sexual Health Clinic,** 484 Adelaide St (☎3227 8666 or ☎3227 7091), offers **free testing.** Open M-Tu, Th-F 9am-5pm, W 8am-noon.

**Internet: State Library** (see above); **Emailplus,** 328 Upper Roma St (☎3236 0433; 15min. $1; open daily 9am-late); **Global Gossip,** 288 Edward St (☎3229 4033; 1hr. $4-5.50; open daily 8am-midnight); and **Café Scene,** corner of Brunswick and Ann St (☎3216 1624), is pricey, but the cheapest in the Valley. 30min $3.30.

**Post Office: GPO,** 261 Queen St (☎3405 1434; *Poste Restante* ☎3405 1448). Half a block from the end of the mall. Open M-F 7am-6pm. *Poste Restante* until 5pm. For weekend mail, try level 2 of the Myer Center (☎3405 1380). Open M-F 8:30am-5:30pm, Sa 9am-4pm, Su 10:30am-4pm. **Postal Code:** 4000; GPO code: 4001.

**Phone Code:** 07.

**MEDIA AND PUBLICATIONS**
**Newspaper:** *The Courier-Mail* (88¢).
**Nightlife:** *Time Off* and *Rave* Magazines (free). For info on gay and lesbian nightlife, check out *BrotherSister*.
**Radio:** Rock, Triple J 107.7FM or Triple M 104.5FM; News, 936AM; Tourist Info, 88FM.

QUEENSLAND

# ▛ ACCOMMODATIONS

Accommodations are clustered in four main areas of the city: the city center, in the middle of the action; South Brisbane and West End, near the riverside parklands, cultural and performance venues, and colorful Boundary St; Fortitude Valley and New Farm, with cafés, art galleries, street festivals, and a funky nightpulse, though it's not always the safest at night; and Petrie Terrace, close to the Transit Centre and Caxton St party scene. Most of the accommodations listed have courtesy pickup. Unless otherwise noted, check-out is 10am and key deposits are $10. Linen and cutlery are usually free with a deposit.

## CITY CENTER

**Palace Backpackers** (☎3211 2433, freecall ☎(1800) 67 63 40). Corner of Ann and Edward St; near the city center and Transit Centre. The former Salvation Army headquarters, this 7-level building is a backpacker landmark. The amazingly efficient staff checks in only international travelers up to the 350 person capacity, so you won't wait in line, but you will yearn for name recognition. Near-nightly after-hour parties make for noisy halls. Three-story veranda, big kitchen, rockin' backpackers pub (see **Nightlife,** p. 312), Internet, and café (meals $3-8). Laundry. Reception 24hr. 7- to 9-bed dorms $17; 4-bed dorms $20; singles $33; twins $48; doubles $45. VIP.

**Explorers Inns,** 63 Turbot St (☎3211 3488, freecall ☎(1800) 62 32 88). At the corner of George St near Transit Centre. Pleasant budget hotel with a gorgeous, affordable restaurant. Ensuite rooms have TVs. Nonsmoking. Reception M-F 24hr., Sa-Su until 10pm. Singles, doubles, twins $75; triples $86; quads $97.

**Annie's Shandon Inn,** 405 Upper Edward St, Spring Hill (☎3831 8684; fax 3831 3073). Like Grandma's house, complete with family snapshots, cozy beds, and pastels. Cold breakfast included. Kitchenette downstairs. Laundry $1.60. Reception 7am-9pm. Check-out 9am. Singles $44, ensuite $55; twins and doubles $55, $66.

**Acacia Inner City Inn,** 413 Upper Edward St, Spring Hill (☎3832 1663; fax 3832 2591). A simple, practical inn that was home to some of American General Douglas MacArthur's men. Recently refurbished. Cold breakfast included. Check-out 9:30am. Singles $40; twins and doubles $55; doubles ensuite or triples $70.

## FORTITUDE VALLEY AND NEW FARM

▨ **Globetrekkers,** 35 Balfour St, New Farm (☎3358 1251; www.globetrekkers.net). Between Brunswick St and Bowen Tce. Friendly, small 100-year-old house with lots of character. Walls may need a lick of paint, but you'll swear that Dennis' "unfinished" sculptures and paintings on the porch need nothing at all. Comfy mattresses and hardwood floors are lovely. Pool, kitchen. Unlimited Internet for $2. Laundry. Dorms $18; twins and doubles $40, ensuite $44. Park your campervan in back and have access to the facilities for $9 per person. Book ahead.

**Bowen Terrace,** 365 Bowen Tce, New Farm (☎3254 0458). On the corner of Barker St, which is off Brunswick St. Warm, welcoming colonial house. Only 16 beds, but worth trying to secure a room. Lounge, small kitchen, new game room, large deck with partial view of downtown, recently refurbished. Motel-like rooms with TV, fridge, and coffee machines. Singles $27.50; twins $33; doubles $38.50, ensuite $49.50.

**Tourist Guest House,** 555 Gregory Tce, Fortitude Valley (☎3252 4171, freecall ☎(1800) 80 05 89; fax 3252 2704). Homespun B&B with front porch. Wonderful rooms with a heritage feel, TV, sink, and fridge. Spacious doubles have couch and desk. Dorm $17; singles $40, ensuite $50; twins and doubles $55, $65; triples $60, $80.

**Homestead,** 57 Annie St, New Farm (☎/fax 3254 1609, freecall ☎(1800) 65 83 44). Giant murals and rooms with names like "Babes in the Woods" or "Great Expectations." Relaxing atmosphere on quiet street. Free bus to airport, Transit Centre, and city. Planned trips, kitchen, back garden, a shamrock-shaped pool, and free bike use. Laundry. Reception daily 7am-7pm. Dorms $17; singles $35; twins and doubles $42. VIP.

QUEENSLAND

# PETRIE TERRACE

**▓Yellow Submarine,** 66 Quay St (☎3211 3424). Painted bright yellow, this little house has a lot of character despite slightly tired rooms. Wonderful owners are eager to show off Brisbane at low prices. Ken cooks at least one free dinner a week. Outdoor TV lounge and a new pool. 6-bed dorms $17, weekly $99; doubles $42, $230. Book ahead.

**City Backpackers,** 380 Upper Roma St (☎3211 3221, freecall ☎(1800) 06 25 72). 400m from the Transit Centre, next to YHA. Completely renovated with enormous kitchen and rooftop dining with fantastic views. Clean, comfortable rooms. Irish pub, **The Fiddler's Elbow,** has live music W and Su. Kitchen, Internet 35min. $2. Laundry $2. Dorms $18; singles $35; twins and doubles $44. YHA, VIP.

**Aussie Way,** 34 Cricket St (☎3369 0711). Pleasant 1872 colonial home offers a quiet escape from raucous Caxton St. Pool, kitchen, Internet access, TV lounge. Laundry. Dorms (max 5-bed) $18; single $27.50; twins and doubles $40. YHA, VIP.

**Brisbane City YHA,** 392 Upper Roma St (☎3236 1004; fax 3236 1947). Private, clean, and low-key, with a friendly staff. Perfect for couples or friends, not for socialites. The new building is best. Café ($5 burgers), kitchen, reading loft. Laundry. 6-bed dorms $17.50; 3-bed dorms $18.50; twins $44; doubles $48, ensuite $66.

# SOUTH BRISBANE

**▓Somewhere to Stay,** 45 Brighton Rd (☎3846 2858, freecall ☎(1800) 81 23 98; fax 3846 4584; www.somewheretostay.com.au). On the corner of Franklin St. Large rooms, some have gorgeous views. Pool, big kitchen, garden, and free bus to city. Laundry $2. Internet (30min. $2.50). Check-out 9:30am. Prices vary based on amenities and view. 4-bed dorms $14-18; singles $23-26; doubles $35-51. YHA, VIP, NOMADS.

**Brisbane Backpackers Resort,** 110 Vulture St (☎3844 9956, freecall ☎(1800) 62 64 52; fax 3844 9295). Near the corner of Boundary St. Large ensuite rooms with TV, fridge, balcony. Tennis court, swimming pool, spa, Internet, nightly movies, and café. Reception 24hr. Check-out 9:30am. 6-bed dorms $18; singles, twins, doubles $52. Cheaper, basic accommodation in their building across the street $14.50. YHA, VIP.

# ⬕ FOOD

The West End has small, trendy sidewalk cafés and Mediterranean-style restaurants, particularly along Boundary St and Hardgrave Rd. Chinatown in Fortitude Valley has lots of cheap Asian food, while trendier New Farm has more expensive eateries. The city center has a variety of options and a Coles Express **supermarket** at the corner of Queen and Edward St (open M-F 6am-9pm, Sa 6am-5pm, Su 10:30am-4pm). In Petrie Tce, many Caxton St pubs have lunch specials and Tu and Th two-for-one. For a memorable ice cream experience, try ▓**Cold Rock** (☎3844 2766), with locations around Brisbane.

# CITY CENTER

**JoJo's,** corner of Queen St Mall and Albert St (☎3221 2113). Perched between chaotic Queen St Mall and majestic skyscrapers, JoJo's attracts travelers, students, and businessmen to its four counters: seafood, Thai, Italian, and pastry. Dishes are cooked to order for $10-25, but daily specials are cheaper. Open M-F 9am-late, Sa-Su 11am-late.

**Govinda's Vegetarian Restaurant,** upstairs at 99 Elizabeth St (☎3210 0255). Hare Krishna owners only serve 1 meal a day (except F), but it's a $7 all-you-can-eat extravaganza with free entertainment. Juice bar mixes $2 lassies. Su: $3 feast with chanting and dancing. Open M-Sa 11:30am-2:30pm, F also 5:30-8:30pm, Su 5-7pm.

**Parrots,** 93 Elizabeth St (☎3229 0187). Serves 15 varieties of thick, juicy gourmet hamburgers ($10-14), with your favorite meat or vegetarian patty. Open Tu-Sa 11:30am-10:30pm, Su 11:30am-9:30pm. Licensed.

QUEENSLAND

## WEST END

▣ **Three Monkeys,** 58 Mollison St (☎3844 6045). On the West End rotary off Boundary St. Walls decked with theater posters, African and Indian art, woven baskets, and statuettes. Dim lighting, jazz music, and comfy seating—this is the living room you always wished you had. Varied, inexpensive menu includes grilled foccaccia ($7.50), *spanako-pitta* ($9), and a delectable choice of cakes and cookies. Open daily 9:30am-late.

**Café Chantann,** 150 Boundary St (☎3844 8808). This small café offers a Mediterranean menu of primarily Greek cuisine. Get there early when mains are $7.50. Belly dancing and plate smashing F-Sa nights. Open daily 5pm-late. BYO.

**George's Seafood,** 150 Boundary St (☎3844 4100). A small seafood shop that will grill, batter, or crumb any filet for $1 extra. Unbeatable deal: grilled Tasmanian salmon filet for $5. Open M-F 9:30am-7:30pm, Sa 8:30am-4pm, Su 10:30am-6:30pm.

## NEW FARM

▣ **Moray Café,** corner of Moray and Merthyr Rd (☎3254 1342). Quiet location off Brunswick St, across the street from the river. Attitude without pretense. Hip, popular, half-outdoor café with bright colors, good music, and international, veggie-friendly fare. Best Caesar salad in Queensland, hands down ($10.50). Sweet potato risotto ($12). Open daily 8:30am-late. Kitchen closes at 10pm. Licensed.

▣ **Himalayan Café,** 640-642 Brunswick St (☎3358 4015). Tibetan and Nepalese delicacies in an unnaturally oxygen-rich environment. Relax in the warm atmosphere created by art, tapestries, and paper covered lights. The back Himalayan Room seats patrons on cushions. Diced goat, lightly spiced, cooked with pumpkin and potato ($12); also many vegetarian options. Open Tu-Su 5:30-10:30pm. Back room must be booked.

**Koffies,** 726 Brunswick St (☎3254 1254). Start your day (or night) with an uplifting brekkie (Big Breakfast $8.50). Coffees and cakes too. Open 8:30am-10pm.

## FORTITUDE VALLEY

▣ **Garuva,** 174 Wickham St (☎3216 0124). A fantastic dining experience. Enter via a narrow passage through several doors in rooms decorated with overhanging trees and full-length mirrors. Once in, sit on a cushioned rug as a white curtain is drawn around you. Meals from six nations, sweet potato and bean curry to cujons of shark ($11.) Open M-F 11:30am-2:30pm, M-Sa 6pm-midnight. Book ahead.

**King of Kings,** 175 Wickham St (☎3852 1889). Halfway between Brunswick St and Chinatown. Waiters constantly bring trolleys filled with a variety of tasty yum cha dishes not even Superman could resist. Big plates cost $3, but the dishes are all designed to be shared. Open M-F 9:30am-3pm, Sa-Su 8:30am-3pm.

## SOUTH BANK

**Chez Laila,** South Bank Parklands on the boardwalk (☎3846 3402). A Lebanese restaurant where "people eat to live longer." Outdoor deck overlooking the river and city skyline. The best Lebanese falafel for miles ($7). Which begs the question: how many Lebanese falafels are there for miles? Open daily 8am-late.

**Capt'n Snapper** (☎3846 4036). Parklands off Tribune St. Delicious fresh seafood and a well-stocked all-you-can-eat salad bar. Open daily 11am-late.

# 🎬 SIGHTS

**CITY TOURS.** One of the best deals for a city tour is **City Sights,** an 1½hr. bus tour of cultural and historical attractions. Tickets allow one day of unlimited access on public bus and ferry networks and can be purchased on the bus, from any customer service center, or at most tourist offices. (*Tours leave every 45min. daily 9am-3:45pm. $16.50, concessions $11, families $33.*) For a tour of the Brisbane River, the large **River Queen** paddlewheel boat departs daily from the Eagle St Pier, with factual commentary of passing sights and accordion music. (☎3221 1300. 1½hr. lunch cruise $22, with buffet $33. Su afternoon tea cruise $22. Buffet dinner cruise $45. Book ahead.) **Tours and Detours** offers several different city and river trips, including half-day ($35) and full-day ($65) city highlight tours, an afternoon float upstream to Lone Pine Koala Sanctuary and Mt. Coot-tha ($40), or a stunning tour of Brisbane after dark ($35). (☎3830 4455.) **Brisbane Historical Walk** leaves from Ann St, under the Old Clock Tower, for a 2hr. meander around city center, squares, public buildings, and Botanic Gardens. (☎3862 2156. Mar.-Dec. Su 3pm. $12, concessions $8.)

**CASTLEMAINE BREWERY.** The womb of XXXX, self-proclaimed "Queensland's beer," is 5min. from Caxton St on Milton Rd. The 45min. walking tour ends (and your day really begins) with you, an hour, and four tall ones. Meet at the Castlemaine Sports Club, at the crest of Heusser Tce behind the brewery. (☎3361 7597. M-W 11am, 1:30, and 4pm; occasionally W 7:30pm. $7, W 7:30pm with BBQ $15. Book ahead.)

**CARLTON BREWHOUSE.** Thirty minutes south of Brisbane are the brewers of VB, Foster's, and Carlton. The tour may be slightly dry, but the four beers at the end sure aren't. (In Yatala. CoachTrans buses to the Gold Coast leave the Transit Centre daily 9:15, 11:15am. ☎3826 5858. Tours 10am, noon, and 2pm. $7.50, concessions $5. Book ahead.)

**CITY HALL.** Opened in 1930, it earned the epithet "Million Pound Town Hall" for its outrageous building cost. The recently restored **clock tower,** a landmark of the city skyline, stands 92m high with an **observation deck.** The **Brisbane City Gallery** inside hosts remarkable changing exhibits. (☎3403 4048. Deck open M-F 8:30am-4:30pm, Sa 10:30am-4:30pm. Art Gallery open M-F 10am-5pm. Free.)

**QUEENSLAND CULTURAL CENTRE.** On the south side of Victoria Bridge, the Cultural Centre contains many of Brisbane's major artistic venues, including the art gallery, museum, performing arts complex, state library, and theater company. (☎3840 7190.) Inside, the **Queensland Art Gallery** has over 10,000 works, primarily Australian and Aboriginal. (☎3840 7303. Open daily 10am-5pm. Free guided tours M-F 11am, 1, 2pm; Sa 11am, 2, 3pm; Su 11am, 1, 3pm. Free admission to the permanent collections; special exhibitions $8-12.) The **Queensland Museum** houses dinosaur skeletons, whale models, and live samples of the largest species of cockroach. (☎3840 7555. Open daily 9:30am-5pm. Free admission to regular collection; special exhibitions $5.50-11.)

**POWERHOUSE CENTRE FOR LIVE ARTS.** Once powering Brisbane's tram system, the New Farm Park's Powerhouse is now an alternative arts venue, housing performances, dining, and galleries. (Brunswick St, New Farm Park. ☎3254 4518.)

**SCIENCENTRE.** With over 170 hands-on exhibits, Sciencentre offers plenty for kids to play with and gives parents a sacred respite. (110 George St. Between Mary and Charlotte St. ☎3220 0166. Open daily 10am-5pm. $8, concessions $6.)

**QUEENSLAND POLICE MUSEUM.** If you are bored and near the Transit Centre, drop in to this exhibit in the Police Headquarters. The highlight is a gruesome but educational model of a murder scene from which to speculate what occurred. Elementary, my dear Watson. (100 Roma St. ☎3364 6425. Open M-F 9am-4pm. Free.)

## PARKS AND GARDENS

**SOUTH BANK PARKLANDS.** Built on the former World Expo '88 site, South Bank offers splendid views of the city, tree-lined and café-dotted boulevards, weekly markets, and a reminder of the relaxed Brizzy way. The **man-made lagoon**—with real sand, shallow and deep ends, and gorgeous night lighting—is ingenious. (Lifeguard on duty 9am-6pm.) There's also a well-stocked **Maritime Museum** with wrecks and models. (At the old South Brisbane Dry Dock, south end of the parklands. ☎3844 5361. Open daily 9:30am-5pm. $5.50, concessions $4.40, families $14.) On the weekends, the park center houses a **crafts village** with crafts, psychics, clothes, and massages. (Open F 5-10pm by lantern-light, Sa 11am-5pm, Su 9am-5pm.) The Parklands also organizes free events, including car shows, fireworks, and weight lifting championships. The **Visitor Information Centre** is toward the Victoria Bridge end of the park, near the Tribune St entrance. *(Just across the river by Victoria Bridge. Accessible by foot, bus—orange B stop on Grey St, CityTrain—South Brisbane or Vulture St Stations, or ferry—terminal stop South Bank. ☎3867 2051; www.south-bank.net.au. Open daily 9am-6pm, except F 9am-10pm. Although there are no official gates, South Bank is "open" 5am to midnight.)*

**BOTANIC GARDENS.** Visitors here stroll among palm groves, camellia gardens, and lily ponds surrounded by many species of birds. *(10min. walk from the city center. City Circle bus #333 stops at Albert or George St, near the entrance on Alice St. Free tours depart the rotunda near the Albert St entrance. ☎3403 0666. Open 24hrs. Tours M-Sa 11am and 1pm.)*

**MT. COOT-THA PARK BOTANIC GARDENS.** Mt. Coot-tha: the other botanic garden. It includes a Japanese Garden, botanical library, tropical dome, lots of Scrub Turkey, and plenty of picnicking green. The park also has Queensland's first **Planetarium.** *(☎3403 8888. 45min. programs W-F 3:30 and 7:30pm, Sa 1:30, 3:30, and 7:30pm, Su 1:30 and 3:30pm. $10, concessions $8.50, families $28; free exhibit in the foyer.)* Hop back on the #471 bus to reach the **Mt. Coot-tha summit,** with a view of greater Brisbane that's spectacular at night. The casual Kuta Café and the fancier Mt. Coot-tha Summit Restaurant both have panoramic views. *(☎3369 9922. Open M-Sa 11:30am-late, Su 8am-late. Meals $11-23.)* To walk back to the gardens, find the JC Slaughter Falls track from the summit, with an optional Aboriginal Art loop. At the bottom of the trail, exit the carpark to the right, and follow the road for 5min. *(7km from the city center. From Town Hall, bus #471 takes 12min. to the gardens, 20min. to the summit; 1 per hr. Gardens: ☎3403 2535. Tours M-Sa 11am and 1pm from the information centre. Open daily Apr.-Aug. 8am-5pm; Sept.-Mar. 8am-5:30pm; gates close at 4:30pm.)*

**BRISBANE FOREST PARK.** You can picnic, camp, birdwatch, cycle, ride horses, and hike on the 28,500 hectares of The Gap. No, not THAT Gap. The *Information Guide* describes a number of walks and has an invaluable map. *(60 Mt. Nebo Rd. Take bus #385 from Albert St. ☎3300 4855.)*

## WILDLIFE

**ALMA PARK ZOO.** The zoo has walk-through kangaroo and deer enclosures, koalas, monkeys, and water buffalo, and allows feeding of some of the friendlier animals. Twenty acres of gardens and BBQs make it an ideal picnic spot. *(Alma Rd, Dakabin. 30min. north of Brisbane. Take the Caboolture train line to Dakabin—leaves Roma St 9:02am, Central 9:04am—where a courtesy bus will meet you. ☎3204 6566; www.almapark zoo.com.au. Open daily 9am-5pm. Hold a koala at 12:30 and 3pm. $17.50, concessions $9.)*

**LONE PINE KOALA SANCTUARY.** The world's largest koala sanctuary has around 130 koalas, including 21-year-old Sarah, the oldest koala in the world. Emus, Tasmanian devils, raucous laughing kookaburras, and lots of hand-feedable 'roos try to raise the average activity level. *(Take bus #430 from the Koala platform in the Myer Centre 8:30am-4:30pm, or take Wildlife Cruise 19km upstream on the Brisbane River to the sanctuary. Cruise: ☎3221 0300. Return $16. Departs North Quay at 10am; free pickup from city accommodation. Sanctuary: ☎3378 1366. $14, concessions $11.)*

**AUSTRALIA ZOO.** The crocs get fed everyday at 1:30pm—a spectacle you won't forget, especially if crocodile hunter Steve Irwin is there. Cuddle a python, feed a kangaroo, and patiently follow the world's oldest Galapagos tortoise. *(In Beerwah. Catch the 7:50am "Crocodile Train" from the Transit Centre, and the zoo's bus will meet you at Beerwah; call ahead to arrange other bus pickups. ☎5494 1134; www.crocodilehunter.com. $15.50, students $13.50. Open 8:30am-4pm.)*

**WALKABOUT CREEK WILDLIFE CENTRE.** An aviary, crocs, platypi (best seen in the morning), and other strange water creatures grace this wildlife park. *(60 Mt. Nebo Rd, the Gap, in Brisbane Forest Park. Take the #385 bus from Albert St. ☎3300 4855. Open Su-F 9am-4:30pm, Sa 10am-4:30pm. $3.50, concessions $2.50.)*

**AUSTRALIAN WOOLSHED.** Sheep are the focus, but clever sheep dogs steal the show. Help out by feeding the baby farmyard animals or milking the cows. *(Samford Rd, Ferny Hills. 800m from the Ferny Grove railway station, 20min. north of Brisbane. ☎3872 1100; www.auswoolshed.com.au. $15, concessions $11, children $10.)*

QUEENSLAND

# ⚠ ACTIVITIES

**ROCK CLIMBING AND SKYDIVING.** Join **Outdoor Adventure** at Kangaroo cliffs, past Southbank towards the Peninsula, for **rock climbing** W 6-10pm. Look for the instructors' bright red shirts. (☎3870 3223. $15.) Think you need some practice first? Try **indoor climbing.** (224 Barry Pde, Fortitude Valley. ☎3216 0492. $12; harness and shoes extra.) A little higher up, **Brisbane Skydiving Centre** will show you the city at 200km per hr. from 12,500ft. (☎(1800) 06 15 55. $220, including free pickup.)

**WATER ACTIVITIES.** Brisbane has many waterways that are perfect for **canoeing.** Written guides to the popular **Oxley Creek** and **Boondall Wetlands** are available from libraries or tourist offices. **Queensland Canoeing** offers canoe and kayak education. (☎3278 1033. Simpson's Playground, Graceville Ave, Graceville. Open M-F 9am-4:30pm.) For rentals, try **Goodtime Surf and Sail.** (29 Ipswich Rd, Woolloongabba. ☎3391 8588. Canoe $25 per day; kayak $20 per day. Deposit $50. Open M-W and F 8:30am-5:30pm, Th 8:30am-8pm, Sa 9am-4pm, Su 10am-3pm.) **Rainbow Safaris** leads canoeing daytrips on weekends. Trips last from 8am-8:30pm and cover 22km of the Brisbane River, but the favorable current makes the trip manageable. (11 Alamanda Dr, Camira. ☎3288 2845. BYO drinks and food $65 per person, all inclusive $90. Book ahead.) **ProDive** offers trips to the area's best reefs and wrecks, including gear and pickup. (☎3368 3766.)

**BUSHWALKING.** **Rob's Rainforest Explorer Day Tours** takes you through Mt. Glorious and Samford Valley (M, Th; in **Brisbane Forest Park,** see above), Glasshouse Mountains and Kondalilla Falls (Tu, F; see p. 341), the Green Mountains of Lamington National Park (W; see p. 326), or the Natural Bridge and Springbrook National Parks (Sa; see p. 327). (☎3357 7061. $48, including transport.)

# 🎭 ENTERTAINMENT AND FESTIVALS

Brisbane may have a reputation for not offering a lot to see, but you will soon realize this just isn't true. Instead, Brisbane has seemingly continuous festivals and diverse theater, arts, and music. Call the **Queensland Cultural Centre** (☎3840 7190) for a current schedule and info on discounts. The **Performing Arts Complex,** just across Victoria Bridge in South Brisbane, is composed of four theaters: the **Concert Hall** hosts symphony and chamber orchestras; the 2000-seat **Lyric Theatre** sponsors drama, musicals, ballet, and opera; the 700-seat **Optus Playhouse** shows drama; and the 315-seat **Cremorne Theater** stages intimate productions. Whether or not you see action on stage, the theaters are gorgeous. (☎13 62 46. $5 guided tours M-F noon from the tour desk at the ticket sales foyer; book ahead.)

The **Queensland Conservatorium** (☎3875 6241, concert inquiries ☎3875 6222) presents university-affiliated concerts for free or very cheap admission. **Opera Queensland** (☎3875 3030), produces three productions a year. For contemporary Australian theater, **La Boite,** 57 Hale St, Petrie Tce (☎3369 1622) offers six plays a year. The **Queensland Ballet** (☎13 62 46), the oldest dance group in the country, is renowned for its neoclassical style. The **Queensland Theatre Company** offers eight shows annually. (☎3840 7000. $20-45.)

Escape the mainstream with Sunday afternoon jazz at **Jazzy Cat,** 56 Mollison St. (☎3846 2544; www.jazzycat.com.au. Su 1:30-4:30pm.) **The Bombshelter,** 200 Main St, Kangaroo Point (☎3391 2266), features great acts Su 3-7pm.

The former state treasury building at the intersection of Queen, Elizabeth, and George St continues to exploit money—but now for "fun"—in the enormous, glitzy **Treasury Casino,** a Brisbane landmark with five restaurants, seven bars, over 100 gaming tables, and more than 1000 gaming machines. (☎3306 8888. Open 24hr.)

The **Entertainment Centre** (☎3265 8111), on Melaleuca Dr in Boondall, is Brisbane's largest indoor complex for sports, concerts, and special events. By Citytrain, take the Shorncliffe line to Boondall Station (27min., departs at least every 30min.). The **"Gabba,"** Vulture and Stanley St, Woolloongabba (☎3896 4555), is Queensland's major **cricket** and **football** stadium. Take the bus to the station on the corner of Main and Stanley St ($2.20) or the train to Vulture St. Tickets for football are available from Ticketmaster (☎13 61 22). For cricket, try Ticketek (☎13 19 31).

QUEENSLAND

The **Brisbane Festival** celebrates spring in August of even years. The **Brisbane International Film Festival** (☎3220 0444; www.biff.com.au) is held annually the last week in July and the first week in August, with alternative and retrospective releases. The **Valley Fiesta** (☎3252 5999), in early September, features street festivals, local bands, and dance performances. Most exciting of all, the **Australia Day Cockroach Races** will be run on Jan. 26, 2001 at the Storybridge Hotel, 196 Main St, Kangaroo Point (☎3391 2266). Root your favorite bug on!

# ⊠ NIGHTLIFE

Brisbane nights roll by in sweaty nightclubs, noisy pubs, and smoky jazz lounges. Fortitude Valley is home to Brisbane's most exciting nighttime scene, with alternative bars and dance clubs, live music, and several gay establishments. Weekends are huge and weeknights sparse on Caxton St in Petrie Terrace, with a decidedly more mainstream set. The city center is a big draw for backpackers, with its many Irish Pubs, drink specials, and rocking Thursday nights.

Be glad you don't have to keep track of the myriad live performances in Brisbane—the W or Sa edition of the *Courier-Mail*, as well as other entertainment guides such as *Rave*, *Time Off*, *Scene*, and *BrotherSister* (a guide to gay and lesbian entertainment and clubs) all take care of this task. They are all free and available at the record store **Rocking Horse**, 101 Adelaide St, and many local nightclubs.

## FORTITUDE VALLEY

**The Empire Hotel,** on the corner of Brunswick and Ann St (☎3852 1216). The truest one-stop party venue in town. **The Empire,** downstairs on the corner, supplies a hard techno beat and industrial, sci-fi decor. Open daily until 5am. ⊠**The Wonder Bar,** upstairs, satisfies a late-nighter of any breed. To the left, comfy couches and alternative tunes; to the right, fresh and funky chemical beats. Cover $7.

**The Zoo,** 711 Ann St (☎3852 1381). A converted warehouse flowing with alternative and indie bands. W: DJs. $3-10 cover disappears late. Open W-Sa 8:30pm-2am.

**Ric's,** 321 Brunswick St (☎3854 1772). Acoustically and electronically eclectic: this café with outdoor seating, live music, and an upstairs techno bar is always packed. Sa-Su: live bands. Open Su-Th 11am-1am, Sa-Su 11am-5am.

**The Beat,** 677 Ann St (☎3852 2661). The techno beat is straightforward, but the scene is anything but. DJs spin electronic and house. The only thing more scandalous than the moves on the dance floor are the unprintable names of the shooters. 11:30pm and 2:30am floor show with gay dancers and a drag queen. Cover $7.

**Hotel Wickham,** 308 Wickham St (☎3852 1301). A gay and lesbian pub that turns into big dance party on weekend nights. Open Su-Th 10am-3am, F-Sa 10am-5am.

## PETRIE TERRACE

**Hotel LA,** 68 Petrie Tce (☎3368 2560). On the corner of Caxton St. A tad upscale with plenty of social climbers, but the only place with a weekday crowd. Tu, Th: 2-for-1 on drinks and meals 6pm-10pm; open 22hr. per day 7am-5am.

**Paddington Tavern,** 186 Given Tce (☎3369 0044). Restaurant **Fibber McGees** has fantastic deals. M: $5 steaks; Tu and Th: 2-for-1. Bands F-Sa. **Saloon Bar** next door has live music (F-Sa $6 cover) and almost as many cowboy hats as specials. Open Su-Th noon-2am, F-Sa noon-3am.

**O'Leary's,** 25 Caxton St (☎3368 1933). Straddling a mix between English pub and acid jazz bar, this new watering hole offers a log fire for the winter and a beer garden for the summer. Great place to watch soccer. W-Sa: DJs; W-Th: $3 pints.

**The Pot Music Bar and Café,** 80 Petrie Tce (☎3876 4456). Mostly a café, but hosts live local acts from electronica to full bands. Th: music jam. Open M-Th 8am-10pm, F-Sa 8am-midnight. $3 occasional cover.

**The Caxton,** 38 Caxton St (☎3369 5544). A little more upscale, drawing a young business crowd. Attached to an always-busy grill with "supper menus" of mainly pizza and

QUEENSLAND

nachos. Tu: 2-for-1 meals and drinks 5pm-close. F: P.O.E.T.S. (piss off early, tomorrow's Saturday), groups of 5 get a $30 bar tab by calling ahead. Open 11am-late.

**Transcontinental Hotel,** 482 George St (☎3236 1366). The Trans spills deals. M: call for hospitality bar tab; Tu: pool competition; W: live music; Th: $1 drinks until 1am (cover $6); F: free drinks 6-7pm (call to register). Open T-Sa 8am-4am, Su-M 8am-3am.

## CITY CENTER AND RIVERSIDE

🖾 **Mary Street,** 138 Mary St (☎3221 1511). User-friendly but distinctly packed. Five scenes, one cover: squeeze your way past a young crowd to the grunge stage, pool room, acoustic den, beergarden, or stylish lounge. Open Th-Sa 5pm-5am.

**Rosie's Tavern,** 235 Edward St (☎3220 1477). A great place to turn dollars into alcohol. W: trivia night and $6 jugs; F: free cocktails 5:30-6:30pm. Open Th-Sa 8pm-5am.

**Downunder Bar,** under the Palace Backpackers (☎3211 9277). Whether you like it or not, it's Brizzy's backpacker central. Have your hostel key ready (they may not let you in without it) and your international mojo working. A modest interior with a small dance floor. Dinners $6-7. Food served noon-2:30pm and 6-9pm. Dance every day until 3am.

**Friday's,** 123 Eagle St, Riverside Centre (☎3832 2122). A young crowd gets classy at this giant riverfront hangout. The maze of rooms offers eclectic entertainment—dance music, modern tunes, and live music. Tu and F-Su: jamout for local bands; Th: $1 drinks 8pm-midnight. Th $6 cover, Sa $8. Open Su-Th 10am-3am, F-Sa 10am-5am.

## SPRING HILL

**Alliance Tavern,** 320 Boundary St (☎3832 7355). On the corner of Boundary and Leichhardt St. A standard bar sandwiched between a drag cabaret upstairs (Playford's) and a nightclub with pool tables and DJs spinning Top-40 dance music downstairs, all drawing a comfortably mixed crowd. Th: karaoke; Su: $1 pots. Bar open daily 8am-2am, nightclub W-Su 9pm-2am. Cover F $5.

**Options,** 18 Little Edward St (☎3831 4214). A mixed scene with dance floors and live entertainment; particularly good F-Sa. F-Sa cover after 10pm. Open Th-Sa 8pm-5am.

# MORETON BAY AND ISLANDS

With the Gold Coast to the south and the Sunshine Coast to the north, one would think, following the coastal logic (e=m x sea²), that Moreton Bay would be filled with travelers. Instead, Brisbane, inexplicably built inland, draws most journeyers away from one of the most spectacular areas in the world. Don't let this happen to you. The forest of masts on Manly's marina promises smooth sailing. Here, at the mouth of the Brisbane River, a comfortable culture thrives in perpetual slow-motion. Across the bay, North Stradbroke Island offers wonderful diving, surfing, whale watching, and swimming. Although this area lacks pre-packaged fun, the natural beauty of Moreton Bay is worth self-motivating.

# NORTH STRADBROKE ISLAND

A fierce cyclone in 1896 cleanly split the land mass once called Stradbroke Island. While South Stradbroke (see p. 325) has remained relatively uninhabited, its northern neighbor, separated by a 200m channel, is now home to 3000 people. With miles of sandy white surf beaches, famous blue inland lakes, and dive sites, "Straddie" is an ideal step off the beaten path and only 20km south of Brisbane.

## ▐ TRANSPORT

Despite its apparent isolation, North Stradbroke can be easily reached from Brisbane by public transportation. Take **Citytrain** to Cleveland (at least every 30min., $3.50). From Cleveland, the courtesy bus **"Bessie"** runs from the train station to meet the **Stradbroke Flyer** ferry, which departs for One Mile Jetty in Dunwich.

(☎3286 1964. 30min., 8-9 per day, 6:30am-6:30pm. Return $12.) Alternately, **Stradbroke Ferries** provides a courtesy bus to its **Water Taxi** service. (☎3286 2666. 30min.; 10-12 per day, 6am-6pm. Return $10.50, students $9.50.) Take the Vehicular Ferry only if you have a car (1hr.; 11-14 per day; return $80 for the car and as many people as can fit in it; book ahead). **Island Transport Services** offers a cheaper vehicular ferry service. (☎3829 0008. $70 per car.) The **North Stradbroke Island Bus Service** runs between Point Lookout, Amity, and Dunwich. (☎3409 7151. 14 per day; M-Su 7:15am-7pm. Return $8.) Most **car rental** companies on the mainland will not rent vehicles to Stradbroke travelers because of salt corrosion.

## ■ ▮ ORIENTATION AND PRACTICAL INFORMATION

North Stradbroke Island has three distinct townships: residential **Dunwich,** the ferry drop off point; **Amity Point,** north of Dunwich, with calm beaches and great fishing; and **Point Lookout,** 22km northeast of Dunwich, with most accommodations. **East Coast Rd** is the main road connecting Dunwich and Point Lookout; its name changes to Mooloomba Rd near the end. The southern end of the island consists of lakes, swamps, national park land, and habitat reserves.

The **tourist office,** which books tours and manages the campgrounds, is the yellow building at the base of the Dunwich green. (☎3409 9555; fax 3409 9789. Open M-F 8:30am-5pm, Sa-Su 8:30am-3pm.) Although there's **no bank** on the island, the three **post office** branches serve as Commonwealth bank agents. **Police:** ☎3409 9020. **Hospital:** ☎3409 9059. **Internet** is available at Straddie Coffee Pot in Dunwich. (☎3409 9311. Open M-Th 8am-6pm, F-Su 8am-8pm. 1hr. $4.)

## ▮ ACCOMMODATIONS

Among the fleet of bed options are two hostels and seven campsites: two in Dunwich, two in Amity, and three in Point Lookout. Camping is permitted on the rest of the island at least 11km from the causeway (shore camping permit $3; tent site $5.50 per person per night, powered $8). Make bookings through the tourist office.

**The Stradbroke Island Hostel,** 76 Mooloomba Rd (☎3409 8679; email straddiehos tel@hotmail.com). Halfway between the Guesthouse and the end of Point Lookout, on the left just past Endeavor Rd. "Straddie Hostel," as it is affectionately known, has a relaxed atmosphere with a funky common room, small kitchen, and ping-pong. Dorms $16; doubles $35; discounts for longer stays.

**North Stradbroke Island Guesthouse** (☎3409 8888). On the left at the entrance to the Point Lookout area, close to Home Beach. Unbeatable $8 transportation from Brisbane. Basic rooms, but attached dive center. Dorms $18; doubles $44. VIP, NOMADS.

**The Islander Holiday Resort** (☎3409 8388; fax 3409 8730). A step up in price and a leap in quality, with pretty grounds, swimming pool, and tennis court. The most basic ensuite rooms have kitchenette, balcony, and TV/VCR for $70, weekly $300; two bedroom suites $110, $500. Two night minimum.

## ◖▮ FOOD AND ENTERTAINMENT

Most food is in Point Lookout, clustered in the **Lookout Shopping Village** and **Centre Point Shopping Centre.** At the top of the hill towards Point Lookout, **Straddie Hotel Pub** has a brasserie with mains for $16 and specials for less. With outdoor pool tables and a bar, it's the local hangout and gets packed on weekends. (Food served 7:30-9:30am, noon-2pm, 6-8pm.) For **groceries,** try Bob's 727 Foodmarket in Centrepoint Shopping Village, Point Lookout. (☎3409 8271. Open 7am-9pm.) Food on the island is not cheap, so bringing food is a good idea.

## ◉ ▮ SIGHTS AND ACTIVITIES

The island is known for its **scuba diving. Stradbroke Island Scuba Center,** below the Guesthouse, has daily trips to among 15 sites. (☎3409 8888. Single dive $72; double $110; 4-day PADI $320; snorkeling $44, including boat trip and gear.) **Straddie**

**Adventures** offers popular adventure tours. (☎3409 8414. Sandboarding $27.50, sea kayaking and snorkeling $50, half-day 4WD tour $50. VIP discount.)

The easiest and cheapest thing to do on North Stradbroke Island is walk—miles of unspoiled beaches and seemingly unexplored bush will keep a spirited traveler busy for days. Heading toward the end of Point Lookout on the left is a "Beach Access" sign for **Frenchman's Beach,** a convenient starting point for any beach walk. Farther up, near the RSL Club, lies the entrance to the **Gorge Walk,** a 15min. stroll past rocky headlands and gorges, white sand beaches, and blue waters. This obligatory walk is famous for **whale-watching** June-Sept. and dolphins, turtles, and manta rays year-round. The Gorge Walk also passes the **Blowhole,** where crashing waves are channeled up a narrow gorge and transformed into fountains of spray. The swimming **lagoon** 4.5km along the beach, is a lovely day hike or picnic spot. **Main Beach** stretches 32km, drawing **surfers** with one of Queensland's best waves during early summer's northerly winds. **Cylinder Beach,** which runs in front of the Straddie Hotel, is more family-oriented with safe swimming, but the break still offers a long fast wall, up to 200m in ideal conditions.

On hot summer days, **Myora Springs,** 4km along East Coast Rd from Dunwich toward Point Lookout, is a refreshing place to cool off. The aptly named **Blue Lake** is a lovely freshwater spot that's part of **Blue Lake National Park.** Drive 8km along Tazi Rd from Dunwich and follow the signs (regular cars must stop 2.7km away and walk the rest, while 4WD vehicles can drive almost all the way, following a sand track). To tour the beaches with your own 4WD, buy an access permit from the tourist office or at most campsites ($7 for 48hr., $12 per week). **Tour de Straddie** (☎3409 8098) operates 4WD tours twice a day.

# MANLY

Manly is a content harborside village where there seem to be more boats than people. A quick trip from Brisbane and near most ferry services, Manly is the perfect accommodations base for exploring the nearby islands as well as a quiet space to return to after a day fishing, sailing, or scuba diving. The main street leads to a jam-packed small craft harbor where you don't have to be the manliest to anchor.

**TRANSPORT.** From Brisbane, take Citytrain to the Manly stop on the Cleveland line (35-40min. from Roma St, 5am-11:54pm; at least every 30min. daily; $2.60). The **Tourist Information Centre,** 43A Cambridge Pde, is across from the Manly Hotel. (☎3348 3524. Open daily 10am-3pm.) **Post office:** 222 Stratton Tce, in the Harbour Village Shopping Centre on Cambridge Pde. (☎3396 2735. Open M-F 9am-5pm, Sa 9am-noon.) **Internet:** Go Video, 11 Cambridge Pde. (☎3396 0554. 30min. $2.50. Open M-Th 10am-9pm, F 10am-10pm, Sa 9am-10pm, Su 9am-9pm.)

**ACCOMMODATIONS AND FOOD.** ▓**Moreton Bay Lodge,** 45 Cambridge Pde, has the best backpacker-style lodging on the Bay. It's a quiet, friendly spot with spacious rooms, TV, kitchen, spotless bathrooms, and helpful owners. (☎3396 3020. Airport and train pickup. Free bike hire. Key deposit $20. Dorms $14, weekly $91; singles $30, ensuite $35; doubles $40, $50; triples $50, $60. VIP.) A neat symmetry divides the hostel from the casual but lovely **Bay Window Café and Bar,** on the second floor, with a gorgeous harbor view and cheap quality food. (☎3396 3020. Open Tu-Su noon-2:30pm and 5:30-8:30pm. Happy Hour daily 5:30-6:30pm.) Across the street, **Manly Hotel,** 54 Cambridge Pde, is a newly remodeled favorite of businessmen paying by company check. Wood paneling, thick patterned rugs, private bath, TV, fridge and leather chairs adorn the lush newer ensuite rooms. The hotel has a bar and a restaurant that serves three meals daily. W, Sa: karaoke; Th-F: bands. (☎3249 5999; fax 3893 1248. Singles $39-$77; doubles $50-$88.)

**SIGHTS AND ACTIVITIES.** A brisk 20min. walk along the Esplanade from the harbor leads to the center of nearby town, **Wynnum by the Bay.** Strolling farther, past the end of the harborwalk and through the soccer fields, leads to the **Wynnum Mangrove Boardwalk,** a 500m walk guided by informative signs. The mangroves grow in dense concentration and it's possible to see clearly their pneumatophores (specialized "breathing roots") protruding through the mud in small clumps. On the Esplanade in Wynnum is a huge **tidal pool** perfect for a dip. Parks with changing rooms and BBQs run along the Esplanade.

If sailing floats your boat, book a trip on **Solo**, a famous Australian ocean racing yacht. A daytrip includes fast sailing around Moreton Bay, lunch, snorkeling, swimming, and either a stop at Peel Island for its isolated beaches and water-tubing, or on Moreton Island for sand tobogganing. Solo also offers a moonlight sail from 6-11pm, including a full dinner. (☎3348 6100. Th, Sa-Su. Daytrip $75. Moonlight $65. VIP and NOMADS discounts.) **Manly Eco Cruises** offers 50min. tours around Moreton Bay from Manly. (☎3396 9400. Sa-Su 11am, noon, 1, 2, 3pm. $13, students $11.) For free sailing, show up at the **Royal Queensland Sailing Club** for the friendly ◙WAGS (Wednesday Afternoon Gentleman's Sailing) races; the winner gets a bottle of rum. Yacht owners are always looking for temporary crew; if you are a beginner, they may teach you. (☎3396 8666. W noon. Women welcome.)

## MORETON ISLAND

Moreton, not usually considered a tourist destination, is a haven for the adventurous. The **Tangalooma Wrecks**, 14 old dredges sunk between 1964 and 1984, are a great diving or snorkeling destination. The striking **Big Sandhills** provide an ideal opportunity for sandboarding. Around the headland is a walking track with whale sightings and outstanding panoramas including the **Cape Moreton lighthouse.** hiking trails lead to the top of **Mt. Tempest**, the world's highest sand mountain.

Civilization on the island is centered around the **Tangalooma Resort** (☎(1300) 65 22 50), which offers day cruises with 9am pickup from Brisbane's Roma St Transit Centre, return departs the resort at 3:30pm ($28, children $14). The resort operates tours of the island, the most popular being the Blue Lagoon ($32) and Desert tours ($16). **Dolphin Wild-Island Cruises** sends a power catamaran from the mainland for a daytrip full of wrecks, dolphins, and sand tobogganing. (☎5497 5628. $79.) Charter the 10-person **Moreton Island Taxi Service 4WD** or join them for a full-day tour of the island's highlights. (☎3408 2661. Charter: about $80 roundtrip to the lighthouse. Tour: F-M, but Su is the longest trip. $75, concessions $60.)

## OTHER ISLANDS IN MORETON BAY

Moreton Bay is dotted with more than 300 islands perfect for daytripping. Cheap accommodation other than camping is sparse, but a day is plenty to sample the islands' offerings: pristine beaches, snorkeling, and an occasional whale sighting.

📷 **COOCHIEMUDLO ISLAND.** A popular getaway for locals, Coochiemudlo entices with shops, restaurants, and occasional crafts markets. **Coochiemudlo Island Ferry Service** runs a passenger and vehicular ferry from Victoria Point Jetty. (☎3820 7227. Passenger: 20min., approx. every 40min. Return $4, children $2. Vehicular: 10 per day. Return $30.) **Bay Islands Taxi Service** (☎3409 1145) also services Coochie from Victoria Point. The **Coochie Bus Service** offers a 30min. tour of the island. (☎3820 7425. $5, children $2.)

📷 **BRIBIE ISLAND.** At the northern end of Moreton Bay, Bribie is the only island accessible by car. From Brisbane, go 45km north to Caboolture, then 19km east. The **tourist office** is just over the bridge from the mainland. (☎3408 9026. Open M-F 9am-4:30pm, Sa 9am-3pm, Su 9:30am-1pm.) Bribie is separated from the mainland by **Pumicestone Passage**, a marine park teeming with mangroves, more than 350 species of birds, sea cows, turtles, and dolphins. Vehicles give easy access to great fishing on the mainland side of the channel and surfing on the east.

📷 **ST. HELENA ISLAND.** Formerly the Alcatraz of Australia, St. Helena now perhaps offers less options to get ashore. In its glory days, it was the first prison in Queensland and the only commercially viable prison in the world. The only way to visit the island is with the **Cat-o'-Nine-Tails** vessel, which offers day and night "tours" to the island—actors put on a show of St. Helena's colorful past and turn tourists into prisoners. Cruises run from **Manly** and **Redcliffe.** (☎ 3396 3994. $48. Evening "ghost tour" is not for children.)

# GOLD COAST

Gorgeous beaches, thumping nightclubs, excellent theme parks, and plenty of accommodations make the Gold Coast Australia's premier holiday destination. The region's permanent population of 390,000 triples to 1.2 million every summer as Australian and foreign tourists flock to the sun, sand, and parties. The term "Gold Coast" has a few possible origins: tourist officials say it's for the stretches of golden sand beaches, but cynics point to high rises and tacky tinsel glitter primarily found in Surfers Paradise. Around Surfers, natural attractions abound—to the south, outstanding point breaks have created some of the world's best surfing beaches and to the north South Stradbroke Island offers a peaceful escape from the bustling coast. A trip to the "Green behind the Gold," the less-touristed but rewarding Gold Coast Hinterland, will complement time spent on the coast.

# COOLANGATTA AND TWEED HEADS

Evidently, the name Surfer's Paradise is taken. However, the outstanding point breaks off the twin towns Coolangatta QLD and Tweed Heads NSW have created some of the best surfing in Australia, if not the world. With three surfing beaches and a huge variety of conditions on any given day, this area is the true surfer's paradise. Summer brings a young crowd of surfers and backpackers as well as families on holiday, but anyway you cut it, the atmosphere is always relaxed. With less neon, fewer skyscrapers, and more pristine stretches of beach, Coolie and Tweed is the perfect place for a break from the up-tempo, artificial Gold Coast scene. As locals like to say, they're near enough to Surfer's Paradise and far enough away. The Tweed-Coolangatta border is only really marked by discrepancies in daylight savings time, most notably at New Year's Eve, when eager partygoers and champagne lovers run across the street and ring in the new year twice.

## ▮ TRANSPORT

The state border divides the settlement down the length of **Dixon St,** which bends right into **Boundary St** and heads out onto the rounded peninsula. At the end of the peninsula is the infamous **Point Danger,** whose cliffs were responsible for Captain Cook's shipwreck. It is now marked by the world's first laser lighthouse

QUEENSLAND

and a 270° view of the ocean. At the **Twin Towns Service Club,** Boundary St meets **Griffith St** and **Wharf St,** the respective main drags of Coolangatta and Tweed Heads.

**Buses:** Coach Trans (☎13 12 30), which honors McCafferty's passes, has service up the coast (about every hr. 5:15am-4pm), including **Brisbane** (2¼hr., $15) and **Surfer's Paradise** (45min., $4). Greyhound, McCafferty's, and Pioneer Motor Services all stop in town on their service to **Brisbane** (2hr., 8 per day, $12-24), and to **Sydney** (15hr., 10 per day, $71). Suncoast Pacific's (☎5531 6000) daily 3:15pm bus ($30) will get you to **Maroochy** (4hr.) and **Noosa** (4¾hr.). Kirklands runs 2-4 buses per day to **Brisbane** (1½hr., $13) and **Byron Bay** (1½hr., $15). Surfside buslines (☎13 12 30) runs the best **public transportation** within the Gold Coast. Route 1 and 1A stop as far south as Kingscliff NSW up to Paradise Point, including, of course, a stop at Surfer's Paradise (45min., every 10-60min., 24hr., $4); a one-day unlimited travel pass is $10, or buy sector tickets. Connections will get you to Gold Coast theme parks, and if you buy your admission ticket from the driver, the bus ride is free.

**Taxi: Tweed Heads Taxis** (☎5536 1144).

**Car Rental: Tweed Auto Rentals,** 4 Wharf St (☎5536 8000, freecall (1800) 819 051), is next to the tourist office. Rentals from $140 per week.

## ✦ ⚡ ORIENTATION AND PRACTICAL INFORMATION

**Tourist Office: Tourist Information Centre,** 4 Wharf St (☎5536 4244, freecall (1800) 67 44 14). At the corner of Bay St. Their free *Tweed-Coolangatta Visitors Guide* is indispensable. Open M-F 9am-5pm, Sa 9am-noon.

**Bus Transit Centre: Golden Gateway Travel,** 29 Bay St (☎5536 1700). Open M-F 7am-5:30pm, Sa 8am-3pm.

**Banks:** Find 24hr. **ATMs** at National Bank, 84-88 Griffith St, at the corner of Warner St, and at Commonwealth Bank in Tweed Mall. Open M-Th 9:30am-4pm, F 9:30am-5pm.

**Internet Access:** Access light meals and the net at **Java Bay Internet Café,** 33 Wharf St (☎5599 3232), at the corner of Bay St. $5 for 30min. Open M-Sa 8am-6pm, Su 10am-6pm. Also, **Coolangatta Internet Café** (☎5599 2001), is on the corner of Griffith and Warner St. Open M-Sa 9am-7pm, Su noon-4pm. $4 for 30min.

**Post Office:** 2 Griffith St. Open M-F 8:30am-5pm.

## ⌐ ACCOMMODATIONS

There are plenty of beds here, but the cheapest are found in the limited hostels, pubs, caravan parks, and motels scattered around town, all near the beach.

**⬛ Sunset Strip Budget Resort,** 199 Boundary St (☎5599 5517). Marvelous, with an enormous kitchen and pool. Huge, clean, nightclub-style lounges. Guests of all ages intermingle happily. Large, yet incredibly cozy and personal. Th night $4 BBQ. Reception 7am-11pm. Singles $30; twins or doubles $40; triples $60; quads $70.

**Kirra Beach Hotel** (☎5536 3311). On the corner of Miles St and Marine Pde. It may be around Kirra Point from Coolangatta, but its clean, bright ensuite rooms are a stone's throw from one of the world's most perfect barrel waves. Singles $30; doubles $40-50.

**Coolangatta YHA,** 230 Coolangatta Rd, Billinga (☎5536 7644). Near the airport, 3km north of Coolie. Management has changed recently, and the hostel enjoyed a facelift. Clean, with large kitchen, laundry, pool, TV lounge. Improvements include 24hr. access, a free all-you-can-eat breakfast, Internet access (10min. $2), daily drop off and pickup to the best waves, and a huge mural that makes the hostel impossible to miss. Courtesy pickup from bus stop with advance notice. Dorms $17-19; twins $19-21; doubles $42; families from $64. Non-YHA members $3 more.

**Kirra Beach Tourist Park,** Charlotte St in Kirra (☎5581 7744), just off Coolangatta Rd, opposite the Kirra Surf shop. Laundry, pool, TV room. Linen $6.50. Office open 7:30am-7pm. Spacious cabin $16-22 per person; tent sites for 2 $17-24.

## 🖼️🎵 FOOD AND ENTERTAINMENT

The **Rainbow Bay Surf Club,** 2 Snapper Rocks, has an incredible view overlooking Rainbow Bay. Family oriented, and packed in the summer, they serve lunch ($6.50-9), dinner ($12), and drinks until late. (☎36 37 36. Food served noon-2pm, 6-8pm.) **Little Malaya Restaurant,** 52 Marine Pde, has a tasty menu, which includes many vegetarian options for around $10. (☎5536 2690. Open noon-2pm and 5:30-10pm.) **Lookout Café** on Point Danger has tasty sandwiches for $3-5, ice cream, and panoramic views of the ocean. (☎5599 2031. Open daily 8am-5pm.) There's a Woolworth's **supermarket** in Tweed Mall on Wharf St (open M-Sa 7am-10pm, Su 8:30am-6pm), and a 24hr. convenience store on Marine Pde at Showcase.

The pink, spaceship-like **Twin Towns Service Club** (☎5536 2277) at Griffith and Wharf St and **Tweed Heads Bowls Club** (☎5536 3800) on Florence St have a plethora of oceanside entertainment, including live music and free Monday night movies. For a younger crowd and a longer night, head to the **Balcony Beach Club** on Marine Pde for a chic nightclub feel. (Open Th-Su 8pm-3am. Bring your passport as ID. No cover.) Downstairs, the **Coolangatta Hotel** has live music Tu-Su, featuring talented cover bands at night, and not-so-talented karaoke performers Sunday afternoon. (Open Sa-Th 9am-midnight, F 9am-2am.)

If you yearn for more, try **The Sands** on McLean St, which features bands F-Sa. (☎5536 3066. $3 cover. Open late.) Across the street, at **Ice,** 23 McLean St, everybody is colored purple and dances to pulsing, popular dance music. (☎5599 3077. Open W-Su 9pm-3am.) If that's still not enough action, Surfer's is a quick bus away on Surfside buslines (45min., runs 24hr., $4). (See **Nightlife,** p. 324.)

For a different sort of entertainment, try the Cosmic Rock 'n' Bowl F-Sa evenings at the Coolangatta-Tweed **Tenpin** (☎5536 1606), across from the Tweed Mall.

## 👁️🎯 SIGHTS AND ACTIVITIES

Tweed Heads-Coolangatta's greatest attractions are the beaches that line its perimeter. **Rainbow Bay** and **Coolangatta Beach,** off of Marine Pde, have the safest swimming on the Gold Coast and are thus family-oriented. **Flagstaff** and **Duranbah Beaches** lie to the southeast; the latter is famous among surfers for its fast waves. The three point breaks, **Kirra, Snapper Rocks,** and **Greenmount,** are some of the best in the world. Surfers are welcoming and surf shops are on every corner. **Kirra Surf,** located where Coolangatta Rd meets Musgrave St, is a landmark surfshop in the area. You can find board rentals at **Point Danger Surfshop** (☎5599 4469) right on the point. For a surfing lesson, call Adam at **Always Summer Surf School** (☎5599 1046). For $35, he'll get you riding within two hours (equipment included).

The walkway that begins to the left of Point Danger, facing the ocean, and continuing to Greenmount, is beautiful with lush greenery on one side, and sand and sea on the other. You'll trip over kangaroos, emus, and gorgeous exotic birds at the fabulous **Currumbin Wildlife Sanctuary,** 7km north along the Pacific Hwy, a Surfside bus stop. See the lorikeet feedings (daily 8am and 4pm), but be sure to duck. (☎5534 1266. Open daily 8am-5pm.) For another pretty view, walk up to the **lookout** on Razorback, via Wharf and Florence St, to view Mt. Warning and some of the world's most special sub-tropical rainforests.

**Tweed Endeavor Cruises** leads terrific river and rainforest cruises on a 150-person double-decker vessel. The 1½hr. tour is fairly uneventful, but the 4½hr. tour is very worthwhile. (☎5536 8800. 1½hr. cruise W and Su $22, concessions $20; 4½hr. with BBQ lunch M, W, F-Su $42, $38; 4½hr. with seafood lunch Tu, Th $50, $47.)

# SURFERS PARADISE

Surfers, partyers, and families may have replaced Adam and Eve, and concrete and neon may have covered the Garden of Eden, but in Surfers Paradise, there's still plenty of bare skin, no hint of embarrassment, and the proverbial apple is near impossible to resist. A narrow urban strip, packed with storefronts, hugs miles of gorgeous sand and rippling waves, though towering hotels shade the very beaches that caused their creation. Surfers Paradise is on nearly every backpacker's itinerary for two reasons: thundering nightlife followed by sleepy daze at the beach—then repeat. Clubs throb with techno, and 5am closing times often just transfer parties to the street. Surfers can also be a convenient base for nearby theme parks, the lush Hinterland, and unspoiled South Stradbroke Island.

# ▐ TRANSPORT

**Buses:** The **Transit Centre** is at the corner of Beach Rd and Ferny Ave, 1 block west of Paradise Centre. Premier Motor Service (☎ 13 34 10) may offer the most comfortable service, but McCafferty's (☎13 14 99 or ☎5538 2700), Coachtrans (☎13 12 30 or ☎5588 8777; best for Brisbane), Kirklands (☎(1300) 36 70 77; best for Byron Bay and NSW coast) and Greyhound (☎13 20 30) also service Queensland. Coachtrans honors McCafferty's passes. There are services to: **Brisbane** (1½-2hr.; at least every 45min. 5:55am-5pm, some later services until 10:25pm; $12-13); **Sydney** (14-15hr., $69-77); **Byron Bay** (1½-2hr., $21-28); and **Cairns** (30hr., $153-170). **Lockers** are available 6am-8:30pm (12hr. $4-8).

**Local Buses: Surfside** (☎ 13 12 30), the local 24hr. bus company, runs very frequently to numerous roadside stops on the Gold Coast Hwy, as well as the Pacific Fair Mall, the theme parks, and Southport. Prices vary, but are inexpensive. Unlimited 1-day pass $12, 1-week $30. With the purchase of a theme park ticket from a Surfside driver you receive free return transport to the park and free unlimited travel for the rest of the day. **Gold Coast Tourist Shuttle** offers transport to all theme parks with pickup and drop off from local accommodations and unlimited travel on Surfside's service. (☎(1300) 65 56 55. $30 per week, 10-day $39.) **Gold Coast Get Around** provides a similar service, with transport to all theme parks and most local destinations (15-day pass $54, children $27).

**Taxis: Regent Taxis** (☎ 13 10 08 or ☎5588 1289). For those not in a hurry, **peddle cabs** (often found on the corner of Cavill Ave and Gold Coast Hwy) make for a romantic ride.

**Car Rental: Red Back Rentals,** in the Transit Centre, offers reliable rental packages. (☎5592 1655. Open daily 8am-5pm.) Also rents **bicycles. Thrifty** (☎5538 6511), on the corner of Enderley Ave and Gold Coast Hwy, rents from $39.

# ✸ ORIENTATION

That maps of Surfers are long and narrow reflects the fact that all the action is squeezed into a strip many kilometers long and just a few blocks wide between the Pacific Ocean and the **Nerang River.** Three main avenues run parallel to the shore: the **Esplanade,** which skirts the beach; the southbound **Gold Coast Hwy,** a block over; and **Ferny Ave,** the northbound Gold Coast Hwy, one more block inland. Central Surfers is marked by the **Paradise Centre** pedestrian shopping mall, enclosed by the Esplanade, the highway, **Cavill Mall** to the north, and **Hanlan St** to the south. The Esplanade continues north past **Main Beach** to the **Marina** and **the Spit,** the end of a peninsula just past Seaworld. To the south is **Broadbeach,** home to the enormous Conrad Hotel Jupiter Casino and the monolithic **Pacific Fair Mall.**

# ▐ PRACTICAL INFORMATION

**Tourist Offices: Gold Coast Tourism Bureau** (☎5538 4419; fax 5570 3259) is the main tourist office, located in a green kiosk on Cavill Mall. Pick up a map and the listings booklet *Wot's On* or *Point Out.* Open M-F 8:30am-5:30pm, Sa 9am-5pm, Su 9am-3:30pm. The **Backpackers Information Centre** (☎5592 2911, freecall ☎(1800) 35 98 30; fax 5538 1282) is located in the transit center. Open daily 8:30am-6pm. After-hours, info and a direct phone to hostels are still available.

**Banks:** Westpac, corner of Cavill Ave and Gold Coast Hwy has a 24hr. **ATM.** Bank open M-Th 9:30am-4pm, F 9:30am-5pm.

**Police:** 68 Ferny Ave (☎5570 7888), opposite the Cypress Ave carpark. There's also a police hut on the corner of Cavill Mall and Orchid Ave (☎5531 5540).

**Medical Services: Gold Coast Medical Transport** (☎ 13 12 33). **Medical center,** Paradise Centre (☎ 5592 3999). Open M-W 8:30am-6pm, Th 11am-6pm, F 8:30am-6pm, Sa 9am-5pm, Su 9am-1pm. **Gold Coast Hospital** (☎ 5571 8211).

**Internet Access: Magic TV,** 50 Cavill Ave, on the corner of Ferny Ave (☎ 5527 6522). 1hr. $4. Open daily 10am-10pm. **Email Centre,** 51 Orchid (☎ 5538 7500). Open Su-Th 10am-11pm, F-Sa 10am-midnight. 30min. $3. Many hostels also have connections.

**Post Office:** Main branch is inside the Cavill Mall. Open M-F 8:30am-5:30pm, Sa 9am-noon. **Postal code:** 4217.

**Phone Code:** 07.

# ▌ ACCOMMODATIONS

In Surfers, hostel staff assume the role of camp counselors, each night leading the troops to cheap meals and the party scene. The symbiotic relationship of hostels and nightclubs makes for plenty of freebies, so any traveler with party intentions should opt for hostel accommodations to help reduce the sucking sound of Surfer's money vacuum. If you didn't come to party,

**Surfer's Paradise**

🏠 ACCOMMODATIONS
Backpackers in Paradise, 3
Cheers, 1
Sleeping Inn Surfers, 4
Surfers Paradise Backpackers, 7
Surf 'n' Sun, 2

🍴 FOOD
Malones, 5
Seafood on the Beach, 6

either get Paradise lost or seek quieter digs at highway hostels. Summer and Easter are peak seasons—book ahead. All hostels have free pickup, 10am check-out, and $10 key deposit.

▨ **Surfers Paradise Backpackers Resort,** 2837 Gold Coast Hwy (☎ 5592 4677, freecall (1800) 28 28 00; www.surfersparadisebackpackers.com.au). A 15min. walk south along the highway to the corner of Wharf Rd in front of the Parkroyal Hotel. Spotless, happy and family-run, "The Resort" also has outstanding facilities: big kitchen, marvelous new bar, TV room, gym, tennis court, pool, laundry, dorms with private bath. 150m to beach. Free board use. Bicycle rental. Sauna (45min. $4). Internet 8min. $2. Reception daily 7:30am-7pm. Dorms $17; doubles $40. Free courtesy bus. YHA, VIP.

▨ **Sleeping Inn Surfers,** 26 Whelan St (☎ 5592 4455, freecall (1800) 81 78 32; www.sleepinginn.com.au). A 5min. walk from the Transit Centre across Ferny Ave. Clean dorms and apartments are spacious and self-contained. All units have kitchens and living rooms with TVs. Friendly, mellow atmosphere. Sa $5 BBQ. Reception daily 7am-9pm. Dorms $16; singles $30; doubles $38; apartments $48-150. YHA, VIP, ISIC.

▨ **Aquarius,** 44 Queen St, Southport (☎ 5527 1300, freecall (1800) 22 99 55). Call for courtesy bus or, from Surfers, follow the Gold Coast Hwy over the bridge and take your first left. Aqua the cat and her top-notch staff take care of their guests with contagious energy in a stylish, colorful setting as they ask: "Can you outparty us?" Clean rooms, TV lounges, glow worm trips, internet, pool, spa, fishpond, and garden. Reception daily 7:30am-9:30pm. Dorms $17; doubles $44. YHA, VIP, ISIC.

QUEENSLAND

**Trekkers,** 22 White St, Southport (☎5591 5616, freecall ☎(1800) 10 00 04). Call for pickup; a 45min. walk north from Surfers on the Gold Coast Hwy. Ten minutes to beach. A beautiful, comfortable, and social hostel. Spotless rooms, most with private bath, all doubles with TV. Pool, free board and bike use, kitchen, laundry. Taco and BBQ nights. Reception daily 7:30am-8:30pm. Dorms $18; doubles $46. YHA, VIP, ISIC.

**Backpackers in Paradise,** 40 Whelan St (☎5538 4344, freecall ☎(1800) 26 86 21). Two blocks down Whelan St off Ferny Ave, the closest hostel to the city center. New, young, and promising management. Large pool, clean spacious rooms, bar, lounge with giant TV. Hostel bistro serves $5 breakfasts and dinners. Reception daily 8am-7pm. 12-bed dorm $14; 8- and 4-bed dorms with bath $17; doubles $44. NOMADS, VIP.

**Surf 'n Sun,** 3323 Gold Coast Highway (☎5592 2363, freecall ☎(1800) 67 81 94). Corner of Ocean Ave, close to beach. Famous for its party atmosphere, but guests can also have quiet if they choose. Private bathrooms, glow worm trips, courtesy bus, pool. Tu: pre-70s night. Reception 7:30am-11pm. Dorms $17; doubles $42. YHA, VIP.

**Cheers,** 8 Pine Ave just off Ferny Ave (☎5531 6539, freecall ☎(1800) 63 65 39). The largest hostel in Surfers. Rooms are basic, but the bar and beergarden are gorgeous. Pool, free Internet. Reception daily 8am-10:30pm. Dorms $17; doubles $38. YHA, VIP.

**Mardi Gras International Backpackers Resort,** 28 Hamilton Ave (☎5592 5888, freecall ☎(1800) 80 12 30). A short walk to the beach and downtown. Clean, small dorms with balcony, TV, and private bath. Bar ($2 beer, $3 spirits), beergarden, carpark, gym, pool table, kitchen, laundry. Reception daily 8am-10pm. Dorms $20; doubles $54.

## ◖ FOOD

Nearly every beach on the Gold Coast has a **Surf Life Saving Club (SLSC)** and an **RSL Club,** where guests can eat cheap meals and play pokies. The **Palm Beach SLSC,** 117 Jefferson Ln (☎5534 2180), end of 7th Ave, off the highway between Surfers and Coolangatta, has meals for $3-7, a courtesy bus, and a beautiful terrace overlooking the beach. A Woolworth's **supermarket** is located in the basement of the Paradise Centre (open M-F 8am-9pm, Sa 8:30am-5:30pm, Su 10:30am-4pm).

### DOWNTOWN SURFERS

Dozens of inexpensive cafés, bistros, and Asian restaurants are in the city center. Classy **Malones,** Shop 306, Paradise Centre on Cavill Mall, serves a $5 pasta dish. (☎5592 6066. Open 24hr.) **Seafood on the Beach,** 4 The Esplanade, lures you from the water for $5 fish-and-chips. (☎5527 5736. Open daily 6am-9pm.)

### MAIN BEACH AND SOUTHPORT

Tedder Ave on Main Beach is lined with bistros, bakeries, classy cafés, and Ferraris. **Senza Nome,** 26 Tedder Ave, has $5 lunch specials. (☎5591 1366. Open 9am-10pm.) **Hook and Chook,** 15 Tedder Ave, baits patrons with $3-5 sandwich and burger takeaways. (☎5532 0097. Open M-Sa 7:30am-8pm, Su 8:30am-8pm.) **Anglers Arms,** 50 Queen St, Southport, has a children's fish-and-chips whose size is quite mature. (☎5532 1677. Open M-W and F-Su 10am-10pm, Th 10am-midnight.)

**WHAT A WHOPPER** Throughout Australia, the yellow and red signs for the fast food joint "Hungry Jack's" provoke a mental double-take. Haven't I seen that logo before? Once inside, the mystery deepens. Whoppers? Chicken tenders? My god, they've ripped off Burger King! If I call right now, maybe they'll give me a cut of the millions they'll sue for! Unfortunately, there's nothing illegal going on. Burger King is well aware of the Hungry Jack's chain—it's theirs. Before Burger King expanded to Oz, some enterprising fellow went to the Australian patent office and got the rights to the name "Burger King," thinking the big boys in the States would pay him off to use the name in Australia. The fast food intelligentsia was not duped, however. Simply changing the name to Hungry Jack's, Burger King set up shop in Australia with the same logo, food, and promotions. And don't even think about it, McDonald's is already here...

QUEENSLAND

## THE SPIT

Towards the Spit, at **Peter's Fish Market**, 120 Sea World Dr, opt for the best fish-and-chips in town ($5), or try your luck cooking their fresh raw seafood. (☎5591 7747. Open daily 9am-8pm.) **Peter's Fish Café** has a larger menu and a small buffet-style option. (☎5531 0077. Open M-Th 11:30am-3pm and 5-9pm, F 11:30am-3pm and 5-9:30pm, Sa-Su 11:30am-9pm.) **Seaway Café**, at the end of the Spit, has milkshakes worth the trek past Seaworld. (☎5591 6970. Open daily 8am-5pm.)

## BROADBEACH

Surf Pde, parallel to the Esplanade, is lined by fairly indistinguishable upscale cafés, which serve delicious breakfasts and keep the cappuccino machines busy all day. **Jo's Brasserie,** on Level 2 in the Oasis Centre, has popular $4-10 meals. (☎5592 2237. Open daily noon-2:30pm and 5:30-9:30pm.) **Cosmopolitan,** on Surf Pde has $5 pizza and pasta dishes and a classy decor. (☎5531 5534. Open 11am-midnight.) **5 Star Kebabs,** 3/88 Surf Parade makes $5 toasted kebabs that are some of the area's best. (☎5592 5240. Open 24hr.)

# 👁️ 🏄 SIGHTS AND ACTIVITIES

A typical day at Surfers is spent lazing on the beach, raising adrenaline levels on thrill rides at the theme parks, or spending money in the huge mall complexes. Tours visit scenery away from the coast, and a couple of museums entertain visitors on the odd rainy day or when beach burnout strikes suddenly. **Aquabus Safaris,** 7A Orchid Ave, offers a 75-min. canal cruise around Surfers and down the Nerang River. (☎5539 0222. $24, children $19, seniors $22.)

## BEACHES, SURFING, AND WATER SPORTS

The beach stretches unbroken 25km from the quiet **Main Beach** on the Spit peninsula all the way south to Coolangatta's Snapper Rocks. Surfers Paradise is a bit of a misnomer, however. The outstanding beach breaks are great for beginners, but the best surfing is to the south. Surfing conditions vary considerably, especially as sand shifts to alter the breaks. Local surfers sometimes drive up and down the coast looking for the best break. Since weather conditions significantly alter an area's quality and level of danger, beginners and experienced surfers alike should ask around first. For more detailed info, hang ten to www.surfcheck.com.au, listen to 90.9 Sea FM's surf reports, or call Mike Perry's surf hotline at ☎(005) 52 29 95.

The most popular beach among boardless beachgoers is **Surfers North.** Near the end of Staghorn Ave and just north of Surfers Paradise, it's the most central hangout off the Paradise Centre Mall and the recipient of blaring music from the local radio station during the summer. Farther south is **Broadbeach,** then **Kurrawa,** near the Pacific Fair Shopping Center. **Burleigh Heads** has a popular surfing area, though it can be mobbed and often has dangerous breaks. For your own safety always swim between the flags, even though the beaches are patrolled by Surf Life Savers.

For equipment, try the **Surfers Beach Club** kiosk on the beach end of Cavill Mall. (☎5526 7077. Long boards $15 per 1hr., $20 per 3hr., $25 per day. Wet suits $5 with a board. Short boards, in-line skates, or baggy boards $10 per 1hr., $15 per 3hr., $20 per day. Lockers $4. Open daily 9am-5pm.) **Cheyne Horan School of Surf,** run by a world champion, guarantees you'll be standing on the board by the end of the first lesson; for those interested in competition, Horan also organizes the **Surfers Paradise Boardriders Club** (☎5538 8550; cheynehoran@hotmail.com). **Cable Ski World** (☎5537 6300), on Oxley Dr in Runaway Bay, offers waterskiing ($30), and bungee jumping ($69); buy their Gold Card for $5 and get a 25% discount.

## THEME PARKS AND THRILL RIDES

Tickets to all parks can be bought at reduced prices from the tourist info booth on Cavill Mall. Surfside, Coachtrans, and Gold Coast Tourist Shuttle provide **transportation** to all parks, except FrozenWorld (see **Transport,** above). Because of the high prices and long lines, arrive early to get the most out of the park.

QUEENSLAND

**DREAMWORLD.** The much trumpeted "Tower of Terror" is the tallest and fastest ride in the world, shooting forward at up to 160kph, then straight up 38 stories, and straight down again, all in a matter of seconds. The rest of the park consists of rides, an IMAX theater, and wildlife shows. *(In Coomera, a 25min. drive from Surfers.* ☎ *5588 1111, freecall (1800) 07 33 00; www.dreamworld.com.au. Open daily 9:30am-5:30pm. $50, concessions and children ages 6-13 $31; $42, $27 at info booth.)*

**WET 'N' WILD.** On hot summer days, the whitewater flumes of this water park will cool you down, while in the winter, the slides and pools are heated. Other attractions include dry courts for volleyball and soccer, a giant 60kph speed slide, an eight lane slide racer, and on summer nights, a movie screen above a wave pool with new release screenings. *(☎ 5573 2255; www.wetnwild.com.au. Open daily from 10am; closing times vary. $25, children $17; $23, $16 at info booth.)*

**SEAWORLD.** Lots of fish, dolphins, sharks, seals, some sad-looking pigeons, a few rides, and a hilarious sea lion show are all on display near the Spit, north of Surfers. Swimming with dolphins is immensely popular, and lets you fully interact with Bottlenoses in a friendly environment. *(On Seaworld Dr. ☎ 5588 2205; www.seaworld.com.au. Open daily 10am-5pm. $50, concessions and children ages 6-13 $31; $42, $27 at info booth. Swimming with dolphins $95, arrive early in the morning to reserve.)*

**MOVIE WORLD.** This Warner Brothers park offers the 6min. *Wild Wild West* ride that climaxes in a 70kph, 20m drop into water; a new Pokemon Island Adventure for the young; and a *Lethal Weapon* roller coaster that suspends passengers from the rail. *(A 25min. drive north of Surfers, on the Pacific Hwy. ☎ 5573 8485; www.movieworld.com.au. Open daily 9:30am-5:30pm. $50, concessions $31; $42, $27 at info booth.)*

**FROZEN WORLD.** Kept at below freezing temperatures, the spacious indoor park has ice slides, snow playing areas, a skating rink, and an ice maze, all of which will cool any sunburn in a hurry. The highlight is the ice carving by Chinese ice sculptors. *(Corner of Gold Coast Hwy and Ocean Ave. ☎ 5570 3633. $16.50, concessions $11.)*

**OTHER THRILLS AND SPILLS.** Indulge James Bond fantasies at the **Australian Shooting Academy** where first-timers can bust some caps under safe, supervised conditions. *(Upstairs in the Paradise Centre, beside Tenpin Bowling. ☎ 5527 5100. Open daily 10am-10pm; must be 18 or bring a legal guardian. $65-105.)* There's **indoor rock climbing** (☎ 5526 2007) for $8 in the Mark Shopping Centre on Orchid Ave; lessons available. Several other **thrill rides,** including various forms of **bungee jumping** and **virtual reality** rides, share a small plot on the corner of the Gold Coast Hwy and Palm Ave. *(Most open daily 10am-10pm. Thrills $5-25.)* The highlight is **Bungee Rocket,** a small, two-person compartment that propels occupants 150 ft. up in 1 second with 5.5Gs. *(On the corner of Palm Ave and Gold Coast Hwy. ☎ 5570 2700. $25.)*

## MUSEUMS AND FESTIVALS

**Ripley's Believe It or Not** museum, in Raptis Plaza on Cavill Mall, a worldly collection of mind-boggling facts, people, and feats, is well worth a visit, especially on a rainy day. *(☎ 5592 0040. Open daily 9am-11pm; $10, backpackers $9, children $7, family discount.)* For more traditional art, visit the **Gold Coast Arts Gallery,** 135 Bundall Rd, 3km from the city center. *(☎ 5581 6567. Open M-F 10am-5pm, Sa-Su 11am-5pm. Free.)* **The Gold Coast Marathon** *(☎ 5527 1363)* will stream down the flat coast June 24 in 2001. Mid-October means **Honda Indy 300** *(www.indy.com.au),* a four day extravaganza of races highlighted by the Indy event, which follows a track around Surfers and down the Esplanade. Crowds pack the streets and hang out of highrises. Airshows, street parties, and fireworks complement the races. Accommodations get booked months in advance for jacked-up prices.

## ♫ ▥ ENTERTAINMENT AND NIGHTLIFE

Aside from partying and drinking, the main nighttime activity in Surfers seems to be getting the best deals on partying and drinking. Most of the hostels provide free passes and cheap meal tickets for several clubs. The majority of clubs are on Orchid Ave, known as the "Avenue," and are open until 5am; it seems that people don't get tired in Paradise. **Bring your passport,** as some clubs won't accept other forms of ID. The Gold Coast Backpackers Association organizes a **club crawl** called the **"magical mystery tour."** (☎(1800) 35 98 30. W and Sa 9:30pm. $15, includes entry to clubs, a free drink at the first three clubs, a photo, and a t-shirt.) High rollers try their luck at **Conrad Jupiters Casino** (☎5592 1133, freecall ☎(1800) 07 41 44).

▨ **Rose and Crown,** Raptis Plaza on Cavill Ave (☎5531 5425). Popular with many crowds, dance music and Top-40 play in one room, and talented live bands perform in the other. Drink specials and prizes. Open Tu-W 8pm-3am, Th-Sa 8pm-5am. Cover $5-6.

▨ **Cocktails and Dreams,** The Mark, Orchid Ave (☎5592 1955). Make like Tom and Cruise to this constantly packed club. Popular with backpackers and more. Organizes events with the hostels, such as M theme night, Tu 70s night, W and Sa Club Crawl. Downstairs, **The Party** plays an alternative songlist. Open daily 8pm-5am. Cover $5.

**The Drink,** 4 Orchid Ave (☎5570 6155). Surfers' new nightclub—euro, stylish, and busy. Open Tu-Su 8pm-5:30am. Cover after 10pm $5.

**Billy's Beach House,** corner of The Esplanade and Hanlan St (☎5531 5666). On the beach, with pool tables, lots of dance space, and plenty of bar. Th $1 stubbies, F $2 Crown Lagers. Dress code.Open Su-W 10am-midnight, Th-Sa 10am-2am. Cover $3 .

**Shooters,** The Mark, Orchid Ave (☎5592 1144). A saloon-style club with bull heads, large pool table area, and regular drink deals. Open 9pm-5am.

**The Mansion,** 5 Beach Rd (☎5538 5525). Talented DJs spin drum and bass and more. Dress code. Open F-Sa, M 9pm-5am. Cover $5-10.

**Fever,** 26 Orchid Ave (☎5592 6222). Popular, relatively new club plays drum and bass. Open F-Su 8:30pm-5am. Cover up to $10.

**Melba's,** 46 Cavill Ave (☎5592 6922). A restaurant turned classy nightclub by dark. Melba's avoids Orchid Ave's meat market feel. Grooves to mainstream and techno. Happy Hour 4-8pm downstairs, 8-10pm upstairs. Restaurant open daily noon-3am. Club open 8pm-5am, W-Th and Da-Su 7pm-5am, F 5pm-5am. Cover $8.

**O'Malley's,** 1 Cavill Ave near The Esplanade (☎5570 4075). Packed Irish pub with a patio over the Mall and The Esplanade. Live music every night. Open Su-Th noon-midnight, F-Sa noon-2am.

**M.P.,** or the **Meeting Place,** Forum Arcade (☎5526 2337). Connects 26 Orchid Ave to 3171 Gold Coast Hwy. Surfers' only **gay club.** Open late. Open Tu-Th 9pm-2am, F 9pm-4am, Sa 9pm-5am, Su 9pm-2am.

## ▓ DAYTRIP FROM SURFERS: SOUTH STRADBROKE

Separated from the Spit by a thin channel, South Straddie is the Gold Coast's hidden gem and a must for any traveler to the area. Largely undeveloped and home to friendly free-roaming wallabies, the long, narrow island (22km by 3km) is blessed with quiet river beaches on the west side and gorgeous empty surf beaches with breathtaking white sand dunes on the east side. The main activity center is the **Stradbroke Island Resort,** which has pools, spas, a sauna, watersports, tennis courts, restaurants, and a monopoly on non-camping accommodation. Individual Fijian style cabins have TVs and fridges. (☎5577 3311, freecall (1800) 07 41 25. Four-person cabin $100.) The island also offers two camping options with toilets, showers, and BBQ. **Tippler's camping area** (☎5577 2849) is just 300m from the resort, while **Currigee camping area** (☎5577 3932) is on the southern end of the island (tent sites for 2 $11). The south end of the island is far from the resort and hubbub (17km), but it is home to one of the region's best surf breaks, The Other Side.

**Ferries** run from Gate C, Runaway Bay Marina, 247 Bayview St, Runaway Bay, off the Gold Coast Hwy past Southport. (☎5577 3311. 20min.; depart Runaway daily 7am and 10:30am, return Su-Th 2:45pm and 5pm, F-Sa 3:30pm and 11:30pm; return

**QUEENSLAND**

$20.) Return from Surfers Paradise transit center to Runaway Bay is $4, but free for those staying at the resort. **Gold Coast Water Taxi** (☎ (018) 75 97 89) leaves from Runaway Bay, Mariner's Cove, or the Spit to anywhere on the island for $25-30.

# GOLD COAST HINTERLAND

Unbelievably, within an hour or so from the bustling coast, you can be bushwalking through lush, subtropical rainforest, enjoying spectacular views, and strolling through laid-back towns. The Hinterland makes a perfect escape from the glitz of the coast; a little exploration will undoubtedly complete your visit to the region.

**▐ TRANSPORT.** Travel by car offers the most flexible means to see the Hinterland. An easy one-day tour from the Gold Coast starts at Murwillumbah, then picks up the road towards Nerang, stops at the Natural Bridge, descends into the valley, ascends to Springbrook for rainforested waterfalls, and finally returns to the Coast via Mudgeeraba. For park info, contact Queensland National Parks (☎ 5544 0634).

Alternatively, buses and tours can get you almost anywhere in the Hinterland. **Mountain Coach Company** has a bus tour to O'Reilly's in Lamington National Park via Mt. Tamborine from Coolangatta, Burleigh, and Surfers. (☎ 5524 4249. $37.50, children $17, including pickup.) **Scenic Hinterland Day Tours** offers a trip to Springbrook and Natural Arch, including Purlingbrook Falls, a thousand year old forest, and subtropical rainforests. (☎ 5531 5536. $36, concessions $33.) **All State Scenic Tours** accesses Lamington National Park from Brisbane, leaving Su-F at 9:30am and returning 3pm. (☎ 3003 0700. Return $44.) Some hostels offer tours to Lamington National Park or to see the nighttime glowworms at Natural Bridge.

## LAMINGTON NATIONAL PARK

The 200 square kilometers of Lamington National Park are split into two sections: **Green Mountains/O'Reilly's** and **Binna Burra.** The park's 160km of well-trod paths lead to spectacular waterfalls, clear springs, subtropical rainforest, and the NSW border ridge, with magnificent views of Mt. Warning's ancient volcanic crater.

**O'RIELLY'S.** O'Reilly's can only be accessed via Canungra along a switchback road which is often one lane. The **info center** books camping for O'Reilly's and for bush campsites accessed only by trails. (☎ 5544 0634. Open M, W, Th 9-11am and 1-3:30pm; Tu, F 1-3:30pm. $3.50 per night.) From **O'Reilly's**, the **Toolona Creek circuit** (17km; 5-6 hr. return) will take you past numerous waterfalls on its way to stunning panoramas. **Python Rock** is another popular route, leading to the Morans Falls.

**BINNA BURRA.** To get to Binna Burra, follow the signs for Beechmont and Binna Burra from Nerang. The **Binna Burra Mountain Lodge,** Binna Burra Rd, Beechmont (☎ 5533 3622), operates a daily bus service to the coast and Brisbane. The ranger and **information center** book camping. (☎ 5533 3622. Open daily 7:30am-3:30pm. $9 per night, student $6.) **Ship's Stern circuit** (19km return) contains unique rainforest species, giant trees, waterfalls, and views of the lush valleys below.

## TAMBORINE MOUNTAIN

Tamborine, a 600m-high plateau, contains nine small national parks of subtropical rainforest. Beautiful waterfalls and native wildlife make this a hiker's paradise. Fresh, cool air, views of the coast and inland mountains, and an attractive town are all just a short drive from the coast.

---

### WILL THE REAL SLIM SHADY PLEASE STAND UP

Throughout the Hinterland one can find a scarce Australian species known as the lyrebird. Capable of copying up to twenty different sounds that they hear in their environment, the lyrebird originally imitated sounds of other birds and animals. Now, as testament to their invaded habitat, the birds are known to make the sounds of chainsaws, rewinding cameras and car horns—proof that you can teach an old bird new tricks.

To get to the park, exit the **Pacific Hwy 1** at Oxenford and follow the steep, twisting **Oxenford-Tamborine Rd;** use low gear. Near the highway exit, check out the **Russel Hinze Park,** a swamp and island refuge for various water birds. Approaching the plateau, the road secretly changes its name to MacDonnell Rd. Turn right onto Long Rd, right at the roundabout, and left at Geissman Dr to reach the **Tamborine Natural History Information Centre,** in Doughby Park. (☎ 5545 3200. Open daily 10:30am-3:30pm.) **Tamborine Mtn Coach Service** picks up at Southport and other points on the Gold Coast at 8:15am and 3:30pm to Tamborine Mtn, and returns at 7:15am and 2:15pm. (☎ 5545 1298. $6, $4 children.)

**MT. TAMBOURINE.** The town of **Mt. Tamborine** offers Devonshire tea houses, B&Bs, and pottery shops. It's just an hour's drive from Brisbane or the Gold Coast, which translates into a constant flow of visitors. Luckily, most visitors don't venture far beyond town, so if you set out on the trails, you'll enjoy relative solitude. For budget travelers, Tamborine is better as a daytrip, because beds are pricey. The **Joalah National Park** circuit (2.3km; 1hr.) offers subtropical rainforest and the picture-perfect Curtis Falls, but no vistas. The track begins on Eagle Heights Rd, either from the carpark off Dapsang St or the shops near Geissmann Dr.

**WITCHES FALLS NATIONAL PARK.** Witches Falls National Park was the first national park declared in Queensland. The **Witches Falls Walking Track** (2.7km; 50min.) runs along the western side of the plateau. This path is stunning at points, but there is more backyard than rainforest at the beginning. The path ends at Witches Chase, from which you can return to the carpark by following this road to Beacon and Main Western Rd (1hr.), or retracing your steps (50min.).

# SPRINGBROOK NATIONAL PARK

Further up Springbrook Rd, find the unattended **Info Centre** in the old schoolhouse, which has color maps of the many walks, lookouts, and camping and picnic areas. (Ranger ☎ 5533 5147. Open 8am-4pm.) Continuing along Springbrook Rd to the Canyon Lookout will lead to the **Twin Falls Circuit** (4km) and the fabulous, day-long **Warrie Circuit** (15km). The Warrie track leads through rock wedge caves and behind, around, and under countless waterfalls. The first accommodation to catch the sun, **Springbrook Mountain Lodge YHA,** 317 Repeater Station Rd, is a small hostel at the top of Springbrook, near the Best of All Lookout. (☎ 5533 5366. Advance notice $10 roundtrip bus from Gold Coast. Dorms $21; twins $24; cabins $44-66. Book ahead.) At the Springbrook Homestead (☎ 5533 5200) on Springbrook Rd, you'll find the only public **observatory** in Southeast Queensland.

To reach the Natural Bridge Section, look for signs after the Springbrook-Mudgeeraba Rd for Natural Bridge via Muwillumbah-Nerang Rd. The **Natural Arch,** Springbrook's most popular sight, is about 1km from the carpark, 3km north of the NSW border. The arch is a gorgeous cavern where a waterfall tumbles through a hole in the hardened lava that was opened by the drill-like force of heavy boulders and swirling water. At night, the cavern comes alive with bats and **glowworms.**

# MT. COUGAL NATIONAL PARK

Just 30min. from the Gold Coast and tucked away in the town of Currumbin are three natural pools with cliff jumps. Signs from the Pacific Hwy between Burleigh Heads (just south of Surfers) and Coolangatta lead there via **Currumbin Creek Rd. Currumbin Rock Pool,** a deep freshwater pool with short cliff dives and smaller pools for lounging above and beneath short falls, is 10min. down the road. Another 6km along Currumbin Creek Rd is **Mt. Cougal National Park,** a rugged part of Springbrook National Park in the Currumbin Creek headwaters (☎ 5532 3032). A 500m walk to **Cougal Cascades** takes you into the rainforest to a **natural water slide,** where cool water cascades over smoothed rocks. Not much farther along the same path is another natural pool with a much higher jump than those at the Currumbin Rock Pool. Only very daring folks attempt these slides and jumps; **use caution** and common sense at all of these risky attractions, and obey posted warnings.

QUEENSLAND

# SOUTHERN AND DARLING DOWNS

West of the Great Dividing Range lie the hills and valleys of the Southern Downs, and the towns of Toowoomba, Warwick, and Stanthorpe. Toowoomba's carefully crafted greenery is only beginning to draw tourists, but the rich agriculture, rustic beauty, and quiet, small town feeling of Warwick and Stanthorpe draw backpackers for seasonal work. For those coming to the Downs with time to spare, Girraween and Sundown National Parks please visitors with their wildflower displays (Sept.-Mar.), granite outcroppings, and spectacular views. Stanthorpe is also the center of Queensland's only wine region, the Granite Belt. The highway transects the region and crosses the border south into the New England region (see p. 150) of New South Wales.

## TOOWOOMBA

With over 150 parks and gardens, many connected by bike and walking paths, Toowoomba has outgrown its name, which is derived from an Aboriginal word meaning "swamp." Using the "Garden City" as a more appropriate alias, Toowoomba consists of a formidable commercial center that fades into a seemingly endless suburbia. The omnipresent stretches of finely manicured greens give the feeling of a city built on a golf course. With different markets every Sunday, the famous Carnival of Flowers in September, and breathtaking views of the Dividing Range, Toowoomba is fighting to become a tourist destination.

**🔁 PRACTICAL INFORMATION.** McCafferty's **buses** leave from 28-30 Neil St (☎4690 9888). Buses run to: **Brisbane** (2hr.; Su-F 13 per day 5:30am-6pm, Sa 11 per day; $12); **Melbourne** (22hr., 2 per day, $130); and **Sydney** (15hr., departs 9pm daily, $62). For northern destinations, connect in Brisbane. Crisps buses, same terminal, are better for travel to **Warwick** (1½hr., 2-3 per day, $12) with immediate connections to **Stanthorpe. Bikeline,** 2 Prescott St, rents bikes. (☎4638 2242. $18 per day, $50 per week.) The **tourist office,** (☎4639 3797) at the corner of James and Kitchener St, has more information, but is not as centrally located as the **tourist information center,** 476 Ruthven St, which also has Internet ($5 for 30min.; open M-F 9am-5pm, Sa 9am-2pm). **Coffee On Line,** 148 Margaret St, also has Internet (☎4639 4686. Open late.) To reach the **post office,** 64 Annand St, take Hall Ln off of Neil St. (☎4632 9888. Open M-F 9am-6pm.) **Commonwealth Bank,** 368 Ruthven St, at the corner of Russell St, provides the closest **ATM** to the bus station.

**🏠 ACCOMMODATIONS.** For inexpensive lodgings close to town and the bus station, the **pubs** around Russell and Ruthven St are the way to go. The best deal in town is **The National,** 63 Russell St. (☎4639 2706. Singles $20 for the first night, $10 each additional night.) The **Gladstone Hotel,** 426 Ruthven St (☎4638 1707), is also a steal with singles for $20 and twins for $35. **The Norville Hotel,** 70 Russell St, is more expensive, but also a stunning, old building with interesting balconies (☎4639 2954. Singles $25; twins and doubles $35.) **Jolly Swagman Caravan Park,** 47 Kitchener St, diagonally opposite the tourist office, is a 15min. walk from town. (☎4632 8735. Reception 7am-8pm. Laundry. Tent sites $11, powered $14; on-site vans $25, for two people $30; 5-person cabin with kitchen $43.)

**🍴 FOOD.** Most of Toowoomba's restaurants, bars, and cafés are around Margaret St, also (appropriately) known as "Eat Street." **Charcoal Chicken,** 183 Margaret St, offers tasty and affordable roast dinners for $7. The **High Court Café,** 169 Margaret St, has elegant gourmet meals ($7-20) and a beautiful wood interior. (☎4632 4747. Open daily noon-2:30pm and 5-9pm.) It also offers a popular nightlife option (W-Sa 9:30pm-3am). The Irish pub **Fibber Magee,** 153 Margaret St (☎4639 2702) is another local nighttime hotspot.

**📷🎷 SIGHTS AND ENTERTAINMENT.** For an incredible view of the Dividing Range, **Picnic Point,** a 30min. walk from the tourist center, is a must (follow James St east to Tourist Rd). A 4hr. hike to Table Top Mountain begins a short way off

QUEENSLAND

**PIES IN THE BACK OF YOUR HEAD** Australia's common magpie birds are well-known to attack humans that venture anywhere near their nests during the spring breeding season. Many Aussies have felt the sting of a swooping beak, often when riding their bicycles. Magpies don't attack, however, when one is looking at them. So, to avoid attack, some cautious natives wear ice cream containers on their heads with eyes painted on the back. But which is more humiliating: to be attacked by an angry bird or wear an ice cream container on your head?

Tobruk Memorial Dr, but is not for the faint-of-heart. For those without a car, Andrew Kidd's **Trident Tours** are a godsend. For $15, he'll pick you up, take you on a 2½-hour tour of all of Toowoomba's highlights as well as its subtleties, and drop you where you wish. (☎4687 6520. Tours daily 10am and 2pm. Book ahead.)

The **Carnival of Flowers** (☎4632 4877) is Toowoomba's biggest draw. Held for a week in mid-September, the carnival features a parade, flower shows, and the exhibition of prize-winning private gardens for the public. In the "Garden City," you'll also find **Ju Raku En,** Australia's most traditional and **largest Japanese Garden,** on the University of Southern Queensland campus. (Open daily 7am to dusk.) The **Botanic Gardens** (officially called the Queen's Park Gardens) on Lindsay St are another floral highlight, especially during spring and summer.

# WARWICK

The second-oldest town in Queensland, Warwick ("WOAR-ick"; pop. 10,000) is mainly known for its annual rodeo (☎4661 9060), attracting a crowd of more than 30,000 fans on the last full weekend in October. It's Australia's most famous rodeo and the culminating event of the month-long Rose and Rodeo Festival.

For those in the market for **livestock** (or just a good show), pig and calf sales (W morning) are at the corner of Fitzroy and Lyons St; cattle sales (Tu at 7:30am) and sheep sales (W 1pm) are at the corner of McEvoy St and Bracher Rd. Another worthwhile stop is the Rosenthal **Lookout** on Glen Rd, about 2km southeast of the town center, which offers stairs to climb and a pretty view.

The **tourist information office** is at 49 Albion St. (☎4661 3122. Open M-Sa 9am-5pm, Su 10am-2pm.) The **transit center,** 78 Grafton St (☎4661 8333) services buses to: **Brisbane** (2¼hr., 2-3 per day, $24); **Toowoomba** (1½hr., 4-5 per day, $12); and **Stanthorpe** (45min., 1-3 per day, $10). Other services include: **National Bank,** 97 Palmerin St, (open M-Th 9:30am-4pm, F 9:30am-5pm); the **post office,** 98 Palmerin St, corner Grafton St (☎4661 1194; open M-F 9am-5pm); and an **Internet café,** 74 Palmerin St, in town hall (1hr. $6; open M-F 9am-5pm, Sa 9am-noon). A Woolworth's **supermarket** can be found on Palmerin St (open M-F 8am-9pm, Sa 8am-5pm).

The **Criterion Hotel,** 84 Palmerin St, has tidy rooms, a TV lounge, a bar whose patrons are watched over by the face of the "Virgin Mary" on the ceiling, a restaurant, and a front veranda overlooking the main street. (☎4661 1042. Breakfast included. $20 per person.) Another bargain, the **Universal Hotel,** 60A Grafton St, is located two blocks away from Palmerin St, on the outskirts of town. (☎4661 1770. $20 per person.) **Kahler's Oasis Caravan Park,** 98 Wallace St, is 1km south of Warwick on the New England Hwy. (☎4661 2874. Sites $12; cabins for 2 from $35.)

**Elle's Coffee Lounge,** 81 Grafton St, has a pleasant setting, a colorful menu, and a brimming bagel sandwich for $3.50. (☎4661 7140. Open daily until late.) The **Condamine Sports Club,** on Palmerin near Grafton St, has $5 specials. (☎4661 1911. Open daily 11:30am-2pm and 5:45pm-8pm.) It also hosts well-frequented nightlife activities (F-Sa until 2am). The Warwick **RSL Club,** 65 Albion St, has an endless menu at reasonable prices. (☎4661 1229. Open noon-2pm and 6pm-8pm.)

# STANTHORPE

As the commercial center for the Granite Belt, Stanthorpe (pop. 5000) offers a pleasant escape from the city. Its cool, crisp climate in winter and location in the

QUEENSLAND

heart of Queensland's best wine country have made it a year-round destination for many Brisbane residents, while its abundant fruit-picking opportunities attract flocks of backpackers in the summer months. The town is an ideal base for visiting the renowned local wineries, exploring the granite formations and wildflowers of the surrounding national parks (Sundown, Girraween, Boonoo Boonoo, and Bald Rock), or enjoying a romantic getaway into the beautiful countryside.

**Ⅶ PRACTICAL INFORMATION.** Coming in from Warwick off the New England Hwy, Stanthorpe's main street, **High St,** turns into **Maryland St** as it bends south in the center of town. The **tourist office,** 28 Leslie Pde, sits by the bridge at Quart Pot Creek. (☎4681 2057; fax 4681 1200. Open M-F 9am-5pm, Sa-Su 9am-4pm.) The **bus station,** 57 Maryland St (☎4681 1434) is inside the Mobil petrol station. Crisps buses run to: **Brisbane** (3½hr., $29), **Toowoomba** (2hr., $22), and **Warwick** (45min., 2 per day, $12). Other services include: **ATMs** at the National and Commonwealth **banks,** 25 and 27 Maryland St (open M-Th 9:30am-4pm, F 9:30am-5pm); the **post office,** 14 Maryland St, whose 1901 clocktower is the tallest building in town (☎4681 2181; open M-F 9am-5pm); **Internet** at Burges, 27 Railway St (☎4681 2917; open M-F 8am-6pm, Sa 9am-11:30am, $2 for 15min.); and a large Woolworth's **supermarket** on the corner of High and Lock St (open M-F 8am-9pm, Sa 8am-5pm).

**Ⅶ☐ ACCOMMODATIONS AND FOOD.** The cheapest and most central accommodation options are in the nearly indistinguishable pub hotels clustered on Maryland St. The rooms are clean and have sinks; most also have a TV lounge upstairs and a fireplace room and bar downstairs. The **Country Club Hotel,** 26 Maryland St, offers the lowest rates in town and an inexpensive restaurant. (☎4681 1033. Singles $15; twins $28; doubles $25.) The **Commercial Hotel,** 11 Maryland St, has slightly bigger rooms and a deck. (☎4681 2244. Singles $20; doubles $35.)

**Top of the Town Caravan Park,** which includes the **Stanthorpe Backpacker's Hostel,** 10 High St, is a friendly, spotless place to stay 15min. north of the town center. For those seeking work, Jason arranges fruit and vegetable picking work and offers transport to the farms. (☎4681 4888. Key deposit $10. Reception 7am-6pm. Campsites $9, for 2 $15; dorms $15; caravans for 2 $30; ensuite cabin with kitchen and TV $50.) Alternative accommodations are available on **"host farms,"** small cattle stations, but you'll need a car to reach them. Most cost $30-40 per person. **Callemondah,** 58km west of Stanthorpe on Texas Rd, charges $30 per night to stay on the sheep and cattle station. (☎4685 6162. Linen $5. Activities extra. Book ahead.)

Coffee and lunch shops are mostly located along the main road. ☒**Il Cavallino,** 130 High St, is an Italian trattoria with exquisite, carefully crafted dishes (try the calamari). Using the Ferrari horse as an emblem, and a racecar-themed decor to match, its higher prices ($10-25) are made worthwhile by its leap in quality and atmosphere. (☎4681 1556. Open Tu-Su.) **The Regal Café,** 159 High St, most days serves sandwiches, fish, and burgers for $3-10, while Friday brings a special seafood night (☎4681 1365. Open M-Th and Sa 7:30am-7:30pm, F 7:30am-8pm.) **The Coffee Spot,** 18 Maryland St, has sandwiches (under $5) and complete breakfasts. (☎4681 3131. Open M-F 8:30am-5pm, Sa 8:30am-noon.) **Anna's Restaurant** (☎4681 1265), on the corner of O'Mara Tce and Wallangarra Rd, just past the tourist office, has beautifully prepared menu options ($10-15) and weekend buffets.

**WINERIES.** The famous Granite Belt **wineries** line either side of the New England Hwy just south (and a little north) of Stanthorpe. Unfortunately, the wineries can't be reached by public transportation or on foot. One option, **Stanthorpe Sports and Camping,** 13 Maryland St, rents mountain bikes. (☎4681 1196. Half-day $10, full $15; $100 deposit.) More popular, however, are tours that provide for a joyful day and a late-afternoon nap. The tourist office has lists of all the local winery tours, but **The Grape Escape,** led by witty, jolly Chris Pascoe, is the best. (☎4681 4761, www.grapeescape.com.au. From $49, including pickup, drop off, and lunch. Book ahead.) Another option is to travel by horse: **Red Gum Ridge** (☎4683 7169) gives lessons and day rides to local wineries. If you're driving (and wishing you weren't), the way to

**BRING IN THE FEDS** In 1917, Australian Prime Minister Billy Hughes was on a whistle stop tour to sell a conscription referendum. While he was speaking from his train to a crowd at Stanthorpe Station, the station master, known for his anti-conscription stance, signaled for Hughes' train to start, ending the speech and sending Hughes on to Warwick. At Warwick Railway station, Hughes was hit by a thrown egg. He asked a Queensland constable to arrest the perpetrator, but the constable responded: "no jurisdiction." The ensuing fights between the conscription and anti-conscription supporters, coupled with the inaction of the Queensland police, caused Hughes to vow to start his own police force. So began Australia's Federal Police.

the wineries is well-marked; most are close to the highway. **Ballandean Estate Wines** (☎4684 1226) is Queensland's oldest family operated winery. **Golden Grove Estate** (☎4684 1291), just across the road, offers a different taste. For a wonderful setting and a unique sparkling Shiraz, try **Mountview Wines** (☎4683 4316). **Heritage Wines,** Cottonvale (☎4685 2197), has a popular Moonshine Madness and free tours.

🎟 **SIGHTS.** For a view of the town and more, walk 30min. up to the **scenic lookout** on Mt. Marlay. From Woolworth's, follow the signs up Lock St. Stanthorpe's gem is the fascinating **Historical Museum,** 15min. up High St from the town center, near the showgrounds. It's a delightful cornucopia of historical oddities: fruit fly catchers, ancient heating devices, and even a handmade TV. (☎4681 1711. Open W-F 10am-4pm, Sa 1-4pm, Su 9am-1pm. $3, children $1.) The more classic **Stanthorpe Regional Art Gallery** is in the same building as the library, across from the Civic Center on Lock St. (☎4681 1874. Open M-F 10am-4pm, Sa 1-4pm, Su 10am-1pm. Free.)

The 1872 discovery of tin in Quart Pot Creek marked the beginning of years of mining around Stanthorpe. Today, amateurs can try **fossicking** (digging for gems); a license is required. **Blue Topaz Caravan Park** in Severnlea, 7km south of Stanthorpe, supplies licenses. (☎4683 5279. $5, families $7.) Strike gold at **Thanes Creek Fossicking Area,** 40 km west of Warwick (☎3237 1435). For those less independent, **South West Safaris** (☎4681 3685) offers fossicking tours.

Stanthorpe has three major **festivals**: the largest is the **Apple and Grape Harvest Festival,** an extravaganza with a gala ball, rodeo, wine fiesta, and museum exhibition (held every even numbered year). The Granite Belt **Spring Wine Festival,** celebrating the release of the new vintage, is held at the wineries during the first three weekends in October. The winter months are devoted to the **Brass Monkey** season, a general and ongoing Downs-wide wine-and-dine celebration of the area's (and particularly Stanthorpe's) position as the coldest winter region in Queensland, featuring traditional Christmas dinners every weekend.

## NEAR STANTHORPE: NATIONAL PARKS

In addition to the parks listed below, two New South Wales national parks, **Bald Rock** and **Boonoo Boonoo,** are easily accessible from Stanthorpe. For more information, see p. 158. None of the National Parks can be reached by public transportation, but **South West Safaris** (☎4681 3685) offers several types of 4WD tours.

**GIRRAWEEN NATIONAL PARK.** Girraween is a popular destination for bushwalkers, birdwatchers, campers, and picnickers. To get there, drive 26km south on the New England Hwy, turn left at the sign, then drive 9km on a sealed road. Massive granite boulders, which seem precariously balanced on top of each other, are interspersed among eucalypt forests, lyre birds, and Queensland's only wombat population. A 1½hr. return hike takes you to the granite **Pyramid,** which offers a breathtakingly expansive view including the famous **Balancing Rock,** and **Bald Rock,** Australia's largest granite rock, just across the border in NSW. The **Castle Rock track** (1½hr. return) is a more moderate climb to a spectacular 360° view from this high summit. The hike to the **Granite Arch** (25min. return) is even more mellow. In the spring, wildflowers sprout from the bases of rocks, hence the park's name—*girraween* is the Aboriginal name for "place of flowers." The Visitor Center, at the

QUEENSLAND

southern end of Bald Rock Creek, is usually open seven days a week; the rangers daringly post the day's hours on an erasable board. Nearby, there are picnic, swimming, and rock-climbing areas. **Camping** is available in designated areas with hot showers, toilets, and barbecue grills. (☎4684 5157. $4 per person, families $15. Self-register upon arrival, but book in advance for Easter and Christmas.)

**SUNDOWN NATIONAL PARK.** Sundown offers rugged terrain, spectacular gorges, high peaks, and panoramic views, as well as swimming holes, fishing, and canoeing in a primitive and underdeveloped area. To get there, drive 75km along Texas Rd north from Stanthorpe and turn left at the signs for Glenlyon. For a longer route with wider roads, take the New England Hwy south to Tenterfield (approx. 40km) and turn right onto the Bruxner Hwy. The 16,000-hectare park has very different geology than neighboring parks, with a mix of sedimentary and igneous rocks that has produced sharp ridges. The **Severn River** cuts the park in two. As there are no graded walking tracks, areas of interest can be reached by following the river and side creeks. The **Permanent Waterhole** is a beautiful large waterhole on a major bend in the river, a 20min. hike upstream along the west bank. The **Split-Rock** and **Double Falls** are well worth the 3-4hr. return hike up McAllisters Creek. Cross the river east into the creek, being careful not to get sidetracked by the old 4WD track. **Camping** is accessible by 2WD vehicles and hikers on the western side of the river. Access from Ballandean to the east is strictly 4WD. Campsites have pit toilets, fireplaces, and BBQ. (☎6737 5235. $3.50 per person, families $14.)

# SUNSHINE AND FRASER COASTS

And the beach just keeps on coming. See surf and sun, bikes and boards, surfers and sophisticates—or see no one at all. With stretches just as beautiful as the Gold Coast, minus the touristy droves, hype, and neon, the Sunshine Coast is a slightly warmer vacationland with 300 days of sunshine per year. Beaches envelop developed resort towns, and waters greet those eager to partake in aquatic pleasures. The largest of the islands that dot Queensland's coastal waters, sandy Fraser Island, reclines paradoxically under a cover of rainforest growing right out of sand. Its legendary dunes and freshwater lakes are frequented by a parade of package tours and bold independent travelers. Farther north, fruit-picking is popular and a bevy of workers' hostels have sprung up to meet the demand.

## MAROOCHY

Maroochy is the general name for an area of coast encompassing the towns of Maroochydore, Alexandra Heads, and Mooloolaba (north to south). Die-hard surfers fill the beaches, and their stereotypically laid-back attitudes permeate the region. Maroochydore is the urban center, heavily oriented toward small industry, and located where the Maroochy River flows into the ocean. About 1km south, Alexandra Heads is best known for great surfing and a safe family beach. Another 2km south, Mooloolaba is lined by beachfront esplanades with nightclubs and an aquarium. Maroochy is a popular base for fruit-picking work, with lychee and ginger season from Feb. to Mar., strawberries from June to Oct., and tomatoes from Nov. to Feb. Average pay is about $11 per hour, and most hostels help find work.

**▐ TRANSPORT.** Suncoast Pacific, Greyhound, and McCafferty's all stop at the Suncoast Pacific terminal in the Scotlyn Shopping Center on First Ave off Aerodrome Rd, Maroochydore. **Buses** run to: **Airlie Beach** (16hr., 1 per day, $111); **Bundaberg** (5¾hr., 1 per day, $42); **Cairns** (26hr., 2 per day, $152); **Hervey Bay** (3¾-4¼hr., 6 per day, $23); **Mackay** (14½hr., 2 per day, $94); and **Rockhampton** (10hr., 2 per day, $63). **Noosa** cannot be accessed from Maroochydore on these coachlines. The local blue **Sunshine Coast Sunbus** (☎13 12 30 or ☎5492 8700) operates hail and ride, connecting the coastal areas fairly effectively; fares range from $1.35 to $8.80. Service #1 and #1A run from the Sunshine Plaza, down Cotton Tree Pde and the Alexandra

Headlands to the Mooloolaba Esplanade (at least every 30min. to Noosa, $5). Service #2 will take you from the Sunshine Plaza to Nambour.

**ORIENTATION AND PRACTICAL INFORMATION.** The main commercial strip in Maroochydore is **Aerodrome Rd. Alexandra Pde** runs from the end of Cotton Tree Pde, past Alexandra Heads, all the way to Mooloolaba, turning into Mooloolaba Esplanade near the end. **The Wharf,** home to many restaurants and shops, is on the right off Parkyn Pde, which is a left off the Mooloolaba Esplanade after it bends around by the Surf Club. The **tourist office** (☎ 5479 1566) is on Sixth Ave just off Aerodrome Rd. Other services include: **taxi** (☎ 13 10 08; about $10 from Maroochydore to Mooloolaba); and **Internet** at **Infoconnect,** 11 Ocean St, Maroochydore (☎ 5475 8555; 30min. $4.50). **Post offices** are at 22 King St, Cotton Tree (☎ 5443 1350) and 1/32 Brisbane Rd, Mooloolaba; **Postal Code:** 4557. There is also a post office at 21 Ocean St, Maroochydore; **Postal Code:** 4558. All open M-F 9am-5pm.

**ACCOMMODATIONS.** Most hostels in Maroochy arrange fruit-picking work. **Maroochydore YHA Backpackers,** 24 Schirmann Dr, is a beautiful hostel just over the river, a few blocks off Bradman Ave, in a quiet residential neighborhood; take Sunbus #1 or call for pickup. Classic red brick rooms have wooden beds, but the nice pool, gardens, enormous kitchen, large common areas, and activities ensure you'll only use your room for sleeping. (☎ 5443 3151. Reception daily 7:45am-1pm and 5-7pm. Laundry $2. Dorms $18, singles $34-40, twins and doubles $40.) **Suncoast Backpackers Lodge,** 50 Parker St, parallel to Aerodrome Dr, is small, friendly, and clean, with a common space, kitchen, pool table, and continuous tunes. (☎ 5443 7544. Reception daily 8:30am-noon and 5-8pm. Courtesy pickup and drop off in Mooloolaba. Dorms $18, weekly $107; twins and doubles $40, $120. VIP.) **Mooloolaba Beach Backpackers,** 75 Brisbane Rd, is new, colorful, and close to the nightlife. Bunk dorms have kitchens on each level. Spacious ensuite doubles with TV are in a separate brightly-colored, motel-like building. (☎ 5444 3399, freecall ☎ (1800) 02 01 20. Dorms $22; ensuite doubles $55; ensuite quads $100. VIP.) **Maroochy Shire Council** (☎ 5479 1566), operates seven caravan parks.

**FOOD AND NIGHTLIFE.** Maroochy has many good Thai restaurants, but the best is **Som Tam Thai,** on the corner of Fifth Ave and Aerodrome Rd. (☎ 5479 1700. Open daily 5-10pm. Mains around $13.) **Krishna's Vegetarian Café,** Shop 2/7 First Ave, Maroochydore, has all-you-can-eat vegetarian meals for under $8 (open M-F 11:30am-2:30pm, F-Su 5:30-8pm). Plush and classy, **Fiszh Resistance,** 1 Venning St, Mooloolaba (☎ 5452 6699), near The Esplanade, makes a $10 backpackers special of what was once irreconcilable—fish, chips, salad, and a glass of wine. **Saltbush Deli,** Shop 6 River Esp, has gourmet sandwiches for $6.50-8. (☎ 5478 0777. Open 8am-4pm.) Franklins Fresh **supermarket** is in the Big Top Shopping Centre (open M-F 8am-9pm, Sa 8am-5:30pm, Su 10:30am-4pm).

Mooloolaba comes alive after dark. **Friday's on the Wharf,** on the River Esp, is modern, but the old weatherboard sheds from the bar retain some of that old coastal Queensland character. (☎ 5444 8383. Restaurant open daily noon-3pm and 5:30-9pm; nightclub open Tu-Su late.) **Secrets 2000,** 89 The Esplanade, knows the recipe for a busy nightclub: 13 TV screens, three bars, a DJ, and a dance floor. A YHA, VIP, or NOMADS card will get you free entry and a free drink. (☎ 5478 3422. Open until 3am.) The walls of **O'Malley's,** 109 The Esplanade, seem to sing: "come ant dance wyt me in Irlaunde." With no less than 15 beers on tap, you'll be dancing in no time. The bistro serves $9-12 Irish fare. (☎ 5452 6344. Open noon-2pm, 6-8pm. Bar open 10am-late. Tu-Su nights and Su 3pm feature live music.)

**ACTIVITIES.** Being in Maroochy means spending time near the water. **Bad Company,** 6-8 Aerodrome Rd, Maroochydore, is a surf shop across the street from a good strip of beach. (☎ 5443 2457. Open M-F 9am-5pm, Sa 8:30am-5pm, Su 8:30am-4pm. Short and body boards half-day $15; longboards half-day $25.) **Maroochydore Beach** offers good beach breaks for shortboard riders. **Alexandra Headlands** can have rips, large swells, and big crowds. If surfing's not your thang, **Maroochy Skate**

**Biz,** 150 Alexandra Pde, offers in-line skates, bikes, skateboards, and scooters. (☎5443 6111. Open daily 9am-5pm. full-day$7.50, full-day $22.)

At **Underwater Adventures,** on the Wharf, the largest oceanarium in the Southern Hemisphere, you can get a kiss from an eccentric seal (11am, 1, 3:30, 5pm) or glide through a wrap-around clear aquarium on a moving walk with sharks, giant rays, and 250kg Moreton Bay gropers swimming inches overhead. (☎5444 2255; www.underwaterworld.com.au. Open daily 9am-6pm, last entry 5pm. $21.50, concessions $14, children $11.) If you're up for it, you can jump right into that seemingly suicidal aquarium pool and **dive with the sharks.** (Operated by Scuba World; 30min.; certified divers $95, tank and wetsuit only $82.50; non-certified, including scuba lesson $110; double dive on the Sunshine Coast reefs $99.)

Crew in sailing races at the **Mooloolaba Yacht Club** (☎5444 1355), near the end of Parkyn Pde, 12:30pm Wednesday and Sunday. Spots aren't guaranteed, but sign up for the "funsail" and bring a six-pack for the skipper.

# NOOSA

Upper-class couples, Australian families, and backpackers all come to Noosa in roughly equal numbers to enjoy the gorgeous beaches, glitzy shopping areas, outdoor dining, and lush, tropical greenery. Some criticize Noosa for catering to upscale vacationers with carefully crafted trendiness, but the area manages to draw backpackers in droves anyway, with high quality and low prices. The cultures intermingle without friction during the day, but stick to their own at night. Weary, hungover backpackers may find welcome relief from the foam and tinsel of the Gold Coast, with activities to suit every whim and bush and rustic inland towns just around the corner. Cooloola National Park, just north of Noosa, is a wilderness ripe for 4WDing, hiking, canoeing, and camping.

## ▐ TRANSPORT

**Buses:** McCafferty's (☎13 14 99), Suncoast Pacific (☎5449 9966), and Greyhound Pioneer (☎13 20 30) run to: **Brisbane** (3hr., 11-13 per day, $16); **Airlie Beach** (15hr., 1 per day, $110); **Bundaberg** (5hr., 1 per day, $38); **Cairns** (25hr., 2 per day, $151); **Hervey Bay** (2¼-3½hr., 5 per day, $19); **Mackay** (12½-13¾hr., 2 per day, $92); and **Rockhampton** (8½-9½hr., 2 per day, $63). For more connections, connect by **Sunbus** to Cooroy or Nambour. Suncoast Pacific runs to **Tin Can Bay** (2hr., 1-2 per day, $16).

**Public Transportation: Sunshine Coast Sunbus** (☎13 12 30 or ☎5492 8700), offers frequent hail-and-ride service around Noosa. Service #1 to **Maroochydore, Mooloolaba,** and **Caloundra.** Service #10 to **Noosa Junction, Noosa Heads, Tewantin, Sunshine Beach,** and **Sunrise Beach.** Service #12 to **Eumundi** and **Cooroy.** Fares $1.35-8.80; buses run approximately 6am-9pm, later on weekends.

**Taxis: Suncoast Cabs** (☎13 10 08) provide 24hr. service.

**Car Rental: Henry's,** 13 Noosa Dr (☎5447 3777), has cars and bicycles. **Thrifty** (☎5447 2299), offers 4WD rentals for Fraser Island, and an esky free of charge. **Noosa Sunrover Rentals,** Noosa Harbour, Tewantin (☎5449 7833), specializes in 4WDs.

## ▐ ORIENTATION

The Noosa area can be a bit confusing to navigate because its distinguishing features all have irritatingly similar names. The three main communities are Noosa Heads, Noosa Junction, and Noosaville; Noosa National Park is also a prime attraction. These areas are connected by Noosa Drive and Noosa Parade, and are located along the Noosa River, which runs into Noosa Sound and Noosa Inlet. Seriously. . . this isn't something to joke about. **Noosa Heads** is the main tourist area, and activity revolves around the sidewalk-chic **Hastings St,** one block north of the **Noosa Parade Bus Interchange.** Many trendy shops, restaurants, and upscale hotels line the street. The entrance to **Noosa National Park** is at the end of Hastings St.

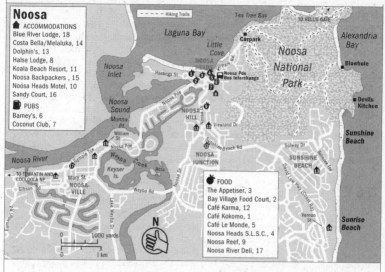

**Noosa**

**ACCOMMODATIONS**
Blue River Lodge, 18
Costa Bella/Melaluka, 14
Dolphin's, 13
Halse Lodge, 8
Koala Beach Resort, 11
Noosa Backpackers , 15
Noosa Heads Motel, 10
Sandy Court, 16

**PUBS**
Barney's, 6
Coconut Club, 7

**FOOD**
The Appetiser, 3
Bay Village Food Court, 2
Café Karma, 12
Café Kokomo, 1
Café Le Monde, 5
Noosa Heads S.L.S.C., 4
Noosa Reef, 9
Noosa River Deli, 17

A 15min. stroll over the hill along the wooden sidewalk ramp leads to the heart of **Noosa Junction,** Noosa's business center. The **post office, supermarket,** and a string of **banks** all lie within 5min. of each other. **Noosaville** is 3km southwest of Noosa Heads (30min. walk), and is the departure point for most cruises to Fraser Island. Its main street, **Gympie Tce,** is filled with international restaurants, motels, and boat hires. The **Sunshine Beach** area is 3km east of Noosa Junction. The cluster of beachfront hostels here are best reached by car, by bus, or by foot along the beach, since the walk along the busy David Low Way takes at least 30min. Both Sunshine Beach and nearby **Sunrise Beach** (another great moment in innovative nomenclature) are popular spots, but the total 40km stretch of sand leaves ample room for bathers to spread out.

## 🛈 PRACTICAL INFORMATION

**Tourist Office: Tourism Noosa Information Centre** (☎ 5447 4988; www.tourism-noosa.com.au), at the T intersection of Noosa Dr and Hastings St, Noosa Heads. This is the most Noosa-focused info center. Among the walls of brochures, *Noosa: The Guide* and *Hello Noosa* are good introductions to the town. Open daily 9am-5pm. **Backpacking Round Queensland,** 9 Sunshine Beach Rd, Noosa Junction (☎ 5474 8530, freecall ☎ (1800) 66 67 20), does bookings and provides Internet (30min. $3) and job listings. Open M-Sa 8am-10pm, Su 9am-10pm.

**Currency Exchange: Banks** are on Hastings St, Noosa Heads; Sunshine Beach Rd, Noosa Junction; and Gympie Tce, Noosaville. Open M-Th 9:30am-4pm, F 9:30am-5pm.

**Police/Air Sea Rescue:** (☎ 5447 5888), on Langura Court, Noosa Junction; also at the corner of Hastings St and Noosa Dr, Noosa Heads.

**Medical Services: Noosa Hospital,** 111 Goodchap St, Noosaville (☎ 5445 9200).

**Internet Access:** The cheapest Internet is available (to non-guests as well) at **Koala Beach Resort** (15min. $1). Also at: **NoosaNetcafé,** 75 Noosa Dr, Noosa Heads (☎ 5474 5770; open M-F 9am-5pm, Sa 9am-4pm, Su 10am-4pm; 10min. $1); and **Backpacking Round Queensland,** see **Tourist Office,** above.

**Post Office: Noosa Post Office,** 91-93 Noosa Rd, Noosa Junction (☎ 5447 3280; fax 5447 5160). Open M-F 9am-5pm, Sa 9am-12:30pm. **Postal Code:** 4567.

**Phone Code:** 07.

QUEENSLAND

# ACCOMMODATIONS

Lodging in Noosa comes in three general categories: hostels, motels or hotels, and "holiday units," which are sometimes private homes. Intense competition for budget travelers makes for low hostel prices and perks such as cheap meals, courtesy shuttle service, surfboards, and on-site bars. With Noosa's increasing popularity there aren't always enough budget beds to go around and during Christmas and school vacations, rates can double; be sure to book ahead. Motel and hotel rooms can top $200 on Hastings St, but are much cheaper without a beachfront view. Families may find it cheaper to rent units or homes; **Accom Noosa** (☎5447 3444, freecall ☎(1800) 07 20 78; www.accomnoosa.com.au) can help find affordable, longer stays. Camping is not allowed in Noosa National Park, but it is possible in **Cooloola National Park** (see p. 339).

## NOOSA HEADS

Lodging here puts you near busy Hastings St and close to the Noosa National Park.

**Halse Lodge (YHA),** 2 Halse Ln (☎5447 3377, freecall ☎(1800) 24 25 67; www.halselodge.com.au). Up the small hill across Noosa Dr from the Noosa Pde bus interchange. This stately, wooden house built in 1880 is relaxed and attracts a quiet crowd. Large common areas. A tiny bar is festive until the 11pm common space lockdown. Laundry $2. Reception daily 7am-8pm. Dorms $19-21; twins and doubles $49.

**Koala Beach Resort,** 44 Noosa Dr (☎5447 3355, freecall ☎(1800) 35 74 57; www.koalaresort.com.au). A 10min. walk from the bus interchange; take a right onto Noosa Dr and follow it over the hill. Popular with a young, hard-partying crowd. Laundry, pool, volleyball court, small kitchen, and outdoor eating area. Internet 15min. $1. Reception daily 7:30am-8pm. Ensuite dorms $20; twins and doubles $45. VIP.

**Noosa Heads Motel,** 2 Viewland Dr (☎5449 2873). On the corner of Noosa Dr, just up the hill from the Noosa Junction rotary. Just minutes away from the action, but a beautiful jungle-like lot makes it feel hidden in the wilderness. Clean ensuite units, all with double beds, kitchen, TV, and covered parking. Closing for a period in 2001 for renovations. Downstairs units $64; upstairs units $75; units with a double and 2 twins $86.

## SUNSHINE BEACH AND SUNRISE BEACH

Although these hostels are removed from the Noosa action (25min. walk from Junction), they are close to the beach. By car, they're off the David Low Hwy.

**◪ Costa Bella/Melaluka,** 7 Selene St (☎5447 3663, freecall ☎(1800) 00 36 63; www.melaluka.com.au). Take the highway to Sunrise Beach; turn at Vernon St and make 2 quick rights down the hill. Although it may lack the communal hostel atmosphere, you'll have to pick your jaw off the floor after seeing the new, spacious Costa Bella units, which are self-contained with ocean views and patios. The other 2 buildings also offer fully equipped units. 2 pools, BBQ, Internet. Laundry in each unit. Frequent 5min. courtesy van to town. Reception M-F 8am-8pm, Sa-Su 9am-7pm. Old building $19 per person; new building $22 per person; Costa Bella $25 per person.

**Dolphins,** 14 Duke St (☎(0417) 60 29 24, freecall ☎(1800) 45 44 56; www.dophins beachresort.com). New hostel near Sunshine Beach shops. Energy and friendliness make this a choice Noosa spot, close to the beach. Self-contained units have TV, kitchen, and bathroom, all around a fun outdoor common area. Internet, table tennis. Dorms $20; twins and doubles $45. YHA, VIP, NOMADS.

## NOOSAVILLE

Most of the travelers who stay in this less glamorous part of town prefer the serenity of the Noosa River to the beaches, which are a 30min. walk away.

**Noosa Backpackers Resort,** 11 Williams St (☎5449 8151, freecall ☎(1800) 62 66 73). Located on a side street 2min. from the river, 25min. from the National Park. A low-key

QUEENSLAND

**A MOVING LOCAL LANDMARK** Betty, of ▨ Betty's Burgers, had to leave her Hastings St shop last year after 20 years of serving Noosa. The city responded by buying her a caravan from which to serve her legendary $1 burgers. The lesson of this experience was not lost on Betty, whose burgers are now $1.65. Follow your nose to the end of Hastings St, away from the national park, turn right at the roundabout, and head towards the beach to the caravan. Open daily 8am-4pm.

hostel driven by the energy and friendliness of its owners. Courtesy van, weekly movie nights, and daily theme dinners ($3.50-7). Discounts offered on their Trailblazers camping tour of Fraser Island. Pool table, swimming pool, Internet. Reception daily 8am-12:45pm and 1:30-8pm. 4-bed dorms $19; doubles $42. VIP.

**Blue River Lodge,** 181 Gympie Tce (☎5449 7564). Directly across from Noosa River. Spotless units with 2 bedrooms, but 1 will remain locked unless you pay $10 for each guest beyond 2. Pickup available. Laundry. Units $60. 7th night free.

**Sandy Court,** 30 James St (☎5449 7225). A half-hostel complex 2min. from the river. Units are ensuite motel rooms with 3-4 bunks installed, which translates into spacious kitchens and TV lounges. Parking, laundry, Internet (1hr. $8). Free pickup. Reception 6:30am-8pm. Check-out 9:30am. Dorms $20; twins and doubles $45.

## 🗗 FOOD

With over 140 restaurants in Noosa, more than 30 of which are on Hastings St, you can be sure to find some great, reasonably priced food. The three main food clusters are Noosa Hill and Junction; Hastings St, Noosa Heads; and Gympie Tce, Noosaville. The surf clubs are a great place for a cheap meal or a sunset beer; try **Noosa Heads Surf Life Saving Club,** 69 Hastings St (☎5447 5395). Backpackers, however, tend to eat at hostels, most of which offer meals for $7 or less. Coles **supermarket** is off Sunshine Beach Rd in Noosa Fair Shopping Centre, Noosa Junction (open M-F 8am-9pm, Sa 8am-5:30pm, Su 10:30am-4pm).

**Café Kokomo,** 5 Hastings St, Noosa Heads (☎5447 2467). A friendly, personal spot for delicious fresh, healthy meals. Great deals before 7pm—grilled lamb cutlets, large pizzas, and Caesar salads all go for $11. After 7pm this is no longer a budget establishment. Indoor and outdoor dining. Open daily 8am-late. Kitchen closes 9:30pm.

**Café Le Monde,** 52 Hastings St, Noosa Heads (☎5449 2366; fax 5449 2108). A local favorite. Classy and comfortable, it's also a breakfast gathering place for local surfer celebs. The express lunch baguettes are delicious and reasonable ($7 for a foot-long; available 11am-5pm), while dinners are tasty, but often pricey (mains $10-23). Live music 5 nights a week. Open daily 7am-midnight.

**Noosa River Deli,** 255 Gympie Tce, Noosaville (☎5474 0404). A pleasant riverside spot for lunch. Sandwiches from $5; light meals $8.50-9.50. Open daily 8am-4pm.

**Café Karma,** 16 Sunshine Beach Rd, Noosa Junction (☎5474 8588). Gourmet sandwiches ($6.50-8.50) in a nice setting with friendly service. Open M-Sa 7am-5pm, Su 7am-3pm.

**The Appetiser,** 47 Hastings St, Noosa Heads (☎5474 9573). Sandwiches, light meals, and breakfast all day, including the Aussie Breakfast for $7. Open 7am-5pm.

**Noosa Reef,** Noosa Dr (☎5447 4477). On the hill between Hastings St and the Junction. Modern and airy, with a family atmosphere. The café deck has great views of the town. Parents can send their kids to the adjoining video/play room for a $9 meal while they enjoy pizza wraps, steaks, and fish-and-chips for $11-17.

## 👁 🎐 SIGHTS AND ACTIVITIES

**NOOSA NATIONAL PARK.** Noosa National Park (☎5447 3243), is a 454-hectare area of tropical vegetation, coastal walking paths, and rare wildlife, which bills itself as the most visited park in Australia with over one million visitors per year. A lovely, koala-strewn path (1.4km) through the woods from the Noosa information booth on Hastings St will land you at the entrance; or follow Hastings St, take a left on Park Dr and follow the boardwalk. The park is ideal for walking and jogging, though it can be dangerous at night or alone. The tourist office provides maps of five interconnected paths, ranging from 1 to 4.2km. The coastal track, which offers elevated views of the ocean and ends at exhilarating **Hell's Gates,** is gorgeous at sunrise, and offers many places to **surf** if you walk your board in. Beautiful stretches of **beaches** (some nude, some gay, some clothed, some straight) are on **Alexandria Bay** on the eastern side of the park, accessible primarily from **Sunshine Beach.** Water and toilets are available, but camping is prohibited. **Little Cove,** hidden discretely between Hastings St and the national park, a 5min. walk from the shops, is a charming and secluded beach.

**SURFING.** With warm water temperatures and a strong surfing community, the Sunshine Coast is a great place to surf. The best season is Nov.-Mar., as the waves in winter tend to be fickle. Noosa is a wave mecca of five right-hand points, with the bonus of a beautiful backdrop. **First Point** is great for longboarders, while **Little Cove** suits beginners. The best waves are perhaps **National Park** and **Tea Tree,** with long lines and barrel sections, but unfortunately this is not a secret we are divulging—in good conditions it can get extremely crowded. For isolation, try **Double Island Point** to the north in Cooloola, but watch out for rips and suspect shadows. On the other side of Noosa National park, try **Sunshine Beach,** with varying conditions, but so much surf there's almost always a good break somewhere.

**Learn to Surf,** with world champion Merrick Davis, guarantees you'll be standing by the end of one lesson. (☎(0418) 78 75 77. 2hr.; $35. Book ahead.) For boards, try **Ozmosis,** 30 Hastings St, Noosa Heads (☎5447 3300; boards half-day $20, full-day $30, deposit $200; bodyboards $10, $15, $150), or **Impact Surf,** Shop 1-7 Sunshine Beach Rd, Noosa Junction (☎5474 9198; short and body boards 4hr. $10; longboards $15; wetsuits $5; open M-F 9:30am-5:30pm, Sa 9:30am-5pm, Su 10am-5pm.)

**OTHER ACTIVITIES. Camel Safaris** offers camel trips through the Noosa Northshore bush and beach. (☎5442 4402. 1½hr., $35.) **Clip Clop Horse Treks** lets you splash through lakes and trot through bush around Lake Weyba for a day. (☎5449 1254. $150.) Tandem skydive over the coast with **Sunshine Skydivers,** one of the least expensive operators in the state. (☎(0500) 52 25 33. 12,000ft $270, backpackers $209; 14,000ft $320, $259.) Cruise around the Great Sandy National Park using thermals and natural lift while **paragliding.** (☎5445 7466. 40m instructional tandem flight $80, full-day lesson $130; full certification courses offered.)

Noosa is also a great departure point for **Great Sandy National Park** (for all the options, see **Cooloola National Park,** p. 339, and **Fraser Island,** p. 343).

## 🎵🍸 ENTERTAINMENT AND NIGHTLIFE

**Barney's,** on Noosa Dr near Hastings St, has an unpretentious surfing mood perfect for a relaxing beer. Get a "huge" beer for $8—you won't mind taking your time. (☎5447 4544. Happy Hour 4-6pm.) **The Koala Bar,** 44 Noosa Dr, in the hostel, is backpackers-central with pool tables, DJ, and nightly specials to spice up the evening, which ends abruptly at the stroke of midnight. The **Coconut Club,** next to Barney's near Hastings St, known as "The Nut," has dancing in a faux tropical setting (open W-Su; $5 cover F-Sa). The brand-new **Reef Bar** (☎5447 4477), a bright surf club look-alike with public bar prices, is underneath the Noosa Reef restaurant on Noosa Dr. This nightspot offers pool tables, sports channels, and accomplished drinkers. Noosa's slightly upscale night spot, **Rolling Rock,** Upper Level, Bay Village on Hastings St, Noosa Heads, is packed with the tragically hip. Thumping techno rocks the house on Thursday, while Sunday features live local bands. (☎5447 2255. Open 9pm-3am every night, but doors strictly close at 1:30am. Cover $5 after 10pm W-Su. M $2 drinks until 2am with $2 entry.)

# NEAR NOOSA

## COOLOOLA NATIONAL PARK

Extending 50km north of Noosa up to Rainbow Beach is the sandy white coast and 64,000 hectares of forest of Cooloola National Park. Together with Fraser Island, Cooloola forms the Great Sandy Region, the largest sand mass in the world. Intrepid explorers and Sunday strollers alike will enjoy this wilderness area. The beaches are generally uncrowded, but in summer months and holidays there's a thick blanket of tents and picnickers on the sands.

**◪ PRACTICAL INFORMATION.** Cooloola National Park stretches 50km along the coast from Noosa in the south to Rainbow Beach farther north. The road from Tewantin, northwest of Noosa, accesses the park and the western side of Lake Cootharaba. Information on the park is available from **Cooloola Shire Council,** 242 Mary St, Gympie (☎5482 1911); **Rainbow Beach Tourist Information Centre,** 8 Rainbow Beach Rd, Rainbow Beach (☎5486 3227); the **Queensland Parks and Wildlife** office in Rainbow Beach (☎5486 3160); and Noosa tourism offices.

**▣ TRANSPORT. Rainbow Beach** accesses the park at its northernmost tip. **Noosa Ferry Cruise** floats between Noosa Heads and Tewantin. (☎5478 0040. Return $10; Noosa Heads jetty is at the Sheraton.) The 2min. Noosa Northshore Ferry (☎5447 1321) leaves from across from Moorindil St in **Tewantin** for the park. **Rainbow 4WD Hire,** 9 Karoonda Crescent, Rainbow Beach (☎5486 3555), rents 4WDs. **Noosa's Cooloola/Everglades Cruises** picks up along the Sunshine Coast for its full-day Everglades BBQ cruise. They also offer a 2-in-1 safari which includes a tour of Cooloola beach. (☎5449 9177, freecall ☎(1800) 65 76 66. M and W-F. Everglades $62, children $40; 2-in-1 $95, $62.) **Polleys Coaches** tours Tin Can Bay ($9) and Rainbow Beach ($11.50) from **Gympie.** (☎5482 9455. Departs M-F 6am and 1:30pm.)

**⚑ ACCOMMODATIONS.** Hidden in the bush, but only 20min. from Noosa, **Gagaju** is a stress-free, focused escape on the border of Cooloola National Park and Noosa River. It's as eco-friendly, welcoming, and in touch with nature as a place could be. Dorm accommodation is in 16- to 18-bed bush bunkhouses—it's like camp, but much better. (☎5474 3522, ☎(1300) 30 22 71. Free pickup from Noosa. Running water and laundry. Tent sites $12 per person; dorms $20. Canoe trips: half-day $20, full-day $30, 2-day $79, 3-day $115.) **The Rocks Backpackers Resort,** Spectrum St, Rainbow Beach, is a clean, modern hostel. (☎5486 3711, freecall ☎(1800) 64 68 67. Dorms $18; doubles $38.) **Camping** is permitted at 14 sites in the park (permits $4 per person, payable at the self-registration stations).

**◪ SIGHTS.** The Cooloola National Park forests hold many natural wonders: rainforests growing from pure sand, winding waterways shaded by mangroves, and characteristic Aussie critters like kangaroos and ground parrots. Even the plants are unusual: endangered *boroniakeysii* (pink-flowered shrubs) mingle with thin, stubborn stalks of blackbutt, and melaluka "tea trees" dye the river a deep black. One of the best ways to enjoy the park is to canoe or motor up to **Lake Cootharaba,** Queensland's largest natural lake, and the **Everglades,** where the dark water creates mirror images of the dense riverbanks lined with sedges. As in any wilderness area, keep **safety** in mind and watch out for the wildlife. Sharks in the

QUEENSLAND

---

**A RUNNING BET** In a Pomona pub in 1957, a bet was made that no one could run up Mt. Cooroora (439m) in less than an hour. In just 40min., Bruce Samuels won himself 40 pounds. The challenge has since become an annual race to be crowned King of the Mountain. The record stands at under 25min. to climb this extremely steep 1.5km path with its loose stones, slippery spots, and caution signs. Most run the race in about 2hr. and then immediately proceed to the pub.

river system occasionally approach the shore, and swim alongside the stingrays, catfish, and jellyfish in the ocean. Use caution when swimming in inland lakes.

The beach in Cooloola is famous for its natural beauty. Extending from Rainbow Beach to Double Island Point are the 200m high cliffs of the **Coloured Sands.** When the weathering of iron-rich minerals in the dune soils formed the cliffs, they were stained in a complex range of tones and hues. If it's raining, you're in luck, for rain intensifies the colors. Aboriginal legend speaks of Rainbow, a representative of the gods, who was killed in an attempt to save the beautiful maiden; as he crashed to the ground, his colors permeated the sand. **Double Island Point** was named by Captain Cook in 1770, when he believed the point was actually islands. The **lighthouse** at the point offers views of the coastline in each direction.

## THE SUNSHINE COAST HINTERLAND

Noosa is more than just the coastal strip. Just inland of the Sunshine Coast lies a veritable smorgasbord of tourist delights: stunning national parks, roadside crafts markets, and kitschy tourist traps. The Hinterland is inaccessible via public transportation, but can be reached by driving or a tour. **Storeyline Tours** offers several options including a tour of Montville, Blackall Range, and Glasshouse Mountains, or a morning trip to the Eumundi Markets. (☎5474 1500. Montville-Glasshouse M half-day $30, concessions $28, children $15; markets W and Sa $12, children $7.) **Noosa Hinterland Tours** hits the same regions. (☎5474 3366. Montville-Glasshouse Tu, F full-day $40; markets $12.) **Off Beat Rainforest Tours** accesses exclusive rainforest for eco-guided walks in Conondale National Park. (☎5473 5135; www.offbeattours.com.au. $115, children $75.)

**POMONA.** Pomona, north of Eumundi, is home to the **Majestic Theatre,** the oldest silent movie theatre in Australia. Movies are accompanied by a Wurlitzer organ. (☎5485 2330. Movie $6; Th evening wine, movie, and supper $9; F morning tea and movie $9. Annual movie festival in early Sept.)

**EUMUNDI MARKETS.** Some hostels in Noosa provide return bus service to the famous **Eumundi Markets,** a bustling collection of just about anything on the cheap, from sweets to sheets and soaps to boats. The markets are Sa 6:30am to 2pm—get there early for the good stuff. A kinder, gentler "upmarket market" appears on Wednesday. For more info, contact Eumundi Historical Association (☎5442 8581).

**YANDINA.** In the town of Yandina, just south of Eumundi, is the **Ginger Factory,** 50 Pioneer Rd, where the zest on your sushi and the bite in your ale most likely originate. The factory is the largest ginger processing plant in the southern hemisphere. If that doesn't impress you, neither will the factory, though the huge vats of multicolored ginger in different stages of processes are worth a free peak. (☎5446 7096. Open daily 9am-5pm.) Across the street is **Granny's Macademia,** with free multi-flavored nut tastings. Six kilometers from the Bruce Highway, south of Nambour, is a big pineapple and **Big Pineapple Plantation,** a working fruit and nut plantation, with small rides and shows. (☎5442 1333. Open daily 9am-5pm.)

**BLACKALL RANGE.** The sheer Blackall Range escarpment rises from the plains to cradle green pastures and rainforests, sprinkled with the old country villages of Mapleton, Flaxton, Montville, and Maleny. Once known for its hippie appeal, Montville is pretty touristy, but for the patchouli-wearing set still offers massage and herbal services, along a couple blocks of antiques, galleries, crafts, teahouses, and a cuckoo clock shop. From Noosa follow the Bruce Hwy to Nambour and then turn toward the Blackall Range. The **Montville Information Centre** (☎5478 5544; www.montvillevillage.com.au) is on Main St.

**KONDALILLA AND MAPLETON FALLS.** Kondalilla and Mapleton Falls National Parks, both on the road north of Montville, have pleasant trails and picnic areas. The 80m Kondalilla Falls (Aboriginal for "rushing water") are especially gorgeous. Although the Picnic Creek walk (1.2km) will technically get you to the lookout and rock pool, the best views of the rushing waters are sprinkled along the Kondalilla Falls circuit track (2.7km) that begins at the lookout. The Wompoo circuit (1.3km) at Mapleton Falls, located just past Mapleton on the Obi Obi Rd, winds its rainforested way to an excellent lookout. The ranger can be contacted at ☎5494 3983.

**GLASSHOUSE MOUNTAINS.** The Glasshouse Mountains rise abruptly from the rolling farmlands south of Landsborough. According to Aboriginal legend, this group of 13 volcanic peaks represents the father Tibrogargan, the pregnant mother Beerwah, and their many children. This distinct landscape was formed by gradual weathering since the last activity 20 million years ago. Walking access is limited, but experienced climbers can ascend Mt. Beerwah and Mt. Tibrogargan.

# HERVEY BAY

For many travelers, Hervey Bay (pronounced "HAR-vee") is little more than a pause before heading to Fraser Island. Going through Hervey Bay is like going through customs: you must stop, however briefly, before venturing into the enticing foreignness beyond. The whale-watching season (Aug.-Oct.) draws crowds, but the local backpacker economy serves only to create an amenable waystation.

## ⌐ TRANSPORT

**Trains:** A shuttle bus links Hervey Bay to **Maryborough Coach Terminal,** on Lennox St, Maryborough ($4.40), leaving Hervey Bay 30min. before trains. Tilt Train (☎13 22 32) departs Maryborough to: **Brisbane** (4½hr., 1-2 per day, $43), **Bundaberg** (1hr., 1-2 per day, $18), and **Rockhampton** (4¾hr., 1-2 per day, $52).

**Buses: Bay Central Coach Terminal,** Bay Central Shopping Center, Pialba (☎4124 4000). Open M-F 6am-5:30pm, Sa-Su 6am-1pm. Greyhound (☎13 20 30) and McCafferty's (☎13 14 99) run to: **Brisbane** (5-6hr., 8 per day, $34); **Airlie Beach** (13hr., 5 per day, $96); **Bundaberg** (1¾hr., 5 per day, $20); **Cairns** (23hr., 6 per day, $143); **Mackay** (11hr., 6 per day, $91); **Maroochydore** (4hr., 2 per day, $23); **Noosa** (3½hr., 2 per day, $19); and **Rockhampton** (6-6½hr., 6 per day, $58).

## ◀▶ ⁊ ORIENTATION AND PRACTICAL INFORMATION

Hervey Bay is actually a clump of suburbs facing north toward the Bay. Named from west to east the suburbs are: **Port Vernon, Pialba, Scarness, Torquay,** and **Urangan**. Most of the action is along **The Esplanade** at the water's edge, where takeaway shops and tour booking agencies seem to repeat endlessly. The harbor extends all the way down the Esplanade and then around to Pulgul St, and is a superb place to pick up cheap seafood fresh from the trawlers.

**Tourist Office:** There are countless booking agents on The Esplanade, but only offices sporting the blue and white "i" sign are bona-fide tourist offices. These offices, run by volunteers, offer unbiased advice. **Bay Central Tourist Information Center,** Bay Central Shopping Center, Pialba (☎4124 8244; fax 4128 1122), next to the coach terminal. Open M-F 9am-5pm. **Hervey Bay Visitor Information Centre,** 10 Bideford St, Torquay (☎4124 9609, freecall ☎(1800) 81 17 28; www.herveybaytourism.com.au).

**Currency Exchange: National Bank,** 415 The Esplanade (☎13 22 65), has an **ATM.** Fee to change traveler's checks or cash $5. Open M-Th 9:30am-4pm, F 9:30am-5pm.

**Emergency:** ☎000.

**Police:** (24hr. ☎4128 5333), on the corner of Queens and Torquay Rd.

**Hospital: Hervey Bay Hospital,** Nissen St, Pialba (☎4120 6666).

**Taxi: Hervey Bay Taxi** (☎13 10 08).

**Bicycle Hire: Rayz Pushbike Hire** (☎(0417) 64 48 14), offers free delivery and pickup. 24hr. $12. Open 7am-5pm.

**Camping Gear: Torquay Disposals and Camping,** 417 The Esplanade (☎4125 6511). Open M-F 8:30am-5pm, Sa 8:30am-4pm, Su 8:30am-noon.

QUEENSLAND

**Internet Access:** 346 The Esplanade, Scarness (☎4124 2289), charges 5¢ per min., which—take out the calculators—is cheap: 1hr. $3. Open M-Sa 8:30am-10pm, Su 9:30am-10pm. **Hervey Bay Email,** 404 The Esplanade (☎4125 6401). 1hr. $5.

**Post Office:** 426 The Esplanade, Torquay (☎4125 1101); 3 Bryant St, Pialba (☎4128 1047); 564 The Esplanade, Urangan (☎4128 9280). Open M-F 8:30am-5pm, Sa 8:30-11:30am. **Postal Code:** 4655.

**Phone Code:** 07.

# ◤ ACCOMMODATIONS

Hostel courtesy buses line up like pigs at a trough to meet incoming buses at the Bay Central Coach Terminal. All hostels except the Friendly Hostel also run Fraser 4WD safaris. While you can book a safari that is not based at your accommodation, you can often get free nights when booked at the same hostel and tour.

▨ **Smuggler's Rest,** 369 The Esplanade, Scarness (☎4128 2122, freecall ☎(1800) 50 21 15). In the old Fraser Magic property. Walk the planks (or down The Esplanade) to great rates and lots of energy. Former backpackers who have just opened up this pirate-themed hostel seem to know what backpackers like and what they don't. Free videos and playstation. Self-contained units with a dorm room and twin or double. Reception daily 8am-10pm. Dorms $15; twins and doubles $38. NOMADS.

**Fraser Roving,** 412 The Esplanade, Torquay (☎4125 4065, freecall ☎(1800) 35 40 65). This hostel looks like a cross between a Roman villa and a hospital, but the staff makes it feel like one of the friendliest hostels on the Bay. Clean rooms, entertainment center, Internet, private lockers. Fantastic bistro with $8 daily specials. Reception 24hr. 6-bed dorm $13.50; 4-bed dorm $15.50; twins and doubles $35, ensuite $40.

**The Woolshed,** 181 Torquay Rd, Scarness (☎4124 0677). 5min. from the beach and shops. This smaller hostel has an outdoor setting featuring waterfalls, ponds, and gardens. Rooms have character: old tools and pictures, corrugated iron walls, and Aboriginal spears and didgeridoos. Co-ed bathrooms. Kitchen and BBQ area. Laundry. Reception daily 6:30am-at least 8pm. Checkout 9:30am. 4-bed dorms $15; new cabins with verandah $36; camping out back $7 per person.

**Friendly Hostel,** 182 Torquay Rd, Scarness (☎4124 4107). The owners are indeed friendly, if a bit firm. The place feels more like a B&B without the second B; lovely wooden-floored rooms, no bunks, cable TV, small reading libraries, and fully supplied kitchen. A quiet backpacker's dream. Pickup on request. Laundry. Reception daily 8am-10:30pm. 3-bed dorms $15; twins $34.

**Colonial Backpackers YHA,** Boat Harbour Dr, Urangan (☎4125 1844, freecall ☎(1800) 81 82 80). Rustic, relaxing, relentlessly spotless, but removed from the center of town. Rooms are basic and tiny, but the common room with cable TV next to an open kitchen is a great social scene. A licensed in-house restaurant sprawls onto the pool deck area, whipping up tasty meals for $5-7. Free pickup and drop off. Laundry $2. Key deposit $10. Reception 6:45am-9:30pm. Dorms $17-19.50; twins and doubles $38-49. Log cabins $17-32 per person; villas $19-43 per person. YHA.

**Olympus,** 184 Torquay Rd, Scarness (☎4124 5331, freecall ☎(1800) 06 31 68). Nothing godly, but nice enough for Zeus in his backpacking days. Eight duplexes have a spacious kitchen, TV lounge, nice bathrooms, and a terrace, with 2 twins or doubles upstairs and 2 tight-packed dorms downstairs. Laundry, small pool. Reception daily 6am-9:30pm. Check-out 9:30am. Dorms $15; twins and doubles $36. YHA, VIP.

**Beaches Backpackers,** 195 Torquay Tce, Torquay (☎4124 1322, freecall ☎(1800) 63 66 30). A pool-centered, partying hostel. 24hr. rockin' bar (Happy Hour 3-4pm and 7-8pm, table-dancing encouraged), and a budget bistro (7am-9pm) pull in backpackers by the busload. Mega-package includes Fraser Island safari, Whitsunday sail, and a smattering of nights at their 2 hostels from $500. Key deposit $10. Reception daily 7am-7pm. 8-bed dorms $13; 6-bed ensuite dorms $16.50. VIP.

**Beachfront Camping:** Three caravan parks on the beach side of The Esplanade: **Pialba** (☎4128 1399), **Scarness** (☎4128 1274), and **Torquay** (☎4125 1578). Free pickup from the bus station. Laundry, showers, BBQ. Tent sites for 2 $12, powered $14.

## FOOD AND NIGHTLIFE

Hervey Bay has the usual spread of fast-food and chippers, along with a handful of prohibitively expensive restaurants. **The Black Dog Café,** 381 The Esplanade, will serve you your bone—sushi rolls $4.50-6, outstanding chicken teriyaki $10.50. Backpackers get 10% off. (☎4124 3177. Open daily 10:30am-2:30pm and 5:30-late; kitchen closes at 9:30pm.) **Curried Away,** 174 Boat Harbour Dr (☎4124 1577), near Main St, Pialba, has some great curries for $9-12. **China World,** 402 The Esplanade, on the corner of Tavistock St, has an $11 all-you-can-eat dinner buffet. (☎4125 1233. Open M-F 11am-2pm and 5:30-9pm.) Hostel eats are quite good and cheap. Many supermarkets are along The Esplanade, including **Express,** 414 The Esplanade (open 6am-midnight). Bigger and cheaper is **Woolworth's,** on the corner of Boat Harbour Dr and Elizabeth St (open M-F 8am-9pm, Sa 8am-5:30pm).

**Marty's On The Beach,** 344 The Esplanade, has two bars: one serves an unbeatable T-bone and a pot of beer for $7.50, the other has wood-carved pool tables and live music. (☎4128 1233. Open daily 10am-2am. Café 11:30am-2:30pm and 5:30-9pm.) **Dolly's,** 406 The Esplanade, is a local bar with live music, free pool (7-9pm), and $6 jugs (9-10pm). Courtesy bus available. (☎4125 5633. Open daily 9pm-3am.)

## ACTIVITIES

**WHALE WATCHING.** Weighing up to 40 tons, the equivalent of 11 elephants or 600 persons, the humpback whale stops in Hervey Bay on its migration back to Antarctica after giving birth in the warmer waters up north. The whales assemble in Platypus Bay, 50km from Urangan Harbour, where sightings are undeniably dramatic. Whale watching is big business from August to November. Thirteen boats in Hervey Bay form the whale-watching fleet: they offer guaranteed whale sightings during the season or your next trip is free. The flagship vessel is the **Spirit of Hervey Bay,** purpose-built for whale watching, including underwater viewing rooms and a whale-listening hydrophone. (☎4125 5131, freecall ☎(1800) 64 25 44. Departs Great Sandy Straits Marina 8:30am and 1:30pm for a half-day cruise. $79, children $44.) **M.V. Princess II** offers an affordable full-day, small-boat experience. This tour is more personalized, though it lacks the glitz of the big, fancy vessels. (☎4124 0400. Full-day $65, includes BBQ lunch.) **Whale Song** offers two cruises daily, at 7:30am and 1pm. (☎4125 6222, freecall ☎(1800) 68 96 10. $70, children $40.)

Every year, the return of the humpback whales is celebrated with the aptly-named **Whale Festival,** held for two weeks in August. It features an ▨Electric Light Parade in which locals carry desk lamps up and down the streets. (☎4124 9609.)

**DIVING.** ▨**Divers Mecca** may be the best place on the coast to do a PADI Open Water certification course. This course is one of the cheapest in Australia, but comprehensive, including four boat dives, not shore dives. (403 The Esplanade. ☎4125 1626, freecall ☎(1800) 35 16 26. Begins M and Th; courtesy pickups. Open daily 9am-5pm. Intro dive $80, PADI certification $164, Advanced Open Water $242.)

**OTHER ACTIVITIES. Splash Safaris** explores the waters off Fraser Island, stopping on deserted beaches and snorkeling among coral reefs. You won't get as much out of the half-day tour, so go for the full-day tour to the tip of Big Woody Island. (☎(0500) 55 55 80. Half-day $59, full-day $69.) **Torquay Beach Hire,** offers beach activities. (The Esplanade, Torquay Beach. ☎4125 5528. Waterskiing $25, big banana $9, catamaran $25.) **Skydive Hervey Bay** includes a scenic flight over Fraser Island. (☎4124 8248. 10,000ft $219; 14,000ft $308.) **Humpback Camel Safari** offers 2hr. rides. (Toogoom, 15min. from Hervey Bay. ☎4128 0055. Pickup available. $38.50.)

# FRASER ISLAND

Fraser Island, the world's largest sand island and a World-Heritage-listed national park, attracts 350,000 visitors every year. Backpackers up and down the coast can't stop talking about the island—an untrammeled wilderness scarred only by a

QUEENSLAND

4WD track. This is the ideal destination for any outdoorsman: 4WDer, bushwalker, or fisherman. Although a sand island, it is covered with dense rainforest and punctuated by over 200 lakes. The winds perpetually resculpt the island's topography, but its unique natural beauty is a constant.

# ▐ GETTING THERE

## BY BOAT

**Fraser Island Vehicular Ferry Services** runs ferries from several locations (return fare: $16.50 walk-on; vehicles $77, $5.50 for each person in addition to the driver): **Fraser Venture,** the most convenient for independent 4WDers, from Riverheads to Wanggoolba Creek (☎4125 4444; 30min.; daily 9, 10:15am, 3:30pm; Sa also 7am); **Fraser Dawn** from Urangan Boat Harbor to Moon Point (☎4125 3325; 50min.; 8:30am, 3:30pm); and **Kingfisher** from Riverheads to Kingfisher (☎4125 5511; 50min.; 7:15, 11am, 2:30pm). The barge **Rainbow Venture,** on the southern tip, connects Inskip Point near Rainbow Beach to Hook Point. (☎5486 3154. 15min.; continuously 7am-4:30pm; walk-on $11; vehicles $66, $2 each additional passenger.)

## BY AIR

**Air Fraser Island** (☎4125 3600) offers one-way or same-day trips ($50) and an overnight trip, including 4WD hire, return flight, and camping equipment $190. They also offer a scenic flight over Fraser (30min. $165).

# ▐ GETTING AROUND

## GUIDED TOURS

A structured, safe, and hassle-free way to see the island is on a tour, assuming you're willing to forego the freedom of a personal 4WD and outdoor camping. Tour options are plentiful, but ignore daytrippers—you'll need at least two days to see the island. The prices are higher than the hostel self-guided specials, but once you've factored in food, permits, and petrol, the tours are a good deal, especially for those traveling alone.

**Trailblazers Tours** operates a 3-day tour through Noosa Backpackers Resort. This is the best guided safari package available for a younger crowd, mixing guiding and camping, including Cooloola National Park's Coloured Sands. (☎5474 1235, freecall ☎(1800) 62 66 73. Departs W, Sa; $190.) **Kingfisher Bay Wilderness Adventure Tours** is the most expensive, but very well run, with accommodation at the spacious Wilderness Lodge. (☎4120 3333, freecall ☎(1800) 07 25 55; www.kingfisherbay.com. 2-day overnight $198; 3-day overnight $270; quad share, twin share extra.) **Fraser Island Top Tours** offers a daytour and two safaris with accommodation in Fraser Island Retreat, Happy Valley. (☎4125 3933, freecall ☎(1800) 06 39 33; www.fraserislandtours.com.au. Daytour $77, children $42. Wilderness Safari leaves Tu, Th, Sa; Northern Adventure leaves Su, W, F; both $165.) **Fraser Venture Tours** attracts a younger set to their daytrips and three-day safaris with accommodation at Eurong Beach Resort. (☎4125 4444, freecall ☎(1800) 24 91 22. Daytour $77; 3-day safari $220.) **Fraser Explorer Tours** also travels from Noosa to Fraser and the Coloured Sands, with accommodation in Eurong Beach Resort. (☎5447 3845. Daytour $99, children $55; 2-day $165; 3-day $220.)

**Clip Clop Horse Treks** (☎5449 1254), at Eumarella Rd, Lake Weyba, Noosa, offers a 6-day horse-riding and camping trek. **Stefanie Yacht Charters** sails with 11 guests for two days and two nights, accommodation and food included. (☎4125 4200, freecall ☎(1800) 65 07 76. Departs Su, Tu, Th. $295, $265 camping on the beach.)

## SELF-DRIVE WITH HOSTELS

Extremely popular with backpackers, these three-day and two-night unguided 4WD tours bring back stories, dirty clothes, and lots of sand. Unlike guided tours, participants camp out at night. Hostel self-drive safaris usually cost $125, plus the hidden costs of fuel (about $5-10 per person) and food and booze ($15-20 per-

**BUT ALL THE COOL KIDS ARE DOING IT...** Although beach driving can be a lot of fun, reckless driving can lead to disaster. The most serious danger is creek cuts in the beach; test the depth of a creek before attempting to cross. Don't cross if the water is higher than your knees—instead, wait for the tide to go down. Also, don't drive at night when it is difficult to see and other drivers are more likely to be drunk and foolhardy. Location is also important; you're tempting fate by driving on the eastern beaches south of Dilli Village and Ungowa, north of the Ngkala Rocks, or on the west side north by Moon Point.

son). The group must also be able to leave a bond of about $500. Packages include 4WD hire, ferry passes, camping permits, access fees, camping equipment, and full preparatory briefing. Usually, the hostel hosts an afternoon meeting on the day before departure, a 4WD briefing the morning of, and a pre-departure supermarket run. To drive on the safari, you must be over 21 years old, but anyone can ride.

**Smuggler's Rest** offers the most attractive Fraser safari. Their $130 package includes fuel, meals, and 4WDs with all forward facing seats for up to eight people. The type of partying you'll get with a group is usually related to the aura at the particular hostel: the Woolshed and YHA attract quieter groups, while Beaches and Fraser Roving party.

### RENT YOUR OWN 4WD

For folks who want the thrill of hurtling down a beach independently, several companies rent 4WDs at comparable costs: Toyota trucks ($130; seats 4), Landcruiser ($150; seats 5), Troopcarrier ($160; seats 8). Hire companies also offer camping kits for $10-14 per person per day. Some good operators include: **Bay 4WD Centre,** 54 Boat Harbour Dr (☎4128 2981); **Aussie Trax,** 56 Boat Harbour Dr (☎4124 4433, freecall ☎(1800) 06 22 75); and **Safari,** 55 Old Maryborough Rd (☎4124 4244, freecall ☎(1800) 68 98 19). All of these companies pickup locally. It's worth asking whether a rental agency belongs to the **Fraser Coast 4WD Hire Association,** the local watchdog. Hostels can also arrange 4WD hire for a private trip.

### DRIVING ON THE ISLAND

Driving on Fraser gives you maximum flexibility but is only possible in a 4WD vehicle or a well-equipped motorcycle. Speed limits are established on the island: 35km per hr. on inland roads and 80km per hr. on the Eastern Beach. Don't rush—allow at least 30min. to travel 10km on inland roads. Inland roads, usually pothole-filled one-lane trails, wind through the forest. The beaches themselves are registered national highways—all normal traffic rules apply. Larger vehicles will occasionally stay on the right, however; in any case, always use your blinker to indicate on which side you plan to pass oncoming traffic.

### 🛈 PRACTICAL INFORMATION

**Tourist Office:** For information, contact the **Hervey Bay tourist offices** (p. 341), or **Fraser Coast Tourism Board,** Maryborough (☎4122 3444).

**Permits:** If you're going over in a car, you'll need a **vehicle permit** ($30, valid for a month; includes map and island details). **Camping permits** ($4) are good for all campgrounds except the privately run Cathedral Beach Resort and Dilli Village, both on the east shore. With the permit comes a packet identifying allowed camping areas; some have curfews. Both permits are available from: **Hervey Bay City Council,** 77 Tavistock St, Torquay (☎4125 0222); **Marina Kiosk,** Buccaneer Ave, Urangan (☎4128 9800; open daily 6am-6pm); and **Hervey Bay Visitor Information Centre,** 10 Bideford St, Torquay (☎4124 9609, freecall ☎(1800) 81 17 28; www.herveybaytourism.com.au). Camping permits can also be picked up in convenience stores on the island.

**General supplies:** Stock up at Eurong Beach Resort, Fraser Island Retreat at Happy Valley, Kingfisher Bay Resort, Cathedral Beach Resort, or Orchid Beach.

QUEENSLAND

**Telephones:** Ungowa, Central Station, Dundubara, Waddy Point, Indian Head.

**Showers:** Cold showers are available at all campgrounds except Lake Allom. Coin-operated hot showers are available at Central Station, Waddy Point, Dundubara.

**Air ambulance:** contact Nambour QAS (☎5441 1333).

**Taxi:** ☎4127 9188.

# ACCOMMODATIONS

Accommodation is included in the guided tour packages, but if you are arranging your trip independently, there are heaps of options. **Cathedral Beach Resort and Camping Park** has camping sites. (☎4127 9177. Sites for 2 $22; for 4 $31.) **Happy Valley** has houses and charges weekly rates. (☎4124 1789. $570 for 4 people.) **Eurong Beach Resort** offers motel units. (☎4127 9122. Twins $88, each additional person $6.) **Fraser Island Retreat** (☎4127 9144) has individual lodges for $53-154 per person. The upscale **Kingfisher Bay Resort** (☎5488 1512, freecall ☎(1800) 07 25 55) is well hidden in the bush on the western side of the island, offering 4-person self-contained cabins for $250. There are eight main **camping** areas on the island, but camping is also allowed on designated beaches (see **Practical Information**, above).

# THE LAY OF THE LAND

**INLAND. Lake McKenzie** is the most popular of the freshwater lakes, with white sands, shady pine trees, and water of various shades of perfect blue. **Lake Wabby** (3½hr. by foot) is at the eastern base of the steep Hammerstone Sandblow, which gradually encroaches this perched lake. Some visitors enjoy sliding down into the lake, but the trip is fast (the drier the sand, the faster) and you hit the water hard— a bad combo for your spine. Walking across the dune feels like crossing a vast desert, perfect for practicing your Lawrence of Arabia impersonation; in fact, Fraser and nearby Cooloola National Park combined have more sand than the Sahara. The southernmost lake, **Boomanjin**, is, like many others, lined with fallen leaves from the overhanging swamp paperbarks and tea trees, which give it tea-colored (but not flavored) water. It's the largest lake on Fraser, and the largest perched lake in the world. There are also a number of freshwater creeks good for swimming, especially **Eli Creek. Wanggoolba Creek** is a silent beauty, muffled by its sandy bottom; the only babbling you'll here is from other tourists or conversations between the eel and catfish inhabitants.

**THE EASTERN BEACH.** There is a *lot* of beach on Fraser Island, and most of it looks the same, bordered by raging surf and low-lying trees announcing the tentative start of island vegetation. The Eastern Beach is perfect for 4WDing, but be careful (see **Driving on the Island**, above). **Don't swim in the ocean,** as tiger sharks, box jellyfish, and riptides are real dangers. Heading north from Eurong, patches of rocks decorate the beach. There are short bypasses at **Poyungan Rocks** and **Yidney Rocks** and a longer route around the **Indian Head** promontory, where one can spot ospreys and whales (in season on calm days). Almost at the top of passable beachland, a collection of shallow tide pools called **The Champagne Pools,** or **The Aquarium,** make prime swimming holes at low tide. Be careful of the **tides;** not only is there a danger of being stranded by high tide, but incoming waves can cause serious injury by crashing up and over the rocks that dam the pools. Other attractions along the beach are the **Coloured Sands,** or **Cathedrals,** massive sand formations of countless shades, and the **Maheno shipwreck,** the remains of a massive cruise liner that washed ashore in a storm in the early part of the century.

# HIKING

Hiking can be cheaper and more rewarding than 4WDing, and is the safest way to access the **Western Beach,** a soft white silica paradise. Consider trying a smaller chunk of the island near Central Station (ranger station ☎4127 9191), **Lake McKen-**

QUEENSLAND

zie, and **Lake Wabby** before attempting a more ambitious itinerary off the beaten track. If hiking really interests you, contact Phil at **Mango Hostel**, 110 Torquay Rd (☎ 4124 2832), for information about setting up itineraries.

# BUNDABERG

Bundaberg is not high on the list of Australia's choice idling spots; most visitors get coffee at the bus terminal, stretch their legs, and hop back on board. However, it is the hottest spot to put in a few weeks on the vegetable-picking circuit, and hostels in town house mainly workers. Backpackers seeking to beef up their bank accounts mix with seasoned life-long workers in the fields. At the end of the day though, it's all about kicking the dirt off your work boots, occasionally splurging on Bundaberg's famous rum, and saving energy for another day in the fields. Some last a day, others months. Despite Bundy's dearth of activities—or because of it— the survivors enjoy some of the purest camaraderie on the coast.

## ◪ TRANSPORT

**Trains:** The **train station** is at the corner of Bourbong and MacLean St. Ticket office open M-F 8:45am-4:30pm, Sa 9:30am-2pm and 3:30-4:30pm, Su 8:45am-2pm. Tilt Trains (☎ 13 22 32) depart for **Brisbane** (1-2 per day, $49.50); **Maryborough** (1-2 per day, $18, with connecting bus to **Hervey Bay** $22); and **Rockhampton** (1-2 per day, $45).

**Buses:** The **Coach terminal** is on Targo St. To get to town from the station, turn right and pass the roundabout and McDonald's to Bourbong St. McCafferty's and Greyhound run to: **Brisbane** (7-7½hr., 8 per day, $46); **Airlie Beach** (11hr., 3 per day, $93); **Cairns** (19-20hr., 7 per day, $125); **Hervey Bay** (1¾hr., 7 per day, $20); **Mackay** (8½hr., 7 per day, $79); **Maroochydore** (5½hr., 1 per day, $42); **Noosa** (5hr., 2 per day, $38); and **Rockhampton** (4-4¾hr., 7 per day, $45).

**Local Bus Transport:** Duffy's City Buses (☎ 4151 4226). Route #4 passes near the Bundaberg rum distillery on the way to Bargara (4 times per day). Route #5 also passes the distillery on its way to Burnett Heads (3-5 times per day). The buses also have several stops in the city center. **Stewart & Sons** (☎ 4153 2646) connects Bundy with Innes Park, Elliott Heads, and Moore Park.

**Taxi:** ☎ 4151 1612.

## ▮ PRACTICAL INFORMATION

**Tourist Office: City Council Visitors Centre,** 188 Bourbong St (☎ 4153 9289; fax 4151 2527; www.bundabergcity.qld.gov.au). Open M-F 8:30am-4:45pm, Sa-Su 10am-1pm. **Tourist Information Centre** (☎ 4151 2306, freecall ☎ (1800) 06 04 99), is only reachable by car. Follow Bourbong St south 2km toward Childers. Open daily 9am-5pm.

**Police:** on Bourbong St (☎ 4153 9111).

**Hospital: Bundaberg Base** (24hr. ☎ 4152 1222), on Bourbong St near Tallon Bridge.

**Internet café: The Cosy Corner,** on Barolin St, opposite the post office. 15min. $1.10. Open M and F 7am-8pm, Tu-Th 7am-10pm, Sa 8am-4pm, Su 11am-3pm.

**Post Office:** (☎ 4153 2700), at the corner of Bourbong and Barolin St. Open M-F 8:30am-5pm, Sa 8:30am-11:45am. **Postal Code:** 4670.

**Phone Code:** 07.

# WORK

Experienced workers will tell you that the first few days are the hardest. If you can bear through three or four days of a sore back though, picking work can be rewarding, especially to the wallet. The wage is generally $11 per hr., before taxes. Under contract work, getting paid for how much you pick can reel in even more.

Usually, you need to pay for a week of accommodation at a hostel before they'll find work for you. Most of the year (except Dec.-Jan.), work can be found within a day or so, and the farm will teach you what to do—anyone (with proper work

QUEENSLAND

**HOSTEL FIRE.** Located 53km south of Bundaberg, Childers struggles to come to terms with the aftermath of the tragic Palace Backpackers fire that killed 15 international backpackers in June 2000.

authorization, see p.73) can do it. The job involves a fair amount of luck—weather, farmers, personality, what you're picking; generally, snowpeas and avocados are good, and zucchinis and chilis are bad, but some people will swear by the latter. Most workers stay 3-4 weeks, seeking to beef up their bank accounts.

## ACCOMMODATIONS

The better hostels in town help find jobs (usually within a day), provide free transport to and from work, have strict alcohol policies, and are equipped with walk-in fridges. For those on a looser budget, or just in town for the night, motels are a dime a dozen down Bourbong St.; the farther from town, the cheaper.

**Bundaberg Backpackers and Travellers Lodge,** 2 Crofton St (☎4152 2080; fax 4151 3355). Across from the bus terminal at the corner of Targo and Crofton St. The Hilton of hostels, this spotless, air-conditioned haven is by far the picker's and 'packer's pick of the litter. Free pickup at train station. Laundry. Bike hire $10 per day. Key deposit $15. Reception daily 8am-8pm. Check-out 8:30am. Dorms $20, weekly $132. YHA, VIP.

**Iluka Gardens Forest Retreat,** 127 Logan Rd, Innes Park (☎4159 3230). For those not working, another great budget option is close by. A relaxing and peaceful getaway is hidden in the bush between fields of sugarcane and the Woongarra Marine Park's fringing reef—a series of cabins, a few people, and lots of wildlife. Free pickup in Bundaberg. Dorms, doubles, and family rooms all $15 per person.

**Workers and Diving Hostel,** 64 Barolin St (☎4151 6097). From the bus station call for a ride, or walk across the street, down Crofton St, and take a left onto Barolin St (10min.). Serious about their picking. Cable TV lounge, small kitchen. Reception daily 8am-noon and 3-7pm. Dorms and ensuite units $16.50, weekly $105. NOMADS.

**Finemore Caravan Park** (☎4151 3663). From Bourbong St, turn onto Burrum St across from the train station, then left at the zoo on Quay St and walk a few blocks. Laundry, pool, showers, toilets, kitchen. Linen $5. Reception daily 7am-7pm. Campsites $8, with a large vehicle $10, powered $14; ensuite cabins for 2 $38.

## FOOD

Bundaberg has a few good spots to fill up your tummy and absorb all that rum. **Numero Uno,** 167A Bourbong St, has big pasta servings, including $4.50 lunch pasta specials. (☎4151 3666. Open M-F 11:30am-2pm and 5pm-late, Sa-Sa 5pm-late.) **The Grand Hotel,** on the corner of Targo and Bourbong St (☎4151 2441), has a bar with cheap eats and cheap beer, as well as live bands Th-F and karaoke Sa-Su.

## SIGHTS AND ACTIVITIES

**Diving** in Bundaberg is rock-bottom cheap. **Salty's,** 208 Bourbong St, offers a 4-day PADI course in an on-site heated saltwater pool with shore dives to the Coral Coast's volcanic rock fringing reef. (☎4151 6422, freecall ☎(1800) 62 54 76; www.saltys.net. Open M-F 8am-5pm, Sa 8am-noon, Su 8-10am. 4-day classes start M, W, F. $164, boat dives on the artificial reef $230. 2 shore dives $45, 2 reef dives $85.) **Bundaberg Aqua Scuba,** 66 Targo St (☎4153 5761), across from the bus terminal, offers two shore dives for $45 and a $164 PADI open water course.

Love it or hate it, Bundaberg **rum** is Australia's best selling spirit. Distillery tours are popular but disappointing—much is on video and only one drink comes with the price. (☎4150 8684. Tours on the hour M-F 10am-3pm, Sa-Su 10am-2pm. $5.50; hostels arrange free transportation.) Indulge in *X-files* and *E.T.* fantasies (or just a picnic lunch) at the scientifically unexplained **Mystery Craters,** 35 giant sandstone craters believed to be over 25 million years old. Take Main Rd 20min. toward Gin Gin and look for the signs. (☎4157 7291. Open daily 8am-5pm.)

Celebrating the start of the turtle nesting season, the week-long **Coral Coast Turtle Festival,** held in November, features a carnival, shows, markets and parades, marking the official start of the **turtle rookery** season. **Mon Repos** (15km from the city center) hosts the largest loggerhead turtle rookery in the South Pacific. Access to the beach is limited during the season, but guided walks operate from the visitor center. (☎4159 1652. Open daily Nov.-Mar.)

# CAPRICORN AND WHITSUNDAY COASTS

From the Tropic of Capricorn, the Bruce Hwy worms its way north through sugarcane fields and along the tropical coast. Between Rockhampton and Townsville, some oceanside towns like Airlie Beach have been shaped into backpacker havens, while others, such as Mackay, still grimace at the sight of sandals and an unwashed t-shirt. The isolated Eungella National Park rewards its few intrepid visitors with tumbling waterfalls and elusive platypi. Off-shore islands vary in size and flavor, but each has its own beaches and possibilities for privacy. Great Keppel Island, almost within sight of Rockhampton's shore, lacks roads entirely; the ferry lets passengers off on the beach. Farther north off Airlie Beach, the Whitsundays are a blizzard of stunning islands. All along the coast there's plenty to see under the water as well, as the Great Barrier Reef is close at hand.

# ROCKHAMPTON

Australia's self-proclaimed "beef capital," Rockhampton is ruled by the human minority (pop. 60,000) while the cattle majority (pop. 3.5 million) bide their time for revolt. Straddling the Tropic of Capricorn, this Great Barrier Beef is a gateway to Great Keppel Island. Many inexplicably stately buildings loom over chain stores and shops on the town's meticulously laid out grid of streets. For the most part Rocky is a serious, very conservative town, with its share of hair salons and saddle shops, but a few interesting cultural activities stir this country town, providing a day's worth of entertainment, that can end—if you wish—with a great steak.

## ◧ TRANSPORT

**Train Station:** At the end of Murray St. From the city center, go south (away from the river) on any street, then turn left on Murray. Lockers $2. Taxi into town about $9.

**Buses:** McCafferty's terminal (☎4927 2844) is behind KFC on Linnet St, off Queen Elizabeth Dr, which becomes Fitzroy St on the other side of the bridge. Lockers $2. Greyhound's terminal (☎4921 1890) is on the south side of Rockhampton, on George St between Fitzroy and Archer St. Both have services to: **Brisbane** (10½hr., 5 per day, $66); **Airlie Beach** (6¼hr., 2 per day, $59); **Bundaberg** (4hr., 5 per day, $45); **Cairns** (14hr., 5 per day, $103); **Hervey Bay** (6½hr., 3 per day, $58); and **Mackay** (4hr., 5 per day, $42). For **Noosa** and **Maroochydore** ($63), connect through Bundaberg (see p. 347). For information on transport to **Great Keppel Island,** see p. 352.

**Public Transportation: Capricorn Sunbus** (☎4936 1002) covers most corners of the city, with a sliding fare scale (usually $2-4).

**Taxi:** ☎ 13 10 08.

## ✳❼ ORIENTATION AND PRACTICAL INFORMATION

On the south side of the **Fitzroy River,** the city has a flawless grid design, with most of the action near the river's edge along **Quay St. East St** runs parallel to Quay and houses a pedestrian mall between **Fitzroy** and **William St.**

**Tourist Office: Rockhampton Tourist Information Centre,** 208 Quay St (☎4922 5339, freecall ☎(1800) 80 58 65; email rdpda@ozemail.com.au). The in-house, constantly updated *Rovin' Round Rocky Region* is one of the most helpful, comprehensive booklets you'll find in Oz. Open M-F 8:30am-4:30pm, Sa-Su 9am-4pm.

**Currency Exchange: Commonwealth Bank** (☎4922 1733). In the mall. Traveler's check exchange for a $5 fee, no fee for cash. Visa checks can be cashed with no fee at **ANZ,** 214 Bolsover St (☎4931 7764). Open M-Th 9:30am-4pm, F 9:30am-5pm.

**Library:** On the corner of Williams and Alma St (☎4936 8265). Free **Internet** terminal. Book ahead for a 30min. session.

**Emergency:** ☎000.

**Police:** (☎4932 1500). On the corner of Denham and Bolsover St. Open 24hr.

**Hospital: Rockhampton Base Hospital** (☎4920 6211, emergency room ☎4920 6270). On top of the hill on Canning St, near North St.

**Internet Access:** Free at the library. The cheapest Internet café is **Rocknet,** 238 Quay St (☎4922 2760). 30min. $2.50. Open M-F 7:30am-6pm, Sa 9am-noon.

**Post Office:** 150 East St (☎4927 6566; fax 4927 6802). Open M-F 8:30am-5:30pm. **Postal Code:** 4700.

**Phone Code:** 07.

# ACCOMMODATIONS

**Yeppoon Backpackers,** 30 Queen St, Yeppoon (☎4939 8080, freecall ☎(1800) 63 68 28). Offers the best means to explore Great Keppel, while being a treasure in itself. Pickup from Rockhampton. Trips to Cooberrie, Koorana, 4WD Fire Rocks, and "Serenade" boat trips. Stay a night and add a Great Keppel day trip $32; 2 days, 1 night $48; 3 days, 2 nights $59; all include bus, ferry, and all the snorkeling you can handle. 4-bed dorms $17, doubles $36.

**Rockhampton Youth Hostel (YHA),** 60 MacFarlane St (☎4927 5288; fax 4922 6040). From the McCafferty's terminal, take a left on the main street, Queen Elizabeth Dr, and a right on MacFarlane St. Kitchen, TV room. Key deposit $10. Reception 7am-noon and 5-10pm. Packages include a night in Rocky, two on Great Keppel, return ferry ticket, and bus to and from the ferry for $96. Free pickup. Dorms $20; twins $40, $46.

**Criterion Hotel,** 150 Quay St (☎4922 1225; fax 4922 1226). Just south of the Fitzroy bridge. Grand, picturesque, and not the slightest bit self-conscious, with plenty of framed pictures showing off the building's colorful past. Laundry, bar, 2 restaurants. Reception 7am-1am. Singles $23-48; twins and doubles $40-53.

**O'Dowd's,** corner of William and Denison St (☎4927 0344). A gorgeous new Irish pub in town. Rooms are squeaky clean and comfortable. Common room has a TV and fridge. Laundry $2. Key deposit $10. Singles $28; twins $40; family room for 4 $60.

**Downtown Backpackers (Oxford Hotel),** corner of Denham and East St (☎4922 1837). Right in the mall. Pubstay in good downtown location with simple rooms but a comfortable TV room. Laundry. $15 per person.

**The Riverside Tourist Park,** on Reaney St just off Bridge St (☎4922 3779). North of the river and city center. This is the only campground in the area. Laundry. Reception 7am-7pm. Tent sites $7 per person; caravan sites for 2 $16.

# FOOD

It's obvious—Rockhampton has many steakhouses serving up phenomenal steak. Or buy your own meat at **Coles** supermarket in City Centre Plaza on Fitzroy St (open M-F 8am-9pm, Sa 8am-5pm), and cook on the free BBQs which line the river.

**Great Western Hotel,** 39 Stanley St (☎4922 1862). The best steakhouse in town just got a real bullriding ring in the back. The Rocky Rump melts in your mouth for $14. Practice Rodeo Rides W 7:30pm. Hosts weekly events including Championship bullrides, rodeos, cutting, and indoor campdrafts. Cover $5.50-16.

QUEENSLAND

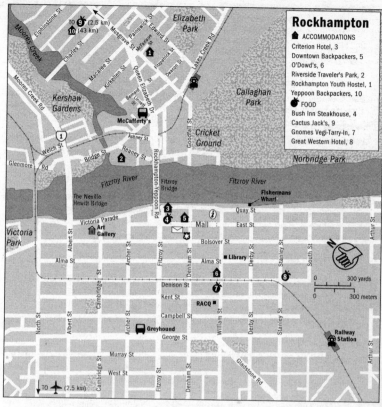

**Rockhampton**

**ACCOMMODATIONS**
Criterion Hotel, 3
Downtown Backpackers, 5
O'Dowd's, 6
Riverside Traveler's Park, 2
Rockhampton Youth Hostel, 1
Yeppoon Backpackers, 10

**FOOD**
Bush Inn Steakhouse, 4
Cactus Jack's, 9
Gnomes Vegi-Tarry-In, 7
Great Western Hotel, 8

Q U E E N S L A N D

**Gnomes Vegi-Tarry-In,** 104 William St (☎4927 4713). Near the intersection with Denison St. The ultimate in vegetarian hideaways: candle-lit tables, small waterfall out back, 2 dozen varieties of tea ($3 a pot), and delicious dishes from an entirely vegetarian menu that changes daily. Mains $11. Open M-Th 10am-10pm, F-Sa 10am-11pm.

**Bush Inn Steakhouse,** Quay St (☎4922 1225). In the Criterion Hotel. A great place to chew some of Rocky's finest for $13-17. W-Sa: live jazz or blues.

**Cactus Jack's,** 243 Musgrave St (☎4922 2062). 20min. north of the city center. Great Mexican. Tu: $7 all-you-can-eat chili; W: $4 Margaritas.

## SIGHTS AND ACTIVITIES

**ZOO.** The zoo has an enormous geodesic dome aviary, chimpanzees, and the usual line-up: 'roos, crocs, cassowaries, dingoes, free roaming peacocks, koalas. Feedings at 3pm. (10min. ride from city center on Sunbus route #4A; departs from the arcade carpark on Bolsover St between Denham and Williams St. $2.85 one-way, usually runs 5min. past the hr.; about every hr. ☎4922 1654. Zoo: open daily 6am-6pm. Aviary: open daily 8am-5pm.)

**BOTANIC GARDENS.** The guided tour of the botanic gardens is a highlight of Rockhampton's sights. (10min. ride from the city center on Sunbus route #4A; departs from the arcade carpark on Bolsover St between Denham and Williams St. $2.85 one-way, usually runs 5min. past the hour, about every hour. ☎4922 1654. Gardens: open daily 6am-6pm. Tours: depart the Info Centre Tu, W, Th 9:30am; $3, bookings essential.)

**GRACEMERE SALEYARDS.** Learn how farmers acquire their stock at the Gracemere Saleyards, the largest stud selling venue in the Southern Hemisphere—but keep your hands in your pockets or you may end up with a thousand slow travel companions. M: prime cattle; Tu: pig and calf; F: store cattle; last Th of each month: horse sales. *(In Gracemere, QLD. ☎4933 1222; www.rockysaleyards.qld.gov.au.)*

**DREAMTIME CULTURAL CENTRE.** The Dreamtime Cultural Centre provides a humble but elegant perspective on the indigenous peoples of Australia and the Torres Strait Islands. The center is set in a park with a meandering trail highlighting different medicinal plants of the area. Get boomerang instructions and a didgeridoo demonstration at the end of the tour. *(5min. north of Rockhampton by car, on the corner of Yeppoon Rd and the Bruce Hwy. Sunbus #10 runs from Rocky. ☎4936 1655. Open daily 10am-3:30pm. Tours regularly 10:30am-1pm. $12, concessions $10.)*

**CAVING.** The **Olsen's Capricorn Caverns** are ancient limestone caves that feature the **cathedral** with its incredible natural acoustics and a natural light spectacle during summer solstice (first two weeks on January). There are both 1hr. and day tours of the caves. Included in the price is an opportunity to take a self-guided tour through a "dry rainforest." The caverns also host **Wild Caving Adventure Tours,** which allow you to spend 4hr. rock-climbing, being sardined in 12cm wide tunnels, and squeezing through "fat man's misery." *(23km from Rockhampton. ☎4934 2883. Open daily 9am-4pm. Admission and basic 1hr. tour $13, concessions $6.50. Day tour $33. Adventure tour $45; book at least 24hr. ahead; call for transportation services.)*

**KOORANA CROCODILE FARM.** At Koorana Crocodile Farm, a daily tour includes watching hungry crocs shoot vertically out of the water to catch their food. *(35km east of Rockhampton along the Emu Park Rd. ☎4934 4749. Tours 1-2:30pm. $13.50, children $7. Croc hatching Feb.-mid Apr.)* **Get-about Tours** offers a tour of Cooberrie Park, Emu Park, and Koorana Crocodile Farm *(☎4934 8555. Su, Tu, Th. $59, concessions $54.)*

**ROCKHAMPTON ART GALLERY.** The gallery has workshops and special exhibits. *(62 Victoria Pde. Beside the river. ☎4936 8287. Open Tu-F 10am-4pm, Sa-Su 11am-4pm. Free.)*

**HIKING.** With its shadowy presence over Rockhampton, **Mt. Archer** stands at 604m, with vast views of the city and the surrounding landscape. From the summit (a $15 cab ride) you can hike back to the base on the walking track (11km; 4-5hr.) to German St, then take German St to Moores Creek Rd to Musgrave St into the city. Standing above rainforests and eucalypts, the lookout also offers a unique perspective on the layout of the city. Especially visible at night, the main streetlights are claimed to spell H-E-L-L, although this spectacle is debatable.

**FARMSTAY.** **Myella Farm Stay** offers a farmstay on 2600 acres for 13 people with activities such as horse and motorbike riding, 4WD tours, cow milking, and, of course, campfires. *(125 km southwest of Rockhampton. Free pickup from Dululu, which is on a McCafferty's route. ☎4998 1290. 3-days, 2-night $198, including gorgeous buffet meals.)*

## ■♫ NIGHTLIFE AND ENTERTAINMENT

The nightlife in Rocky doesn't pack the same punch as Balboa. Still, the **Heritage Tavern,** on the corner of Quay and William St, offers some nighttime entertainment. It houses the gorgeous, sports-themed **Stadium Night Club,** where 20 TVs ensure you won't miss a moment of the action, and the pool tables are rolled out of the way F-Sa for Top-40 dancing. *(☎4927 6996. Open Th-Su 8pm-3am. F-Sa $5 cover after 11pm.)* Also in the tavern, **The Bourbon Bar** has live rock bands F-Sa with no cover. For a pint of Guinness ($6), live Irish and rock music (Th-Sa nights), and some Irish grub ($7-10), good laddies and lasses hit the new pub **O'Dowd's,** 100 Williams St. *(☎4927 0344. Open M-F 8am-midnight, Sa-Su 8am-2am.)*

## NEAR ROCKHAMPTON: CARNARVON GORGE NATIONAL PARK

A mere 500km southwest of Rockhampton and Gladstone, this rugged national park is rich with Aboriginal rock art, deep pools, and soaring sandstone cliffs. The gorges, however, are the main attraction. Camping facilities are available. Winter

QUEENSLAND

is the best time to visit, but be aware that at night temperatures fall below freezing. For information, contact the ranger (☎4984 4505).

# GREAT KEPPEL ISLAND

A trip to Great Keppel is like winning an instant vacation: it's a high-flying resort escape that miraculously falls within your budget. The largely untouched island is surrounded by unbelievably clear waters, 17 beaches with fine snorkeling right off-shore, and a brilliant night sky streaked by shooting stars. While budget accommodations abound, the island's posh resort doesn't mind the odd backpacker crashing its nightlife, or taking its catamaran out for a lazy afternoon. For many visitors, it's enough to curl up on any of the beaches and seize a taste of paradise. The sunset, shimmering off the tranquil waters will make you reconsider the fate of the return boat ticket. If you ever do make it back to the mainland though, don't be surprised if you forgot how to tie your shoes.

## ▐ TRANSPORT

Before arranging your own transport to Great Keppel Island, consider the **packages** offered by some of the hostels (see **Accommodations,** below). If you choose independent transport, to get to the island you will need a ferry (30min. from Rosslyn Bay) and to get to the ferry you will need a bus (40min. from Rockhampton). **The Freedom Flyer** leaves from Keppel Bay Marina, Rosslyn Bay. (☎4933 6244. 9, 11am, 3pm. $29 return, students $22, children $15.) Their **Freedom Cruise** provides lunch and access to secluded beaches on nearby islands ($49, concessions $39, children $29). **Keppel Tourist Services** run a ferry to the island, leaving from the Great Keppel Island Transit Center in Rosslyn Bay. (☎4933 6744, freecall ☎(1800) 35 67 44. F 7:30, 9:15, 11:30am, 3:30, 6pm; $30 return, children $15.) **Young's Coaches'** Route #20 runs to both ferries from the corner of Denham and Bolsover St, Rockhampton. (☎4922 3813. 2-5 per day; $7.) **Rothery's Coaches,** leaving downtown Rocky after accommodation pickups, meets only the Tourist Services' ferry. (☎4933 6744. 8, 10:30am, 1:30pm; $15 return, children $8). For drivers, free parking is available outside the ferry terminals. Safer is **Great Keppel Island Security Car Park** (☎4933 6670), on the Scenic Hwy, which offers a courtesy bus to the harbor.

The ferries let passengers out on the main beach. Parallel to the beach is the island's main (and only) drag, the **Yellow Brick Road** (we are in Oz, but the road's dark brown) that runs the entire commercial strip of Great Keppel, a 5min. stroll.

## ▐ ACCOMMODATIONS

When considering accommodations, look at the big picture—most accommodations on the island offer packages including bus and ferry transfers and rooms on the mainland that manage to ease the price and trouble of arranging transfers yourself. Camping is not allowed on Great Keppel but is increasingly possible on nearby Keppel Group islands. For package information, try: **Yeppoon Backpackers** (☎4939 8080, freecall ☎(1800) 63 68 28), or **Rockhampton YHA** (☎4927 5288; see Rockhampton Accommodations, p. 350).

▧ **Great Keppel Island Backpackers** (☎4939 8655, freecall ☎(1800) 18 02 35). A friendly, relaxed throw-back to the way the island used to be. The staff will have you in stitches with their banter. Canoeing, snorkeling and boat trips are often free bonuses. BBQ. Check-out 9am. Reception daily 8am-5pm. Dorms $19; tents with a large wooden double bed $44; cabins with bath for 2 $100, each extra person up to 7 $10.

**Great Keppel Island Village YHA** (☎4927 5288 or ☎4939 2050). Currently being run by Keppel Haven and affiliated with the Rockhampton YHA. A path-connected, plant-surrounded smattering of "safari tents" with a quality common kitchen. Reception daily 7am-5pm; check-in at ferry. Dorms $18; singles $30; twins and doubles $43. YHA.

**Keppel Haven** (☎4939 2050, freecall ☎(1800) 35 67 44). "Safari tents" make a tent village, while bunkhouses and cabins provide more comfortable, expensive stays. Very few showers and toilets. Linen $5. Key deposit $20. Reception daily 7:30am-5pm. Dorms $17.50; singles $27.50; twins and doubles $40; 4-person ensuite bunkhouses with linen $100; self-contained cabins $120.

## FOOD AND NIGHTLIFE

With a grand total of eleven establishments on the island, Great Keppel has what might be generously termed limited offerings. You're best off buying food on the mainland, but the island has some options. **The Keppel Café,** near the resort, looks like your basic takeaway shop and it is—but it's the best food for your money on the island (open daily 8am-9pm). **Island Pizza** serves lasagna and subs for $6-9 and more expensive pizza. (☎4939 4699. Open Tu 6-9pm, W-Su 12:30-2pm and 6-9pm.) The **Wreck Bar** is a spacious nightclub where the only things wrecked are the patrons. Cover bands perform M and Th-Sa nights and Su 1-6pm. The beach outside is perfect for sharing a few drinks under the night sky (open daily until 2am).

## ACTIVITIES

The resort's **Information and Tour Centre** makes bookings for non-guests, has Internet (30min. $5), and posts a list of daily activities. (☎4939 5044. Open daily 8am-5pm.) Great Keppel has 17 beaches marking its 27km circumference, while all of "civilization" is within an 8min. stroll. **Monkey Beach,** a mere 30min. jaunt south of the hostels, has the best and most accessible **snorkeling. Long Beach,** a 35min. walk past the airstrip, exists in splendid isolation. Hike to ■**Mt. Wyndham** (no relation to the famous editor) for delicious views of your paradise. Other walks go to the **Old Homestead** and the **lighthouse.** *Keppel Haven's Track Map* is helpful for bush walks (free at the Keppel Tourist Services ferry terminal on the mainland, or $1.50 on the island), but Carl Svendsen's map is beautifully detailed ($1.50).

To traverse the inviting water with a bit of speed or sport, visit the fellas at the Resort's **watersports area,** off the Yellow Brick Rd, just before the resort. They offer everything from high-speed banana rides ($10) to catamaran/windsurfer hire ($15 per hr.) to waterskiing ($20) to parasailing (one of the last companies that gives the thrill of beach takeoffs and landings; $50). The **Beach Shed** at Keppel Haven, has jet skis (15min. $40), snorkel gear (24hr. $10), and kayaks (1hr. $10). The **Dive Shop** (☎4939 5022), right next door, offers dive trips for the certified ($77) and the uninitiated ($99); tag along and snorkel for $33. **Sea kayaking,** run by Geoff at Island Backpackers, is another adventurous way to spend the afternoon. Geoff also offers a cheaper canoe and snorkel adventure (sea kayaking $33, for Island Backpackers guests $28; canoeing $15).

For the even more adventurous, **Tandem Skydive** has beach landings (8000ft. $275, 12,000ft. $375). The catamaran **Capricat** offers a 3hr. sail and snorkel trip ($40, children $25), as well as a sunset cruise ($45, children $27). For a slower pace, hop on a dromedary and enjoy **camel riding** on the beach ($44).

## NEAR GREAT KEPPEL ISLAND: THE KEPPEL GROUP

The isolated and largely deserted islands in the Keppel Group provide the possibilities to play Gilligan (with a planned return, of course). The coconut-infested **Pumpkin Island** (those wacky Aussies) offers beautiful revegetation, coral, and white beaches. And it can all be yours—well, nearly yours, I mean who would play the professor, the movie star, Mary Anne. . . A maximum of 28 people on the island choose between one of the five cabins for up to 6 people and camping. The island has toilet, showers, BBQ, drinking water, and plenty of deserted beaches. (☎4939 4413 or ☎4939 2431. Camping $10 per person; cabins $130 per night.) For transport, call Keppel Bay Marina (☎4933 6244) or a water-taxi (☎4933 6133), but it won't come cheap—$260-300 roundtrip on a boat that can carry 6-10 people. **Middle Island, Humpy Island,** and **North Keppel** also offer camping.

# MACKAY

Emerging out of miles and miles of sugarcane, Mackay (pronounced "MICK-eye") serves as a convenient gateway to the hidden treasures of the rainforested national parks inland and the isolated islands offshore. Airlie Beach corners the backpacker market, but Mackay lets its travelers seek something different. The Finch Hatton Gorge, Eungella (pronounced "Yun-guh-lah"), and Cape Hillsborough National Parks reveal a breath-taking beauty too often overlooked. While controlled cane fires glow on the night horizon, the moderate heat of the city's nightlife makes it a reasonable spot to spend an evening, before you take a morning stroll through the city's gardens and strike out for the wilderness.

## ▐ TRANSPORT

**Trains:** The **train station** (☎ 4952 7418) is about 5km south of town on Connors Rd, off Nebo Rd. No public transport, but a taxi costs about $10 and some hostels offer free pickup. Purchase tickets in town at any travel agent. Lockers $2.

**Buses: Mackay Bus Terminal** (☎ 4951 3088) is on Milton St between Gordon and Victoria St. McCafferty's runs to: **Brisbane** (14hr., 5 per day, $102); **Airlie Beach** (1¾-2hr., 5 per day, $27); **Bundaberg** (8¼-9¾hr., 9 per day, $79); **Cairns** (9½-12hr., 9 per day, $81); **Hervey Bay** (10¾hr., 7 per day, $91); and **Rockhampton** (4¼hr., 9 per day, $42). For **Noosa** and **Maroochydore,** connect through Bundaberg (see p. 347) or Hervey Bay (see p. 341).

**Taxis:** Mackay Taxi (24hr. ☎ 13 10 08). **Taxi Transit** (☎ 4951 4990) will take you to the northern beaches (Eimeo Beach $3), but not to local destinations.

**Car Rental: Avis** (☎ 13 63 33, ☎ 4951 1266) is located at the airport. **U-Drive** (☎ 4957 5606, freecall ☎ (1800) 67 01 10) offers courtesy pickup. **Thrifty** (☎ 4957 3677, freecall ☎ (1800) 81 80 50) is at 3 Mangrove Rd. **Budget** (☎ 4951 1400).

## ✳ ⑦ ORIENTATION AND PRACTICAL INFORMATION

Mackay radiates from the sea as it sprawls along the waterfront. The city center rests on the southern bank of the Pioneer River. **River St** runs along the waterfront, and the town's main drag, **Victoria St,** is the next parallel street to the south. Plenty of nightlife and restaurants line **Sydney** and **Wood St,** which are perpendicular to Victoria St. The **Bruce Hwy** comes into the west side of town, and the exit leads to **Gordon St,** parallel to and just south of Victoria St.

**Tourist Office: Mackay Tourism Office,** 320 Nebo Rd (☎ 4952 2677; fax 4952 2034). At the southwestern corner of the city center. Open M-F 8:30am-5pm, Sa-Su 9am-4pm.

**National Parks Office:** (☎ 4944 7800). On the corner of River and Wood St. National park info, videos on the reef, and permits for the Cumberland Islands and other national park camping ($3.85 per person per night). Open M-F 8:30am-5pm.

**Markets: Victoria Street Markets,** city center (☎ 4957 5736). Su 8:30am-12:30pm.

**Currency Exchange: Commonwealth Bank,** 126 Victoria St (☎ 4953 5559). Traveler's check exchange $5 fee, no fee for cash.

**Emergency:** ☎ 000.

**Police:** (24hr. ☎ 4968 3444). On Sydney St, between Victoria and Gordon St.

**Hospital: Mackay Base Hospital** (24hr. ☎ 4968 6000). Follow Gordon St west to the Bruce Hwy, turn right at Bridge St; it's on the left before the bridge.

**Internet: Hong Kong Importers,** Bazzar Arcade, 128 Victoria St (☎ 4953 3188). 1hr. $5. Open M-F 8am-5:15pm, Sa-Su 9am-2pm.

**Post Office:** 69-71 Sydney St (☎ 4957 7333). Between Victoria and Gordon St. Open M-F 8am-5:30pm. **Postal Code:** 4740.

**Phone Code:** 07.

QUEENSLAND

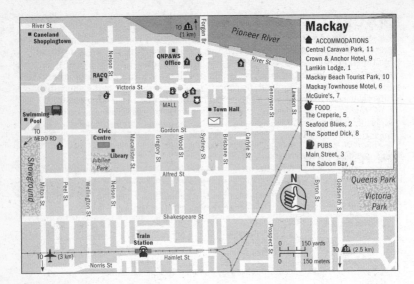

**Mackay**

▲ ACCOMMODATIONS
Central Caravan Park, 11
Crown & Anchor Hotel, 9
Larrikin Lodge, 1
Mackay Beach Tourist Park, 10
Mackay Townhouse Motel, 6
McGuire's, 7

🍎 FOOD
The Creperie, 5
Seafood Blues, 2
The Spotted Dick, 8

🍺 PUBS
Main Street, 3
The Saloon Bar, 4

# ACCOMMODATIONS

Mackay's accommodations won't make you linger here.

**Larrikin Lodge (YHA),** 32 Peel St (☎4951 3728; fax 4957 2978). 200m from the bus terminal. Mackay's only true hostel has new owners and a garden. Laundry $2. Internet. Reception 7-10am and 5-10pm. Dorms $16, twins $37.50, family room $55.

**Crown and Anchor Hotel,** 27 River St (☎4953 1545). A locals pub with spacious twin rooms and a porch overlooking the river. Laundry $2. Share $15, weekly $85.

**McGuire's,** 17 Wood St (☎4957 7464). These are the cheapest beds and lunch specials in town. Rooms are clean, but you get what you pay for, so you may want to see a room first. Dorms $12; singles $25; twins and doubles $35; triples $40.

**Mackay Townhouse Motel,** 73 Victoria St (☎4957 6985; fax 4957 6249). Enter through the Imperial Arcade. Even in the perfect downtown location, this motel remains removed. Clean, spacious ensuite rooms, with fridges and TVs. Laundry $7. Reception 24hr. Singles $44; twins and doubles $55; family units from $66.

**Mackay Beach Tourist Park,** 8 Petrie St, Illawong Beach (☎4957 4021, freecall ☎(1800) 64 51 11). 3km south of the city center, on the beach. BBQ area and pool patrolled by wandering peacocks. Tentsites for 2 $15, powered $20; cabins for 2 $47.

**Central Caravan Park** (☎4957 6141). On Malcomson St. Just over the Forgan Bridge, near the city center. Pool, laundry, and kitchen. Reception 7am-8pm. Tentsites for 2 $13, powered $16; cabin doubles $28; Villa ensuite doubles with A/C $40.

# FOOD AND NIGHTLIFE

**The Spotted Dick,** 2 Sydney St, is not the local herpes clinic; in fact, its wacky decor and crazy cuisine make it one of Mackay's best eateries. Meals run $8-14, and most of the wood-fired pizzas cost less than $10. Catch live music Friday nights or "krazy karaoke" W-Su, kontests Sa. (☎4957 2368. Open 10am-2am. Kitchen open daily noon-2pm and 6-8:30pm. Happy Hour: M-F 5-7pm, Sa 3-5pm.) **The Creperie** (☎4951 1226), on Gregory St near Victoria St, serves up crepe meals with a scrumptious assortment of fillings and a side salad for $10-12. Polish your meal off with what else but crepes—dessert ones, served with ice cream for $6-8. **Seafood**

**Blues,** 171 Victoria St (☎ 4953 5453), has cheap fresh seafood. A Woolworth's **supermarket** is in the Caneland Shopping Centre (open M-F 8am-9pm, Sa 8am-5pm).

The cream of Mackay's **nightlife** crop is **Main Street,** on the corner of Victoria and Gregory St, the biggest club in town where DJ-hosted party madness rages around pool tables and two bars. (☎ 4957 7737. Open Tu-Su. Cover $2 F-Sa.) For a rip-roarin' good time, look for the giant cow clad in country-western attire, above the entrance of **The Saloon Bar,** 99 Victoria St. The interior achieves that delicate balance between saloon and hip nightclub. (☎ 4957 7220. Open Tu-Su. Cover $2 F-Sa.)

## SIGHTS AND ACTIVITIES

While most of Mackay's attractions lie in its surroundings, there are a few things to do in town. For a quick overview, pick up *A Heritage Walk in Mackay* free from the tourist office. The **walk** begins on River St and hits all the historical and cultural hot spots. Don't miss **Queen's Park,** where the lovely **Orchid Gardens** overflow with delectable flowers. To see Mackay in style, hop on a **Harley Trike** with Frank, who's beard is nearly as long as his Mackay loyalty. (☎ (0409) 54 02 61. $25.)

**Mackay Adventure Divers** offers the best way to daytrip around the islands south of the Whitsundays. Snorkel or dive on Cumberland, Scawfell, and the Llewellyn Wreck. Spend your surface interval on a deserted beach. (☎ 4953 1431. Half-day cruise with 2 dives $94.) A few hours with **Reef Flight** and you'll see isolated Bushy Reef from above in a seaplane, from below while snorkeling in its adjacent suspended lagoon, and with your eyes closed while relaxing on the coral beach. (☎ 4953 0220. 35min. flight and 2½hr. on the island. $194.) Sail for a half-day on the **Capricorn Dancer** past tranquil offshore islands. (☎ 4953 3599. M, W, F, Su. $31.)

## DAYTRIPS FROM MACKAY

### CARLISLE ISLAND

Just like Heron Island to the south, Brampton Island is no longer accessible to daytrippers, campers, or anyone not willing to spend $130 per person per night. Fortunately, you can slide by the island's resort and find solitude and isolation on nearby Carlisle Island. This island, fringed by coral, is monitored by the National Parks office in Mackay, which arranges **camping** permits ($4 per person per night). Carlisle has a toilet, BBQ, and lots of shady trees. If the guests-only boat transfer to Brampton Island P&O Resort (☎ 4951 4499) is not full, you may be able to grab a spot ($35 each way), and arrange a boat transfer to Carlisle.

### NEWRY ISLAND

Newry Island is a small, simple spot ideal for swimming and bushwalking. The **Newry Island Resort** consists of basic cabins with a double and three single beds, showers, and bath. (☎ 4959 0214. $30-70 for 1-5 people.) **Camping** is available with access to toilets and showers for $5. The downside is the lack of cooking facilities (BBQ only), which means paying around $12 for the evening meal. Pickup from Seaforth (near Mackay) can be arranged (☎ 4959 0214).

---

**THE BIG LEAP** Twenty minutes north of Mackay along the Bruce Hwy is the small community of **The Leap,** located at the base of a massive stone precipice. In 1866, the local Juipera Aboriginal tribe made a raid on a white man's vegetable garden and killed a farmhand in the process. During the retributive counter-attack, an Aboriginal woman named Kohara was cornered at the edge of the cliff holding her baby in her arms. Rather than submit to capture, Kohara laid her infant daughter on the ground and leapt to her death. In an act of reparation, Jack Barnes, the farmer whose garden was the subject of the initial raid, took the baby from the mountain and raised her as his own child. Many, particularly Aboriginals, attributed the devastating effects of a 1918 cyclone to the vengeance of Kohara's spirit.

# NEAR MACKAY

## CAPE HILLSBOROUGH NATIONAL PARK

About 20km up the Bruce Hwy is the right-hand turn-off to Cape Hillsborough National Park, where rugged, pine-covered mountains tumble into the bright blue Coral Sea. Rocky outcrops protrude through the tropical rainforest, while kangaroos and scrub turkeys roam the landscape.

The brand-new, well-built, must-see **Diversity Trail** (1.2km) is an aptly named jaunt with a boardwalk through many species of mangroves, an area of open woodland with many straight, dowel-like grasstrees (which Aboriginals used for spears), and a massive pile of seashells under a rock where Aboriginals broke open the catch-of-the-day. The **Beachcomber Cove Track** (1.6km) is the steepest trail but provides great views from the top of the ridge. The **Andrews Point Track** (2.6km) begins in sheltered rainforest before exposing onto the ridge with six lookouts.

Down Bruce Hwy, on the left, is the turn-off for **Holiday Hide-away**, a new budget spot next to the ocean. (☎ 4959 0367. Tent sites $10, powered $12; cabins $50.) The road ends at a terrific Council **campsite**, just a few kangaroo hops from the beach. (Self-register for $8 per site.) Next door to the campsite is the **Cape Hillsborough Holiday Resort**, with over 7km of its own walking tracks, a pool, and open BBQ. (☎ 4959 0152. Tent sites $9, for 2 $11; cabins $44; beach huts $55; motel rooms $66. All prices except tentsites increase $11 for one-night stays on the weekend.)

Adjacent to Cape Hillsborough is one of the best northern beaches, **Smalley's Beach**, on a short, but unsealed, road. Its **campsite** has toilets, water, and the beach as its front yard, but no showers ($4 per person; permits from the ranger's office). On the premises are a **ranger station** (☎ 4959 0410; open 7am-4pm), cooking facilities, bathrooms, and showers. Pick up the *Cape Hillsborough Visitor Information Sheet*, which details some of the area's finest walking tracks.

## MACKAY TO EUNGELLA

The road to Eungella heads out from the south side of Mackay, along the Bruce Hwy. At a four-way intersection with a rail crossing, turn right onto the Peak Downs Hwy and follow it to a junction with Eungella Rd. The road leads through the endless sugarcane fields of Pioneer Valley, sometimes ablaze at sunset when unchanging winds make the best time for controlled burning.

After **Marian** is the town of **Mirani** with its **Illawong Sanctuary**, on Eungella Rd 4km after the bridge, a well-maintained wildlife sanctuary populated by the usual suspects and even an ice-cream eating emu. (☎ 4959 1777. Open daily 9:30am-5pm. $11, children $5.50. Croc feeding 2:30pm.) Farther along Eungella Rd, in **Pinnacle**, is The **Pinnacle Hotel**, where stopping for Wendy's famous, scrumptious █home-made pies is a must. (☎ 4958 5207. Open 9am-11pm. Pie $3.50.)

After the hotel is a well-marked turn-off to beautiful **Finch Hatton Gorge** (10km from Eungella Rd). Contact the ranger (☎ 4958 4552) for the latest on trail conditions, as the narrow road dips through several creeks that are often too full to cross Jan.-March. Walking trail maps are available for free at the QPWS office in Mackay. The hike up to **Wheel of Fire Falls** (4.2km; 45min.) is one of the most enjoyable circuits in the area with knockout floral diversity. The shorter trek to **Araluen Falls** (1.6km) winds past two tree trunks remarkably intertwined like licorice strands, and ends at a zig-zag waterfall pouring into a deep, gorgeous pool. Aboriginal legend has it that those who swim nude in the pool will be blessed with healthy children, but you'll likely argue frozen children. In either case, for the sake of tradition, get there early on a summer morn to take a proud paddle for progeny.

Just off the dirt road to Finch Hatton Gorge is the idyllic █**Platypus Bush Camp**, with open-air huts and tent sites that afford great views and sounds of the adjacent creek area burgeoning with platypi, fireflies, and fruit bats. The camp features an open-air kitchen, a gently rocking porch swing, a rainforest-walled shower, and a sauna made with Mackay cedar. A creekside hot tub has just been built out of

## ABBREVIATE TILL YOU DROP
Hearing a bit too many unfamiliar words ending in "y" sounds? The words aren't new, just part of the relentless repertoire of Aussie abreviations. Australians refer to objects, places, and even meals as though they were special friends needing nicknames. Sunglasses are "sunnies", BBQs "barbies", and wind or track pants "trackies". Rockhampton is "Rocky", Tasmania "Tazzie", and Brisbane "Brizzy". The morning meal is "brekkie" and snacks are "nibblies". Feel free to make up your own, as many "Aussies" do. You don't have to have a "uni" education to do so.

rock, but you'll have to rely on gastronomics for bubbles. Doubles, including the Honeymoon Hut, offer platypus viewings from bed and a crisp stream running by your doorstep. Call to arrange a pickup, or have **Jungle Johno** or **Reeforest** (see **Eungella National Park,** below) drop you off. (☎4958 3204. Dorm bunks $15; doubles $45; camping $5 per person; bring your own food.)

## EUNGELLA NATIONAL PARK

Much of 49,610-hectare Eungella National Park, 84km west of Mackay, is a massive range of steep rainforest-covered slopes and deep misty valleys. What you can see from hilltop views or on any of the nine walking trails is gorgeous. The mountains trap clouds, resulting in high precipitation, and serve as natural barriers between this park and other swaths of rainforest in Queensland. Red cedars, palms, and giant ferns coat many slopes, and platypi splash in the water at the bottom of the ravines. Over the years, Eungella has seen a dramatic change of focus—it has been prospected for gold, planted with sugar cane, logged, grazed for dairying, and in 1941 declared a national park.

The cheapest way to see the park is by car, as there is **no public transportation** up the valley. Be careful on the road to Eungella, as it climbs 800m in 3km; take the turns slowly. Alternately, two companies run daytrip bush safaris that are probably the best way to see the park unless you're a botany whiz. **Jungle Johno's Bush, Beach, and Beyond Tours** is led by coal-miner-cum-tour-guide Johno, who is deeply knowledgeable in topics from horticulture to folklore. He'll also take you to the Finch Hatton Gorge and Broken River. (☎4959 1822. $75; concessions $69; children $45. Save $9 by bringing your own food.) His tours also leave from Airlie Beach (☎4948 1144), thus providing no excuse for missing Eungella's beauties. Cole Adamson, who runs **Reeforest Adventure Tours,** offers tours to the Park and Gorge, both including full steak lunches. (☎4953 1000. $75, children $48.50.)

Just outside the entrance to the park, the ◧**Eungella Chalet** has what may be the best location of any accommodation in Queensland. Surrounded by Eungella's green mountains, the chalet overlooks the vast Pioneer Valley, where clouds can settle into a puffy river and sunrises are other-worldly. Venturing onto the hang glider's ramp next to the pool, where the world championships were once held, feels like toeing a diving board over the earth. The licensed restaurant serves breakfast (7-9am), lunch (noon-2pm; $7.50-13) and dinner (6-8:30pm; $15-23) as well as snacks all day. Mountain bike hire $8 per half-day. Backpackers rates are offered only during the week. (☎4958 4509. Singles $28; twin shares $22; twins and doubles $50; motel suites $72; one-bedroom cabin $88.) Near the chalet, **The Hideaway Café,** a delightful restaurant with yet another amazing view, serves vegetarian options or gourmet burgers, for $5-8. (☎4958 4533. Open daily 8am-5pm.)

Five kilometers along the hilltop pastures, meadows, and fields from the Chalet, you'll cross **Broken River,** with excellent platypus-spotting, a picnic area, a campground with toilets and hot showers ($4 per person), and a ranger station (☎4958 4552; open daily 8-9am and 3:30-4:30pm). Nine walking trails depart from trailheads between the chalet and Broken River. The short **Rainforest Discovery Walk** (1km), from Broken River picnic area, is a self-guided track.

QUEENSLAND

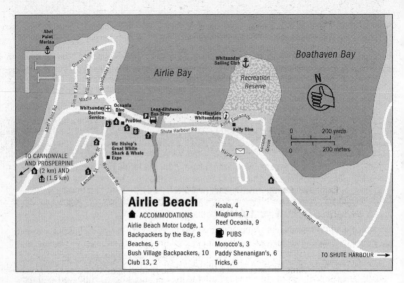

**Airlie Beach**

⌂ ACCOMMODATIONS

Airlie Beach Motor Lodge, 1
Backpackers by the Bay, 8
Beaches, 5
Bush Village Backpackers, 10
Club 13, 2

Koala, 4
Magnums, 7
Reef Oceania, 9

🍺 PUBS

Morocco's, 3
Paddy Shenanigan's, 6
Tricks, 6

# AIRLIE BEACH

Walking down the one-street of Airlie Beach (pop. 3,700; pronounced "AIR-lee") means being bombarded by advertisements, but Airlie was once nothing but mudflats. When a developer's proposal was turned down by the Shire Council in nearby Bowen, he moved his project, and truckloads of Bowen sand, an hour south, putting the "Beach" in Airlie. It was an upscale tourist destination until a pilot strike in the 1980s stalled Queensland's tourism for a year-and-a-half. The resorts became budget in a bid for survival, and backpackers flocked to them in response. The overwhelming array of activities offered on the nearby waters of the Whitsunday Islands and the Great Barrier Reef has turned the town into the biggest backpacker draw between Brisbane and Cairns. A new $8 million waterfront lagoon will be finished in 2001, rendering Airlie even more attractive with year-round swimming, a nice park, and some decent sand. But one look at the blue harbor and beckoning islands explains the true roots of its popularity.

## ▐ TRANSPORT

**Trains:** The rail station is in Prosperine. Whitsunday Transit (☎ (1300) 65 54 49) picks up arriving train passengers and runs down Shute Harbour Rd., stopping in the center of Airlie and at some accommodations (5 per day, $6.50-8.50).

**Buses:** Travel offices and most hostel desks book transport. Greyhound (☎ 13 20 30) and McCafferty's (☎ 13 14 99) drop off in the center of town within walking distance of most hostels; the other accommodations offer courtesy pickups. **Buses** run daily to: **Brisbane** (18hr., 3 per day, $116); **Bowen** (1¼hr., 3 per day, $20); **Bundaberg** (12hr., 2 per day, $93); **Cairns** (10hr., 3 per day, $66); **Gladstone** (9hr., 2 per day, $81); **Hervey Bay** (13hr., 2 per day, $104); **Mackay** (2hr., 3 per day, $27); **Mission Beach** (8hr., 2 per day, $66); **Rockhampton** (7hr., 3 per day, $59); and **Townsville** (4hr., 3 per day, $39). For **Maroochydore** and **Noosa** (both around $100), connect through either **Bundaberg** (see p. 347) or **Hervey Bay** (see p. 341).

**Local Transportation:** Whitsunday Transit (☎ (1300) 65 54 49), runs between Cannonvale and Shute Harbour, daily 6am-6:40pm, at least every 30min., stopping in front of Oceania Dive. Whitsunday Taxi (☎ 13 10 08), serves the whole area.

**Scooter Rental:** Whitsunday Moke and Scooter Hire, Cannonvale (☎ 4948 0700), offers courtesy pickup and drop off. Scooters 1hr. $4.50, mokes 24hr. $32. Open 8am-6pm.

QUEENSLAND

# ✦ ⁊ ORIENTATION AND PRACTICAL INFORMATION

Airlie Beach's layout is simple enough. Its main street, **Shute Harbour Rd,** is where most of the hostels and restaurants are located. Picnic tables line the parallel Beach Walk. Sunbathers entrench themselves along **Airlie Esplanade,** which turns left toward the bay off Shute Harbour Rd heading into the recreation reserve. **Cannonvale** is a suburb of Airlie Beach along the Prosperine-Shute Harbour Rd.

**Tourist Office:** One on every street corner. **Destination Whitsundays** is upstairs on the corner of Shute Harbour Rd and the Esplanade (☎(1800) 64 45 63; fax 4948 0111; email dw@mcs.net.au). Internet 1hr. $5. Open daily 7:30am-10pm.

**Marine Parks Authority Office:** (☎4946 7022), on the corner of Mandalay St and Shute Harbor Rd, 2km out of town toward Shute Harbour. Info on camping and national parks. Open M-F 9am-5pm, Sa 9am-1pm.

**Currency Exchange: Commonwealth Bank** (☎4946 7433), cashes most traveler's checks with a $15 commission. Cash exchange $5 commission. Open M-Th 9:30am-4pm, F 9:30am-5pm. There's an **ANZ Bank ATM** next to the post office.

**Police:** Altman Ave, Cannonvale (☎4948 8888). Open 24hr.

**Medical Services: Whitsunday Medical Centre,** 400 Shute Harbour Rd (24hr. ☎4946 6275). Open M-Sa 9am-6pm, Su 11am-6pm. **Whitsunday Doctors Service** (☎4946 6241), on the corner of Shute Harbour Rd and Broadwater Ave, right next to Oceania Dive. Open M-Sa 8am-5pm, Su 9am-1pm. Both do **dive medicals.**

**Internet Access:** Everywhere. Expect to pay $5 per hr.

**Post Office:** Up the hill along Shute Harbour Rd next to McDonald's (☎4946 6515; fax 4946 7241). Open M-F 8:30am-5:30pm, Sa 9am-12:30pm. **Postal Code:** 4802.

**Phone Code:** 07.

# ▐ ACCOMMODATIONS

Airlie's cornucopia of budget establishments can barely keep pace with backpacker demand, so book ahead. Check into deals if booking tours through your hostel. Check-out is 10am, and key deposit $10, unless otherwise indicated. The nearby Whitsunday Islands offer cheap **camping,** but space is limited (see p. 364).

▨ **Club 13** (a.k.a. **Whitsunday Backpackers Club**), 13 Begley St (☎4946 7376, freecall ☎(1800) 63 39 45; email club13@net-lynx.net). A hostel in a condo—spacious kitchens, gorgeous lounges and patios, and terrific bathrooms, some with tubs. Pool, brilliant views, a friendly modern feel, and the best hostel breakfast in town. Free pickup. Reception daily 7am-6pm. Dorms $18; twins and doubles $45; triples $50. One night free with overnight tour or dive course booking. YHA, VIP.

▨ **Reef Oceania,** 147 Shute Harbour Rd, Cannonvale (☎4946 6137, freecall ☎(1800) 80 07 95; fax 4946 6846; info@reeforesort.com). 3km from town. Sprawls luxuriously across 15 hectares of land including a great pool, volleyball court, free movies, ping-pong, BBQ, bistro, and bar. Free pickup from bus stop, and free hourly bus service to and from town. Reception 24hr. Ensuite cabins for 6 $14.50 per person, with kitchen and TV $16.50; twins and doubles $49.50; overflow to 4-share dorms $7.

**Bush Village Backpackers Resort,** 2 St. Martins Rd, Cannonvale (☎4946 6177, freecall ☎(1800) 80 92 56; fax 4946 7227). 1.5km out of town. The ultimate in cleanliness and goodwill. Self-contained cabins line a driveway that leads to the pool, porch, TV lounge, video library, and troopful of baby 'roos and wallabies. The cabins have kitchens and modern baths. Free bus to town. Laundry ($2), Internet, pool table. Reception 7am-9pm. Check-out 9:30am. Dorms $18-21; twins and doubles $49-55.

**Backpackers by the Bay,** 12 Hermitage Dr (☎/fax 4946 7267; email bythebay@whitsunday.net.au). 650m from town toward Shute Harbour. Bunk-style rooms, chill atmosphere, and amenities galore. BBQ, laundry ($2), pool, game room, free nightly

QUEENSLAND

activities, and a sweet view of the bay. Free pickup and bus to town. Internet 30min. $4. Reception daily 7am-7:30pm. Dorms $18; twins and doubles $44. YHA, VIP.

**Beaches,** 356-62 Shute Harbour Rd (☎4946 6244, freecall ☎(1800) 63 66 30; fax 4946 7764; www.beaches.com.au). Surprisingly nice accommodation in a spot known more for its bars and restaurants. Dorms are in former ensuite motel rooms with balconies, kitchenettes, TVs, and fans. Secured parking, laundry ($2), game room, spacious kitchen, Internet. Free night with overnight tour or dive course booking. Reception daily 7am-8pm. Dorms $14-18; twins $40. VIP.

**Magnums,** 366 Shute Harbour Rd (☎(1800) 624 634; fax 4946 5980; email accomwhi@tpgi.com.au). The biggest party scene in Airlie with an open air bar and bistro and a happening nightclub. All rooms have a kitchen, bathroom, and balcony. Word is that expansion is in the works. Reception 6am-10pm. Dorms $12, with dinner $15.

**Koala,** on Shute Harbour Rd (☎4946 6001, freecall ☎(1800) 80 04 21; fax 4946 6761; email whitwand@whitsunday.net.au). This edition of the famed chain pulls in a party-primed posse with a tiki-torch Polynesian flavor. 6-share ensuite huts have a small kitchen. Pool, volleyball court, laundry. Satellite TV in each room. Meal discounts next door at Morocco's. The only campsite in town. Internet 1hr. $5. Reception daily 7am-8pm. Dorms $15-18; twins and doubles $43-45; camping for 2 $9. VIP.

**Airlie Beach Motor Lodge,** 6 Lamond St (☎4946 6418; fax 4946 5400; email motorinn@whitsunday.net.au). Off Shute Harbour Rd from Abel Point Marina. Classic motel rooms, sauna, saltwater pool, BBQ, and private balconies. Reception daily 7am-8pm. Prices vary with season. Doubles from $79; self-contained units $89.

**Island Gateway Holiday Resort,** corner of Jubilee Pocket Rd and Shute Harbour Rd (☎4946 6228; fax 4946 7125). 1.2km from the center of town. Reception daily 7:30am-7pm. Tent sites $17, powered $20; on-site vans for 2 $35; cabins for 2 $47.

## FOOD AND NIGHTLIFE

With the exception of a few cafés, practically all of Airlie's restaurants double as bars and clubs after 9pm. If you stay around, you'll undoubtedly be treated to entertainment—often a cheeky contest involving various states of undress. Look for discount flyers around town.

**Paddy Shenanigan's,** 352 Shute Harbour Rd (☎4946 5055). A hugely popular, and somewhat less genuine, Irish pub. Artfully presented seafood meals from $10-20. Near nightly entertainment starts around 9pm, and really heats up after midnight. Happy Hour 5-6pm, pints $2.50. Open daily 11am-2am.

**Beaches,** 356-62 Shute Harbour Rd (☎4946 6244). An ever jam-packed backpacker mecca. Dinner at long, communal, wooden tables for $5-13. Get a free drink if you grab a coupon on the street and show up by about 5pm. Party games start daily around 9:30pm and are followed by dancing until midnight.

**Morocco's** (☎4946 6446). Next to Koala on Shute Harbour Rd. Tamer than Beaches, with a slightly more upscale decor and some outdoor tables. Inside, videos play on huge big-screen monitors. Meals cost $10-17, but you can sometimes pick up a $4 discount on the street. Open daily 7-10am and 4:30pm-2am.

**Magnums,** 366 Shute Harbour Rd (☎4946 6266). The newest—and arguably the wildest—joint in town. Stop in and choose from several kinds of entertainment. Live guitar music plays outside, but in the club rages Top 40 music and nightly games, from cane-toad racing to wet t-shirt contests. Open Su-Th 8pm-2am, F-Sa 8pm-5am.

**Tricks,** 352 Shute Harbour Rd (☎4946 6465). This place almost always manages to whip up a lively dance party. No cover. Open daily until 5am.

## SIGHTS AND ACTIVITIES

The best thing to do in Airlie Beach is visit the Whitsunday Islands or dive the Great Barrier Reef, but there is no shortage of other activities.

**BY LAND. Conway National Park** is a few kilometers east of Airlie Beach. A self-guided **walk** lasts just over an hour and passes wrinkled fig trees, mucky mangrove swamps, and a few rare bottle trees. On the way, stop at the **QPWS** for a detailed leaflet. (*QPWS ☎ 4746 7022. Open M-F 8am-5pm, Sa 9am-1pm.*) **Fawlty Tours** has a daily rainforest excursion that features a look at Cedar Creek Falls. (*☎ 4948 0999. $45.*)

**BY SEA.** Reel it in with **M.V. Jillian;** troll for mackerel, cobia, and tuna, and then enjoy lunch on board. (*☎ 4948 0999. Daytrips depart Abel Point 9:15am and return around 6pm. $95.*) If you're looking for a longer fishing trip, **Marlin Blue** has a very experienced captain. (*☎ 4946 5044.*) **Salty Dog Sea Kayaking Tours** offers short tours of nearby islands and the fabulous Bowen beach, including guided bushwalks and all meals. (*☎ 4946 1388 or ☎(0419) 54 48 41. 1-day $65, 2-day $195.*) **Ocean Rafting** offers daytrips on a raft that tops 65km per hr. Trips include a chance to dive and tan on the beach, as well as either visiting aboriginal caves or taking rainforest walks. (*☎ 4946 6848; www.ozadventures.com. $66, children $39.*) Cruise 300ft above Airlie with **Whitsunday Parasail.** After, you can enjoy the resort pool free of charge. (*On the jetty near Coral Sea Resort. ☎ 4948 0000. $45, with jet skis $55.*)

**READY TO RIDE AND SPREAD THE ALARM.** Hand feed kangaroos, ducks, and emus—and carefully, the crocs—at **Barefoot Bushmans Wildlife Park.** The area also features pythons, cassowaries, koalas, and a giant waterslide. (*Lot 2, Shute Harbour Rd, Cannonvale. ☎ 4946 1480. Open daily 9am-4:30pm. $18, children $9, families $48.*) Airlie's only sight is definitely one of Australia's most bizarre. **Vic Hislop's Great White Shark & Whale Expo** is a shrine to the owner's unflagging efforts to document, with clippings, photos, and movies, the "dangers of sharks" and battle against these "monsters." A great white shark sits frozen in a block of ice for your viewing pleasure. (*13 Waterson Rd. ☎ 4946 6928. Open daily 9am-6pm. $15.*)

##  DIVING

The scuba scene is hot in the Whitsunday area. Dolphins, turtles, manta rays, and even small reef sharks prowl these waters. The most popular site for overnight trips are on the outer reefs that lie just beyond the major island groups, including the Bait, Hardy, and Hook Reefs. Occasionally, boats will venture to the Black or Elizabeth Reefs. Mantaray Bay is the best spot nearby. Reasonable prices can be found year-round. All trips incur an extra $4 per day Reef Tax.

**Reef Jet** (☎ 4946 5366; fax 4948 1212; www.reefjet.com.au). This fast boat provides the only daytrip in the area. You and 40 other passengers head to Bait Reef, a good location for both beginners and advanced divers. The trip departs Abel Marina at 8:30am, returning 4:30pm. 2 certified dives $171, 2 intro dives $187.

**Kelly Dive** (☎ 4946 6122; fax 4946 4368; www.kellydive.com.au). A sailing-diving combo: 3 days and 3 nights aboard one of their two luxury sailing ships, squeezing in up to 6 dives. Double your pleasure, double your fun. Sailing $399; each certified dive $50. Intro dives are $60; each additional $50.

**Oceania Dive,** 257 Shute Harbour Rd (☎ 4946 6032; www.oceaniadive.com.au). The brand new 27m boat "Oceania" sets sail Tu and F for a 3-day, 3-night trip to Elizabeth and Kangaroo Reefs. The boat carries 30 passengers. Advanced and specialty courses available. Up to 10 certified dives $500. 5-day course $535.

**Pro Dive,** 344 Shute Harbour Rd (☎ 4948 1888). Runs an all-inclusive 3-day, 3-night trip on the *Stella Maris*. Certified $460; snorkelers $360. PADI courses 6-day $540, 4-day course with only daytrips $300.

# NEAR AIRLIE BEACH: BOWEN

One of Queensland's best kept secrets, Bowen lies just 40min. north of Airlie on the Bruce Hwy. Its gorgeous beaches make the town a strong alternative to Bundaberg (see p. 347) as a place to make some cash. Several hostels will arrange $10.45 per hour (pre-tax) jobs at local farms during picking season (May-Nov.). For more info on working in Australia, see p. 74. Bowen is a stop on every McCafferty's and Greyhound bus. **Bowen Tourism** is at 42 Williams St. (☎4786 4494; fax 4786 4499. Open M-F 9am-7pm, Sa-Su 9am-6pm.)

**Horseshoe Bay** is the town's biggest attraction. To get there, follow Soldiers Rd out of town, take a right onto Horseshoe Bay Rd, and follow it to the end. Although it is sometimes crowded by a large elderly population, the small inlet is the perfect place to spend an afternoon. **Murray Bay** is a less frequented and beautiful beach. Turn right off Horseshoe Bay Rd onto unsealed Murray Bay Rd. The road ends about a 10min. walk from the beach. **Queens Bay** is met directly in the middle by Soldiers Rd. At its far right tip is **Grays Bay,** with calm water and good **fishing.** For the carless, **Bowen Bus Service** runs to the beaches from the library on the corner of Herbert and William St. (☎4786 4414. M-F 3 per day, Sa 2 per day. $2.)

**Harbor Lights Caravan Park,** 40 Santa Barbara Pde, has the town's best back-packer unit, with a big common room, nice bathroom, and a four-person carpeted bedroom. (☎4786 1565. Backpacker units $15, weekly $90; tent sites $20, $79; on-site vans $27.50; self-contained cabins $55.) **Trinity's** is located out of the center of town, on the corner of Soldiers and Horseshoe Bay Rd. It offers a bus to town, laundry, and Internet. (☎4786 4199. $13, weekly $88.) For those not working, the **Horseshoe Bay Resort** is a terrific option. (☎4786 2564; fax 4786 3460. Tent sites for 2 $13, powered $18; on-site vans $39-45; motel-style units $59.)

# WHITSUNDAY ISLANDS

Some rising majestically from the sea, wooded and christened with creeks and waterfalls, others barely poking a tip above water, the Whitsundays are a collection of 74 islands just off the coast of Queensland. Whitsunday Island is the largest and most appealing to campers and hikers, and it's home to the deservedly famous Whitehaven Beach. Other backpacker favorites include Hook Island, with its choice snorkeling spots and Aboriginal cave painting, Day Dream Island, Long Island, and the Molle Island Group, of which South Molle is the best. More creative names include Dead Dog Island and Plum Pudding Island. At the posh resorts on Hayman, Hamilton, and Lindeman Islands many guests arrive by private helicopter, but the islands can make decent daytrips for backpackers, too.

## ▐ TRANSPORT

**Blues Ferries** (☎4946 5111), departing Shute Harbour, is one of the only companies to run direct transfers without trying to turn each trip into a "day cruise" of the islands. Schedules are available at almost any booking office or hostel. Between three and eight ferries leave the harbor daily to: **Daydream** ($16 return), **South Molle** ($16 return), and **Hamilton** ($38 return). **Island Camping Connection** drops campers off at any of the islands. (☎4946 5255. Minimum of 2 campers, $35 per person. Camping equipment available for hire.) Of course, the multiple-island daytrip is an option—though you'll have little time on the islands and plenty on a motorboat. **Whitsunday All Over** ferries passengers to **Daydream Island** or **South Molle.** (☎4946 6900. Both $24 return.) **Reef Express** runs daily from **Abel Point Marina** to **Hood** and **Whitsunday Island** in a **glass-bottom boat.** (☎4946 4447. $55, children $27.50.) **The Whitsunday Dreamer** chugs along to **Long** and **Daydream Islands** as well as **Sun Lovers Reef.** (☎4946 6665. Departs Shute Harbor 9:30am; for 2 $59.) **Mantaray** daytrips stop at **Whitehaven Beach** and **Mantaray Bay.** The trip includes snorkeling and pickup. (☎4946 6665. $50, children $25; dive package $90.)

**Air Whitsunday Seaplanes** flies over the islands. (☎4946 9111. 25min. sight-seeing trip $75, reef sight-seeing $110; 4hr. Reef and Whitehaven Panorama $199.) Flying to individual islands is costly. **Helireef** runs 10 to 35min. scenic flights. (☎4946 9102. $55-139; longer trips with stopovers $165-245.)

## ▐ THE ISLANDS

The island group is rich with cheap camping options. There are 21 campsites on 17 different islands, but before embarking, you must get a permit from **QPWS** at the

**Marine Parks Authority,** on the corner of Shute Harbor and Mandalay Rd, Airlie Beach. (☎4946 7022. Open M-F 9am-5pm, Sa 9am-1pm. Permits $3.50 per night. Walk-in applications are welcome, but book ahead for smaller campgrounds.)

**WHITSUNDAY ISLAND.** The principal draw of the Whitsunday Islands is the famed **Whitehaven Beach,** a 6km-long slip of white along the western part of the beach that resembles the foam on a cappuccino. Sand as pure as talcum powder lies softly at the bottom of ever-clear tidal pools. Behind the beach, a forest clings tenuously to the sand. Across the bay is another beach with the bonus of soft coral framed dramatically by the baby-bottom-white sand. On the other side of the island is **Cid Harbour,** a common mooring site for the 2-night boat trips. Cid Harbor houses the island's three **campgrounds.** The largest is **Dungong Beach** (limit 30 people), which has toilets, drinking water, sheltered picnic areas, and a walking track (1km; 40min.) that leads to the second campground, **Sawmill Beach** (limit 15 people). The same amenities are provided here, but remember to take a water supply if you're camping farther south at **Joe's Beach** (limit 6 people). There is excellent **snorkeling** in the shallow waters not far from the beach.

**HOOK ISLAND.** The beaches on Hook have beautiful stretches of coral just off-shore, literally a stone's throw from **Chalkies Beach** and **Blue Pearl Bay.** *Let's Go* does not recommend throwing stones at beautiful stretches of coral. On the south side of the island lies **Nara Inlet,** a popular spot for overnight boat trips. About 20min. up the grueling path is a cave shelter used by the sea-faring Ngalandji Aboriginals, bordered on both sides by middens (piles of shells). The rare paintings inside date back to 1000 BC and may have given rise to the popular Australian myth that a boatload of exiled Egyptians washed ashore ages ago and left hieroglyphic-like traces in various corners of Queensland. Although the story is unsubstantiated, it is true that at least one glyph in the cave is a good match for "king" in Hieroglyphic Luwian, spoken in ancient Troy. **Maureens Cove** (limit 20 people), on Hook's northern coast, is a popular anchorage and a nice site for really roughing it. Take a sleeping bag and plop down on the beach. Also on the island is **Stonehaven Beach** campground (limit 12 people), a popular sea kayaking site. **Hook Island Wilderness Resort,** just east of Matilday Bay, is definitely the best bargain resort in the islands with a range of activities from volleyball to goanna feeding. (☎4946 9380; fax 4946 9470. Camping $13; hut-style dorms $20; beach-front cabins for up to six people $180.) There is an underwater reef observatory at the end of the jetty. Transfers to the island depart daily from Shute Harbor at 9am on **Seatrek Cruises.**

**SOUTH MOLLE ISLAND.** South Molle offers some of the best **bushwalking** in Queensland. The trek (5km; 1½hr.) from the Resort to ■**Spion Kop,** an enormous rock precipice, is a must. Adventurous hikers scramble up the rocks for an absolutely astounding 360° view of the Whitsundays. **Sandy Beach** (limit 15 people) has over 15km of hiking trails. The trip to the island's resort is 5km through the grasslands. Another 1km will take you to Balancing Rock. Many 2-night sailing excursions moor offshore and guests come ashore to bushwalk or use the pool at the **South Molle Island Resort.** (☎4946 9433, freecall ☎(1800) 07 50 80; fax 4946 9580. 3-share rooms $90 per person, including meals, transfer, and nightly entertainment. Cheaper standby rates are often available.) The island's water activities facility has catamarans (30min. $10) and parasailing ($49; open daily 8am-4:30pm.)

**DAYDREAM ISLAND.** Part of the Molle group, the resort here is the island. **Daydream Island Resort** has seven eating establishments, and tons of water activity toys for hire. (☎4948 8488; fax 4948 8499. Standby twins $85, with meals $123). If you prefer to spend a day at the resort without spending the money for the night, try **Whitsunday All Over,** which offers use of the pool, lunch, and a water activities discount. (☎4946 6900. Daytrip $37, including snorkeling.)

QUEENSLAND

**HAMILTON ISLAND.** Although the **Hamilton Island Resort** is pricey, the property is breathtaking, including a gorgeous pool with a suspended bridge. (☎ 4946 9999; fax 4946 8888. $69 per person for twin or double ensuite bungalows, including transfer.) The endless—though dough-consuming—activities on the island make it worth a daytrip. **Jono's Beach Hire** at the resort rents catamarans (1hr. $20), windsurfers (1hr. $15), and snorkel gear ($8). Soar across a valley on the **Wire Flyer,** a hang glider attached to a 325m long cable. Follow the signs posted around the island to find its hilltop location. (☎ 4946 8780. $30, children $20, 2 runs $50.) **FantaSea** will take you for the day. (☎ 4946 5111. $45 including lunch; children $23.)

**LONG ISLAND.** Only a short journey from Airlie Beach, Long Island has one campground at **Sandy Bay** (limit 6 people) and a backpacker resort called **Club Crocodile.** The resort's special includes a twin-share room, transfer, use of the pool and spa, and plenty of bushwalking. Its launch departs regularly from Shute Harbour. (☎ 4946 9400, freecall ☎ (1800) 07 51 25. Min. 2 nights. $25 per night.)

**OTHER ISLANDS.** On **North Molle Island** lies the mammoth Cackatoo Beach Campground (limit 50 people), fully equipped with facilities. Other fully equipped campsites include **Glouster Island's** Bona Bay (limit 15 people), Northern Spit (limit 40 people) on **Henning Island,** the small-secluded sites at Sea Eagle Beach (limit 4 people) on **Thomas Island,** and **Armit Island** (limit 12 people; closed for seabird conservation Oct.-Mar.). Basic grounds with simple bush camping sites are Geographer's Bay (limit 6 people) on **Tancrea Island,** Burning Point (limit 12 people) and Neck Bay (limit 12 people) on **Shaw Island, Saddleback Island** (limit 6 people), Western Beach (limit 10 people) on **South Repulse Island,** and the four-person sites on **Olden Island, Planton Island,** and **Denmon Island.**

Finally, Boat Port (limit 6 people) on **Lindeman Island** has some terrific walks. The **Mount Odefield walk** (3.6km) goes from the Airstrip Hut to the summit. The **Loop walk** (6.3km) begins in the same spot but runs along the headlands to the northern beaches. The easiest track goes to **Coconut Beach** (5.2km).

## ◖ SAILING THE ISLANDS

Traveling the Whitsundays without sailing the islands is like going to Paris without seeing the Eiffel Tower. A sailing safari is one of the most popular activities in Queensland, but it's also one of the most expensive. There are four classes of boats at play: the uninspiring **motor-powered**—this includes boats that have sails but nonetheless motor everywhere; the stately **tallships,** with rigging of yesteryear and the elegance of age; the **cruising yachts,** which offer more comfort, but come up just shy; and the proper **racing yachts,** called **maxis,** which are close to, if not in, racing shape, generally more expensive, and so much sexier. Travel agents may try to push the maxis (which give higher commissions), with a valid case that these boats will get you to locations faster and thereby give you more time in each place. Then again, the powerboats will get you there even faster, so choose the balance of sail-time vs. location-time that suits you best. During the low seasons (Oct.-Nov. and Feb.-Mar.), when discounts can be found, all sailing trips are usually booked solid a few days ahead of time; unless you **book ahead,** your boat may be decided for you, or you may miss out altogether.

Ask how much time is actually spent on the safari. Many boats offer "three-day, two-night" trips that leave at midday and come back 48hr. later; these boats often offer three such trips a week, making Airlie Beach the only place in Oz with a nine-day week. When the options are overwhelming, try asking a few more questions. How many passengers can the boat take? Are the bunks separate from the common space? Is there an opportunity to dive? How much sailing is done? Can passengers participate in sailing? Is snorkel gear included? Boats generally cater to vegetarians, supply plenty of food, and sell soft drinks and water at a slight mark-up. Finally, keep in mind that it can get chilly and wet out on the waves. Boats usually provide waterproof weather jackets, but quick-dry shorts are also a good idea.

# DAYTRIPS

**On the Edge** (Prosail; ☎4946 5433). Most Prosail 3-day, 2-night trips offer an additional day on this boat for free. Whitehaven M, W, Sa. Hook Island Tu, Th, F, Su. Each trip departs Abel Point Marina 9am; $53. Intro dives $45. Package deals: pre-booked cruise/dive special $89; 2 days of sailing $95; cruise family rate $128.

**Reef Express** (☎(1800) 81 93 66). A motor boat departing 9am for Whitehaven Beach. Includes snorkeling off Hook Island. $55, with a pre-booked dive $90.

**Maxi Ragamuffin** (☎4946 7777). Travels M-W and Sa to Blue Pearl Bay on Hayman Island; Th and Su to Whitehaven Beach on Whitsunday Island. Departs Shute Harbor 8:45am, returns 4:15pm. $78, concessions $69, children $39; dives $54. Pre-booked sail and dive package $116; 2 days to both islands, no overnight $122.

## 48-HOUR TRIPS

**Tallarook** (☎4946 5299). Departs Abel Point. $185 including dive. Each additional dive $30, certified $24. Night dives available.

**Freedom** (☎4946 6922). Includes a visit to Turtle Bay. Departs Abel Point Marina M, W, Sa 4pm; returns M, W, F 2pm. Day and night snorkeling and 1 intro or certified dive included, $185. Each additional dive $30, certified $25.

**Summertime** (☎4948 0999). Extensive bushwalks at anchor sites. Departs from Abel Point Marina W, F, Su 1pm; returns W, F, Su noon. $185.

## THREE-DAY, TWO-NIGHT TRIPS

### MAXIS

◪ **Southern Cross** (☎4946 4999). **Siska,** 80ft., offers the most comfort. Departs Sa and Tu 9:30am; returns M and Th 4:30pm. $285. **Southern Cross,** 68ft., is a former America's Cup finalist. Departs W and Su 9:30am; returns Tu and F 4:30pm. $275.

**ProSail** (☎4946 5433). Offers 4 Maxis. **Matador,** the world's largest maxi, carries 20 guests and 4 crew. Departs Su and W. **Condor** carries 26 guests and 4 crew. Departs Su and Th. **Apollo,** 80ft., has 23 guests and 4 crew. Departs M and F. **Hammer,** 75ft., carries 19 guests and 3 crew. Departs Sa and Tu.

### CRUISING YACHTS

**ProSail** (☎4946 5433). **Indulgence** and **Platinum,** each carry 12 guests and 2 crew. Depart Tu, Th-F, Su. $275. **Otella** and **Iceberg** are ex-racing yachts, which each carry 12 guests and 2 crew. Depart M, W, and F-Sa. $285.

**Great Eagle** (☎4946 5299). Departs Abel Point Marina M and F 9:30am; returns W and Su 4:30pm. $250.

**The Flying Dutchman** (☎(1800) 67 71 19). Offers a round-trip with 8 dives. Departs Abel Point Marina W and Sa 9am; returns F and M 4pm. $299; only snorkeling $260.

**Stargazer** (☎4946 6969). Snorkeling included. Departs Abel Point Marina M and Th 9am, returns W and Sa 4pm. $250.

## TALL SHIPS AND EXTENDED TRIPS

◪ **Solway Lass** (Southern Cross; ☎4946 4999). A gorgeous 127ft., built in 1902. The trip is nothing but luxury, with great meals and A/C cabins. The wooden staircase leading below deck may inspire recreations of *Titanic* scenes, and admiring the full-sailed glory from the bowsprit will bring you back to that era. 3-day, 3-night: twins and doubles $349, 4-share $329. 6-day, 6-night: $629, $569.

**Providence V** (☎(1800) 65 53 46). 3-day, 2-night trips. Diving can be arranged. Departs Abel Point Marina varying days 9:30am, returns third day at 4:30pm. $275.

**The Anaconda III** (☎(1800) 07 50 35). A 101ft. sailing luxury yacht offering a 3-night cruise with up to 6 dives. Departs Tu and F 8pm. $400 before dives.

QUEENSLAND

## DO IT YOURSELF

For reasonably experienced sailors and boaters who can put together a small group, **Queensland Yacht Charters** (☎ (1800) 07 50 13) offers the unbeatable option of chartering your own yacht, catamaran, or power cruiser. The boats come fully equipped and accesorized; sailing boats include fuel, power boats don't. Not including the hefty $500-1000 bond, rates range from $320-670 per night, which, when divided amongst a group, often beats the cost of a cruise.

## ◢ DIVING

Ninety-five percent of diving in this area departs from Airlie Beach (see p. 360). Boats normally venture to Bait, Hook, or Hardy reefs, which lie just beyond the largest island group. Manta Ray Bay, off Hook Island, is limited by 2hr. mooring rules, but it's pristine and postcard perfect. A couple of trips do depart from island resorts, but to get the most bang for your buck, depart the mainland at one of the two harbors. If you are dead set on the full resort experience, a trip to Hardy Reef departs **South Molle Island Resort** daily at 8:30am and returns at 5:30pm. (☎ 4946 9433. $125, families $275.) **Club Crocodile** on Long Island offers packages that are a bit more affordable. (☎ 4946 9400. Cruise $85, intro dive $60, certified $45.)

# NORTH COAST OF QUEENSLAND

The northern Queensland coast sits at the junction of the tropical far north, the rugged frontier of the outback, and the modern cities of the southern coastline. Tall green fields and smoking mills represent the region's greatest agricultural asset, sugar cane. Sunny Townsville is the economic and residential center of the area. Off its shores, Magnetic Island offers solitude and koalas in the wild. Between here and Mission Beach, white beaches glow next to crystalline water, across which the Great Barrier Reef beckons. The miles inland hide swaths of rainforest populated by birds, bugs, and bouncing 'roos, and between it all, the civilization that clings to the coast wrests its existence from the unrelenting wild.

# TOWNSVILLE

Queensland's second largest city, Townsville (pop. 144,000) is primarily a residential and industrial center, but in a way, more authentically Aussie than tourist-ridden Cairns. Not everyone is happy with that balance of tourism, so the city itself was given a recent face-lift—its 2.2km beach-front was landscaped, strung with a bike path, and dotted with parks and restaurants. These public spaces are perfect for sunbathing, rollerblading, or otherwise enjoying one of Townsville's 320 sunny days. Townsville's greatest attractions, however, are off-shore. The city harbor is a gateway to nearby Magnetic Island and the world-famous Yongala wreck, a 100-year-old cargo ship well worth its reputation as a diver's dream.

## ▐ TRANSPORT

**Airplanes:** The **airport** (☎ 4727 3211) is west of town. Qantas flies direct daily to: **Brisbane** (1¾hr.; 4 per day; 5-day advance discount fare $441, student fare $331); **Cairns** (1hr.; 4 per day; $227, $171); and **Mackay** (1hr.; 3 per day; $251, $189). An **airport shuttle bus** (☎ 4775 5544) meets all major flights and runs to town daily 5:30am-9pm. One-way $6, return $10. To drive from the airport to town, take John Melton Black Dr, which becomes Bundock St. Bear right onto Warburton St and again onto Eyre St. From Eyre St, go left on Denham St to the town center.

**Trains:** The **train station** (☎ 4772 8288, reservations ☎ 13 22 32) is at the corner of Flinders and Blackwood St. The *Inlander* train departs W and Su at 6pm, for: **Charters Towers** (3hr., $20); **Cloncurry** (16hr., $75); **Hughenden** (8hr., $43); **Mt. Isa** (20½hr., $91); and **Richmond** (10¾hr., $54). The *Spirit of the Tropics* leaves Tu and F at 8am, heading to: **Brisbane** (24hr., $135); **Bowen** (5½hr., $32); **Mackay** (7½hr., $52); and

**Rockhampton** (13hr., $89). The **Queensland Rail Travel Centre** (☎4772 8358) is to the right of the station. Open M 7:15am-5pm, Tu and F 6:30am-5pm, W 7:15am-6pm, Th 8:30am-5pm, Sa 12:45-4pm, Su 7:15-10:45am.

**Buses:** The **Transit Centre** is on the corner of Palmer and Plume St, a 5min. walk from the city center (open daily 6am-8:30pm). McCafferty's (☎13 14 99; open daily 5:30am-11pm) and Greyhound (☎13 20 30) run to: **Airlie Beach** (4hr., 3 per day, $39); **Brisbane** (20hr., 5 per day, $134); **Cairns** (4hr., 5 per day, $41); **Cardwell** (2¼hr., 5 per day, $26); **Charters Towers** (2hr., 2 per day, $20); **Cloncurry** (10hr., 2 per day, $81); **Hughenden** (4hr., 2 per day, $41); **Ingham** (1½hr., 5 per day, $21); **Innisfail** (4¼hr., 5 per day, $37); **Mackay** (5hr., 5 per day, $53); **Mission Beach** (3½hr., 2 per day, $37); **Mt. Isa** (12hr., 2 per day, $91); **Richmond** (5hr., 2 per day, $52); and **Rockhampton** (9hr., 5 per day, $82). Phew.

**Public Transportation: Sunbus** (☎4725 8482) has its main terminal in the center of Flinders Mall. Most tickets $2.50-3.50. 24hr. bus passes $9.

**Car Rental: Townsville Car Rentals,** 12 Palmer St (☎4772 1093; fax 4721 3678). $38-60 per day, with 100km limited mileage. **Independent Rentals,** 25 Yeatman St, Hyde Park (☎4721 4766). Weekly rentals start at $192.50.

**Automobile Club: RACQ,** 635 Sturt St (24hr. ☎4721 4888). Open M-F 7:30am-5:30pm, Sa-Su 8am-noon.

**Taxis: Taxi Townsville** (☎4713 1008). 24hr. service.

## ⚡🔢 ORIENTATION AND PRACTICAL INFORMATION

Although Townsville is a large city with a complicated lay-out, the downtown area is thankfully easy to negotiate. Buses pull into the Transit Centre on **Palmer St,** which is also where most hostels are located. From there, it's only a 10min. walk over the **Ross River** bridge and up Dean St to the open-air **Flinders Mall.** The beach and many nice restaurants are set along **The Strand,** a street that runs beside the ocean for several kilometers. **Castle Hill** looms to the east, accessible both by road and a relatively steep walking trail.

**Tourist office: Visitor Information Centre** (☎4721 3660), is the big circular kiosk in the Flinders Mall. Open M-F 9am-5pm, Sa-Su 9am-1pm. **Department of Environment Information Centre,** 2-68 Flinders St (☎4721 2399; fax 4771 5578), answers marine and national park questions. Open M-F 9am-5pm.

**Currency Exchange: Bank of Queensland,** 16 Stokes St (☎4772 1799), up from Flinders Mall on the left, often has the best rates with the shortest lines. $5 commission. Open M-Th 9:30am-4pm, F 9:30am-5pm. **Westpac,** 337 Flinders Mall (☎4722 8200), also has great rates, but a $7 commission. Open M-Th 9:30am-4pm, F 9:30am-5pm.

**ATMs:** Machines are in Flinders Mall for both Cirrus and Plus transactions.

**Police:** Corner of Stanley and Sturt St (☎4760 7777). Open 24hr.

**Hospital: General Hospital,** 1 Eyre St (☎4781 9211, emergency ☎4781 9753).

**Internet Access: Internet Den,** 265 Flinders Mall (☎4721 4500). 1hr. $7. Open daily 7am-midnight. **Javanet Café,** on Palmer St (☎4772 5595), in the Transit Centre complex. 1hr. $5.50. Open M-W and F 9:30am-10pm, Th 9:30am-8pm, Sa-Su 11am-7pm.

**Post Office: General Post Office,** 252 Flinders St (☎4771 6133; fax 4721 1219), at the Denham St entrance to Flinders Mall. Open M-F 8:30am-5:30pm. *Poste Restante* open M-F, 9:30am-4:30pm. **Postal code:** 4810.

**Phone Code:** 07

**QUEENSLAND**

## 🏠 ACCOMMODATIONS

As Townsville is more of a transportation hub for backpackers than a tourist destination, its hostels are less luxurious than those elsewhere. Most are near the Transit Centre. Linen is usually free; expect a $10 key deposit.

**Globetrotters,** 45 Palmer St (☎4771 3242; email globe@ultra.net.au). Just east of the Transit Centre. Good deals on Magnetic Island ferry-and-hostel packages. Laundry, pool, BBQ, TV, tropical garden. Reception daily 6:30am-6:30pm. Dorms $18; twins $42, with A/C $44; ensuite triple $57, as a twin $44. VIP.

**Reef Lodge,** 4 Wickham St (☎4721 1112; fax 4721 1405). Off Flinders St East. Cozy rooms have fridges. Free pickup from Transit Centre. Laundry, BBQ. Reception daily 8am-10pm. Dorms $15.50-16.50; doubles $36; motel rooms $49.50.

**Transit Centre Backpackers** (☎(1800) 62 88 36; fax 4721 2328; www.tcback-packer.com.au). Surprisingly quiet for its bus terminal location, Backpackers has spacious dorms and clean bathrooms. The place has little atmosphere, but it's perfect when your backpack's too heavy to carry anywhere else. Laundry, TV room. Reception daily 5:30am-11:30pm. Dorms $16.50; singles $28.50; twins $35.50; doubles $37.50, with bath, TV, and fridge $44. VIP.

**Southbank Village Backpackers,** 35 McIlwraith St (☎4771 5849), across from the bus terminal. Go left out of the terminal and walk through the BP petrol station. This hostel is comprised of 7 stilt houses which show their age, but new management has begun renovation. Reception daily 8am-8pm. Singles $13; twins $30; doubles $28.

**Coral Lodge B&B,** 32 Hale St (☎(1800) 61 46 13; fax 4721 6461; urwelcum @ultra.net.au). From Flinders Mall, follow Stokes St for 4 blocks, turn left on Hale; it's on the left. One of only two B&Bs in town. All rooms have A/C, TV, and fridge. Singles $50; twins and doubles $60. Self-contained singles $65; twins and doubles $75.

**The Rocks,** 20 Cleveland Terrace (☎4771 5700; fax 4771 5711). At this B&B, hardwood floors, 18th century furnishings, and a gorgeous harbor view can bid you good morning—as long as you book well ahead. Singles $87; twins and doubles $97-107.

## ◖ FOOD

Most of the city's restaurants are along The Strand and Flinders St East. Flinders Mall hosts the **Cotters Market,** with fruit, vegetables, and crafts Su 8:30am-2pm. Woolworth's **supermarket,** 126-150 Sturt St, is between Stanley and Stoke St (open M-F 8am-9pm, Sa 8am-5pm, Su 8:30am-1pm).

▧ **C Bar,** on Gregory St (☎4724 0333). At the corner of the Strand. Enjoy a great view of the ocean in this stylish café, where breakfast, lunch, and dinner can be served with a cigar, if you wish. Salmon omelettes $7, tortilla sandwiches from $6, and seafood kebabs $14. Open M-F 8:30am-10:30pm, Sa-Su 7:30am-10:30pm.

▧ **La Bamba Café,** 3B Palmer St (☎4771 6422). Near the corner of Dean St. Bright, colorful walls are filled with local art. Breakfasts start at $3, and huge, overflowing baguettes run $5-7. Open W-M 8am-2pm and 6pm-late.

**Magnetic House Café,** 145b Flinders St East (☎4771 2172). Recently voted the best in Townsville on a radio show, this is the place to enjoy coffee, tea, and breakfast all day. "Feast-size" portions of pasta $11, and salads run between $5 and $11. Open M-Tu and Th-Sa 11am-4pm and 6:30pm until late, Su 9:30am-2pm.

**Cactus Jack's,** 17-21 Palmer St (☎4721 1478). Their famous margaritas are a good deal during Happy Hour (5-7pm) for $4, and even better during "Margaritaville" on W for $3.50. Popular steak sandwich for $10. Open daily 5pm-late.

**Coffee On Sturt,** 254 Sturt St (☎4771 3661). A small café with the best banana splits. Salads and vegetarian options $7-10. Movie deal—dinner, dessert, drink, and cinema voucher for $16.50. Open Su-Th 10am-10pm, F-Sa 10am-midnight.

**Heritage Café 'n' Bar,** 137 Flinders St East (☎4771 2799). A little of the bohemian coffeehouse vibe, with delicious pasta dishes for $8-9 and massive garden salad for $7.50. Thursday after 6pm, a bucket of prawns and a XXXX beer or glass of wine costs only $7.50. Open M-Th 6pm-late, F 11am-3pm and 5pm-late, Sa-Su 5pm-late.

**Caffe Toto,** 51 Palmer St (☎4721 1227). Outstanding Italian meals, with indoor and outdoor dining areas. Plates of pasta ($8.50-12.50) are rich and filling. Before 7pm, backpackers get a free beer with dinner. Open M-F 11:30am-late, Sa-Su 8am-late.

QUEENSLAND

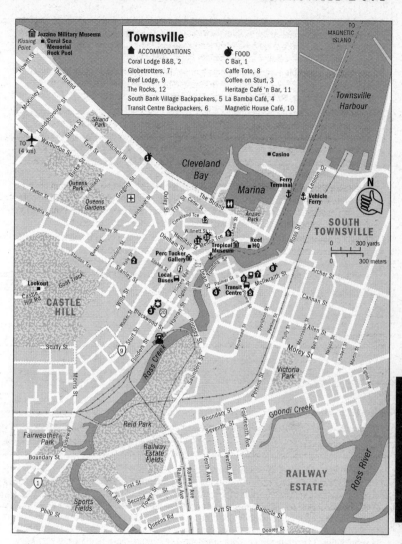

**Townsville**

⌂ ACCOMMODATIONS
Coral Lodge B&B, 2
Globetrotters, 7
Reef Lodge, 9
The Rocks, 12
South Bank Village Backpackers, 5
Transit Centre Backpackers, 6

● FOOD
C Bar, 1
Caffe Toto, 8
Coffee on Sturt, 3
Heritage Café 'n Bar, 11
La Bamba Café, 4
Magnetic House Café, 10

QUEENSLAND

## ◣ DIVING

**Kelso Reef,** Townsville's closest access to the Great Barrier Reef, is home to over 400 kinds of coral and schools of tropical fish. These sites are on the outer reef and are fairly well preserved, but call ahead to dive companies because high winds can obscure visibility. However, Townsville's best dive site isn't on the reef. In 1911, the ◣**S. S. Yongala** went down in the tropical waters off the coast of Townsville; the still-intact shipwreck is considered one of the world's best wreck sites and one of Australia's best dives. But note that the dive requires advanced certification.

**Sun City Watersports** (☎ 4771 6527). A small operation that offers the only daytrip to the Yongala wreck. The boat is functional and nothing more, but the company offers some of the best guided dives in Northern Queensland. The company also makes daytrips to the reef. Yongala trip W and Su; $179, $199 with gear. Reef trips from $120.

**Pure Pleasure Cruises,** Great Barrier Reef Wonderland, Flinders St East (☎4721 3555). Specializes in daytrips to Kelso Reef on a hi-speed catamaran, with snorkeling, fishing, or diving. $122, diving $155. Ask about "Reefpacker" specials, including a day on the reef and 2-nights free lodging at a participating hostel for $125.

**Dancing With Dolphins** (☎4772 4773; www.dancingwithdolphins.com.au). Sailing trip to the reef and Yongala. Departs M and F 6:30am. 3-day trip $435, with gear $485.

**Pacific Dive Services,** Tobruk Pool, The Strand (☎(0417) 77 00 59). NAUI certification courses from $345. 2-day trip from $390. 3-day also available.

## ⊙ SIGHTS

Although Townsville isn't known for its sights, there's enough here to convince travelers to postpone that trip to Magnetic Island for a day.

**REEFHQ.** The center features the world's first indoor coral reef—a 2.5 million liter aquarium that scientists have rigged to work like a reef in the ocean. Tours and shows almost every hour, including a visit to the working sea turtle research facility. (2-68 Flinders St. ☎4750 0800. Open daily 9am-5pm. $16, children $7, families $38.)

**MUSEUM OF TROPICAL QUEENSLAND.** New museum has exhibits on coral and shipwreck archaeology. (78-102 Flinders St. ☎4726 0606. Open daily 9am-5pm.)

**OMNIMAX THEATER.** Shows films on the hour between 10am and 4pm. Check with the theater for current flicks. (In the Great Barrier Reef complex on Flinders St East. ☎4721 1481. $12, students and concessions $10, family $30.)

**BILLABONG SANCTUARY.** Kangaroos wander this sprawling wildlife park. Several daily presentations allow you to get up-close and personal with wombats, pythons, and more. (17km south of Townsville. ☎4478 8344; www.billabongsanctuary.com.au. Open daily 8am-5pm. $20, students and seniors $15, children $10, families $47.)

**AQUARIUS ON THE BEACH.** For the best city view without the challenge of Castle Hill, have a drink at the 14th floor restaurant of this local hotel. (75 The Strand. ☎4772 4255. Restaurant open Tu-Sa from 6:30pm.)

## ◮ ACTIVITIES

Most of Townsville's tourists just take a walk along The Strand looking for excitement, but adventures are a only phone call away. **Right Training,** 53 Cheyne St, Pimlico (☎4725 4571), offers a 2hr. abseiling and rock climbing combo for $54. **Castle Hill** has some challenging **walking paths** that lead to spectacular views of Townsville. Bring water and sturdy hiking boots, because the paths can be steep, slippery, and long. **Coral Sea Skydivers,** 14 Plume St, leads tandem jumps daily, as well as 2-day and 5-day certification courses for solo jumps. (☎4772 4889; www.coralseaskydivers.com.au. Tandem $220-320. Book ahead.) **Detour Coaches,** Shop 5 in the Great Barrier Reef Wonderland Complex (☎4721 5977), jaunts to Billabong Sanctuary for $32. Plan ahead: they have 11 tours, but not all of them leave every day. **White Water Rafting: Raging Thunder Adventures** takes the rapids on Tu, Th, and Su. (☎4030 7990; www.ragingthunder.com.au. Rafting $133; kayaking $120.)

## ◪ NIGHTLIFE

Appropriately called **The Bank,** 166-173 Flinders St East, this bank-turned-nightclub prices drinks at $3 until 10pm, all night for college students. (☎4771 6148. Open W-Sa 8pm-5am. Tu basic spirits $1 until 1am. Cover $3; smart dress. No cover W or Th-Sa before 10pm.) **Mad Cow,** 129 Flinders St East, features less drinking, live music downstairs W and Su, and no strict dress code. More tavern than nightclub, three pool tables contribute to the calm-as-a-cow atmosphere. (☎4771 5727. W "Cowioki" nights. Open M-Th 8pm-3am, F-Sa 8pm-5am, Su 7pm-1:30am. No cover.) A favorite hangout for young locals is **Bullwinkle's Bar & Cabaret,** 108 Flinders St. Every other night drinks are $3 until 11pm, and just one dollar on Tuesdays until

1am. (☎4771 5647. Cover $4-5. Open daily 8pm-5am.) Test your connoisseur skills at **Portraits Wine Bar,** 151 Flinders St East. Wine-tasting occurs the first Tu of every month; members $8; don't worry, membership is free. (☎4771 3335. Open M-F noon-late, Sa 6pm-late. Drinks $2.50 M-F 5-7pm. Live music weeknights 8pm-midnight.) The **Exchange Hotel,** 151 Flinders St East, specializes in beer, and lots of it; pots are only $1. Open jam session Th night for anyone dying to belt out some tunes. (☎4771 3335. Open M-Sa 8am-5am, Su 8am-noon.)

# MAGNETIC ISLAND

"Maggie Island?" Townsville natives will say with a shrug of the shoulders, "that's just a suburb of Townsville." If pressed, however, the source of their contempt will often emerge: envy. After all, it's almost always sunny, the beaches are wide and inviting, and pockets of eucalyptus trees are dotted with wild koalas. The 20km coast on the island's east side is the only inhabited area; most of the island is national park. Transportation involves rolling out of bed and walking into the nearest forest. On less crowded beaches, or when young children aren't around, people bathe in the buff. Understandably, backpackers flock here in huge numbers. But even in the peak season, with the Australian school holiday crowd mixed in, there still seems to be plenty of room to stretch out in solitude.

## TRANSPORT

The quickest way to get to Maggie Island is with **Sunferries Magnetic Island,** 168-192 Flinders St East (☎4771 3855). Ferries depart daily from Flinders St (30min., 11 per day, $15 return) and the Breakwater terminal on Sir Leslie Thieses Dr (20min., 14 per day, $15 return). If you have wheels, the only way to get them across the water is on Capricorn Barge Company's **Magnetic Island Car Ferry,** located all the way down Palmer St. You, your car, and up to five friends can chug to the island for $102 return. (☎4772 5422. 1hr.; M-F 6 per day, Sa-Su 3 per day. Book ahead.)

There are less than 20km of sealed roads on the island, and the bus system does a fine job of covering all of them. **Magnetic Island Buses** (☎4778 5130) runs roughly every 50min; stops are marked by blue signs. Tickets are sold on the bus ($1.80-4.10), but the better deal is a one-day ($11) or two-day ($13) unlimited pass, available from the bus driver. Buses operate M-Sa 5:25am-11:50pm, Su 6:50am-8:50pm. Renting a "moke" (an open-air, golf-cart-like auto) is super-popular. Try **Moke Magnetic,** in the Picnic Bay Mall, $40 per day plus 44¢ per km. (☎4778 5377. Open daily 8am-5pm. $100 deposit.)

## ORIENTATION

The island is roughly triangular in shape, and almost all accommodations, restaurants, and activities are located along the east coast. Instead of having one town that serves as the island center, civilization is spread out. **Horseshoe Bay,** a 30min. bus ride from the ferry, is the island's northernmost populated area and the watersports center. Heading south, **Arcadia** is the next cove of civilization, a 15min. bus ride from the ferry, on the shores of **Geoffrey Bay** and **Alma Bay. Nelly Bay** is next, a 20min. walk from Picnic Bay and home to the island grocery store. **Picnic Bay,** the culinary hub of the island, sits at its southernmost point. The road continues westward (unsealed at the end, no mokes allowed) to **West Point.**

## PRACTICAL INFORMATION

**Tourist Office: Information Centre** (☎4778 5155; fax 4778 5158), next to jetty in Picnic Bay. Tour and transport bookings. Open M-F 8am-4:30pm, Sa-Su 8am-1pm.

**Travel Office: Magnetic Travel,** 55 Sooning St (☎4778 5343), in the shopping plaza at Nelly Bay. Open M-F 8:30am-5:30pm, Sa 8:30am-12:30pm.

**Currency Exchange:** There are **no banks** or **ATMs** on Magnetic Island. The info center does credit card cash withdrawals, charging $2 per $100 withdrawn. The **post office** is also the local agent for Commonwealth Bank.

QUEENSLAND

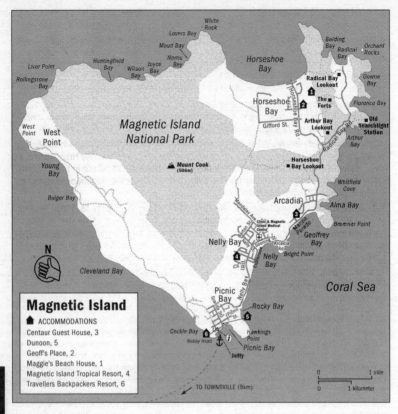

**Magnetic Island**

⛺ ACCOMMODATIONS
Centaur Guest House, 3
Dunoon, 5
Geoff's Place, 2
Maggie's Beach House, 1
Magnetic Island Tropical Resort, 4
Travellers Backpackers Resort, 6

**Police:** On the corner of Granite and Picnic St, Picnic Bay (24hr. ☎4778 5270). Open M 8:30am-noon, W and F 8:30am-2pm.

**Medical Center: Clinic,** 72 Sooning St, Nelly Bay (☎4778 5107). Open M-F 9am-11am, Sa-Su 9am-2pm. The **Magnetic Island Medical Centre,** 68 Sooning St, Nelly Bay (24hr. ☎4778 5614), does diving medical exams for $55. Open M, W, F 9am-12:30pm and 2:30-5pm, Tu 3-6pm, Th 8:30am-12:30pm, Sa 9am-noon.

**Taxi: Magnetic Island Taxis** (☎13 10 08) charges about $15 to cross the island.

**Internet Access: Courtyard Mall Cyber Café,** shop 2 Courtyard Mall, The Esplanade, Picnic Bay (☎4778 5407). 1hr. $7. Open daily 8:30am-5:30pm. Terminals are also available in some hostels and at the **Tourist Information Centre** for $6 per hour.

**Post Office:** Picnic Bay Arcade, The Esplanade (☎4778 5118). Open M-F 8:30am-5pm, Sa 9am-noon. **Postal code:** 4819.

**Phone Code:** 07.

# ▗ ACCOMMODATIONS

Although most hostels offer regular courtesy buses, it can still be inconvenient to move around the island. Consider location when choosing your hostel. Remember that camping is prohibited in the national park, but one hostel (Geoff's Place) has campground facilities. Standard key deposit is $5-10.

**Centaur Guest House,** 27 Marine Pde, Alma Bay (☎4778 5668, freecall ☎(1800) 65 56 80; www.bpf.com.au). The best dorms on the island and believed to be the oldest hostel in Australia. Free activities include wine-and-cheese night (Sa) and pancake and ice cream night (Th). Internet 1hr. $5. Reception daily 7am-8pm; afterhours check-in available. Dorms $18; singles $33; twins and doubles $39; 5th night free. YHA, VIP.

**Magnetic Island Tropical Resort,** 56 Yates St, Nelly Bay (☎4778 5955; fax 4778 5601; tropres@byte-tsv.net.au). A beautiful collection of cabins at various levels of luxury. Family-oriented. A fair trek from the beach, but lots of space with a relaxing atmosphere. Dorms are in large, clean 6-bed ensuite huts. Pool, hot tub, laundry. Internet. Reception daily 7am-10:30pm. Dorms $19; doubles $55, extra person $11. YHA, VIP.

**Dunoon,** corner of The Esplanade and Granite St, Picnic Bay (☎4778 5161; fax 4778 5532). A good deal for groups—beachfront ensuite cottages with full kitchen, dining area, and living room. Reception daily 7:30am-5:30pm. $108; book ahead.

**Maggie's Beach House,** 1 Pacific Dr, Horseshoe Bay (☎(1800) 00 15 44; www.mag giesbeachhouse.com.au). Across the street from the beach, behind the Horseshoe Bay bus stop. Opened in September 1999, Maggie's is the new party place in town. Nightly mixers include toga and rugby parties. Café, laundry, Internet. Reception daily 8am-8pm. Dorms $21-24; doubles $78.

**Travellers Backpackers Resort,** 1 The Esplanade, Picnic Bay (☎4778 5166, freecall ☎(1800) 00 02 90; email travellers@ultra.net.au). Right in front of the pier. A former motel recently converted into a giant hostel with 4 bars and Maggie's only public nightclub. Kitchen, pool, Internet. Meals from $6.50. Reception daily 7:30am-midnight. Ensuite dorms $19; twins and doubles $20; singles $44. YHA, VIP.

**Geoff's Place,** 40 Horseshoe Bay Rd (☎4778 5577; www.geoffsplace.com.au). One of the larger backpacker joints on the island, this hostel is comprised of basic wooden huts 5min. from the beach. If you're looking for nightlife, Geoff's club has guests jamming on the weekend nights. Laundry, pool. Reception daily 8am-8pm. Tent sites $9, powered $18; dorms $13.50-19.50; doubles $44. YHA, VIP.

## FOOD AND NIGHTLIFE

Magnetic Island is known for relaxation, not gourmet cuisine. The center of gastronomical gravity is rather pricey **Picnic Bay.** Magnetic Island **Supermarket,** 55 Sooning St, Nelly Bay is the largest on the island (open M-F 8:30am-7pm, Sa 8:30am-5:30pm, Su 9am-2pm). If you'd like to head out for a night on the town, you really have only one option. **The Shed,** a bar and nightclub in Travellers Backpackers, has DJ dance tunes F-Su. (Open 10pm-3am. No cover.)

**Nelly Bay Bakery Café,** 53 Sooning St, Nelly Bay (☎4758 1400). An extensive menu of baked goods and 15 varieties of pizzas for $12-18. Open daily 8am-9:30pm.

**Possum's Café,** 55 Sooning St, Nelly Bay (☎4778 5409). Besides delectable sandwiches ($3-4), they also make picnic baskets for romantic afternoons ($25 with champagne). Open M-Tu 8am-5pm, W-Sa 8am-7pm, Su 8am-3pm.

**Green Frog Café,** 1 The Esplanade, Picnic Bay (☎4778 5833). Specializes in fruit juices ($4-5) and the island's finest coffee. Open Sa-Tu 8am-4:30pm, W-F 8:30am-4:30pm.

**The Bakery,** 22 McCabe St, Arcadia (☎4778 5800). Always stocked with freshly made patisserie delights. Open daily 7am-4pm.

**Blue Waters Gallery Café,** 5 Bright Ave, Arcadia (☎4778 5645). The walls are lined with local paintings. A full breakfast costs $5.50, made-to-order sandwiches start at $4, and pastas are $10. Open daily 7:30-10am, 11:30am-2:30pm, and 6pm-late.

**Magnetic Mango** (☎4778 5018). At the end of Apjohn St, Horseshoe Bay. This sprawling mango plantation serves fresh mango juice and smoothies for $3. Any purchase from the kitchen gives you free access to the plantation—complete with goats, goldmine, and mini-golf course. Open Sa-W from 10am.

## DIVING

Magnetic Island offers some of the most inexpensive dive opportunities in all of Queensland. A plethora of small wrecks and reefs provide endless exploration.

QUEENSLAND

**Pleasure Dives,** shop 2 in the Arcadia Resort (☎ 4778 5788). Incredible deals on PADI certification classes from the shore (3 days, $149), including an advanced course at the *Yongala* (2 days, 5 dives; $299). They also offer courses on the outer reef (4 days, $299) and dives for advanced divers at the *Yongala* wreck ($170, with gear $205).

**Magnetic Island Dive Centre,** first arcade of Picnic Bay Mall (☎ 4758 1399). Free pickup and drop off from any island accommodation. Four-day PADI island certification classes $175; mixed island and reef course $275. Advanced courses on the outer reef $245. Advanced courses to *Yongala* $325. Certified dives $35, for 2 $55; the company can provide your buddy. Resort dives $60.

**Pure Pleasure Cruises** (☎ 4778 5155), in the tourist office at Picnic Bay. The largest company with the most expensive trips. Outer reef snorkeling daytrip $122, families $305. One resort dive $66 extra; 2 certified dives $33 extra.

# ◪ ACTIVITIES

**TOURS.** Careen around Magnetic Island with ◪**Tropicana Tours** and its zany, awesome owner Steve. On his 4hr. afternoon tour, pile into a 10-seat Jeep Wrangler, cruise to the Beach Boys, feed lorikeets, see beaches—and then finish with a beer at sunset. *(2/26 Picnic St. ☎ 4758 1800; www.tropicanatours.com.au. $75; more mild morning version $45.)* **Sunbird Tours** is a more nature-conscious way of touring Maggie. Visit mangroves, see birds, and learn about ecology with Deborah, the company's owner and a former environmental educator. *(☎ 4758 1211. 3hr. $40.)*

**GREAT OUTDOORS.** The Magnetic Island National Park has several fabulous walking tracks. The most popular is the Forts Walk (4km; 1½hr.), which virtually guarantees koala spotting. It's best to go from 4-6pm, when the critters are just waking up. Another option is to take the island path (8km; 3hr.) that leads from Picnic Bay through wetlands and mangroves to West Point. Make sure you bring water and sturdy shoes. Bluey's Horseshoe Ranch has a bush ride and a popular beach option. *(38 Gifford St, Horseshoe Bay. ☎ 4778 5109. 2hr. $50; half-day $70.)*

**WATER ACTIVITIES. Magnetic Island Sea Kayaks** departs daily at 8:15am and returns about noon. *(93 Horseshoe Bay Rd, Horseshoe Bay. ☎ 4778 5254. $35, including a light tropical breakfast.)* **Jazza** offers sailing tours around Maggie Island on its 12m yacht, featuring a private trumpet concert by the skipper. Bring only a bathing suit and a love of jazz. *(☎ 4778 5530. Open daily 10am-4pm. $60.)*

**OTHER ACTIVITIES.** At **Magnetic Island Mini Golf,** 18 holes of putt-putt can be followed by pool, ping pong, air hockey, and more. Competitive, who's competitive? *(27 Sooning St, Nelly Bay. ☎ 4758 1066. Golf $4.50, children $3. Ask about package deals with other amusements.)* Visit koalas, wombats, emus, and talking cockatoos at the **Koala Park Oasis.** *(Pacific Dr, Horseshoe Bay. ☎ 4778 5260. Open daily 9am-5pm. $10, children $4.)*

# CARDWELL

A small village between Mission Beach and Townsville, Cardwell brushes up against an appealing beach perfect to admire, but don't take a dip unless you're a croc—salties may be lurking. The town is in the middle of several large farming communities, making it an ideal stop to fuel the wallet. Cardwell's hostel owners often arrange **fruit-picking work** ($10-13 per hr.) for their guests.

    **Cardwell Air Charters,** 131 Bruce Hwy, runs scenic flights over Hinchinbrook Island and the **Undara Lava Tubes.** (☎ 4066 8468. 40min.; $75, children $37.50.) In nearby **Ingham** (53km south) roars the towering **Wallaman Falls.** At 305m, it's Australia's **largest waterfall,** and most impressive during the Wet.

    Most of the establishments in town are along Cardwell's patch of the Bruce Hwy, locally known as **Victoria St.** The "transit centre" is just a swath of bitumen in the center of town called Brasenose St. McCafferty's and Greyhound run to **Townsville** (2hr., 9-10 per day, $24) and **Cairns** (3¼hr., 10-11 per day, $20).

The YHA-affiliated **Kookaburra Holiday Park and Hinchinbrook Hostel,** 175 Bruce Hwy, is the best hostel in town. It offers free pickup from the bus stop, kitchen, pool, and Internet. (☎4066 8648; fax 4066 8910; email kookaburra@znet.net.au. Reception M-F 8am-7pm, Sa-Su 8am-6pm. Tent sites for 2 $16.50; dorms $16.50; twins and doubles $40; motel doubles $55.) If your holiday in Cardwell is a working one, the managers of **Cardwell Backpackers Hostel,** 178 Bowen St, behind Muddie's restaurant, arrange farm work for guests and bus them over. Privacy here is sacrificed for a friendly, communal atmosphere; guests sleep in a 12-bed dorm enclosed by a partition. (☎4066 8014. Kitchen, TV room, laundry. Dorms $10; if locally employed $14.) **Pacific Palms Caravan Park and Backpackers,** 186 Bruce Hwy, near the corner of Sheridan St, offers dorms, BBQ, and laundry. (☎4066 8671. Reception 7am-8pm. Dorms $11; tent sites $11, powered $14.)

🍴**Annie's Kitchen,** 107 Victoria St, makes a mean veggie burger for $4 and a huge milkshake for $3. (☎4066 8818. Open daily 6am-8pm.) **Muddies,** 221 Victoria St, is another local favorite. Walk past the big red crab to sample their seafood, which is pricey but elegant. (☎4066 8907. Open daily 10am-9pm, takeaway available. Sandwiches $6-10; full meals $14-20.) The 5-Star **supermarket,** 198 Victoria St, offers a good selection for a small town. Open daily 6am-8pm.

# HINCHINBROOK ISLAND

Across the Hinchinbrook Channel, just 4km from Cardwell, is Hinchinbrook Island and the untrammeled wilderness of its national park, where granite peaks loom above mangrove swamps. A trip to Hinchinbrook is a virtually human-free addition to the Queensland experience. The famous Thorsborne Trail (32km; 4 days) is the most popular hike on the island, but a limit of 40 people are allowed on the trail at one time. Book at least two or three months in advance.

🔋 **PRACTICAL INFORMATION.** Daytrips to the island don't require bookings, but overnight camping trips will not happen spontaneously. Get a permit in advance, read up on various trail options, and piece together a terrific camping trip (camping permits $4 per night). The folks at the QPWS, located at the **Rainforest and Reef Centre,** 142 Victoria St, Cardwell, are anxious to help. Located on the north side of town near the jetty, the center issues camping permits and has a helpful pamphlet on the **Thorsborne Trail,** which includes a map and lots of info on camping, hiking, and wildlife. (☎4066 8601; fax 4066 8116. Open M-F 8am-4:30pm, Sa-Su 8am-4pm. Donations welcome.) Rangers recommend spending two or three nights on the trail. One popular four-day itinerary takes campers to the three main campsites: **Little Ramsay** (6.5km), **Zoe Bay** (17km), and **Mulligan Falls** (24km).

📧 **TRANSPORT.** Luckily, you don't need a camping permit in order to enjoy Hinchinbrook, you can take a daily ferry to enjoy a quick taste of wilderness. **Hinchinbrook Island Ferries,** 131 Bruce Hwy, features sightings of **dugongs,** an endangered sea cow. One-way tickets are useful if you do have a camping permit and want to walk the length of the island. (☎4066 8270. $59, $89 return.) Then **Hinchinbrook Wilderness Safaris** will pick you up at George Point and bring you back to Lucinda, south of Cardwell. (☎4777 8307. $40.)

⛰ **HIKING.** If you crave more rugged terrain, Hinchinbrook also has several impressive mountains. **Nina Peak** is the most accessible, and the only one for which a separate permit isn't required. The hike is 10-15min. each way and features a great view of mangroves. The other mountains have no trails, require permits (book one year in advance), and are quite challenging—even for experienced hikers. The largest is **Mt. Bowen,** where up to four groups are allowed each month. With even more draconian permitting restrictions than the island itself, the other mountains only allow two groups per month. On the south end of the island, the **Mt. Starloch** hike takes you on a wild bushwalk to the remains of an American B-17 bomber which crashed on the island during WWII; **Hinchinbrook Island Safaris** ferries to this difficult hike from Lucinda ($50 return).

QUEENSLAND

# MISSION BEACH

Rapidly becoming a major backpacker destination, this nearly continuous stretch of beach is often confused with Shangri-la. A utopia for those seeking rest during their northern trek, Mission Beach is staggeringly beautiful and so far unmarred by tourism. The untouched corals and sand cays of the reefs off Mission Beach make it one of the best diving spots on the Great Barrier Reef. Divers share virgin sites with manta rays, giant grouper, and dolphins.

## ■ TRANSPORT

Greyhound and McCafferty's stop in Mission Beach several times daily. Both run to **Cairns** (2¼hr., 5 per day, $12) and **Townsville** (3¼hr., 4 per day, $34). Once you arrive in town, a hostel courtesy bus will take you to your accommodation. You can also use these buses to move around during your stay, but at night you'll need to use the $3 **Mission Beach Bus Service** (☎4068 7400), which runs about once per hour. **Island Coast Travel,** in the Homestead Centre at Mission Beach, is a bus and rail ticket agent. (☎4068 7187. Open M-F 9am-6pm, Sa 9am-noon.)

## ✴ ⁊ ORIENTATION AND PRACTICAL INFORMATION

The region known as Mission Beach is actually a group of four communities strung along 14km of waterfront property. From north to south, these towns are: **Bigil Bay, Mission Beach, Wongaling Beach,** and **South Mission Beach.** The main streets are **Porter's Promenade,** which runs through Mission Beach proper, and **Cassowary Drive,** which runs through Wongaling. A popular landmark is the **frighteningly large cassowary,** a statue set in the center of Wongaling Beach. Just off the coast are the **Family Islands,** including the daytrip destination **Dunk Island** (see p. 380).

You'll find the area tourist office in the **Wet Tropics Information Centre** on Porters Promenade, just north of the Mission Beach town. (☎4068 7099; fax 4068 7066. Open M-Sa 9am-5pm, Su 9am-4pm.) Next door, you'll find another valuable resource—the **Community for Coastal and Cassowary Conservation,** which stocks a wealth of brochures. (☎4068 7197. Open daily 10am-5pm.)

Mission Beach services include: the **police** (☎4068 8422), 500m past said frighteningly large cassowary at the corner of Webb Rd and Cassowary Dr in Wongaling Beach; the **medical center,** on Cassowary Dr between Mission and Wongaling beaches (24hr. ☎4068 8174; open Su-F 8am-6pm, Sa 8am-noon); **Beverley's,** Shop 15, Hub Shopping Centre, where foreign currency and traveler's checks can be exchanged for no fee (☎4068 7365; open daily 9am-5pm); and the **post office,** 32 Porter's Promenade, which also serves as the local **bank.** Stop by for credit card withdrawal or Commonwealth Bank services. (☎4068 7200. Open M-F 9am-5pm.) There is also an **ATM** at the Mission Beach Resort. **Postal code:** 4852.

## ⋔ ACCOMMODATIONS

All hostels offer free pickup at the bus station and do tour bookings.

**The Treehouse,** Bingil Bay Rd, Bingil Bay (☎4068 7137; fax 4068 7028). A YHA-affiliate perched on a hill, not a tree. The beach is a bit of a trek (2.5km), but a free hostel courtesy bus runs the route. BBQ, pool, laundry, tiny grocery store, and comfy reading space. Reception 6:30am-8:30pm. Dorms $17; twins and doubles $46.

**Scotty's Mission Beach House,** 167 Reid Rd (☎4068 8676; email scottys@znet.net.au). At the end of Webb St, off Cassowary Dr. Free evening drinks and a pool that permits topless bathing definitely make Scotty's the partygoer's hostel. This accommodation also has a great location—the beach is just across the street, and Wongaling is a 10min. walk. Laundry, TV room, kitchen, and Internet. Reception daily 7:30am-7pm. Dorms $18; twins and doubles $38, ensuite $49. VIP.

**Mission Beach Backpackers Lodge,** 28 Wongaling Beach Rd (☎4068 8317; fax 4068 8616; email mblodge@znet.net.au). From Cassowary Dr, turn onto Wongaling Beach Rd at the aforementioned frightening large cassowary; the hostel is on your left. It's a 2-

story house with spacious rooms, pool, laundry, and Internet. Reception daily 8am-12:30pm and 1:30-8pm. Dorms $18; twins $37; doubles $39. VIP.

**Tropical Hibiscus Caravan Park,** Cassowary Dr, Wongaling Beach (☎ 4068 8138; fax 4068 8778). About 500m from the beach and 100m from the Wongaling shopping center. A peppy family manages this park with a fabulous location. Pool, BBQ, tour bookings, and a shopping plaza practically next door. Linen for cabins $3. Tent sites $13, powered $16.50; cabins for 2 $40, ensuite $60.50.

## FOOD

Most restaurants are concentrated at the village green along Porter's Promenade. If you're looking for **supermarket** staples, check Cut-Price in Mission Beach or Foodstore in Wongaling Beach (both open daily 8am-7pm).

**Toba,** 37 Porter's Promenade (☎ 4068 7852). At the Village Green. Serves a variety of Southeast Asian cuisine including Indonesian fried noodles, Vietnamese, and Japanese specialties (mains $10.50-18). All furniture is authentic Asian, and herbs are grown in the backyard. Open W-M 6pm-midnight.

**The Shrubbery Tavern,** 44 Marine Pde (☎ 4068 7803). One of the town's three licensed bars, this tavern on the water specializes in Greek and Mediterranean dishes (mains $13.50-20). The menu will tell you the restaurant's eggs are from "happy chickens" and that the greens are grown locally. Happy Hour 4:30-6pm. Closed Tu.

**Piccolo Paradise,** David St (☎ 4068 7008). On the Village Green. This café offers pasta, pizza, and a selection of espresso. Open daily 8am-9:30pm.

**Early Birds Coffee Shop** (☎ 4068 7299). At the corner of Campbell St and Porter's Promenade. Slightly less expensive than the other cafés in town with its breakfast special ($6). Open daily 7:30am-4:30pm.

**Ma Donovan's Bakery** (☎ 4068 8944). In Wongaling Beach's shopping center, to the right of our friend, the frighteningly large cassowary. Generously-sized focaccia pizzas ($3-4) and tempting "vanilla slices" ($1.30). Open M-F 6am-4pm, Sa 6am-2pm.

## SIGHTS AND ACTIVITIES

**DIVING. Mission Beach Dive Charters** is the only PADI dive center in town. In addition to a range of scuba courses, it arranges trips to the *Lady Bowen*, a 105-year-old shipwreck discovered in 1997. It also makes outer reef day trips, which include three dives. (☎ 4068 7277. Open water certification $295; shipwreck $125; outer reef $125.) **Friendship Cruises** is a smaller operation and a favorite of budget travelers. (☎ 4068 7262. Cruise $66, with certified dive $101, with intro dive $116.) **QuickCat** also makes trips to Dunk Island and the reef. (☎ 4068 8432. Transport $134; certified dive $55.)

**HIKING.** Several beautiful **walking tracks** are in the area. The incomprehensibly titled, *Walking Tracks in the Mission Beach Area*, a 25¢ pamphlet available at hostels and the tourist center describes several walks in the **Licuala State Forest.** The **Rainforest Circuit Walk** (1.3km; 30min.) is a jaunt through a rainforest under a 15m canopy of Licuala Fan Palms. Start at the carpark of the Tully-Mission Beach Rd. **Licuala Walking Track** (7.8km; 3hr.) stretches north through coastal lowland rainforest to the El Arish-Mission Beach Rd. **The Cutten Brothers Walk** (1.5km; 30min.) snakes through mangroves between Alexander Dr and Clump Point jetty. If you're interested in longer walks, the **Bicton Hill Track** (4km; starts 3km past the Wet Tropics Info Centre) and the **Kennedy Track** (7km; 4hr.) feature mangrove views, beach, and of course, loads of rainforest.

**OTHER ACTIVITIES. Bush 'n' Beach** offers short riding lessons and trotting on the beach. (☎ 4068 7893; bushnbeach@znet.net.au. 1½hr. trip $49.50; half-day $88, including brunch.) Also, whitewater rafting and kayaking packages are available through **R 'n' R** (☎ (1800) 07 90 39) and **Raging Thunder** (☎ 4030 7990; all trips $128). **Mission Beach Nature Tours** has canoe trips. (☎ 4068 8582. $75, including lunch.) **Jump the Beach** offers tandem skydiving several times daily. (☎ (1800) 63 80 05. 8000 ft. $228.)

# ▓ DAYTRIPS FROM MISSION BEACH

## DUNK ISLAND

Just off shore, the Family Islands are perhaps the best and shortest excursion from Mission Beach, and the perfect backdrop for a beach party or evening luau. Dunk Island, a.k.a. the "father island," lies just off-shore. The largest of the nuclear grouping, Papa Dunk is the only day-tripper destination. Nearby Bedarra, also known as "the mother," is uninhabited except for a hoity-toity resort. The "twins" are close together and only slightly farther out. The smaller land masses at the fringe of the group are the brothers, sisters, and the triplets. Big family.

There are two boats that service Dunk Island. Those looking to maximize time on the island should opt for the **Dunk Island Express Water Taxi,** Banfield Parade, near Scotty's on Wongaling Beach. (☎4068 8310. 10min., 6 per day, $26 return.) For lollygaggers wishing to prolong their cruise over to the island, check out **Dunk Island Ferry & Cruises,** which departs from Clump Point Jetty, 1km north of the village green. (☎4068 7211. 30-45min.; daily 8:45am and 10:30am; $26 return.) **Coral Sea Kayaking** has daytrips to Dunk including lunch, environmental interpretation, and snorkeling gear. (☎4068 9154. $80; shorter morning and afternoon trips $45.)

The **Dunk Island Resort** (☎4068 8199) monopolizes all island activities. If the room rates ($200 and up) seem prohibitive, don't despair. Just steps from the jetty are some of the most exquisite and cheapest campsites in North Queensland (permits $3.50 per person per night). The grounds are equipped with hot showers and limited cooking facilities, and the beach doesn't get any better than this. This isn't a well-kept secret, however, and it's small—book about a week in advance during the high season. **Dunk Island Watersports** (☎4068 8199) issues **camping permits** and hire a slew of water toys: paddle skis (1hr. $15), sailboards (1hr. $20), snorkel gear (1hr. $15), and catamarans (1hr. $25). The only place to eat on the island, besides the resort's fancy restaurant (resort guests only, please), is **BB's on the Beach,** next door to Watersports (☎4068 8199; open daily 11am-7pm); but it's cheaper to bring your own food. The main attractions on Dunk, aside from the postcard beaches, are the **walking tracks.** The local favorite is the walk circumscribing most of the island (10km; 2-3hr.), which combines Dunk history with diverse landscapes and a trip to the island's highest point. An easier option is the coastal hike (1km; 1hr.) up to **Muggy Muggy Beach** from the dock. No matter what, this island is a slam dunk.

## PARONELLA PARK

Just a little west of nowhere between Cairns and Mission Beach hides the Moorish castle of Paronella Park (☎4065 3225). Built in the 1930s by Spaniard José Paronella, this is a spot to ooh and aah over. When the main thoroughfare was diverted in the 1960s to what is now the Bruce Hwy, this enchanting park slipped from tourist itineraries into obscurity. New owners and rejuvenated advertising have revived tourist interest, but the crowds haven't swollen enough to cloud its waterfall, Lovers Lane Palm Grove, and the Bamboo Forest surroundings. Romance is in the air here: last year, about 30 couples said "I do" in the castle. The park has been discovered by the entertainment industry and has served as the backdrop for three movies, eight TV shows, a music video, and an international magazine's photo shoot. Enthusiastic park guides give tours of the grounds, and then leave you to explore on your own.

Unfortunately, this place is almost inaccessible via public transportation. If driving, look for signs along the Bruce Hwy for Paronella Park (the South Johnstone exit is the fastest. If you're not tying the knot or gawking at the handmade architecture, take some time to stroll down Kauri Ave or feed the fish and eels in the teeming waterfall pool from the ruins of the castle's grand staircase.The **ticket cottage** at the entrance provides a list of the park's horticultural highlights and some history. (Open daily 9am-5pm. Tours 40min., every 30min.

QUEENSLAND

Admission $13, children $6.50.) An adjacent **caravan park** blends into its surroundings. Caravan park guests get 24hr. access to the grounds, including a guided night walk (tent sites $12, powered $14; cabins from $32).

## INNISFAIL

North of Mission Beach en route to Cairns lies the community of Innisfail. This town offers few tourist attractions, but its unusual juxtaposition of architecture makes it worthwhile to cruise down the main drag, Edith St, where buildings that are run down stand alongside day-glo Art Deco structures. But those who stay in Innisfail are drawn to its year-round labor market, not its architecture.

Just north of Innisfail, the road to the **Atherton Tablelands** (see p. 392) branches off inland toward **Millaa Millaa.** The **railway station** is off the Bruce Hwy west of town, and the **bus stop** is on Edith St. McCafferty's and Greyhound run daily to **Cairns** (1¼hr., 9-10 per day, $12) and **Townsville** (3½hr., 9-10 per day, $34). The **Information Centre,** 24 Bruce Hwy, offers maps, brochures, and tour bookings. (☎4063 2000. Open M-F 9am-5pm, Sa-Su 10am-3pm.) The **post office** is on the corner of Rankin and Edith St. (☎4061 1077. Open M-F 8:30am-5pm.) **Postal code:** 4860.

■**The Codge Lodge,** 63 Rankin St, near the corner of Grace St, is billed as a sport-fishing resort, but non-fishing types need not shy away. Convenient to the town center, the lodge is hands-down the best budget accommodation in town. An immaculate kitchen and beautiful pool area come quite cheaply. (☎4061 8055; fax 4061 8155. Reception daily 7am-10pm. Dorms $18; singles $22; doubles $38. Book ahead during the Dry.) The folks at **The Endeavour International Backpackers Hostel,** 31 Glady St, arrange work on neighboring farms. From the rail station, follow the Bruce Hwy toward town until you reach Glady St, then turn right, and it'll be on the left. The Endeavour is clean and maintains a family atmosphere. (☎4061 6610; fax 4061 6003. Pool, laundry, shuttle to work. Dorms and twins $13 per person.)

**The Tropical Beer Garden,** 25 Ernest St, in The Crown Hotel (see above), has filling meals, outdoor seating, and a tropical mural. (☎4061 4722. Open Su-W 11:30am-2pm and 6-8pm, Th-Sa 6-9pm.) **Roscoe's Pizza and Pasta,** 170 Edith St, is divided into an Italian restaurant and pizza joint. (☎4061 6888. Restaurant open Tu-Su 6-10:30pm. Pizza place open Su-M 5-9:30pm, Tu-Th 5-10pm, F-Sa 5pm-midnight.

# FAR NORTH QUEENSLAND

The northeast corner of the continent, from Cairns north into Australia's last great frontier, is nothing short of heaven for rugged backpackers and outdoor adventurers. The Great Barrier Reef snakes close to shore here, luring divers with boat trips and visits to the spectacular corals on the reef. Vast swaths of tropical rainforest press up close to the Coral Sea by the craggy mountains of the Great Dividing Range. The rich variety of wildlife and untouched landscape prove that the Far North's greatest attraction is its natural beauty.

Cairns now caters to travelers with city comforts, but the more remote parts of this land remain untamed wilderness. The Captain Cook Hwy leads modern-day trailblazers north into the rainforest, which becomes incredibly dense around Cape Tribulation. Wilder yet is the Cape York peninsula, starting beyond Cooktown and stretching to the Torres Strait, which separates the Gulf of Carpentaria from the Coral Sea and Australia from Papua New Guinea. The most formidable of Australian roads dares travelers to make the harrowing journey to the tip.

## CAIRNS

The last sizeable city at the corner of the great tropical outback, Cairns is both the northern terminus of the backpacker route and the premier gateway to snorkeling and scuba diving on the Great Barrier Reef. Palm-lined avenues and lush gardens blossom with colors that rival the reef's coral and fish. While tidal mudflats preclude traditional beach activities, bars and parks provide plenty of diversions for

QUEENSLAND

travelers between forays off the coast. The atmosphere of Cairns (pronounced like beer "cans") is friendly, laid-back, and very touristy. More of a big town than a small city, most backpackers use Cairns as a home base for launching skydiving trips, scuba vacations, bungy jumps, and white-water adventures. In addition to this daredevil crowd, the city also caters to Asian luxury tourists. Often you will find store signs printed in both English and Japanese, and pricey opal stores stand next to cheap kebab stands. But fear not, the backpacker culture is alive and well.

---

### CAIRNS HIGHLIGHTS

**UNDERWATER WONDERLAND.** Scuba diving on the Great Barrier Reef, and learning about it first from Reef Teach (see p. 388).

**CULTURAL CATHARSIS.** Dancing, didgeridoo music, and Aboriginal narratives at Tjapukai (see p. 390).

**CYCLING.** Bandicoot Bicycle Tours through the tablelands (see p. 387).

**STIMULATING.** The pure adrenaline rush of sky diving (see p. 388).

**BIZARRE BAZAAR.** Music, art, and WWII oil tanks at Tank Arts Centre (see p. 386).

---

## ◪ TRANSPORT

**Airplanes:** The **airport** (☎ 4052 9744) is 6km north of Cairns on Captain Cook Hwy. Follow the signs. Domestic carriers Qantas (☎ 13 13 13) and Ansett (☎ 13 13 00) have daily flights to: **Adelaide** (5-8hr., 5-7 per day, $735); **Brisbane** (2hr., 9 per day, $309); **Canberra** (5hr., 10-13 per day, $672); **Darwin** (2-5hr., 6 per day, $523); **Hobart** (6-10hr., 6-7 per day, $795); **Melbourne** (5hr., 9 per day, $753); **Perth** (5-10hr., 6-9 per day, $789); and **Sydney** (3hr., 7-8 per day, $666). Smaller Flight West Airlines (☎ 13 23 92) has domestic flights and also flies to **Papua New Guinea.** Most hostels run a free shuttle bus airport pick-up service; just call from the terminal. Buses also run to town from just outside the terminal ($4.50). **Taxis** to town are about $12 and run 24hr.

**Trains:** The **train station** is wedged between Bunda St and the Cairns Central shopping mall on McLeod St. From the Esplanade, walk west on Spence St and it's on the right. Luggage lockers 24hr. $2. **Travel Centre Office** sells tickets. 10% YHA discount for long-distance trips. (☎ 4036 9341. Open M-F 9am-5pm, Sa 9am-noon, with early hours M-Tu, Th, Sa 6:45am-8am.) The **East Coast Discover Pass** ($249) covers rail from Cairns to **Sydney** and is good for up to 6 months. (See also **By Train,** p. 63.) Travel to **Brisbane** (31-32hr.; M-Tu, Th, Sa 8am; $159).

**Buses:** The **bus station** is at **Trinity Wharf,** on Wharf St. Open daily 6:15am-1am. Leave luggage at the gift shop ($2 per day). Coral Coaches (☎ 4031 7577) goes daily to: **Cape Tribulation** (4hr., 2 per day, $34); **Cooktown** (Inland: 5½hr.; 1 per day W, F-Sa; $53; Coastal: 8hr.; Tu, Sa (and Th June-Oct.); $59); **Karumba** (11½hr.; 1 per day M, W-Th; $139); and **Port Douglas** (1¼hr., 8 per day, $21). McCafferty's (☎ 13 14 99) and Greyhound (☎ 13 20 30) run to: **Brisbane** (26-28hr.; 5 per day; $156, YHA or VIP $140, students $125); **Cardwell** (3hr., 5 per day, $21); **Ingham** (3½hr., 5 per day, $28); **Innisfail** (1¼hr., 5 per day, $13); **Mission Beach** (2¼hr., 2 per day, $13); **Rockhampton** (14-15hr., 5 per day, $103); and **Townsville** (6hr., 5 per day, $41).

**Ferries:** Quicksilver (☎ 4099 5500) departs from The Pier at the Floreat Jetty to **Port Douglas** (1½hr.; 1 per day; $22, return $32).

**Local Transportation:** Sunbus (☎ 4057 7411) depot on Lake St in City Place. Fares $1-6; unlimited day pass $9, families $21. Buses go south into Cairns' suburbs and as far north as Palm Cove.

**Taxis: Black and White** (☎ 13 10 08 or ☎ 4051 5333). 24hr. service.

**Car Rental: Cairns Autorent,** 137 Lake St (☎ 4051 6077). 2WD from $35 per day. Open 7:30am-5pm. **Cairns Leisure Wheels,** 314 Sheridan St (☎ 4051 8988). 2WD start at

$49 per day, 4WD $145. Open 7am-6:30pm. For trips far afield: **National,** 135 Abbott St. (☎4051 4600), weekly rentals start at $39 per day, 4WD $85; **Budget,** 153 Lake St (☎4051 9222), rentals start at $39 per day, 4WD $120.

**Automobile Club:** Royal Automobile Club of Queensland (RACQ), 138 McLeod St (24hr. ☎4051 6543). Open daily 7:30am-5:30pm.

# ORIENTATION

Cairns is tucked between undulating hills on the west, a harbor on the east, and mangrove swamps on the north and the south. In this modern city, the streets are straight and they intersect at right angles, so navigation is a cinch. **The Esplanade,** with its many hostels, runs along the waterfront. At the street's southern end is the **The Pier,** which supports the pricey Pier Marketplace. Farther south, the Esplanade becomes **Wharf St** and runs past the **Trinity Wharf** and **Transit Centre.**

**Shields St** runs perpendicular to The Esplanade to **City Place,** a pedestrian mall with an open-air concert space. From this intersection, **Lake St** runs parallel to the Esplanade. Continuing away from the water, Shields St also intersects **Grafton St** and **Sheridan St** (called Cook Hwy north of the city). The **Cairns Railway Station** is on **McLeod St** in front of the mega-mall.

# PRACTICAL INFORMATION

**Tourist Offices: Tropical Tourism North Queensland,** 51 Esplanade (☎4051 3588; fax 4051 0127), near the The Pier. From the train station, turn left onto Spence St, then take a left onto the Esplanade; 100m down on your left. From the bus station, head right on Wharf St, which will curve and become the Esplanade; the office is on your left, between Spence and Shields St. Open daily 8:30am-5:30pm. **City Council,** 119-145 Spence St (24hr. ☎4044 3044; fax 4044 3022; www.cityofcairns.qld.gov.au), south of Cairns Central. Free *Community Service Guide,* loaded with information and maps. Open M-F 8am-5pm. **Traveller's Contact Point Cairns,** 13 Shields St (☎4041 4677; fax 4041 1338; email cairns@travellers.com.au), upstairs in City Place. Another excellent source for information and bookings. Services include mail forwarding and a job resource center. Internet 30min. $2. Open daily 8am-8pm.

**National Parks Office: The Queensland Parks and Wildlife Service (QPWS),** 10 McLeod St (☎4046 6601; fax 4046 6604). The *Australian Guide to National Parks* is helpful, but pricey ($30). The *Queensland Guide to Camping* is cheaper, but less helpful ($6). Open M-F 8:30am-4:30pm.

**Budget Travel: Flight Centre,** 24 Spence St (☎4052 1077, 24hr. info (1300) 30 77 35), guarantees to beat any quoted price. Open M-F 9am-5pm, Sa 9am-noon. **STA Travel** has two local branches: 9 Shields St (☎4031 4199; fax 4031 6384; open M-F 9am-6pm, Sa 10am-2pm) and shop 39 in Cairns Central Shopping Centre (☎4031 8398; open M-W, F 9am-5:30pm, Th 9am-7pm, Sa 9am-3pm).

**Money:** The best **currency exchange** rates are found at a hostel, of all places. Try **Caravella's 77,** 77 Esplanade (☎4051 2159), for a slap-down, bing-bang zero percent commission. The **American Express Office,** 79-87 Abbott St, 2nd fl (☎4051 8811), at Orchid Plaza, has 1% commission rates. Open M-F 8:30am-5pm, Sa 9am-noon. **Thomas Cook,** 59-63 Esplanade (☎4041 1000), exchanges currency. Open daily 9am-8pm. **ATMs** at virtually every bank accept Visa, MC, Cirrus.

**Library: Cairns City Public Library,** 151 Abbott St (☎4044 3720). Book in advance for free Internet access up to 1hr. Open M 10am-6pm, Tu-F 10am-7pm, Sa 10am-4pm.

**Ticket Agencies: TicketLink** in the **Cairns Civic Centre,** corner of Florence and Sheraton St (☎4031 9555; fax 4031 3102). Call for ticket prices and show listings.

**Police:** (☎4030 7000; fax 4030 7144) on Sheridan St, between Spence and Hartley St. Open 24hr. **Dial 000 if you have an emergency.**

**Hotlines:** Alcohol and Drug Information (☎(1800) 17 78 33). Lifeline (☎13 11 14).

**Pharmacy:** Chemmart Pharmacy, shop 1085 Esplanade. Open daily 9am-10pm. Yes, they do nose piercing.

QUEENSLAND

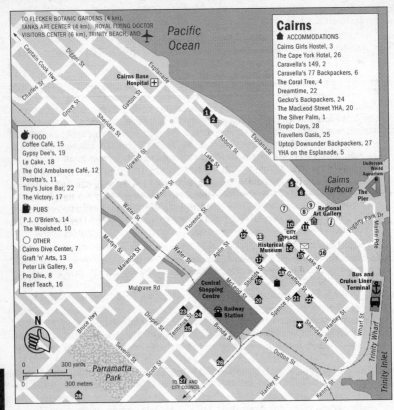

TO FLECKER BOTANIC GARDENS (4 km),
TANKS ART CENTER (4 km), ROYAL FLYING DOCTOR
VISITORS CENTER (6 km), TRINITY BEACH, AND

*Pacific
Ocean*

Cairns Base
Hospital

**Cairns**

🏠 **ACCOMMODATIONS**

Cairns Girls Hostel, 3
The Cape York Hotel, 26
Caravella's 149, 2
Caravella's 77 Backpackers, 6
The Coral Tree, 4
Dreamtime, 22
Gecko's Backpackers, 24
The MacLeod Street YHA, 20
The Silver Palm, 1
Tropic Days, 28
Travellers Oasis, 25
Uptop Downunder Backpackers, 27
YHA on the Esplanade, 5

🍅 **FOOD**
Coffee Café, 15
Gypsy Dee's, 19
Le Cake, 18
The Old Ambulance Café, 12
Perotta's, 11
Tiny's Juice Bar, 22
The Victory, 17

🍺 **PUBS**
P.J. O'Brien's, 14
The Woolshed, 10

⭕ **OTHER**
Cairns Dive Center, 7
Graft 'n' Arts, 13
Peter Lik Gallery, 9
Pro Dive, 8
Reef Teach, 16

Cairns
Harbour

The
Pier

Undersea
World
Aquarium

Regional
Art Gallery

CITY
PLACE

Historical
Museum

Central
Shopping
Centre

Railway
Station

Bus and
Cruise Liner
Terminal

Mulgrave Rd

Parramatta
Park

TO AND
CITY COUNCIL

0    300 yards
0    300 meters

QUEENSLAND

**Hospital: Cairns Base Hospital** (☎4050 6333), on the Esplanade beyond the last couple of hostels (Bel-Air and Caravellers 149). 24hr. emergency department.

**Internet Access:** Internet access is everywhere in Cairns. **The Call Station,** 123 Abbott St. (☎4052 1542). Open 8am-11:30pm. 1hr. $3 before noon and after 6pm. Also, **Traveller's Contact Point Cairns** (see above) and the **Tourist Information Office** on the corner of Aplin and Sheridan St (1hr. $2).

**Post Office: Cairns General Post Office (GPO),** 13 Grafton St (☎4031 4382; fax 4051 3871), on the corner of Hartley St. *Poste Restante.* Open M-F 9am-5pm. Another office (☎4031 2922; fax 4051 9292) is on the 2nd fl of the Orchid Plaza. Open M-F 9am-5:30pm, Sa 9am-12:30pm. **Postal code:** 4870.

**Phone Code:** 07.

## MEDIA AND PUBLICATIONS

Newspapers: Cairns Post (88¢).
Nightlife: Barfly (free), available in hostels, stores, restaurants.
Music: Rock, Hot 103.5, news 846am.

## ACCOMMODATIONS

Though geographically small, Cairns is second only to Sydney as a backpacker's destination, and it's studded with dozens of budget hostels. Most are clustered along the Esplanade, but many others are located in the center of town near Cairns Central. Regardless of location, most hostels have a pool, a large kitchen, and coin operated laundry facilities. Generally, the management will shuttle you from the airport and offer you free or discounted meals at a local bar. Travelers who visit during the Dry can also play in the inter-hostel soccer games. Many hostels offer discounts in the off season (roughly Oct.-May).

## HOSTELS

**Dreamtime,** 4 Terminus St (☎4031 6753; fax 4031 6566). Just off Bunda St behind Cairns Central, a 15min. walk from the Esplanade. Daily shuttles to Pier and bus station. A microcosm of tropical paradise, Dreamtime is, well, a dream come true. Proprietors Steve and Kathy insist on learning guests' first names and offer more than basic amenities. Front office books a myriad of adventure trips, from reef diving to skydiving. Cozy and sociable atmosphere. Pool, BBQ, kitchen. Reception 7:30am-noon and 4-8pm. Dorms $17.50; twins and doubles (some with fridge) $40. Book ahead.

**Tropic Days,** 26-28 Bunting St (☎4041 1521; fax 4031 6576; www.tropic days.com.au). Behind the Showgrounds, north off Scott St; a 20min. walk west from downtown. Despite its slightly inconvenient location, Tropic Days is a travelers' oasis. Meticulously jungle-themed paintings adorn walls amid a neatly tended tropical garden. BBQ hut comprised of palm fronds and origami-style palm mobiles. Free shuttle to City Centre. TV/video lounge. Camping in back $9, 3-bed dorms $16; doubles $35.

**Cairns Girls Hostel,** 147 Lake St (☎4051 2016). Between Florence and Aplin St. A true gem in the morass of accommodations in Cairns, this women-only hostel has provided a safe haven for travelers for over 30 years. No noise after 9:30, but no curfew either—so feel free to party late and tiptoe past your roommates. Refurbished twin rooms are carpeted. 3 kitchens, 3 bathrooms. Reception 7am-9:30pm. Rates on a sliding scale: $16 for the 1st night, $13 by the 4th; weekly: $90.

**Gecko's Backpackers,** 187 Bunda St (☎4031 1344; fax 4051 5150). Gecko's is a newcomer to the hostel scene. Comfy, clean rooms, all with new mattresses. Free meals at the Woolshed. Internet. Reception 7am-noon and 4-8pm. 3- or 4-bed dorms $18; singles $25; doubles $40.

**Travellers Oasis,** 8 Scott St (☎(1800) 62 13 53; fax 4052 1634; travoasis@travoa sis.com.au). One of the bigger operations on this side of town, Travellers Oasis has three main buildings surrounding a courtyard, garden and pool. Management says they've chosen not to buy a television because they'd rather have guests talking to each other. But that's up to you. Complimentary coffee and tea. Internet 30min. $3. Reception 7am-8pm. 3- and 4-person dorms $18; singles $27; doubles $39.

**Uptop Downunder Backpackers Resort,** 164-170 Spence St (☎4051 3636; fax 4052 1211). A 15min. walk west from the edge of town; at night, it's safer to take their courtesy bus. 24hr. pickup service for new arrivals. Though an inconvenient distance from downtown, Uptop delivers in service and style. Spotless rooms equipped with fridges. Pool tables, BBQ, Internet, and mini-cinema with nightly flicks. Reception 6:30am-10pm. Check-out 9:30am. Dorms $15; singles $28; twins and doubles $32.

**Caravella's 77,** 77 Esplanade (☎4051 2159; www.caravella.com.au). Between Aplin and Shields St, 10min. from the bus station. Outside, Caravella's 77 is in the middle of all the action. Inside, things remain pretty clean and colorful. Internet access, movies, pool table. Tour bookings. Linen deposit $5. Key deposit $5. Dorms $18; twins and doubles $50. Some rooms have ensuite and some have A/C, but they're given out randomly so you'll need to ask about them when you book. Flash your *Let's Go* and ask about a $5 discount on your 1st night's stay. VIP.

**Caravella's 149,** 149 Esplanade (☎4031 5680; fax 4051 4097). Across from the playground between Minnie and Upward St. Large dorm blocks equipped with fridges. Internet access for a (large) fee, free videos. Key deposit $10. Reception 7:30am-10:30pm. Check-out 9:30am. Big dorms $15 (one is female-only); small dorms with fan $16, with A/C and bath $17; twins and doubles $36, with A/C $38.

**The McLeod Street YHA,** 20-24 McLeod St (☎4051 0772; fax 4031 3158). Right across from the train station. This YHA has the feel of a motel more than a hostel, with open-air hallways surrounding a pool. Clean, simple dorms $18.50, with A/C $20; twins and doubles $44; family rooms $60. Non-YHA members $3 extra.

QUEENSLAND

**YHA on the Esplanade,** 93 Esplanade (☎4031 1919; fax 4031 4381; email esplanade@yhaqld.org). Near the corner of Aplin St, extremely close to nightclubs and cheap restaurants. Safe, no-frills place to crash. Dorms $18.50; twins and doubles $42.

## HOTELS AND MOTELS

**The Coral Tree,** 166-172 Grafton St (☎4031 3744; fax 4031 3064; www.coral-treeinn.com.au). Next to Kuiyam Hostel. Luxurious, moderately up-market. Pricey, but you get your money's worth. A/C, TV, bath, and balcony. Reception 6:30am-9:30pm. Reservations 24hr. Rooms $106, self-contained suites $136.

**The Cape York Hotel,** 147 Bunda St (☎4051 2008; fax 4031 0331). At the corner of Spence St near the train station. Comfortable rooms with veranda views. Reception 9am-9pm. Singles $33; twins and doubles $44. Book ahead.

**The Silver Palm,** 153 Esplanade (☎4031 6099; fax 4031 6094). Next to Caravella's 149. Apartments behind the motel with 1 or 2 bedrooms, A/C, TV lounge, and kitchen. Reception M-F 7am-7pm, Sa-Su 7am-1pm and 5-7pm. Check-out 9:30am. Two people $65; 4 people $95.

## ⬛ FOOD

Cairns bubbles with good eats, from all-night kebab and pizza stalls on the Esplanade to upscale restaurants that specialize in seafood. For basic **groceries,** try Bi-lo Mega Fresh in Cairns Central (open M-F 8am-9pm, Sa 8am-5:30pm, and Su 10:30am-4pm); or Woolworth's, near the Esplanade, on Lake St next to City Place (☎4051 2015; open M-F 8am-9pm, Sa 8am-5:30pm, Su 1-8pm).

**Coffee Café,** 87 Lake St (☎4041 1899). Offers scones, jam, and a pot o' tea for $5 within earshot of the open-air concert hall. Sit outside and enjoy your breakfast or lunch special, just cause you're special ($6.50-7.50). Open M-Sa 7am-9pm, Su 8am-9pm.

**The Old Ambulance Café and Bistro,** 135 Grafton St (☎4051 0511). Serves a great quiche ($5), fancifully presented cakes ($3.50), and superb, ice cream-laden iced coffee ($3.50). Get salads or pizzas for about $7 each. Lunch until 2pm, dinner after 6pm. Open M 7am-6pm, T-Th 7am-10:30pm, F-Sa 7am-11:30pm.

**Perrotta's,** corner of Abbot and Shields St (☎4031 5899). A mod-looking café; stop in early for elegant french toast ($7) or fluffy scrambled eggs ($5.50). Open 8am-10pm.

**The Victory,** 62 Shields St (☎4051 1883). Featuring new-age music and vegetarian and vegan dishes, Victory is only open for dinner, but does dinner right—soup ($5.50), stuffed mushrooms ($10), pasta ($10). 20% off before 6pm. Open 5:30pm-late.

**Le Cake** (☎4031 7273). In Rusty's Bazaar on the Grafton St side. Croissants ($1), fresh coffee ($2.50 a pot), and uncensored art exhibitions on the wall. Oh la la! Open W-Th 7am-5pm, F 6am-6pm, Sa-Su 6am-1pm.

**Tiny's Juice Bar,** 45 Grafton St (☎4031 4331). At the corner of Spence St. Sports a selection of 50 juices to remedy various ailments, including halitosis, hay fever and gout ($2-4); sandwiches ($2-3) and smoothies ($3-4). Open M-Sa 7:30am-4pm.

**Gypsy Dee's,** 41a Shields St (☎4051 5530). Near the corner of Sheridan St. As if the stylized gypsy wagon just left of center stage weren't enough, this hot spot has generous dinner portions ($11-22), vegetarian entrees ($9-15), and live music or a DJ every night. Open daily 11:30am-2am, closed Sa lunch.

## ⬛ SIGHTS

⬛ **TANKS ART CENTRE.** A trio of WWII deisel tanks have been transformed into a massive art exhibition space. The best local art is on display here, and each show lasts three weeks. The last Sunday of every month June-Nov., Tanks hosts Market Day, a free bazaar with live music and plenty of pottery, crafts, and herbs for sale. *(46 Collins Ave. Accessible from Sunbus #1B ($2). ☎4032 2349. Open daily 11am-4pm.)*

⬛ **PETER LIK GALLERY.** You've probably already bought at least 10 of his postcards—now see his pictures in life-size form. Lik is quickly becoming recognized as one of Australia's best photographers and his fantastic prints of Australian wild-life are showcased in this modern gallery. Well worth 15min. to walk around. *(4 Shields St. ☎4031 8177; www.peterlik.com. Open 9am-10pm. Free.)*

**CAIRNS REGIONAL ART GALLERY.** The exhibits are ever-changing, often featuring the work of Australian artists and international artists working in Australia. The building is beautiful, stop in if you're trying to remember what it was like *not* to live in a hostel. *(Corner of Abbott and Shields St. ☎4031 6865. $6, concessions $3.)*

**UNDERSEA WORLD AQUARIUM.** Houses a small but captivating presentation of the reef's brilliantly colored sea life. Make sure you have time for the shark feedings, scheduled for 10am, noon, 1:30, and 3pm; if you book ahead, you can even dive with the sharks for 30min. After you sign the insurance waiver, of course. *(In the Pier Marketplace, near the wharves. ☎4041 1777. Open daily 8am-8pm. $10, children $6, families $25. Shark diving 3:30-8pm $75.)*

**GRAFT 'N' ARTS.** A youth and community arts center, Graft 'n' Arts offers a variety of workshops, such as African drumming, and Capoiera and Salsa dance. Live musical and theatrical performances pop up from month to month. Check the outside bulletin board or *Barfly* for details. *(124 Grafton St. ☎4051 4023.)*

**FLECKER BOTANIC GARDENS.** The gardens include fern and orchid houses, a Gondwanan (evolutionary flora track) garden, a meandering boardwalk, and a trail that crosses fresh and saltwater lakes. *(Hop on the Sunbus from City Place, #1B ($2.30), or drive north on Sheridan St and take a left onto Collins Ave. ☎4044 3398. Guided walks daily 1pm. Open M-F 7:30am-5:30pm, Sa-Su 8:30am-5:30pm. Free.)*

**MOUNT WHITFIELD ENVIRONMENTAL PARK.** The last bit of rainforest in the Cairns area. The park's shorter Red Arrow circuit takes about an hour, while the more rugged Blue Arrow circuit is a 5hr. return trek up and around Mt. Whitfield. Don't stay after dark because finding a cab or a bus back into Cairns might take a while. *(Wedged between the Tanks Art Centre and the Botanic Gardens on Collins Ave.)*

## 🔊 ADVENTURE ACTIVITIES

Cairns is mostly a tourist town because it's warm in the winter and it's an easy gateway to the Great Barrier Reef. At night, travelers stay in town and drink at the local pubs, but during the day they're outside the city-limits enjoying ghastly thrills, bumps, and spills for relatively reasonable prices. Most companies pickup and drop off free of charge and can be booked from your hostel.

**■ CYCLING.** Ride with **Bandicoot Bicycle Tours** for an amazing day of cycling, sightseeing, swimming, and relaxation in the tablelands above Cairns. Enjoy several short rides (3-7km) between your trips to waterfalls, giant fig trees, and guided nature walks. If you're tired, just catch a lift with the support vehicle. Lunch is included and often features fresh fish and tropical fruit. *(☎4055 0155; email bandicoot01@hotmail.com. Trips M, W, F departing 7:30am, returning 6:30pm. $98.)*

**BUNGY JUMPING. AJ Hackett** is a New Zealander with a death-wish—ask him about bungy jumping the Eiffel Tower (and then getting arrested for it). Or just sign up for one of his (legal) Australian jumps. W: night bungy. *(☎4057 7188; email bungy@internetnorth.com.au. Daily 9am-5:30pm. $95. Extra for videos, photos.)*

**FISHING.** Pull outta whopper. Cast for your own bait and then tow the line with **Fishing The Tropics.** They run their 6m boat in the Cairns estuary and the Daintree River. *(☎4057 8289. Half-day $70, full-day $120.)* **VIP Fishing & Game Boat Services** offers similar packages, along with others that feature fly fishing for black marlin. *(☎4031 4355. Half-day $60, full-day $120, marlin trips from $190.)*

**HORSEBACK RIDING. Blazing Saddles** offers a 3hr. trail ride easy enough for beginners. The half-way point provides a pretty view of the ocean and Scout Island. *(24hr. ☎4051 4055. Daily 8:30am, 1:30pm. $75, children under 14 $55.)*

QUEENSLAND

**HOT AIR BALLOONING.** Ever wanted to ride beneath a big balloon shaped like a koala? Now's your chance (and let's just hope it's your only one). **Hot Air Cairns** will take you up, up, and away. Departs 5am and returns 10am. Packages with skyrail, rafting, and others available. *(☎4031 0999; www.hotair.com.au. 30min. $115, 1hr. $180.)*

**JET BOATING.** This is not your Dad's speed boat. **Cairns Jet Boating** will take you out on a water rocket roaring at 100km per hr. Book ahead. *(☎4057 5884. $65.)*

**PARASAILING.** Cruise 300ft. above Trinity Inlet with **North Queensland Water-Sports.** Jet skiing and bumper tubing also available. *(☎4045 2735. $50, tandem $80.)*

**SKYDIVING.** What goes up must come down, and these two companies let you fall in style. Jump tandem with an instructor from 8000ft. with **Skydive Cairns.** *(☎4035 9667. $228, more for higher.)* Or, for the only beach landing around, try **Skydive Mission Beach.** *(☎4031 0900. $199, transport included.)*

**WHITEWATER RAFTING.** Three companies offer basically the same deal—a day of rafting that's wild but tame enough for beginners. **R n' R Rafting** has several options including multi-day and family packages. The longer your trip, the rougher your rapids. *(☎4051 7777. Half-day $75, full-day $133, and 2-day $395.)* Or check out **Raging Thunder Adventures** *(24hr. reservations ☎4030 7990. Half-day $75, full-day $133.)* **Foaming Fury** has half-day rides ($70) and full-day rides that include a rainforest walk ($99).

**BEACH.** Cairns doesn't really have a beach—it has a mudflat. However, Trinity Beach is nearby with nice white sand and plenty of private cove areas that keep it from feeling inundated with sunbathers. *(Sunbus #1 and 1A run to Trinity Beach from the depot in City Place. M-F every 30min., Sa-Su every hr.)*

> **WARNING. Box jellyfish** are serious business—a single jellyfish may have enough poison to kill three adults, and its sting usually proves deadly. They're out and about between October and May in coastal waters north of Great Keppel Island. Always ask locals about them before swimming. Some beaches install jellyfish-proof nets, and some diving establishments sell jellyfish-proof wetsuits, but stay out of the water if you are at all concerned about your safety. On land, avoid wild mangroves when bushwalking; **saltwater crocodiles** hide out there. Salties can also be found in northern coastal and inland waters.

##  DIVING AND SNORKELING

By far the most popular way to see Cairns is through goggles. Every day, thousands of tourists and locals suit up with masks, fins, and snorkels to slide beneath the ocean surface and glimpse the Great Barrier Reef. The lucky ones attend ▩**Reef Teach**, 14 Spence St, for a 2hr. lecture by Paddy Colwell, an Irish marine biologist who doubles as a comic. In his own unique—and entertaining—way, Colwell teaches divers about the history of the reef, its biodiversity, and how to avoid harming the reef or themselves. Reef Teach is terrific even for advanced divers. (☎/fax 4051 6882. M-Sa at 6:15pm, includes tea, coffee, and chocolate biscuits.)

As the main gateway to the reef, Cairns is studded with an overwhelming number of dive shops and snorkeling outfits. Knowing which one to choose can be tricky and even a little daunting when you're bombarded with brochures and booking agents. So think about some questions: How long do you want to dive—a day-trip or a multi-day trip? How big of a boat do you want? For personal dive instruction and a group atmosphere, smaller boats may be the way to go. Finally, are you going with other divers or with friends who may prefer other water activities? Unless you're all diving, you won't want a dive trip—maybe a cruise with diving options (à la **Passions of Paradise** or **Great Adventures**).

In order to dive in Australia (or anywhere in the world), you have to have an open-water certification, a driver's license for the water. The only way to get this certification is to spend about 4 days and at least $400 in scuba school, where you learn about scuba equipment and diving techniques. However, **introductory dives** offer a taste of scuba diving *without* going to scuba school. For a fee, dive companies will give you a 1hr. crash course in diving basics, and then they'll take you out on a real-life—guided and supervised—scuba dive. These are great opportunities for people who are only going to be on the reef for a short time. But keep in mind you can only (legally) do a few of these before you have to go to school. Also, intro dives usually aren't on the best dive sites, and of course, they're slightly more risky than having all the training. But if they're your only option, they're worth a shot—if only because everyone should see this natural wonder underwater at least once.

## DAY TRIPS

**The Falla**, located in The Pier (☎4031 3488). A swanky, restored pearl lugger boat (a.k.a. sailboat) is chartered by a small crew; with a maximum of 35 passengers, everyone gets tight. The friendly divemasters—eager to help novices—will take you out for a day on Upolo Reef. The boat leaves at about 8:30am and returns about 6pm. The base price is $69, including lunch (children $30, families $180). First intro dive $50, second $30. First certified dive $40, second $20.

**Passions of Paradise** (☎4050 0676). Offers full day cruises to Paradise Reef and Upolo Cay. This boat has a young, vibrant spirit; spontaneous conga dancing is not an unknown occurrence on the deck. The high-speed catamaran can take between 60 and 70 passengers on the 10hr. trip. Departs 8am. Base price for snorkeling, lunch, and transport is $70. Add $55 for an intro dive or 2 certified dives.

**Great Adventures,** 1 Wharf St (☎4051 4444; www.greatadventures.com.au). More expensive, but with good reason. For $139, they will speed you and 300 other passengers out to a humongous floating pontoon on the edge of the reef. There, you can do an intro dive for $85 or a certified dive for $55. You can also snorkel or ride in a semi-submersible free of charge. Departs daily at 10:30am, returns 5:30pm. Also ask about their dive courses, which can be taken at the luxurious Green Island Resort.

## MULTI-DAY TRIPS AND SCUBA SCHOOLS

**Pro-Dive** (☎4031 5255; www.prodive-cairns.com.au). On the corner of Abbott and Shields St. Fun and informed crews lead long trips on a new, luxury vessel. Their most popular trip is the 5-day learn-to-dive course. Although the price tag may seem hefty at $594, it includes all diving, equipment, meals, and housing. Same for their three-day, two-night trips, which include up to 11 dives for $484. Open daily 8:30am-9pm.

**Deep Sea Divers Den,** 319 Draper St (☎4031 2223; www.divers-den.com). Take a 2- or 3-day package to the outlying ribbon reefs of Norman and Saxon. Conveniently, divers can leave for multi-day trips any day of the week. Three-day, 2-night snorkeling packages $365, certified divers $460. Four-day dive course $435.

**Down Under Dive,** 287 Draper St (☎4031 1288; www.downunderdive.com.au). A 2-masted clipper ship with a hot tub takes 2-day (or longer) trips, starting at $210 for snorkelers and $290 for certified divers. The company also offers diver training for those on a budget. A 4-day course starts at $280 for two days of pool training and two days on Hastings and Saxon Reefs. Open daily 7am-5pm. 24hr. reservations.

**Cairns Dive Centre,** 121 Abbott St (☎4051 0294; www.cairnsdive.com.au). Generally the least expensive to the outer reef, with a "floating hotel" catamaran for its flagship and a smaller boat for daytrips. 3-day, 10 certified dives $385; 2-day, 6 dives $275. 4-day course $275, or $418 to also sleep aboard the boat.

 **SHOPPING**

In a city that sports glitzy, high-class shopping malls, finding cheap supplies can be a challenge. Cairns has two main shopping malls: Cairns Central, located in the center of town, has a grocery store and some prices suitable for budget travelers. The Pier, on the Wharf, is most likely too expensive for daily supplies. Beware of purchasing didgeridoos, boomerangs, and spears advertised as "made by true Aboriginals." Sometimes they're not the real thing or the artist hasn't been offered the best price for his work. When it comes to **Aboriginal crafts,** the safest bet is to purchase at stores with signs that say they're "aboriginally owned and operated."

QUEENSLAND

**Rusty's Bazaar,** wedged between Sheridan and Grafton St just south of Shields St. As good a shopping experience as Cairns has to offer. Fruit, honey, and camera equipment are just some of the items up for grabs at this open-air market. Show up early before the good stuff sells out. Open F 6am-7pm, Sa-Su 6am-1:30pm.

**The Night Markets,** on the Pier end of the Esplanade. Cheap food and even cheaper souvenirs (not just in the monetary sense). Open daily 5-11pm.

**Kaotica Secondhand,** 81 Grafton St (☎4051 9386). Near Rusty's Bazaar. Features 50s-90s fashions, theme night anyone? Backpackers flock here to unload excess belongings and pick up jeans ($15-40) or dresses ($8-20). Open M-Tu, Th 10:30am-5:30pm, W 10:30am-5pm, F 9:30am-6pm, Sa 9:30am-2pm, Su 9:30am-1pm.

## ◪ NIGHTLIFE

Despite its widespread and well-deserved reputation as a haven for backpackers, the Cairns nightclub scene is still a few paces behind that of other cities. Some places are crowded with backpackers—resembling what your college dorm parties would be if you went to a school with 10,000 international students. But at least if you get your hand stamped before 10pm, these parties are all free. And your hostel will usually give you a free meal voucher for one of the clubs, too. For the latest local word, pick up a copy of *Barfly* (free) at any café around town. The free *Pink Guide to Cairns,* available at Walker's Book Shop, 96 Lake St, details **gay-friendly** nightlife and accommodations.

There's also another alternative to just going out on your own. **Ultimate Party** is a Cairns pub crawl held every Wednesday and Saturday night. It's sort of like a giant mixer for the twenty-something tourists. Pay $45 for dinner, entry into 4 clubs, a shot in each club, entertainment, transport, and a t-shirt. Crowd size varies, but it can be as large as a couple hundred people. Call ☎4041 0332 if you want to sign up, or look for an Ultimate Party t-shirt on the street.

**The Woolshed,** 24 Shields St (☎4031 6304 for free shuttle bus until 10pm). A rowdy frat party. Backpackers come here to dance on the tables, drink beer, and enter the weekly Mr. and Ms. Backpacker contests. It's all party, all night, with everyone dancin' to top 40 hits. Practically every hostel in town offers meal vouchers for this place, so expect to take a number and wait in line. Happy Hour 9:30-10:30pm. $5 pitchers. Cover $5.50. Open nightly 6-9:30pm for meals, club open until late.

**P.J. O'Brien's** (☎4031 5333). In City Place at the corner of Shields and Lake St. Here it's St. Patrick's Day every day. With tables made from beer barrels, authentic Irish memorabilia, and quotes from Yeats in the murals, this place almost looks like an Emerald Isle museum. The atmosphere is lively and pints of Guinness ($5.50) and tasty food (meals $10-16.50) make P.J.'s the new hot spot in town. A slightly older and more sophisticated crowd than in the Woolshed. Neat dress required.

**Tropos** (☎4031 2530). On the corner of Lake and Spence St. The Cairns version of a Miami dance scene. The club plays a serious techno mix, and the dance floor is a stage where groovers shake their thang. Open until 5am, this is everyone's last stop at the end of the night. You can't miss it—the whirling spotlight can be seen across the street. Neat dress required. W: retro night. Cover $5.50, free before midnight.

**Johnno's Blues Bar** (☎4031 5008). At the corner of Abbott and Aplin St. Red-hot jazz, cool blues, and a dash of rock 'n' roll plays 7 days a week in this rough-around-the-edges club. Cover charge varies depending on the band. Passers-by can enjoy free blues outside the club most Fridays. The back room holds a mechanical bull for anyone who thinks he's jackeroo enough to handle it. Tu: $6 jugs all night. Open 9pm-late.

**The Chapel,** 91 Esplanade, upper level (☎4041 4222). A restaurant in the early evening that loses its religion after 10pm. With an urban feel, dim lighting, surrealistic paintings, and dripping candles, the Chapel is both classy and pseudo-goth. Plays an eclectic mix of tunes with DJs on F and Sa. A welcome relief from the backpacker crowd. Meaty meals $17-25. Stubbies $4.50. No cover. Open daily noon-2am.

**Rattle 'n' Hum,** 67 Esplanade (☎4031 3011). Near the corner of Shields St. Bright lights prevent this place from being a real bar, but it's full on the weekends. Hardwood floors,

QUEENSLAND

**THE GREAT UNDERWATER ORGY** The last thing those immobile little corals seem to be interested in is sex. But every year, for three days in November, the reef turns into a bacchanalian lovefest as coral release sperm and eggs into the water. At night, it seems to be snowing upside-down in the ocean, as the baby-juice floats to the surface. After fertilization, miniature jellyfish-like creatures swim about until they find a hard rock to stick themselves to. These grow to become the luminous coral creatures of the Great Barrier Reef. Needless to say, this oceanic orgy is an amazing time to dive (if you don't mind being covered with coral lovestuff).

pool tables, and video monitors that play Top 40 hits. Brick-oven pizza until midnight at open-air tables perfect for people-watching. No cover. Open daily 11:30am-midnight.

**nu-trix,** 53 Spence St (☎4051 8223). Between Grafton and McLeod St. Hard to miss with its rainbow-colored marquis. A gay bar and dance club with no dress code. Best shows F-Sa; cover varies. Open W-Su 9pm-late.

## 🖪 DAYTRIPS FROM CAIRNS

### TJAPUKAI

Just north of Cairns and off the Cook Hwy in neighboring **Smithfield** is the national coup of Aboriginal cultural parks: **▨Tjapukai.** Pronounced "JAB-a-guy," this is the most wholly rewarding, intelligently presented, and culturally fair presentation of Aboriginal myths, customs, and history in all of Queensland. It has been showered with all kinds of awards, including the 1999 Gold Award from the Pacific Asia Travel Association for the best cultural attraction in the world. Give this experience at least half a day. Learn how to throw boomerangs and spears, see a cultural dance show, view a film on Aboriginal history, and more. (☎4042 9999; www.tjapukai.com.au. Open daily 9am-5pm. $27, children $13.50. Transfers to and from Cairns and the Northern Beaches are available for $7 each way.)

### ZOOS

Farther along the Cook Hwy heading north, a pair of complementary roadside attractions exist under one ownership. **Wild World: The Tropical Zoo,** near Palm Cove on the Cook Hwy, 20min. north of Cairns, lets you get up close and personal with kangaroos and wallabies. There's a comprehensive reptile house, a koala colony, and public crocodile feedings. (☎4055 3669. Open daily 8:30am-5pm. $20, children $10.) Somewhat smaller, **Hartley's Creek Crocodile Farm,** is 40km north of Cairns. The farm has hundreds of crocs, as well as kangaroos and cassowaries. The "crocodile attack show," in which keepers taunt a croc until it eats a hand-fed chicken, begins at 3pm. (☎4055 3576. Open daily 9am-5pm. $16, children $8, families $40.) **Coral Coaches** services the parks. (☎4031 7577. 6 per day, $6-10.)

### GREEN ISLAND

Diminutive **Green Island** (technically a **coral cay;** see p. 29) barely pushes above the water surface; its perimeter can be walked in 15min. Though dominated by the luxury resort in the center, a short boardwalk through the rainforest and a beach path access nature. The more adventurous can forge a trail through the dense rainforest (if you walk long enough, you'll always end up back at the resort).

The cheapest and quickest way to the island is with **Great Adventures,** which offers a 45min. ferry. Extras include diving (intro dive or 2 certified dives $85), and a choice of snorkel equipment or a ride in a dinky glass-bottom boat. (☎4051 0455. Departs Cairns daily 8:30, 10:30am, leaves Green Island at noon, 2:30, or 4:30pm. $45, children $22.50, families $112.50.) The sailboat **Ocean Free** also specializes in trips to Green Island. Travelers aboard the schooner get the chance to explore the island or dive the reef around it. (☎4041 1118. Open 9am-5:30pm. Depart Cairns daily 9am. $60. Intro dive $49, for 2 $79; certified dive $35, $49.)

The real highlight of Green Island is **▨Marineland Melanesia,** 250m northeast of the resort left of the jetty, a combination gallery, aquarium and croc farm. Come at

10:30am or 1:45pm to watch a live feeding of Cassius, the world's **largest crocodile** in captivity. That's 18ft. of pure power, man. You can also hold yearling crocodiles or tour the primitive art collection. (☎4051 4032. Open daily 9:15am-4:15pm. $8.50, children $4.) Just off the end of the jetty is the antiquated **Marine Observatory,** from which you can observe bits of the coral reef from 1.5m below the surface ($3). The resort has a nice pool surrounded by a couple of boutiques and small cafés ($5, children $2.50; free to Great Adventures passengers). Daily 9:30am to 4:15pm, the **dive shop** rents snorkeling gear ($10 per day) and sells underwater cameras ($28). Instructors outfit day-trippers and take them on an intro dive ($88, certified $60). **Michaelmas Cay,** just north of the island on the outer reef, has good diving and is the site of a natural bird sanctuary. Unfortunately, the least expensive accommodation on Green Island runs $250 per person, so you can probably fuggedaboutit.

### FITZROY ISLAND

**Fitzroy Island** is much larger than Green Island, and is generally a better choice for the budget traveler. There are affordable beds, though most people only go for a day. **Sunlover Cruises** does the trip to the island or a combination of the island and Moore Reef. (☎4050 1333. Both cruises depart 9:30am, return 5pm. $36, children $18, families $90. Combo: $142, children $71, families $355.) If a cruise sounds too easy, try traveling to Fitzroy Island via **sea kayak** with **Raging Thunder Adventures.** A high-speed catamaran takes you most of the way, followed by 3hr. of reef kayaking, snorkeling, and lunch. An overnight package includes bunk accommodations at the Fitzroy Island Resort and two days of kayaking. (☎4030 7990. Daytrip $110. Overnight $135.) **The Fitzroy Island Resort** is a place to splurge. (☎4051 9588; 24hr. reservation ☎(1800) 07 90 80. Shared bunks $31; private bunks for 1-3 people $116; family rooms $150.) Forty **campers** are allowed on the island at a time ($10 per site; contact the QPWS on McLeod St, Cairns in advance). The resort has a **kiosk** which serves meals ($3-15) from 9am to 5pm. The **Rainforest Restaurant** is pricier ($10-18).

The resort's **dive shop** offers introductory diving and snorkel gear at bargain rates. (Intro dive $66, certified $60. Snorkel gear $12. Open 9:30am-4pm.) Snorkel and dive trips leave at 10:30am, 12:30, and 2:30pm. To keep busy, try a walk to the **lighthouse** (5km return) starting at a clearing adjacent to the **Reefarm,** a giant-clam breeding farm 1km north of the resort. There are a couple good 500m walks through the rainforest on the northern end of the island as well. Just past the Restaurant, the **Secret Garden track** cuts west into the island while **Nudey Beach track** continues along the coast. The Secret Garden track is easy and has informative nature placards. The Nudey Beach track, a bit more challenging, is made of huge stone slabs leading to boulders at the shore and, regrettably, a non-nude beach.

# ATHERTON TABLELANDS

Although much of northern Queensland is picturesque, nothing quite compares to the Atherton Tablelands. Rolling hills meet unspoiled rainforest, the perfect venue for spotting wildlife and rushing waterfalls. If you have an extra day in Cairns the 50km drive to these a group of high plateaus is well worth it. Traveling northeast on the Kennedy Hwy, you'll find the farming village Mareeba and touristy Kuranda. Opting for a southern route via the Gilles Hwy, you'll encounter the residential township of Atherton, charming Yungaburra, and Malanda. Bring a sweater in the winter; at an elevation of 1000m, you'll forget you're in the tropics.

### ▐ TRANSPORT

The mountainous, lakeside roads give drivers both a mild challenge and verdant panoramas. Although driving provides the fullest experience, the Tablelands are accessible without a car. White Car Coaches, 44 Spence St, Kuranda (☎4091 1855), services: **Atherton** ($21); **Malanda** ($28); **Mareeba** ($16); and **Yungaburra** ($26). The **Skyrail Rainforest Cableway,** the world's longest gondola (7.5km), lifts you up above the rainforest canopy into Kuranda village. A 1½hr. round trip originates in Carovonica Lakes, 10min. northwest of Cairns. (24hr. ☎4038 1555. $27, children $13.50.

Open daily 8am-5pm.) The **Kuranda Scenic Railway** provides an antique train ride from downtown Cairns to Kuranda. Chock-full of camera-toting tourists, this bumpy journey comes with relentless, inflection-free commentary. (☎4031 3636. From Cairns Su-F 8:30 and 9:30am, Sa 8:30am; to Cairns Su-F 2 and 3:30pm, Sa 3:30pm. One-way $25, children $13, concessions $17, families $63.)

## KURANDA

Kuranda is the Disneyland of the Atherton Tablelands. With street performers on giant unicycles, horse-drawn carriages, a giant shooting gallery, and gondolas all around, Karunda makes a business out of entertaining tourists. Its famed **original markets** (open W-Su) and **Heritage Markets** (open daily 8:30am-3pm) transform the cozy village into a bazaar of arts, crafts, and clothing.

**Birdworld,** in the Heritage Markets, has over 50 Australian squawkers as well as 23 "exotic species," including the elusive canary and pigeon. (☎4093 9188. Open daily 9am-4pm; $10, children $3; combination ticket with the Butterfly Sanctuary $18, children $6.) The **Australian Butterfly Sanctuary,** 8 Rob Vievers Dr, next door to the Heritage Markets, bills itself as Australia's largest butterfly farm. (☎4093 7575. Tours on demand. Open daily 10am-4pm. $11.50, children $5.) If plummeting from a 250ft. tower is more your bag, try the **Sky Screamer Thrill Ride.** (☎4041 3280. $44; discounts and shuttles for hostelers at 9:30am and 12:30pm, returns 12:30 and 4pm, $20.) **River Cruise and Rainforest Tours,** on the Barron River just off Arara St, offers 45min. guided riverboat rides. (☎4093 7476. $12, children $6, families $30.)

If you're looking to stay overnight, **Kuranda Backpacker's Hostel** (a.k.a. "Mrs. Miller's"), 6 Arara St, is across the street to the left of the train station. Massive renovations have made this hostel feel like a tropical resort. In the mornings, the proprietor feeds over 50 rainbow lorikeets. Amenities include a kitchen, pool, bike rental (half-day $10), tropical garden, laundry, and free pickup from Cairns. Reception 8am-6pm. (☎4093 7355. Dorms $16; twins and doubles $36; one self-contained flat $49. YHA, VIP.) **Kuranda Bottom Pub Hotel,** on the corner of Coondoo and Arara St just across the street from Skyrail, sports a garden bar, a pool, and tidy rooms. Reception M-Sa 10am-10pm, Su 10am-4pm. (☎4093 7206. Singles $43; doubles $55; each extra person $10.)

Chips and sandwiches are served at the **Jungle Bar** toward the back of the Heritage Markets, across from the entrance to Birdworld. (☎4093 8849. Open daily 8am-2pm; bar open until late.) Locals love **Frog's,** 11 Coondoo St, with outside dining in the middle of the main drag. (☎4093 7405. Open daily 9:30am-4pm.)

## LAKE TINAROO AND DANBULLA FOREST

Saturated with crater lakes and sprinkled with waterfalls, the volcanic soil of the central Tablelands sprouts bizarre forest along the shores of the **Tinaroo, Barrine,** and **Eacham Lakes. Danbulla Forest Drive** circumscribes Lake Tinaroo. The free *Danbulla Forest Drive* visitor's guide, available from the **Department of Natural Resources,** 83 Main St, Atherton (☎4091 1844), lists sights along the 40min. loop. Take care when driving along this circuit, since it's mostly unsealed. Both Lake Eacham and Lake Barrine have walking paths for spotting birds and small animals. Contact the **QPWS Eacham District Office** (☎4095 3786) at Lake Eacham for more information. The 3km Lake Circuit Track around Lake Eacham in Crater National Park is the well-paved way to see muskrat-kangaroos and giant iguanas.

**Camping** in the thick of the forests is the best way to get personal with the Tablelands. There are several state forest campgrounds around Lake Tinaroo ($2 per night, toilets available). The campgrounds are described in the visitor's guide to Danbulla; call the Department of Natural Resources with any questions.

## YUNGABURRA

Tiny Yungaburra (pop. 400; pubs 1) is at the heart of the Tablelands with Lake Tinaroo and the Danbulla forest to the north, waterfalls to the south, Lakes Eacham and Barrine to the southeast, and the volcanic hills of the **Seven Sisters** to the west. The town is handsome, untouched by commercial tourism, yet warm to all visi-

**QUEENSLAND**

**LET'S SEE THE SHOW** Australia's oldest operating cinema, the Magestic Theatre, on the corner of Eachem Place and English St, retains its original canvas seats and projector. The father of current owner built the theater when the movies had to run on a generator because they didn't have wired electricity. Now, see modern movies on the weekends or Cinema Club showing on Sunday at 7pm. But bring pillows and blankets—a show at the Magestic is a still a social affair.

tors. Yungaburra hosts the biggest **markets** in the north on the fourth Saturday of each month. Homemade crafts, fresh produce, and even goats can be bartered at these authentic events. From Cairns, take the Gillies Hwy west about 60km.

Just off the west side of Yungaburra is the **Curtain Fig Tree,** a monstrous strangler fig forming an eerie curtain in the middle of the rainforest. Pick your gaping jaw off the ground and check out the 50m tall, 500 year-old **Cathedral Fig Tree** on the east stretch of the Dunbulla Forest Dr. The best place to spot a **platypus** is at the Atherton Shire Council Pumping Station. From Yungaburra, head past the bridge and turn right onto Picnic Crossing Rd (the road sign is actually 10m ahead of the turn-off). Follow the 2nd right turn. You'll find a concrete picnic table for a late-afternoon snack and platypus families near the bend in the river.

Yungaburra's youth hostel, ⚑**On the Wallaby,** is utterly superb. The common area feels like a mountain hut with rough-edged wood furnishings and a wood-burning stove. The bathrooms and showers are sided with stone and wood, and the bunk rooms are clean and fresh. Enjoy BBQ, kitchen, garden, and laundry. Guests can join tour activities (canoeing and biking) on an individual basis. (☎4095 2031. Reception 8am-1pm and 4-8pm. Tent sites $10; dorms $18; twins and doubles $40. Transport offered to and from Cairns on Su for $15.) One kilometer south of Lake Eacham on the Gillies Hwy is the **Lake Eacham Caravan Park** with showers, laundry, and a small general store. The price includes admission to a garden and petting zoo. (☎4095 3730. Reception 7am-7pm. Tent sites for 2 $10; small cabins available if booked in advance.) **Curtain Fig Motel,** 16 Gillies Hwy, has sparkling rooms. (☎4095 3168. Reception 7:30am-8:30pm. Doubles $72; each extra person $15.)

The **Gem Gallery and Coffee Shop,** 44 Eacham Rd, serves breakfast for under $2. They also have cheap opals and free opal-cutting and gold-working demonstrations, not to mention free **Internet.** (☎4095 3455. Open daily 8am-late.) **Nick's Bella Vista Restaurant,** 33 Gilles Hwy, is a regalia of hat-wearing, dancing and yodeling. At this Swiss-Italian restaurant meals run $10-27 and there's live music F-Sa. (☎4095 3330. Open F-Tu 11am-3:30pm and Th-Tu 6-11pm.) Cut-Price on Eacham St is the local **supermarket.** (☎4095 2177. Open daily 7am-7pm.)

## MALANDA AND AROUND

Only a short distance form Yungaburra, friendly and hospitable Malanda has cows, cows, and more cows, but not much else. Approximately 25km south of Malanda and beyond Millaa Millaa, the **waterfall circuit** leads past a series of spectacular swimming holes. From the north a sign points to the falls. Catch the loop from the south by looking for the "Tourist Drive" sign. **Millaa Millaa Falls** is the perfect waterfall: a straight, even curtain with rocks at the bottom and a bit of green on either side. **Zillie Falls** starts off a sedate creek at the top of the falls; a rocky, slippery-when-wet path through the adjacent rainforest leads to the roaring drop where the cascading **Ellinjaa Falls** look like liquid fireworks.

The little-known ⚑**Platypus Forest Lodge,** 12 Topaz Rd, 6km east of the town center off Lake Barrine Rd, is a stellar B&B that's perfect for nature buffs. The new owners run an immaculate lodge complete with sauna, hot tub, canoe, wood-burning stove, and loads of hospitality. Out back, platypuses, turtles, possums, and tree kangaroos inhabit a swath of rainforest. (☎/fax 4096 5926. Singles $40; doubles $50.) **The Malanda Hotel-Motel,** on the corner of English and James St, has one of Malanda's only pubs where you can drink beer till the cows come home, literally. (☎4096 5101. Open 8am-midnight. Hotel rooms $22 per person, families $55; motel singles $33, twins and doubles $55, families $66.) The **Peeramon Hotel** on Peeramon

QUEENSLAND

Rd, is in (surprise) **Peeramon** between Yungaburra and Malanda. From Atherton, take the first paved road on the right after leaving Yungaburra; from Cairns it's the first paved left after the Lake Eacham exit off the Gillies Hwy. An old lady's **ghost** still floats about the place: a photo above the piano captures her, mid-air and luminescent in a group picture on the front steps. (☎4096 5873. Reception M-Th 11am-midnight, F-Su 10am-midnight. Singles $10-20; doubles $40-60. Book ahead.)

**Granny's Country Kitchen,** 22 James St, on the main drag in Malanda, is a sandwich shop with a burger, chips, and drink for under $6. (☎4096 6506. Open Su-W 7am-7pm, Th-Sa 7am-9pm.) The Five Star Fresh **Market** is at 2-11 English St.

## NEAR THE TABLELANDS: CHILLAGOE

Situated almost 200km west of Mareeba, the drive is half the experience on a day-trip to this old mining town. The road is mostly paved up to Dimbulah, but the last 30km into Chillagoe is bumpy dirt; 4WD is highly recommended. Lush pastoral scenes dissolve into landscapes of rust-colored dirt. Wild cattle meander along, and termite mounds of all sizes dot the landscape like cemetery headstones. When you think you're desperately lost in the middle of nowhere, take heart—you're close to Chillagoe. The Savannahlander **train** from **Cairns** stops in nearby **Almaden** (5½hr.; departs Cairns W 6:30am; $39, concessions $20) from which a bus carts people into town. The main draw is a system of **caves.** Tours run out of **Queensland National Parks and Wildlife Service** office on the corner of Queen and Cathedral St. (☎4094 7163. Open daily 8:30am-5pm. $5.50-8.)

**Chillagoe Caves Lodge,** 7 King St, has a restaurant. (☎4094 7106. Sites $5.50, powered $8; budget beds $11; singles $27.50; doubles $36.) The **Post Office Hotel,** on Queen St, offers new, color-coordinated rooms. (☎/fax 4094 7119. Beds $15; rooms without beds $5.50. Yes, rooms without beds.) Pick up **groceries** at the Chillagoe General Store, 11 Queen St (open daily 7am-6pm).

# PORT DOUGLAS

The coastal road to Port Douglas overlooks a patchwork of indigo and teal waters almost as lovely as the town it will eventually reach. There are no traffic lights in Port Douglas and the sun seems as though it should always be shining there, and it almost always is. Although the city has only 3,500 full-time residents, Port Douglas swells with vacationers from June to September. Easy access to a gorgeous, four-mile beach lures both foreign and native vacationers.

## ▐ TRANSPORT

**Buses: Coral Coaches** (☎4099 5351; fax 4099 4235), on the corner of Grant and Warner St, runs daily to: the **airport** (1¼hr., 10 per day, $22); **Cairns** (1½hr., 11 per day, $16); **Mossman** (30min., 10 per day, $6). Buses run to **Mareeba** via **Mossman** (2hr., Tu-Th 1 per day, $20).

**Ferries: Quicksilver** (☎4099 5500) leaves Port Douglas from the Marina Mirage daily at 5:15pm for **Cairns** (1½hr., $20, YHA 10% discount).

**Taxis: Port Douglas Taxis,** 45 Warner St (☎4099 5345). 24hr. service.

**Car Rental: Crocodile Car Rentals,** #2 50 Macrossan St (☎4099 5555), specializes in **4WD** (from $70 per day for sealed roads, $80 unsealed). **Allcar Rentals,** 21 Warner St (☎4099 4123), rents cars from $39 per day and is one of the only places in Australia that has **automatic 4WD.**

**Bike Rental: Port Douglas Bike Hire,** 42 Macrossan St (☎4099 5799). Half-day $9, full-day $12, weekly $55. Open daily 9am-5pm.

**Road Report:** (☎4033 6711), with all road conditions and closings.

## ◢▪ ORIENTATION AND PRACTICAL INFORMATION

Port Douglas Rd branches off of the Captain Cook Hwy (Hwy 1) 70km north of Cairns and launches out onto the Port Douglas peninsula. Side streets lead to **Four Mile Beach** to the east and to **Marina Mirage** to the west. The town lies on the northern tip of the peninsula where Port Douglas Rd runs into Davidson St and then intersects the main drag, **Macrossan St.**

**Tourist Office: Port Douglas Tourist Information Centre,** 23 Macrossan St (☎4099 5599; fax 4099 5070), between Grant and Wharf St. This office (like all others in Port Douglas) is privately-owned and may have a biased opinion. Open daily 8am-6:30pm.

**Banks:** All banks open M-Th 9:30am-4pm, F 9:30am-5pm. **ANZ,** 36 Macrossan St (☎13 13 14), exchanges currency for a $5 commission and has an **ATM.** If headed north, keep in mind that there are **no ATMs** north of the Daintree River.

**Medical Services: Port Village Medical Centre,** Shop 17 in Port Village Centre on Macrossan St (24hr. ☎4099 5043). Office open M-F 8am-6pm, Sa-Su 9am-noon. The nearest **hospital** (☎4098 2444) is in Mossman, on Hospital St.

**Police:** (24hr. ☎4099 5220), at Macrossan and Wharf St. Open M-Th 8am-2pm.

**Internet: Mega Byte Internet Café,** 48 Macrossan St (☎4099 5568). 1hr. $10. Open daily 9am-10pm.

**Post Office:** 5 Owen St (☎4099 5210; fax 4099 4584). On the corner of Macrossan and Owen St, up the hill. Open M-F 9am-5pm, Sa 9am-noon. **Postal Code:** 4871.

**Phone Code:** 07.

# ACCOMMODATIONS

**Port o' Call (YHA),** 7 Craven Close (☎4099 5422, freecall (1800) 89 28 00; fax 4099 5495; www.portocall.com.au). Take a left off Port Douglas Rd onto Port St as you come into town. Free shuttle bus to Cairns (departs M, W, and Sa 8:30am; call for a 10am lift north from Cairns). Word has spread far and wide that Port o' Call is the fairest YHA of them all. This impeccable hostel has a pool, laundry, bike rental, and Internet. The bistro serves dinner daily (meals $7.50-10.50; open 6-9pm) and swings during Happy Hour (5-7pm). Reception 7:30am-7:30pm. 4-bed dorm with bath $20, non-YHA member $21; deluxe motel rooms are $75, during the Dry $95. VIP, NOMADS.

**Port Douglas Backpackers,** 8 Macrossan St (☎4099 4883; fax 4099 4827; email backpack@internetnorth.com.au). Smack in the center of town and upstairs from a small shopping plaza. Coral Coaches stops in front daily. Groomed for the backpacker crowd, this place feels like an office-turned-dormitory, with fluorescent lighting and carpet tiles. The location is great, but can be noisy. Only 4 showers. 2 lounges. Reception 7:30am-1:30pm and 3:30-7pm. Dorms $18; 1 double $45. Book ahead June-Sept.

**Tropic Breeze Van Village,** 24 Davidson St (☎4099 5299). Just 100m from the beach. Reception 8am-7pm. Sites for 2 $15, powered $18, extra person $5; cabins for 2 $55.

**Marae** (☎4098 4900; fax 4098 4099; www.marae.com.au). 15km north of Port Douglas. If you've come to get away from it all and don't mind a bit of a splurge, this B&B presents a peaceful, romantic escape. With mountain views and lots of wildlife around, you can relax in the salt water pool or chat with the cockatoo. Min. stay 2 nights. Singles $90; doubles $130. Bookings essential.

# FOOD AND ENTERTAINMENT

**Court House Hotel,** on the corner of Macrossan and Wharf St, is the most rockin' joint in town. Locals flock here for the live American music W-M nights. The owner is an American expatriate who says Port Douglas offers "the best blues this side of Chicago." (☎4099 5181; fax 4049 6249. Stubbies $3, counter meals up to $12.) **Ironbar Restaurant,** 5 Macrossan St, just across from Port Douglas Backpackers, sponsors cane toad races every Tu and Th at 9pm. Choose your own amphibian; the winner (human, not toad) gets a free drink. The kitchen offers huge kangaroo burgers, skewered crocodile, and barbecued prawns for $3-24. (☎4099 4776. Open M-F 11am-2am, Sa-Su 8am-2am.) Also keep in mind **Le Petit Café,** 31 Macrossan St, with homemade ice cream, sweets and treats. (☎4099 4287. Open daily 7am-6pm, later during the Dry.)

## 👁 🌀 SIGHTS AND ACTIVITIES

**The Rainforest Habitat** has eight acres, three enclosures, and over 1000 animals without cages or any discernible fear of people. Mingle with the cockatoos and parrots, tickle a fruit bat's tummy, or scratch a wallaroo behind the ears. Early risers can also enjoy 'Breakfast with the Birds,' a full buffet in the aviary 8-11am. (☎4099 3235. Open daily 8am-5:30pm; last entry 4:30pm. $16, children $8. Wheelchair accessible. Coral Coach departs Port Douglas depot hourly, $3 return.)

At the east end of Macrossan St, **Four Mile Beach** never gets full. This gorgeous stretch attracts an array of locals, topless backpackers, and swanky resort-types. (Lifeguard on duty M-Sa 9am-5pm.) **Extra Action Watersports** (☎4099 3175) is just north of Marina Mirage. Steve, the owner and self-defined 'action man,' can set you up with any number of heart-stopping adventures. **Parasailing** lasts 12-15 min. (solo $60, couple $80). You can also try 30min. of **jet skiing** ($60, $80) or a bit o' **bumpa tubing** ($25, $40). Packages for all three activities are available ($100, $150).

Visitors can **snorkel** independently or with several private outfits, most of which depart from Marina Mirage. **Sail Away-Low Isles,** 23 Macrossan St, fits snorkeling, riding in a glass-bottom boat, and **'boom netting'** into one afternoon. Departs daily at 9:30am. (☎4099 5777; www.reefandrainforest.com.au. 7hr. $99, children $49, families $260; call for booking.) **Wavelength,** 18 Macrossan St, is another company that offers daily snorkeling trips. Eight-hour ventures to the outer reef depart at 8:30am. (☎4099 5031. $127, children $87.)

Port Douglas is an excellent destination for **scuba divers.** Portions of the Great Barrier Reef lie just off Four Mile Beach and offer a plethora of marine life. When selecting a dive or snorkel shop, ask plenty of questions. Knowing boat capacity, dive difficulty, and site destinations ahead of time is important.

**Quicksilver Diver** (☎4099 5500). In the Marina Mirage. Like Disney World for

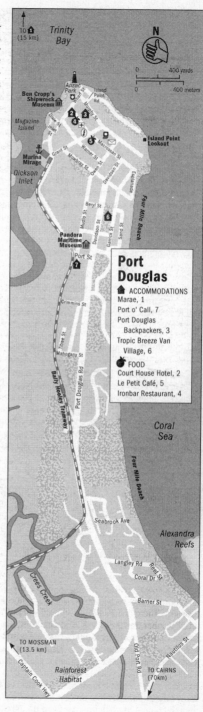

**Port Douglas**

🏠 **ACCOMMODATIONS**
Marae, 1
Port o' Call, 7
Port Douglas
    Backpackers, 3
Tropic Breeze Van
    Village, 6

🍴 **FOOD**
Court House Hotel, 2
Le Petit Café, 5
Ironbar Restaurant, 4

QUEENSLAND

diving families. Ride a high-speed catamaran to the outer reef and spend the day enjoying submersible rides, snorkeling, and lunch buffet. $150, children $77.50. Special snorkeling tours with a marine biologist, additional $31. Introductory dive, additional $107; certified dive, additional $67. All equipment included. Catamaran departs daily at 10am.

**Discover Dive,** 414 Grant St (☎ 4099 6333; www.discoverdive.com.au). Corner of Warner St. This five-star, PADI dive center specializes in small group training. It offers introductory pool dives for $28 and scuba refresher courses for $50. A brand new boat takes groups of 18 to the reef daily. Departs 8:15am and returns 4pm. Open daily 9am-6pm.

**Haba Dive** (☎ 4099 5254). In the Marina Mirage. Offers two or three dives on each of their daily trips. Groups of 40 depart at 8:30am with free pickup and lunch. Intro dives $180; certified dives $160, with equipment $190. Snorkeling $120, children $75.

## ▐ DAYTRIP FROM PORT DOUGLAS: MOSSMAN GORGE

Disgorge yourself from the activity of Port Douglas life at gorgeous **Mossman Gorge.** Part of the **Daintree National Park,** the valley is riddled with hiking paths originating from the visitors' parking lot (follow signs). The shorter paths to the Mossman River are quite easy, but the 2km circuit track in the thick of the rainforest is more challenging. Be prepared to hop over small creeks (and an occasional small lizard). On any of the trails you'll feel engulfed by the magnificent green canopy.

**Coral Coaches** runs to Mossman from Port Douglas. (☎ 4099 5351. 30min., 10 per day, $6.) If driving, take Hwy 1 north from the junction to Port Douglas for about 20km. Follow the signs for Mossman Gorge and turn left across from the high school. Drive about 4km to Kuku Yalanji, 1km more to the carpark at the gorge.

If you want to learn the secrets of the rainforest, spend an hour with an Aboriginal guide from **Kuku-Yalanji Dreamtime Walks,** on the road to the gorge. The tour covers traditional medicines and bush tucker, and includes tea and damper. (☎ 4098 1305. Tours M-F 10am, noon, and 2pm. $15, students $12.) The Aboriginal-owned operation has a shuttle to Port Douglas but it more than doubles the ticket price and requires one day advance notice.

## DAINTREE

Daintree is an excellent gateway to the rougher frontier land of the north. Kingfishers, kookaburras, and friendly faces abound in this tiny forest village of 120 residents. The town's main economic assets are the estuarine crocodiles (or salties) that live in the Daintree River: boatloads of camera-toting croc-seekers pass through the village daily. The town's exit off Coast Hwy can flood. Call ☎ 4033 6711 or one of the local restaurants for road conditions.

If you're not visiting on an all-inclusive tour package from Port Douglas or Cairns, you can book a river tour at the **Daintree General Store**—which also serves as the town watering hole and post office. Most river excursions are similar, varying primarily in length (from 1hr. to 2½hr.). Prices range from $15 to $28; children travel for less. Check out **Daintree Wildlife Safari** (☎ 4098 6192) or **Daintree River and Reef Cruise Centre** (☎ 4098 6115). **Chris Dahlberg** runs excellent morning bird-spotting tours from the Daintree jetty. (☎ 4098 7997. 2hr.; $30. Bookings essential.)

The ▣**Red Mill House** (☎/fax 4098 6233) is reason enough to visit Daintree. A TV room, swimming pool, and BBQ are just some of the extras that convince many guests to stay longer than they originally planned at this lovely B&B. The morning meal is made of fruit from the tropical garden in the backyard. The older part of the house has one single ($35), one double ($66), and one triple ($99) with bathroom facilities and a spa. The newer section offers four ensuite queen-size rooms ($88). **Daintree River View Caravan Park,** smack in the middle of town, rents tent sites. (☎ 4098 6119. Hot showers, BBQ. Sites $12, powered $15.) All restaurants in Daintree line Stewart St. They offer fare ranging from exotic emu burgers (at **The Big Barramundi**) to toasted turkey sandwiches (at the **Daintree Coffee Shop**).

## NEAR DAINTREE: WONGA BEACH

Halfway between Mossman and Daintree is the small seaside hamlet of **Wonga Beach** (pop. 700). Tucked away in this unassuming village lies **Redbacks,** a juggernaut backpacker oasis. Sparkling new rooms and facilities are coupled with a seemingly endless supply of on-site activities. And, of course, it's probably the only spot in Australia with a **giant slingshot for catapulting flaming coconuts. Coral Coaches** from Cairns drops at the door, or follow signs off the Captain Cook Hwy. (☎4098 7871; fax 4098 7520. Reception 6am-8pm. Dorms $15; doubles $65.)

# CAPE TRIBULATION

Travelers continuing up the coast will use the **Daintree Ferry,** which shuttles across the river from 6am-midnight. (Walk-on passengers $1, cars $7). The utterly fantastic road from Daintree to Cape Tribulation is anything but what its name would suggest. The rainforest crashes down on the ocean surf, and every forest inch is teeming with wildlife. Conservationists and capitalists are locked in a heated struggle over the future of these lush forests. The former vie to prevent the Cape from obtaining central electricity, but tourist-minded businesses see modernization as the way to open the wilderness to travelers. Everyone involved can at least agree the lands of Cape Tribulation are some of Queensland's most beautiful.

**▐ ▐ TRANSPORT AND PRACTICAL INFORMATION.** About 15km north of the Daintree River, 'Cape Trib' is in the heart of **Daintree National Park** and is more of a landmark than a township. When locals talk about it, they're usually referring to a large general area served by Cape Tribulation Rd, which runs north past Cow Bay, Alexandra Bay, Thornton Peak, and the Cape itself. Each of these locations is a few kilometers from the others, so moving around is somewhat difficult unless you have a car. However, the two main hostels provide shuttles to various sights and offer a number of adventures on their own premises. Coral Coaches stops in **Cow Bay.** (Cairns ☎4031 7577, Port Douglas ☎4099 5351. Departs Cairns 7am, 3:30pm, Port Douglas 8:15am, 5pm. $24.) There is no official information center in Cape Tribulation. The **QPWS (Queensland Parks and Wildlife Service) ranger station** (☎4098 0052) has public info, but the hours are extremely limited: M-F 9:30-11:30am. Two other sources of info are the Daintree Rainforest Environmental Centre and the Bat House (see **Sights and Activities**).

**▐ ACCOMMODATIONS.** Most accommodations are solar powered, so don't plan to plug in your night-light. ▓**Crocodylus Village** is on Buchanan Creek Rd, east off Cape Tribulation Rd. Coral Coaches (☎4098 2600) runs there from Cairns for $46, and the hostel offers a complimentary bus to the beach four times a day. This hostel is a backpacker oasis organically entwined with the rain forest, with several open-air cabins scattered around a large wooden patio. (☎4098 9166; fax 4098 9131; www.queensland-holidays.com.au. Reception 7:30am-11:30pm. Pool, laundry, horseback riding, sunrise paddle trek in a hybrid kayak/canoe, guided bushwalk. Cabin rooms $18; ensuite hut for 2 $65, each extra person $10. YHA. Book ahead.) More appropriately called "PK's Jungle Party," **PK's Jungle Village** is about 400m after the "Welcome to Cape Tribulation" sign. The nightly entertainment pales in comparison to the weekly theme parties, usually four-keggers. If you miss the first daily Happy Hour, don't worry—there's another. (☎4098 0040; fax 4098 0006. Volleyball, horseback riding, guided bushwalking, and bike rental. Dorms $20; doubles $60; triples $82; quads $104. VIP.) **Cape Trib Beach House** is a rain forest camping ground converted into a rain forest cabin complex. (☎4098 0030. Pristine beach. Bar, restaurant, pool, Internet, laundry. 6-bed dorm $24; family-style cabins for 4 with A/C $30; beach front cabins with queen beds $79-89.)

There are also two accommodations on the way to Cape Tribulation from Daintree. The **Daintree Manor**, 27 Forest Creek Rd, just north of the river, offers breathtaking views, 24hr. power, beautiful handmade furniture, and a TV lounge with good reception. (☎/fax 4090 7041. Ensuite singles $85; doubles $99.) Up the road, **Club Daintree** is set off the main thoroughfare on Cape Kimberly. (☎4090 7500; fax 4090 7501. Reception 6am-midnight. Camping $8; dorms $15; cabins $98.)

**▐ FOOD. Café on Sea,** between Cow Bay and PK's, is right on Thorton Beach with a palm-tree framed view of the sea. Enjoy sandwiches ($4), burgers ($6), or full meals ($12.50) under the tented open-air dining area. (☎4098 9118. Open 9am-

5pm or later depending on bookings.) **Lync Haven** is the most amusing eating establishment, with Snoopy the cockatoo welcoming guests at the door. If the staff isn't overloaded, ask to see the orphaned 'roos that you can feed out of your hand. The menu includes burgers ($4-6) and sandwiches ($2.50-4); the veggie-friendly dinner menu (everything under $12) is expansive. (☎4098 9155. Open daily 7am-7pm.) **The Cow Bay General Store,** on Spurwood Rd just off Buchanan Creek Rd, sells groceries and petrol. (☎4098 9127. Open 7:30am-6pm.)

🔳 **SIGHTS AND ACTIVITIES.** All attractions on Cape Tribulation revolve around the wet tropics. **The Daintree Rainforest Environmental Centre,** just before Cow Bay off Cape Tribulation Rd, is an excellent reference center. A 23m tower allows visitors to view the rainforest from above the canopy. The ticket price includes a guided walk on the rainforest boardwalk (40min.), wet tropic movies, and an exhibit of forest wildlife pickled in jars on the porch. (☎/fax 4098 9171. Open daily 8:30am-5pm. $9 for those lodging in the area; otherwise, $11; families $27.50.) A less extensive source of forest info is the "**Bathouse,**" opposite PK's on the west side of the highway. The all-volunteer staff will be happy to take your picture with their giant flying fox, Rex. (☎4098 0063; www.austrop.org.au. $2 donation.) Just down the road from the Bathouse is 🔳**Dubijee** ("doob-i-gee"), a visitor area with a spectacular 1.2km boardwalk through a variety of coastal forests and mangroves, a must for all visitors. Further south is the **Maardja** ("mar-ja") boardwalk through old growth rainforest, which is near a wonderful mangrove walk.

**Cooper Creek Wilderness Cruises** explores the mangroves in search of crocodiles. (☎4098 9052. 1hr. $16; 1½hr. night cruises $18; bookings essential.) They also offer creek walks and package deals. **Rum Runner** is one of the several tours based out of Cairns that runs daily trips to the reef off the Cape. (☎4050 9988, freecall ☎(1800) 68 64 44. Free bus to beach from all local resorts, snorkeling equipment included. $109, standby for less; certified divers can have two trips out for $66 extra.)

The popular two-day, one-night trip to **Snapper Island** is available at the Crocodylus Village through **Tropical Sea Kayaks** (☎4098 9166) for $159. This excursion features reef walking, snorkeling, beach camping, and fully prepared meals, including all equipment. **Wundu Trail Rides,** between Lync Haven and the Rainforest Village, lets you discover the coral coast on horseback. Wear long pants and covered shoes to take this excursion through the Daintree Tea Plantation. (☎4098 9156. Departs twice daily. 3hr. guided rides $55, 10% discount for groups of 7 or more.)

## ROUTES TO COOKTOWN

There are two routes from Cape Tribulation to Cooktown—one inland, one coastal. The Bloomfield Track is the coastal ro—, well, track. It beats through 150km of bush as it swerves and dips, hugging the sides of precipitously steep mountains. When it's in bad condition, the Bloomfield Track is impassable. When it's in "good" condition, the road is about as much fun as you can legally have in a 4WD. Views of the rainforest and the coastline are amazing, and fording the rivers can be exciting. Expect the trek to take you about 5hr., be prepared to veer, jag, bump, stray, dance—whatever you have to do—to avoid large potholes and fallen trees. Call ahead for road conditions and bring lots of cash, as most places don't take credit. If you'd rather not be the one clutching the steering wheel, **Bloomfield Track 4WD Safaris** (☎4099 5665) will do the dirty work for you. Tours depart from Port Douglas three times per week and stay overnight in Cooktown.

The inland route to Cooktown is not as exciting as the coastal track, but it's mostly paved and can save your heinie a bit of bruising. Better road conditions also allow you to focus less on the next pothole and more on the fantastic views.

**BLOOMFIELD TRACK.** On the southern section of the track lies **Wujal Wujal,** a tiny Aboriginal community with a **convenience store** (open M-Th 8am-4:30pm, F 8am-noon) and a basic **service station** (open M-Th 8am-5pm, F 8am-noon). Off the road are the **Bloomfield Falls,** a terrific place to relax after the hard ride, but watch out for those feisty crocs.

Between Wujal Wujal and Cooktown, the mountains pull back from the coast as you drive on a dirt road through dry savannah. North of the bridge to Wujal Wujal, the road is much less treacherous. Along the way, there are occasional general stores and small-town hotels. The **Bloomfield River Inn** stocks petrol and food. (☎4060 8174. Open Th-Su 8am-8pm.) Just up the road, **Viv's Takeaway** prepares tasty sandwiches for $3. (Open daily 8am-7pm. All meals are under $10.)

The final stretch of road before Cooktown leads to the **Lion's Den Hotel**, where records of countless wayfarers are scrawled over the walls inside. (☎4060 3911. Open daily 8am-whenever everyone leaves. Beer $3.50, pub grub $12 a plate. Campsites with showers $5 per person. **Pay phone** in front.)

**INLAND TO COOKTOWN.** There are a handful of interesting stop-offs on this route. The prettiest, **Mt. Molloy,** is a 10min. drive (27km) southwest of Mossman on the Peninsula Developmental Rd. The **Mt. Molloy National Hotel** is a large, aged building. The rooms are a bit dusty, but homey with comfy beds and a pub downstairs. (☎4094 1133; fax 4094 1045. Reception at pub 10am-midnight. Meals $9-15, special $6. Beds $20, children $10.) The **Mt. Molloy Café & Takeaway** can whip up Mexican fare, sandwiches, and towering burgers for around $5. (☎4094 1187. Open 7am-8pm or until midnight if people are around.) A **picnic area** with hiking information and public restrooms is 500m from the hotel.

**Mt. Carbine** lies 28km north. Once a prosperous mining town, it is now three roadside buildings. The **Mt. Carbine Roadhouse** has petrol, food, and backpacker lodging. (☎4094 3043. Meals $7-12. Open daily 7am-7pm. Singles $15, doubles $25.)

Continuing north, the road begins to literally cut through the hills, with walls of stone outcroppings flanking the pavement. Sixty kilometers north of Mt. Molloy is **Bob's Lookout,** which is more inspiring than it sounds. Stop to see the hills, and you'll be glad you did. **Palmer River Roadhouse,** 110km north of Mt. Molloy, decorated with various murals tracing the area's gold mining history, offers the standard Far North pub fare. (☎4060 2020. Open daily 7am-10pm. Tent sites $5; caravan sites $7. No credit cards; **eftpos** accepted.)

Farther north, the bitumen gives way to a gravelly, snaky descent through the hills with some more beautiful views of the landscape. The **Lakeland Downs Hotel Motel** marks the end of the pavement for the Peninsula Developmental Rd and the last pit stop before Cooktown, 82km away. (☎4060 2142. Dinner $8.50-15. Singles $40; doubles $60; families $10 more per extra person.)

# COOKTOWN

Imbued with legends, folklore, and mystery, Cooktown persists in spite of its nearly deserted streets. Ask residents about the history of their home and they'll gladly shower you with Aboriginal creation myths and other fascinating tales. Europeans arrived here in 1770 when Captain Cook's ship, the *Endeavor*, was grounded on the Great Barrier Reef. The discovery of gold a century later at nearby Palmer's field turned the sleepy town into a port metropolis with thousands of residents. When the gold ran out, almost everyone picked up their stakes and sojourned to the southern goldfields. The tenacity of the 1600 who remain today has created a history-rich, fun-filled place, full of small-town friendliness.

## ▐ TRANSPORT

**Buses:** Coral Coach (☎4098 2600) has service between Cooktown and Cairns. Endeavour Farms Trading Post (see **Food,** below) is the local ticketing agent. To **Cairns,** by coastal route (7½hr., Tu and Sa 11:30am, $52) via **Lion's Den** (30min.), **Cape Tribulation** (4¼hr.), **Cow Bay** (4¾hr.), **Mossman** (6hr.), and **Port Douglas** (6½hr.), or by inland route (5hr., W, F, and Su., 2:30pm, $47) via **Lakeland** (1¼hr.), **Mt. Carbine** (3¼hr.), **Mt. Molloy** (3½hr.), **Mareeba** (4¼hr.), and **Kurada** (4¾hr.).

**Car Rental:** The aptly named **Cooktown Car Hire** (☎4069 5694) is one of the only options this far north, and it has **4WD** from $90.

**Taxis: Cooktown Taxis** (☎4069 5387). Available 6:30am-midnight.

**Automobile Club: RACQ, Cape York Tyres** (☎4069 5233), at the corner of Charlotte and Furneaux St. Open M-F 7am-7pm, Sa-Su 7:30am-6pm.

## ✴ 🛈 ORIENTATION AND PRACTICAL INFORMATION

The Cooktown Development Rd becomes **Hope St** as it runs north toward **Grassy Hill.** Two blocks to the west, **Charlotte St** holds most of Cooktown's shops and services. It's crossed by several streets, including Boundary, Howard, Hogg, and Walker. At the far-north end of town, Charlotte St runs along the water, curves eastward, and becomes **Webber Esplanade.**

**Tourist Office: Cooktown Travel Centre** (☎4069 6100, freecall (1800) 00 17 70; fax 4069 6100; email cooktowntourism@hotmail.com), on Charlotte St next to Anzac Park.

**Currency Exchange: Westpac** (☎4069 5477), on Charlotte St, between Green and Furneaux St, charges $7 for overseas traveler's checks or cash. Credit card advances. No ATMs here or anywhere nearby. Open M-Th 9:30am-4pm, F 9:30am-5pm.

**Medical Center: Cooktown Hospital** (☎4069 5433), on the corner of Ida St and the Cooktown Developmental Rd, on the way out of town heading south.

**Police:** (☎4069 5320), across from the wharf on Charlotte St. Staffed M-F 8am-4pm; afterhours, use intercom at the office door.

**Post Office:** (☎4069 5347), on Charlotte St, across from the Sovereign Hotel. Open M-F 9am-5pm. **Postal Code:** 4871.

**Phone Code:** 07.

## 🏠🍴 ACCOMMODATIONS AND FOOD

**Pam's Place,** at the corner of Charlotte and Boundary St, is the backpacker hub of Cooktown. Perks include a large kitchen, linen, laundry facilities, bar, pool table, swimming pool, and morning shuttles to the bus station and airport. (☎4069 5166; fax 4069 5964. Key deposit $10. Bike rental. Dorms $16.50; singles $35; doubles $45. YHA. V, MC 3.5% surcharge.) **Alamanda Inn,** across from the Ampol station on the corner of Hope and Howard St, offers tidy guest house rooms in a flower-filled setting. (☎/fax 4069 5203. All rooms have A/C, fridge, TV, and sink. Singles $28; doubles $40; motel rooms $40, $50; and luxury rooms $56, $75.) If you are looking to splurge, look into the luxurious **Milkwood Lodge Rainforest Retreat** (☎4069 5007; www.milkwood-lodge.com). It's about a 10min. walk from town, but the accommodations are spacious and impeccable—the lodge has several fantastic cabins each equipped with a double bed, a day bed, kitchen, and bathroom. The $95 per night is steep, but less extravagant if you split it with friends.

For a quick tasty treat, visit the **Endeavour Farms Trading Post,** on Charlotte St between Hogg and Walker St. Barbara, the owner, enjoys helping travelers find their way, having found Cooktown "rough as bags" herself when she first arrived. The fish-and-chips ($5) are Cooktown's finest. (☎4069 5723. Open daily 8am-7:30pm.) The **Cooks Landing Kiosk** at the wharf serves bottomless coffee ($2) and toasted sandwiches ($2-3) that are tiny but scrumptious (open daily 8am-5pm). **Segram's,** on Charlotte and Furneaux, has to-die-for pizza. A personal pie will cost you $12-15, but it might be enough for two.

## 📷 SIGHTS AND ACTIVITIES

The **Cooktown Cemetery,** on McIvor River-Cooktown Rd, is full of legends. Its highly segregated plots are divided into sections for white, Aboriginal, and Jewish residents. The Chinese Shrine lies at the farthest left-hand corner of the cemetery, where 30,000 slaves and their possessions were buried. Pick up a fact sheet on the cemetery at any local accommodation. Twenty years ago, the city brought the **Botanic Gardens,** off Walker St, back to life after having been left to decay after the gold rush. There's a walking path to **Finch Bay** (which can also be reached by following Walker St to its end), which branches into the trail to secluded **Cherry Tree Bay.** Along the road leading to the **lighthouse** is an excellent **lookout.**

# CAPE YORK

One of the last vestiges of the great Australian frontier, Cape York consists of rugged, intense landscape and narrow mountain roads—a journey that's a challenge and a risk. There are three ways to see Cape York: by traveling with a professional guide, by reading about it in a book, or by going with your friends—if y'all have a 4WD, some wilderness experience, an emergency cell phone, and a thirst for adventure. Seriously, this trek is not for the light-hearted, and it wouldn't make a good holiday weekend. (Depending on road conditions, the trip up and back could take you up to 2 weeks.) But those who do make an attempt, or who drive even part of the southern route, are rewarded with gorgeous sunsets, lush savannahs, packs of wild hogs, inquisitive kangaroos, silver-crested cockatoos, and much more. Cape York is nature in its pristine form, for better and for worse. It's spectacular, but also isolated from the services civilization can offer.

## THE BASE OF THE CAPE

Even if you haven't the time, the money, or the stamina for the full journey up the Cape, you can get an exciting sample of wilderness within a reasonable distance of Cooktown. One good two- to three-day trip runs north 62km of Lakeland along the **Peninsula Developmental Rd** to the famed Aboriginal rock art of Split Rock, the outpost town of **Laura,** the truckstop at **Musgrave** (2hr. north, entrance to the **Lakefield National Park**), and then east along the rugged **Lakefield Rd** and **Battle Camp Track** to complete the circuit. Four-wheel-drive is adamantly recommended for the first two-thirds of the journey and imperative for the final leg. Up here the Dry chokes the land with dust, the Wet floods it Noah-style. If you travel on Battle Camp Road, you'll have to ford at least three rivers and skedaddle past crater-sized pot holes.

Just like the roads, Cape York natives are tough as nails. There's close to nothing in these towns, so don't go looking for the Holiday Inn. Laura (pop. 100) has the **Quickan Hotel** (☎ 4060 3255; open daily 10am-midnight; pub grub $15; beds $25; tents $5), and **post office** (open M-F 9am-5pm; **postal code:** 4871). Limited supplies may be purchased next door to the pub at **The Ampol Station Laura** (☎ 4060 3238; open daily 7:30am-5:30pm). Pick up a map, petrol, groceries, or a cheap sandwich ($4) at the **Laura Café** (☎ 4060 3230; open daily 7am-9:30pm). The **Ang-gnarra Visitors Centre** (☎ 4060 3214), across from the Laura Café, has a practically tree-less **Caravan Park** ($5, powered $6) with a pool, laundry, and not quite sparkling bathrooms. Laura's one must-see—and it is amazing—is **Split Rock,** a series of ancient Aboriginal art sites (15min. walk $5; 3hr. walk $10). Bring a hat, sunscreen, hiking shoes, and water. The **Ang-gnarra Aboriginal Corporation** (☎ 4060 3200) offers tours.

An hour southwest of Laura (50km, 4WD only) is the **Jowalbinna Bush Camp,** run by Aboriginals. (☎ 4060 3236; fax 4051 4888. Camping sites $7, children $4; half-day tour of rock art sites $55, full-day $80, meals included.)

The first pitstop north of Laura on the Peninsula Developmental Rd is about 70km away. It's the **Hann River Road House** (☎ 4060 3242), run by Bushy and his sister Sue. Pitch your tent here, fill up on gasoline, or taste a good burger.

On the Peninsula Development Rd, 138km north of Laura, lies **Musgrave** (pop. 2), marked by the **Musgrave Roadhouse** (☎ 4060 3229; open 7:30am-10pm), **Musgrave Roadhouse Pub,** and **Musgrave Roadhouse Lodge** (singles $25; doubles $40; sites $5). Don't blink or you'll miss it altogether. Tiny or not, Musgrave is the perfect juncture for exploring **Lakefield National Park.** This region of mango-lined floodlands, Queensland's second largest national park, features forests, plains, lagoons, and rivers. You can strike its heart by traveling back towards Cooktown along the **Battle Camp Track,** named after a battle between miners and Aboriginals during the gold rush, though perhaps it should be named after your own battle with the elements. During the wet season, the track is submerged in water, but in the Dry, Lakefield is transformed into a bird sanctuary extravaganza. Crocodiles, feral pigs, and wallaroos are also commonly spotted critters—keep that in mind when you drive through its three rivers. After entering the Battle Camp Track, north of Musgrave, travel east along the clearly-marked track past Lowlake. Bring some emer-

QUEENSLAND

gency supplies, and be prepared for a long trip. It could take you 7hr. or more to drive that route. And also be aware that locals avoid the route, so you may be alone for quite a while if something goes wrong.

**Camping** in these areas is by permit only ($3.50), which can be obtained 6-12 weeks in advance by phoning or writing the **Lakefield Ranger Station** PMB 29, Cairns Mail Centre, QLD 4871. Campers can also get permits on the spot at the station. The ranger station is located in the middle of the park, 112km from Musgrave. (☎/fax 4060 3271. Open daily 9am-5pm.) For those wishing to camp in the southern half of the park, you'll need a permit for the New Laura Ranger Station, while the Lakefield base requires a northern camping permit.

## COEN

North of Musgrave, Peninsula Developmental Rd swerves up and down like a hopping 'roo. The frequent dips are often filled with small, impromptu creeks, which can grow to become monstrous rivers during the Wet. After 109km, the road reaches **Coen** (pop. 300 on a busy day). There's not much to do here; most visitors just stop in to refuel on their way to or from the top of the Cape.

Except for the **police station** (☎ 4060 1150; open M-F 9am-noon) on the road leading into town, everything else is found on Regent St. The **Ambrust General Store** offers groceries, petrol, pay phone, camping, and a **post office**. (☎ 4060 1134. Store open daily 7:30am-6pm; post office M-F 9am-5pm, Sa 9am-noon.) Many establishments here do not operate, or only to a limited degree, during the Wet. The office for the **QPWS** has info packets on nearby parks and campgrounds.

**◪Homestead Guest House,** filled with memorabilia of a gold rush era, is a bit of a time capsule. (☎ 4060 1157; fax 4060 1158. Reception 7am-9pm. Laundry, kitchen. Twins and family rooms $25 per person. No credit cards.) The pub and social center of Coen is the **Exchange Hotel,** with beer ($2.20-3.50), pool table and pay phone. (☎ 4060 1133; fax 4060 1180. Reception 10am-10pm. Doubles $60.) For country cookin' after the long ride, try the **Wilderness Café.** Breakfast ($5-10) and burgers ($4.50-7) stay true to the vegetarian's nightmare that is Cape York cuisine. (☎ 4060 1146. Open M-F 7am-8pm, Sa-Su if people are around.)

The only sight worth seeing in Coen is **◪Charlie's Mine,** at the end of the dirt road and on the right just before the grid leading into town (follow the signs). Eccentric miner-artist Charlie Spiteri built his unique home and filled it with reproductions of Rennaissance artworks made from stones and glass bottles. With a bed covered in onions and potatoes, this place is probably the last thing you'd expect to see in isolated Coen. (☎ 4060 1186. Donations welcome.)

## NORTH OF COEN

Another 65km north along the undulating Peninsula Developmental Rd, a track of red earth and white sand filled with dips (read: miniature rivers cutting through the road) at every turn, leads to the **Archer River Roadhouse.** This place is a nexus of travelers venturing to and from the Tip and is a welcome reminder that yes, life exists somewhere along these lonesome roads. The kitchen serves the usual fare of beer ($3.20-3.30), burgers ($4-6, including the famous Archer Burger) and full meals ($10-14). Three-bed units and one double are modern, clean, and well-maintained. A pretty campground is available as well. (☎/fax 4060 3266. Reception 7am-10pm. Singles $35; doubles $50.) Many parts of the nearby **Archer River** get dried-out in the…well, Dry. There's lots of great camping if you can find a spot; it's quite popular from June to September.

Northeast of the Archer River is the **Iron Range National Park** (128km to the Ranger Station), the largest area of tropical lowland rainforest in Australia and filled with cuscus, parrots, butterflies, and the northern native cat.

Beyond the Archer River, the Peninsula Developmental Rd bears west to the bauxite-mining town of **Weipa,** but if you're not into fishing or bauxite ore, you'll probably be bored to pieces in Weipa. **Telegraph Rd** forks off to the north toward the **Jardine River National Park** and the town of **Bamaga** at the very tip of the Cape. If you're headed to the Jardine River, then you must be itchin' to get to the tip.

QUEENSLAND

# WORLDWIDE CALLING MADE EASY

**The MCI WorldCom Card, designed specifically to keep you in touch with the people that matter the most to you.**

MCI WORLDCOM    WORLDPHONE.

1·800·888·8000

J. L. SMITH

## www.wcom.com/worldphone

Please tear off this card and keep it in your wallet as a reference guide for convenient U.S. and worldwide calling with the MCI WorldCom Card.

---

## HOW TO MAKE CALLS USING YOUR MCI WORLDCOM CARD

- **When calling from the U.S., Puerto Rico, the U.S. Virgin Islands or Canada** to virtually anywhere in the world:
1. Dial 1-800-888-8000
2. Enter your card number + PIN, listen for the dial tone
3. Dial the number you are calling :
   **Domestic Calls:** Area Code + Phone number
   **International Calls:**
   011+ Country Code + City Code + Phone Number

- **When calling from outside the U.S.,** use WorldPhone from over 125 countries and places worldwide:
1. Dial the WorldPhone toll-free access number of the country you are calling from.
2. Follow the voice instructions or hold for a WorldPhone operator to complete the call.

- **For calls from your hotel:**
1. Obtain an outside line.
2. Follow the instructions above on how to place a call.
   **Note:** If your hotel blocks the use of your MCI WorldCom Card, you may have to use an alternative location to place your call.

### RECEIVING INTERNATIONAL COLLECT CALLS*

Have family and friends call you collect at home using WorldPhone service and pay the same low rate as if you called them.

1. Provide them with the WorldPhone access number for the country they are calling from (In the U.S., 1-800-888-8000; for international access numbers see reverse side).
2. Have them dial that access number, wait for an operator, and ask to call you collect at your home number.

*For U.S. based customers only.

## START USING YOUR MCI WORLDCOM CARD TODAY. MCI WORLDCOM STEPSAVERS℠

Get the same low rate per country as on calls from home, when you:

1. **Receive international collect calls to your home** using WorldPhone access numbers
2. **Make international calls with your MCI WorldCom Card** from the U.S.*
3. **Call back to anywhere in the U.S. from Abroad** using your MCI WorldCom Card and WorldPhone access numbers.

*An additional charge applies to calls from U.S. pay phones.

**WorldPhone Overseas Laptop Connection Tips —**
Visit our website, www.wcom.com/worldphone, to learn how to access the Internet and email via your laptop when traveling abroad using the MCI WorldCom Card and WorldPhone access numbers.

**Travelers Assist®** — When you are overseas, get emergency interpretation assistance and local medical, legal, and entertainment referrals. Simply dial the country's toll-free access number.

**Planning a Trip?**—Call the WorldPhone customer service hotline at 1-800-736-1828 for new and updated country access availability or visit our website:

## www.wcom.com/worldphone

## MCI WorldCom Worldphone Access Numbers

*Easy Worldwide Calling*

MCI WORLDCOM.

# The MCI WorldCom Card.

## The easy way to call when traveling worldwide.

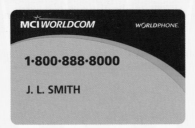

**MCI WORLDCOM**     WORLDPHONE.

**1·800·888·8000**

J. L. SMITH

## The MCI WorldCom Card gives you…

- Access to the US and other countries worldwide.
- Customer Service 24 hours a day
- Operators who speak your language
- Great MCI WorldCom rates and no sign-up fees

For more information or
to apply for a Card call:
## 1-800-955-0925

Outside the U.S., call
MCI WorldCom collect
(reverse charge) at:
## 1-712-943-6839

© 2000, MCI WORLDCOM, Inc. MCI WorldCom, its logo, as well as the names of MCI WorldCom's other products and services referred to herein are proprietary marks of MCI WorldCom, Inc. All rights reserved.

| COUNTRY WORLDPHONE TOLL-FREE ACCESS # | |
| --- | --- |
| Argentina (CC) | |
| Using Telefonica | 0800-222-6249 |
| Using Telecom | 0800-555-1002 |
| Australia (CC) ♦ | |
| Using OPTUS | 1-800-551-111 |
| Using TELSTRA | 1-800-881-100 |
| Austria (CC) ♦ | 0800-200-235 |
| Bahamas (CC) + | 1-800-888-8000 |
| Belgium (CC) ♦ | 0800-10012 |
| Bermuda (CC) + | 1-800-888-8000 |
| Bolivia (CC) ♦ | 0-800-2222 |
| Brazil (CC) | 000-8012 |
| British Virgin Islands + | 1-800-888-8000 |
| Canada (CC) | 1-800-888-8000 |
| Cayman Islands + | 1-800-888-8000 |
| Chile (CC) | |
| Using CTC | 800-207-300 |
| Using ENTEL | 800-360-180 |
| China ♦ | 108-12 |
| Mandarin Speaking Operator | 108-17 |
| Colombia (CC) ♦ | 980-9-16-0001 |
| Collect Access in Spanish | 980-9-16-1111 |
| Costa Rica ♦ | 0800-012-2222 |
| Czech Republic (CC) ♦ | 00-42-000112 |
| Denmark (CC ) ♦ | 8001-0022 |
| Dominica+ | 1-800-888-8000 |
| Dominican Republic (CC) + | |
| Collect Access | 1-800-888-8000 |
| Collect Access in Spanish | 1121 |

| COUNTRY ACCESS # | |
| --- | --- |
| Ecuador (CC) + | 999-170 |
| El Salvador (CC) | 800-1767 |
| Finland (CC) ♦ | 08001-102-80 |
| France (CC) ♦ | 0-800-99-0019 |
| French Guiana (CC) | 0-800-99-0019 |
| Germany (CC) ♦ | 0800-888-8000 |
| Greece (CC) ♦ | 00-800-1211 |
| Guam (CC) ♦ | 1-800-888-8000 |
| Guatemala (CC) ♦ | 99-99-189 |
| Haiti + | |
| Collect Access | 193 |
| Collect access in Creole | 190 |
| Honduras + | 8000-122 |
| Hong Kong (CC) | 800-96-1121 |
| Hungary (CC) ♦ | 06*-800-01411 |
| India (CC) | 000-127 |
| Collect access | 000-126 |
| Ireland (CC) ♦ | 1-800-55-1001 |
| Israel (CC) ♦ | 1-800-920-2727 |
| Italy (CC) ♦ | 172-1022 |
| Jamaica + | |
| Collect Access | 1-800-888-8000 |
| From pay phones | #2 |
| Japan (CC) ♦ | |
| Using KDD | 00539-121 ▶ |
| Using IDC | 0066-55-121 |
| Using JT | 0044-11-121 |

| COUNTRY ACCESS # | |
| --- | --- |
| Korea (CC) | |
| To call using KT | 00729-14 |
| Using DACOM | 00309-12 |
| Phone Booths + | |
| Press red button ,03,then* | |
| Military Bases | 550-2255 |
| Luxembourg (CC) | 8002-0112 |
| Malaysia (CC) ♦ | 1-800-80-0012 |
| Mexico (CC) | 01-800-021-8000 |
| Monaco (CC) ♦ | 800-90-019 |
| Netherlands (CC) ♦ | 0800-022-91-22 |
| New Zealand (CC) | 000-912 |
| Nicaragua (CC) | 166 |
| Norway (CC) ♦ | 800-19912 |
| Panama | 00800-001-0108 |
| Philippines (CC) | |
| Using PLDT | 105-14 |
| Filipino speaking operator | 105-15 |
| Using Bayantel | 1237-14 |
| Using Bayantel (Filipino) | 1237-77 |
| Using ETPI (English) | 1066-14 |
| Poland (CC) + | 800-111-21-22 |
| Portugal (CC) + | 800-800-123 |
| Romania (CC) + | 01-800-1800 |
| Russia (CC) + ♦ | |
| Russian speaking operator | |
| | 747-3320 |
| Using Rostelcom | 747-3322 |
| Using Sovintel | 960-2222 |
| Saudi Arabia (CC) | 1-800-11 |

| COUNTRY WORLDPHONE TOLL-FREE ACCESS # | |
| --- | --- |
| Singapore (CC) | 8000-112-112 |
| Slovak Republic (CC) | 08000-00112 |
| South Africa (CC) | 0800-99-0011 |
| Spain (CC) | 900-99-0014 |
| St. Lucia + | 1-800-888-8000 |
| Sweden (CC) ♦ | 020-795-922 |
| Switzerland (CC) ♦ | 0800-89-0222 |
| Taiwan (CC) ♦ | 0080-13-4567 |
| Thailand (CC) | 001-999-1-2001 |
| Turkey (CC) ♦ | 00-8001-1177 |
| United Kingdom (CC) | |
| Using BT | 0800-89-0222 |
| Using C& W | 0500-89-0222 |
| Venezuela (CC) + ♦ | 800-1114-0 |
| Vietnam + ● | 1201-1022 |

**KEY**

Note: Automation available from most locations. Countries where automation is not yet available are shown in *Italic*

(CC)Country-to-country calling available.

+ Limited availability.

★ Not available from public pay phones.

♦ Public phones may require deposit of coin or phone card for dial tone.

● Local service fee in U.S. currency required to complete call.

▶ Regulation does not permit Intra-Japan Calls.

* Wait for second dial tone.

■ Local surcharge may apply.

**Hint:** For Puerto Rico and Caribbean Islands not listed above, you can use 1-800-888-8000 as the WorldPhone access number.

©2000 MCI WORLDCOM, Inc. All Rights Reserved. The names, logos, and taglines identifying MCI WorldCom's products and services are proprietary marks of MCI WORLDCOM, Inc. or its subsidiaries.

## THE TREK TO THE TIP

North of the Archer River, the Cape's jungle becomes junglier, its heat hotter, its rough tracks rougher, and its wet season wetter. The trip all the way to the Torres Strait that separates Australia from Papua New Guinea is only for the hardest-of-the-hard-core, born-for-the-bush traveler. And what's to do there? Walk a kilometer from the north-ernmost campground, stick your toe in the water, write "___(your name) was here ___(the year)" in the sand, turn around and head back to civilization. Unless you own a car, you can't get to the northernmost point in Australia without shelling out a lot of dough; prices vary depending on duration of trip and mode of transportation, but all options are expensive. Rental companies who insure cars traveling to the Cape are rare. **Britz Rental,** 411 Sheridan St, Cairns, has a four-day minimum rental for 4WDs or campers going to the top of the peninsula. (☎(1800) 33 14 54. In the Dry, 4WD from $175 a day, campers from $195, not including insurance. Open daily 8am-4:30pm.)

**Tour packages** are often the only option. Departing from Cairns, retired bombar-diers air-drop mail over the Cape on **Cape York Air** (☎4035 9399); pilots will let pas-sengers accompany them on their daily runs ($195-390; W tours to the Cape $550). If you can scramble up as far as the Jardine River, **John Charlton's Cape York Boat Adventure** can show you the rest for a very reasonable fare. (☎4069 3302. 2hr. sun-set cruise $30; full-day trips $90). Visiting the Cape is a battle, whether it's against crocs (unlikely) or wallet shock (almost certain). Still, the victory is oh-so-sweet.

# CENTRAL AND WESTERN QUEENSLAND

Queensland's interior is unforgiving—water is scarce and constant threats such as locusts have hardened farmers. There are no "cowboys" here: the correct title for a greenhorn is "jackeroo" (or "jilleroo," as the gender may be). From the third year, workers are called stationhands, and the name "jackeroo" becomes a hard strike against pride. While outback towns can be unkind or indifferent to outsid-ers, the people living here maintain an ethic of trust. A fierce pride in the isolated lands they inhabit is often conveyed in a surprising, peculiar sort of fierce friendli-ness. Folks look you in the eye, and if they don't like what they see, you'll know it.

Queensland's vast interior is traversed by a few highways, unsealed in patches. Generally in better shape than north-south roads, there are several east-west routes: the **Warrego Hwy** (54) from Brisbane to Charleville; the **Capricorn** and **Lands-borough Hwy** (66), from Rockhampton through the Gemfields and Barcaldine to Mt. Isa; the **Flinders Hwy** (78), from Townsville through Charters Towers and Hugh-enden to Mt. Isa; and the **Gulf Development Rd** (1), including part of the **Kennedy Hwy,** from the Atherton Tablelands outside Cairns through the Gulf Savannah to Nor-manton. Connecting them all, the so-called **Matilda Hwy,** the major north-south road, actually encompasses fragments of the Mitchell, Landsborough, and Capri-corn Highways and the Burke Developmental Rd.

# THE WARREGO HIGHWAY

As you head west along the Warrego Hwy from Brisbane, you'll watch the land-scape slowly fade from the sharp contrasts of city lights, black pavement, and green lawns to the subdued copper hues of miles and miles of dust. While passing through the Darling Downs, you'll find Charleville at the intersection with the Mitchell Hwy. South of Charleville, the Mitchell heads through Cunnamulla and across the border to Bourke, New South Wales.

## CHARLEVILLE

Charleville, located at the junction of the Matilda (Mitchell) and the Warrego Hwy, is a worthwhile stop on a trip down either road; it's a sizable and attractive town by outback standards, and offers several interesting diversions. The city's histori-cal sites are well-woven into its modern-day fabric.

From the **train station,** 112 King St (reservations ☎ 13 22 32), two **trains** per week head to **Brisbane** (17hr., $81) via **Roma** and **Toowoomba.** McCafferty's **buses** go to **Brisbane** (14hr., 2 per day, $52) and **Mt. Isa** (15hr., 1 per day, $92). Call **Western Travel Service,** 94 Alfred St (☎ 4654 1260, afterhours ☎ 4654 1029) for bus or train schedules. **Tourist Information Centre:** next to the Graham Andrews Parkland on Cunnamulla Rd. (☎ 4654 3057; fax 4654 3970. Open daily 9am-5pm.) Other services include: **ATM,** at the Westpac on 18 Wills St; **Internet,** at the **library,** 69 Edward St (☎ 4654 1296; open M-F 8:30am-1:30pm and 2:30-4pm, Sa 9am-noon); and **post office** at Wills and Alfred St (☎ 4654 1383; open M-F 9am-5pm; **Postal code:** 4470).

The 🖪**School of Arts Hostel** (☎ 4654 2599), on the corner of Wills and Edward St, shines with wonderful Aboriginal paintings and murals. There's a TV/video lounge, but the best perk is that all prices include three meals a day. (Reception 24hr. Singles, family rooms, doubles $16 per person.) The elegant **Corones Hotel,** 33 Wills St (☎ 4654 1022), has backpacker beds ($20), singles ($35-45), and doubles with bath ($45-55). The dinner buffet at the restaurant costs $12, and the bar stays open until midnight. Within the hotel is **Poppa's Café,** 33 Wills St, with veggie-friendly sandwiches ($4) and *real* coffee ($2-2.50) that will soothe any weary outback traveler's forlorn tastebuds. (☎ 4654 1022. Open M-F 8am-4pm.)

At **Community Development Employment Program,** 111 Sturt St, talented local artist Ernie Adams gives smashing didgeridoo concerts and discusses his murals. (☎ 4654 3016. Open M-F 8am-4pm or by appointment. Free.) At the edge of Graham Andrews Park near Baker St stands the **Stiger Vortex,** a 5.4m high black conical contraption, and the remains of another. In 1902, meteorologist Clement L. Wragge created these "rainmaker guns" believing that shooting them off would, for some reason, bring rain to end a six-year drought. Nope. A visit to Charleville's **Skywatch** on Airport Dr off Cunnamulla Rd east of the info center, allows you to view Mars, Venus, and moon craters, reveals your *real* astrological sign, and explains the whole solar system. (☎ 4654 3057. Shows daily Mar.-Oct. 6:30 pm. $9. Book ahead.)

# CAPRICORN AND LANDSBOROUGH HWYS

The road west from Rockhampton cuts a diagonal through Queensland's Gemfields. Route 66 is called the Capricorn Hwy until its junction with the Matilda Hwy in Barcaldine when it becomes the Landsborough Hwy, which passes through Longreach and Winton and meets the Flinders Hwy two hours east of Mt. Isa.

## GEMFIELDS

Wanna be a millionaire? You might try digging in the dirt in Queensland's Gemfields. Fossicking in this area draws thousands of tourists each year. The income is hardly steady, but it can be lucrative. An unemployed couple recently uncovered a gem worth a million dollars, and a 14-year-old matched that a few years back.

If you want to try your luck, start at the **Naomi Hills Cattle Station** in **Dingo.** Pay $154 for guides, equipment, and a 6hr. dig; professionals will do their best to help you find a sapphire. But luckily, you don't have to find a sapphire to stay at the ranch. (☎ 4925 9121. Beds $18, $38.50 including dinner, continental breakfast, and a tour featuring didgeridoo playing, whip cracking, and boomerang throwing.)

**Emerald,** where no emerald has ever been found, is an affluent town (pop. 10,000) and a major agricultural center with grain, cotton, and mandarin oranges. A convenient stop on McCafferty's (☎ 4982 2755) route to Mt. Isa, the town is also a stepping-off point for the Gemfields. The new **Central Inn,** 90 Clermont St, has rooms with TV. (☎ 4982 0800. Singles $39; doubles $49; including breakfast.)

Forty kilometers west of Emerald, **Anakie** lies in the prime fossicking region. This village holds the last **petrol** station for 125km, and an **info center,** 1 Anakie Rd (☎ 4985 4525; open daily 8am-6pm). Most tourists drive 10-18km further north to **Sapphire** or **Rubyvale,** where you can stop along the road to sort through pre-dug buckets of dirt ($5.50 per bucket). The **Rubyvale Caravan Park** is on Main St. (☎ 4985 4118. Reception 7am-8pm. Tent sites $11, powered $15; cabins for 2 $45.)

# BARCALDINE

Barcaldine (pronounced "bar-CALLED-in") may be the most authentic outback town in Queensland and can be easily reached by car, train, or bus. Most visitors are passing through on their way to Mt. Isa and hang out in the caravan parks outside of town. The locals, however, manage to keep six pubs afloat: one for every day of the week except Sunday, when everyone rolls into church.

Barcaldine's main draw is the **Australian Workers Heritage Centre,** a giant circus tent filled with tributes to Australia's working class. The exhibition's highlight is the history of Australia's Labor Party, which started in Barcaldine. (☎ 4651 2422. Open M-Sa 9am-5pm, Su 10am-5pm. Admission for 1 week $10, concessions $8, children $5.50. Just think how many times you can visit in a week.) When not frequenting the Heritage Centre, visit ■**Mad Mick's Funny Farm,** 84 Pine St. Mick leads folks around his slab hut, where they can meet Ned the Emu and view his wife's collection of 1000 dolls. Entry fee also includes crazy rides on Mick's restored Model T. (☎ 4651 1172. Farm open Apr.-Sept. 9:30am-noon. $8, concessions $7, children $4, includes tea and damper. Book ahead at tourist office.)

The main drag is **Oak St,** where the Landsborough and Capricorn Hwys meet. The **train station,** on Oak St between Beech and Maple St, prefers tickets be booked through the central reservations desk. (☎ 13 22 32. Open M-F 8am-4:30pm.) McCafferty's **buses** stop at the **BP station** on the corner of Oak and Box St. (☎ 4651 1333. Open daily 6:30am-9pm.) Other services include: **RACQ,** 151 Oak St (☎ 4651 1337, afterhours ☎ 4651 1544); **tourist office,** on the corner of Oak and Beech St (☎ 4651 1724; open daily 8:30am-4:30pm); Westpac **bank** with an **ATM,** 103 Oak St (☎ 4651 2993; open M-F 9am-5pm, Sa 9-11:30am); and the **post office,** at the corner of Ash and Beech St (☎ 4651 1147; open M-F 9am-5pm, Sa 9-11am). **Postal code:** 4725.

The **Artesian Hotel,** 85 Oak St, has mostly iron-bar four-poster beds. Reception 10am-noon. (☎ 4651 1691. Beds $20.) **Homestead Caravan Park,** on the corner of Yew and Box St, has a **petrol station.** Reception 7am-8:30pm. (☎/fax 4651 1308. Tent sites for 2 $11, powered $15, each extra person $3; cabins $38-55.)

# BLACKALL

Despite its hot artesian water and affinity for stumps, Blackall (pop. 1800) is a relaxing stop on the Matilda Hwy. Wonderfully bloated bottle trees line the streets like giant Chia Pet bowling pins, but this small town has a surprisingly modern feel.

McCafferty's **buses** pull into Blackall Travel, 68 Shamrock St (☎ 4657 4422), and run daily to: **Brisbane** (departs 7:25pm), **Mt. Isa** (8am), and **Rockhampton** (M, W, F 8am). The **Tourist Information Centre** is on Short St, just off Shamrock St in the center of town. (☎/fax 4657 4637. Open daily 9am-5pm.) Other services include: **ATM** at Commonwealth Bank, 113 Shamrock St; **police** (☎ 4657 4200) on Violet St; **Internet** at the **library,** on the corner of Shamrock and Short St (30min. $1; open Tu-F 10am-12:30pm and 3-5pm, Sa 9:30am-noon); and **post office,** 87 Shamrock St (☎ 4657 4147; open M-F 9am-5pm). **Postal code:** 4472.

The **Prince of Wales Hotel,** 63 Shamrock St, is a steal. (☎ 4657 4731. Reception M-Th 6:30-8pm, F-Sa 6:30-9pm. Twins $11.) A **caravan park** is at the corner of Garden St and Hart Ln. (☎ 4657 4816. Reception daily 8am-7pm. Tent sites $11, powered $14; on-site van for 2 $30; cabins for 2 $49.) The place with the giant kangaroo out front is **The Big Red,** 188 Shamrock St. This souvenir shop sells kangaroo skins, and the café next door serves tasty breakfasts ($3-10), burgers ($4-7), and Smithy's artesian soda. (☎ 4657 4501. Open daily 7am-5:30pm.)

# LONGREACH AND AROUND

The micropolis of Longreach (pop. 4500) is the largest town in the Central West. With its own Pastoral College and School of Distance Education, Longreach acts as the public service and educational center for the area, though priests and rulers can be a dangerous combination. Just ask Pope Gregory VII. Visitors might forget they're in the outback when they walk down **Eagle St,** crowded with cafés, shops, and plenty of pubs and jukeboxes to keep the town hoppin'.

QUEENSLAND

The town's biggest attraction is not actually in town: the **Australian Stockman's Hall of Fame and Outback Heritage Centre** is a massive, multi-media museum off the Landsborough Hwy. (☎4658 2166. Open daily 9am-5pm. $19, concessions $15.) Near the airport is the **Qantas Founders Outback Museum**, housed in the original 1921 Qantas headquarters, with an introductory film and a full-scale model of the first Qantas plane. (☎4658 3737. Open daily 9am-5pm. $8, concessions $5.) For a more grounded historical experience, the **Powerhouse Museum** on the corner of Swan and Ibis St, is filled with hulking gas engines, pumps, tractors, and a complete diesel electric locomotive. (☎4658 3933. Open daily 2-5pm. $4.)

McCafferty's **buses** depart from **Longreach Outback Travel**, 115A Eagle St, with daily service to **Brisbane** and three weekly services to **Rockhampton**. (☎4658 1776. Open M-F 8:30am-5pm, Sa 8:30am-noon and 3:30-4:30pm, Su 10:30-11:30am and 3:30-4:30pm.) The **Information Centre** is at Qantas Park on Eagle St. (☎4658 3555. Open M-F 9am-5pm, Sa-Su 9am-1pm, June-Aug. weekend hours only.) Other services include: **Police** on Galah St (☎4658 2200); **hospital** on Jabiro St (☎4658 4700); Brooksie's **taxi** (☎(1800) 24 25 11); **free Internet access** at the library, 96 Eagle St (☎4658 4104; open Tu and Th 9:30am-1pm, W and F 12:30-5pm, Sa 9am-noon); and **post office** on Duck St. (☎4658 1887. Open M-F 9am-5pm.) **Postal code:** 4730.

The cheapest place to stay is in the **Royal Hotel,** 111 Eagle St, but keep in mind that the pub downstairs hosts a disco from 9pm-2am every F and Sa. (☎4658 2118. Reception Su-Th 10am-11pm, F-Sa 10am-2am. Dorms $11; singles $22; twins $33.) The **Merino Bakery,** 128 Eagle St, sells the freshest bread in town. (☎4658 1715. Open M-F 4:30am-5pm, Sa 4am-noon.)

## WINTON VS. KYNUNA

Two towns duke it out over the matter of *Waltzing Matilda*. Winton's North Gregory Hotel was the site of Banjo Patterson's first performance of Australia's unofficial national anthem, but truckstop Kynuna (163km northwest) is much closer to the actual billabong in the song, and *they've* got the original music score.

Kynuna may be the real deal, but Winton's the site of the brand-new **Waltzing Matilda Centre,** 50 Elderslie St. With statues, holograms, and an underwater "ghost," the only center in the world dedicated to a song is a bit obsessed. (☎4657 1466. Open daily 8:30am-5pm. $14. Café open daily 8am-4pm.) Winton also tries to outdo its neighbors with **Arno's Wall,** behind the North Gregory Hotel, a 70m stretch of home implements, motorcycles, and other flotsam set in concrete. The **Royal Theatre,** on Cobb St, is a large, roofless theatre built in 1918 in which you can watch the stars under the stars. (☎4657 1296. Apr.-Sept. W 8pm. $6.50.)

Staking it's claim, Kynuna's **Swagman Hall of Fame** performs its own history of *Waltzing Matilda* in a two-act show that includes a sing-along followed by a comedy routine. (☎4746 8401. Open daily 8am-10pm. Show: daily 7:30pm, $10.)

Winton's local McCafferty's **bus** station is the Newsagent, 74 Elderslie St. (☎4657 1147. Open M-F 8am-5:30pm, Sa 8am-1pm and 5-6:30pm, Su 10am-2pm and 5-6:30pm.) The **tourist office** is inside the Waltzing Matilda Centre on Elderslie St and sells Mud Maps ($3.50), which describe outback highlights.

The **North Gregory Hotel,** on Elderslie St, was first built in 1878. (☎4657 1375. Reception daily 7am-10pm. Singles $25, ensuite $35; doubles $35, $45. Breakfast included.) On the outskirts of town, **Matilda Country Caravan Park,** 43 Chirnside St, is a friendly place with free pickup from the train and bus stations. (☎4657 1607. Reception 7am-8pm. Tent sites for 2 $12, powered $16; cabins from $60.)

# THE FLINDERS HIGHWAY

A long, lonely route, Flinders Hwy is primarily a straight shot from Townsville to Mt. Isa, on the way though it passes through two towns. Ravenswood and Charters Towers are remote enough to offer a true taste of the outback. As you head further west, towns only get smaller, marked only by a lower speed limit, general store, and petrol pump. Most traffic heads straight to Mt. Isa, a bleak industrial outpost but a gateway to the Northern Territory.

**THE DINOSAUR OUTBACK** It's hard to imagine the dry, dusty outback as the home of giant marine reptiles, but 100 million years ago, much of central Queensland (and some parts of New South Wales and South Australia) was a huge inland sea. This area, called the Great Artesian Basin, has yielded some incredible fossils, including the 12.8m Kronosaurus, Ichthyosaurs, and squid-like ammonites. Fossils are still being discovered today around Hughenden and Richmond.

## RAVENSWOOD

If it's authentic outback you want, Ravenswood (pop. 300) is it. The ghosts of miners past seem to haunt this town, and mining rig skeletons are anchored along the only road in town. Situated about 125km southwest of Townsville, Ravenswood is not serviced by bus so this trip is only for road trippers.

**Macrossan St** is the main road and features Ravenswood's one-man band: the **post office,** on the corner of Raven St, which doubles as a **general store,** triples as a **petrol station,** and quadruples as a **café.** (☎/fax 4770 2136. Open M-F 8am-6:30pm, Sa-Su 9am-3pm.) There are spacious rooms at the **Imperial Hotel** on Macrossan St. (☎4770 2131. Reception 10am-10pm. Singles $45; twins $50; doubles $55.)

The **old jail and courthouse** is now a museum; friendly, knowledgeable curator Woody is the most interesting exhibit. No, its not in the post office. (☎4770 2047. Open W-M 10am-3pm; guided tours 11am and 1:30pm; admission by donation.) On Deighton St is the **White Blow,** a natural quartz crystal mountain.

## CHARTERS TOWERS

South of the Atherton Tablelands, the land dries out and old outback towns begin to punctuate a barren landscape. Once nicknamed "The World" for its cosmopolitan flair, Charters Towers, 1½hr. west of Townsville, was the hub of Queensland, but only traces of its glory days remain.

**█🛈 TRANSPORT AND PRACTICAL INFORMATION.** The **Queensland Rail Station** (☎13 22 32) is on Enterprise Rd on the east side of town. Trains go to **Townsville** (3hr.; Tu and Sa 10:08am; $22) and **Mt. Isa** (17hr.; Su and W 9:16pm; $104). Greyhound, McCafferty's, and Douglas buses depart from the corner of Gill and Church St to **Townsville** for $15-20. Book at **Traveland,** 13 Gill St. (☎4787 2622; fax 4787 7570. Open M-F 8am-5pm, Sa 9am-noon.)

The center of Charters Towers is created by the simple T intersection of Mossman and Gill St, known as the Historic City Centre. Government offices and "The World" theater run along Mosman St, while most shops, restaurants, and banks descend down Gill St. Services include: the **tourist office,** 74 Mosman St at the top of Gill St (☎4752 0314; email tourinfocentre@httech.com.au; open daily 9am-5pm); several **banks** with ATMs strung along Gill St; **RACQ** agents at Gold City Wreckers, 21 Dundee Ln (☎4787 2000); **library** in the Old Bank of New South Wales building, 34 Gill St (☎4752 0338); **Internet** at Charters Towers Computers (open M-F 8:30am-5pm and Sa 8:30am-noon; $8 per hr.); **police station,** 49-55 Gill St (☎4787 1333); **hospital,** 137-139 Gill St near Boundary St (☎4787 1099); and **post office,** 17-19 Gill St (☎4787 1047; open M-F 9am-5pm). **Postal code:** 4820.

**🏠🍴 ACCOMMODATIONS, FOOD, AND NIGHTLIFE.** The **York Street Bed and Breakfast,** 58 York St, is a beautiful place to stay, but far from the center of town. (☎4787 1028. Lodge rooms $28; singles $61; doubles $73.) For something cheaper, try the **Waverly Hotel** at the end of Mossman St. (☎4787 2591. Singles $22; twins $33.) **Charters Towers Caravan Park,** 37 Mount Leyshon Rd, is a 20min. walk south of town. (☎/fax 4787 7944. Reception 7am-7pm. Sites for 2 $11, powered $15.)

The **Stock Exchange Café,** 76 Mosman St, serves somewhat makeshift yet tasty cuisine including quiche, burgers, or lasagna for less than $5. (☎4787 7954. Open M-Th 8:30am-5pm, F-Sa 8:30am-9pm, Su 8:30am-4pm.) **Lawson's Bar and Restaurant,** 82-90 Mosman St, is a classy joint next to the World Theater. (☎4787 4333. Open

W-Su 11:30am-2:30pm and 6pm-late.) Nightlife in Charters Towers is confined to two nightclubs: **Regent Club 96 Bar,** 69 Gill St (☎4787 2600; open F-Sa until 3am); and **Pegasus Night Club,** 33 Gill St, in the White Horse Tavern (☎4787 1064; open F-Sa 10pm-3:30am). The **World Theatre,** 82-90 Mosman St, features concerts, ballets, operas, and plays. (Ticket office ☎4787 4337. Open M-F 10am-1:30pm, Sa 10am-noon.) Two **cinemas** play mostly American films. (Shows W-Su nights. $9, W $6.)

📷 **SIGHTS AND ACTIVITIES.** The big attraction in town is the largest **gold-producing mine** in all of Queensland. Tours are booked through the tourist office (W $13). **Gold Nugget Scenic Tours** runs a 2½hr. sight-seeing tour around town, departing the tourist office daily at 8:30am. (☎4787 4115. $22, children $10.) Two cattle stations nearby hire backpackers for a couple of weeks and offer "City Slicker" holiday packages: **Bluff Downs** (☎4770 4084) and **Plain Creek** (☎4983 5228).

## PRAIRIE AND HUGHENDEN

After a few hours, the road runs through **Prairie,** a town with a pub worth a stretch and a coffee. **The Prairie Hotel,** on the Flinders Hwy, has two rooms, a new motel unit, and camp sites. (☎4741 5121. Sites $11; powered $16.50; singles $22; doubles $39. Motel: singles $50; doubles $61.)

**Hughenden** (HYU-enden) marks the eastern edge of Queensland's marine dinosaur territory: stop into the **Visitor Information Centre,** 37 Gray St, to see the **Muttaburrasaurus skeleton** they've got stashed in the back. (☎4741 1021. Open daily 9am-5pm. $2.) Budget accommodation in Hughenden is limited to the ambitiously-named **Grand Hotel,** 25 Gray St (☎4741 1588; singles $22; twins and doubles $38), and the **Allan Terry Caravan Park** (☎4741 1190; reception M-F 6am-9pm; tent sites for 2 $10, powered $14; cabins $49.50). **Pete's Country Kitchen,** 3 Gray St, serves as the local bus stop and café, with Brontosaurus burgers into the wee hours. (☎4741 1180. Open daily 6:30am-10pm and midnight-2am.) **Porcupine Gorge,** a beautiful natural valley, is 63km north of town. **Adventure Wildlife and Bush Treks** operates from the caravan park, and has full-day trips ($83) and 3-day trips ($330) on demand.

## RICHMOND

West of Hughenden along the Flinders Hwy, Richmond packs an impressive paleological punch. **Kronosaurus Korner,** 93 Goldring St, is both the regional **Visitor Information Centre** and the **Marine Fossil Display,** housing the bones of local cretaceous creatures. (☎4741 3429. Open daily 8:30am-4:45pm. $8.) The brand new **Moon Rock Café,** across from the information counter, cooks up inspired dino-burgers and veggie-friendly sandwiches ($2.50-6.50). The **caravan park** up the street is an exceptional value with A/C, shared bathrooms, and kitchen. (☎4741 3772. Key deposit $10. Tent sites $10, powered $13; donga beds $15.) The **Mud Hut Motel,** 72 Goldring St, has basic pub rooms. (☎/fax 4741 3223. Singles $44; doubles $55.)

# MOUNT ISA

When the subject of Mount Isa comes up, backpackers' conversations sober up and casual laughter dwindles. This is the city where hitchhikers on their way to the Northern Territory break down and buy a bus ticket. Honeymooning couples have been known to sell their campervans in the Isa and head to the airport. No matter what your next destination is, from Mt. Isa you've got a hell of a long trip ahead of you. The city itself has the feel of an intergalactic spaceport; walking down the street, it's possible to tick off dozens of languages in overheard chitchat. Two- and three-trailer road trains crowd the outskirts of town, and in case you forgot to set your watch ahead half an hour after leaving the Northern Territory, you'll be reminded by the sounds of the 8am and 8pm underground mining blasts, part and parcel of the copper mines' 12hr. shifts. There are three types of people who come here: first, copper, silver, zinc, and lead miners; second, graziers (farmers) from outlying areas who need to stock up on food and supplies; and third, you, the traveler, stopping at the biggest urban outpost on the endless haul from the Queensland coast to the tropical Top End or to the Red Centre. So take a deep breath, try not to choke, and get ready to cross the desert.

**TRANSPORT.** The **Train Station** (☎4744 1203) is on Station St near Miles End next to the mines. From town, take Isa St west over the bridge until it ends; the station is on the right. The *Inlander* train departs 6pm Monday and Friday to: **Townsville** (19hr.) via **Cloncurry** (3½hr.); **Richmond** (9¼hr.); **Hughenden** (11¼hr.); and **Charters Towers** (16hr.). McCafferty's, 27-29 Barkly Hwy, is at Campbell's Coaches. From town, take Grace St west over the river until it ends and the terminal is on your right. (☎4743 2006. Open M-F 6am-7:45pm, Sa 6am-noon and 6-7:45pm, Su 6am-8am and 6-7:45pm. YHA.) **Buses** run to: **Brisbane** ($122); **Darwin** ($191); **Alice Springs** ($166); **Cairns** ($132); **Charters Towers** ($86); **Richmond** ($45); **Rockhampton** ($175); and **Townsville** ($91). The Greyhound booking office is at **Downtown Travel** (☎4743 5077), and they travel to the major cities at similar prices.

**ORIENTATION AND PRACTICAL INFORMATION.** The city center is a manageable four-by-four grid, bounded by **Isa St** to the north, **West St** to the west, **Mary St** to the south, and **Simpson St** to the east. The **Barkly Hwy** enters from Northern Territory and runs parallel to the **Leichhardt River** until the bridge at **Miles End,** then turns left over the water into the city center on **Grace St.** From Cloncurry in the east, the Barkly Hwy becomes **Marion St.** This forks to the left, whereas Grace St forks to the right into town after passing the **Riversleigh Interpretive Centre.**

**Traveland,** 27-29 Barkly Hwy, next to the McCafferty's terminal, is a budget travel office. (☎4743 3399; fax 4743 7376. Open M-F 9am-5pm, Sa 9am-noon.) The **Riversleigh Interpretive Centre,** Centenary Park, Marion St, books mine tours. (☎4749 1555; fax 4743 6296. Open M-F 8:30am-5pm, Sa-Su 9am-4pm.) Other services include: **Commonwealth Bank,** 23 Miles St (☎4743 5033; traveler's checks or cash exchange fee $5; open M-Th 9:30am-4pm, F 9:30am-5pm); **Mt. Isa Base Hospital,** 30 Camooweal St (☎4744 4444); **police,** 7 Isa St, at the corner of Miles St (☎4743 1111; open 24hr.); **Internet** at the **library,** 23 West St (☎4744 4256; open M-Th 10am-6pm, F 10am-5pm, Sa 9am-noon; 15min. $2); **United Cab** (24hr. ☎ 13 10 08); **RACQ,** 13 Simpson St (☎4743 4300, afterhours ☎ (0417) 71 41 62); and **post office,** on the corner of Camooweal and Isa St (☎4743 2454; open M-F 8:30am-5pm). **Postal code:** 4825.

**ACCOMMODATIONS AND FOOD.** **Traveller's Haven,** at the corner of Pamela and Spence St, is the only hostel in town, with free pickup and a nice pool. (☎4743 0313. Reception daily 6:30am-1pm and 5-7pm. Linen $2. Key deposit $5. Dorms $15; singles $28; twins and doubles $36. VIP.) **Boyd's Hotel,** 16-20 West St, near the corner of Marion St, is one of the cheapest hotels in Mt. Isa. The basic rooms have A/C and sinks. (☎4743 3000. Singles $40; twins $55.) **Sunset Van Park,** 14 Sunset Dr, is on the corner of Carbine Ave. (☎4743 7668. Reception daily 7am-10pm. Key deposit $10. Sites for 2 $15, powered $17; cabin for 2 $59.)

Fast food has made it to the corner of Queensland's outback, but there are few good places to eat in the Isa. The **Buffalo Club,** on the corner of Grace and Simpson St, offers a $9 all-you-can-eat lunch buffet. Look decent: collared shirt yay, sandals nay. (☎4743 2365. Open Su-Th 10am-11pm, F-Sa 10am-2am.) For herbivores, the **Miner's Hut Café,** 31 Miles St, makes mean meat-free meals. (☎4743 1555. Open M-F 8am-5pm, Sa 8am-2pm.) Woolworth's **supermarket,** 2 Miles St, at Isa St, is in the town center. (☎4743 6888. Open M-F 8am-9pm, Sa 8am-5pm.)

**SIGHTS.** The most exciting thing to do in Mt. Isa is leave. Alternately, a 4hr. **Underground Mine Tour** dives into the belly of the beast. Put on the suit and hat and enter the winding labyrinth of tunnels. Book through the Riversleigh Centre as far

**QUEENSLAND**

**TAIL FROM THE ROAD** Two blokes driving along the endless, dusty outback roads hit and knocked unconscious a kangaroo. Feeling sorry for the critter, they carried it back into the car. Starving for some kind of entertainment in the vast nothing of the outback, the two decided to dress up the kangaroo and put a Yankees jacket on the sleeping marsupial. When it finally woke up, the kangaroo panicked, flailing about the car with its powerful legs. The two 'roo-snatchers got so beat up they had to be hospitalized. They couldn't pay for the medical fees, though—the jacket-wearing kangaroo had pocketed the wallet and credit cards and hopped away.

ahead as possible. (☎4749 1555. 2 per day M-F; $44.) The **Frank Aston Underground Museum,** on Shackleton St, off Marion St across from Kmart, is a hollowed-out hill containing mining machinery, an exhibit on Kalkadoon culture, and a beautiful display of minerals and gems. (☎4749 0610. Open daily 9am-4pm. $5.)

# THE GULF SAVANNAH

The area between the Atherton Tablelands and the Gulf of Carpentaria along the **Gulf Developmental Rd,** the Gulf region revels in remoteness, welcoming the way-ward visitor with respectful indifference. This is the outback's outback. The Gulf's few tourist attractions include historic "nowhere-to-nowhere" trains, gorges, and lava tubes. The Gulf can be an escapist fantasy or a city slicker's nightmare. The sea can be reached by Karumba Point Rd off the Gulf Developmental Rd, 4km before **Karumba** (pop. 600) and 72km northwest of **Normaton.**

The Dry (Apr.-Oct.) is the time to visit, though even then the road conditions can be bad. Road reports are issued by the **Gulf Savannah Tourism** (☎4051 4658) in Cairns, as well as in local info centers and RACQs. The most common route through the region is the **Gulf Developmental Rd,** linking Cairns to Normanton, where it joins the desolate north-south **Burke Developmental Rd.** These are primarily single-lane, cattle-strewn, kangaroo-enticing sealed roads. Conventional vehicles are fine on most roads during the Dry, but caravans should avoid those which are unsealed. If you want to brave the Wet, 4WD is essential. Never drive the Ootann Rd connecting Mt. Surprise and Chillagoe or anywhere along the Mt. Isa-River-sleigh-Lawn Hill National Park route without 4WD.

Several **tours** operate from Cairns. **Cool Croc,** a six-day camping excursion, leaves from **Cairns** and arrives in **Darwin,** or vice versa. (☎(1800) 68 84 58. Apr.-Oct. $549; YHA, VIP, ISIC $489; includes breakfast and dinner.) Stationed throughout the region are **Savannah Guides,** with knowledge of specific areas, including Lawn Hill National Park, Undara Lava Tubes, Cobbold Gorge, and Tallaroo Hot Springs. Book ahead at individual stations or the main office in Cairns (☎4031 7933).

## ROUTE 1 FROM CAIRNS: THE EASTERN GULF

Lying between the Atherton Tablelands and the Carpentaria Coast along Rte 1, **Georgetown** (pop. 350) and **Mt. Surprise** (pop. 65) make for decent stopovers. The towns, along with nearby **Einasleigh** and **Forsayth,** are part of the **Etheridge Goldfield** and popular with amateur fossickers. The *Savannahlander* **train** connects **Mt. Surprise** and **Forsayth,** via **Einasleigh.** (☎(1800) 62 03 24. 6¼hr.; departs Mt. Surprise Sa 8:15am, departs Forsayth F 7:45am. $38.50, concessions $19.)

The eastern Gulf's most awesome attraction is a 40min. drive from Mt. Surprise. The **Undara Volcano** erupted 190,000 years ago, creating 69 **lava tubes** in the middle of dense rainforest, with caverns averaging 10m high and 15m wide. **Undara Experience** visits nine of them. (☎4097 1411. 2hr. tour $33; daily 8am and 1pm. Half-day tours $64; daily 8:30, 10:30am, 1, 3pm.) At Undara, you can camp ($5.50 per person) or stay in the tent village ($16.50 per person; linen $5.50).

## NORMANTON AND CROYDON

**Normanton** (pop. 1200) is the largest town in the Gulf; two-thirds of its population is Aboriginal. The town is as much a relic as its famous **Gulflander train,** 20 Matilda St (☎4745 1391), in the station on Matilda St next to the **info center** (open in the Dry daily 7am-6pm). There's a Westpac **bank** with an **ATM** at the corner of Landsborough and Little Brown St. Normanton's **Brolga Palms Motel** and **National Hotel** are both connected to the **Purple Pub** on the corner of Landsborough and Brown St. (☎4745 1009. Hotel singles $25; doubles $40; motel singles $63; doubles $73.) At the other end of Brown St is the **caravan park.** (☎4745 1121. Tent sites $5 per person; caravan sites $10; powered $13).

The population of **Croydon** increases by nearly 20% when the Gulflander pulls in. The **Club Hotel** is the last of the 122 pubs that once catered to gold-miners. (☎4745 6184. Open daily 10am-10pm. Singles $37; doubles $53.) **Croydon Caravan Park** is on the corner of Brown and Aldridge St. (☎4745 6238. Sites for 2 $10, powered $13.)

QUEENSLAND

# SOUTH AUSTRALIA

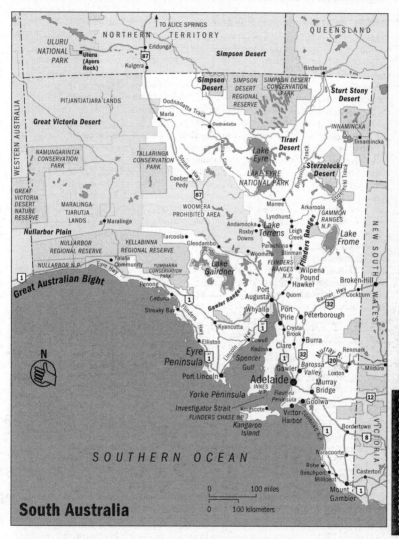

South Australia

Prophets of the Australian backpacking scene are known to wander the deserts of the land, telling all who listen: "There is only one South Australia, and Adelaide is its capital." That said, it's amazing that such a relatively small number of travelers and tourists to the land down under bother to do anything besides race from Melbourne to Uluru via requisite stop-overs in Adelaide and Coober Pedy. For those who take the time to learn and love this state, with its fly-specked, harsh, but beautiful Outback north, the lovely Eyre Peninsula's coast, and the world's biggest country town (Adelaide), a new truth about the east coast will become evident: the best thing about Queensland's touristy beaches is the road out.

The prophets go on: "And then God created the heavens and the Earth." Highway 87, which connects Coober Pedy with Port Augusta to the south and Alice Springs to the north, will remind the most forgetful of city slickers where exactly humanity stands on the scale of things: the stars up above join together in a glowing white choir known as the Milky Way, and the harshest, driest, most sunscorched country this side of the SA-WA border will either capture your heart and imagination, or send you scrambling for the next bus to someplace wetter.

Continuing with their speech, these sages say: "For God so loved the world, He gave it His only Parachilna." That little town may well be one of the most unlikely places to find one of the best pubs in all of SA, but defying expectations, there it is. The ancient Flinders Ranges, a portfolio of spectacular sculpting by five billion years of geological processes, is known more generally for the wildlife than the nightlife (if one discounts all the nocturnal animals roaming the bush), but in nearby Parachilna rages one hell of a good time.

When relating the powers of the South Australian landscape: "And He turned water into wine." Here, in the driest state in the driest continent on earth, the population chants this mantra: save water, drink wine. Although Cooper's line of beers might be the homebrew, a good chunk of the state's economy rests on the fine vintages produced throughout the south of the state: the Barossa and Clare valleys east-northeast of Adelaide, the McLaren Vale and Fleurieu Peninsula region to the south of the capital, the banks of the Murray River, the southeast of the Eyre Peninsula, and the Coonawarra region between Naracoorte and Mount Gambier, down southeast by Victoria, all provide a more refined way to get bloody pissed.

"I will make you fishers of men." South Australia's long coastline offers everything: sheltered bays for swimming; beaches exposed to the great Southern Ocean where the waves roll in high and mighty, ready to be caught by anyone with the willingness and a board; large populations of seals, sea lions, and steel-blue fairy penguins; on-site locations for the filming of some segments of *Jaws*; great fishing from any angle; and a breezy respite from the oft-raging inferno further inland.

South Australia isn't Dante's Paradise, probably, but it sure isn't very far away. Although its veracity is a matter of some debate among scholars of the Torah, there is an apocryphal section of the Book of Genesis that reads:

> 13 And so Adam and Eve were cast out of the Garden. 14 On the way out, Adam asked a seraphim, 15 "Which way is it to South Australia?" 16 To which the angel replied, "Follow me, as I'm going there myself."

Visitors should do themselves a favor: follow the angel, and stay for a while.

## SOUTH AUSTRALIA HIGHLIGHTS

**SENSORY OVERLOAD.** Adelaide's Central Market (p. 423).

**TAKE ONE FOR THE TEAM.** Late nights in pubs with bushies, truckies, and ordinary-blokes.

**SPECTACULAR SPELUNKING.** The formations of the Naracoorte Caves (p. 449).

**REASSESS.** A new perspective on Wilpena Pound from St. Mary's Peak (p. 455).

**CHILL OUT.** Cooling off in the underground hostels of Coober Pedy (p. 458).

**CHUG-A-LUG.** Cooper's line of ales and stouts.

**CULINARY ADVENTURE.** The quadong fruit, an outback original.

# ▣ GETTING AROUND

If you don't have a car, the most practical way to see most of South Australia's attractions is by bus. Greyhound Pioneer (☎ (1800) 80 61 75) runs between **Adelaide** and **Melbourne, Sydney, Alice Springs,** and **Perth,** stopping over at a few destinations in between. McCafferty's (☎ (1800) 07 62 11) is another major bus company. Premier Stateliner (☎8415 5555) services smaller towns throughout South Australia. For **train** information, see p. 418.

Major **car rental** companies with branches in SA include **Hertz** (☎13 30 39), **Avis** (Adelaide ☎8410 5727), and **Thrifty** (☎(1800) 06 40 45); local outfits, often with lower prices, are listed throughout this chapter. A conventional vehicle is fine for wine and beach country, but 4WD is strongly recommended for forays into the outback. Another good option, often more practical for those traveling alone or going to out-of-the-way places, is to book a **tour.** Many choose the jump-on, jump-off flexibility of backpacker buses like **Oz Experience** (☎(1300) 30 00 28) or **Wayward Bus** (☎8232 6646), but plenty of local organizations run excellent trips. Most hostels have ample tour advice and can book for guests, often at a discount. Still the greatest way to see the state is to buy a used car or 4WD upon arrival, and sell it when leaving the country—this provides the ultimate in freedom and flexibility.

# ADELAIDE

To the area's first residents, the Kaurna people, the area in and around Adelaide was "Tandanya," the place of the red kangaroo. To the hundreds of thousands of immigrants who filled the region and over-flowed into the hinterland, this was a place to make a new start. To the many backpackers, this is a spot to get drunk, get some rays, and then, after a week or so, get on a bus to Alice Springs.

Once known only for its inordinate number of churches, Adelaide has emerged as a city with far more to offer than an uplifting Sunday sermon. The first completely planned city in Australia, in the first state not to be settled by convicts, Adelaide has always liked to think of itself as different from the other Australian capitals. The one million people who call the state capital home take pride in the big leafy trees on wide streets, graceful colonial buildings, and flourishing arts scene, and enjoy a big-city lifestyle that belies the lower cost of living.

This city appreciates the good life. With more restaurants per capita than any other city in Australia, Adelaide can satisfy any palate at any budget, and then wash it all down with some of the country's best wines. The city's cultural attractions, headed by the Adelaide Festival of Arts, includes a symphony and chamber orchestra, numerous small experimental theaters, and world-class galleries and museums. For those who prefer a more raucous pace, the nightclubs along Hindley St, the pubs in the city center, and the cafés on Rundle St fit the hedonistic bill.

Some people in the country-side think of Adelaide as a country town, albeit a very large one. Travelers looking for a list of sights comparable to Paris or London will be disappointed; all the must-see sights and must-do museums yield only a few days of exploration. But anyone who appreciates what differentiates a traveler from a tourist—the willingness to live for a while rather than blow in, look at some paintings and some historic buildings, and get out of town—will find Adelaide right up their alley. The beachfront suburb of Glenelg is now one of Adelaide's most popular residences for fisherfolk, yuppies, travelers, and at least a gazillion seagulls. The gardens, playgrounds, and jogging trails in Adelaide's 68 hectares of parkland provide plenty of room to romp. Visually stunning hikes can be found in the Adelaide Hills, and nearly 100 fantastic wineries cluster in three distinct regions within an hour of the city center. And, perhaps most importantly of all, visitors to Adelaide will find that almost anyone here is willing to say hello.

## ◪ GETTING THERE

### BY PLANE

The airport, 7km west of the city center, services domestic and international carriers in separate terminals. A taxi ride to the city runs $12-15, but most hostels in the city or Glenelg offer free pickup from the airport with advance booking. Failing that, the cheapest way is the **Transit Regency Airport-to-City Bus,** which picks up and

SOUTH AUSTRALIA

**IN-LINE SKATING.** The Linear Park Bike Track cooled by sea breezes (p. 419).

**PEOPLE-WATCHING.** The lively Central Market (p. 423).

**SUMMER FARE.** Summer outdoor theater at the Botanic Gardens (p. 424).

**HAUT CULTURE.** The collection at the Art Gallery of South Australia (p. 424).

**AMAZING GRACE.** A beer at the chillest bar, Grace Emily (p. 427).

**DRINK IN.** Spectacular views from Mt. Lofty in Adelaide Hills (p. 429).

drops off near city accommodations. (☎8381 5311. Every 30min. M-F, every 1hr. Sa-Su, 7am-10pm. $6, children $2; return $10. Book ahead for travel to the airport.) Catch the bus in front of the domestic terminal directly in front of the currency exchange, or to the left as you exit the international terminal. **TransAdelaide** public bus #270 will bring you from Currie St in the city to the airport entrance on Burbridge Rd, but from there it is a 15min. walk to the terminal.

Be sure to mention that you're an international traveler when booking domestic flights; on one-way fares it can make a big difference in price. Qantas (domestic flights ☎13 13 13, international ☎13 12 11) and Ansett (☎13 13 00) are the major carriers. Qantas also oversees ASA (Airlines of South Australia; ☎8682 5688, freecall ☎(1800) 01 82 34), servicing the **Eyre Peninsula;** and O'Conner (book through Qantas), servicing **Mt. Gambier.** Kendell Airlines is the major local carrier (book through Ansett), with flights to: **Ceduna** ($280); **Coober Pedy** ($361); **Kangaroo Island** ($90); and **Mt. Gambier** ($194). 17 and under receive a 25% discount, seniors 40%. Emu Airways (☎8234 3711, freecall ☎(1800) 18 23 43) services **Kangaroo Island.**

## BY TRAIN

Train travel is usually pricier than bus travel, but the prospect of sitting on a bus for 34hr. may make one cringe. All interstate or long distance country trains use the **Keswick Interstate Rail Passenger Terminal** (☎13 21 47) in Keswick, a suburb 2km southwest of Adelaide's Central Business District. Only suburban commuter trains use the **Adelaide Railway Station** (☎8210 1000) on North Tce. The Transit Regency Airport-to-City Bus brings rail passengers to and from the Keswick Station. (☎8381 5311. $3, children $1, return $5. Book ahead for travel to the station). The Keswick terminal has free car parking. The *Overland* services **Melbourne** (12-13½ hr.; departs Su-Tu, Th-F 7:15pm, W 9:20am; $58, students $46, children $29, economy car $30). The *Ghan* runs to **Alice Springs** (19hr., departs M, Th 3pm; $170, $136, $85). The *Indian Pacific* runs to **Perth** (39hr.; departs Tu, F 6pm; $248, $198, $124). The *Indian Pacific* and *Ghan* both connect Adelaide with **Sydney** (24-25hr.; departs W, Su 7:45am, Sa 8:50am; $152, students $122, children $76; YHA 10% discount. Confirm times in advance.) International students with an ISIC card usually qualify for student rates; try **Cannon St Travel,** across from the bus station.

## BY BUS

Adelaide's **central bus station** is at 101-111 Franklin St. Across the street stands the pink **Backpacker Travel and Transit Centre** with tour information, free luggage storage, and Internet access. (☎8410 3000. Open M-F 9am-5pm, Sa 10am-2pm. Internet 1hr. $6.) National bus companies provide regular service to and from Adelaide at prices that generally beat rail and air travel. Greyhound Pioneer (☎13 20 30) runs to: **Brisbane** (29hr., 2 per day, $160); **Darwin** (14hr., 1 per day, $280); **Melbourne** (10hr., 2 per day, $45); **Perth** (34hr., 1 per day, $199); **Sydney** (22hr., 3 per day, $96); **Alice Springs** (20hr., 1 per day, $135); **Yulara/Ayers Rock** (20hr., 1 per day, $135), and many places in between. McCafferty's (☎13 14 99), the other major long-distance bus line, services destinations around southern, northern, and eastern Australia. Greyhound Pioneer and McCafferty's prices are usually within a few dollars of each other. Within South Australia, Premier Stateliner (☎8415 5555) is the main

## Adelaide

**ACCOMMODATIONS**

Adelaide Backpackers Inn, 7
Adelaide City Backpackers Hostel, 1
Adelaide Traveller's Inn, 8
The Austral Hotel, 10
Backpack Australia, 4
Backpack Oz, 9
Breckon Inn, 6
Cannon St Backpackers, 2
East Park Lodge, 11
Kiwi 'n' Oz International, 5
Sunny's Backpacker Hostel, 3

SOUTH AUSTRALIA

carrier. See coverage of your intended destination for prices and frequency from Adelaide. The free *State Guide*, available at the tourist office and many hostels, combines all bus info and is indispensable for planning travel around the state.

# ✦ ORIENTATION

Surrounded by parklands, Adelaide proper is only one square mile, which makes it easy to navigate. Bordering the city on all four sides are the four terraces, creatively named North, South, East, and West. The streets running east to west are split by **King William St,** the major north-south thoroughfare in the center of the city, at which point their names change. Streets running north to south retain their names when they meet four smaller squares or **Victoria Sq** in the very center of the city. Although Adelaide is a relatively peaceful city, the parklands are unsafe at night, especially near the River Torrens and in the southwest corner of the city.

**Keswick,** with the railway station, is about 2km southwest of the **Central Business District (CBD).** The airport and the beach suburb of **Glenelg** are southwest of the CBD. Northwest of the CBD, just in from the gulf and on the Port River, is the suburb of **Port Adelaide.** The **Adelaide Hills,** including Cleland Conservation Park and Belair National Park, are east of the city.

# ▐ GETTING AROUND

## BY PUBLIC TRANSPORTATION

Adelaide is serviced by public buses, trains, and one lone tram that make up an integrated public transport system called **TransAdelaide.** The same tickets can be used on any bus, train, or tram. TransAdelaide runs two free bus services around the city: **Beeline** and **City Loop.** These bright yellow buses are easily identified, fully wheelchair accessible, and clearly labeled "Free Ride." Beeline runs in the city center, from the railway station on North Tce down King William St to Victoria Sq and back (every 5min. M-Th 7:40am-6pm, F 7:40am-9pm; every 15min. Sa 8:30am-5pm). City Loop, true to its name, runs both directions around a loop that covers the north half of the city, including stops at North, East, and West Tce. It also stops at most major tourist attractions, Central Market, and near the bus station. (Every 15min. M-Th 8:30am-6pm, F 8:30am-9:30pm; every 30min. Sa 8:30am-5pm.)

To roam farther, you need to tackle the mass of bus and train routes that comprise TransAdelaide's suburban system. Luckily, an info line (☎8210 1000, staffed daily 7am-8pm) can tell you which bus you need and where and when to catch it. The **Passenger Transport Information Centre,** at the corner of King William and Currie St, also has route schedules (open M-Sa 8am-6pm, Su 10:30am-5:30pm).

Single **tickets** to anywhere in the system on any bus, train, or tram are good on any service (including return trip) for 2hr. and can be purchased from bus drivers, tram conductors, and train vending machines (M-F 9am-3pm, single trip $1.60; all other times $2.80). Daytrip tickets ($5.40) allow one-day unlimited travel on any service and can be purchased when boarding buses or trams, but must be bought beforehand for trains. You must **validate** single or daytrip tickets each time you enter a new bus, train, or tram. An option for those staying longer is the Multitrip ticket, which you must buy at a newsagent, post office, or the Passenger Transport Info Centre prior to boarding. It's good for ten 2hr. trips ($19, off-peak $11).

The best way to get to **Glenelg** and the beach from the city is to take the tram from Victoria Sq to Moseley Sq (30min., trams run every 15-20min. M-F 6am-midnight, Sa 7:30am-midnight, Su 8:50am-midnight). Although it's much cheaper to explore on your own, for a fully guided tour of the area, **Adelaide Explorer** does a city to Glenelg hop-on, hop-off tour that takes 3hr. Pick up the small bus, decorated like a tram, anywhere on the route or join at 38 King William St daily at 9am, 10:30am, noon, 1:30, or 3pm. (☎8364 1933. $25 per day, concessions $24, ages 6-14 $15, families $55; second day $7.)

## BY BOAT

**Popeye boats** runs inexpensive cruises on the River Torrens from Sept. to May, weather permitting. They depart Elder Park, behind the Festival Centre, and arrive at Adelaide Zoo (25min.; every 1hr. M-F 11am-3pm, every 20min. Sa-Su 10:30am-4:30pm; $4, children $2). From the same spot, **Elder Park Paddle Boat Hire** charges $6 per 30min. (☎(018) 84 45 88. Open daily 9am-6pm, off-season 9:30am-5pm.)

## BY CAR

**Hertz,** 233 Morphett St (☎13 30 39); **Budget** (☎13 27 27); and **Avis,** 136 North Tce (☎8410 5727), have counters at the airport and agencies in town. **Thrifty** (☎8211 8788, freecall ☎(1800) 06 40 45) is affiliated with **Caudell's Explorer Self-Drive,** Hindley St (☎8410 5552), which offers automatic cars from $50, and manual 4WD from $69-100 per day. **Bush Bashers,** 175 Hart St, Glanville (☎8242 3033) has 4WD hire from $100 with 200km, or from $120 with unlimited km. (minimum age 25).

If you're under 25, it's much cheaper to hire from a smaller agency. These companies are scattered around the suburbs, but will generally pickup and drop off in town. **Smile Rent-a-Car,** 163 Richmond Rd, southwest of town, has excellent rates, no age surcharge for drivers under 25, unlimited kilometers, friendly service, and good quality cars. (☎8234 0655, freecall ☎(1800) 62 44 24. Small manual or automatic from $30-40, plus $10 per day for insurance.) **No Frills Car Rental** is what its name suggests, but it has no age limit and cars from $20 per day. (☎8341 2727. New cars from $35; 2-day min.; $10 flat-rate insurance required).

For campervans or motorhomes, **Britz,** 376 Burbridge Rd, Brooklyn Park (☎8234 4701, freecall ☎(1800) 33 14 54), has two- to six-berth vans and one-way rental with unlimited kilometers to all major cities in Australia. Also ask about relocation deals, where you pay as little as $1 per day, plus petrol costs. **Skippy Camper Rentals,** 1505 South Rd, Darlington (☎8296 2999), has regular campervan rentals (minimum hire 5 days, one-way available) as well as some used camper vans and 4WDs for sale with buy-back schemes available.

## BY TAXI

**Des's** (☎13 13 23), **Diamond** (☎13 24 48), **Yellow** (☎13 22 27), **Adelaide Independent** (☎13 22 11), **Suburban Taxis** (☎31 10 08), and **Access Cabs** (☎(1300) 36 09 40) all provide service. Access Cabs is wheelchair-accessible. Cabs are easy to find.

## BY BICYCLE

Many city streets have designated cycling lanes. The 40km **Linear Park Bike and Walking Track** provides the biking, jogging, or rollerblading enthusiast with beachside breezes and river views in the beautiful Adelaide foothills. Further information is available at bike shops, including **Elder Park Mountain Bike Hire** (☎8223 6271; open behind the Festival Centre M-F 9:15am-5pm, Sa-Su 9:15am-6pm; family rates available); **Linear Park Mountain Bike Hire** (☎8223 6953; 20% backpacker discount); **Freewheelin'** (☎8232 6860); and **Mountain Bike Hire** (☎8212 7800). Rentals start at $15-20 per day, but there are cheaper weekly rates. Some hostels also rent bikes.

# 🔢 PRACTICAL INFORMATION

## TOURIST AND FINANCIAL SERVICES

**Tourist Office: South Australian Travel Centre,** 1 King William St (☎(1300) 65 52 76; www.visit-southaustralia.com.au), at the corner of North Tce, has well-informed staff. Open M-F 8:30am-5pm, Sa-Su 9am-2pm. Wheelchair accessible. **Glenelg Tourist Information Office,** Moseley Square, Glenelg (☎8294 5833). Open daily 9am-5pm.

**National Parks Information: Department for Environment, Heritage and Aboriginal Affairs Information Centre,** 77 Grenfell St (☎8204 1910; fax 8204 1919). **Flinders Ranges and Outback Visitor Centre,** 142 Gawler Place (☎(1800) 633 060).

SOUTH AUSTRALIA

**Budget Travel:** YHA Travel, 38 Sturt St (☎8231 5583). Open M-F 9am-5pm.

**Employment:** 55 Currie St (☎9231 9444) or 12 Durham St, Glenelg (☎8202 6700). Valid working visa only. The W and Sa *Advertiser* has job classifieds.

**Consulates: U.K.** (☎8212 7280). For Australian visa extensions ($135), bring proof of funds (e.g. bank statement) and apply at the **Department of Immigration and Ethnic Affairs,** 4th fl. of the Commonwealth Centre, 55 Currie St.

**Banks:** Generally open M-Th 9:30am-4pm, F 9:30am-5pm. **ATMs** all around the city.

**Currency Exchange:** Almost any time, if you're dressed nicely, at **Adelaide Casino,** North Tce. Passport or driver's license required. Open Su-Th 10am-4am, F-Sa 10am-6am. **Myer Financial Services,** 5th floor, Myer Centre, Rundle Mall. Open M-Th 9am-5:30pm, F 9:30am-9pm, Sa 9:30am-5pm, Su 11am-5pm. **American Express,** 113 Grenfell St. Open M-F 8:30am-5:30pm, Sa 9am-noon. **Thomas Cook,** booth on the Rundle Mall. Open M-Th 9am-5pm, F 9am-7pm, Sa 10am-4pm, Su 10am-2pm.

## LOCAL SERVICES

**Bookstores: Europa Bookstore,** 238 Rundle St (☎8223 2289), for foreign language and travel books (some secondhand). Bookstores of every imaginable stripe line Rundle St and Mall, and some avant-garde (not to mention X-rated ones) are on Hindley St.

**Library: State Library of South Australia,** North Tce at the corner of Kintore Ave (☎8207 7200). Book ahead for free 30min. **email** slots, or wait for free 15min. stints. Open M-W, F 9:30am-8pm, Th 9:30am-5pm, Sa-Su noon-5pm. Just around the corner on Kintore St, the **Lending Library of Adelaide** has free 30min. and 1hr. slots with fewer patrons. Those yearning to learn about history's greatest batsman would do well to investigate the Sir Donald Bradman exhibit. Open M-F 10am-5pm, Sa-Su noon-5pm.

**Ticket Agency:** Most cultural and sporting events are booked through **BASS** (☎13 12 46, M-Sa 9am-8pm; 24hr. info line ☎0055 3330; interstate bookings ☎8400 2205; www.bass.sa.com.au). $2 service charge per ticket.

**MEDIA AND PUBLICATIONS**

**Newspapers:** *The Advertiser* (88¢).

**Nightlife:** "The Guide" the in Th *Advertiser. Rip it Up* and *db* on the alternative club scene (free). For gay nightlife, try *Gay Times* (free).

**Radio:** Rock, 107.1FM; News, ABC 831AM; Tourist Info, 88FM.

## EMERGENCY AND COMMUNICATION

**Emergency:** ☎000.

**Hotlines and Info Centers: Gay and Lesbian Counseling Service** (☎8362 3223, freecall ☎(1800) 18 22 33) can give info on what's on around town. Staffed M-F 7-10pm, Sa-Su 2-5pm and 7-10pm. **Women's Information Switchboard** (☎8223 1244). **Disability Information and Resource Centre,** 195 Gilles St (☎8223 7522).

**Interpreter Services:** ☎13 14 50. Free.

**Late-night Pharmacy: Simpsons Pharmacy** (☎8231 6333), corner of West Tce and Waymouth St. Open M-F 7am-midnight, Sa-Su 9am-midnight.

**Medical Assistance: Crisis Care Service** (☎8272 1222). **Emergency Medical Service** (☎8223 0230 or ☎8275 9911). **Adelaide Medical Clinic** and **24hr. Home Visit Medical Service** (☎8267 3544, afterhours mobile ☎0412 829 904), AMA House, 1st Fl. Ward St, North Adelaide. **Royal Adelaide Hospital,** North Tce (☎8222 4000).

**Internet Access:** See **library** above for free access info. Most hostels have kiosks. **Ngapartji,** 211 Rundle St (☎8232 0839). 30min. $5, or wait in line for 2 free computers on the street. Open M-Th 8:30am-7pm, F 8:30am-10pm, Sa 10am-10pm, Su noon-7pm. **Talking Cents,** 53 Hindley St (☎8212 1266). Cheap international calls and faxes. Open daily 8am-9pm. Internet 1hr. $8. **Young Media Australia,** 69 Hindmarsh Sq (☎8232 1577). Internet 30min. $3. Open M-F 9:30am-4:30pm.

SOUTH AUSTRALIA

**Post Office: General Post Office,** 141 Franklin St (☎8216 2222), at the corner of King William and Franklin St, just north of Victoria Sq. Open M-F 8am-6pm, Sa 8:30am-noon. *Poste Restante* can be picked up M-F 7am-5:30pm, Su 9am-1pm. **Postal Code:** 5000. **Phone Code:** 08.

# ACCOMMODATIONS

Unless otherwise noted, all listed hostels have 24hr. access, kitchen, laundry facilities, free linen, $10 key deposit, 10am check-out, free luggage storage, and helpful tour and bus booking facilities. All take Mastercard and Visa, though some have minimum charge requirements. Adelaide hostels are rarely full in winter, but it's wise to call a day or two ahead in summer, and a week ahead during festivals.

**Backpack Oz,** 144 Wakefield St (☎8223 3551, freecall ☎(1800) 633 307). On the corner of Pulteney St. The closest to the action of Rundle St, this 50-bed hostel has a sociable, chill staff. The building was a pub 120 years ago, and is still true to its roots—guests can buy a $2 beer or $1 softdrink whenever the office is open. A/C in all rooms, and sweets on the pillows. Free pickup. Free dinner on W. Internet 1hr. $4. Reception 6am-10pm. Dorms $16; singles $28; twins and doubles $39. 7th night free.

**Breckon Inn,** 11 Gilbert St (☎8211 8985). Behind the Brecknock Inn, 401 King William St, a good Irish bar in the south part of the city. Just opened March 1999, it's quite modern and clean, with a friendly staff and boisterous guests. Laundry, work board, nice TV lounge. Cutlery deposit $10. Dorms $15. NOMADS. Wheelchair accessible.

**East Park Lodge,** 341 Angas St (☎8223 1228; fax 8223 7772; email eastpark@dove.com.au). A 15-20min. walk from Rundle St. A diverse clientele enjoys airy, newly renovated rooms. The rooftop offers a fantastic nighttime view of Adelaide Hills and the city. This is the only hostel in town with a swimming pool. Make and paint your own didgeridoo for $50. Bike hire; some auto and motorbike hire. Free pickup. Reception 7am-8pm. Check-out 9:30am. Dorms $16; singles $30; twins and doubles $42. VIP.

**Adelaide Backpacker's Inn,** 112 Carrington St (☎8223 6635, freecall ☎(1800) 24 77 25; fax 8232 5464; email abackinn@tne.net.au). A 10min. walk from Victoria Sq. Small, quiet crowd with lots of Japanese travelers. The free nightly apple pie, custard, and ice cream are never rationed, in 1999 alone the hostel management baked 4000 pies. Free pickup and drop off from bus, train, or plane. Internet 15min. $2. Huge breakfast $4. Great Su night BBQ $5. Reception 6am-8pm, but will take phone calls until about 11pm. Dorms $15; singles $28; twins and doubles $40. 7th night free.

**Cannon St Backpackers,** 110 Franklin St (☎8410 1218, ☎/fax (1800) 06 97 31; email info@cannonst.com.au). Across from the bus station. More than 150 beds and a lot of extras wrapped in a youthful, laid-back, if somewhat impersonal attitude. Free ping pong and pool tables, with weekly competitions. Internet 1hr. $6. Backpacker bar and bistro has cheap meals starting at 6:30pm. Happy Hour 8-10pm. 10-bed dorms $13; 4-bed dorms $16; twins and doubles $38. VIP.

**Adelaide City Backpackers Hostel,** 239 Franklin St (☎8212 2668; fax 8212 7974). A few blocks from the bus station. Imagine a plain, sterile, no-frills hostel. Now imagine the opposite, add lots of plants, put chandeliers, paisley carpet, stained glass, and 50 beds into a historic restored home and call it a hostel. This building has ornate furniture, pictures crowding every wall, and a pleasant courtyard. A/C and heat. Free pickup from bus, train, and plane. Breakfast and nightly dessert included; dinner included on your first night. Su: BBQ $3.50-5. Dorms $15; twins and doubles $35-40; family rooms available. Stuffy $10 dorm available, but not when weather is too hot. YHA, VIP, ISIC.

**Sunny's Backpacker Hostel,** 139 Franklin St (☎8231 2430, freecall ☎(1800) 22 57 25 (BAK PAK); fax 8231 0131). Next to the bus station. Small, friendly hostel with 48 beds in standard bunk rooms, very clean communal bathrooms, and a small outdoor patio. Female dorm has separate ensuite facilities. BBQ, kitchen, free email access. Free parking and pancake breakfast. Reception M-F 6am-9pm, Sa-Su 6am-12:30pm and 5-8pm. Dorms $16; twins $35; doubles $39. YHA, VIP.

**Kiwi 'n' Oz International Backpackers,** 130 Wright St (☎8221 5656, freecall ☎(1800) 00 62 51; fax 8221 5858; email kiwioz@senet.com.au). About 10min. from the bus station, near the action of Gouger St. All rooms at this relatively quiet 60-bed hostel are ensuite and have A/C. 2 TV lounges, 1 with VCR; 3 kitchens. Game rooms, movie nights, daytrips. Free pickup. Reception 9am-2pm and 5:30-9pm. Dorms $10-15; twins $28; doubles from $40; luxury doubles with TV and balcony $45.

**Backpack Australia,** 128 Grote St (☎8231 0639, freecall ☎(1800) 804 133; fax 8410 5881). With your back to the pink Backpacker Travel and Transit Centre, walk down the alley half a block and take a right on Grote St. A *Simpsons*-bedecked hangout space and cheap beer hint that this a fun place to be. Cheap meals at pub. Laundry and BBQ facilities on rooftop patio. Rooftop camping $9 per person; dorms $14; doubles $32.

**The Austral Hotel,** 205 Rundle St (☎8223 4660). Situated above a hip pub, which makes it easy to stumble or escort someone home. Spacious, simple rooms. Slightly more expensive than a hostel, but in exchange you get fantastic location, privacy, and a whole lot of fun. Singles $30; twins and doubles $40.

**Adelaide Travellers Inn,** 118 Carrington St (☎(1800) 63 37 47). Joins the ranks of hostels near the bus station and Gouger St fun. An inexpensive hostel with spacious dorms and the expected amenities. A locked carpark is available for guests. Internet 1hr. $4. All rooms with A/C and heat. Camping in yard $8; dorms $12; doubles $30.

# GLENELG

Visitors preferring the sun over the city might consider basing themselves in Glenelg, a tram ride from Victoria Sq in the city. Glenelg is relaxing, beachy, and easily accessible to the city, airport, coast, and Adelaide's outlying attractions.

**◪ Glenelg Beach Resort,** 1 Moseley St (☎8376 0007, freecall ☎(1800) 06 64 22). One block from the shore on your right as you walk up Jetty Rd away from the beach. This full-blown backpackers complex won the 1998 and 1999 South Australia tourism award for best budget accommodation. Licensed, with a lively bar to prove it, pool tables, small stage for local bands, pleasant common area, and game room. It can get loud at night, although quiet time is the rule upstairs after 10pm. Mountain bikes, tours to the wine valleys, and videos. Pickup and drop off at airport, bus, and train. Internet 10min. $2. Dorms $17; singles $34; doubles $48; family rooms $52.

**◪ Albert Hall,** 16 South Esplanade (☎8376 0488, freecall ☎(1800) 06 04 88; fax and guest line 8294 1966). As you face the jetty, turn left and walk 5min. along South Esplanade until the mansion appears on your left. Luxury is defined by high ceilings, marble bathrooms, and a beachside view. Free pickup and drop off. Internet 15min. $2. Dorms $15, with balcony $17; doubles with balcony $42, ensuite $50.

# ◪ FOOD

Adelaide claims to have more restaurants per capita than any other city in the country. **Gouger St,** in the city center near Victoria Sq, offers a wide range of good, inexpensive ethnic cuisine. **Rundle St,** in the northeast section of the city, caters to the young hipster set, as students forgo lectures in nearby Adelaide University in favor of strong cups of espresso and being seen by everyone else walking down the street. Clusters of restaurants can also be found on the upscale **Hutt St** in southeast Adelaide, the equally upscale North Adelaide Melbourne and O'Connell St, and the flashy but cheap Hindley St, across King William St from Rundle St (head here for 24hr. food). **Jetty Rd** in the beachside suburb of Glenelg also bursts with cafés and ice cream shops. Coles **supermarket,** next to Central Market on Grote St, is very near Victoria Sq (open M-Th midnight-6pm, F midnight-9pm, Sa midnight-5pm, Su 11am-5pm). In Glenelg, Coles is down Nile St just off Jetty Rd. There is also a Woolworth's on Rundle Mall, one block east of King William St.

For less formal fare, bakeries, pie carts, and pubs are scattered around Adelaide. For a real Aussie experience, late-night snackers have visited the "Pie Carts" outside the Adelaide Train Station on North Tce since 1915. The infamous pie floater—an Aussie meat pie swimming in a thick pea soup and topped with tomato sauce—is a South Australian original, and potentially habit forming.

## GOUGER STREET

Gouger St (pronounced "goo-jer") houses the █Central Market, with stall after stall of every imaginable edible and free samples to boot. For the most riotous, colorful experience, stop by on Friday evenings or Saturday mornings. Market open Tu 7am-5:30pm, Th 11am-5:30pm, F 7am-9pm, Sa 7am-1pm. **Market Adventure** offers fun Central Market tours with plenty of tastings. Meet at the down escalator in Central Market. (☎8336 8333. Tu and Th 10:30am and 1:30pm, F 10am and 2pm, Sa 8:30am. $22, ages 3-11 $12; minimum 4 people per tour. Bookings essential.)

█**Noodles,** 119 Gouger St (☎8231 8177). Serves exactly that: noodles in every shape, form, and color for just $6. Comes with generous servings of chicken, beef, seafood, or veggies for a few dollars more. Outdoor dining in the summer. Open M 5:30pm-late, Tu-F 11:30am-3pm and 5:30pm-late, Sa-Su 5:30pm-late. BYO.

**Matsuri,** 167 Gouger St (☎8231 3494). Meaning "festival" in Japanese, Matsuri lives up to its name with festive decoration and custom, from a rock garden to a shoes-off rule. Adelaide's best sushi restaurant, but the best never comes cheap. Individual pieces $2-3, 6-piece packs $3-10. For non-sushi eaters, noodle dishes for $7-9. Open M 5:30pm-late, W-Th 5:30pm-late, F noon-2pm and 5:30pm-late, Sa-Su 5:30pm-late.

**Bunga Raya,** 83a Gouger St (☎8231 7790). Dishing out authentic Malaysian laksa and noodles, rice, meat, and seafood dishes ($7-10), this simple, unassuming restaurant is more delicious than most of the simple, unassuming restaurants lining Gouger. Lunch specials $5. Open M-Sa 11am-2pm and 5:30pm-late, Su 5:30pm-late.

## RUNDLE STREET

Rundle St, one block south of North Tce, flows neatly east from Rundle Mall. It is the place to be in Adelaide, day or night, and offers an incredible range of restaurants, cafés, pubs, and holes-in-the-wall.

█**Vego and Love'n It!,** 240 Rundle St (☎8223 7411). Just past Mindfield bookstore, hidden up a set of stairs on the first floor. A huge range of vegan and vegetarian food, large portions, and delicious concoctions make this an extremely popular daytime eating spot. The veggie burgers ($5-6), sandwiches ($5-7), and desserts are original and plentiful. Tofu ice cream, anyone? $1.50. Juices $2. Open M-F 10am-5pm.

█**Amalfi,** 29 Frome St (☎8223 1948). Between Rundle St and North Tce. The plain brick exterior barely hints at the excellent Italian food and fine service inside. This "Pizzeria Ristorante" sneaks onto upscale gourmet dining lists with relatively budget prices. Pasta dishes run $12-13, with meat mains in the $13-16 range. For many locals, it's all about the pizza (small $9-10, large $15-18). Finish it off with tiramisu for $5. Open M-Th 11:30am-3pm and 5:30-11pm, F-Sa 11:30am-3pm and 5:30pm-midnight.

**Al Fresco,** 260 Rundle St (☎8223 4589). An Adelaide landmark and popular at any time of the day or well into the night, Al Fresco serves a tempting range of Italian cakes and biscuits, a wide range of focaccia, dynamite coffee, and the best *gelato* in the city. Eighteen flavors are all made on-site; small $2.50. Pick up a light meal in minutes or linger over a latte for hours. Open daily 6:30am- "hmm...maybe 2 or 3am."

**Ruby's Café,** 225b Rundle St (☎8224 0365). Creative comfort food (most small dishes $8-11, large $11-13) served on chrome tables. Breakfast served all day Su (9am-5pm), with Bloody Marys ($5) topping the menu; fabulous eggs with chilli ($6) are a mouthful or 10. Open M-Sa 6:30pm-late, Su 9am-5pm and 6:30pm-late.

# THE BEST OF THE REST

The rest of the city is a melange of cafés, pubs, and posh restaurants. Many downtown pubs offer cheap meals.

**The Gilbert Place Pancake House** (☎ 8211 7912). Off King William St, between Currie St and Hindley St. Turn into the alley called Gilbert Place and walk to the end. In a city that shuts down early, a sign reading "this door will never close" is a welcome sight for hungry eyes. Gilbert's fanciful $7-9 creations (Jamaican Banana, Ham Steak and Pineapple, Bavarian Apple) and Tu $5 all-you-can-eat specials make this place stand out.

**Quiet Waters BYO,** 75 Hindley St (☎ 8231 3637). Offers a large range of vegetarian dishes for those disgruntled diners in a largely meat-eating state.

**Lizard Lounge,** 172a Hutt St (☎ 8237 0210). This small café and its exciting menu are a mouthful of the utmost fun. Coffee, tea, and hot chocolate are not cheap ($4-6) but you're paying for atmosphere. Liqueur coffees ($6.50) are killer. Light snacks and mind-boggling desserts ($6-9) add to the revelry. Open M-Sa 7pm-late.

# ◉ SIGHTS

Adelaide is perhaps the best city in Australia for spending a day indulging cultural cravings without tiring your legs or opening your wallet. Adelaide's sights and museums are all located along (or just off) North Tce, the city's cultural boulevard.

**▩ SOUTH AUSTRALIAN MUSEUM.** This gracious building holds huge whale skeletons, native Australian animal displays, rocks and minerals, and even an Egyptian mummy. It is renowned for having the largest collection of Aboriginal artifacts in the world. (Next to the State Library, North Tce. ☎ 8207 7500, tour info ☎ 8293 5666. Open daily 10am-5pm. Admission free. Free tours W 2pm, Sa-Su 2 and 3pm. Wheelchair accessible.)

**▩ ART GALLERY OF SOUTH AUSTRALIA.** This gallery showcases Australian, Asian, and European prints, paintings, sculpture, and decorative arts, as well as lots of Southeast Asian ceramics. The collection of Australian art, arranged chronologically by room and ending with a fine 20th-century collection, is especially impressive. There are free audio guides to the Australian collection. (North Tce near Pulteney St. ☎ 8207 7000. Open daily 10am-5pm. Admission free. Free tours: 1hr.; M-F 11am and 1pm, Sa-Su 11am and 3pm. Wheelchair accessible.)

**▩ TANDANYA—NATIONAL ABORIGINAL CULTURAL INSTITUTE.** The first major Aboriginal multi-arts complex in Australia and a good place to begin your education in Australian indigenous culture—this is nothing short of fascinating. The gift shop stocks a broad range of Aboriginal arts and crafts. (253 Grenfell St. At the corner of East Tce on the city loop bus route. ☎ 8224 3200. Open daily 10am-5pm. $4, concessions $3. Guided tours and talks by appointment. Didgeridoo performances daily at noon.)

**MIGRATION MUSEUM.** Combining history, biography, and oral storytelling to explain patterns of immigration that have shaped South Australian society, the museum's graphic stories and photographs make for an excellent, if somewhat sobering, visit. (82 Kintore Ave. Off North Tce, behind the state library. ☎ 8207 7580. Open M-F 10am-5pm, Sa-Su 1-5pm. Free, donations welcome. 1hr. tour $4.50. Book in advance. )

**ADELAIDE BOTANIC GARDENS.** Acres of beautifully landscaped grounds surround heritage buildings, a small lake with black swans, and meandering walkways. The Bicentennial Conservatory, the largest glasshouse in the Southern Hemisphere, is the only section with an entrance fee. The computer-controlled atmosphere simulates a tropical rainforest, complete with misty rain. (North Tce. ☎ 8228 2311. Gardens: open M-F 7am, Sa-Su 9am, close 2hrs. before sunset.; free. Museum of economic botany: open M-Th 11am-3pm, Su noon-4pm. Conservatory: open daily 10am-4pm; $2.50, concessions. $1.25. Free garden tours leave from the restaurant Tu, F, and Su 10:30am.)

**ADELAIDE ZOO.** Now home to more than 1300 animals, the more than 100-year old zoo still has some Victorian buildings, and some of the animal enclosures look as though Queen Victoria herself could have visited them. The Southeast Asian rainforest, the sea lions, and the children's feeding area zoo are some of the most popular exhibits. *(Frome Rd. Less than 2km north of the city in the northern Parkland area, and a 15min. walk from North Tce through the Botanical Gardens or down Frome Rd. Popeye boats from the Festival Centre also run to and from the zoo in summer. ☎8267 3255. Open daily 9:30am-5pm. $12, concessions $10, children $7. Guided tours daily 11am and 2pm.)*

**ADELAIDE GAOL.** The jail was opened in 1841 and closed for prisoners in 1988. Forty-nine prisoners were executed here, but the displays focus on the plight of female inmates and the daily activities of a prisoner (smoking, mostly). *(18 Gaol Rd, Thebarton. A moderate walk just northeast of the city or 5min. ride to Stop 1 on bus #151, 153, 286 or 287 from North Tce. ☎8231 4062. Open M-F 11am-4pm. $6.50, concessions $5, children $4. Guided tours Su 11am-3:30pm.)*

**ADELAIDE-HIMEJI GARDEN.** This garden offers a good look into the art of the Japanese garden, and begins to explain the deep religious and spiritual significance of horticulture to the Japanese. *(South Tce, east of Pulteney St. ☎8203 7483. Open daily 8am to 1hr. before sunset.)*

**ST. PETER'S CATHEDRAL.** The mother of all churches in this city of churches. Built between 1869 and 1904, this Anglican cathedral towers over North Adelaide and swings the "heaviest and finest" bells in the Southern Hemisphere. *(King William St. North of the city; a 10-15min. walk from North Tce up over the river and past the cricket oval. ☎8267 4551. Open daily 9am-4pm. Free. Tours W 11am and Su 3pm.)*

**CARRICK HILL.** This Tudor mansion houses a private art collection and is surrounded by almost 40 hectares of beautifully tended English gardens and native bush. Summer evening outdoor theater here is delightful, though you'll need to take a taxi back to the city. *(46 Carrick Hill Dr, Springfield. A 10min. drive from the city center, at the southern end of Fullarton Rd; or 25min. by bus #171 from King William St. Get off at stop #16 and walk 500m to the main gates on the left. ☎8379 3886. Open W-Su 10am-5pm.)*

**HAIGH'S CHOCOLATES VISITORS CENTRE.** Australia's oldest chocolate maker, Haigh's has been churning since 1915. The company has gained fame as the developer of the original chocolate Easter Bilby in an effort to displace the tyrannical Easter Bunny (the bilby, a type of bandicoot, is a native endangered species; the rabbit is an introduced pest). *(154 Greenhill Rd. One block south of South Tce and just east of Pulteney Rd. ☎8271 3770. Open M-F 8:30am-5:30pm, Sa 9:30am-4:45pm. Free guided tours with tastings M-Sa 1:30 and 2:30pm. Bookings advisable.)*

# ◨ ACTIVITIES

To appreciate the full range of outdoor activities available, travelers should visit the numerous outdoor goods stores on Rundle St.

**MOUNTAIN BIKING. Rolling On Mountain Bike Tours** has guided day tours around Adelaide, its forests and vineyards, or the Barossa Valley. It's a good choice even for those without much riding experience—trails are fairly flat and there's a backup vehicle if you get tired. *(☎8358 2401. $79-99; extended trips also available.)*

**SNOW AND ICE.** At **Mt. Thebarton,** you can ski, snowboard, sled, or skate year-round on South Australia's only real "Permasnow." OK, it's all indoors and the ski run is actually a 150m bunny hill. But where else can you ski for $8? *(23 East Tce, Thebarton. 5min. by bus #151, 153, 286 or 287 to stop 2 from North Tce. ☎8352 7977. Open M-Tu, Th 9:30am-5:30pm, W, F 9:30am-4:30pm and 7-11pm, Sa-Su 12:30-4pm and 7:30-11pm. Skiing or boarding 1hr. $8; equipment $5-10. Skating $7.50, skates $2.)*

**ABSEILING, ROCK CLIMBING, AND CAVING. Rock Solid Adventure** offers abseiling, rock climbing, and a two-night caving trip to Naracoorte Conservation Park on demand. *(☎8322 8975. Abseiling 3hr., $44; rock climbing 4hr. $57; caving $195.)*

**DIVING. Glenelg Scuba Diving** runs daily boat dives to Adelaide's wrecks and reefs, and offers a four-day PADI certification class. *(☎8294 7744. Dives from $30; equipment hire available. 4-day PADI class $225.)*

**SKYDIVING. S. A. Skydiving** is pleased to help you jump out of a plane, free fall for 40sec., and then float to earth, all attached to an instructor. They also offer a full-day solo jump course, which is unusual. *(☎8272 7888. Tandem $240, solo $350.)*

**SWIMMING.** The **Adelaide Aquatic Centre,** Jeffcott Rd, North Adelaide, is a huge, indoor complex with a 50m pool, a diving and water polo area, and small, shallow pools surrounded by potted trees. *(30min. walk from North Tce up King William St; or take bus #231, 233, 235, or 237 from Victoria Sq, or from stop Z3 in front of the Festival Centre on King William St. ☎8344 4411. Pools open daily 5am-10pm; gym M-F 6am-10pm, Sa 6am-6pm, Su 9am-5pm. $4, concessions $3. Gym fees $7.50.)*

**SPECTATOR SPORTS.** International and interstate cricket (Oct.-Mar.); Australian Rules Football (mostly on Sa); and soccer, rugby and rugby union (Apr.-Sept.) are played at the **Adelaide Oval.** "Cricket's Greatest Batsman," Sir Donald Bradman, is key to the tour; visitors to whom this means nothing mayn't want to risk joining a 2½hr. tour. *(Just north of the city along King William Rd. ☎8231 3639. Tours Tu, Th at 10am, Su at 2pm, except on match days. $5. Cricket museum open Tu, Th 10am-1pm. $2. Match tickets and schedules at any BASS outlet, ☎13 12 46.)*

**BEACH ACTIVITIES.** Don't miss the beach suburb of **Glenelg,** with its lovely swimming beach and café culture. **Inline skates** can be hired at the main Glenelg beach on summer weekends, and there's often free outdoor entertainment. During the summer, the smooth sand of Glenelg's Holdfast Bay is also a great spot to try your hand at **beach volleyball** or **parasailing** *(☎(0411) 19 16 53; from $40 per person.)*

# ⚑ ENTERTAINMENT

A 2min. walk north on King William St from its intersection with North Tce at Parliament House will bring you to the huge, white **Adelaide Festival Centre** (☎8216 8600). Situated on the Torrens River, this is the focus of Adelaide's cultural life, with some performance or another on most nights. Throughout the summer and particularly on weekend afternoons, a few outdoor theater events and concerts are free and open to the public. Pick up a calendar of events from inside the Festival Centre complex or call BASS (see **Practical Information,** p. 419). The **State Opera of South Australia** (☎8226 4790), the **Adelaide Symphony Orchestra** (☎8343 4834), and the **State Theatre Company of South Australia** (☎8231 5151) all perform at the Festival Centre; it's also the place for big-name traveling musicals and theater performances. Student rush tickets are sometimes available. **Elder Hall,** North Tce, part of the University of Adelaide, hosts concerts. (☎8303 5925. Lunch hr. concerts F 1:10-2pm; $2.) Something is usually playing at the grand old **Her Majesty's Theatre,** 58 Grote St (☎8216 8600), on the CityLoop bus route.

Adelaide's most accessible **alternative cinemas,** both on Rundle St, are the **Palace Eastend** (☎8232 3434) and **NOVA** (☎8223 6333). Tuesday night is usually discount night at movie theaters across Australia. The **IMAX Theatre,** in Vaughan Place off the east end of Rundle St near the Exeter Hotel, screens four-story-tall, in-your-face movies daily on the hour. (☎8227 0075. Open 10am-10pm. $13, concessions $10, children $9; 3-D movies $14, $11.) Mid-December through mid-February brings **Cinema in the Botanic Gardens,** outdoor showings of popular and classic movies (7:30pm; $11.50, concessions $8; tickets at gate or via BASS).

# ❀ FESTIVALS

**WOMADELAIDE,** a **WO**rld **M**usic **A**rt **D**ance festival, comes to town in mid-to-late February in odd-numbered years. **Arts Project Australia** runs the show in Botanic Park from Friday to Saturday, with dozens of acts from dozens of countries and workshops on six stages, while a "global village" sells international food and crafts.

(☎8271 9905. Weekend tickets \$115, students and concessions \$95; daily ticket prices from \$45.) **The Feast** (late Oct. to mid-Nov.) is Adelaide's annual lesbian and gay festival, with three weeks of masquerades, parties, and concerts.

Although it doesn't occur in 2001, the **Adelaide Festival** (☎8216 8600), is considered one of the world's best arts festivals. Overlapping with the Adelaide Festival, the **Adelaide Fringe Festival** (☎8231 7760) features artists out of the mainstream.

# ⊠ NIGHTLIFE

In this "family" city, most areas shut down promptly at 6pm, and the streets of Adelaide after dark can seem like a post-apocalyptic waste zone. If you know where to look, however, Adelaide maintains a thriving nightlife into the wee hours. The **East End**, which, very roughly, includes Rundle St east of the mall, Pulteney St, and Pirie St, is the center of Adelaide's "pretty" scene. Bouncers here are very mindful of the **dress code** for dance clubs, and enforce it unflinchingly. The café scene dominates all, as uni students and others drink schooners and smoke cigarettes on the sidewalk, waiting for everyone else to walk by and see them. **Hindley St** is, no doubt, home to many X-rated venues and the like, as well as numerous fly-by-night dance clubs, but a slow creep of gentrification is obvious on the blocks near King William St and the Rundle Mall. Denizens of the increasingly residential city center are up in arms about noise, threatening good times with 10pm curfews.

To find out what's on, Thursday's *Advertiser* includes *The Guide*. *Rip it Up* (published weekly) and *db* (published biweekly) are free and highlight the alternative and club scene. *Gay Times* provides information on events and nightlife and lists of gay-friendly establishments. It's free at BSharp Records on Rundle St.

⧆ **Grace Emily,** 232 Waymouth St (☎8231 5500). The chillest bar in Adelaide, for the moment, is not on Rundle or Hindley, but here on Waymouth St where live music happens several times per week, there are no pokies, and everyone is laidback as hell. Open daily 4pm-late.

**Austral,** 205 Rundle St (☎8223 4660). Known affectionately by locals as the "Nostril," this bar draws a large, young crowd to enjoy live entertainment. Encourages the fine art of DJ-ing by hosting one nearly every night. If there's nothing happening here, there's probably nothing happening in town.

**Heaven II,** 7 West Tce (☎8211 8533). This bright purple building at the corner of North and West Tce provides a celestial vision of sorts, if your idea of the afterlife is a hedonistic mix of alcohol, dance music, lycra, and nubile 20-somethings. Features DJs, local bands, and internationally renowned acts (cover varies accordingly). Once a month Heaven floods with soap suds during the foam party. Heaven's gates open at 9 or 10pm W-Su, and there's almost always a line F-Sa and St. Peter can be moody.

**Cargo Club,** 213 Hindley St (☎8231 2327). One of Adelaide's funkier clubs and a strong holdout from recycled Top-40 tunes. Live music ranges from jazz to African and draws a crowd that can't decide whether it is trendy or alternative. DJ with dance music on W. Occasional poetry readings and movies. Cover around \$6. Doors open at 10pm.

**The Planet,** 77 Pirie St (☎8359 2797). If you've come to the land down under looking for tainted love or karma chameleons, tell your hostelmates to wake you up before they go, and go to "Greed," this club's hugely popular Friday tribute to the 80s. W is "Planet Disco," complete with 70s outfits, and Sa means house music and tightly packed, writhing young bodies. An upstairs viewing area can be a welcome escape. Cover \$8.

**G.A.Y.,** 69 Light Square (☎8212 6969). Promises only one thing: to groove all year long. Open F 10pm-late, Sa 10pm-7am, Su 10pm-late.

**The Hampshire Hotel,** 110 Grote St (☎8231 5169). Appearance can be deceiving. This apparently mild-mannered Australian pub, is actually a hub for Adelaide's backpacker scene. W and Su are Karaoke Nights.

**The Mars Bar,** 120 Gouger St (☎8231 9636). A dance club with a mix of straight and gay clientele. Campy surrounds make the Mars Bar a haven for would-be "Queens of the Desert." F and Sa: drag nights; W 12:30am: Gong Show; Th: "Hot Vegas Nights."

**Exeter,** 246 Rundle St (☎8223 2623). A lively pub, a.k.a. "Excreter," has a beer gardens and big, unpretentious, slightly older weekend crowd.

**Aquarium Club Bar,** 41 Currie St (☎8373 0672). This place caught Latin Fever and has spun out Latin music every F since, including salsa and latin dance classes. Cover $8.

**The Earl of Aberdeen,** Carrington St, Hurtle Sq (☎8223 64330). Woodsy, old-style pub with a variety of beers on tap and good pub meals.

**Brecknock Inn,** 401 King William St (☎8231 5467). Offers Guinness to those tired of the Cooper's Brewery, as well as the usual draft beers. F and Sa: live Irish music.

**Edinburgh Castle,** 233 Currie St (☎8410 1211). A mainly gay male clientele. Open M-Th 11am-midnight, F 11am-1:30am, Sa 11am-1am, Su 2pm-midnight.

# ▓ DAYTRIP FROM ADELAIDE

## PORT ADELAIDE

Port Adelaide makes the perfect Sunday daytrip. **Fisherman's Wharf** (☎8341 2040), Lighthouse Sq, Commercial Rd is the place to be Sundays 8am-5pm and Mondays 9am-5pm. At this large indoor market you can get anything from CDs to seafood. Also on Sundays, budget travelers' dreams come true as $2 **river cruises** (1¾hr.)—with occasional dolphin sightings—depart from the wharf. To reach Port Adelaide take bus #151 or 153 from North Tce opposite Parliament house, and get off at stop #40 (about 30min.). Alternatively, the Outer Harbor railway line links the port and the North Tce railway station (20min., every 30min. M-F 9am-midnight). The wharf is a short walk from Port Adelaide Railway Station or from bus stop #40.

# NEAR ADELAIDE

## ADELAIDE HILLS

In a state where much of the terrain is unfriendly at best, the Adelaide Hills provide a haven of lush greenery and a suburban playground within minutes of Adelaide. As you climb toward the Mt. Lofty summit, Adelaide's lights and coastline unfold below you. Huge expanses of national parkland surround the peak, broken up by wineries, orchards, and picturesque towns from a gentler, slower past. For a little taste of Bavaria and surprising cultural opportunities, stop by Hahndorf. Browse in the numerous arts and crafts stores, sample the many family bakeries, and revel in the region's overwhelming sense of peace and relaxation.

▐▓ **TRANSPORT AND PRACTICAL INFORMATION.** Much of the Adelaide Hills is a 20-40min. drive east from the Adelaide city center. The main road through the Adelaide Hills is the South Eastern Fwy (Hwy 1). The Hills are also easy to explore by public transportation; the $1.60 will take you as far as many tours will. Call **Hills Transit** (☎8210 1000) for routes and timetables. Most buses are considered part of the Adelaide system and use the same fare system. Bus #842 and 843 leave from Currie St and run to **Strathlybyn,** #822 to **Cleland Wildlife Park,** and #104 to **Morialta Falls** and **Conservation Park. Gray Line** runs a "taste of the Adelaide Hills" **tour** on Tu and Sa 9:30am-5:30pm. (☎8374 1270, freecall ☎(1800) 63 47 24. Open daily 7:30am-9pm. $49.) The **Adelaide Hills Visitor Information Centre** is at 41 Main St, Hahndorf. (☎8388 1185, freecall ☎(1800) 35 33 23. Open daily 9am-5pm.)

▐ **ACCOMMODATIONS. YHA** maintains a series of five "limited access" hostels in the Adelaide Hills along the Heysen Trail, located at **Para Wirra, Norton Summit, Mt. Lofty, Mylor,** and **Kuitpo.** Bookings must be made in advance at the YHA office, 32 Sturt St, Adelaide (☎8231 5583), or at the YHA hostel in Adelaide, where you will be given a key and a map. These hostels, though well-kept, are unattended and provide bare bones amenities—beds, kitchens, toilets, and showers. Guests must bring linen and food, though blankets and pillows are provided. (Beds $10-15, non-YHA $3 more.) The limited-access ◼**Mt. Lofty YHA,** 20km from Adelaide, is an easy choice for an overnight in the Adelaide Hills, especially for travelers without cars. The 16-bed stone cottage was built in 1880 (and rebuilt after the 1983 bushfires), right in Cleland Conservation Park, on the Heysen Trail and near other good walking trails. It's an excellent getaway, especially in summer. (Beds $15.) **Fuzzies Farm,** Colonial Dr, Norton Summit, provides a glimpse at what post-industrial society might be like. (☎8390 1111. $25 the first night, $15 each additional. Weekly $80, plus chores. Rates include meals. Book ahead.)

◼◪ **SIGHTS AND ACTIVITIES.** The biggest attraction in the Adelaide Hills is **Mt. Lofty,** visited by 500,000 people annually and part of Cleland Conservation Park. Take the South Eastern Fwy out of the city, exit at Crafers, and follow the signs (20-25min.). The summit has spectacular views of the city, especially at night, and an **Information Centre** with extensive info about **hikes** in the surrounding Cleland Conservation Park. (☎8370 1054. Open daily 9am-5pm.)

The **Cleland Wildlife Park,** located within Cleland Conservation Park, is an easy daytrip from Adelaide. (☎8339 2444. Park open daily 9:30am-5pm. $8, concessions $6.) **Night Walks** (☎8339 2444) view some of the rarer and often endangered species of wildlife. Within the park, **Aboriginal Cultural Guided Tours** take place on Yurridla Trail. (☎8339 2769. W, Su 11am and 1:30pm.) **Mt. Lofty Botanic Gardens,** near Mt. Lofty, is about 30min. from Adelaide and accessible by public transport. (☎8228 2311. Open M-F 9am-4pm, Sa-Su 10am-5pm.)

The **Warrawong Wildlife Sanctuary,** Stock Rd, Mylor, offers unforgettable dawn and sunset walks in 85 acres that hold over 50,000 native plants, as well as many rare and endangered mammals. Bettongs, wallabies, birds, platypi, and southern short-nosed bandicoots are all here. (☎8370 9422. Walks 6:30am and 7:30pm; $18.) To get to Warrawong, take the South Eastern Fwy, exit at Mt. Barker Rd, and when you see signs from Stirling, turn right on Longwood Rd and then left on Stock Rd (follow signs). Transportation from Adelaide can be arranged with **Eucalyptours** (☎8339 4507). If you have a car, the limited-access YHA in Mylor Conservation Park is not far from Warrawong Wildlife Sanctuary.

Easy walking trails and waterfalls bring people to **Morialta Falls** and **Conservation Park** (☎8281 4022), 30min. by bus #105 (M-Sa only) from Currie St. Get off at stop #26, and walk 1km to the Falls carpark. The limited-access YHA at Norton Summit is near Morialta Falls.

The **Monarto Zoological Park** is 70km east of Adelaide on the Princes Hwy; take the South Eastern Freeway (Hwy 1) to Callington. The animals are in an open-range park, which can be accessed via walking trails and safari bus tours, both included in the admission price. (☎8534 4100. $13, concessions $11, ages 4-14 $8.)

In Hahndorf, find **The Cedars: Hans Heysen House,** Heysen Rd, which was the home of Australian landscape watercolor artist Hans Heysen (1877-1963) and has been preserved in its original state. (☎8388 7277. Open M-F, Su. $5. 3 tours per day.) Masterpieces of the future could be in progress at the **Hahndorf Academy,** 68 Main St. The academy includes an art gallery, museum, and craft shop; much of Heysen's own stunning collection, stolen in 1995, is now back on show. (☎8388 7250. Open M-Sa 10am-5pm, Su noon-5pm.)

# FLEURIEU PENINSULA

The Fleurieu Peninsula (pronounced "FLOOR-ee-oh") stretches southeast from Adelaide, encompassing rolling hills and sweeping valleys. The peninsula also holds the small-town attractions of Victor Harbor, the luscious vineyards of McLaren Vale, and miles of coastline that include some of the best beaches of South Australia. Those with cars will be entranced by the beautiful drives around these hills; an afternoon in a car with a full tank of gas is as rewarding as a lifetime spent studying Heysen landscapes or a full day at the wineries.

SOUTH AUSTRALIA

## TOURS OF THE FLEURIEU

**Great Southern Tours** offers day or overnight tours covering the highlights of the Fleurieu. (☎8371 3147. May-Oct. Su-Tu and Th-F, Nov.-Apr. Th-Tu. $45.) **Bee-init Tours** also operates a popular tour from Adelaide, with stops at two wineries in McLaren Vale, a train ride, and an evening Granite Island Little Penguin tour. (☎8332 1401. Aug.-June M, Th, and Sa 2:30pm. $39, children $25.) **Camel Winery Tours,** based in McLaren Flat, offers a one-day winery safari with up to seven winery visits. (☎8383 0488. $75.) **Just Cruisin Chauffeur Car** (☎8383 0529) provides the opportunity to tour the peninsula in a 1962 Cadillac Fleetwood, highlighting wineries, nature, galleries, or the history of the region. **Sea and Vine Tours** offers an 8hr. McLaren Vale tour, hitting several wineries. (☎8384 5151. $45.)

## MCLAREN VALE

Just 45min. (37km) south of Adelaide, the idyllic, sleepy set of vineyards in McLaren Vale (pop. 2000) sit in the grassy inland knolls of the Fleurieu Peninsula. Over 45 wineries, the majority of which are still family-owned, operate cellar door sales, and process world-class wines. The beaches of the peninsula and nearby Willunga, are also easily accessed from McLaren Vale.

**TRANSPORT.** Premier Stateliner (☎8415 5555) comes through town from the **Adelaide** central **bus** station (45min., 1-3 per day, $6). If you don't have a car however, getting around once you are in McLaren Vale may be a problem. A better option is a tour of the Fleurieu out of Adelaide (see **Tours of the Fleurieu,** above).

**ORIENTATION AND PRACTICAL INFORMATION.** The best way to get to McLaren Vale is with a group of friends, a car, and a **designated driver.** The Australian police take drink driving seriously; it is not uncommon to find Random Breath Testing Units (known as Breathos) on main roads to and from wine regions. That said, drive out of Adelaide on **Main South Rd.** Follow Hwy A13 off of Main South Rd on to Victor Harbor Rd, and bear left onto Main Rd, McLaren Vale's main drag. **McLaren Vale and Fleurieu Visitor Centre,** on the left and impossible to miss, offers a map of the wineries and a small bistro. (☎8323 9944; fax 8323 9949. Open daily 10am-5pm.) **McLaren Flat,** on Kangarilla Rd, 3km east of McLaren Vale, is the center of the wine-producing area. The **Kangarilla Rd** nearly flows with wine, passing more wineries than an entire fleet of Mickey Mantles could handle. McLaren Vale has everything and anything that a tourist might need (except for a lot of inexpensive accommodations) on **Main Rd,** including **ATMs,** several groceries, numerous restaurants, and even a few wineries, fancy that. There is **Internet access** at the **McLaren Vale Game Scene,** 165 Main Rd. (☎8323 9681. Open daily noon-8pm. 1hr. $5.) As Main Rd runs south, it becomes **Willunga Rd.** Nearby **Noarlunga Centre** (not a town center so much as an administrative complex *cum* shopping mall and tavern) has good facilities, too—a shopping center, **ATMs, hospital** (☎8384 9222), library, swimming pool, and movie theater. Noarlunga Centre is the southernmost spot to catch trains to and from **Adelaide,** with local buses then connecting Noarlunga Centre to **McLaren Vale, Willunga, Aldinga,** and other small towns. The **information desk** on the upper level in the mall has all the route information.

**ACCOMMODATIONS AND FOOD.** The majority of accommodations are old-world B&Bs at new world prices; most people just make the area a daytrip from Adelaide. There are options, however, for the intrepid budget traveler willing to venture a few minutes away from McLaren Vale. In **Willunga,** down Willunga or Victor Harbor Rd from McLaren Vale, the **Willunga Hotel,** on High St, offers classic pub-hotel rooms in a building dating from 1868 and generous counter meals for $8. (☎8556 2135. Singles $20; doubles $40.) **Emu Retreat,** on Hahns Rd, Willunga, is an ecologically-correct, fun-minded "alternative lifestyle" farm, complete with emu egg quiche. (☎/fax 8556 3655. Dorms $10; doubles $80. Book ahead.) Of the penin-

SOUTH AUSTRALIA

sula's many caravan parks, the **McLaren Vale Lakeside Caravan Park,** Field St, is most conveniently located for wine tasting trips. There are lots of extras, including a swimming pool, spa, and tennis courts, not to mention an absolutely gorgeous setting. (☎8323 9255. Tent sites $13; powered $16; ensuite vans $36.)

Most wineries have picnic grounds and some offer tables in idyllic settings. Every square centimeter of wall at ▓**McLaren Vale Bakery** (☎8323 7476), McLaren Vale Shopping Centre on Main Rd, is plastered with awards and newspaper clippings extolling the bakery's fabulous pies. The Wine Pie, Lamb Piquant Pie, and Chicken Champagne Pie are just some of the national winners.

**WINERIES.** McLaren Vale is the best-known wine area in South Australia after the Barossa Valley. The majority of the 45 wineries are small and family-owned, with noted exceptions including **Hardy's, Andrew Garret, Middlebrook,** and **Seaview.** Pick up a map from the Visitor Centre and let your taste buds take the lead.

    **Wirra Wirra Vineyards,** McMurtrie Rd (☎8323 8414). When you see the fence made from giant tree trunks you'll know you've arrived; once you've tasted the "Church Block Red," you won't want to leave. Open M-Sa 10am-5pm, Su 11am-5pm.

    **Dennis of McLaren Vale,** Kangarilla Rd (☎8323 8665). Fancy a drop of hot spiced mead, the oldest alcoholic beverage in recorded history? Made from fermented honey and scented with cloves. Open M-F 10am-5pm, Sa-Su 10:30am-5pm.

    **Marienberg Wines,** 2 Chalk Hill Rd (☎8323 9666). Ursula Pridham, Australia's first female winemaker, founded this winery in 1966. Open daily 10am-5pm.

    **Hardy's Tintara,** Main Rd (☎8323 9185). When the first vines were planted here in 1838, the vintner probably never imagined that more than 150 years later, this would be the largest winery in the area. Reds, whites, sparkling wines, ports, and brandy are all available. Self-guided winery tours are available. Open daily 10am-5pm.

▣ **SOUTHERN BEACHES.** The beaches on the western Fleurieu Peninsula, with high cliffs, occasional dolphin sightings, rocky reefs, miles of clean sand, prime sunsets, and few people, should not be missed. To hit the beaches via public transportation, take the Noarlunga line train from Adelaide Railway Station (North Tce) to Noarlunga. Transfer to bus #741 or 742 at the Noarlunga Interchange for **Maslin** or **Moana Beach.** For **Christies Beach,** transfer to bus #741. For **Port Noarlunga,** take bus #741, 742, or 745. (Full-day ticket for both train and buses $5.)

Closest to Adelaide, **Christies Beach** has a nearby park and many small shops along Beach Rd. For **snorkelers** or **divers,** the **Port Noarlunga Aquatic Reserve** is a shallow reef accessible from the end of the jetty. South again, **Seaford** has a walking and biking track along the cliffs. At the swimming beach **Moana,** cars can park just a few meters from the water. **Maslin Beach,** directly west of McLaren Vale, was Australia's first "unclad" beach and still hosts the **Nude Olympics** one day each January. Farthest south, **Aldinga Beach** is very convenient to Willunga.

# COORONG NATIONAL PARK

Here, where the Murray River hits the sea, huge piles of clean sand have piled up along the coast and created the narrow Younghusband Peninsula, which shelters the shallow lagoon system of Coorong National Park. The shallow, rich estuarine environment is home to the largest permanent breeding colony of Australian pelicans, along with more than 230 other species of water birds. The park is listed in international environmental agreements as being of world significance, and was even named in *Outdoor Magazine's* list of Australia's top ten beaches. The small town of Goolwa is at the top of the peninsula.

▣ **TRANSPORT.** Premier Stateliner (☎8415 5555) runs from **Adelaide** to Goolwa via **McLaren Vale, Victor Harbor, Port Elliot,** and **Middleton** (2hr., 1-3 per day, $13). Goolwa **Taxis** can be reached at ☎8552 8222. The **River Murray Interpretive Centre,** on the wharf in Goolwa, has tourist info. (☎8555 3488. Open daily 9am-5pm.)

SOUTH AUSTRALIA

**▌ ACCOMMODATIONS.** Permits are required for **camping** in the Coorong and are available at Signal Point Interpretive Centre. In Port Elliot, between Victor Harbor and Goolwa, **Port Elliot Caravan and Tourist Park** is poised right on the gorgeous curved beach of Horseshoe Bay. (☎8554 2134; fax 8554 3454. Tent sites for 2 $13, powered $15; sites on the beach foreshore $16; cabins for 2 with bath $48.) Also in Port Elliot is the **Arnella by the Sea YHA**, 28 North Tce, which has 20 beds in a heritage building right near the water. (☎8554 3611, freecall ☎(1800) 06 62 97; email narnu@bigpond.com. Reception daily 8am-2pm and 4-8pm. Dorms $20; singles $30; twins and doubles $50.)

**▟ ACTIVITIES.** Most of **Coorong National Park's** 46,000 hectares are **sand dunes.** The heaped dunes of the **Younghusband Peninsula** create a 145km stretch of beach and shelter a series of lagoons more than 100km long. For a budget snack in season, dig your toes into the sand at the Southern Ocean's edge to find the shellfish **cockles,** which can be pried open and eaten fresh from the ocean. **Goolwa Cruises,** on the Main Wharf in Goolwa, offers adventure and discovery cruises on the waters in Coorong National Park. Pickup about 9am, drop off 6:30pm. (☎8555 2203, freecall ☎(1800) 44 22 03. Adventure cruise $94; Discovery cruise $80.)

## VICTOR HARBOR

Sheltered from the immense Southern Ocean by the sands of Encounter Bay, the seaside town of Victor Harbor (pop. 4600) is neither totally asleep nor wide awake, but it is completely on the beaten track. South Australia's colonial governors chose Victor Harbor as their summer residence, and tourists have been streaming there since. First a whaling port and later a shipping port, Victor Harbor is now both an almost-painfully romantic seaside spot and the serious surf center of Encounter Bay. Besides the little penguin colony, the main draw is its summer temperature, which is as much as 10°C cooler than steamy Adelaide. From May to October, Southern Right Whales capture the attention of tourists' cameras.

**▐ TRANSPORT.** By bus, Premier Stateliner runs from **Adelaide** via **McLaren Vale** to and from Stuart St. (☎8415 5555. 1½-2hr., 1-3 per day, $12.) Services include: **Peninsular Taxi Group** (☎8552 2622, Victor Harbor; ☎8552 8222, Goolwah); **Victor Rent-a-Car,** 66 Ocean St (☎8552 1033; min. age 25); and **RAA** (☎8552 1033). **Sealink,** the service reaching Kangaroo Island, can be booked through **Traveland** (☎8552 8434), on Ocean St, and **Travelworld** (☎8552 1200), in the Harbor Mall on Ocean St.

**▟▐ ORIENTATION AND PRACTICAL INFORMATION.** Victor Harbor is fairly easy to navigate. Flinders Pde runs along the ocean beneath the shade of massive fur trees; Ocean St runs one block behind, becoming Hindmarsh St in the eastern of two roundabouts in city center. Victoria St is the main street on the western side of the city, and leads to the highway to Cape Jervis. Victor Harbor is 85km south of Adelaide on the Main South Rd. **Tourist Information Centre:** near the causeway to Granite Island. (☎8552 5738; fax 8552 5476. Open daily 9am-5pm.) **Police:** Torrens St (☎8552 2088). **Hospital:** Bay Rd (☎8552 1066). There are many **ATMs** on Ocean St.

**▛▜ ACCOMMODATIONS AND FOOD. The Anchorage,** on the corner of Coral St and Flinders Pde, a few blocks east of the main green, is in a clean, bright, cavernous two-house edifice. The hotel also has comfortable budget guest rooms. (☎8552 5970; email victor@anchorage.mtx.net. Key deposit $10. 4- to 6-bed dorms $15 per person. Hotel: singles $35; doubles $50.) The 100-year-old **Grosvener Junction Hotel,** 40 Ocean St, has simple rooms at backpacker rates. The bar is a fun place, although perhaps too excited about greyhound racing for non-gamblers. TV lounge and fridge, but no cooking facilities; bathrooms down the hall. (☎8552 1011. Backpacker singles $20; singles $25; doubles $49.) Sitting Brando-esquely on the waterfront, **Victor Harbor Beach Front Caravan Park,** 114 Victoria St, is on the west side of the city, immediately before the bridge into Encounter Bay. (☎8552

1111; fax 8552 8307. Laundry, BBQ. Key deposit $10. Tent sites for 2 $14, powered $16, each extra person $4; cabins for 2 $42, each extra person $5. Book ahead.)

The **Original Victor Harbor Fish Shop,** 20 Ocean St, has fish-and-chips and a burger. (☎ 8552 1273. Open daily 9am-5pm.) **Ocean Chinese,** on Ocean St, with reasonably priced takeaway, is popular on weekends. (☎ 8552-3994. Open Th-Tu 1pm-late.)

**◨◪ SIGHTS AND ACTIVITIES.** Little Penguins win top billing on **Granite Island.** Entry onto this small island is free if you take the 10min. stroll from the causeway entrance, but you can also take a horse-drawn tram. (May-Sept. daily 10am-3:20pm, Oct.-Apr. 10am-4pm; $4 return; evening run for the penguins, $5 return). **Camel rides** can be had for $3; look for the camels on the mainland end of the causeway. The area around the head of the causeway on the mainland is a kiddie wonderland, with go carts, fairy floss, minigolf, and more. Near the causeway entrance, the **South Australian Whale Centre,** 2 Railway Tce, is a must for anyone interested in marine mammals. (☎ 8552 5644. Open daily 10am-5pm. $4.) The **Penguin Interpretive Centre** is open 30min. before the guided penguin walks, which start daily at dusk on the island side of the bridge. (☎ 8552 7555. Walk and interpretive center admission $7.50; walk only $6.50.) There is an easy walking trail (40min.) on Granite Island which affords excellent views of the mainland and the sea. For the latest **whale-sighting** info, call the center's hotline. (☎ (1900) 93 12 23. 75¢ per min.) To see koalas, wetland birds, and dingoes, check out **Urimbirra Wildlife Park,** 5km from Victor Harbor down the road toward Adelaide. (☎ 8554 6554. Open daily 9am-6pm. Meet koalas at 11am, 2, and 4pm; croc feed 1:30pm. $6.50.)

Between Victor Harbor and Goolwa, Middleton has good **surf** beaches and Port Elliot has a beautiful, though crowded, beach called **Horseshoe Bay,** plus pretty good **surfing** at **Boomer Beach** on the western edge of town. Try your hand at **Parasailing** through **Odyssey Adventures,** on the causeway. (☎ 8277 3233. $50.)

## CAPE JERVIS

Cape Jervis is the jumping-off point for the **Kangaroo Island ferry,** the **Heysen Trail,** and exploration of the entire peninsula. ▨**Cape Jervis Station** looks straight out of a home-decorating magazine, with intricately carved chairs and a tennis court. The Station now occupies several hundred acres, as well as the former Old Cape Jervis Homestead. Wally, the affable owner, can help organize horse back riding and fishing trips. The Sealink bus picks up and drops off at the gate, and guests are entitled to free ferry transfers. (☎ 8598 0288. Station: cots in an outside tent in summer $15; singles $60; doubles $80, each extra person $10; singles in log cabin $40; doubles $60. Homestead: tent sites $20; powered caravan sites $20; backpacker accommodation $20; singles $45. Book ahead.) For those with transportation and the desire to camp in a breathtaking spot, **Deep Creek Conservation Park,** 13km from Cape Jervis on the road to Victor Harbor, provides campgrounds with limited facilities ($10 per car) and bush camping ($5 per car). This park features seacoast views of the **Backstairs Passage** and **Kangaroo Island,** bushwalking, wildlife, and relative solitude. **Blowhole Beach,** a steep 3km from Cobbler Hill picnic area, and **Deep Creek Cove,** 6.4km from Tapanappa Campground, are spectacular walks that cross the **Heysen Trail.** Visit the **Park Headquarters** (☎ 8598 0263) for maps, info, and permits.

# KANGAROO ISLAND

Queensland shows off the Great Barrier Reef, Victoria flaunts the Great Ocean Rd, the Northern Territory struts Kakadu, and South Australia retorts with Kangaroo Island—which means that sometimes the words "touristy" and "bourgeois" don't even begin to describe it. This place gets a lot of east-coast backpackers, fresh from Sydney and Melbourne, who quite likely are still uncertain what a koala, kangaroo, or goanna looks like; the folks coming from Perth are less common, having already seen (and possibly run over) quite a few of the animals along the way. It's expensive to get there and around, but KI (pop. 4000), Australia's third-largest

**WHATCHAMACALLIT** Although much of Australia was claimed on the dubious (and now-repudiated) doctrine of *terra nullus*, Kangaroo Island actually *was* empty of human inhabitants when Flinders and his men arrived in 1802. Eventually, however, evidence of Aboriginal occupation did surface, although none had lived here for thousands of years. The island was avoided because, in the Dreamings of the Kaurna people of the region around Adelaide, it was the gateway to the afterlife and the Isle of the Dead. Therefore all the place names were given by Europeans; one town, American River, actually owes its name to a bunch of seafaring Seppos, who paused there in the early 19th century.

island, has 21 national and local conservation parks, including the sprawling Flinders Chase National Park. Here you can see (and perhaps trip over) kangaroos, passive koalas, and much-hyped little penguins; stroll among a colony of Australian sea lions; watch New Zealand fur seals wave-surf; and climb over and through awesome geological formations.

For visitors going to Seal Bay, Kelly Caves, and Flinders Chase, it's worth picking up an **Island Parks Pass.** Good for one year, it allows unlimited access and lighthouse tours. (Available at any of the locations and the visitors center. $24, children $17, families $65.) Although the park service runs the penguin tours in both big towns, these are not covered by the pass ($6, concessions $4.50, families $16.50).

## ▐ TRANSPORT

Kangaroo Island is accessible by airplane and ferry, but once on the island there is **no public transportation.** Visitors seeking freedom to do and see as they please need to bring a car over on the ferry (return $130) or rent a car ($80-120 per day), bearing in mind that many roads are unsealed. Everyone else will just have to sign up for a tour ($140-250 including coach, ferry, and accommodation).

**BY AIR.** Flights from Adelaide (30min.) rival or even better the ferry's cost. Three airlines depart Adelaide's airport, each 2 to 4 times per day, and land at **Kingscote Airport,** 13km from the town of Kingscote in Cygnet River. An **airport shuttle** service runs between Kingscote and the airport. (☎8553 2390. $10.) **Southern Sky Airlines** often has a special backpackers deal. (☎(1800) 64 33 00, Adelaide ☎8234 3300, Kingscote ☎8553 2296. $90 return; non-hostelers $108 return; book at least 7 days ahead). Another option is **Kendell Airlines,** 61 Dauncey St, Kingscote. (☎13 13 00 or ☎8231 9567. $47-75 one-way on "seasonal saver" or "saver" fares with no advance notice; $66 one-way if purchased 7 days in advance; open daily 8:30am-5pm.) Kendell passengers enjoy a 10% discount on **Budget** car rental. **Emu Airlines** is not as earthbound as its flightless namesake. (☎8234 3711, freecall ☎(1800) 18 23 53. $140 return with no advance notice; $120 return with 2-week notice.)

**BY FERRY AND COACH. Kangaroo Island Sealink** (reservations ☎13 13 01 or ☎8553 1122; open daily 8am-8pm) runs between **Cape Jervis** and **Penneshaw** (45min.; 2-5 per day; one-way $30, cars $65). Sealink offers connecting coach service between Adelaide and the Cape Jervis ferry dock from Adelaide's central **bus station,** 101 Franklin St (1¾hr., 2 per day, return including ferry $90). Sealink also runs coach service on the island to and from the **ferry terminal** in Penneshaw. This can be used as a limited form of transportation to and from Kingscote or American River, even if you're not taking the ferry. Two **coaches** (☎13 13 01) per day leave **Kingscote** (7am and 5:30pm), arriving in **American River** (30min.) and **Penneshaw** (1hr.). Two per day leave Penneshaw (10am and 7pm), arriving in American River (30min.) and Kingscote (1hr.). Kingscote to or from Penneshaw $11 one-way; either town to or from American River $6.50; book ahead.

**BY CAR.** A vehicle is indispensable to those who want to explore Kangaroo Island's remote sights or want to hike in its national parks. Many roads are

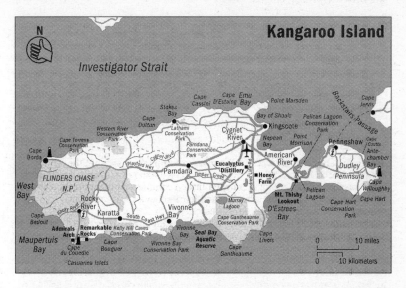

**Kangaroo Island**

*Investigator Strait*

unsealed, but 4WD is only a plus, not a necessity. Most companies only deliver to the Kingscote Airport or to Kingscote itself (making flying a more convenient option); **Budget** offers Penneshaw ferry drop off and pickup (☎8553 3133). All rental companies offer free shuttles between the airport and Kingscote. Hertz-affiliate **Kangaroo Island Rental Cars,** on the corner of Franklin St and Telegraph Rd, Kingscote, has a counter at the airport. (☎8553 2390, freecall ☎(1800) 08 82 96. 2-6 day rental with 200km per day $70 per day for small manual, $105 per day for 4WD.) They can also arrange competitive fly-drive packages. Renters at **Boomerang** (☎8553 9006), also in Kingscote, get unlimited kilometers at competitive prices. **Penneshaw Car Rentals** rents small, late model, air-conditioned cars. (☎8593 0023, freecall ☎(1800) 68 66 20. Half-day with 100km $47, full-day with 240 km $75.)

**TOURS.** Without a car, joining a tour is your only option for experiencing the island's top attractions. To see the best sights and wildlife, be sure your tour includes **Seal Bay** and **Flinders Chase National Park** (home of **Remarkable Rocks** and **Admiral's Arch**). Tours are enjoyable and informative, but usually include just one long day of touring (as in 10hr.) and may rush through the island's natural attractions. If you only have one day to pack it all in, **Kangaroo Island Adventures** (☎8231 1744) joins with **Sealink** (☎13 13 01) to cart travelers to the big sights for $149, leaving Adelaide at 6:45am and returning around 10:30pm. Flying, though more expensive, will give more precious hours on KI. **Kangaroo Island Ferry Connections** offers a day tour with pickup and drop off in Penneshaw, American River, and Kingscote; all the big sights; morning tea and lunch; and a backpacker friendly price. (☎8553 1233, freecall ☎(1800) 01 84 84. $78; children $55.) For sleeping under the stars, **CampWild Adventures** offers a two-day 4WD camping trip. (☎(1800) 44 43 21. Departs Tu, Th, and Sa. $205, including coach and ferry. Max. 10 people.)

**BY BIKE, SCOOTER, OR CAMEL. Penneshaw Youth Hostel** and **Kangaroo Island Central Backpackers,** Kingscote, both rent bikes by the day ($20). **DBS Sales,** 10 Telegraph Rd, Kingscote, rents single and tandem bikes. (☎8553 2349. 24hr. hire single $25, tandem $35.) **Kangaroo Island Mountain Bikes** is a good option for longer bike trips. They will help plan itineraries and deliver bicycles anywhere on the island. (☎(015) 72 16 76. $20 per day for 4 days or more.) For scooter hire, try **Country Cottage,** Centenary Ave, Kingscote. (☎8553 2148. $35 per day.) Finally, if you've always wanted to camp out with your own personal camel, call **Kangaroo Island**

SOUTH AUSTRALIA

**Camel Safaris.** They offer all-inclusive trips for two or more nights exploring Dudley Peninsula. (☎8553 1147. From $98 per person per night.) **Western KI Caravan Park** also has sunset camel rides. (☎8559 7201. 1hr. $25.)

## █ CAMPING

There are four camping sites in Flinders Chase National Park, which are convenient for hiking (see p. 439). But the most beautiful bush camping on the island is in **Cape Gantheaume Conservation Park** on D'Estrees Bay. It's a long way from Flinders Chase National Park and the road is rough, but it has a gorgeous ocean view. No facilities are available. Permits available for $5 at Murray Lagoon ranger station (☎8553 8233), or the Gateway Information Centre (☎8853 1185).

Six caravan parks are scattered around the island, as well as eight other camping grounds. **Western KI Caravan Park,** just 3km from the Flinders Chase entrance, has lots of wildlife, a shower block, powered sites, laundry, and BBQs. (☎8553 1075. On-site vans $35. Book ahead.) Basic camping grounds with toilets but no showers are at **American River, Browns Beach, Vivonne Bay,** and **Western River,** among others. Pick up camp or caravan park advice and permits ($3.50 per site per night) at the Gateway Information Centre just outside Penneshaw.

## ▚ WILDLIFE

Kangaroo Island is one of the best places in the country to see Australia's native fauna in the wild. **Kangaroos** and **wallabies** are omnipresent, especially at dusk in the western half of the island. For **koalas,** head to the **Rocky River Visitors Centre** in Flinders Chase National Park (see p. 439). Three kilometers before the entrance to Flinders Chase NP, the **Western KI Caravan Park** (☎8559 7201) on South Coast Rd welcomes koala-spotters, as well. It takes luck to spot a **platypus,** although any river in Flinders Chase has promise. Your best bet is hiking the **Black Swamp Trail,** which leaves from behind the Flinders Chase visitors center at dusk (it's 45min. along an unused road hopping with kangaroos and wallabies at night). Neither koalas nor platypus are native to Kangaroo Island—they were introduced in the 1920s when it was feared they might go extinct on the mainland.

**Penguin** nesting colonies are conveniently near towns: a larger group is in Penneshaw, but they can be seen in Kingscote as well. Australian **sea lions** waddle around at Seal Bay, and fun-loving New Zealand **fur seals** are the featured attraction at Admiral's Arch in Flinders Chase. Echidnas, rare glossy black cockatoos, are often spotted on the Breakneck River trail, also in Flinders Chase. Emus wander near the visitors center at Flinders Chase. Other birds, including the beautiful crimson rosella, are everywhere—try the short trails around Kelly Caves for good watching. Murray Lagoon in the southeast of the island offers some of the best waterfowl viewing. If all else fails, head for **Parndana Wildlife Park,** 3km west of Parndana on the Playford Hwy, with koalas, 'roos, emus, and even a five-legged sheep not related to Dolly. (☎8559 6050. Open daily 9am-5pm. $4, children $1.)

## ◐▲ SIGHTS AND ACTIVITIES

For general information about the national parks on the island try **National Parks and Wildlife South Australia,** 39 Dauncy St, Kingscote (☎8553 2381; fax 8553 2531). Consider the weather when planning a trip to KI. In summer, although it may be hot inland, it will rarely be anything but moderate on the coast; always bring a wind-proof jacket and a wool sweater, especially for the night-time penguin viewings. This far south, there is only an average of 4½hr. of full sunshine in winter.

**SEAL BAY CONSERVATION PARK.** Arguably Kangaroo Island's finest natural attraction, **Seal Bay Conservation Park** allows visitors to stroll (with a guide) through a colony of Australian sea lions. The park is on the island's southern coast, 60km along a sealed road from Kingscote. A **visitors center** offers general info, toilets, and a few snacks. Hike along the boardwalk, which brings you within viewing range of the sea lions, but guided **tours** are an infinitely better option. Visiting the park between 11am and 1:30pm means more company that just pinnipeds—most tour buses arrive then; in summer, the people on the beach occasionally outnumber the animals. More expensive, and requiring bookings, **sunset tours** reveals what happens in a seal colony when the sun goes down... (☎8553 4207. Open daily Feb.-Nov. 9am-4:15pm; Dec.-Jan. 9am-7pm. Admission $6.50, children $6, families $20. Boardwalk: $6, $4.50, $16.50. Tours every 30-45min. Sunset: $18, $10, $45.)

**LITTLE SAHARA.** Just a short drive from Seal Bay, a jumbo pile of hot, white sand once reminded someone of Africa, so it became known as **Little Sahara.** Surprisingly large dunes are here for the climbing and worth a stop. In the summer, try to avoid midday—this is the Sahara, after all. (From Seal Bay, when you get back to South Coast Rd, turn left. After about 5km, take the first road left; if you cross the small bridge, you've just missed it. The road into the carpark is about a 5min. drive from the main road, but the last stretch is in rough shape; be extra careful if your car is riding low.)

**CAVING.** The **Kelly Hill Caves,** on South Coast Rd about halfway between Vivonne Bay and the Flinders Chase visitors center, are the main attraction of **Kelly Hill Conservation Park.** The largest cave area is accessible on a 40min. guided tour. Translucent stalactites and stalagmites and petrified tree roots please visitors almost as much as the natural air-conditioning on hot summer days. **Adventure Caving tours** require advance booking. (☎8559 7231. Open daily May-Aug. 10am-3pm; Sept.-Apr. 10am-4pm. Tours: 10 and 11am, noon, and 1:30, 2:30, 3:30, and 4:30pm. $6, concessions $4.50, families $16.50. Adventure: $20-30, concessions $12-17, families $52-77.)

**BUSHWALKING.** The **bushwalking** opportunities in Kelly Hill and the neighboring **Cape Bouger W.P.A.** are limited, but good; there is an 8hr. return hike down to the seaside from the Kelly Hill headquarters. The two short trails (20 and 40min. return) near the cave entrance grant walkers a good chance to see the bright red and blue rosella bird, as well as the spiny echidna.

**SURFING.** Kangaroo Island also provides opportunities for the board-toting to hit the **surf.** Visit the Kangaroo Island Gateway tourist information center for the *Surfing Guide,* which details four southern beaches **(Hanson Bay, Vivonne Bay, D'Estress Bay, and Pennington Bay)** and one northern beach **(Stokes Bay).** The water off the island is pretty cool all year; surfers need a full-length wetsuit. **Kangaroo Island Surf Tours** caters for both beginners and experienced surfers, and runs trips including accommodation both in Kingscote and at campsites, with some group concessions available. Fishing, snorkeling, sandboarding, and golf are also possibilities. (☎8553 2882. From $90 per day.)

# KINGSCOTE

Kingscote (pop. 1500) is Kangaroo Island's largest town and was the first European settlement in South Australia. Although everyone comes to KI for points further west, Kingscote contains a beautiful beach, not so much for swimming as walking, and a very pleasant historical site, where settlers began South Australia's first official town and tended what was to become the oldest mulberry tree in the state. More practically, the small, pleasant streets of Kingscote hold the island's only ATM, Internet, and supermarket.

■▪ **ORIENTATION AND PRACTICAL INFORMATION.** The Esplanade runs along the water and becomes Kingscote Tce and then Chapman Tce moving south. Most of the shops and services are one block in from the beach on **Dauncey St,** which is intersected by Telegraph Rd, Commercial St, Murray St, and Drew St. Services include: **tourist info** at the **Kingscote Gift Shop,** 78 Dauncey St (☎8553 2165; open daily 8:30am-5:30pm); **National Parks and Wildlife Office,** 39 Dauncey St (☎8553 2381; fax 8553 2531); an **ATM** at Bank SA, Dauncey St; **police** (☎8553 2018); **RAA** (☎8553 2162 or ☎8553 2197); **free Internet** at the library (M 1-5pm, Tu-F 9:30am-

5pm); and **post office** on Dauncey St (☎8553 2122; open M-F 9am-5pm, Sa 9-11:30am; postal code: 5223). The **hospital** (☎8553 2028) serves the whole island.

**⌐ ACCOMMODATIONS. Ellson's Seaview,** on Chapman Tce across from the ocean swimming pool, has rooms in the guest house that share a clean communal bathroom and are cheaper than those in the main motel. (☎8553 2030; fax 8553 2368. Reception 8am-8:30pm. Singles $44; twins and doubles $51, each extra person $10.) **Kangaroo Island Central Backpackers,** 19 Murray St, is four short blocks from the coast. The extremely budget-conscious who don't mind spartan quarters and a run-down backyard can take advantage of the cheapest beds in town. Reception is next door at the second-hand shop M-F; on weekends a sign posted in the window informs would-be guests of the necessary procedures. (☎8553 2787. Linen $2. Dorms $14; twins and doubles $37; triples $51; family room for 4 $65.)

**⌐ FOOD. Roger's Deli and Café,** 76 Dauncey St, is attached to the news agency, and offers a typical range of pies and hamburgers for $2-5, as well as more interesting Asian cuisine for $10-15. (☎8553 2053. Open M-W 8am-5:30pm, Th-Sa 8am-7:30pm, Su 8am-whenever.) **Blue Gum Café,** across the street from Roger's, serves up snazzy pancakes with ice cream and maple syrup for $5.50 and $4-7 lunch sandwiches in a cheery setting. (☎8553 2089. Open M-F 7:30am-5:30pm, Sa 7:30am-12:30pm.) **A.M. Pizza** (☎8553 3228), at the south end of Dauncey St, opens at 5pm daily. The mighty South Aussies of Foodland **supermarket** hang out on the corner of Commercial and Osmond St (open M-F 9am-5:30pm, Sa 9am-12:30pm).

**◙ SIGHTS.** At dusk, the rocky coast north of the pool and all the way up past the jetty awakens with penguin activity. Guided **tours of the burrows** depart twice nightly from the front of the Ozone Hotel (7:30 and 8:30pm in winter, 9 and 9:40pm in summer; $6, children $4.50, families $16.50). **Pelicans** take center stage at the jetty every day at 5pm, when a feeding brings them together to jostle for fish (time details at Jenny Clapsons Gallery near the jetty; $2 donation requested).

North of town on the Esplanade, a beautiful beach winds 1km toward **Reeves Point Historical Site,** where the first official settlers in South Australia first put down roots—especially when they started planting mulberry trees. The beach here is unspoiled and untraveled, allowing visitors to watch water birds forage for food, scramble down an ancient jetty where boats once loaded basalt for paving roads, and inspect tram tracks from yesteryear. The tallest hill at the point, **Flagstaff Hill,** provides a great view of the bay and the town. **Fishing** is popular with locals, and for anyone hoping to be outdoors and miss some of the tourists—well, put it this way; the tourists aren't here.

# PENNESHAW

The town of Penneshaw (pop. 250) on Kangaroo Island's northeast coast serves as the primary ferry arrival point from Cape Jervis on the mainland. A quick stroll up North Tce from the ferry jetty leads to the pub, petrol station, and a few small restaurants; small Nat Turner St connects North Tce to the post office and to Middle Tce. The **Kangaroo Island Gateway Visitors Centre,** 1km down the road toward Kingscote from Penneshaw's ferry terminus, has maps, camping permits, and a list of tours. (☎8553 1185; fax 8553 1255. Open M-F 9am-5pm, Sa-Su 10am-4pm.)

Penneshaw's main attraction, besides the ferry, is its colony of little **penguins.** Each night after sunset, the 30cm penguins waddle back to their burrows along the coastline. The **Penguin Interpretive Centre** is just east of the ferry dock, off Middle Tce. There's a lighted wooden boardwalk here with public access. Guided tours are worth the money, though, if the penguins are few and far between. (Tours including penguin center admission nightly at 8:30 and 9:30pm; in winter 7:30 and 8:30pm. $5, children $3.50.) To the left as one faces the ferry dock, a several-hundred-meter trail provides interpretive displays of the area's geology.

**⊠Penguin Walk Hostel (YHA)**, 33 Middle Tce, is the nicest hostel on the island, with roomy, colorful six-bed ensuite rooms with stove and refrigerator. (☎8553 1233; fax 8553 1190. Reception M-F 9am-6pm, Sa-Su 9am-1pm. Linen $3. Dorms $14; twins and doubles $40; family rooms $53.) **Penneshaw Pizza** is next door to the YHA. (☎8553 1110. Open daily from 4:30pm until at least 9pm.) **Penneshaw Youth Hostel**, 43 North Tce, offers functional accommodations, kitchen, TV lounge, and a small courtyard. The hostel rents mountain bikes and runs diving tours. The adjoining **Blue Dolphin Café** offers cheap eat-in or takeaway. (☎8553 1284; fax 8553 1295; email adv.host@king.on.net. Reception 7:45am-7:30pm. 8-bed dorms $14; twins or doubles $32. Diving $45. YHA, VIP.) **Welcome Mart**, Middle Tce, has groceries (open M-F 8:30am-6pm, Sa-Su 9:30am-4pm).

# FLINDERS CHASE NATIONAL PARK

Occupying the western end of the island and 17% of its total area, the rocks and animals of Flinders Chase are the highlight of the island. The best attractions are clustered 15-20km south of Rocky River along Boxer Dr. The easternmost sight, on Kirkpatrick Point, is Remarkable Rocks. The rocks, of a type of stone totally unlike that which makes up the cliffs all along the coast of the island, would draw your attention even if it weren't for the work of the grotesque hand of 750 million years of erosion by ice, wind, and water. Just over 105km from Kingscote (much along a dirt track), the Flinders Chase **visitor center** is located at Rocky River, along the South Coast Rd. (☎8559 7235; fax 8559 7268. Open daily Sept.-May 9am-5pm; June-Aug. 10am-5pm. One-day park entry costs $8.50 per car.)

Five kilometers west of Remarkable Rocks, **Cape du Couedic** houses a red-capped sandstone lighthouse. Three lightkeepers lived here with their families early this century, totally cut off from the rest of the world. Four times a year, a steamer brought food, newspapers, and schoolwork, which the families hoisted up the cliffs. Just south of the lighthouse, a footpath winds to the edge of Cape du Couedic and then to the limestone cave of **Admiral's Arch.** More common than the Australian sea lions, a few thousand New Zealand **fur seals** call this area home.

**⌂ CAMPING.** Flinders Chase National Park has **four camping sites,** all non-powered with toilet facilities. The **Rocky River site,** near the visitor center, offers convenience and the only showers, but the sites are in a dirt clearing. Tent campers may prefer to drive 13km into the park to the nicer surrounds of nine cheaper sites at **Snake Lagoon.** The two other sites are in the less frequented northern section of the park. Permits are available for all sites at Rocky River visitor center (☎8559 7235); caravans are not allowed at Snake Lagoon. Rocky River sites cost $12, all other sites $5. Entry fee is $8.50 per car. Book ahead.

You can also rent a rustic **cabin** at one of Flinders Chase's three lighthouse stations, but nobody's going to hoist you food. (Book ahead with Flinders Chase National Park visitor center. Linen $10. Adults $10-30, children $5. Minimum charge: Cape du Couedic $90, Cape Borda and Cape Willoughby $60.)

**⋀ HIKING TRAILS.** Numerous short hikes and excellent 2- to 7-day coastline treks are available for bushwalkers on Kangaroo Island. All hikers should pick up the *Walking Trails in Kangaroo Island Parks* brochure from any visitors center. **Breakneck River Trail,** (6km; 2hr.) in Flinders Chase National Park, is a hidden treasure. It is a fairly easy, almost entirely flat, well-marked hike through a progression of plant communities, and ending at a small beach with huge waves. Look for echidnas and rare glossy black cockatoos. The trailhead is on West Bay Rd, 13km from the visitor center. The **Rocky River Mouth Trail** (3.3km; 1½hr.) is shorter than Breakneck River Trail, but is more demanding and consists of more interesting terrain. This is a fun trail, which runs along the Rocky River and is good for spotting wildflowers in the spring. The trailhead, with toilets and campsites, is at Snake Lagoon on West Bay Rd, 9km from the visitors center.

SOUTH AUSTRALIA

# CENTRAL WINE REGIONS

Wine is South Australia and South Australia is wine, and no more so than 70km northeast of Adelaide in the famous Barossa Valley. The nearby Eden Valley and more northerly Clare Valley (45min. north of Barossa) round out the wine triumvirate that produces many of the country's best wines. Some of the vines have been growing since the 1840s, when the first German settlers planted their cuttings from Europe and prayed they would thrive. More than 150 years later, there's no doubt those prayers have been answered many times over. Sip, swill, gulp, or guzzle: this stuff is liquid joy no matter how you polish it off. For another major wine regions, see Hunter Valley, p. 150; Rutherglen, p. 591; and Yarra, p. 543.

## BAROSSA VALLEY

Arguably Australia's most well-known wine region, the Barossa Valley lives up to its reputation, with wines to suit all palates and budgets. Most of Australia's largest wine companies are based here, along with plenty of excellent small family operations. Barossa is authentically German but does not flaunt it, unlike its Cornish kinsmen in the Yorke. Many residents are descendants of the original settlers—Lutherans who fled religious persecution in Prussia in 1842.

## ▐▀ TRANSPORT

For wine sojourns to the Barossa, a car affords the greatest flexibility, a tour leaves the details and driving to others, and a bicycle makes for an enjoyable day if the weather (and your sense of balance) remain fine; even your own two feet can bring a day of good tasting. Car hire is strongly recommended for those bent on doing a serious wine tour, as many wineries are in out-of-the-way places. Driving parties should always keep a designated driver absolutely alcohol-free and mock the poor sober bastard mercilessly. Barossa Valley's police are diligent and unforgiving when it comes to drunk driving.

**Buses:** Barossa Adelaide Passenger Service (☎8564 3022) sends buses to the Barossa region from **Adelaide** (1-3 per day) to: **Lyndoch** ($8); **Tanunda** ($10); **Nuriootpa** ($11); and **Angaston** ($12). Children and seniors half-price. No reservation required, but confirm times in advance.

**Taxi: Barossa Valley Taxi** (☎8563 3600), Tanunda. Book early.

**Automobile Clubs: Royal Automobile Association** in Gawler (☎8522 2478), Tanunda (☎8563 2123), and Williamstown (☎8524 6268).

**Bike Hire:** Mountain bikes at **Barossa Bunkhaus** (☎8562 2260), Nuriootpa (full-day $10, guests $8); **Tanunda Caravan and Tourist Park** (☎8563 2784), Tanunda (full-day $15); and **Zinfandel Tea Rooms,** Tanunda (full-day $10).

## ▟▐ ORIENTATION AND PRACTICAL INFORMATION

The Barossa Valley encloses several townships. Approaching from Adelaide via **Gawler,** the first town in the Barossa is **Lyndoch** (LIN-dock; pop. 1000). After Lyndoch, the **Barossa Valley Hwy** enters the main town of **Tanunda** (pop. 3900), 70km northeast of Adelaide and changes its name to **Murray St.** It then continues on to **Nuriootpa** (noor-ee-OOT-pah; pop. 3500) and proceeds east to **Angaston. Williamstown** lies south of Lyndoch. If you bypass **Gawler** and take **Sturt Hwy** from Adelaide, the road enters the Barossa at Nuriootpa.

The **Barossa Visitor Information Centre** is in Tanunda. (☎(1800) 81 26 22; fax 8563 0616; http://barossa-region.org. 66-68 Murray St. Open M-F 9am-5pm, Sa-Su 10am-4pm.) It is home to the excellent **Wine Centre** (see p. 442). The banks in Gawler, Nuriootpa, and Tanunda all have **ATMs.**

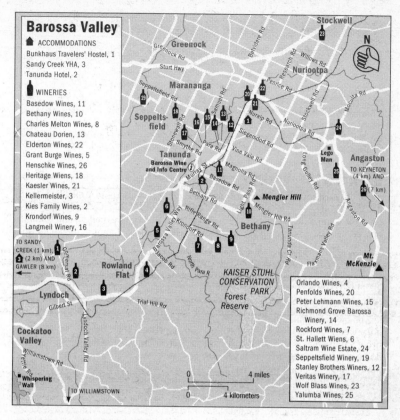

## Barossa Valley

**ACCOMMODATIONS**
Bunkhaus Travelers' Hostel, 1
Sandy Creek YHA, 3
Tanunda Hotel, 2

**WINERIES**
Basedow Wines, 11
Bethany Wines, 10
Charles Melton Wines, 8
Chateau Dorien, 13
Elderton Wines, 22
Grant Burge Wines, 5
Henschke Wines, 26
Heritage Wiens, 18
Kaesler Wines, 21
Kellermeister, 3
Kies Family Wines, 2
Krondorf Wines, 9
Langmeil Winery, 16

Orlando Wines, 4
Penfolds Wines, 20
Peter Lehmann Wines, 15
Richmond Grove Barossa
  Winery, 14
Rockford Wines, 7
St. Hallett Wiens, 6
Saltram Wine Estate, 24
Seppeltsfield Winery, 19
Stanley Brothers Winers, 12
Veritas Winery, 17
Wolf Blass Wines, 23
Yalumba Wines, 25

## ACCOMMODATIONS

**The Bunkhaus Traveller's Hostel** (☎8562 2260). Near Nuriootpa, before the turn-off to Angaston on the Barossa Valley Way from Tanunda to Nuriootpa. The bus will drop off and pickup directly outside. Right in a vineyard—luscious vines 20 paces from the front porch; TV lounge, kitchen. Intimate, with friendly management. Laundry. 12 beds. Book ahead. Dorms $13; doubles $38.

**Tanunda Caravan and Tourist Park** (☎8563 2784). Just outside Tanunda on Barossa Way toward Lyndoch. Convenient location. Leafy trees give welcome shade. BBQ, kiosk, laundry. Grassy tent sites from $13; basic on-site vans from $30; cabins from $38.

**Sandy Creek YHA,** in Sandy Creek Conservation Park, 2km from Lyndoch. You need your own transport and must get the key from the YHA South Australia office, 38 Sturt St, Adelaide (☎8231 5583). Pre-booking is essential. This limited-access hostel has 8 bunks in a renovated stone farmhouse. $15, under 18 $10.

## FOOD

The Barossa is not just about wine—food is also a high priority. Foodland, on Barossa Valley Way just past the turn-off for Angaston, has **groceries.** (Open M-W, F 8am-6pm, Th 8am-9pm, Sa 8am-4pm.)

**Zinfandel Tea Rooms,** 58 Murray St, Tanunda (☎8563 2822). German and Australian breakfasts until 11am, light lunches, and rich desserts for afternoon tea. Excellent apple strudel, rhubarb crumble, and other desserts for $3.50. Soup or small sandwiches start under $3. Open daily 8:30am-6pm.

**Siegersdorf Wine Company and Restaurant,** Barossa Valley Way (☎8563 0773). Between Tanunda and Nuriootpa. Good food and service. Choose a starter such as seafood bisque or a kangaroo sampler, then a main like roast of the day or chicken stir-fry, and finally a dessert like apple strudel or cherry cheesecake. Vegetarians are not top priority. 3-course lunch M-Sa $10, daily 3-course dinner and Su lunch $12.

**La Buona Vita,** 89 Murray St, Tanunda (☎8563 2527). The chef, an award-winning German native, and his wife Vanetta run an excellent place. Pizza ($7-12) in pleasant surrounds, plus pasta ($7.50-8.50), schnitzel, and fish 'n' chips for light meals in the $5-6 range. Fresh baked pies. Take-away and delivery available. Open daily noon-late.

## WINERIES OF THE BAROSSA VALLEY

The complete tour of over 40 wineries requires Bacchanalian spirit, Herculean effort, and Gargantuan ability to hold your liquor. Most people "only" visit four to six in a day, but that is plenty for a nice buzz—each winery has free tastings, with no obligation to purchase. Grapes are harvested from late February into April or early May. This is when tastings are busiest, and when some backpackers find **picking jobs.** Most wineries in Barossa are open daily from 10am to 4 or 5pm.

### WHETTING THE PALATE

If you don't understand what all the fuss over wine is about (and even if you do), start your Barossa visit with an hour at **The Barossa Wine Centre,** 66-68 Murray St, Tanunda. The beautiful exhibits make the craft of wine-making and the etiquette of wine-tasting accessible to skeptical novices, while connoisseurs may appreciate the in-depth displays and filmed discussions with area winemakers. (☎8563 0600. Open M-F 9am-4pm, Sa-Su 10am-3pm. $2.) Two wineries offer tours of their production facilities: **Seppelt,** in Seppeltsfield (M-F 11am, 1, 2, 3pm; Sa-Su 11:30am, 1:30, 2:30pm; $4, children $1) and **Chateau Yaldara** (☎8524 4200), Gomersal Rd, Lyndoch (daily 10:15, 10:45am, 1:15, 2:15, 3:15pm; $4). The tours take about 45min. and are well worth the price. **Wolf Blass Wines,** 97 Sturt Hwy, Nuriootpa, also has a small wine heritage museum near its tasting rooms. (☎8562 1955. Open M-F 9:15am-4:30pm, Sa-Su 10am-4:30pm. Free.)

### STUMBLING AROUND

If you're exploring on foot, start from the main road **(Barossa Valley Way)** in Tanunda, where you'll find the small **Stanley Brothers Winery** with pottery and jams also for sale at the cellar door and a picnic area. (☎8563 3375. Open M-F 9:30am-5pm, Sa-Su 11am-5pm.) Not far away on Para Rd, **Richmond Grove Barossa Winery,** on the banks of the small Para River, specializes in Rieslings and has picnic areas among the gum trees. (☎8563 2204. Open M-F 10am-5pm, Sa-Su 10:30am-4:30pm.)

**A QUICK WINE PRIMER** Wine tasting, like anything else, has its own vocabulary. Australia's, and the Barossa's, most famous red grape varieties are Shiraz (often called Syrah outside Australia) and Cabernet Sauvignon. Riesling, Chardonnay, and Sauvignon Blanc are probably the most well-known whites. Sparkling wines are simply the ones with bubbles (champagne is the most famous kind of sparkling wine). Fortified wines are sweeter wines with added alcohol, often called dessert wines in North America and liqueur wines in Europe. Port, sherry, and vermouth are some of the most well-known fortifieds. Dry is the opposite of sweet. Crisp means the wine has an acidity, roughly the opposite of smooth or soft. In general, taste white before red, dry before sweet, and sparkling before fortified. Aroma, a word usually used with younger wines, is the same as bouquet (used with older wines)—they both mean simply "what the stuff smells like." You needn't use any of these words, though; the important question is whether or not you like what you're tasting. Cheers!

Down Para Rd, **Peter Lehmann Wines** is a larger operation, buying grapes from about 200 growers, crushing more than 10,000 tons of grapes every year, and turning them all into excellent reds, whites, and fortifieds. (☎8563 2500. Open M-F 9:30am-5pm, Sa-Su 10:30am-4:30pm.) **Langmeil Winery,** at the corner of Para and Langmeil Rd, has a good tasting range in a cellar door dating from the 1840s. (☎8563 2595. Open daily 11am-5pm.) ▨**Rockford Wines,** in Tanunda on Krondorf Rd, caters to small groups and ought not be missed; their coopers also enlighten visitors on the role of the barrel in wine-making. (☎8563 2720. Open M-Sa 11am-5pm.) **Henschke,** in Keyneton, is out of the way but is highly regarded by locals. (☎8564 8223. Open M-F 9am-4:30pm, Sa 9am-noon, holidays 10am-3pm.)

## STUMBLING AROUND WITH A DESIGNATED DRIVER

For those not confined to walking distance, the options seem endless.

**Saltram Wine Estate,** (☎8564 3355). On the Nuriootpa-Angaston Rd, just outside Angaston. Smooth, fruity, and fabulously decadent—Saltram's Semillon is the stuff from which dreams are made. This winery has been working on their reds, whites, and ports since 1859. Open M-F 9am-5pm, Sa-Su 10am-5pm. Bistro open daily 11am-3pm.

**Bethany Wines,** (☎8563 2086). On Bethany Rd, between Tanunda and Nuriootpa. High above the rest of the valley with a panoramic vista and lovely picnic areas. The family still uses the old gravity feed method to make excellent reds, whites, ports, and sparkling wines. Open M-Sa 10am-5pm, Su 1-5pm.

**St. Hallett Wines,** (☎8563 2319). On St. Hallett's Rd, Tanunda. Since 1944, St. Hallett has made every drop of their wine exclusively from Barossa fruit. Premium red and white table wines are the specialty. Open daily 10am-5pm. Coopers at the **keg factory** across the road welcome visitors to watch them practice their craft, shaping the huge oak barrels that are as much a part of the best wines as the grapes (☎8563 3012).

**Orlando Wines,** (☎8521 3140). At Rowland Flat. Some 250,000 people each year pay respects at this cellar door. It has built a reputation around its Jacob's Creek wine, Australia's largest wine export brand. One out of every five branded bottles that leaves the country bears the Jacob's Creek label. Open M-F 10am-5pm, Sa-Su 10am-4pm.

**Chateau Dorrien,** (☎8562 2850). At the corner of Seppeltsfield Rd and Barossa Valley Way, Dorrien. Those who appreciate the sweeter things in life will love Dorrien. Five honey meads, ranging from sweet to spicy, are their specialty. Open daily 10am-5pm.

## STUMBLING AROUND ON A TOUR

**Groovy Grape Getaways** is the most popular backpackers tour to the Barossa, running from Adelaide and Glenelg daily, with free hostel pickup. The tour stops at the big rocking horse, the whispering wall, 4 wineries, and Seppelts and includes a BBQ. (☎8395 4422. $39.) If you're more serious about wine, or less than thrilled about spending a day drinking with 22-year-olds, **Prime Mini Tours** runs a small, enjoyable tour which includes a visit to the big rocking horse, whispering wall, and Angas Park Dried Fruits, a gourmet lunch, and stops at four wineries. (☎8293 4900. $38. Free pickup.) If you're staying in the Barossa, **Valley Tours** has the least expensive full-day winery and sights tour. (☎8563 3587. $42 including lunch, with pickup and return to Barossa Valley accommodations.) **Barossa Getabout Tours** goes farther afield, minimum of eight persons. (☎8524 6468. W, F, Sa, including lunch and transfers in the valley $39; Nov.-Apr. Tu and Th twilight dinner tour $45.)

## 👁 🌿 SIGHTS AND FESTIVALS

Designated drivers, take heart: not every attraction in the Barossa requires drinking. **Mengler Hill lookout,** on Mengler Hill Rd outside Tanunda, is definitely worth a stop to see the rows of vines in every direction. Behind its ramshackle exterior, the **SA Museum of Mechanical Music,** Barossa Valley Hwy, Lyndoch, hides musical wonders you never dreamed possible. Tom, the affable guide advises, "if you don't have a sense of humor, don't come in." (☎8524 4014. Open daily 9am-5pm. $5.) The

**THE LEGO MAN** In 1993 Tom Lucieer opened a museum of Danish plastic bricks—a collection worth nearly $100,000. The original Lego toy, which is made of wood, is transported daily by two policeman and an armored car to a local bank for overnight keeping. Her Majesty the Queen has visited the collection twice; maybe she needs to learn you can't hold on, but must lego. This man is in with the Lego company; several of his original designs are slated to be produced commercially, and he gets the new sets before the stores do. So, if the kids (or the inner child) are bored by wineries, bring them to Angaston to see the Lego Man. (☎ 8564 2714. 37 Jubilee Ave, off Schilling St in Angaston. Open daily 10am-5pm. $2.)

road linking Williamstown and Sandy Creek passes **Barossa Reservoir,** with its famous curved **Whispering Wall,** where murmured confidences can be heard meters away. In Tanunda, the ☒**Kev Rohrlach Collection,** on Murray St between Nurioopta and Tanunda, preserves much of Australian history and society through one man's massive collection of stuff; as any visitor will say, it must be seen. (☎ 8563 3407. Open M-Sa 11am-4pm, Su 10am-5pm.)

As if you needed an excuse to drink, festivals abound. During the **Barossa Classic Gourmet Festival** in late August and most of September, wineries invite chefs and accompany their liquid wares with gourmet feasts. Every October, the **Barossa International Music Festival** (☎ 8359 2994) celebrates the arrival of spring.

## CLARE

Between Adelaide and the South Australian outback, Clare (pop. 4000) and its neighbor, Burra, constitute the final outposts of civilization before the Flinders Ranges and the back of beyond. The Clare Valley, running from Auburn up to Clare along the Main North Rd, hosts some 20-odd vineyards. The higher altitude here (about 340m) means a respite from some of the lowland heat associated with places like the Yorke Peninsula, and the more pleasant weather allows soaring pine and fur trees to point skyward over the golden-brown terrain. Golden-brown, that is, except for those lush carpets of vineyard green.

**▯ TRANSPORT.** If you're driving from Adelaide (136km south of Clare), take Main North Rd through Elizabeth and onto the Gawler bypass, then turn left at the exit to Tarlee. Main North Rd runs through the town center and passes most of the wineries. On the road from Auburn to Clare, signs pointing to "Historic Mintaro" lead to an absolutely spectacular 12km drive.

**▯ PRACTICAL INFORMATION.** In Clare itself, Old North Rd runs one block east of Main North Rd, the highway on which visitors enter from Auburn. The **Clare Valley Tourist Information Centre,** in the town hall, stocks free winery and town maps. (☎ 8842 2131. 229 Main North Rd. Open M-Sa 9am-5pm, Su 10am-4pm.) Services include: the **police station** (☎ 8842 2711) and **RAA** (☎ 8842 2172, ☎ 8842 3105). The **hospital** (☎ 8842 2500) is on the main road to Burra, north of the town center, but more convenient is a **clinic** on Old North Rd (☎ 8842 2100, afterhours 8842 2773). **Scan Print,** in the Foodland complex on Old North Rd, has **Internet.** (Open M-F 9am-5pm. 30min. $5, check email for $2.) Thanks be to Mercury, Roman god of merchants, commerce, and bankers, all the banks in town have **ATMs.**

**▯ ACCOMMODATIONS.** A central location in Clare, clean rooms, and low prices make **Taminga Hotel,** 302 Main North Rd (☎ 8842 2808), a good choice for those without their own transport (singles $20; doubles $30). Slightly nicer, the **Clare Hotel** (☎ 8842 2816), also on Main North Rd, has motel rooms with attached baths (singles $45; doubles $50). The award-winning **Clare Caravan Park,** 3km south of town on Main North Rd, has a lake, pool, laundry, and even a small flora and fauna reserve. (☎ 8842 2724; fax 8842 3447. Reception 8am-7pm. Tent sites $13 per person, powered $15; self-contained cabins for 2 $40-$46.)

◻ **FOOD.** Clare, like many larger Australian road-side towns, offers a selection of bakeries and cafés, but heartier feed comes from a counter meal in a pub hotel or the Chaff Mill Country Kitchen (see below). Clare **Foodland** contains a **bakery** and a large **grocery** selection. (☎8842 2416. 47 Old North Rd. Open M-Sa 8am-5pm.) There is another, smaller Foodland on Main North Rd; one ought not confuse them, especially if one is looking for Scan Print and the wonders of the Internet. **Price's Traditional Bakery,** north of the post office, has been churning out pies, pastries, and sausage rolls for more than a century; try the $1.50 honey log with fresh cream. (☎8842 2473. 269 Main North Rd. Open M-F 8am-5pm, Sa 9am-1:30pm.) The staff of the friendly **Chaff Mill Country Kitchen** cooks breakfast, lunch, and dinner of the steak and pasta persuasion (lunches $5-15; dinners $15-21). (☎8842 3055. 308 Main North Rd. Closed M lunch, all day Tu; open M, W-Su 10am-8 or 10pm.) The **Taminga Hotel** (☎8842 2808), on Main North Rd, serves the town's best counter meals, with $5 daily specials, generous portions, and fresh ingredients.

**WINERIES OF CLARE VALLEY.** The Clare Valley is the northernmost wine production area in South Australia, cooler than the much larger Barossa Valley. Around 28 wineries operate here, though not all have cellar doors. If a winery has tastings, however, the folks at the Clare tourist office know. Most are small family operations, and only five Clare wineries crush more than 500 tons of grapes per year. Signs to the wineries tend to be small; it is essential to pick up a guide at Clare's tourist office. An old railway line, parallel to Main North Rd, has been converted into the 27km scenic **Riesling Trail,** named after the most famous style of wine from the region. The trail runs between Clare and Auburn and is suitable for walking and biking (one-way 2hr.). Convenient car parks in Clare, Sevenhill, Watervale, and Auburn allow for walkers to take smaller journeys. The trail passes farms and vineyards, as well a few wineries, including Sevenhill Cellars. Bikes can be hired in Clare from **Clare Valley Cycle Hire,** 32 Victoria Rd (☎8842 2782).

**Sevenhill Cellars,** (☎8843 4222). College Rd, Sevenhill, 6km south of Clare. Made since 1851 by and for the brothers of adjoining St. Aloysius church. Seven Jesuit brothers have continued the 149-year tradition of wine-making. Sacramental wine, sold only for religious purposes, is 25% of the output. Fine reds (including St. Ignatius), whites (including St. Aloysius), and fortified wines may, however, be tasted and purchased. Does this seem a little ironic to anyone? Open M-F 8:30am-4:30pm, Sa 9am-4pm.

**Taylors Wines,** (☎8849 2008). Off Mintaro Rd in Auburn, 25km south of Clare. The largest winery in the Clare Valley, and the largest estate on one site in Australia. All wines are made only from grapes grown on the estate, and all are bottled here. Family-owned, they've won many awards with their lovely, cool whites and hearty reds. Their cabernet sauvignon is particularly excellent. Open M-F 9am-5pm, Sa 10am-5pm, Su 10am-4pm.

**Leasingham Wines,** 7 Dominic St, in Clare (☎8842 2785). Perennial medal-winner and venerable Clare institution. The appeal is rounded out by a lovely setting and friendly service. Riesling was developed here, but the winery is now pushing ahead with reds. Open M-F 8:30am-5pm, Sa-Su 10am-4pm.

# NEAR CLARE: MARTINDALE HALL

Martindale Hall, east of historic Mintaro, about 20min. from Clare by car, was featured in the film *Picnic at Hanging Rock*. The Georgian mansion is now an upscale B&B. Self-guided tours are available. The main road toward Mintaro is south of Clare; follow the signs reading "Martindale" on the Clare-Burra road. (☎8843 9088. Open M-F 11am-4pm, Sa-Su noon-4pm. $5, concessions $3.50.)

# BURRA

The rest of this region may draw tourists with wines and vines, but Burra's tourist economy depends on mines. The historic mining town, 30min. (40km) northeast of Clare and 156km north of Adelaide on the main route to Sydney via Broken Hill, plays up its copper roots for tourists. Seeing it today, it's hard to believe that Burra (pop. 2000) was the largest inland town in Australia in 1851, with almost 5000 people. While the town might not be termed "a thrill a minute," it has latched onto historical tourism with tenacity, and sells its status as a state heritage area with surprisingly fascinating exhibits.

**⚅ PRACTICAL INFORMATION.** The highway spits cars right into **Market Square**, at the intersection of Market and Commercial St. The **Burra Visitor Centre** books copper and gold mining tours and Clare Valley winery tours (☎ 8892 2154; fax 8892 2555. 2 Market Sq. Open daily 9am-5pm. Most are half-day tours, $28-35.) **Internet** is available at Stockman Electronics. ($5 30min. Open M, W, F 1-5pm.)

**▨▨ ACCOMMODATIONS AND FOOD.** In the 1840s, when many miners lived in mud dugouts along the banks of Burra Creek, the South Australian Mining Association built the ▨**Paxton Square Cottages,** on Kingston St, just over the small bridge visible from Market Sq. The 32 ensuite cottages have kitchens and fireplaces. (☎ 8892 2622; fax 8892 2508. Linen $5. $25 per person, each extra person $10.) The 150-year-old **Burra Hotel** is in the town center. (☎ 8892 2389. Counter meals served M-Sa noon-2pm and 6-8pm. Singles $25.)

During the day, or for a light lunch, the **Burra Country Pantry** (☎ 8892 2400) in Market Square offers warm breads and delectable Cornish pasties ($1.50-2). For budget dinners, you're limited to counter meals at any of the handful of hotels. At the **Commercial Hotel** (☎ 8892 2010), $2.50 will get you soup and a fresh roll, $5 a generous, tasty counter meal. Market Square has a small Foodtown **supermarket** (open M-F 8:45am-5:30pm, Sa 8:45-11am).

**▨ SIGHTS.** If you have a car and want to see the town's history, buy the **Burra Passport** at the tourist office, which includes all details for a self-guided driving tour of the area ($10, concessions $8; with both museum entrances $18, $15). The museums have friendly staff who provide necessary background if you've gone this far in life without a detailed knowledge of the history of copper mining. **Morphett's Enginehouse Museum,** on the site of Burra Mine, details the mechanical aspects of the mine and the pumps that brought 15 million liters of water out of the ground each day. (☎ 8892 2154. Open M-F 11am-1pm, Sa-Su 11am-2pm. $4.) The **Burra mine,** known as the **Monster Mine,** was the world's largest copper mine in the 1870s and saved the state from bankruptcy. The museum's highlight is the chance to climb through the adit, a small underground retimbered tunnel. The **Bon Accord Mining Museum** focuses on the social history of the mines by telling the stories of individual miners. (Open M-F 12:30-2:30pm, Sa-Su 12:30-3:30pm. $4.) The best part of the Passport is the key, which you can use to get into the old **Redruth Gaol** (a police lockup), the spooky **Unicorn Brewery cellars** (the archaeological remains of an old township), and miners' dugouts.

For those tired of copper, **Mongolata Gold Mine,** 23km east of Burra, offers a guided tour of the old government battery and an underground tour of the mine. (☎ 8892 2233. $10. Book ahead.) **Burra Trail Rides** (☎ 8892 2627), Basin Farm, 3km northeast of Burra off the road to Morgan, has horse rides starting at $10 (for 1hr.) and stock driving rides for 1-3 days, with meals and camping gear supplied. All skill levels easily accommodated.

# SOUTHEAST OF THE MURRAY RIVER

The majestic Murray River winds west from the Great Dividing Range. Fed by a watershed that spans most of New South Wales and portions of Victoria, the largest waterway in Australia slices through the southeast corner of South Australia and empties into the Southern Ocean. Fruit, especially wine grapes, flourishes along the irrigated river basin, while the Coorong, a 145km stretch of coastal lagoons, supports over 240 species of birdlife. The towns near the Victoria border can be associated with geographic regions within that state. The area around

Naracoorte is an extension of the agricultural Wimmera district (see p. 561) and Mt. Gambier continues the themes of Victoria's southwest coast.

## DRIVING THE PRINCES HIGHWAY

The road from Tailem Bend south toward Mt. Gambier runs along the Coorong, providing excellent access to both the wetlands of the coast and the fishing, swimming, and surfing beaches farther to the south.

**MENINGIE.** Meningie, at the north end of the Princes Hwy, is the last town for 146km before Kingston SE, at the junction of Hwy 1 and Alt 1, the inland and coastal highways respectively. Public bathrooms on the foreshore provide a spot for bathers to change, so even those just cruising through the area can take a dip at the beach. There is a gas station at the south end of the town. Probably most useful to travelers is the office of the **National Parks and Wildlife Service,** 34 Princes Hwy (☎ 8575 1200), where one can pick up the magazine called *The Tattler*, covering the southeastern coastal parks from Goolwa to the Victoria border.

**ROBE.** Robe, 190km south of Meningie, hosts a valuable commodity to accompany its good surf beaches, a **YHA hostel.** Part of the **Robe Long Beach Tourist Park,** 70-80 the Esplanade, it offers backpacker accommodation right on Long Beach. (☎ 8768 2237. Dorms $10; singles $20; twins and doubles $27.) **Foodland** grocery store is on Main Rd. (☎ 8768 2263. Open daily 7:30am-7:30pm.) There is **tourist information** at the **Robe Institute and Library,** on Mundy Tce. (☎ 8768 2465. Open M-F 9am-5pm, Sa-Su 10am-1pm.) **RAA:** ☎ 8768 2006 or ☎ 015 714 204.

## MOUNT GAMBIER

In an obsidian palace deep beneath Mount Gambier's famed Blue Lake, a disgruntled deity lives in permanent exile. The Lake King originally lived with his fellow gods in divine bliss, but betrayed them during a conflict long since forgotten, and was banished. The lake's mercurial hues reflect his shifting moods; it's a shimmering sapphire during summer, but fades to slate gray in colder months.

For historical and cultural precision, it should be noted that *Let's Go* completely made this story up. Still, it's as good an explanation as any for Blue Lake's mysteriously shifting color, a phenomenon which continues to baffle scientists. The lake is Mount Gambier's big draw, but the town's caves and lively downtown are worth a spin, too. Plus, as the largest town in the area (pop. 21,000), Mount Gambier makes a good base for exploring nearby wineries or the caves of Naracoorte.

**TRANSPORT AND PRACTICAL INFORMATION.** V/Line **buses** stop at the Shell Blue Lake service station at 100 Commercial St W., and run to **Adelaide** (6hr., $41) and **Melbourne** (7hr., $50) via the Victorian cities of **Heywood, Portland, Port Fairy, Warrnambool,** and **Geelong.**

The town's main commercial area lies at the intersection of Bay and Commercial St, and extends back to James and Helen St. Here are the **pharmacies, markets, 24hr. ATMs,** and **banks** (open M-Th 9:30am-4pm, F 9:30am-5pm). The **Visitor Information Centre** is part of the Lady Nelson Centre (see **Sights,** below), on Jubilee Hwy E, northeast of the CBD, and is open daily 9am-5pm. Near town hall and the intersection of Bay and Commercial St is the **Civic Centre,** which houses a **library** with free **Internet access.** (☎ 8721 2540. Open M, W, F 9am-6pm, Tu 9am-5pm, Th 9am-8pm, Sa 9-11:30am.) **Post office:** 30 Helen St (open M-F 9:30am-5pm).

**ACCOMMODATIONS.** The Gaol, off Margaret St, promises a unique hosteling experience. As the name suggests, this place is a recently converted jail, "decriminalized" in 1995. The ensuite rooms are very comfortable, but the owners are committed to retaining some of the penitentiary charm. Provision of breakfast is based on good behavior. (☎ 8723 0032, freecall ☎ (1800) 62 68 44. Dorms $18; doubles $39.) The reformed can head for the **Blue Lake Motel,** Kennedy Ave, 500m east of the Lady Nelson centre. The congenial ownership offers clean ensuite rooms with four bunks. Linen $2. (☎8725 5211, freecall ☎(1800) 08 82 91. Beds $12.)

Several hotels stand in the CBD, offering basic ensuite rooms for $40 to $50. There are some less expensive options, too, the best of which is the **Federal Hotel-Motel,** 112 Commercial St E., half of which consists of cozy shared-bath rooms with TV. (☎8723 1099. Singles $20.) **Blue Lake City Caravan Park,** on Bay Rd up by the lake, is a veritable Disneyland of caravan parks. It's spotless, with facilities that include a pool, tennis and basketball courts, and spacious outdoor cooking facilities. (☎8725 9856. Sites from $14.50; caravans from $38.)

⛏️📺 **FOOD AND ENTERTAINMENT.** The Central Business District is packed with chip shops and takeaway joints, supermarkets and greengrocers. Mt. Gambier's hip **Jonties Café,** 13 Commercial St E., opposite the courthouse, is an excellent spot to while away the day. The vibe is chill and the gourmet food reasonably priced at under $12 for dinner. (☎8723 9499. Open M-F 8am-midnight, Sa-Su 8am-6pm.) Fully licensed **Café Luna,** 82 Commercial St W., has a coffee bar featuring a truly superior cappuccino for $2. (☎8725 4887. Open M 10am-3pm, Tu-Th and Su 10am-midnight, F-Sa 10am-1:30am.) The **Pepper Pot Café,** 41 Commercial Rd E., across the street from the town hall, serves a scrumptious breakfast for $8. (☎8724 9220. Open M-F 8:45am-4:45pm, Sa-Su 8:45am-1:30pm.)

A number of pubs congregate in the town center. The **Mount Gambier Hotel,** 2 Commercial St W., has high wooden ceilings, pool tables, video games, and live bands and dancing Th-Sa. (☎8725 0611. Alas, only until midnight.) **Gambier City Bowling,** on Commerical St W., offers a weekend special of two games of ten pin, hot dog, and a drink for $10. (☎8723 2442. Open M-Sa 10am-late, Su 11am-late.)

📷 **SIGHTS.** Bay Rd leads south through the center of town to spots that overlook **Blue Lake** and its resident demons, or whatever the hell makes it change color. The lake itself fills the crater of a volcano that erupted only 4000-5000 years ago, and holds 8 billion gallons of water, which are used to supply the town's thirsty gullets and flush toilets. Just south of the Blue Lake, by the entrance to the Blue Lake City Caravan Park, a clearly marked road leads up to absolutely beautiful walking tracks that access Mt. Gambier, the Devil's Teacup, and Leg of Mutton Lake. Here, the butterflies, crickets, and grasshoppers outnumber the black flies a million to one. The 2.3km walk to the top of the mountain is best attempted in the morning.

Lieutenant James Grant, allegedly the love child of the mythical Lake King, was the first European to sight Mt. Gambier as he sailed on the brig *Lady Nelson* in 1800. A replica of this historic ship now graces the **Lady Nelson Visitor and Discovery Centre** on Jubilee Hwy E. The center highlights the area's history and geological phenomena. (☎8724 9750. Open daily 9am-5pm. $7, children $3.)

Back in town center, there are two caves. The **Cave Gardens,** at Bay Rd and Watson Tce, the original water source for the town, is the centerpiece of the town square park, with flowering vegetation and trickling waterfalls. The flooded **Engelbrecht Cave,** on Jubilee Hwy West between Victoria Tce and Ehret St, is a popular spot for adequately trained **cave divers.** Two of the cave's chambers are open for viewing (tours on the hr. $4; open daily 11am-3pm). A third nifty hole in the ground on Jubilee Hwy E. known as the **Umpherston Sinkhole,** is carpeted with trees, ivy, and flowers, has BBQ and picnic facilities, and is dramatically lit at night.

# NARACOORTE

The best part of Naracoorte is underground. The small town, roughly 125km west of Horsham VIC on the Wimmera Hwy, and 100km north of Mt. Gambier along the Riddoch Hwy, would be a good deal more anonymous if it weren't for residents' cleanliness (the town was Australia's tidiest in 1999) and a nearby network of eerily gorgeous caves, recently designated a World Heritage site.

**▞ PRACTICAL INFORMATION.** The **Sheeps Back Wool Museum and Tourist Information Centre,** northwest of the town center on MacDonnell Rd, has info and a museum. (☎8762 1518, freecall ☎(1800) 24 44 21. Open daily 10am-4pm. Museum $5.) The CBD has the town's **banks** and **ATMs;** a **Foodtown supermarket,** 63 Omerod St (open M-F 8:30am-8pm, Sa 8:30am-5pm, Su 9:30am-5pm); and the **public library** with free **Internet access** (open M 10am-5pm, Tu, W, F 9:30am-5pm, Th 10am-8pm, Sa 8:30am-noon). **Police:** 56 Smith St (☎8762 0466). **Hospital:** Jenkins Tce (☎8762 8100). **Post office:** 23 Ormerod St (open M-F 9am-5pm).

**▞▞ ACCOMMODATIONS AND FOOD.** Two hotels face each other across Naracoorte's town center. The **Kincraig Hotel,** 168 Smith St, offers hotel rooms with sinks. (☎8762 2200. Singles $25; doubles $40.) Its doppelganger, the **Naracoorte Hotel-Motel,** 73 Ormerod St, has the better restaurant, but similar accommodation. (☎8762 2400. Singles $24; doubles $43.) **Camping** is available both at Bool Lagoon and at Naracoorte Caves Conservation Park ($15 per car). The Naracoorte sites feature laundry, BBQ, showers, and toilets. Questions on camping should be directed to the Naracoorte Caves Conservation Park (☎8762 2340). Get **permits** at the Conservation Park ticket office or the permit kiosk at Bool Lagoon (open daily 10am-3pm). **Maddie's Café,** on Goodchild Place at the corner of Smith St, is a friendly spot for light fare and strong coffee. (☎8762 3953. Open M-F 9am-5pm.)

**▣ SIGHTS.** Twelve kilometers south of town is the **Naracoorte Caves Conservation Park,** a well-marked 4km west off the Riddoch Hwy. The **Wonambi Fossil Centre** is next to the carpark. (☎8762 2340. Open daily 9am-5pm.) The **Alexandra Cave** features five chambers full of delicate calcite stalagmites, stalactites, straws, and flowstone. **Blanche Cave** lacks these delicate decorations, but has immense columns and windows caused by a partial collapse of the roof. Back in the 1850s, the local landlord used the cave for lavish parties, and the furniture remains inside. The most famous of the caves, the **Victoria Fossil Cave,** discovered in 1969, contains the remains of nearly 100 different species of Pleistocene fauna from 10,000 to two million years ago. Buried under silt after dying in the cave, the animals' fossils provide important clues to how the Australian marsupial megafauna were affected by the arrival of humans. Infrared bat-cameras have been installed in **Bat Cave** to allow tourists to view the bats without disturbing the breeding grounds. **Wet Cave** isn't quite as spectacular as the others, but it's the only cave you can see without a guide. Excellent **tours** are available daily 9:30am-4pm, on the following routes: Wonambi Fossil Centre and Wet Cave (self-guided); Alexandra Cave and Wet Cave; Bat Centre and Blanche Cave; and Victoria Fossil Cave. (1 tour $8, concession $6, children $5; 2 tours $14, $10, $8; 3 tours $20, $14, $12; 4 tours for the cave-aholic $25, $20, $15.) Also available are **adventure caving trips,** for both novices and advanced spelunkers. Book ahead via the Park's head office.

# YORKE PENINSULA

On Yorke, sandy flats punctuate rolling farmland, and sheer cliffs, looming over the hinterland, storm into the sea. What isn't farmed is covered in scrub forest. The northern half of the Yorke primarily features copper-mining history, centered in the Copper Coast town of Moonta. Copper went bust in the 1920s, so along with historical tourism, fishing—both recreational and industrial—has become increasingly important. Visitors should take heed: in the summer a northern wind that is hotter than hell sweeps the peninsula and the air drips with swarms of Beelzebub's flies. The only refuge—beach towns like Port Vincent and Wallaroo. On Yorke's southern tip, however, Innes National Park offers spectacular ocean views, pleasant surfing beaches, and gorgeous camping.

SOUTH AUSTRALIA

# THE COPPER COAST

A trio of old mining towns known as the Copper Coast (or Triangle)—Kadina, Wallaroo, and Moonta—sprang up as a result of discoveries of large copper deposits in the 1860s. The largest mines closed in 1923 after a worldwide copper glut. The towns may seem dull at first, but every hotel sports a bar (actually, it's the other way around), and in their numerous museums, these settlements retain some of the feel of South Australia's colonial days. At the area's biggest draw, Wallaroo beach, the water's blue, the sand is clean, and the sky is usually clear.

**■ TRANSPORT.** Premier Stateliner runs **buses** to and from **Adelaide** via **Port Wakefield** to all three towns. (☎8415 5555. Buses depart from and return to Adelaide 2 per day M-F, and 1 per day Sa-Su. $16, ages 5-15 $7.) Though they may be triplets, these towns are not identical. Wallaroo is the only one located on the ocean, where grain silos and a shipping jetty point to what those in non-tourist trades do to make a living. Moonta is the most history-oriented town, playing its Cornish and mining heritage to the hilt; the **Moonta Station Visitor Centre,** on Kadina Rd in the old railway station, serves the entire Yorke Peninsula. (☎8825 1891. Open daily 9am-5pm.) About 500m further down the Kadina-Moonta Rd from Kadina, the Moonta Community **library** has Internet. (☎8825 2088. Open in school term M, W-F 9am-4pm; Su 1:30-4pm. During holidays and summer, open Tu 10am-noon and 2-7pm; W-F 2-5pm; Su 1:30-4pm.) Kadina is the most metropolitan of the towns (which isn't saying much), offering modern conveniences including the peninsula's only **ATMs,** Woolworth's **supermarket** (open daily 7am-9pm), and 24hr. **RAA** services (☎8821 1111, ☎8821 1948, mobile ☎(018) 85 90 70).

**▮ ACCOMMODATIONS.** For fine, basic pub accommodation, each town has a winner. Kadina has the **Wombat Hotel,** 10 Taylor St. (☎8821 1108. $19, including light breakfast.) In Moonta, try the **Royal Hotel** at 2 Ryan St. (☎8825 2108. Singles $25; doubles $40; light breakfast included.) Both have cheap counter meals. For freedom from pubs, refuge can be found in the rooms (most with balcony) at the beautiful **Sonbern Lodge Motel,** 18 John Tce, Wallaroo. The pool table and velvet chairs look as though they would be layered in the dust of ages, if only they weren't so clean. The Sonbern also stocks plenty of tourist information. (☎8823 2291; fax 8823 3355. Shared bath. Singles $24; doubles $38, ensuite $40-55.)

**▮ FOOD.** The Yorke Peninsula is famous for its Cornish cuisine, especially the pasty (about $1.50), but only Moonta is bold enough to claim the moniker, "Australia's Little Cornwall." Of the many sit-down restaurants in the Copper Triangle, ▨**Skinner's Jetty Fish Café,** on Jetty Rd, Wallaroo, is easily the best. Fresh seafood is served (mains $12-24) in a dining room overlooking the jetty or outside in a leafy garden. Downstairs is an inexpensive take-away counter. (☎8823 3455. Take-away counter open daily 10am-8pm. Dining room open daily noon-2pm and 6-8pm.) **Price's Bakery,** on Owen Tce in Wallaroo, offers what everybody at the beach wants: a clean store with good sweets ($1.50), ice creams, pasties ($1.60), sandwiches ($2-3), sparklers, and cigarettes. (☎8823 2223. Open M-F and Su 8:30am-5:30pm, Sa 8:30am-3pm.) In all three towns there are ample and obvious delis.

**▨ SIGHTS.** The deepest attraction is the **Wheal Hughes Copper Mine**, on the outskirts of Moonta, on the road to Wallaroo. Tours venture underground to explore the workings of this real-life mine. Reasonable fitness and a pair of socks required; boots and helmet provided. (1½hr. tour 1pm. $12, children $6. Purchase tickets at the Moonta Visitor Centre by 12:30pm.) For something a bit more eccentric and entertaining, head to the multi-award-winning ▨**Banking and Currency Museum,** 3 Graves St, in Kadina. Take a tour through this tribute to tender. Money lines everything, from the walls to the doors. (☎8821 2906; fax 8821 2901. Open July-May Su-Th 10am-4:30pm. $3, children $1.)

## INNES NATIONAL PARK

Gorgeous Innes National Park, on the southwest tip of the peninsula, is the real attraction of the Yorke. It's primarily known as a fantastic spot for surfing, diving, snorkeling, whale watching, and fishing, but there's always plenty of room for folks just driving in to picnic and take in the views. About 9,000 hectares were set aside as national park land in 1970 to encourage the re-population of the rare Great Western Whipbird. Visitors may not catch sight of these rather shy creatures (which make a grating "happy-birthday-to-you" call), but the sculptured headlands and crashing waves justify the drive from up north. And those not planning on fishing may find that the omnipresence of happy anglers changes their minds.

The Yorke Peninsula Passenger Service (☎ (1800) 62 50 99) runs **buses** daily from **Adelaide** to **Yorketown** for $25. However, buses go no farther than **Warooka,** west of Yorketown, and Stenhouse Bay is more than 50km farther, requiring a car for any measure of flexibility in exploring the park. A daypass costs $5 per vehicle (fee waived if camping). The park's main road, 26km long, is sealed and suitable for conventional vehicles; although the side roads to overlooks and beaches are not sealed, many with 2WD cars still drive on them.

The park entrance and **National Park Office** (☎ 8854 4040; fax 8854 4072) are near the town of Stenhouse Bay. The **Innes Park Trading Post** (☎ 8854 4066), at the park entrance, has food, a bar, and information on where fish are biting and on which park areas are safe for swimming and surfing. The Trading Post also rents accommodations in a building at the park entrance ($10 per person), fills SCUBA tanks, and sells unleaded gas at normal prices.

"Beds" in the southern peninsula are usually sleeping bags, best used in the park itself. No bookings are required for **tent sites;** self-register at the office just inside the entrance for camping in designated areas. Sites at **Pondalowie Bay** have water and toilets ($12 per vehicle). All other camping areas cost $5 per vehicle. Several **lodges** and **huts** provide shelter within the park. Some have solar-powered lighting, full kitchens, and flush toilets. Others just have four walls. The lodges sleep four to 12 people ($22-65 per night per person; booking and payment due 2 weeks prior to arrival). The nearest hostel accommodation is about 100km from the park, in Port Vincent on the eastern coast of the peninsula. The **Tuckerway Hostel,** 14 Lime Kiln Rd, provides a simple but clean place to lay your head. The large 52-bed facility is more often used by school groups than by individuals, but the price can't be beat. (☎/fax 8853 7285. No linen. Dorms $10, under 18 $7. YHA. Definitely call ahead.)

# FLINDERS RANGES

This is ancient country, geologically, with soft worn-down mountain ranges in place of huge craggy peaks. The road dribbles through endless hills of colored dust and sagebrush. The Flinders is most popular from autumn to spring, when the nights are chilly and the days sunny. It's hot, hot, hot in summer, but for travelers with A/C, it's definitely still worth the trip. The Flinders Ranges begin at the northern end of the Gulf of St. Vincent and continue 400km into South Australia's vast northern outback, ending near Mt. Hopeless (which is a pretty accurate description of the terrain way out there). The ranges are divided into three sections, each with its own national park: southern, central, and northern.

## ▣ TOURS

Many companies run good backpacker camping trips to the Flinders from Adelaide, and longer tours are generally worth the cash. **Wallaby Tracks Adventure Tours** takes backpackers into the central Flinders, including bush camping and stops at Wilpena Pound, Aboriginal art sites, and Bunyeroo and Brachina Gorges. (☎ 8648 6655 or freecall ☎ (1800) 63 99 33. 1-3 days $79-235.) **Outback 'n' Coastal 4WD Adventures** has three-day Flinders camping trips with a maximum of seven passengers. (☎ 8250 2911. $299.) If your time is severely limited and the thought of a 900km

> **DRIVING IN THE FLINDERS.** Every year, hundreds of visitors success-fully explore the Flinders Ranges in standard 2WD cars. Within Flinders Ranges National Park, the roads to gorges and lookouts are not sealed, but are gener-ally in quite good condition when the weather has been clear. Most rental car companies, however, will not cover any damage to their cars or accidents on unsealed roads. Once you head north of Flinders Ranges National Park, road conditions are much less certain, and 4WD is preferred. The unsealed roads all the way up to Arkaroola are accessible to 2WD and fairly heavily traveled, and locals and even tourist office staff will usually send tourists in conventional cars happily on their way. But locals cannot predict flash floods, which can wipe out sections of the road in a matter of minutes. Sharp rocks can shred tires. A pool of water on the road can actually be hiding deep mud that a 2WD will not be able to handle. No matter how clear the skies, call the Northern Road Conditions Hotline (☎(1300) 361 033), or ask to see the daily road conditions fax at a petrol station in the area before setting out. Mobile phones will not operate in most of the Flinders. Do not think of driving off the bitumen in the central or northern Flinders without a spare tire and a jack, and make sure to take food and water (average 1L per hr. in the hot dry summertime; an esky is handy too.)

daytrip doesn't make your muscles revolt, **Adelaide Sightseeing** offers a one-day return jaunt from Adelaide to Wilpena Pound. (☎8231 4144. $145.)

A local couple operates **Intrepid Tours,** 7 Sixth St, Quorn, offering half-day tours that visit Mt. Arden, overlooking the Flinders, or Depot Creek Gorge with a focus on geology; and full-day tours that head to Wilpena Pound or explore the Blinman and Parachilna areas. (☎8648 6277. Half day $45; leave at 9am, 2pm; full-day $85.) **Quorn Flinders Ranges Eco-Tours,** 2 Railway Tce (☎8648 6016), has half-day 4WD tours into Dutchman Stern Conservation Park ($44), extended tours across the Simpson Desert, and five-day northern Flinders Ranges Tours. Self-driving tours are also available; inquire at the **Mill Motel,** 2 Railway Tce (☎8648 6016).

**Wayward Bus,** 237 Hutt St, Adelaide, has a South Aussie Outback tour covering the Flinders and Coober Pedy. Travelers bus to **Coober Pedy,** then travel to the Wil-liam Creek pub, down the Oodnadatta track, through the Flinders and Wilpena Pound, do wine tasting in the **Clare Valley,** and end in Adelaide four days later. (☎8232 6646. $320, including meals and 3 nights accommodation.) The **Pichi Richi Railway** (☎/fax 8658 1109) travels through the Flinders Apr.-Oct.; between Quorn and Woolshed Flat (2½hr., $24) and between Quorn and Saltia (3½hr., $30).

## PORT AUGUSTA

Port Augusta (pop. 14, 800) promotes itself as the "Crossroads of Australia." There is an element of truth to this; road-weary travelers who stop here are almost all on their way to somewhere else. This town is a place to pause, but not to linger.

Those who do choose to stay can visit **Wadlata Outback Centre,** 41 Flinders Tce, with a hands-on display of the stories, culture, and land of the outback. (☎8642 4511. Open M-F 9am-5:30pm, Sa-Su 10am-4pm. $7, concessions $4.50.) The **Arid Lands Botanic Gardens,** 400m north of town off the Stuart Hwy, offer walking trails with labeled plants. (☎8641 1049. Open M-F 9am-5pm, Sa-Su 10am-4pm. Free.)

Stateliner (☎8642 5055) runs **buses** to: **Adelaide** (4hr., 3-5 per day, $30); **Port Lin-coln** (4½hr., 2 per day); **Whyalla** (1hr., 2-5 per day); and **Wilpena Pound** (2hr.; Su, W, F; $27) via **Quorn** (35min.). The bus station is opposite the library on Mackay St. The *Ghan* and *Indian Pacific* **trains** depart from off of Stirling Rd to **Alice Springs** (15hr.; M, Th 7pm; $136, concessions $68) and **Perth** (33hr.; Tu, F 10:50pm; $224, concessions $112). Contact **Harvey World Travel,** 91 Commercial Rd (☎8642 6699), or call ☎13 22 32 to book. **Budget,** 16 Young St (☎8642 6040), rents vehicles.

If you're just passing through from Adelaide, stick to the highway, which becomes **Victoria Pde.** The city center focuses around **Commercial Rd,** with **post**

office, banks, and ATMs. Services include: Tourist Information Office, 41 Flinders Tce
(☎8641 0793; open M-F 9am-5:30pm, Sa-Su 10am-4pm); National Parks and Wildlife
Service, 9 Mackay St (☎8548 5300); and the library, on the corner of Mackay and
Marryatt St, with free Internet (☎8641 9152; open M and F 9am-6pm, Tu and W
9am-8pm, Th 9am-9pm, Sa 10am-1pm, and Su 2-5pm).

Both hostels in Port Augusta are on Trent Rd, about 2km from the city center.
The Bluefox Lodge, at Trent Rd and Hwy 1, opened in late 1999, offers free bus-sta-
tion pickup, seasonal vegetables, and Internet (15min. $2). Spinifex Nick, the resi-
dent tour guide, provides amusing tours of the Flinders ranges. (☎8641 2960. Beds
$15.) Port Augusta Backpackers, 17 Trent Rd, is not fancy but it does the job. (☎8641
1063. Dorms $12, breakfast included.) Port Augusta Holiday Park, Stokes Tce off Stu-
art Hwy, is over the bridge north of downtown. (☎8642 2974. Dorms $12; tent sites
for 2 $18, powered $19; on-site vans for 2 $44.) Hot Pepper Café, 34 Commercial Rd,
has sandwiches and coffee. (☎8642 2549. Open M-Th 9:30am-5pm, F 9:30am-
5:30pm, Sa 9:30am-noon.) Coles supermarket is on the corner of Jervois and Mary-
att St. (☎8641 1700. Open daily 6am-midnight.)

# SOUTHERN FLINDERS

## MT. REMARKABLE NATIONAL PARK

Between Adelaide and Port Augusta, somewhat near the otherwise uninviting
industrial town of Port Pirie, Mt. Remarkable National Park (15,632 hectares) is
the pride of the southern Flinders Ranges. Whereas this park doesn't have the big
wonders of its northern counterparts, it is only a couple of hours from Adelaide,
has its own quiet splendor, and is perfect for laid-back bushwalking and camping.
On the eastern side, the scenic Alligator Gorge section of the park is accessible at
Wilmington, on Main North Rd between Clare and Port Augusta; or by the cross-
park trail (26km; 10hr.) from Mambray Creek to Alligator Gorge. Mt. Remarkable
itself can be approached on a 4hr. hike from a trail starting 3km north of Melrose
(24km south of Wilmington), also along Main North Rd. The Alligator Gorge trail
(1.2km; 1hr.) has the best scenery on the eastern side of the park.

The park headquarters is on the western side of the park at Mambray Creek,
45km north of Port Pirie, directly off Hwy 1 on a road lined with magnificent eucalypts. Here is a pay station with trail maps, a 54-site campground, and access to
bushwalks through canyons or over ridges. (☎8634 7068. Park fees apply $5 per
vehicle, $12 per vehicle to camp; bushcamping $3 per person). Bush camping is
prohibited during South Australia's total fire ban season, from Nov. 1-Apr. 30.
National Parks and Wildlife (☎8634 7068) in Port Augusta has more details.

# CENTRAL FLINDERS

The Central Flinders includes the most famous attractions of the Flinders. To
reach Quorn, Hawker, Rawnsley Park, or Wilpena Pound via public transport, take
Stateliner (Adelaide ☎8415 5555, Port Augusta ☎8642 5055) connecting through
Port Augusta, but service is limited (departs Adelaide and Port Augusta W, F, Su).
If you have a Greyhound Pioneer bus pass, Stateliner fares into the Flinders are
half-price. Stateliner service to Port Augusta via Hawker and Quorn leaves Wilpena
Pound (Th-F, Su). Connections to Adelaide are available from all three buses. Wil-
pena Pound is as far as you can get into the Flinders with regular public transport.

## QUORN

Smack in the middle of the Flinders Ranges, Quorn (pop. 1400) is the outback
town for the movies. Its historic streets and hilly backdrop have appeared in at
least nine films, and the friendly pubs and country hospitality lack the saccharine
edge. Straightforward inhabitants create a simple, relaxing atmosphere in which
to take in the beauty of the Flinders Ranges.

**TRANSPORT AND PRACTICAL INFORMATION.** Stateliner (☎8415 5555) runs to Quorn from **Adelaide** via **Port Augusta** (1 per day Su, W, F; $39). **Andu Lodge** (☎8648 6655) offers the cheapest and most flexible travel service; they will pickup or drop off, by arrangement, in **Port Augusta, Wilpena Pound, Devil's Peak,** and **Dutchman's Stern.** Quorn lies 40km northeast of Port Augusta and Hwy 1, and 340km north of Adelaide, on Hwy 47. **Railway Tce** is the main street. The **Flinders Ranges Visitor Information Centre,** 3 Seventh St (☎/fax 8648 6419), is open M-F 9am-5pm. There are **no ATMs** in the Flinders. **National Australia Bank,** Railway Tce, is open M-Tu, Th-F noon-4pm. **Police:** (☎8648 6060). **Road conditions:** Northern Roads Conditions Hotline (☎(1300) 36 10 33). A Foodtown **grocery store** is on Seventh St (open M-F 8am-6pm, Sa 9am-4:30pm, Su 9am-2:30pm). **Internet** at the **library,** West Tce. (☎8648 6101. Open M 9am-4pm, Tu and F 9am-6pm, W-Th 9am-5pm, Sa 10am-noon.)

**ACCOMMODATIONS AND FOOD.** ⊠**Andu Lodge,** 12 First St, is an excellent base for a Flinders holiday. Short-term staff are sometimes hired in exchange for accommodation, breakfasts, and a free Flinders trip. Clean rooms, kitchen, Internet, and bike hire. (☎(1800) 63 99 38, ☎/fax 8648 6655. Dorms $14; singles $28; twins $36; doubles $38; families $65.) The **Transcontinental Hotel,** on Railway Tce, is the best of Quorn's four hotels for backpackers. The bar below is a great place to chill out and meet locals. (☎8648 6076. Singles $29; doubles $49. Ask about "backpacker specials.") The **Quandong Café and Bakery,** 31 First St, has wholesome food and doubles as a pleasant art gallery. (☎8648 6155. Open daily 9:30am-4:30pm.)

**HIKING.** Hikers who climb **Dutchman's Stern,** a bluff 10km north of Quorn, are rewarded with views of **Spencer Gulf.** Two main walks include a ridgetop hike (8.2km; 4hr. return) and a loop walk (10.5km; 5hr.). Another hiking option is **Devil's Peak,** 11km south of Quorn, a 697m peak with excellent views and a few fossils (2hr.; open May-Sept.). **Mt. Brown Conservation Park,** 16km south of town on Richmond Valley Rd, contains the usually dry **Waukerie Falls** and **Mt. Brown** itself (open May-Sept.). There is camping in **Warren Gorge,** a beautiful spot owned by the town.

## HAWKER

Hawker, lacking the picturesque qualities of Quorn, provides little more than utilitarian proximity to Wilpena Pound. But if you're not camping, this is the closest budget accommodation to Flinders Ranges National Park. Stateliner **buses** connect from **Adelaide** ($51) via **Port Augusta** and **Quorn. Hawker Motors,** at the corner of Wilpena and Graddock St, is all a petrol station should be and much more, with road reports, tourist info, a small museum, and **Internet.** (☎8648 4014. Open daily 7:30am-6pm.) An unstaffed **info booth** is on the west side of Elder Tce, at Wilpena Rd. The **National Parks and Wildlife Service,** 60 Elder Tce, is combined with the **post office.** (☎8648 4244. Open M-F 9am-5pm.) **Gloede's General Store** has supplies. (☎8648 4005. Open M-F 8am-5:30pm, Sa 9am-6pm, Su 9am-5:30pm.)

The **Hawker Hotel Motel,** across from the Old Ghan Railway Station, has firm beds, clean bathrooms, and A/C in the hotel rooms. (☎8648 4102. Singles $30; twins and doubles from $40.) Just north of town on Leigh Creek Rd, friendly owners run the highly-rated **Flinders Ranges Caravan Park.** (☎8648 4266. On-site vans for 2 from $35, BYO linen.) **Elder Terrace Café,** Elder Tce, opposite the info booth, has inexpensive light meals and friendly service. (☎8648 4101. Open daily 8am-8pm.)

## WILPENA POUND AND FLINDERS RANGES NATIONAL PARK

Wilpena Pound is the stuff of legends. The Pound looks like a huge crater, but is actually a syncline (geological downfold) outlined in quartzite. 450km north of Adelaide (4-5hr. drive), it is the best-known rock formation in the state. The surrounding national park offers spectacular views, challenging hikes, and a glimpse into Aboriginal and geological history. This is some of the best scenery in South Australia, immortalized in many of Hans Heysen's landscapes.

**☎ TRANSPORT.** Most tours through the Flinders stop by Wilpena Pound. You can also take the Stateliner bus (☎ 8415 5555) from **Adelaide** (7hr., $55) or from **Port Augusta** ($27), but be aware that camping is the only budget accommodation. In an emergency, contact park headquarters in Hawker (☎ 8648 4244, afterhours ☎ 8648 4248), police in Hawker (☎ 8648 4028), ranger in Port Augusta (☎ (015) 79 38 28), hospital in Hawker (☎ 8648 4007), or fire service (☎ 8648 4065).

**◪ PRACTICAL INFORMATION.** The helpful **Wilpena Visitor Centre** serves as the park entrance and headquarters, and is the place to get general park and hiking info, buy day-passes ($5), and register to camp. (☎ 8648 0048. Open daily 8:30am-5pm.) The privately-owned **Wilpena Pound Resort** (☎ 8648 0004, freecall ☎ (1800) 80 58 02; fax 8648 0028) also operates a general store, petrol station, restaurant, bar, campground, and up-scale motel with singles from $85. Bar meals are tasty and cheaper ($9-15; meals daily 6:30-8:30pm). Camping in the park at designated sites costs $5 per night per vehicle, including the park entrance fee. A few sites have toilets and water, but most just have dirt. For a shower, hit the refurbished **Wilpena Campground** (tent sites for 2 $12, powered $18, each extra person $4).

**◪ HIKING.** To explore **Wilpena Pound,** you must sweat or spend a bit, since no cars are allowed into the Pound itself. The first 2km of the hike in are a bit monotonous, but check out the burnt-out tree on the right side of the trail that is the spitting image of the Statue of Liberty. After the trail starts climbing a bit, it crosses a creek and then leads to a cabin called **Hill's Homestead** (toilets available). A short, somewhat steep walk up **Wangarra Hill** behind the homestead leads to the lower (5min.) and upper (20min.) lookouts over the Pound. A shuttle **bus service** from the visitors center to the Pound cuts 2km off the trip each way, leaving you about 800m from Hill's Homestead, and making it a 90min. excursion up to Wangarra and back (2-3 per day; $3 return). Visitors should leave pets at home, the park is chock full of traps set to kill foxes, based on a chemical produced by Australian plants, harmless to native animals, but lethal to foxes and dogs. Meat pies, anyone?

A high-intensity scrambling climb for serious hikers is the rocky trail to **St. Mary's Peak** (11.8km return direct route, 5hr.; 16.8km circuit returning via Wilpena Pound, 7hr.). For this, or any longer walk, advise the ranger of your plans and your expected time of return. The helpful brochure, *Bushwalking in the Flinders Ranges National Park*, is available at the visitor center.

Many visitors consider the **drive** through the park's gorges, with their colored walls and geological structures, more beautiful than the walk into the Pound itself, with the drive through Bunyeroo Gorge to Brachina Gorge as the highlight. The turn-off for the gorges is 4km north of the Wilpena junction on the road toward Blinman. These roads are usually accessible to 2WD and 4WD, but it's always a good idea to ask at the visitor center first (see **Driving in the Flinders,** p. 452).

## NEAR FLINDERS RANGES NATIONAL PARK

**RAWNSLEY PARK STATION.** Rawnsley Park Station (☎ 8648 0030 or ☎ 8648 0008), south of the park off the road between Wilpena and Hawker, offers horseback riding (minimum 2 people; 1hr. $30 per person, 2hr. $40, half-day $70, full-day $100), sheep shearing, scenic flights, 4WD tours (half-day $55; full-day $85 includes lunch), and mountain bike hire (1hr. $5, half-day $15, full-day $25). The station also runs a 48-bed bunkhouse ($12; students $10) and has a caravan park.

**PARACHILNA.** Just north of Flinders Ranges National Park, 89km north of Hawker on Hwy 83, Parachilna is a tiny blip of a town, but well worth knowing about. The newly-renovated **▩Prairie Hotel** offers hotel accommodation with A/C. Their scrumptious restaurant has potato and leek soup ($5.50); a hamburger that must have been brought down from heaven by angels ($6); and a feral grill ('roo, camel, venison, goat; $18). The food is excellent, but the scene in the bar is very possibly the best in the state, bringing people on journeys of 250km just for a night of shouts with the mates. (☎8648 4895; email ab@flinders.outback.on.net. Bar open until the crowd leaves. Rooms \$30.) **The Old Schoolhouse Tearooms** are good for a morning tea or light lunch break. (☎8648 4679. Open Tu-Su 10am-5pm.)

**BLINMAN POOLS.** Although the hostel at **Angorichina,** halfway along the unsealed, rocky road between Parachilna and Blinman, caters to groups only, **cabins, campsites,** and a **general store** with fuel are available. (☎8648 4842. Store open M-Sa 8:30am-6pm, Su 9:30am-noon.) From the carpark here, a 4hr. return hike to the permanent spring-fed ⧉**Blinman Pools** is one of the Flinders' most beautiful hikes. **Blinman,** at the northern edge of Flinders Ranges National Park, is not an exciting town (pop. 20), but it has the necessary amenities. The short walk (20-30min.) to the **war monument** at the highest point in town is worthwhile. The 360° view over purple mountain ranges is one of the best in the Flinders.

# NORTHERN FLINDERS

Adventurous travelers with strong legs for hiking, a strong car for driving, and a strong psyche for dealing with isolation will find much challenge and beauty in the rugged, remote terrain that stretches north toward the central deserts. To cover the couple hundred kilometers between Flinders Range National Park and Gammon Ranges National Park, drivers can either come up through Wilpena and Blinman (see above) or stick to the highway from Hawker and follow the pavement as far as Copley. The stops described here are along that highway.

**OLD BELTANA.** Just 35km north of Parachilna and 30km south of Leigh Creek along the sealed highway, the spookily quiet heritage town of Old Beltana (18km east of the highway on unsealed but good quality roads) hosts the small church where, in 1911, Rev. John Flynn developed the idea of the **Royal Flying Doctor Service.** This town was once a railway junction, but now just a handful of people live in a few well-kept houses among crumbling buildings (though the sign in the small outdoor museum proclaims indignantly: "Beltana has never been a ghost town").

**LEIGH CREEK.** After Coober Pedy, Leigh Creek is the second-largest town in the state north of Port Augusta. About 2000 people lived here a few years ago, but now just 600 call it home because the coal mining operation, the town's life-blood, is drying up. The present town, 22km south of the coalfield, was built by the **Electricity Trust of South Australia (ETSA)** between 1979 and 1984. Leigh Creek, therefore, is neatly arranged, obviously planned, and quite new, thus worlds apart from every other South Australian outback town. The landscaped downtown area has a **pub, supermarket, cafeteria, police** (☎8675 2004), **library, theater,** and small **hospital.** There's public **Internet access** at the school library. (Open M, W-Th 8:30am-4:30pm, Tu, F 8:30am-4:30pm and 7-9pm, Sa 9am-noon. Log-on fee \$2, then 1hr. \$3.) **Leigh Creek South Motors** has fuel, tires, showers, and toilets. (☎8675 2016. Open M-Sa 8am-8pm, Su 9am-8pm.) Book ahead for coal mine tours (☎8675 4316). The **hotel** in town isn't cheap. (☎8675 2025. Singles \$50.) The **visitor information office** is next to the hotel. (☎8675 4316. Open M-F 9am-5pm; closed during school holidays.) Leigh Creek is also near the Oodnadatta Track, for more info, see p. 459.

**COPLEY.** Copley, 13km north of Leigh Creek, is 267 sealed kilometers northeast of Port Augusta, and 130 unsealed kilometers west of Arkaroola. **Cookes Outback Motors** (☎8675 2618) has 24hr. RAA towing, tires, and car batteries. **Copley Caravan Park** (☎8675 2288) has caravan and tent sites (\$5 per person) as well as cabins and on-site vans for two (\$40-45). The **hotel** has a busy, friendly pub. (☎8675 2635. Singles \$30; twins \$40.) **Tulloch's Bush Bakery and Quandong Café** is a gourmet aberration with quandong pie (\$2.50; the quandong is a shiny red outback stone fruit like a peach) and unusual meat pies. (☎8675 2683. Open daily 8:30am-4:30pm.)

SOUTH AUSTRALIA

## GAMMON RANGES NATIONAL PARK

This is where Australia gets serious. The 128,228 hectares of the Gammons are more craggy, more exotic, more stunning, and more isolated than the southern Flinders and possibly than anything you've ever seen. The Gammons can only be explored on unsealed 4WD tracks and wilderness experience is advisable. Check in at the **National Parks and Wildlife Service** headquarters in Balcanoona, where the friendly rangers can give advice on bush camping and bushwalking. (☎8648 4829. Park fee $5 per vehicle per night.) Less experienced nature-lovers can camp at **Italowie Camp** or **Weetootla Gorge** and hike in the edges of the park.

# OUTBACK SOUTH AUSTRALIA

North and west of the Flinders, the Australian outback surpasses legend and becomes dirt real. A moisture-deprived basin has created the salt flats of Lake Torrens and Lake Eyre. Much of the sparsely populated outback beyond is encompassed by the Desert Parks area. The famous Oodnadatta Track, a favorite for 4WD TV commercials, is a rough 4WD circuit carving through this area. The Stuart Hwy, which slices the continent in half from Port Augusta up to Darwin, is the quickest, and in most cases, the only option to Ayers Rock and Alice Springs. Visitors should prepare themselves mentally for the 45°C (113°F) that one will find even in the shade. At the same time, if one bothers to stop, one will be blessed with phenomenal views of the salt flats, remnants of dry lakes that only have water in them once in a while, and silence—except in the summer and autumn, when some bush flies can't help but make their presence felt.

 **DRIVE CAREFULLY.** The area off the Stuart Hwy is not for the casual tourist. With most roads unsealed, a 4WD is essential. Keep in mind that this region, though arid, is subject to flash flooding. Talk to national park officials to plan your trip and immediately before setting out, check road conditions, updated daily, on the Northern Road Conditions Hotline (☎(1300) 36 10 33). Carry plenty of water for long drives (both for drinking and for your car), check in with officials, and notify friends or family before and after undertaking a journey. If your car does break down on a remote road, do not panic and do not start walking—people die every year when they make this mistake. Stay with the car, since it provides shade and can be spotted much more easily by search parties.

## FROM ADELAIDE TO COOBER PEDY

Welcome to the outback. As the Stuart Hwy winds its way north and west toward the opal capital of the world, there is little to see other than the harsh reality of the dry, windy terrain.

**PORT AUGUSTA.** Any trip from Adelaide to Outback South Australia must pass through Port Augusta, the "Crossroads of Australia" (see p. 452).

**PIMBA.** The first towns, Pimba, and its larger cohort 10km north of the highway, Woomera, offer basic amenities. **Spud's Roadhouse** (☎8673 7473), in Pimba, is open 24hr., hosts a hotel and a bar, and is the local **RAA** access point. One should keep in mind that from Pimba, the petrol just gets more and more expensive, hitting $1 per liter by the big CP; at the same time, distances are big, so top off at every opportunity. Ever seen a perfectly inelastic demand curve at work?

**WOOMERA.** Woomera is a large Royal Australian Air Force (RAAF) base, and the capital (of sorts) of the Woomera Restricted Area, a bombing range and site for all manner of military and space tests. The **Woomera Heritage Center,** easy to find with the missles, cannons, and jet planes in front, doesn't provide the usual array of

**FORE!** Budget travelers, take heart: *Let's Go* has found a golf course within your price range. And this is no ordinary course: players never have to worry about replacing divots, they never hit trees, they needn't drive little carts, they never land in the rough—and water hazards are nowhere in sight. Impossible? Nope. Welcome to golf in the outback, where land is cheap, water precious, and grass non-existent. The desolate ground may be hard, flat, almost treeless, and bone-dry, but that hasn't stopped Coober Pedy from installing an 18-hole course. There's not a scrap of fairway or tinge of bright green in sight, and so the greens fee is quite literal: $10 gets you a small square of green astroturf. Carry it around and set it down whenever it's time to take a whack at the ball. The "greens" are carefully smoothed sections of dirt, covered in used motor oil to create a smooth surface, centered around a regular golf cup and (sometimes) a tattered flag. Regular cars are allowed on the course, though golfers must give right-of-way to cars when the fairway doubles as the road. Smart golfers use fluorescent orange golf balls both for visibility and because bearded dragons on the course mistake the white balls for their own eggs and steal them. Plaid pants remain optional.

Dreaming stories and natural historical displays, but instead stories of 19th-century homesteaders, explorers, nuclear bombs, and radio astronomy. (☎8671 0788. Open daily Mar.-Nov. 9am-5pm, Dec.-Feb. 10am-2pm.)

**GLENDAMBO.** Glendambo, 270km southeast of Coober Pedy, is the last stop before the mining town, so all drivers should check the petrol level and fill up. The BP here runs backpacker accommodations, but there are not many beds. The motel is expensive (☎8672 1030; budget singles $74). About 100km north of Glendambo, the highway doubles as an emergency landing strip for the Royal Flying Doctor Service. It often also doubles as pasture land, as many of the homesteads do not have fences by the road, allowing sheep and cattle to roam. So keep alert.

# COOBER PEDY

Many towns in Australia have landmarks, beaches, or events that attract tourists; in Coober Pedy, the town itself is the attraction. This remote outpost halfway on the long, dry haul between Alice Springs and Adelaide gets 150,000 tourists each year, partly because there's nowhere else to stop, and partly because the town is utterly unlike anywhere else on earth. More than half of the 3500 residents live underground in homes almost invisible from the outside, except for the occasional ventilator shaft and TV antenna sticking out of a hillside. Homes, churches, shops, even hostels, are carved out of the earth to escape the extreme temperatures, which can reach 50°C (122°F) in the summer and plunge on winter nights. More than 45 nationalities are represented, with many immigrants from southern and eastern Europe. Men outnumber women five to one (in the early days, it was 400 to one), and nearly everybody in town has some connection to opals—eighty percent of the world's opal supply is pulled from the ground in the region. This is a mining town; it's not unusual to see trucks drive through town with big "EXPLOSIVES" signs, indicating homemade fertilizer-and-diesel-fuel bombs. But no worries; this is a fun town in which to spend more time than one originally intended.

**⊏ TRANSPORT.** Greyhound Pioneer and McCafferty's run to Coober Pedy from Adelaide and Alice Springs. Every tour between Adelaide and Alice stops off in Coober Pedy. For **automoblie rental,** compare **Budget** (☎8672 5333; beginning at $88 per day for 4WD) and **Thrifty** (☎8672 5688; 4WD not necessarily available; 2WD $90 per day), at the Desert Cave Hotel. **Taxis:** ☎(1800) 24 32 47.

**▟▐ ORIENTATION AND PRACTICAL INFORMATION.** Outside town boundaries, 1.5 million **abandoned mine shafts** make the danger of carelessly stepping backward and plummeting to your death very real. Signs around town are no joke:

do not explore opal fields by yourself. Coober Pedy is 685km south of Alice Springs (6-8hr.), 730km southeast of Ayers Rock, 538km north of Port Augusta, and 846km north of Adelaide (8-10hr.). The turn-off from the Stuart Hwy leads into **Hutchison St,** the main street and location of virtually every establishment, including all three **backpacker hostels, ATM at Westpac Bank,** the **tourist information center** (☎8672 5298, freecall ☎(1800) 63 70 76; open M-F 9am-5pm), and the **post office** (☎8672 5062) in the miners' store. **Underground Books,** next to Desert Cave just off Hutchison St, has area maps and serves as the booking agent for the **Mail Run** and **Opal Quest tours.** (☎8672 5558. Open M-Sa 8:30am-5:30pm, Su 10am-4pm.) **Police:** (☎8672 5056). **RAA:** (☎8672 5230), at Desert Traders. **Hospital:** (☎8672 5009). The school **library** (turn off Hutchison St at Underground Books and follow the signs) has **Internet access** (1hr. $3; open M-F 8:30am-5pm, Sa-Su 1-5pm).

■ **ACCOMMODATIONS AND FOOD.** ■**Radeka's Backpacker's Inn,** at Hutchison and Oliver St, has bus pickup and drop off. This maze of underground "caves" is clean and comfortable. There are no doors to close, putting privacy at a minimum. (☎8672 5233. Kitchen, pool table, Internet, TV room, bar. Dorms $14; doubles $38. YHA, VIP.) **Joe's Backpacker's** is across from Radeka's. If the owners look familiar, perhaps you saw them in *Priscilla*, carting a kangaroo carcass across the outback. In the film, Joe and Maria refused to give the stranded drag queens a lift. In real life, they're a good bit more friendly. (☎8672 5163; fax 8672 5821. Kitchen, TV lounge. Dorms $14. VIP.) **Riba's Underground Camping** (☎8672 5614), is on William Creek Rd, outside of town. Turn off 4km before Hutchison St, coming from Port Augusta. Above-ground and subterranean campsites for $12, including hot, underground showers. Visitors interested in homestays should call **Underground Books** (☎8672 5558 or mobile ☎041 883 6164).

■**John's Pizza Bar,** Hutchison St (☎8672 5561), makes excellent pizza for $7-8.50, with large piles of toppings. **Trace's Restaurant,** at the top of Hutchison St, is a Greek restaurant with backpacker specials for $7. (☎8672 5147. Open daily 4pm-late.) The Miners Store **supermarket** is on Hutchison St (open daily until 7pm).

■ **SIGHTS AND ACTIVITIES.** More than almost anywhere in Australia, joining an organized tour is worthwhile. **Radeka's Desert Breakaways Tours** is a very good choice, popular with backpackers. The tour includes many humorous stops around town and the opal fields, a trip out to the Breakaways, and a chance to noodle for your own opal. The stop at Crocodile Harry's home, the womanizer who was supposedly the inspiration for Crocodile Dundee, may make some women uncomfortable. (☎8672 5233. 4½hr.; $25.) **Opal Quest Mine Tour** includes noodling and also gives tourists a chance to put on the hard hats and try out some mining machinery. (Book at Underground Books, ☎8672 5558. Departs daily 9am, 2pm; 2hr. $25.) **Riba's Evening Mine Tours** takes guests down into a mine for a 1½hr. tour. (☎8672 5614. Daily 7:30pm. $12.) For an unforgettable look at the outback, join the mail carrier on the 12hr. ■**Mail Run.** (☎(1800) 06 99 11 or at Underground Books ☎8672 5558. Departs M, Th 9am. $70. Book ahead.)

The town's **underground churches** are usually open to visitors. In some, miners with artistic talent have carefully etched religious symbols and beautiful statues into the walls. Outside town, **The Breakaways** are a set of flat-topped mesas rising out of the flatness. To see them yourself, explore the 70km return loop (2hr. drive), over the aptly named **Moon Plain.** At the Breakaways, you can still see tracks where the *Mad Max III* cars raced, and drive along the road where the drag queen in *Priscilla* rode on the roof, arms outstretched, gown trailing in the wind (before Kate Winslet stole the pose).

# OFF THE STUART HIGHWAY: OODNADATTA TRACK

The Oodnadatta Track, one of the most famous outback tracks in Australia, runs 619km from Marree, north of Leigh Creek in the Flinders, through William Creek and Oodnadatta to Marla, 235km north of Coober Pedy on the Stuart Hwy. The

> **THE MYSTERY MAN OF MARREE** One would think that the creation of the world's largest work of art would have gained much publicity. However, an anonymous fax to a local pub simply entitled "tourist attraction" tipped the world off to the awesome and curious spectacle that lay quietly in the South Australian outback: a well-crafted 4km outline of an Aboriginal hunter carved into a plateau 60km northwest of Marree, the only artwork visible from outer space. Many clues, satellite photos, and years later, the tools of inscription, artist(s), and meaning of the giant figure—known as the Marree Man—are still unknown. Controversy ensues as the world continues to scratch its head, wondering when or if the artist will step forward.

outback doesn't get any more authentic. The road is unsealed, suitable for **4WD only,** and can be impassable after rain. Every spark of civilization is worth a stop.

East of Coober Pedy, at **William Creek** (technically on Anna Creek cattle station, which is the world's largest station—almost half the size of Tasmania) airplanes can land and taxi right to the town's only substantial building, the gathering place for everyone from cattle stations far and wide: the ⚄**William Creek Pub** (☎ 8670 7880). Covered with signs, the lively interior mocks every fragment of political correctness that might find its way out here. The public phone outside the pub was supposedly the most expensive telephone ever installed in the Southern Hemisphere. Inexpensive accommodation and camping are also available.

**Oodnadatta** is a sad-looking town, but it has precious amenities, including **car repair facilities.** Check road conditions with the **police** (☎ 8670 7805). The **Transcontinental Hotel** (☎ 8670 7804) has cheap rooms, and the **Pink Roadhouse** is the place to fuel your car and yourself. The huge Oodna Burger for $7 is the local special.

# EYRE PENINSULA

It's a good bet that most international tourists this far west in South Australia are bound for or coming from Western Australia. The tourist folks on the Eyre know this, and they market the peninsula as "Australia's Best Detour" and merely suggest travelers add 295km to their itineraries and pop down for a breath of fresh Eyre. Not a bad idea, for in the driest state on the driest continent on earth, the coast of the Eyre Peninsula provides a welcome belt of coves with pounding, fish-filled surf—all uncrowded and removed from anything resembling urban bustle.

## ▐ TRANSPORT

**Premier Stateliner** (Adelaide ☎ 8415 5555, Whyalla ☎ 8645 9911, Port Lincoln ☎ 8682 1734, Ceduna ☎ 8625 2208) is the only public **bus** carrier on the Eyre with frequent service, though Greyhound stops in **Ceduna** on the way to **Perth.** Stateliner runs between Adelaide and **Whyalla** (M-Th and Sa-Su 5 per day; F 6 per day). Buses also leave Adelaide bound for **Port Lincoln,** stopping in towns along the eastern coast (depart Adelaide M-F 2 per day, Su 1 per day; depart Port Lincoln Su-F 2 per day, Sa 1 per day). Stateliner runs an overnight bus from Adelaide to **Ceduna** via **Streaky Bay** (depart Adelaide Su-F 1 per day; depart Ceduna daily 1 per day ).

By car, traversing the Eyre Peninsula means diverging from the inland Eyre Hwy (Hwy 1), which runs 468km from Whyalla, on the eastern edge of the peninsula due west to Ceduna. The highlights of the Eyre are found instead on a coastal triangular route via the Lincoln Hwy and Flinders Hwy (Alternate Hwy 1), which takes 763km to connect the same two towns.

## WHYALLA

This city, the state's second-largest with just 25,000 people, substantiates how large Adelaide (pop. 1,100,000) is in comparison to the rest of South Australia's towns. Whyalla, billed by town elders, much like Lybia, as a "city of contrasts," is first and foremost a commercial mining port with a slumping economy and many empty storefronts. But contrasts indeed abound, and for the relatively sad-looking shopping centers to the west, there is the pleasant city center, offering shopping, good pub hotels, and easy access to the city's biggest tourist attraction, fishing.

**⛏ PRACTICAL INFORMATION.** The **Whyalla Tourist Centre** is on the left-hand side of Lincoln Hwy (Hwy 1), north of the city and next to a stranded corvette. (☎8645 7900; fax 8645 3620. Open M-F 9am-5pm, Sa 9am-4pm, Su 10am-4pm.) **Westland Shopping Centre,** on the corner of McDouall Stuart Ave and Nicolson Ave, has two **supermarkets** and a food court. To reach the **city centre,** turn left onto Whitehead St immediately upon entering the city from the north; or from the south, follow the Lincoln Hwy to Broadbent Tce. **ATMs** abound on Forsyth St in city center. The **post office** (☎8646 9616) is on Darling Tce in the city center.

**⛏ ACCOMMODATIONS.** The hotels provide the least expensive accommodation, and unlike many pub hotels, all have private baths in all rooms. The rooms at **Hotel Bayview,** on Forsyth St, have A/C, TV and fridges in the rooms. (☎8645 8544. Singles $25; twins and doubles $45; triples $55.) Down the street, **Hotel Spencer,** 1 Forsyth St, offers rooms with roughly the same amenities as the Bayview. (☎8645 8411. Singles $25, with bath $30; twins $30, $40; doubles $40.) **Whyalla Foreshore Caravan Park,** Broadbent Tce, is 2km from the post office and very near the beach. (☎8645 7474. Sites $11, powered $14; on-site vans for 2 $24; cabins for 2 $28-45.)

**⛏ SIGHTS.** North of the city, the **Whyalla Maritime Museum** shares the tourist information complex and is housed in the *HMAS Whyalla.* The first ship built in the Whyalla Shipyard, it is now the "largest permanently landlocked ship" in Australia, 2km from the nearest shore. Well, that's one way to earn a superlative. (☎8645 7900. Open daily 10am-4pm. $6, children $3. Tours at 11am, noon, 1, 2, and 3pm. Allow 1½hr. for visit.) The **Whyalla Conservation Park,** 10km north of the Whyalla info center on Hwy 1, offers a good chance to see the flora and fauna of these arid lands. (☎8645 1704. Open 30min. before dawn to 30min. after sunset.) The town of Whyalla, from an Aboriginal word that means "place of the water," would like guests to know that this is a good place to fish and boat. The **sport fishing club** and the **yachting club** are on the marina, near the city centre.

## WHYALLA TO PORT LINCOLN

As Hwy 1 speeds along the west coast, the gently undulating road hosts a few dots of civilization tucked away in the monotonously rolling plains. At the least, they provide colorful fish-shaped signs and petrol stations; at the most, **Cowell, Arno Bay, Port Neill,** and **Tumby Bay** could be a quiet seaside town in which to crash for a night. All four towns have pub hotels (singles $20; twins and doubles $30) and caravan parks. **Cowell,** 111km south of Whyalla, offers one of the safest and best fishing areas in South Australia at its **Franklin Harbour,** as well as a thriving oyster industry, and Australia's only commercial jade mining. The **District Council Office,** 6 Main St, can give tourist info. (☎8629 2019. Open M-F 9am-5pm.) The livelier of the town's two quiet hotels is the **Franklin Harbour Hotel.** (☎8629 2015. Single $20, including breakfast.) **Tumby Bay,** 50km north of Port Lincoln, has plenty of facilities and, of course, fishing. **Tumby Bayside Holiday Units** has backpacker accommodation with a well-equipped kitchen, BBQ, TV, and laundry. (☎8688 2087. $15.)

## PORT LINCOLN

At the southern tip of the Eyre Peninsula, busy and breezy Port Lincoln lords over Boston Bay, the second-largest natural harbor in the world—more than three times the size of Sydney Harbour. Port Lincoln (pop. 13,000) was to be the state capital, but inadequate fresh water destined today's politicians for Adelaide instead. Aquaculture here is big business. The town ships out the largest tonnage of commercial fish in Australia, as well as huge amounts of grain. Port Lincoln is a frequent port-of-call for vacationers, both as a stopover en route to the more remote attractions of the Eyre Peninsula, and as a decent destination itself.

◪ **PRACTICAL INFORMATION.** Tourist destinations in Port Lincoln are generally close enough to walk comfortably. The main drag is **Tasman Tce** (which becomes London St), along the water, with the major hotels, pubs, cafés, and tourist shops. A few blocks inland, **Liverpool St** provides good shopping, a small movie theater, and some restaurants. The **Visitor Information Centre,** 66 Tasman Tce (☎ 8683 3544), is open daily from 9am to 5pm. Other services include: **ATMs** at Tasman Tce and Liverpool St; **police** (☎ 8688 3020); **hospital** (☎ 8683 2200); **cabs** (☎ 13 10 08). The **library,** in the Spencer Institute of TAFE building, just off Tasman Tce has free 1hr. Internet sessions. (☎ 8688 3622. Open M, F 8:30am-6pm, Tu-Th 8:30am-8pm, Sa 10am-1pm, Su 1-5pm.)

◤ **ACCOMMODATIONS.** The popular **Lincoln Hotel,** at the beginning of Tasman Tce as you enter town from Whyalla, has functional rooms with TV and a pleasant balcony. (☎ 8682 1277. Continental breakfast $3.75. Singles $22, ensuite $27; twins and doubles $38/$48.) **The Pier Hotel** (☎ 8682 1322), at the center of Tasman Tce, incorporates stunning ocean views with show-biz decor. Most rooms have ensuite bathrooms. (Singles $25; twins and doubles $35; weekly rates $100/$130.) **Kirton Point Caravan Park,** at the end of London St (Tasman Tce), has a lovely setting 3km from the town center. (☎ 8682 2537. Tent sites $5 per person; cabins from $22.)

◪♫ **SIGHTS AND ENTERTAINMENT.** Port Lincoln is home to South Australia's magnificent four-day **Tunarama Festival** (☎ 8682 1300), on the Australia Day long weekend in late January. The festival features a rodeo and beauty contest, but fish take the day in the highly competitive tuna-tossing contest. **Yacht Away Cruising Holidays** (☎ 8682 5585) offers a daily tuna farm and Boston Bay cruise (3½hr., $25). At the **Glen-Forest Animal Park,** 15km from Port Lincoln, you can get hands-on with dingoes, kangaroos, wombats, and camels. (☎ 8683 3544. Open daily 10am-5pm.) Six kilometers north of Port Lincoln on Lincoln Hwy, **Boston Bay Wines** turns out first-rate whites and reds. (☎ 8684 6300. Tastings and sales Sa-Su 11:30am-4:30pm.)

A daytrip from Port Lincoln gives plenty of time to take in the gorgeous sea views of **Lincoln National Park,** about 20km south of town. If birds come here all the way from Siberia on their summer migrations, you know it's gotta be good. The very southern tip of the park is a sheltered, almost untouched wilderness named **Memory Cove.** Access is limited to 15 vehicles per day (4WD only). At the bottom of the Eyre and 32km southwest of Port Lincoln, **Whaler's Way** (☎ 8685 6016) is a 14km scenic tourist drive. Interpretive signs give details on the superb coastal scenery, cliff lookouts, and ancient rock caves. For entry or camping permits at either of these places, interested parties must pick up an entry pass and key from the **Port Lincoln Visitor Centre.** For more info, contact **National Parks and Wildlife,** 75 Liverpool St, Port Lincoln. (☎ 8688 3111. Open M-F 8:45am-5pm.)

## PORT LINCOLN TO CEDUNA

The Flinders Hwy (Hwy 1) heads northwest from Port Lincoln to the remote outpost of Ceduna. This road is largely more of the same rolling, mallee-scrubbed land, but various species of reptiles slither and crawl across the road and one can never be sure when a kangaroo will bound by. A mere 47km from Lincoln toward Ceduna, you'll find the lazy town of **Coffin Bay,** the center of the state's oyster industry. Tourist info is available from **Beachcomber Agencies** on the Esplanade. (☎ 8685 4057. Open daily 8am-7:30pm; in winter 8am-6:30pm.) The Port Lincoln tourist center is more convenient for those planning day trips out of that town.

**Coffin Bay National Park** is 17km west of the main highway. This peninsular park is a remote beach heaven; surfers, picnickers, and pelicans coexist peacefully among the dunes, estuaries, and bays. ($5 per vehicle per day.) Most areas are accessible only with 4WD, except **Yangie Bay** (15km from the entrance) and **Point Avoid** (which is much better than it sounds; 18km from the entrance). Bush camping permits and maps are available at the park entrance. **National Parks and Wildlife Service** (☎8688 3111), in Port Lincoln, has further info.

**Mt. Dutton Bay Woolshed,** 52km northwest of Port Lincoln, is a B&B and woolshed museum rolled into one. As many as 1200 sheep were once kept here, but today the owners keep 36 backpackers instead. (☎/fax 8685 4031. Museum open M-Sa 10am-5pm; admission by donation. Dorms $15. Book ahead.) About 25km north of Port Kenny along the Flinders Hwy (watch for a sign), turn toward the coast and drive about 40km to **Point Labatt Conservation Park and Aquatic Reserve,** where Australia's only mainland sea lion colony lounges near the cliffs. Beautiful **Streaky Bay,** the last town before Alt 1 rejoins Hwy 1, offers a peaceful bayside stop before the heat of the mainland and the looming Nullarbor hits like a blast. The **Streaky Bay Community Motel-Hotel** is very nice, if generally expensive, although five basic hotel rooms are available. (☎8626 1008. Singles $20; doubles $30.)

## CEDUNA

At the far west corner of the triangular Eyre circuit, the Flinders Hwy (Alt. Hwy 1) meets up with the more direct and dull Eyre Hwy (Hwy 1) and rolls into Ceduna, civilization's last watering hole before the westward track across the Nullarbor Plain toward Perth. People here don't ask what brought you to town; they ask which way you're heading (answer: 780km east to Adelaide on Hwy 1 or 480km west to the WA border). The **ATMs** in town are the **last ATMs** for 1300km (assuming, of course, one is headed for Western Australia). Ceduna provides the basic beds, beans, and booze, plus a few nice beaches to sit down and rest. **Decres Bay,** 12km from town, is a good swimming beach, and a little farther on is **Laura Bay,** a tranquil beach within the **Wittelbee Conservation Park.** Get maps and directions from the tourist office or follow the signs heading southeast from town.

Stateliner (Ceduna ☎8625 2208, Adelaide ☎8415 5555, Port Augusta ☎8642 5055) runs buses daily to Ceduna via **Port Augusta,** and Greyhound Pioneer (☎13 20 30) also passes through en route to **Perth.** The Eyre Hwy becomes **Poynton St,** briefly, as it passes through the center of town. It intersects Kuhlmann St, which itself becomes McKenzie St as you head toward Adelaide. **Ceduna Gateway Tourist Centre** is at 58 Poynton St. (☎8625 2780, freecall (1800) 63 94 13. Open M-F 9am-5:30pm, Sa 9-11:30am.) **ATMs** are at **ANZ Bank,** 27 Poynton St and at **Bank SA,** 10 McKenzie St.

**Ceduna Greenacres Backpackers,** 12 Kuhlmann St, is marked with a red sign, half-hidden by trees. It has muraled concrete walls, metal bunks, and a free home-cooked dinner. (☎041 881 1241; fax 8625 3811. Dorms $15; twins and doubles $30.) **The Ceduna Community Hotel Motel,** on O'Loughlin Tce, along the waterfront, has hotel rooms and a motel pub with somewhat pricey meals. (☎8625 2008. Singles $25; doubles $29.) Jim's Foodtown **supermarket,** on Thevenard Rd, is southwest of downtown. (☎8625 2175. Open daily 8am-8pm.) **Bill's Chicken Shop** serves fried chicken, fresh fish, and deli sides into the evening. (☎8625 2880. Half chicken $5.)

## CROSSING THE NULLARBOR

Explorer Edward John Eyre minced no words when he described the Nullarbor Plain, calling it "a hideous anomaly, a blot on the face of Nature, the sort of place one gets into in bad dreams." They named the highway after him anyway. Welcome to the Nullarbor—a plain that could contain England, the Netherlands, Belgium, and Switzerland, with 7000 square kilometers to spare. The Ninety Mile Straight (146.6km), from Caiguna, WA to Balladonia, WA, is the longest straight stretch of highway in the country. Robert Frost has no idea what it means to say that there are miles to go before you sleep. Greyhound **bus** drivers do, however, making this grueling desert haul in 26hr. ($199).

The Eyre Hwy is smooth, black bitumen all the way, finally completed in 1976 after construction began during World War II. The road is traveled fairly heavily compared with the empty roads up north; it's rarely more than 100km between

**GOD, IS THAT YOU?** When one is driving through the sandy scrub lands of South Australia, one might notice pillars of dust rising in the distance. These are either blown up by vehicles on unsealed roads, or they are little dust funnels caused by the winds and the sun. However, they are not pillars sent by God to guide wayfarers through the desert. At least, probably not. Should one choose to follow one of these dust clouds, be careful; if it's a road train, one will eventually find a grocery store, but if it's just a funnel, one may find oneself lost in the desert for 40 years to life.

roadhouses with fuel, but repair facilities are few and far between. This is a road train route, so all drivers should brace for the turbulence from passing 25m trucks. Bring along bottled water, warm clothing, and blankets. Drivers should make sure their cars are equipped with a jack, spares, coolant, and oil and should have a mechanic check the vehicle. Each of the **roadhouses** along the way has **eftpos** and major credit card facilities, almost all have a caravan park and camping sites, and most have cheap accommodation. The **automobile association** is at ☎ 13 11 11. **Yalata Medical Service** (☎ 8625 6237) is the best bet for medical service on the Nullarbor. **Police** are at Penong (☎ 8625 1006) and Ceduna (☎ 8628 7020). For details of road-houses and scenic detours, pick up the free brochure *Australia's Great Road Journey: The Nullarbor* at the tourist office in Ceduna if coming from the east, or at the Norseman tourist office if coming from the west. **Commemorative crossing certificates** (now there's something for the mantle) are free at either office after completing the journey, unless you'd rather forget the whole experience.

**Nullarbor Traveller** is a backpacker-oriented camping trip that runs from Perth to Adelaide. Travelers snorkel, explore caves, and camp under the stars. For those with cash and time to spare, this is quite the way to cross old man Eyre's personal hell. (☎ 8364 0407; www.southaustralia.com/nullarbor. 7-9 nights, $450-800.)

## CEDUNA TO BORDER VILLAGE

After leaving Ceduna on the long road west, dozens of windmills and wheat silos signal the approach of **Penong**, 73km west of Ceduna, and its **hotel**. (☎ 8625 1050. Services open 24hr.) Paul Gravelle's **surfboard factory** waits in Penong for the interested. At **Cactus Beach**, 21km south of Penong along a well-maintained gravel road, you can watch top-caliber surfers maneuver along Castles, Cactus, and Caves, the names of the famous breaks at one of Australia's best surfing beaches. Cactus is definitely not for novices; less advanced surfers approve of the sandy bottom and good waves at **Shelly Beach,** east of Point Sinclair. Easing on down the main road, 78km west of Penong, backpacker accommodation is available at the all-encompassing **Nundroo Hotel Motel Inn.** (☎ 8625 6120. Open 7am-10pm.)

**Yalata Roadhouse**, 51km west of Nundroo, has backpacker accommodation. (☎ 8625 6986. Open 7am-10pm, in winter 7am-9pm. Campsites $4 per person, powered $8; singles and twins $10 per person; self-contained units $45.) A permit is required to enter the township of **Yalata** itself, home to an Anangu community (pop. 500). The **Head of Bight**, 78km west of Yalata, has stunning views with sand dunes to the right, sheer cliffs to the left, and blue ocean right in front. Between May and October, the view gets even better, when 60 to 100 **Southern Right Whales** breed, calve, and nurse here before returning to feed in sub-Antarctic waters for the summer. Whale watching **permits** ($7) are required and available from Yalata Roadhouse or from the **White Well Ranger Station** on the road south to Head of Bight (☎ 8625 6201. Open daily 8:30am-5:30pm; whale watching mid-July-Oct.) By the time you reach the fuel stop at Nullarbor, 94km west of Yalata, you're officially on the treeless plain. There's backpacker accommodation at the **Nullarbor Hotel Motel.** (☎ s8625 6271. Open 7am-11pm.) As the booklet says under the "general interest" category for Nullarbor, "you are now standing on one of the largest, flattest, and most enigmatic lumps of limestone on the planet." It's that good.

The first of six gorgeous coastal lookouts is 50km west of Nullarbor. These are often just a few hundred meters off the main road and are well worth a break.

You're looking at where Australia seems to have been chopped off; **Bunda Cliffs** plummet 90m straight down into the Southern Ocean. The cliffs start at Twin Rocks at Head of Bight and extend 200km to just east of Border Village. There's backpacker accommodation at **Border Village** (☎9039 3474), 188km west of Nullarbor, as well as a huge fiberglass kangaroo named Rooey II. As you cross into WA, put your watch back 45min. (45min. forward if you're going east). Daylight savings sometimes requires an additional hour adjustment. This is also the **agricultural roadblock** before entering WA (it's at Ceduna if you're going east), where any fruit, vegetables, honey, and plant material will be confiscated to stop the spread of the fruit fly. For questions on what is allowed across the border, call the agriculture department (☎9311 5333 in WA, ☎8269 4500 in SA).

As you enter Western Australia, it's 13km from Border Village to the roadhouses of **Eucla** (open 6am-10:30pm), another 63km to **Mundrabilla** (open 7am-10:30pm), 115km more to **Madura** (open 6:30am-8pm; swimming pool available), 93km to **Cocklebiddy** (open 7am-7pm), 66km to **Caiguna** (open 24hr.), 182km to **Balladonia** (open 6am-10pm), and 193km to **Norseman,** the official end of the Nullarbor Plain.

## FROM CEDUNA TO PORT AUGUSTA

For those coming from the Nullarbor, the stretch of Hwy 1 running from Ceduna to Port Augusta, the scrub covered plains of the northern Eyre Peninsula are going to give the lush tropics of the Wet-season Northern Territory a run for their money. If **Wirrulla, Poochera,** and **Minnipa,** 92km, 140km, and about 170km respectively from Ceduna, were lumped together to form a mega-town in the Northern Eyre peninsula, it would still only have one horse in it. At any rate, boring or not, anyone going from Perth to Adelaide has little choice but to traverse this road. Grin and bear it; after all, one never knows when a giant Galah is waiting in the distance. People driving straight through at 110km (or *substantially* above, although *Let's Go* cannot condone such behavior) should be able to make the trip in 4.5hrs; anyone wishing to stop along the way should allow at least 6hr.

At one of two area tourist information joints in **Kimba,** a strange creature looms in front. A large, strange creature indeed, which reminds *Let's Go* of a joke: "What's 8m high, 2.5m wide, weighs 2.3 tons, and gelcoated?" "The *HMAS Whyalla*?" "No, stupid, the ∎**Big Galah!**" And so it roams free, cemented on top of its little hill, the Big Galah, always motionlessly celebrating the half-way point across Australia and keeping a watchful eye on all the traversers of the Eyre Hwy below. Tourist center open daily 8am-5pm, although the Big Galah never sleeps.

# TASMANIA

With Australia lying empty in a far corner of the Empire, England seemed to have a perfect solution for its 18th-century prison overflow problem. Parliament members happily sent their rabble across the ocean, washed their hands, and went to tea. But lawlessness was still a huge problem in the new colony, and penal officials in New South Wales decided to ship the troublemakers away once again. Australia was already at the end of the earth, but Tasmania was at the end of Australia. The British considered the wild little island, then known as Van Diemen's Land, the worst punishment available, reserved for the most heartless criminals.

Silly Poms. What was thought to be an inhospitable, weatherbeaten rock was in fact the lushest corner of the continent. Still, the penal settlements in the gorgeous areas near Hobart and Strahan were brutal indeed. Furthermore, the native Aboriginal populations were decimated by the new colony through invasion and outright genocide. During this century, Tasmania has turned from blood red to leafy green. An upsurge of conservation efforts, centralized social policies, and liberal activism mark today's political scene. The struggle against the proposed Franklin Dam on the Gordon River in the early 1980s foreshadowed Tassie's involvement in the Australian conservation movement. Though Tasmania has historically had a politically and socially conservative government, their Green party has been represented in the state's governing coalition twice in the past decade.

Only 3% of the visitors to Australia make it down under down under, but Tassie is well worth the time and money spent getting there. A third of the state is under government protection, mostly under the name Tasmanian Wilderness World Heritage Area, which includes the last great temperate rainforest on the globe. Bushwalkers from around the planet come to Tasmania's mountainous interior to explore the Overland Track, one of the premier hiking trails in the Southern Hemisphere. The uninhabited west coast bears the brunt of the Southern Ocean's fury, but the storms rarely push past the mountains, so the east coast and midlands are pleasant year-round. Tiny holiday villages filled with prosperous fishing fleets and vacationing families speckle the shore. In the southeast, the capital city of Hobart, Australia's second-oldest city, is happily mired in its own history and welcomes yachts from Melbourne and Sydney every December in a glorious internationally famous turnout. Rolling farmland stretches north from Hobart to Launceston, Tasmania's second city and northern hub. But perhaps most spectacular about this magical island is its amazing natural diversity, its uncanny ability to house so many different species and environments in such a small space. In fact, some of Tassie's best known species can only be found within its borders, such as the slow-growing Huon pine, which can live for centuries, and the Tasmanian Devil, a mysterious, scavenging marsupial. Many travelers try to see the island in just a few days, but once they lose themselves in the wilderness and history of Australia's secret stow-away, they may never be able to get enough of Tasmania.

## TASMANIA HIGHLIGHTS

**THANKING GOD.** Not being a convict on the Tasman Peninsula (p. 477).

**SO CLOSE...** The Southern Ocean toward Antarctica from South Cape (p. 482).

**ENVIRO-DEBATE.** The controversial Gordon Dam (p. 484).

**ABANDON HOPE.** The way to Hells Gate and a 2000-year-old Huon Pine (p. 487).

**GO BUSH.** The world-famous Overland Track (p. 489).

**THE WILD.** Eating kangaroo and spying on platypi atop a mountain (p. 499).

**DOING ABSOLUTELY NOTHING.** The aquamarine waters of Blue Lake (p. 499).

**SUNSET.** The granite peaks and white-rimmed shore at Wineglass Bay (p. 503).

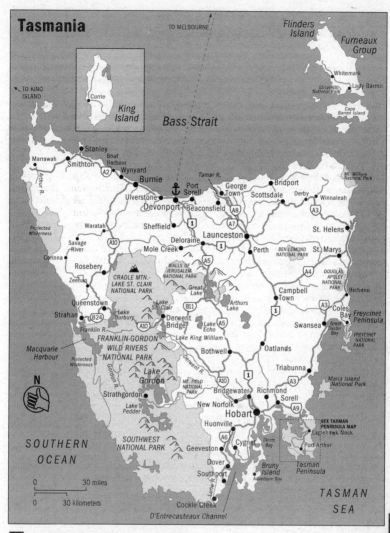

**Tasmania**

TO MELBOURNE

Flinders Island

Furneaux Group

TO KING ISLAND

Currie

King Island

Bass Strait

Whitemark

Strzelecki National Park

Lady Barron

Cape Barren Island

Marrawah

Stanley

Boat Harbour

Smithton

Wynyard

Burnie

Tamar R.

Port Sorell

George Town

Bridport

Scottsdale

Derby

Winnaleah

Mt. William National Park

Arthur R.

Ulverstone

Devonport

Beaconsfield

Waratah

Sheffield

Deloraine

Launceston

Perth

St. Helens

Protected Wilderness

Savage River

Mole Creek

St. Marys

Corinna

Roseberry

WALLS OF JERUSALEM NATIONAL PARK

BEN LOMOND NATIONAL PARK

Zeehan

CRADLE MTN.-LAKE ST. CLAIR NATIONAL PARK

Great Lake

DOUGLAS APSLEY NATIONAL PARK

Campbell Town

Bicheno

Queenstown

Lake Burbury

Lake St. Clair

Arthurs Lake

Coles Bay

Freycinet Peninsula

Strahan

Derwent Bridge

Lake Echo

Swansea

Great Oyster Bay

FREYCINET NATIONAL PARK

Franklin R.

Macquarie Harbour

FRANKLIN-GORDON WILD RIVERS NATIONAL PARK

Lake King William

Bothwell

Oatlands

Protected Wilderness

Derwent R.

Lake Gordon

MT. FIELD NATIONAL PARK

Triabunna

Maria Island National Park

Strathgordon

Lake Pedder

Bridgewater

Richmond

Sorell

New Norfolk

Hobart

SEE TASMAN PENINSULA MAP

N

SOUTHERN OCEAN

SOUTHWEST NATIONAL PARK

Huonville

Cygnet

Geeveston

Storm Bay

Eaglehawk Neck

Port Arthur

Tasman Peninsula

Dover

Bruny Island

Adventure Bay

TASMAN SEA

0   30 miles

0   30 kilometers

Southport

Cockle Creek

D'Entrecasteaux Channel

# ⌂ GETTING AROUND

Tasmania has three principal gateways: Hobart (by air), Devonport (by *Spirit of Tasmania* overnight ferry or air), and Launceston (by air or to its George Town port by *DevilCat* ferry). The state then comfortably divides into south, northwest, and northeast zones as the respective domains of the gateway cities. Getting around on a budget is a bit of a challenge. There is no rail network, and the main bus lines—**Redline** and **TWT's TassieLink**—are expensive, limited, and infrequent. TassieLink offers "Explorer Passes," which are worth the investment when using their buses as a touring service (valid 7-days within any 10-day period $130, 21-days within 30-days $220). On the bright side, there are residents in every corner—including many hostel managers—who are keen to fill the void, offering reasonably priced shuttles and tours on a call-and-request basis. Seek local recommendations and information boards. With a companion or two to share expenses, renting a car is more popular here than on the mainland. The gateway cities have small companies offering cheaper, older cars. Visitors unaccustomed to Tasmania's narrow, winding roads should drive with added caution. Explicitly check with the rental company on their policy regarding travel on unsealed roads (some prohibit it altogether, others increase the liability excess). Four-wheel-drive vehicles, necessary for winter travel and a portion of Tassie's backroads, come with better insurance policies on unsealed roads. Though not recommended by *Let's Go*, **hitchhiking** is relatively popular, but often means sticking to the main roads. **Biking** is a satisfying alternative, especially on the more accessible east coast. *Bicycling Tasmania*, by Terry and Beedham, is trustworthy; the three major gateway cities have rental outfits catering to cycle touring. If you're planning on extensive bushwalking, pick up a copy of *100 Walks in Tasmania*, by Tyrone Thomas, which has detailed track descriptions and excellent maps.

# ◪ NATIONAL PARKS

All of Tasmania's National Parks charge an entrance fee. A 24hr. pass is $3 (vehicles $9). For those planning to visit many parks, there's a 2-month pass for $12 (vehicles $30) or an annual pass for $18 (vehicles $42). Passes are available at most of the park entrances, or from any of the Parks & Wildlife Service offices. For more information, contact the head office in Hobart, 134 Macquarie St (☎6233 6191), or visit their website at www.parks.tas.gov.au.

# HOBART

The capital of Australia's smallest state, Hobart is built at the mouth of the Derwent River, shielded by a scatter of islands and breakwaters at the feet of Mt. Wellington. Founded on February 21, 1804, Hobart is Australia's second oldest city. Since its days as a penal colony, the capital's fortunes have mirrored the state's. Mining wealth helped establish the city, but as a small fish in the federated Australian pond, Hobart has never grown large or complex. Hobart's social strata consists of the conservative establishment, the creative intelligentsia, strong-willed environmental activists, and disaffected alterna-teens. All Hobartians, however, unite in enjoying a slower pace of life than their mainland counterparts, and they seem to like it that way. Almost all of Tassie's travelers take at least a short stop in Hobart, receiving a dose of urbanity before heading out into the great beyond.

> **HOBART HIGHLIGHTS**
>
> **SPENDING MONEY.** Saturday morning's renowned Salamanca Market (p. 474).
>
> **PANORAMA.** Seeing half of Tassie from the summit of Mt. Wellington (p. 474).
>
> **CHARM.** History at Battery Point (p. 474).
>
> **EATING A LOT.** Chocolate at the Cadbury Chocolate Factory (p. 475).
>
> **DRINKING EVEN MORE.** Cascade Brewery tours (p. 475).

# ✈ GETTING THERE

Air and road are the only ways in and out of Hobart. Plan ahead, because buses do not run frequently. Renting a car from another city to Hobart is the most convenient travel option by far. Many visitors travel by hitchhiking.

## BY PLANE

**Hobart Airport** is 18km east of Hobart on Hwy A3. International flights must make connections on the mainland. **Kendell,** Level 3, 118 Queen St, Melbourne (☎(1800) 33 88 94, in Melbourne ☎9670 2677) and **Qantas** (☎13 13 13) fly to Melbourne at least four times per day ($130-260) and Sydney at least twice per day ($188-376). International travelers can get better deals; bring your passport and international ticket. **Redline Airporter Bus** shuttles between the airport and lodgings ($7.50).

## BY BUS

The most helpful thing to do is pick up timetables for Redline, TWT's TassieLink, and Tigerline services from Hobart's main **bus depot**, 199 Collins St. Redline Coaches (☎(1300) 36 00 00) is the all-purpose intercity service running buses 2-6 times per day to: **Devonport** (4½hr., $33), and **Launceston** (2½hr., $19) via **Oatlands** (1hr., $11). Redline also runs once daily Su-F to: **Bicheno** (4¼hr., $22); the **Coles Bay turn-off** (4hr., $22); **St. Helens** (4hr., $32); **St. Marys** (3½hr., $29); and **Swansea** (3½hr., $22). 20% student discount. TassieLink (☎(1300) 30 05 20) offers special bushwalking packages, and runs coaches to: **Bicheno** (3hr.; W, F, Su; $21); the **Coles Bay turn-off** (3hr.; W, F, Su; $20); **Lake St. Clair** (3¼hr.; Tu, Th, F, Su; $29); **New Norfolk** (40min.; Tu, Th, F, Su; $5); **Queenstown** (5hr.; Tu, Th, F, Su; $37); **Sorell** (20min.; W, F, Su; $5); **St. Helens** (4hr.; F, Su; $30); **Strahan** (Tu, Th, F, Su; $42); **Swansea** (2¼hr., Su-F, $17); and **Triabunna** (2hr., M-F, $12). Summer schedule adds: **Cockle Creek** (3¼hr.; M, W, F; $45); **Lune River** (2½hr.; M, W, F; $20); **Mt. Field National Park** (1¼hr., 1 per day, $20); **Scotts Peak** (3¼hr.; Tu, Th, Sa; $47); and **Southwest hiking trails** (2-3hr.; Tu, Th, Sa; $45). Hobart Coaches (☎6234 4077), runs to **Cygnet** (1hr., M-F 5:15pm, $7) and **Kettering** (1hr., 4-5 per day M-F, $6).

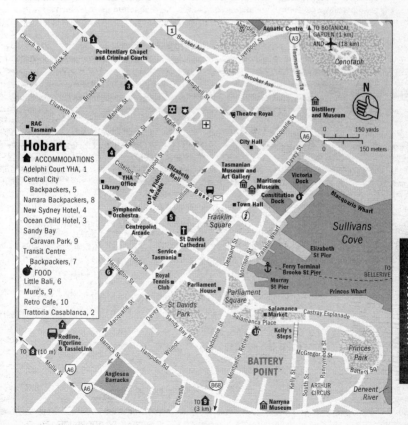

TASMANIA

# F GETTING AROUND

**Ferries and Cruises:** The best deal around is **Captain Fell's Historic Ferries.** (☎6223 5893. 2½hr. dinner cruise departs Franklin Wharf nightly 6pm. $22.) **Roche O'May Ferries** (☎6223 1914) sails from Brooke St Pier to the Wrest Point Casino. Departs daily 10:30am, noon, 1:30, 3pm. $12. The **Lady Nelson** (☎6272 2823) gives less commercial river cruises in a more historical context. 1½hr. tour departs Elizabeth St Pier in summer Sa-Su 11am, 1, 3pm; in winter Sa-Su noon and 2pm. $5.

**Local Transportation:** Metro **city buses** (☎13 22 01) run through Hobart and the suburbs daily 6am-midnight. Purchase tickets on-board; $1.20-2.80 depending on number of sections traveled. "Day Rover" tickets ($3.10) allow unlimited travel M-F 9am-4:30pm and after 6pm, Sa-Su all day. **The Metro Shop,** 9 Elizabeth St, in a corner of the Post Office, has a complete timetable for $2. Open M-F 8am-5:15pm.

**By Tour:** Good if you're short on time, an option is a prearranged day tour organized by **Tigerline,** in the Transit center, 199 Collins St (☎(1300) 65 36 33), or **Experience Tasmania,** 129 Liverpool St (☎6234 3336). Both offer hotel pickup and an array of combination tours to the highlights of the Hobart region. 2hr. to full-day tours $18-105; min. 4 passengers. Book through the tourist office (☎6230 8233) or with a hostel reception. Bottom Bits Bus (☎(1800) 77 71 03) has trips to Mt. Field National Park (full-day, $45) and the Huon Valley (3-days, $195).

**Car Rental:** Car rental agencies are everywhere in Hobart. Off-season rates run as low as $17 per day. The following companies rent to ages 21-24. **Autorent Hertz,** 122 Harrington St (☎6237 1111), rents top-end cars from $40-50 per day. For YHA discount, call ☎13 30 39 and quote Discount Program number 317961. **Thrifty,** 11-17 Argyle St (☎6234 1341, airport ☎6248 5678), from $39. **Range** and **RentABug,** 136 Harrington St and 105 Murray St (☎6231 0678), from $28, including minibuses and campervans. **Selective Car Rentals,** 132 Argyle St (☎6234 3311), from $22.

**Automobile Club: RACT,** corner of Murray and Patrick St (☎6232 6300). Open M-F 8:45am-5pm). 24hr. roadside help (☎13 11 11), insurance queries (☎13 27 22).

**Bikes: Derwent Bike Hire** (☎6268 6161), at Cenotaph on the cycleway at the Regatta Grounds, hires road and mountain bikes, tandems, and roller blades from $7 per hr. Long-term hire also available from $100 per week and $200 per month. Open Sept.-Dec. and Feb.-May Sa-Su 10am-5pm; open Jan. daily 10am-5pm; closed Jun-Aug.

**Taxis: City Cabs** (☎(1800) 80 87 51). 24hr. City to airport $20-23.

# ✴ ORIENTATION

Most tourist attractions and services cluster around the **Elizabeth St Mall,** behind the wharves of Sullivan's Cove. South of the Cove lies **Battery Point,** one of the oldest sections of the city, choked with antique shops and cottages. The northern border of Battery Point is defined by **Salamanca Place,** a row of old Georgian warehouses that have been renovated as shops and restaurants. **Franklin Wharf,** adjacent to Salamanca Place, is the departure point for the many harbor cruises. Hobart is backed by the **Wellington Range,** which affords fine views from **Mt. Nelson,** to the south, or the larger **Mt. Wellington,** to the west. The city proper can be navigated on foot, while public buses run to the outer reaches of the suburbs.

Beyond the **Queen's Domain** north of downtown, the **Tasman Bridge** spans the Derwent River. There, the Tasman Hwy (A3) heads east and connects to the A9 to the Tasman Peninsula. **Brooker Ave** leads north up the Derwent Valley, becoming Hwy 1 to Launceston, and connecting to the A10 for points west. **Davey St** leaves downtown as the A6, heading southward toward the Huon Valley and Bruny Island.

TASMANIA

# 🔁 PRACTICAL INFORMATION

## TOURIST AND FINANCIAL SERVICES

**Tourist Office: Hobart Tasmanian Travel and Information Centre,** 20 Davey St (☎6230 8233), at Elizabeth St. Books accommodation and cars ($2 fee), as well as tours and walks (no fee). Open M-F 8:30am-5:15pm, Sa-Su 9am-4pm (winter Su 9am-1pm).

**Budget Travel Office: YHA's Tasmanian Headquarters,** 2nd floor, 28 Criterion St (☎6234 9617). Travel insurance, passport photos, tickets, and travel advice, in addition to YHA memberships and hostel bookings. Open M-F 9am-5pm.

**Tasmanian Parks and Wildlife Service:** 134 Macquarie St (☎6233 6191; www.parks.tas.gov.au), in the Service Tasmania Bldg. Open M-F 9am-5pm.

**Forestry Tasmania:** 79 Melville St (☎6233 0203). Open M-F 8:30am-5:30pm.

**Currency Exchange:** Mobs of banks, most with **ATMs,** crowd in and around Elizabeth St Mall. **Trust Bank,** 75 Liverpool St (☎6230 3790), changes cash and checks for **no charge.** Most banks have a $5-10 fee. All open M-Th 9:30am-4pm, F 9:30am-5pm.

**American Express:** 74a Liverpool St (☎6234 3711). Basically a travel agency. AmEx sends people to **Trust Bank** to cash their traveler's cheques. Open M-F 8:45am-5pm.

## LOCAL SERVICES

**Bookstores: Hobart Bookshop,** 22 Salamanca Square (☎6223 1803). Richly stocked shelves of new and second-hand books. Open M-F 9am-6pm, Sa-Su 10am-5pm.

**Library:** 91 Murray St (☎6233 7529), at Bathurst St. Reference library open Feb.-Nov. M-Tu 9:30am-6pm, W-F 9:30am-9pm, Sa 9:30am-2:30pm; Dec.-Jan. M-Th 9:30am-6pm, F 9:30am-9pm, Sa 9:30am-12:30pm. Provides **Internet access** 30min. $5.

**Market: Salamanca Place** (☎6233 7529). Open Sa 8am-3pm. See **Sights,** below.

**Laundromat:** Most hostels have coin-operated washers. **Machine Laundry/Café,** 12 Salamanca Sq (☎6224 9922), behind Salamanca Pl; enter through Kennedy Ln or Wooby's Ln. A funky new approach to laundry combines risotto ($8-9), frittata ($8-9), ($5-8) and desserts ($5) with washing machines ($3 each for wash and dry). Open M-Sa 8am-6pm, Su 9am-6pm; winter daily 9am-5:30pm.

**Outdoor Equipment:** Gear stores cluster along Elizabeth St near Liverpool St. **Snowgum,** 104 Elizabeth St (☎6234 7877), sells the usual equipment as well as climbing and kayaking gear. They also rent sleeping bags, packs, and tents ($35 per week, $50 deposit) and kayaks ($80, $300). Open M-F 9am-5:30pm, Sa 9am-2pm.

**Fishing Equipment:** Get info and fishing tackle ($20 per day) at **Bridges Bros.,** 142 Elizabeth St (☎6234 3791). Open M-Th 9am-5:30pm, F 9am-6pm, Sa 9am-1pm. *Angling Code for Inland Fisheries,* available at the tourist office, outlines all regulations.

**MEDIA AND PUBLICATIONS**
*Newspaper:* The Mercury.
*Entertainment:* The Mercury includes Gig Guide on Thursday and EG on Friday.
*Radio:* Rock, Triple J 92.9FM; News, ABC 729AM; Tourist Info, 88FM.

## EMERGENCY AND COMMUNICATIONS

**Emergency:** Dial ☎000.

**Police:** 37-43 Liverpool St (☎6230 2111). **Lost and found,** ☎6230 2277.

**Hospital: Royal Hobart Hospital,** 48 Liverpool St (☎6222 8308).

**Pharmacy: Corby's Everyday Pharmacy,** 170 Macquarie St (☎6223 3044). Open daily 8am-10pm.

TASMANIA

**Hotlines: Crisis Watchline,** (24hr. ☎13 11 14). **AIDS Hotline:** (☎(1800) 00 59 00). Staffed M-F 9am-5pm. **Alcohol and Drugs Hotline,** (24hr. ☎(1800) 81 19 94).

**Internet and Fax: Service Tasmania,** 134 Macquarie St has six **free terminals.** (☎(1300) 13 55 13. Open M-F 8:15am-5pm. 30min. limit.) **Drifters Coffeehouse** is a true Cybercafé (see p. 473). Also try the **library** (see **Local Services,** above).

**Post Office:** 9 Elizabeth St (☎6236 3577; fax 6234 9387), at Macquarie St . Open M-F 8am-5:45pm. **Postal Code:** 7000.

**Phone Code:** 03

# ▐ ACCOMMODATIONS

During the December summer festival, book well ahead.

▨ **Narrara Backpackers,** 88 Goulburn St (☎6231 3191). Turn left off Harrington St. Offering spotless accommodation with a cozy atmosphere, this three-story house proves the newest place is sometimes the best. Off-street parking. Laundry. Internet 10min. $2. Reception daily 8am-10pm. Dorms $16; twins $36; doubles $40.

**Central City Backpackers,** 138 Collins St (☎6224 2404). On the 2nd floor through the Imperial Arcade. A large hostel with a kitchen, common areas, and a great location. Downstairs lounge has billiards, a pub, and bowls of vegetarian goodness ($4; open nightly 6pm-late). Sleepsheet $2, full linen $5. Laundry. Internet 6min. $2. Key deposit $5. Reception daily 8am-10pm. 6-bed dorms $16; 4-bed dorms $18; singles $32; twins and doubles $40. No credit cards.

**Transit Centre Backpackers,** 199 Collins St (☎6231 2400). Above the bus depot. Drab bus station setting, but comfortable. Friendly proprietors live on-site. Fireplace, heaters, extra doonas for the winter chill, TV, kitchen, laundry, billiards. Free storage. No alcohol permitted on premises; free coffee and tea. Reception daily 8am-11pm. Dorms $15.

**New Sydney Hotel,** 87 Bathurst St (☎6234 4516). Rooms and bathrooms are well-maintained despite their age. TV lounge, full kitchen. Downstairs music shuts down by midnight. Internet 6min. $2. Deposit $10. 7-night max. stay. Dorms $16; doubles $35.

**Ocean Child Hotel,** 86 Argyle St (☎6234 6730). On the corner of Melville St, a short walk from the city center. The rooms above this small nautical pub are a bit dark, but orderly. TV in the kitchen. Friendly staff. DJ on W and live music Th-Sa (usually jazz or folk that isn't likely to keep people awake). Linen $2. Laundry $2. Dorms $14; doubles $30. VIP.

**Adelphi Court YHA,** 17 Stoke St, New Town (☎6228 4829). A 25min. walk from the heart of Hobart, off Elizabeth St, or New Town Rd. Take a Metro bus from Argyle St to stop 8A opposite the hostel, or a bus from Elizabeth St to stop 13. Built around a pleasant courtyard, Adelphi is the high-priced mothership of the Tasmania YHA fleet. Large common area with games, booking office, grocery kiosk, wash basins in rooms. Continental breakfast $4. Off-street parking. Internet 30min. $10. Key deposit $10. Reception daily 7:30am-10:30pm. Dorms $19; singles $42; twins $48. Non-YHA add $3.

**Sandy Bay Caravan Park,** 1 Peel St (☎6225 1264). 3km from the city center off Nelson St, which runs into Sandy Bay Rd across from the casino. The Busy Bee bus services the casino M-F 8am-6pm every 10min. Coin-op stove 20¢. Bedding $4. Reception Su-W 8:30am-6pm, Th-Sa 8:30am-7pm. Tent sites $8 per person; powered $17; on-site caravans for 2 $40; self-contained cabins for 2 $60, each extra person $8.

# ◖ FOOD

Hobart has just the international cuisine the two-minute noodle weary have been craving. Good value restaurants downtown serve meals from every pocket of Asia. The pubs and grills at Salamanca Place serve lunch and dinner once brekkie is finished at the hopping cafés. The ultimate Tassie tucker is abalone or salmon with a Cascade beer. **Purity,** 69 King St, Sandy Bay (☎6211 6611) or 189 Campbell St, North Hobart, (☎6234 8077), is an inexpensive **supermarket** (both open M-W, Sa 8am-6pm, Th-F 8am-9pm). Get organic and bulk foods at **Eumarrah**

**Wholefoods,** 45 Goulburn St (☎6234 3229; open M-F 9am-6pm, Sa 9am-2pm). The Saturday **Salamanca Market** has deals on local produce, sauces, spreads, honey, and cheese (open Sa 8am-3pm).

▨ **Retro Café,** 33 Salamanca Pl (☎6223 3073). On the corner of Montpelier Retreat. Regulars enjoy fine food and excellent coffee. On Saturday, there's great people-watching at the Salamanca Market. It can be hard to get a seat, but their all-day brekkie bagel ($9) is worth the scramble. Open M-Sa 8am-6pm, Su 8:30am-6pm.

**Trattoria Casablanca,** 213 Elizabeth St (☎6234 9900). Recently renovated, this classy Italian restaurant has black-and-white photos from its namesake movie on the walls. Pastas in 15 varieties ($8-13.50) and pizzas ($8-19) from A(nchovies) to Z(uccini). Open M-Th 5:15-11:30pm, F-Sa 5:15pm-1am, Su noon-11:30pm.

**Mures Fish Centre,** Victoria Dock (☎6231 2121). A complete seafood complex. The sealevel **Bistro** serves the masses the town's best fish-and-chips ($7.50). Order and pay at the counter, then wait to be called. Separate, licensed beverage counter. Open daily 11am-9pm. The **Upper Deck** has fine dining lunches (noon-2:30pm) and winter dinner specials (6-10pm; both from $13.50). To starboard, **Orizuru** (☎6231 1790) makes fresh sushi (lunches $12; entrees $6-10; mains $16-24). Open M-Sa noon-2:30pm and 6-9:30pm. **Polar Parlor** has ice cream and desserts. Open daily 8am-9pm.

**A Taste of Asia,** 358 Elizabeth St, North Hobart (☎6236 9191). A favorite with locals. Quirky Asian-inspired cuisine, from sushi to stir-fry. The large take-away plates ($9) are a great deal. Open M-W noon-8pm, Th noon-8:30pm, F noon-9pm, Sa 4:30-9pm.

**Drifters Internet Café,** Shop 9, 33 Salamanca Pl, The Galleria (☎6224 3244). Good homemade soups ($4.50), all-day breakfasts ('shrooms and eggs benedict for $6), and cappucino ($2). Even better are the 'zines, great music, and Internet access. (10min. $2; 1hr. $10). Open M-Th 10am-6pm, F 10am-8pm, Sa 9am-6pm, Su 11am-6pm.

**Little Bali,** 84a Harrington St (☎6234 3426). Tiny yellow dining room, bright with wicker lamp-shades and flying animals. Good, quick, cheap Indonesian meals (small $5.50, large $7.50; 50¢ table surcharge). Open M-F 11:30am-3pm and 5-9pm, Sa-Su 5-9pm.

**Steve's Kebab House,** 127 Liverpool St (☎6231 6000). Across from the Elizabeth St Mall. International kebabs are a specialty: Yankee-doodles with mustard and sauce, Aussie kebabs with a fried egg and sauce, and tasty vegetarian falafel. Everything is less than $6.20. Open Su-M 11am-9pm, Tu-Th 11am-10pm, F-Sa 11am-3:30am.

# 👁 SIGHTS

Hobart is brimming with interesting convict history. *Hobart's Historic Places*, *Sullivan's Cove Walk*, and *Women's History Walk*, available from the tourist office, are excellent free brochures that provide information and orientation.

## DOWNTOWN

**TASMANIAN MUSEUM AND ART GALLERY.** Fine displays explore Tasmania's early convict history, unique ecology, and artistic heritage. The modern Australian art section is particularly strong, and the mega-fauna models particularly humbling. *(40 Macquarie St. At Argyle St. ☎6211 4177. Open daily 10am-5pm. Free. Guided tours leave from the bookstore W-Su 2:30pm; tours can also be arranged on demand.)*

**PENITENTIARY CHAPEL AND CRIMINAL COURTS.** One of the oldest, best-preserved buildings in Tasmania, and an excellent example of Georgian ecclesiastical architecture. Within lie the court rooms and gallows of the grim 1830s. *(6 Brisbane St. Enter on Campbell St. ☎6231 0911. Guided tours available M-F 10, 11:30am, 1, 2:30pm. $7.70, concessions $5.50. Ghost tours: ☎(0417) 36 13 92. Daily 8pm. $7. Book ahead.)*

**MARITIME MUSEUM.** This new facility concentrates on Tassie maritime heritage, with a focus on local shipping and whaling. Filled to the gunwales with model boats, ancient photographs, scrimshaw, and other crusty relics. Newspaper clip-

TASMANIA

pings of more recent catastrophic shipwrecks make for some riveting reading. *(16 Argyle St. In the Carnegie Building at Davey St. ☎6223 5082. Open daily 10am-5pm. $6.)*

**TASMANIA DISTILLERY.** This single-malt whiskey distillery offers a museum, shop, and self-guided tour with free spirit tastings. *(2 Macquarie St. In the Gasworks complex. ☎6231 0588. Open daily 9am-7pm; winter 10am-6pm. $5, concessions $4.)*

**CYCLEWAY.** Along the west bank of the Derwent River is a bicycle path with views of and from Mt. Wellington, the Tasman Bridge, the Government House, Regatta Grounds, the Queen's Domain, the Royal Botanical Gardens, and the shipyards in Hobart. The tourist office has a brochure with maps.

**OTHER SIGHTS DOWNTOWN.** The oldest theater and synagogue in the country sit together in Hobart's downtown. The **Theatre Royal,** established in 1834, is still used. *(29 Campbell St. Between Collins and Liverpool St. ☎6233 2299. Open M-F 9am-5pm, Sa 9:30am-1pm.)* The **Synagogue,** on the other hand, is not. Since its construction in 1843 inspired by the Regency Egyptian Revival, Hobart's Jewish community has shrunk such that there isn't one rabbi in all of Tasmania. *(Argyle St. Near Liverpool St.)*

At the cove, the **Elizabeth, Brooke,** and **Murray St Piers** harbor most of Hobart's large vessels. Look for the Antarctic Research Expedition's giant orange ice-breaker, *Aurora Australis.* **Constitution** and **Victoria Dock** are thronged with popular fishmongers and marine restaurants. Several companies run **harbor cruises** from this area (see **Ferries and Cruises,** p. 470).

# SALAMANCA PLACE AND BATTERY POINT

**SALAMANCA PLACE.** This row of famous Georgian warehouses now contains trendy galleries, restaurants, shops, and acts as the backdrop to the Saturday outdoor market. Guaranteed to be busy all day, the much-celebrated Salamanca Market is an excellently chaotic amalgamation of crafts, produce, performers, and good times. *(Open Sa 8am-3pm.)*

**ANTARCTIC ADVENTURE.** An odd but pleasant discovery center-*cum*-amusement park combining facts, fun, and 20min. planetarium shows of the Southern Hemisphere's starry sky. The most popular exhibit, the Blizzard, simulates downhill speed skiing. *(2 Salamanca Sq. ☎6220 8220, freecall ☎(1800) 35 00 28; www.antarc tic.com.au. Open daily 10am-5pm. $16; concessions $13; under 14 $8, families $40. Planetarium show every hour 11am-4pm.)*

**BATTERY POINT.** Salamanca Place butts up against the lovely historic neighborhood of Battery Point where many of Hobart's convict-era buildings have been preserved. The Battery Point National Trust leads tours through the village, or do a self-guided tour by referring to the walking brochures (see **Cycleway,** above). *(Tours depart Franklin Sq Wishing Well Sa 9:30am. 2½hr. $10, children $2.50.)*

**PRINCES PARK.** This pleasant green space just behind the Esplanade on the edge of Battery Point was the site of the Mulgrave Battery. The oldest building on Battery Point, this 1818 signal station was converted to relay messages from Hobart to as far away as Port Arthur.

# THE MOUNTAINS

**MT. NELSON.** Just south of central Hobart, it offers sweeping views of Hobart and the Derwent estuary. A signal station at the top, part of the chain that connected Port Arthur to the capital, also has a restaurant. *(Take the #57 or 58 Mt. Nelson bus to its terminus. Road to the top open daily 9am-9pm. Restaurant open daily 9:30am-4:30pm.)*

**MT. WELLINGTON.** Several kilometers west of Hobart, Mt. Wellington (1270m) is a must-see. The top is extremely windy, cold, and often snowy. On a clear day, you can see the peaks of half the state, all clearly marked on signs in the observation shelter. The summit is also home to a huge telecommunications tower that can become crowded with vehicle visitors, but surrounding walking tracks are spectacular. The road to the top closes occasionally due to snow and ice. **Fern Tree,** on the lower foothills of the mountain, is a lovely picnic area with walking tracks up the slope. *(Take the #48 or 49 Fern Tree bus to stop 27, at the base of the mountain. Getting to the top without a car may involve shelling out some dough for a narrated van trip up the road. Experience Tasmania tours $20, concessions $17. Observation shelter open daily 8am-6pm. For track details, get the Mt. Wellington Walk Map ($4) from the tourist office.)*

# NORTH AND SOUTH

■ **CADBURY CHOCOLATE FACTORY.** One of Hobart's most popular attractions, Cadbury provides tours showing all stages of the chocolate process—most importantly, the free tasting every step of the way. *(In Claremont, north of Hobart and the Derwent River. Take the Claremont service #37, 38, or 39 to the factory. ☎ 6249 0333, freecall ☎ (1800) 62 73 67. Tours M-F 9, 9:30, 10:30am, 1pm. 1hr. $10, concessions $7, children $5. Advanced booking required. Only abbreviated tours mid-Dec. to mid-Jan., $4.)*

■ **CASCADE BREWERY.** This is the place for those who prefer death by beer rather than chocolate. Built in 1832 by a Mr. Degraves, who drew up the plans while in prison for debt default, it's the oldest brewery in Australia, producing 800 stubbies per minute. *(131 Cascade Rd. Take the Claremont service #37, 38, or 39 to stop 17. ☎ 6221 8300. Tours M-F 9:30am and 1pm. 1½hr. $7.50, concessions $5, children $1.50. Free beer at the end. Bookings essential.)*

**FEMALE HISTORIC SITE AND ISLAND PRODUCE TASMANIA FUDGE FACTORY.** Once the Hobart jail and a factory for women and children in the 1820s, the site is now home to building ruins, memorial gardens, and fine confectioners. The poignant tours split their time between the historic site ("lest we forget") and today's small, handmade production of fudge and truffles. Um, did someone say nonsequitur? Free samples. *(16 Degraves St, South Hobart. Near the Brewery. Take bus #43, 44, 46, 47, or 49 bus from Franklin Sq up Cascade Rd to stop 14, turn right onto Apsley St and cross the bridge onto Degraves St. ☎ 6223 3233. Shop and gardens open M-F 8am-4pm. Tours M-F at 10:30am. 1¼hr. $6, concessions $5, children $3. Book a day ahead.)*

**ROYAL TASMANIAN BOTANICAL GARDENS.** With 13 hectares and 6000 species, this is the largest public collection of Tasmanian plants in the world, and the largest collection of conifers in the Southern Hemisphere. Founded in 1818, it is also the second oldest gardens in Australia. The wildly popular Al Fresco Theatre runs an outdoor play in January, and "Shakespeare in the Garden" in February. *(North of the city, near the Tasman Bridge. Take any bus, including the MetroCity Explorer, that's headed to the eastern shore to stop 4 before the bridge; or take the X3-G express to Bridgewater, which stops at the main gate. Or walk 25min. from the city to Queen's Domain past Government House. ☎ 6234 6299. Open daily Oct.-Mar. 8am-6:30pm, Apr. 8am-5:30pm, May-Aug. 8am-5pm, Sept. 8am-5:30pm. Free. Outdoor Theatre $20, concessions $10.)*

**BONORONG WILDLIFE PARK.** See, hear, pet, and feed the beasts that roam the island's wilderness. Tasmanian devils, koalas, quolls, wombats, and injured birds live in enclosures, while 'roos and their joeys bounce independently, emus chuckle, and peacocks strut their stuff. Every visitor gets a bag of kangaroo feed, which will be eaten right out of your hand. Most of the animals were orphaned or injured and will eventually be returned to the wild. *(North of Hobart in Brighton. Metro bus X1 from Hobart to Glenorchy Interchange connects with #125 or 126 to Brighton and takes about 1hr. By car, it's a 25min. drive north on Hwy 1; follow the signs in Brighton. ☎ 6268 1184. Open daily 9am-5pm. $10, children $5. Feeding times: Devils 11:30am and 2pm, koalas 12:30 and 3pm, echidnas 2:15pm, quolls 2:25pm, wombats 2:45pm.)*

**AUSTRALIAN ANTARCTIC DIVISION.** Responsible for organizing Australian Antarctic research expeditions, the Division maintains a small display room on the Australian role in the exploration of the earth's most forbidding frontier. *(South of Hobart in Kingston. Take Tigerline Coaches from St. David's Cathedral on Murray St. It's a 20min. walk from the Kingston Shopping Centre. By car, it's a 15-min. drive on the A6. There are signs directing you from Kingston. ☎ 6232 3209. Open M-F 9am-5pm. Free.)*

**TASMANIA**

# ♫ ENTERTAINMENT

Check out the entertainment listings in the "EG" insert of Friday's *Age* newspaper. The arthouse cinema is the **State**, 375 Elizabeth St, with indie films in glamorous facilities. (☎6234 6318. $9, concessions $6.50; W $6.) **The Theatre Royal**, 29 Campbell St, the oldest theater in Australia, produces reliably good shows. (☎6233 2299. Open M-F 9am-5pm, Sa 9:30am-1pm. $20-35.) The more experimental **Peacock Theatre**, 77 Salamanca Pl, is in the Salamanca Arts Centre. (☎6234 8414. $3.50-15.) The **Tasmanian Symphony Orchestra**, 1 Davey St, in the Hotel Grand Chancellor, is over 50 years old but still holds performances every few weeks. (☎(1800) 00 11 90. $40, concessions $20.) The **Wrest Point Hotel**, 410 Sandy Bay Rd, at Nelson Rd, is the oldest casino in Australia. The emphasis is on pokies and other electronic games; there are few real gaming tables. (☎6225 0112, Tables open Su-Th 2pm- 2am, F-Sa 2pm-3am; other hotel facilities open 1hr. later.)

# ♫ NIGHTLIFE

Hobart is often mocked for its lukewarm nightlife, and while this isn't the place to find a world-class club scene, there are definitely places to party. Once again, Salamanca Place draws the masses.

**The New Sydney Hotel**, 87 Bathurst St (☎6234 4516). An extremely popular Irish pub where margaritas (a dubious Irish tradition) are the most popular beverage ($8.50). Live music Tu-Su, mainly cover bands. No cover. Open M noon-10pm, Tu noon-midnight, W-F 11:30am-midnight, Sa-Su 1pm-midnight.

**'Round Midnight**, 39 Salamanca Pl (☎6223 2491). Part of a 3-story extravaganza, completely packed late nights on weekends. Folks start the night at **Syrup**, on the ground-floor. Open Su-Th 10am-midnight, F-Sa 10am-1am. **Knopwoods**, on the first-floor, is a classy restaurant (kitchen open W-Su 7-11pm) turned nightclub. **'Round Midnight**, on the top floor, is a smoky pub with loud music. Cover $4-7. Open M, W-Th midnight-4am, F 11:30pm-5am, Sa 11:30am-6am.

**Club Surreal**, 86 Sandy Bay Rd (☎6223 3655). At the corner of St. George's, upstairs from St. Ives Hotel. Surreal Saturday nights are jam-packed with an 18+ crowd wanting to boogie. Huge video screens, TVs on the floor, and techno and disco dance floors connected with a slippery slide. Pub open Su-Tu 4-10pm, W 4pm-3am, Th 4pm-midnight, F-Sa 4pm-3am. Club cover W $4, F-Sa $8. Open W, F, Sa 10:30pm-4:30am.

**The Who**, 251 Liverpool St (☎6231 2744). Attracts hipsters of all ages. The modern, abstract architecture distinguishes the place from its surroundings and complements the cuisine ($8-15). Live bands W-Su, featuring mostly rock music. Open Su-M 2pm-midnight, Tu 11am-11pm, W-Th 11am-1am, F 11am-2am, Sa 5pm-2am.

**Sumac Vegetarian Café**, 112 Liverpool St (☎6231 4020). This promising new venue attracts the fringe, eco-artsy community with its groovy curtains, sinking couches, and fabulous food. Live performances or films most nights. Open daily 11am-midnight.

# ⚑ DAYTRIP FROM HOBART: RICHMOND

Richmond, a gracefully preserved 1870s Georgian village less than 30min. northeast of Hobart (B31 off the A9 after 12km), is a popular daytrip. Antiquarians can pass an afternoon looking at a piece of living history, like the state school, on Torres St (built in 1834); Richmond bridge, on Wellington St (built by convict labor in 1823); and St. John's Catholic Church, off Wellington St up the hill (built in 1837). The ⚑**Richmond Gaol**, 37 Bathurst St, built in 1825, confined a generation of criminals, Aboriginals, and bushrangers. Its history is colored with tales of escapes, especially by the notorious Ikey Solomons—thought to be the inspiration behind Dickens' Fagan character. Pacing the same floorboards as convicts, standing in the same corner where they were flogged, and leaning against the same dark walls of solitary confinement create an eerie intimacy with the former inmates. (☎6260 2127. Open daily 9am-5pm. $5, children $2, families $10.50.)

TassieLink runs to: **Hobart** (50min., M-F 7:40am, $5) and the East Coast, including **Triabunna** (1¼hr., M-F 4:55pm, $7) and **Swansea** (1¾hr., $12). **Richmond Cabin and Tourist Park,** 48 Middle Tea Tree Rd, 1km south of town off Bridge St, has a heated indoor swimming pool, playground, small tennis court, and BBQ. (☎6260 2192. Sites for 2 $14, powered $16; on-site vans for 2 $38.) The **Richmond Bakery,** behind Saddler's court on Edward St, serves pastries, pies, and decent coffee. (☎6260 2628. Open daily 7am-7:30pm.)

# THE SOUTH

Anchored by the capital city of Hobart, the southern end of Australia is a mix of convict history and modern hiking. Ninety minutes east of Hobart lies the Tasman Peninsula and historic Port Arthur, the most significant—and commercialized—testament to Tassie's colonial history; ninety minutes to the west lies the entrance to the vast expanse of the Southwest National Park in the Tasmanian Wilderness World Heritage Area. In between, amid the hop vines of the Derwent Valley and the apple orchards of the D'Entrecasteaux Channel, flourish the homes of people who know they've found the good life. Wandering through groves of Huon pines and trekking with camels along Bruny's beaches, you're bound to feel the same.

## TASMAN PENINSULA AND PORT ARTHUR

Pinched to almost nothing, the narrow **Eaglehawk Neck** connects the Tasman Peninsula to the rest of the island. Tourist buses now funnel through the very place guard dogs once ravaged would-be escaped convicts. Initially known as the "Black Line" past which military units forced Aboriginals, the peninsula's steep cliffs, narrow neck, and rumored shark-infested waters made it a natural choice for dumping repeat offenders. From 1830-1877, 12,000 convicts were shipped to **Port Arthur's** cruel colonies for offenses ranging from petty thievery and "skulking without permission" to murder. The inmates were put to work, and Port Arthur eventually became a settlement that exported timber and leather. The ruins of the many convict-built sandstone buildings are Tasmania's most popular tourist attraction, with 250,000 visitors annually. Port Arthur's commercialism could be too much for some; try the surrounding area where you can escape the crowds. The Tasman coastline, now a National Park, is particularly astounding; well-beaten walkways to bushwhacked tracks provide some of the most phenomenal views in Tassie.

**⌷ TRANSPORT.** There is no real Port Arthur town, just services to the site. TassieLink (☎(1300) 30 05 20) is the only **bus** company servicing the tourist attraction, departing the depot in **Hobart** M-F 4:15pm for the YHA and Port Arthur Motor Inn (2¼hr.; $12). Buses depart Port Arthur M-F 6am, holidays 7am. Book at the YHA.

A 1hr. drive north, the uninteresting town of **Sorell** is the main service center en route to the Suncoast (via the A3). Redline **buses** run to **Hobart** (45min.; 9 per day M-F, 2 per day Sa; $4). TassieLink runs up the East Coast (W, F, Su morning; extra summer service) to **Triabunna** (1hr., $7); **Swansea** (2hr., $12); **Coles Bay** turn-off (2¼hr., $15); **Bicheno** (2½hr., $16); and **St. Helens** (3¾hr., F and Su only, $25).

**⁊ PRACTICAL INFORMATION.** By the Eaglehawk Neck Historic Site on the A9, the **Officers Mess** has basic **groceries,** takeaway, and an **information centre.** (☎6250 3722. Open daily 8am-8pm; winter Su-Th 9am-6:30pm, F-Sa 9am-7:30pm.) In Sorell, the **Westpac bank,** with **24hr. ATM,** is at 36 Cole St at the junction of the A3 and A9 (open M-Th 9:30am-4pm, F 9:30am-5pm). **Post office:** 19 Gordon St, Sorell (☎6265 2579; open M-F 9am-5pm). **Postal code:** 7172.

**⌂ ACCOMMODATIONS.** The **Seaview Lodge Host Farm,** 732 Nubeena Back Rd, Koonya has a fairy-tale, hilltop location on 90 acres of land. **Tassie Experience &**

**CURSES—FOILED AGAIN!** On May 17, 1832, Port Arthur escapee George "Billy" Hunt tried to cross Eaglehawk Neck, which was protected by guard stations and a line of savage dogs. He attempted to disguise himself by donning a kangaroo skin and hopping through the blockade. The guards bought the act—and started shooting at him; kangaroo meat was an important supplement to their rations. Hunt threw off the skin, crying "Don't shoot! It's only me, Billy Hunt!"

**Eco Tours** runs out of the farm. TassieLink drops passengers off in Koonya 30min. before arriving in Port Arthur; free pickup available from Koonya or Port Arthur. From the A9 in Taranna, follow the B37 9km to Nubeena Back Rd, and then 1½km up to the farm. (☎6250 2766; www.tassie.net.au/~seaview. Linen $5. Laundry $2. Bike hire $15. Dorms $12-15; twins and doubles $30.) **Eaglehawk Neck Backpackers,** 94 Old Jetty Rd, 1km from the Neck, offers two self-contained beach huts. (☎6250 3248. Bike and canoe hire. Dorms $14. Hut for 2 Apr.-Nov. $40. Limited tent sites $6 per person.) The **Port Arthur YHA,** on Champ St, first left past the entrance to the historic site, sits mere meters from the ruins and has a resident ghost named Alice. (☎6250 2311. Reception daily 8:30-10am and 5-10pm. Dorms $16, non-YHA $19.) The **Port Arthur Garden Point Caravan Park,** is left off the A9 1km before the historic site. (☎6250 2340. Dorms $13; tent sites for 2 $13, powered $15; cabins $60-80.)

 **SIGHTS.** The model prison, lunatic asylum, hospital, and church of the sprawling, over-priced **Port Arthur Historic Site** are a visible reminder of Australia's convict heritage. The downstairs museum area provides the most historical information, while the short **walking tours** of the grounds provide minimal insight. Buy admission tickets and Ghost Tour tickets from the YHA or front desk of the visitor complex. (☎6250 2363; www.portarthur.org.au. Open daily 8:30am-8pm, but most buildings close at 5pm; allow 4hr. to explore. $18, concessions $14.40, children $9; after 4:30pm $9.) A 20min. harbor cruise passing by the **Isle of the Dead,** the colony's cemetery, and **Point Puer,** the convict boys' colony, is included in the price of admission; book at the visitor complex. Cruises that actually land on the Isle of the Dead cost an extra $8. The overwhelmingly popular **Historic Ghost Tour** runs nightly (times vary)—spooky stories, creepy shadows, and minimal history. (30min., $13.)

**RECENT HISTORY**
On Sunday, April 28, 1996, a gunman killed 35 people in Port Arthur historic site and township. The shock to Tasmania and Australia as a whole will last a long time; the violence triggered gun law reform. Information on the tragedy is available in any Tasmanian bookstore and in a free booklet of the court transcription available at the visitors desk. Please be considerate of the Port Arthur community by not asking staff and shopkeepers about the incident.

## AROUND THE TASMAN PENINSULA

As of April 1999, much of the Peninsulas' coastline is encompassed by **Tasman National Park,** and lined by cliff-top **hiking trails.** Peter and Shirley Storey's handy *Tasman Tracks,* available at tourist shops on the peninsula, details about 50 walks and has good maps. One of the region's most intriguing sights is the **Tessellated Pavement,** just before Eaglehawk Neck. The natural platform of sedimentary rock has grooves hatched across the surface caused by unequal erosion, giving it the appearance of tile. The carpark is 500km up Pirates Bay Dr, and it's an easy 15min. return walk to the beach.

Continuing on the A9 just past Eaglehawk Neck is the C338 turn-off to the **Devils Kitchen** and **Tasman Arch** carparks. Both cliffside sights are easy 10-15min. return walks. Continue along the moderate gravel track to **Pattersons Arch**

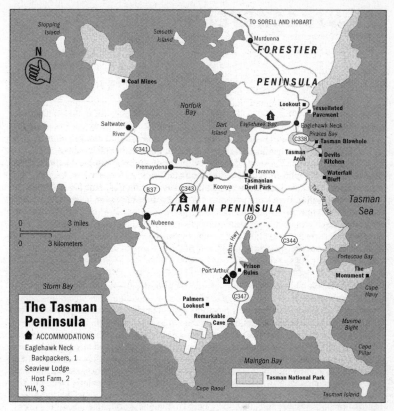

The Tasman Peninsula

▲ ACCOMMODATIONS
Eaglehawk Neck
  Backpackers, 1
Seaview Lodge
  Host Farm, 2
YHA, 3

(15min.) and **Waterfall Bay** (45min.), where it links up with the steep **Tasman Trail** to the **falls** (1¼hr.) and **Waterfall Bluff** (1½hr.). The view out to sea gets better the higher you hike. Walking from Devils Kitchen to **Fortescue Bay** can be a breath-taking 8hr. or overnight walk. Basic **camping** is available with drinking water, showers, and toilets (sites $10; park fees apply). The Fortescue **ranger** has details (☎6250 2433). You can reach Waterfall Bay and Fortescue Bay by car. For Water-fall Bay, take the first right off C338 and follow 4km to the cul-de-sac; for Fortes-cue Bay follow a 12km sign-posted, unsealed road east off A9, south of the B37 Taranna junction.

From Fortescue Bay, the Tasman Trail leads to **Cape Hauy** (4hr.). Starting with a deep descent from the campground, this very difficult trek passes by the spectac-ular **Monument,** featuring the dolorite spires of **The Candlestick, The Needle,** and **The Lanterns,** popular among ambitious **rock climbers.** The 3-day return trip to **Cape Pil-lar** is wicked awesome. Camping is available at **Lime Bay** with pit toilets and spring-fed water ($3). Check with the park office for updates, including summer ranger activities. **Parks and Wildlife** (☎6250 3497) is on the A9 before the Devil Park.

On the way to Port Arthur, the **Tasmanian Devil Park Wildlife Reserve Centre,** in Taranna, is substantially more expensive and more cramped than other wildlife parks, including the excellent Bonorong, just north of Hobart. (☎6250 3230. Open daily 9am-5pm. $11, children $5.50, families $29.50.) For time better spent, head next door to the **World Tiger Snake Centre,** with over 1000 snakes. Did you know a female tiger snake can store sperm in her body for up to 2 years? (Open daily 9am-5pm. Summer $8, children $4, families $19; winter $5, $2, $10.)

TASMANIA

# D'ENTRECASTEAUX CHANNEL

The channels, islands, and caves south of Hobart were first charted by Frenchman Bruni D'Entrecasteaux in 1792, more than a decade before the first English settlement in the area. The Huon River flows gently through the valley, feeding fertile soil in a cool climate perfect for berries, pears, and apples. The pastoral land between the Huon River and the D'Entrecasteaux Channel teems with antiques and vineyards. As with many smaller towns, the hamlet of Cygnet acts merely as a base for exploring the area, while Bruny Island is an adventurous escape into wild nature. South of the Huon River, Geeveston and the Lune River area are launchpads to the southwest. The widely circulated *Southern Tasmania's Waterways and Wilderness* is a useful navigational aid on the entire region.

## CYGNET AND THE HUON VALLEY

Near the mouth of the Nicholls Rivulet on Port Cygnet 60km southwest of Hobart, Cygnet is a friendly, artsy community that hosts seasonal fruit pickers and year-round travelers en route to the Huon Valley. Several testaments to the region's fruit trade lie on the A6 to Huonville from Hobart. **Doran's Jam Factory** has been churning out fruit preserves since 1834. Their spiced apple butter is the local favorite; savor it with scones in their tea room. (☎6266 4377. Open daily 10am-4pm. Free self-guided tours and samplings.) Down the road, **The Huon Apple and Heritage Museum,** in Grove, is filled with memorabilia and technology from the apple industry. The 90-year-old peeling machine is the core of the exhibit, and you're invited to eat the remains. From March to June, 500 varieties of apples are on display. (☎6266 4345. Open Aug.-June daily 9am-5pm. $4.) This region of Tasmania is locally known for its cool-climate wines, many of which are available at the **Hartzview Vineyard and Wine Centre,** 10km south of Cygnet in Gardners Bay (via the B68 and C626). In addition to its own pinot noir and fruit wines, Hartzview sells those of smaller area vineyards without cellar-door sales of their own. (☎6295 1623. Open daily 9am-5pm. Tastings $2, refunded on purchase.)

**Hobart Coaches,** 21 Murray St, leaves **Hobart** for the Cygnet carpark. (☎6234 4077. 1hr., M-F 5:15pm, $7.) **Mary St** holds **Trust Bank** (☎6295 1682; open M-F 9am-noon and 1-5pm); the **library** (☎6295 1800; open Tu 10am-2pm, Th 10am-5pm, F 3-8pm), with **Internet** (30min. $5); and **post office** (open M-F 9am-5pm). **Postal code:** 7112.

The **▓Balfes Hill Huon Valley YHA & Backpackers,** 4 Sandhill Rd, Cradoc, 4.5km north of Cygnet, is a great place. The older building caters to eager workers willing to pick berries or prune orchards November to May. The hostel managers will help find employment and provide transportation ($10 per week or $1 per trip). The new building has comfortable bunks, clean bathrooms, kitchen, video lounge, ping-pong, billiards, laundry, and a phone. Phone ahead for pickup from the bus stop. (☎6295 1551. Twins $30, ensuite $36; ensuite family rooms $50. Non-YHA add $3.) Three **pubs** and the **Red Velvet Lounge** along Mary St provide the only options for eating out. The Red Velvet Lounge, 87 Mary St, is part art gallery, part wholefoods store, and part café. (☎6295 0466. Open daily 9am-6pm.) Of the three **supermarkets,** Value-Plus is open longest (open daily 7:30am-9:30pm).

## BRUNY ISLAND

Bruny was the first bit of land Abel Tasman glimpsed when he "discovered" Tasmania in 1642, and the island has seen more than its share of famous explorers since. Captain Cook and his understudy Captain Bligh (of *Mutiny Onboard H.M.S. Bounty* fame) both visited the island and believed it to be part of the mainland—they were proven wrong when D'Entrecasteaux sailed through the channel in 1792. Bruny once bustled with a great whaling industry, but timber and agriculture reign today. North Bruny is home to 1000-year-old frayed-looking trees called "blackboys;" and South Bruny houses the majority of the island's 500 locals and tourists. The island captures its visitors—families and adventurers alike—with dramatic coastal scenery, remnants of its exploratory past, and plenty of space to bushwalk, bike, paddle, and swim.

TASMANIA

⚡ **TRANSPORT. Ferries** (☎6272 3277) run roughly every hour between Kettering and **Bruny** (15min.; M-Sa 6:50am-6:30pm, F until 7:30pm, Su 8am-6:30pm; return fare for cars $18, motorcycles $11, bicycles $3, pedestrians free). **Hobart Coaches** leaves 21 Murray St in Hobart for the ferry terminal. (☎6234 4077. 1hr., M-F 4-5 per day, $6.) The Lumeah YHA also offers the **Little Island Bus Service,** with pickup and drop off to anywhere in **Hobart** or out to **Bruny.** (☎6293 1265. M, W, F mornings; $25 return, ferry trip included. By booking only.) The island has no public transportation, but a few bikes can be rented at the Lumeah YHA (see below). Bruny's roads are almost entirely gravel, and many rental car companies do not insure travelers.

🔢 **PRACTICAL INFORMATION.** The **Visitor Centre** is across the channel in **Kettering** by the ferry terminal. (☎6267 4494. Open daily 9am-5pm). Park passes to the two new national parks can be purchased here. The **Adventure Bay General Store,** 712 Adventure Bay Rd, has **petrol, eftpos,** and **groceries** (open daily 7:30am-9pm). The Bruny Island **Online Access Centre** has **Internet,** scanning, and fax service at the Bruny Island District School in Alonnah, between the oval and tennis court. (☎6293 2036. Open Tu 2-5:30pm, W 9am-noon, 1-4pm, and 6-9pm, Th 1-4:30pm, F 1-4pm and 6-9pm, Sa 1-4pm. 30min. $5.) The **post office** is at the **Alonnah General Store,** just off the B66 in Alonnah (open daily 7:30am-7pm). **Postal code:** 7150.

🍴🛏 **ACCOMMODATIONS AND FOOD.** South Bruny's **Lumeah YHA,** in Adventure Bay, offers spacious dorms, huge common areas, a brick fireplace, laundry, and BBQ. They loan fishing gear, run tours (half-day $30, by demand), provide bus service (see above), and arrange camel treks (30min. $15, 2½hr. with tea $45). Book ahead for meals, massages (1hr. $40), or ferry pickup ($10). (☎6293 1265. Closed June-Aug. Bike and kayak hire. Linen $2. Sites $10; dorms $15; doubles $42; family rooms $56.) The **Adventure Bay Holiday Villages,** at the end of the road in Adventure Bay, is decorated with bleached whale bones. (☎6293 1270. Coin-op showers. Laundry. Sites for 2 $10, powered $13; on-site vans for 2 $30; cabins for 2 $45.) At the start of the Penguin Island and Grass Point tracks, many of the island's protected lands offer free camping. **Cloudy Bay** on the southern part of the island and **Jetty Beach** near the lighthouse require parks passes. These and **Neck Beach** on the south end of the isthmus between North and South Bruny offer primitive sites with pit toilets, no water, and no firewood. Contact the ranger at the **Labillardiere State Reserve** (☎6298 3229) for more info.

The ▨**Hothouse Café,** 46 Adventure Bay Rd, 6km north of Adventure Bay, is a sheltered outdoor café with fantastic food, perfected by a panoramic view of the sea. (☎6293 1131. Open daily 10am-7:30pm. Gardens and Gumtree maze $3.)

📷🔦 **SIGHTS AND ACTIVITIES.** The ▨**Bligh Museum,** 880 Adventure Bay Rd, contains fascinating old maps, marine photos, and memorabilia concentrating on the region's infamous explorers, such as Cook, Bligh, Flinders, and D'Entrecasteaux. (☎6293 1117. Open M-Sa 10am-4pm. $4.) The **Cape Bruny Lighthouse,** built by convicts between 1836-1838, is 30km southwest of Adventure Bay. (☎6298 3114. Open daily 10am-4pm. Tours by arrangement $10, children $2.) Near the lighthouse, hike down the hills and through the coastal heath and coves of the **Labillardiere Reserve** (7hr.). From Sept.-Feb., fairy penguins and muttonbirds roost on the Neck of the island. Parks and Wildlife runs free nightly tours from the Neck at dusk during the summer. The island is also a haven for rare white wallabies, diverse birdlife, dolphins, seals, and migrating southern right whales. **Cloudy Bay** has some of the best surf in Tasmania. **Jetty Beach** offers more sheltered waters suitable for kids. The **Pine Log Bight Track** (7hr.) from Cloudy Bay beach to Tasman Head is mostly a 4WD track but includes some steep climbs with fantastic views. Heading south from Adventure Bay, turn right onto Lockleys Rd for 2.5km, then right again onto Resolution Rd to the Mavista Picnic Area, where you can walk to **Mavista Creek** (20min.). The easy walk continues up to **Mavista Falls** (2hr.), crossing the creek 12 times. The Falls are quite beautiful, but are home to lots of leeches.

TASMANIA

## FAR SOUTH: GEEVESTON AND GATEWAYS TO WILDERNESS

Below Huonville, the A6 roams south along D'Entrecasteaux Channel to the bottom of the world. About 25km down, **Geeveston** teeters on the edge of the southwest wilderness. In the last Ice Age, Aboriginals lived in the southwest's caves. Today, most of the region is protected as Hartz Mountains National Park, Southwest National Park, and Tasmanian Wilderness World Heritage Area. TassieLink (☎ (1300) 30 05 20) **buses** run from **Hobart** to **Dover** (1½hr., 1 per day M-F, $13), and Dec.-Feb. to **Lune River** (2½hr.; M, W, F; $20) and **Cockle Creek** (3¼hr.; M, W, F; $45).

The Geeveston **Visitor Information** is in the **Forest & Heritage Centre** on Church St. (☎ 6297 1836. Open daily 10am-4:30pm. Museum $4. **Internet** 30min. $2.) Church St has several **supermarkets** (open Su-Th 8:30am-6:30pm, F 8:30am-7:30pm); and a **post office** that's also a **bank** (☎ 6297 1102; open daily 9am-8pm). **Postal code:** 7116.

The **Geeveston Forest House,** at the end of Church St, has free laundry. (☎ 6297 1102. Singles and doubles $12.) **Lune River YHA,** 40km south of Geeveston, is "Australia's most southerly" hostel. (☎ 6298 3163. Pickup from Dover $5; bike hire $15 per day; canoes $10 per half-day; glow worm caves tour $30. Dorms $12.) The region has many **camping** options, with free sites at the **Tahune Forest Reserve,** 27km west of Geeveston; **Hastings Forest,** 13km west of Dover; and **Cockle Creek,** 25km south of Lune River. All are off of unsealed roads and offer pit toilets and drinking water. Cockle Creek also has a phone.

Even if you're not camping, follow the **Arve Road Forest Drive** (unsealed) from Geeveston to the Huon River to see native Huon pines, which take 500 years to mature and live about 2500 years. The easy **Huon Pines Loop Trail** (20min.) starts at the carpark past the Tahune Forest Reserve campground. Nearby, take the Arve Loop Rd to the "**Big Tree,**" an 87m, unbelievably wide swamp gum (or mountain ash). About 10km northwest of Lune River is the **Hastings Newdegate Cave,** dripping with dolomite formations. (☎ 6298 3209. Summer tours every hour 10am-6pm, in winter 11am-4pm. 1hr. $10, concessions $8; includes entry to the thermal springs.) The Lune River area is also known for fresh and saltwater fishing. The carpark past the free camping area in **Cockle Creek** marks the end of Australia's most southerly road. An easy walk (4hr. return) from the campground goes to South Cape Bay, the closest you can get to **Australia's southernmost tip** and neighboring Antarctica. The campground is also the endpoint of **South Coast Track** (85km). Most people hiking the full track fly into **Melaleuca** and walk back out 6-9 days later. Some combine it with the **Port Davey Track,** extending it another five days. For info on flights, which run about $100 per person one-way, contact **Par-Avion Wilderness Tours** (☎ 6248 5390), at the Cambridge Airport in Hobart, or **Tasair Wilderness Flights** (☎ 6248 5088). The area around Cockle Creek is part of the **Southwest National Park.** Park fees apply; passes available from the Geeveston Heritage Complex.

# DERWENT VALLEY AND THE SOUTHWEST

The Derwent River flows into Hobart from the northwest and empties into the Tasman Sea. From the coast, the A10 Hwy traces the river to its source in the forested interior wilderness, separating the south from the agricultural Midlands region above (see p. 505). To the south of the Derwent Valley, stretching to the Southern Ocean, lies the great expanse of Southwest National Park in which the vast Lakes Gordon and Pedder shine like diamonds in the rough. Some of Tasmania's greatest environmental debates have also taken place here. This area has few towns or services, but visitors enjoy many outdoor activities.

# NEW NORFOLK

A misty valley enfolds the small town of New Norfolk, 25km northwest of Hobart on the Derwent River. The climate is perfect for growing hops—regional cultivators harvest up to 45 tons per day. **Oast House,** on the Lyell Hwy before town, was once used to dry the harvest; now it's New Norfolk's most hopping tourist attraction with a hop museum, hop gallery, and hop-house café, but no hip-hop. (☎6261 1030. Open Sept.-Dec. W-Su 9:30am-5pm, Jan.-May daily 9:30am-5pm. $3.50.) Eleven kilometers west of New Norfolk, the **Salmon Ponds** and **Museum of Trout Fishing** constitute the oldest trout hatchery in the Southern Hemisphere. Fish feed will get those (w)hoppers hopping. (☎6261 1614. Open daily 9am-5pm. $5.)

TassieLink (☎(1300) 30 05 20) runs **buses** to: **Hobart** (40min.; Tu, Th, F, Su; $5); **Lake St. Clair** (2½hr.; Tu, Th, F, Su; $26); and **Queenstown** (4¾hr.; Tu, Th, F, Su; $32). The **Derwent Valley Information Centre** is on Circle St. (☎6261 0700. Open M-F 8:15am-5pm.) Believe it or not, inside the **police station,** 14 Bathurst St, is **free Internet access** (open M-F 9am-5pm). The **Bush Inn Hotel,** 49-51 Montagu St, north on the Lyell Hwy, includes full breakfast. (☎6261 2256. Singles $30; twins and doubles $50.) The **New Norfolk Esplanade Caravan Park,** on the river bank, has coin-op showers and laundry. (☎6261 1268. Key deposit $5. Crowded sites for 2 $8, powered $12.) Purity **supermarket** is on Charles St (open M-W, Sa 8am-6pm, Th-F 8am-9pm).

# MT. FIELD NATIONAL PARK

In Mt. Field, an hour from Hobart, summer visitors enjoy bushwalks and waterfalls, while winter visitors head for the slopes to downhill and cross-country ski. No bus company services the park or its ski fields during the winter. TassieLink (☎(1300) 30 05 20) runs **buses** Dec.-Feb. to: **Hobart** (1¼hr., 1 per day, $19); **Lake St. Clair** (2½hr., 1 per day, $25); and **Scott's Peak** (1¾hr.; Tu, Th, Sa mornings; $40). Tour companies lead trips from **Hobart. Bottom Bits Bus** offers well-led, full-day tours during the summer. (☎(1800) 77 71 03. $45.) **Closer to Nature** offers more expensive full-day tours year-round. (☎6288 1477. $100.) Rangers lead free walks, slide shows, and nighttime wildlife-watching trips during the summer. Maps and park passes are available at the entrance station. Continue 100m up the road to the **park shop** (☎6288 1526) for more park info, takeaway food, and souvenirs. The **Mt. Field Information Line** (☎6288 1319) has a recording on ski and road conditions.

The National Park Office administers three basic 6-person **cabins** near Lake Dobson with mattresses, a wood heater, firewood, and cold water. (☎6288 1149. $10 per person; min. $20 per night; book ahead.) The park shop also runs a **campground** near the park entrance. The self-register campsites are equipped with showers, bathrooms, BBQ, and laundry. Its grounds fill with pademelons, and the creek is home to platypi. (Sites $5 per person, powered $7.) Past the park on the B61 (Gordon River Rd), **Mt. Field YHA** provides basic beds. (☎6288 1369. Dorms $15. Linen $1. Laundry.) Food options are scarce; some get **groceries** in New Norfolk. In a pinch, the **pub** across from the YHA has counter meals (daily 6:30-7:30pm). West 12km in Maydena, Harry's **mini-market** closes at 9pm.

The park can be divided into two distinct areas. The lower slopes near the park entrance have picnic and BBQ facilities, a park shop, and easy walks to a trio of waterfalls and the tallest flowering plant in the world. **Russell Falls,** a paved walk (10min.) from the carpark through wet eucalypt forest, has long been the favorite destination. It's definitely worth continuing up along the steep gravel road to **Lake Dobson** (16km) through eucalypts, mixed forest, sub-alpine woodland, and alpine mosaic. The upper slopes offer a network of extended bushwalks amid glassy highland lakes. The easy **Pandani Grove Nature Walk** (1hr.) circles Lake Dobson and introduces unusual wildlife: pineapple grass, bright red scoparia, the endemic conifers, the pencil King Billy pines, and platypi.

TASMANIA

Though snow cover varies, skiers come to walk back in time, travelling up the slope by tow or making their own tracks in the backcountry. Without 4WD, Lake Dobson Road can only be accessed with 2WD and chains; the ski fields are a 40min. walk past the carpark. The ski kiosk rents skis and lift tickets.

## SOUTHWEST NATIONAL PARK AND THE GORDON RIVER DAM

The B61 Hwy, better known as the **Gordon River Rd,** continues through Maydena, winding 86km through the rugged mountains of Southwest National Park. The road passes through the settlement of **Strathgordon** (pop. 15), 12km before its abrupt end at the Gordon River Dam (about 1½hr.). **TassieLink** (☎(1300) 30 05 20) runs summer service between **Hobart** and **Scotts Peak** (3¼hr.; 1 per day Tu, Th, Sa; $47) via **Timbs Track** (2hr., $45), **Mt. Anne** (2¾hr., $45), and **Red Tape Track** (3hr., $45). The park is largely inaccessible by road, stretching south to Melaleuca and Cockle Creek to form the **South Coast Track** (see p. 482). The construction of the Gordon River Dam system brought condemnation from international environmental activists, who argued that the dams would destroy the region's wild beauty. But the dams were built anyway in the early 1970s, and today the power station is the largest in Tasmania's—it alone could support Hobart's power usage for a day.

Carved out of the Tasmanian Wilderness World Heritage Area, the unnatural Lakes Gordon and Pedder are captivating. **Hydro's Visitor Centre,** on a ledge above the dam, has brochures on the dam's construction and history. Take 196 steps down to the top of the dam. Tours go through the 1km access tunnel into the power station and provide some pro-power fodder to the conservation debate (☎6280 1134. Open daily Nov.-Apr. 10am-5pm; May-Oct. 11am-3pm. Tours 1hr. Nov.-Apr. daily 10am, 2pm; May-Oct. 11am; $5.) **Lake Pedder** can be viewed from both the main road and the entirely unsealed **Scotts Peak Rd.** This difficult road forks off of the Gordon River Rd 28km into the park at Frodshams Pass, ending 36km later at the Huon Campground. Just 2.5km into Scotts Peak Rd is the short and sweet **Creepy Crawly Nature Trail** (20min.). Longer walks go from Timbs Track to the **Florentine River** (easy rainforest walk; 4hr.), the **Eliza Plateau** (6hr.; difficult ridge climb to Mt. Eliza), and Lake Judd (unmarked track with difficult river crossings; 8hr.). Picnic and camp sites at the **Huon Campground** grant easy access to the Arthur Plains and Port Davey walking tracks. Other sites are at **Edgar Dam,** 8km before the end of Scotts Peak Rd, and **Teds Beach,** east of Strathgordon. Strathgordon's **Lake Pedder Motor Inn** is the only other park accommodation. (☎6280 1166. Singles $55-80; twins and doubles $65-90.) **Trout fishing** is encouraged in Lake Gordon and Lake Pedder from August to April. (license required). For park info, contact the entrance station (☎6288 2258), or rangers at Mt. Field (☎6288 1141).

# THE WESTERN WILDERNESS

At the upper end of the Derwent Valley, the A10 Hwy crosses the Derwent Bridge and winds past Lake St. Clair and the Franklin River toward Tasmania's west coast. Much of the interior has been set aside to preserve the temperate rainforest. The western coastline of Tasmania is among the most remote, unsettled areas in Australia. Twenty-thousand kilometers of Indian Ocean separate the shore from the nearest landmass and periodically send violent storms crashing in.

The first settlements in the area supported themselves by exploiting timber. Soon thereafter, prospectors began searching the hills and creeks for gold, hoping to strike it rich like their Victorian comrades. Alas, they never reached the end of the rainbow—many hapless diggers departed bankrupt. Eventually, explorers discovered mountains of tin, silver, and copper just beneath the surface. When the lode ran out, the end was at hand for many of the dilapidated mining communities. The logging industry also fell on harder days, which was good news for the forest; today, vast tracts of the West are as wild and pristine as they were when the first European settlers arrived.

TASMANIA

# CRADLE MOUNTAIN

If you haven't seen a picture of mystic Cradle Mountain rising above quiet Lake Dove, you must not be in Tasmania. The mountain is Tassie's most famous landmark, visited by hundreds of thousands of wilderness lovers every year. The area is a complex glacial fabric of creeks and crags that shelter the state's unique jewels: sweet-sapped cider-gum woodlands, rainforest of King Billy and celery-top pine, and carpets of cushion plants. Supposedly, long-extinct species including the freshwater crayfish, mountain shrimp, and velvet worm have been found alive and kicking around Cradle Mountain. *Nothofagus gunnii*, the state's only native deciduous tree, thrives along the mountain's skirt, and thousands throng in late April and May to see the fiery colors of its leaves. Naturalist Gustav Weindorfer called Cradle Mountain the place "where there is no time and nothing matters."

**TRANSPORT. Maxwell's Coach and Taxi Service** (☎6492 1431) makes frequent, unscheduled runs between the campground, the visitors center ($2), and Dove Lake ($8), and offers 24hr. service throughout the northwest region (see **Lake St. Clair,** p. 488; book ahead). **TassieLink** (☎(1300) 30 05 20) departs Tu, Th, Sa from **Cradle Mountain Lodge** and the **Cradle Campground** for **Devonport** (1½hr., $24); **Launceston** (3hr., $37); and **Strahan** (3¾hr., $24).

**PRACTICAL INFORMATION.** Cradle Valley is the northern trailhead for the **Overland Track,** Tasmania's most prominent walk, traversing the length of the **Cradle Mountain-Lake St. Clair National Park** (see **Overland Track,** p. 489). The national park is also the northernmost end of the **Tasmanian Wilderness World Heritage Area.** Park fees apply. The **Visitors Centre,** just past the park entrance, features displays with helpful layouts of the walking tracks and a public telephone. (☎6492 1110. Open daily 8am-6pm, winter 8am-5pm.) A 7.5km gravel road connects the visitors center to **Waldheim** and **Dove Lake.**

**ACCOMMODATIONS AND FOOD.** In peak season, accommodations are booked fast, so call ahead. On the entrance road, 2km outside the park, the **Cradle Mountain Tourist Park** provides tent sites, humorously basic Alpine huts (intended for campers when it's raining), bunk rooms, self-contained cabins, and heaps of amenities. There's an unequipped cooking shelter with BBQ and a kitchen for hostelers. (☎6492 1395. Reception daily 8am-8pm. Sites $5-8 per person; powered $8-10; 3-bed Alpine huts $10-14; bunks $14-20; cabins for 2 $65-80. YHA, VIP.) The visitors center runs the eight **Waldheim Cabins,** 5.5km inside the park, which can bunk up to 8 people each. The Overland Track begins right outside. Heating, basic kitchen, showers, composting toilets, and limited generated power for lighting are provided. (6-bunk cabins $65 for up to 3; each extra person $10-19.) **Bring your own food**—there is no produce at Cradle Mountain. The **Cradle Mountain Lodge General Store**, right outside the park, sells basic supplies at inflated prices. (Open M-F 9am-5pm, Sa-Su noon-4pm, extended summer hours.)

**HIKING.** The Cradle Mountain Area has a web of tracks. Unfortunately, the free park brochure map is of little use for all but the **Dove Lake Circuit** (2hr.). At least it's the most popular and environmentally friendly—a beautiful, mostly boardwalked, lakeside track through old-growth forest. The map for sale at the visitors center ($4) is good for all other day hikes. The first stage of the **Overland Track** and its side tracks offer more arduous climbs: the hike up to **Marions Lookout** (1223m) begins along the Dove Lake track, continues steeply to the summit, and returns via Wombat Pool and Lake Lilla (2-3hr.); the ascent of Cradle Mountain (1545m) is a difficult hike from Waldheim or Dove Lake past Marions Lookout, involving some boulder climbing toward the summit (6hr.). Registration is advised for any walks longer than 2hr. According to statistics, it rains 275 days a year, is cloudless on only 32, and can snow at any time—dress accordingly. Tracks around the visitors center and the Cradle Mountain Lodge include a rainforest walk and

TASMANIA

**MARSUPIALS FROM HELL** It doesn't spin around faster than you can see it, and it's rarely seen in convict stripes. Still, the Tasmanian devil is a remarkable creature. These marsupials are rarely more than 45cm high and aren't built for speed, being far more adept at climbing than at running. Their jet-black coats are occasionally marked with white bands or spots, but the maw is the most striking feature, full of jagged teeth and usually open wide. The powerful jaws can crush bones up to 7.5cm in diameter and allow the devil to eat almost anything. Devils are entirely carnivorous, hunting small mammals as well as scavenging carrion. Once common throughout Australia, they were driven off the mainland by dingoes; however, they thrive in Tasmania to the point of being considered a pest in some areas. While devils' attacks on humans are limited to the occasional theft of souls, they do sometimes kill farm animals. They are also extremely noisy, particularly when feeding, and are very irritating when they take up residence under people's houses. Despite their abundance, you won't often see the nocturnal, secretive critters in the wild; your best hope for spotting one is to try a wildlife park. For info on more Aussie animals, see p. 27.

**Pencil Pine Falls** (10min.). The lodge organizes a number of **activities:** walking tours (2½-3hr., $17), canoe trips (2½hr., $38), fly fishing (2½hr., $40), horse-riding (1hr., $31), abseiling (3hr., $35), and bike hire (half-day $15; full-day $20; deposit $200).

## STRAHAN

Strahan is the only coastal community of any size between Hazard Bay in the northwest and Recherche Bay south of Hobart. The town itself has few attractions; it is primarily a gateway to the Franklin-Gordon Wild Rivers National Park World Heritage Area and the entire southwest wilderness. Franklin-Gordon is accessible only by bushwalking, boat, or plane.

**▐ TRANSPORT.** TassieLink (☎(1300) 30 05 20) runs **buses** through **Queenstown** (1hr., $6) to: **Hobart** (6hr.; Th, Th, F, Su; $42) via **Lake St. Clair** (3hr., $23); **Devonport** (5½hr., $36); and **Launceston** (7hr.; Tu, Th, Sa; $49) via **Cradle Mt.** (45min., $24).

**▐ PRACTICAL INFORMATION.** The **Strahan Visitors Centre,** on the Esplanade, is run by a theater company, an unlikely but tremendously successful association. Sailing into its ninth year and still going strong, the local play *The Ship That Never Was*, humorously explores the last great escape from Sarah Island's Prison. (☎6471 7622. Open daily Nov.-Apr. 10am-8pm; May-Oct. 10am-6pm. Shows daily at 5:30pm, Jan. also 8:30pm; $10.) The **Parks and Wildlife Office,** in the historic customs house on the Esplanade, sells passes to national parks. (☎6471 7122. Open M-F 9am-noon and 1-5pm.) The customs house also has **Internet** access. (☎6471 7788. Open Tu-Th 3-8pm, F-Sa 10am-3pm. 30min. $5.) **Police:** on Beach St (☎6471 8000). **Post office:** at the Customs House (open M-F 9am-5:30pm). **Postal code:** 7468.

**▐▐ ACCOMMODATIONS AND FOOD.** The **Strahan YHA,** 43 Harvey St, one block inland, has kitchens and a resident platypus—don't mix the two. Follow the Esplanade until a path diverges to the caravan park, then take the path (10min.) across the street through cabins to arrive at the rear of the YHA. (☎6471 7255; strahancentral@trump.net.au. Minimal reception hours daily 4-8pm; call transferred to mobile phone afterhours. Dorms $15; twins $36.) The basic **Strahan Caravan Tourist Park** is at the far end of town. (☎6471 7239. Reception daily 8am-7pm. Sites for 2 $12, powered $15, on-site vans for 2 $35, ensuite cabins $45-68.) Standard chippers are everywhere. **Strahan Central** is a posh café and crafts store on the corner of Herald St and the Esplanade. (☎6471 7612. Open M-Th 8:30am-8pm, F 8:30am-430pm, Sa 10am-8pm, Su 10am-7:30pm. Meals $7-13.) A Riteway **supermarket** is also at the far end of the Esplanade (open daily 7:15am-7:30pm).

TASMANIA

**⛰️🏞️ SIGHTS AND ACTIVITIES.** The track to **Hogarth Falls** (40min. return) a few hundred meters from central Strahan, is rampant with wildlife. Accessed through **People's Park,** the track follows **Botanical Creek,** home to aquatic critters, including the elusive platypus. North of town at the end of Harvey Rd, **Ocean Beach** stretches from Macquarie Head in the south to Trial Harbour over 30km north. It's the longest beach in Tasmania with brooding surf and windy dunes; swimming is unsafe. In late Sept., thousands of **mutton-birds** descend on the beach after flying 15,000km from their Arctic summer homes and go about laying their *one* egg of the season. Rangers ask that you observe from the wooden platform to reduce erosion.

From 1822 until 1833, **Sarah Island** was the feared penal colony for recidivist offenders. One of the darkest pits in the British penal system, its convicts were forced to wade chest-deep in the harbor's freezing water pushing giant Huon pine logs. Today, all of Sarah Island's buildings have been reduced to sign-posted ruins.

Most Strahan visitors choose to cruise, sail, speedboat, or fly into the World Heritage Area. **World Heritage Cruises,** on the Esplanade, runs the least expensive trips through the Harbour and up the Gordon River, including passage through Hells Gate, 1hr. at Sarah Island, and 30min. at Heritage Landing to admire a 2,000 year-old Huon pine. (☎6471 7174. 5½hr.; departs daily 9am; $47, children $21; YHA discount; smorgasbord $9.) **West Coast Yacht Charters,** on the Esplanade (☎6471 7422), offers trips to **Sir John Falls, Heritage Landing,** and other sites. **Wilderness Air** seaplanes expensively flies to Sir John Falls, but ventures far beyond cruise-accessible territory. (☎6471 7280. 1½hr., $125.) Paddle the river yourself in a kayak or canoe from **Hells Gates Wilderness Tours,** on Risby Cove (☎6471 7576).

South of Strahan 12km along Lowanna Rd, encasing King River, lies the **Teepookana Forest Reserve,** which suffered the brunt of Queenstown mining. The forest viewing tower explains Huon pine logging (3hr. moderate return walk from **Iron Bridge**). Because the reconstructed Railway (see **Queenstown**) will go through the forest, logistics about access have not been clarified. Contact the visitors center for more info, or try **Forestry Tasmania,** on the Esplanade. (☎6471 7176. Open M-F 9am-noon and 1-5pm.) Wooden crafts are available at shops throughout town, but **Tut's Whittle Wonders,** on Gaffney St, has the most eccentric collection. (☎6471 7329. Admission $1.50.) Some of Teepookana's Huon pine timber is available at the **Huon Pine Sawmill,** on the Esplanade. (☎6471 7244. Open daily 8:30am-5pm.)

## QUEENSTOWN

In 1883, Mick and Bill McDonough, also mysteriously known as the Cooney Brothers, discovered a large outcropping of copper, later termed the Iron Blow (they initially thought they'd struck iron). The Blow was first mined in hope of finding gold, though each ton of rock yielded just two ounces of the precious metal. The **Mount Lyell Gold Mining Company** formed in 1888, but redirected its efforts toward copper in 1891, only after millions of pounds of copper had already slipped away. The company built a smelter to process the copper ore on-site, wreaking environmental havoc. Nearly every large tree in the surrounding hills was felled to feed the smelter, while the young growth was killed by the thick yellow sulphur haze released during the pyritic processing, and the exposed topsoil was washed into the Queen River by heavy rainfall. The town (pop. 2200 and falling) currently resembles lunar wasteland in the midst of dense vegetation.

The **Mt. Lyell Mine** still chugs along, with tours exploring the working areas. All tours leave from the office at 1 Driffield St (☎6471 2388). Daily surface tours visit the old open-cut mines, the working copper mine, and other sites (1hr.; daily Sept.-May 9:15am and 4:30pm, June-Oct. 9:15am and 4pm; $12). Underground tours are more thorough and you don a full miner's get-up (2½hr, $50; book ahead). The old Iron Blow open-cut mine, just off the Lyell Hwy near **Gomanston,** offers broad views of surrounding barren hills and of the water-filled crater. The **Queenstown Scenic Chairlift,** 7 Penghana Rd, and the viewing platform at the top provide a heightened perspective. (☎6471 2338. Open daily morning-sunset. $7, children $5.) Today's hot issue is the **ABT Wilderness Railway Restoration Project.** Construction is underway laying new tracks in the same old spots between Queenstown and Strahan. Contact the chairlift staff or the Mt. Lyell Mine office for updated information.

The road to Queenstown makes for white-knuckled driving (allow 45min. to Strahan and 1½hr. to Derwent Bridge). **TassieLink** (☎(1300) 30 05 20) runs to: **Strahan** (45min., 1-2 per day, $6); **Hobart** (4¾hr.; Tu, Th, F, Su; $37) via **Lake St. Clair** (1¾hr., $18); **Launceston** (5¼hr.; Tu, Th, Sa; $44) via **Cradle Mt.** (3hr., $18); and **Devonport** (4hr., $31). The **Mt. Lyell Mine Office** has info (see below). **Parks and Wildlife** (☎6471 2511) is represented by **Centrelink/Service Tasmania,** 34 Orr St, next to the post office. (☎(1300) 36 67 73. Open M-F 9am-5pm. Free **Internet.**) **Trust Bank,** at Orr and Sticht St, has no-fee currency change (open M-F 9am-5pm). **Police:** 2 Sticht St (☎6471 3020). **Post office:** 32 Orr St (open M-F 9am-5pm). **Postal code:** 7467.

The **Empire Hotel,** 2 Orr St, retains some of the glory of its heyday as a miners' pub. (☎6471 1699. Singles $20; twins and doubles $35; ensuite $45. Meals $9-14.) **Queenstown Cabin and Tourist Park,** 17 Grafton St, is across the river, 2km from the town center. (☎6471 1332. Sites $8, extra person $4; powered $10, $5; backpacker beds $20, $5; on-site caravans $35, $5; self-contained cabins for 2 $55, $7.)

# FRANKLIN-GORDON WILD RIVERS NATIONAL PARK

After the completion of the Gordon River Dam project in the early 1980s, Hydro proposed a new dam along the Gordon, just below its intersection with the Franklin. This proposal sparked environmental activists to create the Wilderness Society. After eight years, massive river blockades, and over 1200 civilian arrests, the conservationists were eventually successful, and the World Heritage Bill came into being. Today, **Lyell Hwy** (A10) runs 86km between Queenstown and the Derwent Bridge, through the Franklin-Gordon Wild Rivers National Park at the heart of the **Tasmanian Wilderness World Heritage Area,** which is otherwise roadless for endless kilometers to the north and south. To use any of the Park's facilities, purchase a National Parks Pass and get a park brochure itemizing points of interest along the highway, before leaving Lake St. Clair or Queenstown.

Three walks in particular stand out. The 10min. **Nelson Falls Nature Trail,** hidden in wet rainforest 25km east of Queenstown, leads to a lovely cataract. **Donaghys Hill Lookout,** 50km east of Queenstown, should not be missed. The 40min. return track holds mind-blowing views of the Franklin River Valley and **Frenchman's Cap** (1443m), its principal peak (3- to 5-day return hike to the top). The **Franklin River Nature Trail,** 60km east of Queenstown, is a well-maintained 20min. circuit through rainforest. Between Queenstown and Nelson Falls, **Lake Burby** has **swimming, boating, trout fishing,** and **camping** surrounded by mountains (camping $5; no showers or laundry). Between Nelson Falls and Donaghys Hill, the **Collingwood River** also has some basic **camping** with fireplaces and picnic facilities (free). Roadside lookouts at **Surprise Valley** and **King William Saddle** (67km and 70km east of Queenstown, respectively) offer views of the eastern side of the wilderness area. The saddle marks a major divide of Tasmania. To the east lie dry plains and highlands, while to the west a 2.5m annual rainfall flows into the Franklin-Gordon rivers, through wet rainforest, and out to Macquarie Harbour.

# LAKE ST. CLAIR

Half of the headline act of the **Cradle Mountain-Lake St. Clair National Park,** Lake St. Clair is Australia's deepest lake as well as the source of the Derwent River. Its Aboriginal name is Leeawuleena ("sleeping water"), a serene juxtaposition of mountain, wood, and water. The lake anchors the southern end of the famous **Overland Track** (see below) with Cradle Mountain at its northern terminus. There are also a number of day hikes and a few family-friendly nature trails near the lake.

**Lake cruises** with commentary run the length of the lake from the Cynthia Bay jetty (daily at 9am, 12:30, and 3pm; stopping at Echo Point $12, and Narcissus Bay $15). A return cruise is also available (1½hr.; $20, children $15; book ahead at the tourist office). **Walking tracks** radiate from **Watersmeet,** 20min. from Cynthia Bay. **Woodlands Nature Walk** and **Platypus Bay Trail** make an easy, enjoyable loop through the woods to the water (1½-2hr.). Longer hikes head west to the sub-alpine forests of **Forgotten** and **Shadow Lakes** (3-4hr.) alongside waratah (flowering Nov.-Dec.); over the ridge, you can tackle steep, weather-beaten **Mt. Rufus** (7hr. return). If you take the ferry out in the morning, the lakeside hike to Cynthia Bay from Narcissus Bay amid rainforest, tea-tree, and buttongrass takes 5hr.; it's 3hr. from Echo Point.

TassieLink (☎(1300) 30 05 20) **buses** depart from **Derwent Bridge Wilderness Hotel** and the visitors center for: **Hobart** (2¾hr.; summer daily, winter Tu, Th, F, Su; $29); and **Launceston** (Direct 3½hr.; in summer M, W, F; $45. With connections 7½hr.; year-round on Tu, Th; $61) via **Queenstown** (1½hr., $19), **Cradle Mountain** (4½hr., $35), and **Devonport** (6hr., $48). Maxwell's Coach and Taxi Service (☎6492 1431) operates a small, **24hr. charter service** in the Cradle Mountain-Lake St. Clair region to: **Hobart** (3hr., $65); **Derwent Bridge** (10min., $6); **Frenchman's Cap** (30min., $15); and **Queenstown** (1¾hr., $35). The **visitors center** is at **Cynthia Bay,** at the southern end of the lake, accessible via a 5km access road that leaves the Lyell Hwy just west of Derwent Bridge. **Register** here for any extended walks, especially the Overland Track. (☎6289 1172. Open daily 8am-5pm; late Dec.-Feb. 8am-7pm). Next door, the **Lakeside St. Clair** is a privately owned tourist information center, restaurant, and booking agency. (☎6289 1137. Open daily 9am-8pm. Fishing gear $15 per day; canoe 2hr. $20; bike half-day $25.)

The park has **free camping** sites within the entrance with walking access only and pit toilets. The closest camping is a 10min. walk from Cynthia Bay toward Watersmeet; other sites are located at **Shadow Lake, Echo Point,** and **Narcissus Bay. Lakeside St. Clair** has several accommodations just outside the park entrance with coin-op showers, a pay phone, and a kitchen with a wood-fire stove (sites $5 per person, powered for 2 $12; doona $5; electrically-heated backpacker bunks $20). Opposite the Lake St. Clair access road on the Lyell Hwy is the barn-sized **Derwent Bridge Wilderness Hotel.** Backpacker rooms are in the cramped, modular units detached from the main hotel building. (☎6289 1144. Singles and doubles $20.) The hotel serves plain meals at reasonable prices (meals noon-2pm and 6-8pm).

**COLD KILLS.** Many people come to Tasmania to hike the endless, untamed wilderness. Make no mistake: Tasmania's wilderness is still wild and can kill you. The greatest hazard in the wilderness is the unruly weather that can shift from zephyr to gale in a heartbeat. Even in the summer, when the weather is hot, carry warm and waterproof clothing to prevent hypothermia, a lowering of the body's core temperature that can be fatal. Dehydration is also a common cause of hypothermia, so take care to stay hydrated. The best treatment for hypothermia is preparation: take the time to plan your trip. Do not attempt bushwalks without the proper equipment and experience. Ask locals about what conditions to expect. Wear wool or fiber pile clothing, including gloves and a hat. Wet cotton, especially denim, is deadly. For more info on treating hypothermia, see **Essentials,** p. 45. The Parks and Wildlife Service can advise on gear.

## THE OVERLAND TRACK

Connecting **Cradle Mountain** and **Lake St. Clair** through 80km of World Heritage Wilderness, the Overland Track is Australia's most famous trail. Every year, approximately 8000 attempt the track, most taking 5-8 days to complete it, depending on the number of side trips along the way. Purists contend that the track has become a congested highway, but its grandeur cannot be denied. The ascent of the state's tallest peak, **Mt. Ossa** (1617m), makes a good day-long side trip. The weather is fickle and will undoubtedly soak some portion of your journey.

The heavy traffic is having a disastrous impact on the path's fragile alpine ecosystems, so practicing minimum-impact bushwalking is crucial. Stay on the track, spread out when there is no track, walk on rocks, wear lightweight walking boots, rotate campsites, and use fuel stoves only. A *Bushwalking Code* brochure is available at the normal brochure bevvies. The track huts fill easily, so hikers must

**TASMANIA**

carry tents. If you are planning to walk the track, write to request an information kit at **Parks and Wildlife Service.** (☎6492 1110; fax 6492 1120. Cradle Mountain Visitor Centre, P.O. Box 20, Sheffield TAS 7306.) A copy of the Cradle Mountain-Lake St. Clair National **Park Map** ($9) is essential. The track itself can be undertaken from either the Cradle Mountain end (see p. 485) or Lake St. Clair (see p. 488), but most opt for Cradle Mountain and the slight downhill advantage of heading toward Lake St. Clair. The national park permit costs $12.

# THE NORTHWEST

The ferry brings most Tasmanian visitors to the Northwest first, and after a week hiking the Overland Track and two more along the Franklin River, many have a hard time leaving. World Heritage wilderness is the big draw, punctuated by seaports on the northwest coast and mining towns on the western highways. As an Aboriginal homeland, a fierce wilderness, an ecotourism jackpot, a mining motherlode, and a land of colonial convict myth-memory, the Northwest sees the currents that dominate Tasmania's identity play out their drama in the starkest relief.

# DEVONPORT

Many people come to Tasmania in search of untouched wildlands, unspoiled rivers, and unending mountains. Many people also arrive in Devonport, which is a bit of a shock: a grim waterfront, dominated by a cluster of huge gray silos. Still, the city is a very useful gateway to the rest of the state.

## ▰ TRANSPORT

**Flights:** The **airport** is 6km east of the city center on the Bass Hwy. Ansett-affiliated **Kendell** (☎13 13 00) and Qantas-affiliated **Southern Australia** (☎13 13 13) operate flights to **Melbourne** (1hr., 3-4 per day, $115-205). **Fox Coaches** shuttle meets all flights and delivers passengers to town. (☎(0418) 14 26 92. $5; book ahead.)

**Ferries:** The **Spirit of Tasmania** departs **Melbourne** (14½hr.; M, W, F 6pm; $119-152, cars $30-40, bikes $20-25); the return departs **Devonport** (Tu, Th, Sa 6pm). Dinner, breakfast, and accommodation are provided. Book ahead at the Visitors Centre or dial ☎13 20 10. A free **shuttle** meets ships and services to the town center.

**Buses: Redline Coaches,** 9 Edward St (☎(1300) 36 00 00), runs daily **buses to: Hobart** (5hr., $33); **Launceston** (1¼hr., $14); and **Stanley** (2hr., $18) or **Wynward** (1hr., $10) via **Burnie** (40min., $8). **TassieLink** (☎(1300) 30 05 20) buses leave the Visitor Centre for: **Cradle Mountain Lodge** (1½hr., $25); and **Strahan** (6¼hr., $36) via **Queenstown** (5hr., $31).

**Public Transportation: Mersey Link** (☎(1300) 36 75 90) buses depart from the Rooke St Mall, running M-F 7:30am-6pm, Sa 10am-5pm. Fares $1.20-3.10.

**Car Rental:** Major companies with counters at the airport and ferry terminals include **Hertz** (☎6424 1013; open daily 8am-6pm; also at 26 Oldaker St;) and **Thrifty** (☎6427 9119; open daily 8am-5:30pm; $50-55 per day; age 21-24 $15 surcharge; also across from the ferry at the Esplanade). Smaller firms are often cheaper; try **Advance** (☎6424 8885; open daily 9am-5pm; at airport and 156 William St.); or **Rent a Bug**, 5 Murray St (☎6427 9034; open M-F 8:30am-5:30pm, Sa 8:30am-noon; rents to those under 21).

**Automobile Club: Royal Automobile Club of Tasmania (RACT),** 5 Steele St (☎6421 1933, 24hr. ☎13 11 11). Open M-F 8:45am-5pm.

## ✴ ORIENTATION

The port of Devonport is the mouth of the **Mersey River,** and the ferry terminal is on its eastern bank. Devonport is bounded to the west by the **Don River** and to the south by the **Bass Hwy** (Hwy 1), which offers the only bridge across the Mersey. The city center lies on the western bank, with **Formby St** at the river's edge, the

TASMANIA

**Rooke St Mall** one block inland, each intersected by **Best St** and **Stewart St** running away from the river; most of the essentials lie within a block of these four streets. North of this center square, Formby St leads to **Mersey Bluff** and **Bluff Beach** at the western head of the river. The Bass Hwy heads west to **Burnie** (46km) and southeast to **Launceston** (97km) and **Hobart** (300km) cutting through **Deloraine** (45km). Drive to **Cradle Mountain** through Spreyton and Sheffield on the B14 (1½hr.).

# 🛈 PRACTICAL INFORMATION

**Tourist Information: Tasmanian Travel and Information Centre,** 92 Formby Rd (☎6424 4466), around the corner from McDonald's, can book accommodations and transport. Open M-F 9am-5pm. **The Backpackers' Barn,** 10-12 Edward St (☎6424 3628; www.tasweb.com.au/backpack/index.htm), specializes in orienting prospective bushwalkers, with locker storage ($1 per day, weekly $5) and equipment sale or hire (tents $7 per day, sleeping bags and packs $5 per day). Open M-F 9am-6pm, Sa 9am-noon.

**Currency Exchange: Commonwealth Bank,** 20 Rooke St (☎6424 1416). Open M-Th 9:30am-4pm, F 9:30am-5pm. **ATMs** lie on Rooke St Mall between Best and Steele St.

**Library:** 21 Oldaker St (☎6424 4255). Open M-Tu 9:30am-5:30pm, W-Th 9:30am-6pm, F 9:30am-9pm, Sa 9:30am-12:30pm. **Internet access** 30min. $5.

**Police:** 17 Oldaker St (☎6421 7511).

**Post Office:** 88 Formby Rd (☎6424 5501). Open M-F 9am-5pm. **Postal Code:** 7310.

**Phone Code:** 03.

# 🛏 ACCOMMODATIONS

**Formby Rd Hostel,** 16 Formby Rd (☎6423 6563). A half-kilometer south of the city center. This brick Victorian house is the new hostel in town, featuring a lovely second-floor porch facing the river, roomy common spaces, and a clean kitchen. Linen provided. Laundry. Reception daily 8-10am and 5-7:30pm. Dorms $11; doubles $30. Cash only.

**Tasman House Backpackers,** 169 Steele St (☎6423 2335; fax 6423 2340). Take Mersey Link bus #20 from Rooke St to stop 173, across from the hostel. Or, from Formby Rd on the river, go west along Steele St, past the sign and then around the block to reach the entrance—left on Lovett St and a quick left on Tasman St. Gigantic common spaces, ping-pong table, and billiards. Free city center pickup; $3 ferry shuttle. Free storage. Laundry. Internet 1hr. $5. Reception daily 8am-10pm. Dorms $10; twins $12; doubles $28, ensuite $35. VIP. **Tasman Bush Tours** operates out of the house, with day-trips from $48, and 6-day Overland Track trips from $580.

**Molly Malone's Irish Pub,** 34 Best St (☎6424 1898). Closest to the city center. Rooms have sink and heater. Well-stocked kitchen and lounge. Downstairs pub's weekend live music carries upstairs. No laundry or parking. Key deposit $10. Check-in at the pub or the Backpackers Barn (see **Practical Information,** above). Dorms $13; doubles $50. 3-night max. Cash only.

**Mersey Bluff Caravan Park,** Bluff Rd (☎6424 8655). On Mersey Bluff beach, 2km from the city center. Sites $7, powered $16; on-site caravans $42; cabins $52.

# 🎬🎵 FOOD AND ENTERTAINMENT

The **Rooke St Mall** overflows with standard chippers, counter meals, and fast food. **The Kitchen,** 2A Stewart St, makes you feel right at home. (☎6424 1129. Open M-F 8:30am-5pm.) **Renusha's Indian Restaurant,** 153 Rooke St, near the corner of Oldaker St, will spice up your diet. (☎6424 2293. Open M-Th 5:30-9:30pm, F-Sa 5:30-11pm, Su 5:30-8:30pm. Takeaway $10-12; eat-in $13-17 with $15 min. charge.) Coles **supermarket** is on Formby and Best St (open M-W 8am-6pm, Th-F 8am-9pm, Sa 8am-6pm). At night, **Spurs,** 18-22 King St, has a country-western American theme, video games, and pool tables that attract a young, casual crowd. (☎6424 7851. Open W-F, Su 4pm-1:30am; Sa 5pm-1:30am. Live music F-Sa.) Next door, the **Warehouse** is a dance club (open F-Sa 10:30pm-3am; cover $5-6).

**TASMANIA**

## ⚑ SIGHTS

**Tiagarra Aboriginal Cultural Centre and Museum,** a 30min. walk from the city center to Mersey Bluff near the lighthouse, is an interpretive center that explores 40,000 years of Tasmanian Aboriginal history. The modern-day souvenir shop sells mainland Aboriginal art and instruments. (☎6424 8250. Open daily 9am-5pm. $3.) A 15min. walk around the bluffs leads to controversial **rock engravings**—a few have been stolen, and of those remaining, some skeptics say wind and rain are the true artisans. The **Devonport Maritime Museum,** on Gloucester Ave off Bluff Rd, preserves local history with old photographs, model boats, and a good archive of family history. (☎6424 8250. Open Apr.-Sept. Tu-Su 10am-4pm, Oct.-Mar. Tu-Su 10am-4:30pm. $3.) An old-fashioned steam train runs to Coles Beach from the museum at Don River Railway, on Forth Rd, 3km west in Don. (☎6424 6335. 30min. return; departs daily on the hr. 10am-4pm. $7, children $4, family $18.)

## ⚑ DAYTRIPS FROM DEVONPORT

The **Leven Canyon Reserve,** about 60km southwest of the city near Nietta, has a lookout with stunning views of Leven Gorge. To get there, take the Bass Hwy west, then the B15 south to Nietta, then C128 to the Canyon. A bit to the north of the canyon via C125 lie the **Gunns Plains Caves,** with a creek that houses platypi and freshwater crayfish in addition to the underground wonders. (☎6429 1388. Tours daily on the hour 10am-4pm. $8, children $4).

The **Aspestos Range National Park,** including Bakers Beach, is a small coastal heathland reserve 40km east of Devonport, popular for swimming, fishing, walking tracks, and abundant wildlife. The park is accessible by car only via three gravel roads. From Devonport take the C740, which heads north from the B71 between Devonport and Exeter. Register to camp at **Springlawn,** just past the park entrance. (Ranger ☎6428 6277. Park fees apply.) Sites have flush toilets, BBQ, tables, water, and a public telephone. Two more scenic camping areas are 3km farther down the road on the beach by **Griffiths Point** and **Bakers Point,** and have pit toilets, fireplaces, tables, and water (sites $4, family $10; firewood included). The easy **Springlawn Nature Walk** (45min.) passes through scrub and lagoons past wallabies and pademelons (their smaller relatives). The track continues up to **Archers Knob** for a view of the surrounding hills and coastline (2hr. return; moderate).

## DELORAINE AND SURROUNDS

In the foothills of the western Tiers, huddled in the agricultural Meander Valley between Devonport and Launceston, Deloraine functions as a perfect base for exploring the World Heritage Wilderness to the southwest.

**🖥 TRANSPORT AND PRACTICAL INFORMATION. Redline** (☎(1300) 36 00 00) runs out of Deloraine Video Library, 29 W. Church St (☎6362 2143) with daily **coaches** to: **Burnie** (1¾hr., $15); **Devonport** (1hr., $10); and **Launceston** (45min., $7). **TassieLink** (☎(1300) 30 05 20) coaches stop at Sullivan's Restaurant by arrangement only en route to **Cradle Visitor Centre** (2½hr.; Apr.-Nov. Tu, Th, Sa; Dec.-Mar. daily; $31); and **Lake St. Clair** (7½hr.; Tu, Th; $66). The **Deloraine Visitor Information Centre,** 98 Emu Bay Rd, doubles as the folk museum. (☎6362 3471. Open M-F 9:30am-4pm, Sa 1-3:30pm, Su 2-4pm. Museum $2.) A **Trust Bank** is at 24 Emu Bay Rd (☎13 18 28; open M-F 9am-5pm). The **library,** 2 Emu Bay Rd, has **Internet access.** (☎6362 2770. Open M-Th 11am-1pm and 2-5pm, F 11am-1pm and 2-7pm. 30min. $5.) **Police:** at Westbury Pl (☎6362 4004). **Post office:** 10 Emu Bay Rd (☎6362 2156; open M-F 9am-5pm). **Postal code:** 7304.

**🖥 ACCOMMODATIONS AND FOOD.** The **Deloraine Highview Lodge YHA,** 8 Blake St, is the best—and only—hostel around, with breathtaking views of Quamby Bluff and the Great Western Tiers, comfy bunks, and lively Scottish propri-

TASMANIA

etors that can arrange tours. Go up Emu Bay Rd, turn right on Beefeater St and left on Blake. (☎6362 2996. Reception 8-10am and 5-10pm. Bike hire $15. Dorms $13, non-YHA $16). The **Apex Caravan Park,** on West Pde, has river sites and showers. (☎6362 2345. Sites for 2 $10, powered $13). A **supermarket** is at 58 Emu Bay Rd (open Sa, M-W 8am-6pm, Th-F 8am-9pm).

◪ **PARKS.** A 1½hr. drive southwest from Deloraine lies the most pristine and awe-inspiring section of the World Heritage Area, the **Walls of Jerusalem National Park.** A hike to the top of Mt. Jerusalem gives an amazing 360° view (8hr. return). Less trafficked than Cradle Mountain, the park contains the same craggy bluffs, vales, and ridges, with stretches of green mosses and lakes. The mostly duck-boarded track begins from a carpark with a pit toilet off the Mersey Forest Rd (C171). The first hour is a steep walk to the park's border and down into the Walls. From there, it's relatively level except for inclines through the gates of the Walls. A compass, a $9 park map, and overnight equipment are required even for dayhikes because of the highly variable weather. The Walls are not to be taken casually; rangers recommend it only for experienced hikers. Park fees apply; call ☎6363 5182 for more info.

About 35km west of Deloraine off the B12, is the **Mole Creek Karst National Park** (☎6363 5182), home to two spectacular caves. **Marakoopa Cave** is cavernous with shawl and flowstone formations, two underground streams, and a glow worms chamber. **King Solomon's Cave** is much smaller with fewer steps and more colorful formations. Temperatures in the caves can be a chilling 9° Celsius. Park fees do not apply, but Parks and Wildlife runs tours for a fee ($8; both caves $12). The **Westbury Maze and Tea Room,** 10 Bass Hwy, between Deloraine and Launceston, has a challenging and disorienting tall hedge maze. (☎6393 1840. Open Oct.-June daily 10am-6pm. $4, children $3, families $14). **Ashgrove Farm Cheese** is 18km north of Deloraine on the Bass Hwy in Elizabeth Town. Learn everything you ever wanted to know about cheese—that probably won't be much. Then eat your heart out with free cheese tastings. (☎6369 1105. Open daily 9am-5pm.)

## THE NORTHWEST COAST

West of Devonport, the Bass Hwy 1 and A2 Hwy trace the northern coast of Tasmania. The Bass Hwy passes through Ulverstone and Burnie before reaching the junction where A2 continues northwest and A10 branches south toward Queenstown, Zeehan, and Strahan. If driving, the scenic coastal route through Penguin is worth the minor diversion. From Burnie, A2 continues past Wynyard (18km) and Rocky Cape National Park (30km) to Smithton (74km) and nearby Stanley (66km).

**BURNIE.** The area's major transport hub is Burnie, a declining paper mill town. **Redline,** 117 Wilson St (☎6434 4488), connects Burnie to: **Boat Harbour** (45min., by booking only, $4.70); **Deloraine** (1½hr., 3-4 per day, $15); **Devonport** (45min., 3-10 per day, $8); **Launceston** (2¼hr., 3-4 per day, $19); **Stanley** (1½hr., 1-3 per day M-Sa, $11); and **Wynyard** (20min., 1-3 per day M-Sa, $2.70). The **Tasmanian Travel and Information Centre** is in the Civic Centre complex. (☎6464 6111. Open M-F 9am-5pm, Sa 10am-1pm.) An **ANZ Bank** with an **ATM** is on the corner of Wilson and Cattley St (open M-Th 9:30am-4pm, F 9:30am-5pm). The only budget accommodation is the **Treasure Island Caravan Park,** 253 Bass Hwy, 4km away in Cooee, with an indoor pool. (☎6431 1925. Sites $8, powered $10; dorms with kitchen $12; caravans $30; cabins $50.) Burnie's most savory sight is the ◪**Lactos Cheese factory,** on Old Surrey Rd. (☎6431 2566. Open for free tastings M-F 9am-5pm, Sa-Su 10am-4pm.)

**WYNYARD.** The self-proclaimed **Tulip Town,** Wynyard is a coastal town with flower bed roundabouts and the public Gutheridge Gardens on the bank of the River Inglis. The annual October Tulip Festival exhibits spring flowers, food, music, and crafts. The main street, **Goldie St,** at the corner with Hogg St, holds: a **tourist info cottage** with walking track brochures and **Internet access** (20min. $3); the **post office,** 33A Goldie St (open M-F 9am-5pm; **postal code:** 7325); a sizeable **supermarket**

(open M-W 8am-6pm, Th-F 8am-9pm, Sa 8am-6pm); and a **library,** in the supermarket parking lot (☎6442 2769; open M-Th 10am-6pm, F 10am-9pm; **Internet** 30min. $5; book ahead). The beachside **Wynyard Caravan and Backpacker Park,** 30B Old Bass Hwy, just off the highway 1km east of the town center, has a kitchen and free airport pickup. (☎6442 1998. Sites for 2 $10, powered $14; singles $14; twins, doubles, triples $12 per person.) The striking **Table Cape** is a mosaic of farmland dotted with a lighthouse on a volcanic promontory, 7km north of Wynyard. The **Table Cape Tulip Farm,** 363 Lighthouse Rd, is open during the flower bloomings. (☎6442 2012. Open Sept.-mid-Oct. daily 10am-4:30pm). The area around Wynyard is also renowned for its phenomenal **diving.** The **Scuba Centre Dive Shop,** 62 Old Bass Hwy is 3km east of Wynyard. (☎6442 2247. Open M-Sa 9am-6pm. Full gear $50-70 per day; 4-day all-inclusive course $355.)

**BOAT HARBOUR.** About 12km west of Wynyard is the turn-off for Boat Harbour, a tiny coastal community with great **surf** and swimming beaches. **Boat Harbour Beach Backpackers,** 64 Strawberry Lane, has free pickup from the bus, kitchen, laundry, and enthralling views of the beach and Rocky Cape National Park. Driving, it's 3km from the highway turn-off to Boat Harbour; turn right off Sisters Beach Rd on Pokes Rd, then right on Strawberry Lane. (☎6445 1273. Reception daily 8am-10pm. Dorms $15; doubles $38.) ▧**Mallavale Farm,** 1 Pokes Rd, on the corner of Sisters Beach Rd, is a family farm that cooks up delicious, reasonably-priced dishes. (☎6445 1171. Open M-Sa 9:30am-4pm, Su 11am-4:30pm.)

**ROCKY CAPE NATIONAL PARK.** Staying true to its name, Rocky Cape National Park (☎6458 1100) features a mountainous coastline, rare flora, and **Aboriginal cavesites.** The two ends of the park are accessible by separate access roads. The 9km eastern access road turns off the A2 12km west of Wynyard and leads to walking tracks and **Sisters Beach.** The 4km western access road, 18km further down the A2, ends at a lighthouse and great views of Table Cape and the Nut (see **Stanley,** below). Aboriginal caves can be accessed from both entrances via short walking tracks; the **Coastal Route** track traverses the length of the park (11km; 3hr.). There is no visitors center nor any other amenities, but the shops near both entrances stock park brochures. The small park is geared toward day use; the low-growing vegetation is still recovering from a severe (campfire-started) bushfire several years ago and offers little protection from the sun during extended walks.

## STANLEY

In the far northwest of the state, Stanley is built at the base of the **Nut,** a huge volcanic plateau first seen by European Matthew Flinders in December 1798. Flinders described it as a "cliffy round lump in form resembling a Christmas cake," Aboriginals referred to it as Moo-Nut-Re-ker, but the sailors' nickname is the one that stuck. Tidy and quiet, Stanley's Church St is lined with flowers, tea rooms, craft shops, a **newsagency** with **limited groceries** (open M-Th 7:30am-8:30pm, F 7:30am-9pm, Sa 8am-9pm, Su 8am-8:30pm), and a **post office** (open M-F 9am-12:30pm and 1:30-5pm; **postal code:** 7331). Most people spend their time fishing, swimming, and **seal** and **penguin spotting.** But the big attraction for daytrips is a steep but short (10-15min.) plod up to the top of the Nut and then a leisurely walk (45min.) around. A **chairlift** makes the climb easy (open summer daily 9:30am-5:30pm, winter 10am-4pm; $6 return, children $4), and the **Nut buggy tour** carts people around the top ($5; closed in winter). The town also houses the **Highfield Historic Site,** marking the settlement that instigated development in the northwest. From the bottom of Church St, follow the scenic route 3km to the site. (☎6458 1100. Open Oct.-Apr. daily 10am-4pm; May-Sept. Sa-Su 10am-2pm. $2-5.) The **Stanley Caravan Park and YHA** is on the waterfront at Wharf Rd, tucked under the Nut. (☎6458 1266. Reception daily 8am-8pm. Sites for 2 $14, powered $16; dorms $16; twins and doubles $36.) **Peggs Beach Coastal Reserve,** 16km west of Stanley, offers primitive, secluded **camping** along the Black River with pit toilets and no amenities (sites $3).

# THE NORTHEAST

Tasmania's northeast is blessed with a sunny disposition. Folks here grow up listening to Melbourne radio, drinking Boag's beer, and disdaining the political antics of the South. The pleasant coastline is dotted by quiet fishing and port towns that make suitable summer holiday spots for families with young children. Both sides of the Tamar ("TAY-mer") River are home to vineyards and fruit farms.

## LAUNCESTON

Built where the North and South Esk rivers join to form the Tamar River, Launceston ("LON-seh-ston") is Tasmania's second-largest city and Australia's third-oldest, founded in 1805. The intense historic rivalry between Hobart and Launceston persists, manifesting most clearly in beer loyalty: Boag's is the ale of choice in the north, Cascade in the south. Though this growing university town has not escaped commercialization, steeple-tops and church spires still rise above the rest, vigilantly guarding Launceston's character, vitality, and old-world charm.

### ⎙ TRANSPORT

**Flights:** Launceston Airport, south of Launceston on Hwy 1 to B41. Ansett (☎ 13 13 00) and Qantas (☎ 13 13 13) fly to **Melbourne** ($203, return $239). Tasmanian Shuttle Bus Services, 101 George St, provides airport **shuttles** that meet flights and will pickup from accommodations. (☎ 6331 2009. $10.)

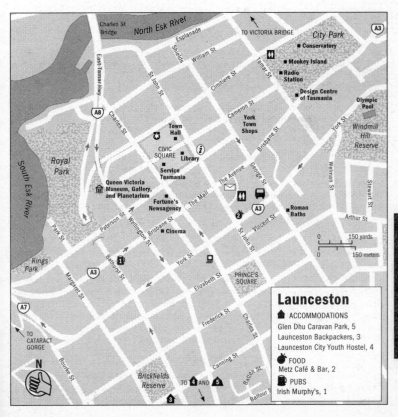

**Launceston**

🛏 ACCOMMODATIONS
Glen Dhu Caravan Park, 5
Launceston Backpackers, 3
Launceston City Youth Hostel, 4

🍴 FOOD
Metz Café & Bar, 2

🍺 PUBS
Irish Murphy's, 1

TASMANIA

**Buses:** A Redline office is at 112 George St (☎ 6336 1444). Their **buses** run to: **Hobart** (2½hr., 2-6 per day, $20); **Bicheno** (2½hr., 3-7 per week, $22); **Burnie** (2½hr., 2-6 per day, $19); **Deloraine** (45min., 3-6 per day, $7); **Devonport** (1½hr., 2-6 per day, $14); **George Town** (45min., 1-3 per day Su-F, $8); **Oatlands** (1¼hr., 3-6 per day, $15); **St. Helens** (2¾hr., 1-3 per day Su-F, $20); and **St. Mary's** (2hr., 1-3 per day Su-F, $16). TassieLink buses (☎ (1300) 30 05 20) leave from Gateway Travel Centre to: **Cradle Mountain Lodge** (3½hr.; Tu, Th, Sa; $37); **Lake St. Clair** (2½hr., 3-7 per week, $50); and **Strahan** ($49) via **Queenstown** (6½hr.; Tu, Th, Sa; $44).

**Public Transportation: Metro** (☎ 13 22 01) buses run daily 7am-7pm. Fares $1-3.

**Taxis: Taxi Combined** (☎ 6331 5555 or ☎ 13 10 08). Fare to airport $18-21.

**Car Rental: Budget,** at the airport, from $38 per day. (☎ 6391 8566. Ages 21-24 $18 surcharge. **Economy,** 27 William St (☎ 6334 3299), from $28, rents to ages 21-24.

**Automobile Club: RACT** (☎ 6335 5633, 24hr. ☎ 13 11 11), at the corner of York St. Open M-F 8:45am-5pm.

**Tours: Devil's Playground Ecotours** (☎ 6343 1787, mobile ☎ (0409) 38 33 71) offers day tours (Waterfalls, Caves, and Wildlife; Tu, Su; $65), and night tours (Historic Pubs, F, $25). For wild adventures, try **Tasmanian Expeditions,** 110 George St (☎ 6334 3463, freecall ☎ (1800) 03 02 30). Rock-climbing $55; 2-day cycling and canoeing $320; 3-day Cradle Mountain and Freycinet National Parks $430.

**Bike Rental: Rent-a-Cycle,** 36 Thistle St W. (☎ 6344 9779) rents for $18 per day. **Rik Sloane Cycles,** 10-14 Paterson St (☎ 6331 9414), rents 21-speeds for $20 per day, weekly $105. Open M-F 8:30am-5:30pm, Sa 8am-2pm.

## ✦ 🔢 ORIENTATION AND PRACTICAL INFORMATION

The town is best explored by foot, since most attractions are within four blocks of the **Brisbane St Mall** and all the streets are one-way. The city center is bounded on the north by the **North Esk River** and on the west by the **South Esk,** which flows through the Cataract Gorge. From here, the A8 runs north to George Town; Hwy 1 heads south to Hobart through the Midlands and west to Deloraine and Devonport; and the A3 snakes east to St. Helens and the east coast.

**Tourist Office: Gateway Tasmania Travel Centre,** corner of St. John and Patterson St (☎ 6331 4844; www.gatewaytas.com.au). A 1hr. $10 walking tour leaves from the Centre M-F 9:45am. Open M-F 9am-5pm, Sa 9am-3pm, Su 9am-noon.

**Currency Exchange: Commonwealth Bank,** 97 Brisbane St (☎ 6337 4432). Open M-Th 9:30am-4pm, F 9:30am-5pm. The mall also has several **ATMs.**

**Hiking Equipment: Allgoods,** 71-79 York St (☎ 6331 3644), at St. John St. Huge, inexpensive, and comprehensive, including army surplus and maps. Basic equipment hire at their Tent City annex, 60 Elizabeth St. Open M-F 9am-5:30pm, Sa 9am-4pm.

**Bookstore: Birchalls,** 118-120 Brisbane St (☎ 6331 3011). Australia's oldest bookshop. Open M-Th 8:30am-5:30pm, F 8:30am-9pm, Sa 8:30am-5pm, Su 10am-4pm.

**Library:** 1 Civic Sq (☎ 6336 2625). Open M-Th 9:30am-6pm, F 9:30am-8pm, Sa 9:30am-12:30pm. **Internet access** (☎ 6334 9559) 15min. $2.50. Book ahead.

**Police:** on Cimitiere St (☎ 6336 3701). Enter through Civic Square.

**Pharmacy: Centre Pharmacy,** 84 Brisbane St (☎ 6331 7777). Open M-Sa 8:30am-10pm, Su 9am-10pm.

**Hospital: Launceston General,** on Charles St (☎ 6332 7111).

**Internet: Service Tasmania** (☎ (1300) 36 67 73), in Henty House, Civic Square, has 3 free terminals. Open M-F 8:15am-4:45pm. **Central City Computers,** 173 Charles St (☎ 6334 9226). 30min. $5. Open M-F 9am-6pm, Sa 9am-4pm. Also, see the **Library.**

**Post Office:** 107 Brisbane St (☎ 6331 9477). Open M-F 9am-5:30pm, Sa 9:30am-1pm. **Postal Code:** 7250.

**Phone Code:** 03.

TASMANIA

# ACCOMMODATIONS

Many of the pubs in the city center have accommodation upstairs, though the noise often carries. Also, look for a new backpackers above the Metz Café and Bar.

**Launceston Backpackers,** 103 Canning St (☎6334 2327). Across from Brickfields Reserve, off Bathurst St, about a 7min. walk from the city center. Large kitchen, off-street parking, free storage, laundry. Key deposit $10. Reception daily 8-10am and 5-10pm. Check-out 10am. 4- to 6-bed dorms $14; twins $30; doubles $32.

**Launceston City Youth Hostel,** 36 Thistle St (☎6344 9779). Opposite the Coats Patons building at Glen Dhu St. Turn right onto Howick from Wellington St, then left onto Glen Dhu St; or take Metro #24 from Allgoods to stop 8. This old mill-canteen has long hallways and dozens of bunks in each room. Coin-op shower (10¢), security lockers, midnight quiet time. Mountain bikes $18 per day, weekly $115; 10-speeds $12, $75; tents $14 per week; boots $20 per week; stoves $7 per week. Dorms $13.

**Glen Dhu Treasure Island Caravan Park,** 94 Glen Dhu St (☎6344 2600). 2km from downtown. Follow directions to City Youth Hostel. Lots of noise from neighboring Hwy 1. BBQ, showers, laundry, outdoor campers' kitchen with kettle, hot plate, and toaster-oven. Sites for 2 $14, powered $16; caravans $34; cabins $56-62.

# FOOD

Launceston has several options. Coles **supermarket** is at 198 Charles St (☎6334 5744; open M-W, Sa 8am-6pm, Th-F 8am-9pm). The organic **Wholefoods Launceston,** is at 54 Frederick St (☎6331 7682; open daily 10am-6pm.)

**Elaia Café-Deli,** 238-240 Charles St (☎6331 3307). Two blocks south of Princes Square. Great Mediterranean decor and classy food. Great tapenade focaccia ($9.50). Busy F-Sa dinner. Mains $10.50-16.50. Open M-Sa 9am-9pm, Su 10am-6pm.

**Homeostasis,** 80 Elizabeth St (☎6334 0440). Healthful meals—what's a vita-soy shake? ($3.50). Open M-Th 8:30am-6pm, F 8:30am-8:30pm, Sa 9am-3pm.

**The Metz Café and Bar,** 119 St. John St (☎6331 7277). Corner of York St. Upscale pizza pub and wine bar attract a mixed crowd of young business folk, couples, students, and travelers. $10 backpacker coupon special for an individual gourmet pizza and a schooner. Open daily 8am-midnight.

**Saloon Bar,** 191 Charles St (☎6331 7355). In Hotel Tasmania. It's hard to find more for your money. Heaping plates of chili, roast, or mixed veggies for $5. Porterhouse steak $9. Live music W, F, Sa; cover $3-7. Kitchen open daily 8am-9pm; bar until 3am.

# SIGHTS AND ACTIVITIES

The most spectacular sight in Launceston is the handiwork of the South Esk River—the Cataract Gorge Reserve. A 20min. walk from Paterson St toward Kings Bridge, it's not exactly pristine wilderness—the First Basin of the gorge has been popular since the town's settlement and now hosts peacocks, an exotic tree garden, a restaurant, and a free swimming pool. Walking tracks run on either side of the river; some climb to the gorge's rim (2hr.) for excellent views of the cataracts. The **Band Rotunda** near the far end of the Alexandra Bridge and the **Duck Reach Power Station** at the far end of the gorge, provide info on the gorge. (☎6337 1288. Rotunda: open M-F 9am-4pm, Sa-Su 9am-4:30pm. Power station: daily dawn-dusk.)

The **Queen Victoria Museum and Art Gallery,** on the corner of Cameron and Wellington St, houses an impressive local and natural history display focusing on Tasmania's wildlife. The central foyer explains mining, mineralogy, and metallurgy. The upstairs gallery offers a brief but sweet peek of Tasmanian sculpture, paintings, ceramics, and textile art. The Planetarium is part of the complex. (☎6323

3777. Open M-Sa 10am-5pm, Su 2-5pm. Free. Planetarium shows Tu-F 3pm; Sa 2 and 3pm. $3, children $2, families $7. No children under 5 admitted.)

For sightseeing from an aerial perspective, **Cable Hang Gliding,** in the Trevallyn State Recreation Area, sails above the Trevallyn Dam Quarry. (☎(0419) 31 11 98. Open Dec.-Apr. daily 10am-5pm, May-Nov. Sa-Su 10am-4pm. $10.) The less dramatic chairlift runs across the First Basin. (☎6331 5915. Open Sept.-May daily 9am-4:30pm, June-Aug. Sa-Su 9am-4:30pm. $6, children $4.)

Launceston is blessed with an abundant supply of parks all around town. The small but notorious **City Park,** at Tamar and Brisbane St, harbors a war memorial, botanical conservatory, and an enclosure teeming with **Japanese macaque monkeys** (open Mar.-Sept. M-F 8:30am-4:30pm, Sa-Su 9am-4:30pm; Oct.-Mar. closes 5:30pm).

## 🎵 ENTERTAINMENT

Many downtown pubs have live music on weekends; the best and most popular is **Irish Murphy's,** 211 Brisbane St, two blocks from the mall. Rest your drinks on barrels of beer while groovin' to live music W-Su. (☎6331 4440. Open daily noon-3am. Cover $3 Th-Sa. Guinness pints $5.50. Happy Hour M-Th 9:30-10pm, F-Su 4-6pm and 9:30-10pm; VB pints $3, 20% off everything else.) The hip ▤**Cucina Simpatica** café, 57 Frederick St, by the Brickfields Reserve, hosts live jazz twice per month Su afternoons. (☎6334 3177. Open daily 10am-10pm.) For more pampered relaxation, the **Aquarius Roman Baths,** 127-133 George St, has an indoor frigidarium (cold bath), tepidarium (warm bath), caldarium (hot bath), and rubarium (heat lamps) in the style of ancient Rome—unfortunately, there are no vomitoriums. (☎6331 2255. Open M-F 8:30am-10pm, Sa-Su 9am-6pm. $20, doubles $30.)

## NEAR LAUNCESTON: GEORGE TOWN

North along the A8 50km, where the east side of the Tamar River meets the Bass Strait, lies George Town. Once considered the capital of the north, George Town now acts more as an historical center and Launceston's port. It does, however, lay claim to the title of the oldest *town* in Australia and the third oldest settlement. A lighthouse was constructed near the shore, but in 1995, the *Iron Baron* still wrecked on the nearby Hebe Reef, spilling countless liters of oil into the sea.

The town's seafaring history has been preserved in the **Pilot Station & Maritime Museum** in **Low Head,** 5km north of the town. Established in 1805, this convict-built estate is the oldest continuously operating facility of its kind in Australia, with displays on communication, navigation, shipbuilding, and **beer bottles** salvaged from shipwrecks. (☎6382 1143. Open daily 8am-8pm. $3.) The road ends at the **Low Head Lighthouse** (☎6382 1211) with great views of the peninsula and the *DevilCat*. **Fairy penguins** and seals use some of the beaches around George Town and Low Head as rookeries during the spring. **Fairy Penguin Twilight Tours** leads nightly tours one hour before sunset. (☎(0418) 36 18 60. $7, children $3.) **Seal & Sea Adventure Tours** offers seal-watching tours of the Hebe Reef and Tenth Island. (☎(0419) 35 70 28. 3-4hr; $200 minimum charge, 3 or more people $75 each, family of 4 $230.)

The DevilCat fast **ferry** departs Dec.-Apr. weather-depending to George Town from **Melbourne** (6hr.; Tu, Th, Sa 8:30am; $125-130, concessions $83, cars $30); and from George Town to Melbourne (W, F, Su 2pm). A **shuttle** bus meets the ferry ($2). Riverline **buses** (☎6382 1484) leave from Cheaper Liquor, 17 Elizabeth St; the Shell Station, 32-36 Main Rd; and the ferry terminal to **Launceston** (45min., M-F 3 per day, $8); and on to **Hobart** (2½hr., $27). But who would ever want to leave cheaper liquor? The **Tourist Information Centre** is a hut on the main road entering town from the south. (☎6382 1700. Open daily Aug.-Sept. 10am-2pm, Oct.-July 10am-4pm.) There's a **supermarket** at 8 Bathurst St (open Sa, M-W 8am-6pm, Th-F 8am-9pm). The **library,** in Regent Sq, has **cheap Internet.** (☎6382 1356. Open daily 9am-8pm. 1hr. $1.) **Banks,** the **police station** (☎6382 4040), and the **post office** cluster on Macquarie St. **Postal code:** 7253.

George Town itself doesn't warrant more than a day's visit, but if you must stay, give the delightful ▨**Traveller's Lodge (YHA)**, 4 Elizabeth St, a try. Turn left at the third roundabout. The lodge doubles as the Heritage Cable Cottage with the oldest tree in George Town in the backyard. (☎6382 3261. Check-out 11am. Bunks $15, non-YHA add $3; doubles $45; tent sites $10.)

# THE A3 EAST FROM LAUNCESTON

The road from Launceston weaves 165km east to St. Helens and the Suncoast through dairy farms, woodlands, and rainforest, close to numerous parks, hiking trails, and lookouts.

**SCOTTSDALE.** Scottsdale is the first major service center out from Launceston. Redline **buses** leave from Roses Newsagency, 12 King St (☎6352 2413), for Launceston (1¼hr., 2 per day M-F, $9) and Winnaleah (2½hr., 1 per day M-F, $7). If you have to spend the night, **Bellows Backpackers & Budget Accommodation,** 65 King St, is a comfy retreat one block off the main road. (☎6352 2263. Reception daily 7:30am-9:30pm. 4-bed dorms $18; twins and doubles $45.) The outgoing managers run the town's **Tourist Information Centre** and **Pepper Bush Peak 4WD Tours.** These outstanding tours cater to backpackers, with specials like Platypus Wildlife—a 4hr. evening tour, mountain-top BBQ, accommodation, and breakfast for $69.

**MT. VICTORIA FOREST RESERVE.** The Reserve is 45min. past Scottsdale. From the A3, follow signs south to Ringarooma and continue 15km on mostly unsealed roads to the carpark. The strikingly thin single-drop **Ralph Falls,** reckoned to be the tallest in Tassie, is a 10min. walk from the carpark, and Cashs Gorge lies 30min. beyond. The tough hike up Mt. Victoria passes a melange of ecosystems and a panorama of the whole Northeast, from Ben Lomond to Flinders Island.

**DERBY.** Derby is a historic tin-mining town. The quirky **tourist centre/butcher shop** (☎6354 2364; open daily 5am-5pm) and the painted fish rock are on the north side of the A3 heading east, past the second bridge. Derby's big draw is the ▨**Tin Mine Centre** with a tea room, museum, reconstructed mining village, and the opportunity to pan for miniscule gemstones. (☎6354 2262. Open daily Sept.-June 9am-5pm; July-Aug. 10am-4pm. $4, children $1.50, families $10.)

**WINNALEAH.** The tiny town of Winnaleah is 2km off the A3. Redline **buses** run to Derby (15min., Su-F 2pm, $2.40) on the way to Launceston (2¾hr., $15). Suncoast Coach Service (☎6376 1753), otherwise known as the mail bus, connects to St. Helens (1hr., M-F 12:30pm, $4). Six kilometers on a side road from town, the **Merlinkei Farm Winnaleah YHA,** 524 Racecourse Rd, is the only hostel before St. Helens, and doubles as a dairy farm—guests are welcome to try their hand at milking. Pickup from town available. (☎6354 2152. Bunks $12, non-YHA add $3.)

**CLOSER TO ST. HELENS. Blue Lake** is in South Mt. Cameron on B82 as you approach **Gladstone** and **Mt. William National Park,** about 12km northeast off the A3. An inadvertent product of mining, Blue Lake's unearthly shade of aquamarine is due to the mineral composition of the soil. The **Weldborough Pass Scenic Reserve,** just beyond Weldborough, offers a rainforest walk guided by "Grandma Myrtle" right by the highway. The 15min. circuit weaves beneath huge tree-ferns and myrtle beeches. About 30min. west of St. Helens, in the middle of a pasture in Pyengana just off the A3, **Pub in the Paddock—St. Columba Falls Hotel** recalls a time before pubs had to be Irish, Western, or have pokies to attract customers. Slops, the beer-drinking pig, draws droves. (☎6373 6121. Open daily 11am-late. Meals served noon-2pm and 6-8pm. Singles $25; doubles $35.) Nearby, the 90m cascading **St. Columba Falls** unleashes 42,000L per minute. To get there, drive 10min. beyond the pub on an unsealed road ending at a carpark and a 10min. walk to the falls.

**TASMANIA**

# BRIDPORT

Bridport lies along the sheltered beach of **Anderson's Bay** at the estuarine mouth of the **Brid River.** Here you'll find many of the joys of an estuary: birds to spot, oysters to dig, and beach cricket to play. With few sights, Bridport lends itself to relaxing walks along the beach.

**▐▊ TRANSPORT AND INFORMATION.** Everything in town is on Main St. **Visitors center: Bridport 2000 Plus** (open daily 10am-4pm). **Library:** (☎6356 0258. Open M, W 10am-1pm; Tu, F 3-7pm; Th 10am-1pm and 4-8pm; Sa 9am-1pm. **Internet access.**) Bridport has **no bank,** and the nearest **ATM** is in nearby **Scottsdale.** Tubby's **supermarket** has eftpos and a **post office** desk (open daily 7am-7pm; post office open M-F 9am-5pm). **Postal code:** 7262.

The Redline **bus** from **Launceston** to **Scottsdale** (1¼hr., M-F 2 per day, $9.30), connects with **Stan's Coach Service** to Bridport. (☎6356 1662. 30min., 2 per day M-F, $3.) By car, the 77km drive northeast from Launceston passes through many **vineyards** in the **Tamar Valley:** take the A8 to the B81 near Rocherlea, and then the B83 to the B82 in Pipers River. Just past Pipers River is the **Delamere Vineyard,** 4238 Bridport Rd (open for tastings daily 10am-5pm; $2). About 2km off the B82 is **Pipers Brook Vineyard,** 1216 Pipers Brook Rd, a much larger operation offering daily tours (open for free tastings daily 10am-5pm; tours 11am, 2pm).

**▐▊ ACCOMMODATIONS AND FOOD.** The ▊**Bridport Seaside Lodge,** 47 Main St, is a budget traveler's dream. There's a large kitchen, tidy rooms, free canoes, and a verandah with expansive views of the estuary beach. (☎6356 1585. Dorms $15.) **Bridport Caravan Park,** on Bentley St, has close-quarter, wooded sites along the beach. (☎6356 1227. Sites $10, powered $13.50.) Bridport has the standard takeaway joints, but the real find for cheap and tasty eats—if you can stomach it— is **Springfield Fisheries,** the fish slaughterhouse, on Main St just before crossing the bridge into Bridport. Brave past the bloody fish guts to buy hot smoked and then frozen vacuum-sealed trout. (☎6356 1104. Open daily 8am-4pm. $2 each.)

**▣ SIGHTS.** A 30min. shoreline stroll north from the Main St bridge past the old pier takes you to the **Mermaids Pool** swimming hole. Extend the walk past **wildflowers** in the spring by heading down Main St, turning right just past Walter St, and looping back around along the coast (2½hr.). Another walk to **East Sandy Point** grants great views and leads to huge dunes (1½hr. return). To get to the start of the track, follow Main St, which turns into Sandy Points Rd, and park at the gateway where the road becomes a rough 4WD track.

# FLINDERS ISLAND

The largest of the Furneaux Group islands, approximately 60km northeast of the state proper, Flinders Island is the Tasmania of Tasmania—exceedingly remote, unpopulated, and blessed with a preponderance of natural beauty. It caters to the enterprising, adventuresome outdoor enthusiast. At 756m, Mt. Strzelecki in **Strzelecki National Park** (☎6359 2217) is the highest point on the island, from which you can see the other 54 Furneaux Islands and, if you're lucky, Wilson's Promontory in Victoria. A manageable walk (3km; 5hr.) traverses fern gullies and craggy outcrops. Park fees apply. Getting to the island can be challenging. **Island Airlines** runs flights out of **Launceston.** (☎(1800) 81 88 26. 40min., 1-4 per day, $172 return.) **Sinclair Air Charter** will take up to 5 passengers from **Bridport.** (☎6359 3641. $250 one-way min. charge.) Southern Shipping can carry up to 12 passengers on their **cargo freight** from **Bridport** to **Lady Barron.** (☎6356 1752. 8hr.; M evening, Tu morning; $70 return, children $40.) Even though Flinders is a Tasmanian municipality, rental companies generally forbid long ferry vehicle transport. **Ann Campbell's Cars** (☎6359 2168), **Bowman & Lees Car Hire** (☎6359 2388), and **Flinders Island Lodge Furneaux Car Rentals** (☎6359 3521) rent cars on the island. **No bike hire** is available on the island. The island has fantastic **camping;**

otherwise, budget stays are in the two major townships. **Nunamina Hostel** over-looks the sound in Lady Barron. (☎6359 3617. Twins $20.) **Interstate Hotel** is in Whitemark. (☎6359 2114. Singles $18.)

## MT. WILLIAM NATIONAL PARK

More of a hill than a mountain, Mt. William overlooks a quiet stretch of coast in the sunny northeast corner. The gentle 180m peak has views of the **Furneaux Islands,** which once provided a bridge between Tassie and the mainland. The major reason to visit Mt. William is to safari among marsupials. Wallabies are everywhere. Echidnas pop up in the daytime. At dusk, chest-high Forester kangaroos are in motion, as well as smaller pademelons, wombats, and chazzwazzers. After dark—with a good flashlight—spot brushtail possums, spotted-tail quolls, and Tasmanian devils. Eagle-eyed visitors might even glimpse the rare New Holland mouse.

Mt. William is a relatively isolated, primitive national park with no facilities. A supply of **drinking water** is essential. In an emergency, call the **ranger** (☎6357 2108) at the north entrance. No buses run to the park, but **Terry's Bus Service** (☎6357 2193) meets Redline coaches in **Derby** and goes to **Gladstone** (1½hr., M-F 12:30pm, $2), about 20km southwest of the park entrance. From St. Helens, the drive takes about 1½hr. The gravel access roads are a bumpy ride even at slow speeds. The turn-off is sign-posted from Gladstone, and the popular north entrance is by the hamlet of **Poole;** the south entrance is by **Ansons Bay.** Both ends of the park offer ample coastal **camping** (free), hiking, and beach walks. Park fees apply. The north-ern access road leads to **Forester Kangaroo Dr,** past the turn-off for **Stumpy's Bay** and its camping areas, and on to the trailhead for the **Mt. William walk** (1hr., moderate).

# THE SUNCOAST

The east coast is Tasmania's softer side where the weather, the seas, and even the locals are mild. A mountainous interior shelters the east coast from the storms that pound the west. The docile climate and tracts of arable land have led to fairly thick settlement, but by mainland standards the area remains quiet year-round and mute in winter. Agriculture and holiday tourism sustain the towns, when summer travelers come for fresh- and saltwater fishing, swimming, and loafing in the sun.

## SAINT HELENS

St. Helens, near Georges Bay, is the largest and northernmost of the east coast vacation villages. Getting to St. Helens treasures about 15km northeast of town requires a car and the ability to handle weaving gravel access roads. **Humbug Point,** via Binalong Bay Rd, offers great walks and views, while **St. Helens Point,** via St. Helens Point Rd, has free camping with pit toilets, decent fishing, and good surf at **Beerbarrel Beach.** North of Humbug Point, the **Bay of Fires Coastal Reserve** has long beaches and primitive campsites. The access road ends at the privately-owned **Gardens** and **Margery's Corner. Leda Falls** is opened to the public at Cerise Brook on Medea Cove Rd. The falls are 1½hr. from Cerise Brook.

Redline (☎6376 1182) **buses** sell tickets at the newsagency at Quail and Cecilia St and run to: **Hobart** (4hr.; 1 per day M, W, F; $32); **Launceston** (2½hr., 1 per day Su-F, $19); and **St. Mary's** (40min., 1 per day Su-F, $4). TassieLink (☎(1300) 30 05 20) runs to: **Hobart** (4hr.; 1 per day F, Su; $31), through **Bicheno** (1hr., $8), the highway **turn-off for Coles Bay** (1¼hr., $10), and **Swansea** (1¾hr., $12). The **St. Helens Travel Centre,** 20 Cecilia St, makes TassieLink bookings. (☎6376 1329. Open M-F 9am-5pm, Sa 9am-noon.) **St. Helens History Room,** 59 Cecilia St, offers plenty of local history and **tourist information.** (☎6376 1744. Open M-F 9am-4pm, Sa 9am-1pm; admission to history room $2.) A rare **24hr. ATM** is at **Trust Bank,** 18 Cecilia St. **Service Tasmania,** 23 Quail St, has 30min. **free Internet** (open M-F 8:30am-4:30pm). **Post office:** 46 Cecilia St (☎6376 1255; open M-F 9am-5pm). **Postal code:** 7216.

The **St. Helens YHA,** 5 Cameron St, off Quail St, has basic facilities. (☎6376 1661. Reception daily 8-10am and 5-10pm. Dorms $16, non-YHA add $3.) The standard

TASMANIA

**St. Helens Caravan Park** is 1.5km from the town center on Penelope St, just off the Tasman Hwy on the southeast side of the bridge. (☎6376 1290. Sites for 2 $12-14, powered $16-18, with bath $20-22; on-site caravans $30-40; cabins $45-70.) Brush up on your chopstick skills at ■**Wok Stop,** 57a Cecilia St. Dishes in all spices and sizes are $3-11. (☎6376 2665. Open M-F 11:30am-3pm and 4:30-8:30pm, Sa-Su 5-8:30pm.) TAS **supermarket** is at 33 Cecilia St (☎6376 1117; open daily 7:30am-7pm.)

# BICHENO

The spectacular 75km drive south from St. Helens along the A3 traces the coastline's sand dunes and granite peaks to the small town of Bicheno. With postcard penguins and national parks (Freycinet and Douglas-Apsley) an easy day-trip, its own rocky shoreline, and a neighborly community, Bicheno ("BEE-shen-oh") is an enchanting town you won't want to leave. It's hard to avoid beach activities in Bicheno. The 3km beach-side track begins at the bottom of Weily Ave, left off Burgess St. This marvelous walk leads past the blowhole, the marine reef around Governor Island, and numerous nooks for swimming, snorkelling, and diving.

Redline **buses** sell tickets at **Value-Plus supermarket** (☎6375 1388) and run to the **Coles Bay turn-off** (10min., 1 per day M-F, $4), continuing to **Swansea** (40min., $7), with connections to **Hobart** (5hr., 1 per day Su-F, $22) and **Launceston** (2¾hr., 1 per day Su-F, $22). **TassieLink** (☎(1300) 30 05 20) runs buses to: **Hobart** (3hr.; 1 per day M, W, F, Su; $21); the **Coles Bay turn-off** (10min.; 1 per day M, W; $2); **Swansea** (40min.; 1 per day M, W; $5); **Triabunna** (1½hr.; 1 per day M, W; $9); **St. Helens** (1hr.; 1 per day F, Su; $8); and **Launceston** (2½hr.; 1 per day M, W, F, Su; $19). **Bicheno Coach Service** (☎6257 0293) runs to **Coles Bay** (40min.; 1-3 per day M-Sa; $6) and **Freycinet National Park** (50min., $7), making Redline and TassieLink connections from the **Coles Bay turn-off.** The **Tourist Information Centre** (☎6375 1333) is a hut in the town center. It books nightly **penguin-spotting** tours year-round (1hr., $15), fishing trips (3hr., $75), hires mountain bikes ($20 per day), and sells surf gear and boogie boards. The **Online Access Centre** is on Burgess St near the Primary School. (☎6375 1892. Open M-Tu 10am-2pm and 5-7pm, W 10am-2pm, Th-F 10am-2pm and 6-8pm, Sa-Su 10am-noon. 30min. $5.) The Value-Plus **supermarket** (open daily 7:30am-6pm) and the **post office** (with limited **banking** services; open M-F 9am-5pm), are at the A3 elbow in the town center. **Postal code:** 7215.

The **Bicheno Hostel,** 11 Morrison St, lies off the A3 behind a little white church near the post office. Guests get 10% off penguin tours, comfortable bunks, coastal views from the kitchen, and access to a free washer. (☎6375 1651. Dorms $15.) **Bicheno YHA** is 3km north of the town center on the A3. Though it has cramped bunks and old furniture, this classic bungalow, 50m from the sea, gets points for character. At night, you can often see the penguins return to their burrows. (☎6375 1293. Dorms $14, non-YHA add $3.) Both **pubs** in town have counter meals.

# DOUGLAS-APSLEY NATIONAL PARK

Douglas-Apsley lacks the poster appeal of a coast, mountain, or rainforest, but it's the last significant dry eucalypt forest in Tasmania. Its 1989 elevation to national park status marked the greening of Tassie politics. No roads lead through the park, enabling hiking and swimming to flourish in this undeveloped ecosystem.

The **Apsley waterhole** is a deep pool in the middle of the slow Apsley River, 10min. from the southern carpark. A loop to the **Apsley River Gorge** (3hr.) follows a track from the north side of the waterhole uphill and back down into the gorge, returning on an undefined track downstream along the river. The return trip includes moderate climbing, rock scrambling, and river crossings, so only attempt it when the river is low and the rocks are dry. A **lookout** on the upper banks of the right-side of the river marks the waterhole. The 3-day **Leeaberra Track,** running from north to south to prevent the spread of root-rot fungus, goes the length of the park. It requires experience, a map, and a compass. Signs along the **lookout walk** introduce the park's tree species, such as the blue gum, black wattle, and native cherry—

springtime brings beautiful wildflowers. An unusual number of reptiles lurk in the park, such as the endangered Tasmanian bettong and southern grayling fish.

The popular southern end of the park (Apsley River), is a 15min. drive from **Bicheno,** the nearest service center—the park has no telephones or drinking water. The obscure southern access road leaves the A3 5km north of Bicheno, heading west along 7km of gravel road. The northern access road from St. Marys, mostly along the **MG logging road,** is even harder to find. There is no bus service to the park, but the Bicheno Coach Service (☎6257 0293) can charter a **minibus** from Bicheno. (☎6257 0293. To southern entrance: 2 people $30 return, $15 each extra person. Northern entrance: 1-4 people $50 return, 5-12 people $100 return.) Free **campsites** with pit toilets are near the carparks, and others are 50m from the Apsley waterhole. The nearest **rangers** (☎6375 1236) are in Bicheno. Park fees apply.

## COLES BAY

The tiny township of Coles Bay is the service center for **Freycinet National Park.** Its sunny shelter in the lap of **Great Oyster Bay** satisfies many summer vacationers, while its remote location (27km south on the C302 off the A3 between Bicheno and Swansea) ensures elevated prices. TassieLink (☎(1300) 30 05 20) and Redline (☎(1300) 36 00 00) **buses** run as close as the **turn-off for Coles Bay** on the A3 south to **Hobart** (3½-5hr., 1 per day Su-F, $20-22) and north to **Launceston** (2½hr., 1-2 per day Su-F, $19-21); from the turn-off, take Bicheno Coaches (☎6257 0293) to town (30min.; 1-3 per day M-Sa; $5), the park (40min., $6), or Bicheno (10min., $1). The **supermarket,** on Garnet Ave, houses the **tourist information office,** the **post office,** and a **coffee shop,** as well as offering limited **banking** and **petrol.** (☎6257 0109. Open daily in summer 8am-7pm, winter 8am-6pm.)

The **YHA-affiliated Iluka Holiday Center** is at the western end of the Esplanade. The interior may be sparsely decorated, but it's just a hop, skip, and jump away from the beach. (☎6257 0115. Reception daily 8am-6pm. Dorms $15, non-YHA add $3; twins and doubles $44; tent sites $14, powered $16; on-site vans for 2 $40.) **Freycinet Backpackers** is part of the **Coles Bay Caravan Park,** 3km north of town off the Coles Bay main road, or an easy 30min. walk round Muir's Beach. They offer a great kitchen, free laundry, and a return bus voucher to walking tracks. (☎6257 0100. Reception daily 8am-9:30pm. Linen $4. Tent sites for 2 $12, powered $14; twin-share dorms $15 per person 1st night, $12 each extra night. Book 3 months ahead for both facilities during peak summer season and holidays.)

## FREYCINET NATIONAL PARK

Show us a promotional brochure of Tasmania without a picture of **Wineglass Bay,** and we'll show you an episode of the Simpsons where Maggie talks. Well, there is one episode—but you get the point. Freycinet National Park ("FRAY-sin-nay") is home to the photogenic bay as well as **Great Oyster Bay** and the stately red granite **Hazards.** Just a 3hr. drive from both Hobart and Launceston, this park is a popular vacation spot.

Coles Bay is the service center for Freycinet, but for information, stop at the **visitors kiosk,** near the park entrance. (☎6257 0107. Staffed M-F varied hours.) **Campsites** with wood, water, and basic toilets are available (tent sites $5, powered $6). Register and pay at the kiosk; park fees apply.

At an outdoor theatre past the kiosk, rangers offer free programs, such as nocturnal walks and Aboriginal land use (Dec.-Jan. 3 per day). A few kilometers down, just past the Freycinet Lodge, there's a turn-off on an unsealed road for **Sleepy Bay** (1.8km) and **Cape Tourville Lighthouse** (6.4km). It's an easy 20min. return walk to the Bay, good for **swimming** and **snorkelling;** the Lighthouse sits atop a cliff with amazing views of the coast. **Honeymoon Bay,** popular for **snorkeling,** and **Richardson's Beach,** popular for **swimming,** lie further down the main road. All major walking tracks begin at the carpark at the end of the road. There is no fresh water on day-hikes; bring your own. The **Wineglass Bay Lookout** walk is the classic choice (1hr.); an equally-pleasing alternative is a half-day loop by **Wineglass Bay** and **Hazards**

**Beach** (11km). The **Mt. Amos** track is taxing, but has spectacular views (3hr.). A moderate 33km hike around the whole peninsula takes 2-3 days.

The long stretch of white-sanded **Friendly Beaches** can be accessed via the 4.5km unsealed Friendly Beaches Rd, 18km north of Coles Bay. There are **free campsites** at **Isaacs Point** (with pit toilets) and **Ridge Camp**. Neither has fresh water.

**Bicheno Coaches** stops in Coles Bay at both hostels and the post office enroute to the park's tracks. (☎6257 0293. Departs M-F morning, Sa-Su and return service by bookings only; $3, return $5.) They also offer service between Coles Bay, the **Coles Bay turn-off** (30min., $5) and **Bicheno** (40min., $6); at the turn-off, you can connect with TassieLink and Redline services to other destinations (see **Coles Bay,** above).

## SWANSEA

Swansea is a calm bayside town, 45km southwest of Bicheno and 135km north-east of Hobart. Most visitors enjoy a relaxing holiday on the coast while taking in the local history. The Council Chambers and Community Center are timber buildings from 1860, and the Morris' General Store has been run by the same family since 1838. Swansea's most interactive historical attraction is the **Mill Complex,** made-up of the **Black Wattle Bark Mill,** the only **bark crusher** in Australia; the **Yesteryear Museum,** chronicling the ecology and changing technology of Swansea from settlement to 1960; and the **Wine and Wool Centre.** (☎6257 8382. Open daily 9am-5pm. $5.)

Redline (☎6257 8118) and TassieLink (☎(1300) 30 05 20) run **buses** to: **Triabunna** (50min., 1-2 per day Su-F, $5); **Hobart** (4¼hr., 1-3 per day Su-F, $17); **Bicheno** (45min., 1-2 per day Su-F, $5-7); **Coles Bay turn-off** (40 min., 1-2 per day Su-F, $6); **Launceston** (2hr., 1-2 per day Su-F, $22-24); and **St. Helens** (2hr.; 1 per day W, F, Su; $12). The Redline "depot" is the **Corner Store.** (☎6257 8118. Open daily 7am-8pm; winter 7am-7pm.) The **Swansea Bark Mill Complex,** 96 Tasman Hwy, operates as the **tourist centre.** (☎6257 8382. Open daily 9am-5pm.) A **supermarket** (open M-F 9am-5:30pm, Sa-Su 9am-4:30pm) is on **Franklin St,** the main drag. **Police:** one block back on Noyes St (☎6257 8044). The **Online Access Centre** is in the Community Centre on Franklin St. (☎6257 8806. Open M 9am-1pm, Tu 4-8pm, W 9am-noon and 1-3pm, Th 10am-2pm, F 6-9pm, Sa 10am-2pm. 30min. $5.) The **post office,** at Arnoll and Franklin St, has limited **banking** (☎6257 8170. Open M-F 9am-5pm.) **Postal code:** 7190.

The **Swansea YHA,** 5 Franklin St, includes a well-equipped kitchen, a piano in the common room, crude metal bunks, and laundry. (☎6257 8367. Reception daily 8-11am and 5-10pm. Dorms $16, non-YHA add $3). The **Swansea-Kenmore Cabin and Tourist Park,** 2 Bridge St, at the south end of town, has a spa-sauna (for 2 $7), doves and parrots, swimming pool, kitchen, and laundry. (☎6257 8148. Limited tent sites for 2 $10-13, powered $13-16; on-site caravans $30-35; cabins $48-60.)

## TRIABUNNA

On **Prosser Bay,** 50km southwest of Swansea and 87km northeast of Hobart, Triabunna ("try-a-BUN-na") is a tiny town in which to stock up on food before heading to **Maria Island.** TassieLink (☎(1300) 30 05 20) runs to **Hobart** (1½hr. 1-3 per day Su-F, $12); **Sorell** (1hr.; 1 per day W, F, Su; $7); **Swansea** (50min., 1-2 per day Su-F, $5); **Bicheno** (1½hr.; 1 per day M, W, F, Su; $9); and **St. Helens** (2½hr.; 1 per day F, Su; $18). They also connect to the **Eastcoaster Island Ferry** in **Orford** (5min.). The **tourist information centre,** at the Esplanade, has **Internet access.** (☎6257 4090. Open daily 9am-4pm. Donation requested.) The **post office** is on Vicary St (open M-F 9am-5pm). **Postal code:** 7190. New managers Don and Fron renovated ◙**Udda Backpackers (YHA),** 12 Spencer St, bringing genuine hospitality with home-baked cookies. Follow Vicary St toward the fire station, turn left after the bridge onto a gravel road, then left onto Spencer St; signs point the way. (☎6257 3439. Free Maria Island ferry pickup. Dorms $14; twins and doubles $28, $34.) **Triabunna Caravan Park** is at 6 Vicary St. (☎6257 3575. Sites $10, powered $12; on-site vans for 2 $25.) Value-Plus **supermarket** is at Charles and Vicary St (open daily 8am-6pm).

TASMANIA

## MARIA ISLAND NATIONAL PARK

Maria ("muh-RYE-uh") Island has housed penal colonies, cement industries, whalers, and farmers. Today, the island national park is almost devoid of civilization, preserved for its historical and biological significance. The ruins of the settlement at **Darlington**—along with abundant wildlife, natural beauty, and isolation—are a main attraction. Walks wander through the **Darlington Township** ruins (1½hr.), over the textured sandstone of the **Painted Cliffs** (2hr.; best done at low tide; check schedule at visitor centre) to the rock-scramble up **Bishop and Clerk** (4hr.) To reach Maria, the **Eastcoaster Express catamaran** departs **Eastcoaster Resort**, 5km between both Triabunna and Orford. (☎6257 1589. 20min.; late-Dec.-Apr. 9am, otherwise 10:30am, 1pm, 3:30pm; daytrip $18, overnight $21, bikes and kayaks $3.) Take the turn for Louisville Pt/Maria Island Ferry off the A3. Brochures about the park are available at the tourist office in Triabunna; the ferry has detailed descriptions of walking tracks. On the island itself, there are no shops or facilities save a **visitor centre,** with maps and brochures, and a **ranger station** (☎6257 1420) with a telephone. Park fees apply. To get beyond the Darlington ferry wharf, walk or bring a mountain bike. The old Darlington prison has been resurrected into 6-bed **units,** each with a table, chairs, and fireplace. Instead of getting booked for this jail, you'll have to book ahead yourself with the ranger. (Shared toilets, sinks, and hot showers. Beds $8, children $4, entire unit $20. Get Out of Jail Free.) The island has three **campsites: Darlington,** with ample grassy space (tent sites $4, families $10); **French's Farm,** 11km south down the main gravel road, with an empty weatherproof farmhouse, pit toilet, and rainwater tanks; and **Encampment Cove,** 3km down a side road near French's Farm, with a small bunkhouse and pit toilet.

# CENTRAL EAST

The Central East lays out the red carpet with its Heritage Hwy Tourism Region—a land of crafts and sandstone architecture. The agricultural Midlands, producing a quarter of Australia's potato crop, roll south to the Lakes region where Ben Lomand's ski peaks spill into the Derwent Valley.

## THE MIDLANDS

The fertile hills between Hobart and Launceston were once garrison towns keeping watch over the colony's convicts. The English settlers decided to make the mid-country of Tasmania look more like the mid-country back home, planting a wealth of English plants and building hedges and narrow lanes. The spirit of the Midlands is captured by the small town of **Oatlands,** a bit closer to Hobart than Launceston. There are no oats anywhere near the place, but lore says that Macquarie was nostalgic for Scotland when he gave the town its name. A walk down High

**THE POINT OF WOOD** Aboriginals crossed over to Tasmania from mainland Australia during the last Ice Age 30,000 years ago. When the ice caps melted, the peninsula connecting Tasmania to the continent flooded with water, isolating the colonists. For 30 millennia, Tasmanian Aboriginal culture thrived. These people pursued a semi-nomadic existence, following seasonal food supplies within a well-established home range. Fire was used to drive game out of the bush onto the spears of waiting hunters, and the periodic burning of vegetation shaped the terrain. Although stones were used as tools, they used no stone-tipped weapons or implements. Instead, spears were fashioned entirely from wood, hardened in fire and sharpened with stone tools. The result was a highly effective weapon that could be thrown with deadly force at a range of 60m. Analysis has revealed that these ancient Aboriginal spears had the same similar weight distribution and aerodynamics as today's Olympic javelins.

TASMANIA

St takes you past 87 old sandstone stores, cottages, and government buildings that have been recycled as antique galleries or cafés.

Redline **coaches** run to: **Hobart** (1¼hr., 1-2 per day, $11); **Launceston** (1½hr., 1-2 per day, $11); and **Ross** (25min., by booking only, $7). The **Tourism Centre** is at 77 High St (☎6254 1212; $1-2 donation requested for library **Internet** access). **Post office:** on High St (open M-F 9am-1pm and 2-5pm). **Postal code:** 7120. The **Oatlands YHA**, 9 Wellington St, is one of the Midlands' gems. (☎6254 1320. Reception daily 8:30-9:30am and 5-8:30pm. Bunks $14.) Don't miss Oatland's nightly **Ghost Tour,** from Callington Mill. (☎6254 1135. 2hr. $8; departs summer 8 and 9pm.)

## BEN LOMAND NATIONAL PARK

Tasmania's premier **ski resort** and largest Alpine area, **Ben Lomand National Park** (☎6336 5312, infoline ☎(190) 2229 0530) is about 60km southeast of Launceston. The lifts are nothing to brag about, the slopes (1300m at peak) are easier than those on the mainland, and there's less snow. Still, if you're in Tassie and you need to ski, this is where to go. During the summer, regular park fees apply; during the winter, entry costs $12 per car. To reach the park, follow the A3 3km east out of Launceston, then take the Blessington Rd (C401) 40km to the Ben Lomand Rd and the park entrance. From here, a steep 18km unsealed access road leads up to the ski village; rent chains at the base ($15, fitting $5). TassieLink runs a **charter service** from **Launceston.** (☎(1300) 30 05 20. 12-seater $390). **Ski rental** costs $38 per day. (☎6372 2574. Snowboards $50, with equipment $80, deposit $100.) Lift tickets run $20-28, students $10-15; beginner packages are available from $75. Plateau walks are suitable in spring and summer for wildflower photo-ops and views from **Jacobs Ladder Lookout.** The **Creek Inn,** at the top of the access road, offers accommodation year-round. (☎6372 2444. Dorms $20.) There is **free camping** with pit toilets and drinking water, 1km outside the park entrance.

# VICTORIA

Victoria may be mainland Australia's smallest state, but it's blessed with far more than its share of fantastic cultural, natural, and historical attractions. Its environment runs the gamut from the dry and empty western plains of the Mallee to the inviting wineries along the fertile banks of the Murray River, from the ski resorts of the Victorian Alps to the forested parks of the Gippsland coast. Nowhere else in Australia is so much ecological diversity only a daytrip away. The capital of the state and the cultural center of the nation, sleek and sophisticated Melbourne overflows with eclectic ethnic neighborhoods, seaside strips, and student haunts. With acres of verdant gardens, countless artspaces, and a vibrant never-tiring atmosphere, it's no wonder that many Aussies claim that the best-kept secret about Sydney is Melbourne.

Victoria's most distinctive attractions are found on the coast. West of Melbourne, the breathtaking Great Ocean Road winds its way along the roaring ocean. Hand-cut between 1919 and 1931 from the limestone cliffs, the road passes surfing beaches, coastal getaways, temperate rainforests, and geological wonders, including the Twelve Apostles rock formations, which poke precariously from the sea like ancient, jagged fingers. East of the capital, the coastline unfolds past Phillip Island's penguin colony and the beach resorts on Mornington Peninsula, heading into Gippsland. Here, crashing waves collide with granite outcroppings to form the sandy beaches at the edge of majestic Wilsons Promontory National Park. East Gippsland's beaches slowly give way to stony, sandy bird-filled tidal estuaries.

Most of Victoria's interior is remarkable less for its natural grandeur than for its historical significance. The mountainous exceptions are the ranges of the Grampians National Park, whose mammoth beauty evokes gazes of awe and humble moments of cosmological contemplation. North of the Grampians, the river-wrought lands of the Wimmera and the scraggly plains of the Mallee don't overwhelm at first sight, but the subtleties of the bush have their own delicate, small-scale beauty. Victoria's historical heart beats to the drum of the mid-19th century gold rush, which flooded central Victoria with seekers of the sweet stuff. When the ore waned, a host of dusty country towns were left in its wake, today preserved in tourist-oriented nostalgia—the Goldfields and the Murray river towns in north and Central Victoria live fondly in a fascinating past of mangled miners and rugged riverboats. In his wanderings throughout the Hume corridor, legendary bushranger Ned Kelly had a plan to stick it to the man. Today, this area is a fertile land of small-scale wineries cast pale by Australia's ski mecca, the High Country. The 20th century has brought extensive agricultural and commercial development, including several massive hydroelectric public works projects that continue to impact the state's ecosystems. Still, Victoria's physical beauty remains, tempered by a refined sensibility and cosmopolitan flair that add a touch of class and culture to Australia's down-to-earth grit.

Like most visitors' experiences, this chapter begins with Melbourne. It then moves clockwise through the spokes of the Victorian wheel, starting with the area south of Melbourne and continuing through the Great Ocean Road, Victorian Outback, Goldfields, Murray River, Hume Corridor, High Country, and Gippsland. Within each region, towns are ordered moving outward from the center.

# █ GETTING AROUND

Getting around Victoria is a breeze, thanks to the very complete, super-efficient system of intrastate trains and buses of **V/Line** (☎ 13 61 96; www.vlinepassen ger.com.au), which runs an information center at its main terminal in Melbourne's Spencer Street Station. V/Line has a few interstate options, but more complete national service is offered by **McCafferty's Bus Lines** (☎ 13 14 99; www.mccaffertys.com.au) and **Greyhound Pioneer** (☎ 13 20 30; www.greyhound.com.au). Renting a car allows considerably more freedom, and Victoria's highway system is the most extensive and easily navigable in the country. To cut down on occasionally prohibitive rental costs, check ride-share boards at any hostel. The **Royal Automobile Club of Victoria (RACV),** on Bourke St between William and Queen St, Melbourne (☎ 13 19 55 or ☎ 9703 6363; emergency roadside assistance ☎ 13 11 11; www.racv.com.au), has great maps and sells short-term traveler's insurance. Members of automobile clubs in other countries may already have reciprocal membership. To join in Victoria, the basic RACV Roadside Care package (including 4 free service calls per year and limited free towing) costs $50, plus a $30 first-time-joiner's fee for those over 21 (for more information, see p. 66).

Victoria's short internal distances make **cycling** a feasible means of travel. A series of byways criss-cross the state, traversing the more remote regions along mountain trails and abandoned train tracks. **Bicycle Victoria (BV),** 19 O'Connell St, North Melbourne, across from the north side Victoria Market, is the optimal resource for cyclists. They offer *Discovering Victoria's Bike Paths* ($14), which focuses mostly on the Melbourne area but covers a few regional tracks. Nonmembers can pick up free brochures on the state's many bike trails, and the very helpful staff will gladly answer all questions and make referrals. (☎ 9328 3000; email bicyclevic@bv.com.au. Open M-F 9am-5pm.)

## VICTORIA HIGHLIGHTS

**GROOVING.** Always-happenin' eclectic street culture in Melbourne (p. 508).

**GOING SPORTS-MAD.** The local footy fans at Melbourne's MCG (p. 537).

**BLATANTLY STARING.** Dusk feedings at the Koala Conservation Centre (p. 545).

**PLAYING UNABASHED TOURIST.** The spectacular Twelve Apostles (p. 555).

**PLUMMET.** The 60m abseil at The Ledge in Grampians National Park (p. 562).

**HERE BIRDIE BIRDIE...** The Malleefowl at Little Desert National Park (p. 567).

**COMMERCIALIZED HISTORY.** Sovereign Hill in Ballarat (see p. 572).

**AUSTRALIA'S FINEST.** A day or a lifetime at Taggerty Bush Settlement (p. 588).

**PAMPER YOUR PALETTE.** Free tastings at Rutherglen Wineries (p. 591).

**A SIMPLE SUNRISE.** Wilsons Promontory's wind-swept lighthouse (p. 599).

# MELBOURNE

The capital of Victoria and Australia's second-largest city, Melbourne is frequently thought of more as an ideal place to live than a great place to visit. This is half true; as Melburnians themselves are likely to tell you, there are countless reasons why this metropolis deserves the oft-touted designation as the planet's most liveable city. But Melbourne's bad rap as a travel destination stems from its lack of a singular, Kodak-moment icon like the Sydney Opera House or Uluru (Ayers Rock). Instead, the city is a sleek and stylish cosmopolitan collage of sights and sounds. Many would-be tourists fall prey to the "a city is just a city" mentality and rumble on to Sydney; but Melbourne is so much more than just another city. Both ultra-modern skyscrapers and ornate neogothic edifices line its wide streets, and the rumble of the green-and-gold trams that run down them is penetrated now and then by the roar of a hundred thousand sports nuts at the MCG. You might spend one hour window-shopping at Southbank's chic boutiques, and the next comparing fruit amid the bustling clamor of the Queen Victoria Market or strolling through yet another expansive city garden. Students enjoying late-night caffeine sessions in smoky Fitzroy cafés coexist with clubhoppers raging until 6am in South Yarra and Prahran. Sprawling over 6200 square kilometers and home to over three million denizens, Melbourne needs to be savored, not just seen.

VICTORIA

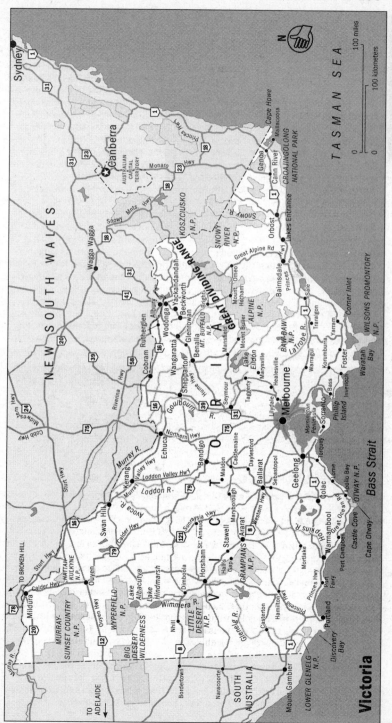

Victoria

It all began rather inauspiciously in 1825, when John Batman sailed a skiff up the Yarra, got stuck on a sandbank, then justified his blunder by claiming that he had found the "place for a village." Then named Batmania (Gotham City was already taken), the diminutive burg underwent a phenomenal growth spurt at the onset of the Victorian Gold Rush three decades later. "Marvelous Melbourne" celebrated its coming-of-age in 1880 by hosting the World Exhibition, which attracted over a million people. When the Victorian economy crashed in the 1890s following a series of bank failures, Melbourne's infrastructure collapsed, and its fetid open sewers earned it the nickname "Marvelous Smellbourne." By the early part of the 19th century, though, things were up and running again, and Melbourne posed a legitimate challenge to Sydney for the honor of being named Australia's capital. While the Canberra compromise ultimately deprived both metropoli of this status, Melbourne was more than happy to serve as temporary home to the government until the Parliament House was completed. The city's 20th-century apex was the 1956 Olympic Games, which brought Melbourne's love for sport to an international audience.

The subsequent years have seen even more population growth and an increasingly international flavor; most of the recent immigrants hail from China, Southeast Asia, Italy, and Greece (Melbourne has the world's third-largest Greek population after Athens and Thessaloniki). Today, Melbourne's various neighborhoods—the frenetic Central City, alterna-funky Fitzroy, Italianate Carlton, mellow St. Kilda, chic South Yarra, and more—invite exploration and lie within minutes of each other via tram. The weather is temperate, though beware of frequent rainstorms; most of the time, it's great for beach-going or walking along the Yarra at night with the reflection of the banana-yellow Flinders St Station shimmering on the water. With picturesque waterfronts, numerous parks, famous sporting events, and a world-class cultural scene, Melbourne invites visitors to relax and enjoy all the attractions of a large city with none of the hype.

## MELBOURNE HIGHLIGHTS

**FOOTY.** Aussie Rules at the MCG, Melbourne's sports obsession (p. 531).

**SCARED OF THE DARK?** Night tours of Old Melbourne Gaol (p. 532).

**HAWKING.** Tremendous bargains in the Queen Victoria Market (p. 532).

**OLD-SCHOOL GRANDEUR.** The Art Deco elegance of the Astor Theatre (p. 537).

**CITY VIEWS.** Cycling the waterfront of the Yarra and Port Philip Bay (p. 537).

**UNBRIDLED PANDEMONIUM.** The Moomba Festival (p. 538).

**PARTYING LIKE A ROCKSTAR.** Upscale South Yarra and chiller Fitzroy (p. 539).

# ◪ GETTING THERE

## BY PLANE

Boomerang-shaped **Tullamarine International Airport,** 22km northwest of Melbourne, has three terminals. The central terminal houses all international arrivals and departures. The first floor serves **United Airlines** (☎ 13 17 77), **Cathay Pacific** (☎ 13 17 47), **Singapore Airlines** (☎ 13 10 11), Qantas, and Ansett Airlines. The two major domestic carriers lie on each side of the international terminal: **Qantas** (☎ 13 12 11; www.qantas.com.au) to the left and **Ansett** (☎ 13 13 00; www.ansett.com.au) to the right. Each flies to all Australian capitals at least once a day, and they have similar fares. Return fares with three weeks advance purchase include: **Adelaide** ($283); **Alice Springs** ($623); **Brisbane** ($444); **Cairns** ($670); **Canberra** ($255); **Darwin** ($811); **Hobart** ($300); **Perth** ($656); and **Sydney** ($267). Winter specials are even cheaper.

**Travellers Information** (☎ 9297 1805; fax 9297 1051), directly in front of arriving international passengers as they exit, books same-day accommodations, provides maps and brochures, and has a useful backpacker bulletin board. Lockers ($4-8 per day) are located on either end of the international terminal.

**Skybus** (☎9335 2811) provides ground transport to Melbourne's city center. It stops at the Queensberry Hill YHA and at the Spencer St bus and train station downtown. The bus departs from the station for the airport at a quarter past and a quarter to the hour, and from the **Melbourne Transit Centre,** 58 Franklin St, every 30min. ($10, return $18). Taxis to the city center cost roughly $28 and take about 30min. **Car rental** companies are clustered to the left when exiting international arrivals (see **Getting Around,** below).

## BY BUS AND TRAIN

**Spencer Street Station,** at the intersection of Spencer and Bourke St, is the main intercity **bus** and **train station.** (☎9619 2139. Open daily 6:30am-10pm.) Both **V/Line** (☎13 61 96; www.vline.vic.gov.au) and **Great Southern** (☎13 21 47) run out of here.

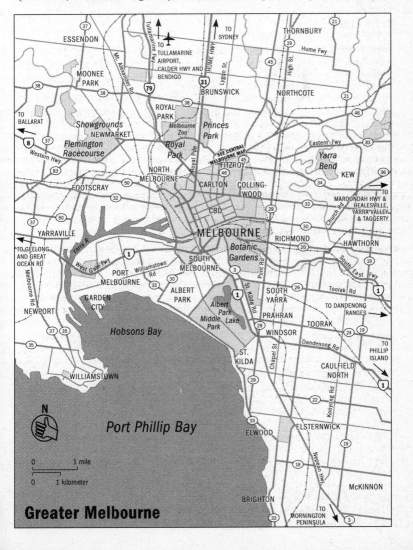

**Greater Melbourne**

In addition to its regular fares, **V/Line** offers unlimited travel passes within Victoria for seven days ($75) to overseas tourists only. **McCafferty's** (☎13 14 99 or ☎9670 2533; www.mccaffertys.com.au), is located in the barrel-shaped **coach station** adjoining the main Spencer St station, and offers bus service to most major Australian cities, as well as longer unlimited passes (see p. 63). The **Melbourne Transit Centre**, 58 Franklin St, near Elizabeth St, is the main terminal for **Skybus** (☎9335 2811) and **Greyhound Pioneer** (☎13 20 30; www.greyhound.com.au).

## FROM MELBOURNE TO:

| DESTINATION | COMPANY | DURATION | TIMES | PRICE |
|---|---|---|---|---|
| Adelaide | McCafferty's | 11hr. | 2 per day | $45 |
| Adelaide | V/Line | 11hr. | 1 per day | $52 |
| Adelaide | Greyhound | 8½hr. | 2 per day | $52 |
| Albury | V/Line | 3½hr. | 4-6 per day | $40 |
| Alice Springs | Greyhound | 28hr. | 1 per day | $205 |
| Alice Springs | McCafferty's | 30hr. | 4 per week | $207 |
| Alice Springs | Great Southern | 20hr. | 1 per week | $292 |
| Ararat | V/Line | 3hr. | 3-5 per day | $27 |
| Ballarat | V/Line | 1½hr. | 7-12 per day | $14 |
| Bendigo | V/Line | 2hr. | 5-7 per day | $21 |
| Bright | V/Line | 4½hr. | 1 per day | $39 |
| Brisbane | McCafferty's | 23hr. | 2 per day | $141 |
| Brisbane | Greyhound | 24hr. | 2 per day | $149 |
| Brisbane | Countrylink | 34hr. | 1 per day | $177 |
| Cairns | McCafferty's | 51hr. | 2 per day | $297 |
| Cairns | Countrylink | 70hr. | 4 per week | $332 |
| Canberra | V/Line | 8½hr. | 1 per day | $50 |
| Canberra | Greyhound | 8hr. | 2 per day | $62 |
| Castlemaine | V/Line | 1½hr. | 5-7 per day | $16 |
| Darwin | McCafferty's | 50hr. | 4 per week | $348 |
| Darwin | Greyhound | 50hr. | 1 per day | $370 |
| Echuca | V/Line | 3½-4hr. | 4-6 per day | $27 |
| Geelong | V/Line | 1hr. | 8-17 per day | $9 |
| Mildura | V/Line | 7-9hr. | 2 per day | $55 |
| Perth | Greyhound | 42½hr. | 1 per day | $277 |
| Perth | Great Southern | 54hr. | 2 per week | $340 |
| Sydney | McCafferty's | 13hr. | 3 per day | $54 |
| Sydney | Greyhound | 11hr. | 4 per day | $63 |
| Sydney | Countrylink | 11hr. | 2 per day | $110 |
| Uluru (Ayers Rock) | McCafferty's | 29hr. | 4 per week | $196 |

# ◈ ORIENTATION

The heart of one of the world's largest urban sprawls, Melbourne's lively, dense core comprises a geometrically precise city center surrounded by a slew of distinctive suburbs. The city center alone could take up the whole of an abbreviated visit, but the surrounding neighborhoods are where the true spirit of Melbourne lives. For those keen to conquer the entire polis, think about investing in the *Aha! Map of Melbourne* ($11), an enormous, hand-drawn, marvelously accurate map that details every single suburb.

## CITY CENTER

The city center, also known as the Central Business District (CBD), is composed of a well-arranged rectangular grid of streets bordered by **Spencer St** on the west,

La Trobe St on the north, **Spring St** on the east, and **Flinders St** (which borders the Yarra River) on the south. Five major streets run east to west: La Trobe (the northernmost), Lonsdale, Bourke, Collins, and Flinders. To the north of all but La Trobe are "little" streets—roads named after their southern superior (for example, Little Collins St is just north of Collins St; and Flinders Ln is just north of Flinders St). Nine streets cross this grid running north to south: Spencer (the westernmost), King, William, Queen, Elizabeth, Swanston, Russell, Exhibition, and Spring. Spencer St runs by the primary bus and train depot, bridges the Yarra River to South Melbourne, and carries trams #12, 48, 75, 95, 96, and 109. Directly in the middle, **Elizabeth St** carries major northbound tram lines (#19, 57, 59, and 68). One block east, **Swanston St** is a pedestrian walk but also carries important north-south tram routes (#1, 3, 5, 6, 8, 16, 22, 25, 64, 67, and 72). On the east end, Spring St borders Parliament and both Treasury and Carlton Gardens.

The eastern half of the city contains most restaurants and sights. **Bourke St Mall** (a pedestrian stretch of Bourke St between Elizabeth and Swanston St, traversed by trams #86, 95, and 96) swarms with people every day; the giant screen "alt.tv" at Bourke and Swanston St marks the heart of the city. The area just north of the city center bordered by La Trobe, Queen, Elizabeth and Victoria St borders Queen Victoria Market and is a hive of budget accommodations, while East Melbourne contains **Fitzroy Gardens** (p. 531) and Victoria's sporting shrine, the **Melbourne Cricket Ground** (p. 531; accessible by trams #48, 70, and 75 from Flinders St).

# NORTH MELBOURNE

North Melbourne is a pleasant mix of bungalows, flats, refurbished residences, and neighborhood shops and eateries, all easily reachable from the city center. Forming its eastern edge, **Elizabeth St** heads north from the city center and passes the **Queen Victoria Market** with its abundant, inexpensive food stocks and wares; travel west along Victoria St (traversed by tram #57) to find lots of cool budget eateries. William St heads north from the city center past **Flagstaff Gardens** and becomes **Peel St.** Peel and Elizabeth St intersect near the University of Melbourne with Elizabeth continuing northwest under the name **Flemington Rd** (along which trams #55 and 59 continue), ultimately leading to the **Melbourne Zoo** (p. 533). At this intersection, Peel St becomes **Royal Pde** (tram #19), which borders the University and continues on as **Sydney Rd** to the northern suburb of Brunswick.

# CARLTON

Dominated by Italiana, Carlton begins at **Nicholson St** and extends west through the Carlton Gardens and to the **University of Melbourne.** Its primary thoroughfare is **Lygon St,** where upmarket Italian bistros, somewhat cheaper *gelaterias* and *pasticcerias*, and a smattering of ethnic and eclectic food cater to a crowd of crusty old Mediterranean types and college students alike. Public transportation doesn't go along Lygon St in Carlton. Either take a tram up Swanston St (#1, 3, 5, 6, 8, 16, 22, 25, 64, 67, or 72) and then walk east along Queensberry or Faraday St, or take #96 up Nicholson St and walk west along Faraday St.

# FITZROY

Fitzroy, Melbourne's bohemian district, is a shopping mecca for those looking for new or used clothes, music, or eclectic books, but it also has Melbourne's best café society and excellent restaurants of all stripes. While it's packed with style and populated with "ferals" (Australians' term for the nose-ring crowd), Fitzroy is blessedly low on attitude, and its establishments house a healthy mix of freaks, families, and everyone in between. Tram #11 runs the length of **Brunswick St,** the main artery of Fitzroy. **Smith St** makes the boundary between Fitzroy and its eastern neighbor, **Collingwood,** and is home to a number of fine eateries and factory outlet stores. Just east of Smith are a handful of **gay bars** (and a fair number of straight ones too). The blocks of **Johnston St** between Brunswick and Nicholson St in Fitzroy form the smallish Latin Quarter, with lots of Iberian stores, restaurants, tapas bars, and dance clubs.

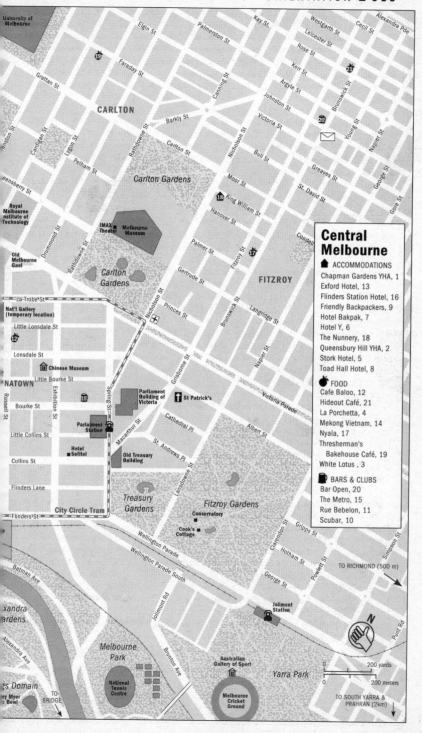

**Central Melbourne**

🏠 ACCOMMODATIONS
Chapman Gardens YHA, 1
Exford Hotel, 13
Flinders Station Hotel, 16
Friendly Backpackers, 9
Hotel Bakpak, 7
Hotel Y, 6
The Nunnery, 18
Queensbury Hill YHA, 2
Stork Hotel, 5
Toad Hall Hotel, 8

🍴 FOOD
Cafe Baloo, 12
Hideout Café, 21
La Porchetta, 4
Mekong Vietnam, 14
Nyala, 17
Thresherman's
  Bakehouse Café, 19
White Lotus , 3

🍷 BARS & CLUBS
Bar Open, 20
The Metro, 15
Rue Bebelon, 11
Scubar, 10

## SOUTH MELBOURNE

The Yarra divides Melbourne into the more working-class suburbs of the north and the fancier ones to the south. South Melbourne, west of St. Kilda Rd and stretching south from the West Gate Freeway to **Albert Park,** is an exception. More blue-collar than adjacent communities, this neighborhood has some quality restaurants and nightspots along its main drag, Cecil St. It's also a quick walk to the park, the **Royal Botanical Gardens** (p. 534), the city center, or the **beach** at Port Phillip Bay. Take tram #96 or 12 from Spencer St to get there.

West of South Melbourne along Port Phillip Bay are three of Melbourne's quietest, most posh suburbs. Port Melbourne is the most commercial and least impressive. Ferries to **Tasmania** depart from Station Pier at the terminus of tram #109. Bay St (City Rd near the CBD), marks the division between Port Melbourne and more urbane Albert Park, an upscale residential neighborhood with stately bungalows along the seaside. Middle Park, just south of Albert Park and Kerferd Rd, is a quiet bayside community, less showy and more liveable than its northern neighbor.

## SOUTH YARRA AND PRAHRAN

South Yarra and Prahran ("pruh-RAN") span the area enclosed by the Yarra to the north, St. Kilda Rd to the west, Dandenong Rd to the south, and William St to the east. The focus of gay Melbourne, **Commercial Rd** runs east-west, separating South Yarra from its southern neighbor Prahran. The district's main street is **Chapel St;** the section of the boulevard that lies in South Yarra is the commercial incarnation of the fancy suburbs south of the river. On sunny Sundays, the beautiful people come here to shop for Prada and Versace and then snipe about the catty salesgirls in sleek, pricey sidewalk bistros. Yet as in all multicultural Melbourne, good deals can be found between competing extravagances. Chapel St gets a little more down-to-earth south of Commercial Rd in Prahran, which is closer in spirit to St. Kilda. **Greville St** branches west from Chapel and is a den for second-hand clothing, record stores, and bizarre restaurants. Trams #78 and 79 run slowly along Chapel St. By tram from Flinders St Station, #8 travels waywardly below the Botanical Gardens, then along Toorak Rd to its intersection with Chapel St, while #5 and #64 head south along St. Kilda Rd, and then go east along Dandenong Rd to Chapel. The quickest way to get to the area from the central city, though, is to hop a Sandringham Line train from Flinders Station and take it to South Yarra, Prahran, or Windsor Stations, each of which lies only a few blocks west of Chapel St.

## ST. KILDA

Though it's a bit removed to the southeast of the city center (and officially in the city of **Port Phillip,** see p. 545), St. Kilda is a budget hotspot with cheap accommodations and popular eateries. Trams #12 and 96 bring people to St. Kilda from Spencer St Station, while #16 attacks from Flinders Station. Tram #16 travels along **St. Kilda Rd,** and passes Melbourne's two largest green spaces, the **Royal Botanical Gardens** and **Albert Park,** en route. At **St. Kilda Junction,** St. Kilda Rd intersects Fitzroy St, which runs west toward the beach where it curves south to follow the waterfront and becomes the Esplanade. **Barkly St** runs south from the junction toward the beach, completing a triangle with Fitzroy St and the Esplanade. A half-kilometer toward the beach from St. Kilda Junction, **Grey St** links Fitzroy and Barkly St, and is the focus of St. Kilda's budget accommodations. The last street that branches south from Fitzroy St before it turns into the Esplanade is **Acland St,** the southern end of which is one of Melbourne's many excellent café districts, distinguished by its superlative old-time cake shops.

# ◪ GETTING AROUND

## BY PUBLIC TRANSPORTATION

Melbourne's superb public transportation system, the **Met,** comprises light-rail trains, buses, and trams (☎ 13 16 18, open daily 7am-9pm for inquiries; www.vic

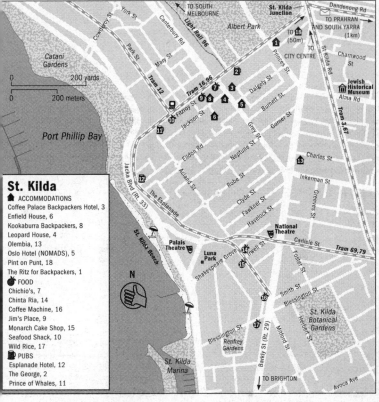

**St. Kilda**

**ACCOMMODATIONS**
Coffee Palace Backpackers Hotel, 3
Enfield House, 6
Kookaburra Backpackers, 8
Leopard House, 4
Olembia, 13
Oslo Hotel (NOMADS), 5
Pint on Punt, 18
The Ritz for Backpackers, 1

**FOOD**
Chichio's, 7
Chinta Ria, 14
Coffee Machine, 16
Jim's Place, 9
Monarch Cake Shop, 15
Seafood Shack, 10
Wild Rice, 17

**PUBS**
Esplanade Hotel, 12
The George, 2
Prince of Whales, 11

trip.com.au). **Tram** routes criss-cross the metropolitan area and are the most useful for navigating the city and its proximate outskirts. Weekdays they run every 3-12 min., nights and weekends every 20min. or longer. The burgundy-and-gold **City Circle Tram** circumnavigates the **Central Business District (CBD)**, provides running commentary on the city's sights and history, and is totally **free.** Many Melburnians hop on all the trams without paying, since you don't actually have to show your pass to ride them—but if an inspector decides to make a spot check and you're without a valid ticket, expect a hefty $100 fine. The bus and light-rail train systems are mostly for commuters going to farther-afield residential areas, and you can't board without a valid Metcard. There are **train stops** at **Melbourne Central, Flagstaff Gardens, Parliament,** and **Spencer St,** though the main rail hub is the beautiful banana-colored **Flinders St Station** at the southern foot of Swanston St, identifiable by its big clock—and, um, it's beautiful bana...you get the point.

The entire network comprises three Met zones, though you'll only be in Zone 1 unless you travel out to a distant suburb. **Tickets** within Zone 1 can be used on any of the three types of transportation, and are valid for unlimited travel for a 2hr. period ($2.40), a day ($4.60), a week ($20), or a month ($75). Concession rates are roughly half-price; you qualify if you are under 15 years old, or have a valid Australian university ID (ISIC cards or international university IDs not accepted). Only 2hr. tickets can be purchased from coin-operated machines on board trams and buses; if you're going to be in town for a while, the long-term passes save a lot of time and hassle. If you purchase your ticket anywhere but on a tram itself, you must validate it by putting it in any of the electronic green boxes on the tram; otherwise, even if you have a ticket, you can be fined if you forget to do this. Obviously these instances are rare, but right now the government is in the midst of privatizing the Met; commercial interests may be more pronounced than government laxness. Tickets are sold at stations, on board trams and buses (coins only), and at the **Met Shop,** 103 Elizabeth St (☎13 16 38; open M-F 8:30am-5pm, Sa 9am-1pm.) For more info and route maps, grab the free Met *Fares and Travel Guide.*

## BY CAR

The usual national car rental chains mostly have offices in the Melbourne city center and at the airport. They tend to rent only to people over age 25, though some accept renters aged 21-24 with a surcharge. National agencies include: **Budget,** 398 Elizabeth St, on the corner of A'beckett St (☎9203 4844, airport ☎9293 2355; open M-F 8am-6:30pm, Sa-Su 8am-5pm; from $60 per day, $18 extra per day for drivers aged 21-24); **Hertz,** 97 Franklin St (☎9663 6244, airport ☎9338 4044; open M-Th 7:30am-6pm, F 7:30am-7pm, Sa 7:30am-5pm, Su 8am-5pm; from $56, $15); **Thrifty,** 390 Elizabeth St (☎9663 5200, airport ☎9241 6100; open daily 7:30am-6pm; from $54, $15); and **Avis,** 20-24 Franklin St (☎9663 6366, airport ☎9338 1800; open M-Th 7:30am-6:30pm, F 7:30am-7pm, Sa-Su 8am-5pm; from $60, $25).

Local firms tend to have cheaper rates, though if you're traveling around the state or the country, you may find it inconvenient that they don't have lots of locations. **Delta Rent-a-Car** (☎9600 9025; www.deltacars.com.au), on the corner of A'Beckett and Elizabeth St across from the Transit Centre, starts at $49 per day, $12 surcharge for ages 21-24. **Backpacker Car Rental,** 103 Railway Ave, in Werribee, charges $100 per week with unlimited kilometers and free delivery. (☎9731 0700. Must be at least 23 years old.) A good but out-of-the-way option for long-term rental is **Car Connection** (☎5473 4469; email car@carconnection.com.cau) in Castlemaine, 120km northwest of Melbourne. They offer a station wagon for up to six months for $1950 plus insurance, and full camping equipment for two people for the duration of the rental for $250. There are also tons of **bargain agencies** with names like Rent-a-Bomb that are only half-joking about the quality of their cars. The deals can run as cheap as $10 per day, but weigh the savings against the potential costs of breaking down in the middle of nowhere. The **Royal Automobile Association of Victoria (RACV)** (☎13 19 55 or ☎9703 6363), at their new location on Bourke St just east of William St, is a comprehensive driving resource. Anyone can buy good maps from them; members get towing and emergency roadside assistance. For further information, see **On The Road,** p. 66.

## BY TAXI

If you're out after the Met stops running at midnight, a cab is the only option. All companies have a $2.60 base charge plus 96¢ per km. There's a $1 surcharge when you arrange cab pickup by phone and if you ride between midnight and 6am. The misnamed **Silver Top** (☎13 10 08) and **Black Cabs** (☎13 22 27) are both yellow.

## BY BICYCLE

Melbourne's central city is compact, though traffic congestion makes it difficult to navigate by bike. The streets in the outer suburbs are flat and broad enough to make biking a convenient transit option, and there are loads of bike tracks for recreation. For more information, see **Melbourne Recreation,** p. 537.

# ▐ PRACTICAL INFORMATION

## TOURIST AND FINANCIAL SERVICES

**Melbourne Tourism Services: City Experience Center,** Melbourne Town Hall (☎9658 9658; www.melbourne.org). On Swanston St between Little Collins and Collins St. Features interactive virtual tours of the city. Open M-F 9am-6pm, Sa-Su 9am-5pm. The office includes the **Melbourne Greeter Service**, a great—and *free*—way to get acquainted with the city, with 2-4hr. individual tours tailored to your personal interests. Arrange one by filling out a brief application 3 working days in advance; you can also do this via email (greeter@melbourne.vic.gov.au). There are also info booths at **Bourke St Mall** (open M-Th 9am-5pm, F 9am-7pm, Sa 10am-4pm, Su 11am-4pm) and **Flinders St Station** (open M-Th 9am-5pm, F 9am-6pm, Sa 10am-4pm, Su 11am-4pm).

**Victorian Tourist Offices: Victoria Visitor Information Centre** and **AUSRES** booking service, Melbourne Town Hall (☎9658 9658; fax 9650 6168; 24hr. info ☎13 28 42). On the corner of Little Collins and Swanston St. Open M-F 9am-6pm, Sa-Su 9am-5pm. **Information Victoria**, 356 Collins St (☎(1300) 36 63 56). Open M-F 8:30am-5:30pm.

**Disabled and Elderly Travelers Information: Travellers Aid**, 2nd fl., 169 Swanston St (☎9654 7690; fax 9654 1926). Open M-F 9am-5pm, Sa-Su 11am-4pm. Also at Spencer St Station (☎9670 2873). Will meet and assist elderly and disabled travelers on trains and buses M-F 7:30am-7:30pm, Sa-Su 7:30am-11:30am; arrange ahead.

**Outdoors Information: Natural Resources and Environment (NRE)**, 8 Nicholson St, East Melbourne (☎9637 8325; email publication.sales@nre.vic.gov.au). Maps and info on licenses. Open M-F 8:30am-5pm. Also call **Parks Victoria** (☎13 19 63) for all park info.

**Budget Travel: YHA Victoria**, 83-85 Hardware Ln (☎9670 9611; fax 9640 0540; email travel@yhavic.org.au), provides a full listing of YHA hostels and a booking service. International booking surcharge $5, non-YHA member domestic surcharge $2. Attached budget travel agency. Open M-F 9am-5:30pm, Sa 10am-1pm. **STA Travel's Victorian headquarters**, 222 Faraday St, Carlton (☎9349 2411), and all over the city center, including 208 Swanston St (☎9639 0599). Open M-Th 9am-6pm, F 9am-7pm, Sa 10am-4pm. **Backpackers World**, 167 Franklin St (☎9329 1990), in Hotel Bakpak. **Backpackers Travel Centre**, Shop 19, Centre Place, 258 Flinders Ln (☎9654 8477).

**Consulates: Canada**, 123 Camberwell Rd, East Hawthorne (☎9811 9999). Open M-F 8:30am-5:30pm. **Great Britain**, Level 17, 90 Collins St (☎9650 4155). Open M-F 9am-4:30pm. **United States**, Level 6, 553 St. Kilda Rd (☎9526 5900). Open M-F 9am-noon and 1-4pm.

**Currency Exchange:** All banks will exchange money during regular operating hours: M-Th 9:30am-4pm, F 9:30am-5pm. The currency exchange at 190 Collins St (☎9654 2768) is open daily 8am-8:40pm. **Thomas Cook Foreign Exchange**, 330 Collins St (☎9602 3811), at the corner of Elizabeth St. No commission when exchanging Thomas Cook traveler's checks; $7 on other checks and cash. Open M-F 9am-5pm, Sa 9am-2pm. Several banks have offices at the airport. ANZ, Commonwealth Bank, Westpac and National Bank **ATMs** accept V, MC, AmEx, Cirrus, and Plus. Their 24hr. outlets swarm like locusts all over the city.

**American Express Travel Center:** 233 Collins St (☎9633 6333), and inside the GPO (☎9203 3001). Buys all traveler's checks, changes cash commission-free (1% on cash exchanges over $300), and provides letter holding service to holders of AmEx cards or traveler's checks. Wire transfers available. Open M-F 9am-5:30pm, Sa 9am-noon.

# LOCAL SERVICES

**Bookstores:** Duh. They're all over the city. **Reader's Feast** (☎9662 4699), in the basement of the Midtown Plaza at the corner of Bourke and Swanston St, has the latest fiction. Open M-W 9:30am-6pm, Th 10am-6pm, F 9:30am-9pm, Sa 10am-5pm, Su noon-5pm.

**Library: State Library of Victoria**, 382 Swanston St (☎9669 9888), on the corner of La Trobe St. Open M-Th 10am-9pm, F-Su 10am-6pm.

**Ticket Agencies: Ticketek** (☎13 28 49, freecall ☎(1800) 06 28 49; www.ticketek.com.au), and **Ticketmaster** (☎13 61 00; www.ticketmaster.com.au), for sports, performances, and other events. Handling fee for phone booking. Both open M-Sa 9am-9pm, Su 10am-5pm. **Halftix** (info ☎9650 9420), Bourke St Mall opposite Myer Department Store, sells half-price tickets on performance day only and often sells out by 2pm. Cash only. Open M 10am-2pm, T-Th 11am-6pm, F 11am-6:30pm, Sa 10am-2pm.

**Employment Assistance:** Most *Let's Go* listed accommodations help find temp jobs free of charge. Some particularly good ones are the Exford Hotel and Flinders Station Hotel. **Backpacker's Resource Centre** (BRC; ☎(1800) 15 46 64), in the lobby of Hotel Bakpak (see **Accommodations,** p. 520), usually comes up with work within a week for no registration fee. Melbourne's biggest daily paper, *The Age*, has extensive classifieds on Saturday and can be accessed online at www.theage.com.au.

### MEDIA AND PUBLICATIONS

**Newspapers:** The main newspapers are *The Age* ($1) and *The Herald Sun* (90¢) for local coverage and *The Australian* for national news.

**Nightlife:** *InPress* and *Beat,* released on Wednesday (free). For gay nightlife, check out *MSO* and *Brother Sister.*

**Entertainment:** *Age*'s Entertainment Guide and *Herald Sun*'s Gig Guide, found in Friday's paper.

**Radio:** Alternative, Triple R 102.7FM; Rock, Triple J 107.5FM and Triple M 105.1FM; News, 1026AM; Tourist Info, 88FM.

## EMERGENCY AND COMMUNICATIONS

**Emergency:** ☎000.

**Police:** 637 Flinders St (☎9247 6666).

**Crisis Lines: Victims Assistance and Referral Hotline** (☎9603 9797). **Centre Against Sexual Assault** (☎9344 2210). **Lifeline Counseling Service** (☎13 11 14). **Poison Information Service** (☎13 11 26). **Emergency Surf Life Saving** (☎9534 8400).

**Other numbers:** Directory assistance ☎12 23, international ☎12 25; reverse charge calls ☎12 550; translation and interpretation ☎13 14 50.

**Pharmacy: The Block Pharmacy,** Shops 7 and 8, The Block Arcade, 282 Collins St (☎9650 6688). Open M-F 7:30am-5:30pm, Sa 8:30am-12:30pm.

**Hospital: St. Vincent's Hospital,** 41 Victoria Pde, Fitzroy (☎9288 2211). Take any tram east along Bourke St to stop #9. **Royal Melbourne Hospital,** Grattan St, Parkville (☎9342 7000). Take tram #19 from Elizabeth St to stop #16.

**Internet Access:** There are 8 free terminals at the **State Library** (see above); sign up in advance for 30min. sessions. In the city itself, prices tend to hover around 15¢ per minute. A major exception is **Traveller's Uni-Net Stop,** 211 Victoria St (☎9326 4418), one block west of Vic Market, promising the "cheapest Internet access in Victoria"— 1min. 7¢. Open daily 9am-midnight. Another good deal is **Backpacker's World,** 167 Franklin St (☎9329 1990), in Hotel Bakpak. 1hr. $6. St. Kilda's backpacker trade keeps competitive pricing of about 7¢ per minute everywhere; multitudes of Internet shops line Fitzroy St.

**Post Office:** General Post Office (☎13 13 18), at the corner of Elizabeth and Little Bourke St. *Poste Restante.* Open M-F 8:15am-5:30pm, Sa 10am-1pm. Also at Melbourne Airport VIC 3045 (☎9338 3865) with full fax, photocopy, and Poste Restante services. Open M-F 9am-5pm, Sa-Su 10am-4pm. Postal Code: 3000.

**Phone Code:** 03

# ▐ ACCOMMODATIONS

Melbourne's tourist industry supports numerous budget accommodations to host its backpacker population. The two biggest hostel hives are **St. Kilda** and the area just **north of the city center** enclosed by La Trobe, Queen, Elizabeth and Victoria St. The mostly YHA-affiliated hostels in **North Melbourne** tend to be quieter and more sedate, popular with at least as many school groups and elderly travelers as 20-something backpackers, while the accommodations in the **city center** are as boisterous as they are conveniently located. **South Yarra** and **Prahran** lie farther afield but are preferred by those who enjoy the proximity to these districts' shopping

**GETTIN' IT ONLINE IN MELBOURNE ;-)**

**www.visitvictoria.com** Contains a search engine with all sorts of info on food, nightlife, accommodations, and events in Melbourne and all of Victoria. Events searchable by type, town, and date.

**http://melbourne.citysearch.com.au** An eating and drinking guide, up-to-date entertainment listings, and a comprehensive business directory.

**http://melbourne.sidewalk.com.au** The latest entertainment options, restaurant listings, shopping guides, and gay and lesbian information.

**http://members.ocean.com.au/conwaywn** An illustrated overview of the city, plus a guide to Melbourne's nature sanctuaries.

and nightlife. The St. Kilda options, with one notable exception, generally make up for what they lack in cleanliness with an unquenchable thirst to party.

Availability drops during the **high season** (roughly Nov.-Feb.) when most accommodations raise their prices a tad ($2-4). The more popular hostels tend to be booked solid during these periods (and are also in demand during school holidays, from June-Aug.), so be sure to book as far in advance as possible. During summer holiday, you can usually find accommodation at universities (varies, usually between Christmas and mid-February). Try **Melbourne University** (Ormond College, ☎9344 1110; $45 per night) and **Monash University** (Halls of Residence, ☎9905 4000; from $30). Further north of the city, in Bundoora, **LaTrobe University** (☎9479 1357) offers accommodation at each of its three colleges in basic dorm rooms with bathroom, laundry, and kitchen on most floors: **Chisholm College** caters the most toward backpackers (☎9479 2875; singles $16, weekly $98, doubles $25, weekly, $161; available Dec.-mid-Feb.); **Glenn College** includes an evening meal and breakfast, but may be booked-up with conferences (☎9479 5100; singles $23, weekly $160; Dec.-Jan.); and **Menzies College** is the cheapest option, but you must have a full-time student ID card (☎9479 1075; singles $11; Dec.-Jan.). To get to LaTrobe Uni, catch bus #350 (45min.) or #250 (1hr) from Flinders Station.

Unless noted otherwise, all accommodations have a common room with **TV, hall baths, 24-hour access, luggage storage, a guest kitchen, laundry machines** ($2-3 wash, $1-2 dry), and **no chore requirements.** An increasingly popular form of deposit is an international passport in lieu of cash. This policy, which has been adopted by some of Melbourne's major hostels, can be inconvenient, though you can generally get your passport back for the evening should you need it for ID purposes. Remember that prices generally rise a few dollars during the summer.

# CITY CENTER

**The Greenhouse Backpacker,** 228 Flinders Ln (☎9639 6400; fax 9639 6900; email friendlybpacker@optusnet.com.au). Near Swanston St. Reception is on the 6th Floor. The same owners as Flinders and the Friendly B (see below) opened the first-rate Greenhouse in July 2000. Most rooms are 4-share with spring mattresses and large lockers. Sparkling bathrooms, cable TV, funky dining room, industrial-size kitchen. Roofdeck with BBQ and inspiring city views. Free Internet. Linen included. Dorms $22, weekly $140; singles $45; doubles $60. Wheelchair accessible.

**Flinders Station Hotel Backpackers,** 35 Elizabeth St (☎9620 5100; fax 9620 5101; www.flindersbackpackers.com.au). One block north of Flinders Station, on the corner of Flinders Ln. Glistening hostel gives excellent safe haven from the bustling city just out the door. Quick-and-true job placement, Internet access, large kitchen with gigantic walk-in refrigerator, and 24hr. supermarket across the street. On-site bar open daily until 3am, bottleshop until midnight. Linen included. Passport or driver's license key deposit. Check-out 11am. No heat or A/C, but rooms retain warmth well in winter. 8-bed dorms $13, in summer $16; 4-bed dorms $14, $21; twins and doubles $57, $60, ensuite $81, $88. $10-12 discount and free jug of beer on weekly payment. Wheelchair accessible.

**The Friendly Backpacker,** 197 King St (☎9670 1111, freecall ☎(1800) 67 11 15; fax 9670 9911; email friendlybpacker@optusnet.com.au). One block east of Spencer St Station at the corner of Little Bourke St. Cheery atmosphere, heaps of local scene info, loads of amenities, and inner-spring mattresses. Small lounges on each of 4 floors; two TVs and a VCR with movie collection. Heat and A/C. Linen included. Key deposit $10. Reception 7:30am-11pm. Check out 10am. Free pickup from bus station, Tassie ferry, and airport. Dorms $20, weekly $126; singles $40; twins and doubles $56. Breakfast with first night stay. Book one week in advance Oct.-May. Wheelchair accessible.

**Exford Hotel,** 199 Russell St (☎9663 2697; fax 9663 2248; www.exfordhotel.com.au). At the corner of Little Bourke St, in Chinatown. Same owners as Flinders Station Hotel, but not quite the same par. The peeling paint on many walls detracts from the otherwise handsome wooden floors and winding stairwell that give the Exford a stately feel. A few rooms offer sweeping views of the Chinatown gates. Solid job placement. Locals and travelers party in the lively hotel pub until the wee hours. Internet (10min. $2). No heat or A/C. Linen included. Passport, driver's license, or $50 key deposit. Check-out 11am. Dorms $12-15; twins and doubles $39-45.

## JUST NORTH OF THE CITY CENTER

Walk uphill past La Trobe on Elizabeth St or take tram #19, 55, 57 or 59 to some of the nicest budget accommodations in town.

■ **Hotel Bakpak,** 167 Franklin St (☎9329 7525, freecall ☎(1800) 64 52 00; fax 9326 7667; www.hotelbakpak.com). Between Elizabeth and Queen St. This cavernous 6-level facility can sleep up to 780 and has established itself as a pulsing, party-hearty nerve center for Melbourne's backpacker scene. Dubious wall murals and a blaring intercom don't do much for atmosphere, but no one beats Bakpak's cornucopia of amenities, which include a budget travel agency, free airport pickup, employment service, basement "Roo Bar," café, Internet access (1hr. $6), free passes to the nearby city baths (see **Recreation,** p. 537), small movie theater, and unique "Cabana style" showers. Roo Bar parties offer amazingly cheap drinks and provide a great way to meet fellow travelers. No smoking. Linen included. Passport key deposit. Spare but spruce 10- to 16-bed barrack $17; smaller dorms $18-$19; singles $35; twins and doubles $50. VIP.

■ **Toad Hall,** 441 Elizabeth St (☎9600 9010; fax 9600 9013; www.toadhall-hotel.com.au). Between A'beckett and Franklin St. A classier, more reserved place, several cuts above the frenetic backpacker scene, Toad Hall's appealing Victorian structure combines the intimacy of a B&B with the conveniences and attentive staff of a large inn. Airy, crystal-clean kitchen, plant-filled patio, and basement Victorian bluestone den with cable TV, VCR, and stereo. Inner-spring mattresses, refrigerator, and tea in every room. Linens and cushy quilt included. Parking $5. Key deposit $20. Reception daily 7am-10pm. Dorms $25; twins $50; doubles $60, ensuite $90. Bookings advised. YHA, VIP.

**Stork Hotel,** 504 Elizabeth St (☎9663 6237; fax 9663 8895). At the corner of Thierry St. The Stork dates back to the Victorian gold rush, when it was the last stop on the line between Port Melbourne and the Goldfields. It remains a genial gathering place for travelers, retaining its history without seeming worn. The family that runs the Stork has traveled extensively and can empathize. Ground-floor pub closes early in deference to sleepers; attached restaurant has meals for $7-10. Linen and towel included. 4-person dorm $20; singles $42; twins and doubles $54. Flexible weekly rates; ask manager.

**Hotel Y,** 489 Elizabeth St (☎9329 5188, freecall ☎(1800) 24 91 24; fax 9329 1469; email hotely@ywca.net). Between Thierry and Franklin St, less than a block from the Transit Center. The Y has the feel of a luxury hotel with stellar rooms, swimming pool, and the sleek Café Y. The bathroom tiles, designed by Deb Halpern, the creator of Melbourne's Ophelia statue (p. 533), have been photographed for architectural journals. Second floor women only. Ensuite 4-bed dorms $33; singles $77; doubles $88. YMCA/YWCA 10% discount. Book several weeks ahead; credit card or one-night's stay deposit.

# NORTH MELBOURNE

Residential North Melbourne is quieter and more relaxed than the city center, and though its accommodations are quite a hike from downtown, it's made accessible by tram #57 and 59 from Elizabeth St and tram #55 from William St.

**Queensberry Hill YHA,** 76-86 Howard St (☎9329 8599; fax 9326 8427; email queens berryhill@yhavic.org.au). Take tram #55 north from William St to stop 11 on Queensberry St, then go 2 blocks west to Howard St. This YHA grand dame overflows with 314 bunks on three colorful floors, glistening communal bathrooms, and tons of amenities in a nearly-new facility. Free parking and bike hire, rooftop patio with BBQ and sweeping view of city, travel agency, huge kitchen, pool tables, Internet (1hr. $4), and currency exchange. What it lacks in personal warmth, it makes up for in unbridled functionality. Dorms $20-21, non-YHA members $23-24; singles $55, $58; doubles $62, $68; family rooms $72, $78; ensuite rooms $10-16 extra. Two-week max. stay. Book ahead in summer. Wheelchair accessible.

**Chapman Gardens YHA Hostel,** 76 Chapman St (☎9328 3595; fax 9329 7863; email chapman@yhavic.org.au). Take tram #57 north to stop 18, turn right onto Chapman St, and the hostel is on the left. The C-Gardens' landscaped estate and pleasant gazebo are in a quiet, tree-lined residential neighborhood. Clean, heated rooms (mostly tiny twins). Free parking and bike hire. Key deposit $10. Luggage storage $2. Reception daily 7:30am-12:30pm and 1-10pm. 4-bed dorms $20, non-YHA $23; twins $21, $24; singles $37, $40. Seventh night free. Book ahead.

# FITZROY

**The Nunnery,** 116 Nicholson St (☎9419 8637, freecall ☎(1800) 03 26 35; fax 9417 7736; www.bakpakgroup.com/nunnery). Stop 13 on tram #96, at the northeast corner of Carlton Gardens. Housed in the former convent of the Daughters of Mercy, this heavenly hostel has large dorms, halls that are snazzily decorated with an incongruous mix of religious paraphernalia and psychedelia, a breezy wooden deck with BBQ, and rooms with balconies overlooking Carlton Gardens. Linen and towel included. Internet (8min. $2). Reception 8am-8pm. Check-out 9:30am. Passport or $20 key deposit. Free soup W night and wine-and-cheese Su night. Dorms $18, weekly $112; smaller dorms $19-20; singles $40; twins and doubles $45-60. Discounts for stays over 3 nights. VIP.

# MIDDLE PARK

**Middle Park Hotel,** 102 Canterbury Rd (☎9690 1882; fax 9645 8928; email mid dlepark@ozemail.com.au). Across from the Middle Park stop on trams #95 and 96. 1km from St. Kilda. Beautiful budget accommodation in a restored 1890s building with high ceilings, clean rooms, and large terrazzo bathrooms. Job placement assistance. No heating, though thick doonas are provided. Free linen and towel. Nightclub, upscale bistro, and casual neighborhood bar downstairs (pub meals $7-12, backpacker specials $5). Key deposit $10. Reception M-F 7:30am-7:30pm, Sa 9am-1pm, enquire at the bar afterhours. Dorms $17, weekly $98; singles $35, $195; doubles $50, $250.

# SOUTH YARRA AND PRAHRAN

🌑 **Chapel St Backpackers,** 22 Chapel St, Prahran (☎9533 6855; fax 9533 6866; www.csbackpackers.com.au). Just north of Dandenong Rd, on tram routes #78 and 79, and across from Windsor train station. One of the best places in town, just a stumble from both Melbourne's best nightlife and St. Kilda. The banal building front belies the fresh and modern facilities inside. Very friendly staff; reception common area leads to close ties with other guests that spill from the heated bunk rooms. Most rooms have ensuite bathrooms. Internet (1hr. $6). Linen and doona included. Key deposit $20. Check-out 10:30am. 4- to 6-bed dorms $18, weekly $119, in summer $20, $125; twins and doubles $48-50, $329, summer $55-60, $343; breakfast included.

**Claremont B&B,** 189 Toorak Rd, South Yarra (☎9826 8000; fax 9827 8652). One block east of the South Yarra train station, and on tram route #8. A stylish budget B&B set in an elegantly refurbished 1886 Victorian building. Central staircase with mahogany banisters is brilliantly lit by stained-glass skylight. Rooms with hardwood floors, wrought-iron beds, and TVs. Spotless hall baths. Singles $60, weekly $295; doubles/twin $75, $395; additional person $10, $60; continental breakfast included.

**Lord's Lodge,** 204 Punt Rd, Prahran (☎9510 5658; fax 9533 6663). Take tram #3, 5, 6, 16, 64, or 67 south on St. Kilda Rd to stop 26 and walk east 2 blocks along Moubray St. It doesn't look like much from the outside—and it's removed from both Prahran and St. Kilda—but for a $15 fee, they guarantee work for the duration of your stay. Reception M-Sa 8:30-11:30am and 5-6pm, Su 8:30-11:30am. Dorms $17. 7th night free.

## ST. KILDA

St. Kilda is **backpacker heaven,** with dirt cheap and often unkempt, grungy hostels—but hey, you get what you pay for. The hostels, centered around Grey St, largely mirror the precinct's fun-loving, gritty flavor. Though removed from the city center, it's easily accessed by tram (stop 133 on lines #16 and 96). The beach, restaurants, and lively nightlife of St. Kilda are in easy reach. If you're coming in March, book way ahead to avoid the hassle of the Grand Prix crowd (see p. 538).

**▨ Olembia,** 96 Barkly St (☎9537 1412; fax 9537 1600; www.olembia.com.au). Tucked behind a small canopy near the intersection with Grey St. Alone, it's a cut above the usual budget digs; compared to the gritty St. Kilda backpacker options, it's a 5-star resort. Gorgeous living room with sofas and fireplace, perfect for curling up with a book. Spacious dining room. Ornate, high-ceilinged rooms with comfy mattresses are impeccably clean, as are the bathrooms. Free parking. Bike hire $12 per day. Reception 7am-1pm and 5-8pm. Linens and doona included. Key deposit $10. 3- to 4-bed dorms $20-21; singles $44; twins and doubles with box-springs $60-64. Book ahead in summer.

**Pint on Punt (NOMADS),** 42 Punt Rd (☎9510 4273, freecall ☎(1800) 83 50 00; fax 9529 5518; email admin@pintonpunt.com.au). Just north of St. Kilda Junction. Take tram #3, 5, 16, 64, or 67 from Flinders Station. New and clean, the Pint has large rooms with new mattresses. Free continental breakfast, and 30% discount offered on pub meals downstairs; guest kitchen under construction. Free city pickup. Satellite TV. Soundproof boundary between bar and accommodations. Passport or Aussie student ID key deposit. Reception 7am-noon and 5-9pm, or at the bar until 1am. Check-out 10am. 4- to 6-bed dorms $16-17; singles $35; twins and doubles $40. VIP, NOMADS.

**Enfield House,** 2 Enfield St (☎9534 8159, ☎freecall (1800) 30 21 21; fax 9534 5579). Take tram #16 or 96 to stop 30 by Fitzroy and Grey St. Walk half a block down Grey, turn right on Jackson St, then left onto Enfield St. In a sprawling mansion that once was a popular brothel, Enfield provides mellow, worn surroundings. Big-screen cable TV, funky rooftop deck, and daily events such as trivia and soccer. Rooms and bathrooms are basically clean. Reception 8am-1pm (3pm in summer) and 5-9pm. Four week max. stay. Dorms $17-18, weekly $105-110; singles $35, $315; twins and doubles $50-55, $280-$315. Breakfast included. Book ahead in summer.

**Coffee Palace Backpackers Hotel,** 24 Grey St (☎9534 5283, freecall ☎(1800) 65 40 98; fax 9534 5724; email backpaca@ozemail.com.au). One block off Fitzroy St. The Coffee Palace gang downs java by day, VB by night, and then sleeps it all off in century-old worn but liveable digs. The top-floor deluxe ensuite rooms are significantly better, with heaters and inner-spring mattresses. Really popular, but only with partiers who don't mind the grungy atmosphere. Passport key deposit. Dorms $14-16, deluxe $16; twins and doubles $32-36, $40. Renovations planned for mid-2001. Book ahead in summer. Free bus station or airport pickup. VIP.

**The Ritz for Backpackers,** 169 Fitzroy St (☎9525 3501, freecall (1800) 67 03 64; fax 9525 3863). Tram #16 lets off at stop 132 out front. The minimalist aesthetic confounds the name. Don't come here if you don't want to party. Tons of activities, including video and wine-and-cheese nights. Bathrooms aren't hyper-clean, but the shower stalls are luxuriously big. Linen included; doona $2. Free morning pancakes. Reception 7am-10pm. Checkout 9:30am. Dorms $13-17, weekly $90-110; twins and doubles $38-40, $250-$260. Prices rise in summer. VIP.

**Leopard House,** 27 Grey St (☎9534 1200). Recently purchased by the owners of the **Kookaburra Backpackers,** 56 Jackson St (☎9534 5457), down the street. When your trusty *Let's Go* researcher arrived, both properties were undergoing extensive renovations set to be completed by Oct. 2000. When finished, both will reportedly have larger rooms (many ensuite) and be wheelchair accessible. Driver's license key deposit. Check out 9:30am. 4-bed dorms $15, $17 in summer; 8-bed dorms $18, $20.

**Oslo Hotel,** 38 Grey St. Very sparse and somewhat grungy accommodation offers large backpacker dorm ensuites with TV lounge suitable for groups on extended stays. Dorms $15. Prices negotiable based on length of stay.

# ⊡ FOOD

Melbourne hosts an array of restaurants dazzling in both diversity and number, from steamy Chinatown holes-in-the-wall to Fitzroy café *couture* to Carlton Italian cuisine to South Yarra sidewalk bistros to St. Kilda's mix of backpacker-targeted and upscale eateries to everything else and then some. Multicultural influences give rise to Chinese restaurants with french fries and sushi bars with cappuccino. The city's restaurants constitute a scene in and of themselves; on most nights, Melburnians pack into their favorite eateries until closing time (which is whenever the proprietors feel like shutting the doors). Enjoy.

## CITY CENTER

Amid the bustling urban jungle of Melbourne's CBD lurk what seem like a million fantastic eateries, hidden away in labyrinthine corridors or diminutive crannies between high-rise buildings. Most are Asian, including Chinese, Japanese, Indian, Nepalese, Sri Lankan, Malaysian, Indonesian, and Vietnamese. Neon-pulsing **Chinatown** fills the stretch of Little Bourke St hemmed in by colorful red gates between Swanston and Exhibition St. At the **Midtown Plaza,** on Swanston St between Bourke and Little Bourke St, you can get a filling sushi or noodle-soup meal for around $5. Blink and you'll miss the **Greek Precinct,** on Lonsdale St between Swanston and Russell St. It's only a half dozen or so pricey Hellenic restaurants and taverns, but the baklava is divine. Many of the coolest cafés, most with an Italian twist, call the CBD home as well; they often lurk in narrow arcades (such as the Block Arcade, between Collins and Little Collins St) that snake through the city. Above all, the city center rewards the adventurous gourmet; wander around with only your nose and palate as a guide and you're sure to find a culinary treasure.

▨ **Mekong Vietnam,** 241 Swanston St (☎9663 3288). Their specialty is *pho',* a Vietnamese noodle soup served in all shapes and sizes. The more adventurous can get soup with beef balls, bone marrow, or chicken livers, but there are less exotic versions (scrumptious sliced beef and chicken) as well as vegetarian-friendly ones at almost half price. A mere $5-7 will get you a massive, steaming tureen of the stuff, along with bottomless tea. Informal and bustling. Open M-Sa 9am-10pm, Su 10am-10pm.

▨ **Café Baloo,** on Russell St (☎9663 3226). Between Little Lonsdale and Lonsdale St. A great bargain, the Baloo mixes South Asian fare with pasta and sandwiches in classy, mellow environs. Smooth jazz and fertility figures give background to heaping portions of curry and biryani served in heaping portions with your choice of fish, chicken, beef, lamb, chickpea, or tofu ($7-9). Pasta basics seem out of place but offer variety ($7-8). 50¢ table charge per person; no alcohol. Open M-F noon-10pm, Sa-Su 5-10pm.

**Nudo,** 187 Russell St (☎9639 8998). Not much on service or atmosphere (think bustling and orange), but for $6.50 you get a huge platter of stir fried noodles, rice, or noodle soups with your choice of meat. Dishes will make you forget you've been trying to get your waiter's attention for 20min. Open Su-Th 11am-11pm, F-Sa 11am-1am. BYO.

**Krome Kafe,** 273 Swanston St (☎9663 8199). Vervy, nervy, swervy café with a cutting-edge caffeine scene and surprisingly little attitude. Oddly, the interior has little chrome, but brekkie is served all day, and there's a range of meaty options ($8-15). Live entertainment F night. Open M-Th 8am-8pm, F 8am-11pm, Sa 11am-8pm, Su noon-7pm.

**Shark Fin,** 131-135 Little Bourke St, Chinatown (☎9663 1555). A standout distinguished by elegant decor and truly superior cuisine. Pricey (basic mains around $14-18, can go up of $30), but you get what you pay for; portions are huge and served with the perfect amount of delicately spiced sauce. Best Szechuan chicken around. Open M-Sa 11:30am-3pm and 5:30-11pm, Su opens 11am. Dim sum at lunch time.

**Stalactites,** 177-183 Little Lonsdale St (☎9663 3316). On the corner of Russell St. Somewhat pricey like most of its Greek Precinct counterparts, but a bit less upscale. The $10 appetizer sampler gives a taste of nearly every little dip, snack, and meat the Mediterranean has to offer. $6 souvlaki and giros. Licensed and BYO. Open 24hr.

**Curry Bowl,** Shop 41, Myer House Arcade, 250 Elizabeth St (☎9639 0868). Sri Lankan and South Indian fare served hot, fresh, and quickly. A "small" curry will feed even the hungriest backpacker. Meals $3-6. Open M-F 9:30am-5:30pm, Sa 10:30am-3:30pm.

**Fast Eddy's Café,** 32 Bourke St. A fave-rave with the late-night crowd for its 24hr. food.

# NORTH MELBOURNE

**The Queen Victoria Market (QVM;** see **Sights,** p. 532) serves as the focal point of culinary North Melbourne. In fact, much of the city congregates here, where you can get all the fresh ingredients you need to cook up a fabulous dinner cheaply. The surrounding area is home to some fine eateries as well. From the city, take any tram north on William or Elizabeth St.

**▨ La Porchetta,** 302-308 Victoria St (☎9326 9884), across from the QVM. Hundreds of tantalizing wood-fired pizzas served daily (small $4.40, medium $5.60, large $6.60). When you've received the check, you'll think they've undercharged you. Open Su-Th 11am-midnight, F-Sa 11am-1am. Takeaway available. BYO wine only.

**▨ The White Lotus,** 185 Victoria St (☎9326 6040). One block west of QVM. Entirely vegan menu attempts to guide the "way to heaven," following the Buddhist tenets of Tien Tao. All meals prepared without meat, animal products, or even onions or garlic. Carnivores will be placated—nay, amazed—by the excellent imitation meat dishes, like mock abalone made from soy and wheat gluten or the spicy Mongolian "beef." Meals $8-14. Open M-F noon-2:30pm and 5:30-11pm, Sa-Su 5:30-11pm. BYO.

**The Queen Vic** (☎9320 5822). In the QVM. The food court has excellent budget fare, mostly made from fresh goods sold next door. **Victoria Fish** serves fish-and-chips ($7-8). **Afghan** purveys souvlaki, doner kebab, and many vegetarian dips ($4-6). The **Consciousness Café** has healthy salads and sandwiches ($4-6). Hours vary, but usually open market hours: Tu and Th 6am-2pm, F 6am-6pm, Sa 6am-3pm, Su 9am-4pm.

**Red Gum,** 312 Victoria St (☎9329 7156). Offers major backpacker bargain: $2 dinner from 6:30-9pm. They pick the meal for the day, you pick meat or veggie, hand over some change, and that's that. It's the only thing they serve, and they attract backpackers by the hordes. Bar open daily 10am-11pm.

**The Traveller's Café,** 229 Victoria St (☎9328 1118). Two blocks west of QVM. Well-traveled owners have festooned the walls with pictures and kitsch from around the globe. The menu is similarly cosmopolitan, ranging from Hokkien noodles to eggs Manhattan ($6-10). Full juice and coffee bar. $1 discount with an international passport. Open M-F 7:30am-5pm, Sa-Su 8:30am-5pm.

# CARLTON

The best known street in Carlton is **Lygon St,** Melbourne's Little Italy, where tons of Italian pizzerias, cafés, and gelaterias are juxtaposed with Thai and Vietnamese joints along the five-block stretch between Queensberry St to the south and Elgin St to the north. Despite Carlton's proximity to the University of Melbourne and its attendant student traffic, most of the Italian eateries (whose *maitre d's* aggressively recruit would-be patrons in the evenings) are out of the budget range. There are, however, a fair number of affordable non-Italian places, and a few cafés where you can get a cheap pasta that's still *delicioso*.

■ **Threshermans Bakehouse Café,** 221 Faraday St (☎9349 2319). Aptly named, with one counter serving food, the other an extensive array of pastries and cakes. Lunch and dinner are probably the best value on Lygon St: $5.50 for a plate of mix-and-match pastas, veggies and potatoes. Thick lasagna $5.50, foccacia pizzas $3.40. With all the money you've saved on dinner, head over to the other counter for a delicious canoli ($2.50). Restaurant open daily 11:30am-3pm and 5-11pm; café open daily 6am-midnight.

**Tiamo,** 303-305 Lygon St (☎9347 0911). Diminutive but elegant adjoining Italian joints, Tiamo and Tiamo2. The first is dark and flavorful, offering basic Italian pastas. Tiamo2 is light and blithe with a more sophisticated menu. Cheap breakfasts ($4-9) and tasty desserts ($5.50). *"Ti amo"* means "I love you" in Italian, and perhaps you'll fall in love with this place. If you do, you're utterly desperate. It's just a restaurant—get a grip. Tiamo open M-Sa 7:30am-11pm, Su 8am-10pm; Tiamo2 open M-Sa 9:30am-10pm.

**Jive,** 131 Lygon St (☎9347 6666). Very popular with the uni crowd, Jive's walls are splashed with big bold colors, and its sound system reverberates with American soul tunes. The food is basic, but good and cheap: Asian noodles, pasta, and pizza in all kinds of varieties ($5-10). Nothing's more than $14. The bar gets funky F-Sa. Open Su-Th 3pm-1:30am, F-Sa 3pm-3:30am, maybe earlier on uni holidays. Free delivery.

**Toto's,** 101 Lygon St (☎9437 1630). You're not in Kansas anymore—and it doesn't seem like Australia either. Toto's has the feel of a large Italian villa. They just do the basics but they do them well—pastas and pizzas in various sizes ($6-10). Licensed and BYO wine. Restaurant open Su-Th noon-3pm and 5-10pm, F-Sa noon-3pm and 5-11pm. Adjoining bistro open daily 11am-10pm.

# FITZROY AND COLLINGWOOD

The heart of Melbourne's bohemian scene and café society lies in Fitzroy, along **Brunswick St** between Gertrude and Princes St. Particularly on sunny weekend days, hippies, post-hippies, ferals, and freaks of every ilk frequent the countless artsy coffeehouses and eateries. As always, though, much mainstream and wannabe chic intermingles with their opposites in an attempt to feel cutting edge. The area gets progressively posher as you go south along Brunswick, closer to the city. The stretch of Johnston St just west of Brunswick St is Melbourne's Latin Quarter, with Latin dance clubs, Iberian grocers, and great—but pricey—tapas bars. There are also dining options galore along **Smith St** in Collingwood.

■ **Nyala,** 113 Brunswick St (☎9419 9128). FYI: Nyala is moving a few doors down Brunswick St in late 2000. Nyala's menu samples the best of Africa. Start with a selection of delicious dips, such as deberja, a combination of eggplant, chili, garlic, and yogurt ($6). Mains are split evenly between meaty and veggie. The house specialty is the ridiculously savory Gambian lamb Domeda ($13.50), but even better is the luscious curried chicken Kuku Na Nazi ($14). For dessert, Tafach Mooz (sweet banana and ice cream, $4.50) may in fact cause an orgasm. Open Tu-Sa 6pm-late. BYO (corkage $1).

■ **Hideout Café,** 389 Brunswick St (☎9436 5688). J.D. Salinger should be eating the huge portions at this sprawling café. The menu has breakfast, mains, and a long list of "Snax" (served from noon); even the smallest sized nachos ($8.50, large $12.50) could feed a small developing country—which could probably fit in the gigantic, colorful booths that line the side wall. The thick milkshakes are liquid bliss (now that's a $5 milkshake, indeed). Open Su-Th 7am-1am, and F-Sa 24hr.

**Mario's,** 303 Brunswick St (☎9417 3343). This small café is hard to spot—only a small neon sign in the window bears its name—but it sports some of the best breakfast buys in town. Poached eggs on thick toast only $5.50; for $1-1.50 you can add a side item like thick, juicy mushrooms. Lighter options like porridge and yogurts ($5). Those who spurn the first meal of the day can grab $9-14 pasta dishes. Full coffee bar. Licensed.

**Vegie Bar,** 380 Brunswick St (☎9417 6935). A converted warehouse where Fitzroy's large meat-averse population gathers to chow guilt-free. They promise "food for the body and soul" and serve it up in heaping portions. Mains all under $8.50. The rich veggie-filled risotto is the all-star ($8.50). Crowded and lively even on weeknights. Lots of vegan and wheat-free options. Open daily 11am-10pm. Fully licensed.

**Retro Café,** 413 Brunswick St (☎9419 9103). While not particularly retro in design (except the mesmerizing indoor waterfall), this somewhat upmarket eatery is nothing if not eclectic. An intriguing fusion of Southeast Asian, modern Italian, Mediterranean, and nouveau Australian influences; the turkish breads and dips run a hefty $8.50, and the house specialty, BBQ lamb cutlet, is baaaad to the bone ($15). Sunday "Famous Retro Brekkie" is a see-and-be-seen Fitzroy tradition—bacon, poached eggs, toast, mushrooms, and tomato, all mopped in rich hollandaise ($9.90). Open daily 8am-late.

**Robert Burns Hotel,** 376 Smith St (☎9417 2233). Just north of Johnston St. Behind the uncharacteristic non-Iberian name hides great value Spanish fare. Eat in the bright, friendly bar or in the large, simple adjacent restaurant. Chicken dishes run $11-12 and steak $15-20, but at the bar you can get them for about half-price. The chicken *shasliks* ($7) is doused in creamy, tangy sauce with fries and salad. Paella $14 per person, min. 2 people. Kitchen open M-F noon-2:30pm and 6-10pm, Sa-Su noon-3pm and 6-10pm.

## SOUTH YARRA AND PRAHRAN

Preened, pricey South Yarra aggressively markets itself as the place to see and be seen, and its mod-Oz bistros with sidewalk seating see their share of black-clad fashion mavens after a day of shopping in Chapel St's boutiques. There are some excellent budget options though, particularly south of Commercial St in more down-to-earth Prahran. The ubiquitous coffee bars are a wallet-friendly way to sample the scene (cappuccino around $2.50). Check out the Prahran Market, on Commercial Rd at Izett St, for cheap, fresh produce, meat, and ethnic foodstuffs.

▨ **Gurkha's Brasserie,** 190-192 Chapel St (☎9510 3325). Delicious Nepalese cuisine comes at a very reasonable price in an ornate restaurant bedecked with lanterns and peaceful South Asian music. It might take you a while to figure out what to order, but a good bet is the *Dal Bhat Masu*, which comes with your choice of meat curry (the goat is wonderfully tender), soup, and rice or bread for only $12.50. Vegetarian version available for $11.90. For all you exhibitionists, the front window has a low table with pillows to sit on. Open daily 5:30-10:30pm. Licensed and BYO wine. 10% takeaway discount.

▨ **Jamon Sushi,** 205 Greville St (☎9510 2928). This place is not cheap, but the sushi is absolutely divine. Around the corner from the bustle of Chapel St, this hip eatery will have you moaning with delight—think Meg Ryan—and wondering why Japanimation is projected on the wall. The chef is surrounded by the eating counter, and if he's got time, he'll give you a sushi primer. After two bites of the sushi and roll combo platter, the $20 you just forked over will be but a distant memory. Sushi or sashimi platters $12, deluxe $20. Open Tu 6:30pm-late, W-F 12:30-3pm and 6:30pm-late, F-Su 6:30pm-late.

**Gratzi,** 534 Chapel St (☎9824 0099). Artsy decor belies the low prices of the mod-Italian potpourri mixed with French and American influences. Breakfast is served all day; try the Greek yogurt, a creamy, honey-flavored concoction with muesli and strawberries ($6). Various crepes ($4.50-8) bulge with fresh fruit or roasted eggplant, ham, cheese, and tomato, or design your own. Open M-F 7:30am-6pm, Sa-Su 8am-6pm. BYO.

**That Little Noodle Place,** 565 Chapel St (☎9827 3148). The name says it all: noodles, done in a ton of Asian varieties. Design your own from a selection of all kinds of meat, veggies, and sauce. The *Bum Bo Xao* is a specialty, incorporating beef, peanuts, vegetables, and garlic fish sauce on a bed of rice *vermicelli*. All noodle dishes $9. Lightning-fast service. Open 11:30am-11pm. Fully licensed.

**Amigos,** 7/478 Chapel St (☎9826 1653). You and this Tex-Mex place will quickly become friends. All the basics. Crowded environs benefit from a fully-stocked margaritas bar ($7). One catch: where are the free chips and salsa? Open daily noon-late.

## ST. KILDA

With all the hipness of South Yarra and Chapel St but far less pretense, St. Kilda offers diverse and exciting menus with quality affordable eateries interspersed with many decidedly non-budget options. The result is a delightful mix of value and vogue. You can't go wrong with the holes-in-the-wall or fancier bistros on

Fitzroy St; Acland St, legendary among locals for its divine cake shops, also has a menagerie of great cuisine of all ethnic stripes.

■ **Chinta Ria,** 94 Acland St (☎9525 4664). The "soul" incarnation of a three-restaurant Malaysian consortium (the "jazz" is at 9/176 Commercial Rd, Prahran, and "blues" at 6 Acland St, St. Kilda). Meat and seafood main courses ($14-17) might damn your wallet, but the cheaper and equally divine fried rice and noodle selections ($8.50-9.50) will lead you to eternal salvation. The Singapore *Mee Hoon* is a winner. Open M-Sa noon-2:30pm and 6-10:30pm, Su noon-2:30pm and 6-10pm. Delivery $3; $20 min.

■ **Monarch Cake Shop,** 103 Acland St (☎9534 2972). The oldest cake shop on Acland St (est. 1934) and still the best. All-stars are Polish cheesecake, tartalicious plum cake, and sacrelicious chocolate *kugelhof* ($11-13). Slices $2.50-3. Open daily 7am-9pm.

**Wild Rice,** 211 Barkly St (☎9534 2849). This place doesn't look like much, but enter to find a nice vegan selection. Rice or tofu balls, sweet potato fillers, and Nori pyramids ($3) can be combined to produce an eclectic meal or taken as an appetizer for large roll-ups, foccacias, casseroles, or curries ($5-10). Lush garden courtyard enclosed out back. Open daily noon-10pm; kitchen closes at 9pm.

**Chichio's,** 109 Fitzroy St (☎9534 9439). Vast Italian menu offering pasta, seafood, salads, grilled meats, and wood-fired pizzas. Backpacker menu is a budget feast: extra large pizza or pasta and pesto foccacia, Italian salad, and wine or soft drink ($9 per person, 2 person minimum). "Small" means large and "large" means enormous.

**Seafood Shack,** 47 Fitzroy St (☎9534 7777). This little place is more than a hole-in-the-wall and less than a restaurant. We all know that size is all that matters: $5.50 for a heaping helping of the fish-and-chips. Defying its name, the best thing about the Shack is its burgers, from Aussie to gourmet ($5.50, with salty fries). Open daily 11am-late.

**The Coffee Machine,** 191 Acland St (☎9525 5166). This machine is actually a full café and manufactures some of the finest breakfasts on either side of the Yarra. Many consider the coffee the best in Melbourne. Hot sandwiches and pastas for lunch ($9–12). Breakfast served until 4:30pm. Open daily 8am-6pm.

**Jin's Place,** 89B Fitzroy St (☎9534 1488). Small, sleek and sparkling, Jin's serves some of Melbourne's cheapest raw fish. There are lots of other options too: Korean-style pizza, tofu steak, *tsukune* (tasty mushroom turnovers), and teriyaki chicken. It's all perfectly fresh, and nothing costs over $5. Sounds fishy, huh? Open daily 12:30pm-midnight.

# ◉ SIGHTS

## CITY CENTER

■ **RIALTO TOWERS.** Rising 253m above the city center, the Rialto Towers is the tallest office building in the Southern Hemisphere. The 55th floor observation deck provides absolutely spectacular 360° views of the city and surrounds. "Zoom City" live-action video cameras are very much an example of a method of surveillance so crucial to the Foucaultian analysis of the techniques of disciplinary power. Ahem, er, they, uh, allow you to zoom in and literally see people crossing the street all the way across town. **Rialtovision Theatre** plays a 20min. film, *Melbourne, the Living City* (to distinguish it from all those cities populated entirely by perambulatory corpses) that highlights Victoria's tourist spots with cheesy music and dramatic, wide-angle shots. *(525 Collins St. 1 block east of Spencer St station between King and William St. ☎9629 8222. Open Su-Th 10am-10pm, F-Sa 10am-11pm. Film every 30min. Film and deck admission $10, concessions $8, child $5.50, family $27.50.)*

**HOTEL SOFITEL.** You can get a less impressive but entirely free view of the city on the other end of Collins St from the Rialto Towers, where it intersects Exhibition St. Ascend to the 35th floor restaurant and stare at the abyss beyond the full-wall bathroom windows to eyeball the Melbourne skyline.

**IMMIGRATION MUSEUM.** Chronicling the experiences of 200 years of Australian immigration, the museum combines excellent pictures and interactive technology with compelling testimony. A mock ship in the main room shows typical living quarters aboard ocean-going ships from the 1840s to the 1950s. The top floor is home to the ambiguously related **Hellenic Antiquities Museum,** hosting occasional exhibits on loan from museums in Greece. Outside, the **Tribute Garden** preserves family names under a thin veil of running water for those who chose to pay to become a part of history instead of earn it. *(400 Flinders St. In the Old Customs House on the corner of William St. A City Circle Tram stop. ☎ 9927 2700. Open daily 10am-5pm. Joint admission $8, concession and YHA $6; garden free. Wheelchair accessible.)*

**ST. PAUL'S CATHEDRAL.** The Anglican cathedral, completed in 1891, impresses not in its scale but in the intricacy of its detail. The exquisite floor tiling has simpler patterns throughout the nave but more intricate mosaics near the altar. The beautifully stenciled pipes of the 19th-century Lewis organ are also worth a look. *(Presides over the corner of Flinders and Swanston St, diagonal Flinders St Station. Enter on Swanston St. Open daily 7am-6pm. Free.)*

**MELBOURNE CENTRAL MALL.** This six-level megamall houses some of Australia's swankiest boutiques and cafés alongside tourist shops selling cheesy koala-and-kangaroo merchandise at outrageous prices. In the central atrium stands the 50m-tall Coop's Shot Tower, built in 1889-90, then Melbourne's highest structure. Today it houses shops and is enclosed by a soaring 20-story, 490-ton glass cone, an iconic feature of Melbourne's skyline. A huge fob watch in the atrium in front of the Shot Tower has an automated Waltzing Matilda display on the hour—that tourists love and locals hate. A central stage enraptures hordes of schoolkids with shows and sing-alongs; Sundays see local caricature artists working their magic. *(At La Trobe and Swanston St. Open M-Th and Sa 10am-6pm, F 10am-9pm, Su 11am-6pm.)*

**STATE LIBRARY OF VICTORIA.** A great space to read or work, and equipped with all manner of international newspapers, the State Library is worth a visit if just to marvel at the spectacular interior design. The whole place is undergoing a $190 million renovation that will most notably reinstate glass to the roof of the Domed Reading Room (to be renamed the La Trobe Australiana Reading Room), a spectacular octagonal space soaring 35m high. An eastern section of the building along Russell St, formerly the home of the Museum of Victoria (see graybox, p. 532), holds a fraction of the permanent collection of the **National Gallery of Victoria** (p. 533) while the gallery undergoes renovations. *(At La Trobe and Swanston St. Library ☎ 9669 9888 or evenings and weekends ☎ 9669 9810; www.slv.vic.gov.au. Free tours M-F 2pm. Open M-Th 10am-9pm, F-Su 10am-6pm.)*

**CHINATOWN.** The pagoda gates at the corner of Swanston and Little Bourke St indicate your arrival at a two-block stretch of Asian restaurants, groceries, and bars that was first settled by Chinese immigrants in the 1870s. A block and a half east, the **Chinese Museum,** slightly worn and in need of a paint job, houses *Dai Loong* (Great Dragon), the **biggest imperial dragon in the world** (not the longest, which is in Bendigo VIC), a staple of Melbourne's Moomba festival (p. 538) that is so huge it has to be wound around two entire floors. The third floor provides a brief but honest look at ethnic discrimination as well as contributions that Chinese merchants, veterans, and sportsmen have made to Australia. *(22 Cohen Pl. ☎ 9662 2888. $6, concessions $4. Open daily 10am-4:30pm. Wheelchair accessible.)*

**PARLIAMENT OF VICTORIA AND OLD TREASURY.** Victoria's parliament is a stout, pillared 19th-century edifice every bit as stolid and imposing as a seat of government should be. Free tours detail the workings of the Victorian government and the architectural intricacies of the parliament chambers. *(Spring St north of Bourke St. A City Circle Tram stop. ☎ 9651 8567. Tours when Parliament is not in session 10, 11am, noon, 2, 3, and 3:45pm. No self-guided tours.)* Designed in Italian Palazzo style by a 19-year-old prodigy, the **Old Treasury Building** contains a museum chronicling Melbourne's past, including some great stories about the idiosyncrasies of the city's first years. The gold vaults in the basement were built to prevent a crime wave that plagued the Treasury during the Victorian Gold Rush; by themselves they're not much to see, but free tours running daily at 1 and 3pm bring the site to life. *(2½ blocks south on Spring St. Open M-F 9am-5pm, Sa-Su 10am-4pm. $8, concessions $4.)*

**FITZROY GARDENS.** These gardens, originally laid out in the shape of the Union Jack, bloom year round. On the south end is Cook's Cottage, a small stone home constructed by Captain James Cook's family in England in 1755 and moved to Melbourne in 1934 to celebrate the city's centennial. Cook never actually reached the site and may not even have spent time in this house, but it's a well-preserved—if dull—domicile filled with period stuff. Next door is the Conservatory, a colorfully stocked greenhouse with seasonal plants and flowers. *(Gardens bordered by Lansdowne, Albert, and Clarendon St, and Wellington Pde. Tram #48 or 75 from Flinders St. Cook's Cottage: ☎ 9419 4677. $3, concessions $2. Conservatory: Free. Both open daily 9am-5pm.)*

**ST. PATRICK'S CATHEDRAL.** A beautiful product of Gothic revival, St. Patrick's comes replete with grotesque gargoyles, stained glass, and a magnificent altar. Just inside lies the baptismal font, housing a fine example of 17th-century religious narrative painting, *The Finding of the Child Jesus in the Temple.* ◼The cathedral is most spectacular by night, when its 106m spires are illuminated by floodlights. *(West of the Fitzroy Garden's northwest corner on Cathedral Place. Open 6am-6pm. No tourists during mass M-Sa 7-8:45am and 12:45-1:45pm, Su 7am-12:30pm and 6:15-7:30pm.)*

**YARRA PARK AND THE MELBOURNE CRICKET GROUND (MCG).** First established in 1853 and expanded in 1956 and again in 1992 to seat 92,000, the MCG functions as the sanctum sanctorum of Melbourne's robust sporting life. It houses Aussie Rules Football every weekend in winter, including the Grand Final the last Saturday in Sept. There are also, of course, cricket contests, from Oct.-Apr., highlighted by test matches between Australia and strong competitors from South Africa, England, New Zealand, Pakistan, and the West Indies. The best way to see the stadium is to take a guided tour from the northern entrance, which offers unique insight into the MCG's history, allowing you to step inside the player's changing rooms, the **Melbourne Cricket Club Museum,** and onto the hallowed turf itself. Entertaining guides make the 1hr. tour worth the price even if you don't have the slightest idea what the hell a wicket, over, or googlie are. *(☎ 9657 8879. Tours run on all non-event days at regular intervals, at least every 30min. 10am-3pm. $13, concessions $9, families $33. MCG and museum admission without tour half price.)* The north side of the MCG contains the **Australian Gallery of Sport and Olympic Museum** further celebrating Australia's love for sport. The venue houses the **Australian Cricket Hall of Fame** (which requires some understanding to appreciate), a new AFL exhibition, and the **Olympic Museum,** with a focus on Australian achievements and the '56 Melbourne games. *(☎ 9657 8879. Admission included with MCG tour. Admission without tour half price. Open daily 9:30am-4:30pm.)* **AFL games** are also a must—tickets about $16, concessions half price (available at Ticketmaster, ☎ 13 61 00)—and allow you to experience firsthand an essential aspect of Melburnian culture. Be sure to order a meat pie and beer, and if you don't get the rules (start by checking out **Sports,** p. 24), just cheer along with the passionate fans. Berating the referees as loudly as possible is always a good move. *(All in Yarra Park, southeast of Fitzroy Gardens across Wellington Pde. Accessible via trams #48, 70, and 75.)*

**NATIONAL TENNIS CENTRE (MELBOURNE PARK).** To the west across the railroad tracks from the MCG and Yarra Park sits the ultramodern Tennis Centre, now called **Melbourne Park.** The stadium's retractable domed roof shelters the **Australian Open** Grand Slam every January. You can wander around and see the trophies and center court for free or take a 40min. guided tour. You can't follow in their footsteps on the center court, but the outer courts give proximity to greatness for a roughly $20 playing fee. In the neighboring **Olympic Park,** the Melbourne Storm play its **rugby** matches. *(Take tram #70 from Flinders St. Tennis Centre open M-F 9am-5pm. Tours $5, concession $2.50. Bookings required at ☎ 9286 1600.)*

VICTORIA

**BEMUSING MUSEUMS** With all the renovations and name-changes under way with Melbourne's myriad museums, it's easy to lose track of what's going on. Ma *Let's Go* is here to help. A quick breakdown: Museum Victoria is the over-arching state museum organization that operates several Melbourne museums, including the Scienceworks Museum (2 Booker St, Spotswood), the Melbourne Planetarium (in the Scienceworks Museum), the Immigration Museum (400 Flinders St), and the crown jewel, the Melbourne Museum (in Carlton Gardens). Not to be confused, just south of the Yarra River is the National Gallery of Victoria, which is currently under renovation. The National Gallery's Australian collection will be moved into the new Museum of Australian Art at Federation Square. If that's not enough for you, what is now the Melbourne Museum used to be the Museum of Victoria, located behind the library. Now, the library is home to a portion of the National Gallery's collection during renovation, but once the construction is complete, it will go back to being just a library. And the game of museum musical chairs will be over. Instead of watching this game though, you could always just sit back with a VB watchin' some footy.

## NORTH OF THE CITY CENTER

**CARLTON GARDENS AND MELBOURNE MUSEUM.** Spanning three city blocks, the verdant gardens criss-crossed with pathways and spectacular fountains deliver peaceful sobriety between Spring St and Victoria Pde. Standing starkly within the gardens is the sprawling **Melbourne Museum,** newly reopened in October 2000 as the **largest museum complex in the Southern Hemisphere.** This six-year $300 million project replaces the old Museum of Victoria. The Melbourne Museum comprises two buildings: the **Royal Exhibition Building,** which was home to Australia's first parliament and now hosts major expositions and temporary exhibits; and a new, stunning facility next door that contains the museum's permanent galleries—a forest, an Aboriginal center, a children's museum, a science and technology wing, and an IMAX theatre (see **Film,** p. 537). *(Bordered by Victoria, Rathdowne, Nicholson, and Carlton St, on the city circle tram. Museum ☎ 8341 7777; www.museum.vic. gov.au. $12, concessions $9, families $30. Open daily 10am-6pm.)*

**■ OLD MELBOURNE GAOL.** This stalwart prison was completed in 1864 and housed a total of 50,000 prisoners in its 84 years. The main structure has three levels of cells linked by iron catwalks. The tiny cells each house small displays about everything from the history and specifications of the jail to fascinating stories about **Ned Kelly's gang,** though the creepiest displays feature the stories and death masks of the most notorious criminals executed here. Kelly, Australia's most infamous bushranger, was hanged in the jail, and the trap door and scaffold are still here, as is the suit of armor that he wore in his final shoot-out with police. Wonderfully spooky evening tours led by professional actors provide a chillingly vivid sense of how horrible it was. Or satiate your thirst with a Ned Kelly soda (pretty tasteless, eh?) in the gift shop on your way out and be thankful you've escaped—no criminal ever did. *(On Russell St just north of La Trobe. ☎ 9663 7228; www.nattrust.com.au. Admission $10, concessions $8. Night tours W, Su 7:30pm. $19, children $11. Bookings essential for night tours; call Ticketmaster ☎ 13 61 00. Open daily 9:30am-4:30pm.)*

**QUEEN VICTORIA MARKET.** The modernizing development that brought the rest of Melbourne into the 20th century somehow passed over the Market. It remains an old-fashioned, open-air market, abuzz with hundreds of vendors hawking their wares to the thousands of Melburnians who pack in for excellent bargains on produce, dairy products, and meat. Saturdays and Sundays see the market at its frenetic best. Don't be afraid to bargain with the vendors; good deals can turn into amazing ones after noon, when sellers are anxious to empty their stock. Walking tours explore the market's history and cultural importance, and include plenty to eat. From late Nov. to early Mar., the market is also open at night 6:30-10:30pm, and the focus becomes multicultural. *(On Victoria St between Queen and Peel St. Open Tu, Th 6am-2pm, F 6am-6pm, Sa 6am-3pm, Su 9am-4pm. Tours ☎ 9320 5822. Depart from 69 Victoria St, near Elizabeth St. Food tour Tu, Th-Sa 10am; $18. History 10:30am; $12. )*

Spend less,
EXPLORE MORE!

LOW STUDENT AIRFARES
EURAIL PASSES
BUS PASSES
STUDY ABROAD

800.272.9676

www.studentuniverse.com

**Why wait in line when you can go online?**
Low student airfares the easy way.
Go ahead... put your feet up and
plan your trip.

student universe .com
IT'S YOUR WORLD. EXPLORE IT

# Here's your ticket to freedom, baby!

**Wherever you want to go...
priceline.com can get you there for less.**

- Save up to 40% or more off the lowest published airfares every day!

- Major airlines serving virtually every corner of the globe.

- Special fares to Europe!

If you haven't already tried priceline.com, you're missing out on the best way to save. **Visit us online today at www.priceline.com.**

## priceline.com℠
*Name Your Own Price*℠

CST 2040530-50     ©2000 priceline.com Incorporated

**MELBOURNE ZOO.** Many sections of this world-class zoo are expertly recreated native habitats that allow visitors to view animals much as they live in the wild. The African Rainforest—with pygmy hippos, arboreal monkeys, and gorillas—is first-rate. A darkened platypus area lets you watch the bizarre monotreme swim about. The aviary's birds zoom overhead, but the residents of the butterfly house may even land on you. *(On Elliott Ave, north of the University of Melbourne. Take tram #55 from William St to the Zoo stop.* ☎ *9285 9300. Free tours daily 10am and 3pm. Open Apr.-Dec. daily 9am-5pm, Jan.-Mar. 9am-9:30pm. $16, concessions $12, ages 4-15 $8, families $43.)*

## SOUTH OF THE YARRA RIVER

**SOUTHBANK.** The riverside walk that begins across Clarendon St, Southbank has an upmarket shopping and sidewalk-dining scene. It's most crowded on sunny Sundays, when an odd mix of skater kids, toned health nuts, and the Armani-clad gather here to relax, show off, and conspicuously consume. The area extends along the Yarra for two very long city blocks, and while you could easily squander your entire budget here within a day, you can window-shop, people-watch, and get some great views of the Flinders St Station and the city skyline for free. There are also some cool fountains where water performs more tricks than you thought possible, as well as two of Melbourne's most famous icons: a four-story-high Victoria Bitter sign (unfortunately just a sign...), and Deb Halpern's strange, Y-shaped sculpture *Ophelia*, with big eyes, two noses, and a fat-lipped smile.

**VICTORIAN ARTS CENTRE.** This enormous complex is the central star of Melbourne's performing arts galaxy. The 115m white-and-gold latticed spire of the **Theatres Building** is a landmark in itself, and inside there's more room for performance than most cities can handle. This eight-level facility holds three theatres (see **Performing Arts,** p. 536) that combined can seat over 3000 and are home to the **Melbourne Theatre Company, Opera Australia,** and the **Australian Ballet.** As if that weren't enough, next door is the 2600-seat **Melbourne Concert Hall,** which hosts the renowned **Melbourne Symphony** and the **Australian Chamber Orchestra.** The Theatres Building also houses an extensive permanent collection of Australian and Aboriginal art on display in the various foyers, as well as the **Performing Arts Museum,** a collection of shoes, outfits, and photos. *(100 St. Kilda Rd. At the east end of Southbank, just across the river from Flinders St Station.* ☎ *9281 8000; www.artscentre.net.au. Open M-Sa 9am-11pm, Su 10am-5pm. Free. Guided tours leave from Arts Center shop, Level 6, Theatres Bldg. M-Sa noon and 2:30pm. $10, concessions $7.50. Special Su 12:15pm backstage tour $13.50.)*

**NATIONAL GALLERY OF VICTORIA.** Constructed in 1968, the National Gallery is undergoing a $136 million renovation (see graybox, p. 532). Scheduled to reopen some time in 2002, the NGV is showing a small piece of its massive collection (generally regarded to be the finest in the Southern Hemisphere) at the Russell St entrance of the **State Library of Victoria** (p. 530). Many of the Australian pieces will be permanently moved to the brand new **Museum of Australian Art** at Federation Square, opposite Swanston St from Flinders Station, opening in May 2001. Most of the major pieces will be in Victorian regional museums, or maybe even in your home town abroad, until the distant grand-reopening. *(180 St. Kilda Rd. Temporary location 285-321 Russell St.* ☎ *9208 0222; www.ngv.vic.gov.au. Open daily 10am-5pm. Free guided tours M, W-F 11am, 1, 2pm; Tu 1, 2pm; Sa 2pm; Su 11am, 2pm.*

**▨ SHRINE OF REMEMBRANCE.** A wide walkway lined with tall, conical Butan cypresses leads to this imposing temple with columns and a ziggurat roof, that commemorates fallen soldiers from WWI. The central space is crowned by a stepped skylight and the **stone of remembrance,** which bears the inscription "Greater Love Hath No Man." The skylight is designed so that at 11am on November 11 (the moment of the WWI armistice), a ray of sunlight shines onto the word "Love" on the stone. Don't worry about missing this impressive solar-architectural feat: the effect is simulated every 30min. with artificial light, after which volunteer guides give excellent talks about the site's significance. At the back of the Shrine, read about Anzac Day—April 25—which commemorates the bloody battle of Gallipoli that Australian and New Zealand troops fought during WWI. Ascend to the shrine's balcony for spectacular views of the Melbourne skyline and the neighboring suburbs. Or venture down into the crypt and view the colorful division flags and memorial statue. Outside, veterans of subsequent wars are honored with a memorial that includes the **perpetual flame,** burning continuously since Queen Elizabeth II lit it in 1954. *(St. Kilda Rd. www.shrine.org.au. Open daily 10am-5pm. $2 donation.)*

**ROYAL BOTANICAL GARDENS.** Over 49,000 plants fill the 36 acres stretching along St. Kilda Rd east to the Yarra and south to Domain Rd. The gardens first opened in 1845, and the extensive array of mature species reflects 150 years of care and development. Stately palms unique to Melbourne share the soil with twisting oaks, rainforest plants, possums, wallabies, and even a pavilion of roses. A number of walking tracks highlight endemic flora; the **Australian Rainforest Walk** is right inside Gate F just southeast of the visitors center and provides an overview of wetlands vegetation from Tasmania to Queensland. There's also a steamy **rainforest glasshouse** and lake where you can have tea and feed ducks and geese. *(Open daily 10am-4:30pm.)* Special events, such as outdoor film screenings, take place on summer evenings (see **Cinema,** p. 536). The **Aboriginal Heritage Walk** explores the use of plant-life by local Aboriginal groups in ceremony, symbol, and food. *(Heritage walks Th 11am and alternate Su 10:30am. $10, concession $7.50. Book ahead.)* Near the entrance closest to the Shrine of Remembrance are the **Visitor's Centre** and the **observatory.** The visitor's center houses an upscale café and a garden shop. *(Open M-F 9am-5pm, Sa-Su 9:30am-5pm.)* The observatory includes an original 1874 telescope but is closed to the public except for weekly tours, which detail 19th century time-keeping methods. *(Tours Su 2pm; $6, concession $4. Night tour Tu 7:30pm, $13, concessions $9. Book ahead.)* The small cottage by Gate F is the **La Trobe Cottage,** home of Victoria's first lieutenant governor, Charles Joseph La Trobe. *(Open M, W, Sa-Su 11am-4pm. $2.)* Tours leave from the cottage to **Government House,** the home of the governor of Victoria, the Queen's appointed representative. *(4 Parliament Place. ☎ 9654 4711. Tours $11, concessions $9, children $5.50. Book ahead. Hecklers beware: House not otherwise open to public. Gardens: ☎ 9252 2300. Tours depart the Visitors Centre Su-F 11am and 2pm; $4, concessions $2. Open daily Nov.-Mar. 7:30am-8:30pm; Apr.-Oct. 7:30am-5:30pm. Free. Wheelchair accessible.)*

**SIDNEY MYER MUSIC BOWL.** This open-air concert bowl in Kings Domain gardens, north of the Shrine of Remembrance, features concerts in the summer months and a small ice-skating rink during the winter. Particularly popular is the Christmas-time concert series "Carols by Candlelight." The bowl is undergoing an extensive renovation that will be complete by December 2000. *(☎ 9281 8360.)*

# ST. KILDA

Bayside St. Kilda lies just far enough away from the city to be relaxed, but close enough to maintain a lively—if mellow—vibe during the day; at night more of the same citywide scene of black-clad bar hoppers hatches. There aren't a lot of tourist sights per se, but the offbeat shops, gorgeous sandy shoreline, and comfortably mixed population of the weird and the ordinary are indeed a sight to behold. St. Kilda Beach is easily accessed by any number of trams (see **Orientation,** p. 512), and swarms with swimmers and sun-worshippers during summer. The **Esplanade,** along the length of the strand, is a great place for in-line skating and jogging. On Sundays, the Esplanade craft market sells art, toys, housewares, and everything else, all impressively handmade by the stall holders.

**LUNA PARK.** The entrance gate of this St. Kilda icon is a grotesque, mammoth funhouse face. Venture through its mouth to find classic carnival rides: a roller coaster, Ferris wheel, and tunnel of terror, all permanently protected by the historical commission. *(☎ 9525 5033. On the Lower Esplanade. Free entry. Ride tickets $1; most rides require 3 tickets. Open F 7-11pm, Sa 11am-11pm, Su 11am-dusk. Public and school holidays Su-Th 11am-5pm, F-Sa 11am-11pm.)*

**WHAT'S THAT ON THE SIDEWALK?** Part of Melbourne's oft-cited liveability is the attention paid to public art. Deb Halpern's **Ophelia** on Southbank, is the fat-lipped, multi-colored, Y-shaped visage that has become one of the city's most prominent icons. On the pavement in front of Halpern's work, look for the ephemeral chalk drawings of Bev Isaac. North along Swanston St in front of the State Library of Victoria, a stone cornice with part of the word **"library"** protrudes from the pavement. This random work of Petroneous Sponk will keep you guessing "What the...? Why?" Perhaps the most popular of the sculptures is the group of **three businessmen** cast in bronze standing at the corner of Swanston and Bourke St. Their emaciated frames and wild-eyed expressions inspire amusement in most onlookers, though the work was originally underwritten by the government of Nauru and meant to reflect the greed and spiritual impoverishment of the Australian businessmen who plundered the tiny Polynesian country's natural resources.

**ALBERT PARK.** Opposite Fitzroy St lies Albert Park, the southern extension of Melbourne's vast park system, with ample green space, free BBQs, tennis courts, and groups of kids playing footy. The Grand Prix course is here (see **Recreation,** p. 537). The huge interior lake is great for sailing or paddleboating, but no swimming is allowed. *(For info call Parks Victoria ☎ 13 19 63.)*

**JEWISH MUSEUM OF AUSTRALIA.** The Jewish Museum outlines both the history of the Jewish people as a whole and the experience of Australia's 90,000 Jews from the time of the First Fleet. A stunning hallway draws a timeline of Jewish history, complete with fascinating and state-of-the-art multimedia displays. The Belief and Ritual Gallery provides a thorough overview of Judaism's basic tenets, including a painfully detailed French woodcut of a circumcision ceremony. There are also rotating displays of art and Judaica. *(26 Alma Rd. ☎ 9534 0083. www.jewishmuseum.com.au. East of St. Kilda Rd by stop 32 on tram #3 or 67. Museum open Tu-Th 10am-4pm, Su 11am-5pm. $7, concessions $4. Tours of the adjacent synagogue are free with admission and take place Tu-Th 12:30pm and Su 12:30 and 3pm. Wheelchair accessible.)*

## OUTSKIRTS OF THE CITY

**SCIENCEWORKS.** This extension of the Museum of Victoria is a big hit with kids, who arrive in droves on weekends and school holidays. The displays are designed to trick children into thinking learning is fun (two words: fake feces). There are multiple exhibitions, including one called Sports Works that affords the opportunity to engage in simulated competition against Olympians. (Don't try too hard; you will lose, and the kids will laugh at you for taking it too seriously.) The new digital Planetarium brings the stars as well as special shows to your comfortably seated self, but requires a few more dollars. *(2 Booker St. 5km from downtown in the suburb of Spotswood. Take the Werribee or Williamstown line from Flinders St Station, get off at Spotswood, and follow the ample signs; the walk takes about 10-15min. A better option on a sunny day is to take the Williamstown Seeker ferry from Southgate walk; departs every 2hr. 11am-5pm; $12 return. Scienceworks: ☎ 9392 4800. Open daily 10am-4:30pm. Admission $8, with Planetarium $13; concessions $6, $10; children $4, $7, family $20, $34.)*

**MUSEUM OF MODERN ART AT HEIDE.** A meeting place for artists, writers, and poets during the emergence of Australian modernism in the 1930s and 40s, the Museum of Modern Art has since been converted into an excellent venue for contemporary Australian and international art. Featuring work by Charles Blackman, Arthur Boyd, Joy Hester, and Sidney Nolan, the museum also has rotating exhibits of cutting-edge art from international makers. Perhaps most impressive is the five-hectare sculpture park. *(7 Templestowe Rd. In the northern suburb of Bulleen, 20min. from the city center by train to Heidelberg Station on the Hurstbridge line from Flinders St Station; then take National Bus 291 to Bulleen Rd and Manningham; then a 5min. walk. ☎ 9850 1500. Open Tu-F 10am-5pm, Sa-Su noon-5pm. $11, concessions $6. Sculpture park free.)*

# 🎵 ENTERTAINMENT

Melbourne prides itself on its style and cultural savvy, and nowhere is this more evident than in its entertainment scene. The range of options can seem overwhelming: there are world-class performances at the Victorian Arts Centre, edgy experimental drama in Carlton and Fitzroy, the popular dramas and musicals of the moment, and a panoply of independent and avant-garde cinema. The definitive website for performance events is http://melbourne.citysearch.com.au.

## PERFORMING ARTS

Book for larger shows through **Ticketek** (☎ 13 28 49, freecall ☎ (1800) 06 28 49), or try **Halftix** for half-price same day tickets (see **Ticket Agencies,** p. 519); for smaller productions, call the theater companies directly. The **Victorian Arts Centre,** 100 St. Kilda Rd (☎9281 8000; www.artscentre.net.au), is hard to miss—the large spire right across the Yarra from Flinders St Station. The center houses five venues: the **State Theatre** for major dramatic, operatic, and dance performances; the **Melbourne Concert Hall,** for symphonies; the **Playhouse,** for recent dramatic hits; the **George Fairfax Studio,** mainly for plays; and the **Black Box,** for musicals and productions targeted at an under-35 audience. (Tickets range from free-$140. Box office open M-Sa 9am-9pm.)

   **La Mama,** 205 Faraday, Carlton (info ☎9347 6948, bookings ☎9347 6142). About halfway up Lygon St, head east on Faraday; La Mama is very near the intersection, hidden down an alleyway and behind a parking lot. New, esoteric Australian drama in a diminutive, black-box space. Similar cutting-edge work is performed at the affiliated **Carlton Courthouse Theatre,** 349 Drummond St (same ☎ as La Mama), just around the corner in the old courthouse building, across from the police station. Tickets $8-16.

   **Last Laugh,** 380 Lygon St, Carlton (☎9419 4611). Melbourne's biggest comedy club scene, with big-name international jokesters. Ticket prices vary depending on the act.

   **National Theatre,** corner of Barkly and Carlisle St, St. Kilda (☎9534 0221). Offbeat, cosmopolitan fare, like modern dance, opera, and "world music." Tickets prices run the gamut.

   **Palais Theatre,** on the Esplanade, St. Kilda (☎9537 2444). The Palais holds the largest chandelier in the southern hemisphere. Seats 3000. Tickets $40-50.

   **Princess Theatre,** 163 Spring St (☎9299 9800). Popularly successful musicals in a 1500 seat venue. Tickets $50-70. Book through Ticketmaster (☎13 61 00).

   **Regent Theatre,** Collins St between Swanston and Russell St (☎9820 0239). Dazzlingly ornate. Hosts big-name touring shows, especially celebrity acts. Seats 2000. Tickets $35-70. 2hr. tours of Regent and Forum available Tu, Th 10am. $20. Book ahead.

   **The Forum,** corner of Russell and Flinders St (☎9299 9700). Looks like an Arabian palace and Florentine villa combined, with a few gargoyles thrown in for good measure. Big-budget dance and drama. Frequent mature cabarets provide a bawdier show.

   **Universal Theatre,** 19 Victoria St, Fitzroy (☎9419 3777). Mixed theatrical bag between mainstream and the wacked-out fringe (comedy, experimental, and drama).

## CINEMA

Melbourne has long been the center of Australia's independent film scene, and there are tons of old theaters throughout the city that screen artsy and experimental fare as well as old cinema classics. The arthouse crowd logs on to www.urban cinefile.com.au, which features flip reviews of the latest stuff. The annual **Melbourne International Film Festival** (see **Festivals,** p. 538) showcases the year's indie hits. Plenty of theaters in the city center show mainstream first-run movies as well; **Hoyts Cinema Centre,** 140 Bourke St (☎9663 3303), has a bar in the lobby if the flick isn't entertaining enough. **Movieline** (☎13 34 56) has a ticketing service and recorded info on showtimes and locations. At the theater, try a "choc-top," the chocolate-dipped ice-cream cone that's a staple of Melbourne movie-going ($2-3).

**Astor Theatre,** corner of Chapel St and Dandenong Rd, St. Kilda (☎9510 1414; www.astor-theatre.com). Spectacular 1936 Art Deco theater that still bears many of its original furnishings and all of its stately beauty. Mostly repertory and re-issues. Seats 1100. Many double features. $11, concessions $10; book of 10 tickets $80.

**Cinema Nova,** 380 Lygon St, Carlton (☎9347 5331). In Lygon Court. Indie and foreign fare; small theater with wonderfully comfortable purple arm chairs. $12, concessions $9.50, students $8. Before $4.50; all-day Bargain M $6.50.

**Flicks in the Park,** Fitzroy Gardens, East Melbourne. As part of the "Summer Fun in the Parks" program, the city offers free movies on the lawn stage beginning at 9:45pm. For more info, ☎9658 9658 or check www.melbourne.vic.gov.au.

**IMAX,** Melbourne Museum, Carlton (☎9663 5454). Off Rathdown St in the Carlton Gardens (see p. 532). Gigantic movie screen (23m x 31m) located in a mammoth subterranean theater. Shows are short on content (50min.) but more than make up for it with astounding visuals—some even offer 3-D action viewed through space-age liquid crystal glasses. $15, concessions $12, children $10; 3-D shows $1 extra. Daily screenings of seven films happen on the hour Su-Th 10am-10pm, F-Sa 10am-11pm. Slate of films changes seasonally. YHA 20% discount, NOMADS 10%.

**Moonlight Cinema,** in the Royal Botanical Gardens (☎9428 2203; www.moonlight.com.au). From mid-Dec. to early-Mar., movies are shown on the central lawn. Films start at sundown, approximately 8:45pm. $13, concessions $10.

**The Kino,** 45 Collins St (☎9650 2100). Downstairs in the Collins Place complex. Quality independent and foreign films. $13.50, concessions $10.50. M special $8.50.

## SPORTS AND RECREATION

Melburnians refer to themselves as "sports mad," but it's a good insanity, one that causes fans of footy (Aussie Rules Football), cricket, tennis, and horse racing to skip work or school, get decked out in the costumery of their favorite side, and cheer themselves hoarse. Their main asylum is the **Melbourne Cricket Ground (MCG),** adjacent to the world-class **National Tennis Centre** (now called **Melbourne Park;** see p. 531). A new ward, **Colonial Stadium,** right behind Spencer St station, has begun to share footy-hosting responsibilities with the more venerable MCG. The lunacy peaks at various yearly events: the **Australian Open,** a Grand Slam tennis event, in late January; the **Grand Prix** Formula-One car-racing extravaganza in March; the **AFL Grand Final** in late September; the **Melbourne Cup,** a "horse race that stops a nation," in early November; and cricket's **Boxing Day Test Match** on Dec. 26. (See **Festivals,** p. 538, for more information.)

Melbourne's passion for sport is not limited to spectator events. City streets and parks are packed with joggers, skaters, and footy players. The newly refurbished, crushed gravel tan track that circles the Royal Botanical Gardens is best for **running.** Other great routes include the pedestrian paths along the Yarra, the Port Phillip/St. Kilda shore, and the Albert Park Lake. All of these wide, flat spaces make for excellent **in-line skating** as well. **City Skate,** Wednesday at 9pm, draws local bladers together at the Victorian Arts Centre near the waterfall; folks convene and break into smaller groups based on preferred route and skill level. You can rent equipment at the **Skate Warehouse,** 354 Lonsdale St. (☎9602 3633. 1hr. $7.50, 3hr. $12.50, full-day $17.50, F-M weekend $27.50.) **Skateboarders** should check out the public **skate park** at the corner of Swanston and Lonsdale St next to the State Library, which has a decent selection of half-pipes.

An extensive **bike trail** runs along the Yarra, and others loop through Albert Park and Middle Park, along the Port Phillip beaches, and around North Melbourne's gardens. Southern Melbourne's flat bayside roads make for low-impact, scenic cycling. **St. Kilda Cycles,** 11 Carlisle St, has good rates. (☎9534 3074. Open M-F 9am-6pm. Half-day $15, full-day $20). Or try **Fitzroy Cycles,** 224 Swanston St (☎9639 3511. Open M-Th 9am-6pm, F 9am-7pm, Sa 9:30am-5pm. 1hr. $9, full-day $35.) Rates include helmets and locks. Many hostels rent bikes for little or no charge. **Bicycle Victoria (BV),** 19 O'Connell St (☎9328 3000), provides insurance for members ($51 per year) and free info for non-members (see **Getting Around Victoria,** p. 507).

If you're not quite so active, and the weather is agreeable, there is a **beach** in St. Kilda accessible by tram #16 and 96. It's not Australia's finest, but it'll do for sun and swimming. **Albert Park** has a lake good for sailing, but not for swimming. Just inside the Clarendon St entrance to the park, **Jolly Roger** rents sailboats for $25-35 per hr. and paddleboats for $36 per hour. (☎9690 5862. Open Tu-Su 9:30am-5pm.) The **Melbourne City Baths,** 420 Swanston St, on the corner of Franklin St, offer two pools, sauna, spa, squash courts, and a gym in a restored Neoclassical building. (☎9663 5888. Open M-F 6am-10pm, Sa-Su 8am-6pm; pool $3; sauna and spa $7.)

## GAMBLING

The Australian penchant for "having a flutter" (betting) reaches its neon-lit apotheosis at **Melbourne's Crown Casino,** 8 Whiteman St, at the western end of South Bank. A little slice of Las Vegas down under, this $1.6 billion complex houses the most gaming tables of any casino in the world (which could translate to the most pathetic losers...see **Pokies vs. The People,** p. 125), plus five-star accommodations, luxury shopping, Elvis impersonators, fog-filled, laser-lit jumping fountains, a perennially packed Planet Hollywood, and three nightclubs: Heat, Club Odeon, and the Mercury Lounge. While you're nearby, sneak over to Café Greco on the waterfront for a slice of their knee-weakening mixed berry cheesecake ($6.50, and yes, it's *that* good.) Minimum bets are around $5, though the more cautious can start at the less cut-throat "how to play" tables. (☎9292 8888. Open 24hr., and busy just about every one of those hours.)

## ✿ FESTIVALS

Melburnians create excuses for city-wide street parties any time of the year. Below are the city's major events, but there are too many to list. For a complete guide, grab a free copy of *Melbourne Events* at any tourist office, or look under "Festivals and Events" at www.visitmelbourne.com. All dates listed are for 2001.

**Midsumma Gay and Lesbian Festival,** Jan. 13-Feb. 4, 2001 (☎9415 9819; www.midsumma.org.au). Three weeks of homosexual hijinks all over the city ranging from the erotic (a "Mr. Leather Victoria" contest) to the educational (a Same-Sex Partners Rights workshop), with lots of parades, dance parties, and general pandemonium.

**Australian Open,** Jan. 15-28, 2001 (☎9286 1234). One of the world's elite 4 Grand Slam tennis events, held at Melbourne Park's hard courts. Day passes cost around $20.

**Qantas Australian Grand Prix,** Mar. 1-4, 2001 (☎9258 7100; www.grandprix.com.au). Albert Park, St. Kilda. Formula One frenzy holds the city hostage.

**✿Moomba,** Mar. 9-12, 2001 (☎9699 4022; www.melbournemoombafestival.com.au). Named after the Aboriginal word for "party," Moomba is basically a non-stop 4-day city-wide fête amid food, performances, and events.

**Melbourne Food and Wine Festival,** Mar. 16-Apr. 18, 2001 (☎9628 5008; www.foodwine.yellowpages.com.au). A free and delicious way to celebrate Melbourne as Australia's "culinary capital" or just to get stuffed and trashed.

**International Comedy Festival,** Mar. 29-Apr. 22, 2001 (☎9417 7711; www.comedyfestival.com.au). Huge 3-week international and Aussie laugh-fest, with over 1000 gut-busting performances.

**International Flower and Garden Show,** Apr. 4-8, 2001 (☎9639 2333). Royal Exhibition Building and Carlton Gardens, Carlton.

**Anzac Day Parade,** Apr. 25 each year (☎9650 5050). ANZAC vets in the Commemoration March head down Swanston St and St. Kilda Rd to the Shrine of Remembrance.

**Federation Festival,** May 9-27, 2001 (☎9666 4242; www.melbournefestival.com.au). New event celebrates the centenary of the first opening of parliament with concerts, plays, exhibitions, lectures, and dance.

**St. Kilda Film Festival,** late May to early June (☎9209 6699). Palais Theatre and George Cinemas, St. Kilda. The country's best short films: documentary, experimental, comedy.

**International Film Festival,** July 18-Aug. 5, 2001 (☎9417 2011; www.melbournefilmfestival.com.au). 2001 marks the 50th anniversary of the cream of the international cinematic crop (plus top-level local work) playing at various swish venues around the city.

**Royal Melbourne Show,** Sept. 20-30, 2001 (☎9281 7444; www.royalshow.com.au). At Ascot Vale. Sideshow alleys, rides, entertainment, and, of course, animal exhibitions and judging.

**Melbourne Fringe Festival,** Sept. 23-Oct. 14, 2001 (☎9481 5111; www.melbournefringe.org.au). Opening parade on Brunswick St, Fitzroy. Street parades, performance art, and parties all across town.

**Melbourne Festival,** Oct. 10-Nov. 3, 2001 (☎9662 4242; www.melbournefestival.com.au). A 3-week celebration of the arts, attracting world-famous actors, writers, and dancers for over 400 performances, workshops, and parties in 30 different venues.

**Qantas Australian Motorcycle Grand Prix,** late-Oct., 2001 (☎9280 7100; www.grandprix.com.au). Phillip Island. Fast bikes (instead of fast cars). Going around a track. Fast.

**Spring Racing Carnival,** Nov. 3-10, 2001 (☎9258 4666; www.melbournecup.net.au). Flemington Racecourse. Australia's love for horse racing reaches fever pitch, punctuated by the **Melbourne Cup** on Nov. 8.

**Chapel St Festival,** Nov. 4, 2001 (☎9529 6331). 250,000-300,000 people crowd Chapel St from Dandenong to Toorak Rd for entertainment and mayhem.

**Melbourne Boxing Day Test Match,** Dec. 26 each year (☎9653 9999; www.baggygreen.com.au). More than 100,000 cricket fans pack the MCG to root for the boys in green and gold against top cricketers from around the world.

# ⚓ NIGHTLIFE

Melbourne pulses with a world-class nightlife scene. Only a handful of venues play the standard bass-heavy club remixes of familiar mainstream dance hits. Most feature DJs (some of whom have international followings) who spin funky, mind-bending original selections of techno, house and deep house, trance, drum 'n' bass, jungle, garage, and breakbeats. You probably won't recognize any of it, but it's eminently danceable. Tons of retro nights feature 70s and 80s faves, with crowds in campy period wear. Covers are ubiquitous outside of Fitzroy and range up to $20, but you get your money's worth—few clubs close earlier than 3am, and some rage nonstop from Thursday all the way until Sunday night.

There are three main areas for **nightclubs.** Downtown tends to be straighter (as in less gay and more mainstream), though you'll find a little bit of everything. South Yarra and Prahran have the trendiest venues and the best **gay scene.** Though most clubs in the area are gay-friendly, predominantly gay places are concentrated along Commercial Rd, with a smattering in Collingwood. Fitzroy and St. Kilda are pretty much the anti-Chapel St—much more casual, tending toward grungy but good music shows and charging the cheapest covers, if any at all. The more you pay, expect to get that much attitude at the door. Rude treatment often comes free of charge at fading venues. Another curiosity is that even places that are gritty during the day are, at night, host to black-clad hipsters seeking the ever-changing cutting edge. Venues, genres, and cover charges change with bewildering rapidity. To keep up, read *In Press* and, to a lesser extent, *Beat* magazines, both of which are free, released every Wednesday, and have exhaustive weekly listings. For music shows, the best coverage is in The Age's *Entertainment Guide* (*EG*) or the Herald-Sun's *Gig Guide*, both of which come out in their Friday papers.

There is a blurry but important distinction between **bars** and **pubs** in Melbourne. The bars tend to be a bit more chill but no less slick than their nightclub cousins; they don't have covers, though. Drinks are expensive (beer bottles $4-4.50, wine and mixed drinks $4.50-5.50), and wine and spirits are the intoxicants of choice; many bars don't have beer taps at all. Most pubs, on the other hand, charge less for drinks (half-pint pots $2.30-2.80, pints $4.50-5, mixed drinks $3.50-4.50), are loud and raucous, and have live entertainment on weekends (cover $3-8), making the distinction between pub and club somewhat blurry as well. So might your mind be after a night of hitting local watering holes, as most of them try to lure backpackers with cheap drink specials (pots as low as $1-1.50) and often keep taps flowing until early in the morning, or even 24 hours. Basically, almost anywhere you go you're bound to have a damn good time.

## BARS AND PUBS

### CITY CENTER

▨ **Rue Bebelons,** 267 Little Lonsdale St (☎9663 1700). There's no sign outside; you have to be in the know. The consummate Melburnian bar, relaxed and understatedly stylish, with an excellent selection of wines ($2.50) and spirits ($4-5). The deep house music and dim lighting create the ideal atmosphere for a silent, brooding solitary drink or an intimate *tête-a-tête*. Open Tu-F 8am-3am, Sa noon-3am, Su 2-8pm.

**Club UK,** 169 Exhibition St (☎9663 2075). Year-old dance-pub brings the best of Britain to the backstreets of Melbourne with ubiquitous Union Jacks, English ales on tap ($6), and pulsating Brit beats. Very inclusive; particularly popular among British expatriates and backpackers, Club UK attracts outrageous dress and a mixed gay-straight crowd. A small library near the stairwell gives patrons a classy break from the groovin' upstairs balcony and the dungeon dance floor in the basement. W: $2 pints; Su: $1 beer and champagne until 8pm. Occasional $5 cover. Open W-Th, Su until 3am, F-Sa until 5am.

**Up Top Cocktail Bar,** 1st fl, 163 Russell St (☎9663 8990). Enter via the alleyway off Russell St. The *Swingers* aesthetic's first tentative foray down under. Smallish lounge decked out with disco ball, brocade-framed mirrors, and other lounge-daddy accoutrements. Lines F-Sa. Excellent music, with groove, house (both the deep and progressive varieties), latin, and UK indie. Mixed drinks from $5, bottled beer from $4, snacks from $2. Open W-Th 4pm-3am, F 4pm-5am, Sa 6pm-5am, Su 6pm-3am.

**Pugg Mahones,** 106-112 Hardware St (☎9670 6155). Between Little Lonsdale and Lonsdale St. Irish pub packs in a lively all-ages crowd with live music on weekends. Oddly, the bar area is fashioned as a bookshelf, with books next to booze. Take the time to study their selection of Irish beers on tap (pints $5.50, pots $2.60). M: backpacker night with $3 pints of the Aussie brews. No cover. Open daily until 4 or 5am.

### FITZROY AND COLLINGWOOD

▨ **Bar Open,** 317 Brunswick St (☎9415 9601). Edgy urban chic tempered by a solid dose of post-hippie haziness. Portraits of the Queen Mum abound, offset by minimalist black barstools and a baffling sign that reads "Tofu and Drinks." Younger crowd chats comfortably downstairs in intimate environs, including cushy chairs near the fireplace. Upstairs Th-Sa houses an eclectic mix of international fusion acts, earnest folk singers, and soulful blues bands—not rock, but groove. No cover. Open daily noon-2am.

**Labour in Vain,** 197 Brunswick St (☎9417 5955). The name of this pre-gold rush era hotel laments the back-breaking work of the early settlers and convicts; today, it's been remodeled to celebrate their hard-drinkin' after-work antics. Lined with one of Oz's best antique beer bottle collections, it's part watering hole, part history museum. Great home-brewed Fitzroy Amber Ale, tinged with a soft honey flavor. Open daily 1pm-1am.

> **IF HE HAD ONLY CALLED HER...** The upstairs of Young & Jackson bar across from Flinders Street Station is called Chloe's Bar, after the subject of the titillating painting of a nude 14-year-old girl that was unveiled at the 1880 Melbourne Exhibition. It caused a great stir at the time, which was later surpassed when its maker, Jules Lefebvre, ditched Chloe for her sister, and the distraught model killed herself by drinking a cocktail of match heads and champagne. Always remember the "half your age +7" year rule for dating legitimacy.

**The Tote,** 71 Johnston St (☎9419 5320). At Wellington St, one block east of Smith St. The bar isn't much, but sneak to the back room to experience one of Melbourne's best rock venues—the band is right in your face, and the room's rockin' energy will have even the most languid soul bouncing and thrashing in no time. Plus the booze is cheap (spirits $3.60). Bar area is free but to go to the back will run you $4-10, if anyone is actually manning the door. Open M-Th noon-1am, F-Sa noon-3am, Su 6-11pm.

**Builder's Arms,** 211 Gertrude St (☎9419 0818). At Gore St, halfway between Brunswick and Smith St. Large and lively, this versatile bar brings in an all ages and orientations. The crowd interestingly ages about 5-10 years going from the back room to the front—but it's anyone's territory in the red-draped dance room with standard-issue disco ball. Very gay-friendly; popular Th "Q&A" (Queer and Alternative night) night. W: live acoustic music; Th-Sa: DJs and disco. Open M-Th 5pm-1am, F-Su 3pm-1am.

**Standard Hotel,** Fitzroy St (☎9419 4793). Isolated on an ill-populated road one block west of Brunswick St, this neighborly joint attracts a host of locals and a slew of *artistes.* Adorned with kitsch, including a shot of a mohawked Robert DeNiro from *Taxi Driver,* the Standard's not-so-standard features include a stately dining room with eclectic menu ($10-17) and an extensive, lush beergarden with ponds, plants, bar, and BBQ. Live music W and Su. Open M-Tu 3-11pm, W-Su noon-11pm.

**Rainbow Hotel,** 27 St. David St (☎9419 4193). Like the Standard, a little off the beaten path (one block east of Brunswick) but worth the 1min. trek. There's live music everyday—blues, country, jazz, and R&B. Dance if you can around the crowded island bar, but don't knock into the band: there's no stage, just a small section of floor right in the thick of things. Cheap drinks (pots $2.20, spirits $3.60), but prices rise slightly during showtime (around 9:30pm). Cover? Not a chance. Open daily 3pm-1am.

**Evelyn Hotel,** 351 Brunswick St (☎9419 5500). Bare black floors make great space to bust a move; add in the red curtains and throbbing music and the mood becomes seductively plutonic. Live acts every night. Cover ranges widely. Open daily noon-2am.

## ST. KILDA

**▓ Esplanade Hotel,** 11 Upper Esplanade (☎9534 0211). Multifaceted seaside hotel, known fondly as the "Espy." First floor down-to-earth Lounge Bar carries 2-3 live music acts every night; no cover except F-Su $2 after 9pm. Drink prices rise slightly when the bands are on. Downstairs is a gritty public bar; upstairs the ornate Gershwin Room, which once housed sumptuous fêtes for the Melburnian elite, now hosts special live music acts Th-Sa and comedy nights Tu and Su (cover up to $15). The new attached restaurant serves midrange meals ($13-17). Happy hour in public bar Tu-Th 5-7pm. Lounge Bar open M-W noon-midnight, Th-Sa noon-1am, and Su noon-11:30pm.

**The Elephant and Wheelbarrow,** 169 Fitzroy St. (☎9534 7888). A very fun "traditional English pub" and one of a handful of places you won't feel uncomfortable not wearing all black. Alternates every other Monday with **Inflation** (p. 542) as home to *"Neighbors* Night," where the cast of this popular Aussie soap opera mingles with patrons and helps with trivia games...for $25. Occasional weekend bands play to a mixed age group; alternately, the stereos blow pop dance music with actual words. No cover.

**The George Public Bar,** 129 Fitzroy St (☎9534 8822). Not to be confused with the next door **George Melbourne Wine Room** that carries over 500 wines ($18-500), the George Public bar is a well lit subterranean neighborhood bar that perfectly follows St. Kilda's unpretentious attitude, even with its popularity. Inspirational alcoholic messages posted on the chalkboard outside, like "Beauty is in the eye of the Beer Holder." Often standing room only, The George draws a 25-35 year-old crowd to friendly times and prices ($2.40 pots, $4.50 pints). Open M-Th noon-1am, F-Su noon-3am.

**Sunset Strip,** 16 Grey St (☎9534 9205). Much-beloved haunt in the heart of St. K's backpacker district with wildly varied—and just plain wild—theme nights. Hard-core industrial DJ nights, "funk 'n' flat-out retro," mellow jazz trios, and outrageous drag acts. No pots, just bottles ($4) and spirits ($5). Usually rages Th-Sa until 5am.

**Prince of Wales,** 29 Fitzroy St (☎9536 1177). Longstanding local haunt divided into two downstairs bars: the side closer to the beach attracts a blue collar, grungy crowd, while the other side is a pleasant gay bar. M nights are a backpacker haven with $1 pots. Upstairs, there's a live DJ or band Th-Su nights; cover is $10 and up, provided you get past the attitude-laden security. Su night upstairs is gay night; 1st F of every month is for lesbians. Downstairs bar open until 3am.

**Mink,** 2b Acland St (☎9536 1199). Considered one of Melbourne's best cocktail bars, Mink has enough vodka variations to make you sing like an old Russian sailor.

# NIGHTCLUBS

## CITY CENTER

▨ **Metro,** 20-30 Bourke St (☎9663 4288). Simply unbelievable. The largest club in the Southern Hemisphere, the Metro packs in a younger (18-25), straight crowd on week-ends for a major scope-and-scam scene. Eight bars and 3 floors of dance action; the ground floor's the most frenetic, with fog, flashing lights, and a triangular plane of green laser that cuts above heads in the main dance pit. DJs are enclosed in protective glass casing, a wise choice since this place is constantly on the verge of exploding. Second floor has live music and catwalks, third floor an observation deck with plush and private booths. Th: "Goo," alternative-grunge; F: "Discotech"; Sa: "Pop," mainstream dance hits. Phone ahead for dress code, and come before midnight. Cover $6-10.

▨ **Scubar,** 389 Lonsdale St (☎9670 2400). Shagadelic, baby! Prototype for the space-age bachelor pad, this smallish downstairs venue is befitted with groovalicious furni-ture, mohair wall coverings, a translucent bar, a leopard-print pool table, and a big ceil-ing aquarium with tropical fish. Open M-Sa; most active Th-Sa, with DJs spinning trancy beats until 3am for a healthy mix of gays and straights, suits and shafts, that dance not for show but because they love the vibe. Th: hip-hop, break dancing; F: band until 11pm; Sa: 70s funk/house. Tapas bar serves light food. Cover $5 after 10pm Th-Sa.

**Arizona Bar,** Russel at Little Lonsdale St (☎9654 5000). Opened May 2000 in a former topless dance club, Arizona is quickly becoming a major alternative venue. Young, slightly unkempt grunge crowd rocks through two sprawling, labyrinthine stories mauled by Southwest U.S. motifs. Heavier beats and dancing on upper floor; downstairs a bit more blithe but still bumpin'. Especially popular on Sa night ($3 bourbon or vodka spe-cial). Open F-Sa until 6am (expanding soon to Th and Su nights). Cover $7.

**Club 383,** 383 Lonsdale St (☎9670 6575). Pool tables and a big dance floor on the 1st fl., a more intimate dance area and black-lit lounge space on the second. A large video screen plays squeaky-clean 50s-era films to contrast with the jaded 90s nihilism of the music. F: "Retro," slightly older crowd; Sa: "Collision," indie-alternative, slightly younger, $1 pots and $2 spirits 10-11pm. Cover $5, students $3. Open until 5am.

**Inflation,** 60 King St (☎9614 6122). Throws the city's biggest backpacker party Tu nights with free 1-liter buckets of beer from 9-10pm and 11pm-midnight. Alternate M: "Neighbors night" (see **Elephant and Wheelbarrow,** p. 541). Cover $6-10.

## SOUTH YARRA & PRAHRAN

▨ **Revolver,** 1st fl., 229 Chapel St (☎9529 1117). One of the most happening alternative clubs in the city, with a mixed crowd of uni kids, slick, black-clad club-goers, and edgy, multiple-pierced skate-punk types. Everyone is around 22 years old, either in age or in spirit. Performance/dance area frequented by various alternative bands on weekends; afterwards a DJ takes over for groovy late-night dancing. The calmer lounge has pool, campy table arcade, and retro furniture. Lines can get long; no bogans. Beer $4.50, spirits $5.50. Occasional cover $5-10. Open Tu-W noon-3am, Th noon-M 3am nonstop.

**Chasers,** 386 Chapel St (☎9827 6615). If you're 21 and want to feel old, this might be the place for you. Massive two-story complex with six bars and a vast dance floor offset by smaller spaces to lounge and chill. Be careful when table dancing because the bass might knock you over. Dress casual but sharp. Cover $10-12. Open F-Su 10pm-7am.

**Salt,** Daly St (☎9827 8333). At the end of the street, just off Chapel St north of Toorak Rd. Away from the brouhaha and shrouded in a crowd of mist inside, the Salt pumps penetrating bass amid the glowing blue lights that emanate from all corners of this two-story complex. Featured in Madison Avenue's "Who the Hell are You?" music video. W: retro; Th: commercial house; F: techno and R&B funk; Sa: progressive and happy house. Dress sharp and come early. Cover $5-20. Open W-Sa 11pm-around 7am.

**The Market,** 143 Commercial Rd (☎9826 0933). Styled as the "total venue," this is Melbourne's hippest gay club (straight-friendly). Formerly the Three Faces club; new ownership has taken it a bit up-market. Sassy queens strut their stuff in the top floor cocktail lounge, while patrons play pool and scope the dance floor from the balcony. The ground floor is all about bodies grinding to serious techno beats and bass-heavy remixes of gay anthems. Th: some of the best drag shows in town. Cover $5 after 10pm.

**Diva,** 153 Commercial Rd (☎9824 2800). Small but very popular gay bar (straight-friendly) with tons of themes and drink specials. W: Mayhem drag show; Th: Disco DNA; F: Live and intimate; Sa: Retro. No cover, ever. Lines after 1am. Open W-Sa until 3am.

**Xchange,** 119 Commercial Rd (☎9867 5144). Almost exclusively gay men frequent this more pub-like venue. Small interior houses pool table and cramped dance floor. Happy hour daily 5-7pm with $1.50 pots and $3 spirits. Open daily 2pm-late.

**Dome,** 19 Commercial Rd (☎9529 8966). Melbourne's most popular and expensive nightclub, and the place to be seen. Sa: self-proclaimed "Number 1 dance party in Melbourne," which purportedly attracts upwards of 2500 people. Hordes wait outside for hours; metal detector greets you at the door. The main arena is a vast, crowded, sweaty vortex of dance action, with box-dancing glowstick mavens. Off to the side is "Jane's Bar," where the gay/lesbian crowd generally congregates; drag shows Sa at 3am. Cover $12-15. Show up early or don't bother. Dress sharp. Open F-Su 10pm-way late.

**Frost Bites,** 426 Chapel St (☎9827 7401). By day a pizza and pasta restaurant, by night a blaring club that attracts a young crowd and long lines. Frozen cocktail specialty (from Blue Hawaiian to Mango Splice)—like slurpees with booze. Beware: servings are small and expensive (diminutive regulars $5, non-large large $8). W backpacker night: half-priced pizzas (7-9pm), and $1.50 pots, $4 spirits, and $4 regular slushees (7pm-midnight). Live music W, Th, Su. Smart casual dress. No cover. Open until 3am.

# ◪ DAYTRIP FROM MELBOURNE: YARRA

## YARRA VALLEY WINERIES

Though not as well known or as heavily visited as the Hunter Valley NSW (p. 150) or the Barossa Valley SA (p. 440), the Yarra Valley produces some top-grade wines. Located about 60km from Melbourne, the Yarra's vineyards were started in 1835 with 600, um, procured vinecuttings from the Hunter Valley. After a depression in the 1890s decimated wine demand, the Yarra basically shut down. Grapes were replanted in the 1960s, and today the Yarra has more than tripled its size from its peak in the 1800s. The Yarra's cool climate makes it ideal for growing Chardonnay, Pinot Noir, and Cabernet Sauvignon grapes; virtually every one of the over 30 wineries produces wines of these varieties. Quality sparkling wines (not champagne, silly—you can only get that in Champagne, France) abound, as the Chardonnay and Pinot Noir grapes are two of the principal grapes used to make the bubbly.

◪ **PRACTICAL INFORMATION.** Public transportation options to the wineries are limited; Lilydale, 10-20km outside the Yarra, is on the Met train line, but after that there's no way to get to the wineries without hiring a car (remember *Let's Go* does not recommend drinking and driving, and perhaps more importantly, neither do the police). Pick up a free *Wineries of the Yarra Valley* or *Wine Regions of Victoria* at the Melbourne tourist office, or check out www.yarravalleywineries.asn.au. There are several tour options from Melbourne, though the best and most affordable is the unimaginatively named Backpacker Winery Tours (☎9329 8599; www.backpackerwinerytours.com.au). The $65 tour offers pickup at major hotels, free tastings at four wineries, and a gourmet lunch, not to mention knowledgeable commentary and lessons on wine quality and tasting technique.

⌚ **WINERIES.** You can't go wrong with any of the options, especially at the normal price of $2 for a taste of their whole selection (tasting fee generally refundable upon purchase). Hours vary, but wineries are generally open daily 10am-5pm.

> **Yering Station,** (☎9730 1107). Victoria's first vineyard? (see **Gehrig Estate**, p. 592.) The tasting area has a delightful art gallery, and the multi-million dollar complex next door has a top-notch restaurant with a huge glass wall overlooking the Valley. Open M-F 10am-5pm, Sa-Su 10am-6pm.

> **St. Huberts,** (☎9739 1118). Founded in the 1860s by Hubert de Castella, this winery has a crisp, intense Pinot Noir and a very popular Cabernet.

> **Yarra Ridge,** (☎9730 1022). This Foster's-owned winery has a small and unadorned tasting area, apparently to emphasize that their focus is on wine, not tourism. The Greg Norman Chardonnay and Cabernet Merlot are as of yet only sold in the United States, and the winery is the only spot you can grab a bottle in Australia.

> **Domaine Chandon,** (☎9739 1110; www.domainechandon.com.au). This is the most polished spot in the Yarra, with a walk-through exhibit on the process of producing sparkling wine. No free tastings, though—only $5 flutes with a free bread plate.

# ⚿ OTHER DAYTRIPS FROM MELBOURNE

**HEALESVILLE SANCTUARY.** An open-air zoo, the Healesville Sanctuary lies in the Yarra Valley. Its minimum-security environs keep the Aussie menagerie steps from visitors. In the platypus habitat, you can walk through the enclosure where the oviparous monotremes splash in waterfalls. The zookeepers oversee close-up encounters with the animals between 11am and 3:30pm; check signs for display times. *(From Melbourne, take the Met's light rail to Lilydale, then take bus #685 for about 35min. Only two buses go directly from the station weekdays at 9:40am and 11:35am. ☎5957 2800. Open daily 9am-5pm. Admission $16, concessions $12, children $8, families of 6 $44.)*

**WERIBEE PARK AND OPEN RANGE ZOO.** For a relaxing daytrip from Melbourne, the mansion at **Werribee Park** is a good bet, with serene sculptured gardens, an imposing billiards room, and an expansive nursery wing. Built between 1874-77 by a Scottish sheep tycoon determined to move beyond his working-class heritage, the estate fell into disrepair after the owner's death and was taken over by a monastery. Since being purchased by the Victorian government, it's become a popular tourist stop. *(K Rd. 40min. west of Melbourne along the Princes Hwy. ☎9741 2444. Open M-F 10am-3:45pm, Sa-Su 10am-4:45pm. $11, concessions $7. Wheelchair accessible.)* You can go on safari among animals from the grasslands of Australia, Africa, and Asia at Victoria's **Open Range Zoo,** just behind the mansion on K Rd. To explore on your own, take the two 30min. walking trails; a tour of the 200-hectare park takes about 3hr. *(☎9731 1311. Open daily 9am-5pm; entrance closes at 3:30pm. 50min. safaris daily between 10:30am-3:40pm. $16, concessions $12, families $43. Wheelchair accessible.)*

**ORGAN PIPES NATIONAL PARK.** Oz is all about unique geological formations, and the Melbourne area features one of its own: the Organ Pipes National Park. Although the 6m metamorphic landmarks look more like french fries than organ pipes, they're still a good daytrip or stop en route to the central Goldfields. Plus, french fries taste good. To reach the pipes, walk 15min. down the gulch. Also look for the **Rosette Rock,** which resembles a flowing stone frozen in time (10min. down the path). The park is also a laboratory for environmental restoration and has been largely repopulated with native plants and trees since the early 1970s, when weeds concealed the pipes. The park has picnic and BBQ facilities and charges no entrance fee. *(Just off the Calder Hwy (Hwy 79), 20km northwest of Melbourne. Public transport from Melbourne is slightly tricky: take tram #59 from Elizabeth St to Essendon Station, then switch to bus #483 to Sunbury. Organ Pipes: ☎9390 1082. Wheelchair accessible.)*

VICTORIA

**HANGING ROCK NATIONAL PARK.** It's more than just a movie. The unique rock formations featured in the famous *Picnic at Hanging Rock* are nearly as curious as the protagonists' fate (if you don't want to know the ending, read no further…they vanished without a trace!). *(Enter from Calder Hwy, past Organ Pipes National Park; follow the signs and enter at the south gate on South Rock Rd. Or take V/Line from Spencer St Station to Wood End, and walk or take a cab the 6km from the station. ☎ 5427 0295. Open daily 9am-6pm. $7 per car.)*

**PUFFING BILLY STEAM RAILWAY.** The train is a relaxing way to see the interior of northeast Victoria's Dandenong Ranges. The billowing vapor reminds of simpler times, but quickly dissipates in the verdant rainforest terrain. Try not to think of it as just a train ride through the forest or you might be disappointed—but your kids will love it. *(40km east of Melbourne on the Burwood Hwy to Belgrave. Or, take a Hillside Train from Flinders Station. Puffing Billy: ☎ 9754 6800. Train from Belgrave to Lakeside: 1hr., 3 per day, $20.50, family $57.50; from Belgrave to Gembrook: 1¾hr., 1 per day, $28.50, family $80.50.)*

# PORT PHILLIP AND WESTERNPORT BAYS

Two pincers of land curve south from Melbourne around Port Phillip and Westernport Bays: the Bellarine Peninsula to the west and the Mornington Peninsula to the east. The bays were the site of the first white settlement in Victoria in 1803 (near Sorrento), a squalid effort that lasted less than a year. By the latter 19th century, however, spectacular coastal views and a sunny, temperate climate made the bays the site of choice for summer homes of the goldfield-spawned *nouveau riche*. With the exception of Phillip Island and its notorious Little Penguins, this area remains largely a wealthy getaway, a fact that deters most backpackers. There are, however, enough budget opportunities here to allow everyone to enjoy the awesome scenery, sandy beaches, and excellent surfing.

## PHILLIP ISLAND

Phillip Island has become synonymous with the endearing Little Penguins that inhabit its southwest corner and scamper back to their burrows nightly in a "Penguin Parade." The Parade is massively popular—drawing some 3.5 million visitors each year—so be prepared for a touristy crowd. A plethora of other wildlife, such as koalas, wombats, seals, and hundreds of species of birds also call Phillip Island home; spot them in the wild on one of a number of nature walks, or visit the island's two wildlife centers. Large breakers crashing against the island's southern shore create a surfers' mecca in summer, and the Grand Prix motorcycle race draws racers and their fervent followers in early October. Despite the crowds, the rolling hills and vibrant blue Bass Strait waters make Phillip Island a great place to relax for a few days.

**⊡ TRANSPORT.** Phillip Island lies across a narrow strait from San Remo, 120km southeast of Melbourne. Numerous backpacker-oriented tours take groups to the island. The best value is the **Duck Truck Tours,** run by the folks at Amaroo Park Hostel. The tour includes Melbourne transfers, up to three nights at the hostel, a guided tour of the Penguin Parade and the whole island, meals, and a half-day of bike use. (☎ 5952 2548. $106, YHA or VIP $97.) By car, Phillip Island is just two hours from Melbourne; take the South Eastern Arterial (M1) to the Cranbourne exit to the South Gippsland Hwy (M420), then turn onto the Bass Hwy (A420), and finally onto Phillip Island Tourist Rd (B420). This road leads straight into **Cowes**, the island's biggest township, where it turns into Thompson Ave. V/Line buses serve Cowes from **Melbourne** (3hr., 1 per day, $14). To purchase V/Line tickets in town, head to Cowes Travel or Going Places Travel, both on Thompson Ave.

**⛴ PRACTICAL INFORMATION.** Once on Phillip Island, you'll see the **Phillip Island Information Centre** over the bridge. (☎5956 7447; www.phillipisland.net.au. Open daily 9am-5pm.) Buy tickets for the Parade here to avoid long queues. Other services include: **police** (☎5952 2037); **hospital** (☎5952 2345); **ATMs** on Thompson Ave; and **post office,** 73-79 Thompson Ave (open M-F 9am-5pm). **Postal code:** 3922.

**⛴⛴ ACCOMMODATIONS AND FOOD.** The most popular budget lodging on Phillip Island is the **Amaroo Park Hostel (YHA),** 97 Church St, Cowes; head down Thompson St and hang a left on Church St. Though mostly a trailer park, the back-packer accommodations are lovely, with nice wooden furniture, a pool table, a pub with cheap drinks, and an outdoor veranda with BBQ. The friendly staff runs all kinds of tours and serves $5 dinner and a $5 cooked or $3 cold breakfast. (☎5952 2548. Internet. Dorms $14, non-YHA $17; doubles $34, $40; tentsites $10. Call to inquire about pickup in Melbourne. Book ahead.)

Your best bet for lunch is the **Phillip Island Bakery,** at the corner of Thompson and Chapel; sandwiches and hot pies run under $4. (☎5952 2027. Open M-F 7am-5pm, Sa-Su 7am-4:30pm.) For more upmarket eats, sample **Café Terrazzo,** 5 Thompson Ave, a whimsically painted bistro with a range of pasta and wood-fired pizza. (☎5952 3773. Open daily noon-3pm and 5-9pm; winter open daily 5-9pm. Meals $8-15.) An IGA **supermarket** is at the corner of Thompson and Chapel St. (☎5952 2244. Open 7:30am-5:30pm, summer until 8pm.)

**⛰ ACTIVITIES AND WILDLIFE.** Phillip Island's tourist magnet is the **Little Penguin Parade,** at the Phillip Island Nature Park. Each night, anywhere between a handful and 1000 penguins return to their burrows after lengthy fishing expeditions to rest or attend to their hungry chicks. The **Visitors Centre** provides extensive information about the penguins, including interactive exhibits on their life cycle, diet, and behavior. A boardwalk provides beach access from the center and allows you to watch the penguins burrow after they arrive. Most people await the penguins from a large grandstand along the boardwalk. To grab a good seat, arrive by sunset (bring warm clothing). After a 30min. to 1hr. wait, the penguins emerge; their parade lasts nearly an hour. (☎5956 8300; www.penguins.org.au. Open daily 10am-10pm. $10.50, children $7.50, families $26.50. Wheelchair accessible.)

Although the penguins are the main draw, several other animals make cameos. On the island's western extreme, past the penguin parade, Australia's largest colony of **Australian fur seals** lives just offshore from the **Nobbies** rock formation. A boardwalk approaches the Nobbies, enabling you to take in the beautiful eroded hills and crashing sea (open 7:30am-dusk). The **Seal Rocks Sea Life Centre** is costly for the experience. Inside you'll find displays on local marine life, a video of the seals, and a Disneyesque boat ride past animated displays tracing the area's seal hunting and conservation history. If you pop $1 in the binoculars on the board-walk, you'll see the coolest thing this place has to offer—the seals themselves. (☎(1300) 36 73 25. Open 10am-dusk. $15, students $12, children $7.50, families $38.) The **Koala Conservation Centre,** south of Cowes on Phillip Island Rd, is a sanctuary housing 23 koalas in eucalypt canopies. The nocturnal marsupials are most active at feeding time, 1½ hours before dusk. (☎5952 1307. Open daily 10am-6pm, until 7pm in the summer. $5, children $2, families $12.)

Throughout the year—but particularly in summer—Phillip Island offers great outdoor recreation. Surfers swarm to the island's southern coast; ask the staff at the information center for the *Surfing Guide to Phillip Island.* **Island Surfboards,** 147 Thompson Ave and 65 Smith's Beach Rd, can set you up with a board and provides excellent instruction. (Bookings ☎5952 3443. Boards 1hr. $8, $25 per day. 2hr. lesson $25.) If surfing's not your bag, but you still love the water, the beaches are spectacular. Cape Woolamai, on the southeast corner, has the island's highest point, numerous walking trails, and a patrolled beach for swimming between the flags. Bushwalking trails cover the island, ranging from casual to hard; the info center's pamphlet *Discover Phillip Island Nature Park* is a good place to start.

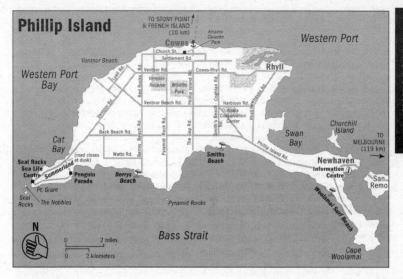

Phillip Island

TO STONY POINT & FRENCH ISLAND (10 km)

Western Port

Cowes
Church St.
Settlement Rd.
Amaroo Caravan Park

Western Port Bay

Ventnor Beach
Ventnor Rd.
Lyall Rd.
Red Rocks Rd.
Ventnor Reserve
Wildlife Park
Cowes-Rhyll Rd.
Rhyll

Ventnor Beach Rd.
Phillip Island Rd.
Coghlan Rd.
Harbison Rd.
Smith's Beach Rd.
Koala Conservation Center

Cat Bay
Back Beach Rd.
Pyramid Rock Rd.
The Gap Rd.
Berrys Beach Rd.
Watts Rd.
Swan Bay
Churchill Island

Seal Rocks Sea Life Centre
Summerland
(road closes at dusk)
Penguin Parade
Berrys Beach
Smiths Beach
Phillip Island Rd.
Newhaven
Information Centre (i)
Woolamai Surf Beach
San Remo
TO MELBOURNE (119 km)

Pt. Grant
Seal Rocks
The Nobbies
Pyramid Rocks

Bass Strait

Cape Woolamai

N

0 ___ 2 miles
0 ___ 2 kilometers

# SORRENTO

South of Melbourne and St. Kilda, lying on the Mornington Peninsula along Port Phillip Bay, Sorrento is an area rich in history, accessible to nearby parklands, and defined by its distinctive rocky coastline. Though home to a year-round population of only 1500 people, this resort town buzzes with activity throughout the holiday season and offers a chance for visitors on various budgets to relax amid the old limestone buildings and ponder the sea.

**TRANSPORT AND PRACTICAL INFORMATION.** From Melbourne, take a **train** to Frankston (1hr., every 15min., $9.50), then bus #788 to stop 18 (1½hr., 6 per day, $7). If you're coming from the Great Ocean Road, you can reach Sorrento via **ferry** from Queenscliff, on the Bellarine Peninsula (1hr.; 12-18 per day; $7, vehicles $34). The **information center** (☎5984 5678) is on St. Aubins Way, on the shore next to the boat launch. Along **Ocean Beach Rd,** Sorrento's main street and a traffic nightmare, you'll find numerous **ATMs,** and a **post office,** 16 Ocean Beach Rd (open M-F 9am-5pm). **Postal code:** 3943.

**ACCOMMODATIONS AND FOOD.** From the roundabout at the inland end of Ocean Beach Rd, follow the YHA signs up Osset St to the **Sorrento Hostel,** 3 Miranda Rd. This backpacker retreat has an outdoor patio with BBQ, an outdoor shower, kitchen, and basic groceries. The hostel operators will eagerly lead you to beautiful walking tracks, and can secure discounts on everything from horse rides to swimming with dolphins. (☎5984 4323. Dorms $16, non-YHA $19. Book 1 week ahead in summer.) Ocean Beach Rd is lined with eateries; **Stringer's Café,** 2-8 Ocean Beach Rd, offers made-to-order sandwiches and salads. (☎5984 2010. Open daily 8am-5pm. Meals $3-8.) There's also a **supermarket** next door (open M-Sa 8am-7pm, Su 8am-6pm). Perched atop the hill, **Hotel Sorrento,** 5 Hotham Rd (☎5984 2206), provides a chance to enjoy a beer ($2.50) watching the sunset on the bay.

**SIGHTS.** The town's main attraction is its bottle-blue bay at the bottom of Ocean Beach Rd, popular for swimming and sailing in summer. For an unforgettable experience, swim with dolphins and seals with **Polperro Dolphin Swims.** The Muir family runs this eco-friendly service to help fund their dolphin research, promoting conservation through education. (☎5988 8437. 4hr.; 2 per day Sept.-Apr.;

VICTORIA

VICTORIA

**CALLING THE SHOTS** Mornington Peninsula National Park is the site for a few notable events in Australian history. Fort Nepean's guns fired Australias first shots of World War I and World War II. The first time around, Britain had just declared war, and Australia followed suit immediately. It just so happened that a German ship was heading out to sea, and the fort fired at it to get it back to shore, imprison the crew, and refit the boat for Australia's efforts in the war. The second time around, the chaps at the fort were a little trigger happy from WWI, and as Britain declared war, the fort shot at a friendly ship coming into harbor that had failed to identify itself. The park is also home to the beach where a former Australian prime minister went for a swim and never came back.

$60, YHA $54.) The most popular area to hang out and **surf** is **Back Beach,** on the west of the peninsula. You can learn to surf with the **Sorrento Surf School,** on Ocean Beach Rd. (☎ 5988 6143. 2hr., $25.) Take caution: the riptides here change rapidly.

## NEAR SORRENTO: MORNINGTON PENINSULA

Mornington Peninsula National Park spans across more than 40km of coastline and bush country. The park is separated into different regions, each of which has a particular draw. Point Nepean, located on the western tip of the peninsula, consists of 6km of nearly undeveloped land only recently opened to the public. The best way to see this part of the park is by bus from the visitors center, located at the end of Pt. Nepean Rd. (☎ 5984 4276. Buses depart daily every 30min. from 9:30am-3pm. $8, concessions $4.50; park fees included.) Disembark at the first stop and walk the rest of the way (allow 2hr.) to Fort Nepean, an historical military base (see **Calling The Shots,** below), and take the bus back home from there.

There are also a plethora of **vineyards** on the peninsula. The **Dromana Estate Vineyards,** on Harrisons Rd in Dromana, is open for tastings daily 11am-3pm (☎ 5987 3800. $2.). Pick-your-own fruit farms also abound; check out **Sunny Ridge,** on the corner of Mornington-Flinders Rd and Shands Rd. (☎ 5989 6273. Open Nov.-Apr. daily 9am-5pm; May-Oct. weekends only 10am-5pm; $6-7 per kg. of strawberries.)

## QUEENSCLIFF

Upscale in inhabitants and swathed in Victorian architecture, Queenscliff is bucolic, relaxing and maybe even a little romantic. Prepare to browse on **Hesse St,** take twilight strolls, or sit on the beach. Queenscliff perches perilously on the easternmost tip of the **Bellarine Peninsula,** 120km southwest of Melbourne, attached to the mainland by a thin spit of tea-tree covered land. The town has undergone a series of incarnations, first as a major fishing village, then as a military outpost, and finally as a resort for Victoria's elite. Today, many travelers use Queenscliff as a peaceful place to start, or end, their journey on the Great Ocean Rd (see p. 550).

**Queenscliff Dive Centre** conducts snorkeling tours to swim with a colony of playful fur seals and dolphins. They also run scuba certification classes. (☎ (1800) 81 42 00. 2hr. tour from $35. Book ahead.) The **Marine Discovery Centre** runs informative events throughout the summer. (☎ 5258 3344. Tours $4.)

You can reach Queenscliff from Melbourne by taking the **train** to Geelong (1hr., 15 per day, $9), and then a **bus** from there (45min., on schedule with trains, $4). Or take a **ferry** from the Sorrento Pier (1 hr.; 6-7 per day; $7, vehicles $34). The **Visitor Information Centre,** 55 Hesse St (☎ 5258 4843), is open daily from 10am-4pm. **Hospital:** ☎ 5266 7111. **Post office:** 47 Hesse St (open M-F 9am-5pm). **Postal code:** 3225.

The jewel in the crown of hosteling, YHA-affiliated ▮**Queenscliff Inn B&B,** 59 Hesse St, offers an elegant but affordable taste of the town's luxury. In a red brick 1906 Edwardian building, the Inn is centered around a gorgeous drawing room with an open fire. The delectable breakfast ranges from home-baked breads ($5.50) to full cooked meals ($12.50). There's a kitchen and laundry available, too. (☎ 5258 4600. Linen $2. Dorms $15; singles $20; doubles $20; family rooms around $70. ) If you can't get a bed here, some of the scuba diving outfits rent out bunk-beds. Try the **Queenscliff Dive Centre,** 37 Learmonth St, opposite Town Hall. (☎5258 1188. Bunks from $25; private rooms from $50.)

For a light lunch (from $4) or a milkshake ($3), rub elbows with locals at the **Promenade Café,** 1 Symonds St. (☎5258 2911. Open daily 8am-5:30pm, winter 10am-5pm.) The grand **Queenscliff Hotel,** presiding regally over the bay with stained glass and intricately patterned tiles, has served as a summer resort since the town's earliest days. You probably can't afford the rooms or the main dining room, but the casual restaurant, **Mietta's,** 16 Gellibrand St, provides a chance to pretend you can. Menu options range from a delicate tomato bruschetta to a hearty meat lasagne. (☎5258 1066. Open daily 10am-8pm. Meals $8-10.) There's a **supermarket** at 73 Hesse St. (☎5258 1727. Open M-F 9am-6pm, Sa-Su 9am-5pm.)

# GEELONG

Geelong (pronounced "ja-LONG"), an hour southwest of Melbourne on the Princes Hwy (Hwy 1) at the western end of Port Philip Bay, is an important transportation hub for the **Great Ocean Road** and other points west. While most people just pass through, there are pleasant attractions, as befits the second-largest city in Victoria.

**TRANSPORT AND PRACTICAL INFORMATION.** The **V/Line Station** (☎13 61 96), on Brougham St, remains Geelong's most important building for most travelers. Trains run to: **Melbourne** (1hr., departs every hr., $9); **Ballarat** (1½hr.; M-Sa 3 per day, Su 2 per day; $10); and **Warrnambool** (2¼hr., 3 per day M-F, 2 per day Sa, 3 per day Su, $24). V-Line also has buses to **Bendigo** (M-F 12:30pm, $29). Navigating Geelong is fairly easy. The Princes Hwy runs north-south through town, and assumes the alias of Latrobe Tce in Geelong. Moorabool St also runs north-south, from the pier; its intersection with Malop and Little Malop St host most of the town's action. The **tourist information center** is in the Wool Museum. (☎5222 2900. Open daily 9am-5pm.) Other services include: **banks** with **ATMs** on Moorabool and Malop St (open M-Th 9:30am-4pm, F 9:30am-5pm) and a **post office,** 99 Moorabool St (open M-F 9am-5:30pm, Sa 9am-noon). **Postal code:** 3220.

**ACCOMMODATIONS. NOMADS National Hotel,** 191 Moorabool St, on the corner of Little Ryrie and Moorabool St, is a new hostel with complete facilities. Downstairs, the pub serves up wok-prepared noodle dishes and live music. (☎5229 1211 or ☎(0410) 52 99 35. Key deposit $10. Dorms $17.) **Irish Murphy's,** 30 Aberdeen St, located above a great Celtic pub, has small but clean kitchen facilities, renovated bathrooms, and a deck with fab views of the bay. The pub is a classic hotbed of Irish fun, with beautiful wood finishing attracting the eye as the Guinness does the palate. (☎5221 4335; fax 5223 3055. Pub open M-Th 11am-midnight, F-Sa 11am-1am, Su 11am-11pm. Bunks $14-17; twins $34; doubles $40.) There are also many B&Bs and motels southwest of the V/Line station on Aberdeen St.

**FOOD. Gilligan's,** 100 Western Beach Rd, across from the Cunningham Pier, has cheap fresh seafood. (☎5222 3200. Open M and W-Th 11am-7:30pm, F-Su 11am-8pm.) **Pizza Lovers,** 87 Ryrie St, offers excellent pizza from $5. (☎5221 8858. Open M-Th 11:30am-11:30pm, F-Sa 11:30am-4am, Su 5-11:30pm.) At the corner of Gheringhap and Little Melop St, the **Courthouse Café** is a cool spot with outstanding salads and free **Internet.** (☎5229 3470. Open M-F 10am-6pm.)

**SIGHTS.** The main attraction in town is the **Wool Museum,** 26 Moorabol St, east along Brougham St. It's surprisingly fascinating, with live weaving demonstrations, interactive displays illustrating the centrality of the wool industry in Australian history and folklore, and excellent traveling exhibitions. (☎5227 0701. Open daily 9:30am-5pm. $7, concessions $6, children $3.50.) **Johnston Park,** just across from the station, has many shady trees, and is home to the **Geelong Art Gallery,** which specializes in Australian art. (☎5229 3645. Open M-F 10am-5pm, Sa-Su 1-5pm. $3.) There is a family **beach** toward the northwest corner of town; head down Moorabal, on your right after you pass the Wool Museum on your left.

## BELIEVE IT OR NOT, I'M WALKING ON HARES

It doesn't take very long for most visitors to Australia to realize how hated cute little bunny rabbits can become. The presence of rabbits down under owes itself to one very foolish Thomas Austin, of Barwon Park. On Christmas Day, 1859, Austin imported 10 pairs of the little hopping buggers via the waters of Corio Bay off the shores of Geelong. Little did he know that ecological catastrophe was near at hand—in the absence of predators they multiplied quickly, causing widespread destruction of native crops. Farmers have tried everything from the 1950 introduction of the Myxoma virus to the less scientific means of poisoned carrots and rifle rounds to wipe the bouncing blight off the Australian landscape.

# GREAT OCEAN ROAD

The Great Ocean Road is one of life's greatest vehicular experiences. The entire serene and spectacular southwestern coast of Victoria, from Torquay to Portland, is encompassed by the Great Ocean Road region, though the road itself is just the 200km stretch that links Torquay to Warrnambool before being absorbed by the Princes Hwy. The Victoria government, in tribute to Australians who died in World War I, commissioned the coastal highway with the intention of creating one of the world's greatest drives. They succeeded, carving a route that winds between misty temperate rainforests and the unearthly pillars, stone arches, and gorges sculpted by the Southern Ocean. Almost too notable, the road attracts heavy tourist traffic.

Heading west, the first part of the Great Ocean Road is called the **Surf Coast**, stretching from Torquay to Lorne, where, unsurprisingly, surfers enjoy the excellent breaks. Not only surfers take advantage of this area, however; swimming beaches also cluster near the larger towns. Moist ocean winds confront the forest barrier of the **Otway Ranges** on the 73km stretch from Anglesea to Apollo Bay. This cool, rainy climate nurtures tree ferns, large pines, waterfalls, and a range of fauna; a stop here promises an extensive network of walking trails. After Apollo Bay, the hub of the Otways, the drive turns inland across Cape Otway, rejoining the shoreline at the **Shipwreck Coast.** Here, unrelenting winds, unpredictable offshore swells, and inconvenient limestone formations turned the region into a graveyard for 19th-century vessels, but also shaped the famous **Twelve Apostles** rock formations. Moving farther west, discover whales off **Warrnambool,** mutton birds in **Port Fairy,** and estuary fishing in **Lower Glenelg National Park.**

## ▐ GETTING AROUND ON THE GREAT OCEAN ROAD

If you have a **car** to explore the Great Ocean Road, you're lucky, as public transport probably won't get you everywhere you want to go. **Bicycling** along the highway is a possibility, but make sure you are in shape for it: the hilly topography between Torquay and Lorne will tone your butt faster than you can say "billabong." **Public transportation** from Melbourne via V/Line (☎13 61 96) requires a pitstop in **Geelong,** from which buses head to points west: **Apollo Bay** (3 per day M-F, 2 per day Sa-Su), and **Torquay** and **Lorne** (4 per day M-F, 2 per day Sa-Su). On Fridays throughout the year and Mondays in December and January, the "coast link" V/Line bus services **Lorne, Apollo Bay, Port Campbell,** and **Warrnambool,** with brief stops at tourist lookouts along the Shipwreck Coast. You thus stand a good chance of getting stranded in Lorne until Friday if you arrive early in the week. **Bellarine Transit** (☎5223 2111) sends about three buses a day from Geelong to Torquay.

Several **bus tours** from Melbourne to Adelaide allow travelers to take their time sampling the southwest coast, with layovers en route. **Oz Experience** runs one-day or multi-day tours, including Mornington Peninsula or the Grampians. The Road is also part of their regular journey from Melbourne to Adelaide, allowing you to hop on and off for up to six months. (☎(02) 9368 1766. $180; 5% YHA discount.) **Wayward Bus** operates a three-day adventure with more structure. (☎(08) 8232 6646,

VICTORIA

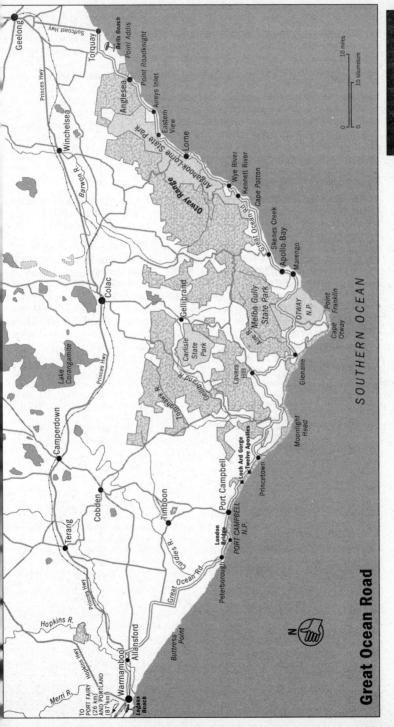

Great Ocean Road

freecall ☎(1800) 88 28 23. $170, includes lunches, planned pitstops, and accommodations.) Short day and overnight trips that cover lots of ground quickly are also very popular. **Let's Go Bush Tours** gives you dinner, breakfast, and accommodation. (Cool name, but no affiliation. ☎9662 3969. Tours Jan.-July M, W, Sa; Aug.-Dec. Sa only. $85.) **Otway Discovery Tours** guarantees a koala sighting in its one-day, pack-your-own-lunch tour. (☎9654 5432. $50.) The two-day 4WD **Natural Discoveries Ecotour** limits its groups to nine people; the rainforest-by-night tour and log cabin accommodations are highlights. (☎9629 3848. Tu, Th, Sa. $135, including meals.)

Several useful publications on the Great Ocean Road are available at tourist offices and bookstores throughout Victoria. The free glossy *The Great Ocean Road* provides just the facts, ma'am, just the facts. The National Park Service's *Map Guide: SouthWest* has reliable maps and sample short-term itineraries. *Great Ocean Road: A Traveller's Guide* is another option.

## TORQUAY

Wave seekers and beach bums who feel like they've wandered too far from Byron Bay, take heart: there's great surfing in Victoria, and Torquay, at the eastern end of the Great Ocean Road, is the center of the action.

**▐▌ TRANSPORT AND PRACTICAL INFORMATION.** V/Line **buses** (☎13 61 96) leave from outside the Bernell Caravan Park by the NOMADS hostel on the Great Ocean Road for: **Melbourne** (1½hr., 4 per day, $14); **Geelong** (45min.; 4 per day M-F, 2 per day Sa-Su; $5); **Lorne** (1hr., $5); and points west. **Bellarine Transit** (☎5223 2111) provides additional bus transport to Geelong. Most commercial activity takes place along the aptly named Surfcoast Hwy., a continuation of the Great Ocean Road, or just off the highway on Gilbert St, where there is a well-marked shopping district with **ATMs** and several food options.

**▐▌ ACCOMMODATIONS AND FOOD.** NOMADS **Bell's Beach Backpackers,** 51-53 Surf Coast Hwy, is a brightly painted bungalow-style bunkhouse with a pronounced surfing mood set by posters, magazines, and nearly constant screenings of surf documentaries. Also has immaculate bathrooms, lockers, bikes, and good vibrations. (☎5261 7070, freecall ☎(1800) 81 98 83. Key and linen deposit $15. Reception 8-10am and 4-10pm. Dorms $17; doubles $40; higher during school holidays.) Close to Bell's Beach and Jan Juc, but correspondingly farther from town, is **Pointbreak Backpackers,** 185 Addiscott Rd, about 8km southeast of Torquay via the Great Ocean Rd. Brand-spanking-new, this hostel has a full kitchen, BBQ nights, and a courtesy bus to town center and the beach. (☎5261 5105 or ☎(0418) 52 18 55. Dorms $17; winter rates lower.) Book two weeks in advance for a bed during the Easter surfing competition.

Hordes of surfers with the munchies provide a large market for the takeaways and chippers that dominate Torquay's food scene, centered on Gilbert St. **Spooner's,** 57 Geelong Rd, a cheap and friendly coffeehouse, provides a dash of the oh so popular café scene. (☎5261 3887. Open daily 9am-5pm.) There's a Food-Works **supermarket** on Gilbert St (open daily 7am-midnight).

**◪ SURFING.** Peak **surfing** season spans from March to August. The reef breaks at **Bell's Beach** attract top professional surfers for the Easter **Rip Curl Pro Classic.** It's a 10min. drive from town, a 30min. bike ride, or a 1hr. walk along the **Surf Coast Walk** past stunning cliff views to **Airey's Inlet.** The walk also passes **Jan Juc,** the second-best surfing site around (also safe for swimmers). For closer swimming beaches, cross the highway from NOMADS and continue straight for 10min. to **Cozy Corner, Torquay Front Beach,** or **Fisherman's Beach.**

The colossal **Rip Curl World Headquarters,** 101 Surfcoast Hwy (☎5261 0000), is just the beginning of a string of surfer retailers. Hang a left before the big buildings to find the bargains at one of several seconds shops, which sell "imperfect" goods at closer to perfect prices (most open daily 9am-5pm). Behind Rip Curl, **Surfworld** has a hall of fame of Australia's most venerated surfers, as well as interactive displays on wave physics, different kinds of breaks, and surfing history. (☎5261 4606. Open daily 10am-4pm. $6, concessions and NOMADS $4.) Surfworld's lobby also plays host to the town's **Visitor Information Centre** (open daily 9am-5pm).

## FROM TORQUAY TO LORNE

The turn-off to **Point Addis** appears abruptly about 5km out of Torquay. The point offers outstanding views of Victoria's western coastline, serrated by silty clay and gray cliffs. Between Point Addis and the highway is the beginning of the recently cleared **Koorie Walk,** (2km; 1hr. return) which leads through the **Ironbark Basin Reserve.** Displays along the walk elucidate the ways of life of the Koorie Aboriginals who once inhabited the area. Red ironbarks and peregrine falcons are natural highlights; the park is best in the early morning or late afternoon.

Enroute, **Anglesea** is still close enough to the surf for plenty of aquatic action, but is much quieter than the typical beach town, providing a place to escape and recharge batteries. For immaculate accommodation, try **Anglesea Backpackers,** 40 Noble St. The owner, Tony, will book surfing lessons and horseback rides and rent boards and bikes. (☎5263 2664; www.anglesea-backpackers.com.au. Internet 1hr. $5. Dorms $20, off-peak $17, winter $15; doubles $60, $55, $40.)

## LORNE

Someone once decided to sell Lorne as "the place of well-being"; that tourism mastermind could just as easily have chosen "the place of the well-dressed" or "the place of the well-to-do." This trendy town is flanked by a popular beach and a temperate rainforest, and it's café scene rivals any town to the west. Although it's been a tourist destination since the 1860s, when the Mountjoy brothers first understood its potential, Lorne's roots aren't so chic. The town started as a timber exporter, felling and shipping logs from what is now **Angahook-Lorne State Park.** Today, the park is great for bushwalking, horseback riding, and fishing.

The Great Ocean Rd morphs briefly into the Mountjoy Pde as it passes through town. **Buses** depart daily from the Commonwealth Bank on Mountjoy Pde to **Melbourne** (2½hr., $22) and **Geelong** (1½hr., $12). Buses to **Apollo Bay** leave on Friday only (1hr., $5). The **Visitor Centre,** 144 Mountjoy Pde, is in the middle of town. (☎5289 1152. Open daily 9am-5pm.) The **post office** is in the Cumberland Resort complex on Mountjoy Pde. (☎/fax 5289 1405. Open M-F 9am-5pm.)

**Erskine Backpackers,** 4 Mountjoy Pde, is at the bend at the west end of town. The sincerely friendly owners offer shared rooms that open on to a lovely veranda. (☎5289 1496. Doonas $3. Bunks $17.) **Great Ocean Backpackers,** 10 Erskine Ave, is a colony of wood cabins set on a hillside in the midst of the forest. The staff knows every walk in the park, and will even give guests a lift to trailheads. (☎5289 1809. Dorms $16. Book ahead.) **Campgrounds** without amenities are available inside the park (☎5289 1732; $6, payable to a roving ranger), or 10km west at the beautiful riverside **Cumberland River Camping Reserve** (☎5289 1790; sites $10; cabins $35-45).

Pick up the best fresh fish on the **pier** toward the west end of town (open daily 9am-6pm). Ridgeway's **supermarket,** 1 Great Ocean Road, is on the Melbourne side of the Erskine River (open M-Th and Su 8am-7pm, F-Sa 8am-8pm).

## NEAR LORNE: ANGAHOOK-LORNE STATE PARK

The National Parks service has routed several manageable walking tracks through the **Angahook-Lorne State Park,** a 21,000-hectare reserve known for its waterfalls and bird variety. The two most popular stops in Lorne's forest reserve are **Teddy's Lookout,** a sweeping view of the countryside, and **Erskine Falls.** Teddy's is a 30min. walk from Lorne up Bay St and left on George St. Erskine Falls is for the more ambitious, requiring a fairly steep 3hr. climb with several river crossings. The walk only takes 5min. from the Erskine Falls carpark via William St and Erskine Falls Rd, although it is still a steep 300-step descent to the riverbed. Various simple tracks begin at the **Sheoak Picnic Area,** a 1hr. walk or 15min. drive up Allenvale Rd from Lorne; off the main road, take the first right after the bridge and turn off the rotary after circling 270°. **Lower Kalimna Falls Walk** (1hr.) leads beneath a waterfall, which can be seen from above on the **Upper Kalimna Falls Walk** (1½hr.). A fairly easy walk (1½hr. return) connects the **Blanket Leaf** carpark to **Cora Lynn Cascades;** after the cascades, the walk becomes more difficult, crossing through the Cora Lynn Creek several times as well. Along Allendale Rd, inside the park, you can visit **Qdos,** an art studio and gallery of humorous and bizarre pieces, with a very chill café. (☎5289 1989. Open M-Tu, Th-Su 10am-6pm; winter open M-Tu, Th-Su 10am-5pm. Sa: live music.) **Otway Ocean Tours** offers **4WD tours** through forest and hinterland, or on the Great Ocean Rd. (☎5244 0944. $55.) **Otwild Adventures** runs canoeing tours that potentially paddle past platypi. (☎5236 2119. $65.)

## APOLLO BAY

According to Greek mythology, the god Helios drags the sun across the sky each day in the back of his chariot, giving us mortals our daily light. Apollo Bay would have been aptly named after this sun god because when there's no sun in this beach town, there isn't much fun either. But, hey, one sun god is as good as another for symbolic purposes. Apollo Bay serves as the gateway to Otway National Park and Cape Otway to the west. The Otway Ranges, one of the highest rainfall areas in the country, provide a lush, hilly backdrop to this resort town.

**■? TRANSPORT AND PRACTICAL INFORMATION. Buses** leave from the **Westpac bank** on Collingwood St once per day to: **Melbourne** (3½hr., $21); **Geelong** (2½hr., $18); and **Lorne** (1hr., $5). Buses to other points along the Great Ocean Rd operate on Fridays only. The above average **Tourist Information Centre,** 157 Great Ocean Road, books accommodations and tours. This is also a good place to begin planning a trip to the Otways, as they advise on road closures and help with campsite availability. (☎5237 6529; fax 5237 6194. Open daily 9am-5pm.) On the highway there are also a FoodWay licensed **supermarket** (open daily 9am-6pm) and a **post office** (open M-F 9am-5pm). **Postal code:** 3233.

**▚▞ ACCOMMODATIONS AND FOOD.** The YHA-affiliated **Surfside Backpackers,** on the corner of the Great Ocean Rd and Gambier St at the west end of town, is a stone's throw from the beach and has one of the friendliest, most helpful hostel owners around. Bonfires are a common occurrence. (☎5237 7263, freecall ☎(1800) 35 72 63. Reception daily 8-10am and 5-10pm. Sites $4; dorms $13; doubles $32-42. Non-YHA $3 more. Book ahead.) Farther from the beach is **Apollo Bay Backpackers,** 47 Montrose St, off Pascoe St, a fine place on a quiet residential street. (☎(0419) 34 03 62. Dorms $15. Reception daily after 5pm, or stop in at the Top Pub on the main drag and ask for Craig.) Twenty kilometers west of Apollo Bay, 7km south of the Great Ocean Rd on the Cape Otway Rd, stands a hostel ideally located for those hoping to thoroughly explore the Otway Ranges. **Cape Otway Backpackers,** part of the accommodation menagerie at **Bimbi Park,** puts its guests right on the edge of the great outdoors; the beach is a 20min. walk through the national park, and horseback riding can be arranged. (☎5237 9246. Dorms $12-15. Book ahead.) **Pisces Caravan Park** is on the east side of town, just off the Great Ocean Road. (☎5237 6749; fax 5237 6326. BBQ, laundry, kitchen. Linen $2. Key deposit $10. Sites $15-20, each extra people $5; dorms $15.) **Raj's,** 151 Great Ocean Rd, at the intersection with Hardy St, has inexpensive meals that are justifiably popular. (☎5237 6452. Open daily from breakfast time). The **Apollo Bay Spaghetti** restaurant, on Moore St, has Italian fare. (☎5237 6551. Open daily noon-2pm and 5pm on.)

**▨ SIGHTS.** Apollo Bay's most luminating feature are its **glow-worms,** which are actually the larval stage in the life-cycle of a local fly. To see the light, try your luck in Otway National Park, or take a tour and be led right to them. **Lloyd's Glow Worms** tours leave from Willow Bryn at the end of the Barham Valley Rd, north of Apollo Bay. (☎5237 6791. $10; bookings preferred; coffee and pancakes included.) For a quiet getaway, **Triplet Falls,** near Laver's Hill (40km west of Apollo Bay on the Great Ocean Rd), is a three-tiered waterfall reached by taking Beach Forest Rd from

VICTORIA

Lavers Hill, turning right onto Phillips Rd, then following signs on unsealed roads. Picnic tables and BBQ facilities are available. Just west of Lavers Hill is tiny **Melba Gully State Park,** with a temperate rainforest. The walk through the park is short (30min. return), but promises exposure to a truly unique environment.

## NEAR APOLLO BAY: THE OTWAYS

The Otway Range stretches 60km west of Apollo Bay and encompass three major parks: **Otway National Park, Otway State Forest,** and **Melba Gully State Park.** Within the cool, temperate rainforest, myrtle beech trees provide shade while tree ferns dominate the eye-level scenery, occasionally animated by swamp wallabies, ring-tailed possums, and gray kangaroos. Misty waterfalls cascade down steep hillsides to form clear creeks. **Mait's Rest** walk (30min.) is one of the best known rainforest walks in Victoria, beginning 17km west of Apollo Bay along the Great Ocean Rd. It's a Disneyesque approach to the bush: informative, convenient, clean, and touristy. Shortly after Mait's Rest is the turn-off for the **Cape Otway Lightstation,** built in 1848. (☎ 5237 9240. Open daily 9am-5pm. $6. Tours 1hr.; every 30min.)

Maps of the Otways' many well-marked walks are available at the Apollo Bay Tourist Information Centre (see above). A 4WD can make exploring the rough-then-sandy, pot-hole filled tracks of the park much easier to navigate. There are three recommended **camping** areas in Otway National Park. In summer, pitch at **Blanket Bay;** follow Lighthouse Rd, then watch signs for a left turn. (☎ 5237 6889. Sites $8.) The **Aire River West** camping area is reached from the Great Ocean Rd another 5km west by way of the Horden Vale turn-off. The Aire River is suitable for swimming, and three walks diverge from the grounds. For **surfing,** check out **Johanna Beach,** which also has free camping, but swimming is ill-advised. Take the sealed Johanna Rd from the Great Ocean Rd.

## PORT CAMPBELL

Port Campbell, the only safe harbor from Apollo Bay to Warrnambool, is a sleepy fishing village on one of the nastiest yet most picturesque coastlines in the world. This most treacherous stretch of the Shipwreck Coast was once feared by mariners around the world. The town provides a good base for diving, fishing, or scenic boat charters. It also holds the headquarters of the **Port Campbell National Park,** which preserves strange and wondrous rock formations.

The ⬛**Twelve Apostles** (though today there are only seven) are the most famous of the rock formations in the area. Try and see them at sunset—though you'll have to jockey aggressively for prime photo-ops. The Gibson Steps, just before the Twelve Apostles, allow a descent to the beach and a view from sea level. Other eroding sandstone monoliths dance between the waves. The **Razorback,** for example, is a long spine of rock, perforated in many places and serrated along the top. The **Bay of Martyrs** and **Bay of Islands** have many tall columns of rock which, like some of the Apostles, occasionally tumble into the sea. The gentle Port Campbell **Discovery Walk** (2.5km) begins at the cliff base at the western end of the beach or at the carpark west of the bay. Or, just hang on the town's beach—a calm, picturesque, perfect place to take a dip. The small **Shipwreck Museum** (☎ 5598 6463; $2) on the highway does bookings for **Port Campbell Boat Charters,** which offers crafts for diving, fishing, or sightseeing expeditions, and for **Port Campbell 4WD Tours** ($25).

The Great Ocean Rd becomes **Lord St** in town, and is the center of all the action: the takeaway joints, restaurants, tourist attractions, and the beach. Buses arrive from Melbourne once a week, on F (also M Dec.-Jan.). The **National Park Information Centre,** on the corner of Morris and Tregea St, one block from Lord St, serves as the town's information center, too. (☎ 5598 6382. Open daily 9am-5pm.) The **post office** is in the **Port Campbell Shopping Centre,** on the Great Ocean Rd. (☎ 5510 6255. Open daily 8am-8pm.) **Postal code:** 3269.

The **YHA Hostel,** 18 Tregea St, one block south of Lord St, has a large kitchen, a lounge with a wood stove, and laundry. (☎/fax 5598 6305. Key deposit $5. Reception 8-10am and 4-8pm. Dorms $14, non-YHA $17.) The **Port Campbell National Park**

VICTORIA

**WHY LONDON BRIDGE FELL DOWN** The bizarre rock formations around Port Campbell are a relatively recent geological phenomenon. Port Campbell National Park is founded upon layers of soft limestone which have amassed from marine animal remains. In the process of forming the Twelve Apostles, waves curling into the sides of jutting cliffs bored tunnels, which in turn left archways. These archways eventually collapsed, leaving the solitary stacks that still stand. The London Bridge formation displays an intermediate stage of this erosion process. It was once conjoined with a second arch that linked it to the mainland. In 1990 the other arch collapsed—leaving two tourists stranded—explaining why it is no longer really a bridge. So before you climb carelessly about, remember: Peter may have been called the Rock, but these Apostles represent only the shakiest of foundations.

**Cabin and Camping Park,** with BBQ, showers, and laundry is next to the National Park Information Centre on Morris St. (☎5598 6492. Reception 8:30am-9pm. Sites for 2 $13-18; powered $15-25; ensuite cabins for 6 $55-95.)

The best place to get some casual eats is the **Kooaah Shop,** in the same building as the museum on the Great Ocean Road. Along with the usual sandwiches, good vegetarian, chicken, and beef burgers can be had for $6. (☎5598 6408. Open daily 10:30am-late.) More upscale, **Emma's** is right across the street, with good value homemade tucker. (☎5598 6458. Open daily 10am-5pm and Th-Su 6:30pm-late. BYO). The only local **pub** is on the corner of Morris and Lord St.

# WARRNAMBOOL

Warrnambool is the self-proclaimed capital of the Shipwreck Coast. The city may lack the historical charm of burgs farther west, but as the biggest city on the coast, it provides a bowling alley, movie theatre, and other such amenities that the other towns lack. From May to October, southern right whales are visible without even leaving the docks. The whales combine with the sand, surf, and (oh yeah) that highway to make Warrnambool a popular holiday destination.

**E TRANSPORT.** The **West Coast Railway Station** is just north of Lake Pertrobe on Merri St, with **trains** to **Melbourne** (3½hr., 2-3 per day, $34) and **Geelong** (2½hr., 2-3 per day, $25). V/Line **buses** depart from South Western Roadways on Raglan Pde for: **Ballarat** (2½hr., M-F 1 per day, $18); **Mt. Gambier** (2½hr., 1 per day, $27); **Port Fairy** (30min., M-F 1 per day, $5); and **Portland** (1½hr., 1 per day, $13). **Buses** to the eastern towns on the Great Ocean Road run on F (also M Dec.-Jan.).

**⬛🈯 ORIENTATION AND PRACTICAL INFORMATION.** The city is built around the Princes Hwy, **Raglan Pde** in town, and envelops Warrnambool Bay (a.k.a. Lady Bay). The bay is bounded by the Merri River on the west and the Hopkins River on the east. The **Visitor Information Centre,** 600 Raglan Pde, provides free maps of the area. (☎5564 7837; fax 5561 2133. Open daily 9am-5pm.) Warrnambool's main drag is **Liebig St,** with most of the restaurants, pubs, **banks,** and **ATMs. Postal code:** 3280. **RACV:** 24hr. ☎5561 5444. **Hospital:** ☎5563 1666. **Big E's,** 517 Raglan Pde, near the corner of Raglan and Banyon, has inexpensive **Internet.** (☎5561 1793. Open daily noon-9pm. 1hr. $8.) **Post office:** corner of Timor and Gilles St (open M-F 9am-5pm).

**⬛ ACCOMMODATIONS.** To ensure a place in summer, book ahead. **Warrnambool Beach Backpackers,** 17 Stanley St, has comfortable dorm beds just a short walk from the beach. The management runs free and discounted tours to Tower Hill, as well as **Great Ocean Roads Trail Rides** (1½hr. $25). The front room has a licensed bar, but the back bunkrooms are quiet. (☎5562 4874. Reception 7:30am-10pm. Key deposit $10. Internet 30min. $5. Dorms $16.) The **Stuffed Backpacker,** 52 Kepler St, is in the middle of town, near the Raglan Pde; reception is in the chocolate shop next to the cinema. It's a no-nonsense, no-frills establishment with clean showers, ample parking, small kitchen, lounge with a fireplace and TV, and a *laissez-faire* attitude. Apple pie and ice cream is free nightly and Leo, the manager, helps guests find jobs. (☎5562 2459. Reception 9am-midnight. Key deposit $5. Dorms $14.) Just down the street, the **Western Hotel Motel,** 45 Kepler St, offers hotel singles with a communal kitchen; an IGA supermarket is next door. (☎5562 2011; fax 5562 4324. Singles $25; weekly with no breakfast $85; twins $40 including breakfast.) The **Backpackers Barn,** 90 Lava St, at the Victoria Hotel, puts guests right in the heart of Warrnambool. (☎5562 2073; fax 5561 3775. $14 per person.)

▢▣ **FOOD AND NIGHTLIFE.** For a sit-down meal, you can't go too wrong in any of the restaurants at the bottom of Leibig St. Brunch is fantastic at hip **Fish-tales,** 63-65 Liebig St, which specializes in fish, vegetarian pasta, and Asian food for under $10. (☎5561 2975. Open daily 8am-8pm. BYO.) The inventive woodfires pizzas for $10.50-13 at **Bojangles,** 61 Liebig St, are delicious. (☎5562 8751. Open daily from 5pm till late.) Coles **supermarket** is on Lava St (open daily 24hr.)

The neighborhood around Leibig St is also where Warrnambool hits the pubs. Perennial favorites include **Seanchai Irish Pub,** across from Bojangles, where you can usually catch a local band and always nurse a pint of Guinness. Open a bit later, **The Whaler's Inn,** across the street, is the same scene minus the Guinness.

▢▣ **SIGHTS AND ACTIVITIES.** The most popular thing to do in Warrnambool is to watch whales. The info center has booklets on the continuously tracked **southern right whales.** Every winter in late May or June, a population of whales stops just off **Logans Beach,** to the east of Warrnambool Bay, to give birth to their calves. They stay until September or October, when they return to the Antarctic to break their five-month fast. Tourists gather on viewing platforms built above the beach to protect the delicate dune vegetation to watch the beasts roll, blow, and breach. These right whales used to be hunted in large numbers all along the Victorian coastline, but have been protected for several decades. Whale watching is much more fun if you have some sort of visual amplification. A common error is to look too far out to sea; they often swim very close to shore.

Warrnambool's other great tourist attraction is the **Flagstaff Hill Maritime Museum,** on Merri St. The museum is a re-creation of a late 19th-century coastal village, including original edifices and artifacts from wrecked ships. The **Loch Ard peacock,** taken from the wreck of the *Loch Ard* in 1878, is located in the Public Hall. Only two people survived the wreck, but this giant ceramic fowl escaped with only slight beak damage. This museum, however, is best for those truly intrigued by Australian maritime history. (☎5564 7841. Open daily 9am-5pm. Lighthouse open 11am-5pm. $9.50, concessions $8, children $4.50.) The **Warrnambool Art Gallery,** at the corner of Liebig and Timor St, is worth a morning's browse. (Open daily noon-5pm. $3.50, concessions $2, students free.)

On the road between Warrnambool and Port Fairy, the main attraction is the **Tower Hill State Game Reserve,** situated in a volcanic crater. The reserve swarms with koalas, kangaroos, emus, possums, echidnas, and Cape Barren geese. It is possible to drive right through the crater, but to really get a good look at the wildlife, try one of the many walking paths around the reserve.

# PORT FAIRY

In 1826, Captain James Wishart sailed the cutter *Fairy* into the mouth of the River Moyne in search of potable water. His search was to no avail, but the 1843 port settlement still commemorated his voyage. From the 1850s to the 1880s, Port Fairy was the busiest Australian port outside Sydney, loading ships headed for the Motherland. Activity has, however, slowed considerably since the late 1800s.

▣▣ **TRANSPORT AND PRACTICAL INFORMATION. Buses** leave from the Tourist Information Centre on Bank St for: **Melbourne** (1 per day, $36); **Geelong** (1 per day, $29); **Portland** (3 per day, $9); and **Warrnambool** (3 per day, $5). A booklet

> **WANTED! REWARD $250,000** In 1522, **Cristovao de Mendonca,** a Portuguese adventurer, may have sailed a mahogany caravel along the east coast of Australia and mapped much of the coastline. Thus, some historians argue that the Portuguese were in fact the first Europeans to discover Australia. But thanks to 16th-century diplomatic arguments and the Lisbon earthquake of 1755, the Portuguese records are lost forever. A French map of a southern land called Java la Grande was published in Dieppe in 1547, but since many of the names appear in Portuguese, some think that the French map was actually plagiarized from de Mendonca's original charts. But de Mendonca lost more than his potential claim to the first map of Australia; his ship crashed on the coast somewhere between Warrnambool and Port Fairy. Since the first sighting of the wreck in 1836, many claim to have spied it, but the constantly shifting coastline has kept it obscured and it has drifted into legend. So when walking this stretch of coastline, keep alert, and perhaps the legend will be verified. The ship's finder, after all, can collect the $250,000 reward still posted by authorities.

with historical details and a walking tour map is available from the **Tourist Information Centre,** on Bank St. (☎ 5568 2682. Open daily 9am-5pm.) The **post office,** 25 Sackville St, has **Internet.** (Open M-F 9am-5pm. 1hr. $6.) **RACV:** ☎ 5568 2700, after-hours ☎ 5568 1017. **Hospital:** ☎ 5568 1303.

**▛▟ ACCOMMODATIONS AND FOOD.** The **YHA Hostel,** 8 Cox St, in a house built by Port Fairy's first official settler, William Rutledge, has TV, Internet, and a kitchen.(☎ 5568 2468. Reception daily 8-10am and 5-10pm. Beds $13, non-YHA $16. Book ahead for March.) **Eumarella Backpackers** is 20km west of Port Fairy in Yambuk, 200m south of Hwy 1. The hostel, in a converted 19th-century schoolhouse, is run by the Peek Whurrong people of the Framlingham Aboriginal Trust. It's next to the Deen Maar, Victoria's first Indigenous Protected Area, with outstanding coastal scenery and wetlands. (☎ 5567 1003. Kitchen, laundry, bike and canoe hire. $15; children $10.)

Port Fairy's whaling days are gone, but there is still a large fishing fleet. Rebuking this culture, the town has recently become an artists' haven, and therefore has a fledgling café scene. The sticky date pudding at **Cobb's Port Fairy Bakery,** 25 Banok St, will change your life for the better. (☎ 5568 1713. Open daily 8am-5pm.) Goodfellows **supermarket** is on Banks St. (☎ 5568 1711. Open daily 8am-9pm.)

**▨ SIGHTS.** Visits can be arranged to **Lady Julia Percy Island,** 19km out in the Bass Strait, where seals, fairy penguins, and peregrine falcons dwell. Contact **Mulloka Cruises** (☎ 5568 1790) stationed at the harbor. **Kitehouse,** 27 Cox St (☎ 5568 2782), sells any kind of kite or wind sock a windy day deserves (and rents bicycles). Almost every bed on the Shipwreck Coast is hired out in March during the **Port Fairy Folk Festival,** held over Australia's Labor Day weekend. (☎ 5568 2227; order tickets months in advance to avoid disappointment.)

## NEAR PORT FAIRY: MT. ECCLES NATIONAL PARK

Some 20,000 years ago, igneous activity formed Mt. Eccles, and the volcanic turbulence continued until about 7000 years ago. Because the volcano is relatively young, many of its topographical features are in excellent condition, not yet muted by time. Maybe the last thing one would expect in a volcanic crater, Lake Surprise is a beautiful place to walk or swim—although if the volcano decided to erupt again, any swimmers would be quickly boiled alive. Maybe that's the surprise.

**Macarthur,** the point of entry to the park, is about 40km north of Port Fairy and 30km south of **Hamilton.** The latter township is on the Hamilton Hwy, which runs west from Geelong. Within the park, well-marked walking tracks lead to several relics of the mountain's volcanic past. Thick manna gum woods cover parts of the slope, providing habitat for elusive, crabby koalas, who are most active in the evening. About 50 years ago, the northwest slope of the mountain was quarried for scoria (the porous volcanic rock that makes up much of the slope); this destructive land use was put to an end when the area was declared a national park in 1960. The **Crater Rim Nature Walk** passes all of the topographical features, and is detailed in a pamphlet available from the tourist info center, but is not the most interesting or rewarding hike in the park. The **Lake Surprise** trail (45min.) descends from the parking lot into the crater, making a loop of the water. The walk is rarely challenging, except for the ascent out, which is fairly steep. For the more adventurous visitor, the **Natural Bridge via the Lava Canal Walk** (2½hr.) follows the broad, deep lava canal south through a clear forest with little undergrowth for about 1.5km, and then gets wild. The trail follows the canal and a stone wall, so it's difficult to get lost, but it looks overgrown and untraveled. After arriving at the Natural Bridge, the trail visits the Dry Crater and ascends Mt. Eccles to an excellent view of the terrain just covered: from the head of the canal, to the dense forest, to the crater at the end. Rangers can provide camping permits and info about the bushland surrounding the park (sites for up to 4 people $14; self-serve registration).

# PORTLAND

Maritime history buffs may take pleasure in Portland's storied past, but most travelers focus more on the beds and parking spaces that make it a hub for the Great South West Walk, Discovery Bay National Park, and Lower Glenelg National Park. This area was once a base for whalers, sealers, and escaped convicts, before the Henty brothers and their sheep enterprise permanently settled it in 1834.

◪ ☲ **PRACTICAL INFORMATION AND TRANSPORT.** Two V/Line **buses** per day connect to: **Port Fairy** (1hr., $9) and **Warrnambool** (1½hr., $12). On Fridays (and Mondays Dec.-Jan.), buses run to: **Apollo Bay** (4hr., $34); **Lorne** (5hr., $38); and **Port Campbell** (2½hr., $22). Beach-front **Bentinck St** runs by the harbor, park, Information Centre, and main hotel. **Julia St** connects Bentinck with **Percy St,** which is where the **ATMs** are located. The **Portland Maritime Discovery Centre** has informative displays on the region, as well as a café with nice views of the water. (☎5521 7708. Open daily 9am-5pm. $7.) The **Portland Visitor Information Centre** is in the same building as the Maritime Discovery Centre on the waterfront at the bottom of Henty St. (☎5523 2671; fax 5521 7287. Open daily 9am-5pm.) More info on to the Lower Glenelg and Discovery Bay can be obtained from the **Parks Victoria** office, 8-12 Julia St. (☎5523 1180. Open M-F 9am-4:30pm.) Other services include: **police** (☎5523 1999); **hospital** (☎5521 0333); **RACV** (24hr. ☎5523 2111); **taxis** (☎5523 2022); and **post office** 108 Percy St (open M-F 9am-5pm). **Postal code:** 3305.

▐▜◪ **ACCOMMODATION AND FOOD.** The **Gordon Hotel,** 63 Bentinck St, provides excellent accommodation close to the waterfront and the center of town. (☎5523 1121. $25.) **Port O' Call,** 85 Bentinck St, has good coffee. (☎5523 1335. Open daily from 7am.) **Sunstream,** 49 Julia St, is a healthy choice with bins of oddities, a tasty lentil burger, and assorted salad roll-ups for under $5. (☎5523 4895. Open M-F 9am-5:30pm, Sa 9am-1pm.) The **IGA supermarket** is behind the Gordon Hotel, on Percy St (open M-W 7am-9pm, Th-F 7am-10pm, Sa-Su 7am-8pm).

▣▟ **SIGHTS AND HIKING.** Although reliable today, many ships came to grief in or near the Portland Harbor. They are now memorialized along **Historic Shipwreck Trail,** beginning at Moonlight Head and stretching to the South Australia border (brochures available at the info center). Shipwrecks, kelp forests, and delicate corals make the waters near Portland a delight for snorkelers and **divers.** Many shops, including **Duck Dive Scuba,** 57 Bentinck St (☎/fax 5523 5617), offer equipment and instruction. For a very different kind of tour (☎9923 2071), check out the **gigantic aluminum smelter** cunningly landscaped to soften the aesthetic blow delivered by metal-processing plants. This "Smelter in the Park" is a great example of environmentally conscious design.

**WORK IT, BABY, WORK IT** Short-tailed shearwaters, fed on by the early colonists during starvation years, still colonize Griffith's Island from the end of September-April. Their nesting rituals, visible just after dusk from a viewing platform and at the less crowded Pea Soup Colony down the road, are a popular spectacle. Every year, thousands of birds fly back and forth over the Pacific, spending eight months of the year on the island. After the 15,000km flight to North America the birds rest briefly, then fly right back. And you think you work hard to get some.

Starting and ending at Portland's information center, the looping, 250km **Great South West Walk** rambles along the coast, then doubles back through the Lower Glenelg National Park. The walk traverses a variety of terrains and provides a grand introduction to the wildlands of southwest Victoria. Daytrips access sections ranging from 8-20km in length. For safety, register with the info center.

**Cape Nelson State Park,** a 243-hectare reserve southwest of Portland, provides some beautiful bush walks as well as good surfing beaches, and the **last manned lighthouse** in Victoria. The black-emu-marked Great South West Walk intersects the park, but other trails, marked with red triangles, abound; one of the best is the **Enchanted Forest** walk (3km return). As one wanders through the groves of short claw-like trees, with the edges clothed in vines, it doesn't take much imagination for this place to become magical. The small white butterflies turn into gossamer-winged fairies; the scrambling sounds of lizards in the underbrush become the teasing giggles of puckish elves; the small caves in the steep seaside cliffs are the stomping grounds of goblins; and one can never be certain if the voices around the next bend are fellow travelers or scurrilous brigands. Anyway, even for the realists who prefer Henry James to Alfred Lord Tennyson, this is a good walk.

**Yellow Rock** in Cape Nelson is a dream for experienced **surfers.** For more info on surfing opportunities, beach boys and girls can consult with "Surfs Up in Portland," compiled by the Portland *Observer,* available at the Maritime Centre.

# NEAR PORTLAND
## LOWER GLENELG NATIONAL PARK

Visitors who are driving the park by car or 4WD can access Lower Glenelg National Park via the Nelson Winnap Rd, which intersects with the Princes Hwy southeast of Dartmoor and northeast of Portland. Limestone dominates the topography of the park and many caves have been formed by percolating rainwater or underground watercourses. The largest and most spectacular of these (and the only ones open to the public) are the **Princess Margaret Rose Caves,** 2km east of the South Australia border and about 15km south of the Princes Hwy. (☎ (08) 8738 4171. Tours daily 10, 11am, noon, 1:30, 2:30, 3:30, and 4:30pm. $5.50.) This area also features a few nature walks, a large, wooded picnic area with BBQ, and limited camping facilities. Camping arrangements must be made before 5pm with the ranger at the **Caves Information Center** (tentsites $8.50; on-site cabins $35).

The **Glenelg estuary,** the longest in Victoria, is one of the prime **fishing** spots in the country, populated by mulloway, bream, mullet, salmon, trout, and perch. Boats can be rented in **Nelson,** the nearest settlement to the park, though fishing gear can be a problem. **Nelson Boat Hire** (☎8738 4048) rents canoes, kayaks, and boats and can help plan trips along the river. The Glenelg River is usually calm, deep, and wide, making it ideal for tranquil canoeing. Four days of paddling will bring the water-born from Dartmoor, on the Princes Hwy, to the mouth of the river at Nelson. This 75km stretch of river supports 11 campsites, only three of which can be reached by automobile. The **Department of Conservation,** at the **Forests and Lands Information Center** (☎ (08) 8738 4051), on Forest Rd, Nelson, provides camping permits and answer questions about river conditions and canoe rental.

The main **information centre** (☎(08) 8738 4051) is on Glenelg Dr, a largely unsealed road that runs through most of the length of the park. The road, heading east from the info centre, is unsealed but very smooth for the first 8km, and a good deal bumpier for the last 14km; this is a rewarding drive, despite shaking automobiles. The tracks that branch off are in considerably worse condition.

## DISCOVERY BAY COASTAL PARK

Discovery Bay Coastal Park stretches 55km from Portland to the South Australia border. For hikers, red emu markers point the way along the Great South West Walk. The park has plentiful **surf fishing** at **Nobles Rocks**, 7km from Nelson. Connecting the sea to freshwater lakes and swamps are mobile dunes up to 20m high; be sure to stay on the marked walking tracks. An extensive lakes system also welcomes fishing, as well as swimming, boating, and close views of pelicans, swans, and ducks. Look for Bridgewater Lakes, by the road from Portland; Swan Lake, up a steep gravel road off the Portland-Nelson Rd; and Long Swamp, 3km from Nobles Rocks. Fickle weather makes it important to plan adventures carefully.

A few kilometers west of Portland at Cape Bridgewater, the Great South West Walk passes through an occasionally steep, always undulating cliff trail leading to a **seal colony.** The access point to the seal colony is a 17km drive west of Portland, heading up Otway St and out of town on Bridgewater Rd. Just after the town of Bridgewater and its awesome beach, there is a parking lot on the left for the **Spindrift Tearoom,** which is the best carpark for a direct, but occasionally steep walk (2hr. return) to the seal colony. **Seals By Sea** tours run 45min. cruises from Cape Bridgewater, but you see seals for less than 5min. (☎5526 7247. $20.)

At the end of Bridgewater Rd is a parking lot with access to the three other sights for which the park is chiefly known: the **Springs,** the **Blowholes,** and the **Petrified Forest.** There is an information board here, and bathrooms, but no ranger station. Walking between the sights, the landscape becomes strangely lunar as the persistent waves and seaspray make it nearly impossible for plant life to colonize the local environment. The volcanic cliffs and surf facing directly west make this a superb place to watch the sunset. To the left is the Petrified Forest (20min.), eerie rock formations in cavities left behind when trees rotted away. Back toward the carpark, the Blowholes are at the foot of the sea cliffs. These can be spectacular if the tidal and meteorological conditions are right. Or they can, well…blow. The Springs (1hr.) are virtually indistinguishable from tidal pools, but in fact are freshwater springs caused by rainwater seeping through the limestone farther inland.

# THE GRAMPIANS AND OUTBACK VICTORIA

The Victorian Outback exemplifies the natural diversity that makes Victoria one of the only places in Australia where so many varying ecosystems are only a daytrip away. Several ill-defined, overlapping regions, Outback Victoria encompasses mountains, lakes, swamps, wildlife reserves, rich farmland, and rugged bushland. West of the Goldfields, inland Victoria rises among the rugged peaks of Grampians National Park before slowly settling into an immense plain that stretches to the west into South Australia and north into New South Wales. The **Wimmera** region draws its name from the river that finds its source in the Grampians and wanders north past the surprisingly lush Little Desert National Park. In neighboring South Australia, the Coonawarra wine region, the Naracoorte cave system, and Mt. Gambier (see p. 440) are also traditionally considered part of the Wimmera. West of Horsham on the Wimmera highway, **Mt. Arapiles** draws rock climbers to its 1300 thrilling ascents. North of Little Desert and west of the Sunraysia Highway, all the way up to Mildura, lies the semi-arid expanse of the **Mallee,** named for the *mallee eucalypt,* a hardy water-hoarding tree that thrives in the rugged plains. Agricul-

**GHOST OF THE GRAMPIANS** Though you might not know it now, the Grampians Hotel in Ararat was a 5-star establishment during the heady days of the Australian gold rush, housing ore millionaires and other hoity-toity types who passed through town. It was also the site of several mysterious deaths, most notably that of a robust prospector from Holland by the name of Jorge. After striking gold at the nearby Canton Lead, Jorge made merry (got wasted) at the hotel pub and was last seen alive climbing the stairs to his ill-fated room, the notorious number 51. The next morning, Jorge was found dead at the base of the stairs, and all the gold in his room was missing. His killer was never found, but in the years that followed, hotel guests and workers began to suspect that Jorge's restless soul still roamed the halls. There have been countless reports of guests (especially in number 51) waking up to the sounds of footsteps at night only to find no trace of any person; some have even claimed that they were pursued down the halls by phantom footfalls. Disturbances range from the ephemeral (uncanny sensations of being watched) to the unmistakable (barstools being violently overturned by an unseen hand). You can still stay at the Grampians Hotel, if you don't mind the hint of a preternatural presence. Just steer clear of room 51—Jorge might enjoy your company.

tural pressure, increasing salinity, and the introduction of alien species like goats, cats, and bees are steadily eroding the once vast areas of mallee scrub. But sanctuaries like the Big Desert Wilderness Park, Wyperfield National Park, Murray Sunset National Park, and Hattah Kulkyne National Park seek to preserve the unique beauty of this seemingly desolate habitat.

## ARARAT

There's little here to justify any sort of detour; treat the town as a base camp for the **Grampians National Park** (see p. 562). If you're stuck for a couple hours between buses, check out the infamous **J-Ward,** next to the hospital, two blocks north of the town center. Built in the 1860s, it served as Ararat's jail until taken over by the Lunacy Department in 1887 and made into a prison for the criminally insane. It served in this capacity until 1991, when its creepy innards were opened to the public. (☎5352 3621. 1½hr. tours M-Sa 11am and 2pm; Su hourly 11am-3pm. $6.)

The volunteer-run **visitor information center,** 91 High St, is in the train station two blocks north of Town Hall Sq. (☎5355 0287, freecall ☎(1800) 65 71 58; fax 5355 0280. Open daily 9am-5pm.) V/Line **buses** run from out front to: **Melbourne** (3hr., 5 per day, $27); **Ballarat** (1¼hr., 3-6 per day, $12); **Nhill** (3-4hr., 1-2 per day, $24); and **Halls Gap** (1hr., 1 per day, $12) via **Stawell** (25min., $4). **Barkly St,** the strip of the Western Hwy that runs through town, is Ararat's main drag. **Post office:** 93 Barkly St (open M-F 9am-5pm). **Postal code:** 3377.

Ararat's pub hotels have comparable minimal amenities and hall bathrooms (rooms $20-25). A **supermarket** is across from the BP (open daily 8am-11pm).

# GRAMPIANS (GARIWERD) NATIONAL PARK

In 1836, Major Mitchell, in command of a British expedition, "discovered" the range of mountains he designated the Grampians after a range in his home country of Scotland. Ensuing hordes steadily pushed the Aboriginals out of their ancestral home they called Gariwerd. A visit to the Grampians now promises both the rich history of Aboriginal culture and the beauty that led white settlers to claim the land as their own. A popular holiday getaway for Victorians and South Australians, and the joy of school and scout groups, the park has something for both those looking to conquer rough terrain and those who just want a respite from the world beyond the ranges. Absolutely vast (half the size of Ireland), the 167,000-hectare park, located 260km west of Melbourne and 400km east of Adelaide, holds breathtaking ranges, abundant wildlife, rare birds, a springtime carpet of technicolor wildflowers, and 80% of the Aboriginal rock art sites in Victoria.

VICTORIA

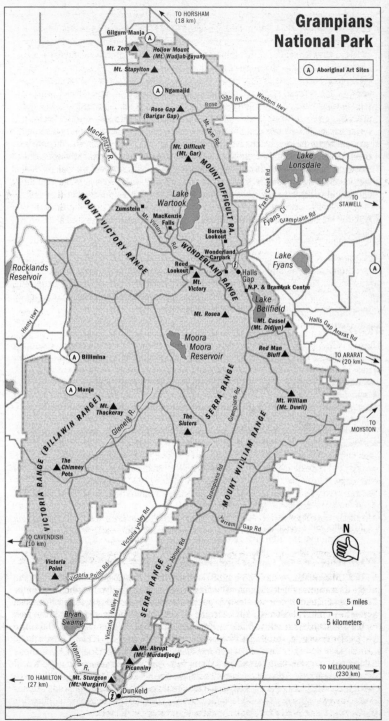

# Grampians National Park

Ⓐ Aboriginal Art Sites

TO HORSHAM (18 km)

Gilgurn Manja
Mt. Zero
Hollow Mount (Mt. Wudjub-guyun)
Mt. Stapylton
Ngamajid
Rose Gap (Barigar Gap)
Rose Gap Rd
Western Hwy
Mt. Zero Rd

Mt. Difficult (Mt. Gar)
Lake Lonsdale
Frats Creek Rd

MOUNT DIFFICULT RA.

Lake Wartook
Zumstein
MacKenzie Falls
Mt. Victory Rd
Boroka Lookout
Wonderland Carpark
Reed Lookout
Mt. Victory
Halls Gap
N.P. & Brambuk Centre
Lake Bellfield
Mt. Rosea
Mt. Cassel (Mt. Didjun)
Red Man Bluff
Fyans Ct
Grampians Rd
Lake Fyans
TO STAWELL
Halls Gap Ararat Rd
TO ARARAT (20 km)

MOUNT VICTORY RANGE
WONDERLAND RANGE

Rocklands Reservoir
Mackenzie R.
Henty Hwy

Moora Moora Reservoir
SERRA RANGE

Billimina
Manja
Mt. Thackeray
The Sisters
Mt. William (Mt. Duwil)
TO MOYSTON

VICTORIA RANGE (BILLAWIN RANGE)
Glenelg R.
Grampians Rd
MOUNT WILLIAM RANGE

The Chimney Pots

TO CAVENDISH (10 km)

Victoria Point
Victoria Valley Rd
Victoria Point Rd
Mt. Abrupt Rd
Yarram Gap Rd

N

Bryan Swamp
Victoria Valley Rd
Wannon R.
SERRA RANGE

0        5 miles
0        5 kilometers

Mt. Abrupt (Mt. Murdadjoog)
Picaninny
Mt. Sturgeon (Mt. Wurgarri)
Dunkeld

TO HAMILTON (27 km)
TO MELBOURNE (230 km)

# TRANSPORT

The northern approach passes through the seemingly empty town of **Horsham,** at the junction of Western and Henty Hwy, roughly 80km north of the park. From the south, the town of **Dunkeld,** on the Glenelg Hwy, provides access via Mt. Abrupt Rd. From the east, the closest town is **Stawell,** 26km away. The most convenient point of entry is on the eastern edge of the park at **Halls Gap.** This is the park's only town, and it's a small one; but it has the basic amenities and is within walking distance of many of the park's points of interest. When reading about the town's offerings remember that, unless otherwise noted, everything is bunched together in a small strip on Grampians Rd, also called Dunkeld Rd, which runs from Halls Gap to (you guessed it) Dunkeld. One V/Line **bus** per day leaves across from the newsagent for: **Melbourne** (4½hr., $40); **Ararat** (1hr., $12); **Ballarat** (2½hr., $25); and **Stawell** (30min., $8). Several companies also run multi-day tours from Melbourne and Adelaide, often incorporating the Great Ocean Road along the way.

# PRACTICAL INFORMATION

The **National Park and Brambuk Centre,** 2.5km south of Halls Gap's town center on Dunkeld Rd, is the best resource for would-be hikers and bush-campers. The helpful rangers provide excellent information on the Grampian's flora, fauna, and history. (☎5356 4381. Open daily 9am-5pm. Hiking maps $3; donations appreciated.) From outside Halls Gap, **Parks Victoria** (☎13 19 63; www.parks.vic.com.au) can answer most questions. The Halls Gap **visitors centre** in the town center has official Halls Gap info. (☎5356 4616, freecall ☎(1800) 06 55 99. Open 9am-5pm.) The **newsagent** next door also has plenty of maps, as well as an **Internet** kiosk (10min. $2; open daily 7am-7pm). The Mobil **petrol station** has camping supplies and an **ATM.** (☎5356 4206. Open daily in summer 6am-10pm; winter 7am-7:45pm.) The **post office** is hidden in the well-marked "Coffee Shop" (open M-F 9am-5pm).

# ACCOMMODATIONS, CAMPING, AND FOOD

The quality of the accommodations here is as high as the Grampians themselves.

▧ **Grampians YHA Eco-Hostel** (☎5356 4544; email hallsgap@yhavic.org.au). A 10min. walk north of the town center on Grampians Rd, at the corner of tiny Buckler St. Brand-spanking-new, this energy efficient hostel opened in July 2000 and is more luxurious, scenic, and sharply decorated than your everyday budget digs. State-of-the-art kitchen, dining area, plush sofas, TV room with VCR, adventure booking office, Internet (10min. $2). Reception daily 8-10am and 5-10pm. Dorms with lockers and heaters $18; singles $38; twins and doubles $45; family rooms $62.

▧ **Brambuk Backpackers** (☎5356 4250; http://brambuck.tourvic.com.au). Across from the Park Centre. Recently refurbished, all rooms are ensuite and have heaters. The single-sex dorms are a tad congested, but less cramped mixed dorms are available. Friendly staff, large lounge areas, BBQ, Internet (10min. $2) Affiliated with the **Brambuk Cultural Centre.** Dorms $22; singles $39; doubles $50; includes brekkie.

**Tim's Other Place** (☎/fax 5356 4288; www.timsplace.net). On Grampians Rd north of the town center, about 100m away from the YHA. This homey 20-bed hostel is easily the most intimate of the three, and has the most backpackers. Free tea and coffee, heat, Internet (1hr. $4). Dorms $18; twins and doubles $44; includes brekkie. The original **Tim's Place** (☎/fax 5384 0236), is located at Mt. Arapiles, near Horsham. Tim runs a free shuttle between his two facilities, and has regular pickup and drop-off in Melbourne and Adelaide ($50 return or through to Melbourne or Adelaide).

**Halls Gap Caravan Park** (☎5356 4251). In Halls Gap center. Powered sites for 2 $22, off-season $18.70; on-site caravans for 2 $45, $40.

**Camping.** There are 13 major camping areas in the national park, all with toilets and fireplaces. All sites are first-come, first-served; campers must pay a $10.20 fee (up to 6 people or 1 vehicle, additional vehicles $5), through self-service permits available at the Park Centre and at most camping areas. Rangers advise stopping at the Centre first for a complete map of the park's campsites and new relevant information. **Bush camping** is free but is forbidden in the Wonderland Range, the Lake Wartook watershed, and any other areas demarcated accordingly on maps. See the Park Centre for details.

Halls Gap's town center has a handful of unspectacular eateries. The **Halls Gap Tavern,** toward the Park Centre, has expensive mains but bargain daily specials. (☎ 5356 4416. Open M-F 8am-9pm, later Sa-Su. $4 brekkie special 8:30-11am, $12 3-course set menu noon-2:30pm and 5-7pm.) The **Brambuk Café,** in the Brambuk Living Cultural Centre (see **Sights and Hiking,** below), specializes in bush tucker, such as emu lasagna and kangaroo steak sandwiches. (Open daily 9am-5pm. Meals around $10.) There's a Friendly **Grocer** next to the newsagent in the town center (open daily 7am-9pm), but its exorbitant prices are decidedly misanthropic.

## ▓ SIGHTS AND LOOKOUTS

Before you head into the park, go to the **Brambuk Living Cultural Centre,** adjacent to the Park Centre in Halls Gap, which has small but excellent displays on the culture and history of the **Koori,** southwest Victoria's native people. Two documentaries run constantly and provide unflinching insight. The new **Dreaming Theatre** shows a 15min. light-and-sound show of a traditional Koori story. The Cultural Centre runs several workshops, including boomerang throwing, didgeridoo-playing and Koori traditional dancing. (☎ 5356 4452. Open daily 9am-5pm. Free entry. Theatre $4.40.)

Unfortunately, the following sights are a good distance from Halls Gap and require a car to reach. Many tourists frequent the spots, though—hikers report catching rides at the Park Centre or their accommodations. Alternately, **Halls Gap Taxis** (☎ (019) 94 36 91) offers pickup and drop off at almost anywhere around the park. The **Balconies,** the Grampians' predominant icon, lie about 1km up from the Reed Lookout carpark off Mt. Victory Rd. The mostly flat approach (20min.) ends in sweeping panoramas and the Balconies themselves, a pair of parallel slabs of sandstone jutting out over the steep sides of Mt. Victory. Those who brave the steep, slippery path to **MacKenzie Falls,** which begins at the carpark just off Lake Wartook Rd, are rewarded with one of Victoria's—and perhaps Australia's—most spectacular waterfalls, a cacophonic 11m wall of crashing water. A new wheelchair-accessible approach was recently opened. **Zumstein recreation area,** west of Lake Wartook on Mt. Victory Rd, is extremely popular because it crawls with kangaroos. Kangaroo herds also wander just about everywhere in the park.

## ▓ HIKING

Although extremely rugged, the Grampians is a very user-friendly national park; most of its highlights can be reached via relatively easy walking trails, without the need to camp overnight in the bush. Thus it's a fave among families and nature lovers of the less-hard-core variety, while at the same time catering to the hard-core hiker with more difficult tracks. The **Wonderland Range** adjacent to Halls Gap in the park's eastern end holds the bulk of the park's main attractions. The strip of **Mt. Victory Rd,** in particular, is loaded with phenomena to impress even the staunchest urbanite. Pick up the indispensable *Wonderland Walks* map ($3.30) in the Park Centre for details on hiking and driving routes.

The Grampians is fertile with hikes of varying difficulty from 30min. to 6hr. to several days. The following trails start relatively near Halls Gap accommodations:

**Wonderland Loop,** (9.6km; 5hr.). Starts in back of the town center carpark. A medium difficulty hike taking in many of the most touristed sites, though strenuous detours are available off the main route. A perfect family outing, the half-day loop along well-formed tracks leads through the lush forest along a river, then up the ironically meager **Grand**

**Canyon,** to the narrow rock tunnel called **Silent Street** (not a street). At the awe-inspiring **Pinnacle,** sweeping views of three valleys enrapture even the acrophobe. The quick descent through stringy-bark forests is mildly steep at times, though the unobstructed ridge-line views are worth every aching knee joint.

**Boronia Peak Trail,** (6.6km; 2-3hr.). Starts past the kangaroo fields next to the Park Centre carpark. A little harder than the Wonderland Loop, but shorter. The dense trees add to the tranquil solitude of this much less touristed route, yet don't obscure bird and other fauna watching. The mostly medium-grade terrain ends in a short unmarked rock scramble to the peak. With a large lake to the south, flat bush country to the east, and the jagged Wonderland range to the west, the view is nothing short of spectacular.

**Boroka Lookout Trail,** (12.4km; 4-5hr.). The toughest hike from Halls Gap. An unrelentingly steep ascent to this lookout in the Mt. Difficult Range rewards with spectacular views of the Fyans Valley and the Mt. William Range, the rough, wrinkly slopes of which have been aptly named the Elephant's Hide (also viewable from the nearby carpark).

**Chatauqua Peak Loop,** (5.6km; 2-3hr.). Starts from behind the Recreation Oval on Mt. Victory Rd, 100m from the intersection with Grampians Rd. The hike opens with an up-close view of the tranquil Clematis Falls, best after rain. The final 400m boulder climb to the peak is long and strenuous, but the views of Halls Gap and the valley are perfect. Those less mobile can skip the boulder hop; the main trail continues on through to Bullaces Glen, a lush fern gulley, ending in the botanical gardens in Halls Gap.

Other Wonderland walks lead to serene waterfalls, curious rock formations, and the occasional hookah-smoking caterpillar. To the south, **Victoria Valley** is carpeted with redgum woodlands and is home to emus and kangaroos. **Manja** and **Billimina,** at the park's western border, contain some of the Grampian's best **Aboriginal art sites.** Experienced hikers might want to tackle some of the steep trails on the Gramps' highest peak (1168m), **Mt. William,** at the park's extreme eastern end; the actual "trail" to the summit is disappointingly fully-paved and well-traveled.

## ⚠ BEYOND HIKING: OTHER ADVENTURE

There are adventure opportunities galore and enough companies that you won't have trouble booking your requisite adrenaline rush. All companies offer free pickup in Halls Gap, and group rates are usually cheaper. The **Adventure Company** (☎5356 4540, mobile ☎(0408) 82 84 32; www.adventurecompany.com.au), with an office in the Grampians YHA, has recently expanded its offerings to appeal to the burgeoning backpacker market: a 6hr. winery tour ($65) and a 17km downhill bike ride ($35), canoeing and kayaking ($30-45), and a range of rockclimbing and abseiling courses ($30-85). The advanced abseil drops you 60m over ❒The Ledge. It's all 10% off if you stay at the YHA (see p. 564). Climbing pioneers **Base Camp & Beyond** (☎5356 4300; www.grampians.net.au), have specialized in rockclimbing and abseiling since 1982. The above two companies can be booked directly or through the **Grampians Central Booking Office,** in the Halls Gap newsagent. (☎5356 4654; email gbcnoeln@netconnect.com.au. Open daily 9am-5pm.) The Booking Office also runs the **Grampians Nature Tours,** with 4WD tours focusing on wildlife or visual highlights (half-day $54, full-day $82.50; popular warm-weather sunset tour with dinner $65; 1-1½hr. night walk $11). **Grampians Adventure Services,** in Shop 4 of the Stony Creek stores in Halls Gap center, can book the above companies, as well as mountain bike tours. (☎5356 4556; email grampadv@netconnect.com.au. Open daily 10am-5pm. Tours: night $20, day $30-40. Rental: full-day $35, includes drop off with the bike anywhere in the Wonderland Range.)

For an exhilarating and 100% free adventure (not for the timid), just walk along any of the roads (preferably unlit) at night and be awed as kangaroo and deer mill all around. Bring a flashlight, because it can get eerie—and to alert any approaching vehicles to your presence.

# LITTLE DESERT NATIONAL PARK

The Little Desert is not, in fact, a desert. So-christened because early settlers found the land ill-suited for farming, the Desert's 134,000 hectares are covered with diverse vegetation and wildlife. In the late 1960s, the government announced that 80,000 hectares of the park would be subdivided and cleared for farmland, sparking one of Australia's first major preservation campaigns. The harsh environment won't wow you with sweeping vistas or spectacular wonders like the Grampians, but it beckons with a subtle micro-beauty: a delicately blooming wildflower here, a rare species of bird there, and a sense of rugged survival everywhere.

**TRANSPORT.** The Little Desert is best approached from **Nhill** (pronounced "nil"—guess why? pop. 1900), north of the central parkland; or from **Dimboola** (pop. 1600), on the Wimmera River to the east. Two V/Line (☎ 13 61 96) **buses** per day Sunday to Friday and one bus Saturday depart Nhill from the station opposite ticket-seller **Rintoule's Travel Service,** 37 Victoria St (☎ 5391 1421). To: **Melbourne** (6-7hr., $46); **Ararat** (3-4hr., $24); **Ballarat** (4-5hr., $37); **Dimboola** (30min., $4.30); **Horsham** (1-2hr., $9); and **Stawell** (2½-3hr., $20). Trips from Dimboola are 30min. shorter and include an additional departure Monday to Saturday. The daily V/Line Daylink service from Melbourne to Adelaide runs through both Nhill and Dimboola and stops in, among other places, **Melbourne** (6¼hr., $45); **Bendigo** (4hr., $21); **Horsham** (1¼hr., $9); and **Adelaide** (4hr., $45). Dimboola's **bus station** is at the Caltex Roadhouse, on the corner of Lochiel and Hindmarsh St.

**PRACTICAL INFORMATION.** The best place to go for park info is the **ranger station** on Nursery Rd in **Wail.** (☎ 5389 1204. Open M-F 8am-4:30pm.) Or call **Parks Victoria** (☎ 13 19 63). Somewhat sparse **tourist information centers** can be found in Nhill, on Goldsworthy Park along Victoria St (☎ 5391 3086; open daily 10am-4pm); and Dimboola, 119 Lloyd St (☎ 5389 1290; open M, W-F 9:30am-5:30pm, Sa 9:30am-4pm, Su 11am until they feel like closing). **Commonwealth Bank,** 14 Victoria St, Nhill, has an **ATM.** (☎ 5391 1033. Open M-Th 9:30am-4pm F 9:30am-5pm.)

**Nhill Online Solutions,** 121 Nelson St, has **Internet access.** (☎ 5391 1910; open M-Tu, F 10am-6pm; Sa 9am-2pm; Su 10am-8pm. 30min. $2.) **Post office:** in Nhill, 98 Nelson St (open M-F 9am-5pm; **postal code:** 3418); Dimboola, 65 Lloyd St (☎ 5389 1542; open M-F 9am-5pm; **postal code:** 3414).

**ACCOMMODATIONS, CAMPING, AND FOOD.** The complete Little Desert experience can be had at the **Little Desert Lodge,** set on over 600 acres of bush, owned and operated by Malleefowl expert Whimpey Reichelt and his wife Maureen. Take Nhill Harrow Rd 16km south of the Nhill town center; signs point the way. The lodge and aviary are a bird- and nature-lover's mecca (see **Sights and Activities,** below). The licensed main kitchen has $16-20 full courses. (☎ 5391 5232; email littledesertlodge@wimmera.com.au. Bunk $18, with linen $29; ensuite twins $77; campsites $11, powered $14. Popular with school groups; book well ahead.)

The **Commercial Hotel,** at Victoria and Nelson St, Nhill, lacks that authentic desert feel but is still a good deal. (☎ 5391 1500. Singles $22.) In Dimboola, along Horshoe Bend Road 4km from the Dimboola post office, **Little Desert Log Cabins and Cottage** is right in the bush, a stone's throw from the park entrance. (☎ 5389 1122. Self-contained cabins with the works $70-80.)

There are two **camping areas** in the National Park, one just south of **Kiata,** a hamlet on the Western Hwy between Nhill and Dimboola, and the other at **Horseshoe Bend,** south of Dimboola. Both campgrounds have fireplaces, tables, and toilets. The $8.30 fee covers 6 people and 1 vehicle (payable at any of the ranger stations, or in the pay receptacles at the campsites; additional vehicle $3.50). Bush camping is allowed in the western and central blocks only and must be vehicle-based.

**NO SMALL FEAT** Most birds sit on their eggs and use the heat of their bodies to warm their unborn young. But the endangered **Malleefowl** have come up with a way to save on baby-sitting and still get out of the nest. Of the family Megapodiidae, meaning "large feet," these grey, beautifully patterned, pheasant-like birds use their great clonkers to build a mound out of dirt, sticks, and tree litter, in which the female deposits her eggs. Each mound takes weeks or months to build, and the fowl often reuse mounds that have been around for more than a century. Once completed, the mound garners warmth from the sun and the fermentation of the tree litter. Over the next few months, the parents build-up and repair the natural incubators until they are nearly one meter high and five meters wide. By changing the depth of the sand and litter layers, the Malleefowl can control the temperature of the eggs. In studies of the Malleefowl hatching cycle, researchers have found that the temperature of a mound's interior varies by fewer than two degrees over a span of several months. Once the eggs hatch, the chicks dig themselves out of their nurseries and are immediately on their own, receiving no assistance or even recognition from their parents. These hatchlings are born nearly mature and can fly within a few hours, though survival rates are low.

Besides a few pubs with counter meals, Nhill's restaurant pickings are slim. Get **groceries** at the Foodway, 17 Victoria St, or the IGA across the street (both open M-F 8:30am-6:30pm, Sa 8:30am-6pm, Su 9am-6pm). In Dimboola, Kay's Foodworks is at 15-19 Nochiel St (open M-F 9am-5:30pm, Sa-Su 9am-12:30pm).

**◼◭ SIGHTS AND ACTIVITIES.** Little Desert's unique Mallee ecology is best explored on foot, although 4WD drivers can usually use the rough, unpaved roads (often closed in winter) to reach remote corners. An excellent 30min. introductory walk leads to the lookout on **Pomponderoo Hill,** showing off typical Little Desert terrain. Go through the gate marked "Gateway to Little Desert" at Dimboola (not the official park entrance), turn left immediately after crossing the Wimmera River bridge, and go south, following the "National Park" signs; the trailhead is 1km past the actual park entrance. Other **walks** begin at the campground south of Kiata and at the Gymbouen Rd south of Nhill; large map boards at each campground show the trails. The truly hard-core may wish to take on the 84km **Desert Discovery Walk,** a one- to four-day trek (depending on what you're made of) across the eastern section of the park that can be tackled in parts or all at once. Detailed brochures on all the walks are available at ranger stations and tourist offices. The well-marked walk is best attempted in spring, when the weather is mild and the wildflowers are in bloom. Overnight campers should register at Wail's Park Office (☎5389 1204).

The **Little Desert Lodge** provides direct access to bushwalks, including the Lodge Loop (1hr.) and the Stringybark Loop (45min.). They also run 4WD tours in vintage 1960s Land Rovers, including a visit to Whimpey's **Malleefowl block,** a fowl sanctuary that attracts international birdlovers to marvel at these birds' trademark mounds (see **No Small Feat,** above; half-day tour $27.50, three-quarter-day $44, full-day $55; min. 6 people). The **Malleefowl Aviary,** at the Little Desert Lodge offers a more pampered, up-close view (open M-Sa 9:30am-4:30pm, Su 1:30-4:30pm; $5.50).

**Oasis Desert Adventures** (☎(0419) 39 49 12), at the eastern entrance of the park in Dimboola, offers many activities, including day tours, flower walks, fishing trips, boomerang and spear throwing, raft and hut building, orienteering, and yabbying (from $15; prices vary based on type and duration of activity; book ahead).

# GOLDFIELDS

In 1851, the first year of Victorian statehood and just two years after the California gold rush, this most precious of metals was discovered in the unassuming burg of Clunes. A year later, the *London Times* reported that 50,000 diggers had already converged on Victoria's goldfields. To the chagrin of Victorians, who had taken pride in the fact that free persons had settled in Victoria before convicts had, ex-convicts from Van Diemen's Land (present-day Tasmania) floated over to join the crowds. Gold was to prove the great equalizer of classes, as convicts hardened by years of manual labor and rugged immigrants from all corners of the world dug-up ore more efficiently than their effete bourgeois counterparts, and the silk-clad landed gentry soon found themselves having to rub elbows with an unpedigreed nouveau riche. The established classes did not allow this social shake-up willingly, forcing the government to invoke mining taxes and grog prohibition, factors that ultimately led to the brief and bloody Eureka Rebellion of 1854 (see p. 12). The Victorian prospectors eventually extracted more ore than even the Californian '49ers, but by the end of the 19th century, the mines were largely exhausted, and most of the boom towns withered away to ghost towns. A few, such as Ballarat and Bendigo, remain substantial cities, and others, such as Castlemaine and Maldon, have been preserved as historical relics. These remaining cities and townships of the Goldfields region, occupying the central area of western Victoria, afford travelers the opportunity to enjoy the recreated gold rush spectacles, a handful of wineries, and the hurly-burly frontier spirit that grew out of this short wave of settlement but went so far in shaping Australia's national character.

# BALLARAT

Victoria's second largest inland city (pop. 83,000), Ballarat is the self-appointed capital of the Goldfields. The most important of the boom towns during the gold rush, it clings to its gracious 1850s image. When miners first started working the Ballarat goldfields, the pickings were easy; alluvial gold, weathered from upstream rocks, was visible to the naked eye in the riverbeds. Although the gold is long gone, much of the 19th-century architecture has been preserved, and the city's golden past has been channeled into a bustling tourist trade that centers on Sovereign Hill, a replica of an old gold town, replete with townspeople dressed in 1850s attire. Huge, elegant Victorian buildings line the main street, and the begonias win the town fame among gardeners. Ballarat was also the site of Australia's closest brush with civil war, on December 3, 1854. A classic case of taxation without representation became an uprising over miners' rights. The bloody Eureka Rebellion that ensued remains an emblem of Australian populism. Ballarat retains this memory by billing itself "the birthplace of the Australian spirit."

## ▐ TRANSPORT

**Trains and Buses:** V/Line (☎ 13 61 96) operates **trains** and **buses** from **Ballarat Station,** 202 Lydiard St N, reached by bus #2. Frequencies vary Sa-Su. To: **Melbourne** (1½hr., 12 per day, $14); **Ararat** (1¼hr., 5 per day, $12); **Bendigo** (2¼hr., 1 per day, $18); **Castlemaine** (1½hr., 1 per day, $14); **Daylesford** (1hr., 1 per day, $9); **Geelong** 1½hr., 3 per day, $10); and **Maryborough** (1hr., 1 per day, $11).

**Public Transportation:** (☎ 5331 7777). $1.45 ticket valid for two hours. Purchase from driver. Most routes depart from Bridge Mall. Helpful transit guide (20¢) from tourist office or on bus. Services typically run every 35min. M-F 7am-6pm; Sa limited schedule.

**Taxis:** Ballarat Taxis (☎ 13 10 08) operates 24hr. Service from the city center to Sovereign Hill is about $6. Up to 5 people can share a cab. Call or catch next to post office.

**Car Rental: Avis,** 1104 Sturt St (☎ 5332 8310). $55 per day, 200km. **Budget,** 106 Market St (☎ 5331 7788). $52 per day, 200km. **Hertz,** 47 Mair St E (☎ 5331 5354). $55 per day, 250km.

## ◤ ⋈ ORIENTATION AND PRACTICAL INFORMATION

Ballarat straddles the Western Hwy, called **Sturt St** as it runs through town east to west. The **train station** is a few blocks north of Sturt on **Lydiard St.** From the station, turn left on Lydiard and cross **Mair St** to get to Sturt St. At its eastern end, Sturt becomes **Bridge Mall,** a pedestrian mall with shops, restaurants, and supermarkets.

**Tourist Office:** 39 Sturt St (☎5320 5741; freecall (1800) 64 84 50; fax 5332 7977; www.ballarat.com), at the corner of Albert St. From the V/Line station, walk left along Lydiard to Sturt St, turn left, and walk one block downhill to the corner of Albert St. Blue signs point the way. Good free maps available. Open daily 9am-5pm.

**Banks:** Banks and **ATMs** line Sturt St. **National Bank,** 329 Sturt St (☎5331 1700). $5 exchange fee. **Commonwealth Bank** (☎5337 7500), on the corner of Sturt and Lydiard St. $7 exchange fee. Both open M-Th 9:30am-4pm, F 9:30am-5pm.

**Laundromat: Ballarat Laundry,** 711 Sturt St. Wash or dry $2. Open daily 6am-10pm.

**Police:** (☎5337 7222). Behind the tourist center on Albert St.

**Hospital: St. John of God,** 101 Drummond St N (☎5331 6677).

**Internet Access: Vic West,** 3 Camp St (☎5331 7602), across from the Tourist Center. 1hr. $5. Free access at the **library,** 178 Doveton St N (☎5331 1211).

**Post Office:** (☎5331 4744; fax 5331 7642), on the corner of Lydiard and Sturt St. **Fax** services. Open M-F 9am-5pm. Poste Restante available. **Postal Code:** 3350.

**Phone Code:** 03

# ACCOMMODATIONS

Ballarat's accommodations market is aimed more at Melburnian families on weekend trips, but has a fair number of budget options as well. Rooms tend to be in short supply because of the city's popularity with school groups, so book well in advance. If you happen to strike it rich while in Gold Country, try one of the palatial B&Bs on Lydiard St. Hapless diggers will have to make do with one of several cheaper options; the tourist office offers a list.

**Sovereign Hill Lodge YHA,** (☎5333 3409; fax 5333 5861). On Magpie St at Bourke St. Take bus #9 or #10 from Bridge Mall to Sovereign Hill ($1.45), or walk for about 20 minutes up a steep hill by following Peel St south at the eastern end of Bridge Mall, then left on Grant St, then right on Magpie St. By car, follow signs to Sovereign Hill, then to the lodge from Geelong Rd, a continuation of Main St. The buildings retain an 1850s style but have recently been refurbished and are in excellent condition. Laundry, kitchen, TV lounge, pool and ping-pong tables, and bar (VB $3.50). Courteous staff issues tickets for all Sovereign Hill events. Reception 24hr. except closed Su 10:30pm-M 7am. Dorms $17.50, non-YHA $20.50. Private motel doubles $105. Book one week in advance due to hordes of school groups. Limited wheelchair access.

**Irish Murphy's,** 36 Sturt St (☎5331 4091; fax 5332 2389). Just across from the tourist office. A relatively authentic Irish pub with live music Th-Sa nights (cover $3 F-Sa after 10pm). Clean, unadorned doubles at the top of the stairs might be a tad loud for the light dozer. Solution: drink downstairs until the bar closes. Kitchen. Communal unisex bathroom. No heat or A/C. No bookings; rooms go to the "first in and the best dressed." Check in after noon. $14 per person, with a cozy comforter $17.

**Robin Hood Hotel,** 33 Peel St N (☎5331 3348). Fairly basic pub bunk accommodations with good location one block from Bridge Mall. Not quite as crystal-clean as Irish Murphy's, but bigger rooms and fanciful red carpets in hallway offer touch of class. $20 key deposit. Book several days in advance. Bunks $20; singles $25.

**Ballarat Goldfields Holiday Park,** 108 Clayton St (☎5332 7888; fax 5332 4244; email goldpark@cbl.com.au). 300m from Sovereign Hill. Kitchens, recreation rooms, playground, heated pool. Reception daily 8am-8pm. New heated communal bathrooms. Key deposit $10. Tent sites for 2 $17.45, powered $19.60; cabins $53.40 and up.

# FOOD AND ENTERTAINMENT

Sturt St is lined with fish-and-chips shops, milk bars, and other takeaway places. The best **cafés** are up the hill, especially at the corner of Dawson and Sturt St. Two 24-hour **supermarkets,** a produce shop, and a bakery are at the far eastern end of Sturt St behind the Bridge Mall. Several cheap eats rest just east of Sovereign Hill.

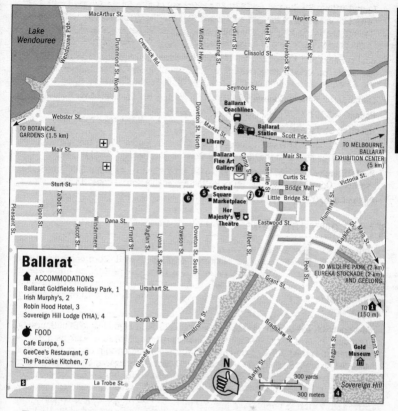

**Ballarat**

🏠 ACCOMMODATIONS
Ballarat Goldfields Holiday Park, 1
Irish Murphy's, 2
Robin Hood Hotel, 3
Sovereign Hill Lodge (YHA), 4

🍎 FOOD
Cafe Europa, 5
GeeCee's Restaurant, 6
The Pancake Kitchen, 7

**The Pancake Kitchen,** 2 Grenville St South (☎5331 6555). On the corner of Lewis St in a restored 1870s building. Not your basic IHOP, the Pancake Kitchen offers pancakes and crepes in assorted fruit or meat incarnations ($8-14). The bottom floor features a gigantic chess set. Sample nights W 6-10pm. Takeaway available. Open M 10am-10pm, Tu-Th 10am-late, F-Sa 7:30am-late, Su 7:30am-10pm. Fully licensed or BYO.

**Gee Cees,** 427 Sturt St (☎5331 6211). Bright, big, and busy, Gee Cees serves gourmet food in an informal yet upscale setting. Order food (mains $12-17, pastas $10-12, pizzas $12-15) at the counter and drinks at the bar; attractive, black-clad waitstaff brings it out lickety-split. Gigantic, deliciously sinful Mars Bar cheesecake $5. Food served until 9:30pm daily; bar open until 11pm on weeknights, midnight on weekends.

**Europa Café,** 411 Sturt St (☎5331 2486). A mix of Mediterranean fare and New York artistic mood. Chalkboard menu changes weekly—an informality of the youthful staff. Most meals around $10. The large window counter is a great place to try one of their 79 Aussie wines. Open Su-W 8:45am-6pm, Th-Sa 8:45am-late. Fully licensed or BYO.

For evening entertainment on weekends, the **Bridge Mall** at the east end of Sturt St fills with pedestrians and street musicians. Numerous hotels and pubs serve as venues for live bands. Locals report the present night scene hops at **Irish Murphy's** (see above) for drink, **Battle and Hum** for live music, and **21 Arms** and **The Chapel** for dance. The historic **Her Majesty's Theatre,** 13 Lydiard St (☎5333 5888), presents live drama nightly. **Blood on the Southern Cross,** a twice-nightly dazzling 80min. sound and light show at Sovereign Hill, is worth the price. It introduces miners' lives on Sovereign Hill and recounts the bitter Eureka Rebellion. Deep-voiced recorded narrator and delightfully melodramatic music add to the mood. (☎5333 5777. M-Sa, plus Su during holiday periods. $27, concessions $21. Bookings essential.)

VICTORIA

**OUR PROUDEST DEFEAT.** The story's told ad nauseum in Ballarat, but to be in the know, you should have the basics down. The colonial government in Melbourne set up a system of gold licenses to milk the hard-working miners of their daily spoils. The miners had to pay the license fee regardless of whether they found gold, and the governor ordered regular license hunts to check up on his charges. The police, though, were not the enlightened, civilized patrolmen of our day, but ex-convicts who were drafted to "keep order" in the bustling gold towns. When a digger was found without a license, he was ordered to pay a fine of 10£ or was chained to a log until he could pay (to keep the arrested man's hands in the cuffs, they often smashed them with a mallet so they would bruise and swell). Needless to say, the miners were less than pleased. When James Scobie, a Scottish miner, was murdered outside the hotel of a government supervisor, the already tense situation began to boil over. The miners formed a reform league to abolish the licenses and soon set up a stockade on the Eureka Lead. They burned their licenses, swore allegiance to the Southern Cross flag, and defended themselves valiantly—albeit briefly—when government forces attacked the next day. Thirty miners were killed and 114 taken prisoner, but the brutal invasion outraged the rest of Australia, and reforms were soon passed abolishing the licenses and giving miners the right to vote. All those charged with High Treason were acquitted. The miners' leader, Peter Lalor, later became Australian Speaker of the House. Sometimes a little revolution now and then is a good thing.

## SIGHTS

Portions of Ballarat retain their gold rush charm and are excellent for evening walks (particularly the Victorian streetscape of **Lydiard St**). Several companies offer tours of Ballarat's historic areas. **Timeless Tours** offers 2hr. architectural tours for groups of four or more; smaller groups should call F-Su to find a tour on which to tag along. (☎5342 0652. $20.) The **Ballarat Begonia Festival,** in early March, is an open-air arts and crafts fair. The **Royal South Street** music, debate, and performance competitions (August to November) attract top talent.

**▧SOVEREIGN HILL.** People have long come to Ballarat with gold on their minds. While a reconstructed gold town built around a mine won't make you rich, Sovereign Hill, Ballarat's biggest tourist draw, is a living museum that will at least give you a feel for what life was like here back in the day. Actors playing miners and townfolk mill about in period garb, and you can salivate as a $50,000 gold ingot is poured before your eyes (and ruminate as the process of extracting pure gold from crushed ore is explained). Exhibits include candle-making, smelting, musket-firing, and a 40min. tour of the mine that reveals the harsh conditions of mining life. Pan for gold yourself or ride the horse-drawn carriage past shops masquerading as old frontier stores. *(Take bus #9 or 10. Signs throughout Ballarat point the way.* ☎5331 1944. *Open daily 10am-5pm. Combined admission to Sovereign Hill and the Gold Museum $22, concessions $16, families $59.)*

**GOLD MUSEUM.** Kitschy, futuristic displays trace the function and importance of gold from the pharaoh's slave pits to today's microcircuitry. Only worth a visit since it's included in the Sovereign Hill ticket (and is just across the street). The museum devotes permanent space to Aboriginal and Chinese influences, Aussie sports, and replicas of the two largest gold nuggets ever found. Cool, small collection of World War I postcards. *(Adjacent to Sovereign Hill, on Bradshaw St.* ☎5331 1944. *Open daily 9:30am-5:20pm. Admission to Gold museum alone $6.50, concessions $3.50.)*

**EUREKA STOCKADE.** Not long ago, the stockade's flimsy remains were meagerly propped up on Eureka St. Now, a sleek $4 million multimedia adventure commemorates the miners' resistance in the Eureka Rebellion. If you've already seen **Blood on the Southern Cross** (see p. 571), the stockade is a little redundant, but the building itself, with its symbolic architecture and giant Southern Cross flag in the shape of a sail, might be worth a look. *(Eureka St at Rodier St. Take bus #8.* ☎5333 1854. *Open daily 9am-5pm. $8, concessions $6, children $4.)*

**BALLARAT FINE ART GALLERY.** The Eureka rebels fought under the Southern Cross flag, the remains of which are kept here. For many years, foreign dignitaries who visited Ballarat were presented with pieces of the flag, leaving this symbol of Australian patriotism tattered. The gallery also houses a comprehensive collection of regional and national artwork, notably a large Lindsay family collection. Keep your eyes peeled for the one Picasso lithograph; it's inconspicuously mixed in with the rest of the lesser-known works. A $5 million expansion will be completed in June 2001; the museum remains open in the interim. *(Lydiard north of Sturt St.* ☎*5331 5622. Open daily 10:30am-5pm. $4, students $2. Tours available. Wheelchair accessible.)*

**BALLARAT WILDLIFE PARK.** The park's 14 acres of open bush are home to some of Australia's diverse fauna, including fearsome saltwater crocodiles and Tasmanian devils, and less imposing emus, goannas, wombats, koalas, and free-roaming 'roos. Take bus #8 or 9 or drive down York St off Main Rd midway between Sovereign Hill and Eureka St. *(York at Fussel St.* ☎*5333 5933. Tours at 11am. Open daily 9am-5:30pm. $12, students $10, children $6.)*

**BALLARAT EXHIBITION AND ENTERTAINMENT CENTER.** With 25% of world wool production, Australia has the world's largest sheep industry, and this gigantic shed is its shrine. See rams on parade, speedy shearers unceremoniously stripping lambs, and an eerie Waltzing Matilda 3D holographic historical diorama. *(5km east of Ballarat toward Melbourne on the Western Hwy.* ☎*5334 7877. Taxis cost about $12. Open Sept.-Apr. daily 9:30am-5pm. $9, students $7.)*

## 🎒 DAYTRIPS FROM BALLARAT: WINERIES

Most vineyards in the Ballarat wine region began production in the 1980s. With cool climate Chardonnays increasingly popular, this region is regarded as an up-and-coming area. Pick up the *Wine Regions of Victoria* pamphlet in local tourist offices. At **Dulcinea Vineyard,** owner Rod Stott says: "I believe in education." He is on site to answer questions and urge visitors to roam through his small cellar and vineyard, tasting his delectable blends on the way. Take the Glenelg Hwy 15min. south from Ballarat toward Creswick. (☎5334 6440. Open daily 9am-5pm. Bottles $12-18.) **St. Anne's Vineyards** is 22km from Ballarat and 77km from Melbourne off the Western Hwy. Free tastings are available in a cool, cobwebbed blue stone cottage. A peppery red Shiraz and a fortified tawny port top the list. (☎5368 7209. Open M-Sa 9am-5pm, Su 10am-5pm.)

## DAYLESFORD AND HEPBURN SPRINGS

There's just something to be said about a place where there's a scale to weigh yourself in front of town hall. Most visitors come to Hepburn Springs seeking the curative properties of its waters; this region contains the largest concentration of mineral springs in Australia. Aboriginals revered the springs long before European settlement, but the scores of guest cottages and B&Bs have sprung up only recently. New Age commercialism has infused these quiet communities with healing crystals, essences, oils, and aromatherapy. The **Hepburn Spa Resort,** next to the springs, provides the works. Services range from the normal pool and spa (weekdays $9, weekends $11) to floatation tanks ($35-38), the civilian version of the torturous sensory-deprivation tank. Spring waters are free. (☎5348 2034. Open M-F 10am-8pm, Sa 9am-10pm, Su 9am-8pm. Partial wheelchair access.) If you plan to do any walking in the surrounding **Hepburn Regional Park** take care to avoid plunging into abandoned mine shafts (maps at info center).

Daylesford is 107km northwest of Melbourne and 45km northeast of Ballarat. V/Line **buses** depart for **Melbourne** (1¾hr.; 3 per day M-F, 2 per day Sa, 1 per day Su; $13) and **Ballarat** (1hr., 3 per day M-F, $9) from Little's Garage, 45 Vincent St, in the heart of Daylesford. While most of the restaurants and services are in Daylesford, the spa complex is in Hepburn Springs, 4km north. Buses run between the two towns ($1.50), but it is a pleasant 40min. walk. A taxi costs about $7. Daylesford's volunteer-run **Tourist Information Centre,** located several blocks south of the

Garage, has a list of accommodations and info on masseurs, healers, and other indulgences. (☎5348 1339. Open daily 9am-5pm.) Daylesford's one main street is home to many **ATMs** and the **post office** (open M-F 9am-5pm). **Postal code:** 3460.

Most of the area's lovely guest cottages and B&Bs will set you back $80-100 per night. **Continental House,** 9 Lone Pine Ave (☎5348 2005), described by some of its patrons as a living work of art (others as a hippie hideout), is secluded behind an impressively dense 5m tall hedge just a few hundred meters from the spa. Refresh yourself at this strictly vegetarian, strictly relaxed guest house with tranquil common areas and basic bunkrooms. Next door, the more mainstream **Golden Springs Lodge** offers the use of a modern kitchen, laundry, common areas, TV, and volleyball net. (☎/fax 5348 4199. $50 per person per night; breakfast included.)

# CASTLEMAINE

Castlemaine, 120km northwest of Melbourne in the central Goldfields, peaked early as a boom town in the heady gold rush days. Since then, with a fairly static population of 7500 for the last 140 years, it has faded into a sleepy, provincial town. While it can't offer the bustle of Bendigo or Ballarat, it does have some good—if mellow—drawing points: fantastic polychromatic gardens blossoming in spring, a quiet historical charm, and a fine array of art displays and boutiques.

▐ **TRANSPORT.** Originating from the **railway station** (open M-F 6am-8pm, Sa 7am-3pm, Su 9:30am-7:30pm), at the north end of Kennedy St, V/Line (☎13 61 96) has **bus** and **train** service to: **Melbourne** (1½hr., 12 per day, $16); **Ballarat** (1½hr., 1 per day, $14); **Bendigo** (25min., 14 per day, $5); **Maldon** (20min., 2 per day, $2); and **Maryborough** (1hr., 3 per day, $7). To get to Castlemaine by **car,** take Hwy 79 (Calder Hwy) to Elphinstone, then Hwy 122 (Pyrenees Hwy).

▐ **PRACTICAL INFORMATION.** In the heart of town, Kennedy, Barker, Hargraves, and Urquhart St run north-south, and Templeton, Lyttleton, Mostyn, and Forest St run east-west. **Barker St** is the main drag, and its intersection with **Mostyn St** forms the corner of Victory Park. The **visitor information center** has moved into the **Castlemaine Market Building** on Mostyn St between Barker and Hargraves, and has a pretty standard display about the town's gold mining past. (Open daily 9am-5pm). Free **Internet access** is available at the **library.** (☎5472 1458. Open M-Tu, Th 10am-6pm; W and F 10am-8pm; Sa 9am-noon. Book ahead.) **Post office:** 202 Barker St (open M-F 9am-5pm). **Postal Code:** 3450.

▐▐ **ACCOMMODATIONS AND FOOD.** It's not as tough as it used to be to grab a cheap bed in Castlemaine, but you'll probably fare better in nearby Bendigo. Like most of the Goldfield towns, the bulk of accommodations are $80-100 B&Bs. If you've got money to spare, and you don't mind human agony being converted into novelty accommodation, incarcerate yourself in the **Old Castlemaine Gaol,** on Bowden St, overlooking the town atop the hill to the west of the railroad station. The 1861 jail held inmates until 1990, when it was renovated as a well-heated and ventilated B&B. The Gaol primarily hosts conventions and groups over 20, and won't take individual guests unless another large group is staying and there's room. The iron catwalks and small cells have been preserved. The dungeons, once the site of horrific torture, now house a wine bar and lounge. If you're not staying here, it's worth taking a self-guided tour anyway. (☎5470 5311; fax 5470 5097; gaol@castlemaine.net.au. Tours $4, not allowed when school groups are staying; call ahead. Doubles $75 per person. Continental breakfast included; dinner $20 extra.) The urban **Carracourt Caravan Park,** 103 Barker St, has squash courts, BBQ, and a swimming pool. (☎/fax 5472 2160. Tent sites for 2 $9, powered $16; single ensuite cabins with kitchenette $40, each extra person $11.) Quieter **Botanic Gardens Caravan Park** provides laundry facilities, a 50m pool, and BBQ. (☎/fax 5472 1125. Tent sites for 2 $11, powered $13; on-site caravans for 2 $33; ensuite cabins without linen $50, each extra person $5.50.)

**INCONSEQUENTIAL FAME** Maryborough VIC is a zippy, modern town that contrasts pleasantly with its sleepy central goldfields neighbors. But there's nothing touristy to do here whatsoever. The town remains in guidebooks, and will be preserved in history, because of a line randomly spoken by a famous American. Mark Twain remarked that Maryborough was a railway station with a town attached. ⊠ Let's Go recommends making something of your life such that someone else's comment isn't your only glory.

Chippers, cafés, and markets run the length of Barker and Mostyn St. **Capone's Pizzeria,** 50 Hargraves St, relives the memory of the bloodthirsty American crime lord through fancifully named Italian cuisine, such as the "No Legs' Lasagna." (☎ 5470 5705. Open daily from 5pm. Meals under $9.) **Screaming Carrot Café,** 16 Lyttleton St (☎ 5470 6555), dishes out alterna-food such as tempeh burgers— "aaaaaaah!" (says the carrot). There's a Rainbow **supermarket** on Hargraves and Mostyn St. (Open M-F 7am-10pm, Sa 7am-9pm, Su 9am-8pm.)

⬛ **SIGHTS.** The **Botanic Gardens,** seven blocks north of the railway station at the end of Kennedy St, are a fine assemblage of flora, with cypress trees, rose bushes, and a central pond. The **Castlemaine Art Gallery and Historic Museum,** 12 Lyttleton St, between Kennedy and Barker St, is a spirited attempt at a strong small-town gallery. (☎ 5472 2292. Open M-F 10am-5pm, Sa-Su noon-5pm. $3, concessions $2.) Several blocks north of the city center, the **Buda Historic House and Garden**, on the corner of Hunter and Urquhart St, displays the intricate craftwork of Ernest Leviny and his daughters in their perfectly preserved late-nineteenth century home. Call ahead to set up a tour; guides have an encyclopedic knowledge of silver, glass, and embroidery patterns. The garden is 3.5 acres of delicate landscaping that includes Australia's largest cypress hedge. (☎ 5472 1062. Open daily 9am-5pm. $8, concessions $5.50.) Combining the elements of a junk yard and a flea market, the **Restorer's Barn,** 129 Mosten St, offers 10,000 sq. ft. of knick-knacks for sale from the mundane to the fascinating. (☎ 5470 5669. Open daily 9am-5:30pm.) Down the road, **Morrell's Studio Glass,** on Mostyn at Urquhart St, hosts an exquisite set of hand-blown glassware. Visitors can watch the blowing take place whenever the artist is at work. (☎ 5470 9800. Open M-Sa 10am-5pm, Su 11am-4pm.)

In November of even years, the **Garden Festival** celebrates the blossoming of the city, and alternates with the Castlemaine **Arts Festival,** held at the end of March in odd years. Both festivals attract visitors from all over Victoria.

# MALDON

A veritable ghost town by weekday, Maldon (pop. 1200) attracts weekend Victorian tourists clutching cameras and mineral water. Still, if history is your thing (and if it isn't, then get the hell out of the Goldfields!), Maldon, 17km northwest of Castlemaine, is a small but necessary stop on the itinerary. After all, it has been declared "Australia's First Notable Town," for whatever that's worth. Main Street's 19th-century buildings with corrugated iron roofs and hand-painted wooden signs present the best preserved array of gold rush era buildings in the state.

▐▊ **TRANSPORT AND PRACTICAL INFORMATION.** Close to town, the highway splits into High St (left) and Main St (right). To get to Maldon, take the V/Line (☎ 13 61 96) from **Castlemaine** (2 per day M-F, $2.50). The ever-friendly **Visitors Information Centre,** on the corner of High St in the cream brick building, offers innumerable brochures and has a list of all available rooms. (☎ 5475 2569; maldon@netcon.net.au. Open daily 9am-5pm.) Although Maldon **lacks ATMs,** the **Bendigo Bank,** attached to the visitors center, will **exchange currency.** (Open M-F 9am-5pm, Sa 9am-noon. 1% commission.) **Post office:** Francis St, opposite the info center. (Open M-F 9am-5pm, Sa 8:30-11am.) **Postal Code:** 3463.

**ACCOMMODATIONS AND FOOD.** Maldon's B&Bs can be pricey ($75-90) but may be worth a splurge for visitors enamored with the period feel and small town atmosphere. The **Maldon Caravan and Camping Park,** on Hospital St, northwest along High St, has toilets and BBQs. (☎/fax 5475 2344. Tent sites $6.60 per person; on-site caravans for 2 $33; cabins for 2 $50.) Behind Main St, the **Derby Hill Accommodation Centre** (☎5475 2033), on Phoenix St, provides weekend lodging in a funky and functional wood and concrete youth camp. Units include bathroom, TV, and kitchenette. (Singles $30; F-Su only. Bookings preferred.) Virtually all restaurants and stores are on a short strip of Main St between Phoenix and High St. **Historic Bakery** on Main St is all the rage but lacks space (meat and other flavored pies $2). A **Friendly Grocer** is on High St. (Open M-F until 6pm, Sa until 4pm, Su until 3pm.)

**SIGHTS.** Amateur historians may enjoy the **Maldon Museum and Archives,** which displays local artifacts from the 1850s to the early 20th century. (☎5475 1633. Adjacent to the visitor's center. Open M-F 1:30-4pm, Sa-Su 1:30-5pm. $2, children 50¢.) For a bird's-eye view of Maldon—and, on a clear day, more than 50km in all directions—follow High St north to the signs for **Mt. Tarrangower,** which rises 571m above sea level from the geographic center of Victoria. The windblown iron **poppet lookout tower** enables daring souls to ascend an additional 24m. October brings a **vintage car race** and a **folk festival** to town. Like every other Goldfields city, there's a mine to visit: go south of Maldon, toward Newstead off the Pyrenees Hwy, to **Carman's Tunnel Goldmine.** (☎5475 2667. Open Sa-Su 1:30-4pm. $4.) The vintage **Victorian Goldfields Railway steam train,** off Hornsby St north along Main St, runs the 8km trip to Muckleford and gives riders a chance to see how an old train works. (☎5475 1427. 2 trips W, 3 Su; $10 return, students $8, ages 4-16 $6, families $29.) The **Newstead Winery** is 15km south of town. (☎5476 2733. Open weekends and holidays 10am-5pm.)

# BENDIGO

Like almost all the towns in the Victorian goldfields, Bendigo (pop. 85,000) sprung into existence in the 1850s when scores of miners flooded in, lured by the promise of some of Australia's most lucrative mines. But while many of its neighbors were tossed from prosperity to obscurity by the boom and bust cycle, Bendigo endured due to the longevity of its gold output (25 million ounces of gold were removed from the area between 1851 and 1954) as well as its status as town of choice for many gold magnates. These same magnates used their early fortunes to indulge their Victorian fancies, creating public buildings in grandiose Gothic style and forging wide thoroughfares with names like Pall Mall and Charing Cross. These vestiges of its wealthy past imbue Bendigo with a certain Anglophilic nostalgia, but its continuing status as a major regional social and economic center lends the city a vitality that many of its gold rush relic neighbors lack. Neither too touristy nor too bland, Bendigo is a fun and laid-back place to visit, offering something for everyone with its authentic historical charm in an indisputably modern setting.

## TRANSPORT

**Trains and Buses:** V/Line (☎13 61 96) runs out of the **Transit Centre** in the Market Place Discovery Centre at the south end of Mitchell St. **Train** and/or **bus** service to: **Melbourne** (2hr., 11 per day, $21); **Adelaide** (8½hr., 1 per day, $51); **Ballarat** (2hr., 1 per day, $18); **Castlemaine** (22min., 11 per day, $5); **Daylesford** (1¼hr., 1 per day, $9); **Geelong** (3¾hr., 1 per day, $30); **Maldon** (via Castlemaine train; 1.5hr., 2 per day, $36); **Maryborough** (1hr., 3 per day, $12); **Mildura** (5hr., 2 per day); and **Swan Hill** (3½hr., 2-3 per day, $24). More infrequent service on weekends.

**Public Transportation:** Local **buses** leave from the corner of Hargreaves and Mitchell St.

**Car Rental: Hertz** (☎5443 5088). At the corner of High and Thistle St. From $42 for 300km per day. **Thrifty,** 29 Myers St (☎5441 6448). $55 per day for 300 km per day.

## 🔢 PRACTICAL INFORMATION

Bendigo is a combination of well-planned streets and winding gold gullies originally packed down by diggers' feet. Most points of interest are near the city center, bounded on the south and east by the railroad tracks and on the north by Rosalind Park. The **Calder Hwy** from Melbourne runs into the center of town and then veers northwest to Mildura. At **Charing Cross, High St** (the stretch of Calder Hwy in town) becomes **Pall Mall,** which eventually turns into **McCrae St** and then into **Midland Hwy,** which leads to Elmore and Echuca. The popular pedestrian **Hargreaves Mall** extends one block along Hargreaves between Mitchell and Williamson St.

**Tourist Office:** 51-67 Pall Mall (☎5444 4445; fax 5444 4447; www.bendigotour ism.com). Located in the ornate Victorian gothic post office building (no longer a post office). Mini-museum setup with slick, rather cheesy interactive computer displays that tell Bendigo's story. Tons of food and accommodations info. Open daily 9am-5pm.

**Currency Exchange: National Bank,** corner of Queen and Mitchell St (☎5443 9399). Open M-Th 9:30am-4pm, F 9:30am-5pm. $5 exchange commission. 24hr. **ATM.**

**Public Library:** 259 Hargreaves St (☎5443 5100; fax 5441 2247). Books, magazines, and free **Internet access;** book ahead if you can. Open M-F 10am-7pm, Sa 10am-5pm.

**Laundromat: View Street Laundry,** 41 View St (☎5441 8877), next to Rosalind Park. Open daily 6am-9pm. Wash $3, dry 10min. $1.

**Police:** ☎5440 2510.

**Medical Assistance:** ☎5441 0440 (for hospital) or ☎000 (for general emergency).

**Internet Access:** In the public library, see above. **AnyKey Internet & Co,** 39 Mitchell St (☎5443 2049; fax 5443 2127). Open M-F 10am-6pm, Sa 10am-2pm. $6 per hour, students $4.50. Printing, scanning, and faxing services also available.

**Post Office:** Corner of Hargreaves and Williamson St (☎5443 0755). Open M-F 9am-5pm, Sa 9:30am-12:30pm. Post Restante available. **Postal Code:** 3550.

**Phone Code:** 03.

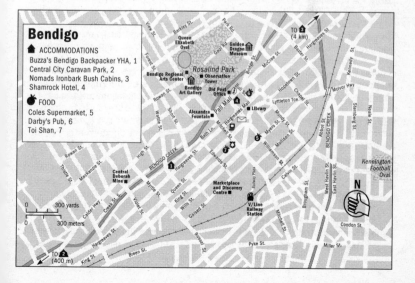

**Bendigo**

🏠 ACCOMMODATIONS
Buzza's Bendigo Backpacker YHA, 1
Central City Caravan Park, 2
Nomads Ironbark Bush Cabins, 3
Shamrock Hotel, 4

🍴 FOOD
Coles Supermarket, 5
Darby's Pub, 6
Toi Shan, 7

# ■ ACCOMMODATIONS

The strip of High St (Calder Hwy, or Hwy 79) running south of town is loaded with cookie-cutter chain motels. You can find some nicer motels and B&Bs along McCrae and Napier just northeast of the city center. Rooms run $50-90. Most fancy hotels downtown will disembowel your wallet, but a few provide a good deal with a gold rush feel. Across from the tourist office, the **Shamrock Hotel** (☎ 5443 0333; fax 5442 4494) offers doubles with shared bathroom ($65; see **Sights,** below).

■ **Nomads Ironbark Bush Cabins,** Watson St (☎ 5448 3344; fax 5448 3787; email ibt.horse@bigpond.com). A refreshing and pleasant taste of the bush. Located 5km from the city center, the Ironbark is out of walking distance, but the owners will pick you up from as far away as Melbourne and Echuca and will shuttle you from the cabins to the city at your request. The six small, tidy cabins each sleep five and have ensuite bathrooms, refrigerators, coffee machines, towels, and linen at no extra charge. Free bush breakfast from the barbie; BBQ (dinner $12) and bar (beer $2.50) in evenings around the campfire. On-site horseback riding center $20 per hr. Special weekend package deals include horseback riding and meals. Bunks $18; doubles $40.

**Buzza's Bendigo Backpacker YHA,** 33 Creek St S (☎/fax 5443 7680; buzza@bendigo.net.au). A nice homey feel, with 24 beds in a small, converted house in a quiet residential area close to the center of town. Three individual shower/bathrooms offer some welcomed privacy. Free coffee and tea, use of kitchen and BBQ, and cozy living room with TV. Laundry $2. Internet 30min. $2. Bike hire $3 per day. Dorms $15; singles $17; doubles $38.

**Central City Caravan Park,** 362 High St at Birch (☎/fax 5443 6937). About 2.5km south of the Alexandra Fountain. Take bus #1 from Hargreaves Mall. The CCCP, a former YHA affiliate, is the cheapest place in town, offering minimalist hostel accommodation, comrade. Bunks or shaded tent sites $12.

# ■ FOOD

Most of the popular restaurants are near the tourist office, especially on Bull St and Pall Mall. **Darby's Pub** at the corner of Bull and Hargreaves St offers selections from all corners of the world—from Ireland to Asia, Spain to Greece, and then some. (☎ 5443 4916. M-Sa noon-2:30pm and 5:30-9:30pm.) You can grab a pitcher of homemade brew at **Rifle Brigade,** at the corner of View and Rowen St (☎ 5443 4092), to wash down standard grille fare ($8-9) or more extensive dishes ($14-17). Cheaper restaurants are all around town but for centralized budget dining, **Hargreaves Mall,** the pedestrian mall along Hargreaves between Williamson and Mitchell St, is the place to be during lunch hours or for a snack. Bendigo's own **Gillie's Famous Pies** (☎ 5443 4965), at the corner of Hargreaves Mall and Williamson St, makes a mean steak-and-kidney pie, but their mini dim sims are even meaner. The **Loaded Dog** doesn't refer to a pooch that's had too many Victoria Bitters; it's an excellent hot dog joint with a vast selection of gourmet sausages and toppings. (Open M-F 9am-5:30pm, Sa 9am-2pm.) The strong Asian presence in Bendigo, with a history that dates to the gold rush migrant labor days, is heralded by numerous Chinese restaurants with heavily Australianized products. **Toi Shan,** 65-67 Mitchell St (☎ 5443 5811), offers a good deal with an all-you-can-eat "smorgasbord" (Tu-F noon-2:30pm, $8.50, F night $9.50) and self-serve take-away packs ($3.20-6). Just try not to wonder why a Chinese restaurant has a Swedish smorgasbord. Coles **supermarket,** at the corner of Myers and Williamson St, is open 24hr.

# 👁 SIGHTS

**CENTRAL DEBORAH MINE.** See the real deal at the last mine to stop operating commercially in Bendigo. On the surface, much of the original processing equipment has been preserved and displayed, including a gigantic, evil-looking stamper battery. Tours take visitors 61m down where mining history and techniques are explained and often demonstrated. It's worth the trip, if only for the lessons in geology and the descriptions of the harsh life of the miners. Real thrill-seekers can try the Underground Adventure Tour, in which participants don miner's garb and go down extra levels to use real mine equipment for two hours. Miner's lunch or tea included. Book in advance. Discounts available for groups bigger than six. *(76 Violet St. ☎ 5443 8322. The Central Deb tourist empire is open daily 9am-5pm. Regular Tour: six daily, every 70min. $15.50, concessions $13; combined mine and tram tickets $21, $19. Underground Adventure: lunch tour $45, $40; morning/afternoon tea tour $38, $33.)*

**HISTORIC SIGHTS.** Tours, complete with recorded commentary, cover the town using the restored 19th-century tram system (1hr., $8, concessions $7). Trams run hourly, picking up from the Alexandra Fountain (see below) near the tourist office or from the Central Deborah Mine. The late-Victorian feel of Bendigo's architecture is most pronounced along **Pall Mall** (pronounced "Pell Mell"), which is littered with more neo-Gothic touches than you can shake a spire at. The most impressive buildings are the **old post office building** (which now houses the visitors center) and the **Shamrock Hotel** at the corner of Williamson St and Pall Mall. The hotel, built for prospectors in 1897, has recently been redone in period style down to the last stone archway. Be nice and quiet and they'll let you sneak into the lobby decked out in stained glass, hoary portraits, and mahogany banisters. The **Alexandra Fountain** at Charing Cross, where High St turns into Pall Mall, is an ornate stone piece over 25ft. high, adorned with fanciful horses and small lions' heads that delicately stream water over the outstretched arms of topless maidens. It's most impressive at night when illuminated by floodlights.

**ROSALIND PARK.** The Park, on the northwest corner of Alexandra Fountain, is a vast expanse of greenery scattered with winding pathways, trees, and statues—including a particularly unflattering likeness of Queen Victoria. One could easily spend an hour getting lost here and in the contemplative fernery in the southeast corner, but don't miss the incline on the park's west end, where a steep path leads to an observation tower. Fashioned after a poppet, a device used to extract miners from caves, the tower resembles a gargantuan three-dimensional trapezoid made out of white and maroon steel girders. If you brave the 124-step climb to the top, the prize is sweeping views of Bendigo and the surrounding gold country.

**GOLDEN DRAGON MUSEUM.** This collection provides a decent overview of both Chinese culture in general and its influence on Bendigo. Displays offer a look at the Chinese-Australian experience in the place they dubbed "Dai Gum San" (Big Gold Mountain), but do gloss a bit over the racism that Chinese-Australians often faced. The collection's highlight is the fantastically ornate Sun Loong, the **longest imperial dragon in the world**, a ceremonial piece that's in full effect during the big parade of the annual **Bendigo Easter Fair**. Adjacent to the museum are the tranquil **Classical Chinese Gardens** and **Kuan Yin Temple**. *(59 Bridge St. ☎ 5441 5044. All open daily 9:30am-5pm. $7, concessions $5, children $4. Garden alone $2.60, children 60¢.)*

**BENDIGO ART GALLERY.** Bendigo is an artistic haven; get the free *Studios and Galleries* from the tourist center. The city's major museum houses an extensive national collection, a host of European works, and various rotating exhibits. You probably won't recognize the names of most of the artists, except from Feb. 3-Mar. 18, 2001, when a Matisse exhibit comes to town. *(42 View St. ☎ 5443 4991. Open daily*

*10am-5pm. Free admission. Free tours daily 2pm.)* If that's not enough culture for you, the **Bendigo Regional Arts Center,** just up the road, houses a full schedule of plays. *(50 View St. ☎ 5441 5344. Box office open M-F 10am-6pm. Shows generally $20+.)*

**DISCOVERY CENTRE.** Kids and kids-at-heart would hate to miss this hands-on exhibit hall that makes science fun, succeeding where high school failed. With Australia's only **vertical slide** (7m high), Discovery is a hidden gem in plain sight. *(7 Railway Place, in front of the V/Line station. ☎ 5444 4400. Open daily 10am-5pm. $8.25, concessions $7.15, children $5. Wheelchair accessible.)*

## 🎵 🏛 ENTERTAINMENT AND NIGHTLIFE

Pubs are everywhere. Most are tame local hangouts that close around midnight. The main late-night entertainment options are on the few blocks of Pall Mall and Hargreaves from Williamson to Mundy St. Friday and Saturday are the big nights to go out. The **Old Crown,** 238 Hargreaves St, is a neighborhood haunt filled with families by day and burly locals at night. On weekends, it's open later than most pubs. (Closes 2-3am. F: live music, occasional cover $3; Sa: karaoke.) **Darby's,** corner of Bull and Hargreaves St, offers a selection of Irish beers on tap ($3) and live music Th-Sa starting at 10pm. (No cover. Open until 1-2am.) Another live music option is the **Sundance Saloon** on Pall Mall and Mundy St, which hosts top Melbourne cover bands on Thursdays. (☎ 5441 8222. Open Th-Sa 8:30pm-late.) For the dancing crowd, the glitz-o-rama **Eclipse** pulsates with two DJs—R&B and dance on the second floor, hits from the last three decades on the third. It's open to all ages before 11pm; if you're over 20, enjoy it when the teenage hordes depart. (☎ 5441 4399. Cover $2-5. Open until 5am.) The **Albert Hotel,** Pall Mall and Mundy St, attracts an 18-25 crowd with a DJ and band downstairs, a "chill room" upstairs, and a beer garden out back. (Open Th-Sa until 3am. F no cover, Th $2, Sa $4.)

# MURRAY RIVER

Australia's longest river, the Murray, rambles along the New South Wales-Victoria border for 2600km before meeting the sea in South Australia's Encounter Bay. The river became an essential transportation artery in the late 19th century, its waters plied by giant freight-toting paddlesteamers. But extensive rail and road networks rendered these boats obsolete by the end of the 1930s, and they have since been reincarnated as tourist attractions. Today the river feeds a productive agriculture of vegetables and fruits (including wine grapes) through a complex irrigation system. It's also a favorite spot for picnicking, water sports, and fishing, drawing travelers for a day or a week of relaxation along the banks of the grand old Murray.

## ECHUCA

As the closest point to Melbourne along the Murray, Echuca was once Australia's largest inland port, a clearinghouse for the wool and agricultural products of southern New South Wales. A massive redgum wharf was built to accommodate the paddlesteamers and barges, and a lively array of hotels, brothels, and breweries was built to accommodate the men who sailed them. Although river traffic declined in the late 1800s, many boats have been preserved, and Echuca now possesses the world's largest flotilla of side-wheel paddlesteamers—its major industry is now nostalgia. Old-time facades dominate its main streets, and a late-19th century feel pervades the town. Despite its exterior, Echuca has the bustle of an entirely modern city, and its tourist industry—though not exactly exciting—avoids the theme-park hokiness of other historic river towns, making this the best place to immerse yourself in the Murray riverboat culture.

## ⌐ TRANSPORT

V/Line **buses** run from the Visitors Centre or the Ampole Road House on the Northern Hwy. To: **Melbourne** (3½ hr., 4-6 per day, $27); **Bendigo** (1¼hr., 1-3 per day, $7); **Kerang** (1¼-2h.r., 1-2 per day, $8); **Mildura** (5hr.; 1 per day M, W, Th, Sa; $35); **Swan Hill** (2hr., 1-2 per day, $16); and **Albury** (3-4hr., 1-2 per day, $22-35). A **steam locomotive** (not V/Line) from Melbourne is scheduled to be running by the end of 2000.

## ⚡ ❓ ORIENTATION AND PRACTICAL INFORMATION

Echuca lies about 200km north of Melbourne at the intersection of two highways, the **Murray Valley Hwy** and **Northern Hwy,** and two rivers, the **Campaspe** (north-south) and the **Murray** (east-west). Echuca's main drags are **Hare** and **High St,** parallel roads that run from the Murray River to the Murray Valley Hwy. Follow the **Cobb Hwy** past the Visitors Centre across the Murray to Echuca's twin city of **Moama** in New South Wales, notable predominantly for its vast array of pokies clubs.

The **Visitor Information Centre,** 2 Heygarth St, is on the Echuca side of the Echuca-Moama bridge. (☎5480 7555, freecall ☎(1800) 80 44 46; fax 5482 6413; www.echucamoama.com. Open daily 9am-5pm.) **ANZ, National,** and **Commonwealth banks** with **24hr. ATMs** are on Hare St (all open M-Th 9:30am-4pm, F 9:30am-5pm). The **library,** at the corner of Heygarth and High St across from McDonald's, offers **Internet access** (30min. $2; book ahead; open M-Tu, Th-F 10am-5:30pm, W noon-9pm, Sa 10am-1pm, Su 2-4pm). **Post office:** on the corner of Hare and Anstruther St (open M-F 9am-5pm). **Postal code:** 3564.

## ⌐ ACCOMMODATIONS

Echuca's accommodation scene consists mostly of luxury riverside B&Bs and pricey motels, but there are a few budget options.

▨ **Echuca Gardens Hostel (YHA),** 103 Mitchell St (☎5480 6522, mobile ☎(0419) 88 10 54; email echucagardens@origin.net.au). An easy 8 block walk east from the city center. Think you're well traveled? The engaging owners are more so. Dazzlingly ornate garden with fountains, fruit trees, murals, and a sauna and spa ($5 per use). Small kitchen, cozy lounge, open fireplace, and welcoming atmosphere. Reception daily 8-9:30am and 5-8pm. 4-bed dorms, twins, doubles $17.50; singles $25.

**NOMADS Oasis Backpackers,** 410-424 High St (☎5480 7866; fax 5480 7867; email nomads@river.net.au). In town and quite well-kept, but with loads less flavor than the YHA. Kitchen, TV lounge, Internet access (1hr. $5). Reception 24hr. Dorms $17; ensuite rooms for 2 $44, $8 per additional person.

**Echuca Caravan Park,** Crofton St (☎5482 2157; fax 5480 1551). Due to its idyllic location right on the Murray, this gigantic facility is choked with campervans, especially during holidays. Tent sites $18, powered $19; off-peak $16, $18; on-site caravans $44, $39.; 5-6 person ensuite cabins $68-83, $55-66.

## ◌▨ FOOD AND NIGHTLIFE

The standard Australian array of chip shops, grub-serving pubs, and fast-food joints line High St, and there are some more upmarket riverfront spots on the Murray Esplanade. Large, cheap meals can be had in the four licensed clubs across the river in Moama. The omnipresent, omni-cheap, budget-friendly **La Porchetta** pizza and pasta chain beckons at 192-202 Annesley St. (☎5480 1130. Open daily 11:30am-9:30pm.) **River Palace,** 614 High St, offers over 100 Szechuan and Malay dishes. (☎5482 3152. Takeaway daily noon-2:30pm; and dine-in from 5pm.) The eclectic **Tic Toc Café,** 129 Hare St, has cheap sandwiches, curries, and well-priced all-day breakfasts. Portions are a bit small, but well prepared. (☎5482 6344. Bacon and eggs $6.50. Open M-Th 9am-5pm, F 9am-11pm, Sa 9am-3pm.) For a splurge, visit **Giorgio's On the Port,** 527 High St, which is not actually on the port, but serves awesome Italian fare nevertheless. (☎5482 6117. Meals from $15.)

The numerous pubs on High and Hare St are peopled by friendly locals. The **Harvest Hotel,** 183 Hare St, offers a brief opportunity for cheap non-sobriety with $1 pots F 5:30-6:30pm. (☎5482 1266. Open M-F 11am-11pm, Sa 11am-4am. Sa: live music, $5 cover after 11pm.) A younger crowd chills at the **Atomic Pool Bar Café,** 207 Darling St, where eight pool tables take up most of the room. (☎5480 2227. Open Tu-F 5pm-2am, Sa-Su noon-2am.)

## 🔱 SIGHTS

If you're not into history, don't expect to be wowed by Echuca's sights. This is definitely a place you come to for a specific purpose, not as a detour off your trip.

**HISTORIC PORT.** The main attraction in Echuca is its historic port, which consists of the wharf and several historic buildings. The 1865 redgum wharf has three levels to accommodate the changing river conditions. Blacksmith and woodturning shops sell handmade wares, and a steam display explains the workings of that portentous invention that brought on the Industrial Revolution. Several old hotels are on display as well. The **Star Hotel** is equipped with every fraternity's dream: a secret underground tunnel that allowed drinkers to escape police raids after the place was de-licensed in 1897; the **Bridge Hotel,** Echuca's first, has a carefully preserved suite and gallery upstairs. *(Historic Port Area, along Murray Esplanade. ☎5482 4248; www.portofechuca.org.au. Open daily 9am-5pm. $10, concessions $8.50.)* The other end of the port is marked by the old **Customs House** where tariffs were exacted from passing watercraft when Echuca was the commercial hub of the Murray. Today, the Customs House building houses **Murray Esplanade Cellars,** which exacts a tariff of zero dollars for sampling its excellent wines and spirits. There's also a small display of historical artifacts that seem much more interesting after a few glasses of tawny port. *(2 Leslie St. ☎5482 6058. Open daily 9:30am-5pm. Free entry.)*

**PADDLESTEAMERS.** Several paddlesteamers still ply the waters off the old port, and are now open to the public for leisurely cruises. The Port Authority runs 1hr. cruises on **P.S. Pevensey** or **P.S. Alexander Arbuthnot.** *(Buy tickets at 52 Murray Esplanade. ☎5482 4248. 5 daily cruises: $15, concessions $12. Joint port and cruise: $20, $17.)* A private company runs the paddlesteamers **Pride of the Murray** and **Emmylou;** a cruise on the Emmylou is worth the slightly higher price. *(Buy tickets at 57 Murray Esplanade. ☎5482 5244. Pride of Murray: 6 daily cruises 1hr. $12.50, children $6. Emmylou: 5 daily cruises 1-1½hr. $15-18, children $7.50-9.)*

**WORLD IN WAX MUSEUM.** Although not particularly relevant to the history of the Murray, the wax museum in front of the port could be the most fun place in town. Figures include dignitaries both foreign and domestic, arranged by era and disposition (amusingly, Stalin, Hitler, and Castro share a case with Churchill). The "sect macabre" contains a set of miniature wax dioramas chronicling torture devices throughout the ages. Er, did we say fun? *(630 High St. ☎5482 3630. Open daily 9am-5:30pm. $9, concessions $8, children $4. $1 YHA discount.)*

**SHARP'S MAGIC MOVIE HOUSE AND PENNY ARCADE.** Adjacent to the port, this small building houses Australia's largest collection of working penny arcade machines, from strength tests to fortune readers. An array of antique cinematic equipment continuously screens old newsreels, comedy shorts, and historical documentaries. It's a bit pricey considering how quickly you run out of things to do. *(☎5482 2361. Open daily 9am-5pm. $11, children $7.)*

**NATIONAL HOLDEN MOTOR MUSEUM.** For car-lovers or those who want a fascinating perspective on an iconic slice of Australiana, the Holden Motor Museum is a must-see. It showcases "Australia's Own" automobile, the GM-affiliated Holden, with over 40 lovingly restored models. The amusing video retrospective spotlights not only the car, but also Australia's love for it through Holden ads. *(7-11 Warren St. ☎5480 2033. Open 9am-5pm. $6, concessions $4.50, children $4, families $14.)*

**OZMAZE.** After living in the past all day, you may want to get lost for awhile. This huge wooden maze is constructed in the form of Australia. If it starts getting dark, at least there's ample firewood to be found… *(On the Echuca side of the Moama bridge.* ☎5480 2220. *Maze: $6.60. Mini golf: $5.50. Open W-M 10am-4pm.)*

## ☑ DAYTRIP FROM ECHUCA: BARMAH PARK AND FOREST

Just 31km from Echuca, the **Barmah State Park and State Forest** is the largest redgum forest in Victoria. The 22,000 hectares are well-endowed with roads and walking tracks, but rain and high water levels render many impassable. The **Dharnya Centre,** on Sand Ridge Rd near the park entrance, 5km north of the township of Barmah, provides maps and info on road conditions, and presents an engaging display on white treatment of Aboriginals. (☎5869 3302. Open daily 10:30am-4pm.) **Camping** is free and abundant in the park, and fishing is excellent (fishing licenses required for ages 18+). When water levels are high enough, the wetlands can be explored by boat or canoe. **Kingfisher Wetland Cruises** offers 2hr. trips. (☎5480 1830. M, W, Th, Sa, Su 12:30pm. $18, children $12.) **Gondwana Canoe Hire,** on Moira Lakes Rd on the way to the park entrance from Barmah, oddly enough, hires canoes. (☎5869 3347. 1hr. $25, half-day $35, full-day $50, 2 days $75.) There is no public transport to the park; V/Line has inconveniently timed service that drops off once per day in **Barmah** town, 10km away. Kind-hearted locals headed toward the park have been known to lend the occasional ride, though *Let's Go* does not recommend hitchhiking. Ask at the youth hostel about ride-sharing.

## NEAR ECHUCA: KERANG

This place is for the birds. Literally. The tiny township of **Kerang,** between Echuca and Swan Hill, has a ratio of about 1000 birds to every human. The entire area comprises one of Australia's most important wetland reserves for avian life. A few kilometers north on the Murray Valley Hwy, **Middle Lake** is a rookery for huge flocks of ibis and has a viewing shelter. The **Gunbower Creek,** a few kilometers east of Kerang, is another popular area for bird-watching and swamp-rambling. For Kerang info, call **Golden Rivers Tourism,** in Barham (☎(1800) 62 18 82; www.goldenrivers.com), or stop in at the **Old Water Tower,** right on the Murray Valley Hwy on the edge of town. The tower houses a **visitor information center** and a small but cool museum. It's well worth the $1 admission to climb the four-story tower, which holds a trippy fluorescent rock display with black light and looks out over Kerang's wetlands and attendant flocks of fowl. To see the wetland in style, book a cruise on the **Wetlander,** off Koondrook-Cohuna Rd on Orr's Rd. (Also called Southern Rd. ☎5453 3000. Cruises run Aug. 15-May 15; Tu 2pm 2hr. cruise $18.50, concessions $16.50; Sa 6:30pm 3½hr. meal cruise, in summer 7pm, $38.50, children $15-25.) In Kerang, across from the visitors center and set back from the road, the **Kerang Caravan Park** lies along the Loddon River, on Riverwood Dr. (☎/fax 5452 1161. Sites for 2 $11; on-site caravans $33; cabins $39-46.)

# SWAN HILL

Swan Hill, located on the Murray River about 340km northwest of Melbourne, is a tranquil rural town, ideal for families, caravaners, and anybody else who values peace over pace. Swan Hill's style of activities matches its tenor of life; the area is thick with nurseries, craft shops, tea rooms, wineries, and other serene pastimes. This part of the Murray has great fishing, and its relaxing cruises on rented houseboats are especially popular among seniors.

**◪ TRANSPORT.** V/Line **trains** leave daily for **Melbourne** (4½hr., $43) from the station on Curlewis St, between McCrae and Rutherford St, near the Giant Murray Cod. **Bus** service is available to: **Adelaide** (6½hr., 1 per day, $41); **Sydney** (14hr., 1 per day, $85-110); **Albury** (6hr., 1 per day, $32-40); **Echuca** (2hr., 2 per day, $18); **Kerang** (45min., 2 per day, $7); and **Mildura** (3½hr., 2 per day, $30).

**⌗ PRACTICAL INFORMATION.** Swan Hill's civic activity centers on the manicured strip of Campbell St between Rutherford and McCallum St. The **Swan Hill Development and Information Centre,** 306 Campbell St, on the corner of Rutherford St, is one block west of the river. (☎ 5032 3033, freecall ☎ (1800) 62 53 73; fax 5032 3032. Open daily 9am-5pm.) Lots of banks with 24hr. **ATMs** face one another at the intersection of Campbell and McCallum St (all banks open M-Th 9:30am-4pm, F 9:30am-5pm). The **library,** 53-67 Campbell St, offers **free Internet access.** (☎ 5032 2404. Open Tu, Th-F 10am-5:30pm; W 10am-5:30pm and 7-8:30pm; Sa 10am-noon; book ahead.) **Post office:** 164 Campbell St (open M-F 9am-5pm). **Postal code:** 3585.

**⌂⌂⌂ ACCOMMODATIONS, FOOD, AND NIGHTLIFE.** The **White Swan Hotel,** 182 Campbell St, offers that wonderful combination of Irish bar and budget accommodation. The rooms are spare but clean, and the bathrooms are simply serviceable. The downstairs saloon rocks nightly until 3am, but the upstairs is soundproofed. (☎ 5032 2761. Singles $25; twins and doubles $40, ensuite $45.) The **Pioneer Settlement,** on Horseshoe Bend, has one of its three lodges reserved for backpackers and has a TV room, BBQ, and fully stocked kitchen—but you might find oh-so-lovable school groups hanging from the rafters next door. (☎ 5032 1093. 4- to 8-bed dorms $15 first night, each extra night $10. Book ahead.) The **Riverside Caravan Park,** 1 Monash Dr, on the river adjacent to the Pioneer Settlement has a pool, BBQ, and small grocery. (☎ 5032 1494. Sites for 2 $15.50, powered $18-20; onsite caravans $42-64; cabins $56-112.) **Café Allure,** 147 Campbell St, serves up an eclectic mix of gourmet breakfasts, smoothies, and rich, large foccacias for under $10. (☎ 5032 4422. Open daily 8am-4pm. Meals $5-9.) Alternately, try the Italian fare at **Quo Vadis,** 255-259 Campbell St (☎ 5032 4408; open daily 6pm-late).

**◨ SIGHTS.** The **Horseshoe Bend Pioneer Settlement,** on Horseshoe Bend, is the oldest outdoor museum in Australia. Follow Campbell St south, hang a left at McDonald's, and head across the railroad tracks to the settlement. A full century (1830-1930) of the history of frontier agricultural settlement is represented by original buildings and olde-tyme equipment. The period-costumed employees of some shops perform uproarious slapstick street theater; paddlesteamers cruise the river along the banks of the settlement, and nighttime brings the **Mallee Heritage Sound and Light Show,** a family-friendly, if slightly hokey, extravaganza. (☎ 5032 1093. Settlement: open daily 9am-5pm; admission $16.50, children $8.50. Cruises: daily 10:30am and 2:30pm; $10, children $6. Mallee Show: nightly $10, children $6. Joint passes available.) Smaller than the Pioneer Settlement, but almost as engaging, is the **Swan Hill Art Gallery,** housed in a modern mud-brick structure next door. Three rotating galleries showcase local work. There's also a permanent collection of contemporary Australian art, concerts, films, and lectures. (☎ 5032 9744. Open Tu-F 10am-5pm, Sa-Su 11am-5pm. $3, concessions $2.)

Swan Hill is also proud of its excellent **fishing.** That pride has resulted in the **Giant Murray Cod.** Towering over its living brethren, it is quite possibly the largest Murray Cod in the world. The statue measures 6m by 11m by 6m, and was originally built as a prop for the movie *Eight Ball*. It now guards the north end of the rail station on Curlewis St, complete with a placard featuring a mawkish paean to the noble fish. The best fishing holes (mainly cod and carp) are 20min. away; ask for updates at the **Natural Resources and Environment** office, 324 Campbell St, when you pick up a **required fishing license.** (☎ 5033 1290. License $10 per month.)

Like most cities on the Murray, Swan Hill has its share of outlying vineyards. **Buller Winemakers** is 14km north on the Murray Valley Hwy. (☎ 5037 6305. Open M-F 9am-5pm, Sa 10am-5pm.) **Best's Winery** is to the south near Lake Boga. (☎ 5037 2154. Open M-Sa 10am-5pm.) Both offer tastings. If game's your game, head out to the **Pheasant Farm,** 20min. northwest of town on Chillingollah Rd, Australia's largest free-range pheasant farm. (☎ 5030 2648. Open daily 9am-5:30pm.)

# MILDURA

With its wide, palm-lined streets and bustling riverside wharf, Mildura is an oasis in dry Mallee country. The area, in the extreme northwest corner of Victoria, was settled in 1887 by the Chaffey brothers, Canadians who had established irrigation communities in California and repeated their success here. The cleverly harnessed waters of the Murray support thriving citrus groves and make Mildura one of Australia's most productive fruit-growing areas; as such, it attracts hordes of backpackers seeking itinerant work (best time of year is Feb.-Mar.). It's also one of the sunniest parts of Australia, and were it not for the massive irrigation system, the landscape would be as arid as the outback that stretches to the horizon. Enjoy it while you're here; Mildura is the last bastion of green for a long, long time.

## ⌐ TRANSPORT

The **train and bus station** is on 7th St, near the river, across from the northern end of Langtree Ave. V/Line runs to: **Melbourne** (7-9hr., 2 per day, $54), via **Swan Hill** (2½-3hr., $30) and **Bendigo** (6hr., $48); **Echuca** (5hr.; 1 per day Tu, W, F, Su; $35); and **Albury** (9hr.; 1 per day Tu, W, F, Su; $56). Tom Evans coaches (☎5022 1415) services **Broken Hill** (3½hr.; M, W, F 9am; $50). McCafferty's runs daily service to **Adelaide** (8:20am, $38) and **Sydney** (6:25pm, $80).

## ✦❓ ORIENTATION AND PRACTICAL INFORMATION

A thoroughly planned city, Mildura is laid out in a grid on the southern bank of the Murray. The commercial center is the strip of Langtree Ave from 7th to 10th St, including a **pedestrian mall** from 8th to 9th with speakers blaring an endless array of Barry White's greatest hits. The **Mildura Visitor Information and Booking Centre,** 180-190 Deakin Ave, is housed in the brilliant Alfred Deakin Centre; look for the silvery tornado sculpture out front. Inside, the **library** has **free Internet access.** Extended visitors and those seeking **work** should ask for the thorough and free *Working Holiday and Backpacker Information Sheet.* (☎5021 4424; fax 5021 1836; www.murrayoutback.org.au. Info center: open M-F 9am-5:30pm, Sa-Su 9am-5pm; Library: Su-M 1-5pm, Tu-F 10am-7pm, Sa 10am-2pm.) Banks and 24hr. **ATMs** are everywhere. All the major **car rental** companies are located in the airport, 8km out of town on the Sturt Hwy, with rentals from $55-65 per day. **Police station:** on Madden St, between 8th and 9th St (☎5023 9555). **Post office:** on the corner of 8th and Orange Ave (open M-F 9am-5pm). **Postal code:** 3500.

## ⌐ ACCOMMODATIONS

The best place to stay is the YHA-affiliated **Rosemont Guest House,** 154 Madden Ave, one block east of Deakin Ave off 11th St. A traditional guest house with fragrant gardens and a swimming pool, Rosemont combines hostel and B&B-style rooms. The affable manager can book tours of the outback and nearby national parks, and provides job search assistance during the fruit-picking seasons. All rooms are singles or twin share. (☎/fax 5023 1535. Kitchen, cozy dining room, plus TV lounge, electric blankets. Generous breakfasts $5. $17, weekly $102; non-YHA add $3. Two-person B&B ensuite rooms with TV, fridge, and full breakfast from $60.) The rest of Mildura's several backpacker hostels are designed with the migrant worker in mind. Basic rooms, work placement, and transport to work run about $15 per night (weekly $90-100); the proletarian demeanor is minimally masked by cable TV, swimming pools, and the occasional ping-pong table. The most centrally located are the **Zippy Koala,** 206B 8th St (☎5021 5793); the **Riverboat Bungalow,** 27 Chaffey Ave (☎5021 5315); the **NOMADS Mildura International Backpackers,** 5 Cedar Ave. (☎/fax 5021 0133); and the **Riviera Motel,** corner of 7th St and Pine Ave (☎5023 0521). You can often find squatter's work in the *Sunraysia Daily's* employment section without having to stay in squatter's quarters.

## FOOD AND NIGHTLIFE

Mildura's food offers more variety than your typical country city. The **Langtree Avenue Mall,** one block west of Deakin St between 8th and 9th St, has a few super-cheap takeaway joints, while the strip of Langtree between 7th and 8th St is a veritable international bazaar. For a town the size of Mildura, it's a wonder they have a Japanese restaurant as authentic as **Gin Za,** 40 Langtree Ave. (☎5023 0203. Open Su-Th 5-10pm, F-Sa 5-11:30pm. Meals $11-17; takeaway discount.) **Siam Palace,** 35 Langtree Ave, serves up Chinese and Thai dishes. The steal is the $5 lunch special, which offers a choice of dishes with steamed rice. (☎5023 7737. Open M-Th noon-2pm and 5:30-10pm, F-Sa noon-2pm and 5:30-11pm, Su noon-2pm.) A 24hr. **supermarket** is at the corner of 8th St and Lime Ave.

A few nightclubs are at 8th and Langtree St. The **Sandbar** warms even the chilliest of winter nights with its tropical motif. Live music starts at 10:30 with no cover. (☎5021 2181. Open Tu-Sa until 3 or 4am. Tu: comedy night, $5; W: drink specials; Th-F: free bar snacks.) The **Sunraysia Jazz and Wine Festival** combines the two mellowest things on earth (Nov. 2-6, 2001).

## SIGHTS

Mildura is the base camp for a variety of tours into nearby national parks and the outback. The visitors center has info on and books for all the commercial tours. For nearly 30 years Tom Evans has been running tours in the Mildura area, bringing his encyclopedic knowledge on his **Junction Tours** (☎5027 4309) to **Mungo National Park** (see p. 241; W, F, Su $66); local hotspots (Tu, Th, Sa; $50-68); or Broken Hill (Su-Tu, 3 days and 2 nights of camping for $462). **Mallee Outback Experiences** (☎5024 6007) operates daytrips to Mungo (W, Sa; $50, families $120); the **Hattah Kulkyne National Park** lakes system (F only; $50, families $120); and various local wineries (Tu, Th; $45, children $30). **Harry Nanya Tours** (☎5027 2076, freecall ☎(1800) 63 08 64), runs half- and full-day trips focusing on Aboriginal history and the Dreaming, including Mungo ($50-55), Wentworth ($50) and wineries ($40).

The ground is nice, but no view's like the one you get on a **hot air balloon** ride from **Camerons.** The pilot, Alan Cameron, points out local landmarks, tells great jokes, and deftly notes parallels between your ride and the first balloon trip ever. (☎5021 2876. 45min. ride $195, allot 3hr. total.) He'll also take unrepentant landlubbers for a ride on his **Harley** motorcycle (30min. $35, 1hr. $55).

The **P.S. Melbourne,** one of Australia's last steam-powered watercrafts, passes through historic Lock 11 (2hr.; daily 10:50am and 1:50pm; $18.50, children $7.50). The 1881 paddlewheeler **Rothbury** cruises to Trentham Estate winery. (☎5023 2200. 5hr., Th 10:30am, $42.) As you probably guessed, local wineries are abundant and excellent. Of the seven in the immediate area, the most internationally famous is **Lindemans** (☎5051 3285). Of the many ways to get there, the easiest is the Mallee Outback's Experience (see above; $45; winery open daily 10am-4:30pm).

The **Mildura Arts Centre,** 199 Cureton Ave, has a decent permanent collection highlighted by a chunky-but-funky Degas, and rotating Australian avant-garde exhibits. The gallery adjoins the grandiose **Rio Vista mansion,** built in 1889 by W.B. Chaffey and preserved with its original furnishings and exquisite Italian marble fireplaces. (☎5023 3733. Open daily 10am-5pm. $3, concessions $2.) Twelve kilometers southeast of town off 11th St, the **Psyche Bend Pumping Station** houses the restored steam pumps that kept Mildura alive and irrigated in the early days. The station is secluded in **King's Billabong,** a bird-filled wetland reserve. (☎5023 2350. Open Tu, Th 1-4pm, Su 11am-1pm. $3, families $8.)

If you've always wanted to learn how to tell the good fruit from bad, **Orange World** beckons you to the "land of the living orange," more commonly known as the town of **Buronga,** 8km north of town on the Silver City Hwy, across in New South Wales. Orange World offers tastings and tours of its panoply of fruit. (☎5023 5197. Open Su-F 9am-4pm. Tours 10:30am and 2:30pm. $8, concessions $7; children $4.)

# HUME CORRIDOR

The Hume Hwy links Melbourne and Sydney, shuttling visitors 872km through relatively unspectacular scenery. However, intrepid travelers who venture an hour or two off the Hume will be rewarded with world-class wineries, dusty hamlets, and quietly inviting country towns. Don't blink or you'll miss Glenrowan and Ned Kelly's Last Stand. Stray a bit from the highway, and you can snowboard or ski on Mt. Buller's excellent powdery slopes, or check out the wineries of the Rutherglen Valley. Sun worshippers can laze away by heading west along the Murray Valley Hwy to fish, swim, or snooze on the Murray's banks in Yarrawonga and Cobram. Across the Murray River, the Hume continues north into New South Wales.

## MARYSVILLE AND LAKE MOUNTAIN

A precocious small town only 1½ hours northeast of Melbourne, Marysville is best known as the closest town (22km) to cross-country ski mecca Lake Mountain.

**TRANSPORT AND PRACTICAL INFORMATION.** McKenzie's **buses** (☎5962 5088) depart for **Melbourne** (2¾hr., 1 per day, $12) from the bus stop across from the general store at 4 Murchison St. The Mystic Mountains **Tourist Information Centre,** on Marysville's main thoroughfare **Murchison St,** posts Lake Mountain snow reports and road conditions, arranges accommodations, and posts a list of available places to stay. (☎5963 4567; fax 5963 4444; www.mmtourism.com.au. Open daily 9am-5pm.) Local **snow and road conditions:** ☎5963 3205 or ☎(1902) 24 05 23 (50¢ per min. www.snowreport.vic.gov.au). The Marysville post office, at the intersection of Murchison St and Pack Rd, has an **ATM** (open M-F 8am-5pm, Sa 9am-4pm, Su 10am-4pm). **Postal code:** 3779.

**ACCOMMODATIONS AND FOOD.** While the area's best lodging lies 21km up the road at Taggerty's YHA-affiliated Australian Bush Settlement (see below), the **Marysville Caravan Park,** on Buxton Rd, is by the Steavenson River on the edge of town. (☎5963 3443; fax 5963 3531. Powered sites for 2 $21; cabins $38-65; cheaper off-season.) No disrespect to Mentos, but **Marysville Country Bakery,** at the corner of Murchison St and Pack Rd, is the real "freshmaker," with delectable sandwiches ($3-4.50) and 20 types of pies and pasties ($2-3)—the best is the chunky Bushman's Pie. (☎5963 3477. Open daily 7am-6pm.) **Uncle Fred and Aunty Val's Old Fashioned Lolly Shop,** 8 Murchison St (☎5963 3644), won't give refunds when you get a toothache from their tasty sweets.

**SIGHTS AND SKIING.** The 31km of regularly groomed cross-country ski trails are packed in season (entry fee $20; trail fee $9, children $4.50). By car, take the Maroondah Hwy (Hwy 34) to Hwy 172. Chains are required for the drive up Lake Mountain during the winter. Back in Marysville, **Lake Mountain Ski Hire** rents skis, skates, toboggans, and chains. (☎5963 3444. Open M-F 8am-6pm, Sa-Su 7am-6:30pm. Everything $5-25.)

Also near Marysville, **Steavenson Falls** lies 4km down Falls Rd. Several lush, hilly bushwalks lead off the path to the soaring cataracts, which are illuminated at night. There's a 30min. ascent to the top of a nearby peak with a view of the falls, and a 40min. trail downhill through the town. In the town itself, and absolutely not to be missed, ◨**Bruno's Art & Sculpture Garden,** 51 Falls Rd, has beautiful gardens and an extensive collection of paintings and collages. The real treats are the sculptures; often whimsical, the subtle creations are powerfully expressive and show great imagination. (☎5963 3513. Gallery open Sa-Su 10am-5pm. Garden open daily 9am-5pm. Gallery and garden $5, garden alone $3.)

## TAGGERTY

The ▨**Taggerty Australian Bush Settlement** (☎5774 7378; fax 5774 7442; www.green.net.au/australian_bush_settlement), provides a splendorous stay for a one-night guest or a several-month visitor. This 30-hectare, YHA-affiliated farm, located by the Cathedral Range National Park, simulates an early pioneer village. The remarkable host, Bronwyn Rayner, is the embodiment of selfless sacrifice. She has operated Taggerty for more than 20 years and built it into a combination B&B, hostel, campsite, working farm, classroom, museum, and youth development facility. Rayner cultivates an organic vegetable garden and cares for a variety of unwanted, misfit, or orphaned animals ranging from sheep and horses to wombats and kangaroos. Guests and visitors can interact with the endearing animals, and the working farm and bush settlement serve as a backdrop for educational programs run for special-needs and at-risk kids. Taggerty also houses an extensive collection of 19th-century bush memorabilia, including costumes, carriages, and an 1853 Norwegian slab hut. Providing its guests an authentic bush adventure, Taggerty integrates the experiences and traditions of both Aboriginals and white settlers. Rayner's work here has been the subject of several TV specials.

Accommodations come in four degrees of comfort and privacy. Tent sites run only $10, while the cheapest beds come in small, rustic cabins donated by the Australian Football League. More hostel-like environs can be had in the cozy, well-kept lodge ($17, non YHA $20). The cream of the crop is the richly decorated homestead, which was *Home Beautiful's* 1990 Home of the Year and Design of the Year. A private double room with king-size bed and classic free-standing bath is sublime ($80). All lodgings come with excellent kitchen and toilet facilities in-room or nearby.

For reasonable prices, guests can take advantage of a board plan or bush activities, with longer and more involved excursions offered for groups of six or more. The Th-Su four-day tour is a fantastic bargain and an unforgettable experience; it includes most meals, bushwalks, chances to visit nearby Marysville, visits to the animal nurture center, chances to grind wheat and churn butter, and lessons about local Aboriginal culture ($89, non-YHA members $99). But best of all, it gives you a chance to interact with the warm, intriguing people that make Taggerty such a special place. The Bush Settlement usually has vacancies, but takes reservations. If you are anywhere in or near the state of Victoria, it is inexcusable to miss this opportunity. Taggerty is 104km east of Melbourne on the Maroondah Hwy (Hwy. 34), 4km after Buxton. If you ask, the V/Line **bus** from **Melbourne** to **Eildon** will also stop at Taggerty YHA at the 104km marker of the Maroondah Hwy (1 per day, $14).

## MANSFIELD

Mansfield's *raison d'être* is its convenient location near the foot of Mt. Buller, which allows tourists to stop and rent skis and chains before making the 45km ascent to Victoria's most popular ski resort. The **Mansfield Passenger Terminal,** 137 High St (☎5775 2606), is the V/Line agent, with service to **Melbourne** (3hr., 1-3 per day) and **Mt. Buller** (1hr., 6-8 per day) in ski season. Law requires all vehicles heading to Mt. Buller to carry **snow chains** from the Queen's Birthday (the second week of June) until the end of the ski season. You can leave them in the trunk, but there are spot checks and hefty fines ($170) for not carrying them at all.

**Ski Centre Mansfield,** 131 High St (☎5775 2859), and its nearby affiliate, **PJ's Ski Hire,** 149 High St (☎5775 1624), rent chains (full-day $15) and a wide range of ski equipment and clothing. (Open in season Sa-Th 6am-7pm, F 6am-midnight.) Similar ski hire joints illuminate High St with attention-grabbing lights; shopping around is easy, but they all offer comparable deals (full-day skis, boots, poles $25-30; snowboard and boots $45-50).

The **Mansfield Visitors Centre** is just outside town at 167 Maroonah Hwy. (☎5775 1464; bookings ☎(1800) 06 06 86; fax 5775 2518; email infocent@mansfield.net.au. Open daily 9am-5pm.) Heading east into town on **High St,** the town's main drag, you'll find ski rental places and a few **ATMs. Internet access: Mansfield Internet and Computers,** 21 Highett St (☎5775 3066; 15min. $2.50). **Post office:** 90 High St (open M-F 9am-5pm). **Postal code:** 3722.

The best budget beds are at the **Mansfield Backpackers Inn,** 112-116 High St, part of the Mansfield Travellers Lodge. (☎5775 1800; fax 5775 2396. Reception 24hr. Dorms $16.50; triples $105-120; family rooms $70-75. Book 1-2 weeks ahead.) All three of Mansfield's pub hotels are near the intersection of High and Highett St and offer similar accommodations (singles $28). The **Mansfield Bus Stop Café,** 141 High St (☎5775 1277), is a great quick-eats place with low prices and a twist of class. The Caribbean Banana pancake special ($7.70) is outrageously good. For family dining a few doors down, **Mingo's Bistro** has great pastas deals from $8. (☎5775 1766. Open daily from 6pm.) Move fast, because the fruit sells out quickly at the **Mansfield Fruit Palace,** 68 High St. (☎5775 2239. Open M-F 8:30am-6pm, Sa 8am-2pm.) You can also stock up on food at the IGA **supermarket,** 47 High St. (☎5775 2014. Open M-F 8am-8pm, Sa 8am-5pm, Su 9am-5pm.)

# MOUNT BULLER

Victoria's largest ski resort, Mt. Buller is a 3hr. drive from Melbourne. Buller's terrain is arguably the best in Victoria, and though it's not the Alps or Rockies, it's still a mecca for Aussie skiers and snowboarders from the Queen's Birthday (the second week of June) through early October.

**◨ TRANSPORT.** Mansfield-Mt Buller Bus Lines (☎5775 2606) **buses** to Mt. Buller depart from **Melbourne** (3hr.; 2-3 per day; return $97.50, including resort entry fees; students $75) or from **Mansfield** (1hr., 6-8 per day, $34). **Snowcaper Tours,** also departing from Melbourne, offers tour packages that include return transport, entrance fees, and an unlimited lift ticket. (☎5775 2367, bookings ☎(1800) 03 30 23. Mid-week $110, weekend $120.) Buses pull into the **Cow Camp Plaza,** in the center of Mt. Buller village. If going by car, bring **snow chains** (it's the law) and take Hwy 164 (Buller Rd) east to Mt. Buller. (Car admission $20 per day; overnight fee Su-Th $3.30 per night, F-Sa $6.60 per night.) Free parking is on the side of the mountain; to get to the village from here, visitors can take a free shuttle, but visitors with luggage must take a taxi ($10). Beware: these daily charges add up fast. Consider taking the bus, especially if you're staying for some time.

**▨ PRACTICAL INFORMATION.** The village is the hub of accommodation, food, and ski services. The Cow Camp Plaza houses **Cow Camp Alpine Ski Rentals** (though renting in Mansfield is cheaper; see p. 588), lockers, and restaurants. Opposite the plaza is the **information tower,** with maps of the resort and slopes, as well as info on work and long-term accommodations options. (☎5777 6622; fax 5777 6655; www.mtbuller.com.au. Open daily during ski season 8:30am-6pm. In summer, visit the post office.) **Toll-free accommodation bookings:** ☎(1800) 03 90 49. The **lift ticket office** sits across the village center from the info tower. (1-day weekday $55, weekend $66.) Call the **Buller Report** (☎5533 3333) for the latest snow conditions or tune into 93.7FM. **Post office:** at the foot of Summit Rd in the Resort Management Building. (☎5777 6077. Open daily 8:30am-5pm.) **Postal code:** 3723.

**▨▨▨ ACCOMMODATIONS, FOOD AND NIGHTLIFE.** Mt. Buller YHA Hostel **Lodge** is the least expensive lodging on the mountain, and you can literally ski to the front door. The lodge has blessedly well-heated dorms. Ski lockers are available. Book at least 3 weeks ahead in July and August. (☎5777 6181; fax 5777 6691; email yha@yhavic.org.au. Reception daily 8-10am and 5-10pm. Dorms $49, non-YHA $53; Sept.-June $39, $42.) Next door to the YHA, the **Kooroora Hotel** has more intimate four-person dorms with baths. Guests get breakfast in the fully licensed pub, which also hosts late-night entertainment. There is a 15% guest discount for on-site ski hire. (☎5777 6050; fax 5777 6202. Dorms M-Th $70, F-Su $80, weekly $510. Reservations require a 50% deposit and should be made months in advance.)

**ABOM,** on the Bourke St slope (Summit St for those on foot), couldn't be further from its full name (abominable). Despite the menacing Polar Bear over the doorway, this European-style ski resort is the perfect refuge from the cold. The bistro

VICTORIA

fare is affordable. (☎5777 6091. Pizza slice $4, toasted sandwich with 3 fillings $3.50.) The Cow Camp Plaza houses several upstairs eateries. The **Pancake Parlour** (☎5777 6540) is done up in faux-1890s style and serves up mean pancakes in crazy varieties like Hot Bavarian Apple and Jamaican Banana ($6.50-10). Upstairs on the opposite side of the Cow Camp, **Café Moguls** is slightly more upmarket, offering pastas and salads for the health-conscious. (☎5777 6882. Open 11:30am-late. Pastas $10-11, focaccia $10.)

**Kooroora's pub** is hands-down the place to go for nightlife on the mountain; live cover bands rage into the wee hours of the morning. **ABOM** (see above), home to **Mooseheads Bar,** is beginning to compete with Kooroora's as a popular watering hole with skiers. With $4.50 stubbies of Toohey's New, the happy hour (4:30-6:30pm) might be the happiest time to visit (open 3pm-late).

**☏ SKIING.** Intermediate runs predominate, though several expert trails are sprinkled on the southern slopes; beginning skiers have plenty of long runs to choose from too, as well as numerous lesson packages. On the south face, **Fanny's Finish** and **Chute 1, 2, and 3** separate the skiers from the snowbunnies. The lift capacity is excellent and lift lines are usually not too long. Those ready for an aerobic challenge will find 75km of cross-country skiing trails and an entire mountain, **Mt. Stirling,** set aside for their use. (☎5777 3541. Car entry $17; trail $8; telemark and cross country ski hire $34.) The slopes can be fun without snow, too; mountain biking is all the rage in the summer. The **Summit Walk** (return 1.5hr., moderate difficulty), beginning at the clock tower to the peak, rewards hikers with views of the High Country below.

**☏ MOUNTAIN BIKING.** In the summer, mountain biking is the thing to do at Buller, with a plethora of tracks and lift access to the top. Lifts operate daily from December 26 to the end of January, then on long weekends until Easter. **Raw NRG** (☎5777 6887), will set you up with information and equipment. Before taking bikes up the lift, which you can do during "expression sessions" (10am-1pm and 1:15-4:15pm), a lesson is required. Group lessons plus two sessions cost $65. Lift passes, if you've already been trained, cost $45 for both sessions in one day. Bike and helmet hire starts around $18 per hour for front suspension; more for dual suspension. Cheaper biking without the chairlift is available.

# GLENROWAN

A small stop heading north up the Hume Hwy (Hwy 31) between Benalla and Wangaratta, Glenrowan owes its fame entirely to the notorious bushranger Ned Kelly and the authorities who finally corralled him here. Upon entering the town, visitors are greeted by the 6m-tall Kelly statue, clad in an iron mask like the one he wore on that fateful day. The primary attraction is the $2.5 million animatronic tourist extravaganza, **Ned Kelly's Last Stand,** located at the **Glenrowan Tourist Centre,** a corny, cultish narrative presentation—entertaining to kids and at least appreciated by adults—in which Ned's outlaw exploits are presented in a self-described "40 minutes of rip-snorting action." (☎5766 2367. Every 30min. 9:30am-4:30pm. $16, concession $14, ages 5-15 $10.) Next door, the **Ned Kelly Memorial Museum and Homestead** offers a small gold prospector style shack as a re-creation of Kelly's headquarters. (☎5766 2448. $2.75, children 60¢.)

# WANGARATTA

With expansive brick sidewalks and 19th-century edifices, Wangaratta is a quiet, rural respite at a crossroads along the Hume Hwy. Although the town has few tourist attractions as such, it can be a sound base for exploring Victoria's alpine country and the vineyards in the surrounding snowfields.

**[E·7] TRANSPORT AND PRACTICAL INFORMATION.** V/Line (☎5721 3641) runs from the station on Norton St to: **Melbourne** (2½hr., 4-6 per day, $30); **Albury-Wodonga** (50min., 4-6 per day, $10); **Rutherglen** (30min.; W, F, Su evenings and daily 3:45pm during school holidays; $4.30); and **Bright** (1½hr., 1 per day, $10). Countrylink runs to **Sydney** (8hr., 2 per day, $90).

The main street, **Tone Rd,** is called **Murphy St** downtown, and intersects Ford, Ely, Reid, and Faithfull St as you proceed north. **Oven St** basically runs parallel and to the north of Murphy St. The **Visitors Centre** is on the Hume Hwy (Tone Rd), 1km southwest of the city center. (☎5721 5711. Open daily 9am-5pm). The **post office** is at the intersection of Murphy and Ely St (open M-F 9am-5pm). Postal code: 3677.

**[ᴬᴵ] ACCOMMODATIONS AND FOOD.** The **Billabong Motel,** 12 Chisholm St, a block east from Murphy on Reid St, has basic heated rooms. (☎5721 2353. Singles $30-35; doubles $40-45). Across the river on Pinkerton, just north of Faithfull St, is **Painters Island Caravan Park.** (☎5721 3380. Reception 8am-8pm. Sites $7, powered $8; on-site caravans $27.50; cabins $40-60.)

The **Scribbler's Café,** 66 Reid St, serves budget-friendly breakfast, sandwiches, and heavier stuff, and offers **Internet access.** (☎5721 3945. Open daily 8am-6pm.) **Vespa's Café,** at Reid and Ovens St, has a bar specializing in local wine and an eclectic menu in a jazzy Mediterranean bistro setting. (☎5722 4392. Open Tu-Sa 10am-late, Su 10am-5pm. Lunch $6-9, dinner $11-16.) Safeway **supermarket** is on Ovens St between Reid and Ford St (open daily 7am-midnight).

**[◉] SIGHTS AND WINERIES.** The best day trip is 15km southeast on the Oxley Flats Rd at the **Milawa Gourmet Region.** The classy **Brown Brothers Vineyard,** on Snow Rd, could sate a small island nation with its five tasting bars. Every course at their Epicurean Centre restaurant includes its own accompanying wine. (☎5720 5547. Open daily 9am-5pm; restaurant open daily 11am-3pm.) Around the corner on Factory Rd, the lactose-loving ■**Milawa Cheese Company** has free samples of gourmet cheeses and sinfully sweet preserves. (☎5727 3589. Open daily 9am-4:45pm.) **Milawa Mustards,** at the Old Emu Inn on Snow Rd, concocts an awe-inspiring set of the condiment. (☎5727 3202. Open daily 10am-5pm. Free tastings.) Varieties range from the sweet (honey, ginger, orange) to the hot (chili, super fine hot) to the alcoholic (bourbon).

Another real treat is **Air World** (☎5721 8788), 7km down Greta Rd. An aviation museum holding the world's largest collection of flying vintage aircraft, the single hangar also shows off tanks, torpedoes, and other military weapons of mysterious function. Wangaratta's renowned **jazz festival** (☎(1800) 80 39 44; www.wangaratta-jazz.com.au), the first weekend of November, ranks among Australia's best.

# RUTHERGLEN

At the heart of Victoria's most renowned wine region, Rutherglen is an excellent base for touring the surrounding wineries. The Murray Valley Hwy, called Main St in Rutherglen, runs from Yarrawonga (45km west) through Rutherglen to Albury (50km east). V/Line buses leave Rutherglen's BP service station for **Melbourne** via **Wangaratta** (3½hr.; M, W, F 6:35am, Su 5:15pm; $35). To make more V/Line connections while school is in session, take the Wangaratta-bound school bus from the post office around 8am. Pay the driver upon boarding. Kelly's Bus Service shuttles to **Albury** at 9:30am on weekdays from the BP station west of the city center. (☎6033 2459 or ☎(0419) 24 48 97. $6.50.) The **tourist office,** in the Jolimont Cellar building on the corner of Drummon and Main St, down the hill from the city center, is the place to go for a potentially dangerous combination of winery literature and bicycle rental. (☎6032 9166, freecall (1800) 62 28 71; fax 6032 9167. Open daily 9am-5pm. One-day rental $20.) **Post office:** Main St (open M-F 8am-5pm). **Postal code:** 3685. The region uses New South Wales' **phone code 02,** not Victoria's 03.

The only budget beds in town can be found in the hotels along Main St (singles $25, doubles $50; book ahead during holidays and wine festivals). The IGA **supermarket,** 95 Main St, has plenty of provisions. (☎6032 9232. Open M-W 7:30am-6pm, Th-F 7:30am-7:30pm, Sa 7:30am-1pm, Su 8:30am-1pm.)

VICTORIA

## NEAR RUTHERGLEN: WINERIES

Rutherglen's temperate climate allows vineyards to keep grapes on their vines longer, favoring full-bodied red wines and fortified varieties like Tokay and Muscat. Choosing from among the excellent local wineries can be quite difficult, especially since they all offer free tastings. For those traveling by car, the *Rutherglen Touring Guide,* available at the visitors center and most wineries, is an indispensable free map. Or grab a free *Muscat Trail Map* for help navigating by bike. For a campier tour, take a horse-drawn stagecoach from **Poachers Paradise Hotel,** 120 Main St. (☎ 6032 9502. Daily 10am and 1pm; three wineries in 2hr. $15 per person; bookings essential.) **Grapevine Getaways** runs a daily tour from Albury at 9:30am. (☎ 6023 2599. From $30; bookings essential.)

The Rutherglen vineyards sponsor several festivals throughout the year. The most popular is the carnival-like **Rutherglen Winery Walkabout** (on Queen's Birthday weekend, the second weekend in June) featuring food and entertainment at the estates and a street fair downtown. True connoisseurs would probably prefer to skip the big production and instead sample the impressive food and wine combinations Rutherglen offers during the **Tastes of Rutherglen** (March 9-18, 2001).

**All Saints Estate** (☎ 6033 1922, freecall (1800) 02 16 21; www.allsaintswine.com.au). Head east of Rutherglen via Corowa Rd, then north on All Saints Rd; just outside of Corowa. If you're only going one place, go here. The most polished, tourist-oriented winery-going experience around. All Saints confirms romantic visions of what wineries should look like, with towering elms lining the driveway, a red-brick castle tasting room, and a sculptured rose garden with central fountain. A marked, self-guided tour leads past immaculate gardens, huge display casks, and a playground. Their **Terrace Restaurant** provides succulent but expensive lunches. A peek into the **Chinese Dormitory and Gardens** on the grounds gives a sense of the early laborers' living conditions. Adjacent to the parking lot, the **North East Victoria Winemakers Hall of Fame** is an informative display of the region's leading figures and wineries. Winery open M-Sa 9am-5:30pm, Su from 10am; restaurant open daily 10am-5pm, Sa from 7pm; book ahead on weekends.

**Chambers Rosewood Winery** (☎ 6032 8641). The opposite cellar-door experience from All Saints. An easy-to-miss building on Barkley St 1km from the tourist office. Unpretentious and easygoing, the winery's simple tasting area gives no hint of the international praise lavished on its rare Tokays and Muscats. Open M-Sa 9am-5pm, Su 11am-5pm.

**Fairfield Vineyards** (☎ 6032 9391). Head west on the Murray Hwy. Their idyllic old cellar building is even better than their selection of wines. Open M-Sa 10am-4:30pm.

**Cofield Wines** (☎ 6033 3798). Offers sparkling whites and reds and some great dining at the adjoining **Pickled Sisters Café** (☎ 6033 2377). Both open W-M 10am-4pm.

**Gehrig Estate** (☎ 6026 7296). East of town on the Murray Hwy. Like **Yering Station** in the Yarra Valley (p. 544), Gehrig's claims to be Victoria's oldest winery. Open M-Sa 9am-5pm, Su 10am-5pm.

# HIGH COUNTRY

Victoria's High Country, tucked between the Murray River and Gippsland's thick coastal forest, is an unusual contrast to Australian sights like Surfer's Paradise or the Red Centre. Here, ancient forests display dazzling autumn colors, and rambling valleys nurture spring flowers that would shame Crayola into turning a deep crimson. In winter, Mt. Hotham and Falls Creek offer the continent's best skiing around the charming village of Bright. In the summer, paragliding, abseiling and mountain biking find shelter beneath Mt. Buffalo's soaring peak.

 **CHAIN ME**. All vehicles heading into the mountains must carry tire chains from Queen's Birthday (June 12, 2001) until October 1.

# BEECHWORTH

The bustle of the goldfield days has abated, but they left their mark on this peaceful country town. Victoria's best preserved gold town, Beechworth produced over $2 billion of gold back in its heyday, but now the town is the kind of place Aussies go for a romantic getaway.

**TRANSPORT AND PRACTICAL INFORMATION.** The V/Line bus stop is on Camp St, just west of Ford St; tickets should be purchased at **Beechworth Animal World,** 34-36 Camp St. (☎5728 1374. Open M-F 9am-5:30pm, Sa 9am-4pm, Su 11am-4pm.) **Buses** run to: **Melbourne** (3½hr., 2-3 per day, $35); **Bright** (30min., 1 per day, $5); and **Wangaratta** (30min., 1-3 per day, $5). The **Visitors Information Centre** is located in beautifully preserved Shire Hall on **Ford St,** Beechworth's main north-south street. (☎/fax 5728 3233. Open daily 9am-5pm.) Clustered together along Ford St near the main intersection with Camp St are an **ATM,** an IGA **supermarket.** (☎5728 1055; open M-F 8:30am-5:30pm, Sa 8:30am-5pm, Su 10am-5pm), and the **post office** (open M-F 9am-5pm). **Postal code:** 3747.

**ACCOMMODATIONS AND FOOD.** Beechworth overflows with B&Bs. The visitors center can help you select accommodation based on price (starting at $45 per double), theme, or amenities. A reasonable hotel-style accommodation with B&B charm is the **Hibernian Hotel,** 40 Camp St, on the corner of Loch St, one block west of the town center. (☎5728 1070. Reception at bar 10am-11pm. Singles $35; twins and doubles $50.) A similar larger pub hotel is the **Tanswells Commercial Hotel,** 30 Ford St. (☎5728 1480. Singles Su-Th $30, F-Sa $40; doubles $50, $60.) The award-winning **Beechworth Bakery,** 27 Camp St, should not be missed by those who prize anything leavened. (☎5728 1132. Open daily 6am-7pm.)

**SIGHTS.** Behind the information center, on Loch St, the **Burke Museum** displays all the gold rush era artifacts you could ever want to see. In the back of the museum sits a row of period shops with displays that simulate the 1860s with an amusement-park feel. (☎5728 1420. Open daily 10:30am-3:30pm. $5.50.) Beechworth **cemetery,** north of the town center on Cemetery Rd, houses the **Chinese Burning Towers;** the simple headstones are all that remain of the Chinese presence in gold-rush Beechworth. Chinese miners once outnumbered whites five to one, but their tightly packed grave sites testify to the discrimination they faced.

The folks at 130-year-old brewery **M.B. Historic Cellars,** 29 Last St, a three blocks west of the town center, produce non-alcoholic cordials in 12 turn-of-the-century flavors, taking you back to the soft-drink world before Coke. (☎5728 1304. Open daily 10am-4pm. Free tastings.) If all that non-alcoholic drinking gives you the munchies, a stop at the bakery and a tour around the old goldfields on the **Woolshed Falls Historic Walk** (1hr.) makes a perfect afternoon picnic. The walk commences at the visitor center where you can pick up a free guide.

Bushranger **Ned Kelly** was first detained in a cell you can visit behind Shire Hall (admission by donation). Proceedings commenced here against Kelly for the killing of constables Lonigan and Scanlon in the infamous Glenrowan siege before moving to Melbourne in search of an impartial jury. Inside the **Beechworth Historic Court House,** 94 Ford St, the courtroom has been preserved in its 19th-century condition, right down to the dock where Kelly stood during his trials. (☎5728 2721. Open daily 10am-3:30pm. $2.50.)

## NEAR BEECHWORTH: YACKANDANDAH

A small gold rush town with a funny name, Yackandandah, or "Yack," can be less touristy and less expensive than better-known Beechworth. Craft shops, fragrant tea rooms, and historic buildings give the town its character. With over 9000 plants and 40 varieties of lavender cultivated, **The Lavender Patch,** 5km west of Yackandandah on Beechworth Rd (called High St in the town center), soothes and delights the senses. Natural lavender products including soaps and potpourri can be purchased in the shop, and the hosts encourage guests to roam the aromatic hillside. (☎6027 1603. Open daily 9am-5:30pm. Free.) To relive the gold rush, take a goldmine tour with **Yack Track Tours,** 2 Kars St, who will provide torches, hardhats, and commentary for your 1hr. tour through an underground gold tunnel. (☎6027 1757. Tours leave Sa-Su 10:30am, noon, 1:30, and 3:30pm, by appointment during the week. $11, families $27.50.)

From Beechworth (23km) or Wodonga (27km), Hwy C315 leads to a turn-off for Yackandandah. In town, shops and services are on High St. The **Visitors Information Centre,** on High St in the Athenaeum building, is the old social and intellectual center of town. (☎6027 1988. Open daily 10am-4pm.) There are **no ATMs. Post office:** on High St (open M-F 9am-5pm). **Postal code:** 3749. **Phone code: 02,** not 03.

Although a night in the nearby town of Albury is probably preferable, the **Yackandandah Hotel,** on High St and Isaacs Ave, makes a good but basic alternative to Beechworth's pricier digs. (☎6027 1210. Reception at bar 11am-8pm. Singles $25; doubles $45.) The sandwiches, pies, and loaves from the **Yackandandah Bakery,** 20 High St, make excellent breakfasts or lunches. (☎6027 1549. Open 8am-5:30pm.) For those with a car and a sweet tooth, it's worth a trip out to the award-winning **Vienna Patisserie Chalet,** 7km north towards Wodondga from downtown, at the Allan's Flat turn-off, where an Austrian couple, decked out in traditional garb, serve delicious tortes and strudels with a real sense of good food. (☎6027 1477. Open Aug.-June daily 10am-6pm. Coffee $3, desserts $4.40.) Just down the road from the Patisserie, slightly closer to town, is **Schmidt's Strawberry Winery,** at the Osborne Flat Rd turn-off. The Schmidts made wine for generations, and began strawberry production and winemaking in 1968. They produce dry and semi-sweet wines, popular with spicy food, and sweet dessert wines ($14 each, all 3 varieties $33). A luscious strawberry liqueur is also available for $22. (☎6027 1454. Open for sales and free tastings M-Sa 9am-5pm, Su 10am-4pm.)

## MOUNT BUFFALO NATIONAL PARK

The sheer face of Mt. Buffalo rises imposingly alongside the Ovens Hwy (Great Alpine Rd), signaling the site of a rich sub-alpine ecosystem with plenty of outdoor adventure opportunities throughout the year. Though the mountain's craggy walls look intimidating from a distance, the ski slopes that draw people here in winter are gentle. If you're a serious downhill skier or looking for nightlife, you'd be better off elsewhere. Mt. Buffalo's slopes are primarily for beginner and intermediate skiers, and are heavily family-oriented.

🛈 **PRACTICAL INFORMATION.** The **park entrance gate** (☎5756 2328) serves as the primary information source on site, though the actual **Parks Victoria office** is located 20km beyond the entry. (☎5755 1466; 24hr. info ☎13 19 63. Open daily 8am-4pm, usually staffed weekday mornings and afternoons.) Entrance to the national park is just off the Great Alpine Rd roundabout by Porepunkah, 5km north of Bright and 320km from Melbourne. The per-car entrance fee is waived for guests of mountaintop lodging ($12.50, off-season $9; concessions $6, $4.50).

🛏 **ACCOMMODATIONS.** The clean, simple lines of the main lounge and bistro at the **Mt. Buffalo Lodge,** 7km along the main road from the visitors center, overlook the slopes (meals $4-10). Inside, a ski shop and ski hire serve visitors for both cross-country and downhill skiing (rates comparable to those in Bright). Guests have access to laundry, a games room, and a TV lounge. Dorms contain basic bunks, a kitchen, no linen and shared facilities. Two meals are included for lodge rooms. (☎5755 1988; fax 5750 1194. Dorms July-Sept. $37, less in off-season. Twin lodge units $108.) Great **campsites** lie beside Lake Catani, 2km beyond the park office. Some are caravan-accessible, and there are toilets, water, hot showers, and laundry. (Sites for 4 $12-16.50. Book at entrance station. Open Nov.-Apr.)

**SKIING. Lift passes** are available for the **Cresta Valley site** adjacent to the Mt. Buffalo Lodge, and the price is a steal. (Morning $30, afternoon $35, full-day $39. Ages 8-15 $19, $23, $25. Lift ticket and lesson package $36, under 16 $25.) In the park, a 13km network of cross-country ski trails lie across the road from the Mt Buffalo Lodge parking lot at Cresta Valley. There's no fee for cross-country skiing; ask for the information sheet at the entrance gate. (On-site rental of cross-country skis and boots $16 per day.)

The drive up to Mt. Buffalo is one of its most dramatic ascents, as **waterfalls** snake over the craggy face of the mountain. There are some spectacular lookouts as well as numerous walking tracks. The most challenging is **"The Big Walk,"** (11.3km) which spans much of the ascent to the summit. The moderate to steep **Eurobin Falls** track (1.5km; 45min.) is a short hike off to the left of the road about 2km from the park entrance. Beginning with an amble and ending in a steep clamber, the walk features spectacular views of the falls careening down the bare rock. In the car, you will pass through dense eucalypt forests on the winding mountain road. A left turn just before the park office leads toward the Mt. Buffalo Chalet and **Bent's Lookout.** This stunning view provides a panoramic sweep across the Buckland Valley, with Australia's tallest peak, **Mt. Kosciuzsko,** visible on clear days.

Driving past the park office toward the Mt. Buffalo Lodge, you'll see numerous marked **walking trails.** Opposite the office, the tremendous view from the Monolith rock outcropping is definitely worth the short walk (750m; part of a 1.5km, 1hr. circuit). Mt. Buffalo's warm-weather activities are as popular as its winter ones. **Abseilers** go over the edge near Bent's Lookout year-round. **Rock climbing, caving,** and rugged mountaineering expeditions, coordinated through Bright's hostels, are run through the **Mt. Buffalo Chalet Activities Centre.** (☎5755 1500. Half-day $55, full-day $110.) The climbing on the north wall of the Gorge is world renowned. Mt. Buffalo is also excellent for hang-gliding and was the site of the world championships in 1986. Lake Catani is a man-made lake but perfect for swimming, fishing and canoeing, as well as bushwalking.

# BRIGHT

Bright is an apt name for this town of radiant natural beauty and glowing hospitality. With excellent budget accommodations and proximity to snowfields, wineries, and larger cities, Bright is a good starting point for skiing in winter, and bushwalking, paragliding, abseiling, and other eco-tourism opportunities in summer.

**TRANSPORT. Buses** leave the post office for **Melbourne** (4½hr., 1-2 per day, $39) and **Wangaratta** (1½hr., 1-2 per day, $10). Tickets sold at the visitors center.

 Info on current road, weather and slope conditions is available at ski rental shops throughout the region, as well as in accommodations, on www.hotham.net.au, and at ☎(1902) 24 05 23 (50¢ per minute).

**ORIENTATION AND PRACTICAL INFORMATION.** Bright is 79km southeast of Wangaratta along the **Ovens Hwy (Great Alpine Rd).** The town center lies hidden behind the highway, by a roundabout with an Art Deco clock tower. Both **Barnard** and **Anderson** link **Gavan St** (the **Great Alpine Rd Hwy** as it's called through most of Bright) to one side of this roundabout; from the other side, the main street, **Ireland St,** extends several blocks. The **Bright Visitors Centre,** 119 Gavan St, is also the place to go for V/Line and Rail Australia tickets. (☎5755 2275; fax 5750 1655; email brightvc@netc.net.au. Open daily 8:30am-5pm.) Other services include: **banks** with **ATMs** on Gavan St; **post office,** on Ireland St (open M-F 9am-5pm); and **Internet access** at **Bright Hikers Backpackers Hostel** (see below; 1hr. $10).

**▐▜▐ ACCOMMODATIONS AND FOOD.** Bright's centrally located backpacker accommodation is ▐Bright Hikers Backpackers Hostel (VIP), 2nd floor, 4 Ireland St, across from the post office. Comfy common areas have great lounge furniture, drying room, pool, a video library, and a Coke machine constructed by the owner from a refrigerator. Guests can borrow a limited selection of snow chains and skiing gear. Kitchen, dorms, and bathrooms are sparklingly clean. (☎5750 1244; fax 5750 1246; email hikers@netc.net.au. Reception 9am-10pm. Mountain bikes $12 per day. Laundry, and Internet. Linen $2.75. Dorms $17, winter $18; weekly $98, winter $105. Doubles $37, $39; $231, $245.) Coming from the visitors center on the Great Alpine Way, turn right on Hawthorne St. and then left onto Coronation St, and just before the bridge lies **Bright & Alpine Backpackers.** The old school camp turned hostel/campground is filled with nostalgia but does show its age. (☎5755 1154. Reception 24hr. Kitchen, laundry. Linen $4. Singles $14.30; doubles $28.60. Sites $7, powered $8.) **Bright Caravan Park** offers budget cabins and shaded sites ideal for summer campers. (☎5755 1141; fax 5750 1077. Sites $14-21, powered $17-25. Cabins $40-72, weekly $240-440. Prices vary seasonally. Book ahead.)

Bright is blessed with quite a few good restaurants. **Tin Dog,** 94 Gavan St (☎5755 1526), dishes up Mexican and Italian fare, including excellent wood-fired pizza. The **Alpine Hotel** is about the only place in town open for breakfast and also has a lively bar that gets a little crazy on Saturday nights when local bands perform. (☎5755 1366. Open daily 10am-late. Breakfast from 8am.) There's a **supermarket** at 16 Ireland St. (☎5755 1666. Open M-Th 8am-8pm, F 8am-9pm, Sa-Su 9am-7pm.)

**▣▐ SIGHTS AND ACTIVITIES.** While it's merely a base for winter skiing at Mt. Hotham, Falls Creek, and Mt. Buffalo, Bright stands alone as the undisputed local king of summer adventure activities. At the center of town, a handful of ski hire establishments will outfit you with **ski and snowboard equipment,** snow chains, and clothing. **Adina Ski Hire,** 15 Ireland St, offers a budget line of older skis to rent, which are a great deal but an unfortunate reminder of the days when fluorescent colors were in. (Open Sa-Th 7am-7pm, F 7am-9pm. Budget skis, boots and poles 1-day $22, weekly $76; snowboard and boots $50, $125. 20% YHA discount.)

Warm thermal air currents make the valleys surrounding Bright ideal for hanggliding and paragliding—the area was home to the 1986 World Championships. **Alpine Paragliding,** 6 Ireland St, next to Bright Hikers, offers tandem paraglides. (☎5755 1753. $120. Flights last at least 10-15 min.) The **Eagle School of Hang Gliding and Microlighting** offers an introductory Bright Flight (15min. $95). The Mt. Buffalo flight takes you over the gorge and silently glides back to earth. (☎(04) 2857 0168. $125, 20min.) The local ranges are ideal for mountain biking during warm, dry weather; **Mountain Thunder Bike Tours** offers full- and half-day trips that include thrilling descents (☎5755 2275. $50-90, with your own bike $33-60. Summer only.) **Adventure Guides Australia** (☎5728 1804) conducts **abseiling** (full-day from $95), night caving ($66), rock climbing (full-day from $100), and bushwalking and camping excursions. All adventure activities are year-round, though they're subject to weather and are much more sporadic in winter.

## FALLS CREEK

An hour's drive from Bright, along roads with sweeping views of the Victorian Alpine country, **Falls Creek Ski Resort** (☎5754 4718; fax 5754 4287; www.ski-fallscreek.com.au) lifts guests as high as 1780m. The ample snowfall, both natural and man-made, is a selling point, and the spread of trails means that bad weather conditions from one direction leave good skiing elsewhere on the mountain. Few trails are very long and are mostly intermediate runs; more advanced skiers can expect to spend more chairlift time than snow time. As snowfall permits, an area of black-diamond trails is opened (called The Maze), as is a snowboarding terrain park with a half-pipe. Falls' ambience is a bit more family-oriented than nearby Mt. Hotham (see p. 597), though their partnership (lift tickets are priced the same and allow access to both resorts) gives multi-day skiers the chance to try both.

Driving to the slopes mandates carrying **snow chains** (rental $18-22 in Bright or almost anywhere around the mountains) and paying a hefty entrance fee. (First day entry fee $20, overnight $29. Price does not include lift tickets.) It is not practical to stay in Bright and use public transport to reach the resort for the day. Pyle's Falls Creek Coach Services (☎5754 4024) runs a ski-season service from **Melbourne** (6hr., 1-2 per day, $110 return), **Albury** (3½hr., 1-3 per day, $58.30 return), and **Mt. Beauty** (50 min., 2-4 per day, $33 return). All prices include entrance fee, but not **lift tickets** (full-day $68, 2-day $133, weekly $382; children $35, $68, $194; lifts plus lesson $95, students $73, children $64).

An active summer resort as well, Falls Creek has bushwalking, horseback riding, tennis, and water activities from October to June. A smaller number of lodges are open for housing during the summer (call central reservations for current openings and tariffs), but prices are lower. During Victoria school holidays in summer, conditions permitting, a small number of lifts are opened (tickets about $15) for **mountain biking;** take the chair up and then bike down the snow-free trails.

Activity is concentrated at the edges of the village. The **Falls Creek Information Centre** sits at the bottom of town, just opposite the first-day parking lot, and keeps information on lessons, lift packages, and accommodations. (☎5758 3490; fax 5758 3585; email fallsinfo@fallscreek.albury.net.au. Open daily 8am-5pm.) Staying on the mountain will let you sleep longer, party later, and make snow angels outside, but the privilege does not come cheap. A horde of small, independent lodges offers varying styles of accommodation. The folks on the **Central Reservations line** (☎5754 4718, freecall ☎(1800) 03 30 79) are affiliated with almost all of them and direct you to the kind you're after. The cheapest beds are in pleasant but basic dorms at the **Frying Pan Inn**, 4 Village Bowl Circle, at the top of the Gully chairlift and at the west end of the village, for $40-72 (weekdays on the margin of the season are cheapest). It's also the Inn place to be on weekends, when there are live bands, dance parties, and drink specials to fuel the debauchery. (☎5758 3390; fax 5758 3416. Open daily 5pm-late.) **The Man,** 20 Slalom St. (☎5758 3362), is the heart of the nightlife with live local bands and crazy staff parties on Mondays.

Up on Slalom St is the **Snowland** complex, housing the **Wombat Café,** an inexpensive snack bar. (☎5758 3666. Open daily 9am-6pm.) Also in the complex is the **post office** (open M-F 9am-5pm; **postal code:** 3699) and a mini-market. There are **ski rental places** everywhere, but it's cheaper to rent in Bright (see p. 595).

# MOUNT HOTHAM

With Victoria's highest average snowfall, 13 lifts, and a partnership with nearby Falls Creek, Mount Hotham is Victoria's intermediate- and advanced-skiing and snowboarding headquarters. Mt. Hotham is considered the hottest place in Victoria for thrill-seekers, and especially for **snowboarders.** The slopes are more challenging than in the rest of Australia, with short but steep double black diamonds cutting through the trees in the **"Extreme Skiing Zone."** Beginner skiing is limited, though lessons are available. With a constant stream of uni groups filling club lodges in the ski season, the mountain is a little younger and a little more hip than nearby Falls Creek, though après-ski offerings are more or less on par with its rival. In the summer, Hotham is relatively quiet, with nature trails and a few shops and lodgings open for visitors.

▐ **TRANSPORT.** From the north, Mt. Hotham is accessible in the winter by a sealed road. Entrance from Omeo to the south is safer and more reliable, but inconvenient for those in Melbourne or Sydney. To get to Mt. Hotham by **bus,** depart from **Melbourne's** Spencer St Station (6¼hr., 1-2 per day, $115 return); **Wangaratta** Railway Station (3¼hr., 1-2 per day, $85 return); or **Bright's** post office (1½hr.; 2-3 per day; $35 return). Contact **Trekset Tours** (☎9370 9055, freecall ☎(1800) 65 90 09) to book.

**⚡ ORIENTATION AND PRACTICAL INFORMATION.** There's a fee to enter the resort, not covering lift tickets, payable at the tollbooth located 1½hr. from Bright on the Great Alpine Rd (cars $23, overnight $36, season pass $160). If you're driving through without skiing, it's free. From mid-October to Queen's Birthday in June, resort admission is free. Drivers heading from Bright can rent mandatory **snow chains** from **Hoy's A-Frame Ski Centre** (☎5759 2658), a right after the second bridge in Harrietville, for $22 with a $30 deposit. These can be returned to **Les and Betty's Mobil Service Station** in **Omeo** on the south side of Mt. Hotham.

The resort is constructed around the Great Alpine Rd, which climbs the mountain. The lodges cluster to the south, with ski lifts and services farther north. Village buses transport folks for free around the resort. The **information center** (☎5759 3550; www.mthotham.com.au) is on the first floor of the Resort Management building, just above the Corral carpark. Directly across the street, Hotham Central houses a **snow sports school office,** ski rental places, a small **grocery store** and a **lift ticket** office, which sells passes valid both here and at Falls Creek (full-day ticket $68-72, children $35-37; lift and lesson packages start at $95 per day, children $64). Tickets for round-trip **helicopter rides** to Falls Creek are $59. The Big D lift hosts night skiing. (Open W, Sa 6:30-9:30pm. $11, upgrade from valid lift ticket $6.)

**▌ ACCOMMODATIONS.** Lodging on Mt. Hotham is pricey, and Bright's excellent hostels offer an inexpensive alternative. If you want to stay where the action is, the plethora of on-mountain lodges are most easily investigated through one of the several bookings agencies, which have access to the current pricing and availability in all 60-80 lodges or at least will send you in the right direction. One such agency is the **Mt. Hotham Accommodation Service** (☎5759 3636; www.mt-hotham-accommodation.com.au), which can sometimes place you in a club lodge for as low as $35 from late July to mid-September, or $20 in the off-season.

**▐ FOOD.** To the south of both the resort and the Big D chairlift sits **Big D,** a complex housing a ski boutique, and the **Isobar,** a trendy joint with cheap food for dine-in or takeaway. (☎5759 3066. Open daily 9am-9pm, later on night ski days.) Next door is **The General,** a general store with a mini-market, pub, bistro, and mailbox. (☎5759 3523. Market open daily in ski season 8am-9pm; bistro and bar open daily noon-late.) The 11km **cross-country track** to Dinner Plain begins just beyond the store. The **Swindler's Balcony Bar & Restaurant,** downstairs in the back of Hotham Central, serves hearty meals by its open fireplace; the bar is a post-ski hotspot with live music on weekends. (☎5759 4421. Open daily 7am-late. Pizza $4 per slice, full meals $8-10.) A couple good **bars** are opposite Hotham Central. The **Snowbird/Summit** bar (☎5759 3503) offers 5-drink jugs for $7.50 and lively crowds.

# GIPPSLAND

Southeast of Melbourne, the Princes Hwy loosely follows the contours of the Victoria coast through verdant, rolling wilderness interspersed with extensive lake systems and small towns on its way to the border of New South Wales. Undeveloped and sparsely populated, this belt hosts eco-tourists and inspires frequent struggles among developers, loggers, and environmentalists. National parks pepper the region; highlights include backpacking through Wilsons Promontory and Croajingalong, boating on the Snowy River, and paying homage to the Den of Nargun in Mitchell River. Though these parks receive far fewer visitors than those further west, this lush land and crystalline coastline promise both solace and adventure.

# WILSONS PROMONTORY NATIONAL PARK

Whether it's an echidna sighting in the woods, or the 360° view of granite headlands from Mt. Oborst, chances are you will leave Wilsons Promontory with some unforgettable experiences. Though one of Australia's most famous parks, receiving 400,000 visitors each year, **the Prom** is also one of the most unspoiled and diverse natural reserves in the world. Jetting out to form the continent's southernmost extreme, the Prom consists of 49,000 hectares of parkland and an additional 8300 hectares of marine and coastal parks and reserves. Tidal flats and marshland meet clusters of heath and towering gum forests. Rich fern gullies follow the contours of the land. This diversity of flora creates habitats for scores of native marsupials, reptiles, birds, insects, and sea creatures. Partially preserved as a national park back in 1897 and now declared a UNESCO World Biosphere Reserve, the Prom is off limits to human settlement and most public transportation.

The Boonerwrung tribe believed that this area was sacred, protected by Lo'han, the ancient guardian spirit, and was visited only for special occasions. Later, when English Naval Officer Tobias Furneaux first spotted the coastline in 1773, the area quickly gained world-wide appeal. In the early days of Australia's settlement, sealers and whalers exploited the waters offshore. The immigration booms of the Gold Rush (1850s) and Federation (1900s) brought an active forestry industry, as timber was needed to support new development elsewhere in Victoria. During World War II, the government sealed off the Prom for commando training. Meanwhile, the park's geological history took some turns, too. Now connected to the mainland by parallel sandy ridges, at various points in its history the peninsula was an island, while at another time, these ridges extended south all the way to Tasmania. For more **information** on Wilsons Promontory, call ☎ (1800) 35 05 52, or visit the Parks Victoria web site (www.park.vic.gov.au).

## FOSTER: GATEWAY TO WILSONS PROMONTORY

From gold rush to gateway, Foster has long been a place where people come looking for supplies and a warm bed. Most of today's visitors are headed to the park; its entrance is just 30km to the south. While in town, take a moment to relax by the creek, or head up the hill behind the hotel for a lovely view of the land.

To reach Foster by car from Melbourne (170 km), take the South Eastern Arterial (M1) to the South Gippsland Hwy (M420), following signs first to Phillip Island, then to Korumburra (changing numbers to A440), and finally to Foster. Alternatively, V/Line (☎ 13 61 96) **buses** run from **Melbourne** (2¾hr.; M-F 4:30pm, Sa 6:50pm, Su 5:35pm; returns M-Sa 7:45am, Su 3:20pm; $22), requiring that you spend the night in Foster before shuttling to the Prom with the **Prom Postie** (see below). **Tourist information** is available inside the Stockyard Gallery at the end of Main St toward the Prom. (☎ 5682 1125. Open daily 10am-4pm, off-season Th-Su 10am-4pm.) **Parks Victoria** staffs an office in the same building. (☎ 5682 2133. Open M-F 8am-4:30pm.) Other services include: **Internet** at Raider's Pizza, 10 Station Rd (1hr. $6); **laundromat**, 6 Station Rd ($3 wash and dry; open daily 8am-9pm); **police** (☎ 5682 2407); **hospital** (☎ 5683 9777); and the award-winning ▨Post office, corner of Main and Bridge St (☎ 5682 2597; open M-F 9am-5pm, Sa 9am-1pm). **Postal code:** 3960.

Accommodations in Foster are both cozy and convenient. The **Foster Backpackers Hostel,** 17 Pioneer St, is the most affordable option, with shared kitchen and outdoor BBQ. (☎ 5682 2614. Dorms $14; adorable clay house double $40; triples and quads from $45.) You can also rent **camping gear** ($10 per night). Ask the owners about their upcoming **farm hostel.** Arriving from the S. Gippsland Hwy, turn right onto Main St, then left on Bridge St; Pioneer St is on the right. Margaret, from the tourist information office, also kindheartedly rents out the "Rose Cabin" behind her house, which is surrounded by grapefruit groves and blueberry bushes and includes a solar-powered shower (1 person $30, 2 people $60).

The best option for meals is one of the town's two bakeries. There are two **supermarkets** in town, where you can buy your last food before getting into the park. **Foodway,** 28 Main St, has longer hours (open daily 8am-8pm, winter 8am-6pm).

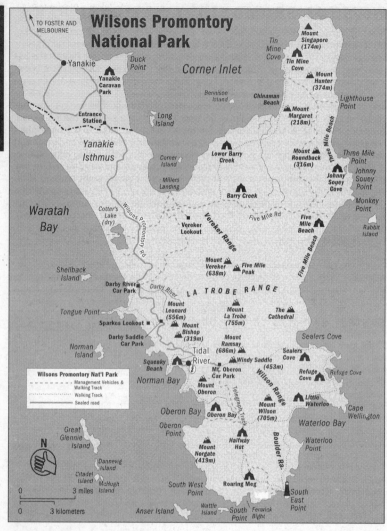

## Wilsons Promontory National Park

TO FOSTER AND MELBOURNE

Yanakie
Duck Point
Corner Inlet
Yanakie Caravan Park
Tin Mine Cove
Mount Singapore (174m)
Tin Mine Cove
Mount Hunter (374m)
Entrance Station
Bennison Island
Chinaman Beach
Lighthouse Point
Long Island
Yanakie Isthmus
Mount Margaret (218m)
Three Mile Beach
Corner Island
Lower Barry Creek
Mount Roundback (316m)
Three Mile Point
Johnny Souey Cove
Johnny Souey Point
Millers Landing
Barry Creek
Monkey Point
Waratah Bay
Cotter's Lake (dry)
Wilsons Promontory Rd
Vereker Lookout
Vereker Range
Five Mile Rd
Five Mile Beach
Rabbit Island
Sheilback Island
Mount Vereker (638m)
Five Mile Peak
LA TROBE RANGE
Five Mile Beach
Darby River Car Park
Darby River
Mount Leonard (556m)
Mount La Trobe (755m)
The Cathedral
Tongue Point
Sparkes Lookout
Mount Bishop (319m)
Sealers Cove
Darby Saddle Car Park
Tidal River
Mount Ramsay (686m)
Sealers Cove
Norman Island
Squeaky Beach
Mt. Oberon Car Park
Windy Saddle (453m)
Refuge Cove
Refuge Cove
Norman Bay
Mount Oberon
Wilson Range
Little Waterloo
Cape Wellington
Oberon Bay
Oberon Bay
Mount Wilson (705m)
Waterloo Bay

**Wilsons Promontory Nat'l Park**
- - - Management Vehicles & Walking Track
······· Walking Track
— Sealed road

Great Glennie Island
Oberon Point
Boulder Ra.
Waterloo Point
N
Dannevig Island
Halfway Hut
Citadel Island
McHugh Island
Mount Norgate (419m)
Telegraph Track
Roaring Meg
South East Point
0    3 miles
0    3 kilometers
South West Point
Wattle Island
South Point
Fenwick Bight
Anser Island

## ✦ 🛈 PARK ACCESS AND TOURIST INFORMATION

Coming from Foster, turn left at the end of Main St onto the **Foster Promontory Rd,** which snakes 30km to the park entrance, nearly 10km past **Yanakie** (entry $8 per car; free if you have arranged for accommodations at **Tidal River,** but not for outstation campers). Without access to a car, the only transport option into the park is by the **Prom Postie,** run by Anne at the Foster Backpackers Hostel (see above), which delivers mail and passengers from **Foster.** (☎5682 6614. Departs Foster M-F 9am; returns from the Prom M-F 11am. $20 return; no entrance fee if traveling with the Postie.) Some touring companies offer day-trips into the park; try **Duck Truck Tours,** which carts people over from **Phillip Island.** (☎5952 2548. $99; see p. 545.)

From the entrance station, the park's only sealed road, **Wilsons Promontory Rd,** winds 30km along the Prom's western extremity, providing many opportunities to turn off for picnics, pictures, and hikes. The road ends at **Tidal River,** a township that does little justice to the park's natural splendor. Many take overnight hikes or daytrips from this area. During its busiest periods, the park runs a **free shuttle bus** between the Norman Bay carpark, at the far end of Tidal River, and the Mt. Oberon carpark (leaves Norman Bay every 30min. from 8am-7pm, arriving at Mt. Oberon for drop off and pickup 15min. later).

Visitors who wish to stay overnight, obtain a fishing license, or get weather updates, should go to the **Tidal River Information Centre,** at the end of the main road. The Centre also has exhibits and a video on the Prom's geology and diverse plant and animal populations. All visitors must register their intentions to bushwalk and camp with park officials here. (☎ 5680 9555. Open Nov.-Easter Sa-Th 8am-7:30pm, F 8am-9:30pm; Easter-Oct. daily 8am-5pm.) Tidal River also has the last toilets, pay phones, and food before setting off into the bush. During peak season, Tidal River's amenities include an **open-air cinema,** with a 9:15pm nightly screening of a recent release. Purchase tickets at the cinema 45min. before showtime ($7.50, children $5). A 24hr. **Blue Box** for contacting a ranger is outside the info center.

# ACCOMMODATIONS

Securing a place to spend the night at the Prom during the summer months is notoriously difficult, though significantly easier for overseas travelers than locals. While Victorian residents lottery for spots, the park reserves last-minute, first-come **campsites** for non-residents of Victoria at Tidal River (2 nights max; $15.50 peak, off-peak for up to 3 people $13.50). For outstation camping, there's usually no need to book in advance, but you must obtain a permit and pay nightly fees ($4.40, children $2.20). All sites have a one-night max. stay, except **Roaring Meg** campsite and northern sites (2-night max.). You can bounce from site to site, though this must be registered with the info center. Toilets in outstation sites have no toilet paper, and no sites are powered.

Finding an accommodation with a non-canvas roof in the summer months is as hard to come by as a good movie on an international flight, but it's worth a shot. Try to reserve three to six months in advance, and even sooner for summer weekends. There are ensuite **cabins** with kitchen and living room (singles and twins Sept.-early Apr. $115, late Apr.-Aug. $105); bunk-style **lighthouse units** (Su-F $36, Sa $56), and 4- to 6-bed **huts** ($44 and $66). Book through the **Tidal River Info Centre** (☎ 5680 9555; email wprom@parks.vic.gov.au).

# HIKING

To best experience the Prom's natural majesty, tackle a few bushwalking trails and take a dip in its crystal-clear water. Although most visitors sample the Prom in a day, allow three to five days to savor it. The information center's *Discovering the Prom* ($13) details the over-100km of trails that criss-cross the Prom, and *Down Under at the Prom* ($17) points to dive sites for scuba and snorkeling. One of the most popular swimming beaches is at **Norman Bay,** past Tidal River.

**SHORT HIKES.** Past the Yanakie entrance to the park, the first left leads to the **Five Mile Track Car Park,** accessing the less-visited northern reaches traversed mostly by overnight hikers. A short detour along the Five Mile Track leads to the **Miller's Landing Nature Walk.** The easy walk (4km; 1½hr.) leads through banksia woodlands to the dwarf mangroves and mudflats of Corner Inlet. Several short walks (1-2km) depart from Tidal River, including: **Whale Rock** (0.7km; 30min.), a loop track winding gradually uphill to a delightful view of Mt. Oberon; and **Loo-ern Track** (2km; 1hr.), a boardwalk designed for those with limited mobility, leading through swamp paperbark to an overlook. For a slightly longer hike, try **Squeaky**

**Beach Nature Walk** (5km; 1½hr.), which passes through dunes, coastal scrub, and beautiful granite outcroppings. Look for wombats in the scrub, and once on the beach, slide your feet to hear the remarkably uniform white-grained quartz sand squeak. **Lilly Pilly Gully Nature Walk** (4.7km; 3hr.), starting from the Lilly Pilly car-park 2km up the road from Tidal River, follows a mellow uphill through coastal woodlands into the rainforest. This walk can be extended by leaving from Tidal River (6.7km; 4hr.); the section between Tidal River and Lilly Pilly Gully is wheel-chair accessible. About 5 km up the main road is a turn-off for the Mt. Oberon car-park, where the **Mt. Oberon Nature Walk** begins. The walk (6.8km; 2-3hr.) climbs steadily up to the summit, leading to one of the best sunrise spots in the park.

**DAY-HIKES.** For more ambitious hikers, three incredible day hikes cover some of the most beloved spots in the Prom. In the southern half of the park, **Tongue Point Track** (11.2km; 4hr.) starts from Darby Saddle (6.7km north of Tidal River) and pro-ceeds, sometimes steeply, past two sweeping lookouts to a small granite peninsula with a stunning view of the coast. The **Oberon Bay Track** (12.4km; 5hr.) leaves from Tidal River, mirroring the scenic coastline along yellow sand beaches of the west-ern bays. In the opposite direction, departing from the Mt. Oberon carpark, the ⬛**Sealers Cove Track** (19km; 5-6hr.) takes you across nearly every environment in the Prom. This popular route passes through eucalypt, stringy bark, and Messmate forest, rising up to Windy Saddle, 3km from the carpark, before descending into Sealers Swamp and through fern gullies en route to **Sealers Cove**. The park bills this as one of the most spectacular beaches in the world—it's hard to disagree.

**OVERNIGHT HIKES.** The overnight hikes in the south are absolutely worth the time and extra preparation, as they allow hikers to savor the multitude of terrains and spectacular secluded spots. The most popular two- to three-day hike sweeps 36km around the eastern coastal areas along well-maintained trails to Sealers Cove (9.6km, see above), Refuge Cove (16.6km), and Waterloo Bay (24km). From Sealers, the track rises to a steep, stunning overlook of the sea before descending into Refuge Cove. This campsite is popular with **boaters** from around the world, and also offers **diving** opportunities. The next bit up Kersops Peak (2.3km) is chal-lenging, but short; it's worthwhile to take the 300m detour up to the summit, with views extending all the way to the lighthouse. The track then dips back down and shadows the coastline, where the varying hues of azure, sapphire, and turquoise water will continue to have you agape. Turning from the sea, you go along a flat section of boardwalks through swampy areas until meeting up with the **Telegraph Track** (29.4km), where it follows this dirt road up to the carpark. It is possible to do this walk in two days, but it's far more enjoyable to spend two nights—preferably at **Refuge Cove** and **Little Waterloo**—to spread the hiking out. There are toilets and drinking water at each site. And don't forget your bathers—the bays are great for **swimming** and offer a well-earned treat after a day on the track. To slip off the beaten path for a truly invigorating experience, try the **Lighthouse Walk** (33km). Departing the Mt. Oberon carpark, head south on the **Telegraph Track** past the **Half-way Hut** through stands of eucalypts. From here, a rugged walking trail through tea-tree groves, temperate rainforest, and wind-blown plateaux proceeds past **Roaring Meg** before making a final steep descent along the old telegraph line. The fury of gale and surf combine with the majestic 1858 vintage lighthouse to frame an unparalleled bushwalk. If you can get a bed at the lighthouse, it's doubly worth-while (bookings through Tidal River). The lighthouse can also be reached via a new track from Waterloo Bay (14.4km; 4½hr.), though this section is difficult and quite steep, allowing you to do both of these popular overnights routes in one trip.

# PORT ALBERT

Bring two things with you to Port Albert: an interest in maritime antiquity and a hunger for fish-and-chips. The oldest fishing town in Victoria, and one of the few still working, Port Albert is 50km east of Foster and 15km south of Yarram off the S. Gippsland Hwy (A440). Walk around town and soak up the salty seafaring aura.

The **Maritime Museum,** on Tarraville Rd (☎5183 2520), attests to the town's deep connection to the sea, containing details on the famous *Clonmel* shipwreck of 1841 (which led to the settlement of Port Albert), old navigational instruments, and a fabulous collection of sea-shells. Take a walk by the **Nooramunga Marine and Coastal Park,** which extends along the coast near town. This park protects a fragile wetland environment, full of marine sediments that support a wonderland of worms, sand fleas, burrowing crabs, mollusks, sea anemones, and other jelly-like translucent creatures. To access the park on foot or bike, pick up the **Old Port Trail** across from Port Albert Fish and Chips. The track winds toward Seabank along inlets and coastal wetlands (11.3km; 4hr. return). By car, look for the anchor on the roundabout outside of town and take the nearest road, labelled "No Through Road." Though unsealed, the first 2km to the park is adequate for 2WD vehicles.

The portside **Port Albert Hotel,** on Wharf St, claims to be the oldest licensed hotel in Victoria. Though perhaps showing its age, the hotel has a lovely veranda. (☎5183 2212. Bunks $15.) For something a bit newer, try **Port Albert Caravan Park,** 9 Bay St. (☎5183 2600. Sites from $14, on-site van $35, self-contained units from $52.) The ⬛**Port Albert Fish and Chips** shop (☎5183 2431), at the end of Wharf St, serves the best fish-and-chips in Australia. If you'd rather catch your dinner, rent **fishing** gear and a boat from **Winch House,** on Wharf St along the pier. (☎5183 2022. Open daily 6:30am-dusk. Tackle $5 per day; canoe $30; kayak $20.)

# YARRAM

Yarram's most outstanding feature is its proximity to the **Tara-Bulga National Park.** A 15km turn-off in Toora, about a third of the way between Foster and Yarram, will lead you to **Agnes Falls,** the highest single-span waterfall in Victoria, dropping 59m into the Agnes River. In the other direction, about 30km east of Yarram, you can access the southern portion of **Ninety Mile Beach,** an unusually long, and quite exceptional, stretch of white-sanded coastline extending past Lakes Entrance. To reach **Woodside Beach,** popular for **swimming** and **surfing,** follow the S. Gippsland Hwy to Woodside and turn right onto Woodside Beach Rd.

Yarram is 50km east of Foster on the South Gippsland Hwy, which turns into Commercial Rd as it passes through town. The **Toppa Coffee Lounge,** 275 Commercial Rd, sells V/Line **bus** tickets to **Melbourne** via **Foster.** (☎5182 6066. 3½hr.; departs M-Sa 7am, Su 2:35pm; $27.) The **Tourist Information Centre** is in the old Court House, at Commercial Rd and Rodgers St. (☎5182 6553. Open M-F 10am-4pm, Sa-Su 10am-2pm.) **Banks** and **ATMs** are everywhere. The **library,** on Grant St, has free **Internet access.** (☎5182 5135. Open M-Tu 2-6pm, Th-F 10am-6pm, Sa 10am-noon; book ahead.) **Post office:** a block from the info center, on the same side of Commercial Rd. (☎5182 5109. Open M-F 9am-5pm.) **Postal code:** 3971.

The accommodations in Yarram center leave much to be desired. Instead, head 1km south of town to the **Ship Inn Motel,** on the S. Gippsland Hwy. Though these pleasant, flowery rooms may be a bit over your budget, they're your best bet for a comfortable night's sleep. (☎5182 5588. Singles $55, doubles $65.) For food, the **Federal Coffee Palace,** 305 Commercial Rd, is definitely the hippest place in town, with cushioned chairs, books and board games. (☎5182 6464. Open W-F noon-10pm, Sa 9am-10pm, Su 9am-4pm. Great latte $2.20; chicken fillet with apricots and camembert $13.) There's an IGA **supermarket** inside the Yarram Plaza. (☎5182 6033. Open M-F 8am-6pm, Sa 8am-1pm.)

# NEAR YARRAM: TARRA-BULGA NATIONAL PARK

At Tarra-Bulga National Park, if it's a sizzler of a day, the fronds of overhanging fern trees nod their welcome and wave away the oppressive heat of the valley. Driving west on the South Gippsland Hwy, turn left at the edge of **Yarram,** following signs to the national park. From here, take either the **Tarra Valley Rd** through the Tarra Valley, or the unsealed **Balook Yarram Rd,** which passes through the Bulga Forest. Both roads connect to the perpendicular **Grand Ridge Rd,** forming a great loop through the forest. The ascent through the **Tarra Valley,** along a narrow and windy 25km stretch of sealed road, passes through lush fern and eucalypts, with occasional patches of yellow wildflowers. Unless you've got a 4WD, don't take any unmarked roads, as they are rarely patrolled and conditions are variable. About 20km up the road lies the superb **Tarra Falls,** visible just after getting out of the car. Another kilometer up the road at the Tarra Valley picnic area, follow the easy **Tarra Valley Rainforest Walk** (1.2km) through the rainforest to **Cyathea Falls.**

At the junction of the Grand Ridge Rd and the Balook Yarram Rd is the **Tarra Bulga Visitor Centre,** with maps and info on day walks and driving tracks. (☎5196 6166. Open Sa-Su and holidays 10am-4pm.) From here you can follow the Lyrebird Ridge Track to the Ash Track (1km) to access the **Fern Gully Nature Walk** (500m). This short walk is the site of the infamous **Suspension Bridge,** which enables you to stand high above a breathtaking fern gully housing birds, wallabies, bats, and bush rats. To reach the Fern Gully Walk directly, head down Grand Ridge Rd about 1km past the Visitor Centre to the Bulga carpark. For a slightly longer walk through the park, try the **Forest Track** (4.3 km; 1½hr.). Leaving from the Visitor Centre, this moderate loop goes through lush fern gullies into a stand of Hazel Pomaderries.

Tarra-Bulga fills a section of the **Strzelecki Ranges,** named after the neurotic Polish explorer Count **Paul Strzelecki.** During his 1840 expedition from New South Wales to the Victoria coast, the Count insisted on maintaining a direct line through any and all terrain by using a compass, sextant, and chronometer. His Aboriginal guide, **Charlie Tarra,** saved the expedition from starvation. The Tarra Valley is named for him ("bulga" is an Aboriginal word for mountain).

There is no bush camping in the park, but there are two **caravan parks** along the Tarra Valley Rd inside the forest. If you're coming into the park from Yarram, the first one you'll hit is the **Nangeela Tourist Park,** 1369 Tarra Valley Rd. (☎5186 1216. Sites for 2 $12-14; cabins for 2 $50.) About 2km further up the road, the **Tarra Valley Caravan Park,** 1385 Tarra Valley Rd, is slightly plusher. (☎5186 1283. Sites for 2 $12-14; cabins for 2-10 from $45.) Both parks have some powered sites, bathrooms, showers, laundry, game room, and a small grocer in the office.

## BAIRNSDALE

Though perhaps not a fascinating destination itself, Bairnsdale is a useful place to refuel before venturing into **Mitchell River National Park** or **the Australian Alps.** About 275km east of Melbourne and 35km west of Lakes Entrance, Bairnsdale is accessible by the Princes Hwy (A1), called **Main St** in town. Bairnsdale is the starting point of the **Great Alpine Rd,** a 300km drive that takes you through the **Australian Alps,** near the **Falls Creek Ski Resort,** to **Wangaratta.** You can also walk in the Alps on the **Australian Alps Walking Track,** which begins in Walhalla (approximately 50km from Bairnsdale) and goes all the way (655km) to Mt. Tennent, outside of Canberra. This massive bushwalk over many of the area's highest mountains can be completed in 10 weeks. For more info, call the **National Parks Service** (☎13 19 63).

**LEGENDS OF THE GUNAI** For at least 18,000 years, the Gunai (or Kurnai) Aboriginal people have inhabited Gippsland. According to legend, Borun, "the Pelican," was the first Gunai. He descended from the northwest mountains carrying his canoe on his head. As he crossed the Tribal River by Wayput (now Sale), a tapping noise began to follow him. Finally, he reached the ocean inlet, still bothered by the incessant tapping. When he put down the canoe, Borun found sitting in it the woman he would wed—Tuk, "the Musk Duck," who would become the mother of all Gunai people. In order to discourage their children from disobeying tribal laws, the Gunai told them fables. One explains the fallen link between Tasmania and the mainland (at Wilsons Promontory). One day, the story goes, two children at play removed a sacred object from the land and brought it back to their mother. The ground rapidly crumbled into the sea, breaking up families and drowning many Gunai. The moral of this story for you: don't remove anything from Australia's National Parks.

Bairnsdale has a **train station with no trains,** though there are plenty of V/Line **buses,** on MacLeod St (☎5452 1711), across from the tourist office and down Pyke St. Buses run to: **Melbourne** (4hr.; 4 per day M-F, 1 per day Sa-Su; $35) via **Sale** where you switch to an actual train (1hr.); and to **Lake's Entrance** (45min., 1 per day, $8). For **bike rental,** visit Marriott's Cycles, 209 Main St, opposite McDonald's. (☎5152 3783. Open M-F 8am-5:30pm, Sa 8am-12:30pm. $15 per day.) **Bairnsdale Visitors Centre,** 240 Main St, has a knowledgeable staff. (☎5152 3444. Open daily 9am-5pm.) In the same building, you can surf the **Internet** at the **Gateway Café** (1hr. $8; open M-F 7:30am-5pm, Sa-Su 9am-5pm). **Post office:** corner of Nicholson and Baily St. (☎5152 4152. Open M-F 9am-5pm.) **Postal code:** 3875.

The accommodations in Bairnsdale are less than exceptional. Try camping in Mitchell River National Park or staying at the **Espas Arts Resort** on Raymond Island (see below). Locally, you can try **Mitchell Gardens Caravan Park,** at the east end of Main St, where there are clean showers, kitchen, laundry, and a pool. (☎5152 4654. Sites $13; cabins $35.) If you're desperate, there is a hostel in town, **Bairnsdale Backpackers,** 119 MacLeod St (☎5152 5097). IGA **supermarket** is behind McDonald's (open M-W 8am-7pm, Th 8am-8pm, F-Sa 8am-9pm, Su 9am-7pm).

## NEAR BAIRNSDALE: RAYMOND ISLAND

If you're looking for a bit of solitude, Raymond Island is the place. **Buses** run from Bairnsdale to nearby Paynesville (30min.; 4-5 per day M-F, 1 per day Sa; $6), from where you can take a 2min. ferry to the island. (☎(0418) 51 79 59. Ferry runs Su-Th 7am-7pm and 9:30-9:55pm, F-Sa 7am-7:10pm and 10:30pm-11:55pm. Cars $3.)This tiny island serves as a wonderful retreat for bushwalking, cycling, and spotting koalas. And though Raymond Island has no stores, there is the good fortune of the **Espas Arts Resort,** a sparkling new budget facility. From the ferry, head left toward the yellow complex. (☎5156 7275. Bunks $15. Call ahead.)

## MITCHELL RIVER NATIONAL PARK

The Mitchell River flows from the alpine high country down to the Gippsland Lakes, bisecting the 11,900 hectares of rainforest that comprise the park. Canoeing, rafting, and hiking through the **Mitchell River Gorge** is the best way to see the park's splendors. To reach the park from Bairnsdale (45km), turn right about 3km west of town onto Lindenow Rd, which becomes Dargo Rd; a number of well-labelled right-hand turns leads from here. Most roads through the park are unsealed and navigated more safely in a 4WD.

In addition to visiting the several gorges and high cliffs looming over the river, most daytrippers venture into the park to pay respect to the **Den of Nargun.** Gunai legend describes Nargun as a giant stone female creature who destroyed intruders with spears or boomerangs and abducted kids who strayed from camp. The cave is said to have been used for initiation ceremonies for women. To reach the Den, turn right off Dargo Rd onto Waller Rd, and then follow a 15min. downhill track through the forest. Sit by the side of the water and absorb this site's mystical energy, but please do not enter the cave because it contains fragile stalagmites.

There are two places to **camp** in the park. One is at the far north end, in Angusvale, reached by turning right off Dargo Rd onto the unsealed Mitchell Dam Rd (free; river water only; pit toilets). The other, at **Billy Goat Bend,** is accessible only by foot; turn right off Dargo Rd onto Billy Goat Bend Rd, follow to picnic area, and then hike in about 1km (free). Bairnsdale Parks Victoria (☎5152 0400) has info.

## METUNG

There's something about Metung. Perhaps it is the uniformity of structure and color in the architecture, or their stylish oblique plane of the condos with sun-streaked sliding doors opening onto a blue lake. Or it may just be that it's easy to lose track of time strolling by the yachts or lying on the beach. Whatever the reason, Metung is a perfect place to rig up and unwind. From Bairnsdale, drive 20km east on the Princes Hwy (A1) and 10km south on Metung Rd (C606). A good diversion in this quiet hamlet is to hire a boat; visit **Metung Cruisers** at the jetty. (☎5156 2208. Open daily 8:30am-5pm. Three-meter inboard with half-cabin half-day $50, full-day $90.) Most people take a boat out to the beaches and wilderness islands; the bird observatory **Rotamah Island** (☎5156 6398) is a full-day trek. If you want to stay closer, **Back Beach**, along the coast in town, is a popular area for swimming, prawning, floundering, waterskiing, and parasailing. **Legend Rock**, in the waters by the yacht club, is the last standing of three rocks that, according to Gunai/Kurnai Aboriginal lore, were hunters turned to stone for hoarding their spoils.

Though not a tourist hot-spot, Metung is a popular holiday retreat, so there are many more up-scale rental units than budget accommodations. Try the **Metung Tourist Park**, at Mairburn and Stirling Rd, a right off Metung Rd just before town. (☎5156 2306. Open daily 8am-9pm. Tent sites $15-25; cabins for 4 $70-120. Reserve 5 months in advance for Christmas.) When hunger strikes, you'll find an ice-creamery, bakery, and a posh café in town; pick up essentials at the **Village Store** on Metung Rd (open daily 7:30am-6pm). The **post office** is across the street from the general store (open M-F 9am-5pm). **Postal code:** 3904.

# LAKES ENTRANCE

Lakes Entrance is the unofficial capital of the Gippsland Lakes region, the largest inland waterway in the Southern Hemisphere. Lakes Entrance is extremely touristy, crowded during summer holidays, and full of caravan parks and mini-golf courses. Fortunately, its expansive beaches, excellent fishing, and numerous boating opportunities enable land-locked visitors to get out of town and into the water.

## ▐ ▐ TRANSPORT AND PRACTICAL INFORMATION

V/Line **buses** leave near the post office and head to **Melbourne** (5hr., 2 per day, $42) via **Bairnsdale** (30min., 2 per day, $8); and **Narooma**, NSW (5½hr., 1 per day, $49). Greyhound runs to **Melbourne** (daily 12:20am, $47). For reservations, call **Esplanade Travel**, 309 Esplanade. (☎5155 2404. Open M-F 9am-5pm, Sa 9am-noon.)

The Princes Hwy, called the **Esplanade** in town, becomes a waterfront strip full of less-than-quaint shops. The **Lakes Entrance Visitors Centre,** on the western end of the Esplanade, has plenty of regional information. (☎5155 1966. Open daily 9am-5pm.) The part of town a few blocks east from the visitors center houses most **banks** and **ATMs**. The **library**, 55 Palmers Rd, up the hill at the east end of town, offers **free Internet** access. (☎5150 9100. Open M-F 8:30am-5pm. Book ahead.) **Post office:** 287 Esplanade (open M-F 9am-5pm, Sa 9am-noon). **Postal code:** 3909.

## ▌ ACCOMMODATIONS

Beach camping may be fun, but it's illegal, and the area is frequently patrolled.

**▨ Riviera Backpackers (YHA),** 5 Clarkes Rd (☎5155 2444; e-mail riviera@net-tech.com.au). Off the eastern end of the Esplanade. Ask the bus to stop near the hostel, or arrange for station pickup in advance. This excellent motel-style YHA earns high marks for its sparkling new facilities and off-street parking. Large lounge with TV, solar-heated pool, billiards, bike rental (1hr. $1, full-day $5), laundry, kitchen, Internet (12min. $2), and safe storage. Reception 24hr. Heated dorms, twins, and doubles all $15 per person, weekly $78. Book a few weeks ahead for Dec.-Jan.

**Echo Beach Holiday Park,** 33 Roadknight St (☎5155 2238). Across from the Esplanade. Four-star park with kitchen, BBQ, laundry, spa, TV, and billiards. Reception 8am-10pm. Powered sites $26, off-season $15; cabins $80-100, off-season $45-60.

**Silversands Tourist Park,** 33 Myer St (☎5155 2343). A few blocks down from the Esplanade. Friendly and clean; travelers can opt to share a van with others. Pool, kitchen, BBQ, spa. Sites $9, for 2 $16; beds $15; doubles $28.

# ◘ FOOD

The Esplanade is overflowing with take-away food shops, and the hotels in town tend to have good bistros in the mid-price range. Get **groceries** at Foodworks, 30-34 Myer St. (☎5155 1354. Open daily 8am-9pm in summer, 8am-7pm otherwise). Or for **bulk foods,** try Lakes Health Bar, 10 Myer St (open M-F 8am-5pm, Sa 9am-noon).

**Caffe 567,** 567 Esplanade (☎5155 1144). Some of the best coffee this side of the Pacific. Sip a café latte ($2.40), while indulging in a devilishly divine dessert, like cherry cheesecake ($4.50). Or enjoy sun-dried tomato and olive bread ($3.50) and—of course—a bottle of beer. Open daily 11am-10pm.

**Pinocchio Inn Restaurant,** 569 Esplanade (☎5155 2565). Noch's usually has a spe-cial—all-you-can-eat pasta or 2 large pizzas for $20. 10% YHA discount. Open daily in summer noon-3am; otherwise Su-M 5-10pm, Tu-Th 5-11pm, F-Sa 5pm-midnight.

**Riviera Ice Cream Parlour** (☎5155 2972). Opposite the footbridge on the Esplanade. Award-winning farm-produced ice cream in 35 flavors. Try the "frog on a log." Generous portions $2-4. Open daily 9am-5pm, summer until 11pm.

# ◉ ◮ SIGHTS AND ACTIVITIES

The **Kalimna Lookouts** above town at the western end afford a perfect view of the patchwork Gippsland Lakes. The lake's biggest attraction is its expansive beach-front. To reach **Ninety Mile Beach,** cross the footbridge opposite Myer St. From the snack bar and toilet area, a walking track (1hr.) follows the coast to the man-made boat entrance to the deep, blue waters of the Bass Strait. Most visitors **hire boats** from one of the jetties along Marine Pde. Try **Victor Hire Boats,** on the north arm of Marine Pde. (☎5155 3988. 8-passenger half-cabins 1hr. $20, each extra hour $15.) A bit further down, **Portside Boat Hire** has more options. (☎5155 3832. 6- to 8-passen-ger half-cabins 1hr. $25, 3hr. $50. 12-passenger BBQ boat $30 per hr. plus fuel; canoes $8 per hr.) Both places are generally open during daylight hours. **Barrier Landing** is the western strip of land created by the entrance. Only accessible by boat, the landing has great fishing and rests by both a lake beach and a **surf beach.** Contact **Mulloway,** on the Marine Pde, for a 3hr. **fishing** trip. (☎(014) 94 31 54. Trips 9am-noon and 1-4pm. $25.) To find out where to fish, pick up the *East Gippsland Fishing Map* ($7) at the visitors center. For action on land, the **Lakes Entrance Wil-derness Trail Rides,** on the corner of Princes Hwy and Bruces Rd in Kalimna West, 10km west of Lakes Entrance, provides horse-riding in the Colquhoun Forest. (☎5156 3288. 1hr. beginner bush ride $22, 2hr. $40; overnights also arranged.)

The **Wyanga Park Winery,** on Baades Rd, is less active and more alcohol-related. Drive there by following the signs from Myer St or take a cruise to the vineyard on *The Corque* for lunch or dinner at **Henry's Café.** (☎5155 1508. Open Su-W 9am-5pm, Th-Sa 9am-8pm for free tastings. Cruises 2-5hr. including tea or meal $18-45; book ahead.) **Lake Tyers Boat Trips,** 10km east of town in Lake Tyers, offer relaxing and virtually silent afternoon cruises on Victoria's largest electric boat. (☎5155 1283. $15, children $9.) The **Griffith Sea Shell Museum,** just east of Centrepoint on the Esplanade, is a fantastically bizarre rainy-day stop with shells in an unbelievable number of shapes, colors, and sizes. Don't miss the psychedelic, black-light coral exhibit. (☎5155 1538. Open daily 9am-5pm. $4, children $2.)

# NEAR LAKES ENTRANCE: BUCHAN

Just 58km north of Lakes Entrance and 50km northeast of Bruthen, Buchan (rhymes with "truckin'"; pop. 200) is surrounded by rolling hills at the base of the Snowy River Valley. Buchan is best known for its spectacular Buchan Caves.

**◪◪ TRANSPORT AND PRACTICAL INFORMATION.** Since no public trans-port serves Buchan, most backpackers arrive on touring buses, such as Oz Experi-ence (☎(1300) 30 00 28) or Wayward Buses (☎(1800) 88 28 23), bound for

**Melbourne** or **Sydney.** When driving from Lakes Entrance, take the Princes Hwy 23km east to Nowa Nowa, turn left onto C620, then right onto C608, following signs to Buchan and the caves.

Just south of the Buchan Caves, the small town center contains a **general store** with basic food and **tourist information** (open M-F and holidays 8:30am-6pm, Sa 8:30am-1pm, Su 9am-1pm). The **Parks Victoria office** has the most information on camping and the national parks area, as well as tickets for the caves and reservations for the 100 closely-packed campsites by the main attraction. (☎5155 9264. Sites $10-13, powered $14-17.) The **Buchan Outreach-Resource Centre,** 6 Davidson St, over the bridge onto Orbost Rd and then right again onto Davidson, has **Internet access.** (☎5155 9294. Open M-Th 9am-4:30pm. Internet 1hr. $3.) **Post office:** across the street from the general store (open M-F 9am-5pm). **Postal code:** 3885.

**▐▜▐▛ ACCOMMODATIONS AND FOOD.** The **▨Buchan Lodge,** left after the bridge on Saleyard Rd just north of the town center, provides outstanding budget accommodation in a beautifully constructed wooden building. The grand main room houses a lounge, dining area, wheelchair facilities, and a well-equipped kitchen. Guests can swim, watch for platypi in the Buchan River, play volleyball, practice the piano, or just relax and have a laugh with Dick, the proprietor, and Casey, his dog. (☎5155 9421. Bunks $17, breakfast included; complimentary tea and coffee all-day.) **Willow Café,** the muralled house a few doors down from the post office, has tasty meals. (☎5155 9387. Open daily 9am through dinner.) Afterward, amble across the street to the **Caves Hotel,** a.k.a. the **pub.** (☎5155 9203. Open M-Sa 11am-between 10pm and 1am, Su noon-8pm.)

**▩ SIGHTS.** The 260-hectare **Buchan Caves** reserve just past the town center before the bridge may be up to 25 million years old, might reach depths of over 50m, and will definitely dazzle their entrants with stalactites and stalagmites. The two big caves, **Fairy Cave** and **Royal Cave,** are open for guided tours (1hr.; 3-5 tours daily 9:30am-3:30pm; $10, children $5, families $25). For a bit more of a challenge without all the railings and floodlights, you can book a group tour of Federal Cave ($15; min. 5 people; book through Parks Victoria or Buchan Lodge).

# SNOWY RIVER NATIONAL PARK

Shrouded in mythic Australiana, Snowy River National Park surrounds the once mighty Snowy River with jagged hills dressed in green. This is some of the most extreme wilderness in Australia. The rugged beauty of the landscape inspired Banjo Paterson, author of *Waltzing Matilda*, to pen his bush ballad *The Man From Snowy River*, which idealizes the harsh bush life and those who choose to take on the challenge. Once an underwater landmass, the park stretches across 98,700 hectares, and includes vastly distinct ecosystems, from rainforest to rainshadow. Many rare species call it home, including the brush-tailed rock wallaby and the tiger quoll. Whether you bushwalk, white-water raft, camp, or canoe, the Snowy River and its surrounding mountainside remain an impressive wonder.

**▐⊏ TRANSPORT**

A car can circumnavigate the park in 6hr. The road is mostly unsealed, and becomes increasingly windy and narrow as it heads north. It is suitable for 2WD vehicles, depending on your confidence as a driver, and weather and road conditions. Call **Parks Victoria** in Orbost (☎5161 1222) or Buchan (☎5155 9264) for up-to-date reports. If you are driving from Buchan, you can take either the Buchan-Gelantipy Rd (C608) through the countryside, or the unsealed Tulloch Ard Rd through the forest, both of which end in Gelantipy. To reach the Tulloch Ard Rd, head north out of Buchan and take a right on Orbost Rd, continuing straight on Basin Rd, then left on Tulloch Ard Rd. The Buchan-Gelantipy Rd leads through

**THE MAN FROM SNOWY RIVER** The wild brumbies of the Snow Mountains and the hard men who braved the unforgiving land inspired the legendary Australian ballad, The Man from Snowy River. A.B. Paterson, writing under the pen name of Banjo, wove the story of a young horseman who outrode even the most experienced of mountain riders to round up a herd of wild mountain horses. While Banjo wasn't writing with a particular rider in mind, once the ballad was released, dozens of stories came pouring in—as he had expected—about men exactly fitting the description. It is widely believed in the Upper Murray country in Victoria that Jack Riley was the man forever immortalized in the epic tale. The ballad stands as a tribute to all bold mountain riders who conquered the harsh territory and tamed its beasts.

**Wulgulmerang,** the last place to get petrol and supplies until you reach Bonang east of the park. About 1km down the road, take the right fork onto Bonang-Gelantipy Rd, which follows a steep descent to MacKillop Bridge, and continues east until its intersection with Bonang Main Rd. You can either take this all the way to Orbost, or turn right onto Yalmy Rd to reach the eastern sections of the park. **Eastour,** out of Orbost, drives people through the Snowy River region. (☎5154 2969. 1-day $118; for more info see **Errinundra National Park,** p. 611.)

## ACCOMMODATIONS

The **Karoonda Park YHA,** 1½hr. from the Princes Hwy and 40km north of Buchan on the Buchan-Gelantipy Rd (C608), has a swimming pool, ping-pong, billiards, darts, tennis, bar, wheelchair facilities, and Internet access. After two nights as a paying guest, useful hands can stay longer as farm workers in exchange for room and board. The YHA has many adventure options: overnight rafting trips (seasonal; $110, backpackers $75); overnight horseback trips ($110, backpackers $75); abseiling (intro $10, full 40m $25); and indoor rock climbing ($4). (☎5155 0220. Rooms $16, non-YHA $18, with board $30; non-backpackers $45. Motel units: singles $25; doubles $45.) About 30km farther north along the dirt track en route to Suggan Buggan and Jindabyne NSW, is the tranquil mountain retreat of **Candlebark Cottage,** at "Springs" along the Snowy River-Jindabyne Rd. On a hill 1km from the main house, this secluded cottage sleeps 8 with a double bed and six loft bunks. Popular with cyclists and families, the cottage is ideal for bushwalking, trout fishing, or winter expeditions. (☎5155 0263. $25, for 2 $50, each extra person $20.) The most popular places to **camp** within the park are **MacKillop Bridge, Raymond Falls,** and **Hicks Campsite.** Raymond Falls and Hicks Campsite can be reached off Yalmy Rd, on dirt tracks suitable for 2WD. All sites have pit toilets, and only MacKillop Bridge has a fee ($8). Camping is also allowed away from designated sites.

## SIGHTS AND HIKING

The region surrounding the Snowy River is well worth a few days exploration. From Buchan along Tulloch Ard Rd, start your journey at Ash Saddle, halfway to Gelantipy. From here, the Betts Creek Track (1-2km; 30min.) begins an easy loop through a magnificent stand of massive, old-growth mountain ash. Follow the Betts Creek 4WD track to the sign for Snowy River National Park, then look on your left for a narrow trail leading through a break in the trees. Continuing further north, the Seldom Seen Track is a left-hand turn 15km north of Gelantipy. This 7km uphill track is suitable for 4WD vehicles or walkers only, and leads to the Mt. Seldom Seen Fire Tower. If the platform is locked for viewing, the base still provides an impressive panoramic view.

Heading into the park on Bonang-Gelantipy Rd, the first sight is Little River Falls. A 400m walking track leads to a viewing platform. Returning to the main road, just over the bridge, a sign for Alpine National Park leads left to a steep unsealed road.

This road goes to Hanging Rock, or World's End, one of the most fantastic and least known lookouts in the park. To reach Hanging Rock, turn left after the bridge (Milky Creek Track), left at Rocky River Ridge Track, and left again at Hanging Rock Track (5km, 4WD vehicles only). The rock is a 10min. descent, jutting out over a 400m valley with a 270° view of the countryside. Returning to the main road, 1km further into the park lies the 400-million-year-old Little River Gorge, the steepest gorge in Victoria (500m). A 400m trail leads down to the gorge from the carpark. MacKillop Bridge, spanning the Snowy at the north of the park, is the starting point of the most traveled (which is not a lot) walking track in the park. The Silver Mine Walking Track (18km; 6hr.) allows glimpses of the glimmer of silver in the surrounding hills, and spectacular views of the river and mountains to the west. The track starts along the 4WD Deddick Track, passing through native pine stands, rising steadily to viewpoints, then dropping down on a walkers-only track as it follows the banks of the Snowy. There is a campsite here for overnight hikers. The walk ascends again to a lookout before heading back down toward the bridge. For the less ambitious, the Snowy River Track (1.5km; 30min.), leaving from MacKillop Bridge, is a self-guided nature walk through the forest and then along the Snowy.

**MacKillop Bridge** is the second structure to span the banks of the Snowy. The original bridge rose 22m above the river, but on the day before the scheduled opening, the great river flooded it out, showing the bridge who was boss. The current bridge soars 30m above the luxuriously warm and clear waters, though damming for hydroelectricity has cut water flow to less than 5% of its original levels; it is unlikely the Snowy will ever tackle another bridge. This is the source of some debate in the vicinity, as community activists rally to "Let the Snowy Flow Again!" Even so, the beauty depicted in the legendary film *The Man From Snowy River* (actually filmed in Mansfield, p. 588) is only slightly muted. Whitewater rafting, canoeing, and kayaking are quite popular, water levels permitting. Contact Snowy River Expeditions, run out of Karoonda Park YHA (see **Accommodations,** above).

## ORBOST AND AROUND

Orbost is a logging town 60km northeast of Lakes Entrance that mostly serves only as a pitstop on the way to nearby beaches and national parks. About an hour from Orbost are two worthy sights, neither of which gets many visitors. To the north, **Errinundra National Park** houses Victoria's largest stand of rainforest. To the south, **Cape Conran** offers beautiful beaches away from the tourist hubbub. Ensuring minimal tourism, no buses go to either.

V/Line **buses** run to Orbost from **Melbourne** (5½hr., 1-2 per day, $47); **Bairnsdale** (1½hr., 1-2 per day, $19); and **Canberra** (5hr., 2 per week, $47); buy tickets at **Orbost Travel Centre,** 86 Nicholson St (☎5154 1481; open M-F 9am-5:30pm). By car, Orbost is just off the Princes Hwy via Lochiel St or Salisbury St; both exits intersect with **Nicholson St.**

The **Snowy River Orbost Visitors Centre,** on Lochiel St, just off the Princes Hwy, creates an all-senses-activating experience, including comparative forest displays, an audiovisual show, info on East Gippsland's national parks, and two outdoor paths that snake through manicured rainforest. (☎5154 2424. Open daily 9am-5pm.) In town, there are **ATMs;** the **Business Centre library,** just off Nicholson on Ruskin St, with **free Internet** (☎5150 9100; open M-F 8:30am-5pm); and a **post office,** on the corner of Nicholson and McLeod St (open M-F 9am-5pm). **Postal Code:** 3888.

Orbost is not the most picturesque of Gippsland's towns, but it is a reasonable place to stay if Cape Conran is full. Try the **Orbost Club Hotel,** 63 Nicholson St, an average budget stay with standard Australian-Chinese menu options (☎5154 1003. Singles $20; doubles $25.) The **Snowy River Kingfruit Shopping Complex,** 28 Salisbury St, is the best option for food and supplies. (☎5154 1577. Open M-Sa 8am-5:30pm.) Or try **Foodway,** on the corner of Browning and Raymond St. (☎5154 1206. Open M-Th and Sa 8:30am-6:30pm, F 8:30am-9pm, Su 9am-6:30pm.) The **Snowy River Caf,** 100 Nicholson St, has basic cheap food. (☎5154 1054. Open M-Sa 7:30am-5pm.)

# ERRINUNDRA NATIONAL PARK

Normally, cool rainforests like the Errinundra are dominated by ancient myrtle beeches, as in the Otway Ranges of southwestern Victoria. Here, however, black olive berry and cinnamon-scented sassafrass cover the forest floor, while a wet eucalypt overstory extends through much of Errinundra Plateau. Approach the forest either by the winding Bonang Rd from the north (from Snowy River), or by the Princes Hwy from the south. About 11km south of Bonang and 54km east of Orbost, these roads intersect with the two ends of Errinundra Rd, which leads into the park. Most of the roads in the park are unsealed, but navigable in a 2WD vehicle on a good day. However, they can be closed after a lot of rain; call the **Parks Victoria** office in Orbost. (☎5161 1222. Open M-F 8am-5pm.) There are a few operators in Orbost with tours to Errinundra, but they tend to be pricey. **Eastour** leads trips upon request, including an Errinundra 4WD day tour. (☎5154 2969. $118.)

To tackle the park independently, get a map and the *Guide to Walks and Tours* at the info center in Orbost and inquire about which tracks are in good condition. Most visitors make their first stop at **Errinundra Saddle,** where Errinundra Rd passes through the plateau. For more of an uphill challenge, climb to the top of **Mt. Ellery** more than 1000m above sea level for a grand view of the forest (2.5km return). To get there, take Errinundra Rd to Big River Rd at the Mt. Morris picnic area, and follow signs to Mt. Ellery. The **Coastal Range** track (25km; 6hr.) is an easy-moderate day trip along an old 4WD track that shows off the forest's unique features. Farther down the road, you'll hit the **Goonmirk Rocks** track (1km; 30min.), which leads through mountain plum pines, silver wattle, and in springtime, the red flowers of the Gippsland waratah. The most popular place to **camp** near the park is **Ada River,** on the southern section of Errinundra Rd. If you want to be within the park, go to **Frosty Hollow,** a remote camping area in the park's eastern reaches; take Bonang Rd to Gap Rd to Gunmark Rd to Goonmirk Rocks Rd to Hensleigh Creek Rd. Both locations are **free** and have pit toilets and a water source.

# CAPE CONRAN

Cape Conran and its Coastal Park are just 35km southeast of Orbost through Marlo. This area offers a solitary and rugged melange of dunes, heath, wetlands, swamps, and woods. From Orbost, go south down Nicholson St to **Marlo-Cape Conran Rd** and follow it to the end. From points farther east, turn left off the Princes Hwy onto Cabbage Tree Rd, 30km east of Orbost, and avoid the right fork to Marlo. The road ends at the Marlo-Cape Conran Rd.

Coming from Orbost, there are some especially serene spots on the road past **Marlo.** One of the best is **French's Narrows,** where the Snowy River meets the sea, about 5km east of Marlo. Two thin strips of land divide the murky river's end from its shallow estuary and the breaks of the Bass Strait. The variety of birds—pelicans, herons, swamp hens, and more—is astounding. Five kilometers farther down the road is **Point Ricardo,** a secluded beach popular for fishing. A short jaunt from the accommodations options is the main **East Cape Beach.** There are two primary walking options; both begin at the carpark on the beach at the end of the road, where there is a map. The mainly coastal **Dock Inlet Walk** is for the fit and ambitious (25km; 6-8hr.). The **Cape Conran Nature Trail** goes inland (2.5km; 1hr.). Because of occasional **flooding,** check with rangers (☎5154 8438) before setting out. The **Yeerung River** is popular for **fishing** and **swimming.** The best places to **swim** are **Sailors Grave** (East Cape Beach) and **Salmon Rocks** (near West Cape Beach).

If you plan to spend the night on the Cape itself, the only options are the Parks Victoria **cabins** or **camping** at **Banksia Bluff,** left off Cape Conran Rd onto Yeerung River Rd just before East Cape Beach. The eight self-contained cabins are comfortable, and one is handicapped accessible. Bring sleeping gear, towels, and food, though the Marlo supermarket drops by daily around 11:30am with groceries.

(☎5154 8438. Cabins for 4 $66, peak $96. Book well in advance.) **Campsites,** though more plentiful, are also in demand (sites for 4 $12, peak $16). If they're booked, try the **Burbang Caravan Park,** tucked in the forest about 3km back up the road toward Marlo. (☎5154 8219. Sites $12-14, vans for 6 $26-40, new cabins for 6 $50-80.)

# CROAJINGOLONG NATIONAL PARK

Tickling Victoria's eastern coastline from the New South Wales border to Sydenham Inlet is Croajingolong ("crow-JING-a-long") National Park. Scamper amid boulders lodged into the park's sandy beaches, frolic in one of the rivers that empties into the ocean, hike out to (and maybe even stay at) the lighthouse, or tumble down one of the massive sand dunes. This phenomenal national park, recognized by UNESCO as a World Biosphere Reserve, extends nearly 100km and covers 87,500 hectares. While the park gets busy in the peak season, it remains uncrowded the rest of the year, and there's always plenty of space to find your own stretch of sand or heathland.

## GATEWAY TOWNS: CANN RIVER AND MALLACOOTA

East of Lakes Entrance, the coast of Victoria becomes a seemingly endless stretch of wilderness punctuated by secluded lakes and estuarine inlets. The Princes Hwy surrenders the coast to this length of wild and retreats 10-20km inland. The highway passes through Cann River and Genoa before crossing the border into New South Wales; a smaller highway winds south to Mallacoota. Cann River and Mallacoota are good bases for a venture into the park if you are unprepared to camp.

**CANN RIVER.** Cann River is a one-road-town with nary a red light to stop the **bus** to **Melbourne** (7hr.; 1 per day M, Th, holiday Sa; $49) or **Canberra** (4hr., same schedule, $39). The handy **Parks Victoria Information Centre,** on the Princes Hwy near the east end of town, has info on accommodations and the park's road conditions. (☎5158 6351. Open daily 9am-5pm, shorter hours off-peak.) **Cann River Hotel,** on the Princes Hwy toward the west of town, is a standard pubstay. (☎5158 6221. Singles $20.) **Pelican Point Coffee Lounge,** a few doors down from the Info Centre, offers perfect pre-wilderness meals. (☎5158 6328. Open daily 9am-4:30pm.) There is a **supermarket** across from the hotel (open M-F 8am-6pm, Sa 8am-1pm, Su 9am-1pm).

**MALLACOOTA.** Mallacoota stays true to its slogan as "Victoria's hidden treasure"—public transportation approaches only as close as **Genoa,** 23km north on the Princes Hwy. The town does, however, have a **Parks Victoria Office,** on the corner of Buckland and Allan Dr. (☎5158 0219. Open M-F 9:30am-3:30pm, closed noon-1pm.) A 24hr. **laundromat** is at 57 Maurice Ave. **Post office:** on Maurice Ave (open M-F 9am-5pm, Sa 9-11am during holidays). **Postal Code:** 3892.

The **Mallacoota Lodge YHA,** 51-55 Maurice Ave, is a motel-style hostel connected to a bistro and a pub that fills after 9pm. (☎5158 0455. Bunks $13, non-YHA $16.) There is also the massive, 600-site **Mallacoota Camp Park,** at the bottom of Maurice Ave on Allan Dr, with waterfront spots looking out at the Howe Range. (☎5158 0300. Sites $12-18, powered $15-22.) There are two **supermarkets** at the top of Maurice Ave (both open daily 8:30am-6:30pm). For eats, your best bet is **Corner Café and Take-Away,** 43 Maurice Ave, which uses many ingredients from their farm in Genoa. (☎5158 0998. Open M-Sa 9am-3:30pm, longer holiday hours. Meals $4-5.)

**Scotty's Boat Charter** offers exceptionally reasonably priced fishing trips. (☎5158 0597. 3hr. trips $25; available Dec.-Apr.) For the best **swimming,** head to **Quarry Beach,** clearly marked on Betka Rd 1km after the road becomes unsealed.

## SIGHTS AND HIKING

If you're unprepared to tackle the bush alone, the best way to navigate the park from Mallacoota is with **Natural Adventures,** which coordinates activities from **kayaking** and bushwalking to 4WD adventures and evening spotlight walks. (☎5158

0166. Full-day $100, including everything. Self-guided kayak trip $45.) If you are going solo, your first stop should be the **Parks Victoria Office** in Cann River or Mallacoota (see above) to pick up maps and check the road conditions.

From Cann River it's a 45km drive down an unsealed road to the **Thurra** and **Mueller Rivers,** where you can splash about, head to the beach, or ▒camp ($12 per night). The campgrounds are now run by the folks at Point Hicks Lighthouse, so Parks Victoria has no info on availability. Both campgrounds have fireplaces, pit toilets, and river water; Thurra is more popular because of its private sites and overnight parking. From Thurra River there are also several worthwhile bushwalks. Highlights include the 2.2km easy walk out to **Point Hicks Lighthouse,** built in 1888, with a great beach to **swim** at on the way. You can also stay at one of two cottages beside the lighthouse. (☎5158 4268. Cottages for 8 $160-190. Linen $10. Call to arrange vehicle access.) Another great walk (4km; 2hr.) leads through tea-tree forest to 150m high dunes, the second highest in the Southern Hemisphere. There are no sign-posts in the dunes, however, so you've either got to play Hansel and Gretel with your footprints on the way back, or return along the river.

In between Cann River and Genoa, there is the turn-off for **Wingan Inlet,** another campsite with popular bushwalking. These sites also have fireplaces, pit toilets, a water source, and fantastic fishing (inquire at Parks Office for permit; sites $10-12). Out of Wingan, there is the idyllically named Lake Elusive Walk (4km 2hr.), which heads to the lake through **wildflowers.**

Fifteen kilometers southwest of Mallacoota, heading out along Betka Rd, is the **Shipwreck Creek Campsite** (fireplaces, pit toilets, limited tank water; sites $7.50-10). While there aren't as many bushwalking tracks out of this site, you can always head out to the beach for the day (not a recommended swimming beach), or start the **Wilderness Coast Walk.** This walk takes you along the beautiful, sandy shoreline, punctuated by grassy outcroppings and immense algae-coated boulders at the water's edge. There are 10 campsites along the 70km trek, starting with Shipwreck Creek and terminating at Bemm River. Do a piece, or, if you're lucky, do it all. To minimize impact on the environment, all overnight hikers must receive a **permit** from the Parks Victoria office in Cann River or Mallacoota before hitting the trail.

## ▓ OFF CROAJINGOLONG: GABO ISLAND

To really head off the beaten path, create a wave to **Gabo Island,** 13km from Mallacoota. Connected to the mainland until the isthmus eroded away at the turn of the century, Gabo Island's vibrant, exotic red granite composes Victoria's easternmost isle. Quarried from the island in a Herculean feat in 1862, the **lighthouse** (Australia's second-tallest at 47.5m) continues to steer ships clear of the coast. Gabo Island also houses the world's largest colony of **Little Penguins,** with over 40,000 adult birds. Accommodation on the island is at the **Light Station,** which can hold up to eight people (for 6 people $70, peak $90; each additional person $10). Book through Parks Victoria in Mallacoota (☎5158 0219). Transport to the island can be tricky. If you don't want to sea-kayak, the **Mallacoota Air Service** (☎5158 0102) will take three adults for $60.

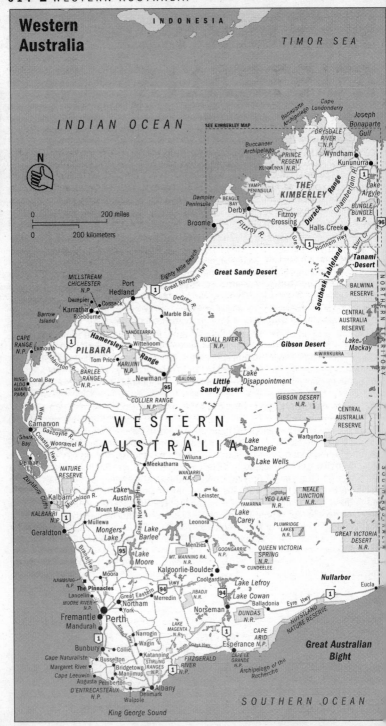

Western Australia

INDONESIA

TIMOR SEA

INDIAN OCEAN

SEE KIMBERLEY MAP

N

0        200 miles
0        200 kilometers

Bonaparte Archipelago
Cape Londonderry
Joseph Bonaparte Gulf

DRYSDALE RIVER N.P.

Buccaneer Archipelago

PRINCE REGENT N.R.
KUNMUNYA N.R.

Wyndham
Kununurra

YAMPI PENINSULA

THE KIMBERLEY Range

Lake Argyle

Dampier Peninsula

BEAGLE BAY
Derby

Fitzroy Crossing

Durack

BUNGLE BUNGLE N.P.

96

Broome

Fitzroy R.

Halls Creek

Great

Northern Hwy

Tanami Desert

Eighty Mile Beach

Great Sandy Desert

Southesk Tableland

BALWINA RESERVE

MILLSTREAM CHICHESTER N.P

Port Hedland

1

Great Northern Hwy

DeGrey R.

CENTRAL AUSTRALIA RESERVE

Dampier
Karratha
Cossack
Roebourne

Marble Bar

Lake Mackay

KIWIRRKURRA

Barrow Island

Hamersley

YANDEEARRA

Wittenoom

RUDALL RIVER N.P.

Gibson Desert

CAPE RANGE N.P.
Exmouth

PILBARA
Range

Ashburton R.

Tom Price
KARIJINI N.P.

BARLEE RANGE N.R.

Newman

JIGALONG

Little Sandy Desert

Lake Disappointment

GIBSON DESERT N.R.

CENTRAL AUSTRALIA RESERVE

NING ALOO MARINE PARK

Coral Bay

95

COLLIER RANGE N.P.

WESTERN

Carnarvon
West
Gascoyne R.
Wooramel R.

AUSTRALIA

Lake Carnegie

Warburton

Shark Bay

Coastal Hwy

Lake Wells

Denham

Meekatharra

Wiluna

NATURE RESERVE

WANJARRI N.R.

YEO LAKE N.R.

NEALE JUNCTION N.R.

Zuytdorp Cliffs

Kalbarri

Murchison R.

Lake Austin

Leinster

KALBARRI N.P.

1

Mount Magnet

YAMARNA

Lake Carey

PLUMRIDGE LAKES N.R.

Mullewa

Leonora

Great Northern Hwy

Geraldton

Mongers Lake

Lake Barlee

Menzies

GOONGARRIE N.P.

QUEEN VICTORIA SPRING N.R.

GREAT VICTORIA DESERT N.R.

95

Lake Moore

MT. MANNING RA. N.R.

CUNDEELEE

Moora

Kalgoorlie-Boulder

NAMBUNG N.P.

The Pinnacles

Coolgardie

Lake Lefroy

Nullarbor

Eucla

Lancelin

MOORE RIVER N.P.

Great Eastern

94

JIBADJI N.R.

Lake Cowan

1

Northam

Hwy

Merredin

94

Balladonia

Eyre Hwy

Fremantle
Perth
Mandurah

York

Norseman

DUNDAS N.R.

NUYTSLAND NATURE RESERVE

Avon R.

Narrogin

LAKE MAGENTA N.R.

CAPE ARID N.P.

Great Australian Bight

Bunbury
Collie

Wagin

South Coast Hwy

Esperance

Cape Naturaliste
Busselton
Margaret River
Cape Leeuwin

Katanning

STIRLING RANGES N.P.

FITZGERALD RIVER N.P.

1

CAPE LE GRANDE N.P.

Bridgetown
Manjimup

1

Archipelago of the Recherche

D'ENTRECASTEAUX N.P.

Augusta
Pemberton

Albany
Denmark

Walpole

SOUTHERN OCEAN

King George Sound

# WESTERN AUSTRALIA

Western Australia is distinct from the rest of the country in many ways, but the most glaring is its overwhelming size. WA covers about a third of Australia, which seems like an obvious and useless observation, but visitors soon realize that simply getting from place to place will occupy much of their time in the state. Tiny pieces of the map translate into draining full days of driving or busing on empty roads. The upside of WA's immensity is a collection of landscapes and activities that no other area in Australia can match. Yet most visitors, like most Australians, don't bother to explore the west, believing that it's just a desolate backwater. Even native Westralians usually only see a fraction of their state. Of WA's 1.8 million people, 1.4 million live in the Perth area, and most of the rest are close to the coast, along the vineyards of the south or the surf-pounded capes of the north. Perth, WA's capital, is a modern city complete with shiny skyscrapers, four universities, and several suburbs. People in Perth and throughout the state have a friendly, relaxed interest in the hardy tourists that do make it out west, and with good reason: tourism has become one of the state's economic mainstays, and a lot of effort has gone into making WA a tourist-friendly destination.

From quokkas in the south to camels and saltwater crocs in the north, WA is home to a range of Australian wildlife. The state's interior is covered with miles of bushland, spinifex grass, and sandy plains, and between August and November the land comes alive as 8000 wildflower species bloom in carpets along the coast south from Exmouth into the Great Southern. The Southwest is the domain of old-growth forests. One of the world's largest trees, the majestic karri reaches heights of 80m and stands in defiance of the state's thriving wood-chipping industry. In the north, the desert gives way to the rugged tropical vegetation of the Kimberley. A few rough roads carve through the huge expanses of rainforest, unearthly rock formations, and spectacular waterfalls that cascade into the Indian Ocean.

Through long years of isolation from the rest of the country, Westralians have developed an independent nature. In 1933, a state referendum revealed a two-to-one preference to separate from the Commonwealth of Australia. Secession never became a political reality, but the self-sufficient spirit remains a subtle undercurrent. While many proud Westralians depend on heavy industry for their livelihood, a growing number are fighting for the protection of their state's natural resources. Ecotourism and promotion of natural attractions have begun to edge out the fishing and animal husbandry industries; tourists certainly prefer visiting the dolphins at Monkey Mia to visiting the massive open-pit mines of the outback. Best of all, West Australia has for the most part avoided the overdevelopment and tourist saturation that some find so distasteful about the east coast. So here's the take-away message: the time is right to go west. You can thank us when you get back.

## ▆ GETTING AROUND

Because of the distances between attractions, and the dearth of long-haul transportation, many travelers—even budget travelers—**buy a car** for long visits (see **Buying and Selling Used Cars,** p. 67). A thriving gray market exists for used cars, 4WDs, and campervans, fueled by hostel message boards and the *West Australian* classifieds. **Used car dealerships** line Beaufort St several kilometers north of Northbridge, outside Perth. Before paying, have the car checked by a mechanic. Some unscrupulous car dealers prey on backpackers and don't honor warranties. Be wary and do your homework before investing. The **Royal Automobile Club (RAC),**

## WESTERN AUSTRALIA HIGHLIGHTS

**I SEE YOU.** Dolphins swimming by the wind-beaten cliffs of Rottnest Island (p. 628).

**UNWINDING.** Local wine after a long day exploring Margaret River's caves (p. 632).

**SERENITY.** Humpback whales jumping past your boat in Augusta (p. 635).

**DON'T LOOK DOWN.** The Valley of the Giants Treetop Walk (p. 637).

**TEST YOURSELF.** Windsurfing the gales at Geraldton (p. 649).

**UNEARTHLY.** The Pinnacles rising from desert-like dunes (p. 649).

**IT'S SAFE, REALLY.** Swim with whale sharks at Ningaloo Reef, Exmouth (p. 654).

**NOW, THIS IS WHAT I CALL A BATH.** The Circular Pool (p. 659).

**LIFE AT A CANTER.** Sunset camel rides on Cable Beach, Broome (p. 664).

**A STRETCH AND A SWIM.** Tropical gorges along the Gibb River Road p. 669).

228 Adelaide Tce, Perth, at the corner of Hill St, offers inspections for members. As WA's branch of AAA, RAC also provides roadside assistance. (☎9421 4400; roadside assistance ☎ 13 11 11. 1-year membership $130; inspections from $100.) For more information see **On the Road,** p. 66.

If you plan to **drive through the desert,** bring plenty of water, petrol, a spare tire, and a fanbelt. Winter and early spring are the safest times of year to drive the Great Northern Hwy because temperatures are lower and traffic more frequent. Throughout WA, you'll share the highway with **road trains,** massive tractor-trailers. Don't assume their turn signal is an attempt to communicate with you that it's ok to pass them; several people have been killed making this mistake.

*Let's Go* does not recommend **hitchhiking,** but some people do it. The most reliable way to get a ride is to check **hostel message boards.**

With the exception of the Kalgoorlie and Perth stops on the *Indian Pacific* line, passenger **rail** service is essentially non-existent. **Greyhound Pioneer** (☎ 13 20 30) is the only **bus** company that runs north of Exmouth. The seasonal Greyhound timetable book is indispensable. Try to book at least a day ahead; space may be limited and the bus might not even stop unless the driver knows you're waiting. If you plan on a lot of bus travel, Greyhound has cheaper passes. For more information see **By Bus,** p. 63. South of Perth and Kalgoorlie, Greyhound service ends, and **South West Coach Lines, Westrail,** and **EasyRider** take over.

Portions of Western Australia can be toured by **bicycle,** but you must carry significant amounts of water. In northern WA, it's not advisable to bike in the hotter, wetter months. Advise regional police and, in the north and outback, the **Royal Flying Doctor Service** of your itinerary. The **Ministry of Sport and Recreation** (☎9387 9700) has more info, as does **Bikewest** (☎9320 9301).

A bewildering range of guided group **tours** are available around Perth and throughout the state. Tourist officials, travel agents, and hostel managers can help narrow the options. Standard prices for four- to five-day tours through the Southwest are around $400. This sum will also get you to Monkey Mia, Kalbarri, and the Pinnacles. Longer and pricier tours are also available.

# PERTH

If Western Australia could be embodied in one city, Perth would be it. It is a big, sophisticated metropolis that's been dropped into a stunning landscape of green hills and quiet farming communities. WA is truly the land of 'no worries,' and this mellow attitude is a point of pride in the state's capital city. Rumor has it that WA spurns daylight savings time so that folks can fit in a quick surf before work.

Perth may also be the world's most isolated capital city (Adelaide is at least two days away by car), but isolation does not mean desolation. Perth is home to 88% of the state's population, and continues to grow steadily. This development

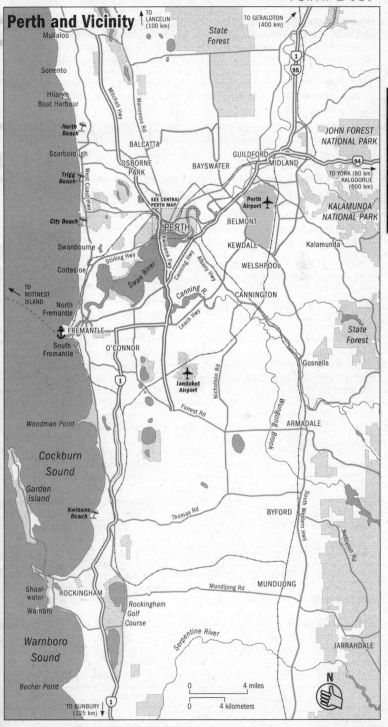

# Perth and Vicinity

TO LANCELIN (100 km)

TO GERALDTON (400 km)

Mullaloo

State Forest

Sorrento

Hilary's Boat Harbour

North Beach

JOHN FOREST NATIONAL PARK

Scarborough

BALCATTA

OSBORNE PARK

GUILDFORD

MIDLAND

TO YORK (80 km) KALGOORLIE (600 km)

BAYSWATER

Trigg Beach

SEE CENTRAL PERTH MAP

KALAMUNDA NATIONAL PARK

City Beach

Perth Airport

PERTH

BELMONT

Kalamunda

Swanbourne

Stirling Hwy

KEWDALE

Cottesloe

Swan River

WELSHPOOL

TO ROTTNEST ISLAND

Canning Hwy

Canning R.

CANNINGTON

North Fremantle

Leach Hwy

State Forest

FREMANTLE

South Fremantle

O'CONNOR

Gosnells

Woodman Point

Jandakot Airport

Nicholson Rd

Forrest Rd

Wungong Brook

ARMADALE

Cockburn Sound

Garden Island

Kwinana Beach

South Western Hwy

BYFORD

Netleton Rd

Thomas Rd

Shoal-water

ROCKINGHAM

Rockingham Golf Course

Mundijong Rd

MUNDIJONG

Warnbro

Warnboro Sound

Serpentine River

JARRAHDALE

Becher Point

TO BUNBURY (125 km)

0    4 miles

0    4 kilometers

N

is easy to understand given the clean air, accessible beaches, gorgeous sunsets, and mild climate. However, there are those who miss the slower pace of the city's past, and these folks look to Fremantle to provide a link to the area's history. Funds flowing into "Freo" have been spent on historic, restorative face-lifts rather than skyline lifts. In between Freo and the city center lie parks, beaches, and plenty of happy souls content to share with visitors the lifestyle for which Perth is famous. Those who make the effort to get here always find that Perth is worth the trip.

---

### PERTH HIGHLIGHTS

**JUST MINDING MY BUSINESS.** Bike paths, wildflowers, and a vista of the Swan River in Kings Park (p. 624).

**HANG TEN.** Perfect breaks in the challenging surf of Trigg Beach (p. 625).

**CULTURAL OASIS.** Modern Australian artwork at Perth's Art Gallery (p. 625).

**BOO.** Ghostly, macabre candlelight tour of Fremantle Prison (p. 626).

**FLOATING ALONG.** Perth Harbour and a view of the city skyline (p. 626).

**VYING FOR THE GOODS.** The funky finds at the Fremantle Markets (p. 627).

**JUNGLE BOOGIE.** DJ tunes at the nightclubs of Northbridge (p. 627).

**DAYTRIPPING.** Bike and whale-watch on relaxing Rottnest Island (p. 628).

---

# ◼ GETTING THERE

## BY PLANE

Local tourist flights around Perth fly from **Jandakot Airport,** south of the city; air traffic into and out of the region arrives at and departs from **Perth Airport,** east of the city. The terminals are small and easy to navigate, but the international terminal is several kilometers away from the domestic terminals. Keep this in mind if you're planning a connection. **Qantas** (☎ 13 13 13) and **Ansett** (☎ 13 13 00) fly daily to: **Adelaide** (2¾hr., $176); **Darwin** (3½hr., $297); **Melbourne** (3¼hr., $231); **Sydney** (4hr., $242); and **Cairns** (indirect, $264). Qantas flies to **Brisbane** daily (4½hr., $341) and Ansett flies there twice a week. For trips within the state, try Ansett, Qantas, or regional carrier **SkyWest.** Qantas' **Airlink** network offers direct flights between **Perth, Broome, Kalgoorlie, Karratha, Port Hedland,** and **Tom Price.**

There are many transport options between the city and airport. **TransPerth** buses #200, 201, 202, 208, and 209 run between the domestic terminals and St. Georges Tce in the city center (35min.; every 30-50min.; $3, concessions $1). The bus from Perth to the airport leaves from the north side of St. George Tce, stop 39. An **Airport City Shuttle** (☎ 9479 4131) runs frequently to a number of stops in Perth from both the domestic ($9) and international ($11) terminals, and also picks up travelers from accommodations. The **Fremantle Airport Shuttle** goes to both Perth Airport terminals, departing daily from the Fremantle Railway Station regularly until midnight; pickup at Fremantle accommodations is available 24hr. when booked in advance. (☎ 9383 4115. $12.) A **taxi** from the airport to the city center costs around $18-21 from domestic terminals and $25-30 from international terminals.

## BY TRAIN

Intercity trains run from the **East Perth Terminal,** off Lord St on Summer St, a 25min. walk northeast from the Perth tourist center. TransPerth trains transport between the station and the city center every 15min. on weekdays and every 30min. on weekends. Westrail (☎ 13 10 53; www.westrail.wa.gov.au) has service to **Bunbury** (2hr., 2 per day, $19) and **Kalgoorlie** (8hr., 1-2 per day, $53) via **Midland.** The *Indian Pacific* runs to **Sydney** (65hr., $459).

## BY BUS

Westrail (☎ 13 10 53) runs buses from the East Perth Terminal. The more expensive Greyhound departs from 250 Great Eastern Hwy in Belmont. (☎ 13 20 30. VIP or YHA 10% discount, students 20%.) To reach the Belmont station, take bus #52 or call ☎ 9479 4131 for a shuttle service from the hostels ($8). Southwest Coach Lines (☎ 9324 2333) departs from the **Perth City Bus Port,** Mounts Bay Rd.

## FROM PERTH TO:

| DESTINATION | COMPANY | DURATION | TIMES | PRICE |
|---|---|---|---|---|
| Adelaide | Greyhound | 36hr. | daily 6:30am | $226 |
| Albany (via Bunbury) | Westrail | 6hr. | 1-2 per day | $38 |
| Albany (via Mt. Barker) | Westrail | 6hr. | 1-2 per day | $38 |
| Augusta | Southwest | 5½hr. | 1 per day | $30 |
| Broome | Greyhound | 32hr. | 1 per day (F, Su 2) | $226 |
| Bunbury | Southwest | 2½hr. | 3 per day | $18 |
| Busselton | Southwest | 3½hr. | 1 per day | $22 |
| Carnarvon | Greyhound | 12hr. | 1 per day (W, F, Su 3) | $105 |
| Darwin | Greyhound | 56hr. | 1 per day | $496 |
| Dunsborough | Southwest | 4hr. | 1 per day | $24 |
| Esperance | Westrail | 10hr. | Su-F 1-2 per day | $56 |
| Exmouth | Greyhound | 16½hr. | 1 per day | $199 |
| Geraldton | Greyhound | 6hr. | 1 per day (W, F, Su 3) | $38 |
| Geraldton | Westrail | 6-8hr. | 1-2 per day | $39 |
| Kalbarri | Greyhound | 6hr. | 1 per day (W, F, Su 2) | $78 |
| Kalbarri | Westrail | 8hr. | M,W,F 8:30am | $49 |
| Kalgoorlie | Greyhound | 8hr. | 1 per day | $101 |
| Kalgoorlie | Westrail | 8hr. | M,W,F | $53 |
| Margaret River | Southwest | 5hr. | 1-2 per day | $25 |
| Monkey Mia | Greyhound | 10hr. | 1 per day (W, F, Su 3) | $133 |
| Pemberton (via Bunbury) | Westrail | 7hr. | 1-2 per day Su-F | $33 |
| Port Headland | Greyhound | 21hr. | 1-2 per day | $186 |
| York | Westrail | 1½hr. | 1-2 per day Su-F | $10 |

## BY CAR

There are several cheap **car rental** agencies in town. **Bayswater,** 160 Adelaide Tce (☎ 9325 1000), or 13 Queen Victoria Ave, Fremantle (☎ 9430 5300), rents to drivers age 20 and up. **Cottlesloe Car and Lite Hire,** 2 Servetus St, Swanbourne (☎ 9383 3057), is another good option and rents to drivers 21 and up. **Atlas Rent-a-Car,** 36 Miligan St (☎ 9481 8866, freecall ☎ (1800) 65 99 99), sometimes has backpacker specials. Although costs will vary depending on distances and vehicle, rates in the city are reasonable: between $30 and $40 a day ($20 off-season); weekly rates are cheaper. An $8-13 per day surcharge generally applies to drivers under 25. The **Travellers' Club,** 499 Wellington St (☎ 9226 0660), across from the train station, helps backpackers with rentals. In addition, many hostels have deals with local companies for lower rates. The **Royal Auto Club,** 228 Adelaide Tce (☎ 9421 4400), offers roadside assistance (call ☎ 13 11 11) to members of RAC or several automobile associations from other countries, including AAA.

# ✳ ORIENTATION

Although Perth's streets are not quite aligned north-south and east-west, it helps to think of them as such, and locals will understand what you mean if you refer to them that way. The rail line functions as the northern boundary of the city, and the

**WESTERN AUSTRALIA**

**Swan River** the southern. The east-west avenues run parallel with **Wellington St** from the railroad tracks to the river. The north-south streets run parallel with **William St.** Between William and Barrack St, east-west streets Hay and Murray St become **pedestrian malls.** Shopping arcades and overhead walkways connect the malls to each other and to the **Perth Railway Station.** The **Wellington St Bus Station** is one block west of the railway station, across William St. Downtown Perth is relatively safe, but not well-lit. At night, it's probably best not to walk around alone.

**Northbridge,** the city's nexus of culture and nightlife, is a 2min. walk north of the railway station. Most activity and budget accommodation are clustered in a square formed by Newcastle St on the north and James St on the south, and between Beaufort St on the east and Russel Sq on the west. Great, green **Kings Park** rises just southwest of downtown, overlooking the city and the Swan. The TransPerth Fremantle line runs west out of the city through the older Perth suburbs. **Subiaco** is a hot spot for cafés and cuisine, and has weekend market stalls on either side of the Subiaco train stop on the Fremantle line. The Fremantle train also passes through **Swanbourne** and **Cottlesloe,** both lively beach suburbs. Although technically its own city and 30min. away, **Fremantle (Freo)** is best thought of as a part of greater Perth. Perth is the central business district, Freo is the laid-back, lucrative fishing port, and everyone frequents both all the time. TransPerth buses and trains run frequently between the two (30min.). **Leederville,** one stop north of Perth on the Currambine line, is another popular area, with plenty of pubs, cafés, and funky shops.

# ▛ GETTING AROUND

Like all cities of a million plus people, Perth takes up quite a bit of space. However, the downtown area is compact and easy to navigate on foot. Most sights are within walking distance of one another, and the **CAT bus service** whisks passengers around downtown for free. The blue CAT runs in a north-south loop from the Swan River to Northbridge, and the red CAT runs east-west from West Perth to East Perth. (☎13 62 13. Blue CAT: every 5-15min., M-Th 7am-6pm, F-Sa until 1am, Su 10am-5pm. Red CAT: every 15min., M-Th 7am-6pm; hourly 10am-6pm on weekends.)

The **TransPerth** network of **buses, trains,** and **ferries** connects to outlying areas. The system is divided into eight **fare zones;** a two-zone ride costs $2.70 and will get you from the city center to the airport or Fremantle. **All-day passes** and **multi-ride cards** are available at TransPerth InfoCentre machines and newsagents and can save you up to 25% (unlimited usage day pass $7). Save your **ticket stub**—it can be used to transfer between bus, train, and ferry services. Tickets for up to four zones are valid for 1½hr. Additional info, as well as maps and timetables for bus and rail service, is available by phone (☎13 62 13) or at all four TransPerth InfoCentres: Plaza Arcade, Wellington St Bus Station, City Busport, and the train station.

It's also easy to get around by taxi; a taxi ride between the international airport terminal and Northbridge costs between $25 and $30. **Swan Taxi,** 1008 Wellington St (☎9444 4444), or **Black and White Taxi** (☎13 10 08) offer taxi service around the city. It's possible to hail a cab around the city, especially along Wellington St or William St, but it's best to call. **Bikes** are also a good option; the tourist office has free maps of bike routes. **Bikewest,** 441 Murray St (☎9320 9301; email bikewest@transport.wa.gov.au), has more information, maps, and advice on bike routes. Bikes can be rented from Kings Park or at a few stands around the city.

# ▟ PRACTICAL INFORMATION

Basic business hours are 9am to 5pm, but shops and services in the suburbs often have extended hours on Thursday, staying open until around 9pm, and shops in the city center frequently stay open until about 9pm on Friday nights. On Sunday stores are open noon until 5 or 6pm.

## TOURIST AND FINANCIAL SERVICES

**Tourist Offices: Perth Visitors Centre,** on the corner of Wellington and Forrest Pl (☎(1300) 36 13 51; fax 9481 0190), has free bus and tour booking. Open M-Th 8:30am-6pm, F

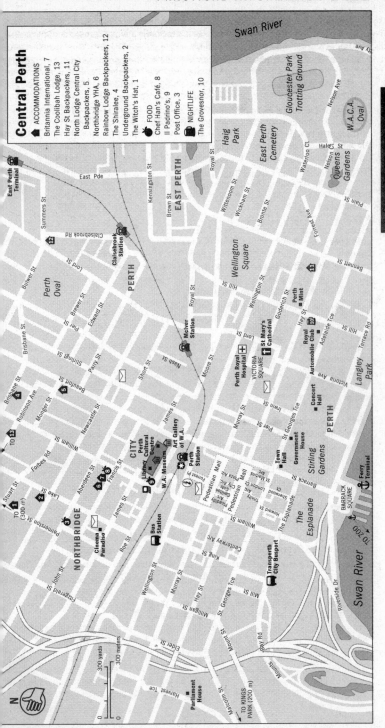

**Central Perth**

▲ ACCOMMODATIONS
Britannia International, 7
The Coolibah Lodge, 13
Hay St Backpackers, 11
North Lodge Central City
Backpackers, 5
Northbridge YHA, 6
Rainbow Lodge Backpackers, 12
The Shiralee, 4
Underground Backpackers, 2
The Witch's Hat, 1

✦ FOOD
Chef Han's Café, 8
Il Padrino's, 9
Post Office, 3

🎬 NIGHTLIFE
The Grovesnor, 10

WESTERN AUSTRALIA

WESTERN AUSTRALIA

8:30am-7pm, Sa 8:30am-5pm, Su 10am-5pm; off-season M-Th 8:30am-5pm, F 8:30am-6pm, Sa 8:30am-4:30pm, Su 10am-3pm. **Fremantle Tourist Bureau,** on the corner of High St and William St, Kings Sq (☎9431 7878). Open M-Sa 9am-5pm, Su noon-5pm.

**Budget Travel: YHA Western Australia,** 236 William St, Northbridge (☎9227 5122; fax 9227 5123; www.yha.com.au). Arranges travel with discounts for YHA members. Membership info available (international travelers $30). **STA Travel,** 100 James St (☎9227 7569). Open M-W, F 9am-5pm, Th 9am-6pm, Sa 10am-3pm.

**Currency Exchange: Thomas Cook,** Piccadilly Arcade on Hay St (☎9481 7900). Open M-F 8:30am-5pm, Sa 10am-2pm. **American Express,** 645 Hay St (☎9221 0777). Hay St Mall in London Court. Foreign exchange open M-F 9am-5:30pm, Sa 9am-noon. **ATMs** and banks are everywhere, especially on William St in Northbridge and on Hay St in the mall area between Barrack and William St. Most machines accept Cirrus and Plus.

**Embassies and Consulates: Britain,** 77 St. Georges Tce (☎9221 5400); **Canada,** 267 St. Georges Tce (☎9322 7930); **Ireland,** 10 Lilika Rd (☎9385 8247); **United States,** 16 St. Georges Tce (☎9231 9400).

## LOCAL SERVICES

**Outdoors Information Centers: CALM** has a customer service center at 50 Hayman Rd. (☎9334 0333; open M-F 9am-5pm) and Freo, 47 Henry St (☎9430 8600; open W-M).

**Public Markets: Subiaco** has markets at the Pavilion at the corner of Rokeby and Roberts Rd on Th-F 10am-9pm, Sa-Su 10am-5pm; **Fremantle** has markets at 84 South Tce on F 9am-9pm, Sa 9am-5pm, Su 10am-5pm.

**Library: The Alexander Library Building** (☎9427 3111), at the north end of the Perth Cultural Centre. **Internet** for research only. Open M-Th 9am-9:45pm, F 9am-5:30pm, Sa-Su 10am-5:30pm. Wheelchair accessible.

**Ticket Agencies:** For sporting events, try **Ticketmaster,** Perth Entertainment Centre, at Wellington St and Miligan St (☎13 61 00). Open M-F 9am-5:30pm, Sa 9am-1pm. For theatrical and musical events, reach **Bocs Tickets,** Perth Concert Hall, 5 St. George's Tce (☎9484 1133; fax 9221 2241). Open M-F 8:30am-5:30pm.

---

**MEDIA AND PUBLICATIONS**

**Newspapers:** *The West Australian.*

**Nightlife:** The free entertainment weekly *XPress*, has the lowdown. For gay nightlife, try the *Westside Observer* (free).

**Radio:** Rock, 96FM and 92.9FM; News, ABC 720AM; Tourist Info, 88FM.

---

## EMERGENCY AND COMMUNICATIONS

**Emergency:** ☎000.

**Police:** ☎9222 1111; Fremantle: ☎9430 1222.

**Hotlines: Sexual Assault** (24hr. ☎9340 1828). **Crisis Line** (☎(1800) 19 90 08). **Sea, Search, and Rescue Line** (☎9442 8600). **AIDS/STD Line** (☎9429 9944).

**Late Night Pharmacy: Beaufort St 24hr. Chemist,** 647 Beaufort St, Mt. Lawley (☎9328 7775). **City Pharmacy,** Wellington St bus depot (☎9321 4441). Open M-F 7:30am-6pm, Sa 9:30am-2:30pm.

**Hospital: Royal Perth Hospital,** on Wellington St near Lord St (☎9224 2244). **Fremantle Hospital,** on the corner of South Tce and Alma St (☎9431 3333).

**Internet Access:** Budget travel offices (see above) offer 15-20min. free. **Internet Go Go,** 150 William St, Northbridge (☎9226 3282). 1 hr. $2.50. **net.CHAT,** shop 14, Wesley Way Arcade, Market St, Freo (☎9433 2011). 1hr. $4. Open daily 8-11am and 9-11pm.

**Post Office: General Post Office (GPO),** 3 Forrest Pl (☎9237 5460). *Poste Restante* pickup M-F only. Open M-F 8am-5:30pm, Sa 9am-12:30pm, Su noon-4pm. **Fremantle GPO,** 13 Market St (☎9335 1611). Open M-F 8:30am-5pm. **Postal Code:** 6000.

**Phone Code:** 08.

# ACCOMMODATIONS

Perth has accommodations of all sorts, from basic backpacker joints to pricey luxury hotels. Most hostels are in Northbridge and the city center. If you are in town for more than a few weeks, check the classified section of the *West Australian* for listings of rooms and flats to lease; they can be cheaper than hostels. All hostels listed offer free luggage storage, on-site laundry facilities, and kitchens. There are no lock-out times, but it's a good idea to call ahead with your estimated time of arrival so someone will be there to greet you. Booking ahead is also wise.

## CITY PROPER

■ **Underground Backpackers,** 268 Newcastle St (☎9228 3755; fax 9228 3744). A newcomer to town, this hostel has huge dorms with big windows and high ceilings. There's also a bar, pool, and a brick basement lounge area just a few steps from the best of the city's nightlife. Internet 1hr. $5. Dorms $18; singles, twins, doubles $55. NOMADS.

■ **The Coolibah Lodge,** 194 Brisbane St, Northbridge (☎9328 9958; fax 9227 6231). A maze of lounges, dorms, and kitchens in a beautifully remodeled colonial home. The bathrooms get a bit cramped, but otherwise it's a great spot close to Northbridge nightlife. Free pickup. Internet 20min. $2. Dorms $17.50; singles $30; doubles $44. VIP.

**Britannia International,** 253 William St, Northbridge (☎9328 6121; fax 9227 9784; email britannia@yhawa.com.au). Between Aberdeen and Francis St. A massive place, with nice rooms and dining space is located "right in the heart of it," with a noise level to match. Internet 1hr. $5. No smoking. Reception 24hr. Dorms $16; singles $22; doubles 1st night $45, $40 each additional; family rooms $70. Non-YHA $3 more.

**Hay St Backpackers,** 266-268 Hay St, East Perth (☎/fax 9221 9880). Clean and freshly painted rooms with heat and A/C are nice, but far from the bustle of Northbridge. Knowledgeable staff will help arrange tours. Two clean kitchens, pool table, small swimming pool. Internet 1hr. $6. Dorms $15-16; doubles $40, ensuite $45.

**The Witch's Hat,** 148 Palmerston St, Northbridge (☎9228 4228; fax 9228 4229; email witchs_hat@hotmail.com). This beautiful pointed building will cost you a bit extra, but you will get a bit extra too: hardwood floors, leather couches, free tea and coffee, and an adorable dog. Dorms $20, weekly $112; singles, twins and doubles $55, $329. VIP.

**The Shiralee,** 107 Brisbane St, Northbridge (☎9227 7448; fax 9227 7446). A mellow atmosphere pervades simple but clean rooms and lounge. A/C, kitchen. Free pickup. Internet 1hr. $4. Dorms $17, weekly $110; twins $42, $280. VIP.

**Northbridge YHA,** 46 Francis St, Northbridge (☎/fax 9328 7794). Basic rooms in a massive building. Be ready for jarring but helpful intercom announcements on travel opportunities that briefly interrupt the social atmosphere. Internet 1hr. $3. Reception 7am-10pm. Dorms $15, weekly $90; twins $35; doubles and triples $45. Non-YHA $3 more.

**Rainbow Lodge Backpackers,** 133 Summers St, Northbridge (☎9227 1818; fax 9227 0719). East of the Perth Oval, cross Lord St to Summers St. A hike from the town center and most nightlife, 3min. from the intercity railway station. Colorful and social. Kitchens, Internet, free in-line skates, fishing rods, and didgeridoos. Free pickup. Dorms $13, weekly $80; singles $25, $150; twins $17 per person, $95. YHA, VIP, ISIC.

## FREMANTLE

■ **YHA Backpackers Inn Freo,** 11 Pakenham St (☎9431 7065; fax 9336 7106). From the train station, turn right onto Phillimore St, then left onto Pakenham. The renovated warehouse space is beautiful, but the corrugated roof can be loud when it rains. Relaxed atmosphere and normally plenty of quiet. Reception 7am-11:30pm; 24hr. check-in available. Dorms $18; singles $22; doubles $44. Non-YHA $3-5 more.

■ **Cheviot Marina Backpackers,** 4 Beach St (☎9344 2055; fax 9433 2066). Turn left down Elder St from train station (becomes Beach St). A big, sunny place offers a beautiful lounge upstairs and discounted drinks at the bar next door. Free Internet. Dorms $15; singles $30; twins and doubles $39. Peak season, up to $10 more. YHA, VIP.

**Old Firestation Backpackers,** 18 Phillimore St (☎9430 5454; fax 9335 6828). Turn right from the train station. Friendly management presides over an array of kitchens and lounges. The rooms are basic, but where else can you try an original firepole? Free Internet and washing machines. Dorms $16.50; twins and doubles $44.

# 🍴 FOOD

Perth is chock-full of great restaurants, food halls, and bakeries. Coles, SupaValu, and Foodland are Perth's major **supermarket** chains. For cheap, quality, imported bulk pasta, cereals, and deli foods, elbow your way through the crowds into **Kakulas Brothers Wholesale Importers,** 185 William St (open M-F 8am-5:30pm, Sa 8am-5pm). In Fremantle, **Kakulas Sister** emulates her Perthite sibs on the corner of Market and Leake St (open M-F 9am-5:30pm, Sa 9am-2pm).

A number of pubs and clubs cater specifically to the backpacker set (even vegetarians), taming the crowds with free meals and drink specials. The determined can find free food almost every night. Su: **The Good, the Bad, and the Ugly,** 69 Aberdeen St (☎9328 9133); M: **The Deen,** 84 Aberdeen St (☎9227 9361); Tu and Th: **hip-e club** (☎9227 8899), on Newcastle and Oxford St in Leederville; W: **⬛The Post Office** (☎9228 0077), on Aberdeen and Parker St.

## CITY PROPER

⬛ **Chef Han's Café,** on the corner of Francis and William St (☎9328 8122). Delicious, fast heaps of vegetarian-friendly noodle and stir-fry for $6-8. Open daily 11am-10pm.

⬛ **Il Padrino,** 198 William St (☎9227 9065). Widely recognized as the best pizza in Perth and a crowd to prove it. Lunch and dinner Tu, lunch W, Th, Fr: half-price pizza and $7.50 pasta. Open Tu-F 11am-late, Sa-Su 5pm-late.

**Boxx Café,** on the corner of Lake and Francis St (☎9228 1400). Offers a wide variety of Asian dishes, including a bunch of vegetarian options. 'Meals in a Boxx' are only $8.

**Villa Italia,** 279 William St (☎9227 9030). The best of the area's numerous Italian restaurants, with a casual atmosphere and flamenco music in the air. Pasta dishes are $8.50 Su-Th; the great desserts will run you extra. Open daily until late.

**Icon Café,** 110 Aberdeen St (☎9227 9216). A stylish and comfortable restaurant with delicious but pricey food. On M and Tu nights there is a $10 pizza and pasta special.

**The Moon,** 323 William St (☎9328 7474). Several veggie options in a spaceship themed diner. Pasta for $5-7 with a coupon. Open M-F 5pm-late, Sa-Su 11am-late.

**Luke's,** 77 James St, Northbridge (☎9328 4159). A quiet and tasty lunch choice with outdoor seating. Sandwiches and burgers are $5-9. Open M-F 8am-2:30pm.

## FREMANTLE

⬛ **Hara Café,** 33 High St (☎9335 6118). Good, cheap vegetarian meals. Indian curries $7, teas $3 a pot. Open M-Tu 11am-4pm, W-F 11am-9pm, Sa-Su noon-9pm.

**Fiorelli,** 19C Essex St (☎9430 6119). Tasty Italian restaurant. On Tu and W nights there is a $10 all-you-can-eat pizza/pasta special. Open daily noon-late.

# 👁 SIGHTS

## CITY PROPER

**KINGS PARK.** You have not experienced Perth until you have visited Kings Park. It's a welcome glimpse of the wild just outside the city center. The 400 hectares are criss-crossed with foot and bike paths and, in the spring, covered with wildflowers. On sunny days its picnic lawns and playgrounds are filled with families and groups of schoolkids, but weekdays are less crowded. Perched atop **Mt. Eliza,** the park offers a great view of the Swan River and city below. (*By foot head west from the city center up St. George's Tce and bear left as it becomes Malcom St and heads to the roundabout at the north end of the park. Or, take the free red CAT to stop #25. Free parking.*)

WESTERN AUSTRALIA

WESTERN AUSTRALIA

**Fremantle**

🏠 ACCOMMODATIONS
Cheviot Marina Backpackers, 6
Old Firestation Backpackers, 1
YHA Backpackers Inn Freo, 2

🍎 FOOD
Fiorelli, 4
Hara Café, 3

🍺 PUBS
The Bog, 5

**WESTERN AUSTRALIAN BOTANIC GARDEN.** In King's Park, next to the war memorial as you face the river, the Botanic Gardens are home to over 1700 native species. Free bush walks and heritage walks depart from the karri log opposite the memorial. *(Tours daily 10am; also W, Su 2pm July-Oct.)*

**BEACHES.** Perth wouldn't be in Australia without its assortment of beaches. **Cottlesloe Beach,** on the Fremantle train line, is a popular family spot with safe swimming. **City Beach** is another swimming spot with a long shore and good facilities. **Scarborough** has bigger surfing waves and crowds of twenty-somethings that make for excellent people-watching. **Trigg Beach,** just north of Scarborough, is a surfer's dream, but the waves can get a bit rough for swimming. Take note that **Swanbourne Beach,** also on the Freo train, is a nude beach.

**THE ART GALLERY OF WESTERN AUSTRALIA.** In the **Cultural Centre** complex along with the **Alexander Library,** the **Perth Institute of the Contemporary Arts (PICA),** and the **Western Australian Museum,** the art gallery has several collections of Australian and international art, including some beautiful Aboriginal carvings and paintings. Exhibits in 2001 include an installation of modern Australian female artists. *(North of the railway station between William St and Beaufort St. Open daily 10am-5pm. Free guided tours Tu-F 12:15pm, Sa-Su 2pm. Free, except to rotating special collections.)*

**PERTH INSTITUTE OF THE CONTEMPORARY ARTS (PICA).** PICA shows contemporary and student art and hosts evening performances. Pick up a booklet of events or call for current happenings. *(☎ 9227 6144. Open Tu-Su 11am-7pm. Gallery free, but performance prices vary.)*

**THE WESTERN AUSTRALIAN MUSEUM.** The museum has exhibits on WA's natural history and culture. Discovery Center has drawers of shells, jewelry, bugs, old shoes, anything and everything else. Don't miss the blue whale skeleton, Aboriginal exhibit, or butterfly gallery. (☎9427 2700. Open daily 9:30am-5pm. Free.)

**THE ZOO.** The zoo houses native and exotic fauna and conducts endangered species breeding programs. The Australian section has frilled lizards, crocodiles, and wallabies, while the African Savannah has lions, meerkats, and rhinos. If you can avoid all the strollers, it's a pretty good time. (On Labouchere Rd in South Perth. Walk across the river from the city center, or take the blue CAT to stop #19 and then ferry across the river (ferry $1.10). ☎9367 7988. Open daily 9am-5pm. $13, children $7, families $36.)

**UNDERWATER WORLD.** Leafy sea dragons, four kinds of sharks, and saltwater crocodiles live here. Walk through a tunnel surrounded by fish and feed animals in a pool. Grownups can book ahead to dive with the sharks for $85, or swim with the seals for $75. (North of Perth along the West Coast Hwy at Hillary's Harbour. Take the Joondalup train to Warwick, then the #423 bus to Hillary's ($3). ☎9447 7500. Open daily 9am-5pm. $17.50, concessions $13.50, children $9.)

**PERTH MINT.** Watch as 200 oz. of liquid gold is poured into bar form. Visitors can also purchase a variety of medallions with custom engravings. (310 Hay St., Take the red CAT to stop #10. ☎9421 7223. Open M-F 9am-5pm, Sa-Su 9am-1pm. $7, children $3.)

**ABOVE, BELOW, AND BEYOND THE CITY.** A **river cruise** from Perth or Freo features local sights along the river and a view of the city skyline from the water. (Captain Cook Cruises departs Pier 3, Barrack St Jetty, daily 9:45am and 2pm; departs East St Jetty, Fremantle, daily at 11am. $27, children under 14 $13, families $67.) Hire catamarans and windsurfs on the south bank off Mill Point Rd, opposite the city center, to further enjoy Swan River. **Malibu City Dive** has diving tours to **Rottnest Island,** noted for its unique corals and fish, and also offers scuba certification classes. (☎9225 7555. Rottnest trips start at $95.) **Planet Perth** has several tour options, including a night tour of a wildlife park with kangaroos, koalas, and Tasmanian devils. (☎9342 2829. Tours start at $40.) For **Pinnacles** tours (see **Nanbung NP,** p. 649), the most popular options are **West Coast Explorer** (☎9418 8835), **Redback Safaris** (☎9275 6204), and **Travelabout Outback Adventures.** (☎9244 1200. All tours from $90.) **Easyrider Backpackers** offers longer tours and the option of leaving the tour and staying for a while before jumping back on later. (☎9226 0307. 5-day tour $300.) For the most adventurous the **W.A. Skydiving Academy** offers tandem jumps. (193 William St, Northbridge. ☎9227 6066, freecall ☎(1800) 24 50 66. From $190.)

# FREMANTLE

**FREMANTLE PRISON.** Get a thorough look at the workings of a maximum security prison without committing a felony. The prison was closed in 1991, three years after nearly burning down during a prisoner-incited riot. (Along Hampton Rd, take Parry to Fairbairn St. ☎9430 7177. Tours every 30min., last tour 5pm. Spooky candlelight tours W and F; book ahead. Open daily 10am-6pm. $11, concession $9, children $4, families $26.)

---

**PRIDE GOETH BEFORE THE ESCAPE** Although its colonial keepers regarded Fremantle Prison as escape-proof, one man managed not only to escape but to dramatically embarrass British authorities in the process. John Boyle O'Reilly and six of his comrades were sentenced to imprisonment at Fremantle for their role in the 1868 Fenian uprising in Ireland. O'Reilly broke out of the prison and hitched a ride to North America aboard a whaling ship. He moved to Boston, where the Irish-American community raised money for him to outfit a new ship, the *Catalpu.* O'Reilly then sailed for Australia to rescue his brethren. When British ships fired on the *Catalpu* off Fremantle, O'Reilly raised the American flag, reminding his attackers that they were in international waters, whereupon his aggressors grudgingly backed off. O'Reilly made his rendezvous with his fellow Fenians and returned to Boston.

**FREMANTLE MARKETS.** One can find just about anything in the markets, from clothing to a massage. There's even a cold beer lurking in the corner at the Market Bar. Fresh veggies abound; prices hit rock bottom around closing time on Sunday. *(On the corner of South Tce and Henderson St. Open F 9am-9pm, Sa 9am-5pm, Su 10am-5pm.)*

**MARITIME MUSEUM.** The Western Australia Maritime Museum explains the history of Fremantle, port trading, and marine archaeology, with several pieces from area shipwrecks. The museum also runs tours of the *HMS Ovens*, a decommissioned Australian submarine. *(At the corner of Cliff St and Marine Tce. ☎9431 8444. Open daily 10:30am-5pm. Tours M-F 11:30am and 2pm. Admission by donation, tours $9.)*

**FREMANTLE ARTS CENTRE.** The Centre is home to the **Fremantle History Museum**, which focuses on the history of European settlement in the area, and also to several art galleries. The building was formerly an asylum, and ghost sightings are apparently a regular occurrence. *(Corner of Ord and Finnerty St. ☎9430 7966. Open Su-F 10:30am-4:30pm, Sa 1-5pm. Admission by donation.)*

**TOURS.** The **Fremantle Trams** runs on several different routes through the city. *(Depart on the hour from in front of Town Hall on High St. $8, concessions $7, children $3.)* **Fremantle Ghost Walks** offers evening tours of the old asylum and the West End of town, both of which are reputed to be haunted. *(Depart from Town Hall. ☎9484 1133. Asylum tour M 8pm, West End tour W 8pm. $12, concessions $10, children $8.)*

# ◪ NIGHTLIFE

Perth has heaps of good pubs, clubs, and cafés, with laid-back, friendly crowds. The best of the scene is in Northbridge, but everything's open much later on weekend nights than during the week. The free entertainment weekly *XPress*, with the lowdown on what's happening, can be picked up at news agents, record stores, and hostels. The new website *perthtribe.com* is another resource for nightlife listings. Covers and dress codes are rare, but a few places will give you nasty looks if you're in jeans, and most places require closed-toed shoes—for feet's sake.

Perth is a reasonably **gay- and lesbian-friendly** city; for up-to-date event info, listen to *Sheer Queer*, a gay and lesbian radio program on 92.1FM (W 9-10am) or check out the free *Westside Observer*, a gay and lesbian newspaper. The **Arcane Bookshop**, 212 William St, is friendly and full of info and publications on Perth's gay scene. *(☎9328 5073. Open M-W 10am-6pm, Th-Sa 10am-9pm, Su noon-5pm.)*

## NORTHBRIDGE AND CITY PROPER

**The Grovesnor,** 339 Hay St (☎9325 3799). The place to go for original live music. A laid-back bar, dripping with music—CDs and records hang from the ceiling. Relaxing house music on W; live band Th until 11:15pm. Weekly local band contest F-Sa; live bands Su. Open daily for dinner, W-Sa until midnight, Su until 10pm.

**The Brass Monkey,** on the corner of James and William St, Northbridge (☎9227 9596). A fun place for drinking tasty, pricey brews. It makes a good beginning or end of the pub crawl that is Northbridge at night. Pool tables downstairs; mellow upstairs with fireplace and balcony. Open M-Sa 11am-midnight, Su noon-10pm.

**Connections Nightclub,** 81 James St, Northbridge (☎9328 1870). A popular gay-owned club with DJ-spun dance, house, and techno beats. Theme nights like Hawaii night, and shows F and Su. Cover: M-Th $3, F-Sa $10, Su $5. Tu: Men only night. Open Tu-W, F 10pm-6am, Sa 9pm-6am, Su 9pm-1am.

**Bar Universal,** 221 William St, Northbridge (☎9227 9596). With *sake*, live jazz, and the slightly older crowd that comes with these things. On weekends, the better you dress, the more likely you are to get in. Open M-Th 11:30am-midnight, F 11:30am-1am, Sa 4pm-1am, Su 4-10pm.

**Metropolis Club** (☎9228 0500). Two locations at 146 Roe St in Perth and 58 South Tce in Fremantle. Glitzy, big time dance clubs that occasionally have name acts. Cover $5 after 10pm. Open F-Sa 9pm-4am. Freo location also open Th 9pm-3:30am.

WESTERN AUSTRALIA

**The Court Hotel,** 50 Beaufort St, Northbridge (☎9328 5292). Near the corner of James St. Off-the-wall theme nights like "bears' night"—for big hairy men and their fans. During summer, live bands play outside in the beer garden. Weekly drag shows featuring acts like Star Whores. Everyone welcome. Open M-Sa 11am-midnight, Su 3pm-10pm.

**Paramount,** 163 James St (☎9228 1344). This noisy bar is open until late on weekends and features live music that tends to the heavy side of the spectrum. There's also an outdoor bar if the smoke (or the music) is too much for you.

**Redheads,** 44 Lake St (☎9228 2888). A great assortment of fish are entertained by hard-core dance music downstairs F-Sa; trendy lighter fare on W; and hip-hop night upstairs Sa. Open W 9pm-4am, F-Sa 7pm-6am downstairs; F-Sa 8pm-1am upstairs.

## FREMANTLE

**The Bog,** 189 High St (☎9336 7751). There's almost always something happening here, so it's a worthwhile first stop. Tu: free food, $6 jugs of beer, and $4 bourbons. Open Su-Th 6pm-midnight, F-Sa 6pm-late.

**Sail and Anchor,** 64 South Tce (☎9335 8433). British pub with a wide variety of intoxicating poisons. Freo is the home of Redback beer; this is a good place to hoist one. Open M-Th 11am-midnight, F 11am-1am, Sa 10am-1am, Su 10am-10pm.

**The Newport,** 2 South Tce (☎9335 2428). Pool room, 2 live bands, an outdoor area, and a dark smoky area. Cover Su for local original music varies. Open M-Th 11am-midnight, F-Sa 11am-1am, Su noon-10pm.

**Rosie O'Grady's,** 23 William St, Freo (☎9335 1645) or 195 James St, Northbridge (☎9328 1488). Dancing to live music nightly and a healthy supply of old Guinness advertisements. Open M-Th 11am-midnight; F-Sa 11am-1am, Su 11am-10pm.

# NEAR PERTH

## ROTTNEST ISLAND

Called a "rat's nest" by Dutch explorers who mistook the island's wallabies (quokkas) for giant rats, Rottnest Island is a hunk of limestone about 19km off the coast near Fremantle (30min. by ferry). The island was settled by farmers in 1830 but was turned into a prison for Aboriginals in 1838. The prison was closed in 1903, but many stone buildings built by the prisoners remain. Today, the island is a class-A nature reserve, and tourists and locals flock there to cycle, swim, snorkel, surf, and relax. The quokkas, Rottnest's unofficial mascot, roam about the island unafraid of humans. Watch out if you're carrying food—quokkas have voracious appetites, but feeding the critters is prohibited because it's harmful to their health.

**E TRANSPORT.** Several companies offer **ferry service** to Rottnest from Perth, Fremantle, and Hillary's. The cheapest is **Oceanic Cruises** (☎9325 1191), which departs from Pier 2 of the Barrack St Jetty (daily 8:45 and 10am; $47 same-day return, children $14; extended stay $10 more) and from the East St Jetty, Fremantle (daily 9:45 and 11:45am; $34, $10); they offer free pickup from Perth hotels and Freo train station. **Rottnest Express** has several daily departures from Victoria Quay, Fremantle. (☎9335 6406. Same-day return $38, children $15; extended stay $5 more.) Both ferries offer $5 VIP and YHA discounts. Courtesy buses depart from the main jetty roughly every hour and head to Geordie Bay, Kingstown, and the airport. The **Bayseeker Bus** is the best way to get around the island (45min. loop around the island; every hr. 9am-4:30pm; day-ticket $5.50). **Bus tours** of the island are available, but are not very exciting ($13, student $10, children $7).

**⛟⛟⛟ PRACTICAL INFORMATION, ACCOMMODATIONS, AND FOOD.** The **Visitors Information Centre** is just up the road from the jetty, at the corner of Colebatch Ave, Thomsons Bay. (☎9372 9752; fax 9372 9755. Open daily 8am-5pm.)

# Hmm, call home or eat lunch?
## With **YOU** <sup>SM</sup>
### you can do both.

Nathan Lane for YOU<sup>SM</sup>.

No doubt, traveling on a budget is tough. So tear out this wallet guide and keep it with you during your travels. With YOU, calling home from overseas is affordable and easy.

If the wallet guide is missing, call collect 913-624-5336 or visit www.youcallhome.com for YOU country numbers.

**Dialing instructions:**
*Need help with access numbers while overseas? Call collect, 913-624-5336.*

Dial the access number for the country you're in.
Dial 04 or follow the English prompts.
Enter your credit card information to place your call.

| Country | Access Number | Country | Access Number | Country | Access Number |
|---------|---------------|---------|---------------|---------|---------------|
| Australia ᴠ | 1-800-551-110 | Israel ᴠ | 1-800-949-4102 | Spain ᴠ | 900-99-0013 |
| Bahamas ✚ | 1-800-389-2111 | Italy ✚ ᴠ | 172-1877 | Switzerland ᴠ | 0800-899-777 |
| Brazil ᴠ | 000-8016 | Japan ✚ ᴠ | 00539-131 | Taiwan ᴠ | 0080-14-0877 |
| China ✚ ▲ ᴠ | 108-13 | Mexico ᴜ ᴠ | 001-800-877-8000 | United Kingdom ᴠ | 0800-890-877 |
| France ᴠ | 0800-99-0087 | Netherlands ✚ ᴠ | 0800-022-9119 | | |
| Germany ✚ ᴠ | 0800-888-0013 | New Zealand ▲ ᴠ | 000-999 | | |
| Hong Kong ᴠ | 800-96-1877 | Philippines ᴛ ᴠ | 105-16 | | |
| India ᴠ | 000-137 | Singapore ᴠ | 8000-177-177 | | |
| Ireland ᴠ | 1-800-552-001 | South Korea ✚ ᴠ | 00729-16 | | |

**YOU** <sup>SM</sup>
*Service provided by Sprint*

ᴠ Call answered by automated Voice Response Unit. ✚ Public phones may require coin or card.
▲ May not be available from all payphones. ᴜ Use phones marked with "LADATEL" and no coin or card is required.
ᴛ If talk button is available, push it before talking.

# Pack the Wallet Guide

## and save 25% or more* on calls home to the U.S

It's lightweight and carries heavy savings of 25% or more*
over AT&T USA Direct and MCI WorldPhone rates. So take this
YOU wallet guide and carry it wherever you go.

### To save with YOU:

- Dial the access number of the country you're in (see reverse)
- Dial 04 or follow the English voice prompts
- Enter your credit card info for easy billing

*Service provided by Sprint*

*Based on AT&T USA Direct rates, Tariff 24.1.3.A, April 8, 2000 and MCI WorldPhone rates, Tariff 3.07341,
May 1, 2000. 25% discount applies for calls less then 100 minutes. Promotion subject to change. Restrictions may apply.
Copyright ©Sprint 2000. All rights reserved. All trademarks referenced herein are the property of their respective owners.

There is an **ATM** opposite the **grocery store** in the shopping area. The **Rottnest Youth Hostel** is on Bickley Point, a 20min. walk or a quick bike ride from the Visitors Centre at Kingstown—follow the YHA signs. A free shuttle bus runs from the settlement every 30min. The hostel is inside an old army barracks with bland, spacious rooms. Reception 8am-5:30pm. (☎9372 9780; fax 9292 5141. Dorms $18; doubles $42; non-YHA members $21, $49.) Though there are meals available in the barracks complex ($7), it's a good idea to bring food to the island. The Thomsons Bay settlement has a **grocery store** in the pedestrian mall behind the visitors center, but prices are considerably higher than on the mainland.

◪ **ACTIVITIES.** The best way to see Rottnest is by bike. The army of bikes zipping around the island is decidedly funny when everyone is packed into the small town area, but biking is peaceful and fun. **Rottnest Island Bike Hire** has a wide selection, including bike buses for family groups. (☎9292 5105. 1-speed $15 per day; 18-speed $20; locks and required helmets included; $25 deposit.) The beaches become emptier as you head away from the settled areas—go far enough and you may have the luxury of a cove all to yourself. **Narrow Neck** and **Salmon Bay** offer good **fishing**, and **Longreach Bay** and **Geordie Bay** are among the many good swimming spots close to the settlement. **Parker Point** has good snorkeling, and **Strickland Bay** has good surfing. Whales and dolphins are frequently seen from the windy, breathtaking cliffs at **West End.** Ask at the visitors center for maps of "snorkel trails" in the island's bays. **Rottnest Malibu Dive** (☎9292 5111) is the only dive shop on the island and has snorkel, diving, and surf tours as well as equipment rentals.

# THE DARLING RANGE, YORK, AND THE AVON VALLEY

Heading east from Perth, the city's suburbs gradually give way to the gently rolling orchards and verdant forest of the **Darling Range,** also called **Perth Hills.** Take the M1 train from Perth to Midland, then buses #317-320 or #327-330 from Midland Station. **John Forrest National Park** offers miles of shaded hiking trails, a colorful **wildflower** season, and kangaroos, parrots, and kookaburras galore. **Wayunga National Park** is filled with walk trails, wallabies, and Aboriginal sites, and known for its whitewater rafting. **Avon Valley National Park** is also in the area, with more trails and rivers for canoeing. (Each park has an $8 per day entrance fee.) For questions on the national parks, check with the **CALM** office, 51 Mundering-Weir Rd. (☎9295 1955. Open M-F 8am-5pm.) **Lake Leschenaultia** affords peaceful swimming, canoeing, BBQ, walking trails, and **camping.** (☎9572 4248. Gate open until anywhere from 4:30 to 9pm. Day entry $7 per car; book ahead.)

Undulating hills, misty dales, and wildflower fields make the **Avon Valley,** 100km east and somewhat north of Perth, a great place for a drive or a bicycle ride. WA's first inland settlement, **York** is home to several restored historical buildings and makes a good lunch spot. Westrail **buses** leave for **Perth** from the railway station (2hr., 1 per day, $10). The **tourist bureau** is in the Town Hall on Avon Tce. (☎9641 4301; fax 9641 1787. Open daily 9am-5pm.)

# YALGORUP NATIONAL PARK

About 100km south of Perth is Yalgorup National Park, marked by a sign 500m before you reach the turn-off. If coming from the north, do not mistakenly turn at Yalgorup Eco Park or Yalgorup Park Rd, which come before the correct turn-off. There is an obvious sign for the National Park. The park, featuring tent sites, nature reserves, miles of dunes, and a forest of jarrah and tuart trees with peppermint undergrowth, is a popular summer weekend destination for Perth residents. Emus, grey kangaroos, and wallabies frolic here, and in the winter the beaches make for good bird-watching, when the speedboats aren't scaring off the wildlife.

# SOUTHWEST

The Southwest coast of Australia is experiencing a boom in both tourism and year-round residency. It's not hard to understand why—Mother Nature has indeed been kind to the Southwest, and its spectacular scenery, with the world's greatest variety of wildflowers, makes it a favorite for travelers. Hikers rave about the Stirling and Porongurup Ranges, and surfers swear by the Southwest's gorgeous beaches and pounding waves. Visitors can bushwalk in the region's karri and jarrah forests, and spot whales from the shore or a tour boat in the winter. The climate is ideal for vineyards, it's worth a trip just to tour these wineries and try some native vintages.

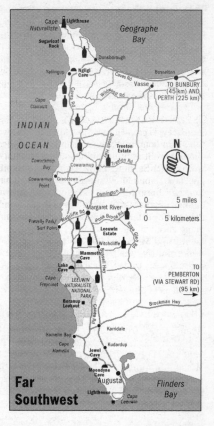

## ⌐ TRANSPORT

The easiest way to see the Southwest is by car; many sights are well off the bus routes, and public transportation in many of the towns is either nonexistent or inadequate. The 3hr. drive south from Perth toward Margaret River takes you through forests, farms, cattle stations, and the occasional limestone quarry. While the road is cluttered with a few too many small businesses for the first hour, the rest of the drive offers open fields, forests, shoreline, and picnic areas. Tours of many sights can be arranged, but costs are high. Nevertheless, several options exist for the auto-less. Some travelers use the **Easy Rider Backpackers** bus. A 3-month pass ($200) covers bus service among most regional hostels. (☎9226 0307; 24hr. notice for pickup. Southbound buses leave Perth Tu-W, F, and Su; buses return to Perth M, W-Th, and Sa.) Another option is **Westrail's** 28-day Southern Discovery Pass ($130). The pass allows for bus and train travel to most southern and eastern destinations including Albany, Esperance, and Kalgoorlie. An option for the rugged and diehard hiker is the **Bibbulmun Track,** which goes from Kalamunda, outside Perth, to Albany through North Bannister, Dwellingup, Collie, Balingup, Bridgetown, Manjimup, Pemberton, Northcliffe, Walpole, and Denmark. If the whole 964km trek seems a bit daunting, it is easy to pick it up and hike a smaller section, or even do short day hikes along the track and back again. The trail passes campsites and shelters with bunks, and towns with hostels and B&Bs that will pick up hikers from the trail. Contact the **Bibbulmun Track Office** (☎9334 0265; fax 9334 0100; www.calm.wa.gov.au).

## BUNBURY

Two hours south of Perth, Bunbury (pop. 28,000) was built around an early Aboriginal settlement. Although the city has other attractions, Bunbury shares in Western Australia's obsession with dolphins. However, for those who tire of dolphin-sighting, as though that is possible, Bunbury offers a laid-back atmosphere in which to amble along the coast or a base from which to visit nearby parks.

**TRANSPORT.** If heading south by train, Bunbury is 3km from **Wollaston,** the southern terminus of WA's **train** network. Transit buses will honor a train ticket stub for a free lift to Bunbury. **South West Coachlines** (☎9791 3222), Carmody Pl, Old Railway Station on Carmody and Haley (open daily 8am-7pm) runs to: **Perth** (2½hr., 3 times per day, $16, students $8); and **Augusta** via **Busselton** and **Margaret River** (2½ hr., departs 6:20am on weekdays, 6:20am and 4:20pm on weekends, $28, students $14). **Transit buses** circle the city regularly (M-F 7am-6pm, Sa 7am-1:15pm; $1.70, $2.50 for outlying areas).

**PRACTICAL INFORMATION. Bunbury Visitor Information Centre,** Carmody Pl and Haley, is conveniently located next door to the bus station. (☎9721 7922. Open M-Sa 9am-5pm, Su 9:30am-4:30pm.) The **police** (☎9791 2422) are on the corner of Wittenoom St at Stephen St, and the **hospital** (☎9722 1000) is on Bussell Hwy following Blair St south out of town. The **post office,** 153 Victoria St (☎9792 9906; fax 9792 9907; open M-F 8:30am-5pm), several **banks,** and a handful of cafés and restaurants share the strip with boutiques and art shops. **Internet** is available at the **Bunbury Internet Café,** on the corner of Carmody Pl and Hayes St next to the bus station. (☎9791 1254. Open M-Sa 8am-4:30pm. 30min. $5.)

**ACCOMMODATIONS AND FOOD.** The **Wander Inn,** 16 Clifton St, is friendly and popular, with ping-pong and pool tables, BBQ, and bright, clean rooms. (☎9721 3242. Dorms $16; singles $20-30; twins and doubles $38. YHA, VIP.) The quiet and tidy **Bunbury YHA,** 55 Sterling St at the corner of Stirling and Moore St, provides free shuttle service from the train station. It also features several private bathrooms, a rare luxury. (☎9791 2621; fax 9791-4742. Internet 1hr. $8. Reception 8-10am and 5-10pm. Dorms $14; doubles $35; family rooms from $50. YHA.) Both hostels rent **bikes** and can arrange **dolphin tours, bushwalking,** and **kayaking.** The shopping center behind the tourist office houses **Coles Supermarket** (open M-W and F 8am-6pm, Th 8am-9pm, Sa 8am-5pm). Victoria St between Wellington and Symmons St is known as 'Cappuccino Strip' for its restaurants and cafés.

**SIGHTS.** Bunbury has managed to avoid the crowds that plague Monkey Mia, but it may not stay quiet for long. The town is growing rapidly, new houses are springing up and public spaces are being revitalized and expanded. The dolphin tours that draw so well in other towns are advertised all over the city, and the **Dolphin Discovery Centre** on Koombana Dr offers a place to swim with these popular creatures and boat tours. The center also offers a theater and interactive exhibits. (☎9791 3088. Open daily Oct.-Apr. 8am-5pm; May-Sept. 9am-2pm. $5, children $2, families $12. Tours daily 11am, 2pm; $18, children $12.) **Dolphin-sighting tours** also run from the jetty on Koombana Dr through **Naturaliste Charters.** (☎9755 2276. 1½hr. daily 9:30, 11am, 2pm. $25, students $22, children $12.)

Non-dolphin related attractions like **Big Swamp Wildlife Park** and **Wellington National Park** can serve as a nice change of pace. The **Marlston Hill Lookout** on the east end of town offers an amazing view of the town on one side and of the Indian Ocean on the other. A walk along Ocean Drive on the north side of town passes basalt rocks, remnants from an ancient volcanic era.

# FROM BUNBURY TO MARGARET RIVER

Small towns dot the Southwest coast toward Margaret River.

**BUSSELTON. Busselton** is a bit tame, but is a pleasant place to relax, walk out along the 2km Busselton Jetty (one of several good seasonal dive spots in the area), fish, swim, or visit an Aboriginal garden. **Buses** run through Busselton en route to **Augusta** from **Perth,** but there is little transportation available within the town itself. The **Busselton Tourist Information Centre,** Peel Tce and Queen St, is helpful, and a small Aboriginal garden is located in their backyard. (☎9752 1288; fax 9754 1470. Open M-F 8:30am-5pm, Sa 9am-4pm, Su 10am-4pm, off-season 10am-2pm.) The **Busselton Backpackers,** 14 Peel Tce, is simple but adequate with free

WESTERN AUSTRALIA

laundry and kitchen facilities. (☎9754 2763. Dorms $14; singles and doubles $25; family room $40.) There are restaurants and dive shops lining Queen St.

**YALLINGUP.** Yallingup Beach was one of the first breaks surfed in WA in the 1950s and remains famous among Australian surfers. The best time for surfing is Oct.-Apr., though it gets very crowded, especially in Dec. and Jan. The two best spots are **Yallingup Beach** itself, right in front of Yallingup's Surf Shop at the bottom of Yallingup Beach Rd, and Smith's Bay, just south of Yallingup Beach. Direct questions to Caves Park Store (☎/fax 9755 2042), on Yallingup Beach Rd.

**Yallingup Cave,** also known as Ngilgi's Cave after an Aboriginal legend about two battling spirits (Ngiligi was a good spirit who fought Wlgine, an evil one; it's not like you would name your starship after Darth Vader) is part of a system of caves descends as much as 37m below the surface. The caves are at the end of a well-marked turn-off to the right off Caves Rd when traveling from Dunsborough to Yallingup. (Tours daily every 30min. from 9:30am-3:30pm. $12, children $5, family $34.) Adventure tours of more difficult sections of the caves are available, but require booking 24hr. in advance. (☎9755 2152. $35.) A number of hiking trails from 2-14km run between the caves and the stark **Cape Naturaliste Lighthouse.** (Open daily 9:30am-4pm. Tours $10, children $2.50.)

Yallingup has little in the way of public transportation or cheap accommodations, so Dunsborough is the best place to stay. In Yallingup, however, there is the somewhat hard to find **Hideaway Holiday Homes,** 24 Elsegood Ave, which has big ensuite cabins that are simple and cheap with several bedrooms and a kitchen, but no linen. (☎9755 2145. Doubles from $55, 6-bed from $77.)

**DUNSBOROUGH. Dunsborough,** with sandy beaches and somewhat sheltered swimming, is another popular holiday destination for Perth residents. Eagle and Meelup Bays both have great beaches for snorkeling and surfing; turn-offs are well marked on Cape Naturaliste Rd, north of town. **Bay Dive and Adventures,** 26 Dunn Bay Rd (☎9756 8846), offers diving, diving classes, and snorkeling trips. For **whale watching,** call **Naturaliste Charters;** tours depart daily from the Boat Ramp on Geographe Bay Rd. (☎9755 2276. 3hr., $45, children $25, under 4 free.) The **Dunsborough YHA,** 285 Geographe Bay Rd, is spacious and looks out over the water. Buses between Augusta and Perth will drop off in Dunsborough upon request. The hostel manager can book tours and has info about bike rentals, canoes, and wind-surfing equipment. (☎9755 3107. Dorms $15-16; doubles $36. YHA, VIP.) Camping is available at **Dunsborough Lakes Caravan Park,** 2-48 Commanage Rd. (☎9756 8300; fax 9756 8333. $12 per person, off-season $8. Cabins $30-130.) Dunn Bay Rd runs through the center of town, with small restaurants and a Newmart **Supermarket.**

# MARGARET RIVER

Among vineyards and forests, washed by the rolling surf of the Indian Ocean, Margaret River (pop. 7000) is a small community of wine makers, artisans, and surfers. The laid-back attitude of locals is so contagious, most visitors adopt the pace and take a few days to relax here—the sights will be seen in their own good time. "Margaret's" also makes a convenient base from which to explore much of the southwestern coast; Cape Leeuwin (to the south) and Cape Naturaliste (the north) are each about 40min. from town by car. Margaret River can be reached by heading south from Busselton on Bussell Hwy or by the more scenic but slower Caves Rd.

▐ **TRANSPORT.** The South West Coachlines **bus stop** in Margaret River is on the Bussell Hwy across the street from the tourist office. Buses leave for Perth (4½ hr., 1-2 per day, $23). Westrail uses **Harvey World Travel,** 109 Bussell Hwy, as its Margaret River agent. (☎9757 2171. Open M-F 9am-5pm, Sa 9am-noon.)

▐ **PRACTICAL INFORMATION.** The **Bussell Hwy** serves as Margaret River's main thoroughfare. The **tourist office** (☎9757 2911; fax 9757 3287; open daily 9am-5pm)

**DON'T QUIT YOUR "WINING"** Who would ever think that the downest of the down under would be comparable to Bordeaux in the elegant business of wine making? And yet it makes perfect sense. The Margaret River area is at latitude 33° south, while Bordeaux wine grapes grow at 40° north. They are practically inverses of each other. And the southwestern Australian coast has a helpful maritime influence, plenty of rain in the winter, and a long and healthy growing season. Do not make the mistake of missing the wineries and their free tasting hours while you are in this area, but be mindful of the blood alcohol level limit (.05%) for drivers.

and **supermarket** are just up the hill from Tunnbridge St. Other services include: **police station,** 42 Willmott Ave (☎9757 2222); **hospital** (☎9757 2000), on Farrelly St off Wallcliffe Rd; **post office,** 53 Townview Tce (☎9757 2250; open M-F 9am-5pm), one block up Willmott Ave from Bussell Hwy; and **Cyber Corner Café,** 72 Willmott Ave, across the street (☎9757 9388; 30min. $5).

**⌐ ACCOMMODATIONS.** Though hostels are cheapest, the area's B&Bs can be a sweet deal for those traveling in pairs or larger groups. The friendly **Margaret River Lodge** is 1½km southwest of the Bussell Hwy off Wallcliffe Rd on Railway Tce. The rooms don't sparkle, but the Lodge offers a number of amenities, including free pickup from the bus station, bike and bodyboard rentals, a swimming pool, and a vegetable garden. (☎9757 9532; fax 9757 2532. Internet 30min. $4. Dorms $16; singles $35; doubles $49. YHA, VIP, NOMADS, ISIC.) **Surf Point Lodge,** on Riedle Dr south of Prevelley, is just above Gnarabup Beach and within walking distance of the Rivermouth area. Clean, spacious rooms and perks including free pickup from the bus station, bikes ($12 per day), boogie boards ($10 per day), and BBQ. (☎9757 1777; fax 9757 1077. Internet 30 min. $5. Dorms $21. Doubles $52, off-season $47; ensuite with fridge $68, $63. Book ahead in summer.) **Matan's Lodge** is on Caves Rd, after a right turn-off of Wallcliffe Rd going away from town. A bohemian, relaxed place, the lodge has an art gallery and small but pretty rooms. (☎/fax 9757 2936. Doubles $65.) **Prevelly Park Beach Resort,** on the way into Prevelly Park taking Wallcliffe west out of town, offers camping. (☎9757 2374; fax 9757 2790. Tent sites $8-12; van sites $45-55; $5 for each extra person. Cabins $55-75.)

**⌂ FOOD.** Margaret River's restaurants are good but pricey. Many are BYO, perfect for enjoying the fruit of the local vineyards. **Sails Café,** 117 Bussell Hwy, is the place to go for breakfast—at breakfast, lunch, or dinner. Pancakes, eggs, it's all here, and so good it can sometimes be hard to get a table. (☎9757 3573. Open daily 8am-5pm.) **Café 111,** 111 Bussell Hwy, features a constantly changing menu which usually includes seafood or pasta from $8.50, comfortable chairs, and lots of reading material in a colorful space. (☎9758 7222. Open daily 8:30am-5pm.) **Goodfellas Café Woodfire Pizza,** 97 Bussell Hwy, offers huge bowls of pasta and exotic pizzas in an elegant candlelit setting. (☎9757 3184. Open daily 5:30-9:30pm. Meals $10-15.) Several of the vineyards on Caves Rd towards Yallingup also have restaurants for those who wish to get out of the center of town.

**◧◫ SIGHTS AND NIGHTLIFE.** There are about 50 wineries in the Margaret River area, and some produce premium quality Australian wines. Several wineries are accessible by bike or foot from town. **Chateau Xanadu,** 3km southwest of town on Terry Rd, is run by friendly folk offering free tastings. Atmosphere is created by the local artwork displayed and sold. (☎9757 2581. Open daily 10am-5pm.) Just behind Xanadu, the **Cape Mentelle** winery, just off Walcliffe Rd, also offers free tastings in a less relaxed atmosphere. (☎9757 3266. Open daily 10am-4:30pm.) For those with a car, Caves Rd north of town is covered with vineyards.

The **Eagles Heritage Raptor Wilderness Centre,** on Boodjidup Rd, is Australia's largest collection of birds of prey and is dedicated to education, rehabilitation of injured birds, and breeding projects. (☎9757 2960. Flight displays daily 11am and

1:30pm. $7, seniors $5, children $3, families $17. Wheelchair accessible.) **Biking** is a good way to travel in and around Margaret River; free area maps are available in the tourist office. Margaret's **beaches** and **surf** are a major tourist draw. Packs of grommets (young surfers) learn the ropes in the relatively tame surf at **Rivermouth;** more experienced surfers delight in the breaks off of Gracetown or at Surf Point. There are tons of other surf spots in the area, but levels of safety and difficulty vary depending on the weather and the size of the swell, so stop at **Beach Life Surf Shop,** 117 Bunbury Hwy, just up from the tourist office, for information and advice or to set up a surfing lesson. (☎9757 2888; 24hr. surf report ☎(1900) 92 29 95. $30 for group lessons, $55 for individual.)

The locals booze it up at the **Settler's Tavern,** 97 Bussell Hwy. The tavern also serves grub and hosts live bands of all sorts (every night but M); on W nights anyone is welcome to grab an instrument and join in the making of music, all the merrier under the influence of alcohol. (☎9757 2398. Cover comes and goes. Open M-Th noon-midnight, F noon-2am, Sa 10am-1am, Su 11am-10pm.)

## NEAR MARGARET RIVER: CAVES ROAD

Caves Rd south of Margaret's is one of the area's most spectacular drives. Winding through the karri forests of **Leeuwin-Naturaliste National Park,** the road passes hundreds of hidden **caves,** though only four are open to the public. They're difficult to access without a car; a taxi from Margaret's to Mammoth Cave (the nearest to town) costs about $25 each way, or hostels can usually help arrange transport. Still, the caves are amazing natural phenomena, and worth the trouble of getting there. The **Cave Works Eco Centre,** at **Lake Cave** about 15km south of Margaret's, has educational exhibits, but the caves themselves are much more interesting. (☎9757 7411. Open daily 9am-5pm; $3, children $2; free with cave entrance fee.) Tours at Lake Cave and **Jewel Cave,** which is the real gem of the four caves, take about an hour each (every hr. on the half hour 9:30am-3:30pm; $13, kids $5, family $34). The **Mammoth Cave** tour is self guided, with CD headset provided ($13, children $5). More serious cavers will want to visit **Moondyne Cave,** where 2hr. tours start daily at 2pm ($27.50, kids 10 and up $19; book in advance). Jewel and Moondyne are about 25km farther south on Caves Rd, closer to Augusta than to Margaret's. The Cave Works **Grand Pass** covers all the caves except for Moondyne, and is valid for 7 days ($30, children $12, families $84). Go spelunking crazy.

Follow the gravel Canto Rd 5km past Lake Cave to get to **Conto Spring** and **Merchant Rock,** a spot with crashing waves and well-weathered trees. The road down can be rough on a 2WD. About 25km south of Margaret's on the left side of Caves Rd is the **Boranup Maze,** a shrub labyrinth that loses its mystery in winter ($2, children $1). Just south of the maze a right turn off Caves Rd leads to the **Boranup Lookout,** a windy spot with views out to the Indian Ocean. Technically, you need a National Parks Pass to visit these sights, but there is rarely anyone checking. On the other hand, a hefty $50 fine awaits those who are caught. (Passes $8 per day, 4-week $20, 1-year $45. Available all over, try CALM centers.)

Several companies can organize half- or full-day tours of **wineries** and other local sights. One of the most popular is the **Great Wine, Food, Forest Bushtucker Tour.** In five hours, this tour packs in a drive through the karri forest, a gourmet lunch, and a tour of six local vineyards. (☎9757 9084. Tours daily at noon. $40, children $30.) Also popular are **Boranup Eco Walks** tours, guided walks through karri and jarrah

---

**90-TON THREESOME!** If you do take one of the many worthwhile whale watching trips in the Southwest, watch for groups of Humpback Whales traveling in threes. Why three? These mammals, each weighing around 30 tons as adults, are too big for private sexual intercourse. Male sexual organs are large and unwieldy; they are 14% the length of the entire body. Thus, an interested couple must get help from another whale for everything to work properly. These threesomes are commonly spotted in the winter around Augusta and Dunsborough.

forests. (☎9757 7576. Daytime walks 1½-3hr. $10-15; children $5-8; night walks 1½hr. in summer $12, children $6; book ahead.) **Margaret River Tour Company** will arrange sight-seeing, winery tours, and surfing trips. (☎041 991 7166. Half-day $40, full-day $65-70; free pickup.) **Milesaway Tours** (☎(1800) 81 81 02) offers similar tours at similar prices and departs from a number of towns in the region; call for details. **Outdoor Discoveries** (☎015 084 945) organizes abseiling outings and other adventurous expeditions from $65 per person.

# AUGUSTA

About 45km south of Margaret River lies the small, pleasant community of Augusta. It's a good base for exploring the surrounding area and (in season) cruising on a whale-watching tour.

**⚑ PRACTICAL INFORMATION.** The **tourist office** is on Blackwood Ave. (☎9758 0166; fax 9758 0174. Open M-F 9am-5pm, Sa-Su 9am-1pm; off-season M-F 9am-4pm, Sa-Su 9am-1pm.) The **post office** is across the street. (☎9758 1570. Open M-F 9am-5pm.) A **fruit market** and **grocery store** are before the tourist office. An **ATM** is just up the street.

**⚑⚑ ACCOMMODATIONS AND FOOD.** The best lodging in town is the ▓**Baywater Manor Resort**, a.k.a. **Augusta YHA**, 88 Blackwood Ave. It's spacious and perfectly maintained, and visitors tend to relax and enjoy the ocean rather than stay out partying. The owners arrange whale-watching and sight-seeing tours and rent cars and bikes. (☎9758 1290; fax 9758 1291. Dorms $17; doubles $42, with bathroom $53; non-YHA members $2 more.) If you can't get a bed in town, the **Hamelin Bay Caravan Park** has camping and van sites in a beautiful location. Eat breakfast on the beach and keep an eye out for the stingrays. (☎9758 5540. Sites $16, powered $20.)

The **Cosy Corner Café** (☎9758 1408) serves tasty breakfast and lunch fare, including burgers and sandwiches for $5-10. Across the street is the **Augusta Bakery** (open daily 8am-5pm). **Cumberland Restaurant,** in the **Augusta Hotel,** is a more expensive alternative for dinner. (☎9758 1944; fax 9758 1227. Meals $10-20.)

**⚑⚑ SIGHTS AND ACTIVITIES.** Nine kilometers south of the town is ▓**Cape Leeuwin**, Australia's southwestern-most point, where the Indian and Southern Oceans meet. A **lighthouse** built in 1895 stands guard over the spot. ($4, children $2. Open daily 9am-4pm.)

**Whales** can often be spotted off the coast from June to October, as they stop in Flinders Bay on their way to the warm waters of the north. Humpback, Southern Right, and Pygmy Blue Whales are all abundant in season, and at times there are as many as 80 whales in the bay. **Naturaliste Charters** runs whale-watching tours from Augusta in the winter, departing daily at 10am. (☎9755 2276. 3hr. $45, children $25.) Be sure to confirm the tour to make sure the weather isn't too rough.

About 12km north of Augusta at the southern tip of Caves Rd lies **Hamelin Bay,** which has a lovely beach. Indeed, the bay may be beautiful to the point of distraction: the areas has seen 11 shipwrecks since 1882. Independent scuba and snorkeling outings to the four visible wrecks are welcome, but there's no boat, so you have to swim from shore. Swimming here is relatively sheltered, and fishing in the area is superb. Check with someone before going on a dive; the wrecks are old and shift around a bit depending on the weather. **Augusta Hardware and Scuba Supplies,** on the main Blackwood Ave stretch across from the post office, has information on dives, renting gear, and filling tanks. (☎9758 1770. Open daily 8:30am-5:30pm.)

# PEMBERTON

The eastern spur of Hwy 10 runs from Karridale, north of Augusta, out to Pemberton, a good 1½hr. drive. Make sure the tank is full before you leave Karridale, and watch for signs—an easily missed right turn onto Stewart Rd, about 40km from Karridale, leads to the last 69km stretch to Pemberton. As the nude hills attest, tiny

**PROTECTING THEIR OWN** The towering karri trees of WA's southwest fear fire like any other trees, but they also once served to fight flames. Rangers the world over erect fire towers to catch signs of forest fire as early as possible, but those in WA decided to construct cabins in the tops of the trees themselves. Rather than attempt to build 60m-tall observation towers up to the lofty canopy from the forest floor, the rangers drove pegs into the karri trunks so that they could climb to these treetop dwellings. From here, the fearless (and vertigo-resistant) firefighters remained vigilant from the 1930s to 1970s, when they switched to aircraft. Today, the towers are open to visitors. Tremendous views reward those who can muster the courage to ascend a mammoth eucalypt. The highest such treehouse, at 75m, is in the **Bicentennial Tree** in Warren National Park.

Pemberton is first and foremost a timber town. Logging trucks rumble at a steady rate along the Vasse Hwy through town, and Pemberton is home to the largest hardwood sawmill in the southern hemisphere. Fortunately, much of the area's spectacular karri forest is safe in designated national parklands.

**⊠ PRACTICAL INFORMATION.** The **Karri Visitors Centre** has information on the surrounding forest, a pioneer museum, and a "Discovery Centre" ($2, children $1, families $5). More practically, it has showers ($2) and toilets for campers. Walk or hike through the forest of karri trees, which are unique to southwestern WA. The Visitors Centre sells useful bushwalking guides and car passes for the nearby national parks. (☎9776 1133; fax 9776 1623. Open daily 9am-5pm.)

**⊠⊠ ACCOMMODATION AND FOOD. Pemberton YHA Pimela Chalets,** on Stirling Rd in the middle of the forest, has clusters of rooms in small cabins that share a kitchen and bathroom. It's charming, but don't try to walk to town—it's almost 10km. (☎9776 1153; fax 9776 1819. Internet 30min. $3. Dorms $16; twins $35; doubles $40; families $55; non-YHA members $3-6 extra.) **Pemberton Backpackers** is right on the main strip, and offers small, cheery rooms in a friendly atmosphere. (☎9776 1105. Internet 30min. $5. Dorms $16.50; twins $19; doubles $49.50.) The **Shamrock Restaurant** is right in the center of town and serves lunch and dinner for reasonable prices. (☎097 761 186. Open daily 11:30am-late.) The aptly named **Chinese Restaurant** is up the hill on Dean St (open W-M 5:30-9:30pm).

**⊠ ACTIVITIES.** The **Gloucester Tree,** one of the tallest fire lookouts in the world, is a prime attraction in Pemberton. Steel dowels wind 61m up the trunk to the platform, from which the brave-hearted get a breathtaking view of the forest canopy and distant sand dunes. Miles of walking trails criss-cross the surrounding **Gloucester National Park** ($8 per vehicle; there is an attendant at the Gloucester Tree). Scenic rail tours of the area may be booked in the tourist office or by phone. (☎9776 1322. Tours 1¾-5½hr. Prices start at $13, children $6.50.) **Pemberton Hiking Company** (☎9776 1559) offers guided hikes, including wheelchair accessible options.

West of Pemberton on the road to Augusta is **Beedelup National Park,** home to the **Beedelup Falls** and a karri tree with a hole cut in its middle through which you can walk. Roads inside the park are unsealed; 2WD cars have access, but drivers should be careful. The ascent to the falls is quite dangerous after dark.

# GREAT SOUTHERN

Sprawling karri and tingle forests, rugged mountain ranges, and the vast nothingness of the Nullarbor Plain are all part of the diverse and beautiful region known as the Great Southern. The South Western Hwy serves to link the region's many parts together, and it's fascinating to watch the land change as one drives along. Albany functions as an urban hub for the sparsely populated southern coast, but by the time you reach Esperance, Perth's cosmopolitanism seems a world away.

The largely agricultural Great Southern is home to a number of respected vineyards, many of which offer complimentary wine-tastings. Tourism has become an economic mainstay, peaking in the spring wildflower season and in the summer, when the beaches around Denmark, Albany, and Esperance are most inviting. Winters in the Great Southern can be chilly, so be sure to bring a warm jacket.

# WALPOLE

Tiny and congenial, Walpole (pop. 450) is experiencing a tourism boom primarily because of its proximity to **Walpole-Nornalup National Park** and the highly popular **Valley of the Giants** Tree Top Walk, 14km out of town.

**? PRACTICAL INFORMATION.** The friendly, volunteer-run tourist bureau, on the north side of the highway, hands out information on the surrounding tingle and karri forest and the beautiful coast of Walpole and Nornalup Inlets and also sells Tree Top Walk tickets. (☎ 9840 1111; fax 9840 1355. Open M-F 9am-5pm, Sa-Su 9am-4pm.) Walpole's **post office** (☎ 9840 1048; open M-F 9am-5pm) and **grocery store** can be found across the highway on parallel Nockolds St.

**╏╏ ACCOMMODATIONS AND FOOD.** The soon to be YHA-affiliated **Tingle All Over**, on Nockolds St, has clean accommodations, a BBQ, and a huge chess set with two-foot-high wooden pieces in the yard. All rooms have sinks, but showers are a short walk outdoors. (☎ 9840 1041. Dorms $16; singles $28; twins and doubles $42. Non-YHA add $2.) Not far away, on Church St, is **Walpole Backpackers**, a newcomer to town. (☎/fax 9840 1222. Laundry and kitchen facilities. Reception 24hr. Dorms $16; singles $25; twins and doubles $38; family rooms $50.) Camping is available at **Valley of the Giants Ecopark**, 13km east of Walpole to the left of the Hwy. (☎/fax 9840 1313. Camping sites $6 per person, powered $11; van site for 2 people $35-50.) Info on camping in the national park is available at the tourist bureau or the **CALM** center in Walpole. (☎ 9840 1027. Open M-F 8am-5pm.) The **Wooz and Suz Café**, along Nockolds St, serves delicious sandwiches and burgers ($5-10) with seating inside or out. (☎ 9840 1214. Open daily 8am-8pm; off-season 9am-7pm.)

**╏┆ ACTIVITIES.** The area's biggest draw is the **Tree Top Walk,** a 600m metal catwalk passing through the canopy of tingle trees. The views are incredible, but those scared of heights be forewarned—the swaying walkways reach as high as 40m. (☎ 9840 8200. Open daily 9am-5pm, last admission 45min. before closing. $6, children $2.50, families $12.) The **Ancient Empire** boardwalk, a short, pleasant walk, departs from the Tree Top Walk info center and passes through a grove of giant red tingle, which can reach 16m in circumference.

Fifteen kilometers east of Walpole is the right turn down Conspicuous Beach Rd leading to **Conspicuous Cliff,** a popular stretch of beach with an information board, picnic space, and public restrooms. It is wheelchair accessible up to the first lookout. About 6km east of town is the left-hand turn-off to the **Giant Tingle Tree,** 24m in diameter and the largest known living eucalypt in the world. Walpole is also famous for its diversity of **wildflowers,** including more than 90 species of orchids; prime viewing runs between August and November.

**WOW Wilderness Services** offers cruises through the Walpole Inlet to a beach and some coastal forest. (☎ 9840 1036. 2½hr.; daily 10am, in summer also 2pm. $22, children $11.) **Walpole-Nornalup National Park** has several hiking trails. The **Bibbulmun Track** runs through Walpole, and it's easy to pick up around town. Both the tourist bureau and the CALM office are along the track, so hikers can leave from there and then come back or turn left from the South Coast Hwy onto Tinglewood Rd (10-15km east of Walpole) to get to a carpark. Safety conditions vary; check with the **CALM** office before heading out. Some shorter hikes around the area include the **Coalmine Beach Heritage Trail,** a flat 3km hike from the tourist bureau in Walpole through melaleucas, ferns, and sheaoak to Coalmine Beach (2hr.); and a short but steep hike (1½hr.) through wildflowers to the top of **Mount Frankland.**

## DENMARK

Located 66km east of Walpole along the South Coast Hwy, Denmark is green, squeaky clean, and proud of it. Originally a timber town, Denmark rapidly exhausted its trees and has since become quite an earth-friendly place. Winner of the 1998 national "Tidy Town" title for its appearance and progressive environmental policies, Walpole has a thriving organic farming scene. Denmark has more than a small town's fair share of organic produce shops, health food stores, and whole-grain bakeries, and a friendly population to boot.

**TRANSPORT AND PRACTICAL INFORMATION.** Westrail buses run to **Perth** (7hr.; daily 8:52am, M and Th 9:27am; $45) and **Albany** (40min., $7). **Strickland St,** Denmark's main thoroughfare, intersects the **South Coast Hwy.** Heading east, turn right on Strickland to reach the **bus stop** and adjacent **tourist office.** (☎9848 2055; fax 9848 2271. Open daily 9am-5pm.) The volunteer-run **Denmark Environment Centre,** also on Strickland St, has plenty of info on the local community and on national environmental issues. (☎9848 1644. Open M-F 10am-4pm, Sa 10am-1pm.) The **post office** is across the street from the tourist office. (☎9848 1302. Open M-F 9am-5pm.) There's **Internet** at **Telecentre** next to the tourist office. (☎9848 2842. Open M-F 10am-4pm. 1hr. $8.) BancWest has an **ATM.**

**ACCOMMODATIONS.** The **Denmark Waterfront,** 63 Inlet Dr, contains simple wood rooms for backpackers as well as laundry, kitchen, and BBQ. (☎9848 1147; fax 9848 1965. Internet 30min. $5. Rooms $15, weekly $85.) The **Wilson Inlet Holiday Park** (☎9848 1267) is located on a beautiful spot 4km down Ocean Beach Rd right on the inlet. There are cabins available for backpackers to share ($15 per person). The **Figtree Café** (☎9848 2051) is one of several small restaurants on Strickland St, and on summer weekends there's live music in a courtyard known as "the Spot."

**SIGHTS AND ACTIVITIES.** Denmark's coastline has good fishing, surfing, boating, and swimming. Shores of **William Bay** are the most scenic, but **Waterfall Beach** to the east runs a close second. **Greens Pool, Elephant Rocks,** and **Madfish Bay** are all sheltered enough to swim. Take William Bay Rd off the South Coast Hwy west of Denmark. The tourist office has a good map of the area and info on **West Cape Howe** and **Walpole-Nornalup National Parks.** Hikes for all skill levels abound, and the ever-present **Bibbulmun Track** runs along the coast. Denmark has an active **arts and crafts** scene, with wares for sale at a number of shops around Strickland St. The town holds four market days each year with live music. There are also several **wineries** in the area; ask at the tourist office about tastings.

## MOUNT BARKER

Mt. Barker (pop. 1700), 47km north of Albany along Albany Hwy, is the sleepy gateway to the floral paradise that is Porongurup National Park. The park is filled with karri trees and wildflowers and views of the Porongurup Range, the oldest volcanic formation in the world, dating back more than 1100 million years. To get there from town, follow Lowood Rd north and turn right on Albany Hwy, then left on Porongurup Rd (tourist drive 252). Westrail **buses** run to Perth and Albany once per day. The **tourist office** is in the old train station on the Albany Hwy. (☎9851 1163; fax 9851 1919. Open M-F 9am-5pm, Sa 9am-3pm, Su 10am-3pm.)

Most lodging and restaurants are located along the Albany Hwy and the Muir Hwy, which becomes Langton Rd as it enters town. **Chill Out Backpackers,** 79 Hassell St, off the very start of Porongurup Rd, is in a beautiful wooden A-frame building. (☎9851 2798. Dorms $15; singles $20; doubles $35.) About 20km outside of town on Porongurup Rd is the homey **Porongurup Shop and Tearoom,** which offers clean, spacious rooms and fresh vegetables from the garden. Upon request, owners will try to arrange pickup from Mt. Barker or Albany. (☎9853 1110. Internet 1hr. $5. Rooms $16.) The **Mt. Barker Caravan Park** is at the north end of town. (☎9851 1691. Singles $17, weekly $88; campers for 2 $40-55.) The food options in

> **PICK ON SOMEONE YOUR OWN SIZE** If you are walking along a sandy path and find a mound with a few large holes in it, you may want to knock gently with your foot to see who is home. But stand back, because it is likely the home of the bullet ant. Or several bullet ants, to be more exact. Each ant is over an inch long, extremely aggressive, and has the ability to inflict excruciating pain. These ants come streaming out to see who has come to call, and when they figure out where you are, they will stand facing you in a fighting stance. If they do manage a bite, the pain is terrible, and rumored to last a week. If you doubt the power of the bullet ant, feel free to test the theory and get back to us with the results...

town are somewhat limited. The **Mt. Barker Hotel** (☎9851 1477) has lunch daily between noon and 2pm, and **Wing Hing Chinese Restaurant** (☎9851 1988) is open for dinner 5:30pm-late. For **groceries,** head across the street to SupaValu.

Two of the most popular hikes are the short but very photogenic **Castle Rock** walk (1½hr.) and the longer **Tree in the Rock** hike (2½hr.). Both are accessible by right-hand turns from Porongurup Rd. Hundreds of varieties of **wildflowers** have been identified in Porongurup and the nearby **Stirling Range National Park.** Peak season is Sept.-Nov., but in the high mountains there are still flowers in Dec.

## STIRLING RANGE NATIONAL PARK

The Stirling Range National Park should not be missed. The rugged, rocky 1000m peaks are a dramatic contrast to vast farmlands, making the drive from Albany undoubtedly one of the Great Southern's most scenic routes. The Stirling Range is the only place in Western Australia that regularly sees snow, and high winds and rain are common near the top—be sure to carry food, water, and warm clothing. Visitors can buy an $8 day pass to the park at an honor box on the road to the trail. Enter yourself in the registration book, but don't forget to fill out the time on your way out—unless you want to dispatch a search team. Four-week holiday passes, valid at all of Western Australia's parks, are available for purchase from a park ranger ($20 per car). Though a **shuttle** (☎9827 9229) travels to Bluff Knoll from the Stirling Range Retreat ($11), the best way to see the area is by car. **Car rental** is easily arranged in Albany: try **King Sound Vehicle Hire** (☎9841 8466), **Crossroads Autos** (☎9842 2993), or **Albany Car Rentals** (☎9841 7077). Prices range $25-50 per day.

Along Chester Pass Rd, 90km north of Albany and just across the road from the turn-off to Bluff Knoll, the **Stirling Range Retreat** has comfortable, immaculate rooms and a swimming pool. Owners have seasonal slide shows and guided nature walks ($10). Trailers are well-heated and roomy. (☎9827 9229. Campsites $7 per person; trailers $33, for 2 $33, for 3 $38.50; backpackers units $17; cabins for 5-6 with kitchen $54. Book ahead Sept.-Nov.) Across the street, the **Bluff Knoll Café** serves a variety of quick, inexpensive meals. (☎9827 9293. Open daily 8am-9pm.)

Try any of the hikes to enjoy the spectacular scenery and nearly 1600 species of **wildflowers.** The most popular is the 3.1km ascent to **Bluff Knoll,** the highest peak in southwestern Australia, which is rated as one of Australia's top 25 climbs. The Aboriginals labeled this knoll Bullah Meual (Great Many Face Hill) for its mercurial climate and face-like appearance. Though marked as a 3-4hr. return, experienced hikers can make the moderately strenuous ascent in an hour. A rockier, less-manicured trail ascends 2km to **Toolbrunup,** the Range's second highest peak.

## ALBANY

Established in 1826, Albany was the first colonial settlement in what is now Western Australia. Albany is proud of its history, and the tourist office has info on buildings of historic interest. Also the commercial center of this region, Albany has all the conveniences of a small city, with the traffic to match. Fortunately the coastline remains pristine, and a lovely view waits around each corner.

WESTERN AUSTRALIA

**▤ TRANSPORT.** Westrail buses (☎9813 1053) depart from in front of the tourist office to **Perth** (6 hr., $35) and **Bunbury** (6hr., 1 per day, $34) via **Walpole, Pemberton, Augusta,** and **Margaret River.** The Bays bus heads to **Esperance** (6 hr., M and Th, $46). **Hitchhikers** usually wait by the "Big Roundabout" on the Albany Hwy, 2km west of the north end of York St. *Let's Go* does not recommend hitchhiking. The two hostels in town also have a steady stream of travelers sharing rides. For the lazy, Love's Bus Service (☎9841 1211) provides **city transport** for $1.80 a trip (M-Sa), but it's not hard to get around Albany on foot.

**◪ PRACTICAL INFORMATION. York St** runs north-south through the center of town. The **tourist office** is in the Old Railway Station, just east of the southern end of York St near Stirling Tce. (☎9841 1088; fax 9842 1490. Open M-F 8:15am-5:30pm, Sa-Su 9am-5pm.) Other services include: **ATMs,** on York St; **police,** on Stirling Tce (24hr. ☎9841 0555); **hospital,** on Hardie Rd (☎9892 2222); **Internet** at the **Yak Café,** 38 Sterling Tce (☎9842 9399; open 9am-late; 30min. $5); **post office,** 218 York St at Peels Place (☎9842 5877; open M-F 8:30am-5pm).

**▥▤ ACCOMMODATIONS AND FOOD.** Albany has two hostels near the center of town. The **Albany Backpackers,** on Spencer St, just around the corner from Stirling Tce and one block east of York St, has spacious, colorful rooms in which a cheery atmosphere prevails. There's info about tours of local sights, including snorkeling and kite flying. In June-Sept. they have a deal with **Esperance Backpackers:** stay two nights between the two hostels and the third night is free. (☎9842 5255. Reception 8am-9pm. Internet 30min. $5. Dorms $17; doubles $42. YHA, VIP, ISIC, NOMADS.) The **Albany Bayview YHA,** 49 Duke St, two blocks west of York St, is another good option with a nice view of the bay. Visitors can rent cars ($39-50 per day), bikes, boogie boards, and fishing gear. Free movies and popcorn. (☎/fax 9842 3388. Dorms $19; twins $38. YHA, VIP.) **Middleton Beach Holiday Park,** at the end of Middleton Rd, is farther from the center of town, but right on the beach. (☎9841 3593, fax 9842 2088. Sites $21, powered $22; off-season $18, $19.)

Somewhat pricey restaurants and cafés dot the main streets in town. Local favorites include **Dylan's on the Terrace,** 82 Stirling Tce (☎9841 8270), and **Eatcha Heart Out** (☎9841 6263) on York St, which has an extensive breakfast menu and great sandwiches. There's also lots of fast food available at the top of York St. For **groceries,** head east on Albany Hwy to the **Coles** supermarket, about 100m from York St. (☎9841 2544. Open M-W and F 8am-6pm, Th 8am-9pm, Sa 8am-5pm.)

**▧ SIGHTS.** Albany has the dubious distinction of being home to the world's largest whaling museum. **Whaleworld,** on Frenchman Bay Rd past the Gap and Blowholes, is on the site of Australia's last whaling station, which closed in 1978 because it was no longer profitable. Check out the former blubber vats, harpoons, and the docks where whales were cut up and processed. (☎9844 4021. Open daily 9am-5pm. 30min. tours every hr. 10am-4pm. $11, concessions $9, families $25.) If live whales are more your speed, try **whale watching** in the winter. Whales can be seen from May-Oct., though peak season is June-Sept. Several tour outfits run cruises; book at the hostels. **Southern Ocean Charters** (☎(0409) 10 71 80), a.k.a. **Big Day Out,** departs daily at 9:30am ($30).

Apart from whales, Albany's most impressive natural sight is the **Natural Bridge,** a rock formation bridging 24m above crashing waves. Nearby **blowholes** only work in rough weather, when spray from below the rock shoots out through a crack, earning the classy nickname, "blowjob." Take care on the rocks—it's a long way to the water below. Do not go beyond the blowhole itself; people have died trying to get a good photo. No Kodak moment is worth that. Both these sights are located in **Torndirrup National Park,** 20km south of town along Frenchman Bay Rd. Another natural beauty, the protected **Middleton Beach** lies just outside of town. The **Middleton Bay Scenic Path** is a pretty walk from the beach out to Emu Point. For those with access to a 4WD vehicle, **West Cape Howe National Park** (about 30km west of Albany) is worth exploring. The roads, which are more like trails, are treacherous even with 4WD, but the beaches (especially **Shelley** and **Dunsky**) are near perfect.

**⚥ NIGHTLIFE.** Albany has chill nightlife options. The **Earl of Spencer Inn,** on Dulce St, is an English-style pub with a beer garden popular among backpackers. Ask about the backpacker special—pie and a pint for $6. (☎9841 1322. Open M-Sa noon-midnight, Su 2-9pm.) The **White Star Hotel** has a bar, café, and pool table, catering to a younger crowd. (☎9841 1733. Closes at midnight.) In the summer, **Legends Bar** (☎9842 1711), at Middleton Beach on Flinders Pde, is hopping and **1912** (☎9841 7688) on York St is the dance center of the late night scene.

# FROM ALBANY TO ESPERANCE

As the South Coast Hwy slices eastward, rolling farmland slowly gives way to brush, and massive trucks known as road trains comprise most of the traffic. Give them a wide berth; they're unlikely to do the same for you. Fuel up in Albany before heading out because petrol stations only appear every 50-75km. The highway is low and fast and the temptation to speed will be great, but take care: the 500km stretch to Esperance is subject to high crosswinds and winter flooding. Jerramuhgup and Ravensthorpe are small towns en route, good for a stretch.

For those without a car, Westrail buses (☎13 10 53 or ☎9326 2813) run between **Albany** and **Esperance** via **Ravensthorpe** (M and Th $41). The **Ravensthorpe/Hopetoun Tourist Bureau** periodically publishes a newsprint guide to the area; check the tourist offices in Albany or Esperance. (☎9838 1277. Open daily when possible; summer 9am-5pm; winter 9am-4:30pm.) **Eftpos** is available at most petrol stations and at the **Hopetoun general store.** (☎9838 3052. Open daily 7:30am-6pm.) Other services include: **police** (☎9838 1004) and **hospital** (☎9838 1006). Ravensthorpe also has a few small restaurants and a grocery store.

About halfway between Albany and Esperance lies the enormous **Fitzgerald River National Park.** This park can be be accessed via **Bremer Bay** (the western end) or **Hopetoun** (the eastern end), or one of several unsealed roads running south from the South Coast Hwy. To get to Bremer Bay from the South Coast Hwy, turn right onto Bremer Bay Rd about 120km east of Albany, then travel 65km east. Hopetoun is 50km south of Ravensthorpe on Ravensthorpe Hopetoun Rd.

Named a Biosphere Reserve due to its abundance and diversity of wildlife, Fitzgerald River National Park hosts rare creatures like the **Malleefowl,** a bird that builds nests out of mounds of dirt that can reach 1m high and 4m wide, the **Chuditch,** a spotted carnivorous marsupial, and the **Dibbler,** a marsupial once thought to be extinct. **Whales** also can be seen from the reserve. To reach **Point Ann,** a particularly good spot, take Pabelup Dr from the north or Devils Creek Rd from the west. Hikes for all skill levels abound; the **East Mount Barren Walk** (3hr.), starting about 12km west of the Hopetoun entrance, is a good one of medium difficulty with great views of the beach. The park is also home to thousands of species of plants and wildflowers; spring (Sept.-Nov.) is the best time for viewing.

Parts of the park require a 4WD, but many areas are reachable on 2WD gravel roads. Caravans should not attempt park roads. Passes for the park are available at CALM offices in Albany (☎9842 4500) or Esperance and the tourist office in Ravensthorpe. Day passes can be deposited in an honor box at the entrance ($9 per vehicle). Camping is allowed at certain spots: **Four Mile Beach** (just west of Hopetoun) and **Saint Mary Inlet** (at Point Ann) are the easiest to access by car (2 people $8, each extra adult $5, children $3). Fires are not allowed, but gas barbecues are available free of charge at Mylies, Point Ann, Quoin Head and Fitzgerald Inlet. There are no reliable sources of water in the park, so be sure to bring enough. **Mt. Madden, Mt. Short,** and **Mt. Desmond** are not in the park itself, but all near Ravensthorpe, and offer excellent views of the area. **Cheynes Beach** in **Waychinicup National Park** is also highly recommended.

## ESPERANCE

Though blessed with a spectacular bay and some of the best beaches and diving Australia has to offer, Esperance (pop. 10,000) is far from Perth, Albany, and even Kalgoorlie, and thus isn't as popular as other spots along the southwest coast. But come summer, the town hops with tourists who flock to the area to swim, fish, dive, and explore nearby Stokes, Cape Le Grand, Peak Charles, and Cape Arid National Parks. Esperance itself is a pleasant, though rather ordinary town—the key to enjoying your stay is to escape to the surrounding natural splendor.

**TRANSPORT. Buses** (☎13 10 53) stop near the tourist office and run to: **Albany** (6-10hr.; Tu-W, F-Sa 8am; $42); **Kalgoorlie** (5hr.; W, F 10:15am, Su 5pm; $36); and **Perth** (10hr., M-Sa 8am, $56). Arriving by **car** from the west, the South Coast Hwy (Monjingup Rd) intersects Harbour Rd, which runs south into town. Several **car rental** companies have offices in town: **STOPOVER** (☎9071 0100) and **Avis** (☎9071 3998) have various deals for around $50 per day. **Hitchhikers** report luck at the north end of Dempster St and on Norseman Rd. Some travelers also check at the hostels for people coming or going. *Let's Go* does not recommend hitching.

**ORIENTATION AND PRACTICAL INFORMATION.** The **Esplanade** flanks the bay, and **Dempster St** snakes along roughly parallel to it. The **tourist office** is inside an old train station near the center of town on the corner of Dempster and Kemp St. (☎9071 2330; fax 9071 4543. Open M-F 8:45am-5pm, Sa-Su 9am-5pm.) **Banks** with **ATMs** accepting Cirrus and Plus cards lie along Andrew St and the block of Dempster St immediately to the north. Other services include: **hospital** (☎9071 9222) on Hicks St; **police** (☎9071 1900), half a block away on Dempster St; and **post office** (☎9071 1470; open M-F 9am-5pm), at Dempster and Andrew St.

**ACCOMMODATIONS.** The colorful **Esperance YHA Blue Waters Lodge,** 299 Goldfields Rd, is across the street from the ocean. Formerly a hospital in Queensland, the entire building was transported to Esperance, reassembled, and spruced up. The hostel is a 15min. walk from the city center along the harbor bike path. Perks include pool table, ping-pong table, Internet (30min. $4), and book exchange. Free bus station pickup and drop off. (☎/fax 9071 1040. Dorms $16; twins $40; families $55. Non-YHA $3 more.) **Esperance Backpackers,** 14 Emily St, just outside the end of town, has spacious rooms and a comfy lounge. Even the kitchen has personality with a huge slab of local wood as the table. They can arrange a wide variety of tours at reasonable prices. Free pickup from the bus stop. (☎9071 4724. Internet 30min. $4. Dorms $15; twins and doubles $38. YHA, VIP, NOMADS.) **NOMADS Shoestring Stays,** 23 Daphne St, is also a good option. Clean and ready to please, this hostel offers tours, hot tub, Internet, free bike hire, and lockers in the rooms. Free pickup and drop off are available. Best of all, there's a kangaroo who was taken in after being orphaned. She mostly concerns herself with soaking up rays in the back yard. (☎9071 3396. Dorms $16; doubles $38; family unit $50-60 depending on season. YHA, VIP, NOMADS.)

There is good **camping** in Cape Le Grand National Park, 60km east of town, and on **Woody Island** in Esperance Bay (entry to each park $8 per car per day). For up-to-the-minute info on camping on Woody Island, contact **Mackenzie's Island Cruises,** 71 The Esplanade (☎9071 5757). Sites from $9 per person.

**FOOD. The Tin Shed** (☎9071 2172), on Andrew St, is a great place for a sandwich or a simple dinner. They're open until late on F and Sa. Among Andrew St's bizarre plethora of bakeries, the burgeoning chain **French Hot Bread** offers the best prices on lamingtons, doughnuts and, of course, hot french bread (open M-F 6am-6pm, Sa-Su 6am-4pm). **Taylor St. Tearooms** offers more expensive dinner fare, but $10 will still get you some good pasta and a nice view of the bay. (☎9071 4317. Open daily 7am-10pm.) A **supermarket** is in the shopping center at the corner of Pink Lake Rd and Dempster St (open M-W, F 8am-6pm, Th 8am-8pm, Sa 8am-5pm).

WESTERN AUSTRALIA

**PRETTY IN PINK** Why are many of the lakes in Western Australia pink? Because these lakes are full of salt, making perfect homes for salt lovers like the Dunaliella salina algae and bacteria called Halobacterium cutirubrum. These tiny bits of life can live in water with salinity as high as 35% NaCl—the ocean is usually around 3%. The bacteria are naturally pink in color and live along the salt crust at the bottom of the lake. When the salinity, temperature, and sunlight are all at high levels, the life forms produce beta carotene to protect themselves. And we see pink from the shores. The algae is even farmed in some places to make food coloring or dietary supplements.

**SIGHTS AND ACTIVITIES.** Drivers or bikers with strong legs should try the 38km loop along the **Great Ocean Dr,** which snakes along the coast and by the algae-tinged **Pink Lake.** The tourist office has a decent map and the road is clearly marked. Take care if you're biking; the road can be narrow and curvy. To begin the drive, start at the southern end of Dempster St and turn right onto Twilight Beach Rd. This drive also passes some great beaches, **Blue Haven** and **Twilight** are especially pretty. In town, the main beach along Esperance Bay is where **sea lions** put on a show below the big tanker jetty—they know where the big fish are.

**Merivale Farm,** 25km east of Esperance along Merivale Rd, serves lush desserts and coffees. (☎9075 9020. Open in summer Sa-W 10am-5pm.) **Mt. Ridley,** about 65km from Esperance, has some **Aboriginal paintings** in the hollowed out boulders at its periphery, as well as a miniature wave rock. To reach it, go east from Esperance along Fisheries Rd, turn-off at Dempster Rd and follow it to a 4WD road about 250m before Ridley Rd. At this point, drive or walk 1.5km to Mt. Ridley.

**Cape Le Grand National Park** lies 60km east of Esperance and should not be missed. Take Goldfields Rd north to Fisheries Rd, turn right onto Marivale Rd, and right again onto Cape Le Grand Rd. For transportation to the park, ask at Esperance Backpackers or Shoestring Stays about tours. Even driving to the park from Esperance, along the 40km stretch of beach, is beautiful. Once in the park, try the short (3km; allow 1½hr.) but direct ascent up **Frenchman Peak.** At the top, phenomenal natural topology allows for completely sheltered views of coast and sea. Down the road, **Lucky Bay** offers incredible white sands and glowing aquamarine water, some surf, and very friendly 'roos. **Hellfire Bay** is equally stunning. In summer there is good snorkeling, possibly with dolphins. But beware of riptides and undertows, and if you are driving on the beach, do not park your car above squishy patches of sand that can suck your car in like quicksand.

**Diving** around Esperance is quite good. **Sanko Harvest,** the second largest **wreck dive** in the world, is popular among experienced divers. **Esperance Diving and Fishing** guide dives and charter fishing trips. (☎9071 5111. Diving from $75. Fishing charters from $120.) **Peak Charles National Park,** north of Esperance along the Coolgardie Esperance Hwy, has **rock climbing;** ask at the CALM office, 92 Dempster St for details. (☎9071 3733. Open M-F 8:30am-4:30pm.)

# GOLDFIELDS

A few hundred kilometers east of Perth, a handful of towns cling tenaciously to a precarious existence in the middle of WA's harsh interior. Two things keep these towns from disappearing altogether: water, piped in from the coast, and gold. In 1893 a group of Irish prospectors stumbled onto an area that would come to be known as the Golden Mile, and the city of Kalgoorlie was born. Today, would-be miners continue to migrate to Kalgoorlie, now the unofficial capital of the Goldfields, in search of work. For the casual traveler however, Kal is a long way from anything and not much of a destination in itself. The Goldfields are barren and dry, and if you're heading west to Perth from Eyre, you may consider heading south along the South Coast Hwy. Unless you mine, or even if you do, the scenic coastal towns will most likely make for a more enjoyable trip.

# NORSEMAN

About 100 years ago, "Hardy Norseman" was tethered overnight in this area as his rider slept. The restless horse pawed at the dusty ground, uncovering a chunk of gold. Prospectors rushed to the area, and the town of Norseman was born. Today, however, Norseman serves more as a waystation than a destination. For travelers heading north from Esperance, Norseman is the first encounter with the Goldfields. For those heading east across the desolate Nullarbor Plain, it is the last taste of civilization for over 1000km.

The **tourist office** on Robert St, one block east on the highway between Sinclair and Richardson St, has information about Norseman and traveling the Eyre Hwy. They also offer free showers, which is a dream come true for Nullarbor survivors. (☎9039 1071. Open daily 9am-5pm.) Next to the office is a small welcome park, one of the few green spots in town (open daily 7am-6pm). In late-breaking news, the people of Norseman were shocked when ANZ bank recently installed an **ATM**. "What do we do with this new-fangled gadget?" an anonymous bank customer cried. Other services include: **police** (☎9039 1000), at the corner of Prinsep and Ramsey St; **hospital** (☎9039 1100), on Talbot St; and **Internet** at the Telecentre on Robert St (☎9039 0400; open M-F 9am-3pm; 15min. $2.50).

The charming, family-run **Norseman Guest House and Backpackers Lodge** on Prinsep St offers comfortable accommodations for visitors who are inevitably on their way somewhere else. Backpackers can use a small kitchen and an outdoor sheltered lounge area. (☎9039 1541. Dorms $16.50; twins $22; singles $27.50.) Norseman's **food** options are limited. The town's hotels and motels have restaurants, but there are no great budget options. The SupaValu, 89 Robert St, has **groceries** (open M-F 8:30am-6pm, Sa 8:30am-5pm, Su 9:30am-1pm). The **BP 24-hour Travelstop** offers a diner, convenience store, and **petrol.**

# CROSSING THE NULLARBOR

The **Eyre Hwy,** running between Norseman and Adelaide across the **Nullarbor Plain,** is a grueling desert haul by car or bus; on a Greyhound **bus,** it's a mind-boggling 26hr. trek ($225, 10% discount with YHA card). The one noteworthy sight is the pink **Lake McDonald** near Penong. **90 Mile Straight,** the longest completely straight stretch of highway in Australia and possibly the world, begins just west of Cocklebiddy. For questions on what is allowed across the border into SA, call the agriculture department (☎9039 3227 in WA, ☎8625 2108 in SA). The **tourist office** in Norseman has helpful info and handles bus bookings. When you reach **Ceduna** at the eastern corner of SA's **Eyre Peninsula,** pick up a Nullarbor certificate of completion at the tourist office. That's a keeper. For more info on this highway, see p. 463.

# GREAT EASTERN HIGHWAY

The drive from Perth to Kalgoorlie along the Great Eastern Hwy is long (nearly 600km) and uneventful. The first hour heading east from Perth winds through the city's suburbs and the **Swan River Valley;** travelers may encounter nasty **traffic** near the city. Driving through the **Darling Range** offers beautiful fields and forests full of wildflowers in season. Road trains rule the road; beware of wide loads bearing machinery, farm equipment, and even buildings. The last stretch between the tiny town of **Southern Cross** (really no more than a wide spot in the highway) and **Coolgardie** is a very desolate 200km. This part of the highway is not as well maintained, so fuel up whenever possible. **Merredin** (pop. 3700) is the largest town on the Great Eastern between Coolgardie and Perth. It's a good spot for lunch—the comfortable **Hay Loft Coffee Lounge** is one of several nice spots in town. Merredin also has a claim to fame: the world's longest road train (over 600m) was driven along this stretch of highway by one of Merredin's own. Fortunately, the tourist bureau is fully stocked with commemorative posters.

**Coolgardie** has exceedingly little to offer the average traveler. It's a dusty frontier town that serves mainly as a residential satellite for families of Kalgoorlie miners. The main street (94 Hwy, known as Bayley St in town) houses a **tourist office**

WESTERN AUSTRALIA

## ENGINEERING A TRAGEDY
Ask any WA local for the story of the Kalgoorlie pipeline, and you'll likely hear a popular Westralian yarn. The tale concerns an engineer who claimed he could build a conduit which would carry water from Perth all the way to Kalgoorlie. Since Kalgoorlie is over 500km away from Perth and over 400m higher in elevation, no one believed that it could be done. But he insisted, and finally someone gave him the money to try. The local legend relates that after he designed and built this huge pipeline, the engineer went to Kalgoorlie and turned on the tap. When nothing happened, the broken man shot himself in the head. No one bothered to turn off the tap, and about an hour later, water flowed out of the pipe and into Kalgoorlie. This account is a myth, but the real story of the engineer's death is tragic as well. After proposing the project in 1898, C. Y. O'Connor, frustrated by delays in construction and plagued by faithless critics, took his own life in 1902, one year before his visionary pipeline became a successful reality.

(☎9026 6090; open daily 9am-5pm), **police station** (☎9026 6000), and **post office** (☎9026 6060). There are no **ATMs** in town, but most roadhouses have **eftpos.** If you must spend the night in Coolgardie, the **Caltex Roadhouse,** on Bayley St, rents simple, clean rooms. (☎9026 6049; fax 9026 6756. Singles $38.50; doubles $48.50.)

# KALGOORLIE-BOULDER

The twin towns of Kalgoorlie and Boulder (total pop. 30,000) cling together as if to escape the isolation of the surrounding outback. Their reason for survival is simple—more than a century after panning began here, the region's gold mines are still going strong. These days, folks don't come to town hoping to stumble upon a lode, stake a claim, and strike it rich—gold doesn't come in chunks anymore; it's in microscopic particles. Mammoth mining interests run the show, and the work is backbreaking and dirty. However, pay can be quite high, and so workers flood the area and its hostels, creating an atmosphere that backpackers may find a bit gritty.

> ### HI HO HI HO, OFF TO WORK I DON'T GO
> The main reason people come to Kal is to work, but finding a job is not as easy as one might expect, especially in mining. Many mining companies will only hire employees with previous experience, and require safety training and certification, which takes time and costs money. It can be done, but it isn't a breeze.

##  TRANSPORT

The **airport** is south of Boulder off Gatacre St. Airlink, Ansett, and Skywest offer daily service to Perth (1-3 times per day, times and prices vary; check with tourist bureau). The **bus stop** is between the tourist office and the post office on Hannan St. Greyhound Pioneer heads to **Perth** (8hr., daily 10:45am, $101; book at tourist office). From the tourist office, Goldfields Express serves **Perth** (8hr.; M, W, and F 10:05pm; T, Th 2pm; $77, with YHA $59). Westrail Prospector trains depart from the **train station** on the corner of Forrest and Wilson St for **Perth** (8hr.; 1-2 per day; $53) and **Esperance** via Norseman (5hr.; departs M, W, F 5pm; $34).

## ORIENTATION AND PRACTICAL INFORMATION

Where the Great Eastern Hwy (National 94 from Coolgardie) ends at the Goldfield Kalgoorlie's main commercial boulevard tumbleweed rolls by; a hard-looking man with a ruddy complexion exits the saloon and spits out some blood from the brawl he just won; women and children scamper from the street. Hannan St looks like a movie set for an old Western and it is about as warm and welcoming as its story hero. Hannan St runs parallel to Hay St and perpendicular to Lionel St, Wilson St, and **Boulder Rd.** The residential district of Boulder lies several kilometers southeast. To reach Boulder from downtown Kalgoorlie, turn right on Boulder Rd at the north end of Hannan and follow it into **Lane St.**

The **tourist office** is at 250 Hannan St. (☎9021 1966; fax 9021 2180. Open M-F 8:30am-5pm, Sa-Su 9am-5pm.) Other services include: **police** (☎9021 9777), on Brookman St; **hospital** (☎9080 5888; 24hr. sexual assault hotline ☎9091 1922), off Maritana St on Picadilly St, several blocks north of city center; **Internet,** at **Netzone,** 109 Maritana St (☎9091 4178; open M-Sa 9am-7pm; 1hr. $10); and **post office,** on Hannan St, south of city center (open M-F 8:30am-5pm).

The police maintain that no areas of Kalgoorlie-Boulder are particularly unsafe, although they do warn to be careful of deep mining holes when bushwalking in the area. However, much of the city is poorly lit, and it is a good idea to exercise caution after dark. The center of Kal's notorious red-light district, **Hay St,** lined with tawdry, neon-adorned tin shacks advertising sauna and spa services, is home to several working brothels. **Women may not want to walk alone in this area after dark.**

## ACCOMMODATIONS

Most low-cost accommodation is geared toward those who have come to town for work and to stay several weeks or months. The two hostels on Hay St are smack in the middle of Kal's red-light district, an area that tends to be noisier at night. Both offer tours or at least transportation around the city for a small fee.

**Goldfields Backpackers,** 166 Hay St (☎9091 1482, mobile ☎(0412) 11 00 01; fax 9091 1484). Near the intersection with Lionel St. Shared kitchen, swimming pool in summer, lounge, and laundry. Call the cell phone if nobody is at reception. More oriented towards travelers than long term workers. Dorms $16; doubles $18; singles $20.

**Gold Dust Backpackers,** 192 Hay St (☎/fax 9091 3737). About a block down Hay St. from Goldfields. Clean, with big kitchen and nice lounge spaces. Slightly rowdier crowd. Internet 1hr. $8. Dorms $15.50; twins and doubles $40. YHA, VIP, ISIC, NOMADS.

**The Palms,** (☎9093 1620). In Boulder at the corner of Wittenoom and Hamilton St. Far from central Kalgoorlie, but free drop off to trains, buses, or planes. Clean rooms in a stylish old building that has seen better days. Free bicycles available. Shared kitchen, spa, BBQ. Dorms $15; singles $27.50; doubles $50; family unit with bath $72.

**Gold Inn,** 147 Hannan St (☎9091 1482). Same management as Goldfields, in a tired building in the center of town. Rooms are simple but adequate. Kitchen and laundry facilities. Singles and twins $16.50; doubles $33.

## FOOD AND NIGHTLIFE

**Monty's,** at the corner of Hannan and Porter, is open 24hr. and has various deals (Tu: $8 pasta). The **Star and Garter Hotel,** 479 Hannan St, another local favorite, has a daily roast for $9. (Open until 9pm.) **Cafés** line Hannan St and many open early or close late to serve the miners. Kal is a hard-working, hard-drinking town. Many **pubs** cluster around Hannan St in the city center. **Paddy's Ale House,** on Hannan St,

---

**FOURTEEN CARAT ASPHALT** Kalgoorlie, like all cities, originally had dirt streets, and one of the city's biggest problems was that whenever it rained, the streets immediately turned into impassable mudpits. Meanwhile, the town's miners were digging up huge amounts of a black stone called telluride in their search for gold, and didn't know what to do with it all. Eventually it occurred to the town's leaders that the telluride could be used to pave the streets, thereby killing two birds with one stone. It wasn't till after the job was done that a prominent scientist determined that telluride itself was composed largely of gold. Kalgoorlie's street had literally been paved with gold, but it didn't take them long to become unpaved once word got out. The town had to wait a little longer to solve its mud problem for good.

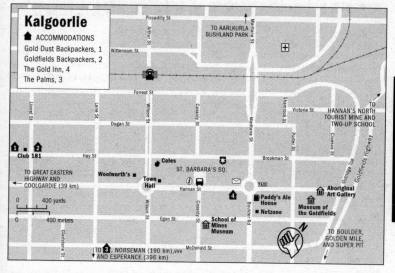

**Kalgoorlie**

▲ ACCOMMODATIONS

Gold Dust Backpackers, 1
Goldfields Backpackers, 2
The Gold Inn, 4
The Palms, 3

WESTERN AUSTRALIA

is a popular choice, serving food from 11:30am into the evening (sandwich and chips $6). They often have live bands at night. Coles **supermarket** is at the corner of Wilson and Brookman St (open M-F 8am-6pm, Sa 8am-5pm).

## SIGHTS AND ACTIVITIES

**Hannans North Historic Mining Reserve,** a right turn off Goldfields Hwy 2km north of Hannan St, offers demonstrations of gold panning and underground mining techniques. The gold pouring and drilling demonstrations are worthwhile, but don't plan on striking it rich panning for gold. The underground tour gives some insight into just how demanding mining work is; plug your ears tight for "the screamer" and the drill. (☎9091 4074. Open daily 9am-4:30pm. $16.50, concessions $12, children $8.50, families up to 6 $42.) The **Super Pit,** an immense open-pit working mine, is the largest hole in the Southern Hemisphere. Do not miss this amazing look into the heart of Kalgoorlie; you will be awed by the size of this pit. Really, it's a marvelous pit, and it doesn't even smell like B.O. The look-out is just outside town; turn towards Boulder on the Goldfield's Hwy, then turn left at the sign for the pit. (Open daily 6am-7pm, except when closed for further blasting. Free.) The **Museum of the Goldfields,** on Hannan between Porter and Outridge Tce, offers even more information about the history of gold mining in the area, tools, and samples of the product. (☎9021 8533. Open daily 10am-4:30pm. Suggested donation $2.) For a unique experience, you can visit one of Kalgoorlie's **brothels. Langtree's Club 181,** 181 Hay St (☎9021 5384), recently received a $2.5 million dollar face-lift and the tour shows just what that money bought. Yes, $20 is steep for views of a few bedrooms, but it's a lot cheaper than the "hands-on" tours.

To explore the area beyond the towns, take a drive or walk along the old railway. The woodlines mark the limits of the clear-cutting that took place in the early 1900s; the forest has not yet fully recovered. Some sheep stations allow visitors; ask at the tourist office. Several outfits have **bush tours;** Aboriginal guide Geoff Stokes (☎9093 3745; Geoffstokes@bigpond.com) runs day tours ($80) and camping trips ($170 per night) focusing on Aboriginal culture and native plants and animals. **Karlkurla Bushland Park,** on the northern border of town, has 200 hectares of regrown bushland, shielding the town from dust storms. **Goldrush tours** has half- and full-day tours of Kalgoorlie and surrounding areas. (☎9021 2954. $15-55.)

# BATAVIA COAST AND MIDLANDS

Renowned as much for its seas of bright autumn wildflowers as for its beautiful coast, this region depends on fishing, agriculture, and tourism to earn its keep. The Batavia Coast stretches from just north of the Pinnacles up as far as the red cliffs of Kalbarri, and takes its name from the most famous of the many shipwrecks that litter its waters. The wheat-growing Midlands extend hundreds of kilometers inland from the coast. The Brand Hwy is the main artery of the region, and runs north from Perth a few dozen kilometers from the coast. However, within the next several years a sealed coastal highway will be completed. In fact, most of it is already in use. The notable exception is the stretch between Lancelin and Cervantes, the gateway to the Pinnacles. These changes will undoubtedly bring more travelers to a region that is already a year-round attraction: the wildflowers peak in the autumn, the world-famous windsurfing is best in summer, and Kalbarri is busiest in winter, when many try to escape the colder weather of the south.

## LANCELIN

Considered by many to be the windsurfing capital of Australia, Lancelin (pop. 700) is a small fishing village about 120km north of Perth. The windsurfing season runs roughly from October through March, with the famed Ledge Point Sailboard Classic in January. But even in the off-season there's almost always some breeze.

**TRANSPORT AND PRACTICAL INFORMATION.** There is no public transportation to Lancelin, but Coastal Coachlines runs **buses** from Perth to nearby **Regans Ford.** (☎9652 1036. 2hr.; departs the Perth train station M-F 4:30pm; $14. Book ahead.) The easiest way to reach Lancelin is by car; from Perth, take Bulwer St to Charles St, which becomes Hwy 60 (Wanneroo Rd). The YHA will pickup its guests from Perth for $25. A **4WD vehicle** can drive the beach, and it's possible to drive along the dunes up the coast to **Cervantes.** Check with the **tourist information centre,** 102 Gingin Rd, to see if the beach is suitable. (☎9655 1100. Open daily 9am-6pm.) **Email** from the hostel or the **Telecentre** above the surf shop. (☎9655 2033. Open M-F 10am-4pm, Sa 10am-1pm. 1hr. $8.)

**ACCOMMODATIONS AND FOOD.** The sparkling, well-run **☒YHA Lancelin Lodge,** 10 Hopkins St, has a comfy lounge, free bikes and boogie boards, and a lovely kitchen. It's only a short walk to Lancelin's beautiful beach, and the people couldn't be nicer. (☎9655 2020; fax 9655 2021. Internet 1hr. $6. Dorms $17; doubles $45, family rooms $60, rates higher in peak season.) The other budget alternative is the **Lancelin Caravan Park,** just around the corner from the YHA—you can't miss the sign. (☎9655 1056. Tent sites $8, powered $10; on-site vans $20.) There's a **supermarket** on Gingin St. (☎9655 1172. Open daily 7am-7pm.)

**ACTIVITIES.** There are several coastal nature walks in the area; pick up trail maps at the hostel or tourist center. No matter where you are, the beach is never far away, and it's up to Western Australia's high standards. Lancelin's coral reefs are unusually close to shore, which makes for good snorkeling and diving. Lancelin Island, a bird sanctuary in swimmable distance, is one of the best spots. More experienced divers enjoy the **Key Biscayne Dive** around an old drilling rig. **Lancelin Surfsports,** 127 Gingin Rd, rents scuba, snorkeling, sandboarding, and surfing gear. (☎9655 1441. Open daily 8am-4pm, later in summer.) **Lancelin Dive and Charter** (☎(0417) 72 77 22) runs **fishing charters,** which leave at 7am from the Lancelin jetty. Charters are seasonal, so call ahead. More casual anglers cast right off the jetty.

Lancelin's other main tourist attractions are the sand dunes which extend for miles to the north and east of town. The dunes are a 4WD playground, and also a practice area for the Australian **military.** They're accessible by car, and many tour operators out of Perth bring travelers here to sandboard (like snowboarding, but on... well, you get the idea). **Bigfoot Bus Adventure Tours** offers a trip over the dunes in a schoolbus with monster truck tires and an equally monster stereo. You don't crush any cars, but it's a fun trip all the same. (☎9655 2550. $28, children $18.)

# NANBUNG NATIONAL PARK: THE PINNACLES

Though it doesn't deserve the hype that surrounds it, the Pinnacles Desert, located in Nanbung National Park, is nevertheless worth a visit. The park isn't really a desert at all, but a sand dune with thousands of wind-eroded limestone pillars, up to 4m tall. Dutch sailors sighting the jagged rocks from the sea mistook them for the ruins of an ancient city. From up close the park looks more like a graveyard, and is quite beautiful in its own desolate way. To avoid the crowds and to see the Pinnacles in the best light, come in the early morning or early evening.

The park is a good 250km north of Perth, and driving is definitely the easiest way to get there. Greyhound drops off in Cataby, which is east of **Cervantes,** the main base for park visitors (2hr.; 1 per day; $20). **HappyDay Tours** picks up from Cataby for a 2hr. walking tour of the Pinnacles. This is much more pleasant after an overnight in Cervantes. (☎9652 7244. Departs daily 8:30am. $33, from Cervantes $20.) The friendly **Pinnacles Beach Backpackers,** 91 Seville St, on the corner of Seville and Barcelona St, offers clean, sunny rooms up the street from the beach. Baby pinnacles decorate the garden. (☎9652 7377; fax 9652 7318. Dorms $17, doubles $44.)

Some popular one-day and over-night packages to the Pinnacles are given by **West Coast Explorers** (☎9418 8835), which arrives at sunset, and **Redback Safaris** (☎9275 6204). Prices range $80-100. If you're driving, allow 1hr. for the drive west to Cervantes from the left turn off the Brand Hwy, about 20km north of the Cataby Roadhouse. The last stretch of road before the Pinnacles is unsealed but relatively smooth ($9 vehicle fee). **Camping** is not allowed in the park, but there are picnic areas and a beach at **Hangover Bay,** a few kilometers from the Pinnacles site. **Turquoise Coast Enviro Tours** offers tours of the area's other natural attractions, such as the **Stockyard Tunnel Cave** and **Lake Indoom.** (☎9652 7047. $66-100.)

# GERALDTON

For a town sprawled along the stunning Indian Ocean, Geraldton (pop. 24,000) pays surprisingly little attention to its coastline. Most restaurants, shops, or hotels in town actually face away from the nearby beach. Windsurfers eager to test their skill in the strong southerly winds flock to Geraldton every summer, but there aren't many sights worth noting back on land. Nevertheless, the many restaurants, several movie theaters, and quality budget accommodations make Geraldton a good place to stop for a day on your way somewhere else.

**⬛❼ TRANSPORT AND PRACTICAL INFORMATION.** If you're arriving by car from the Brand Hwy, head straight through the rotary up Cathedral Ave to get to the town center. The town's main drag, Chapman Rd, and the shop-lined Marine Tce both run parallel to the coast and intersect Cathedral Ave. Greyhound and Westrail run to **Perth** (2-3 times per day, $38). Greyhound also runs to **Broome** (daily 4:25pm, $267) via **Carnarvon** ($61) and **Exmouth** ($182). The **tourist office** is located inside the massive Bill Sewall Complex at the corner of Bayly St and Chapman Rd, about 1km north of Cathedral Ave. (☎9921 3999; fax 9964 2445. Open M-F 8:30am-5pm, Sa 9am-4:30pm, Su 9:30am-4:30pm.) Other services include: **police,** on the corner of Chapman Rd and Forrest St (☎9923 4555); **hospital,** on Shenton St, one block from Cathedral Ave (☎9956 2222); and the **post office** on Durlacher St near Chapman Rd (☎9964 5962; open M-F 8:30am-5pm).

**▮▮▯ ACCOMMODATIONS AND FOOD.** ⬛**Geraldton YHA Foreshore Backpackers,** 172 Marine Tce, one block southwest of Cathedral Ave, has a homey atmosphere with super-friendly owners and a refreshing lack of bunk beds. (☎9921 3275; fax 9921 3233. Free pickup and drop off. Internet 1hr. $7. Dorms $15; singles $22; twins and doubles $37; family rooms for 2 adults $37, each child $5.50; non-YHA $1-3 extra). **Batavia Backpackers,** next to the tourist office, is a friendly, convenient place

WESTERN AUSTRALIA

**THE LITTLE PRINCIPALITY** Along the North Coast Hwy between Geraldton and Kalbarri, Australia takes a hiatus. **Hut River Province** is a 75 square kilometer area that claims to be its own principality. This island of royalty was created by Prince Leonard George Casley with a few twists of the law for a few benefits of tax evasion. Visitors of Prince Leonard (a former farmer) and his very own principality can get a special stamp in their passport, Hut River postage stamps (that need additional Australian stamps to work), and Hut River currency.

to stay with basic rooms and a view of the ocean. (☎9964 3001; fax 9964 3611. Dorms $15.50; singles $21; twins $36. YHA, VIP, ISIC.)

The **Sun City Food Hall,** 56 Durlacher St, near the post office, has Indian, Italian, Mexican, and Chinese meals for $5-6. (☎9964 2313. Open W-M 11:30am-2pm and 5-9pm.) **Tanti's Restaurant,** 174 Marine Tce, next to the YHA, serves excellent Thai food and takeaway is relatively cheap. (☎9964 2311. Open M-W 5:30-10pm, Th-F 11am-2pm and 5:30-10pm, Sa 5:30-10pm.) Woolworth's, on Sanford and Durlacher St, has cheap **groceries** (open M-F 8am-6pm, Th 8am-9pm, Sa 8am-5pm).

**⬛⬛ SIGHTS AND ACTIVITIES.** Most people come to Geraldton for one reason: **windsurfing.** The best conditions are Oct.-Nov. and Mar.-Apr., though it is good year-round. Bring your own gear or rent it at the **Blue Planet Mega Surf Shop,** in the Northgate Plaza on Chapman Rd, which also has a host of info about good windsurfing locations around Geraldton. (☎9964 5533. Open M-F 9am-5:30pm, Sa 9am-5pm.) **Point Moore,** the windiest spot in the area, is for the most experienced. **St. George's Beach** has tamer breezes. In the town itself, **Back Beach** is the surfing hot spot and also has reasonably good swimming. The **Abrolhos Islands,** an archipelago about 60km off of Geraldton, were the site (and cause) of the Batavia wreck. These islands are rich in marine life; some say the diving is as good as on the Great Barrier. **Eco Abrolhos Tours** (☎9964 7887) offer a wide variety of trips to the islands, and **Abrolhos Air** (☎9923 3151) takes visitors on sight-seeing flight from $66.

# KALBARRI

Originally home to Australia's earliest Europeans—two Dutch settlers marooned just south of town for their role in the Batavia mutiny—Kalbarri (pop. 1700) is a vacation hot spot for both Australian and international tourists. Seniors and backpackers alike flock to this tiny town for its mild winter climate and spectacular natural surroundings. During rock lobster season (Nov.-June), crayfishing boats bob in the calm waters off the mouth of the Marchison River. The main reason to come here, though, is to hike in the wonderland of Kalbarri National Park.

**⬛ TRANSPORT.** The access road from the North West Coastal Hwy connects to **Grey St,** which skirts the coast and runs to the town center. Greyhound **buses** (☎13 20 30) run to **Ajana** for connections to **Perth** (2 per day, $78) and **Carnarvon** (2 per day, $67). Westrail **trains** (☎13 10 53) service **Perth** (Tu, Th, and Sa 6:15am, $49). Both depart from the tourist bureau, which does bookings.

**⬛ PRACTICAL INFORMATION.** The **tourist bureau** is on Grey St to the left of Woods St when facing the ocean. (☎9937 1104; fax 9937 1474. Open daily 9am-5pm.) The **Department of Conservation and Land Management (CALM)** office (☎9937 1140) is on Ajana Kalbarri Rd, 1km out of town. Other services include: **police** on Porter St (☎9937 1006); **pharmacy** near Grey and Porter St (24hr. ☎9937 1026); **doctor** (☎9937 1159; afterhours ☎9937 0100); **post office** at Grey and Porter St (open M-F 8:30am-5:30pm, Sa 8:30am-12:30pm); **Internet** at **Explorer Ocean Charters,** next to the post office (☎9937 2027; open daily 9am-4pm; 30min. $5).

**⬛⬛ ACCOMMODATIONS AND FOOD.** For an easy stay, the **YHA Rock Lobster Lodge,** 52 Mortimer St, offers clean rooms, a swimming pool, BBQ, and free use of snorkel gear and boogie boards. From the tourist bureau, turn right on Grey St, then right on Woods St. (☎9937 1430; fax 9937 1563. Dorms $17; doubles $42. 7th night free. Non-YHA or VIP $2 extra.) **Kalbarri Palm Resort,** 8 Porter St, is a minimally disguised Best Western. As such, it has all the expected perks and the expected price. (☎9937 2333; fax 9937 1324. Ensuite doubles $60; family rooms $75.) **Murchison Park Caravan Park,** at the corner of Grey and Wood St, is in a central spot. (☎9937 1005; fax 9937 1415. Sites for 2 $16.50, powered $17; on-site vans $39.)

**Finlay's Fresh Fish BBQ,** on Magee Crescent, serves healthy portions of tasty seafood for around $10 in a huge outdoor shed with picnic tables and campfires. (☎9937 1260. Open daily 5:30-8:30pm.) Foodland **supermarket** is in the Ampol station on Grey St. (☎9937 1100. Open daily 7am-6pm.)

**☎ SIGHTS.** The town of Kalbarri is dwarfed by the surrounding 183,000 hectares of wilderness. The dramatic oceanside cliffs, red river gorges, and wildflowers of **Kalbarri National Park** are well worth exploring. The park's unsealed roads are generally in good condition and 2WD-accessible, but check with **CALM** (☎9937 1140) for updates. Admission to the inland river gorge area costs $9 per vehicle; the machine doesn't accept bills, so bring $1 and $2 coins. From town, travel 11km east along the Ajana-Kalbarri Rd to reach the park; but it's a 25km drive to all the good stuff. The park is easily explored by car, but for those without wheels there are also tours. **Kalbarri Adventure Tours** has a day-long "Canoe the Gorges" trip stopping at Nature's Window and the Z Bend. The hikes in and out are tough at spots but worth it. (☎9937 1677. M, Tu, Th, Sa. $55.) **Kalbarri Safari Tours** runs a full-day trek along Z Bend. (☎9937 1011. Tu, W, F, Su. $55.) **Kalbarri Bush and Wildflower Tours** offers half-day tours to the Z Bend and Nature's Window. (☎9937 1742. $40.)

Scenic lookouts at **The Loop** and **Z Bend** are great photo-ops. The best circuit is unmarked, but heads east along the cliff top from **Nature's Window** to the first riverbank, then down along the ledges and floodplain at water level; keep the river to your right. Along the coast, the banded sandstone and limestone cliffs have been worn into fantastic formations. The cliffside hike (8km; 4hr.) from **Eagle Gorge** to the **Natural Bridge** is also recommended. **Pot Alley** and other lookouts along Red Bluff Rd have beautiful views of the coast and dolphins. The 38km trek from the **Ross Graham Lookout** to the Loop is for the diehard hiker. It takes about four days, and CALM recommends hiking with at least five people.

**Kalbarri Explorer Ocean Charters** has sunset dolphin and whale trips, seasonal morning whale watching trips, and deep sea fishing on demand. (☎9937 2027. Sunset 2hr., $44. Morning $49. Fishing 6hr., $120.) Plant lovers will appreciate the herbarium and nature trail at the **Kalbarri Wildflower Centre** on the North West Coastal Hwy, 1km before Kalbarri. (☎9937 1229. Open June-Nov. daily 9am-5pm. $4. Free bus service daily 10am from tourist office. Guided 1hr. walks Aug.-Oct. daily 10:30am, $3.) **Rainbow Jungle,** on Red Bluff Rd. about 3.5km south of town, is a parrot breeding center. (☎9937 1248. Open Tu-Sa 9am-5pm, Su 10am-5pm. $8.)

# OUTBACK COAST AND GASCOYNE

The Outback Coast is one of WA's most beautiful areas, and although the distances between towns are daunting, the amazing scenery helps pass the time. The coast stretches from the dolphins of Shark Bay north to the whale sharks of Ningaloo Marine Park. Winter is peak season, when caravanning Perthites, young and old, park themselves along the sunny coast to wait out the cold down south.

# SHARK BAY

Shark Bay, Western Australia's much-touted World Heritage area, was the site of the earliest recorded European landing in Australia. In 1616, Dutch Explorer Dirk Hartog came ashore at Cape Inscription on the island that now bears his name. Today, Shark Bay is known mainly for the dolphins at Monkey Mia, tranquil shell beaches, and the "living fossils" (stromatolites) at Hamelin Pool. The best way to see the area is by car or on a tour; taking a bus may involve spending much more time in the area than is necessary or desirable.

**DENHAM.** With around 500 permanent residents, the westernmost town in Australia is just a speck on the Peron Peninsula. The main street, **Knight Tce,** runs parallel to the town's narrow beach. It seems as though you can see the ocean from any point in town. Most stay here because it's the closest town to Monkey Mia, but its natural beauty makes it worthwhile even for those who aren't into dolphins.

The **bus** departs for the Overlander Roadhouse from the Shell station on Knight St at the corner of Denham-Hamlin Rd (M, Th, F 5:20am, 6:15pm). The **tourist bureau,** 71 Knight Tce, is a few doors down from the Shell station. (☎9948 1253; fax 9948 1065. Open daily 8am-6pm.) The staff books bus tickets to **Monkey Mia** (departs 8am, $9; ask for a lift at the hostel first). A few doors down, the **Department of Conservation and Land Management (CALM),** 67 Knight Tce, sells National Park passes. (☎9948 1208. Open M-F 8am-5pm.) The **post office** is two doors down from the tourist office. (☎9948 1220. Open M-F 9am-5pm.)

The **YHA Denham Bay Lodge,** on Knight Tce, 100m south of the bus stop, is nicer than the typical backpacker joint. A "dorm" is actually an individual ensuite unit with a kitchen. Free bus to Monkey Mia daily 8am. (☎9948 1278; fax 9948 1031. Dorms $16.50; twins and doubles $44. YHA, VIP, ISIC.) **Tradewinds Supermarket** is at the BP Station (open daily 7am-7pm). The **Loaves and Fish Bakery,** on Knight Tce, has pasties and sweets. (☎9948 1442. Open M-F 8:30am-5pm, Sa 8:30am-1pm.)

**MONKEY MIA.** No monkeys here. People come to Monkey Mia to see dolphins. The Indian bottlenose dolphins of Shark Bay swim right up to the shore to be fed and scratched by herds of tourists. Some think Monkey Mia provides an unparalleled opportunity to interact with intelligent, sociable animals; others find it a contrived, exploitative, and downright tacky show.

One-day access to the site is $6; a family pass costs $12, and four-week passes are $9, although it only takes an hour or two to "do" the Monkey Mia dolphin bit. Generally there are three feedings between 8am and 1pm each day. The reserve is home to an **information center** and the **Department of Conservation and Land Management (CALM) office** with videos and talks. (☎9948 1366. Open daily 8am-4pm.) **Aristocat 2** offers cruises of various lengths to see marine life, with underwater windows and a short talk about the dugong, an endangered species of seacow (☎9948 1446. $27-43, children $13-16.)

The **Monkey Mia Dolphin Resort** has backpacker beds in campervans that are well past their peak and tent sites. (☎9948 1320; fax 9948 1034. Linen $11. Campsites $8, vans $16.) Bring food with you to Monkey Mia; the restaurants and the mini-mart food shop (open 7am-6pm) are expensive.

**HAMELIN POOL.** About 100km south of Denham and 27km west of the Overlander Roadhouse lies the striking Hamelin Pool, with a white shell beach and **stromatolites.** Stromatolites are formed over thousands of years by microbes, and are the oldest known form of life on Earth. To reach these sights, you need a car or tour. **Shark Bay Car Hire** (☎9948 1247) on Knight Tce rents cars from Denham. **Majestic Tours** has daytrips including Shell Beach and the stromatolites and half-day trips to Shell Beach. (☎9948 1247. Full-day $75; half-day $39.)

---

**FAMILY FEUD** The infamous Vegemite that pops up all over Australia for breakfast—just when you think you are safe with plain toast and butter—was not always vegemite. It was originally called Parwill, as a competitive move against Marmite, another splendid spread of yeastiness. When you've got an Australian accent, Marmite sounds like "Ma might." And Parwill sounds like "Pa will," as though whatever confidence Ma lacks, Pa possesses. Nobody got this complicated joke, though, so the spread was renamed vegemite.

Though not the most thrilling of sights, the Hamelin Pool stromatolites are one of only two living colonies in the world. A short boardwalk extending into the pool's crystal clear, salty waters allows for a closer look. Back on shore, a short walking trail winds along the beach and through a small quarry where chunks of sedimentary shell "rocks" were cut and used to construct many of the area's early buildings. **Camping** is available at the **Hamelin Pool Caravan Park.** (☎9942 5905. Sites for 2 $11, powered $13; each extra adult $5, extra child $2.) Fifty kilometers north of the turn-off to the Hamelin Pool along the Denham-Hamelin Rd is the turn-off for **Shell Beach,** a dazzling 60km expanse of billions of tiny white shells, up to 10m deep. Bring something to sit on if you intend to do any sunbathing.

# CARNARVON

Even though it's near the ocean, Carnarvon (pop. 7000) is at best a place to catch your breath and break up the long distances between destinations on the West coast. Most people who come here are looking for work at the many local fruit plantations, and without a job to fill the days, the town gets boring pretty quickly.

**TRANSPORT.** Greyhound buses depart from the tourist bureau for: **Perth** (1-2 per day, $95); **Darwin** (1 per day); and **Broome** (1 per day) via **Coral Bay** ($143) and **Exmouth** ($97). Integrity has buses to **Perth** (M, W, F; $100); and **Exmouth** (8:30am Su, Th; $75) via **Coral Bay** ($60). Integrity and Greyhound both offer student and backpacker discounts.

**ORIENTATION AND PRACTICAL INFORMATION.** A big yellow plastic banana welcomes visitors to Carnarvon as they head into town along Robinson St from the North West Coastal Hwy. The center of Carnarvon is **Robinson St** between **Babbage Island Rd** and **Olivia Tce.** The **tourist bureau** is at 11 Robinson St, in the Carnarvon Civic Centre at the corner of Stuart St. (☎9941 1146; fax 9941 1149. Open M-F 8:30am-5pm, Sa 9am-noon.) Several **banks** with **ATMs** are on Robinson St. Other services include: **police,** next door to the tourist bureau (☎9941 1444); **hospital,** two blocks down Francis St (☎9941 0555); **post office** on Stuart St across from the Civic Centre (open M-F 9am-5pm); and **Internet** at Gascoyne Express Photographics, 24 Robinson St (☎9941 3366; 30min. $5). Woolworth's, on Robinson St, has cheap **groceries.** (☎9941 2477. Open daily 8am-8pm.)

**ACCOMMODATIONS.** Carnarvon Backpackers, 9790 Olivia Tce, is around the corner from the tourist office. You can stay in self-contained units that were built for American astronauts on the Apollo and Gemini missions—remember when those were? But the friendly management has heaps of info on jobs, and the atmosphere is warm and social. There's BBQ, off-street parking, A/C or fans, and canoe use. (☎/fax 9941 1095. Dorms $17, weekly $108; doubles $45, $293.) The **Carnarvon Tourist Centre Caravan Park,** 108 Robinson St, is five blocks down Robinson St from the tourist office. (☎9941 1438. Tent sites $14, powered $16.50; clean cabins with TV and A/C for 2 $49; each extra person $5; book ahead in winter.)

**SIGHTS.** Babbage Island Rd along the coast toward **Pelican Point** is a pleasant bike ride among mangroves. The mile-long jetty has good fishing and crabbing. **The Blowholes,** 73km north of town, are water jets that reach as high as 20m in choppy weather; a lovely beach is 1km south. To get there, go 24km north on the North West Coastal Hwy and turn left at the sign. This is a limestone road that can get pretty choppy; ask after conditions at the tourist bureau. About 40km farther north is the visible wreck of the huge **Korean Star,** victim of the May 1988 cyclone Herbie. Experienced divers can explore the wreck.

A drive or bike ride through the outskirts of town is worthwhile—the back roads are jammed with banana and mango plantations. Fresh fruit and veggies are plentiful and cheap; ask if you can collect the non-saleable fruits lying on the ground. **Carnarvon Bus Charter** (☎9941 1146) also visits the plantations, as well as the shrimp factory, boat harbor, salt mine, blowholes, and jetty.

Carnarvon is a popular base for trips to **Mt. Augustus,** the largest rock in Australia; it's twice the size of Ayers Rock. The trip is 460km by car on a rough unsealed road; check on road conditions at the tourist bureau before leaving. **Lindsay Orr's Outback Adventure** has a four-day tour. (☎9943 0550. $495.)

## CORAL BAY

Coral Bay is a popular stopover en route to Exmouth, 160km north. The town itself is just a small collection of dive shops and caravan parks, but the beach is a good spot for snorkeling and swimming and the town is one of the main gateways to the Ningaloo Marine Park. The Ningaloo Reef, over 250km long, starts south of Coral Bay and stretches north around the Northwest Cape and back into Exmouth Gulf.

**Sub-sea Explorer** (☎9942 5955) and **Ecology Cruises** (☎9942 5885) run coral-viewing glass-bottom boat and snorkeling trips for $22-30. **Ningaloo Reef Dive Centre** offers 2-dive trips from $132, and a certification course that starts Saturdays for $335. **Snuba Tours** are available for people who want to dive but aren't certified; an air hose connects you to the surface and you can go down to 6m. Just be careful not to choke on your pride. (☎9942 5889. $50.)

The Perth-Exmouth Greyhound **bus** and Integrity buses head to **Perth** ($180) and **Exmouth** ($55) a few times a week. On the right side of the road toward town, the shopping complex houses a small **supermarket** (☎9942 5988; open daily 8am-6pm), the **post office** disguised as a NewsAgent (☎9942 5995; open M-F 8:30am-5pm), and the **Ningaloo Reef Dive Centre** (☎9942 5824, open daily 8am-5:30pm). **The Mermaid's Cave,** also in the shopping center, has tourist info and books tours. (☎9942 5955. Open M-Sa 9am-5pm, Su 9am-1pm.) Another good resource for tourist information is at **Ningaloo Experience,** in town. (☎9942 5877. Open daily 8:30am-5pm.) **Internet** is available in the café next door (30min. $5.50).

The friendly **Bayview Coral Bay Backpackers** has small but colorful twins and doubles, with a BBQ and a large resident lizard. The resort also has cabins and self-contained duplexes and chalets that can be a good deal for groups (☎9942 5932. Twins and doubles $18 per person. Caravans from $60. VIP. Book ahead.)

## EXMOUTH

The scuba diving epicenter of the west coast, Exmouth (pop. 3500) is the place to swim with giant, easygoing whale sharks and manta rays. The wonders of the colorful Ningaloo Reef are complemented on land by the dry, dramatically beautiful Cape Range National Park. The main township area is inland and not much to look at, but as a diving and fishing destination Exmouth can't be beat.

**◨◪ TRANSPORT AND PRACTICAL INFORMATION.** Most action takes place around **Maidstone Crescent,** which intersects **Murat Rd** (the highway) at both ends. Greyhound **buses** to **Perth** (1-2 per day, $204) and **Broome** (1 per day, $229). **Integrity** also runs to Perth ($165). The **tourist bureau** is on Murat Rd. (☎9949 1176; fax 9949 1441. Open M-F 8:30am-5pm, Sa 9am-4pm.) The **CALM office,** on Nimitz St a few blocks from Murat Rd, has more detailed info on Cape Range. (☎9949 1676. Open M-F 8:30am-5pm.) **Challenge Bank,** on Learmouth St, is home to Exmouth's only **ATM.** The shopping center just off Maidstone houses a **pharmacy** (open M-F 9am-5:30pm, Sa 9am-12:30pm) and two **supermarkets** (open daily 7am-7:30pm). The **hospital** is two blocks west, on Lyon St near Fyfe St. (☎9949 1011. Dive medicals $60; call ahead.) **Internet** is available at the **Exmouth Telecentre** on Lermont St behind the shopping complex. (☎9949 2004. Open M-F 9am-5pm. 30min. $6.)

**◤ ACCOMMODATIONS.** Fierce competition between Exmouth's hostels has led hostel owners to offer backpackers lots of freebies, including free bike hire, BBQ, swimming pools, and A/C. Many of the dive shops in town have deals with hostels; indeed, several hostel have dive shops on-site. **Exmouth Base Lodge,** 6km north of town inside the refurbished old naval base, offers twins with free linen. The bathrooms and kitchens are spotless, and there is free use of the tennis courts and

WESTERN AUSTRALIA

ym. (☎9949 1474; fax 9949 1440. Internet 30min. $6. Laundry. Free pickup and drop off and frequent transport to town. Rooms $18. YHA, VIP.) **YHA Pete's Exmouth Backpackers,** on Truscott Cr between town and the beaches, has clean cabins with kitchens. Village Dive operates out of the same building. (☎9949 1101; fax 9949 1402. Internet 30min. $6. Reception until 7pm. Tent sites $8; dorms $16.50; twins and doubles $40. Non-YHA, VIP $2-3 more.) **Excape Backpackers** rooms are somewhat cramped, but tons of space outdoors and a nice lounge area. Reception is at the Exmouth Diving Center on Payne St. (☎(1800) 65 51 56. Dorms $16.50, $13 with a SCUBA class at the dive center; twins $50. YHA, VIP.) **Winston's Backpackers,** on Murat Rd, has tiny rooms in a well-kept building with a kitchen, pool table, and boat hire. (☎9949 2377; fax 9949 2577. Dorms $16.50.) **Camping** is permitted in designated sites within Cape Range National Park (2 people $10 per night, $5.50 each additional person; does not include vehicle entry fee), but don't camp elsewhere—fines are high, and rangers patrol. Fires are strictly prohibited and there is no water in the park, so come prepared.

**⊓ FOOD.** The restaurants in town are expensive, but the seafood is as good as one could expect. The **Rock Cod Café,** just after the Ampol station on Maidstone Crescent, has seafood specials, pasta, and burgers. (☎9949 1249. Open daily 5-10pm.) Another popular choice is the **Golden Orchis Chinese Restaurant,** in Ross St Mall off Maidstone Crescent. (☎9949 1740. Th 5:30-9pm $15 all-you-can-eat buffet.) The only nightlife in town is at **Vance's Bar** (☎9949 1200) in the Potshot Resort. Relatively speaking, Friday is the big night, when beer flows until midnight.

**⊿ WATER ACTIVITIES.** Most people come to Exmouth to see the impressive **Ningaloo Reef,** and the town is full of dive shops catering to all experience levels. Introductory PADI courses cost $300-330, take four or five days, and include at least four ocean dives. Shop around before choosing a dive shop; all have certified instructors and good equipment, but class size and quality of instruction vary tremendously. **Coral Coast Dive,** at Ningaloo Backpackers with training facilities at the naval base, has intro and advanced courses with a maximum class size of six. (☎9949 1004. Dives from $105; classes $292.) **WAGS Diving** (☎9949 2661) is slightly more expensive, but has a maximum class size of four and access to underwater scooters. **Ningaloo Deep** (☎9949 1663) has luxurious, expensive live-aboard diving trips. **Village Dive** has resort pier dives, as well as computer-oriented PADI classes. (☎9949 1101. Pier dive $80; PADI $330). **Exmouth Dive Centre** (☎9949 1201) has pier and island dives from $121.

**Whale shark** snorkeling is very pricey, but incredible. The Ningaloo is one of the few areas in the world where the world's biggest fish visit consistently; they appear most frequently between March and June. **Diving Ventures** offers a package of whale shark snorkeling and a reef dive. (☎9949 2635. $295 including equipment, $250 without the dive.) Similar whale shark snorkel deals are offered with **Ningaloo Blue** (☎9949 1119) or some of the other dive shops listed above. The best surfing is found at **Surfers Beach** at Vlamingh Head, at the northern end of the cape.

Several operators run tours of the Exmouth area and Cape Range National Park. **Ningaloo Ecology Cruises** offers snorkeling and coral-viewing tours on glass-bottom boats. (☎9949 2255. 1hr. tours from $25; 2hr. snorkeling trips from $35, backpackers $30, children $10.) **West Coast Safaris** (☎9949 1625), **West Treks Safaris** (☎9949 2659), and **Pete's Backpackers** offer tours including snorkeling at Turquoise Bay, a boat cruise up Yardie Creek, and a 4WD trek over the top of Cape Range, as well as longer tours to Karijini and Mt. Augustus. **Ningaloo Reef Retreat** (☎9949 1776) has day tours ($44) and an overnight package ($99).

**⚟ HIKING.** With rugged limestone cliffs, canyons, and gorges, **Cape Range National Park** lies 39km from Exmouth, full of bungarras, emus, and Stuart's desert peas. The park has several walking trails, from the **Yardie Creek Track** (1.5km) to the more difficult **Badjirrajirra Route** (8km, leaves from the Thomas Carter Lookout carpark on Charles Knife Rd, 23km south of Exmouth along the Minilya-Learmonth Rd). The solar-powered **Milyering Visitor Centre,** 52km from Exmouth, hands out maps and info on the parks. (☎9949 2808. Open daily 10am-4pm. National Park day pass $9 per car. No water.) A 4WD is the best vehicle for exploring the area, but a 2WD will get you as far as **Turquoise Bay,** a popular snorkeling spot. The main road into the park leads to the north to the tip of the cape and then south along the west coast of the cape, which makes it a relatively long trip. There are unsealed roads (Shothole Canyon Rd and Charles Knife Rd) running across the cape into the park, which is a more direct route, but they can be rough going—check with CALM before heading in this way. If you don't have a car, try the Cape's excellent shuttle service, **Ningaloo Reef Bus,** which stops at the lighthouse, Yardie Creek, Turquoise Bay, Reef Retreat, the Milyering Visitor Centre, and Tantabiddi Reef (F-W $22 to Turquoise Bay, children $11; includes park entry and snorkel gear).

# THE PILBARA

The Pilbara has not traditionally been much of a tourist destination, and on one level it's not hard to understand why. Distances between sights are substantial, the region's small towns don't have too much to offer in and of themselves, and the weather conditions can be extreme. But despite all this, the Pilbara holds tremendous rewards for those that make the effort to come here. The region has a unique allure, and the sight of white-barked gum trees glowing through dusty red twilight tends to make believers out of doubters. Indeed, the seemingly bland landscape of the Pilbara actually includes some of Australia's most dramatic scenery. Armed with the gorges of Karijini National Park and the crystalline waters of the Dampier Archipelago, the region can hold its own in any Aussie beauty pageant. They say that if you haven't seen the west, you haven't seen the real Australia; one could add that if you haven't seen the Pilbara, you haven't seen the real west.

## KARRATHA

The commercial and administrative center of the Pilbara, Karratha (pop. 10,500) was born in the late 1960s as a base for local industrial projects. Today, it houses WA's largest shopping center north of Perth and all the services of a small city. Travelers can find work around town and on the trawlers and prawn boats operating off-shore. From Karratha you can explore the nearby Burrup Peninsula, Dampier Archipelago, Pt. Samson, and Millstream-Chichester National Park.

**▮▪ TRANSPORT AND PRACTICAL INFORMATION.** Greyhound **buses** leave Karratha daily from the Shell station at the corner of Searipple and Welcome Rd (northbound 7:30am, southbound 7:30pm; book at the tourist bureau). Most of Karratha's services are clustered in the town center, bounded by Warambie Rd to the north, Searipple Rd to the east, Welcome Rd to the south, and Balmoral Rd to the west. The **tourist bureau** is on Karratha Rd, 1km south of town. (☎9144 4600; fax 9144 4620. Open Mar.-Oct. M-F 8:30am-5pm, Sa-Su 9am-4pm; Nov.-Feb. M-F 9am-5pm, Sa 9am-noon.) The **shopping center** (☎9185 4288) takes up a block on Welcome Rd and Sharp Ave. Inside is a **chemist.** (☎9185 1316. Open M-W, F 9am-5:30pm, Th 9am-9pm, Sa 8:30am-5pm.) Other services include: **post office,** next to the shopping center (open M-F 9am-5pm); **police,** on Welcome Rd (☎9144 2233); and **hospital,** on Dampier Rd (☎9144 0330).

**▮▪ ACCOMMODATIONS AND FOOD.** The management of **Karratha Backpackers,** 110 Wellard Wat, is immensely knowledgeable about the surrounding area and willing to help you explore. Orphaned kangaroos bounce around. (☎9144 4904. Free bus pickup. Internet 1hr. $8. Dorms $16.50; singles $33; twins and doubles $44.) There are **supermarkets** in the shopping center (open daily 7am-9pm).

**▨ SIGHTS.** The **Burrup Peninsula** was originally the home of the Yaburrara people, and their legacy remains in over 10,000 rock carvings on piles of loose rocks

WESTERN AUSTRALIA

**TAKE ME TO YOUR LEADER** Deep Gorge is a remarkable site with dozens of Aboriginal engravings on the rust colored rocks. There are pictures of people dancing, and indications that emu were present in the area, which is no longer the case. Among the garden-variety pictures however, are two mysterious engravings. The first is of a man who seems to be wearing a sort of wide brimmed hat. The hat is reminiscent of the silly hats that European mariners used to wear (picture the stereotypical pirate—yeah, that's the one). Some people think that this could be a picture of an early European visitor, and a sign that Aboriginal culture was about to change dramatically. The other remarkable picture is of a man with a dome covering his head who looks exactly like an astronaut. Perhaps the Aboriginals had visitors from much farther away than Europe, or perhaps someone is toying with us; or perhaps the Aboriginals are the aliens themselves...Was this on X-files last week?

and boulders. The Burrup also has a handful of safe **swimming beaches,** and a drive out to the peninsula makes a good daytrip from Karratha. There is **no public transport** to the Barrup Peninsula, but you can rent a car in Karratha (☎9185 1003; from $35 per day.) To get there, head toward Dampier on the Dampier Rd and after about 18km turn right on the Burrup Rd. The turn-off for **Hearson's Cove** is marked on the right. On this beach you can see the "staircase to the moon," a natural phenomenon that occurs when a full moon rises over a low tide: the ripples on the water look like steps running up to the moon. About 1km before Hearson's Cove, a dirt track heads into **Deep Gorge,** an area rich in Aboriginal engravings.

Another major natural attraction in the area is the **Dampier Archipelago.** The 42 islands are fringed by coral reefs and the ocean floor is littered with shipwrecks, making for excellent fishing and snorkeling. Unfortunately there is no regular transport to any of the islands, the only way to get there is a tour or hired boat. **Western Waters Aquatic Adventures** is an excellent local tour operator that has fishing, "eco" snorkeling and wildlife tours, and sunset cruises. (☎9185 2141. Half-day trips $75-85; the dolphins that chase the boat don't need to be tipped.)

**Snappy Gum Safaris** offers a variety of trips into the park that depart from the Karratha area. Among these is a three-day adventure tour that includes **Karijini National Park's** "miracle mile" to the bottom of one of the gorges. Climbing a 30m waterfall is one of this route's many challenges. (☎9185 1278. $320.)

## NORTH WEST COASTAL HIGHWAY

These little towns are essentially satellites of Karratha, and in reality they're barely big enough to be called towns. Dampier is about 20km west of Karratha on the Dampier Rd on the other side of the Burrup peninsula. Roeburne, Cossack and Point Samson are east of Karratha and quite close to each other. To get to this area from Karratha take the Karratha Rd south, back to the North West Coastal Hwy, and then go east about 35km to Roeburne. Cossack and Point Samson are north of Roeburne; take the Point Samson Roeburne Rd north from the Hwy. The turn-off to Cossack off this road is about 11km in; Point Samson is another 8km.

**DAMPIER.** Dampier was established as a loading port for the local industrial factories, and that continues to be its main function. The huge ships that arrive to be loaded with salt and iron ore are a sight to behold. Even though the town is home to heavy industry, it remains beautiful, with rocky beaches and great views of the islands. The **Dampier Caravan Park** overlooks the ocean. (☎9183 1109. Max. stay three nights. Tent site for 2 $11, powered $13; caravan sites from $13.)

**ROEBOURNE.** The oldest existing town in the Pilbara and once a thriving capital of the northwest, Roeburne today is a shadow of its former self. The Roeburne **tourist bureau,** inside the old jail, has info on Roeburne and nearby Cossack and Pt. Samson. (☎9182 1060. Open M-F 9am-5pm; Sa-Su 9am-4pm; off-season M-F 9am-3pm, Sa 9am-noon.) **Sandy's Shellhouse** (☎9182 1510) is a fun place to stop on the road from Roebourne to Cossack. Full of birds, fish, kangaroos, emus, and sea-shells, the place acts as a museum, gift shop, and rehabilitation center for orphaned or injured animals. They'll soon open a more official wildlife sanctuary.

**COSSACK.** Twelve kilometers north of Roebourne lies historic Cossack, the first port to be established in the Northwest and once the center of a thriving pearling industry; today it's more a relic than a living town. **Settler's Beach** is gigantic and has safe swimming; Aboriginal carvings can be found in the surrounding cliff faces. The town's **hostel** building dates back to 1897—it shows, but the rooms are clean. (☎ 9182 1190; fax 9182 1132. Beds $16.50; rooms for 2-6 $38.50.) There are no groceries in Cossack, but the **Cossack Tearooms** in the old Customs House has cof-fee, cakes, and light lunches (open M-F 10am-2pm, Sa-Su 11am-4pm). **Getaway Boat Hire** (☎ 9182 1190) will get you on the water from $70 per half day.

**POINT SAMSON.** North 10km on the main road past Cossack lies sleepy little Point Samson and its swimming and fishing beach. Just around the point is **Honeymoon Cove,** which is relatively well attended on nice days.

# MILLSTREAM-CHICHESTER NATIONAL PARK

Once a watering hole for weary Afghan camel drivers, Millstream is a lush green oasis in the midst of thousands of acres of rock and dry, spinifex-covered hills. Date, cotton, Millstream palms, and water lilies thrive in and around the park's freshwater pool, and the surrounding wetlands support a diverse range of fauna.

The turn-off to Millstream-Chichester is 28km east of Roebourne, 175km south-west of Port Hedland on the North West Coastal Hwy; head 60km south along the unsealed but well-maintained Roebourne-Wittenoom Rd. You can also take the winding, unsealed rail service road with a free permit; ask at the Karratha tourist bureau or in Tom Price at Hamersley Iron. The park has **no petrol.** The **Millstream Homestead,** near the southwest corner of the park, is the park's **visitors center,** with displays on local flora and fauna, early settler life, and the culture of the Yin-jibarndi Aboriginals (open daily 8am-4pm).

**Camping** is permitted in the park only at the designated sites of **Crossingpool, Deep Reach Pool,** and **Snake Creek** (sites for 2 $10). The **park entrance fee** is $9 per car. **Python Pool,** about 25km to the north along the Wittenoom Roebourne Rd, is a beautiful spot to swim. The **Cameleers Trail** (6km) uphill from the pool has a rewarding view at the top. **Snappy Gum Safaris** runs tours from Karratha, Dampier, or Roebourne. (☎ 9185 1278. $90, children $30.)

# TOM PRICE

At 747m above sea level, Tom Price is the tallest town in Western Australia. Named after an American mineral surveyor, the town gained its independence from the Hamersley Iron Company in 1988 and since then has worked hard to turn itself into a popular destination. It's a tidy little place that bears no resemblance to the rough and tumble mining towns of the Goldfields. Tom Price is becoming part of the tourist circuit as the closest town to the amazing Karijini National Park. The park is easily explored by car and maps are available in town. **Design-A-Tour** has daytrips from both Tom Price and the Auski Roadhouse. (☎ 9188 1670. May.-Oct. daily. $90, children $45.) **Lestok Tours** daytrips depart from the Tom Price Caravan Park and the tourist bureau. (☎ 9189 2032. $80, children $40.)

There is **no public transportation** to Tom Price. The town lies about 300km east of the Nanutarra Roadhouse and 250km south of the Millstream visitors center. From the Northwest Coastal Hwy, head east on Hwy 136 just north of Nanutarra. The well-maintained, paved road passes through some spectacular country, but no ser-vices are available until **Paraburdoo,** 276km away, so fuel up before you go. After about 220km, the road forks. Both ways are scenic and 2WD-accessible except after heavy rain; the left fork is 70km shorter but unsealed. From Millstream take the Roeburne Wittenoom Rd to the Nanutarra Wittenoom Rd. The very friendly **tourist bureau** is on Central Rd. (☎ 9188 1112. Open M-F 8:30am-5pm.) Across the

**HOLD YOUR BREATH** About 40km west of the Auski Roadhouse lies the town of Wittenoom, incorporated in 1947 as a home for asbestos miners. Asbestos tailings were used extensively as landfill in town, and the road from Wittenoom through Wittenoom Gorge is actually paved with the stuff. Despite the early warnings of health researchers, asbestos mining continued until 1966. Many residents of Wittenoom have contracted mesothelioma, and government officials still warn against travel to the area. Despite this, a handful of die-hard Wittenoomans continue to hang on. The government ordered the shut-off of water, electricity, and phone service to the 25 or so remaining residents on January 1, 1997. But the holdouts arranged a deal with Telstra for phone service, and a court challenge has kept power and water flowing. Though area tourist bureaus refuse to distribute information about Wittenoom or even to give directions, a handful of still-healthy residents push Wittenoom as a destination, trying to preserve the memory of the town that Western Australia would like to forget.

street, the shopping center complex houses a **supermarket** (open M-Sa 8am-8:30pm, Su 8am-6pm); a **bank** with an **ATM;** and a **post office** (open M-F 9am-5pm).

The best beds in town are at the **Tom Price Caravan Park,** 4km west of town. Showers and a swimming pool help beat the summer heat. They plan to install a backpackers unit sometime in 2001. (☎9189 1515. Tent sites $8 per person, powered $20 per site; cabins for 6 and chalets for 4 $83 per night.) On the northeastern corner of Karijini, and just before the dusty turn-off to Wittenoom, the **Auski Roadhouse** has very basic accommodations. (☎9176 6988. Singles $45; doubles $50.)

## KARIJINI NATIONAL PARK

Karijini has not attained as much notoriety as other parks in WA, and the fact that it's not awash in people is but another selling point of this magnificent place. Homeland to the Banjima, Innawonga, and Kurrama Aboriginal people, the park takes its name from their traditional name for the Hamersley Range. Originally an ancient sea floor, the area is decorated by colorful bands of sedimentary rock that are visible in the sheer faces of the massive gorges that slice through the range.

Karijini is easily reached from both Tom Price and the Great Northern Hwy; a recently completed access road bisects the park south of the gorges. The park's northern entrances, through Yampire Gorge and Wittenoom, are not recommended. Both are contaminated by asbestos, inhalation of which can cause cancer and death (see **Hold Your Breath,** above), and the road through Yampire Gorge has been closed. The other park roads are unsealed but mostly well-kept and 2WD-accessible. There are rough spots, especially after rains, so a 4WD is probably a safer bet. The one-day park fee is $9 per car. Carry plenty of **water;** it's scarce in the park and the heat can be oppressive. **Petrol** and supplies are available west of the park in **Tom Price** and at the **Auski Roadhouse** to the northeast. **Maps,** updates on **road conditions,** and **weather** forecasts can be found at area tourist bureaus, as well as at Karijini's **visitors center** near Fortescue Falls. The temporary visitors center is open Apr.-Nov. daily 9am-4:30pm; construction will soon begin on the new and improved center. For more info, contact **CALM** (☎9189 8157) in Tom Price. **Camping** is permitted in designated areas near Weano Gorge, Joffre Falls, and Fortescue Falls (sites for 2 $10, $5.50 for each additional person).

At **Dales Gorge,** the short, steep trail (3hr.) plummets to **Fortescue Falls** and the **Circular Pool,** which is great for swimming. The falls at **Joffre Gorge** are usually dry, but become impressive after a good rain. At **Weano Gorge,** a steep, winding track leads down into ▧**Handrail Pool.** This spot is the end of the miracle mile, and although the water is freezing, it's worth getting wet to explore what must be some of the most beautiful pools on the planet. Other highlights include the **Junction Pool Lookout,** where four gorges converge, and **Kalamina Falls,** which is another serene swimming spot. There are walking trails for all fitness (and bravado) levels in the park, ranging from the easy path overlooking the **Marandoo mine site** to the 9km route up **Mt. Bruce,** which is the highest peak in the area at 1235 meters.

## PORT HEDLAND

Industry is definitely king in Port Hedland: salt mines, refineries, shipping docks, and red dust rule the skyline of this narrow city sandwiched between the Indian Ocean and the Great Northern Hwy. Even the pigeons in town are pink with dust. Though the city gets its share of visitors, most either come to work or just pass through on their way to more pleasant spots.

For those who stay, the **Pretty Pool,** a massive tidal mudflat, is a popular shell-collecting and swimming spot—but wear shoes, as toxic rockfish hide in rocky areas. In the summer, several species of **sea turtles** may be seen, especially Aug.-Oct., at the Pretty Pool, **Cooke Point,** and **Cemetery Beach.** If you're lucky, from Nov.-Apr., you might spot babies making their way to the sea.

Port Hedland has an infrequent **bus service.** (☎9172 1394. M-F 7am-5pm; $2.50 one-way to South Hedland.) Most of the action takes place around the intersection of **Wedge** and **Richardson St.** Greyhound **buses** bound for **Perth** (3:20pm), **Darwin,** and **Broome** (both 10:15am) stop beside the **tourist bureau,** 13 Wedge St, near the corner of Anderson St. (☎9173 1711; fax 9173 2632. Open M-F 8:30am-5pm, Sa 8:30am-4pm, Su noon-4pm; off-season Sa closes 1pm, closed Su.) Several **banks** with **ATMs** cluster around this area. The **shopping center,** 3km from Wedge St east along Wilson St, has a **supermarket** and **pharmacy.** The **post office** is opposite the tourist office on Wedge St (open M-F 9am-5pm).

Port Hedland doesn't offer a lot of choice as far as budget accommodation goes, but the two places in town with backpacker rooms are very friendly. **Port Hedland Backpackers,** 20 Richardson St, has basic rooms, some with A/C. (☎/fax 9173 3282. Dorms $16; twins $32.) **Dingo Oasis Backpackers,** 59 Kingsmill St, has just moved to a great new spot overlooking the ocean. Free bus pickup. (☎9173 1000; fax 9173 5149. Dorms $16; twins and doubles $36-40; A/C extra.)

### PORT HEDLAND TO BROOME

Six hundred kilometers of empty Great Northern Hwy separate Port Hedland and Broome. By bus, the trip takes 7hr.; by car it should be a bit less. It's nearly 300km between the Sandfire Roadhouse and the Roebuck Roadhouse outside Broome, so it is essential to fuel up at either end of this stretch and bring plenty of water. Many travelers head from Port Hedland to Broome, and there's only a few hostels in Port Hedland, so it's not difficult to find traveling companions. The surrounding scrubland is full of strange driving perils, including cows, sheep, goats, kangaroos, and perhaps a camel or two. **Pardoo Station** (☎9176 4930), about 130km east of Port Hedland, offers simple rooms in a delightfully calm setting; call ahead.

# THE KIMBERLEY

Pressed between the Indian Ocean and the Great Sandy Desert, the Kimberley's 320,000 square kilometers of raw, semi-desert bush has hardly changed since its settlement by non-Aboriginals a century ago. Hailed by explorers as a great open cattle land, cowboys flocked to this region, only to encounter tremendous hardships. Driving through barren, striking landscape, one wonders how anything could thrive here, but the boulder-stacked cliffs, unpredictable rivers and gorges, and the proud pockets of settlement attest to the Kimberley's hidden wealth. Increasing numbers of travelers are venturing beyond the beaches of Broome, and those who do are rewarded with unforgettable wilderness. Occupying the north end of Western Australia, the Kimberley is accessible from the rest of the state by flights to Broome or via the long, lonely desert highway from Port Hedland and Rtes 1 and 96, which branch off the Stuart Hwy from the Northern Territory. The Kimberley's only major paved road is the Great Northern Hwy. Most others, including the Gibb River Rd and its offshoots in the north, are unsealed 4WD tracks. Flooded rivers during the Wet (Nov.-Mar.) often close these roads. Call ahead for road conditions (☎(1800) 01 33 14), and register with the police before leaving. The Kimberley's high season is the Dry (Apr.-Oct.).

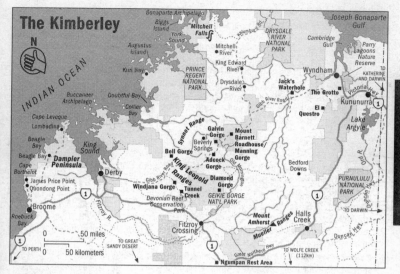

The Kimberley

# BROOME

Sprawling gracefully between the ocean and mangroves, Broome (pop. 14,000) has an immaculate shoreline and happy-go-lucky aura that feel surreal after driving through the dusty interior of the Kimberley. The tropical town's fame grew as a result of a thriving pearling industry in the 1880s. Today, the seaside mecca attracts vacationers seeking to sink their toes into the cool sands of the pristine beaches. Visitors may find themselves lingering over an iced cappuccino or strolling at twilight down endless Cable Beach, reluctant to leave the romantic oasis.

## TRANSPORT

**Airport: Broome International Airport** (☎9193 5455). Take a right from Frederick onto Coghlan St, then a left on McPherson St. Ansett and Qantas fly to: **Perth** ($376); **Adelaide** ($542); **Brisbane** ($716); **Darwin** ($275); **Melbourne** ($635); **Sydney** ($644); **Alice Springs** ($342); and **Uluru (Ayers Rock)** ($342).

**Buses: Greyhound** (☎13 20 30), at the Tourist Bureau. To **Perth** (32½hr., daily 8am, $246) and **Darwin** (26½hr., daily 7:30pm, $213).

**Public Transportation: Town Bus** (☎9193 6585) has an hourly shuttle running to (7:10am-5:10pm) and from (7:45am-6:15pm) **Cable Beach** which also covers **Chinatown** and **Gantheaume Point** (first service only). Fare $2.50, concessions $1; day pass $8, children $4.

**Taxis: Broome Taxis** (☎9192 1133). **Roebuck Taxis** (☎(1800) 88 03 30).

**Car Rental: Broome Discount Car Hire** (☎9192 3100), 100m from the airport on McPherson St. Sedans from $45. Broome Discount rents to drivers at least 21. **Woody's 4WD Hire** (☎9192 1791), Lot 24, Dampier Tce in Chinatown. Sedans from $40. **Hertz**, 69 Frederick St (☎9192 1428), does not rent to drivers under 25. Both Hertz and **Budget** (☎9193 5355, freecall ☎(1800) 64 98 00), at the airport, have one-way 4WD rentals from $100 per day, plus a one-way rental charge ($400-500).

## ORIENTATION

Broome is sprawled out on the peninsula, with the business area on sheltered Roebuck Bay to the east and the beaches on the Indian Ocean to the west. The **Great**

**Northern Hwy** (**Broome Rd** in town), curls into Roebuck Bay from the north. It becomes **Hamersley St** at its intersection with **Napier Tce.** This is **Chinatown,** the oldest part of Broome and the closest thing it has to a downtown. **Paspaley Shopping Centre,** the **Johnny Chi Ln** arcade, and most restaurants and services are scattered on a few blocks of **Carnarvon St,** the parallel **Dampier Tce,** and Napier Tce which intersects them. A block south of Napier Tce, Frederick St heads west; a right on Cable Beach Rd, right on Gubinge Rd, and a mysterious left on Cable Beach Rd leads to the aptly-named **Cable Beach** on the other side of the peninsula. East of Broome, the Great Northern Hwy enters the Kimberley proper and commences its grueling haul toward the Northern Territory.

# ⁊ PRACTICAL INFORMATION

**Tourist Office: Broome Tourist Bureau** (☎9192 2222; fax 9192 2063). Well marked on Broome Rd at the corner of Bagot St. Open during Apr.-Oct. 8am-5pm, Sa-Su 9am-4pm; Nov.-Mar. M-F 9am-5pm, Sa-Su 9am-1pm.

**Budget Travel: Harvey World Travel** (☎9193 5599). In Paspaley Shopping Centre in Chinatown. Serves as the broker for Qantas and other carriers. Open M-F 8:30am-5:30pm, Sa 9am-1pm. **Traveland,** 9 Johnny Chi Ln (☎9193 7233). Off Carnarvon across from the movie theater. Open M-F 8:30am-5pm, Sa 9am-1pm.

**Currency Exchange: ANZ Bank,** 16 Carnarvon St (☎13 13 14). Open M-Th 9:30am-4pm, F 9:30am-5pm. **Commonwealth Bank** (☎9192 1103). On Hamersley and Barker St. Open M-Th 9:30am-4pm, F 9:30am-5pm.

**Books: Woody's Book Exchange** (☎9192 8999). In the Johnny Chi Ln. Open M-F 9:30am-4:30pm, Sa 9:30am-2pm, Su 10am-2pm. **Kimberley Bookshop,** 6 Napier Tce (☎9191 1944). Just east of Carnarvon. Open M-F 10am-5pm, Sa-Su 10am-2pm.

**Markets: Courthouse Market,** near the courthouse on the corner of Hamersley and Frederick St. Open Sa 8am-1pm. **Sunday Market** inside Sun Pictures is open Su 9am-1pm.

**Emergency:** ☎000.

**Police:** (☎9192 1212). At the corner of Frederick and Carnarvon St.

**Pharmacy: Chinatown Pharmacy** (☎9192 1399). Shop 2 in Paspaley Shopping Centre. Open M-F 8:30am-5:30pm, Sa 8:30am-2pm.

**Hospital: Broome District Hospital** (☎9192 1401). On Robinson St, left off Frederick St heading away from downtown.

**Internet Access: Telecentre,** 51-53 Dampier Tce (☎9193 7153). 1hr. $8. Open M-F 9am-5pm, Apr.-Nov. also Sa 9am-1pm. **Fieldstar Consulting** (☎9193 7898). Napier Tce just east of Carnarvon. 1hr. $10. Open M-F 9am-5pm.

**Post Office: Australia Post** (☎9192 1020), in Paspaley Shopping Centre. Open M-F 9am-5pm. **Postal Code:** 6725, Cable Beach 6726.

**Phone Code:** 08.

# ⚑ ACCOMMODATIONS

During the high season (Apr.-Oct.), it is essential to book in advance, even at campgrounds. Most of Broome's backpackers have their own in-house bars, which means that BYO is strictly prohibited. All hostels in Broome are very communal, and most host an international mix of young backpackers.

▨ **Kimberley Klub** (☎9192 3233; fax 9192 3530). On Frederick St between Robinson and Herbert. From the tourist office, take a right on Frederick and it's 3 blocks on the left. Free pickup from Greyhound depot. This popular, spacious hostel has successfully inserted a bit of luxury into budget travel. The Klub is social and family-friendly, with an enormous sparkling pool, bar, modern kitchen, ping-pong, billiards, an open-air TV den, and sand volleyball court. Coin operated A/C for some rooms. $10 deposit each for cutlery and linen. Reception daily 6:30am-7pm. Dorms $17; twins and doubles $62; quads $19 per person. NOMADS $1 discount.

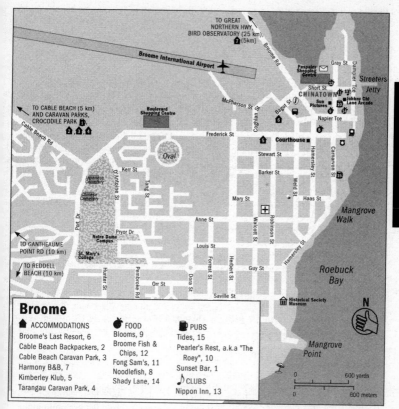

**WESTERN AUSTRALIA**

## Broome

🏠 **ACCOMMODATIONS**
Broome's Last Resort, 6
Cable Beach Backpackers, 2
Cable Beach Caravan Park, 3
Harmony B&B, 7
Kimberley Klub, 5
Tarangau Caravan Park, 4

🍎 **FOOD**
Blooms, 9
Broome Fish & Chips, 12
Fong Sam's, 11
Noodlefish, 8
Shady Lane, 14

🍺 **PUBS**
Tides, 15
Pearler's Rest, a.k.a "The Roey", 10
Sunset Bar, 1

♪ **CLUBS**
Nippon Inn, 13

**Cable Beach Backpackers** (☎9193 5511; fax 9193 5532; email meyo@tpgi.com.au). On Lullfitz Dr. Free pickup from Greyhound and airport. Visitors may hesitate to visit the hostel close to the beach but far from Chinatown. But a free shuttle to town five times a day puts everything within reach. Once the sun sets a crowd of Aussies and backpackers congregate to play cards. Kitchen, laundry, billiards. Pushbike hire half-day $5. Scooters $25 per day. Surfboards $10 per day. Four-bed dorms $15; twins $40. VIP.

**Broome's Last Resort** (☎9193 5000; fax 9193 6033; email lastresortyha@smart-chat.com). Left from the cul-de-sac at the end of Bagot St. A wide range of travelers enjoys the atmosphere of a tropical treehouse in this lively hostel. Patrons relax in the tropical pool by day and chill at the in-house bar by night. Wooden walkways create a shady treehouse feel. Theme party nights, like "Mexican" or "Beach." Kitchen, free luggage storage, coin-op A/C, laundry. Dorms $16-18; twins and doubles $50. YHA, VIP.

**Tarangau Caravan Park,** 994 Millington Rd (☎9193 5084; fax 9193 7551). Relaxed, quiet atmosphere reminds you that you're a stone's throw from the sea. Tent sites for 2 $14, powered $20.

**Cable Beach Caravan Park** (☎9192 2066; fax 9192 1997). Behind the Cable Beach Resort, a 20min. walk from the coast. Turn onto Lullfitz St from the Cable Beach Rd, then left on Millington Rd. Good location compensates for the crowds. Sites $7.50-8.50 per person, powered sites for 2 $18-20.

**Harmony Bed & Breakfast** (☎9193 7439; fax 9193 7429). Five km out of town on Broome Rd. This quiet B&B provides retreat from the noisier hostel scene. Though not luxurious, the rooms are clean and comfortable and relaxing. Perfect for couples. Tropical pool, patio, laundry. Singles $50; doubles $80.

##  FOOD

Chinatown possesses only a smattering of Chinese restaurants, but the area is packed with tasty outdoor cafés. **Coles Supermarket** (☎9192 6299), in the Paspaley Shopping Centre, is open 24 hours.

**Fong Sam's Café** (☎9192 1030). On Carnarvon St across from the cinema. Delicious baked goods for bargain-basement prices bring throngs of tanned visitors to this sunny street café. Various pies and pasties run under $2 each. Fresh quiche and salad are $8.50; pasta of the day $9.50. Open daily 6:30am-5:30pm.

**Blooms Café and Restaurant,** 31 Carnarvon St (☎9193 6366). Near Napier Tce in Chinatown. Despite your best efforts to finish a meal, you'll find yourself thwarted by good food in large portions. Choose from pastas, pizzas, and Thai curries, all in the $10-$16 range. At lunch grab a sandwich with intriguing ingredient combinations ($8-10). BYO. Open 7:30am-10:30pm.

**Noodlefish** (☎9192 5529). At the corner of Frederick and Hamersley St. Locals and tourists crowd around to sample dishes of...noodles and fish. *Thai* noodles and fish, that is. Very creative, fresh meals, but a bit pricey. Spicy, succulent seafood *laksa* is $12. Veggie pad thai $10.50. Open daily 5:30-9pm; Apr.-Oct. 11:30am-2:30pm.

**Shady Lane Café** (☎9192 2060). In the Johnny Chi Ln arcade, in a shady lane. Flap jacks for $6.50, 4-filling toasted focaccia for $8, and fruity smoothies for $4 make it a wallet-friendly eatery. Open daily 7am-4:30pm.

**Broome Fish & Chips** (☎9192 1280). On Napier Tce just west of Carnarvon. Fish (snapper, barramundi, etc.) and chips fried before your eyes, and only $6.50 for this magic trick. Also does a side business in 20L oil drums, 30¢ apiece for those who can't get enough grease. Open M-F 11am-2pm and 4:30-8pm; Sa-Su 5-8pm.

## SIGHTS AND ACTIVITIES

**CABLE BEACH.** At Broome's paradise, 22km of clear Indian Ocean laps against the pearly white sand. Despite the claims of camel, sailing, hovercraft, and 4WD tours alike, the superlative-defying sunsets are always free and inspire philosophic speculation. If a nudist beach never has any naked people on it, will it still draw teenage boys? See for yourself past the rocks on the north end of the beach. On Port Dr south of Cable Beach Road is the **Japanese Cemetery**, a stark yet peaceful memorial to over 900 Japanese divers who lost their lives in the perilous pearling industry. Just south lies its friendly neighbor the **Chinese Cemetery.**

**WATER ACTIVITIES.** If lounging the day away on the beach makes you itch to get moving, you may have too much sand in your bathing suit. If that's not the case, then Cable Beach offers plenty of get-up-and-go activities. Surfboard rental is available on the beach, near the main facilities (*$8 per hr.*). Parasailing, jet skiing, and tubing operators work from Cable Beach. Keep your eyes peeled for the vans that stop by the beach to rent out equipment. Would-be mermen, or those who are just curious, turn to **Broome Adventure Diving** (*☎9192 2233*) for scuba diving.

**REPTILES OLD AND NEW.** Do crocodiles scare you? How about 1500 of 'em? Throw in countless warning signs and more chain-link fence than you can shake a stick at, and you've got **Malcolm Douglas Broome Crocodile Park.** (*200m from the beach access on Cable Beach Rd. ☎9192 1489. Feedings W-Su 3pm. Guided tours M-Tu 3pm. Open M-F 10am-5pm; Sa-Su 2-5pm. $14, concessions $10, children $7, families $35.*) If live lizards aren't your thing, how about dead ones? One set of **dinosaur footprints** is preserved in the rocks at **Gantheaume Point,** the western tip of the Broome Peninsula about 4km from Cable Beach. Take a left onto Gubinge Rd, where Cable Beach Rd turns to the right. The 120-million-year-old prints surface at very low tide and can be difficult to find. A plaster replica is at the top of the cliff.

**WHALE OF A TALE** One day in 1878, a mother whale gave birth to her calf right off the coast of Taiji Hamlet in Wakayama Prefecture, Japan. The people of Taiji, whose economic livelihood depended on whaling, could not believe their luck and quickly sent out their whaling boats loaded with 60 men (almost the entire working male population) to capture the calf. However, Mother Whale overturned the boats, having her revenge. Most of the men became entangled in their own nets and drowned, leaving behind a village of poor children, women, and elders. Wrought with poverty and despair, long-distance tales of prosperous pearling lured the boys left behind to Broome and the Torres Strait. These young men became the mainstay of Broome's pearling industry for the next half-century.

**OTHER BEACHES. Town Beach** is farther south on the Roebuck Bay shore, at the southern end of Robinson St. To the left of the jetty, for three consecutive days each month from March to October, Broome's massive 10m tide is so low that the exposed mudflats stretch for miles, reflecting shimmering moonlight in a staircase pattern. The city celebrates with the **Staircase to the Moon Market** at the Town Beach. At the lowest tides, the waters off Town Beach uncover the skeletons of boats sunk in WWII. **Reddell Beach,** at the southern tip of the peninsula, is covered with rocky outcroppings and red cliffs. The **Mangrove Walk,** on the east coast between Chinatown and the Historical Society, weaves its way through over 10 species of mangroves. Beware of broken glass.

**BIRD OBSERVATORY.** The **Broome Bird Observatory** is an excellent place to spy 40% of Australia's total bird species—it's one of only four such observatories in the country. (☎9193 5600. Located 25km outside of town. Take Broome Rd for 9.2km and watch for the turn-off. Self-guided tours by donation; half-day tours $28, with pickup $50. Open daily Apr.-Oct. 7am-5pm; Nov.-Mar. Tu-Su 8am-5pm.)

**TOURS.** For the most romantic and breathtaking experience Broome has to offer, ride camels down Cable Beach at sunset, threading your way up the dunes to reach the hilltop at twilight. **Ships of the Desert** has morning, afternoon, sunset, and twilight camel tours. (☎9192 6383. 1hr. $30, full-day $75.) Also try **Red Sun Camel Safaris** (☎9193 7423; 2:15pm and 4pm tours). **Land tours** are costly, but if you lack a strong 4WD, they may be the best way to see the rugged terrain of the Kimberley and the remote shorelines to the north. **Discover the Kimberley Tours** runs daytrips to the pristine beaches of the Dampier Coast, north of Broome. (☎(1800) 63 68 02. Tours depart W and F. $125, with Pearl Farm tour $155.) **Over the Top Adventures** offers one- and two-day tours to the Dampier Peninsula and Windjana Gorge and Tunnel Creek. (☎9192 3977. Dampier one-day $175, two-day $275; Windjana Gorge and Tunnel Creek $160, $275. Five-day trip with stops along the Gibb River Rd, Windjana Gorge, and Tunnel Creek $720.) The priciest tours are **scenic flights,** some of which travel all the way to Mitchell Falls and the Buccaneer Archipelago. Such flights are the best way to get a bird's-eye view of otherwise unreachable sights. Soar through the air with the greatest of ease—thanks to a much lighter wallet—on extended flights from **Broome Aviation** (☎(1300) 13 66 29) or **King Leopold Air** (☎(1800) 63 71 55; from $260).

##  NIGHTLIFE

Broome's beaches and clubs seduce bacchants into brief affairs with beer and fellow backpackers. Most accommodations have in-house bars that encourage it. Before the pubs, stop by **Sun Pictures Outdoor Cinema,** on Carnarvon St, the oldest operating outdoor film theater in the world. It spun its first reel in 1916 and spins the newest flicks every night. (☎9192 1077. $10, concessions $8.) At Cable Beach, you'll find the locals playing pool at **Divers Camp Tavern,** a bar and bistro that gets jovial on weekends. (☎9193 6066. Open M-Sa 10am-midnight, Su 11am-10pm. Brews $4.) For a classy splurge, the **Sunset Bar** at the Cable Beach Resort, right at

**WESTERN AUSTRALIA**

Cable Beach, serves heavenly $10 cocktails to match the heavenly ocean view. (☎9192 0400. Open daily 4pm-midnight. Beers $4.50.) **Pearler's Bar a.k.a. "The Roey,"** in the Roebuck Hotel on Carnarvon north of Napier Tce, is a popular place for backpackers and locals. Free ping-pong. Internet access after six beers? Here if you want. (☎9192 1221. Open Su-W 10am-midnight, Th, Sa 10am-1am, F 10am-2am.) **Tides,** in the Mangrove Hotel on Carnarvon, two blocks south of the business district, is distinctly more laid-back than the Roey. Even better, skip the bar and head straight for the outdoor deck in the back with its sprawling view of the mangrove maze below. (☎9193 5169. Open M-Sa 10am-midnight, Su 10am-10pm.) **Nippon Inn,** on Dampier Tce near Short St, is Broome's only nightclub. Immerse yourself in purple walls and techno beats. When other bars wind down around midnight, the most integrated spot in town starts thumping. (☎9192 1941. Open M-Sa 9am-4am, Su 9am-midnight. Victoria Bitter $4. Cover F-Sa $5.)

##  FESTIVALS

Horse racing is big in June and July when the town starts hopping for the **Broome Cup.** Mid-April features the aquatic **Rotary Dragon Boat Classic.** The end of May features the bigger **Broome Fringe Arts Festival,** when the non-mainstream, aesthetically inclined display their stuff. Much of the art is Aboriginal. The late August **Shinju Matsuri Festival** ("Pearl Festival") celebrates the natural beauty of pearls with a Japanese twist. In late November, the **Mango Festival** pays homage to the harvest and includes a Mardi Gras celebration.

## NEAR BROOME: DAMPIER PENINSULA

North of Broome, pristine white beaches stretch all along the Dampier Peninsula. Four-wheel-drive access roads promise striking views of the Indian Ocean. James Price Point, with its contrast of red cliffs and white beaches, and Quandong Point are two closer destinations to Broome. Ask the tourist center in Broome for road and weather conditions and tide charts before you leave. Allow at least two days to visit. The roads are tricky, so carry plenty of spare parts, water, and rations.

Once the sites of Catholic missions, several Aboriginal communities inhabit the Peninsula, welcoming travelers with a glimpse into a rich history. (Entry to most sites $5. Open M-Sa.) **Beagle Bay,** 118km up a rough 4WD track, has petrol and houses the **Beagle Bay Church,** sporting an unusual mother-of-pearl altar. (☎9192 4913. Open M-Th 8am-4:30pm, F 8am-3pm.) Fifty kilometers farther north, the mellow waters of the **Middle Lagoon** offer swimming, snorkeling, and accommodations. (☎9192 4002. Sites $12 per person, powered $15; beach shelters for 2 $40; cabins for 4 $100.) The **old mission church,** built from corrugated iron and paperbark, is the highlight of **Lombadina,** 200km from Broome. You can fuel up, buy **groceries,** and sleep. (☎9192 4936. Dorms $35; cabins $120.) At **Kooljaman,** the end of the Peninsula, tourists can swim, fish, and dive. (☎9192 4970. Tent sites $11 per person, powered $14.50; beach shelters $30.) **Flak Track Tours** departs Broome with a 4WD tour to Beagle Bay, Lombadina, and Cape Leveque or Middle Lagoon. (☎9192 1487. Full-day $187, includes entry and meals.)

# GREAT NORTHERN HIGHWAY

Crossing the Kimberly on the way to the Northern Territory, you have two options. The Great Northern Hwy leaves Broome, continuing along in a tame, mostly sealed fashion. However, in Derby, 220km east of Broome and just north of the highway, a more adventurous option opens—the unparalleled Gibb River Rd (p. 669).

## DERBY

"As the sun sank below the horizon, he stared out into the distance, and as far as he could see, it was all mud. And yet it was beautiful." Okay, we made that quote up, but such is life in Derby (pop. 5000). The expanse of mudflats and water make ▧sunsets at the Derby wharf unforgettable. Off the highway 8km south of town, the **Prison Boab Tree** was the natural jail for Aboriginal prisoners in the 1800s. Derby has the regional headquarters for the **Royal Flying Doctor Service** (☎9191 1211) on Clarendon at Fairbairn St.

The Derby Hwy becomes **Loch St** in town. **Clarendon St** runs parallel and contains most of the sites of interest. Greyhound **buses** stop here twice daily (Darwin-bound at 10:20pm, Perth-bound at 4:55am). Derby's **tourist office**, with **Internet access**, is at the foot of Clarendon St, on the west end of town. (☎9191 1426. Open M-F 8:30am-4:30pm, Sa 9am-noon; also Apr.-Sept. Su 9am-1pm.) An **ANZ bank** with an **ATM** is on Loch St. (☎13 13 14. Open M-Th 9:30am-4pm, F 9:30am-5pm.) Other services on Loc St include: **police** (☎9191 1444); **hospital** (☎9193 3333); and **post office** (open M-F 9am-5pm). **Postal code:** 6728.

The **West Kimberley Lodge,** at the corner of Sutherland and Stanwell St, has clean, quiet rooms, kitchen, and laundry. (☎9191 1031. Twins $50; suites $65.) The grassy **Kimberley Entrance Caravan Park,** on Rowan St, around the curve from the tourist office, overlooks mudflats. (☎9193 1055. Sites $12, for 2 $15; powered $15, $18.)

Join the rest of Derby after sundown at **Derby Takeaways,** next to the tourist office. (☎9191 1131. Open M-F 11am-11pm, Sa-Su 5-11pm.) Woolworth's **supermarket** is at the corner of the Derby Hwy and Waycott St (open M-W, F 8am-6pm, Th 8am-8pm, Sa 8am-5pm, Su 10am-4pm). What little nightlife Derby has coalesces at the sports bar in the **Spinifex Hotel,** on Clarendon St, east of the tourist bureau.

# FITZROY CROSSING

Fitzroy Crossing (pop. 1500), near the **Fitzroy River** right off the Great Northern Hwy 270km east of Derby, is used primarily as a base for nearby **Tunnel Creek, Windjana Gorge,** and **Geikie Gorge.** Geikie Gorge ("GEEK-ee"), 18km from town on the sealed Russ Rd, is a set of awe-inspiring sheer faces of black, white and rust-colored rock towering over the Fitzroy river. **Boat tours** take you right up to the rock faces and also let you see many freshwater crocs. Buy tickets in the gorge parking lot. (1hr.; June-Sept. 3 per day, Apr.-May and Oct.-Nov. 1-2 per day; $17.50.) The **reef walk** (3km; 1½hr.) misses the crocs and shows you the gorges from farther away, but affords a panoramic perspective that becomes downright dumbfounding at sunset. There are toilets and water but no camping at the gorge. (Geikie gorge open daily in the Dry 6:30am-6:30pm.) Day tours for Windjana Gorge and Tunnel Creek leave from Fitzroy Crossing ($85); book at the tourist office.

The **Greyhound bus** runs daily to **Perth** (1:25am, $290) and **Darwin** (1:10am, $135). The **tourist center,** left off the highway at Forrest Rd, has maps of the gorges. (☎9191 5355. Open in the Dry daily 9am-5pm; in the Wet M-F 9am-5pm, Sa 9am-1pm.) Farther down Forrest Rd is the **supermarket** (open M-F 8:30am-5:30pm, Sa-Su 8am-1pm) and the **police** (☎9191 5000); and around the corner is the **hospital** (☎9191 5001) and the **post office** (open M-F 9am-5pm). **Postal code:** 6765.

A resort community unto itself, the **Fitzroy River Lodge** offers motel rooms, "safari lodges," and camping. (☎9191 5141. Sites for 2 $16, powered $19; motel rooms and lodges from $100.) **Darlngunaya Backpackers** is 4km from town on the way to Geikie Gorge; take Forrest Rd and turn right on Russ Rd. Or a $5 shuttle meets the Greyhound. It's soothing, with high ceilings, porches, a spacious kitchen, and laundry. (☎9191 5140. Sites $10; dorms $15; 2-bedroom house $90.)

The best (read: only) bets for food once the supermarket closes are the takeaway stands at the two gas stations (open until 10pm), or the pricey **Fitzroy River Lodge** restaurant (open until 8pm). For a taste of gritty local nightlife, grab a friend (a big, burly friend) and head over to the rowdy pub at the **Crossing Inn.** Take Sanford Rd to Skuthorp. (☎9191 5080. Open M-Sa 10am-10pm, Su noon-6pm.) Alternatively, high-class it at the **Fitzroy Lodge** bar (open until midnight).

# HALLS CREEK

The small, arid town of Halls Creek (pop. 1300), 280km east of Fitzroy Crossing, is a low-key desert town with a dry Dry and a wet Wet. The town is on the way to Bungle Bungle (Purnululu National Park), 109km north. However, it can act as a somewhat distant base for another natural spectacle: the Wolfe Creek Meteorite Crater, 150km south of town along the rumbly Tanami Rd.

The unsealed Duncan Hwy near town has many worthwhile sites—but the road itself steals the show with breathtaking views and 2WD-jarring holes. **China Wall** is a quartz formation 3km from town. The **Caroline Pool,** 14km down, is a popular swimming spot; **Palm Springs,** 40km down, is off-limits for a dip but offers pretty picnicking. **Sawpit Gorge,** 500m past Palm Springs, has a swimming hole beneath a dramatic stone cliff. **Old Halls Creek,** 16km down the Duncan Highway, marks the origin of the gold rush in Western Australia. All that remains are some old street signs and some commemorative plaques.

Services on the highway include: the **tourist center** (☎9168 6140; open M-F 7am-6pm, Sa-Su 8am-5pm), **grocery store** (☎9168 6186; open M-F 8am-6pm, Sa 8am-noon, Su 9am-noon), **Shell station** (☎9168 6060; open daily 6am-10pm), **police** (☎9168 6000), **hospital** (☎9168 6003), and **post office** (☎9168 6111; open M-F 9am-5pm; **postal code:** 6770). While most travelers stop in Halls Creek just long enough to fill the petrol tank, accommodations do exist. For adventurous sunset-seekers, **The Lodge** is located at Old Halls Creek. (☎9168 8999. Sites $8; caravan sites $12, powered $15; singles $25.) The **Shell** has beds and A/C but no linen (dorms $15; singles $50; doubles $75). **Halls Creek Caravan Park** is a block south of the highway on Roberta. (☎9168 6169. Sites $7; powered $9.)

## PURNULULU (BUNGLE BUNGLE) NATIONAL PARK

If the mountain ranges here could be captured in a word, it would be the lilting, roly-poly sound of "Purnululu"—not the choppy name "Bungle Bungle," thought to be either a corruption of the Aboriginal word *purnululu,* meaning "sandstone," or a misspelling of a commonly found grass in the area, *Bundle Bundle.* The ranges were created 360 million years ago and have since been weathered by wind and rain into a smooth egg-carton mattress of orange "beehives," striped with black bands of algae. The Kija Aboriginal people have inhabited the gorges between the mountains for nearly 20,000 years. In fact, it was only in the early 1980s that the existence of the Purnunulu range became widely known to non-Aboriginals; their inaccessibility and remoteness kept them hidden.

■■ **TOURS AND PRACTICAL INFORMATION.** Many visitors choose to avoid the tough tracks into the park and view the natural spectacle from above. **Alligator Airways** (☎9168 1333), in Kununurra, offers tours of the Purnululu area as does **SlingAir Heliwork** (☎(1800) 09 55 00), which runs flights from Kununurra and Turkey Creek (both 2hr.; from $160). To enter the park by car requires a 4WD, tires, rope, water, a jack, and chutzpah—or a 4WD tour. **Desert Inn 4WD** (☎(1800) 80 50 10) and **Kununurra Backpackers** (☎(1800) 64 19 98) offer 2- and 3-day tours that hit the main gorges in the park ($260 and $390, respectively). Kununurra Backpackers and **Gondwana Safaris** offer tours for small groups willing to walk and camp. (☎(0407) 97 37 16. 4-day $520.) If driving without a tour, bring your own topo maps, which can be purchased for $7.50 in Kununurra at the **Department of Land Administration** on Messmate Way at the traffic circle. (☎9168 0255. Open M-F 8am-4:30pm.) The park closes January through March. Vehicle access to the Park is via the 4WD-only **Spring Creek Track,** off the Great Northern Hwy 109km north of Halls Creek and 250km south of Kununurra. Spring Creek Track rumbles east from the highway 53km to the **ranger station** in Purnululu. (☎9168 7300. Open in the Dry daily 7:30am-4:30pm.) Entry fees (vehicles $8) and overnight camping fees ($7 per person) are payable near the station.

■■ **CAMPING AND HIKING.** At the ranger station, another 4WD track creates a three-way intersection with the Spring Creek Track. Seven kilometers to the left is the **Kurrajong campsite,** with untreated water, toilets, and firewood. Thirteen kilometers to the right is the **Walardi campsite** (all sites $7). Camping is allowed only at established campsites, unless with a tour or if registered to bushcamp. Fires are allowed only at sites listed above.

A handful of **walking tracks** meander along the edge of the Purnululu massif (the interior is off-limits). The most popular is the reasonably easy hike through **Cathedral Gorge** (3km; 1-2hr.), starting from a carpark 25km south of the ranger station. The **Piccaninny Gorge hike** (30km) requires more stamina and a night in the bush. Register with the rangers before setting out from the Cathedral Gorge lot. The fairly easy **Echidna Chasm walk** (2km; 1-2hr.) starts 21km north of the ranger station and scrambles over some large boulders. Two walks leave from a carpark 2km south of Echidna Chasm: the more challenging **Froghole** walk (1.4km; 1-2hr.) leads to a small seasonal pool, and the **Mini Palms** (5km; 3hr.) walk ends at a natural amphitheater surrounded by palms.

**Warmun** (formerly Turkey Creek) is the last "town" north of the Spring Creek Track turn-off. Less than 100km from the park, it can serve as a stopover for travelers from Kununurra. The **Turkey Creek Roadhouse** offers petrol, takeaway, and a variety of accommodations. (☎9168 7882. Reception daily 6:30am-7:30pm. Dorms and singles $20; sites $6; on-site caravans $15, powered $20.)

# GIBB RIVER ROAD

The Gibb River Road is a rugged and unforgettable 4WD track that begins 8km south of Derby off the Derby Hwy and is only open from April to October when weather permits. Though technically a 660km "shortcut" between Derby and Kununurra, "doing the Gibb" will take 4 to 5 days to enjoy the primary gorges, and longer to tackle the severe turn-offs. The experience promises dips into pristine, saltie-free gorges, cliff jumping for the super-brave, and unpopulated walks.

▪ **TRANSPORT.** The Gibb is severely corrugated in parts, and many of the turn-offs to the gorges are bumpy and hole-filled. Rental companies in Derby and Broome will rent 4WDs that can do most of the road. Travelers should have plenty of water and food, at least two spare tires, a high clearance jack, tool box, first-aid kit, and a hearty helping of grit and self-sufficiency. Tourist offices in Derby and Fitzroy Crossing sell copies of the *Traveller's Guide to the Gibb River and Kalumburu Roads*, which has detailed information on distances, accommodations, and limited services along the roads ($2; write to Derby Tourist Bureau, PO Box 48, Derby WA 6728 or email derbytb@comswest.net.au). Travelers should register with tourist offices at either end before starting the journey and consider renting a walkie-talkie, CB radio, or cell phone. Traffic can be scarce and you could get stuck for a while. Many people do the Gibb River Rd via small group tours, which can actually be cheaper than renting your own 4WD. **Wilderness 4WD Adventures** offers a trek from Darwin to Broome or vice-versa. (☎(1800) 80 82 88. Nine days $1150, YHA and VIP $50 off.) **Desert Inn 4WD Adventures** does the trip from Kununurra or Broome (☎(1800) 80 50 10. 5 days, $715.)

▪ **HIKES AND GORGES. Windjana Gorge** can be reached from either the Great Northern Hwy (turn onto a gravel road 40km west of Fitzroy Crossing and travel 107km north) or from the Gibb along a 21km gravel road 123km from Derby. This 3.5km limestone crevasse looms as high as 100m over the Lennard River and is part of the 350-million-year-old Devonian Reef. The freshwater crocs are the main attraction, and swimming is permitted. A walk (8km) skirts the river to the right, past the sheer walls of the gorge. There are **campsites** with facilities ($7).

A little over 40km south of Windjana is **Tunnel Creek.** During the Dry, the creek is shallow, and wading through the thigh-deep water in the pitch-black tunnel is a thrill. The walk is over 1km; upon reaching the daylight on the other side, people simply turn around and head back through. A flashlight and shoes are essential. Most sedans can usually tolerate this beginning section of the Gibb River Rd, but be prepared for neck-jarring corrugated roads.

Popular and perfectly shaped **Bell Gorge** lies 100km farther east of the Windjana Gorge turn-off at kilometer 223. A series of falls meet a deep plunge pool, accessible via a 1km walk from the carpark. The turn-off for the gorge is a tough 29km.

**WESTERN AUSTRALIA**

**Camping** is available with bush toilets at Silent Grove or Bell Creek on the turn-off ($7). The next major attraction after Bell Gorge is **Old Mornington** (☎9191 7035), 90km down a turn-off road at kilometer 255 (2½hr.). Nearby **Diamond Gorge** and **Sir John Gorge** are worthwhile, and there is riverside camping ($8). Back on the Gibb, the tropical **Adcock Gorge** and the intimate **Galvin Gorge** are at kilometers 275 and 286 respectively with short turn-offs. At kilometer 306 is **Mt. Barnett Roadhouse** (☎9191 7007) and access to the **Manning Gorge** hike (1hr.) which warrants a stop and is a good place to camp ($7).

One-hundred more fierce kilometers will lead you to the junction of the Gibb with the unforgiving but spectacular **Kalumburu Rd.** The Kalumburu is an entire 267km journey in itself, branching north towards the **Mitchell Plateau** and **Mitchell Falls,** a four-cataract waterfall plunging into the Indian Ocean. This region is one of the most isolated and stunning sights in the Kimberley, but is even more bone-jarring than the Gibb—complete self-sufficiency is absolutely a must.

**Jack's Waterhole,** 120km past the Gibb-Kalumburu junction, has quiet sites and hot showers. (☎9161 4324. $7.) **El Questro Station,** 16km down an access road at kilometer 614, gives boat tours through **Chamberlain Gorge** ($37) and 3-4hr. bushwalks to **El Questro** and **Amalia Gorges.** (☎9161 4318. Sites Apr.-Aug. $15 per person, Sept.-Oct. $11.) ▨**Emma Gorge** (10km away on the Gibb; a 45min. walk) is a perfect pool. The crescent, fern-covered cliffs rise high above the chilly pool, and a droplet waterfall on the right side gives the semblance of rain. There is no camping at Emma Gorge, though pricey cabins are available. (Reservations ☎9169 1777. $50-60 per person.) From there, it's only 25km to the end of the Gibb, at its intersection with the Great Northern Hwy near Kununurra and Wyndham.

# KUNUNURRA

Five hundred kilometers west of Katherine, NT, the little oasis of Kununurra ("cun-ah-NUR-ah") sleeps lazily beneath the sandstone formations of the eastern Kimberley. The name means "big waters," appropriate for a town that accesses the Ord River and grew tremendously during the effort to reroute that river for irrigation. Most travelers use Kununurra (pop. 6000) as a base to explore the dramatic attractions in the eastern Kimberley region, such as Purnululu (Bungle Bungle) National Park, Lake Argyle, and the Gibb River Rd. Kununurra is worth an overnight stay, if only for the sunset on Kelly's Knob or in Mirima National Park.

## ▣ TRANSPORT

**Airport:** The airport is 5km down the Victoria Hwy towards Wyndham. Ansett (☎13 13 00) flies daily to **Darwin** ($127), **Perth** ($473), and **Broome** ($186).

**Buses:** Buses arrive at the tourist bureau at the corner of Coolibah Dr and White Gum St. Greyhound Pioneer (☎13 20 30) departs for **Broome** (14hr., daily 5:45pm, $144) and **Darwin** (12hr., daily 10:05am, $108).

**Cars: Budget,** 947 Mango St (☎9168 2033), and at the airport. **Avis,** 6743 Coolibah Dr (☎9169 1258), and at the airport.

**Taxis: Spuds Taxis** (☎9168 2553).

## ▣ ORIENTATION AND PRACTICAL INFORMATION

From the Northern Territory, **Messmate Way** turns off the Victoria Hwy at a petrol station and heads into town, where it crosses Konkerberry Dr and ends at Coolibah Dr. The **Kununurra Shopping Centre** is on Konkerberry Dr. Most restaurants and the two hostels are on or near Konkerberry as it heads away from Messmate.

**Tourist Office: Tourist Bureau** (☎9168 1177), on Coolibah Dr. Open in the Dry daily 8am-4pm; in the Wet M-F 8am-4pm, Sa-Su 8am-noon.

**National Park Information: Conservation and Land Management** (☎9168 4200). On Messmate Way at the traffic circle. Open M-F 8am-4:30pm. Sells Western Australia park vehicle passes (annual $45; 4-week $20; Purnululu and Mirima only $15). Across the hall is the **Department of Land Administration** (☎9168 0255), which sells topographic maps of the Kimberley ($7.50). Open M-F 8am-4:30pm.

**Banks: Commonwealth Bank** (☎13 22 21), on the corner of Coolibah Dr and Cotton Tree Ave, has a 24hr. **ATM.** Open M-Th 9:30am-4pm, F 9:30am-5pm.

**Police:** at Coolibah and Banksia St (24hr. ☎9166 4530).

**Kimberley Road Conditions:** ☎(1800) 01 33 14.

**Hospital/Ambulance:** (☎9168 1522), on Coolibah Dr, toward Ivanhoe Rd.

**Internet Access: Telecentre** (☎9169 1868), on Banksia St near Coolibah Dr. 1hr. $9. Open in the Dry M-F 10am-6pm, Wet M-F noon-5pm.

**Post Office:** (☎9168 1395), across from the police station at Coolibah and Banksia. Open M-F 9am-5pm. **Postal Code:** 6743.

**Phone Code:** 08

# ACCOMMODATIONS

**Desert Inn** (☎(1800) 80 50 10). Two blocks from the shopping center near the corner of Konkerberry and Tristania St. This cozy, lively place performs hip decorating miracles with scrap metal and the color purple. Friendly staff, pool, patio, shaded lounge areas, spacious kitchen, laundry. Free transport to and from the bus station and to Kelly's Knob for sunset. Dorms $18; doubles $46; triples and quads $19 per person. YHA.

**Kununurra Backpackers,** 111 Nutwood Crescent (☎9169 1998). A 10min. walk from the tourist office; follow Konkerberry away from the highway, then turn right on Nutwood. In a quiet neighborhood, with A/C, pool, kitchen, VCR, and laundry. Free transport to and from the bus station. Key deposit $10. Dorms $18; twins and doubles $45. VIP.

**Kimberleyland Holiday Park** (☎9168 1280). On the Victoria Hwy west of Messmate Way. Pool, laundry. Canoe hire for the Lake (half-day $25). Sites for 2 $16, powered $18.50.

**Town Caravan Park** (☎9168 1763). On Bloodwood St. Despite its proximity to town there's not much privacy. Laundry, kitchen. Sites for 2 $16, powered $18.

# FOOD AND ENTERTAINMENT

Kununurra's scenery may be spectacular, but the food is not. For **groceries,** head to **Coles** in the shopping center. (☎9168 2711. Open 24hr.) The **Kununurra Bakehouse,** at Konkerberry Dr and Ebony St, has cheap sandwiches and fresh pies. (☎9168 3583. Open M-F 5am-3:30pm, Sa 5am-12:30pm.) **Hot Gossip Café,** in the shopping center, serves semi-conventional fare and has cheap, passable Chinese takeaway. (☎9169 1377. Open M-F 8am-9pm, Sa-Su 8am-1pm and 5-8:30pm.) For juicy tidbits, try **Rumours Patisserie,** in the shopping center, where the burger bar does it all, from barra to lentil. (☎9168 2071. Open M-F 6:30am-5:30pm, Sa 7am-4pm, Su 8am-3pm.) **Gulliver's Tavern,** on Konkerberry Dr at Cotton Tree Ave, is the main pub. The patio bar with Aussie pints for $5 is relaxed and uncrowded, like Kununurra itself. (☎9168 1666. Open M-Th noon-11pm, F noon-1am, Sa noon-midnight, Su 1-9pm.) **Kelly's,** in the Country Club Hotel, is a slightly classier option.

# SIGHT AND ACTIVITIES

**Kelly's Knob,** at the north end of town, has views of the stunning topography around Kununurra. Take Konkerberry Dr to the end; turn left on Ironwood, right on Speargrass, and right again at the large stone tablet reading "Kelly's Knob." **Mirima (Hidden Valley) National Park** (☎9168 0200), 2km east of town, looks like a miniature Purnululu range (but without the 6hr. drive). Three short paths wind past the 350-million-year-old formations. Ranger-led walks meet at the carpark at the end of

Hidden Valley Rd. The Derdebe-gerring banan lookout trail (800m) ascends a steep hill for a view over the Ord Valley and nearby sandstone ranges. Try your hand abseiling with **Wild Abseil Tours.** (☎ (019) 45 66 43. Half-day $25-60.)

## ⏸ DAYTRIP FROM KUNUNURRA: LAKE ARGYLE

The largest freshwater body in the southern hemisphere was created by humans. Sandwiched between ancient orange sandstone hills, the 850 square kilometer lake was created in the early 1970s as part of the ambitious Ord River Irrigation Project. While it looks eerily out of place, Lake Argyle is brilliantly blue and still strikingly massive (it can hold 18 Sydney Harbours). To get there, drive 35km south of Kununurra on the Victoria Hwy and turn onto the access road.

Cruises are a popular way to see a fraction of the lake. Though expensive, they are a worthwhile splurge for the amazing views. **Lake Argyle Cruises** has a booking office at the **Lake Argyle Tourist Village** on the lake. (☎ 9168 7361. Tours daily May-Sept., by demand in the Wet; 2hr. wildlife morning cruise $30; 2½hr. sunset cruise $38; 6hr. mountain and island cruise $100. Pickup in Kununurra $16.) **Triple J Tours** provides cruises of Lake Argyle and the Ord River. (☎ 9168 2682. Full-day $120, including pickup.) For adventure-seekers, **Kimberley Canoeing** offers self-guided tours that depart Lake Argyle Dam and meander down the Ord River, stopping at established camps. (☎ (1800) 80 50 10. Full-day $105; 2-day $160; 3-day $120.)

The **Lake Argyle Tourist Village** has accommodations. The **caravan park** has showers and laundry. (☎ 9167 1050. Sites $7, powered $11.) The **motel** next door has a pool and restaurant. (☎ 9167 7360. Singles $65; doubles $70.)

## WYNDHAM AND AROUND

The tiny port town of Wyndham (pop. 1000) lies 100km north of Kununurra, wedged between the Bastion Range, the tidal waters of the Cambridge Gulf, and expansive mudflats. The few stores and locals remain unfazed by an influx of visitors. Wyndham is neatly divided in two: most of the attractions and indoor accommodations are located in the northern wharf area, and the first smattering of stores and houses are in the south section, 4km south of the wharf.

The southern section of town holds the **tourist office** in the Mobil station (☎ 9161 1281; open daily 6am-6pm; in the Wet M-F 6am-6pm, Sa-Su 6am-3pm); **grocery store** (open M-F 7am-6pm, Sa 7am-1pm, Su 8am-1pm); **hospital** (☎ 9161 1104); and **post office** (open M-F 9am-5pm, Sa 9am-2:30pm, Su noon-3pm). The northern section has the **police** (☎ 9161 1055) and **Internet** at Telecentre.

Follow the signs east from the highway for the ◪**Five River Lookout,** 7km up a steep road, with an expansive view of the Gulf, mudflats, and distant mountains. Sunsets here are fabulous. The **Wyndham Zoological Gardens and Crocodile Park,** 4km north on the access road, offers views (or $200 skins) of the name-tagged crocs "Hi! I'm David. I'm 6m long and I eat people and tip over boats. I mate with all the females." (☎ 9161 1124. Open daily in the Dry 8:30am-4pm, in the Wet call ahead. $12, concessions $9. Daily feedings 11am.) **Dreamtime Statues,** in Warriu Park, a block to the right off the highway before the tourist bureau, features larger-than-life statues of the Aboriginal lifestyle. The implications are unclear. A 2000-year-old boab tree graces the **Wyndham Caravan Park,** in the southern section of town, near the Mobil station. (☎ 9161 1064. Sites $8, powered $11). **Gulf Breeze Guest House,** on the highway before the wharf, has a kitchen and shady patio. (☎ 9161 1401. Singles $20; doubles $45; families $50.)

# APPENDIX

## BEER TERMINOLOGY

Nothing's more Australian than beer, and accordingly, the language used for it has an Aussie twist too. Because of the hot climate, Australian pubs generally eschew the British pint in favor of smaller portions which stay cold until you're done. Thus, size is a major variable in the argot of ale. If you're too drunk to think of the proper terms, ordering by size, in ounces, usually works. On the mainland, try a "5," "7," "10," or "15." In Tasmania, order using the numbers "6," "8," "10," or "20." Most importantly, don't forget to **shout** your new-found mates a round, that is, to buy them all a drink.

| BRING ME A... | |
|---|---|
| **Beer:** 7 oz. in QLD and VIC; 15 oz. in NSW; 10 oz. elsewhere | **Middy:** 285mL (10 oz.), used in NSW and SA |
| **Bludger:** a weak drinker who can't finish a full cycle of shouts | **Pint:** 425mL (15 oz.) in SA, smaller than the British or American pint |
| **Butcher:** 200mL (7 oz.) in SA | **Pony:** 140mL (5 oz.) |
| **Darwin Stubbie:** 1.25L bottle in NT | **Pot:** 285mL (10 oz.) in QLD and VIC |
| **Glass:** 200mL (7 oz.) in QLD and VIC | **Real Pint:** 560mL (20 oz.); used in SA or TAS to get a proper glass of beer |
| **Handle:** 10 oz. glass with a handle | **Schooner:** 425mL (15 oz.) in NSW; 285mL (10 oz.) in SA |
| **Jug:** pitcher | **Stubbie:** 375mL bottle |
| **Long neck:** 750mL bottle | **Tinny:** 375mL can |

## GLOSSARY OF 'STRINE

**'Strine** is 'stralian for "Australian." The first trick to speaking Australian slang is to abbreviate everything: **Oz** for Australia, **brekkie** for breakfast, **cuppa** for cup of coffee, **sammy** for sandwich (for more help on how to **Abbreviate Till You Drop,** see p. 359). The term **pommie,** meaning English person, has a debatable origin. Some say it comes from "pomegranate," referring to stereotypically rosy cheeks, while others point to the acronym worn on the early convicts' uniforms: POHME, or Prisoners Of Her Majesty in Exile. The second, less ubiquitous aspect of Aussie slang is **rhyming. Noahs** are sharks (shark rhymes with ark, Noah built an ark), while **I'm on the dog** means "I'm on the phone" (bone rhymes with phone, and then the whole dog-bone thing). Get it? American travelers may be disturbed to be called **seppos,** for good reason: Yanks rhymes with tanks, and the worst kind of tanks are septic tanks. Ouch! Australian **pronunciation** is harder to learn than the lingo—with Aboriginal words especially, but even with English-derived proper nouns it can seem impossible. Americans and Canadians generally have particular difficulties, as much of 'strine has distinctly Anglo origins. Smile, and don't be embarrassed— yes, you're a tourist, but in Australia that's not such a mark of shame. One rule to note: when Australians spell a word out or pronounce a number, they always use the expression "double" (or "triple"), as in the phone number "nine-three-double-seven-five-triple-one" (9377 5111).

**ablution block:** shower/toilet block at a campground
**abseil:** rappel
**ace:** awesome
**ANZAC:** Australia-New Zealand Army Corps

**ANZAC biscuits:** honey-oat cookies
**arvo:** afternoon
**Aussie:** Australian (pronounced Ozzie— thus, Australia is Oz)
**backpackers:** hostel

**barbie:** barbecue
**bathers:** bathing suit/swim-suit
**belt bag:** fanny pack (don't say "fanny" in Oz: it's a crude word for a part of the female anatomy)

**beyond the black stump:** *really* far away

**billabong:** a water hole

**biro:** pen

**biscuit:** cookie

**bitumen:** a rough black asphalt used to pave roads (BICH-uh-min)

**bloke:** guy, man (familiar)

**bludger:** moocher, grifter, lazy person

**bluey:** someone with red hair (seriously)

**bonnet:** hood of a car

**book:** make reservations

**boot:** trunk of a car

**bottle shop:** liquor store

**brekkie:** breakfast

**bush:** wilderness

**bush tucker:** traditional Aboriginal wild foods

**bushwalking:** hiking

**busk:** (verb) to play music on the street for money

**BYO:** bring your own alcohol

**campervan:** mobile home, RV

**capsicum:** bell peppers

**caravan:** trailer, like a cab-less campervan

**carpark:** parking lot

**chap:** guy, man; see **bloke**

**chazzwazzer:** bullfrog

**chips:** thick french fries, usually served with vinegar and salt

**chippers:** fish and chips or fish and chips shops

**chockerblock:** very crowded

**chook:** chicken

**chunder:** vomit

**coffee:** beer (yes, Marge)

**coldie:** a cold beer

**concession:** discount; usually applies to students, seniors, or children, sometimes only to Australian students and pensioners

**cordial:** concentrated fruit juice

**dag:** one who is daggy (usage is common, often benevolent)

**daggy:** unfashionable, unhip, goofy, silly

**damper:** traditionally unleavened bread

**dear:** expensive

**Devonshire tea:** tea and scones, often served in the late afternoon

**dodgy:** sketchy

**doona, duvet:** comforter, feather blanket

**dramas:** problems. "No dramas" is interchangeable with "no worries."

**drier than a dead dingo's donger:** very thirsty

**dummy:** pacifier (for infants)

**ensuite:** with bath

**entree:** appetizer ("main" is a main dish)

**esky:** a cooler (originally from the brand name Eskimo)

**excess:** deductible (as in car insurance)

**fair dinkum:** genuine

**fairy floss:** cotton candy

**fancy:** to like; as in "would you fancy...?"

**feral:** wild, grunge-style (a common slang term)

**flash:** fancy, snazzy

**flat out like a lizard drinking:** doing nothing

**flat white:** coffee with hot milk and a touch of foam

**free call:** toll-free call

**franger:** condom (colloquial, somewhat crude)

**fossicking:** gem-hunting and gold-sifting

**furphy:** tall tale, exaggerated rumor (tell a furphy)

**g'day:** hello

**glasshouse:** greenhouse

**grommet:** young surfer

**ground floor:** American first floor ("first floor" is second floor, etc.)

**grog:** booze

**hire:** to rent

**hoon:** loud-mouth, show-off

**icy-pole:** popsicle (sweet frozen treat on a stick)

**jersey:** sweater, sweatshirt

**jackaroo:** stationhand-in-training

**jillaroo:** female jackaroo

**jumper:** see **jersey**

**keen:** term of respect ("a keen surfer")

**Kiwi:** New Zealander

**lad:** guy, man; see **chap**

**licensed:** serves alcohol

**like hen's teeth:** rare (when did you last see a hen with teeth?)

**lollies:** candies

**magic:** really wonderful, special: "that beach is magic"

**mate:** friend, buddy (used broadly)

**milk bar:** convenience store

**moke:** an open-air, golf-cart-esque vehicle

**mozzie:** mosquito

**nappy:** diaper

**newsagent:** newsstand/convenience store

**no worries:** sure, fine, or "you're welcome"

**ocker:** hick, Crocodile Dundee-type

**odds and sods:** odds and ends

**off like a bucket of prawns in the sun:** leaving like lightning

**ordinary:** bad; an "ordinary" road is full of potholes.

**Oz:** Australia

**pavlova:** a creamy meringue dessert garnished with fruit

**pensioner:** senior citizen

**petrol:** gasoline

**piss:** beer (usually)

**pissed:** drunk (usually)

**pokies:** gambling machines

**powerpoint:** outlet (also electrical hookup at campsites)

**pram:** stroller (for a baby)

**prawn:** jumbo shrimp

**pub:** bar

**push bike:** bicycle

**return:** round-trip

**'roo:** as in kanga-**roo**

**roundabout:** traffic rotary

**rubber:** eraser

**sandgroper:** a West Australian (also Westralian)

**sauce:** Usually tomato sauce. Aussie's closest equivalent to ketchup.

**serviette:** napkin

**sheila:** slang for a woman

**shout:** buy a drink or round of drinks for others. Also a noun, as in an evening's worth of everyone buying rounds for each other.

**side:** team

**singlet:** tank top or undershirt

**skivvie:** turtleneck sweater

**sang or sanger:** sausage

**spider:** ice cream float or nasty arachnid (use context clues here)

**squiz:** a look (to take a squiz at something)

**stone the crows!:** an expression of surprise

**'strine:** Aussie dialect (from Australian)

**swimmers:** swimsuit

**suss:** figure out, sort out

**ta:** short for thank you—usually muttered under breath. Rhymes with la.

**TAB:** shop to place bets, sometimes in pubs

**TAFE:** Technical and Further Education. Community adult education; cooking schools often produce fabulous budget meals.

**takeaway:** food to go, takeout

**Tassie:** Tasmania (TAZ-zie)

**that's a boomerang:** that's something very important to me I don't want you to steal

**torch:** flashlight

**touch wood:** knock on wood

**track suit:** sweat suit, jogging suit

**tucker:** food.

**uni:** university (YOU-nee)

**unsealed:** unpaved roads, usually gravel, sometimes dirt

**ute:** utility vehicle, pick-up truck

**upmarket:** upscale, expensive

**Vegemite:** yeast-extract spread for toast and sandwiches

**walkabout:** to spontaneously set off across the countryside

**wanker:** jerk (very rude term)

**XXXX:** pronounced four-ex, a brand of beer

**yakka:** hard work

**yute:** see **ute**

**zed:** Z (American "zee")

# TEMPERATURE CHARTS

To convert from °C to °F, multiply by 1.8 and add 32. For a rough approximation, double the Celsius and add 25. To convert from °F to °C, subtract 32 and multiply by 0.55. For a rough approximation, subtract 25 and cut it in half.

| °CELSIUS | -5 | 0 | 5 | 10 | 15 | 20 | 25 | 30 | 35 | 40 |
|---|---|---|---|---|---|---|---|---|---|---|
| °FAHRENHEIT | 23 | 32 | 41 | 50 | 59 | 68 | 77 | 86 | 95 | 104 |

| Av. Temp. lo/hi Precipitation | January | | | April | | | July | | | October | | |
|---|---|---|---|---|---|---|---|---|---|---|---|---|
| | °C | °F | mm | °C | °F | mm | °C | °F | mm | °C | °F | mm |
| Adelaide | 16/28 | 61/82 | 19 | 12/22 | 54/72 | 43 | 7/15 | 45/59 | 65 | 10/21 | 50/70 | 43 |
| Alice Springs | 21/36 | 70/97 | 40 | 13/28 | 55/82 | 17 | 4/19 | 39/66 | 12 | 15/31 | 59/88 | 20 |
| Brisbane | 21/29 | 70/84 | 161 | 17/26 | 63/79 | 89 | 10/20 | 50/68 | 57 | 16/26 | 61/79 | 77 |
| Cairns | 24/31 | 75/88 | 407 | 22/29 | 72/84 | 200 | 17/26 | 63/79 | 27 | 20/29 | 68/84 | 38 |
| Canberra | 13/28 | 55/82 | 58 | 7/20 | 45/68 | 53 | 0/11 | 32/52 | 40 | 6/19 | 43/66 | 67 |
| Darwin | 25/32 | 77/90 | 393 | 24/33 | 75/91 | 103 | 20/31 | 68/88 | 1 | 25/34 | 77/93 | 52 |
| Hobart | 12/22 | 54/72 | 48 | 9/17 | 48/63 | 52 | 4/12 | 39/54 | 54 | 8/17 | 46/63 | 64 |
| Melbourne | 14/26 | 57/79 | 48 | 11/20 | 52/68 | 58 | 6/13 | 43/55 | 49 | 9/20 | 48/68 | 68 |
| Perth | 18/30 | 64/86 | 9 | 14/25 | 57/77 | 46 | 9/18 | 48/64 | 173 | 12/22 | 54/72 | 55 |
| Sydney | 18/26 | 64/79 | 98 | 14/23 | 59/72 | 129 | 8/16 | 46/61 | 100 | 13/22 | 55/72 | 79 |

# DISTANCE CHART (IN KILOMETERS)

| | Adelaide | Alice Springs | Brisbane | Broken Hill | Broome | Cairns | Canberra | Coffs Harbour | Darwin | Hobart | Melbourne | Perth |
|---|---|---|---|---|---|---|---|---|---|---|---|---|
| Alice Springs | 1533 | | | | | | | | | | | |
| Brisbane | 2045 | 2990 | | | | | | | | | | |
| Broken Hill | 508 | 1667 | 1612 | | | | | | | | | |
| Broome | 4270 | 2740 | 4464 | 4407 | | | | | | | | |
| Cairns | 3524 | 2411 | 1716 | 3017 | 4085 | | | | | | | |
| Canberra | 1201 | 2731 | 1265 | 1105 | 5227 | 2664 | | | | | | |
| Coffs Harbour | 2084 | 3207 | 417 | 1577 | 5152 | 2142 | 925 | | | | | |
| Darwin | 3020 | 1489 | 3414 | 3157 | 1880 | 2835 | 3977 | 3902 | | | | |
| Hobart | 1010 | 2540 | 1952 | 1131 | 5280 | 3357 | 935 | 1798 | 4670 | | | |
| Melbourne | 731 | 2261 | 1674 | 852 | 5001 | 3078 | 648 | 1519 | 4391 | 279 | | |
| Perth | 2706 | 3626 | 4457 | 2845 | 2388 | 5862 | 3909 | 4359 | 3718 | 3718 | 3434 | |
| Sydney | 1412 | 2822 | 990 | 1155 | 5235 | 2697 | 286 | 640 | 4821 | 1158 | 872 | 4110 |

# AREA CODES

Two-digit phone-code prefixes precede eight-digit numbers when calling beyond the local area. They do not correspond exactly to state borders.

| Prefix | Designation | Regions Included |
|---|---|---|
| 02 | Central East | **ACT,** most of **NSW,** and some Victoria and Queensland towns |
| 03 | South East | **Tasmania, Victoria,** and some NSW border towns |
| 07 | North East | **Queensland** and some NSW border towns |
| 08 | Central and West | **Northern Territory, South Australia, Western Australia,** and some NSW border towns |

APPENDIX

**Council** *Travel*

America's Student Travel Leader for over 50 years

*The journey is the reward...*
-Tao saying

Student/youth airfares -
International Identity Cards - Insurance -
Railpasses - Gear - Foreign language programs -
Work exchanges - Youth hostel memberships -
'Round the World desk - Adventure tours & more.

Visit us at your nearest office
or online @
www.counciltravel.com

Or call: 1-800-2COUNCIL

INDEX

# INDEX

## A

AAA 67
Aboriginal
  art 21
  art in galleries 116
  carvings 625
  crafts 389
  cultural centers 156, 352, 391, 424, 492
  garden 631
  hand stencils 139
  history 9, 11
  land 17
  literature 20
  music 20
  plants 117, 534
  rights 18
  rock art sites 132, 136, 237, 263, 266, 285, 287, 403, 492, 562, 566, 643
  seasons 257
  tales 9, 144, 210, 257, 260, 357, 604, 605
  tours 398, 647
  weapons 210, 227, 358, 505
abseiling
  Adelaide, SA 425
  Bright, VIC 596
  Coffs Harbour, NSW 185
  Cradle Mountain, TAS 486
  Grampians National Park, VIC 566
  Katoomba, NSW 144
  Kununurra, WA 672
  Margaret River, WA 635
  Snowy River National Park, VIC 608
  Tindabyne, NSW 215
  Townsville, QLD 372
AC/DC 20
acacia 26
accommodations 48–52
  bed and breakfasts 51
  camping 52–55
  dorms, college 51
  home exchange 51
  hostels 48

adapters 48
Adelaide Hills, SA 428–429
Adelaide River 255
Adelaide, SA 415–428
  accommodations 421–422
  activities 425–426
  entertainment 426
  festivals 426
  food 422–424
  getting around 418–419
  getting there 415–418
  Glenelg 418, 422
  media and publications 420
  nightlife 427–428
  orientation 418
  practical information 419–421
  sights 424–425
aerogrammes 56
AFL 25
African elephants 232
AIDS 44, 46
Aileron, NT 277
Airlie Beach, QLD 360–363
airplane. See planes.
Albany, WA 639
Albury, NSW 220–222
alcohol
  beer and wine 24
  drinking age 24, 43
  drunk driving 43
  See also breweries, wineries.
Alexandra Heads, QLD 332
Alice Springs, NT 277–284
Almaden, QLD 395
American Express 38, 39, 40, 66
Anakie, QLD 406
Angahook-Lorne State Park, VIC 553
Anglesea, VIC 553
Angourie, NSW 187
animals. See environment.
Ansett Airlines 63
Anzac Day 13, 534
ANZUS 13
APEC 14
Apollo Bay, VIC 554
Apsley and Tia Gorges, NSW 156

Ararat, VIC 562
area codes 57, 675
Armidale, NSW 155–156
Arnhem Land, NT 266–267
arts 18–22
  literature 18–20
  movies 21
  music 20–21
  visual arts 21
Ashes, the 25
Aspestos Range National Park, TAS 492
Atherton Tablelands, QLD 392–395
ATM cards 39
Augusta, WA 635
Austrail Pass 63
Australia and New Zealand Army Corps (ANZAC) 13, 534
Australia Rock 210
Australia Telescope 235
Australian Alps, VIC 604
Australian Automobile Association (AAA) 67
Australian Capital Territory 76–87
Australian Democrats 16
Australian Hotel 211
Australian Open 26, 531, 538
Australian Rules Football 25
Australian Tourist Commission 37
automobile assistance 67
Avon Valley, WA 629
Ayers Rock Resort (Yulara), NT 289

## B

B&Bs 51
Baal, Temple of 147
Back o' Bourke, NSW 232–241
backpacks 53
bad dreams 463
Bairnsdale, VIC 604
Balancing Rock, QLD 331
Bald Rock National Park, NSW 159, 331
Balladonia, WA 465
Ballarat, VIC 12, 569–573
Ballina, NSW 188
bandicoots 27
Bangalow, NSW 193

Barcaldine, QLD 407
Barmah, VIC 583
Barossa Valley, SA 24, 440–444
Barrow Creek, NT 277
Batavia Coast, WA 648–651
Batchelor, NT 268
Batemans Bay, NSW 208
Bathurst Island, NT 255
Bathurst, NSW 226
Batman
  Batmania, QLD 510
  John 510
  jumping crocodiles 256
Battery Point, TAS 474
Bay of Fires Coastal Reserve, TAS 501
Bay of Islands, VIC 555
Bay of Martyrs, VIC 555
Beazley, Kim 16
bed and breakfasts 51
Beechworth, VIC 592
Beedelup National Park, WA 636
beer 24
  Beer Can Regatta 254
  terminology 673
  See also breweries.
beer-drinking pig 499
Bega, NSW 211
Bellarine Peninsula, VIC 548
Bellingen, NSW 179
Bells Line of Road, NSW 147
Ben Lomond National Park, TAS 506
Bendemeer, NSW 156
Bendigo, VIC 576–580
Bermagui, NSW 211
best
  Caesar salad 114
  museum 533
  non-reef diving 206
  rock climbing 205
  wreck dive 209, 371
  See also Let's Go Picks.
beverages. See drinks.
Bibbulmun Track 630
Bicentennial Tree, WA 636
Bicheno, TAS 502, 504
Bicycle Federation of Australia (BFA) 69
bicycle travel. See cycling.
Big Galah, SA 465
Big Merino 219
Bilpin, NSW 148

birds 28
birdwatching 583
birth control 46
Blackall Range, QLD 340
Blackall, QLD 407
Blackheath, NSW 145–146
Blanchett, Cate 22
Bledisloe Cup 25
Bligh, Captain William 11, 480, 481
Blinman, SA 456
*Bliss* 20
Blood on the Southern Cross 571
Bloomfield Track, QLD 400
blowhole 204
Blue Lake National Park, QLD 315
Blue Mountains, NSW 138–150
Bluey's Beach, NSW 170
Boat Harbour, TAS 494
Bobbin Head, NSW 136
Bond, James Bond 324
Bondi Beach, Sydney 98, 115, 122
Booderee National Park, NSW 207
boomerang pass 62
Boonoo Boonoo National Park, NSW 159, 331
Booti Booti National Park, NSW 170
boots 53
Border Ranges National Park, NSW 199, 200
Border Village, SA 465
Botany Bay, NSW 10, 132–134
Bourke, NSW 236–237
Bowen, QLD 363
Bowral, NSW 218
Bowraville, NSW 178
box jellyfish 2, 30, 54, 251, 346, 388
Boyd, Arthur 83, 535
Bradman, Sir Donald 218, 426
*Braveheart* 22
Bremer Bay, WA 641
breweries
  Beechworth, VIC 593
  Carlton, QLD 309
  Castlemaine, QLD 309
  Goulburn, NSW 219
  Hobart, TAS 475
Bribie Island, QLD 316

Bridport, TAS 500
Bright, VIC 595–596
Brisbane Water National Park, NSW 137
Brisbane, QLD 298–313
  accommodations 306–307
  activities 311
  City Center 306, 307, 313
  entertainment 311
  festivals 311
  food 307–308
  Fortitude Valley 301, 306, 308, 312
  getting around 304
  getting there 299–300
  Kangaroo Point 301
  media and publications 305
  New Farm 301, 306, 308
  nightlife 312–313
  orientation 300
  Petrie Tce 307, 312
  practical information 305
  sights 308–310
  South Bank 301, 308
  South Brisbane 301, 307
  Spring Hill 301, 313
  West End 301, 308
Broadwater National Park, NSW 187
Broken Hill, NSW 237–240
Broome, WA 661–666
brothels 111, 524
Bruny Island, TAS 480
Buchan Caves, VIC 607
Budderoo National Park, NSW 205
Buffet, Jimmy 198
Buladelah, NSW 169, 171
Bulga State Forest, NSW 172
Bulga, NSW 149
*Bulletin, The* 19
Bunbury, WA 630
Bundaberg, QLD 347–349
Bundanoon, NSW 218
Bundeena, NSW 131
Bundjalong National Park, NSW 187
Bungle Bungle. See Purnululu National Park.
Burnie, TAS 493

Burra, SA 445
buses 63
bush ballad 19
bush tucker 23
Busselton, WA 631
BYO 24
Byron Bay, NSW 192–198

**C**

Cahills Crossing, NT 266
Caiguna, WA 465
Cairns, QLD 381–391
  accommodations 384
  activities 387
  diving 388
  food 386
  media and publications 384
  nightlife 390
  orientation 383
  practical information 383
  shopping 389
  sights 386
  transport 382
calling cards 56
Camden, NSW 218
camel capital 282
camp stove 53
Campbelltown, NSW 218
camping 52–55
  campervans 55
  dangerous wildlife 54
  equipment 52
Canberra, ACT 12, 76–86
  accommodations 81–82
  camping 82
  consulates 79
  entertainment 85
  festivals 85
  food 82
  getting around 79
  getting there 76
  High Court 84
  media and publications 80
  nightlife 86
  orientation 78
  Parliament House 83
  practical information 79
  sights 83–85
Cann River, VIC 612
Cape Conran, VIC 611
Cape Hillsborough National Park, QLD 358
Cape Jervis, SA 433

Cape Le Grand National Park, WA 643
Cape Leeuwin, WA 635
Cape Otway, VIC 554
Cape Range National Park, WA 655
Cape Tribulation, QLD 399–400
Cape York, QLD 403–405
Capone, Al 575
Capricorn Coast, QLD 349–368
Capricorn Highway, QLD 406–408
car 65–69
  automobile assistance 67
  driving permits 68
  insurance and registration 68
  purchasing 67–68
  rental 65–67
  renting 518
caravans 55
Cardwell, QLD 376
Carey, Peter 19
Carlisle Island, QLD 357
Carlton, VIC 513, 526
Carnarvon Gorge National Park, QLD 352
Carnarvon, WA 653
cash cards 39
cassowaries 28
Castlemaine, VIC 574–575
Castlereagh, NSW 135
Cathedral Range National Park, VIC 588
Caves Road, WA 634
CDC 43
Ceduna, SA 463, 644
Centers for Disease Control (CDC) 43
Central Flinders, SA 453–456
Central Tilba, NSW 210
Central West, NSW 150–232
Central Wine Regions, SA 440–446
Cessnock, NSW 151
changing money 37
Channon, the, NSW 190
Charles Darwin National Park, NT 253
Charleville, QLD 405
Charters Towers, QLD 409
Childers, QLD 15, 348
children and travel 73

Chillagoe, QLD 395
Chinatown, Sydney 96
Chinese immigration 12
cider 24
Circular Quay, Sydney 99
Cirrus 39
Citicorp 38
CityRail, Sydney 98
Clare Valley, SA 24
Clare, SA 444–445
climate 31, 675
    See also seasons.
Cobourg Peninsula, NT 266
cockies 232
Cockle Creek, TAS 482, 484
Coen, QLD 404
coffee 24, 114
Coffin Bay National Park, SA 462
Coffs Harbour, NSW 181–186
Coles Bay, TAS 503
concessions 36
condoms 46, 48
cone shell 30
Conondale National Park, QLD 340
constitutional monarchy 16
consulates 32
    Canberra, ACT 79
    Melbourne, VIC 519
    Perth, WA 622
    Sydney, NSW 101
contact lenses 48
contraceptives 46
converters 48
converting currency 37
convict system, history of 10
Conway National Park, QLD 363
Coober Pedy, SA 458–459
Coochiemudlo Island, QLD 316
Cook, Captain James 10, 132, 401, 480, 481, 531
cookie
    cookie? 191
    death 212
Cooktown, QLD 400–402
Coolangatta, QLD 317–319
Cooloola National Park, QLD 334, 339
Cooma, NSW 212
Coonabarabran, NSW 233–234
Cooney Brothers 487

Cooper's Ale 24
Coorabakh National Park, NSW 172
Coorong National Park, SA 431
Copley, SA 456
Copper Coast, the, SA 450
Coral Bay, WA 654
corals 29
corkage fee 24
Cossack, WA 658
Council Travel 59
country music 21, 153
CountryLink 63
courier flights 61
Cowell, SA 461
Cowra, NSW 228
Cradle Mountain, TAS 485–486
Cradoc, TAS 480
credit cards 39
cricket 25, 531
Croajingolong National Park, VIC 611–613
Crocodile Dundee 180, 459
crocodiles 27, 54, 255
    meat 23
Crowded House 20
Crowdy Bay National Park, NSW 171
crown of thorns 30
Croydon, QLD 412
culture 18–26
    arts 18–22
    drinks 24
    food 22–23
    sport 24–26
currency exchange 37
current events 14–15
Currumbin Rock Pool, QLD 327
customs 36
Cutta Cutta Caves Nature Park, NT 274
cybercafés 58
cycling 69
    Canberra, ACT 79
    Mt. Buller, VIC 590
    Simpson's Gap, NT 284
    Sydney, NSW 100
Cygnet, TAS 480

**D**

D'Entrecasteaux Channel, TAS 480
Daguragu 17
Daintree National Park, QLD 398, 399
Daintree, QLD 398
Dampier Peninsula, WA 666
Dampier, WA 657

Dampier, William 10
Danbulla Forest, QLD 393
Dandenong Ranges, VIC 545
Dangars Gorge, NSW 157
dangerous wildlife 28, 30
    Cairns, QLD 388
    precautions 54
Darling Range, WA 629, 644
Darlinghurst, Sydney 114
Darlington, TAS 505
Darwin, Charles 248
Darwin, NT 244–255
    accommodations 249–250
    activities 253
    bombing 13
    entertainment 253
    festivals 253
    food 250
    getting around 248
    getting there 246
    nightlife 254–255
    orientation 246
    practical information 248–249
    sights 251–253
Davenport Range National Park, NT 276
Daydream Island, QLD 365
Daylesford, VIC 573
Deane, William 16
death cookies 212
Death in Brunswick 22
Deep Creek Conservation Park, SA 433
Degas, Edgar 586
dehydration 44
Deloraine, TAS 492
Den of Nargun, VIC 605
Denham, WA 652
Denmark, WA 638
Derby, TAS 499
Derby, WA 666
Derwent Valley, TAS 24, 482
Devil's Marbles, NT 275
Devonport, TAS 490–492
diabetes 44
Dibbler 641
Dickens, Charles 476
didgeridoos 277
dietary concerns 73
dim sims 23
Dimboola, VIC 567

dingoes 28
disabled travelers 72
Discover Card 39
Discovery Bay Coastal Park, VIC 561
diseases 45–46
distance chart 675
diving 29
    Adelaide, SA 426
    Airlie Beach, QLD 363
    Bateman's Bay, NSW 208
    Botany Bay National Park, NSW 133
    Broome, WA 664
    Bundaberg, QLD 348
    Byron Bay, NSW 197
    Cairns, QLD 388
    Carnarvon, WA 653
    Coffs Harbour, NSW 183
    Coral Bay, WA 654
    Darwin, NT 253
    Esperance, WA 643
    Exmouth, WA 655
    Great Barrier Reef, QLD 295
    Great Keppel Island, QLD 354
    Green Island, QLD 392
    Hervey Bay, QLD 343
    Jervis Bay, NSW 206
    Mackay, QLD 357
    Magnetic Island, QLD 375
    Mission Beach, QLD 379
    North Stradbroke Island, QLD 314
    Port Douglas, QLD 397
    Portland, VIC 559
    Sydney, NSW 122
    Townsville, QLD 371
    Ulladulla, NSW 208
    Whitsunday Islands, QLD 368
Dog House, The 170
dolphins 30
Dooragan National Park, NSW 172
dorms, college 51
Dorrigo National Park, NSW 179, 180
Douglas-Apsley National Park, TAS 502
Dreaming. See Aboriginal tales.
drinking age 24, 43
drinks 24
driving permits 68
    See also car.
drugs, illegal 42

Nimbin, NSW 191
drunk driving 43
dry rainforest 157
Dry, the 2, 258
Drysdale, Russell 222
Dubbo, NSW 231–232
Dunk Island, QLD 380
Dunkeld, VIC 564
Dunsborough, WA 632
Durras North, NSW 208
Dusty, Slim 21, 154, 179
duty-free 36

# E

East MacDonnells, NT 286
Eastern Gulf, QLD 412
echidnas 28, 436
Echuca, VIC 580–582
Eftpos 40
Eight Ball 584
Elcho Island, NT 266
electric current 48
Electronic Travel Authority (ETA) 34
*Elizabeth* 22
Elizabeth II, Queen 115
Ellenborough Falls, NSW 172
Elsey National Park, NT 274
email 58
embassies. See consulates.
Emerald, QLD 406
emergency medical services 44
emergency number dial 000
emu 28
  ice-cream eating 358
environment 26–30
  animals 27–29
  dangerous wildlife 28, 30, 54, 388
  Great Barrier Reef 29
  marine life 29–30
  plants 26
Errinundra National Park, VIC 610
Esperance, WA 642
ETA 34
Etheridge Goldfield, QLD 412
Ettamogah Pub, NSW 223
eucalypts 26
Eumundi, QLD 340
Eungella National Park, QLD 359
Eureka Stockade

Rebellion, Ballarat, VIC 12, 569
Eureka Stockade, Ballarat, VIC 572
Eurobodalla National Park, NSW 209
Evans Head, NSW 187
everlastings 27
exchange rates 37
Exmouth, WA 654–656
Eyre Highway, WA 644
Eyre Peninsula, SA 460–465

# F

Fagan (Charles Dickens) 476
Fairfax, John 146
Falls Creek, VIC 596
Family Islands, QLD 380
fastest
  growing town 255
  ride 324
Faulconbridge, NSW 140
Federal Express 40, 56
Federal Parliament 16
federation 12
ferals 513
festivals 31
  country music 153
  in Adelaide, SA 426
  in Alice, NT 283
  in Barossa Valley, SA 444
  in Brisbane, QLD 311
  in Broome, WA 666
  in Canberra, ACT 85
  in Darwin, NT 254
  in Melbourne, VIC 538
  in Sydney 126
  in Warwick, QLD 329
  jazz 126, 164, 180
Field, Barron 18
financial matters. See money.
Fingal Bay, NSW 166
Finke Gorge National Park, NT 285
first
  collection of cartoons 184
  shots 548
  winery 544, 592
First Fleet 10
  Jewish immigrants 535
first-aid kit 48
fish 29
fish-and-chips 22
fishing 222
Fitzgerald River

National Park, WA 641
Fitzroy Crossing, WA 667
Fitzroy Falls, NSW 206
Fitzroy Island, QLD 392
Fitzroy, VIC 513, 523, 540
five-legged sheep 436
flag 13, 573
Fleurieu Peninsula, SA 429–433
flights
  domestic 62
  international 58–62
Flinders Chase National Park, SA 439
Flinders Highway, QLD 408–412
Flinders Island, TAS 500
Flinders Ranges National Park, SA 454
Flinders Ranges, SA 451–457
flying doctors 456, 616, 667
food and drink 22–24
Forbes, NSW 229
Forster, NSW 169
Foster, VIC 600
Fosters 24
Foucault, Michel 529
Franklin, Miles 19
Franklin-Gordon Wild Rivers National Park, TAS 488
Fraser Coast, QLD 332–349
Fraser Island, QLD 343–347
Fraser, Malcolm 14
Fremantle, WA 626
Frenchman's Cap, TAS 488
freshies. See crocodiles.
Freycinet Peninsula, TAS 503
frostbite 45
fruit 23

# G

Gabo Island, VIC 613
Gallipoli 13, 534
*Gallipoli* 21
Garden of Eden
  Northern Territory 288
  South Australia 414
Gardners Bay, TAS 480
Gariwerd National Park, VIC 562–566
Gascoyne Region, WA 651

gay travelers 71
Geelong, VIC 549
Geeveston, TAS 482
Gemfields, QLD 406
General Delivery 56
Genoa, VIC 612
George Town, TAS 498
Geraldton, WA 649
giardia 46
Gibb River Road, WA 669–670
Gibson, Mel 21
Giles, Ernest 291
Ginninderra Falls, ACT 87
Gippsland, VIC 598–613
Giraween National Park
  in NSW 159
Girraween National Park
  in QLD 331
*Gladiator* 22
Glasshouse Mountains, QLD 341
Gledswood, NSW 218
Glen Innes, NSW 158
Glenbrook, NSW 139
Glendambo, SA 458
Glenrowan, VIC 590
glossary 673
Gloucester National Park, WA 636
glow worms 149, 218, 327, 482, 554
GO 25 card 36
goannas 23, 28
Gold Coast Hinterland, QLD 326–327
Gold Coast, QLD 317–327
gold rush 12
Goldfields, VIC 568–580
Goldfields, WA 643–647
Goods and Services Tax (GST) 36, 41
Goolwa, SA 431
Gordon River Dam, TAS 484
Gordon Wild Rivers National Park, TAS 486
Gordon, Adam Lindsay 18
Goulburn, NSW 218
Gove Peninsula, NT 266
government 16
Governor General 16
Govett's Leap, NSW 146
Grampians National Park, VIC 562–566

Grand Canyon 139, 565
Grand Prix 535, 538
Great Alpine Road, VIC 604
Great Barrier Beef 349
Great Barrier Reef, QLD 2, 29, 295–298, 381
Great Eastern Highway, WA 644
Great Keppel Island, QLD 353–354
Great Lakes, NSW 170
Great Ocean Road, VIC 550–561
Great Southern, WA 636–643
Green Island, QLD 391
Green Party 14, 16, 466
Gregory National Park, NT 274
Greyhound Pioneer 63
Griffin, Walter Burley 76, 83, 224
Griffith, NSW 224–226
Groote Island, NT 266
GST 36, 41
Gulf Savannah, QLD 412
gum trees. See eucalypts.
Gundabooka National Park, NSW 237
Gundagai, NSW 219
Gunns Plains Caves, TAS 492
Gurig National Park, NT 267

**H**

Half-way point 465
Hall, Ben 230
Halls Creek, WA 667
Halpern, Deb 522, 533, 535
Hamelin Pool, WA 652
Hamilton Island, QLD 366
Hamilton, VIC 558
Hanging Rock National Park, VIC 545
Hansel and Gretel 612
Hanson, Pauline 15
Harbour Bridge, Sydney 96
Harbour National Park, NSW 117
Hat Head National Park, NSW 177
Hattah Kulkyne National Park, VIC 586
Hawke, Bob 14
Hawker, SA 454

health 43–47
dietary concerns 73
diseases 45–46
emergency medical services 44
environment 44
immunizations 43
poisonous animals 55
STDs 44, 46
women 46
Heathcote National Park, NSW 131
heatstroke 45
heaven 86, 381, 524
Helfgott, David 180
hell 132, 338
Hepburn Springs, VIC 573
Hervey Bay, QLD 341–343
Heysen, Hans 429, 454
Hidden Valley National Park, WA 671
High Country, VIC 592–598
High Court 16, 84
highest
sand mountain 316
treehouse 636
hiking equipment 52
Hinchinbrook Island, QLD 377
His Natural Life 19
history 9–18
Aboriginal rights 17–18
current events 14–15
European settlement 10–12
government 16
twentieth century 12–14
hitchhiking 69
HIV 44, 46
Hobart, TAS 468–476
accommodations 472
entertainment 476
food 472
getting around 470
getting there 468
media and publications 471
nightlife 476
orientation 470
practical information 471
sights 473–475
Holden cars 582
Holiday Coast, NSW 159, 192
holidays 31
See also festivals.

Home and Away 111
home exchange 51
Homebush Bay Olympic Site, Sydney 121
Hook Island, QLD 365
hookah-smoking caterpillars 566
Hopetown, WA 641
Horsham, VIC 564
Hostelling International (HI) 49
hostels 48
hotels 48
House of Representatives 16
Howard, John 16
Hughenden, QLD 410
Humbug Point 501
Hume Corridor, NSW 218–223
Hume Corridor, VIC 587–592
Hunt, Billy 478
Hunter Valley, NSW 24, 150–153
Huon Valley, TAS 480
Huonville, TAS 480
Huskisson, NSW 206, 207
Hut River Province 650
Hutchence, Michael 20
hypothermia 45

**I**

identification 35
IDP 68
Imbruglia, Natalie 20
Immigration Restriction Act 13
immunizations 43
in your face livestock 232
Ingham, QLD 376
Injalak, Arnhem Land 267
Innes National Park, SA 451
Innisfail, QLD 381
inoculations 43
insects 45, 55
See also diseases.
Insider, The 22
insurance 47, 66
International Driving Permit (IDP) 68
International Student Identity Card (ISIC) 35
International Teacher Identity Card (ITIC) 35
International Youth Discount Travel Card (IYTC) 36
Internet 58

INXS 20
Iron Blow, TAS 487
Iron Range National Park, QLD 404
ISIC card 35
Isle of the Dead, TAS 478
ITIC card 35
IYTC card 36

**J**

Jabiru, NT 260
Jardine River National Park, QLD 404
jazz. See festivals.
Jenolan Caves, NSW 146, 147, 149
jet lag 44
Jindabyne, NSW 213
JJJ 20
Joalah National Park, QLD 327
Johanna Beach, VIC 555
John Forrest National Park, WA 629
Julian Rocks Marine Park, NSW 197
Jurassic Park 255

**K**

Kadina, SA 450
Kakadu National Park, NT 257–266
accommodations and camping 261
food 262
hikes 262
in the Dreaming 260
orientation 260
practical information 261
seasons 258
sights 262
transport 258
Kalbarri, WA 650
Kalgoorlie-Boulder, WA 645–647
Kalumburu Road, WA 670
Kanangra-Boyd National Park, NSW 138, 147, 149
Kangaroo 203
Kangaroo Island, SA 433–439
Kangaroo Valley, NSW 206
kangaroos 27
impersonating 478
meat 23
Karijini National Park, WA 659
Karratha, WA 656
karri 26, 636

Kata Tjuta, NT 293
Katherine Gorge
  National Park, NT
  272–274
Katherine, NT 270–
  272, 274
Katoomba, NSW 141–
  145
Keating, Paul 14, 16
Keep River National
  Park, NT 274
Kelly, Ned 21, 87, 507,
  532, 590, 593
Kempsey, NSW 177
Kendall, NSW 172
Kerang, VIC 583
Khancoban, NSW 215
Kiama, NSW 204–205
Kidman, Nicole 22
Kimberley, the, WA
  660–672
King William Saddle,
  TAS 488
Kings Canyon, NT 288
Kings Cross, Sydney
  96, 104, 112, 128
Kingscote, SA 437–
  438
koalas 27, 436
kookaburra 28
Koori 565
Kosciuszko National
  Park, NSW 215–217
kosher 73
Kuku Yalanji, QLD 398
Kununurra, WA 274,
  670–672
Kuranda, QLD 393
Ku-Ring-Gai Chase
  National Park, NSW
  136–137
Kynuna, QLD 408

**L**

*L.A. Confidential* 22
Labillardiere State
  Reserve, TAS 481
Labor Party 14, 16
Lake Argyle, WA 672
Lake Burley Griffin 83
Lake Jindabyne, NSW
  213
Lake Macquarie, NSW
  165
Lake Mountain, VIC
  587
Lake Pedder, TAS 14,
  482
Lake St. Clair, TAS 488
Lake Tinaroo, QLD 393
Lakefield National
  Park, QLD 403
Lakes Entrance, VIC
  606–607
lamington 23

Lamington National
  Park
  in NSW 199
  in QLD 326
Lancelin, WA 648
Landsborough
  Highway, QLD 406–
  408
Laperouse, Count de
  132
largest
  Aboriginal rock art
    collection 257
  Buddhist Temple
    203
  butterfly farm 393
  cassowary 378
  cattle station 460
  chandelier 536
  chess set 637
  collection of
    Aboriginal artifacts
    424
  collection of native
    animals 134
  crocodile in captivity
    392
  electic boat, VIC 607
  exposed granite rock
    159
  flotilla 580
  fur seal population
    546
  ginger processing
    plant 340
  glasshouse 424
  hardwood sawmill
    636
  hole 647
  imperial dragon 530
  inland waterway 606
  Japanese Garden
    329
  koala sanctuary 310
  Little Penguin colony
    613
  mall in Southern
    Hemisphere 134
  Maxi 367
  Merino sheep 219
  movie screen 125
  Murray cod 584
  museum 119, 532
  nightclub 542
  oceanarium 334
  optical telescope
    234
  penny arcade 582
  perched lake 346
  permanently
    landlocked ship
    461
  pheasant farm 584
  rainforest 610
  rock 654
  sand dune 165

sign 104
single rock in the
  world 290
slingshot 399
species of cockroach
  309
stud selling venue
  351
sundial 153
telescope array 235
waterfall 376
waterway 446
whaling museum
  640
Launceston, TAS 495–
  498
Lawrence, D.H. 203
Lawson, Henry 19
Lee, Shannon 170
leeches 481
Leeuwin-Naturaliste
  National Park, WA
  634
Lego Man 444
Leigh Creek, SA 456
Lennox Head, NSW
  198
lesbian travelers 71
*Let's Go Picks* 5
Leura, NSW 140
Leven Canyon Reserve,
  TAS 492
Liberal Party 14, 16
Licuala State Forest,
  QLD 379
Lincoln National Park,
  SA 462
Lindeman Island, QLD
  366
Lindsay, Norman 140
lion fish 30
Lismore, NSW 188–
  190
Litchfield National
  Park, NT 268–269
literature 18–20
Lithgow, NSW 149
Little Desert National
  Park, VIC 567–568
Liverpool, NSW 218
Loftus, NSW 131
Logans Beach, VIC 557
London Bridge, VIC
  556
Long Island, QLD 366
longest
  beach 487
  gondola cableway
    392
  imperial dragon in
    the world 579
  Olympic torch relay
    122
  road train 644
  straight stretch of
    highway 463

Longreach, QLD 407
Lord Sydney 10
Lorne, VIC 553
Lost City, NT 288
lost passports 33
Low Head, TAS 498
Lower Glenelg National
  Park, VIC 560
Lucas, George 22
luggage 47

**M**

Mabo decision 17
Macarthur, John 11
Macarthur, VIC 558
MacDonnell Ranges,
  NT 284–287
Mackay, QLD 355–357
Macksville, NSW 179
Macquarie Towns,
  NSW 135
Macquarie, Lachlan 11
*Mad Max* 22, 240,
  459
Maggie talks 503
Magnetic Island
  National Park, QLD
  376
Magnetic Island, QLD
  373–376
mail 55
Maitland, NSW 152
Malanda, QLD 394
Maldon, VIC 575, 576
Mallacoota, VIC 612
mallee 26
Malleefowl 568, 641
*Man From Snowy
  River, The* 608
mangrove 26
Manly, QLD 315
Mansfield, VIC 588
Mantaray Bay, QLD
  363
Mapleton Fall National
  Park, QLD 340
maps 52
Mardi Gras, Sydney
  126
Mardi Grass, Nimbin
  192
Mareeba, QLD 392
Margaret River, WA 24,
  632–634
Maria Island National
  Park, TAS 505
Marlo, VIC 611
Maroochy, QLD 332–
  334
Maroochydore, QLD
  332
Marree, SA 459, 460
marsupials 27
Martindale, SA 445
Maryborough, VIC 576

Marysville, VIC 587
MasterCard 38, 39
Mataranka, NT 274
Matrix (what is the) 120
Maydena, TAS 484
McCafferty's 63
McCarthur, General Douglas 306
McCubbin, Frederick 21
McLaren Vale, SA 430–431
meat pies 23
Medic Alert 44
medical assistance 44
megafauna 28, 118, 233, 241
Melaleuca, TAS 484
Melba Gully State Park, VIC 555
Melbourne Cup 26, 537
Melbourne, VIC 508–543
  accommodations 521–525
  bars 540–542
  Carlton 513, 526
  cinema 536
  City Center 512, 521, 525, 529, 540, 542
  Collingwood 513, 527, 540
  consulates 519
  Cricket Ground 531
  daytrips 543–545
  emergency and communications 520
  entertainment 536–538
  festivals 538
  film festival 539
  financial services 518
  Fitzroy 513, 523, 527, 540
  food 525–529
  gay and lesbian 513, 538, 539
  getting around 516–518
  getting there 510–512
  local services 519
  media and publications 520
  Middle Park 523
  nightclubs 542–543
  nightlife 539–543
  North Melbourne 513, 522, 526
  orientation 512–516
  performing arts 536
  practical information 518–520
  Prahran 516, 523, 528, 542
  pubs 540–542
  recreation 537
  St. Kilda 516, 524, 528, 534, 541
  sights 529–536
  South Melbourne 516
  South Yarra 516, 523, 528, 542
  sports 537
  tourist information 518
  websites 520
Melville Island, NT 255
Men At Work 20
Mendonca, Cristovao de 558
Meninigie, SA 447
Mersey River, TAS 490
Metung, VIC 605
Middle Brother State Forest, NSW 172
Midlands, WA 648–651
Midnight Oil 20
Mildura, VIC 585–586
Millsteam-Chicester National Park, WA 658
Mimosa Rocks National Park, NSW 212
Minnie Water, NSW 186
Minogue, Kylie 20
minority travelers 72
Mirima (Hidden Valley) National Park, WA 671
Mission Beach, QLD 378–380
*Mission Impossible II* 22, 120, 133
Mitchell River National Park, VIC 605
Mittagong, NSW 218
Mogo, NSW 209
Mole Creek Karst National Park, TAS 493
Molle Island Group, QLD 365
money 37–41
  ATM cards 39
  credit cards 39
  currency exchange 37
  getting money from home 40
  taxes 41
  traveler's checks 38
Monkey Mia, WA 652
monotremes 28
Mooloolaba, QLD 332
Moomba 538
Moonta, SA 450
Moreton Bay, QLD 313–317
Moreton Island, QLD 316
Mornington Peninsula National Park, VIC 548
Morton National Park, NSW 206, 218
Moruya, NSW 210
mosquitoes 45
Mossman Gorge, QLD 398
movies 21
Mt. Augustus, WA 654
Mt. Barker, WA 638
Mt. Buffalo National Park, VIC 594
Mt. Buller, VIC 589–590
Mt. Cougal National Park, NSW 199
Mt. Cougal National Park, QLD 327
Mt. Eccles National Park, VIC 558
Mt. Field National Park, TAS 483
Mt. Gambier, SA 447–448
Mt. Hotham, VIC 597
Mt. Isa, QLD 410–412
Mt. Kaputar National Park, NSW 235, 236
Mt. Lofty, SA 429
Mt. Oxley, NSW 237
Mt. Selwyn, NSW 217
Mt. Victoria Forest Reserve, TAS 499
Mt. Victoria, NSW 145
Mt. Warning National Park, NSW 200
Mt. Warning, NSW 192, 199
Mt. Wellington, TAS 474
Mt. William National Park, TAS 499, 501
Mt. Wilson, NSW 148
Mudgee, NSW 230–231
Mullumbimby, NSW 199
Mungo National Park, NSW 241, 586
*Muriel's Wedding* 22
Murramarang National Park, NSW 208
Murray River, SA 446
Murray River, VIC 580–586
Murwillumbah, NSW 199
music 20–21
Muswellbrook, NSW 153
Muttonbird Island, NSW 184
*My Brilliant Career* 19, 22
Myall Lakes National Park, NSW 168

**N**

N'Dhala Gorge, NT 287
Nabiac, NSW 169
Namadgi National Park, ACT 87
Namatjira, Albert 281, 285
Nambucca Heads, NSW 177–179
Nanbung National Park, WA 649
Naracoorte, SA 448
Narellan, NSW 218
Narooma, NSW 209
Narrabri, NSW 235–236
Narrandera, NSW 224
NASA 230
nasties 28, 30, 187
national anthem 228
National Parks
  Aspestos Range, TAS 492
  Bald Rock, NSW 159
  Ben Lomond, TAS 506
  Blue Lake, QLD 315
  Booderee, NSW 207
  Boonoo Boonoo, NSW 159, 331
  Border Ranges, NSW 200
  Broadwater, NSW 187
  Budderoo, NSW 205
  Bundjalong, NSW 187
  Cape Hillsborough, QLD 358
  Cape Le Grand, WA 643
  Cape Range, WA 655
  Carnarvon Gorge, QLD 352
  Cathedral Range, VIC 588
  Charles Darwin, NT 253
  Coffin Bay, SA 462
  Cooloola, QLD 339
  Coorabakh, NSW 172
  Coorong, SA 431

Croajingolong, VIC 611–613

Crowdy Bay, NSW 171

Daintree, QLD 398, 399

Doorgan, NSW 172

Dorrigo, NSW 179, 180

Douglas-Apsley, TAS 502

Errinundra, VIC 610

Eungella National Park 359

Eurobodalla, NSW 209

Fitzgerald River, WA 641

Flinders Chase, SA 439

Flinders Ranges, SA 454

Franklin-Gordon, TAS 488

Giraween, NSW 159

Girraween, QLD 331

Grampians, VIC 562–566

Gregory, NT 274

Gurig, NT 267

Hanging Rock, VIC 545

Innes, SA 451

Kakadu, NT 257–266

Karijini, WA 659

Katherine Gorge, NT 272–274

Keep River, NT 274

Kosciuszko, NSW 215–217

Lamington, QLD 326

Litchfield, NT 268–269

Little Desert, VIC 567–568

Lower Glenelg, VIC 560

Magnetic Island, QLD 376

Maria Island, TAS 505

Millstream-Chichester, WA 658

Mimosa Rocks, NSW 212

Mirima (Hidden Valley), WA 671

Mitchell River, VIC 605

Mole Creek Karst, TAS 493

Mornington Peninsula, VIC 548

Morton, NSW 206, 218

Mt. Buffalo, VIC 594

Mt. Cougal, QLD 327

Mt. Eccles, VIC 558

Mt. Field, TAS 483

Mt. Remarkable, SA 453

Mt. Warning, NSW 200

Mt. William, TAS 501

Mungo, NSW 241

Murramarang National Park 208

Myall Lake NSW 168

Namadgi, ACT 87

Nanbung, WA 649

New England, NSW 158

Nightcap, NSW 192

Nitmiluk (Katherine Gorge), NT 272–274

Noosa, QLD 337

Organ Pipes, VIC 544

Otway, VIC 555

Oxley Wild Rivers, NSW 156, 157

Peak Charles, WA 643

Porongurup, WA 638

Port Campbell, VIC 555

Purnululu (Bungle Bungle), WA 668

Rocky Cape, TAS 494

Royal, NSW 131–132

Snowy River, VIC 608–610

Southwest, TAS 484

Springbrook, QLD 327

Stirling Range, WA 639

Strzelecki, TAS 500

Sundown, QLD 332

Sunset, VIC 562

Sydney Harbour, NSW 117

Tamborine, QLD 326

Tarra-Bulga, VIC 603

Tasman, TAS 478

Tomaree NSW 165

Torndirrup, WA 640

Uluru-Kata Tjuta, NT 290–293

Walls of Jerusalem, TAS 493

Walpole-Nornalup, WA 637

Warren, WA 636

Warrumbungle, NSW 234

Watagans NSW 165

Watarrka, NT 288

Waychinicup, WA 641

Werrikimbe, NSW 157

West Cape Howe, WA 641

Wilsons Promontory, VIC 598–602

Witches Falls, QLD 327

Wyperfield, VIC 562

Yalgorup, WA 629

Yuragyir, NSW 186, 187

National Party 16

National Rugby League final 25

native title 17

Native Title Amendment Bill of 1997 18

Nauru 535

Neighbours bar night 541

Nelson Bay, NSW 165

New Age commercialism 573

New England National Park, NSW 158

New England, NSW 150–155

New Norfolk, TAS 483

New South Wales 88–241

getting around 89

New South Wales Corps 11

Newcastle, NSW 160–165

Newry Island, QLD 357

Nhill, VIC 567

Nick Cone and the Badseeds 20

Nightcap National Park, NSW 192, 199

Nimbin, NSW 191–192

Ninety Mile Beach, VIC 607

Ningaloo Reef, WA 655

Nitmiluk (Katherine Gorge) National Park, NT 272–274

Nolan, Sidney 21, 87, 535

NOMADS 51

Noosa National Park, QLD 337

Noosa, QLD 334–338

Normanton, QLD 412

Norseman, WA 465, 644

North Coast, QLD 368–381

North Molle Island, QLD 366

North Stradbroke Island, QLD 313–315

Northern Flinders, SA 456–457

Northern Territory 242–293

getting around 244

Northern Yuragyir, NSW 187

Northwest Coast, TAS 493

Northwest, NSW 232–241

novels 19

NRL 25

nuclear testing 15

nudity
bars 540
for healthy children 358
not in children's books 140
Olympics 431
on beaches 117, 132, 164, 168, 338, 431, 625
sheep 573

Nullarbor Plain, SA 463

Nullarbor Plain, WA 644

Nut, the, TAS 494

**O**

Oatlands, TAS 505

Oberon, NSW 147

Old Bar, NSW 171

Old Beltana, SA 456

oldest
alcoholic beverage 431
bookstore 496
brewery 475
casino 476
chocolate maker 425
continually inhabited site 241
fishing town 602
form of life on Earth 652
Galapagos tortoise 310
koala 310
mainland bridge 140
mulberry tree 437
national park 131
outdoor museum 584
pub 135
remaining Homo sapiens relic 241
river on the planet 285
synagogue 474

theater 476
town 498
trout hatchery 483
volcanic rock
  formation 638
Olgas, the, NT 293
Olympics
  medals 228
  nude 431
  venues 119, 121,
  135
One Nation Party 15,
  16
only collection of
  cartoons in Australia
  184
only in Australia 343
Oodnadatta Track, SA
  459
Oodnadatta, SA 460
operator, phone 58
*Ophelia* 533, 535
Optimus Prime 28
Orange, NSW 227
Orbost, VIC 610
Organ Pipes National
  Park, VIC 544
Otford, NSW 131
Otway National Park,
  VIC 555
Otways, VIC 555
Outback Coast, WA
  651–656
Outback Victoria 561–
  568
Outback, SA 457–460
Overland Track, TAS
  489
Oxenford, QLD 327
Oxley Highway, NSW
  156
Oxley Wild Rivers
  National Park, NSW
  156, 157
Oz Experience 65, 93,
  550

**P**

Pacific Palms, NSW
  170
Pacivica 136
packing 47, 52
Paddington, Sydney
  128
Palmerston, NT 255
Parachilna, SA 455
parasites 46
Parkes Radio
  Telescope, NSW 230
Paronella Park, QLD
  380
Parramatta, NSW 134
passports 33–34
pastoral lease 17
Paterson, Banjo 19,

227, 228, 408, 608
Patonga, NSW 136
pavlova 22
Peak Charles National
  Park, WA 643
Peeramon, QLD 395
Pemberton, WA 635
Penguin Parade 545
penguins 28, 210,
  436, 438, 481, 498,
  545
Penneshaw, SA 438
Penong, SA 464
Penrith, NSW 134
Perisher Blue, NSW
  216
Personal Identification
  Number (PIN) 39
Perth, WA 15, 616–
  628
  accommodations
    623–624
  consulates 622
  food 624
  Fremantle 620, 623,
    624, 626, 628
  getting around 620
  getting there 618–
    619
  media and
    publications 622
  nightlife 627–628
  orientation 619
  practical information
    620–622
  sights 624–627
pests 28
Peter, Paul, and Mary
  20
Phillip Island, VIC
  545–547
Phillip, Arthur 10, 11
phone codes 57, 675
phonecards 58
*Picnic at Hanging
  Rock* 21, 445, 545
Pigeon House Walk,
  NSW 208
Pilbara, the, WA 656–
  660
Pimba, SA 457
PIN numbers 39
Pine Creek, NT 269
Pink Lake, WA 643
Pinnacles, WA 649
Pitt Town, NSW 135
planes 58–63
  airlines 62
  courier flights 61
  domestic flights 62
  international flights
    58–62
  travel agencies 59
plants and animals.
  See environment.
plastic banana 653

platypus 28
PLUS 39
Point Addis, VIC 553
Point Samson, WA 658
poisonous animals.
  See dangerous
  wildlife.
Pomona, QLD 340
population 15
Porepunkah, VIC 594
Porongurup National
  Park, WA 638
Port Adelaide, SA 428
Port Albert, VIC 602
Port Arthur, TAS 15,
  477
Port Augusta, SA 452,
  457
Port Campbell, VIC
  555
Port Douglas, QLD
  395–398
Port Elliot, SA 432
Port Fairy, VIC 557
Port Hedland, WA 660
Port Jackson, NSW 10,
  89
Port Lincoln, SA 461
Port Macquarie, NSW
  172–176
Port Phillip, VIC 516,
  545–549
Port Pirie, SA 453
Port Stephens Bay
  Area, NSW 165–168
Portland, VIC 559–560
Portugese Man-O-War.
  See box jellyfish.
Poste Restante 56
Prairie, QLD 410
prescription drugs 42
Prime Minister 16
Prince, artist formerly
  known as 178
*Priscilla, Queen of
  the Desert* 22, 130,
  283, 459
Protestor's Falls, NSW
  190
public holidays. See
  holidays.
Pumpkin Island, QLD
  354
Purnululu (Bungle
  Bungle) National Park
  668
Pyengana, TAS 499

**Q**

Qantas 62
Queen Victoria Market,
  Melbourne 513
Queenscliff, VIC 548
Queensland 294–412
  Great Barrier Reef 29

Queensland Rail 63
Queenstown, TAS 487
*Quintus Servinton* 19
quolls 27
Quorn, SA 453

**R**

rabbits 28
Racial Discrimination
  Act of 1975 18
rainfall 31, 675
raingear 53
Ravenswood, QLD 409
Rawnsley Park Station,
  SA 455
Rayner, Bronwyn 588
Red Centre, NT 277–
  293
reef sharks 30
regurgitated nectar
  231
religion 16
renting a car 67
repetitive names
  Cutta Cutta, NT 274
reptiles 27
Republican Movement
  14
republicanism 14
restaurants 22
Richmond, NSW 135
Richmond, QLD 410
Richmond, TAS 476
Ringarooma, TAS 499
Riverina, NSW 223–
  226
Robe, SA 447
Roberts, Tom 21
Rockhampton, QLD
  349–352
Rocks, The, Sydney 96,
  115, 128
Rocky Cape National
  Park, TAS 494
Roebourne, WA 657
*Romeo and Juliet* 22
Rottnest Island, WA
  628
Royal National Park,
  NSW 131–132
rugby 25
Rush, Geoffrey 22
Russell Crowe 22
Rutherglen, VIC 591–
  592

**S**

safety and security
  41–43
  alcohol and drugs
    42
  gay and lesbian
    travelers 71
  hitchhiking 69
  insurance 47

minority travelers 72
self defense 42
traveling alone 70
valuables, protecting 42, 49
women travelers 70
sailing 26
  Magnetic Island, QLD 376
  Manly, QLD 316
  Maroochy, QLD 334
  Melbourne, VIC 535
  Sydney, NSW 122
  Whitsunday Islands, QLD 366
St. Helens, TAS 501
Salamanca Place, TAS 474
Sale, VIC 604
salties. See crocodiles.
Sandbar, NSW 171
Sandy Creek, Arnhem Land 267
Sanko Harvest shipwreck, WA 643
Sarah Island, TAS 487
Savage Garden 20
school holidays. See holidays.
School of the Air 283
Scone, NSW 153
Scotts Head, NSW 178, 179
scuba. See diving.
sea life. See environment.
sea snakes 30
Seal Rocks, NSW 171
seals 29
seasons 1
self defense 42
Senate 16
senior travelers 71
sex
  on the Great Barrier Reef 29
  underwater 391
  whales 634
  with rocks 640
sexually transmitted diseases. See STDs.
Shady Camp Billabong, NT 257
*Shakespeare in Love* 22
Shark Bay, WA 10, 651–653
sharks 30
sheep 12, 29, 218, 228, 241, 449, 455, 463, 544, 559, 588, 647
*Shine* 22
Shipwreck Coast, VIC 550
Shoal Bay, NSW 165

Shoalhaven, NSW 205–208
short story 19
shout 24
Siberia 164
Silverton, NSW 240
Simpson Desert, NT 287
Simpson's Gap, NT 284
ski season 2
skiing
  Buchan, VIC 607
  Cooma, NSW 212
  cross-country 215, 217, 587, 594, 598
  Falls Creek, VIC 596
  Mt. Buffalo National Park, VIC 594
  Mt. Buller, VIC 589
  Mt. Hotham, NSW 597
  Mt. Selwyn, NSW 217
  night 216, 598
  Perisher Blue, NSW 216
  Thredbo, NSW 215
skydiving
  Adelaide, SA 426
  Brisbane, QLD 311
  Byron Bay, NSW 197
  Cairns, QLD 388
  Coffs Harbour 185
  Great Keppel Island, QLD 354
  Hunter Valley, NSW 152
  Mission Beach, QLD 379
  Port Macquarie, NSW 176
  Sydney, NSW 123
  Townsville, QLD 372
Skyrail Rainforest Cableway, QLD 392
sleeping bags 52
sleepsacks 48
Smithton, TAS 493
smoking 43
snakes 28, 54
snorkeling 29
Snowy Mountains, NSW 212–217
Snowy River National Park, VIC 608–610
Solitary Islands Marine Park, NSW 183
Solitary Islands, NSW 179, 186
solo travel 70
Sorell, TAS 477
Sorrento, VIC 547
South Australia 413–460
  getting around 414

South Molle Island, QLD 365
South West Rocks, NSW 177
Southern and Darling Downs, QLD 328–332
Southern Flinders, SA 453
Southwest National Park, TAS 484
Southwest, WA 630–636
spider orchids 27
spiders 55
spinifex 26
sport 24–26
Springbrook National Park, QLD 327
Springwood, NSW 140
St. Helena Island, QLD 316
STA Travel 59
Stanley, TAS 494
Stanthorpe, QLD 329–331
*Star Wars* 22
  Darth Vader 632
  Help me, Obi-Wan 120
State of Origin 25
Stawell, VIC 564
STDs 44, 46
sting rays 30
Stirling Range National Park, WA 639
Stockton Bight, NSW 165
stolen children 17, 21
stone fish 30
Stonehenge Down-Under 158
*Story of the Kelly Gang* 21
Strahan, TAS 486–487
Strathgordon, TAS 484
*Strictly Ballroom* 22
Strine (Australian) 15, 673
Strongbow 24
Strzelecki National Park, TAS 500
Strzelecki Ranges, VIC 604
Strzelecki, Paul 604
Stuart Highway, NT 255
studying abroad 73
sunburn 45
Sundown National Park, QLD 332
sunken treasure 558
Sunset National Park, VIC 562
Sunshine Coast Hinterland, QLD 340–341

Sunshine Coast, QLD 332–349
Super 12 25
superlatives
  deepest lake 488
  easternmost point 196
  greatest engineering feat (of its kind) 213
  largest, flattest, and most enigmatic lumps of limestone 464
  most expensive phone installation 460
  second-largest playable guitar in the world 224
  southernmost tip 482
  steepest railway 144
  westernmost town 652
  See also largest, longest, and oldest
Surf Coast, VIC 550
Surfers Paradise, QLD 319–325
surfing
  Austinmer, NSW 203
  Batemans Bay, NSW 209
  Bondi Beach, NSW 122
  Boomerang Beach, NSW 170
  Booti Booti National Park, NSW 170
  Botany Bay National Park, NSW 133
  Bruny Island, TAS 481
  Bulli, NSW 203
  Byron Bay, NSW 192, 196
  Cactus Beach, SA 464
  Celito Beach, NSW 171
  Coffs Harbour, NSW 184
  Coolangatta and Tweed Heads, QLD 319
  Denmark, WA 638
  Dunsborough, WA 632
  Geraldton, WA 650
  Gosford, NSW 137
  Innes National Park, SA 451
  Kangaroo Island, SA 437
  Kiama, NSW 204

Lake Macquarie, NSW 165
Lake's Entrance, VIC 607
Lennox Head, NSW 198
Margaret River, WA 634
Maroochy, QLD 332, 333
Nambucca Heads, NSW 179
Newcastle, NSW 164
Noosa, QLD 338
North Stradbroke Island, QLD 315
Otways,The, VIC 555
Perth, WA 625
Phillip Island, VIC 546
Port Macquarie, NSW 176
Port Stephen Bay Area, NSW 168
Port Stephens, NSW 165
Royal National Park, NSW 132
Sorrento, VIC 548
South Stradbroke Island, QLD 325
South West Rocks, NSW 177
Surfers Paradise, QLD 323
Torquay, VIC 552
Ulladulla, NSW 208
Victor Harbor, SA 433
Wollongong, NSW 203
Yallingup, WA 632
Yamba and Yuragyir, NSW 187
Surprise Valley, TAS 488
Swan Hill, VIC 583–584
Swan River Valley, WA 24, 644
Swansea, TAS 504
*Swingers* 540
Sydney, NSW 89–131
  accommodations 104–111
  activities 122–124
  bars 128–130
  Bondi Beach 98, 108, 115, 122
  Bondi Junction 98
  Chinatown 96
  cinemas 125
  Circular Quay 96, 115, 116
  City Center 96, 106, 112, 117, 129

Collaroy 110
consulates 101
Coogee 98, 109, 115, 122, 129
Cove 96
cricket 120
Curl Curl 122
Darling Harbour 96, 119
Darlinghurst 97, 114
Dee Why 122
Double Bay 98
Elizabeth Bay 97
emergency services 102
employment 103
entertainment 124–126
ferries 99
festivals 126
financial services 101
food 112–115
football 120
gay and lesbian 120, 126, 127, 130
getting around 98–101
getting there 89
Glebe 96, 107, 113, 129
Harbour Bridge 96, 116
Harbour National Park 117
Haymarket 96
Homebush Bay 121
Kings Cross 96, 104, 112, 128
Kirribilli 111
local services 102
Manly 98, 109, 115, 120, 122, 129
Mardi Gras 126
markets 126
Maroubra 122
media and publications 102
Mrs. Macquaries Point 96
Newport Reef 122
Newtown 96, 108, 113, 129
nightlife 127–131
North Narrabeen 122
North Shore 120, 129
Olympics 119, 121
Opera House 96, 115
orientation 93–98
Paddington 97, 114, 128
Palm Beach 122
performing arts 124

post and communications 103
Potts Point 97
practical information 101–103
*Priscilla* 130
pubs 128–130
Pyrmont 96
Redfern 96
Rocks, The 96, 115, 116, 128
Rose Bay 98
shopping 126–127
sights 115–122
sports 124
subway 99
Surry Hills 97, 114, 128
Tamarama 122
tourist and travel Information 101
Ultimo 96
websites 103
Woollahra 98
Woolloomooloo 97
work 103

**T**

Taggerty, VIC 587
taipan 28
takeaway 22
tallest
  building 117
  fire lookout 636
  office building 529
  ride 324
Tamborine National Park, QLD 326
Tamworth, NSW 153–155
Taree, NSW 171
Tarra-Bulga National Park, VIC 603
Tasman National Park, TAS 478
Tasman Peninsula, TAS 477
Tasman, Abel 10, 480
Tasmania 466–494
  Getting Around 467
  National Parks 468
Tasmanian devils 28
Tasmanian tiger 28
taxes 41
Taylors Arm, NSW 179
telephones 56
temperature 31, 675
  See also seasons.
Tennant Creek, NT 274, 275–276
Tennant, Kylie 172
Tenterfield, NSW 158
tents 53
*terra nullius* 11, 17

Terrigal, NSW 137
theme parks
  Dreamworld, QLD 324
  Ettamogah Pub, NSW 223
  Frozen World, QLD 324
  Movie World, QLD 324
  Seaworld, QLD 324
  Toboggan Hill Park, NSW 168
  Wet 'n' Wild, QLD 324
  Wonderland Sydney, NSW 134
Thirroul, NSW 203
Thomas Cook 38
Thorsbone Trail, QLD 377
Thredbo, NSW 215
Three Sisters, NSW 141
ticks 45
tiger shark 30, 346
Tilba Tilba, NSW 210
time zones 32
tipping 22, 41
Ti-Tree, NT 277
Tiwi Islands, NT 255
Tjapukai, QLD 391
Tom Price, WA 658
Tomaree National Park, NSW 165
Tooraweenah, NSW 234
Toowoomba, QLD 328
Top End, NT 256–267
Torndirrup National Park, WA 640
Torquay, VIC 552
tourism. See Australian Tourist Commission.
Tourist Refund Scheme (TRS) 36, 41
Tower Hill State Game Reserve, VIC 557
Townsville, QLD 368–373
trains 63
transportation
  buses 63
  car 65–69
  hitchhiking 69
  planes 58–63
  trains 63
travel agencies 59
traveler's checks 38
Tree Top Walk, WA 637
Triabunna, TAS 504
Tri-nation 25
Triple J 20
trout 222
TRS 36, 41

*Truman Show, The* 22
Tucki Tucki Nature Reserve, NSW 190
Tumby Bay, SA 461
Tumut, NSW 217
Tuncurry, NSW 169
turtles 30
Tweed Heads, QLD 317–319
Twelve Apostles, VIC 550
Two-ply toilet paper 163

## U

Ulladulla, NSW 207
Uluru, NT 291
Uluru-Kata Tjuta National Park, NT 290–293
Ulverston, TAS 493
Umbrawarra Gorge, NT 270
Undara Volcano, QLD 412
UNESCO
  World Biosphere Reserve 598, 611
  See also World Heritage Sites.
Upper Hawkesbury, NSW 135
Uralla, NSW 156
Utzon, Jørn 115

## V

V/Line 63
vaccinations 43
Valla Beach, NSW 178
Valley of the Giants, WA 637
valuables, protecting 42, 49
van Diemen, Anthony 10
VB 24
Vegemite 23, 652
vegetarians 22, 73
vertical slide 579
Victor Harbor, SA 432–433
Victoria 507–613
  getting around 507
Victoria Bitter (VB) 24
Victoria Highway, NT 274
Victoria, Queen 118, 579
Vietnam 13
  memorial 153
vineyards. See wineries.
VIP 49
Visa 38, 39
visas 34

visual arts 21
volunteering 75
*Voss* 19
voting 16

## W

Wagga Wagga, NSW 223
Wail, VIC 567
Walcha, NSW 156
Walhalla, VIC 604
Wallabies 25
wallaby 27
Wallaman Falls, QLD 376
Wallaroo, SA 450
Walls of Jerusalem National Park, TAS 493
Walpole, WA 637
Walpole-Nornalup National Park, WA 637
Waltzing Matilda 19, 227, 228, 408, 530
  3D hologram diorama 573
  See also Patterson, Banjo.
Wangaratta, VIC 590
Warramurrungundji 257, 260
Warrego Highway, QLD 405
Warren National Park, WA 636
Warrnambool, VIC 556–557
Warrumbungle National Park, NSW 234
Warwick, QLD 329
Watagan State Forests, NSW 165
Watarrka National Park, NT 288
Waterfall Way, NSW 157–159
Waterfall, NSW 131
water-purification tablets 53
Wauchope, NT 277
Waychinicup National Park, WA 641
Wayunga National Park, WA 629
weather 31, 675
  See also seasons.
websites
  Melbourne, VIC 520
  Sydney, NSW 103
  travel 75
Weir, Peter 21
weird
  giant VB sign 533

gigantic aluminum smelter 559
museums that deal too lightly with serious subjects 232
overstated awards 215
skulking without permission 477
tuna-tossing 462
UFOs 277
Weldborough Pass Scenic Reserve, TAS 499
well-endowed 583
Wellington National Park, WA 631
Werrikimbe National Park, NSW 157
West Cape Howe National Park, WA 638, 641
West MacDonnell National Park, NT 286
Western Australia 615–672
  getting around 615
Western Union 40
Westernport Bays, VIC 545–549
Westrail 63
WET 41
Wet, the 2, 258
whale watching 165, 168, 184, 185, 343, 433, 451, 464, 557, 629, 632, 635, 640, 641
whales 30
Whian Whian State Forest, NSW 199
White Australia 13
White, Patrick 19
Whitham, Edward Gough 14
Whitsunday Coast, QLD 349–368
Whitsunday Island, QLD 365
Whitsunday Islands, QLD 364–368
Whyalla, SA 460
Wiangaree, NSW 200
Wik decision 17
Wilberforce, NSW 135
wildflowers 2, 26, 132, 187, 282, 331, 500, 503, 562, 613, 629, 637, 639, 641, 648, 651
William Creek, SA 460
Willunga, SA 430
Wilpena Pound, SA 454
Wilpena, SA 456

Wilsons Promontory National Park, VIC 598–602
Windsor, NSW 135
windsurfing
  Geraldton, WA 650
  Lancelin, WA 648
Wine Equalisation Tax (WET) 41
wineries 24
  Albury, NSW 223
  Barossa Valley, SA 442
  Clare Valley, SA 445
  Denmark, WA 638
  Hunter Valley, NSW 150–153
  Huon Valley, TAS 480
  Margaret River, WA 633
  McLaren Vale, SA 431
  Mornington Peninsula, VIC 548
  Mudgee, NSW 230
  near Ballarat 573
  Rutherglen, VIC 591
  Stanthorpe, QLD 330
  Swan Hill, VIC 584
  Wangaratta, VIC 590
  Yarra, VIC 543
Wingham, NSW 171
Winnaleah, TAS 499
Winton, QLD 408
Witches Falls National Park, QLD 327
Witchetty grubs 23
Wittenoom, WA 659
Wodonga, VIC 220
Wolfe Creek Meteorite Crater, WA 668
Wollemi National Park, NSW 138, 148, 149
Wollemi pine 26, 143, 148, 218
Wollongbar, T.S.S. 198
Wollongong, NSW 201–203
wombats 28
Wombeyan Caves, NSW 218
women travelers 70
  health 46
women's suffrage 12
Wonga Beach, QLD 398
Woolgoola, NSW 186
Woolloomooloo, Sydney 97
Woomera, SA 457
work
  abroad 74
  Barossa Valley, SA 442

Bourke, NSW 236
Bowen, QLD 363
Bundaberg, QLD 347
Cardwell, QLD 376
Carnarvon, WA 653
Charters Towers,
  QLD 410
Cradoc, TAS 480
Darling Downs, QLD
  328
Griffith, NSW 225
Innisfail, QLD 381
Jindabyne, NSW 214
Kalgoorlie-Boulder,
  WA 645
Karratha, WA 656
Leeton, NSW 225
Maroochy, QLD 332
Melbourne, VIC 524
Mildura, VIC 585
Nimbin, NSW 191
Orange, NSW 227
Quorn, SA 454
Riverina, NSW 223
Snowy River

National Park, VIC
  608
Sydney, NSW 103
Tamworth, NSW 154
Warrnambool, VIC
  557
See also visas.
working holiday visa
  35
World Heritage Sites
  52
  Fraser Island, QLD
    343–347
  Great Barrier Reef
    295–298
  Kakadu National
    Park 257–266
  Naracoorte caves,
    SA 448
  Shark Bay, WA 651–
    653
  Uluru 291
  Willandra Lakes 241
World Wars 13
Wunyu Beach, Arnhem

Land 267
WWOOF 75
Wycliff Well, NT 277
Wyndham, WA 672
Wynyard, TAS 493
Wyperfield National
  Park, VIC 562

**X**

XXXX 24

**Y**

yabbies 23
Yackandandah, VIC
  593
Yalata, SA 464
Yalgorup National
  Park, WA 629
Yallingup, WA 632
Yamba, NSW 187
Yandina, QLD 340
Yarra Valley, VIC 543
Yarram, VIC 603
Yarrangobilly Caves,

NSW 217
Yarrawonga, VIC 591
*Year of Living
  Dangerously, The* 22
Yellow Brick Road, OZ
  353
YHA 49
Yongala wreck, QLD
  371
York, WA 629
Yorke Peninsula, SA
  449–451
Yulara (Ayers Rock
  Resort), NT 289–290
Yungaburra, QLD 392,
  393
Yuragyir National Park,
  NSW 186, 187

**Z**

Zee end 672

# MAP INDEX

Adelaide 417
Airlie Beach 360
Albury 221
Alice Springs 279
Australia vi-vii
Ballarat 571
Bendigo 577
Brisbane 302-303
Broken Hill 239
Broome 663
Byron Bay 193
Cairns 384
Canberra 77
Central Darwin 247
Central Melbourne 514-5
Central Perth 621
Coffs Harbour 181
Far Southwest 630
Glebe 107
Grampians NP 563
Great Ocean Road 551
Greater Melbourne 511

Greater Sydney 97
Hobart 469
Kakadu National Park 259
Kalgoorlie 647
Kangaroo Island 435
Kata Tjuta (The Olgas) 292
Katoomba and Leura 142
The Kimberley 661
Kings Cross 105
Launceston 495
The MacDonell Ranges
  284-285
Mackay 356
Magnetic Island 374
Manly 110
New South Wales 90-91
Newcastle 161
Noosa 335
Northern Territory 243
Perth and Vicinity 617
Phillip Island 547
Port Douglas 397

Port Stephens 167
Queensland 296-297
Rockhampton 351
South Australia 413
St. Kilda 517
Sunshine Coast and Gold
  Coast 317
Sydney 94-95
Tasmania 467
The Tasman Peninsula 479
The Top End 245
Townsville 371
Uluru (Ayers Rock) 292
Uluru-Kata Tjuta NP 290
Victoria 509
Western Australia 614
Wilsons Promontory NP
  599
Wollongong 201
Yulara 289

INDEX

# If I had my life to live over again,

I would relax. I would limber up. I would take more chances.

## I would take more trips.

I would climb more mountains, swim more rivers, and watch more sunsets.

I would go places and do things and travel lighter than I have.

## I would ride more merry-go-rounds.

*Excerpt from Nadine Stair, 85 years old / photo> John Norris*

technical packs & apparel

# Find Yourself. Somewhere Else.

Don't just land there, do something. Away.com
is the Internet's preferred address for those
who like their travel with a little something
extra. Our team of travel enthusiasts and
experts can help you design your ultimate
adventure, nature or cultural escape. Make
Away.com your destination for extraordinary
travel. Then find yourself. Somewhere else.

away.com
1.877.769.2929

Will you have enough stories to tell your grandchildren?

Yahoo! Travel

Do You
YAHOO!
?